Lipo Wang Ke Chen Yew Soon Ong (Eds.)

Advances in Natural Computation

First International Conference, ICNC 2005
Changsha, China, August 27-29, 2005
Proceedings, Part II

Volume Editors

Lipo Wang
Nanyang Technological University
School of Electrical and Electronic Engineering
Block S1, 50 Nanyang Avenue, Singapore 639798
E-mail: elpwang@ntu.edu.sg

Ke Chen
University of Manchester
School of Informatics
P.O. Box 88, Sackville St., Manchester M6O 1QD, UK
E-mail: k.chen@manchester.ac.uk

Yew Soon Ong
Nanyang Technological University
School of Computer Engineering
Blk N4, 2b-39, Nanyang Avenue, Singapore 639798
E-mail: asysong@ntu.edu.sg

Library of Congress Control Number: Applied for

CR Subject Classification (1998): F.1, F.2, I.2, G.2, I.4, I.5, J.3, J.4

ISSN   0302-9743
ISBN-10   3-540-28325-0 Springer Berlin Heidelberg New York
ISBN-13   978-3-540-28325-6 Springer Berlin Heidelberg New York

This work is subject to copyright. All rights are reserved, whether the whole or part of the material is concerned, specifically the rights of translation, reprinting, re-use of illustrations, recitation, broadcasting, reproduction on microfilms or in any other way, and storage in data banks. Duplication of this publication or parts thereof is permitted only under the provisions of the German Copyright Law of September 9, 1965, in its current version, and permission for use must always be obtained from Springer. Violations are liable to prosecution under the German Copyright Law.

Springer is a part of Springer Science+Business Media

springeronline.com

© Springer-Verlag Berlin Heidelberg 2005
Printed in Germany

Typesetting: Camera-ready by author, data conversion by Scientific Publishing Services, Chennai, India
Printed on acid-free paper   SPIN: 11539117   06/3142   5 4 3 2 1 0

Preface

This book and its sister volumes, i.e., LNCS vols. 3610, 3611, and 3612, are the proceedings of the 1st International Conference on Natural Computation (ICNC 2005), jointly held with the 2nd International Conference on Fuzzy Systems and Knowledge Discovery (FSKD 2005, LNAI vols. 3613 and 3614) from 27 to 29 August 2005 in Changsha, Hunan, China. In its budding run, ICNC 2005 successfully attracted 1887 submissions from 32 countries/regions (the joint ICNC-FSKD 2005 received 3136 submissions). After rigorous reviews, 502 high-quality papers, i.e., 313 long papers and 189 short papers, were included in the ICNC 2005 proceedings, representing an acceptance rate of 26.6%.

The ICNC-FSKD 2005 featured the most up-to-date research results in computational algorithms inspired from nature, including biological, ecological, and physical systems. It is an exciting and emerging interdisciplinary area in which a wide range of techniques and methods are being studied for dealing with large, complex, and dynamic problems. The joint conferences also promoted cross-fertilization over these exciting and yet closely-related areas, which had a significant impact on the advancement of these important technologies. Specific areas included neural computation, quantum computation, evolutionary computation, DNA computation, chemical computation, information processing in cells and tissues, molecular computation, computation with words, fuzzy computation, granular computation, artificial life, swarm intelligence, ants colonies, artificial immune systems, etc., with innovative applications to knowledge discovery, finance, operations research, and more. In addition to the large number of submitted papers, we were blessed with the presence of four renowned keynote speakers and several distinguished panelists.

On behalf of the Organizing Committee, we thank Xiangtan University for sponsorship, and the IEEE Circuits and Systems Society, the IEEE Computational Intelligence Society, and the IEEE Control Systems Society for technical co-sponsorship. We are grateful for the technical cooperation from the International Neural Network Society, the European Neural Network Society, the Chinese Association for Artificial Intelligence, the Japanese Neural Network Society, the International Fuzzy Systems Association, the Asia-Pacific Neural Network Assembly, the Fuzzy Mathematics and Systems Association of China, and the Hunan Computer Federation. We thank the members of the Organizing Committee, the Advisory Board, and the Program Committee for their hard work in the past 18 months. We wish to express our heartfelt appreciation to the keynote and panel speakers, special session organizers, session chairs, reviewers, and student helpers. Our special thanks go to the publisher, Springer, for publishing the ICNC 2005 proceedings as three volumes of the Lecture Notes in Computer Science series (and the FSKD 2005 proceedings as two volumes of the Lecture Notes in Artificial Intelligence series). Finally, we thank all the authors and participants for their great contributions that made this conference possible and all the hard work worthwhile.

August 2005

Lipo Wang
Ke Chen
Yew Soon Ong

Organization

ICNC 2005 was organized by Xiangtan University and technically co-sponsored by the IEEE Circuits and Systems Society, the IEEE Computational Intelligence Society, and the IEEE Control Systems Society, in cooperation with the International Neural Network Society, the European Neural Network Society, the Chinese Association for Artificial Intelligence, the Japanese Neural Network Society, the International Fuzzy Systems Association, the Asia-Pacific Neural Network Assembly, the Fuzzy Mathematics and Systems Association of China, and the Hunan Computer Federation.

Organizing Committee

Honorary Conference Chairs	Shun-ichi Amari, Japan
	Lotfi A. Zadeh, USA
General Chair	He-An Luo, China
General Co-chairs	Lipo Wang, Singapore
	Yunqing Huang, China
Program Chairs	Ke Chen, UK
	Yew Soon Ong, Singapore
Local Arrangements Chairs	Renren Liu, China
	Xieping Gao, China
Proceedings Chair	Fen Xiao, China
Publicity Chair	Hepu Deng, Australia
Sponsorship/Exhibits Chairs	Shaoping Ling, China
	Geok See Ng, Singapore
Webmasters	Linai Kuang, China
	Yanyu Liu, China

Advisory Board

Toshio Fukuda, Japan
Kunihiko Fukushima, Japan
Tom Gedeon, Australia
Aike Guo, China
Zhenya He, China
Janusz Kacprzyk, Poland
Nikola Kasabov, New Zealand
John A. Keane, UK
Soo-Young Lee, Korea
Erkki Oja, Finland
Nikhil R. Pal, India

Witold Pedrycz, Canada
Jose C. Principe, USA
Harold Szu, USA
Shiro Usui, Japan
Xindong Wu, USA
Lei Xu, Hong Kong
Xin Yao, UK
Syozo Yasui, Japan
Bo Zhang, China
Yixin Zhong, China
Jacek M. Zurada, USA

Program Committee

Shigeo Abe, Japan
Kazuyuki Aihara, Japan
Davide Anguita, Italy
Abdesselam Bouzerdoum, Australia
Gavin Brown, UK
Laiwan Chan, Hong Kong
Sheng Chen, UK
Shu-Heng Chen, Taiwan
YanQiu Chen, China
Vladimir Cherkassky, USA
Sung-Bae Cho, Korea
Sungzoon Cho, Korea
Vic Ciesielski, Australia
Keshav Dahal, UK
Kalyanmoy Deb, India
Emilio Del-Moral-Hernandez, Brazil
Andries Engelbrecht, South Africa
Tomoki Fukai, Japan
Lance Fung, Australia
Takeshi Furuhashi, Japan
Hiroshi Furutani, Japan
John Q. Gan, UK
Wen Gao, China
Peter Geczy, Japan
Fanji Gu, China
Zeng-Guang Hou, Canada
Chenyi Hu, USA
Masumi Ishikawa, Japan
Robert John, UK
Mohamed Kamel, Canada
Yoshiki Kashimori, Japan
Samuel Kaski, Finland
Andy Keane, UK
Graham Kendall, UK
Jong-Hwan Kim, Korea
JungWon Kim, UK
Irwin King, Hong Kong
Natalio Krasnogor, UK
Vincent C.S. Lee, Australia
Stan Z. Li, China
XiaoLi Li, UK
Yangmin Li, Macau
Derong Liu, USA
Jian-Qin Liu, Japan
Bao-Liang Lu, China
Simon Lucas, UK
Frederic Maire, Australia
Jacek Mandziuk, Poland
Satoshi Matsuda, Japan
Masakazu Matsugu, Japan
Bob McKay, Australia
Ali A. Minai, USA
Hiromi Miyajima, Japan
Pedja Neskovic, USA
Richard Neville, UK
Tohru Nitta, Japan
Yusuke Nojima, Japan
Takashi Omori, Japan
M. Palaniswami, Australia
Andrew P. Paplinski, Australia
Asim Roy, USA
Bernhard Sendhoff, Germany
Qiang Shen, UK
Jang-Kyoo Shin, Korea
Leslie Smith, UK
Andy Song, Australia
Lambert Spannenburg, Sweden
Mingui Sun, USA
Johan Suykens, Belgium
Hideyuki Takagi, Japan
Kay Chen Tan, Singapore
Kiyoshi Tanaka, Japan
Seow Kiam Tian, Singapore
Peter Tino, UK
Kar-Ann Toh, Singapore
Yasuhiro Tsujimura, Japan
Ganesh Kumar Venayagamoorthy, USA
Brijesh Verma, Australia
Ray Walshe, Ireland
Jun Wang, Hong Kong
Rubin Wang, China
Xizhao Wang, China
Sumio Watanabe, Japan
Stefan Wermter, UK
Kok Wai Wong, Australia

Hong Yan, Hong Kong
Ron Yang, UK
Daniel Yeung, Hong Kong
Ali M.S. Zalzala, UK
Xiaojun Zeng, UK

David Zhang, Hong Kong
Huaguang Zhang, China
Liming Zhang, China
Qiangfu Zhao, Japan

Special Sessions Organizers

Ke Chen, UK
Gary Egan, Australia
Masami Hagiya, Japan
Tai-hoon Kim, Korea
Yangmin Li, Macau
Osamu Ono, Japan
Gwi-Tae Park, Korea
John A. Rose, Japan
Xingming Sun, China

Ying Tan, Hong Kong
Peter Tino, UK
Shiro Usui, Japan
Rubin Wang, China
Keming Xie, China
Xiaolan Zhang, USA
Liang Zhao, Brazil
Henghui Zou, USA
Hengming Zou, China

Reviewers

Ajith Abraham
Wensen An
Yisheng An
Jiancong Bai
Gurvinder Baicher
Xiaojuan Ban
Yukun Bao
Helio Barbosa
Zafer Bingul
Liefeng Bo
Yin Bo
Gavin Brown
Nan Bu
Erhan Butun
Chunhong Cao
Huai-Hu Cao
Qixin Cao
Yijia Cao
Yuan-Da Cao
Yuhui Cao
Yigang Cen
Chunlei Chai

Li Chai
Ping-Teng Chang
Kwokwing Chau
Ailing Chen
Chen-Tung Chen
Enqing Chen
Fangjiong Chen
Houjin Chen
Jiah-Shing Chen
Jing Chen
Jingchun Chen
Junying Chen
Li Chen
Shenglei Chen
Wei Chen
Wenbin Chen
Xi Chen
Xiyuan Chen
Xuhui Chen
Yuehui Chen
Zhen-Cheng Chen
Zhong Chen

Jian Cheng
Il-Ahn Cheong
Yiu-Ming Cheung
Yongwha Chung
Lingli Cui
Jian-Hua Dai
Chuangyin Dang
Xiaolong Deng
Hongkai Ding
Zhan Ding
Chao-Jun Dong
Guangbo Dong
Jie Dong
Sheqin Dong
Shoubin Dong
Wenyong Dong
Feng Du
Hai-Feng Du
Yanping Du
Shukai Duan
Metin Ertunc
Liu Fan

Gang Fang
Hui Fang
Chen Feng
Guiyu Feng
Jian Feng
Peng Fu
Yongfeng Fu
Yuli Fu
Naohiro Fukumura
Haichang Gao
Haihua Gao
Zong Geem
Emin Germen
Ling Gong
Maoguo Gong
Tao Gong
Weiguo Gong
Danying Gu
Qiu Guan
Salyh Günet
Dongwei Guo
Tian-Tai Guo
Xinchen Guo
Xiu Ping Guo
Yi'nan Guo
Mohamed Hamada
Jianchao Han
Lixin Han
Soowhan Han
Xiaozhuo Han
Fei Hao
Jingsong He
Jun He
Liqiang He
Xiaoxian He
Xiping He
Yi He
Zhaoshui He
Xingchen Heng
Chao-Fu Hong
Chi-I Hsu
Chunhua Hu
Hai Hu
Hongying Hu
Hua Hu

Jianming Hu
Li Kun Hu
Tao Hu
Ye Hu
Bingqiang Huang
Gaoming Huang
Min Huang
Yanwen Huang
Yilun Huang
Siu Cheung Hui
Changha Hwang
Jun-Cheol Jeon
Hyuncheol Jeong
Guangrong Ji
Mingxing Jia
Sen Jia
Zhuang Jian
Chunhong Jiang
Dongxiang Jiang
Jijiao Jiang
Minghui Jiang
Mingyan Jiang
Quanyuan Jiang
Li Cheng Jiao
Liu Jie
Wuyin Jin
Xu Jin
Ling Jing
Peng Jing
Xing-Jian Jing
Tao Jun
Hosang Jung
Jo Nam Jung
Venu K Murthy
Jaeho Kang
Kyung-Woo Kang
Ali Karci
Hyun-Sung Kim
Jongmin Kim
Jongweon Kim
Kee-Won Kim
Myung Won Kim
Wonil Kim
Heeyong Kwon
Xiang-Wei Lai

Dongwoo Lee
Kwangeui Lee
Seonghoon Lee
Seunggwan Lee
Kaiyou Lei
Xiongguo Lei
Soo Kar Leow
Anping Li
Boyu Li
Cheng Li
Dahu Li
Guanghui Li
Guoyou Li
Hongyan Li
Huanqin Li
Jianhua Li
Jie Li
Jing Li
Kangshun Li
Qiangwei Li
Qian-Mu Li
Qingyong Li
Ruonan Li
Shouju Li
Xiaobin Li
Xihai Li
Xinchun Li
Xiumei Li
Xuming Li
Ye Li
Ying Li
Yongjie Li
Yuangui Li
Yun Li
Yunfeng Li
Yong Li
Bojian Liang
Jiuzhen Liang
Xiao Liang
Yanchun Liang
Yixiong Liang
Guanglan Liao
Yingxin Liao
Sehun Lim
Tong Ming Lim

Jianning Lin
Ling Lin
Pan Lin
Qiu-Hua Lin
Zhi-Ling Lin
Zhou Ling
Benyong Liu
Bing Liu
Bingjie Liu
Dang-Hui Liu
Feng Liu
Hehui Liu
Huayong Liu
Jianchang Liu
Jing Liu
Jun Liu
Lifang Liu
Linlan Liu
Meiqin Liu
Miao Liu
Qicheng Liu
Ruochen Liu
Tianming Liu
Weidong Liu
Xianghui Liu
Xiaoqun Liu
Yong-Lin Liu
Zheng Liu
Zhi Liu
Jianchang Lu
Jun Lu
Xiaobo Lu
Yinan Lu
Dehan Luo
Guiming Luo
Juan Luo
Qiang Lv
Srinivas M.B.
Changshe Ma
Weimin Ma
Wenping Ma
Xuan Ma
Michiharu Maeda
Bertrand Maillet
Toshihiko Matsuka

Hongling Meng
Kehua Miao
Teijun Miao
Shi Min
Hongwei Mo
Dhinaharan Nagamalai
Atulya Nagar
Mi Young Nam
Rongrong Ni
Rui Nian
Ben Niu
Qun Niu
Sun-Kuk Noh
Linlin Ou
Mayumi Oyama-Higa
Cuneyt Oysu
A. Alper Ozalp
Ping-Feng Pai
Li Pan
Tinglong Pan
Zhiming Pan
Xiaohong Pang
Francesco Pappalardo
Hyun-Soo Park
Yongjin Park
Xiaomei Pei
Jun Peng
Wen Peng
Yan Peng
Yuqing Peng
Zeng Peng
Zhenrui Peng
Zhongbo Peng
Daoying Pi
Fangzhong Qi
Tang Qi
Rong Qian
Xiaoyan Qian
Xueming Qian
Baohua Qiang
Bin Qin
Zhengjun Qiu
Wentai Qu
Yunhua Rao
Sundaram Ravi

Phillkyu Rhee
Lili Rong
Fuhua Shang
Ronghua Shang
Zichang Shangguan
Dayong Shen
Xisheng Shen
Daming Shi
Xiaolong Shi
Zhiping Shi
Noritaka Shigei
Jooyong Shim
Dongkyoo Shin
Yongyi Shou
Yang Shu
Valceres Slva
Daniel Smutek
Haiyan Song
Jiaxing Song
Jingyan Song
Wenbin Song
Xiao-Yu Song
Yan Yan Song
Tieming Su
Xiaohong Su
P.N. Suganthan
Guangzhong Sun
Huali Sun
Shiliang Sun
Wei Sun
Yuqiu Sun
Zhanquan Sun
Jin Tang
Jing Tang
Suqin Tang
Zhiqiang Tang
Zhang Tao
Hissam Tawfik
Hakan Temeltas
Nipon Theera-Umpon
Mei Tian
Chung-Li Tseng
Ibrahim Turkoglu
Juan Velasquez
Bin Wang

Chao-Xue Wang
Chaoyong Wang
Deji Wang
Dingcheng Wang
Gi-Nam Wang
Guojiang Wang
Hong Wang
Hongbo Wang
Hong-Gang Wang
Jigang Wang
Lin Wang
Ling Wang
Min Wang
Qingquan Wang
Shangfei Wang
Shaowei Wang
Teng Wang
Weihong Wang
Xin Wang
Xinyu Wang
Yan Wang
Yanbin Wang
Yaonan Wang
Yen-Nien Wang
Yong-Xian Wang
Zhanshan Wang
Zheng-You Wang
Zhurong Wang
Wang Wei
Xun-Kai Wei
Chunguo Wu
Fei Wu
Ji Wu
Qiongshui Wu
Qiuxuan Wu
Sitao Wu
Wei Wu
Yanwen Wu
Ying Wu
Chen Xi
Shi-Hong Xia
Guangming Xian
Binglei Xie
Li Xie
Tao Xie

Shengwu Xiong
Zhangliang Xiong
Chunlin Xu
Jianhua Xu
Jinhua Xu
Junqin Xu
Li Xu
Lin Xu
Shuxiang Xu
Xianyun Xu
Xin Xu
Xu Xu
Xue-Song Xu
Zhiwei Xu
Yiliang Xu
Jianping Xuan
Yaofeng Xue
Yuncan Xue
Hui Yan
Qiao Yan
Xiaohong Yan
Bo Yang
Chunyan Yang
Feng Yang
Guifang Yang
Guoqqing Yang
Guowei Yang
Huihua Yang
Jianwei Yang
Jing Yang
Li-Ying Yang
Qingyun Yang
Xiaohua Yang
Xiaowei Yang
Xuhua Yang
Yingchun Yang
Zhihui Yang
Jingtao Yao
Her-Terng Yau
Chaoqun Ye
He Yi
Ling-Zhi Yi
Li Yin
Rupo Yin
Liang Ying

Chen Yong
Eun-Jun Yoon
Xinge You
Changjie Yu
Fei Yu
Fusheng Yu
Guoyan Yu
Lean Yu
Mian-Shui Yu
Qingjun Yu
Shiwen Yu
Xinjie Yu
Mingwei Yuan
Shenfang Yuan
Xun Yue
Wu Yun
Yeboon Yun
Jin Zeng
C.H. Zhang
Changjiang Zhang
Chunkai Zhang
Da-Peng Zhang
Defu Zhang
Fan Zhang
Fengyue Zhang
Hong Zhang
Hong-Bin Zhang
Ji Zhang
Jiang Zhang
Li Zhang
Liyan Zhang
Li-Yong Zhang
Min Zhang
Ming-Jie Zhang
Rubo Zhang
Ruo-Ying Zhang
Weidong Zhang
Wei-Guo Zhang
Wen Zhang
Xiufeng Zhang
Yangsen Zhang
Yifei Zhang
Yong-Dong Zhang
Yue-Jie Zhang
Yunkai Zhang

Yuntao Zhang	Tiejun Zhao	Zhiheng Zhou
Zhenya Zhang	Liu Zhen	Zongtan Zhou
Hai Zhao	Guibin Zheng	Chengzhi Zhu
Jian Zhao	Shiqin Zheng	En Zhu
Jianxun Zhao	Yihui Zheng	Li Zhu
Jianye Zhao	Weicai Zhong	Wen Zhu
Lianwei Zhao	Zhou Zhong	Yaoqin Zhu
Lina Zhao	Dongming Zhou	Xiaobin Zou
Wencang Zhao	Gengui Zhou	Xiaobo Zou
Xingming Zhao	Hongjun Zhou	Zhenyu Zou
Xuelong Zhao	Lifang Zhou	Wenming Zuo
Yinliang Zhao	Wengang Zhou	
Zhidong Zhao	Yuren Zhou	

* The term after a name may represent either a country or a region.

Table of Contents – Part II

Neural Network Applications: Pattern Recognition and Diagnostics

Monitoring of Tool Wear Using Feature Vector Selection and Linear Regression
  Zhong Chen, XianMing Zhang 1

Image Synthesis and Face Recognition Based on 3D Face Model and Illumination Model
  Dang-hui Liu, Lan-sun Shen, Kin-man Lam 7

Head-and-Shoulder Detection in Varying Pose
  Yi Sun, Yan Wang, Yinghao He, Yong Hua 12

Principal Component Neural Networks Based Intrusion Feature Extraction and Detection Using SVM
  Hai-Hua Gao, Hui-Hua Yang, Xing-Yu Wang 21

GA-Driven LDA in KPCA Space for Facial Expression Recognition
  Qijun Zhao, Hongtao Lu 28

A New ART Neural Networks for Remote Sensing Image Classification
  AnFei Liu, BiCheng Li, Gang Chen, Xianfei Zhang 37

Modified Color Co-occurrence Matrix for Image Retrieval
  Min Hyuk Chang, Jae Young Pyun, Muhammad Bilal Ahmad, Jong Hoon Chun, Jong An Park 43

A Novel Data Fusion Scheme for Offline Chinese Signature Verification
  Wen-ming Zuo, Ming Qi 51

A Multiple Eigenspaces Constructing Method and Its Application to Face Recognition
  Wu-Jun Li, Bin Luo, Chong-Jun Wang, Xiang-Ping Zhong, Zhao-Qian Chen 55

Quality Estimation of Fingerprint Image Based on Neural Network
  En Zhu, Jianping Yin, Chunfeng Hu, Guomin Zhang 65

Face Recognition Based on PCA/KPCA Plus CCA
  Yunhui He, Li Zhao, Cairong Zou 71

Texture Segmentation Using Intensified Fuzzy Kohonen Clustering
Network
    Dong Liu, Yinggan Tang, Xinping Guan 75

Application of Support Vector Machines in Reciprocating Compressor
Valve Fault Diagnosis
    Quanmin Ren, Xiaojiang Ma, Gang Miao 81

The Implementation of the Emotion Recognition from Speech and
Facial Expression System
    Chang-Hyun Park, Kwang-Sub Byun, Kwee-Bo Sim 85

Kernel PCA Based Network Intrusion Feature Extraction and Detection
Using SVM
    Hai-Hua Gao, Hui-Hua Yang, Xing-Yu Wang 89

Leak Detection in Transport Pipelines Using Enhanced Independent
Component Analysis and Support Vector Machines
    Zhengwei Zhang, Hao Ye, Guizeng Wang, Jie Yang 95

Line-Based PCA and LDA Approaches for Face Recognition
    Vo Dinh Minh Nhat, Sungyoung Lee 101

Comparative Study on Recognition of Transportation Under Real and
UE Status
    Jingxin Dong, Jianping Wu, Yuanfeng Zhou 105

Adaptive Eye Location Using FuzzyART
    Jo Nam Jung, Mi Young Nam, Phill Kyu Rhee 109

Face Recognition Using Gabor Features and Support Vector
Machines
    Yunfeng Li, Zongying Ou, Guoqiang Wang 119

Wavelet Method Combining BP Networks and Time Series ARMA
Modeling for Data Mining Forecasting
    Weimin Tong, Yijun Li 123

On-line Training of Neural Network for Color Image Segmentation
    Yi Fang, Chen Pan, Li Liu 135

Short-Term Prediction on Parameter-Varying Systems by Multiwavelets
Neural Network
    Fen Xiao, Xieping Gao, Chunhong Cao, Jun Zhang 139

VICARED: A Neural Network Based System for the Detection of
Electrical Disturbances in Real Time
  *Iñigo Monedero, Carlos León, Jorge Ropero, José Manuel Elena,
  Juan C. Montaño* 147

Speech Recognition by Integrating Audio, Visual and Contextual
Features Based on Neural Networks
  Myung Won Kim, Joung Woo Ryu, Eun Ju Kim 155

A Novel Pattern Classification Method for Multivariate EMG Signals
Using Neural Network
  Nan Bu, Jun Arita, Toshio Tsuji 165

Data Fusion for Fault Diagnosis Using Dempster-Shafer Theory Based
Multi-class SVMs
  Zhonghui Hu, Yunze Cai, Ye Li, Yuangui Li, Xiaoming Xu 175

Modelling of Rolling and Aging Processes in Copper Alloy by
Levenberg-Marquardt BP Algorithm
  Juanhua Su, Hejun Li, Qiming Dong, Ping Liu 185

Neural Network Applications: Robotics and Intelligent Control

An Adaptive Control for AC Servo System Using Recurrent Fuzzy
Neural Network
  Wei Sun, Yaonan Wang 190

PSO-Based Model Predictive Control for Nonlinear Processes
  Xihuai Wang, Jianmei Xiao 196

Low Cost Implementation of Artificial Neural Network Based Space
Vector Modulation
  Tarık Erfidan, Erhan Butun 204

A Novel Multispectral Imaging Analysis Method for White Blood Cell
Detection
  *Hongbo Zhang, Libo Zeng, Hengyu Ke, Hong Zheng,
  Qiongshui Wu* 210

Intelligent Optimal Control in Rare-Earth Countercurrent Extraction
Process *via* Soft-Sensor
  Hui Yang, Chunyan Yang, Chonghui Song, Tianyou Chai 214

Three Dimensional Gesture Recognition Using Modified Matching Algorithm
Hwan-Seok Yang, Jong-Min Kim, Seoung-Kyu Park 224

Direct Adaptive Control for a Class of Uncertain Nonlinear Systems Using Neural Networks
Tingliang Hu, Jihong Zhu, Chunhua Hu, Zengqi Sun 234

Neural Network Based Feedback Scheduler for Networked Control System with Flexible Workload
Feng Xia, Shanbin Li, Youxian Sun 242

Humanoid Walking Gait Optimization Using GA-Based Neural Network
Zhe Tang, Changjiu Zhou, Zengqi Sun 252

Adaptive Neural Network Internal Model Control for Tilt Rotor Aircraft Platform
Changjie Yu, Jihong Zhu, Zengqi Sun 262

Novel Leaning Feed-Forward Controller for Accurate Robot Trajectory Tracking
D. Bi, G.L. Wang, J. Zhang, Q. Xue 266

Adaptive Neural Network Control for Multi-fingered Robot Hand Manipulation in the Constrained Environment
Gang Chen, Shuqing Wang, Jianming Zhang 270

Control of a Giant Swing Robot Using a Neural Oscillator
Kiyotoshi Matsuoka, Norifumi Ohyama, Atsushi Watanabe, Masataka Ooshima 274

Neural Network Indirect Adaptive Sliding Mode Tracking Control for a Class of Nonlinear Interconnected Systems
Yanxin Zhang, Xiaofan Wang 283

Sequential Support Vector Machine Control of Nonlinear Systems via Lyapunov Function Derivative Estimation
Zonghai Sun, Youxian Sun, Yongqiang Wang 292

An Adaptive Control Using Multiple Neural Networks for the Position Control in Hydraulic Servo System
Yuan Kang, Ming-Hui Chua, Yuan-Liang Liu, Chuan-Wei Chang, Shu-Yen Chien 296

Neural Network Applications: Signal Processing and Multi-media

Exon Structure Analysis via PCA and ICA of Short-Time Fourier Transform
Changha Hwang, David Chiu, Insuk Sohn 306

Nonlinear Adaptive Blind Source Separation Based on Kernel Function
Feng Liu, Cao Zhexin, Qiang Zhi, Shaoqian Li, Min Liang 316

Hybrid Intelligent Forecasting Model Based on Empirical Mode Decomposition, Support Vector Regression and Adaptive Linear Neural Network
Zhengjia He, Qiao Hu, Yanyang Zi, Zhousuo Zhang, Xuefeng Chen 324

A Real Time Color Gamut Mapping Method Using a Neural Network
Hak-Sung Lee, Dongil Han 328

Adaptive Identification of Chaotic Systems and Its Applications in Chaotic Communications
Jiuchao Feng 332

A Time-Series Decomposed Model of Network Traffic
Cheng Guang, Gong Jian, Ding Wei 338

A Novel Wavelet Watermark Algorithm Based on Neural Network Image Scramble
Jian Zhao, Qin Zhao, Ming-quan Zhou, Jianshou Pan 346

A Hybrid Model for Forecasting Aquatic Products Short-Term Price Integrated Wavelet Neural Network with Genetic Algorithm
Tao Hu, Xiaoshuan Zhang, Yunxian Hou, Weisong Mu, Zetian Fu 352

A Multiple Vector Quantization Approach to Image Compression
Noritaka Shigei, Hiromi Miyajima, Michiharu Maeda 361

Segmentation of SAR Image Using Mixture Multiscale ARMA Network
Haixia Xu, Zheng Tian, Fan Meng 371

Brain Activity Analysis of Rat Based on Electroencephalogram Complexity Under General Anesthesia
Jin Xu, Chongxun Zheng, Xueliang Liu, Xiaomei Pei, Guixia Jing 376

Post-nonlinear Blind Source Separation Using Wavelet Neural Networks
and Particle Swarm Optimization
  Ying Gao, Shengli Xie 386

An MRF-ICA Based Algorithm for Image Separation
  Sen Jia, Yuntao Qian 391

Multi-view Face Recognition with Min-Max Modular SVMs
  Zhi-Gang Fan, Bao-Liang Lu 396

Texture Segmentation Using Neural Networks and Multi-scale Wavelet
Features
  Tae Hyung Kim, Il Kyu Eom, Yoo Shin Kim 400

An In-depth Comparison on FastICA, CuBICA and IC-FastICA
  Bin Wang, Wenkai Lu 410

Characteristics of Equinumber Principle for Adaptive Vector
Quantization
  Michiharu Maeda, Noritaka Shigei, Hiromi Miyajima 415

ANFIS Based Dynamic Model Compensator for Tracking and GPS
Navigation Applications
  Dah-Jing Jwo, Zong-Ming Chen 425

Dynamic Background Discrimination with a Recurrent Network
  Jieyu Zhao 432

Gender Recognition Using a Min-Max Modular Support Vector Machine
  Hui-Cheng Lian, Bao-Liang Lu, Erina Takikawa, Satoshi Hosoi 438

An Application of Support Vector Regression on Narrow-Band
Interference Suppression in Spread Spectrum Systems
  Qing Yang, Shengli Xie 442

A Natural Modification of Autocorrelation Based Video Watermarking
Scheme Using ICA for Better Geometric Attack Robustness
  Seong-Whan Kim, Hyun Jin Park, HyunSeong Sung 451

Research of Blind Deconvolution Algorithm Based on High-Order
Statistics and Quantum Inspired GA
  Jun-an Yang, Bin Zhao, Zhongfu Ye 461

Differential Demodulation of OFDM Based on SOM
  Xuming Li, Lenan Wu 468

Efficient Time Series Matching Based on HMTS Algorithm
  Min Zhang, Ying Tan 476

3D Polar-Radius Invariant Moments and Structure Moment Invariants
  Zongmin Li, Yuanzhen Zhang, Kunpeng Hou, Hua Li 483

A Fast Searching Algorithm of Symmetrical Period Modulation Pattern
Based on Accumulative Transformation Technique
  FuHua Fan, Ying Tan 493

A Granular Analysis Method in Signal Processing
  Lunwen Wang, Ying Tan, Ling Zhang 501

Other Neural Networks Applications

Adaptive Leakage Suppression Based on Recurrent Wavelet Neural
Network
  Zhangliang Xiong, Xiangquan Shi 508

New Multi-server Password Authentication Scheme Using Neural
Networks
  Eun-Jun Yoon, Kee-Young Yoo 512

Time Domain Substructural Post-earthquake Damage Diagnosis
Methodology with Neural Networks
  Bin Xu 520

Conceptual Modeling with Neural Network for Giftedness Identification
and Education
  Kwang Hyuk Im, Tae Hyun Kim, SungMin Bae, Sang Chan Park ... 530

Online Discovery of Quantitative Model for Web Service Management
  Jing Chen, Xiao-chuan Yin, Shui-ping Zhang 539

Judgment of Static Life and Death in Computer Go Using String Graph
  Hyun-Soo Park, Kyung-Woo Kang, Hang-Joon Kim 543

Research on Artificial Intelligence Character Based Physics Engine in
3D Car Game
  Jonghwa Choi, Dongkyoo Shin, Jinsung Choi, Dongil Shin 552

Document Clustering Based on Nonnegative Sparse Matrix Factorization
  C.F. Yang, Mao Ye, Jing Zhao 557

Prediction Modeling for Ingot Manufacturing Process Utilizing Data
Mining Roadmap Including Dynamic Polynomial Neural Network and
Bootstrap Method
  Hyeon Bae, Sungshin Kim, Kwang Bang Woo 564

Implicit Rating – A Case Study
  Song Wang, Xiu Li, Wenhuang Liu 574

Application of Grey Majorized Model in Tunnel Surrounding Rock
Displacement Forecasting
  Xiaohong Li, Yu Zhao, Xiaoguang Jin, Yiyu Lu, Xinfei Wang 584

NN-Based Damage Detection in Multilayer Composites
  Zhi Wei, Xiaomin Hu, Muhui Fan, Jun Zhang, D. Bi 592

Application of Support Vector Machine and Similar Day Method for
Load Forecasting
  Xunming Li, Changyin Sun, Dengcai Gong 602

Particle Swarm Optimization Neural Network and Its Application in
Soft-Sensing Modeling
  Guochu Chen, Jinshou Yu 610

Solution of the Inverse Electromagnetic Problem of Spontaneous
Potential (SP) by Very Fast Simulated Reannealing (VFSR)
  Hüseyin Göksu, Mehmet Ali Kaya, Ali Kökçe 618

Using SOFM to Improve Web Site Text Content
  *Sebastián A. Ríos, Juan D. Velásquez, Eduardo S. Vera,
  Hiroshi Yasuda, Terumasa Aoki* 622

Online Support Vector Regression for System Identification
  Zhenhua Yu, Xiao Fu, Yinglu Li 627

Optimization of PTA Crystallization Process Based on Fuzzy GMDH
Networks and Differential Evolutionary Algorithm
  Wenli Du, Feng Qian 631

An Application of Support Vector Machines for Customer Churn
Analysis: Credit Card Case
  Sun Kim, Kyung-shik Shin, Kyungdo Park 636

e-NOSE Response Classification of Sewage Odors by Neural Networks
and Fuzzy Clustering
  Güleda Önkal-Engin, Ibrahim Demir, Seref N. Engin 648

Using a Random Subspace Predictor to Integrate Spatial and Temporal
Information for Traffic Flow Forecasting
  Shiliang Sun, Changshui Zhang 652

Boosting Input/Output Hidden Markov Models for Sequence
Classification
  Ke Chen 656

Learning Beyond Finite Memory in Recurrent Networks of Spiking
Neurons
  Peter Tiňo, Ashley Mills 666

On Non-Markovian Topographic Organization of Receptive Fields in
Recursive Self-organizing Map
  Peter Tiňo, Igor Farkaš 676

Evolutionary Learning

Quantum Reinforcement Learning
  Daoyi Dong, Chunlin Chen, Zonghai Chen 686

Characterization of Evaluation Metrics in Topical Web Crawling Based
on Genetic Algorithm
  Tao Peng, Wanli Zuo, Yilin Liu 690

A Novel Quantum Swarm Evolutionary Algorithm for Solving 0-1
Knapsack Problem
  *Yan Wang, Xiao-Yue Feng, Yan-Xin Huang, Wen-Gang Zhou,
  Yan-Chun Liang, Chun-Guang Zhou* 698

An Evolutionary System and Its Application to Automatic Image
Segmentation
  Yun Wen Chen, Yan Qiu Chen 705

Incorporating Web Intelligence into Website Evolution
  Jang Hee Lee, Gye Hang Hong 710

Evolution of the CPG with Sensory Feedback for Bipedal Locomotion
  Sooyol Ok, DuckSool Kim 714

Immunity-Based Genetic Algorithm for Classification Rule Discovery
  Ziqiang Wang, Dexian Zhang 727

Dynamical Proportion Portfolio Insurance with Genetic Programming
  Jiah-Shing Chen, Chia-Lan Chang 735

Evolution of Reactive Rules in Multi Player Computer Games Based on Imitation
Steffen Priesterjahn, Oliver Kramer, Alexander Weimer, Andreas Goebels 744

Combining Classifiers with Particle Swarms
Li-ying Yang, Zheng Qin 756

Adaptive Normalization Based Highly Efficient Face Recognition Under Uneven Environments
Phill Kyu Rhee, InJa Jeon, EunSung Jeong 764

Artificial Immune Systems

A New Detector Set Generating Algorithm in the Negative Selection Model
Xinhua Ren, Xiufeng Zhang, Yuanyuan Li 774

Intrusion Detection Based on ART and Artificial Immune Network Clustering
Fang Liu, Lin Bai, Licheng Jiao 780

Nature-Inspired Computations Using an Evolving Multi-set of Agents
E.V. Krishnamurthy, V.K. Murthy 784

Adaptive Immune Algorithm for Solving Job-Shop Scheduling Problem
Xinli Xu, Wanliang Wang, Qiu Guan 795

A Weather Forecast System Based on Artificial Immune System
Chunlin Xu, Tao Li, Xuemei Huang, Yaping Jiang 800

A New Model of Immune-Based Network Surveillance and Dynamic Computer Forensics
Tao Li, Juling Ding, Xiaojie Liu, Pin Yang 804

A Two-Phase Clustering Algorithm Based on Artificial Immune Network
Jiang Zhong, Zhong-Fu Wu, Kai-Gui Wu, Ling Ou, Zheng-Zhou Zhu, Ying Zhou 814

Immune Algorithm for Qos Multicast Routing
Ziqiang Wang, Dexian Zhang 822

IFCPA: Immune Forgetting Clonal Programming Algorithm for Large Parameter Optimization Problems
Maoguo Gong, Licheng Jiao, Haifeng Du, Bin Lu, Wentao Huang .. 826

A New Classification Method for Breast Cancer Diagnosis: Feature
Selection Artificial Immune Recognition System (FS-AIRS)
  Kemal Polat, Seral Sahan, Halife Kodaz, Salih Günes 830

Artificial Immune Strategies Improve the Security of Data Storage
  Lei Wang, Yinling Nie, Weike Nie, Licheng Jiao 839

Artificial Immune System for Associative Classification
  Tien Dung Do, Siu Cheung Hui, Alvis C.M. Fong 849

Artificial Immune Algorithm Based Obstacle Avoiding Path Planning
of Mobile Robots
  Yen-Nien Wang, Hao-Hsuan Hsu, Chun-Cheng Lin 859

An Adaptive Hybrid Immune Genetic Algorithm for Maximum Cut
Problem
  Hong Song, Dan Zhang, Ji Liu 863

Algorithms of Non-self Detector by Negative Selection Principle in
Artificial Immune System
  Ying Tan, Zhenhe Guo 867

An Algorithm Based on Antibody Immunodominance for TSP
  Chong Hou, Haifeng Du, Licheng Jiao 876

Flow Shop Scheduling Problems Under Uncertainty Based on Fuzzy
Cut-Set
  Zhenhao Xu, Xingsheng Gu 880

An Optimization Method Based on Chaotic Immune Evolutionary
Algorithm
  Yong Chen, Xiyue Huang 890

An Improved Immune Algorithm and Its Evaluation of Optimization
Efficiency
  Chengzhi Zhu, Bo Zhao, Bin Ye, Yijia Cao 895

Simultaneous Feature Selection and Parameters Optimization for SVM
by Immune Clonal Algorithm
  Xiangrong Zhang, Licheng Jiao 905

Optimizing the Distributed Network Monitoring Model with Bounded
Bandwidth and Delay Constraints by Genetic Algorithm
  *Xianghui Liu, Jianping Yin, Zhiping Cai, Xueyuan Huang,
  Shiming Chen* 913

Modeling and Optimal for Vacuum Annealing Furnace Based on
Wavelet Neural Networks with Adaptive Immune Genetic Algorithm
  Xiaobin Li, Ding Liu 922

Lamarckian Polyclonal Programming Algorithm for Global Numerical
Optimization
  Wuhong He, Haifeng Du, Licheng Jiao, Jing Li 931

Coevolutionary Genetic Algorithms to Simulate the Immune System's
Gene Libraries Evolution
  *Grazziela P. Figueredo, Luis A.V. de Carvalho,
  Helio J.C. Barbosa* 941

Clone Mind Evolution Algorithm
  Gang Xie, Xinying Xu, Keming Xie, Zehua Chen 945

The Application of IMEA in Nonlinearity Correction of VCO Frequency
Modulation
  Gaowei Yan, Jun Xie, Keming Xie 951

A Quick Optimizing Multi-variables Method with Complex Target
Function Based on the Principle of Artificial Immunology
  Gang Zhang, Keming Xie, Hongbo Guo, Zhefeng Zhao 957

Evolutionary Theory

Operator Dynamics in Molecular Biology
  Tsuyoshi Kato 963

Analysis of Complete Convergence for Genetic Algorithm with Immune
Memory
  Shiqin Zheng, Kongyu Yang, Xiufeng Wang 978

New Operators for Faster Convergence and Better Solution Quality in
Modified Genetic Algorithm
  Pei-Chann Chang, Yen-Wen Wang, Chen-Hao Liu 983

Fuzzy Programming for Multiobjective Fuzzy Job Shop Scheduling
with Alternative Machines Through Genetic Algorithms
  Fu-ming Li, Yun-long Zhu, Chao-wan Yin, Xiao-yu Song 992

The Study of Special Encoding in Genetic Algorithms and a Sufficient
Convergence Condition of GAs
  Bo Yin, Zhiqiang Wei, Qingchun Meng 1005

The Convergence of a Multi-objective Evolutionary Algorithm Based on Grids
Yuren Zhou, Jun He 1015

Influence of Finite Population Size – Extinction of Favorable Schemata
Hiroshi Furutani, Makoto Sakamoto, Susumu Katayama 1025

A Theoretical Model and Convergence Analysis of Memetic Evolutionary Algorithms
Xin Xu, Han-gen He 1035

New Quality Measures for Multiobjective Programming
Hong-yun Meng, Xiao-hua Zhang, San-yang Liu 1044

An Orthogonal Dynamic Evolutionary Algorithm with Niches
Sanyou Zeng, Deyou Tang, Lishan Kang, Shuzhen Yao, Lixin Ding 1049

Fitness Sharing Genetic Algorithm with Self-adaptive Annealing Peaks Radii Control Method
Xinjie Yu 1064

A Novel Clustering Fitness Sharing Genetic Algorithm
Xinjie Yu 1072

Cooperative Co-evolutionary Differential Evolution for Function Optimization
Yan-jun Shi, Hong-fei Teng, Zi-qiang Li 1080

Optimal Design for Urban Mass Transit Network Based on Evolutionary Algorithms
Jianming Hu, Xi Shi, Jingyan Song, Yangsheng Xu 1089

A Method for Solving Nonlinear Programming Models with All Fuzzy Coefficients Based on Genetic Algorithm
Yexin Song, Yingchun Chen, Xiaoping Wu 1101

An Evolutionary Algorithm Based on Stochastic Weighted Learning for Constrained Optimization
Jun Ye, Xiande Liu, Lu Han 1105

A Multi-cluster Grid Enabled Evolution Framework for Aerodynamic Airfoil Design Optimization
Hee-Khiang Ng, Dudy Lim, Yew-Soon Ong, Bu-Sung Lee, Lars Freund, Shuja Parvez, Bernhard Sendhoff 1112

A Search Algorithm for Global Optimisation
  S. Chen, X.X. Wang, C.J. Harris 1122

Selection, Space and Diversity: What Can Biological Speciation Tell Us About the Evolution of Modularity?
  Suzanne Sadedin 1131

On Evolutionary Optimization of Large Problems Using Small Populations
  Yaochu Jin, Markus Olhofer, Bernhard Sendhoff 1145

Membrane, Molecular, and DNA Computing

Reaction-Driven Membrane Systems
  Luca Bianco, Federico Fontana, Vincenzo Manca 1155

A Genetic Algorithm Based Method for Molecular Docking
  Chun-lian Li, Yu Sun, Dong-yun Long, Xi-cheng Wang 1159

A New Encoding Scheme to Improve the Performance of Protein Structural Class Prediction
  Zhen-Hui Zhang, Zheng-Hua Wang, Yong-Xian Wang 1164

DNA Computing Approach to Construction of Semantic Model
  Yusei Tsuboi, Zuwairie Ibrahim, Nobuyuki Kasai, Osamu Ono 1174

DNA Computing for Complex Scheduling Problem
  Mohd Saufee Muhammad, Zuwairie Ibrahim, Satomi Ueda, Osamu Ono, Marzuki Khalid 1182

On Designing DNA Databases for the Storage and Retrieval of Digital Signals
  Sotirios A. Tsaftaris, Aggelos K. Katsaggelos 1192

Composite Module Analyst: Tool for Prediction of DNA Transcription Regulation. Testing on Simulated Data
  Tatiana Konovalova, Tagir Valeev, Evgeny Cheremushkin, Alexander Kel 1202

Simulation and Visualization for DNA Computing in Microreactors
  Danny van Noort, Yuan Hong, Joseph Ibershoff, Jerzy W. Jaromczyk 1206

Ants Colony

A Novel Ant Clustering Algorithm with Digraph
Ling Chen, Li Tu, Hongjian Chen 1218

Ant Colony Search Algorithms for Optimal Packing Problem
Wen Peng, Ruofeng Tong, Min Tang, Jinxiang Dong 1229

Adaptive Parallel Ant Colony Algorithm
Ling Chen, Chunfang Zhang 1239

Hierarchical Image Segmentation Using Ant Colony and Chemical Computing Approach
Pooyan Khajehpour, Caro Lucas, Babak N. Araabi 1250

Optimization of Container Load Sequencing by a Hybrid of Ant Colony Optimization and Tabu Search
Yong Hwan Lee, Jaeho Kang, Kwang Ryel Ryu, Kap Hwan Kim 1259

A Novel Ant Colony System Based on Minimum 1-Tree and Hybrid Mutation for TSP
Chao-Xue Wang, Du-Wu Cui, Zhu-Rong Wang, Duo Chen 1269

Author Index 1279

Table of Contents – Part I

Neural Network Learning Algorithms

A Novel Learning Algorithm for Wavelet Neural Networks
   Min Huang, Baotong Cui 1

Using Unscented Kalman Filter for Training the Minimal Resource Allocation Neural Network
   Ye Zhang, Yiqiang Wu, Wenquan Zhang, Yi Zheng 8

The Improved CMAC Model and Learning Result Analysis
   Daqi Zhu, Min Kong, YonQing Yang 15

A New Smooth Support Vector Regression Based on ϵ-Insensitive Logistic Loss Function
   Yang Hui-zhong, Shao Xin-guang, Ding Feng 25

Neural Network Classifier Based on the Features of Multi-lead ECG
   Mozhiwen, Feng Jun, Qiu Yazhu, Shu Lan 33

A New Learning Algorithm for Diagonal Recurrent Neural Network
   Deng Xiaolong, Xie Jianying, Guo Weizhong, Liu Jun 44

Study of On-Line Weighted Least Squares Support Vector Machines
   Xiangjun Wen, Xiaoming Xu, Yunze Cai 51

Globally Exponential Stability Analysis and Estimation of the Exponential Convergence Rate for Neural Networks with Multiple Time Varying Delays
   Huaguang Zhang, Zhanshan Wang 61

Locally Determining the Number of Neighbors in the k-Nearest Neighbor Rule Based on Statistical Confidence
   Jigang Wang, Predrag Neskovic, Leon N. Cooper 71

Fuzzy Self-organizing Map Neural Network Using Kernel PCA and the Application
   Qiang Lv, Jin-shou Yu 81

An Evolved Recurrent Neural Network and Its Application
   Chunkai Zhang, Hong Hu 91

Self-organized Locally Linear Embedding for Nonlinear Dimensionality Reduction
Jian Xiao, Zongtan Zhou, Dewen Hu, Junsong Yin, Shuang Chen ... 101

Active Learning for Probabilistic Neural Networks
Bülent Bolat, Tülay Yıldırım 110

Adaptive Training of Radial Basis Function Networks Using Particle Swarm Optimization Algorithm
Hongkai Ding, Yunshi Xiao, Jiguang Yue 119

A Game-Theoretic Approach to Competitive Learning in Self-Organizing Maps
Joseph Herbert, JingTao Yao 129

A Novel Intrusions Detection Method Based on HMM Embedded Neural Network
Weijin Jiang, Yusheng Xu, Yuhui Xu 139

Generate Different Neural Networks by Negative Correlation Learning
Yong Liu 149

New Training Method and Optimal Structure of Backpropagation Networks
Songyot Sureerattanan, Nidapan Sureerattanan 157

Learning Outliers to Refine a Corpus for Chinese Webpage Categorization
Dingsheng Luo, Xinhao Wang, Xihong Wu, Huisheng Chi 167

Bio-kernel Self-organizing Map for HIV Drug Resistance Classification
Zheng Rong Yang, Natasha Young 179

A New Learning Algorithm Based on Lever Principle
Xiaoguang He, Jie Tian, Xin Yang 187

An Effective Method to Improve Convergence for Sequential Blind Source Separation
L. Yuan, Enfang. Sang, W. Wang, J.A. Chambers 199

A Novel LDA Approach for High-Dimensional Data
Guiyu Feng, Dewen Hu, Ming Li, Zongtan Zhou 209

Research and Design of Distributed Neural Networks with Chip Training Algorithm
Bo Yang, Ya-dong Wang, Xiao-hong Su 213

Support Vector Regression with Smoothing Property
Zhixia Yang, Nong Wang, Ling Jing 217

A Fast SMO Training Algorithm for Support Vector Regression
*Haoran Zhang, Xiaodong Wang, Changjiang Zhang,
Xiuling Xu* 221

Rival Penalized Fuzzy Competitive Learning Algorithm
Xiyang Yang, Fusheng Yu 225

A New Predictive Vector Quantization Method Using a Smaller Codebook
Min Shi, Shengli Xie 229

Performance Improvement of Fuzzy RBF Networks
Kwang-Baek Kim, Dong-Un Lee, Kwee-Bo Sim 237

Neural Network Architectures

Universal Approach to Study Delayed Dynamical Systems
Tianping Chen 245

Long-Range Connections Based Small-World Network and Its Synchronizability
Liu Jie, Lu Jun-an 254

Double Synaptic Weight Neuron Theory and Its Application
Wang Shou-jue, Chen Xu, Qin Hong, Li Weijun, Bian Yi 264

Comparative Study of Chaotic Neural Networks with Different Models of Chaotic Noise
Huidang Zhang, Yuyao He 273

A Learning Model in Qubit Neuron According to Quantum Circuit
Michiharu Maeda, Masaya Suenaga, Hiromi Miyajima 283

An Algorithm for Pruning Redundant Modules in Min-Max Modular Network with GZC Function
Jing Li, Bao-Liang Lu, Michinori Ichikawa 293

A General Procedure for Combining Binary Classifiers and Its Performance Analysis
Hai Zhao, Bao-Liang Lu 303

A Modular Structure of Auto-encoder for the Integration of Different Kinds of Information
  Naohiro Fukumura, Keitaro Wakaki, Yoji Uno 313

Adaptive and Competitive Committee Machine Architecture
  Jian Yang, Siwei Luo 322

An ART2/RBF Hybrid Neural Networks Research
  Xuhua Yang, Yunbing Wei, Qiu Guan, Wanliang Wang, Shengyong Chen 332

Complex Number Procedure Neural Networks
  Liang Jiuzhen, Han Jianmin 336

Urban Traffic Signal Timing Optimization Based on Multi-layer Chaos Neural Networks Involving Feedback
  Chaojun Dong, Zhiyong Liu, Zulian Qiu 340

Research on a Direct Adaptive Neural Network Control Method of Nonlinear Systems
  Weijin Jiang, Yusheng Xu, Yuhui Xu 345

Improving the Resultant Quality of Kohonen's Self Organizing Map Using Stiffness Factor
  Emin Germen 353

A Novel Orthonormal Wavelet Network for Function Learning
  Xieping Gao, Jun Zhang 358

Fuzzy Back-Propagation Network for PCB Sales Forecasting
  Pei-Chann Chang, Yen-Wen Wang, Chen-Hao Liu 364

An Evolutionary Artificial Neural Networks Approach for BF Hot Metal Silicon Content Prediction
  Zhao Min, Liu Xiang-guan, Luo Shi-hua 374

Application of Chaotic Neural Model Based on Olfactory System on Pattern Recognitions
  Guang Li, Zhenguo Lou, Le Wang, Xu Li, Walter J. Freeman 378

Double Robustness Analysis for Determining Optimal Feedforward Neural Network Architecture
  Lean Yu, Kin Keung Lai, Shouyang Wang 382

Stochastic Robust Stability Analysis for Markovian Jump Neural Networks with Time Delay
Li Xie 386

Neurodynamics

Observation of Crises and Bifurcations in the Hodgkin-Huxley Neuron Model
Wuyin Jin, Qian Lin, Yaobing Wei, Ying Wu 390

An Application of Pattern Recognition Based on Optimized RBF-DDA Neural Networks
Guoyou Li, Huiguang Li, Min Dong, Changping Sun, Tihua Wu 397

Global Exponential Stability of Cellular Neural Networks with Time-Varying Delays
Qiang Zhang, Dongsheng Zhou, Haijun Wang, Xiaopeng Wei 405

Effect of Noises on Two-Layer Hodgkin-Huxley Neuronal Network
Jun Liu, Zhengguo Lou, Guang Li 411

Adaptive Co-ordinate Transformation Based on a Spike Timing-Dependent Plasticity Learning Paradigm
QingXiang Wu, T.M. McGinnity, L.P. Maguire, A. Belatreche, B. Glackin 420

Modeling of Short-Term Synaptic Plasticity Using Dynamic Synapses
Biswa Sengupta 429

A Chaotic Model of Hippocampus-Neocortex
Takashi Kuremoto, Tsuyoshi Eto, Kunikazu Kobayashi, Masanao Obayashi 439

Stochastic Neuron Model with Dynamic Synapses and Evolution Equation of Its Density Function
Wentao Huang, Licheng Jiao, Yuelei Xu, Maoguo Gong 449

Learning Algorithm for Spiking Neural Networks
Hesham H. Amin, Robert H. Fujii 456

Exponential Convergence of Delayed Neural Networks
Xiaoping Xue 466

A Neural Network for Constrained Saddle Point Problems: An
Approximation Approach
   Xisheng Shen, Shiji Song, Lixin Cheng 470

Implementing Fuzzy Reasoning by IAF Neurons
   Zhijie Wang, Hong Fan 476

A Method for Quantifying Temporal and Spatial Patterns of Spike Trains
   Shi-min Wang, Qi-Shao Lu, Ying Du 480

A Stochastic Nonlinear Evolution Model and Dynamic Neural Coding
on Spontaneous Behavior of Large-Scale Neuronal Population
   Rubin Wang, Wei Yu 490

Study on Circle Maps Mechanism of Neural Spikes Sequence
   Zhang Hong, Fang Lu-ping, Tong Qin-ye 499

Synchronous Behaviors of Hindmarsh-Rose Neurons with Chemical
Coupling
   Ying Wu, Jianxue Xu, Mi He 508

Statistical Neural Network Models and Support Vector Machines

A Simple Quantile Regression via Support Vector Machine
   Changha Hwang, Jooyong Shim 512

Doubly Regularized Kernel Regression with Heteroscedastic Censored
Data
   Jooyong Shim, Changha Hwang 521

Support Vector Based Prototype Selection Method for Nearest
Neighbor Rules
   Yuangui Li, Zhonghui Hu, Yunze Cai, Weidong Zhang 528

A Prediction Interval Estimation Method for KMSE
   Changha Hwang, Kyung Ha Seok, Daehyeon Cho 536

An Information-Geometrical Approach to Constructing Kernel in
Support Vector Regression Machines
   Wensen An, Yanguang Sun 546

Training Data Selection for Support Vector Machines
   Jigang Wang, Predrag Neskovic, Leon N. Cooper 554

Model Selection for Regularized Least-Squares Classification
  Hui-Hua Yang, Xing-Yu Wang, Yong Wang, Hai-Hua Gao 565

Modelling of Chaotic Systems with Recurrent Least Squares Support
Vector Machines Combined with Reconstructed Embedding Phase Space
  Zheng Xiang, Taiyi Zhang, Jiancheng Sun 573

Least-Squares Wavelet Kernel Method for Regression Estimation
  Xiangjun Wen, Xiaoming Xu, Yunze Cai 582

Fuzzy Support Vector Machines Based on λ—Cut
  Shengwu Xiong, Hongbing Liu, Xiaoxiao Niu 592

Mixtures of Kernels for SVM Modeling
  Yan-fei Zhu, Lian-fang Tian, Zong-yuan Mao, Li Wei 601

A Novel Parallel Reduced Support Vector Machine
  Fangfang Wu, Yinliang Zhao, Zefei Jiang 608

Recurrent Support Vector Machines in Reliability Prediction
  *Wei-Chiang Hong, Ping-Feng Pai, Chen-Tung Chen,
  Ping-Teng Chang* 619

A Modified SMO Algorithm for SVM Regression and Its Application in
Quality Prediction of HP-LDPE
  Hengping Zhao, Jinshou Yu 630

Gait Recognition via Independent Component Analysis Based on
Support Vector Machine and Neural Network
  Erhu Zhang, Jiwen Lu, Ganglong Duan 640

Uncertainty Support Vector Method for Ordinal Regression
  Liu Guangli, Sun Ruizhi, Gao Wanlin 650

An Incremental Learning Method Based on SVM for Online Sketchy
Shape Recognition
  Zhengxing Sun, Lisha Zhang, Enyi Tang 655

Eigenspectra Versus Eigenfaces: Classification with a Kernel-Based
Nonlinear Representor
  Benyong Liu, Jing Zhang 660

Blind Extraction of Singularly Mixed Source Signals
  Zhigang Zeng, Chaojin Fu 664

Application of Support Vector Machines in Predicting Employee
Turnover Based on Job Performance
  *Wei-Chiang Hong, Ping-Feng Pai, Yu-Ying Huang,
  Shun-Lin Yang* 668

Palmprint Recognition Based on Unsupervised Subspace Analysis
  Guiyu Feng, Dewen Hu, Ming Li, Zongtan Zhou 675

A New Alpha Seeding Method for Support Vector Machine Training
  Du Feng, Wenkang Shi, Huawei Guo, Liangzhou Chen 679

Multiple Acoustic Sources Location Based on Blind Source Separation
  Gaoming Huang, Luxi Yang, Zhenya He 683

Short-Term Load Forecasting Based on Self-organizing Map and
Support Vector Machine
  Zhejing Bao, Daoying Pi, Youxian Sun 688

A Multi-class Classifying Algorithm Based on Nonlinear Dimensionality
Reduction and Support Vector Machines
  Lukui Shi, Qing Wu, Xueqin Shen, Pilian He 692

A VSC Scheme for Linear MIMO Systems Based on SVM
  Zhang Yibo, Yang Chunjie, Pi Daoying, Sun Youxian 696

Global Convergence of FastICA: Theoretical Analysis and Practical
Considerations
  Gang Wang, Xin Xu, Dewen Hu 700

SVM Based Nonparametric Model Identification and Dynamic Model
Control
  Weimin Zhong, Daoying Pi, Youxian Sun 706

Learning SVM Kernel with Semi-definite Programming
  Shuzhong Yang, Siwei Luo 710

Weighted On-Line SVM Regression Algorithm and Its Application
  Hui Wang, Daoying Pi, Youxian Sun 716

Other Topics in Neural Network Models

Convergence of an Online Gradient Method for BP Neural Networks
with Stochastic Inputs
  Zhengxue Li, Wei Wu, Guorui Feng, Huifang Lu 720

A Constructive Algorithm for Wavelet Neural Networks
Jinhua Xu, Daniel W.C. Ho 730

Stochastic High-Order Hopfield Neural Networks
Yi Shen, Guoying Zhao, Minghui Jiang, Shigeng Hu 740

Predicting with Confidence - An Improved Dynamic Cell Structure
Yan Liu, Bojan Cukic, Michael Jiang, Zhiwei Xu 750

An Efficient Score Function Generation Algorithm with Information Maximization
Woong Myung Kim, Hyon Soo Lee 760

A New Criterion on Exponential Stability of a Class of Discrete Cellular Neural Networks with Time Delay
Fei Hao, Long Wang, Tianguang Chu 769

A Novel Local Connection Neural Network
Shuang Cong, Guodong Li, Yisong Zheng 773

An Unsupervised Cooperative Pattern Recognition Model to Identify Anomalous Massive SNMP Data Sending
Álvaro Herrero, Emilio Corchado, José Manuel Sáiz 778

A Fast Nonseparable Wavelet Neural Network for Function Approximation
Jun Zhang, Xieping Gao, Chunhong Cao, Fen Xiao 783

A Visual Cortex Domain Model for Illusory Contour Figures
Keongho Hong, Eunhwa Jeong 789

Cognitive Science

ANN Ensemble Online Learning Strategy in 3D Object Cognition and Recognition Based on Similarity
Rui Nian, Guangrong Ji, Wencang Zhao, Chen Feng 793

Design and Implementation of the Individualized Intelligent Teachable Agent
Sung-il Kim, Sung-Hyun Yun, Dong-Seong Choi, Mi-sun Yoon, Yeon-hee So, Myung-jin Lee, Won-sik Kim, Sun-young Lee, Su-Young Hwang, Cheon-woo Han, Woo-Gul Lee, Karam Lim 797

Comparison of Complexity and Regularity of ERP Recordings Between Single and Dual Tasks Using Sample Entropy Algorithm
  Tao Zhang, Xiaojun Tang, Zhuo Yang 806

Representation of a Physio-psychological Index Through Constellation Graphs
  Oyama-Higa Mayumi, Tiejun Miao 811

Neural Network Based Emotion Estimation Using Heart Rate Variability and Skin Resistance
  Sun K. Yoo, Chung K. Lee, Youn J. Park, Nam H. Kim, Byung C. Lee, Kee S. Jeong 818

Modeling Belief, Capability and Promise for Cognitive Agents - A Modal Logic Approach
  Xinyu Zhao, Zuoquan Lin 825

PENCIL: A Framework for Expressing Free-Hand Sketching in 3D
  Zhan Ding, Sanyuan Zhang, Wei Peng, Xiuzi Ye, Huaqiang Hu 835

Blocking Artifacts Measurement Based on the Human Visual System
  Zhi-Heng Zhou, Sheng-Li Xie 839

A Computation Model of Korean Lexical Processing
  Hyungwook Yim, Heuseok Lim, Kinam Park, Kichun Nam 844

Neuroanatomical Analysis for Onomatopoeia and Phainomime Words: fMRI Study
  Jong-Hye Han, Wonil Choi, Yongmin Chang, Ok-Ran Jeong, Kichun Nam 850

Cooperative Aspects of Selective Attention
  KangWoo Lee 855

Selective Attention Guided Perceptual Grouping Model
  Qi Zou, Siwei Luo, Jianyu Li 867

Visual Search for Object Features
  Predrag Neskovic, Leon N. Cooper 877

Agent Based Decision Support System Using Reinforcement Learning Under Emergency Circumstances
  Devinder Thapa, In-Sung Jung, Gi-Nam Wang 888

Dynamic Inputs and Attraction Force Analysis for Visual Invariance
and Transformation Estimation
  Tomás Maul, Sapiyan Baba, Azwina Yusof 893

Task-Oriented Sparse Coding Model for Pattern Classification
  Qingyong Li, Dacheng Lin, Zhongzhi Shi 903

Robust Face Recognition from One Training Sample per Person
  Weihong Deng, Jiani Hu, Jun Guo 915

Chinese Word Sense Disambiguation Using HowNet
  Yuntao Zhang, Ling Gong, Yongcheng Wang 925

Modeling Human Learning as Context Dependent Knowledge Utility
Optimization
  Toshihiko Matsuka 933

Automatic Text Summarization Based on Lexical Chains
  Yanmin Chen, Xiaolong Wang, Yi Guan 947

A General fMRI LINEAR Convolution Model Based Dynamic
Characteristic
  Hong Yuan, Hong Li, Zhijie Zhang, Jiang Qiu 952

Neuroscience Informatics, Bioinformatics, and Bio-medical Engineering

A KNN-Based Learning Method for Biology Species Categorization
  Yan Dang, Yulei Zhang, Dongmo Zhang, Liping Zhao 956

Application of Emerging Patterns for Multi-source Bio-Data
Classification and Analysis
  Hye-Sung Yoon, Sang-Ho Lee, Ju Han Kim 965

Nonlinear Kernel MSE Methods for Cancer Classification
  L. Shen, E.C. Tan 975

Fusing Face and Fingerprint for Identity Authentication by SVM
  Chunhong Jiang, Guangda Su 985

A New Algorithm of Multi-modality Medical Image Fusion Based on
Pulse-Coupled Neural Networks
  Wei Li, Xue-feng Zhu 995

Cleavage Site Analysis Using Rule Extraction from Neural
Networks
  Yeun-Jin Cho, Hyeoncheol Kim 1002

Prediction Rule Generation of MHC Class I Binding Peptides Using
ANN and GA
  Yeon-Jin Cho, Hyeoncheol Kim, Heung-Bum Oh 1009

Combined Kernel Function Approach in SVM for Diagnosis of Cancer
  *Ha-Nam Nguyen, Syng-Yup Ohn, Jaehyun Park,
  Kyu-Sik Park* 1017

Automatic Liver Segmentation of Contrast Enhanced CT Images Based
on Histogram Processing
  *Kyung-Sik Seo, Hyung-Bum Kim, Taesu Park, Pan-Koo Kim,
  Jong-An Park* 1027

An Improved Adaptive RBF Network for Classification of Left and
Right Hand Motor Imagery Tasks
  Xiao-mei Pei, Jin Xu, Chong-xun Zheng, Guang-yu Bin 1031

Similarity Analysis of DNA Sequences Based on the Relative Entropy
  Wenlu Yang, Xiongjun Pi, Liqing Zhang 1035

Can Circulating Matrix Metalloproteinases Be Predictors of Breast
Cancer? A Neural Network Modeling Study
  *H. Hu, S.B. Somiari, J. Copper, R.D. Everly, C. Heckman,
  R. Jordan, R. Somiari, J. Hooke, C.D. Shriver, M.N. Liebman* 1039

Blind Clustering of DNA Fragments Based on Kullback-Leibler
Divergence
  Xiongjun Pi, Wenlu Yang, Liqing Zhang 1043

Prediction of Protein Subcellular Locations Using Support Vector
Machines
  Na-na Li, Xiao-hui Niu, Feng Shi, Xue-yan Li 1047

Neuroinformatics Research in China- Current Status and Future
Research Activities
  *Guang Li, Jing Zhang, Faji Gu, Ling Yin, Yiyuan Tang,
  Xiaowei Tang* 1052

Australian Neuroinformatics Research – Grid Computing and
e-Research
  G.F. Egan, W. Liu, W-S. Soh, D. Hang 1057

Current Status and Future Research Activities in Clinical
Neuroinformatics: Singaporean Perspective
  Wieslaw L. Nowinski 1065

Japanese Neuroinformatics Research: Current Status and Future
Research Program of J-Node
  Shiro Usui 1074

Neural Network Applications: Communications and Computer Networks

Optimal TDMA Frame Scheduling in Broadcasting Packet Radio
Networks Using a Gradual Noisy Chaotic Neural Network
  Haixiang Shi, Lipo Wang 1080

A Fast Online SVM Algorithm for Variable-Step CDMA Power Control
  Yu Zhao, Hongsheng Xi, Zilei Wang 1090

Fourth-Order Cumulants and Neural Network Approach for Robust
Blind Channel Equalization
  Soowhan Han, Kwangeui Lee, Jongkeuk Lee,
  Fredric M. Ham 1100

Equalization of a Wireless ATM Channel with Simplified Complex
Bilinear Recurrent Neural Network
  Dong-Chul Park, Duc-Hoai Nguyen, Sang Jeen Hong,
  Yunsik Lee 1113

A Novel Remote User Authentication Scheme Using Interacting Neural
Network
  Tieming Chen, Jiamei Cai 1117

Genetic Algorithm Simulated Annealing Based Clustering Strategy in
MANET
  Xu Li 1121

Neural Network Applications: Expert System and Informatics

A Gradual Training Algorithm of Incremental Support Vector Machine
Learning
  Jian-Pei Zhang, Zhong-Wei Li, Jing Yang, Yuan Li 1132

An Improved Method of Feature Selection Based on Concept Attributes
in Text Classification
Shasha Liao, Minghu Jiang 1140

Research on the Decision Method for Enterprise Information Investment
Based on IA-BP Network
Xiao-Ke Yan, Hai-Dong Yang, He-Jun Wang, Fei-Qi Deng 1150

Process Control and Management of Etching Process Using Data
Mining with Quality Indexes
Hyeon Bae, Sungshin Kim, Kwang Bang Woo 1160

Automatic Knowledge Configuration by Reticular Activating
System
JeongYon Shim 1170

An Improved Information Retrieval Method and Input Device Using
Gloves for Wearable Computers
Jeong-Hoon Shin, Kwang-Seok Hong 1179

Research on Design and Implementation of the Artificial Intelligence
Agent for Smart Home Based on Support Vector Machine
Jonghwa Choi, Dongkyoo Shin, Dongil Shin 1185

A Self-organized Network for Data Clustering
*Liang Zhao, Antonio P.G. Damiance Jr.,
Andre C.P.L.F. Carvalho* 1189

A General Criterion of Synchronization Stability in Ensembles of
Coupled Systems and Its Application
Qing-Yun Wang, Qi-Shao Lu, Hai-Xia Wang 1199

Complexity of Linear Cellular Automata over $\mathbb{Z}_m$
Xiaogang Jin, Weihong Wang 1209

Neural Network Applications: Financial Engineering

Applications of Genetic Algorithm for Artificial Neural Network Model
Discovery and Performance Surface Optimization in Finance
Serge Hayward 1214

Mining Data by Query-Based Error-Propagation
Liang-Bin Lai, Ray-I Chang, Jen-Shaing Kouh 1224

The Application of Structured Feedforward Neural Networks to the
Modelling of the Daily Series of Currency in Circulation
  Marek Hlaváček, Josef Čada, František Hakl 1234

Time Delay Neural Networks and Genetic Algorithms for Detecting
Temporal Patterns in Stock Markets
  Hyun-jung Kim, Kyung-shik Shin, Kyungdo Park 1247

The Prediction of the Financial Time Series Based on Correlation
Dimension
  Chen Feng, Guangrong Ji, Wencang Zhao, Rui Nian 1256

Gradient-Based FCM and a Neural Network for Clustering of
Incomplete Data
  Dong-Chul Park 1266

Toward Global Optimization of ANN Supported by Instance Selection
for Financial Forecasting
  Sehun Lim 1270

Other Applications of Natural Computations

FranksTree: A Genetic Programming Approach to Evolve Derived
Bracketed L-Systems
  Danilo Mattos Bonfim, Leandro Nunes de Castro 1275

Data Clustering with a Neuro-immune Network
  *Helder Knidel, Leandro Nunes de Castro,
  Fernando J. Von Zuben* 1279

Author Index 1289

Table of Contents – Part III

Evolutionary Methodology

Multi-focus Image Fusion Based on SOFM Neural Networks and Evolution Strategies
  Yan Wu, Chongyang Liu, Guisheng Liao 1

Creative Design by Chance Based Interactive Evolutionary Computation
  Chao-Fu Hong, Hsiao-Fang Yang, Mu-Hua Lin 11

Design of the Agent-Based Genetic Algorithm
  Honggang Wang, Jianchao Zeng, Yubin Xu 22

Drawing Undirected Graphs with Genetic Algorithms
  Qing-Guo Zhang, Hua-Yong Liu, Wei Zhang, Ya-Jun Guo 28

A Novel Type of Niching Methods Based on Steady-State Genetic Algorithm
  Minqiang Li, Jisong Kou 37

Simulated Annealing Genetic Algorithm for Surface Intersection
  Min Tang, Jin-xiang Dong 48

A Web Personalized Service Based on Dual GAs
  Zhengyu Zhu, Qihong Xie, Xinghuan Chen, Qingsheng Zhu 57

A Diversity Metric for Multi-objective Evolutionary Algorithms
  Xu-yong Li, Jin-hua Zheng, Juan Xue 68

An Immune Partheno-Genetic Algorithm for Winner Determination in Combinatorial Auctions
  JianCong Bai, HuiYou Chang, Yang Yi 74

A Novel Genetic Algorithm Based on Cure Mechanism of Traditional Chinese Medicine
  Chao-Xue Wang, Du-Wu Cui, Lei Wang, Zhu-Rong Wang 86

An Adaptive GA Based on Information Entropy
  Yu Sun, Chun-lian Li, Ai-guo Wang, Jia Zhu, Xi-cheng Wang ... 93

A Genetic Algorithm of High-Throughput and Low-Jitter Scheduling
for Input-Queued Switches
  Yaohui Jin, Jingjing Zhang, Weisheng Hu 102

Mutation Matrix in Evolutionary Computation: An Application to
Resource Allocation Problem
  Jian Zhang, Kwok Yip Szeto 112

Dependent-Chance Programming Model for Stochastic Network
Bottleneck Capacity Expansion Based on Neural Network and Genetic
Algorithm
  Yun Wu, Jian Zhou, Jun Yang 120

Gray-Encoded Hybrid Accelerating Genetic Algorithm for Global
Optimization of Water Environmental Model
  Xiaohua Yang, Zhifeng Yang, Zhenyao Shen, Guihua Lu 129

Hybrid Chromosome Genetic Algorithm for Generalized Traveling
Salesman Problems
  *Han Huang, Xiaowei Yang, Zhifeng Hao, Chunguo Wu,
  Yanchun Liang, Xi Zhao* 137

A New Approach Belonging to EDAs: Quantum-Inspired Genetic
Algorithm with Only One Chromosome
  Shude Zhou, Zengqi Sun 141

A Fast Fingerprint Matching Approach in Medicare Identity Verification
Based on GAs
  Qingquan Wang, Lili Rong 151

Using Viruses to Improve GAs
  Francesco Pappalardo 161

A Genetic Algorithm for Solving Fuzzy Resource-Constrained Project
Scheduling
  Hong Wang, Dan Lin, Minqiang Li 171

A Hybrid Genetic Algorithm and Application to the Crosstalk Aware
Track Assignment Problem
  *Yici Cai, Bin Liu, Xiong Yan, Qiang Zhou,
  Xianlong Hong* 181

A Genetic Algorithm for Solving Resource-Constrained Project
Scheduling Problem
  Hong Wang, Dan Lin, Minqiang Li 185

Evolutionary Algorithm Based on Overlapped Gene Expression
  Jing Peng, Chang-jie Tang, Jing Zhang, Chang-an Yuan 194

Evolving Case-Based Reasoning with Genetic Algorithm in Wholesaler's Returning Book Forecasting
  *Pei-Chann Chang, Yen-Wen Wang, Ching-Jung Ting,
  Chien-Yuan Lai, Chen-Hao Liu* 205

A Novel Immune Quantum-Inspired Genetic Algorithm
  *Ying Li, Yanning Zhang, Yinglei Cheng, Xiaoyue Jiang,
  Rongchun Zhao* 215

A Hierarchical Approach for Incremental Floorplan Based on Genetic Algorithms
  Yongpan Liu, Huazhong Yang, Rong Luo, Hui Wang 219

A Task Duplication Based Scheduling Algorithm on GA in Grid Computing Systems
  Jianning Lin, Huizhong Wu 225

Analysis of a Genetic Model with Finite Populations
  Alberto Bertoni, Paola Campadelli, Roberto Posenato 235

Missing Values Imputation for a Clustering Genetic Algorithm
  *Eduardo R. Hruschka, Estevam R. Hruschka Jr.,
  Nelson F.F. Ebecken* 245

A New Organizational Nonlinear Genetic Algorithm for Numerical Optimization
  Zhihua Cui, Jianchao Zeng 255

Hybrid Genetic Algorithm for the Flexible Job-Shop Problem Under Maintenance Constraints
  Nozha Zribi, Pierre Borne 259

A Genetic Algorithm with Elite Crossover and Dynastic Change Strategies
  Yuanpai Zhou, Ray P.S. Han 269

A Game-Theoretic Approach for Designing Mixed Mutation Strategies
  Jun He, Xin Yao 279

FIR Frequency Sampling Filters Design Based on Adaptive Particle Swarm Optimization Algorithm
  Wanping Huang, Lifang Zhou, Jixin Qian, Longhua Ma 289

A Hybrid Macroevolutionary Algorithm
  Jihui Zhang, Junqin Xu 299

Evolutionary Granular Computing Model and Applications
  Jiang Zhang, Xuewei Li 309

Application of Genetic Programming for Fine Tuning PID Controller
Parameters Designed Through Ziegler-Nichols Technique
  *Gustavo Maia de Almeida, Valceres Vieira Rocha e Silva,
  Erivelton Geraldo Nepomuceno, Ryuichi Yokoyama* 313

Applying Genetic Programming to Evolve Learned Rules for Network
Anomaly Detection
  Chuanhuan Yin, Shengfeng Tian, Houkuan Huang, Jun He 323

A Pattern Combination Based Approach to Two-Dimensional Cutting
Stock Problem
  Jinming Wan, Yadong Wu, Hongwei Dai 332

Fractal and Dynamical Language Methods to Construct Phylogenetic
Tree Based on Protein Sequences from Complete Genomes
  Zu-Guo Yu, Vo Anh, Li-Quan Zhou 337

Evolutionary Hardware Architecture for Division in Elliptic Curve
Cryptosystems over $GF(2^n)$
  Jun-Cheol Jeon, Kee-Won Kim, Kee-Young Yoo 348

An Evolvable Hardware System Under Varying Illumination
Environment
  In Ja Jeon, Phill Kyu Rhee 356

An Evolvable Hardware Chip for Image Enhancement in Surface
Roughness Estimation
  M. Rajaram Narayanan, S. Gowri, S. Ravi 361

Evolutionary Agents for n-Queen Problems
  Weicai Zhong, Jing Liu, Licheng Jiao 366

Fictitious Play and Price-Deviation-Adjust Learning in Electricity
Market
  Xiaoyang Zhou, Li Feng, Xiuming Dong, Jincheng Shang 374

Automatic Discovery of Subgoals for Sequential Decision Problems
Using Potential Fields
  Huanwen Chen, Changming Yin, Lijuan Xie 384

Improving Multiobjective Evolutionary Algorithm by Adaptive Fitness
and Space Division
    Yuping Wang, Chuangyin Dang 392

IFMOA: Immune Forgetting Multiobjective Optimization
Algorithm
    Bin Lu, Licheng Jiao, Haifeng Du, Maoguo Gong 399

Genetic Algorithm for Multi-objective Optimization Using GDEA
    Yeboon Yun, Min Yoon, Hirotaka Nakayama 409

Quantum Computing

A Quantum-Inspired Genetic Algorithm for Scheduling Problems
    Ling Wang, Hao Wu, Da-zhong Zheng 417

Consensus Control for Networks of Dynamic Agents via Active
Switching Topology
    Guangming Xie, Long Wang 424

Quantum Search in Structured Database
    Yuguo He, Jigui Sun 434

Swarm Intelligence and Intelligent Agents

A Fuzzy Trust Model for Multi-agent System
    Guangzhu Chen, Zhishu Li, Zhihong Cheng, Zijiang Zhao,
    Haifeng Yan 444

Adaptive Particle Swarm Optimization for Reactive Power and Voltage
Control in Power Systems
    Wen Zhang, Yutian Liu 449

A Dynamic Task Scheduling Approach Based on Wasp Algorithm in
Grid Environment
    Hui-Xian Li, Chun-Tian Cheng 453

A Novel Ant Colony Based QoS-Aware Routing Algorithm for MANETs
    Lianggui Liu, Guangzeng Feng 457

A Differential Evolutionary Particle Swarm Optimization with
Controller
    Jianchao Zeng, Zhihua Cui, Lifang Wang 467

A Mountain Clustering Based on Improved PSO Algorithm
  Hong-yuan Shen, Xiao-qi Peng, Jun-nian Wang, Zhi-kun Hu 477

Multi-agent Pursuit-Evasion Algorithm Based on Contract Net Interaction Protocol
  Ying-Chun Chen, Huan Qi, Shan-Shan Wang 482

Image Compression Method Using Improved PSO Vector Quantization
  Qian Chen, Jiangang Yang, Jin Gou 490

Swarm Intelligence Clustering Algorithm Based on Attractor
  Qingyong Li, Zhiping Shi, Jun Shi, Zhongzhi Shi 496

An Agent-Based Soft Computing Society with Application in the Management of Establishment of Hydraulic Fracture in Oil Field
  Fu hua Shang, Xiao feng Li, Jian Xu 505

Two Sub-swarms Particle Swarm Optimization Algorithm
  Guochu Chen, Jinshou Yu 515

A Mobile Agent-Based P2P Autonomous Security Hole Discovery System
  Ji Zheng, Xin Wang, Xiangyang Xue, C.K. Toh 525

A Modified Clustering Algorithm Based on Swarm Intelligence
  Lei Zhang, Qixin Cao, Jay Lee 535

Parameter Selection of Quantum-Behaved Particle Swarm Optimization
  Jun Sun, Wenbo Xu, Jing Liu 543

An Emotional Particle Swarm Optimization Algorithm
  Yang Ge, Zhang Rubo 553

Multi-model Function Optimization by a New Hybrid Nonlinear Simplex Search and Particle Swarm Algorithm
  Fang Wang, Yuhui Qiu, Naiqin Feng 562

Adaptive XCSM for Perceptual Aliasing Problems
  Shumei Liu, Tomoharu Nagao 566

Discrete Particle Swarm Optimization (DPSO) Algorithm for Permutation Flowshop Scheduling to Minimize Makespan
  K. Rameshkumar, R.K. Suresh, K.M. Mohanasundaram 572

Unified Particle Swarm Optimization for Solving Constrained
Engineering Optimization Problems
  K.E. Parsopoulos, M.N. Vrahatis 582

A Modified Particle Swarm Optimizer for Tracking Dynamic Systems
  Xuanping Zhang, Yuping Du, Zheng Qin, Guoqiang Qin, Jiang Lu .. 592

Particle Swarm Optimization for Bipartite Subgraph Problem: A Case
Study
  Dan Zhang, Zeng-Zhi Li, Hong Song, Tao Zhan 602

On the Role of Risk Preference in Survivability
  Shu-Heng Chen, Ya-Chi Huang 612

An Agent-Based Holonic Architecture for Reconfigurable Manufacturing
Systems
  Fang Wang, Zeng-Guang Hou, De Xu, Min Tan 622

Mobile Robot Navigation Using Particle Swarm Optimization and
Adaptive NN
  Yangmin Li, Xin Chen 628

Collision-Free Path Planning for Mobile Robots Using Chaotic Particle
Swarm Optimization
  Qiang Zhao, Shaoze Yan 632

Natural Computation Applications: Bioinformatics and Bio-medical Engineering

Analysis of Toy Model for Protein Folding Based on Particle Swarm
Optimization Algorithm
  Juan Liu, Longhui Wang, Lianlian He, Feng Shi 636

Selective Two-Channel Linear Descriptors for Studying Dynamic
Interaction of Brain Regions
  Xiao-mei Pei, Jin Xu, Chong-xun Zheng, Guang-yu Bin 646

A Computational Pixelization Model Based on Selective Attention for
Artificial Visual Prosthesis
  Ruonan Li, Xudong Zhang, Guangshu Hu 654

Mosaicing the Retinal Fundus Images: A Robust Registration Technique
Based Approach
  Xinge You, Bin Fang, Yuan Yan Tang 663

Typing Aberrance in Signal Transduction
M. Zhang, G.Q. Li, Y.X. Fu, Z.Z. Zhang, L. He 668

Local Search for the Maximum Parsimony Problem
Adrien Goëffon, Jean-Michel Richer, Jin-Kao Hao 678

Natural Computation Applications: Robotics and Intelligent Control

Optimization of Centralized Power Control by Genetic Algorithm in a DS-CDMA Cellular System
J. Zhou, H. Kikuchi, S. Sasaki, H. Luo 684

Cascade AdaBoost Classifiers with Stage Features Optimization for Cellular Phone Embedded Face Detection System
Xusheng Tang, Zongying Ou, Tieming Su, Pengfei Zhao 688

Proper Output Feedback H_∞ Control for Descriptor Systems: A Convex Optimization Approach
Lei Guo, Keyou Zhao, Chunbo Feng 698

Planning Optimal Trajectories for Mobile Robots Using an Evolutionary Method with Fuzzy Components
Serkan Aydin, Hakan Temeltas 703

Hexagon-Based Q-Learning for Object Search with Multiple Robots
Han-Ul Yoon, Kwee-Bo Sim 713

Adaptive Inverse Control of an Omni-Directional Mobile Robot
Yuming Zhang, Qixin Cao, Shouhong Miao 723

Other Applications of Natural Computation

A Closed Loop Algorithms Based on Chaos Theory for Global Optimization
Xinglong Zhu, Hongguang Wang, Mingyang Zhao, Jiping Zhou 727

Harmony Search for Generalized Orienteering Problem: Best Touring in China
Zong Woo Geem, Chung-Li Tseng, Yongjin Park 741

Harmony Search in Water Pump Switching Problem
Zong Woo Geem 751

A Selfish Non-atomic Routing Algorithm Based on Game
Theory
  Jun Tao, Ye Liu, Qingliang Wu 761

Clone Selection Based Multicast Routing Algorithm
  Cuiqin Hou, Licheng Jiao, Maoguo Gong, Bin Lu 768

A Genetic Algorithm-Based Routing Service for Simulation Grid
  Wei Wu, Hai Huang, Zhong Zhou, Zhongshu Liu 772

Clustering Problem Using Adaptive Genetic Algorithm
  *Qingzhan Chen, Jianghong Han, Yungang Lai, Wenxiu He,
  Keji Mao* 782

FCACO: Fuzzy Classification Rules Mining Algorithm with Ant Colony
Optimization
  Bilal Alatas, Erhan Akin 787

Goal-Directed Portfolio Insurance
  Jiah-Shing Chen, Benjamin Penyang Liao 798

A Genetic Algorithm for Solving Portfolio Optimization Problems with
Transaction Costs and Minimum Transaction Lots
  Dan Lin, Xiaoming Li, Minqiang Li 808

Financial Performance Prediction Using Constraint-Based Evolutionary
Classification Tree (CECT) Approach
  Chi-I Hsu, Yuan Lin Hsu, Pei Lun Hsu 812

A Genetic Algorithm with Chromosome-Repairing Technique for
Polygonal Approximation of Digital Curves
  Bin Wang, Yan Qiu Chen 822

Fault Feature Selection Based on Modified Binary PSO with Mutation
and Its Application in Chemical Process Fault Diagnosis
  Ling Wang, Jinshou Yu 832

Genetic Algorithms for Thyroid Gland Ultrasound Image Feature
Reduction
  Ludvík Tesař, Daniel Smutek, Jan Jiskra 841

Improving Nearest Neighbor Classification with Simulated Gravitational
Collapse
  Chen Wang, Yan Qiu Chen 845

Evolutionary Computation and Rough Set-Based Hybrid Approach to Rule Generation
  Lin Shang, Qiong Wan, Zhi-Hong Zhao, Shi-Fu Chen 855

Assessing the Performance of Several Fitness Functions in a Genetic Algorithm for Nonlinear Separation of Sources
  F. Rojas, C.G. Puntonet, J.M. Górriz, O. Valenzuela 863

A Robust Soft Decision Mixture Model for Image Segmentation
  Pan Lin, Feng Zhang, ChongXun Zheng, Yong Yang, Yimin Hou ... 873

A Comparative Study of Finite Word Length Coefficient Optimization of FIR Digital Filters
  Gurvinder S. Baicher, Meinwen Taylor, Hefin Rowlands 877

A Novel Genetic Algorithm for Variable Partition of Dual Memory Bank DSPs
  Dan Zhang, Zeng-Zhi Li, Hai Wang, Tao Zhan 883

Bi-phase Encoded Waveform Design to Deal with the Range Ambiguities for Sparse Space-Based Radar Systems
  Hai-hong Tao, Tao Su, Gui-sheng Liao 893

Analytic Model for Network Viruses
  Lansheng Han, Hui Liu, Baffour Kojo Asiedu 903

Ant Colony Optimization Algorithms for Scheduling the Mixed Model Assembly Lines
  Xin-yu Sun, Lin-yan Sun 911

Adaptive and Robust Design for PID Controller Based on Ant System Algorithm
  Guanzheng Tan, Qingdong Zeng, Shengjun He, Guangchao Cai 915

Job-Shop Scheduling Based on Multiagent Evolutionary Algorithm
  Weicai Zhong, Jing Liu, Licheng Jiao 925

Texture Surface Inspection: An Artificial Immune Approach
  Hong Zheng, Li Pan 934

Intelligent Mosaics Algorithm of Overlapping Images
  Yan Zhang, Wenhui Li, Yu Meng, Haixu Chen, Tong Wang 938

Adaptive Simulated Annealing for Standard Cell Placement
  Guofang Nan, Minqiang Li, Dan Lin, Jisong Kou 943

Application of Particle Swarm Optimization Algorithm on Robust PID Controller Tuning
Jun Zhao, Tianpeng Li, Jixin Qian 948

A Natural Language Watermarking Based on Chinese Syntax
Yuling Liu, Xingming Sun, Yong Wu 958

A Steganographic Scheme in Digital Images Using Information of Neighboring Pixels
Young-Ran Park, Hyun-Ho Kang, Sang-Uk Shin, Ki-Ryong Kwon ... 962

Noun-Verb Based Technique of Text Watermarking Using Recursive Decent Semantic Net Parsers
Xingming Sun, Alex Jessey Asiimwe 968

A Novel Watermarking Scheme Based on Independent Component Analysis
Haifeng Li, Shuxun Wang, Weiwei Song, Quan Wen 972

On Sequence Synchronization Analysis Against Chaos Based Spread Spectrum Image Steganography
Guangjie Liu, Jinwei Wang, Yuewei Dai, Zhiquan Wang 976

Microstructure Evolution of the K4169 Superalloy Blade Based on Cellular Automaton Simulation
Xin Yan, Zhilong Zhao, Weidong Yan, Lin Liu 980

Mobile Robot Navigation Based on Multisensory Fusion
Weimin Ge, Zuoliang Cao 984

Self-surviving IT Systems
Hengming Zou, Leilei Bao 988

PDE-Based Intrusion Forecast
Hengming Zou, Henghui Zou 996

A Solution to Ragged Dimension Problem in OLAP
Lin Yuan, Hengming Zou, Zhanhuai Li 1001

Hardware Implementations of Natural Computation

A Convolutional Neural Network VLSI Architecture Using Sorting Model for Reducing Multiply-and-Accumulation Operations
Osamu Nomura, Takashi Morie, Masakazu Matsugu, Atsushi Iwata 1006

A 32-Bit Binary Floating Point Neuro-Chip
Keerthi Laal Kala, M.B. Srinivas 1015

Improved Blocks for CMOS Analog Neuro-fuzzy Network
Weizhi Wang, Dongming Jin 1022

A Design on the Vector Processor of 2048point MDCT/IMDCT for MPEG-2 AAC
Dae-Sung Ku, Jung-Hyun Yun, Jong-Bin Kim 1032

Neuron Operation Using Controlled Chaotic Instabilities in Brillouin-Active Fiber Based Neural Network in Smart Structures
Yong-Kab Kim, Jinsu Kim, Soonja Lim, Dong-Hyun Kim 1044

Parallel Genetic Algorithms on Programmable Graphics Hardware
Qizhi Yu, Chongcheng Chen, Zhigeng Pan 1051

Fuzzy Neural Systems and Soft Computing

A Neuro-fuzzy Approach to Part Fitup Fault Control During Resistance Spot Welding Using Servo Gun
Y.S. Zhang, G.L Chen 1060

Automatic Separate Algorithm of Vein and Artery for Auto-Segmentation Liver-Vessel from Abdominal MDCT Image Using Morphological Filtering
Chun-Ja Park, Eun-kyung Cho, Young-hee Kwon, Moon-sung Park, Jong-won Park 1069

Run-Time Fuzzy Optimization of IEEE 802.11 Wireless LANs Performance
Young-Joong Kim, Myo-Taeg Lim 1079

TLCD Semi-active Control Methodology of Fuzzy Neural Network for Eccentric Buildings
Hong-Nan Li, Qiao Jin, Gangbing Song, Guo-Xin Wang 1089

Use of Adaptive Learning Radial Basis Function Network in Real-Time Motion Tracking of a Robot Manipulator
Dongwon Kim, Sung-Hoe Huh, Sam-Jun Seo, Gwi-Tae Park 1099

Obstacle Avoidance for Redundant Nonholonomic Mobile Modular Manipulators via Neural Fuzzy Approaches
Yangmin Li, Yugang Liu 1109

Invasive Connectionist Evolution
Paulito P. Palmes, Shiro Usui 1119

Applying Advanced Fuzzy Cellular Neural Network AFCNN to
Segmentation of Serial CT Liver Images
Shitong Wang, Duan Fu, Min Xu, Dewen Hu 1128

New Algorithms of Neural Fuzzy Relation Systems with Min-implication
Composition
Yanbin Luo, K. Palaniappan, Yongming Li 1132

Neural Networks Combination by Fuzzy Integral in Clinical
Electromyography
Hongbo Xie, Hai Huang, Zhizhong Wang 1142

Long-Term Prediction of Discharges in Manwan Hydropower Using
Adaptive-Network-Based Fuzzy Inference Systems Models
Chun-Tian Cheng, Jian-Yi Lin, Ying-Guang Sun, Kwokwing Chau .. 1152

Vector Controlled Permanent Magnet Synchronous Motor Drive with
Adaptive Fuzzy Neural Network Controller
Xianqing Cao, Jianguang Zhu, Renyuan Tang 1162

Use of Fuzzy Neural Networks with Grey Relations in Fuzzy Rules
Partition Optimization
Hui-Chen Chang, Yau-Tarng Juang 1172

A Weighted Fuzzy Min-Max Neural Network and Its Application to
Feature Analysis
Ho-Joon Kim, Hyun-Seung Yang 1178

A Physiological Fuzzy Neural Network
Kwang-Baek Kim, Hae-Ryong Bea, Chang-Suk Kim 1182

Cluster-Based Self-organizing Neuro-fuzzy System with Hybrid
Learning Approach for Function Approximation
*Chunshien Li, Kuo-Hsiang Cheng, Chih-Ming Chen,
Jin-Long Chen* 1186

Fuzzy Output Support Vector Machines for Classification
Zongxia Xie, Qinghua Hu, Daren Yu 1190

Credit Rating Analysis with AFS Fuzzy Logic
Xiaodong Liu, Wanquan Liu 1198

A Neural-Fuzzy Based Inferential Sensor for Improving the Control of
Boilers in Space Heating Systems
  Zaiyi Liao 1205

A Hybrid Neuro-fuzzy Approach for Spinal Force Evaluation in Manual
Materials Handling Tasks
  *Yanfeng Hou, Jacek M. Zurada, Waldemar Karwowski,
  William S. Marras* 1216

Medicine Composition Analysis Based on PCA and SVM
  Chaoyong Wang, Chunguo Wu, Yanchun Liang 1226

Swarm Double-Tabu Search
  Wanhui Wen, Guangyuan Liu 1231

A Meta-heuristic Algorithm for the Strip Rectangular Packing Problem
  *Defu Zhang, Yanjuan Liu, Shengda Chen,
  Xiaogang Xie* 1235

Music Composition Using Genetic Algorithms (GA) and Multilayer
Perceptrons (MLP)
  Hüseyin Göksu, Paul Pigg, Vikas Dixit 1242

On the Categorizing of Simply Separable Relations in Partial
Four-Valued Logic
  Renren Liu, Zhiwei Gong, Fen Xu 1251

Equivalence of Classification and Regression Under Support Vector
Machine Theory
  Chunguo Wu, Yanchun Liang, Xiaowei Yang, Zhifeng Hao 1257

Fuzzy Description of Topological Relations I: A Unified Fuzzy
9-Intersection Model
  Shihong Du, Qiming Qin, Qiao Wang, Bin Li 1261

Fuzzy Description of Topological Relations II: Computation Methods
and Examples
  Shihong Du, Qiao Wang, Qiming Qin, Yipeng Yang 1274

Modeling and Cost Analysis of Nested Software Rejuvenation Policy
  Jing You, Jian Xu, Xue-long Zhao, Feng-yu Liu 1280

A Fuzzy Multi-criteria Decision Making Model for the Selection of the
Distribution Center
  Hsuan-Shih Lee 1290

Refinement of Clustering Solutions Using a Multi-label Voting
Algorithm for Neuro-fuzzy Ensembles
  Shuai Zhang, Daniel Neagu, Catalin Balescu 1300

Comparison of Meta-heuristic Hybrid Approaches for Two Dimensional
Non-guillotine Rectangular Cutting Problems
  Alev Soke, Zafer Bingul 1304

A Hybrid Immune Evolutionary Computation Based on Immunity and
Clonal Selection for Concurrent Mapping and Localization
  Meiyi Li, Zixing Cai, Yuexiang Shi, Pingan Gao 1308

Author Index 1313

Monitoring of Tool Wear Using Feature Vector Selection and Linear Regression

Zhong Chen and XianMing Zhang

College of Mechanical Engineering,
South China University of Technology, 510640 Guang Zhou, China
mezhchen@scut.edu.cn

Abstract. An approach for tool wear monitoring is presented, which bases on the Feature Vector Selection with Linear Regression (FVS-LR). In this approach, feature vectors are used to capture the geometrical characteristics of tool wear samples, and detection of tool wear is performed by using the model derived from the feature vectors in linear regression method. The signals of cutting force under the condition of tool non-wear and tool wear in 0.6 mm are used to testify the FVS-LR based method for monitoring of tool wear. The results indicate that tool wear can be successfully detected in this method, which is more suitable for the on-line detection in real time because of its efficient algorithm in learning stage and high computing speed in utilization stage.

1 Introduction

Although many non-traditional processing techniques have been emerging, many manufacturing processes still involve some aspects of metal cutting operations. In order to maximize the manufacturing processes in any typical metal cutting process, it is necessary to develop tool condition monitoring systems because tool failures adversely affect the surface finish of the workpiece and damage the machine tools.

Due to the complexity of metal cutting process, an accurate model for wear and breakage for cutting tools can not be obtained, so many researches present computation intelligent method for tool condition monitoring. These methods include fuzzy inference [1], neural networks [2], wavelet transforms [3], genetic algorithm, etc.. Resorting to the benefits of both fuzzy systems and neural networks, fuzzy neural networks (FNN) had been used successfully for tool condition monitoring [4]. But because of the opaque on neural networks and requirements in on-line monitoring in real time, it is necessary to develop new methods which embrace the on-line learning capability and on-line computation capability in real time. For supporting on-line learning of tool condition, the learning algorithm for small sets of samples should be utilized. Many kernel-based learning methods can be applied in the situation of small sets of samples , which include support vector machine (SVM) and feature vector selection with linear regression (FVS-LR) etc.. Because the model for tool wear is highly non-linear, its related sensor signals will embrace intrinsic non-linear characteristics. Hence, the learning algorithm for extraction of non-linear features of tool wear should be adopted. The support vector machine method has been presented in tool wear conditioning [5]. Other kernel-based algorithms also satisfy these requirements, such as kernel principal analysis (KPCA). But the KPCA is not suitable to on-line tool wear conditioning in real time because the KPCA needs to consume a lot of computation of matrix. According to the requirements of rapidity of learning and making decision, we will adopt the FVS-LR because of its less computation time with high performance of learning and making decision as the SVM does according to [6].

In the following, a kernel-based learning algorithm, FVS-LR [6], which characterizes in its learning efficient and rapidity in application stage will be detailed firstly. Then a research on detection of cutting tool wear using the PCA and the FVS-LR will be presented. Finally, a discussion of analytical results is also put forward.

2 Kernel-Based Method with the Feature Vector

Many linear learning methods can be used to solve the learning problem for non-linear features when the kernel method is adopted, for example, the kernel principle analysis, kernel fisher discrimination and SVM. Another kernel-base learning method like the SVM is the FVS-LR, which can efficiently captures the geometric characteristics with the selected feature vector also using kernel trick, and classifies the samples in a linear regression method. The FVS-LR will be described in the following.

2.1 Feature Vector Selection and Kernel-Based Projection [6]

Many kernel based learning method often consume many computation time, such as kernel principle analysis which refers to computation of kernel matrix and its centering in size of samples in learning and utilization stage. G. Baudat [6] presented a feature vector selection and linear regression (FVS-LR) method because the subspace in the mapping space exists, which has highly similar geometric characteristics in the feature space. The basic idea of the FVS-LR is that the feature vector selection in the subspace of the feature space can control the complexity of learning models which make a less generalization error.

The FVS-LR includes two parts: feature vector selection (FVS) and linear regression (LR). The FVS is a core of the FVS-LR, and the LR is a traditional mathematical method. In the algorithm of the FVS, the feature subspace is defined according to a global criterion, and then a searching process is iterated to find feature vectors. After the feature vectors of training samples is obtained, the input vectors can be projected into the feature space using the feature vectors and new data having high dimensional characteristics is obtained. Finally, the task of classification and function approximation can be implemented by only using traditional linear learning method for these new mapped data. The algorithm of the FVS presented by Baudat will be described simply in the following.

For a given set of the feature vectors, we can define the global fitness as

$$J_S = \frac{1}{M} \sum_{x_i \in \mathbf{X}} J_{Si} \quad (1)$$

where M is the size of the original samples and J_{Si} is the local fitness. According to [6], the feature selection can be expressed as an optimization problem in the following:

$$\max_S(J_S). \quad (2)$$

According to (1) and (2), the feature vectors of the training samples can be found iteratively. The feature vectors are selected according to the criterion, which is to minimize the minimal local fitness, keeps orthogonal of the feature vectors, and in every iteration, the global fitness increases gradually. The detail algorithm can be found in [6].

Finishing the feature vector selection, the input vector will be projected into the feature space F by (3):

$$z_i = \Phi_S^t \phi(x_i) \quad (3)$$

where Φ_S is the matrix of the selected vectors in F and $\phi(x_i)$ is real mapping of the original sample x_i.

2.2 Feature Vector Selection with Linear Regression (FVS-LR)

After projecting the input vectors into the feature subspace defined by the selected feature vectors, we can get the mapping z_i. Then we perform a linear regression analysis to data pair (z_i, y_i) according to (4), which y_i is an observation:

$$\hat{y}_i^t = z_i^t \mathbf{A} + \beta^t \quad (4)$$

where $\mathbf{A}$ is a coefficient matrix and β^t is a coefficient vector, which had been detailed in [6].

When the observation y_i satisfies the (4), we can make a decision boundary:

$$y_{ic} = \begin{cases} 1 & z_i \in \mathbf{C} \\ 0 & z_i \ni \mathbf{C} \end{cases} \quad (5)$$

where $\mathbf{C}$ is a kind of data class.

Hence, the important characteristic of the FVS-LR is high efficiency of learning and less consumption of computation in utilization stage. So the FVS-LR can be applied in on-line monitoring of tool wear in an embedded environment.

3 Analysis of Force Signals for Monitoring Tool Wear

3.1 The Setup

The setup is constructed of an old numerically controlled machine tool using a four toothes tool in diameter of 5 mm and a signal acquiring system with a force sensor of Kistler 9441 and a charge amplifier of Kistler 5006. The data set is acquired in the processing condition of main axle rotary speed in 700 RPM, feed rate in 10 mm per rotation and backing depth in 0.8 mm. In order to simulate the tool wear condition, we artificially wear the back lane of tool in 0.6 mm, simply noted as tool wear in 0.6 mm. So we prepare two data sets, which are data sets of tool wear in 0.6 mm and data sets of tool non-wear. From above, the important parameters are the frequency related to tool tooth which is 46.7 Hz and the frequency related to rotary speed of main axle which is 11.7 Hz. This paper will utilize the input vectors constructed by the power spectrum density at these frequencies.

3.2 Principle Component Extraction of Tool Wear Based on KPCA

Because the FVS-LR is considered as the approximation of the KPCA, we should analyze the training samples using the KPCA in order to get the more information for in-depth pattern recognition of tool wear before implementing the pattern recognition of tool condition using the FVS-LR.

There are 16 samples of tool wear in 0.6 mm and tool non-wear respectively. After analyzing the 32 samples using the KPCA, the principle component of first and second can be acquired. Meanwhile, the first principle component with eigenvalue 6.39 can extract the main geometric characteristics of the training samples and indicate clearly that the two class of tool wear in 0.6 mm and tool non-wear can be discriminated visually. And other principle components, such as second principle component, can be considered as the unrelated component with these two classes of training samples. Obviously, based on the principle component related to tool wear mode extracted by the KPCA, the discriminating models for tool wear conditioning can be built. But utilization of the KPCA in tool wear monitoring in real time is not suitable because it needs more computation consumption and computation power in its utilization stage.

3.3 Detection of Tool Wear Based on the FVS-LR

As above, the 16 training samples including 8 training samples for tool wear in 0.6 mm and 8 training samples for tool non-wear will be taken in the research of tool wear detection using the FVS-LR . In training stage, 1 feature vector could be captured in stop condition with global fitness in 0.9; 2 feature vectors in stop condition with global fitness in 0.99; 3 feature vectors in stop condition with global fitness in 0.999. So a few feature vectors can describe the input samples using the FVS-LR. This paper adopts the detection model in feature space while the stop condition with global fitness is 0.999. Then we utilize this model to recognize the tool wear for all 32 samples including 16 training samples. The result is depicted in fig.1. When 0.5 and 0.2-0.8 threshold is used to gate the value obtained from the model, the detection result is shown in table 1, where the non-hit percentage is based on all 32 samples.

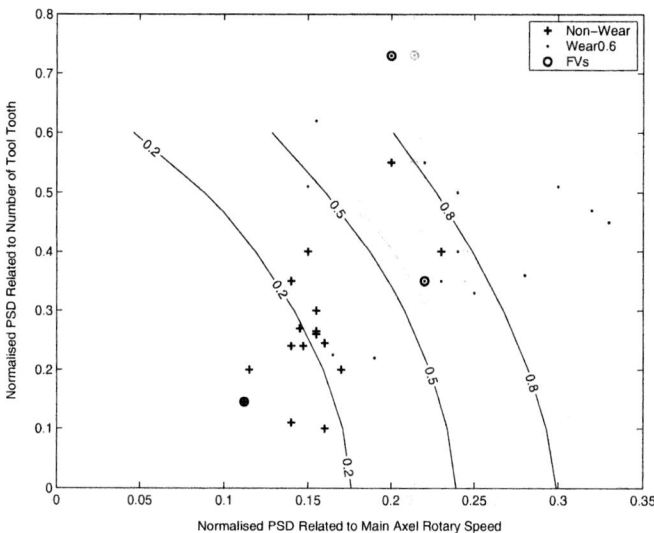

Fig. 1. Pattern Recognition of Tool Wear Based on the FVS-LR. The number on the solid line represents the decision level of recognition of tool wear. This figure indicates that there are 3 feature vectors selected with a global fitness in 0.999.

Table 1. Statistical Results of Detection of Tool Wear

Threshold	0.5	0.2-0.8
Tool wear in 0.6mm		
Hit%	85.72%	100%
Non-hit%	9.38%	21.88%
Tool non-wear		
Hit%	81.25%	100%
Non-hit%	6.25%	25%

3.4 Discussions

As above, the KPCA and the FVS-LR are same in some aspects that they both exploit the kernel trick and refers to learning in the mapped feature space, and they can extract the nonlinear geometric component of the original samples. The result indicates that detection precision of tool wear satisfied even if the size of training samples is small. More training samples, more high precision of detection of tool wear. And Extending the training samples makes a little affect on the rapidity of detection of tool wear because the FVS-LR doesn't need much computation of matrix in utilization stage, and the number of feature vectors is similar with the number of support vectors of the SVM while keeping the same learning performance [6].

4 Conclusions

After analyzing the cutting force signals using the KPCA and the FVS-LR respectively, the conclusions could be drawn as the following:

1. It is not suitable for on-line real time tool wear monitoring by directly utilizing the KPCA.
2. Implementing the algorithm of the FVS-LR in analysis of tool cutting force signals, less feature vectors could be captured and these feature vectors could be used to detect tool wear failure successfully in the experiment.
3. The FVS-LR is suitable for tool wear monitoring in real time because of its characteristics that is high efficiency in learning stage and rapidity in utilization stage.

Acknowledgement. The financial support from the National Natural Science Fund of China under the grant No.305B5580 is gratefully acknowledged.

References

1. Du, R.X., Elbestawi, M.A., Li, S.: Tool Condition Monitoring in Turning Using Fuzzy Set Theory. International Journal of Machine Tools and Manufacture, Vol.32, No.6, (1992) 781–796
2. Brezak, D., Udiljak, T., Mihoci, K., Majetic, D., Novakovic, B., Kasac, J.: Tool wear monitoring using radial basis function neural network. Proceedings of 2004 IEEE International Joint Conference on Neural Networks, Vol.3, (2004) 1859 – 1862
3. Tansel, I.N., Mekdeci, C., McLaughlin, C.: Detection of Tool Failure in End Milling with Wavelet Transformations and Neural Networks (WT-NN), International Journal of Machine Tools and Manufacture, vol.35, no.8 (1995) 1137–1147
4. Li, S., Yao, Y., Yuan, Z.: On-line Tool Condition Monitoring with Improved Fuzzy Neural Network, High Technology Letters, vol.3, no. 1 (1997) 30–33
5. Sun, J., Hong, G. S., Rahman, M., Wong, Y. S.: The Application of Nonstandard Support Vector Machine in Tool Condition Monitoring System. Second IEEE International Workshop on Electronic Design, Test and Applications (2004) 295-300
6. Baudat G., Anouar F.: Feature vector selection and projection using kernel. Neurocomputing, Vol.55 (2003) 21–38

Image Synthesis and Face Recognition Based on 3D Face Model and Illumination Model

Dang-hui Liu[1,2], Lan-sun Shen[1], and Kin-man Lam[3]

[1] Signal and Information Processing Laboratory, Beijing University of Technology,
Beijing, China 100022
liuliu_1998@yahoo.com, slx@bjut.edu.cn
[2] The Academy of Equipment, Command and Technology, Huairou District,
Beijing, China 101416
[3] The Centre for Multimedia Signal Processing, The Hong Kong Polytechnic University,
Hong Kong, China
enlamkm@polyu.edu.hk

Abstract. The performance of human face recognition algorithms is seriously affected by two important factors: head pose and lighting condition. The effective processing of the pose and illumination variations is a vital key for improving the recognition rate. This paper proposes a novel method that can synthesize images with different head poses and lighting conditions by using a modified 3D CANDIDE model, linear vertex interpolation and NURBS curve surface fitting method, as well as a mixed illumination model. A specific Eigenface method is also proposed to perform face recognition based on a pre-estimated head pose method. Experimental results show that the quality of the synthesized images and the recognition performance are good.

1 Introduction

As human beings discriminate different persons mostly by face appearances, the face is therefore the most natural biometric other than fingerprint, palmprint, iris, voice, and handwriting. Nevertheless, research on automatic machine recognition of a human face did not obtain a revolutionary breakthrough until the 1990's [1].

In fact, the appearance of a face will vary drastically when its pose and lighting conditions change. Variations in head pose and lighting conditions make face recognition a very challenging and difficult task. In recent years, many researchers have focused on investigating some more efficient and reliable algorithms for automatic machine recognition of a face [2]. Pentland et al. [3] first proposed a view-based method for solving the head-pose variation problem. Yan et al. [4] adopted a view-based method for face recognition by means of a complicated 3D wireframe face model generated from two orthogonal photos. However, no illumination variation was considered in these methods. Georghiades et al. [5] proposed an illumination cone method for solving the variations of head pose and lighting conditions, but many images captured under different lighting conditions were required to reconstruct a 3D facial surface. Blanz et al. [6] proposed a 3D morphable model method based on a special 3D face database captured by a 3D laser scanner, but the computational burden is very large. Moreover, the 3D morphable model cannot be generated without the special 3D face database.

However, a frontal and a profile photo can be easily obtained by using common cameras in many real applications. Our method uses these two orthogonal photos to create a 3D facial model. Differently from [4], however, our algorithm adopts a simple 3D wireframe model so as to make it computationally efficient. More importantly, the difficult problem of combined variations of head pose and lighting conditions can be solved with our method.

2 Generation of 3D Face Model

A 3D wireframe face model can generally be created by using five different approaches: (1) 3D laser scanner, (2) two orthogonal photos [7], (3) only one frontal photo [8], (4) multiple images from video [9], and (5) 3D morphable model [6]. The second approach can usually obtain a good visual effect and requires simple operations for generating the 3D wireframe face model. The CANDIDE model is a parameterized face model specifically developed for the model-based coding of human faces [10]. For face recognition, we further modify the CANDIDE-3.1.6 model by adding or deleting some feature points, and the new modified model is illustrated in Figure 1. The detection algorithm for the facial feature points [11] can locate some prominent points in both a frontal face image and a profile image. A reference 3D face wireframe model can be adjusted for different image pairs based on the inverse distance interpolation method [12]. A realistic 3D synthesized face image is then generated by means of the texture mapping.

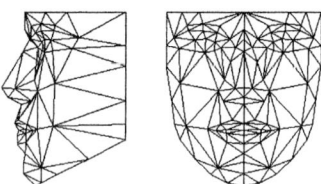

Fig. 1. A new modified model

3 Curve Surface Fitting and Image Synthesization

Due to the discontinuity of the surface directions of neighboring triangles in the simple 3D wireframe face model, the discontinuous changes of illumination on synthesized images become very obvious when a ray is cast onto the model surface. This causes an unrealistic visual effect on the synthesized images. The Phong light and shade processing [13] can be used to smooth the illumination variation, but it is not good for the simple model. A local quadratic Bezier surface-fitting algorithm [14] has been proposed, but it is only good for complex 3D wireframe face models consisting of a large number of vertexes. We therefore propose to use the NBURS function to fit the whole 3D face surface, rather than using local 3D curve surfaces. Moreover, the NBURS function has many merits over the Bezier function [13].

The modified 3D wireframe face model consists of a series of irregular vertexes. However, a 2D control point array is required to fit the facial surface by using a

NURBS surface function. We propose a linear interpolation approach to generate some new accessional vertexes from the irregular vertexes. The array of control points for NURBS surface fitting consists of both the accessional vertexes and original vertexes. Fig.2 (a) shows all the vertexes and the triangular meshes, while the big black dots denote the original vertexes in the 3D wireframe face model and the small black dots denote the interpolated vertexes. In the experiments, we use a thrice NURBS function that can fit an arbitrary surface. Fig.2 (b) and (c) shows the reflection characteristics of the original triangular surfaces and the new NURBS fitting surface when a frontal point light source is employed. It is clear that the NURBS fitting surface is very smooth and has a better reflection effect.

An object is usually illuminated by both the environmental light and a certain light source without considering the object's irradiance. Therefore, the reflected light from an object can be considered to consist of the reflection of ambient light, the diffused reflection of incidence light, and the mirror reflection of incidence light. For a point light source, the reflection light Y is computed as follows [13]:

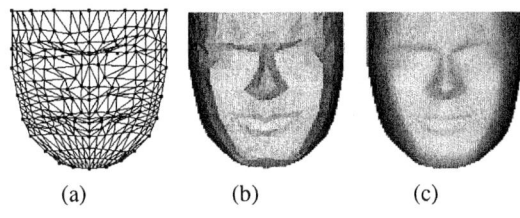

Fig. 2. (a) Regularized control points, (b)The reflection characteristics of the original triangular surface, and (c) The reflection characteristics of the NURBS surface

$$Y = Y_a + Y_d + Y_s = K_a I_a + K_d I \cos\theta + k_s I (\cos\phi)^{n_s}. \tag{1}$$

If a certain directional point-light source illuminates a face, cast shading will exist in the face image since the ray is possibly sheltered by the facial convexity characteristics. The cast-shading region can be located by means of the height of each surface point and the incidence light direction. Only reflection of the ambient light is computed for the cast-shading region, and Eq. (1) is used to compute the total reflection light at other facial surface points. Two synthesized images with cast-shading region and arbitrary head pose are illustrated in Fig. 3.

Fig. 3. Two synthesized images with cast-shading region and arbitrary head pose

4 Face Recognition

Ten persons were selected in the experiments. A frontal view and a profile view of each person are used to generate a specific 3D wireframe face model. Fig. 4 shows these images.

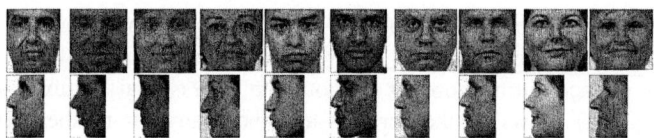

Fig. 4. The frontal and profile photos of ten persons

We need to synthesize some images illuminated by a single point-light source. Let θ_{ly} and θ_{lx} be the angle between the point-light source and the y-axis and x-axis, respectively. Let θ_{py} and θ_{px} be the rotation angles of the 3D facial model around the y-axis and x-axis, respectively. Considering the symmetrical characteristic of human faces, we only synthesize images of 70 different head poses by varying θ_{py} in the range of (0°, 90°) and θ_{px} in the range of (-30°, 30°) in the experiments. A mirror image can then be obtained from a synthesized image by using a mirror operation. For each of the head poses of each person, PCA [4] is applied to the 248 images synthesized under the different lighting conditions to obtain eigenface ϕ_{ij} (i denotes the i-th person and j denotes the j-th head pose), which capture over 99% of the image variations of the synthesized images. We also pre-estimate the head pose in a query image so as to effectively reduce the computational burden. The proposed face recognition algorithm is described as follows:

(1) A query image is first projected onto the ϕ_{ij} s ($1 \le i \le M, 1 \le j \le 70$) of the first M persons.

(2) For each of the first M persons, K ϕ_{ij} s is recorded when the mean squared errors between the query face image and its constructed images based on these ϕ_{ij} s are smaller than based on other ϕ_{ij} s.

(3) The (M*K) ϕ_{ij} s of the first M persons is re-ordered by the mean squared errors. The first P head poses corresponding to the ϕ_{ij} s are recorded. That is, the head pose in the query image belongs to one of the P possible head poses that are estimated by the ϕ_{ij} s ($1 \le i \le M, 1 \le j \le 70$) of the first M persons.

(4) The query image is then projected only onto all the remaining ϕ_{ij} ($M < i \le N$, where N is the number of persons in the gallery; $j \in P$, where P are the possible head poses estimated in step (3)) to largely reduce the computational burden.

Our proposed method was evaluated using 1,000 query images of the ten persons under different lighting conditions and head poses. That is, each person has 100 query images and the lighting conditions and head poses are random. The individual recognition rates are given in Table 1. The average recognition rate is 96.5%.

Table 1. The individual recognition rates (IRR) for the ten test subjects

No.	1	2	3	4	5	6	7	8	9	10
IRR(%)	96	97	99	99	96	94	94	98	94	98

5 Conclusions

We propose a modified CANDIDE model, a linear interpolation method of the vertexes, a NURBS fitting method, and a ray-tracing method for synthesizing images and face recognition. Experimental results demonstrate that our proposed method is effective under different head poses and lighting conditions.

Acknowledgements

The work was supported by National Natural Science Foundation of China (60172045, 60402036), Beijing Natural Science Foundation of China (4042008), Beijing Education Council (200410005022), and by a grant from the Research Grants Council of the Hong Kong Administrative Region, China (Project No. PolyU 5208/04E).

References

1. Chellappa, R., Wilson, C.L., Sirohey, S., SiroheyHuman, S.: Machine recognition of faces: a survey. Proceedings of the IEEE, Vol. 83, No. 5, (1995) 705-740
2. Liu, D.H., Shen L.S., Lam, K.M.: Face Recognition: A Survey. Chinese Journal of Circuits and Systems, Vol. 9, No. 2, (2004) 85-94
3. Pentland, A., Moghaddam, B. Starner, T.: View-based and modular eigenspaces for face recognition. IEEE Computer Society Conference on CVPR, (1994) 84-91
4. Yan J., Zhang, H. J.: Synthesized virtual view-based eigenspace for face recognition. Fifth IEEE Workshop on Applications of Computer Vision, (2000) 85-90
5. Georghiades S., Belhumeur, P.N., David J.K.: From few to many: illumination cone models for face recognition under variable lighting and pose. IEEE Trans. on PAMI, Vol. 23, No.2, (2001) 643-660
6. Blanz, V., Vetter, T.: Face Recognition Based on Fitting a 3D Morphable Model. IEEE Trans. On PAMI, Vol. 25, No. 9, (2003) 1-12
7. Tang, L., Huang, T.S.: Automatic construction of 3D human face models based on 2D images. In Proceedings of IEEE ICIP, 10 (1996) 467-470
8. Chung J.K., Huang,R.S., Lin, T.G., 3-D Facial model estimation from single Front-view Facial Image, IEEE Trans. on CSVT, Vol. 12, No. 3, (2002) 183-192
9. Siu, M., Chan, Y.H., Siu, W.C.: A robust model generation technology for model-based video coding. IEEE Trans. on CSVT, Vol. 11, No. 11, (2001) 1188-1192
10. Ahlberg, J.: CANDIDE-3—An updated parameterized face, http:// www.icg.isy.liu.se.
11. Wu L.F.: Researches on Image Retrieval Based on Face Object, PHD Thesis, Beijing University of Technology (2003)
12. Li M.D., Ruan Q.Q.: An interactive adaptation method of 3-D facial wireframe model. Chinese Journal of Image and Graphic, Vol. 7A, No. 8, (2002) 818-823
13. Hearn D., Baker, M.P.: Computer Graphic. Prentice Hall Press (2000)
14. Yan J.: Two Methods of Displaying Realistic Three Dimensional Synthesized Human Face Graphics, Chinese Computer Engineering, Vol. 24, No. 1, (1998) 49-52

Head-and-Shoulder Detection in Varying Pose

Yi Sun, Yan Wang, Yinghao He, and Yong Hua

School of Electronic and Information Engineering,
Dalian University of Technology, Dalian, P.R.C. 116024
lslwf@dlut.edu.cn

Abstract. Head-and-shoulder detection has been an important research topic in the fields of image processing and computer vision. In this paper, a head-and-shoulder detection algorithm based on wavelet decomposition technique and support vector machine (SVM) is proposed. Wavelet decomposition is used to extract features from real images, and linear SVM and non-linear SVM are trained for detection. Non-head-and-shoulder images can be removed by the linear SVM firstly, and then non-linear SVM detects head-and-shoulder images in detail. Varying head-and-shoulder pose can be detected from frontal and side views, especially from rear view. The experiment results prove that the method proposed is effective and fast to some extent.

1 Introduction

Head-and-shoulder detection plays an important role in object detection especially in face detection and human motion detection. It can be used in a wide range of applications such as visual surveillance, virtual reality, advanced human-interface system, motion analysis and model-based coding, etc [1]. In recent years, the typical approach in head-and-shoulder detection is template matching. Hyeon [2] built a model by using curvature for upper body of human. Broggi [3] and Beymer [4] used a Ω model which had different scales to describe the upper body. Govindaraju et al [5-8] proposed the method of facial detection based on the geometry properties of face profile. It was used to detect head-and-shoulder, but needed prior information and had high error. And to some extent, profile extraction was difficult for complex background images. Besides template matching, statistical learning theory is a recent popular topic in object detection. It has higher reliability and is independent of prior information and parameter models. Papageorgiou's system had reported successful results detecting frontal, rear and side views of people by using Support Vector Machine (SVM) classifiers. Details were presented by Papageorgiou etc [9, 10, 11]. However, the system's ability to detect people whose body parts had little contrast with the background was limited. The method presented in reference [12] was useful to detect head-and-shoulder and partially occluded people. This system detected people who were slightly rotated in depth, while it did not determine the extent of this capability. Fang and Qiu [13] proposed a new method for face detection based on angular radial transform and support vector machine. They also presented a fast processing scheme, but this fast processing scheme was based on skin color detection. Most algorithms mentioned above detected people only from frontal views, so detecting people from an arbitrary viewpoint is also interesting to study. In this paper, we propose an algorithm based on wavelet decomposition technique and combined support vector machines (SVMs). This system can detect head-and-shoulder of varying poses in the cluttered scenes, and it improves detection speed and reduces dimensionality. We use wavelet transform to extract features and reduce the dimension of feature vectors. The combination of the linear SVM and the non-linear SVM ensures the accuracy and speed of the detection system. The system can detect head-and-shoulder from frontal, and side views of people, especially from rear view. The goal of head-and-shoulder detection in this paper is to determine the location and dimension of head-and-shoulders in the image.

2 Head-and-Shoulder Detection

2.1 System Framework

Fig.1. shows the SVM training and head-and-shoulder detection framework. The left part is the training procedure of linear SVM and non-linear SVM, and right part is head-and-shoulder detection procedure.

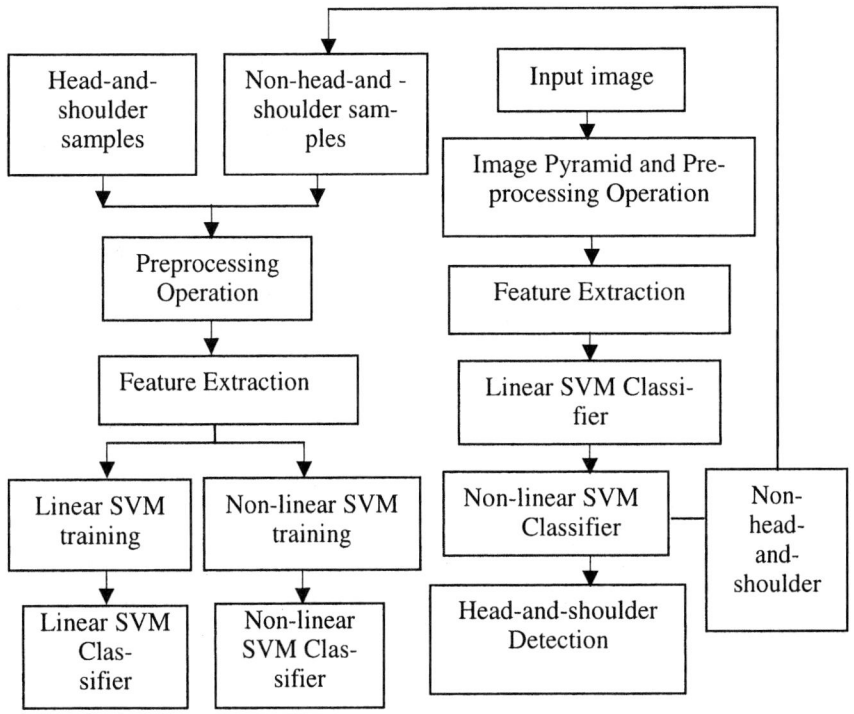

Fig. 1. System Framework

In training procedure, lots of head-and-shoulder samples and non-head-and-shoulder samples are collected to train the Linear SVM and non-linear SVM. Before Training, we have preprocessed these samples and extracted features from them. We can use the trained SVMs as the linear SVM classifier and non-linear SVM classifier.

In the detecting procedure, we generate the image pyramid and preprocess it, and then extract features from the preprocessed image. Input this image features into the linear SVM classifier, we can get rid of non-head-and-shoulder image. Then we input head-and-shoulder image from linear SVM classifier into non-linear SVM classifier. If the result from non-linear SVM classifier is the head-and-shoulder, we show the location and dimension of the head and shoulder in the image. If non-head-and-shoulder images are detected from the non-linear SVM classifier, these non-head-and-shoulder images are regarded as non-head-and-shoulder samples to train the SVMs again.

2.2 Feature Extraction

It is difficult to extract the object from a complex scene. According to the shape properties of head-and-shoulder, the image is preprocessed by a shape filter firstly, and a part of its background can be removed. Fig.2. shows the preprocessing procedure.

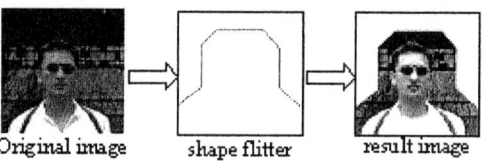

Fig. 2. Shape Filter

In order to process the image effectively and fast, we often transform the image data into a special space. This transformation should have enough initial information to ensure the accuracy and small dimension to simplify the calculation. After preprocessing, we choose wavelet transformation and use the decomposed wavelet coefficients as the features of the image.

Wavelet has good multi-resolution function [14]. We can use wavelet transformation to decompose an image into many "subbands" which are located in frequency and orientation. In this paper, we use Haar wavelet to decompose the image into four subbands: LL, HL, LH, HH. Each subband can be considered as a version of the original image which represents different image properties. The LL subband includes low-frequency information of original image, so the edge of the image is not clear. The detail information is represented by the LH, HL, HH subbands.

Fig.3. shows the result of the wavelet decomposition. Because the LL subband includes most of original image information, we choose the coefficients of LL subband to train the linear SVM and non-linear SVM. These coefficients represent the shape information and gray level distribution of image. Then according to these coefficients, we can classify images to two patterns—head-and- shoulder (from frontal, rear and side views) and non-head-and-shoulder.

Fig. 3. Result of Wavelet Decomposition

2.3 Support Vector Machine

2.3.1 Support Vector Machine Training

Support vector machine (SVM) is a new classifier which provides a novel approach for pattern recognition. SVM is based on a new statistical learning technique which is developed by Vapnik and his team at AT&T Bell Labs [15, 16, 17]. The theory of SVM has been developed in the past 20 years, while their application to real-life pattern recognition [9, 10, 18, 19] is developed recently. The experts pay more attention to this. SVM is a maximum margin classification tool based on Structural Risk Minimization (SRM) principle. In theory it is better than those methods based on Empirical Risk Minimization (ERM) principle. SRM minimizes an upper bound on the expected risk, as opposed to ERM that minimizes the error on the training data [20].

Given samples (x_i, y_i), $x_i \in R^n$, $y_i \in \{-1, +1\}$, $i = 1, ..., l$ (where l is the total of the samples, x_i is the element of the samples, and y_i is the classification result of x_i) and a kernel function $K(x_i, x_j)$. We can get α_i ($i = 1, ..., l$) by computing the maximum of W as formula (1).

$$W(\alpha) = \sum_{i=1}^{l} \alpha_i - \frac{1}{2} \sum_{i,j=1}^{l} \alpha_i \alpha_j y_i y_j K(x_i, x_j) . \tag{1}$$

The α_i is the Lagrange multiplier and it must accord with $0 \leq \alpha_i \leq C$ and $\sum_{i=1}^{l} \alpha_i y_i = 0$, where C is a defined constant which controls misclassification errors. All the x_i in the case of $\alpha_i \neq 0$ compose the Support Vectors (SVs). Then we can get the classifier function as following:

$$f(x) = Sign(\sum_{x_i \in SVs} \alpha_i y_i K(x_i, x) + b) . \tag{2}$$

$$b = -\frac{1}{2} \sum_{x_i \in SVs} \alpha_i y_i [K(x_r, x_i) + K(x_s, x_i)] \tag{3}$$

Where x_r, x_s are different types of SVs [20].

Table 1. Common Kernel Function

Kernel Function	Type of Classifier
$K(x, x_i) = (x^T x_i + 1)^d$	Polynomial of degreed
$K(x, x_i) = \exp(-|x - x_i|^2 / \sigma^2)$	Gaussian RBF
$K(x, x_i) = \tanh(v(x \bullet x_i) + c)$	Sigmoid

In Table 1 we list common kernel function.

Plat [21] developed a fast algorithm for training SVM called SMO (Sequential Minimal Optimization) which makes it possible for PC users to practice on complex applications. In this paper, we implement this algorithm for head-and-shoulder detection. The procedure detail is described in the following steps:

Step 1): Initialize the vector α. In general, $\alpha = 0$.

Step 2): Choose two elements in the vector α at random at the beginning and label them as α_1^{old} and α_2^{old}. Then calculate E_1 and E_2:

$$E_1 = f(x_1) - y_1 . \qquad (4)$$

$$E_2 = f(x_2) - y_2 . \qquad (5)$$

where $f(x)$ is classifier function; x_1 is the sample corresponding to α_1; y_1 is the classification result of x_1; x_2 and y_2 are same as x_1 and y_1. If E_1 and E_2 are less than the defined error, finish the training; otherwise go to step 3.

Step 3): In the next step of recursion, choose two elements in the vector α at random again, and label them as α_1^{new} and α_2^{new}. We can get α_1^{new} and α_2^{new} as following:

$$\alpha_2^{new} = \alpha_2^{old} + \frac{y_2(E_1 - E_2)}{\kappa} \qquad (6)$$

$$\alpha_1^{new} = \alpha_1^{old} + y_1 y_2 (\alpha_2^{old} - \alpha_2^{new}) \qquad (7)$$

$$\kappa = \|\Phi(x_1) - \Phi(x_2)\|^2 \qquad (8)$$

Where $\Phi(\bullet)$ is the kernel function.

Step 4): Calculate E_1 and E_2 using α_1^{new} and α_2^{new} as formula (4) and formula (5). If E_1 and E_2 are not according with the defined error, go to step 2; otherwise finish the training.

2.3.2 Combined SVMs

To some extent the speed of the detection system is decided by the complexity degree of SVM. The complexity degree of non-linear SVM is higher than the linear SVM, while its accuracy is also higher. Combined the linear SVM and non-linear SVM, we can get new SVMs, which can ensure the speed and accuracy of the detection system. Table2 gives the complexity degree of linear SVM and non-linear SVM.

Table 2. The Complexity Degree of Linear SVM and Non-linear SVM

	classifier function	complexity degree
Linear SVM	$\text{sgn}(\omega \bullet x + b)$	N
non-linear SVM	$\text{sgn}(\sum_{i=1}^{L} \alpha_i K(x \bullet x_i) + b)$	$L \times N + O(L)$

Where N is the dimension of model vector, and L is the number of support vectors. N is independent of L and in fact, it is the total numbers of the pixels of per sample image. For example, if the sample image is 16×16 pixels, N is 256. Generally, when the number of support vectors increases, the complexity degree of non-linear SVM is much higher than the linear SVM, which leads to lower speed of the detection system, while the single linear SVM can not get good accuracy.

Based on the analysis above, we propose to use a linear SVM to classify the head-and-shoulder images roughly, so a lot of non-head-and-shoulder images can be removed. The rest images are detected carefully by the non-linear SVM with Gaussian RBF kernel function. The ideal result is to get rid of the non-head-and-shoulder images as possible as we can by the linear SVM, moreover, the good accuracy is obtained as well. To some extent the combined SVMs are the ideal classifier which we find. It has not only the fast speed of linear SVM but also the good accuracy of the non-linear SVM. The detection steps using the combined SVMs in this paper are described as following:

(1) Extract the features from the preprocessed sample images using the wavelet decomposition, and then use these features to train the combined SVMs which include a linear SVM and a non-linear SVM with Gaussian RBF kernel function.

(2) Detect all the images roughly using the linear SVM, so the most of non-head-and-shoulder images are removed.

(3) Detect the head-and-shoulder in the rest images in detail and give the location and dimension of the head-and-shoulder.

3 Experiments and Results

The linear SVM and non-linear SVM are trained on 1532 positive images and 2340 negative images(32×32 pixels). The positive examples are head-and-shoulders of people in various environments, both indoors and outdoors and in various poses. The negative examples are taken from scenes that do not contain any people. In detecting

Fig. 4. Result of Detection

procedure, we have detected 85 gray images including 153 heads-and-shoulders. The background of these images is from simple to complex, and people in the images have different poses. We can detect not only single person but also multiple people. It takes 39.32 seconds to detect 400×112 pixels image, which includes loading the image, detecting and showing the location and dimension. All the experiments are made under circumstance as follows: 1) Matlab language; 2) P4 CPU; 3)256M RAM. Fig.4. shows the detecting result of different images.

In Fig.4, the detecting result demonstrates the capability of the system. It can detect running people, people who are rotated, people whose body parts blend into the background (first row, third from left), and people under varying lighting conditions. Out of 153 head-and-shoulders in 85 images, 134 head-and-shoulders (87.58%) are correctly detected. There are 19 missing persons (second row, first from left) because of selection of samples. And there are two windows on one head-and-shoulder (second row, fifth and seventh from left) because the data in the two windows are all according with the pattern of head-and-shoulder. The system can shows all the windows in which the image data are classified as the pattern of head-and-shoulder.

In order to compare the capability of combined SVMs with the single linear SVM and non-linear SVM, we experiment with 171 head-and-shoulder images and 122 non-head-and-shoulder images (32×32 pixels) and record the time and accuracy. The single linear SVM costs 0.312 seconds and its accuracy is 69.6%. The detecting time of non-linear SVM is 0.391 seconds and the accuracy is 89%. If we use combined SVMs, it takes 0.344 seconds to detect images and 88% images are correctly detected.

4 Conclusions

In this paper, a head-and-shoulder detection algorithm is presented. We use wavelet decomposition to extract features and use linear SVM and non-linear SVM to detect. Wavelet transformation ensures the accuracy and simplification of calculation for training. In detecting, we first use linear SVM to get rid of non-head-and-shoulder images, and then use non-linear SVM to detect head-and-shoulder in detail. Accordingly, we not only ensure the accuracy, but also improve the speed of detection. The detecting images include simple background、complex background、single person and multiple people from front and back. And we get a higher accuracy, especially from back. The training samples are images from different views, which ensures the detecting accuracy of images from frontal and rear views are the same. Through experiments, we get the accuracy of 87.58 %. On the other hand, there are also missing persons in detection. The error rate is 12.42%. Perhaps, this can be attributed to selection of the samples.

Future research should be directed toward addressing the following issues:

(1) In detecting color images, we can use other coarse methods. For example, extract human area according to skin color.

(2) Multi-classifiers is a focus in this field. How to combine the different classifiers is an important problem. Whether the multi-classifier is better than single classifier needs further research.

References

1. Yi Sun et al: 2D Recovery of Human Posture. Proceedings of the First International Conference on Machine Learning and Cybernetics, Beijing (2002)1638-1640.
2. D. H. Hyeon et al.: Human Detection in Images Using Curvature Model. International Conference on Circuits/Systems Computers and Communications (ITC-CSCC) (2001).
3. A. Broggi et al: Shape-based Pedestrian Detection. Proceedings of the IEEE Intelligent Vehicles Symposium, (2000) 215-220.
4. D. Beymer, K. Konolige: Real-time tracking of multiple people using continuous detection . Proceedings of IEEE International Conference on Computer Vision (1999).
5. Venu Govindaraju, Sargur. N. Srihari, David B. Sher: A computational model for face location. Proceedings of the IEEE Third International Conference on Computer Vision, (1991) 718-721.
6. Venu Govindaraju, David B. Sher, Rohini K. Srihari: Locating human faces in newspaper photographs. Proceedings of IEEE Computer Society Conference on Computer Vision and Pattern Recognition, (1989) 549-554.
7. Venu Govindaraju, Sargur. N. Srihari, DavidS her: A computational model for face location based on cognitive principles. Proceedings of the American Association for Artificial Intelligence (AAAI), (1992)350-355.
8. Venu Govindaraju: Locating human faces in photographs. International Journal of Computer Vision, Vol.19. (1996) 129-146.
9. C. Papageorgiou, T. Poggio: A Trainable System for Object Detection. International Journal of Computer Vision, Vol.38. (2000)15-33.
10. Micheal Oren et al: Pedestrian detection using wavelets templates. Proceedings of Computer Society Conference on Computer Vision and Pattern Recognition, (1997) 193-199.
11. C. P. Papageorgiou, M. Oren, T. Poggio: A general framework for object detection. Sixth International Conference on Computer Vision, (1998)555-562.
12. A. Mohan, C. Papageorgiou, T. Poggio: Example-based object detection in images by components. IEEE Transactions on Pattern Analysis and Machine Intelligence, Vol.23. (2001) 349-361.

13. J. Fang, G. Qiu: Human face detection using angular radial transform and support vector machines. Proceedings of International Conference on Image Processing, Vol.1. (2003) 669-672.
14. S. G. Mallat: A Theory for Multiresolution Signal Decomposition: The Wavelet Representation. IEEE Transactions on Pattern Analysis and Machine Intelligence, Vol.11. (1989) 674-693.
15. B. E. Boser, I. M. Guyon, V. N. Vapnik: A training algorithm for optimal margin classifier. Proceedings of 5th ACM Workshop on Computational Learning Theory, (1992)144-152.
16. C.J.C. Burges: Simplified support vector decision rules. International Conference on Machine Learning, (1996)71-77.
17. C. Cortes, V. Vapnik: Support vector networks. Machine Learning, Vol.20. (1995)1-25.
18. E. Osuna, R. Freund, F. Girosi: Training support vector machines: an application to face detection. Proceedings of IEEE Computer Society Conference on Computer Vision and Pattern Recognition, (1997)130-136.
19. T. Joachims: Text Categorization with Support Vector Machines: Learning with Many Relevant Features. Proceedings of 10th Conference on Machine Learning, (1998).
20. S.R. Gunn: Support Vector Machines for Classification and Regression. Technical Report, Image Speech and Intelligent Systems Research group, University of Southampton, (1997).
21. J.C. Platt: Sequential Minimal Optimization: A Fast Algorithm for Training Support Vector Machines. Technical Report MSR-TR-98-14(1998).

Principal Component Neural Networks Based Intrusion Feature Extraction and Detection Using SVM

Hai-Hua Gao[1], Hui-Hua Yang[1,2], and Xing-Yu Wang[1,*]

[1] School of Information Science and Engineering,
East China University of Science and Technology, Shanghai 200237, China
hhgao@tom.com, xywang@ecust.edu.cn
[2] Department of Computer Science, Guilin University of Electronic Technology,
Guilin 541004, China
yang98@gliet.edu.cn

Abstract. Very little research on feature extraction has been taken in the field of network intrusion detection. This paper proposes a novel method of applying principal component neural networks for intrusion feature extraction, and then the extracted features are employed by SVM for classification. The adaptive principal components extraction (APEX) algorithm is adopted for the implementation of PCNN. The MIT's KDD Cup99 dataset is used to evaluate the proposed method compared to SVM without application of feature extraction technique, which clearly demonstrates that PCNN-based feature extraction method can greatly reduce the dimension of input space without degrading or even boosting the performance of intrusion detection system.

1 Introduction

With the development of computer network technology and application, network security is becoming increasingly important. Despite the effort devoted to carefully design and implementation of intrusion prevention techniques such as encryption, network security is still difficult to guarantee because there are always exploitable weakness or bugs in system and application software. Intrusion Detection Systems (IDS), act as the "second line of defense" is becoming a critical technology to protect computer network systems [1]. Intrusion Detection is defined as "the process of identifying that an intrusion has been attempted, is occurring, or has occurred" [2], and there are two main categories for its method. One is misuse detection and the other is anomaly detection. In the anomaly detection method, a model called a profile is developed based on the normal access patterns and any activity that deviates from the predefined profile is regarded as intrusion.

In order to evaluate and compare the performance of applying varied machine learning methods to anomaly detection, the 1998 DARPA network intrusion detection evaluation project was conducted by MIT Lincoln Lab. They set up an environment to

---

* Author for Correspondence. This work was supported by National Science Foundation (No. 69974014) and Doctorate Foundation of the Education Ministry of China (No.20040251010), China.

dump raw TCP/IP data from a local-area network simulating that of a typical U.S. Air Force. These data were reduced and processed by domain experts to form a data set for 3rd KDD competition. Many researches that apply machine learning methods such as artificial immune theory [3], Bayesian parameter estimation [4], Fusion of multiple classifiers [1], clustering [5], data fusion [6] and neural networks [7] to KDD Cup 99 dataset classification have been conducted.

However, among most researches above mentioned, classification algorithms were applied directly on the rough data, which caused high consuming time. Furthermore, some features may be irrelevant or redundant and may have a negative effect on the accuracy of the classifier. Therefore feature analysis is an important preprocessing step for improving intrusion detection performance.

Feature extraction is a main kind of feature analysis technique. Very little research that applies feature extraction to anomaly detection has been done. In this paper, we intend to explore the feasibility of applying feature extraction methods to the anomaly detection task. We evaluate this by adopting principal component neural network (PCNN), specifically, the adaptive principal components extraction (APEX) algorithm [8] for feature extraction. With application of PCNN, the original inputs are transformed into new lower-dimensional features, which are then used as the inputs of SVM classifier to solve anomaly detection problems.

The rest of paper is organized as follows. In section 2, feature extraction using PCNN is presented, and the basic SVM theory and granularity-based grid search method for obtaining optimal SVM parameters are described. In section 3, the experimental results using KDD 99 are presented. Finally, the conclusion and discussion are given in section 4.

2 Feature Extraction and Anomaly Detection

In our proposed approach, we firstly employ a simple t–statistics method to exclude the fields that correspond to low expression for class. Then the APEX algorithm is adopted for feature extraction. After that, we use SVM for classification. Owing to its remarkable characteristics such as good generalization performance, the absence of local minima and the sparse representation of solution, SVM has become a popular research method in anomaly detection. However among most SVM based intrusion detection researches, the SVM parameters were predefined [7], which caused weak flexibility. In this paper we use a validation dataset and adopt granularity based grid search method to obtain optimal SVM parameters, which is described in section 2.3.

2.1 t-Statistics Based Field Selection

In this process, the fields that correspond to low expression for class are removed from the feature space using the simple t-statistics methods. For two-class classification, selection and ranking of fields can be based on the simple t-statistics:

$$t = (\overline{x}_0 - \overline{x}_1) / \sqrt{s_0^2 / N_0 + s_1^2 / N_1} \tag{1}$$

where $N_i, \bar{x}_i, s_i^2$ is the size, mean and variance respectively of class k, k=1, 2. For each field, a t-value is computed. We retain a set of the top n fields, by taking $n/2$ fields with the largest positive t-values (corresponding to high expression for class 1) and $n/2$ fields with smallest negative t-values (corresponding to high expression for class 2). Through field selection, the computational costs of PCNN would be reduced.

2.2 PCNN Based Feature Extraction

In this step, we employ APEX algorithm to extract multiple principal components. The algorithm is iterative that the jth principal component is computed based on the first j-1 principal components. The extraction procedure is described as follows. The detailed description about APEX can be seen at [8].

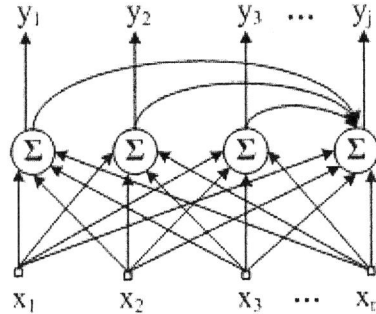

Fig. 1. Network with feedforward and lateral connections for deriving the APEX algorithm

1. Initialize weight $\mathbf{w}_j$, $\mathbf{a}_j$ to small random values at time n=1, where j=1, 2, ..., m (m is the desired number of principal components, $\mathbf{w}_j$ is feedforward connections from input nodes to each of neurons 1,2,...,j. $\mathbf{a}_j$ is lateral connections from the individual outputs of neurons 1,2,..., j-1 to neurons j). Initialize learning-rate parameter η.
2. Set j=1 and for n=1, 2 ... compute:

$$y_1(n) = \mathbf{w}_1^T(n)\mathbf{x}(n) \qquad (2)$$

$$\mathbf{w}_1(n+1) = \mathbf{w}_1(n) + \eta[y_1(n)\mathbf{x}(n) - y_1^2(n)\mathbf{w}_1(n)] \qquad (3)$$

3. Set j=2, and for n=1, 2 ... compute:

$$\mathbf{y}_{j-1}(n) = [y_1(n), y_2(n), \cdots, y_{j-1}(n)]^T \qquad (4)$$

$$y_j(n) = \mathbf{w}_j^T(n)\mathbf{x}(n) + \mathbf{a}_j^T(n)\mathbf{y}_{j-1}(n) \qquad (5)$$

$$\mathbf{w}_j(n+1) = \mathbf{w}_j(n) + \eta[y_j(n)\mathbf{x}(n) - y_j^2(n)\mathbf{w}_j(n)] \qquad (6)$$

$$\mathbf{a}_j(n+1) = \mathbf{a}_j(n) - \eta[y_j(n)\mathbf{y}_{j-1}(n) + y_j^2(n)\mathbf{a}_j(n)] \qquad (7)$$

4. Increment j by 1, go to step 3, and continue until j=m

2.3 SVM and Parameter Optimization

SVM implements the Structural Risk Minimization Principle which seeks to minimize an upper bound of the generalization error rather than minimize the training error. The detailed description about SVM can be referred from [9].

In this paper, we adopt a Gaussian RBF kernel function:

$$K(x_i, x) = \exp(-\gamma \|x_i - x\|^2) \qquad (8)$$

In the Gaussian kernel-based SVM algorithm, C and γ (kernel width) are two adjustable parameters. In some SVM based intrusion detection researches, they are fixed beforehand [7]. In our algorithm, we use a validation set and adopt granularity based grid search method to obtain optimal SVM parameters. We set (C, γ) to an N×M parameter combination with a very coarse grid covering the whole search space. The grid point with the best classification performance is chosen. Subsequently, we decrease the grid granularity to refine the grid resolution, and divide the above chosen grid point into an N×M parameter combination for further optimization, until the termination condition (such as reaching the maximum predefined search round or the performance changes little) is satisfied.

3 Experimental Results

3.1 Data

The data we used for experiment is the KDD Cup 99, which is available with a complete description from the UCI data mining repository [10]. The dataset has 41 features and the total number is about 500 million. The records are labeled with attack types, which fall into the following categories: denial of service (DoS), probe, user to root (u2r), and remote to local (r2l). We merge the four categories into one category "Attack", and try to differentiate them from those "Normal" connections. Upon this simplification, we transform the original multi-class classification problem to a much simpler one, i.e. a two-class problem, which helps us focusing on the effect evaluation of feature extraction.

We chose 11000 unique records randomly from the dataset, 3000 records are used to train the model, and 4000 records are used for SVM optimal parameter search and determination of optimal value of principal component number, and 4000 records are used to test. The attack samples are 1500, 2000, 2000 respectively. In this sampling processing, we found there are many identical records, i.e. all 42 fields have the same values. We kick redundant samples for the purpose of more accurately evaluating our proposed method. In the process of selecting attack samples, we reduced the portion of the easily detected "Probe" attack and included more hard-to-detect attack such as "U2R" and "R2L", which makes our dataset more challenging for classification.

3.2 Data Preprocessing

Among the 42 fields of connection record, the symbolic fields such as *protocol_type* are encoded by numeric values, data are normalized into means of zero and standard deviations of 1. Then the simple t-statistics method is employed for field selection, as depicted in Fig1. We retain the 70% fields for the next step's feature extraction.

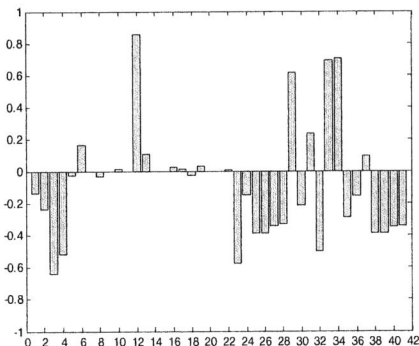

Fig. 2. t-value of each field for the sampled train data, according to the t-value rankness, the 29 fields are selected as input space features for the next step's feature extraction

3.3 Results

The anomaly detection simulation experiment was carried out within a Matlab 7.0 environment, which was running on a PC powered by a Pentium IV 2.5GHz CPU and 512MB RAM. The results are summarized in Fig3 and Table 1.

Table 1. Performance comparison of intrusion detection algorithms for test dataset

Algorithm (Feature number)	Confusion matrix			Accuracy (%)	False alarm rate (%)	Detecting time (ms/sample)
C-SVM(41)	N 1941 118	A←Predicted as 59 1882	N A	95.58	3.04	0.74
APEX-SVM(7)	N 1992 104	A←Predicted as 8 1896	N A	97.20	0.42	0.23

It shows that, for C-SVM algorithm, 1941 of the actual "normal" test set were detected to be normal, for the attack class 1882 of the actual "attack" test set were correctly detected, the total correct classification rate is 95.58%. While for APEX-SVM, 1992 of the actual "normal" test set were detected to be normal, for the attack class 1896 of the actual "attack" test set were correctly detected, the total correct classification rate is 97.2%. Furthermore, with the adoption of PCNN-based feature extraction technique, the intrusion detection algorithm can decrease the false alarm

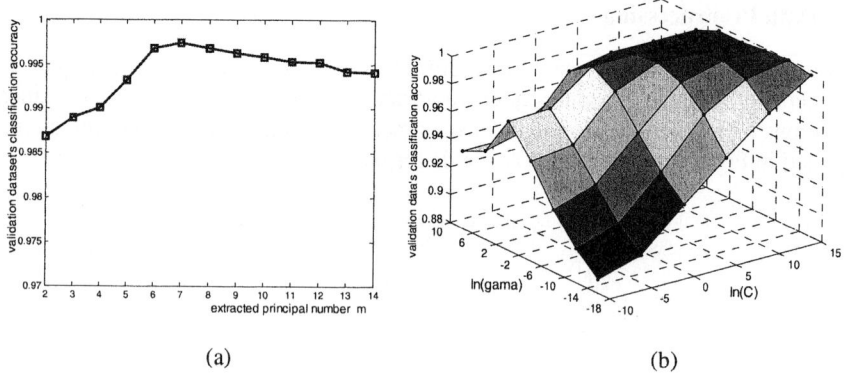

Fig. 3. (a) is the validation dataset's classification accuracy vs. the number m of extracted features adopted by APEX-SVM algorithm, which is used to determine the optimal value of m. It shows that validation data's classification accuracy reaches maximum when m=7, therefore we let m=7 in our intrusion detection algorithm. (b) is the surface plot of validation dataset's classification accuracy when m=7, which illustrates SVM's optimal parameter search process.

rate and average detection time. The results clearly demonstrate that through PCNN-based feature extraction, the SVM-based intrusion detection performance could be improved obviously.

4 Conclusions

In this paper, we proposed a PCNN based approach for anomaly detection from the viewpoint of feature extraction. The APEX algorithm was applied to extract effective features for SVM. The simulation results show that SVM with PCNN feature extraction can achieve better generalization performance than that without feature extraction. This demonstrates that applying feature extraction technique can be an efficient way to boost the performance of intrusion detection system.

References

1. Giacinto, G., Roli, F., Didaci, L.: Fusion of multiple classifiers for intrusion detection in computer networks. Pattern Recognition Letters. 24. (2003) 1795–1803
2. NSTAC Intrusion Detection Subgroup: Report on the NS/EP Implications of Intrusion Detection Technology Research and Development: http://www.ncs.gov/nstac/FIDSGREP.pdf
3. Yang, X.R., Shen, J.Y., Wang, R.: Artificial immune theory based network intrusion detection system and the algorithms design. In: Proceedings of 2002 International Conference on Machine Learning and Cybernetics. 1(2002) 73-77
4. Cho, S., Cha. S.: SAD: web session anomaly detection based on parameter estimation. Computers & Security. 23 (2004) 312-319
5. Oh, S.H., Lee, W.S.: An anomaly intrusion detection method by clustering normal user behavior. Computers & Security. 22 (2003)596-612

6. Wang, Y., Yang, H.H., Wang, X.Y., et al.: Distributed Intrusion Detection System Based on Data Fusion Method. In: The 5th World Congress on Intelligent Control and Automation. New Jersey, IEEE Press. (2004) 4331-4334.
7. Sung, A.H., Mukkamala, S.: Identify important features for intrusion detection using support vector machines and neural networks. In: IEEE Proceedings of the 2003 Symposium on Application and the Internet. (2003) 209-216.
8. Haykin, S.: Neural Networks: A comprehensive foundation. Prentice Hall (1999)
9. Vapnik, V.N.: The Nature of Statistical Learning Theory, Springer, New York (1995)
10. KDD Cup 99 Data: http://kdd.ics.uci.edu/databases/kddcup99 /kddcup99.html.
11. Kim, W., Oh, S.C., Yoon, K.: Intrusion Detection Based on Feature Transform Using Neural Network. ICCS 2004, LNCS 3037(2004) 212–219

GA-Driven LDA in KPCA Space for Facial Expression Recognition

Qijun Zhao and Hongtao Lu

Department of Computer Science and Engineering,
Shanghai Jiao Tong University, Shanghai 200030, P.R. China
qijunzhao@hotmail.com
lu-ht@cs.sjtu.edu.cn

Abstract. Automatic facial expression recognition has been studied comprehensively recently, but most existent algorithms for this task perform not well in presence of nonlinear information in facial images. For this sake, we employ KPCA to map the original facial data to a lower dimensional space. Then LDA is applied in that space and we derive the most discriminant vectors using GA. This method has no singularity problem, which often arises in the traditional eigen decomposition-based solutions to LDA. Other work of this paper includes proposing a rather simple but effective preprocessing method and using Mahalanobis distance rather than Euclidean distance as the metric of the nearest neighbor classifier. Experiments on the JAFFE database show promising results.

1 Introduction

Automatic facial expression recognition has many potential applications such as more intelligent human-computer interface and human emotion interpretation. Along with hot researches in this field, many methods have been proposed. Samel and Iyengar gave an overview of the early work on this topic [1]. More recent work can be found in the surveys of Pantic and Rothkrantz [2], Fasel and Luettin [3].

Six basic emotions, i.e. happiness, sadness, surprise, fear, anger and disgust, are agreed on by most scholars in this realm. In order to recognize these expressions, Elkman et al. [4] proposed the facial action coding system (FACS), which uses 44 action units (AUs) to describe facial actions with regard to their locations as well as their intensities. Instead of dividing the whole face into different units, Lyons et al. [5] chose 34 feature points (e.g., corners of the eye and mouth) on a face for the purpose of analyzing its expression. Another method is to base analysis and recognition directly on the whole facial image rather than its segmentations or so-called feature points [6]. Such method is typically fast and simple. For this sake, we take the last method in this paper. But before further processing, we first make all face images have the same inter-ocular distance and an average face shape so that there is more correspondence among the features on them.

As a classic statistical method, linear discriminant analysis (LDA) is widely used as a way of both feature extraction and dimensionality reduction in the recognition of facial expressions [5][7]. The basic idea of LDA is to maintain the cluster property of the data after their projection to the discriminant space. Traditionally, the LDA model is solved as a problem of generalized eigenvalue problem [8]. But because the dimensionality of a typical image (i.e. the number of pixels in it) is usually much larger than the number of available samples, the scatter matrices might be singular and the LDA works poor. This is called the singularity problem.

Principal component analysis (PCA) is often used as a preprocessing step to reduce the dimensionality of the original data. LDA is then applied in the lower dimensional space. This relieves or eliminates the singularity problem[9]. However, PCA only uses the second order statistical information in data. As a result, it fails to perform well in nonlinear cases. Recently, with the idea of kernel methods, Scholkopf [10] extended PCA to the nonlinear case, called Kernel Principle Component Analysis (KPCA). Its application to face recognition [11] shows excellent performance. This is due to the nonlinear essence of kernel methods and the substantive nonlinear information in facial images. In this paper, we employ KPCA as the first step for dimensionality reduction.

LDA is essentially an optimization problem. Therefore Genetic Algorithm (GA), an effective optimization algorithm, can be incorporated into LDA. In fact, GA has already been applied to the recognition of faces [11][12]. In this paper, based on GA, we propose a new solution for LDA. The proposed algorithm avoids the singularity problem and the experiments on the JAFFE database prove its effectiveness.

The remainder of this paper is organized as follows. KPCA is reviewed in section 2. After a simple introduction of LDA, section 3 specifically presents the GA-driven LDA algorithm. To complete the facial expression recognition system, we give the preprocessing method and classifier in section 4. Then section 5 shows the results of our experiments on the JAFFE database. Finally, we concludes this paper in section 6, where further research directions are also presented.

2 Kernel Principal Component Analysis

When mapped into a higher dimensional space, a non-linearly separable problem may become linearly separable. This underlies the basic idea of KPCA as well as other kernel methods. Denote such mapping as

$$\Phi : R^n \mapsto F, \; x \mapsto \Phi(x), \qquad (1)$$

where F is a higher dimensional space and it could be infinite. Assume $\Phi(x_i), i = 1, 2, \cdots, M$, are centered, i.e. $\sum_{i=1}^{M} \Phi(x_i) = 0$. Then the total scatter matrix of these samples in F is $S_t^{\Phi} = \frac{1}{M} \sum_{i=1}^{M} \Phi(x_i)\Phi(x_i)^T$, where T denotes the transpose operation. PCA is applied in F, i.e. to solve the following eigenvalue equation:

$$S_t^{\Phi} w^{\Phi} = \lambda^{\Phi} w^{\Phi}, \qquad (2)$$

where w^{Φ} is a column of the optimal projection matrix W^{Φ} in F. Substituting S_t^{Φ} into (2), we get

$$w^\Phi = \frac{1}{\lambda^\Phi} \frac{1}{M} \sum_{i=1}^{M} (\Phi(x_i) \cdot w^\Phi) \Phi(x_i), \tag{3}$$

where '·' denotes the inner product. From (3) we can see that all solutions w^Φ with $\lambda^\Phi \neq 0$ lie in the span of $\Phi(x_1), \Phi(x_2), \cdots, \Phi(x_M)$. Thus, (2) is equivalent to the set of equations:

$$(\Phi(x_i) \cdot S_t^\Phi w^\Phi) = \lambda^\Phi (\Phi(x_i) \cdot w^\Phi), \qquad for\ all\ i = 1, 2, \cdots, M, \tag{4}$$

and there exist coefficients α_i $(i = 1, 2, \cdots, M)$ such that

$$w^\Phi = \sum_{i=1}^{M} \alpha_i \Phi(x_i). \tag{5}$$

According to (4) and (5), we have

$$\lambda^\Phi \sum_{i=1}^{M} \alpha_i (\Phi(x_k) \cdot \Phi(x_i)) = \frac{1}{M} \sum_{i=1}^{M} \alpha_i (\Phi(x_k) \cdot \sum_{j=1}^{M} \Phi(x_j)(\Phi(x_j) \cdot \Phi(x_i))), \tag{6}$$

for all $k = 1, 2, \cdots, M$. Defining an $M \times M$ matrix K with its element in the i_{th} row and j_{th} column as

$$K_{ij} := (\Phi(x_i) \cdot \Phi(x_j)), \tag{7}$$

this reads

$$M\lambda^\Phi K\alpha = K^2 \alpha, \tag{8}$$

where α denotes the column vector with entries $\alpha_1, \alpha_2, \cdots, \alpha_M$. As shown in [10], all its solutions are given by the eigenvectors of K:

$$M\lambda^\Phi \alpha = K\alpha. \tag{9}$$

With these α's and (5), we get the optimal projection matrix for the samples in F. And for a test sample x, we can calculate its k_{th} principal component in F by

$$(w_k^\Phi \cdot \Phi(x)) = \sum_{i=1}^{M} \alpha_i^k (\Phi(x_i) \cdot \Phi(x)), \tag{10}$$

where w_k^Φ is the k_{th} column of W^Φ and α^k is the eigenvector of K corresponding to its k_{th} largest eigenvalue.

Generally, m eigenvectors corresponding to the m largest eigenvalues are chosen to span the KPCA space and in order to normalize them, we take the whitening procedure as following:

$$\alpha^i = \frac{\alpha^i}{\sqrt{\lambda_i^\Phi}}, \qquad i = 1, 2, \cdots, m. \tag{11}$$

According to the Mercer condition, the dot product in these equations can be replaced by

$$k(x_i, x_j) = (\Phi(x_i) \cdot \Phi(x_j)), \tag{12}$$

where $k(*,*)$ is called a kernel function. The polynomial function

$$k(x,y) = (x \cdot y + 1)^d, \qquad (13)$$

where d is any positive integer, and the radial basis function or Gaussian kernel function

$$k(x,y) = \exp(-\frac{\|x-y\|^2}{\sigma^2}), \qquad (14)$$

where $\sigma > 0$, are among the commonly used kernel functions [10].

3 GA-Driven LDA

Suppose there are M samples, $x_1, x_2, \cdots, x_M \in R^n$, which are categorized into L classes with N_j samples of the class $j (j = 1, 2, \cdots, L)$. Let I_j denote the set of indexes of the samples belonging to the class j, c denote the mean of all these samples, and c_j denote the mean of the class j. The within-class scatter matrix $S_w = \frac{1}{L}\sum_{j=1}^{L} \frac{1}{N_j} \sum_{i \in I_j}(x_i - c_j)(x_i - c_j)^T$ and the between-class scatter matrix $S_b = \frac{1}{L}\sum_{j=1}^{L} N_j(c_j - c)(c_j - c)^T$. The quotient of the determinants of the between-class and within-class scatter matrices of the projected samples is a common criterion of LDA and the optimal projection matrix of LDA is to maximize it:

$$W_{LDA} = \arg\max_W \frac{|W^T S_b W|}{|W^T S_w W|}. \qquad (15)$$

To apply GA, the optimal discriminant vectors, i.e. the column vectors in W_{LDA}, are viewed as the rotation of the basis of the KPCA space [12]. We start the evolution with the identity basis of the KPCA space and rotate them two by two with randomly selected angles. A random number of vectors are then chosen as discriminant vectors from the rotated vectors.

Definition of Chromosome. Referring to Liu and Wechsler's work [12], binary chromosome, i.e. a bit string, is defined for GA-driven LDA. As we have discussed above, the solutions (discriminant vectors) are derived from the pairwise rotation of the identity basis of the KPCA space: $\epsilon_1, \epsilon_2, \cdots, \epsilon_m$, where $\epsilon_i \in R^m$ with '*1*' as its i_{th} element and '*0*' the others. Because two of the basis are rotated together once, the total number of rotation angles for m basis vectors is $\frac{m(m-1)}{2}$. Thus the chromosome should depict the following rotation angles: $a_1, a_2, \cdots, a_{\frac{m(m-1)}{2}}$. Each angle a_k ($k = 1, 2, \cdots, \frac{m(m-1)}{2}$) is represented by 10 bits, thus the rotation interval is $\frac{\pi}{2^{11}}$ (the rotation angles are confined to $[0, \frac{\pi}{2}]$ for simplicity). And a_k corresponds to the i_{th} and j_{th} vectors (suppose $i < j$), where $k = \sum_{t=1}^{i-1}(m-t) + j - i$. The corresponding rotation matrix Q_k is an $m \times m$ identity matrix but $Q_k(i,i) = \cos(a_k)$, $Q_k(i,j) = -\sin(a_k)$, $Q_k(j,i) = \sin(a_k)$ and $Q_k(j,j) = \cos(a_k)$. And the total rotation matrix is $Q = Q_1 Q_2 \cdots Q_{\frac{m(m-1)}{2}}$. Let $\xi_1, \xi_2, \cdots, \xi_m \in R^m$ be the result vectors after rotation:

$$[\xi_1 \xi_2 \cdots \xi_m] = [\epsilon_1 \epsilon_2 \cdots \epsilon_m] \times Q. \qquad (16)$$

Not all these vectors are chosen as discriminant vectors. Instead, we randomly select l vectors from them. This leads to another m bits in the chromosome. These bits, $b_1, b_2, \cdots, b_m$, demonstrate which vectors are selected: if $b_i=1$, then ξ_i is chosen; otherwise, discarded.

Genetic Operators. Two genetic operators, crossover and mutation, are employed. Both of them are conducted with a given probability. If crossover is taken on two individuals, a random position is selected. Then the bits before this position in one individual and those after this position in the other individual are combined to form a new individual. So are the rest of them. As for mutation, if one bit of an individual is supposed to be mutated, then it is converted from '0' to '1' or from '1' to '0'; otherwise, keep it unchanged.

Fitness. The fitness in GA-driven LDA is based on the criterion of LDA. Take an individual $D = (a_1 a_2 \cdots a_{\frac{m(m-1)}{2}}; b_1 b_2 \cdots b_m)$ as an example. Assume the vectors after rotation are $\xi_1, \xi_2, \cdots, \xi_m$ and l vectors $\eta_1, \eta_2, \cdots, \eta_l$ are selected from them as the discriminant vectors. Then the sample $x_{KPCA} \in R^m$ in the KPCA space will be mapped to $x_{GA-LDA} \in R^l$ in the GA-LDA space:

$$x_{GA-LDA} = [\eta_1 \eta_2 \cdots \eta_l]^T \cdot x_{KPCA}, \qquad (17)$$

where x_{KPCA} can be obtained from the original sample $x \in R^n$ according to (10).

Project all samples into the GA-LDA space by (10) and (17) and calculate the within-class scatter matrix S_w^G and the between-class scatter matrix S_b^G for the projected samples in the GA-LDA space. Then the fitness of the individual D is defined as

$$\zeta(D) = tr(S_b^G)/tr(S_w^G). \qquad (18)$$

Once the fitness of all individuals in the population has been worked out, choose those individuals with larger fitness and form a new generation. Unless the stopping criterion is met, for example, the maximum number of trials is reached, GA is run on the new generation again. When GA stops, the individual with the largest fitness in the last generation gives the result, i.e. l optimal discriminant vectors: $W_{GA-LDA} = [\eta_1^* \eta_2^* \cdots \eta_l^*]$.

4 Facial Expression Recognition

4.1 Preprocessing Facial Images

Firstly, we manually mark the centers of eyes on each face with two points and the face region with a rectangle. Let's denote the centers of left and right eyes as El and Er. And the left-most, the right-most, the upper-most and the bottom-most points of the face are denoted by L, R, T and B respectively. Secondly, calculate the average Y coordinate $\bar{E}_y$ of eyes, the average X coordinates $\bar{El}_x$ and $\bar{Er}_x$ of the left and right eyes, and the average Y coordinates $\bar{T}_y$ and $\bar{B}_y$ of the top-most and bottom-most points. Hereafter, the subscripts 'x' and 'y' represent the X and Y coordinates. Thirdly, calibrate the eyes to make them have the same average inter-ocular distance $\bar{d} = \bar{Er}_x - \bar{El}_x$. This is implemented through scaling in three intervals along the horizontal direction on the face: $[L_x, El_x]$, $[El_x, Er_x]$ and $[Er_x, R_x]$. These intervals are scaled, respectively, to the average ones, $[0, (w-\bar{d})/2]$, $[(w-\bar{d})/2, \bar{d}+(w-\bar{d})/2]$ and $[\bar{d}+(w-\bar{d})/2, w]$, where $w = R_x - L_x$ is the width of the face. Fourthly, calibration along the vertical direction is conducted on each facial image, i.e., vertically divide the face into two intervals, $[T_y, E_y]$ and $[E_y, B_y]$, and scale them to two average intervals, $[0, h*(\bar{E}_y - \bar{T}_y)/(\bar{B}_y - \bar{E}_y)]$ and $[h*(\bar{E}_y - \bar{T}_y)/(\bar{B}_y - \bar{E}_y), h]$, where $h = B_y - T_y$ is the height of the face. Lastly, the face is scaled to the standard width W and height H.

After the calibration and standardization, we work out the average images of each expression and average these average images to get another average image, which we call the BLANK one. Then it is subtracted from all facial images so that we get the difference images as the final input data of the facial expression recognition system. Here the philosophy lies in the belief that information really helpful for the recognition task is included in the difference, thus with these difference images we can perform the recognition task well and the redundant information is reduced. Fig. 1 shows this procedure.

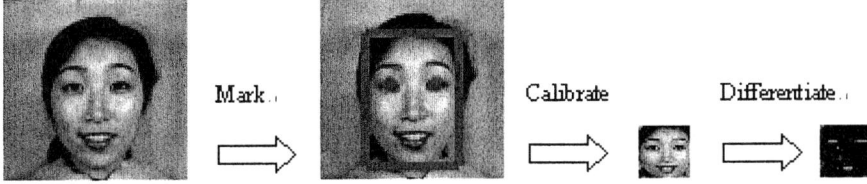

Fig. 1. Preprocessing facial images: $H=24$ and $W=24$

4.2 Facial Expression Classifier

Generally, the nearest neighbor classifier [8] is taken when the features of facial images are extracted. And the common metric is Euclidean distance. However, in the view of probability and statistics, the Euclidean distance does not make use of the deviation or covariance of samples. In this paper, we take the Mahalanobis distance as the metric of the nearest neighbor classifier. Take a sample X from a cluster, whose mean is μ and covariance matrix is Σ, as an example, the distance between X and the cluster center μ is defined as

$$d_m^2 = (X-\mu)^T \times \Sigma^{-1} \times (X-\mu), \tag{19}$$

where the superscript '-1' denotes the inverse matrix.

5 Experimental Results

We test the proposed algorithm with the Japanese Female Facial Expression (JAFFE) database. The database contains 213 images of 7 facial expressions

Fig. 2. Samples from the JAFFE database

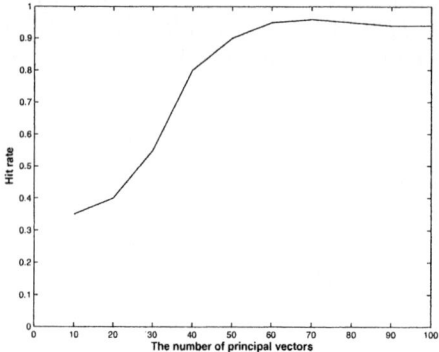

Fig. 3. The hit rate in relation to the number of principal vectors

(angry, depressed, fear, happy, normal, sad, surprised) posed by 10 Japanese female models. Fig. 2 shows some samples of one model.

The experiments are conducted in two ways: leave-one-image-out and leave-one-subject-out. In the 'leave-one-image-out' test, one image is randomly selected out from each expression category. As a result, the whole image set is divided into two sets. One has seven images as the testing set and the other consists of the rest ones as the training set. The whole training and testing process is conducted 10 times and every time a new testing set is selected. Finally we average the results to get the hit rate, or recognition rate, of the proposed scheme. In the 'leave-one-subject-out' test, all images of one subject are selected out to form the testing set with the rest ones as the training set. We also conduct the process 10 times and take the average result as the final hit rate over identity.

We first take the Gaussian kernel function with its $\sigma = 10$ to perform the 'leave-one-subject-out' test. In Fig. 3 we give the hit rate over identity in relation to the number of principal vectors (PVs). From the diagram we can see the best hit rate is 96%, which is apparently better than that of Lyons, 92% [5]. We also perform the tests using the polynomial kernel function. Table 1 shows the average hit rates in the 'leave-one-image-out' and the 'leave-one-subject-out' tests. And the result of 'leave-one-image-out' test, 80%, is also better than Lyons' result, 75% [5].

6 Conclusions and Further Considerations

In this paper, an effective algorithm is proposed for facial expression recognition. The proposed facial image preprocessing procedure improves the performance of

Table 1. Average Hit Rates

Kernel Function	Leave-one-image-out	Leave-one-subject-out
Polynomial, $d=1$	72%	85%
Polynomial, $d=2$	75%	90%
Gaussian, $\sigma=10$	80%	96%
Gaussian, $\sigma=1000$	78%	92%

the following KPCA and LDA. This algorithm avoids the singularity problem of LDA through applying KPCA before LDA and acquiring the optimal discriminant vectors by GA iterations rather than by solving the generalized eigenvalue problem. Moreover, the nearest neighbor classifier using Mahalanobis distance also performs well in recognizing facial expressions. Experiments on JAFFE database testify the effectiveness of this GA-driven LDA scheme in KPCA space for the task of facial expression recognition. A possible explanation to the excellence of this proposed algorithm is that it deals well with the nonlinear properties in facial images by using KPCA and taking into consideration the variances of different facial expressions.

However, the proposed preprocessing method is conducted by hand. This makes it laborious. What we are considering now is how to accomplish it automatically. Actually, both the segmentation of faces and the location of facial features, eyes and mouths for instance, are other hot but difficult topics in the literature of face and facial expression recognition. The complexion-based method [13] works well for segmenting faces in color images. Its basic idea is to distinguish human faces from other objects in images by their different optical properties, for example colors, and shape information. This method as well as other methods used in face detection are in our consideration. As for marking eyes in human faces, we intend to make use of such characteristics of eyes as the apparent difference in gray level between the area of eyes and its surroundings. Our primary goal is either to develop new algorithms or to enhance the accuracy of existent automatical face segmentation and face feature location methods.

Apart from the automatical marking of faces and eyes, we are also interested in the effect of the number of retained principal components as well as discriminant vectors on the final recognition rate. How to choose a proper number of such components and vectors is another direction for further researches.

References

1. A. Samel, P. A. Iyengar: Automatic recognition and analysis of human faces and facial expression: a survey. Pattern Recognition, Vol. 25, No. 1 (1992) 65-77
2. Maja Pantic, Leon J. M. Rothkrantz: Automatic analysis of facial expression: the state of the art. IEEE Trans. on Pattern Analysis and Machine Intelligence, Vol. 22, No. 12 (2000) 1424-1445
3. B. Fasel, Juergen Luettin: Automatic facial expression analysis: a survey. Pattern Recognition, Vol. 36, No. 1 (2003) 259-275

4. P. Elkman, W. V. Friesen: Facial action coding system (FACS), Manual. Palo Alto: Consulting Psychologists Press (1978)
5. M. J. Lyons, S. Akamatsu, M. Kamachi, J. Gyoba: Coding facial expressions with Gabor wavelets. Proceedings of Third IEEE International Conference on Automatic Face and Gesture Recognition, IEEE Computer Society (1998) 200-205
6. C. Padgett, G. Cottrell: Identifying emotion in static face images. Paper presented at the proceedings of the 2nd Joint Symposium on Neural Computation, San Diego, CA: University of California (1995)
7. Xuewen Chen, Thomas Huang, Facial expression recognition: a clustering-based approach. Pattern Recognition Letters, Vol. 24, No. 9-10 (2003) 1295-1302
8. Keinosuke Fukunaga: Introduction to statistical pattern recognition (second edition). Academic Press, Inc. (1990)
9. A. J. Calder, A. M. Burton, Paul Miller, Andrew W. Young, Shigeru Akamatsu: A principal component analysis of facial expressions. Vision Research, Vol. 41, No. 9 (2001) 1179-1208
10. B. Scholkopf, Alexander Smola, KlausRobert Muller: Nonlinear component analysis as a kernel eigenvalue problem. Neural Computation, Vol. 10, No. 5 (1998) 1299-1319
11. Y. Zhang, C. Liu: Face recognition using kernel principal component analysis and genetic algorithms. Proceedings of the 2002 12th IEEE Workshop on Neural Networks for Signal Processing (2002) 337-343
12. C. Liu, H. Wechsler: Evolutionary pursuit and its application to face recognition. IEEE Trans. on Pattern Analysis and Machine Intelligence, Vol. 22, No. 6 (2000) 570-582
13. Yoo T. W., et al.: A fast algorithm for tracking human faces based on chromatic histograms. Pattern Recognition Letters, Vol. 20, No. 10 (1999) 967-978

A New ART Neural Networks for Remote Sensing Image Classification

AnFei Liu, BiCheng Li, Gang Chen, and Xianfei Zhang

Information Engineering University,
No. 306, P.O. BOX 1001, Zhengzhou, Henan 450002, China
liu_anfei@163.com

Abstract. A new ART2A-C algorithm based on fuzzy operators to cluster the remote sensing images and aerials is proposed in this paper. By combining two ART ANNs with higher performance, the traditional ART2A-C is developed with the fuzzy operators introduced in matching rule. Then the proposed method is applied to the classification and the new network is implemented as well as two other existed ARTs respectively. Experimental results show that the new method outperforms the traditional ones.

1 Introduction

Automatic classification of remote sensing images is an important item in remote-sensing image manipulation. It achieves extensive applications in both military and civil affairs. The essential object of remote sensing technology is to obtain the information of targets, which firstly refers to the recognition of various ground truths, therefore, we must classify individuals by type of ground truths. However, during the recognition of ground truths in remote sensing images, the early manual explanation exposes several shortcomings, such as tardiness, hard repetition, influences of professional knowledge of recognizers, experiences, scales, quality and so on, which makes the accurate identification of single pixel difficult. Furthermore, recognition is completely determined by the understanding of the recognizer, introducing subjectivity inevitably. These considerations enlighten us on the illumination that before the classification, we should carry out the automatic clustering using as much objective information of the image as possible. Unsupervised classification needs no training data with its results completely determined by rank. It is always applied to the cases when the exact information of truth samples is absent. Traditional methods include Isodata and K-Means algorithms.

Unfortunately, the most key advantage of manual explanation is not inherited by traditional computer recognition and it gives a poor performance in exertion of expert knowledge. As a kind of non-parameter classifier, ANN (Artificial Neural Network) owns parallel processing ability in a large scale as well as an adaptive capability. It has been introduced to trend analysis, pattern recognition and remote sensing image-classification recently [3][6]. ANN method needs no prior knowledge, which shows its superiority in comparison with other statistical methods. Self-organized ANN employs a non-teacher mode, remaining competition both in learning and classifying. ART (Adaptive Resonance Theory) proposed by Carpenter and Grossberg(U.S.A) [1] is a recognizer in the vector mode and it carries out the clustering in accordance with the existed patterns. ART can learn in real-time without desired labels in training sets, and adapt instationary conditions well. Because of its similarity to the cognizance of brains, ART preserves particular advantages in considerable data clustering and classifying, playing an importance part in artificial intelligence, trouble diagnosis and data compression.

ART2A is a more perfect version of ART. With an easy implementation, it stands for a general fruit of ART algorithms from 1991 up to the present. In this paper, we adopt two fast continuous algorithms—ART2A-E and ART2A-C to cluster various ground truth types in remote sensing images and aerials which act as the reference methods. By combining the ART2A-C with fuzzy ART, a new ART2A-C algorithm based on fuzzy operators is proposed, which improves performance of our classifier.

The remainder of the paper is organized as follow: Section 2 first introduces several ART2A networks and fuzzy ART in brief, and then presents the new algorithm in detail. Section 3 describes the specific clustering processing. Analysis of the experimental results is discussed in Section 4. Finally, Section 5 provides a conclusion and some future work.

2 ART Neural Networks

ART is an unsupervised network using competition mechanism. It inducts a Self-Stabilization mechanism making full use of memory resource of the system, and gets a better clustering performance and stability.

In the development of ART, there exist three types of products where ART-1 and ART-2 aim to binary and continuous inputs respectively with ART-3 a multi-layer network.

2.1 ART2As [2]

The most popular editions of ART are ART2A, ART2A-E and ART2A-C. The last two inherit the fast competition-self-stabilization mechanism of ART2A, where computation of matching degree is combined with competition. Such a mechanism avoids the searching iterative, resulting in the much reduction of computation and a faster speed. To overcome the ART2A's shortcoming in lack of amplitude information, ART2A-E adopts a different match rule, while ART2A-C develops a complement-expansion method instead. The latter method considers $\|W_j(k)\|$ in the competition rule, making the composition of competition and matching possible. The specific algorithms are available in related references [2][4].

2.2 Structure Learning of Fuzzy ART [4][5]

The structure learning rule in Fuzzy ART covers preprocessing expansion, choosing, matching and adaptive adjustment four steps. Choosing is according to the value of

$$t_i = \frac{|X^C \wedge W^i|}{\alpha + |W^i|}, \quad i = 1 \sim \mu(k)$$

while the fuzzy operator "$\wedge$" being defined as follow:

If $X = [x_1, x_2, \cdots x_N]$, $Y = [y_1, y_2, \cdots y_N]$, $X \wedge Y = Z[z_1, z_2, \cdots z_N]$ (1)

then $z_i = \min\{x_i, y_i\}, i = 1 \sim N$. (2)

$|\bullet|$ is so-called vector-model defined as $|X| = \sum_{n=1}^{N} |X_n|$. As a safe parameter, α is always set to 0. The competition rules were presented in [4]: $j^*(k)$ and η represent the winner and matching degree respectively:

$$j^*(k) = \arg\max_{j=1 \square \mu(k)} \{t_j\}$$ (3)

$$\eta = \frac{|X^C \wedge W^i|}{|X^C|}$$ (4)

when $\eta \geq \rho$, W^j will be adjusted, where ρ is the threshold:

$$W^j(k+1) = \beta(X^C \wedge W^j(k)) + (1-\beta)W^j(k)$$ (5)

The learning in some extent is controlled by β ($0 \leq \beta \leq 1$).

2.3 The New ART2A-C Algorithm

We deal with the structure learning in fuzzy ART in 2.2, where fuzzy conjunction, vector-model is introduced. It displaces the traditional cosine rule of two vectors with member-function in fuzzy theory. With simple minimization and model addition operations, this not only provides simplicity in computation but also offers a reasonable explanation for the relationship between the input vector and the given pattern. However, matching degree in 2.2 does not take the magnitude of the weight vectors in consideration, which needs a searching phase including repeated competition and matching.

In the new network, the idea of fuzzy ART is introduced to the ART2A-C. With $\|W_j(k)\|$ in consideration, a new rule $\frac{|\hat{X}(k) \wedge W_j(k)|}{|\hat{X}(k)||W_j(k)|}$ is constructed. Having this new matching rule we succeed in combining the bottom-up competition and top-down matching into one step.

Procedure of the new algorithm is similar to the old one:

Preparation

Firstly, the input elements must comply with this presupposition— $x_i(k) \in [0,1]$. After producing the complement of $X(k)$— $X^C(k) = [x_1^C, x_2^C, \cdots x_N^C]$, we feed a

2N dimensional vector $\hat{X}(k)$ comprised by $X(k)$ and $X^C(k)$ to the neural network:

$$\hat{X}(K) = \left[X^T(k), \{X^C(K)\}^T \right]^T, \quad x_i^C(k) = 1 - x_i(k), \quad i = 1 \sim N \tag{6}$$

Initialization

When $k = 1$, let $W_1(1) = \hat{X}(1)$, $\mu(2) = 1$ \hfill (7)

Competition and Adaptive Learning
Competition and matching run at the same time according to the following formula:

$$j^*(k) = \arg\max_{j=1 \square \mu(k)} \left[\frac{|\hat{X}(k) \wedge W_j(k)|}{|\hat{X}(k)||W_j(k)|} \right]$$

$$\eta = \frac{|\hat{X}(k) \wedge W_j(k)|}{|\hat{X}(k)||W_j(k)|} \tag{8}$$

If $\eta < \rho$, add another class along with the settings as follow:

$$W_{\mu(k)+1}(k) = \hat{X}(k), \quad \mu(k+1) = \mu(k) + 1 \tag{9}$$

or stop the current iterative, else if $\eta \geq \rho$, go to the adaptive resonance state and start up the adjustment:

$$W_j(k+1) = \begin{cases} \alpha(X^C \wedge W_j(k)) + (1-\alpha)W_j(k), & j = j^*(k) \\ W_j(k), & j \neq j^*(k) \end{cases} \tag{10}$$

Notice that W_j is a 2N dimensional vector. It is the center of each class in fact. In above formulas, $\mu(k)$ denotes the number of the neuron used in the k th iterative.

3 Remote Sensing Image Classification Based on Modified ART Neural Networks

Three classifiers are implemented in this paper i.e. ART2A-E, ART2A-C and new ART2A-C. The number of the input nodes is determined by the features fed to the classifiers while each output node corresponds to a class. In our experiments, the RGB value of each pixel feed in the network and the corresponding result refers to its type label. Natural ground truths primarily contains six classes: water, soil, manmade buildings, residential area, vegetation and so on, which results in the number of the output nodes: 6. What is worthy of mentioning is that here 6 implies the capacity of the classifier, and the exact number of classes is determined by the input image itself. We assign a color for each possible output. Therefore, every color in the result images represents a type of ground truth.

Number of the inputs and outputs in the ANN are 3 and 6 respectively, thresholds and training constants are chosen by training the sub-images repeatedly. The exact value of parameters in ART2A-E and new ART2A-C are $\alpha = 0.35$, $\rho = 0.935$ and $\alpha_{new} = 0.31$, $\rho_{new} = 0.99$ respectively with $\alpha_{new} = 0.35$, $\rho_{new} = 0.315$ in the new ART2A-C.

4 Experimental Results and Performance Comparison

Clustering aiming to an aerial and a remote sensing image are implemented here. Source in Figure 1 is got from USC-SIPI image repository (ID: 2.1.01) and Figure 2 is a remote sensing image of Boston [6]. Image-groups present the test images and the effect images after clustering. We train sub-images to choose the best parameters as presented in 3, then clustering on the whole image is carried out. It can be seen from

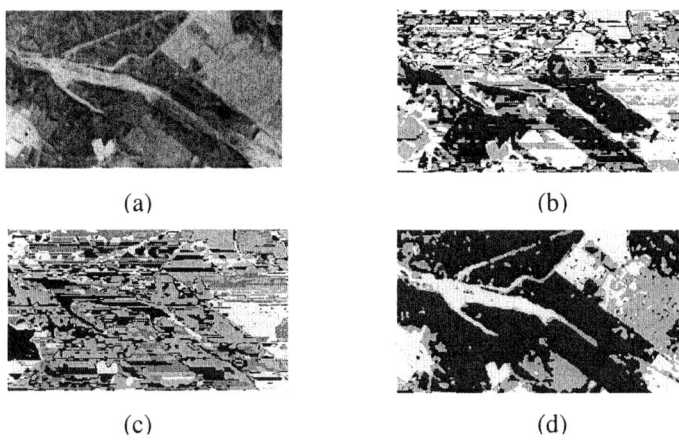

(a) (b)

(c) (d)

Fig. 1. The aerial and classification results

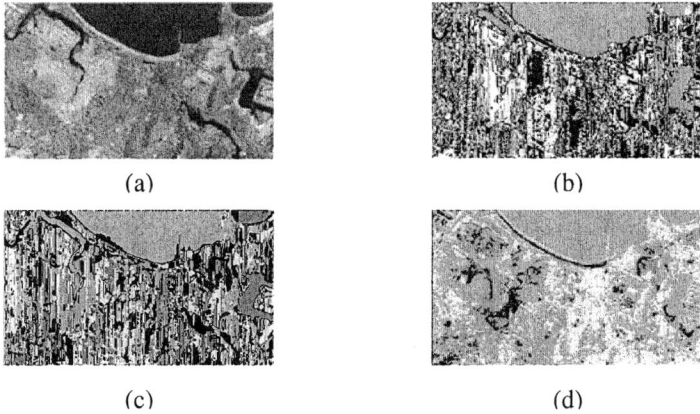

(a) (b)

(c) (d)

Fig. 2. The remote sensing image and its classification results

Fig. 1(b)(c) and Fig. 2(b)(c) that the two original methods achieves similar effects and the contour of classes is not clear with lots of error classifications. From Fig. 1 (d) and Fig. 2(d), it can be observed that the classifier based on the proposed ART2A-C can distinguish the basic classes and produces a better visual effect. Compared with the old ART, we conclude that the classification effect of the whole image is improved obviously in despite of some lack in the area with much details, while for a more completed image like Fig. 2(a), this new method show some deficiency in classifications when compared with the traditional one i.e. K-Means, but achieving a faster speed.

In **Fig. 1,** (a) shows the original test image, (b) is the classification result of the original test image after a ART2A-E[4] neural network classifier, while (c) presents classification result of ART2A-C. Classification result of the new ART2A-C ANN classifier is showed in (d).

In **Fig. 2,** (a) shows the original remote sensing image, (b) is the classification result of the original test image after a ART2A-E[4] neural network classifier, while (c) presents classification result of ART2A-C. Classification result of the new ART2A-C ANN classifier is showed in (d).

5 Conclusion and Future Work

The ANN technology was studied in this article theoretically and experimentally. Several popular ART networks were introduced. A new ART2A-C algorithm based on fuzzy operator was proposed. Experiments show that the proposed algorithm is superior to the traditional algorithms for remote sensing image classification.

Additionally, from experiments, we can see that the best parameters of ART NN vary with the test image, and they are basically decided by trial. In despite of the high speed of ART, the lasting time remains a little longer when the size of the test image is larger. All the lacks, more or less, have brought inconveniences in practice. So in future, more work should be done in an adaptive learning algorithm of the best parameters and speed.

References

1. Carpenter, G, A., Grossberg S.: self-organization of stable category recognition codes for analog input patterns. Appl. Opt, (1987) 4919-4930
2. Carpenter, G, A., et al.: an adaptive resonance algorithm for rapid category learning and recognition, Neural Networks, May, (1998) 544-559
3. Chen, G., Li, B.C., and Guo, Z.G.: Remote sensing image classification based on evidence theory and neural networks. International Symposium on Neural Networks, (2004) 971-976
4. Yang, X.J., Zheng, J.L.: Artificial Neural Network and Blind Signal Processing Beijing Qinghua Publisher (2002)
5. Carpenter, G, A., et al: fast stable learning and categorization of analog patterns by an adaptive resonance system. Neural Networks, (1991) 759-771
6. Gail A., Carpenter, Siegfried Martens, Ogi J., Ogas: Self-organizing Hierarchical Knowledge Discovery by an ARTMAP Image Fusion System, (2004)
7. Huang, D.S.: Systematic Theory of Pattern Recognition using Neural Networks Beijing Publishing House of Electronics Industry (1996)

Modified Color Co-occurrence Matrix for Image Retrieval

Min Hyuk Chang[1], Jae Young Pyun[1], Muhammad Bilal Ahmad[2],
Jong Hoon Chun[3], and Jong An Park[1]

[1] Dept of Information & Communications Engineering,
Chosun University, Gwangju, Korea
{millcre, jypyun, japark}@chosun.ac.kr
[2] Signal and Image Processing Lab, Dept. of Mechatronics,
Gwangju Institute of Science and Technology,
Gwangju, Korea
bilal@gist.ac.kr
[3] Dept. of Computer Information & Communication Eng.
Jeonnam Provincial Collage, Jeonnam, Korea
owl7026@kornet.net

Abstract. Color correlogram for content-based image retrieval (CBIR) characterizes not only the color distribution of pixels, but also the spatial correlation of pairs of colors. Color not only reflects the material of surface, but also varies considerably with the change of illumination, the orientation of the surface, and the viewing geometry of the camera. The invariance to these environmental factors is not considered in most of the color features in color based CBIR including the color correlogram. However, pixels changed their color with almost same proportions with change of environmental factors. This fact is taken into consideration, and new algorithm is proposed. The color co-occurrence matrix for different spatial distances is defined based on the maximum/minimum of color component between the three components (R,G,B) of a pixel. The proposed algorithm has less number of features, and the change of illumination, etc. is also taken into account.

1 Introduction

The rapid growth of multimedia computing and applications has brought about an explosive growth of digital images in computer systems and networks. This development has remarkably increased the need for image retrieval systems that are able to effectively index a large amount of images and to effectively retrieve them based on their visual contents.

Content-based image retrieval (CBIR), a technique which uses visual contents to search images from large scale image databases according to users' interests, has been an active and fast advancing research area since the 1990s. During the past decade, remarkable progress has been made in both theoretical research and system development. However, there remain many challenging research problems that continue to attract researchers from multiple disciplines.

In developing a visual content-based image retrieval system, the first critical decision to be made is to determine what image feature, or combination of image features are to be used for image indexing and retrieval purpose. Image feature selection is critical because it largely affects the remaining aspects of the system design, and greatly determines image retrieval capabilities of the eventual system.

The basic idea of image retrieval by image example is to extract characteristic features from target images which are then matched with those of the query image [1,2]. These features are typically derived from shape, texture, or color properties of query and target images. After matching, images are ordered with respect to the query image according to their similarity measure and displayed for viewing [3].

Color is widely used to represent an image [4]. The color composition of an image, which is usually represented as a histogram of intensity values [5], is a global property which does not require knowledge of the component objects of an image. Moreover, color distribution is independent of view and resolution, and color comparison can be carried out automatically without human intervention. However, it has become clear that color alone is not sufficient to characterize an image. Two very different images might have very similar color distribution (histogram). Therefore, spatial distribution of colors is also very important. To facilitate a more accurate retrieval process, integrated color-spatial retrieval techniques that employ both the color information as well as the knowledge of the colors' spatial distribution for image retrieval have been explored in the literature [6]. However, these schemes are either computationally expensive or storage inefficient.

Color not only reflects the material of surface, but also varies considerably with the change of illumination, the orientation of the surface, and the viewing geometry of the camera. This variability must be taken into account. However, invariance to these environmental factors is not considered in most of the color features. Invariant color representation has been introduced to content-based image retrieval recently. In [7], a set of color invariants for object retrieval was derived based on the Schafer model of object reflection. In [8], specular reflection, shape and illumination invariant representation based on blue ratio vector (r/b, g/b,1) is given. In [9], a surface geometry invariant color feature is provided. These invariant color features, when applied to image retrieval, may yield illumination, scene geometry and viewing geometry independent representation of color contents of images, but may also lead to some loss in discrimination power among images.

In this paper, color distribution, spatial correlation and the environmental changes are taken into consideration. With the change of the environmental factors, pixels changed their color with almost same proportions with respect to each other. If one pixel has maximum, say, red component in one view, and after change of illumination, that pixel will most probably have again maximum red component with change of its value. This fact is taken into consideration, and new algorithm is proposed.

This paper is organized as follows. Section 2 describes the color based image features for CBIR and their shortcomings. Section 3 describes the proposed algorithm. Simulation results are presented in section 4.

2 Color Based Image Features

Color is the most extensively used visual content for image retrieval. Its three dimensional values make its discrimination potentially superior to the single dimensional gray values of images. Before selecting an appropriate color description, color space must be determined.

Each pixel of the image can be represented as a point in a 3D color space. Commonly used space for image retrieval include RGB, Munsell, CIE L*a*b*, CIE L*u*v*, HSV (or HSL, HSB), and opponent color space. There is no agreement on which is the best. RGB color space is widely used color space for image display. It is composed of three color components red, green, and blue. These components are called 'additive primitives' since a color in RGB space is produced by adding them together. In this paper, we have considered RGB color space.

Various color-based image search systems have been proposed based on various representation schemes such as color histograms, color moments, color edge orientation, color texture, and color correlograms [6],[10],[11].

Color histograms are commonly used as image features by many image retrieval systems[12]. Color histogram serves as an effective representation of the color content of an image if the color pattern is unique compared with the rest of the data set. The color histogram is easy to compute and effective in characterizing both the global and local distribution of colors in an image. In addition, it is robust to translation and rotation about the view axis and changes only slowly with the scale, occlusion and viewing angle. However, color histograms have many inherent problems in indexing and retrieving images.

Since any pixel in the image can be described by three components in a certain color space (for instance, red, green and blue components in RGB space, or hue, saturation, and value in HSV space), a histogram, i.e., the distribution of the number of pixels for each quantized bin, can be defined for each component. Clearly, the more bins a color histogram contains, the more discrimination power it has. However, a histogram with a large number of bins will not only increase the computational cost, but will also be inappropriate for building efficient indexes for image databases. The most common size of histograms consists of from 64 to 256 bins. Furthermore, a very fine bin quantization does not necessarily improve the retrieval performance in many applications. One way to reduce the number of bins is to use clustering methods to determine the K best colors in a given space for a given set of images. Each of these best colors will be taken as a histogram bin. In addition, color histogram does not take the spatial information of pixels into consideration, thus very different images can have similar color distributions. This problem becomes especially acute for large scale databases. To increase discrimination power, several improvements have been proposed to incorporate spatial information. A simple approach is to divide an image into sub-areas and calculate a histogram for each of those sub-areas. Increasing the number of sub-areas increases the information about location, but also increases the memory and computational time.

The color correlogram [6] was proposed to characterize not only the color distributions of pixels, but also the spatial correlation of pairs of colors. The first and second dimensions of the three-dimensional histogram are the colors of any pixel pair and the third dimension is their spatial distance. Conventional color co-occurrence matrix (CCM) also represents three-dimensional matrix where the colors of any pair are along the first and second dimension and the spatial distance between them along the third. So the conventional CCM and the color correlogram are same. A color correlogram is a table indexed by color pairs, where the k-th entry for (i, j) specifies the probability of finding a pixel of color j at a distance k from a pixel of color i in the image. Compared to the color histogram, the color autocorrelogram provides the best retrieval results, but is also the most computational expensive due to its high dimensionality.

3 The Proposed Algorithm

In this paper, color co-occurrence, spatial distances and the environmental changes are taken into consideration. With the change of the environmental factors, pixels changed their color with almost same proportions with respect to each other. If one pixel has maximum, say, red component in one view, and after change of illumination, that pixel will most probably have again maximum red component with change of its value. This fact is taken into consideration, and new algorithm is proposed. In this paper, RGB is selected as the color space. The maximum of a color pixel is defined as the color component that has maximum value between the three components (R,G,B) of the pixel. Similarly the minimum of the same color pixel is defined. The color correlogram is redefined based on the maximum/minimum of color component of a pixel for different spatial distances. The proposed algorithm has less number of features, and the change of illumination, etc. is also taken into account.

Before explaining the proposed algorithm, the mathematics of the color histogram and color correlogram are presented. Let I be an N x M image quantized into m colors $c_1,...,c_m$. For a pixel $p = (x, y) \in I$, let $I(p)$ denote its color. Let $I_c \equiv \{p | I(p) = c\}$.

The color histogram h of I is the histogram of quantized color and is defined as

$$h_{c_i}(I) \equiv N.M . \Pr_{p \in I}[p \in I_{c_i}] \quad (1)$$

A color correlogram is a table indexed by color pairs, where the k-th entry for (c_i, c_j) specifies the probability of finding a pixel of color c_j at a distance k from a pixel of color c_i in the image. Let a distance d be fixed a priori. Then, the color correlogram is defined as:

$$\gamma_{c_i,c_j}^{(k)} = \Pr_{p_1 \in I_{c_i}, p_2 \in I}\left[p_2 \in I_{c_j} \Big| |p_1 - p_2| = k\right] \quad (2)$$

where $c_i, c_j \in \{c_1,...,c_m\}, k \in \{1,...,d\}, and |p_1 - p_2|$ is the distance between pixels p1 and p2. If we consider all the possible combinations of color pairs the size of the color correlogram will be very large $(O(m^2 d))$, therefore a simplified version of the feature called the color autocorrelogram is often used instead. The color autocorrelogram only captures the spatial correlation between identical colors and thus reduces the dimension to $(O(md))$ and is defined as

$$\alpha_{c_i}^{(k)}(I) \equiv \gamma_{c_i,c_i}^{(k)}(I) \qquad (3)$$

A large d would result in expensive computation and large storage requirements. A small d might compromise the quality of the feature. But the main concern is the quantized colors m. Generally m is chosen from 64 to 256 quantized colors, which is quiet big number for correlogram.

To reduce the number of quantized colors, we adopt the following procedure. Let the color of a pixel be expressed into its three components as triplet order $I(p) \equiv (R(p), G(p), B(p))$. The maximum color component of a pixel I(p) is determined as:

$$I^{max\,com}(p) = ARG \max_{R,G,B}(I(p)) \equiv ARG \max(R(p), G(p), B(p)) \qquad (4)$$

where $I^{max\,com}(p)$ has one of three values from the set $\{R_{max}, G_{max}, B_{max}\}$ depending on the maximum color components of I(p). Similarly the minimum color component of a pixel I(p) is determined as:

$$I^{min\,com}(p) = ARG \min_{R,G,B}(I(p)) \equiv ARG \min(R(p), G(p), B(p)) \qquad (5)$$

where $I^{min\,com}(p)$ has value from the set $\{R_{min}, G_{min}, B_{min}\}$. The quantized colors m in the cases of the color histogram and the color correlogram is here reduced to set

$$A = \{R_{max}G_{min}, R_{max}B_{min}, G_{max}R_{min}, G_{max}B_{min}, B_{max}R_{min}, B_{max}G_{min}\} \qquad (6)$$

The modified color correlogram is now a table indexed by color pairs, where the k-th entry for (c_i, c_j) specifies the probability of finding a pixel of color c_j from set A at a distance k from a pixel of color c_i from set A in the image. The modified color correlogram has the complexity of the order $(O(6^2 d))$.

4 Simulation Results

4.1 Similarity Measures

Instead of exact matching, content-based image retrieval calculates visual similarities between a query image and images in a database. Accordingly, the retrieval result is not a single image but a list of images ranked by their similarities with the query image. Many similarity measures have been developed for image retrieval based on empirical estimates of the distribution of features in recent years. Different similarity/distance measures will affect retrieval performances of an image retrieval system significantly. The most popular distance measure in the literature is normalized distance intersection proposed by Swain and Ballard [4], and is also used here for the matching. It has been shown that the histogram intersection is fairly insensitive to changes in image resolution, histogram size, occlusion, depth and viewing point.

Let Q be the query image and I be the image from the database. Then, the similarity measures between query image Q and image I from the database for the different described algorithms are given as:

$$S^{hist}(Q,I) = \frac{\sum_{i=1}^{m}\min\{h_{c_i}(Q),h_{c_i}(I)\}}{\sum_{i=1}^{m}h_{c_i}(Q)} \quad (7)$$

$$S^{correl}(Q,I) = \frac{\sum_{c_i,c_j\in[m], k\in[d]}\min\{\gamma_{c_i,c_j}^{(k)}(Q),\gamma_{c_i,c_j}^{(k)}(I)\}}{\sum_{c_i,c_j\in[m], k\in[d]}\gamma_{c_i,c_j}^{(k)}(Q)} \quad (8)$$

$$S^{auto}(Q,I) = \frac{\sum_{c_i\in[m], k\in[d]}\min\{\alpha_{c_i}^{(k)}(Q),\alpha_{c_i}^{(k)}(I)\}}{\sum_{c_i\in[m], k\in[d]}\alpha_{c_i}^{(k)}(Q)} \quad (9)$$

$$S^{prop}(Q,I) = \frac{\sum_{c_i,c_j\in A, k\in[d]}\min\{\gamma_{c_i,c_j}^{(k)}(Q),\gamma_{c_i,c_j}^{(k)}(I)\}}{\sum_{c_i,c_j\in A, k\in[d]}\gamma_{c_i,c_j}^{(k)}(Q)} \quad (10)$$

4.2 Performance Measures

For performance measure, the criteria proposed by Gevers and Smeulders [3] are used. Let rank r^{Q_i} denote the position of the correct match for query image $Q_i, i=1,...,N_2$, in the ordered list of N_1 match values. The rank r^{Q_i} ranges from r = 1 from a perfect match to $r = N_1$ for the worst possible match. The average ranking $\bar{r}$ and its percentile are defined by

$$\bar{r} = \frac{1}{N_2}\sum_{i=1}^{N_2}r^{Q_i}, \text{ and} \quad (11)$$

$$\bar{r}\% = \left(\frac{1}{N_2}\sum_{i=1}^{N_2}\frac{N_1 - r^{Q_i}}{N_1 - 1}\right)100\% \quad (12)$$

4.3 Experimental Results

In this section, the retrieval performance of the proposed algorithm and the comparison with other color based algorithms are investigated. We select $N_2 = 90$ query images from the $N_1 = 3,000$ database images. The retrievals based on the

Table 1. Performance measure for Color based features extraction algorithms

Method	# of features	$\bar{r}$ measure	$\bar{r}$ % measure
S^{hist}	64	61.2	92.1
S^{correl}	64x64x1	55.0	96.5
S^{auto}	64x2	58.1	95.2
S^{prop} with d = 1	6x6x1	59.0	93.0
S^{prop} with d = 2	6x6x2	53.0	97.1

proposed algorithm S^{prop} with d = 1 and d = 2, color histogram S^{hist} with m = 64 quantized colors, color correlogram S^{correl} with m = 64, d = 1 and auto-correlogram S^{auto} with m = 64, d = 2 are used for the comparison.

The performance measures for different color based features extraction algorithms are shown in table 1. The proposed algorithm shows better results, especially when the spatial distance d = 2. The proposed algorithm has less number of features as compared to the rest of algorithms.

5 Conclusions

In this paper, color based feature extraction algorithms are studied. The color histogram does not take into account the spatial relationship among the pixels. The color correlogram takes care of the spatial correlation of pairs of colors. Color not only reflects the material of surface, but also varies considerably with the change of illumination, the orientation of the surface, and the viewing geometry of the camera. This variability must be taken into account. However, the invariance to these environmental factors is not considered in most of the color features in color based CBIR including the color correlogram. In this paper, the color features extraction based on the maximum and minimum of color components are presented. The color correlogram is defined based on the maximum/minimum of color component of a pixel for different spatial distances. The proposed algorithm has less number of features, and the change of illumination, etc. is also taken into account.

Acknowledgements

This study was supported by research fund from the Chosun University, 2004.

References

1. Arnold W.M. Smeulders, Marcel Worring, Simone Santini, Amarnath Gupta, and Ramesh Jain: Content-based image retrieval at the end of the early years. IEEE Transactions of Pattern Analysis and Machine Intelligence, vol. 22, No. 12, December (2000) 1349-1380

2. Yong Rui and Thomas S. Huang: Image retrieval: Current technologies, promising directions, and open issues. Journal of Visual Communication and Image Representation, vol. 10 (1999) 39-62
3. Theo Gevers and Arnold W.M. Smeulders: PicToSeek. Combining color and shape invariant features for image retrieval. IEEE Transactions on Image Processing, vol. 9, No. 1 January (2001) 102-119
4. M. Swain and D. Ballard, "Color indexing: International Journal of Computer Vision, 7(1) (1991) 11-32
5. Brian V. Funt and Graham D. Finlason: Color constant color indexing. IEEE Transactions on Image Processing, vol. 17, No. 5 May (1995) 522-529
6. Jing Huang, S Ravi Kumar, Mandar Mitra, Wei-Jing Zhu and Ramin Zabi: Image indexing using color correlograms. Computer Vision and Pattern Recognition. (1997) 17-19
7. Jan-Mark Geusebroek, Rein van den Boomgaard, Arnold W.M. Smeulders, and Hugo Geerts: Color invariance. IEEE Transactions of Pattern Analysis and Machine Intelligence, vol. 23, No. 12, December (2001) 1349-1380
8. G. C. Gotlieb and H.E. Kreyszig: Texture descriptors based on co-occurrence matrices. Computer Vision, Graphics, and Image Processing 51. (1990)
9. N.R. Howe and D.P. Huttenlocher: Integrating color, texture, and geometry for image retrieval. Proc. Computer Vision and Pattern Recognition. (2000) 239-247
10. D.A. Forsyth: A novel algorithm for color constancy. International Journal of Computer Vision, vol. 5, No. 1 (1990) 5-36
11. J. Huang and S.R. Kumar, M. Mitra, W.-J. Zhu and R. Zabih: Spatial color indexing and applications. International Journal of Computer Vision, vol. 35, No. 3 (1999) 245-268
12. A.K. Jain and A. Vailaya: Image retrieval using color and shape. Pattern Recognition, vol. 29, No. 8 (1996) 1233-1244

A Novel Data Fusion Scheme for Offline Chinese Signature Verification

Wen-ming Zuo and Ming Qi

School of Electronic Business, South China University of Technology,
Guangzhou, P.R. China 510640
wmzuo@yeah.net

Abstract. A novel data fusion signature verification scheme which combines two schemes is proposed. The first scheme with static features described with Pseudo-Zernike invariant moments and some dynamic features is built with a BP (back-propagation) network. In another scheme, 40 values computed with SVD(singular value decomposition) on thinned signature image and thinned high-density image compose the feature vector and another BP network is built for every kind of signature. Then these two BP networks are connected and their outputs are competitively selected to achieve the final output result. A collection of 290 signatures is used to test the verification system. And experiment shows that FAR (False Acceptance Rate) and FRR (False Rejection Rate) can achieve 5.71% and 6.25% respectively.

1 Introduction

Due to the style complexity of Chinese character writing and specialty of Chinese character structure, it is still difficult to verify offline Chinese signatures. Many verification systems were proposed for off-line English signatures, and few were presented for Chinese signatures[1-5]. And features extracted by these schemes can not reflect the specialty of Chinese signatures well[6]. This paper proposes a novel data fusion scheme for off-Line Chinese signature verification based on [6].

The scope of this paper includes a description of data collection and image preprocessing, two schemes for signature verification, a data fusion scheme, experiment results and a final conclusion.

2 Data Collection and Image Preprocessing

150 genuine signatures were collected from 15 volunteers. Two of them simulated other's signatures and wrote 5 skillful forgeries for every other volunteer. These two people were high educated with relatively high levels of literacy, and the forgeries they produced were very similar to genuine ones. In total, there were 290 signatures collected. They were written on a piece of white paper and then scanned into 8-bit gray level images at resolution of 100 dpi by Uniscan e40.

In preprocessing, we found that Ammar's method[7] did not work well in our case. To separate the signatures from the background, we directly used Ostu's algorithm to set a threshold (THD) automatically, and the gray level signature image $S_g[i,j]$ was successfully obtained. Dynamic features were extracted based on $S_g[i,j]$.

$$S_g[i] = \begin{cases} 255 & if\ (S[i,j] > THD) \\ S[i,j] & otherwise \end{cases} \quad (1)$$

When static features were extracted, the signature image was transformed into a binary image $S_b[i,j]$, and then it was thinned to $S_t[i,j]$ using a parallel algorithm [8].

3 Scheme Based on Invariant Moments and Wavelet Transform

In this scheme, static features are described with Pseudo-Zernike invariant moments[6]. Dynamic features include global and local HDFs, relative gravity center of global HDR and a ratio feature extracted using wavelet transform on the weighted and normalized histogram of the gray signature image.

With these features, a BP network is constructed. There are 17 neurons in the input layer, ten in the hidden-layer, and two in the output layer. An object error is set as 0.01. When an output result is [1 0]' that means true and [0 1]' means false. Then the network is trained with 5 genuine samples and other signature samples as forgery ones. When a unknown sample is input, the verification result is output.

4 Scheme Based on SVD

In this paper, two schemes are proposed and further a novel data fusion scheme for offline handwritten signature verification is presented. The algorithm based on SVD is as followed:

a) Gray level signature image is extracted. And it is binarized and then thinned. Object pixel is as 1, and background pixel is as 0. Then a signature image matrix is obtained. And then SVD is processed on it. The first 20 singular values compose the first feature vector.

b) A high-density image namely high-pressure area image is calculated[6]. And it's thinned to decrease influence of stroke width. Then singular values of the matrix are calculated. The first 20 values compose another feature vector.

c) So the final vector including 40 values is obtained through composing these 2 vectors.

d) A 3-layer BP network is built for every kind of signature. There are 40 neurons in the input layer, ten in the hidden-layer, and two in the output layer. An object error is set as 0.0001. If an output result is [1 0]' that means true and [0 1]' means false.

e) This network is trained with 5 genuine samples and other signature samples as forgery ones.

f) An input unknown sample is verified.

5 Data Fusion Scheme

Actually the neuron network is as a kind of data fusion method[9]. In this paper, a novel data fusion scheme based on the BP network is proposed.

These two schemes are effective for offline signature verification. In our research, the method based on SVD is useful for verifying simple forgeries and the method based on invariant moments and wavelet transform is effective for verifying skillful forgery ones. Two BP networks are connected, and their outputs are fused using competitive selection. So with this data fusion scheme, the final result is obtained. This is described as Figure 1.

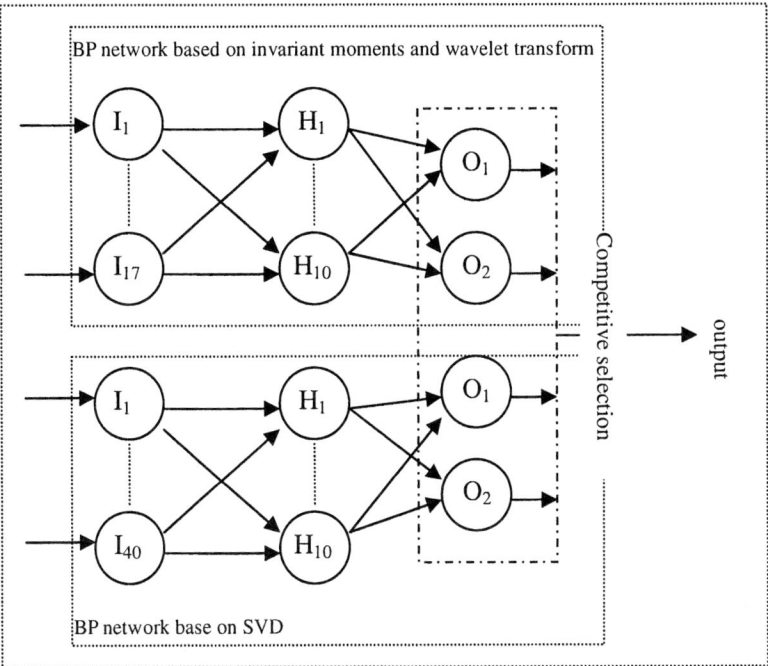

Fig. 1. Data fusion scheme for signature verification

6 Verification and Experiment Result

With this data fusion scheme, a novel system is built to test samples. Experiment results are shown in Table 1.

Table 1. Experiment results

	Scheme based on invariant moments and wavelet transform	Scheme based on SVD	Data fusion scheme
FAR	7.84%	14.28%	5.71%
FRR	6.89%	6.25%	6.25%

From the experiment results, it is shown that this data fusion scheme is more effective than any of the two schemes involved.

7 Conclusion

The study on Chinese signatures shows that some areas of individuals' signatures remain constant, even though every signature written by the same person is different. So we focus on these regions and they are described with several dynamic features. When they are structurally described, we use matrix and extract features with SVD.

In conclusion, a novel data fusion scheme is presented with an aim to characterize offline handwritten Chinese signatures, and our experiment results have demonstrated the effectiveness of this scheme.

References

1. Jun Lin and Jie-gu Li: Off-line Chinese signature verification. 1996 International Conference on Image Processing (1996) 205-207
2. Hai Lin, Hai-Zhou Li: Chinese signature verification with moment Invariants. 1996 IEEE International Conference on Systems, Man., and Cybernetics (1996) 2963-2966
3. Yaqian Shen, Qinghua Qiang, Jingui Pan: Off-line signature verification using geometric features specific to Chinese handwritten. 24th Int. Conf. Information Technology Interfaces (2002) 229-235
4. Peter Shaohua Deng, et al.: Wavelet-based off-line handwritten signature verification. Computer Vision and Image Understanding 3(1999) 173-190
5. Yuanyuan Ding et al.: Offline Chinese signature verification system with information fusion. Proceedings of SPIE, Third International Symposium on Multispectral Image Processing and Pattern Recognition (2003) 875-878
6. Wen-ming Zuo, Shao-fa Li, Xian-gui Zeng: A hybrid scheme for offline Chinese signature verification. 2004 IEEE Conference on Cybernetics and Intelligent Systems (2004) 1401-1404
7. M. Ammar, Yuuji Yoshida and Teruo Fukumura: Off-line preprocessing and verification of signature. International Journal of Pattern Recognition and Artificial Intelligence 4(1988) 589-602
8. Bin He, et al.: Visual C++ digital image processing. Ren Min You Dian Press, Beijing (2001) (in Chinese)
9. S.P. Chaudhuri, S. Das.: Neural networks for data fusion. 1990 IEEE International Conference on Systems Engineering (1990) 327 – 330

A Multiple Eigenspaces Constructing Method and Its Application to Face Recognition

Wu-Jun Li, Bin Luo, Chong-Jun Wang,
Xiang-Ping Zhong, and Zhao-Qian Chen

National Laboratory for Novel Software Technology,
Nanjing University, Nanjing 210093, P.R. China
{liwujun, chjwang}@ai.nju.edu.cn
{luobin, chenzq, chjwang }@nju.edu.cn

Abstract. The well-known eigenface method uses a single eigenspace to recognize faces. However, it is not enough to represent face images with large variations, such as illumination and pose variations. To overcome this disadvantage, many researchers have introduced multiple eigenspaces into face recognition field. But most of these methods require that both the number of eignspaces and dimensionality of the PCA subspaces are a priori given. In this paper, a novel self-organizing method to build multiple, low-dinensinal eigenspaces from a set of training images is proposed. By *eigenspace-growing* in terms of low-dimensional eigenspaces, it completes clustering images systematically and robustly. Then each cluster is used to construct an eigenspace. After all these eigenspaces have been grown, a selection procedure *eigenspace-selection* is used to select the ultimate resulting set of eigenspaces as an effective representation of the training images. Then based on these eigenspaces, a framework combined with neural network is used to complete face recognition under variable poses and the experimental result shows that our framework can complete face recognition with high performance.

1 Introduction

Face recognition is to identify or verify one or more persons in the given still or video images of a scene using a stored database of faces [1]. Due to various applications in the areas of pattern recognition, image processing, computer vision, and cognitive science and so on, face recognition has gained much attention in recent years. Existing approaches for face recognition can be classified into two categories [2]: geometric feature-based methods and appearance-based methods. The geometric feature-based methods, such as elastic bunch graph matching [3] and active appearance model [4], make use of the geometrical parameters that measure the facial parts; whereas the appearance -based methods use the intensity or intensity-derived parameters. As a representative of this approach, the eigenface approach [5] has become the benchmark of face recognition techniques.

The FERET evaluation [6], however, shows that the performance of a face recognition system may decrease seriously with the change of illumination condition or pose. To recognize faces under variable pose, Pentland et al [7] have proposed a multiple eigenspaces method, which builds view-specific eigenspaces. For recognition of human faces with any view in a certain viewing angle range, Huang et al [8] have introduced neural network ensemble to multiple eigenspaces. To address the variable illumination issue, Li et al [9] [10] have proposed illumination invariant methods by building multiple eigenspaces in terms of illumination directions. Kim et al [11] proposed a mixture-of-eigenfaces method to recognize face images with pose and illumination variations. All these approaches with multiple eigenspaces outperformed those using a single eigenspace when the face images are of variations in illumination, pose, and expression and so on.

Nevertheless, all these methods require that both the number of eignspaces and dimensionality of the PCA subspaces are a priori given. But in real world, when imaging conditions are affected by a diversity of factors, it is unreasonable to manually divide the images into several groups and then construct an eigenspace for each. Leonardis et al [12] have proposed a self-organizing framework to construct multiple eigenspaces with two procedures called *eigenspace-growing* and *eigenspace-selection*, and tested it on a number of standard image sets with significant performance. In this paper, a novel self-organizing method to build multiple, low-dinensinal eigenspaces from a set of training images is proposed. Using the same terminology as [12], we divide the process into two procedures named *eigenspace-growing* and *eigenspace-selection*. Procedure *eigenspace-growing* of our method is similar to the corresponding one in [12]. Procedure *eigenspace-selection*, however, is novel which is simpler and more understandable. By *eigenspace-growing* in terms of low-dimensional eigenspaces, it completes clustering images systematically and robustly. Then each cluster is used to construct an eigenspace. After all these eigenspaces have been grown, a selection procedure *eigenspace-selection* is used to select the ultimate resulting set of eigenspaces as an effective representation of the training images. Subsequently based on these eigenspaces, a framework combined with neural network is used to complete face recognition. Experimental result indicates that the multiple eigenspaces constructing method of this paper is very effective and our face recognition framework can recognize face images of huge variations with a high recognition ratio.

The rest of this paper is organized as follows. In section 2, we present our self-organizing method to construct multiple eigenspaces. In section 3, we propose a face recognition framework based on neural network and multiple eigenspaces. Section 4 is the empirical study. Finally in section 5, we summarize the contributions of this paper and discuss future work.

2 Construct Multiple Eigenspaces

Given a set of training images, in order to divide them into several groups each of which can be effectively represented by a low-dimensional eigenspace, there are two parts of the problem that have to be solved: to decide the number of eigenspaces and the effective dimension number of each eigenspace. This paper introduces a novel self-organizing method to construct multiple, low-dinensinal eigenspaces from a set of training images systematically and robustly. The method is divided into two procedures: *eigenspace-growing* and *eigenspace-selection*. Procedure *eigenspace-growing* completes grouping images and constructs an eigenspace for each attained cluster while procedure *eigenspace-selection* is used to select a subset of these attained eigenspaces which can effectively represent the training images.

To describe our method conveniently, we first explain some notations. X is a given set of training images and the number of images in X is n, namely, $|X| = n$. $G_j^{(t)}$, $E_j^{(t)}$ and $p_j^{(t)}$ denote, respectively, the jth subset of X, the jth eigenspace, and the effective dimension number of the jth eigenspace, where the superscript $^{(t)}$ denotes that the *eigenspace-growing* procedure is at the tth iteration. δ_{ij} is the distance between the original image x_i and its reconstruction $\hat{x}_{ij}$ from the eigenspace j, $\delta_{ij} = \|x_i - \hat{x}_{ij}\|$. ρ_j is the reconstructive error of the jth eigenspace,

$$\rho_j^2 = \frac{1}{|G_j|} \sum_{x_i \in G_j} (x_i - \hat{x}_{ij})^T (x_i - \hat{x}_{ij}) = \frac{1}{|G_j|} \sum_{x_i \in G_j} \delta_{ij}^2.$$

2.1 Seed Formation

To initiate the growing, a large number of initial subsets of images (seeds), denoted by $G_j^{(0)}$ (assume $|G_j^{(0)}| = k_j (k_j \square n)$), are randomly selected from X and the number of seeds is also random but within a reasonable range according to n. The smallest effective dimension $p_j^{(0)} = 0$ which means that the seed's eigenspace $E_j^{(0)}$ is the mean image $\bar{x}_j = \frac{1}{|G_j^{(0)}|} \sum_{x_i \in G_j^{(0)}} x_i$.

Not all of the generated seeds are useful for the *eigenspace-growing* procedure. So before growing, some of them must be ruled out based on the comparison of the reconstructive error ρ_j with a predefined threshold value. The closer the images included in one seed are, the smaller ρ_j is, hence only seeds with similar images get small ρ_j and are accepted for further growth.

2.2 Eigenspace Growing

For every eigenspace $E_j^{(t)}$, procedure *eigenspace-growing* finds images in X which is compatible to it and adds the image into $G_j^{(t)}$. For every image not included in $G_j^{(t)}$, it is projected onto $E_j^{(t)}$ and the feature coefficients are attained. Then, we reconstruct it from the feature coefficients, and calculate the reconstructive error δ. After all the reconstructive errors are gotten, we sort all the images with respect to the error δ. If the lowest error is above a threshold value, it indicates that there is no image compatible to this eigenspace and the growth of this eigenspace is terminated. Otherwise, we temporarily add the image with the lowest error into $G_j^{(t)}$, and get the temporary $G_j^{(t+1)}$. Then, we construct the temporary eigenspace and calculate its corresponding reconstructive error $\rho_j^{(t+1)}$ based on current effective dimension number.

Then we can decide:
- If $\rho_j^{(t+1)}$ is below a threshold value, we accept current eigenspace as the permanent $E_j^{(t+1)}$ and use it as the base for the growth of next iteration.
- Otherwise, we increase current eigenspace's dimension by one and recalculate the error $\rho_j^{(t+1)}$:
  - ➢ If the error decreases significantly, we accept current eigenspace and current increased dimension with current set of images.
  - ➢ Otherwise, the temporarily added image is rejected, $G_j^{(t+1)} = G_j^{(t)}$, $E_j^{(t+1)} = E_j^{(t)}$, and the growth of this eigenspace is terminated.

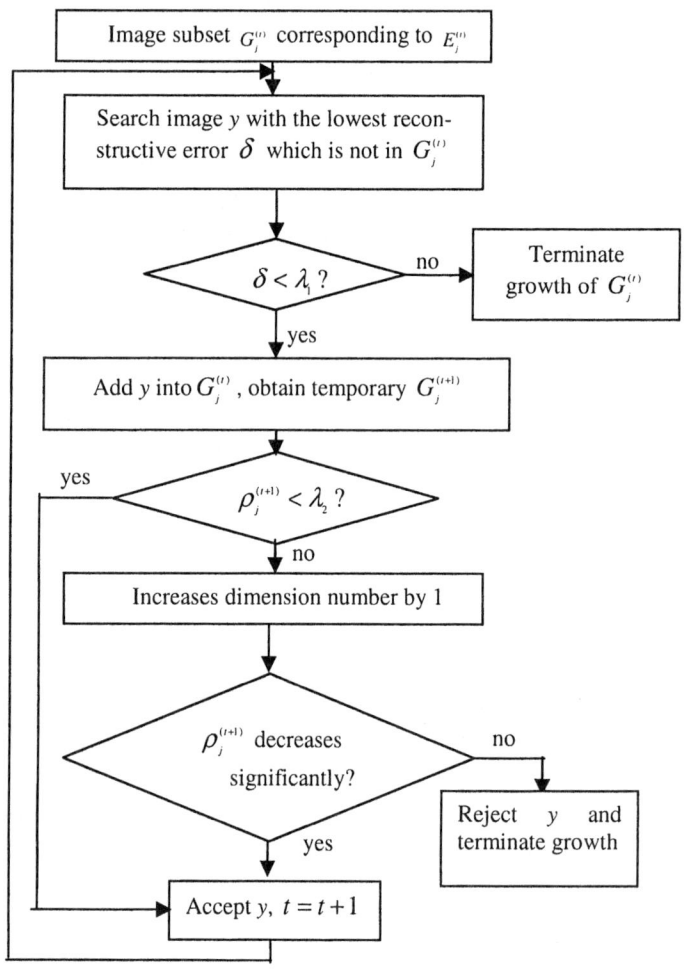

Fig. 1. Eigenspace growing for an individual eigenspace

This completes one iteration of the procedure *eigenspace-growing* which will terminate in a finite number of iterations since n is finite. The procedure *eigenspace-growing* is depicted in Fig.1.

2.3 Eigenspace Selection

Because the eigenspaces are initiated with a large number of random seeds and every seed grows independently, several of the eigenspaces are partially or even completely overlapped in terms of the constituting subsets of images. So certain redundant eigenspaces must be ruled out.

In order to select a set of eigenspaces with large variation in terms of the constituting subsets of images among them, we propose a method based on the idea: If most images in a subset corresponding to an eigenspace are included by the union of subsets corresponding to the other eigenspaces, that eigenspace is rejected. The *eigenspace-selection* procedure is described as follows:

Assume that ultimately k eigenspaces are constructed by procedure *eigenspace-growing*. We sort all of the eigenspaces in an ascending order with respect to the number of the images included in the subset corresponding to each eigenspace. We assume the sorted result is $E_1, E_2, E_3, \ldots, E_k$ and the corresponding subsets are $G_1, G_2, G_3, \ldots, G_k$. For i = 1 to k, let $G_u = [G_{i+1} \ldots G_k]$, where G_u is the union of $G_{i+1} \ldots G_k$. If G_i is a subset of G_u or there are only a small number of images in G_i not included by G_u, G_i is ruled out.

After *eigenspace-selection* procedure is completed, we can attain the necessary eigenspaces that effectively represent the training set.

3 Face Recognition Framework

If the number of eigenspaces is l, the framework for face recognition is shown in Fig.2. Extracting the feature vectors of each image in all l eigenspaces, we can get l eigenvectors. Then by combining all l eigenvectors one by one, we can get the combined eigenvector of the image which is used as the input of a BP-neural network with one hidden layer whose output points out the identity of the image.

At the test phase, given a probe image p, if it belongs to one of the objects in the gallery, the output should tell its identity, otherwise the output is *unrecognizable*. So the output is a binary vector in which one bit stands for a specific object. If the framework is designed to recognize k people, the output vector has $k+1$ bits in which the first k bits stand for k objects to recognize and the last bit stands for *unrecognizable* objects rejected by the framework (also called negative samples). If the identity of the face image is j, the jth bit of the output vector is 1 and the other k bits are 0. And if the identity of the face image is *unrecognizable*, the $(k+1)$th bit is 1 and the other k bits are 0.

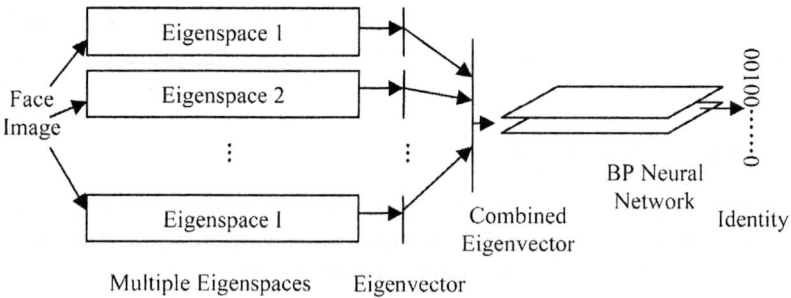

Fig. 2. Framework for face recognition

4 Experiment

To evaluate our framework, we apply it to recognize faces under variable poses. However, it is suitable for recognizing faces with more complex variation, such as arbitrary variations in pose, illumination, and expression and so on.

4.1 Data Acquisition and Preprocessing

In our experiment, we have collected indoor face images using a Logitech QuickCam® Pro 3000 camcorder. To collect face images with different poses, we let subjects sit in front of the camcorder and rotate their heads horizontally from the left side to the right side between ±40 degrees so that in the face images both eyes are always visible. We collected face images of 15 subjects. For all the 15 subjects, we collected 60 images for each subject. Several face images with both eyes being visible in FERET face base [6] are added into the training set for constructing multiple eigenspaces.

To eliminate the effect of the non-face region variations on the recognition performance, we crop the face area from the whole image and perform recognition on the cropped face area. After locating the face and the eyes, we use the method in [8] to estimate the pose of the face in the image. Fig.3 shows a human head seen from above, the distance a between the projection of the mid-point of two eyes and the center of the face, and the radius of the head r (suppose the head has the same shape as a circle) can be attained through face and eye detection. Then we estimate the pose θ by $\theta = \arcsin(a/r)$. First we calculate the mid-point of the two eyes, then extend from the mid-point to the left side by $w(1-\sin\theta/2)/\cos\theta$, extend to top by $w/\cos\theta$, and crop a $3w/\cos\theta$ by $3w/\cos\theta$ area as the face image, then resize it to an image of 80 by 80 pixels, and eliminate its background with a mask of 80 by 80 pixels shown in Fig.4. Fig.5 is some cropped images with various poses from one of the persons in our face base. All training set and test set of this paper are the normalized images just like those shown in Fig.5.

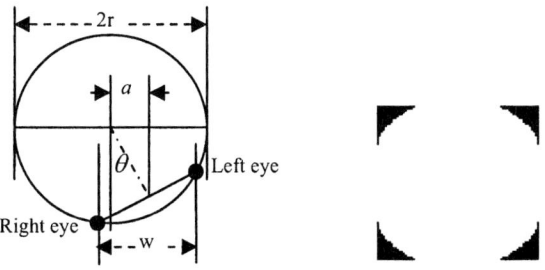

Fig. 3. Pose estimation   **Fig. 4.** Mask image

Fig. 5. The cropped face areas

4.2 Experimental Result

Our experiment is designed to recognize 5 subjects in our database, and use another 5 subjects as a *"rejection"* subject, i.e., negative examples. In the test phase, if the given image is from the first 5 subjects, the output will tell the identity of the subjects or else if the image is from the second 5 subjects, the system will simply reject the image, marking it as *"unrecognizable"*.

As a comparison experiment, we also test the conventional method, which uses neural networks trained on face images with specific poses. In order to train these neural networks, we separate face images into different views using the method in [8]. We group the images into 7 sets: (-35 to -25), (-25 to -15), (-15 to -5), (-5 to +5), (+5 to +15), (+15 to +25), (+25 to +35), and label images falling into each set as -30, -20, -10, 0, +10, +20, and +30 degrees, respectively. That is to say, in this paper, when we say that one image is of 10 degrees, we actually mean that the pose of the face in the image is between 5 and 15 degrees.

Then we create an individual eigenspace with 20 dimensions for each different view by the standard eigenface method in [5], namely, we construct 7 eigenface sets for the -30, -20, -10, 0, +10, +20, and +30 degrees images, respectively. The average faces of seven eigenspaces are shown in Fig.6.

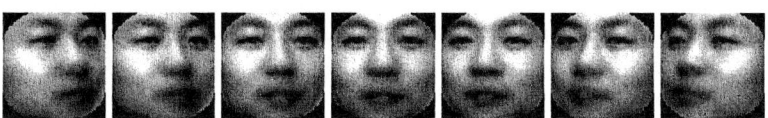

Fig. 6. Average faces of eigenspaces

Table 1. Recognition performance of conventional neural network

Test set / Neural network	-30	-20	-10	0	10	20	30	All
Num of images	18	26	18	34	19	25	21	161
-30 network	100%	88%	78%	62%	63%	72%	62%	74%
-20 network	94%	100%	94%	65%	63%	64%	67%	77%
-10 network	83%	85%	100%	82%	74%	64%	62%	78%
0 network	83%	69%	89%	97%	95%	72%	76%	83%
10 network	72%	77%	89%	85%	100%	92%	76%	84%
20 network	72%	69%	67%	74%	95%	100%	95%	81%
30 network	61%	50%	61%	53%	53%	84%	100%	65%

Table 2. Recognition performance of our framework

Test Set	-30	-20	-10	0	10	20	30	All
Num of images	18	26	18	34	19	25	21	161
Our framework	83%	92%	89%	94%	95%	92%	90%	91%

After the seven eigenspaces are constructed, we train seven back-propagation (BP) neural networks, with training data of -30, -20, -10, 0, +10, +20, and +30 degrees images, respectively. All these networks have 20 input units, 15 hidden units and 6 output units. The training set includes 10 subjects' 542 face images in all and the test set includes 161 face images of the same 10 subjects. The training set and the test set have no intersection. Each column in Table 1 stands for the test images of a specific view, and each row shows the recognition ratio of each neural network tested on images with different poses.

We applied our method presented in section 2 to construct multiple eigenspaces on the training set with various poses including 300 images from FERET face base [6] and 100 images collected by us. Through *eigenspace-growing* and *eigenspace-seletion*, six eigenspaces are finally constructed. The subsets of images corresponding to different eigenspaces have some images with the same pose. So the eigenspaces constructed by our method represent the training set with a globally consistent description. After the six eigenspaces are constructed, we use the same training set (542 images) to train the framework described in section 3 and test it on the same test set (161 images). The recognition result is shown in Table 2.

From Table 1, we can see that if there is an accurate pose estimator and the test image is fed to the right neural network, the recognition rate is above 99% on average, as shown by the diagonal line of Table 1. However, the recognition performance will decrease seriously if the pose estimation is not accurate enough. For example, if the images of -20 degree are fed to the 30 degree network, the recognition ratio is as low as 50%. Furthermore, in real world, the imaging condition is very complex, with arbitrary illumination, pose and expression variations and we do not know which one puts the most significant impact on one specific image. So we do not know how many eigenspaces should be constructed and what the dimension number should be to effectively represent the distribution of face images.

Nevertheless, in our framework, the pose (or other variations) estimation can be skipped. The input image with arbitrary pose can be fed into the framework directly to complete recognition. Moreover, in spite of whatever conditions under which the images are collected, the eigenspaces that represent the images effectively can be constructed in a self-organizing way. In the experiment of this paper, the recognition ratio (91%) of our framework is much higher than the average recognition ratio (77%) of the conventional method without pose estimation. This indicates that our face recognition framework combined with the multiple eigenspaces constructing method is very effective.

5 Conclusion

We have proposed a novel method to construct multiple eigenspaces from a set of training images and applied it to a face recognition framework combined with neural network. The experimental result indicates that our face recognition framework can complete recognition with a high accuracy.

There are many works left to do in the near future. Firstly, the face base is too small and the images in it only have pose variation. We will collect a large face base with more complex imaging conditions to evaluate the multiple eigenspaces constructing method and the face recognition framework. Secondly, the method proposed by Leonardis et al in [12] is not used to recognize faces and our method is also not tested on their image base. We plan to do comparisons with other methods on more data sets. Moreover, we will compare our face recognition framework with some other face recognition methods. Thirdly, the thresholds, such as λ_1, will affect the final resulting set of eigenspaces. We hope to find out the relationship between these thresholds and the ultimate result.

Acknowledgements

The research in this paper used the FERET database of face images collected under the FERET program. The National Natural Science Foundation of P.R.China under grant No. 60273033 and the Natural Science Foundation of Jiangsu Province of China under grant BK2003067 supported this research.

References

1. Zhao, W., Chellappa, R., Rosenfeld, A., Phillips, P. J.: Face Recognition: a Literature Survey. ACM Computing Surveys 35 (2003) 399-458
2. Brunelli, R., Poggio, T.: Face Recognition: Features Versus Templates. IEEE Transactions on Pattern Analysis and Machine Intelligence 15 (1993) 1042-1052
3. Laurenz, W., Jean-Marc, F., Norbert, K., Christoph, v. d. M.: Face Recognition by Elastic Bunch Graph Matching. IEEE Transactions on Pattern Analysis and Machine Intelligence19 (1997) 775-779

4. Edwards, G. J., Cootes, T. F., Taylor, C. J.: Face Recognition Using Active Appearance Models. In: Proceedings of the 5th European Conference on Computer Vision, vol. 2. Freeburg, Germany (1998) 581-595
5. Turk, M., Pentland, A.: Eigenfaces for Recognition. Journal of Cognitive Neuroscience 3 (1991) 71-86
6. Phillips, P. J., Wechsler, H., Huang, J., Rauss, P. J.: The FERET Database and Evaluation Procedure for Face-recognition Algorithms. Image and Vision Computing 16 (1998) 295-306
7. Pentland, A., Moghaddam, B., Starner, T.: View-based and Modular Eigenspaces for Face Recognition. In: Proceedings of the IEEE Conference on Computer Vision and Pattern Recognition, Seattle, WA (1994) 21-23
8. Huang, F. J., Zhou, Z.-H., Zhang, H.-J., Chen, T.: Pose Invariant Face Recognition. In: Proceedings of the 4th IEEE International Conference on Automatic Face and Gesture Recognition, Grenoble, France (2000) 245-250
9. Li, W.-J., Wang, C.-J., Xu, D.-X., Chen, S.-F.: Illumination Invariant Face Recognition Based on Neural Network Ensemble. In: Proceedings of the 16th IEEE International Conference on Tools with Artificial Intelligence (ICTAI 2004), Boca Raton, Florida (2004) 486-490
10. Li, W.-J., Wang, C.-J., Xu, D.-X., Luo, B., Chen, Z.-Q.: A Study on Illumination Invariant Face Recognition Methods Based on Multiple Eigenspaces. Lecture Notes in Computer Science, Vol. 3497. Chongqing, China (2005) 131-136
11. Kim, H.-C., Kim, D., Bang, S. Y.: Face Recognition Using the Mixture-of-eigenfaces Method. Pattern Recognition Letters 23 (2002) 1549-1558
12. Leonardis, A., Bischof, H., Maver, J.: Multiple Eigenspaces. Pattern Recognition 35 (2002) 2613-2627

Quality Estimation of Fingerprint Image Based on Neural Network[*]

En Zhu, Jianping Yin, Chunfeng Hu, and Guomin Zhang

School of Computer Science, National University of Defense Technology,
Changsha 410073, China
nudt_en@263.net, jpyin@nudt.edu.cn

Abstract. Quality estimation of fingerprint image can be used to control image quality at the enrollment stage of automatic recognition system and guide the enhancement of fingerprint image. This paper proposes a neural network based fingerprint image quality estimation method. It estimates the correctness of ridge orientation of each local image block using neural network and then computes the global image quality based on the local orientation correctness. The proposed method is used to guide the fingerprint enrollment and improves the accuracy of the automatic fingerprint recognition system.

1 Introduction

An automatic fingerprint recognition system typically consists of two stages: enrollment and recognition. At the stage of enrollment, several fingerprint image of the same finger is usually inputted, and the system chooses one or several of them as the template fingerprint. Quality estimation plays an important role in controlling the quality of template fingerprint: the system may choose the fingerprint of the best quality as the template. And besides, quality estimation is important to enhancement [1] and minutiae detection [2]. Images of low quality, which is measured by some way, have to be preprocessed [3] before detecting minutiae. Ratha [4] proposed a method to estimate fingerprint image quality from the wavelet compressed image. This method is not suitable for images which need not to be compressed. Bolle [5] and Shen [6] estimated fingerprint image quality by computing the ratio of regions of different types: the ratio of directional regions to unidirectional regions [5] and the ratio of high quality region to poor quality region.

Correct estimation of local ridge orientation is the base of feature extraction (e.g. minutiae detection) of fingerprint image. The incorrect estimation of local ridge orientation typically indicates that the local ridge is noisy and its structure is unrecoverable. This paper proposes a neural network based fingerprint image quality estimation method. It estimates the correctness of local ridge orientation using neural network and then computes the global image quality based on the local orientation correctness. The proposed method is used to guide the fingerprint enrollment and improves the accuracy of the automatic fingerprint recognition system.

---

[*] This work was supported by the National Natural Science Foundation of China under Grant No. 60373023.

2 Quality Estimation

Let I denote a gray-level fingerprint image of size $m \times n$, where $I(x, y)(0 \le x < m, 0 \le y < n)$ is the intensity of the pixel at the xth row and yth column. Divide I into non-overlapping blocks of size $w \times w$ (15×15). Each block is denoted as $W(i, j)$ where (i, j) is the location of W. The center coordination of $W(i, j)$ is $(i \times w + w/2, j \times w + w/2)$. $O_{W(i,j)}^I \in [0, \pi]$ is defined as the orientation of $W(i, j)$.

The main steps of our quality estimation are as follows:

(1) Compute local ridge orientation of each block;
(2) Compute correctness of the estimated local orientation using a trained BPNN;
(3) Estimate the global image quality based on the correctness of local orientation.

Some methods about orientation estimation are reported in literatures. The orientation computation method used in our scheme is the method in Ref [7].

The estimated local orientations are trained using a BPNN. For a specific image block containing ridge structure with correct estimated local orientation, the neural network should respond to it with a large value. And if the block contains no ridge or has incorrect estimated local orientation, the network should respond with a small value. For a block containing ridges, correct estimation of orientation indicates the block quality is high, and incorrect estimation indicates that the quality is poor. Thus the network responding value is related to the quality of the image block. The larger the responding value, the higher quality the image is of. For each image block 11 features, denoted as $\langle C_1, C_2, ..., C_{11} \rangle$, are computed to input to the neural network that outputs a responding value to indicate whether the estimated local orientation is correct or not. Let $\langle G_x(u,v), G_y(u,v) \rangle$ be the gradient at the pixel (u,v). Let (i, j) be the center of $W(k, l)$. The feature vector $\langle C_1, C_2, ..., C_{11} \rangle$ for image block $W(k, l)$ is computed as follows:

(1) C_1, the normal of the sum of the squared gradient vector in the block $W(k,l)$, is computed as

$$C1 = \left| \sum_{u=i-w/2}^{i+w/2} \sum_{v=j-w/2}^{j+w/2} \langle G_x(u,v), G_y(u,v) \rangle^2 \right| \quad (1)$$

(2) C_2, the sum of the normal of the squared gradient vector in the block $W(k,l)$, is computed as

$$C2 = \sum_{u=i-w/2}^{i+w/2} \sum_{v=j-w/2}^{j+w/2} \left| \langle G_x(u,v), G_y(u,v) \rangle^2 \right| \quad (2)$$

(3) C_3, the mean gray of the block $W(k,l)$, is computed as

$$C3 = \sum_{u=i-w/2}^{i+w/2} \sum_{v=j-w/2}^{j+w/2} I(u,v) \Big/ (w \cdot w) \qquad (3)$$

(4) C_4, the gray variance of the block $W(k,l)$, is computed as

$$C4 = \sum_{u=i-w/2}^{i+w/2} \sum_{v=j-w/2}^{j+w/2} (I(u,v) - C2)^2 \Big/ (w \cdot w - 1) \qquad (4)$$

(5) C_5 is the variance of the projected signal along the direction orthogonal to the estimated local ridge orientation as shown in Fig.1(a). The projection window is of size LxH and with the side L parallel to the estimated local orientation. And the center of the window and the center of the block $W(k,l)$ are overlapped. C_5 is computed as equation (5) and (6).

$$Pv[k] = \frac{\sum_{h=-H/2}^{H/2} I(i - h \cdot \sin(O^I_{W(i,j)}) + k \cdot \cos(O^I_{W(i,j)}), j + h \cdot \cos(O^I_{W(i,j)}) + k \cdot \sin(O^I_{W(i,j)}))}{H'} \qquad (5)$$

$$C5 = \sum_{l=-L/2}^{L/2} \left(Pv[l] - \sum_{k=-L/2}^{L/2} Pv[k] \Big/ L \right) \Big/ (L-1) \qquad (6)$$

(6) C_6 is the variance of the projected signal along the direction parallel to the estimated local ridge orientation as shown in Fig.1(b). The projection window is of size LxH (41x15) (side H is parallel to the estimated local orientation) and its center is overlapped with the center of lock $W(k,l)$. C_6 is computed using equation (7) (8).

$$Pv[k] = \frac{\sum_{h=-H/2}^{H/2} (i - h \cdot \sin(O^I_{W(i,j)}) + k \cdot \cos(O^I_{W(i,j)}), j + h \cdot \cos(O^I_{W(i,j)}) + k \cdot \sin(O^I_{W(i,j)}))}{H'} \qquad (7)$$

$$C5 = \sum_{l=-L/2}^{L/2} \left(Pv[l] - \sum_{k=-L/2}^{L/2} Pv[k] \Big/ L \right) \Big/ (L-1) \qquad (8)$$

The features are computed using the smoothed signal, by Guass filter, of $Ph[k]$ $(-L/2 \leq k \leq L/2)$. Fig.2 gives out an example of computing from C_7 to C_{11}.

(7) C_7 is average inter-ridge distance.

(8) C_8 is the variance of the peak heights of the signal.

(9) C_9 is the variance of the valley heights of the signal.

(10) C_{10} is the average amplitude of the signal.

(11) C_{11} is the variance of inter-peak-valley distance.

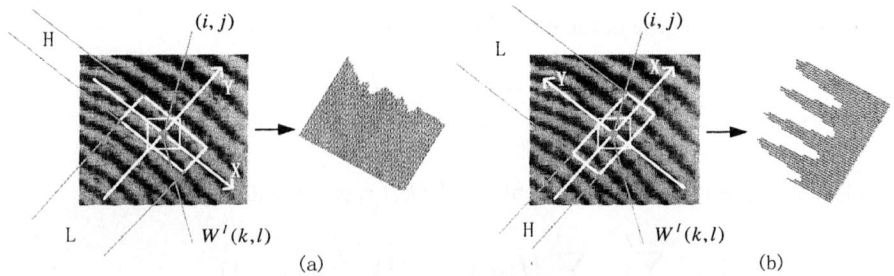

Fig. 1. Projection. (a) Projection along the direction orthogonal to the estimated ridge orientation. (b) Projection along the direction parallel to the estimated ridge orientation.

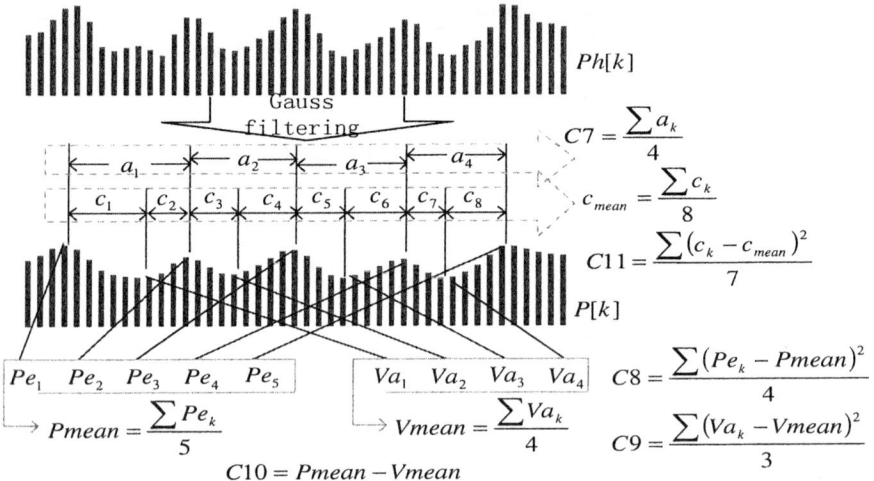

Fig. 2. An example of computing the features of projected signal

When training the neural network, use $\langle C_1, C_2, ..., C_{11} \rangle$ as the input. If the current image block contain ridge structure and the estimated local orientation is correct, the network outputs 1, else outputs 0. At the stage of quality estimation, sum the output value, which is over a certain threshold t_s, of the network at each local image block. The summed value represents the image quality to be estimated.

3 Experiments

Fig.3 gives out some examples of our quality estimation results. The figure shows us that high quality images are of large quality values, which is accordant with our visual judgment.

Quality Estimation of Fingerprint Image Based on Neural Network 69

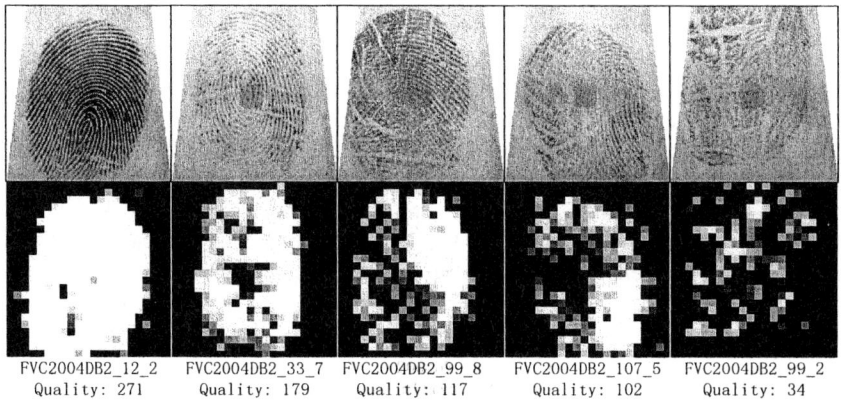

FVC2004DB2_12_2   FVC2004DB2_33_7   FVC2004DB2_99_8   FVC2004DB2_107_5   FVC2004DB2_99_2
Quality: 271   Quality: 179   Quality: 117   Quality: 102   Quality: 34

Fig. 3. Examples of quality estimation results. The first row is the original images from fvc2004db2; The second row is the responding images by the trained neural network; .The quality values are listed below the responding images.

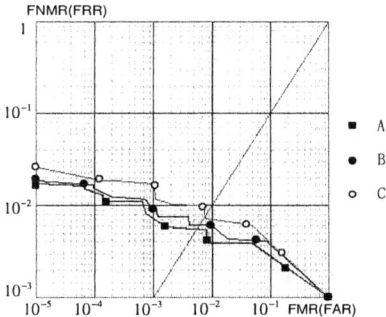

Fig. 4. ROC curve of 3 enrollment methods

Fingerprint image quality estimation should be able to guide template fingerprint selection. At the enrollment stage of automatic fingerprint recognition system, several impressions of the same finger are input to be typically selected one of them as the template. In order to validate the proposed method, we use 3 template selection methods for comparison. Method A selects the fingerprint of the largest quality value, estimated by the proposed, as the template. Method B selects the template similarly, but the quality value is computed by Shen method [6]. Method C chooses the first input fingerprint as the template. FVC2004_DB4, which contain 100 fingers, 8 impressions per finger, is used in the experiments. When testing, the first 3 impressions of each finger are used for enrollment input, and the other 5 impressions are used to match with the template: the last 5 impressions are matched with the template of the same finger to compute FNMR(FRR) and the 4th impression are matched with the templates of other fingers to compute FMR(FAR). The experiments get the ROC curves as shown in Fig.4, which shows us that the proposed method can effectively guide the enrollment and improve the system performance.

4 Conclusion

This paper proposed a fingerprint image quality estimation method based on neural network. Experiments show that the estimated quality value can effectively guide the template selection at the enrollment stage. The quality value of the neural network based method is computed from the local ridge orientation correctness, which is computed using the trained neural network, of each local image block. The local correctness represents the quality of the local image block, and can be used for fingerprint enhancement and segmentation, which will be discussed in our following works.

References

1. E. Zhu, J.P. Yin, and G.M. Zhang. Fingerprint Enhancement Using Circular Gabor Filter. Proc. Int. Conf. Image Analysis and Recognition, LNCS 3212, 2004:750-758.
2. X. Jiang, W.Y. Yau, and W. Ser. Detecting the Fingerprint Minutiae by Adaptive Tracing the Gray-level Ridge. Pattern Recognition, 2001, 34: 999-1013.
3. O. Bergengruen. Preprocessing of poor quality fingerprint images, in XIV intl. Conf. of the Chilean Computer Science Society, October 1994.
4. N.K. Ratha and R.M. Bolle. Fingerprint Image Quality Estimation. IBM Computer Science Research Report RC 21622, 1999.
5. Bolle. System and Method for Determining the Quality of Fingerprint Images. United State Patent number, US596356, 1999.
6. L.L. Shen, A. Kot, and W.M. Koo. Quality Measures of Fingerprint Images . Proc. Int. Conf. on AVBPA 2001, 2001:182-271.
7. A.M. Bazen and S.H. Gerez. Systematic Methods for the Computation of the Directional Fields and Singular Points of Fingerprints. IEEE Transactions on Pattern Analysis and Machine Intelligence, 2002, 24(7): 905-919.

Face Recognition Based on PCA/KPCA Plus CCA

Yunhui He, Li Zhao, and Cairong Zou

Department of Radio Engineering, Southeast University,
Nanjing 210096, P.R. China
heyunhui@seu.edu.cn

Abstract. Based on the equivalence between canonical correlation analysis (CCA) and Fisher linear discriminant analysis (FLDA), two methods for feature extraction of face images are proposed in this paper. In the first approach, the high-dimensional face images are first mapped into the range space of total scatter matrix using principle component analysis (PCA). Then CCA is performed to extract the linear optimal discriminant features without losing Fisher discriminatory information. In the second approach, nonlinear features are extracted using KPCA+CCA which is equivalent to KFDA in nature. The experimental results upon ORL face database indicate that the proposed PCA/KPCA+CCA significantly outperform the traditional Fisherface method.

1 Introduction

The canonical correlation analysis (CCA) equivalent to Fisher linear discriminant analysis (FLDA [1]) [4] has not been applied in face discriminant analysis. Therefore, two methods based on CCA are proposed to extract linear/nonlinear discriminant features of face image in this paper. These two methods employ PCA and KPCA respectively to reduce the dimension of original samples before performing CCA, which overcome the small sample size (SSS) problem in FLDA for face recognition.

2 Equivalence Between CCA and FLDA

Let $u = X^T a$ and $v = Y^T b$ denote the linear combination of the rows of X and Y respectively. The goal of CCA is to determine vector a and b to maximize correlation between two vectors u and v $(u, v \in R^d)$. This problem is equivalent to solve the following eigenvalue problem [2]

$$\Sigma_x^{-1}\Sigma_{xy}\Sigma_y^{-1}\Sigma_{yx}a = r^2(t,u)a = \lambda^{CCA}a \qquad (1)$$

where $\Sigma_x, \Sigma_y, \Sigma_{xy}, \Sigma_{yx}$ are estimated as follows using data matrices X and Y where each row is a sample

$$S_x = X^T X/(n-1),\ S_y = Y^T Y/(n-1),\ S_{xy} = X^T Y/(n-1),\ S_{yx} = Y^T X/(n-1) \qquad (2)$$

The direct connection between CCA and FLDA was given in [3] by coding a dummy matrix $\mathbf{Y}$. Suppose that there are C classes, and n_i samples in class C_i. Total number of samples is $n = \sum_{i=1}^{C} n_i$. The dummy matrix $\mathbf{Y}$ is denoted as

$$\mathbf{Y} = \begin{bmatrix} \mathbf{1}_{n_1} & \mathbf{0}_{n_1} & \cdots & \mathbf{0}_{n_1} \\ \mathbf{0}_{n_2} & \mathbf{1}_{n_2} & \cdots & \mathbf{0}_{n_2} \\ \vdots & \cdots & \ddots & \vdots \\ \vdots & \cdots & \cdots & \mathbf{1}_{n_{C-1}} \\ \mathbf{0}_{n_C} & \mathbf{0}_{n_C} & \cdots & \mathbf{0}_{n_C} \end{bmatrix}_{n \times (C-1)} \quad (3)$$

where $\mathbf{1}_{n_i}$ denote $n_i \times 1$ vector of all ones, $\mathbf{0}_{n_i}$ denote $n_i \times 1$ vector of all zeros. $\mathbf{Y}$ denotes the class labels of samples in matrix $\mathbf{X}$. In FLDA, the total scatter matrix $\mathbf{S}_t$, $\mathbf{S}_x$, between and within class matrix $\mathbf{S}_b$ and $\mathbf{S}_w$ have following relationship

$$\mathbf{S}_b + \mathbf{S}_w = (n-1)\mathbf{S}_x = \mathbf{S}_t \quad (4)$$

The FLDA is equivalent to solve the following eigenequation [1]

$$\mathbf{S}_b \mathbf{a} = \lambda^{LDA} \mathbf{S}_w \mathbf{a} \quad (5)$$

The discriminant vectors in FLDA are the eigenvectors corresponding to the nonzero eigenvalues. The equivalence between CCA and FLDA was presented as follows in [3], which was yet not proofed. In this paper, we give a brief proof based on two theorems in appendix. The vector $\mathbf{b}$ in CCA is useless in discriminant analysis.

$$\mathbf{S}_x^{-1}\mathbf{S}_{xy}\mathbf{S}_y^{-1}\mathbf{S}_{yx}\mathbf{a} = \lambda^{CCA}\mathbf{a} \Leftrightarrow \mathbf{S}_b \mathbf{a} = \lambda^{LDA} \mathbf{S}_w \mathbf{a} \quad (6)$$

3 Feature Extraction Using PCA/KPCA+CCA

The rank of d by d covariance matrix $\mathbf{S}_x$ is $n-1$ which is always singular due to $d > n-1$ in face recognition, so CCA can not be performed directly. To solve this problem, we reduce dimension of original face image sample using PCA into range space of the total scatter matrix. Because face image samples are independent, this space has $n-1$ dimensions. Furthermore, projecting samples into range space of total scatter matrix does not lose any Fisher discriminatory information [5]. The PCA+CCA method is summarized as follows: (1) Compute the nonzero eigenvalues λ_k and corresponding eigenvectors $\mathbf{v}_k$ of $\mathbf{XX}^T$; (2) Obtain the eigenvectors $\mathbf{u}_k$ of $\mathbf{S}_t$ corresponding to nonzero eigenvalues as in Eigenface method [1], where $\mathbf{u}_k = \mathbf{X}^T \mathbf{v}_k / \sqrt{\lambda_k}$ $(k=1,2,...,n-1)$. (3) Project original samples into range space of $\mathbf{S}_t$ to obtain low dimensional features $\mathbf{X}_{PCA}$, and code dummy matrix $\mathbf{Y}$. (4) Compute $\mathbf{S}_x, \mathbf{S}_y$ and $\mathbf{S}_{xy}$ using $\mathbf{X}_{PCA}$ and $\mathbf{Y}$, and solve eigenequation (1) to obtain $C-1$ eigenvectors corresponding to nonzero eigenvalues.

The second method performs KPCA [6] instead of PCA which is described as

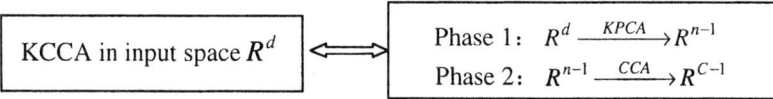

In our experiments, polynomial kernel $k(\mathbf{x},\mathbf{y}) = (\mathbf{x}^T\mathbf{y}+1)^2$ is used in KPCA. Because KPCA+FLDA was proved equivalent to KFDA in [7] and CCA is equivalent to FLDA, the proposed KPCA+CCA is equivalent to KCCA in nature. In PCA/KPCA transformed space, the ill-posed problem of CCA is solved, and the computational cost is reduced. All linear/nonlinear principle components are used for CCA, so linear/nonlinear features are extracted without losing any discriminatory information.

4 Experiments

The proposed KPCA/PCA+CCA methods are tested on ORL face database which contains images from 40 individuals, each providing 10 different images. For each person training samples are randomly selected and the remaining samples are used for testing. The recognition rate is estimated by using a ten-run average. The performance of KPCA/PCA+CCA is compared with Fisherface [1]. The nearest neighbor classifier is used. All 39 discriminatory features are extracted in Fig.1-left. In Fig.1-right, the number of optimal discriminatory features varies from 9 to 39, and five samples are randomly selected per person for training and remaining samples for testing. The Experiment results show that KPCA/PCA+CCA significantly outperform Fisherface and KPCA+CCA is a little better than PCA+CCA. In Fisherface, PCA is first employed to reduce the dimension of samples to make within-class scatter matrix nonsingular, which may lose the discriminatory information. However, performing KPCA/PCA does not lose any discriminatory information. Therefore PCA+CCA can achieve better results than Fisherface, although CCA was proved equivalent to FLDA.

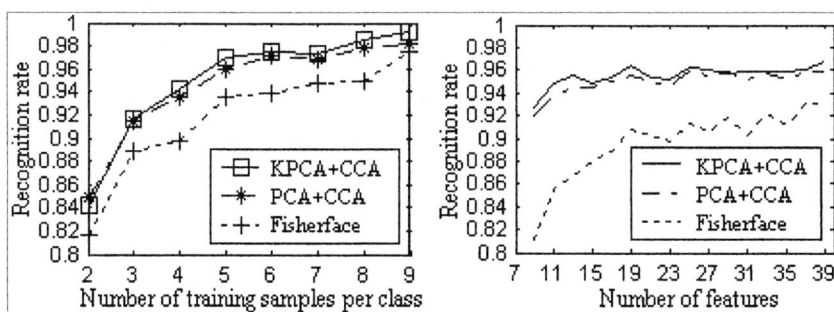

Fig. 1. Comparison of three methods

5 Conclusion

In this paper, we propose PCA/KPCA+CCA methods to solve SSS problem in face recognition, which obtain the linear/nonlinear optimal discriminatory features without losing any discriminatory information. The KPCA+CCA is equivalent to KCCA in nature. Experimental results show that the proposed methods significantly outperform the traditional Fisherface method in the case of SSS problem for face recognition.

References

1. Belhumeur P.N., Hespanha J.P.: Kriegman D.J.. Eigenfaces vs. Fisherfaces: Recognition using class special linear projection. IEEE Trans. PAMI. 19(1997)711–720
2. Lattin J.M., Carrol J.D., Grean P.E.:Analyzing Multivariate Data.Brooks/Cole Press (2003) Barker M., Rayens W.: Partial least square for discrimination. Journal of Chemometrics, 17(2003)166–173
3. Bartlett M.S.: Further aspects of the theory of multiple regression. Proc. Camb. Philos. Soc, 34(1938)33–40
4. Yang J., Yang J.Y.: Why can LDA be performed in PCA transformed space? Pattern Recognition, 36(2003):563–566
5. Scholkopf B., Smola A.: Muller K R. Nonlinear component analysis as a kernel eigenvalue problem. Neural Computation, 10(1998)1299–1319
6. Yang J., Jin Z., Yang J.Y.: Essence of kernel Fisher discriminant: KPCA plus LDA. Pattern Recognition 37(2004) 2097–2100

Appendix

Theorem 1 [2]: Suppose that d eigenvalues obtained using (1) and (5) is $0 \leq \lambda_1^{CCA} \leq \lambda_2^{CCA} \leq ... \leq \lambda_d^{CCA}$ and $0 \leq \lambda_1^{LDA} \leq \lambda_2^{LDA} \leq ... \leq \lambda_d^{LDA}$ respectively, then we have

$$\lambda_i^{CCA} = \frac{\lambda_i^{LDA}}{1+\lambda_i^{LDA}} \text{ and } \lambda_i^{LDA} = \frac{\lambda_i^{CCA}}{1-\lambda_i^{CCA}} \quad (i=1,2,...,d)$$

Theorem 2 [3]: $\mathbf{S}_{xy}\mathbf{S}_y^{-1}\mathbf{S}_{yx} = \frac{1}{n-1}\mathbf{S}_b$, where $\mathbf{S}_{xy}, \mathbf{S}_y, \mathbf{S}_{yx}$ is defined in (2).

Theorem 3: $\mathbf{S}_x^{-1}\mathbf{S}_{xy}\mathbf{S}_y^{-1}\mathbf{S}_{yx}\mathbf{a}_i = \lambda_i^{CCA}\mathbf{a}_i \Leftrightarrow \mathbf{S}_b\mathbf{a}_i = \lambda_i^{LDA}\mathbf{S}_w\mathbf{a}_i$

Proof: suppose that S_x is invertible, we have

$$\mathbf{S}_x^{-1}\mathbf{S}_{xy}\mathbf{S}_y^{-1}\mathbf{S}_{yx}\mathbf{a}_i = \lambda_i^{CCA}\mathbf{a}_i \Leftrightarrow \mathbf{S}_{xy}\mathbf{S}_y^{-1}\mathbf{S}_{yx}\mathbf{a}_i = \lambda_i^{CCA}\mathbf{S}_x\mathbf{a}_i$$

According to theorem 2 we have $\mathbf{S}_{xy}\mathbf{S}_y^{-1}\mathbf{S}_{yx}\mathbf{a}_i = \frac{1}{n-1}\mathbf{S}_b\mathbf{a}_i = \lambda_i^{CCA}\mathbf{S}_x\mathbf{a}_i$.

Using (4) we obtain $\mathbf{S}_b\mathbf{a}_i = \lambda_i^{CCA}(\mathbf{S}_b+\mathbf{S}_w)\mathbf{a}_i$, according to theorem 1 we have

$$(1+\lambda_i^{LDA})\mathbf{S}_b\mathbf{a}_i = \lambda_i^{LDA}(\mathbf{S}_b+\mathbf{S}_w)\mathbf{a}_i$$

Thus $\mathbf{S}_b\mathbf{a}_i = \lambda_i^{LDA}\mathbf{S}_w\mathbf{a}_i$ is obtained. This completes the proof of theorem.

Texture Segmentation Using Intensified Fuzzy Kohonen Clustering Network*

Dong Liu, Yinggan Tang, and Xinping Guan

Institute of Electrical Engineering,
Yanshan University, Qinhuangdao 066004, P.R. China
ysu609@yahoo.com.cn

Abstract. Fuzzy Kohonen clustering network(FKCN) shows great superiority in processing the clustering in image segmentation. In this paper, an intensified Fuzzy Kohonen clustering Network (IFKCN) is proposed for texture segmentation. The method adjusts fuzzy factors to accelerate the speed of convergence. It intensifies the biggest membership and suppresses the other. By using this network in Brodatz texture segmentation, its iteration is fewer and the speed of convergence is quicker than FKCN and AFKCN(Adaptive Fuzzy Kononen clustering Network), and segmentation results are as well as FKCN.

1 Introduction

Texture segmentation is one of the basic fields of image processing, it is an essential precondition for visual analysis and pattern recognition. The goal of texture segmentation is to partition image into several meaningful regions according to some features, so that the features within one region are similar and those of different regions are dissimilar. There have been a lot of algorithms proposed up to now, including recently appeared neural network and fuzzy set based methods[1,2].

Texture segmentation is a feature classification procedure which is based on pixel or region, so the clustering analysis is a reasonable way to implement it. Kohonen clustering network(KCN) is a kind of self-organizing neural network, which contains two layers(input layer and output layer). It shows great superiority in processing the clustering, and it is a useful tool for image segmentation, but this method can't get good accurate result when used for feature clustering which contains ambiguity and uncertainty. To overcome this defect, Bezdek proposed a fuzzy Kohonen clustering network model[3], it improves partition performance and reveals the classification of data more reasonably by using fuzzy factors. But the speed of FKCN convergence is more slowly than the KCN. In order to improve the convergence speed of FKCN, many researchers proposed modified algorithms[4,5,6]. In this paper, intensified fuzzy Kohonen clustering network(IFKCN) is proposed to adjust fuzzy factors to let the convergence more

---

* This work is supported by NNSF of China(Grant No.60404022) and Foundation of Department of Education of Hebei Province(Grant No.2002209).

quickly. The result shows that the number of iterate is less than FKCN and convergence speed is quickly than the FKCN.

The organization of the rest of the paper is as follows. Section 2 briefly introduces a method of texture feature description. Section 3 presents FKCN algorithm and our proposed IFKCN algorithm. Simulation results and comparison on other Kohonen neural networks are presented in section 4, the results show the performance of IFKCN is super than FKCN and AFKCN.

2 Texture Feature Extraction

There are many methods to describe texture image and capture its feature. Spatial gray level co-occurrence matrix (GLCM) is a classical method which can capture the second order statistics properties of texture. It contains information about the positions of pixels having similar grey level values. The ideal is to scan the image and keep track of how often pixels that differ by value are separated by a fixed distance d in position.

We derived feature images through the technique described below. The matrix $M(i,j)$, displacement vector $\mathbf{d} = (dx, dy)$, the value (i,j) of M is the pair of gray level i and j which are a distance d apart. GLCM is given as follow:

$$M(i,j) = \|\{((r,s),(t,v)) : I(r,s) = i, I(t,v) = j\}\| \qquad (1)$$

where $(r,s), (t,v) \in N \times N$, $(t,v) = (r+dx, s+dy)$, $\|\cdots\|$ is the pair of gray level which satisfy the condition. The co-occurrence matrix reveals certain properties about the spatial distribution of the gray levels in the image. A number of useful texture features could be obtained from the GLCM. Some of these features give as follows:

$$Energy = \sum\sum M(i,j)M(i,j) \qquad (2)$$

$$Entropy = -\sum\sum M(i,j)\log M(i,j) \qquad (3)$$

$$Contrast = \sum\sum (i,j)^2 M(i,j) \qquad (4)$$

$$Homogeneity = \sum\sum \frac{M(i,j)}{1+\|i-j\|} \qquad (5)$$

these techniques suffer from a number of difficulties such as the method of selecting the displacement vector $\mathbf{d}$ and finding the most relevant feature.

3 IFKCN Algorithm

3.1 FKCN Algorithm

FKCN is the heuristic learning neural network. The algorithm of FKCN is summarized as following:

Step1: Given sample space $X = \{x_1, x_2, x_3, \cdots, x_n\}$, distance $\|\cdot\|$, cluster number c and error threshold $\varepsilon > 0$.
Step2: Initialize the weight vector $\omega(0)$, set fuzzy parameter m_0, iteration limit $t_{\max}$, initial iteration counter $t = 0$.
Step3: Update all memberships $\{u_{ij}\}$ and calculate learning rate $\{\alpha_{ij}\}$

$$u_{ij} = \frac{1}{\sum_{K=1}^{c} \left(\frac{\|x_j - \omega_i\|}{\|x_j - \omega_K\|}\right)^{\frac{1}{(m_t - 1)}}} \quad (6)$$

$$\alpha_{ij}(t) = (u_{ij}(t))^{m_t} \quad (7)$$

where $m_t = m_0 - t\delta m$, $\delta m = \frac{m_0 - 1}{t_{\max}}$.
Step4: Update all the weight vectors

$$\omega_i(t) = \omega_i(t-1) + \frac{\sum_{j=1}^{n} \alpha_{ij}(x_j - \omega_i)}{\sum_{s=1}^{n} \alpha_{js}(t)} \quad (8)$$

Step5: compute the energy function

$$E(t) = \|\omega(t) - \omega(t-1)\|^2 = \sum_{i=1}^{c} \|\omega_i(t) - \omega_i(t-1)\|^2 \quad (9)$$

Step6: If $t + 1 > t_{\max}$ or if $E(t) < \varepsilon$, and terminate the iteration; otherwise, return step 3.

FKCN can find the cluster's center and partition the feature by distance. It is clear that when m_t in Eq.(6) is fixed and greater than 1, Fuzzy Kohonen SOFM equals the Fuzzy K-Means algorithm.

3.2 IFKCN Algorithm

Fuzzy method is useful in noise image, it can improve partition performance and reveals the classification of data more reasonably. Unfortunately, the convergence speed of the fuzzy Kohonen network is lower than Kohonen clustering network. So it needs to improve the convergence speed. In this paper, we introduce an intensified method into of FKCN, and call it Intensified Fuzzy Kohonen clustering Network(IFKCN). Intensified method is used to adjust the fuzzy factors in order to get the cluster's centers quickly, it not only stands out the chief fuzzy factor, but also suppresses the subordinate factors. The main approach is the same as the FKCN, but the approach of geting the fuzzy factors is different. We replace step3 in FKCN with step3' as followed:
Step3': Update and modify all memberships $\{u_{ij}\}$ and calculate learning rate $\{\alpha_{ij}\}$

$$u_{i,j} = \frac{1}{\sum_{K=1}^{c} \left(\frac{\|x_j - \omega_i\|}{\|x_j - \omega_K\|}\right)^{\frac{1}{(m_t - 1)}}} \quad (10)$$

considering x_j, if the degree of the membership of x_j belonging to Pth cluster is the biggest of all the clusters, the value is noted as u_{Pj}. (If there are two or more biggest memberships, choose the one randomly). Set the Intensified factor $\beta\,(0 \le \beta \le 1)$. After modified, the membership is

$$u_{Pj} = 1 - \beta \sum_{i \neq P} u_{ij} = 1 - \beta + \beta u_{Pj} \qquad (11)$$

$$u_{ij} = \beta u_{ij}, i \neq P \qquad (12)$$

learning rate $\{\alpha_{ij}\}$:

$$\alpha_{ij}(t) = (u_{ij}(t))^{m_t} \qquad (13)$$

where $m_t = m_0 - t\delta m$, $\delta m = \frac{m_0 - 1}{t_{\max}}$.

This modification does not disturb the original order of fuzzy factors. When $\beta = 0$, the algorithm is equal to Kohonen network; when $\beta = 1$, the algorithm becomes Fuzzy Kohonen network algorithm. So it establishes more meaningful than method in [4]. If the selection of β is reasonable, the IFKCN will have the advantages of fast convergence speech and good partition performance.

The "fuzzy intensification" operator in [4] is

$$\begin{cases} \alpha_{ij}(t) = u_{ij}^4, & u_{ij} \le 0.5 \\ \alpha_{ij}(t) = 1 - (1 - u_{ij})^2, & u_{ij} > 0.5 \end{cases} \qquad (14)$$

It intensifies the fuzzy factors when it is lager than 0.5, and suppress all fuzzy factors smaller than 0.5. When all fuzzy factors are smaller than 0.5, or there may be two or more biggest fuzzy factor, this method is not reasonable. Our algorithm prizes the biggest membership and suppresses the other. Even all the membership is lower than 0.5, our method can choose the biggest membership and enhance it, and suppress other membership accordingly, so it is more reasonable than AFKCN.

4 Experimental Results and Conclusions

Several 256 × 256 Brodatz textures are used for segmentation, simulations are carried out under the environment of MATLAB 6.5 on AMD2500+ PC. We set the initial center randomly, comparing the IFKCN and FKCN on the same initial value. The segmentation results(Fig.1)are almost the same.

β is a fuzzy intensified factor , the selection of β have an import effect on the speed of convergence. Fig.2 shows the relationship between β and iterations. From these figures $\beta = 0.4$ can get better results. Using $\beta = 0.4$ in IFKCN and compare the speed of convergence. From the Table.1, we can see that in order to calculate the intensified fuzzy factors, the time cost on each iteration is larger in IFKCN, but the number of iteration is much smaller than FKCN, so using IFKCN the whole time cost is smaller than FKCN in texture segmentation. The number of iteration using in IFKCN is less than the AFKCN, because of the

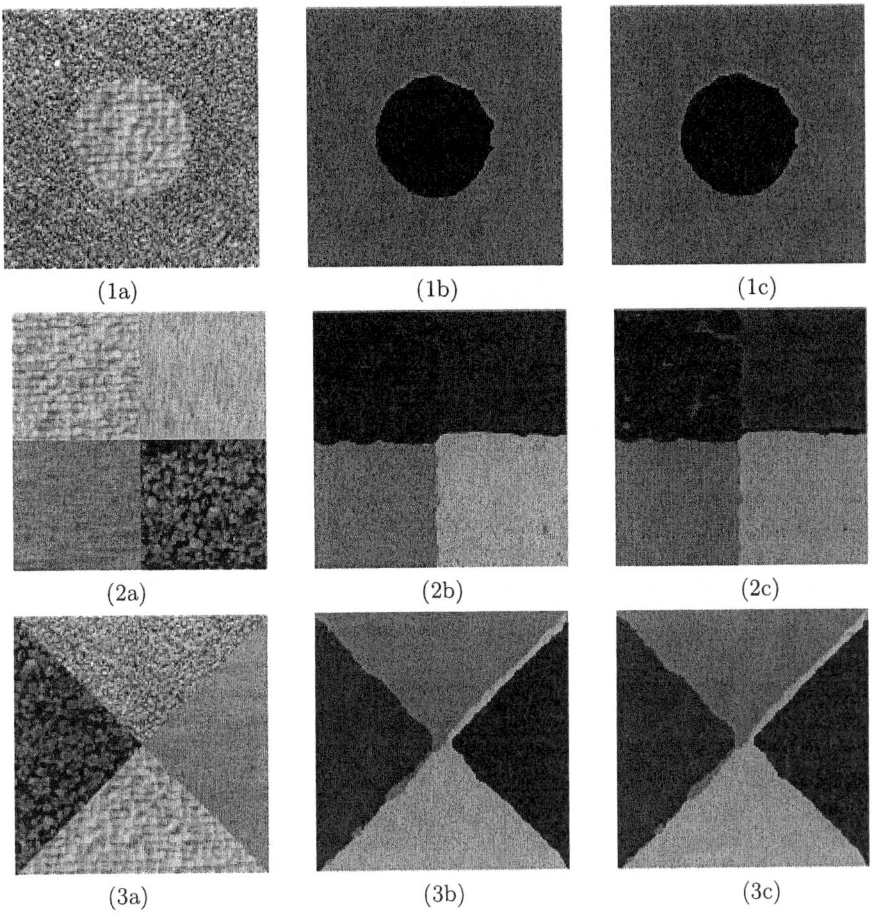

Texture Segmentation Using Intensified FKCN   79

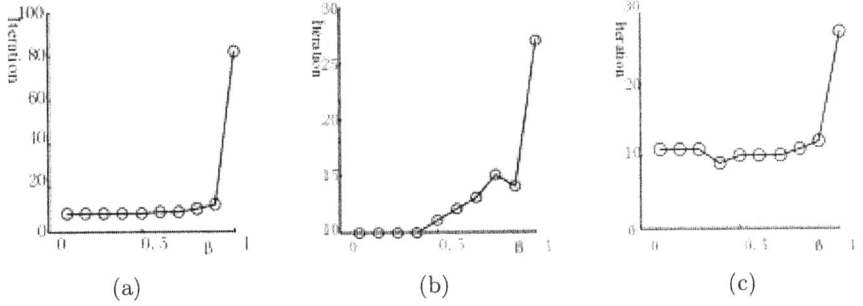

Fig. 1. (1a)(2a)(3a)Original textureA, textureB, textureC, (1b)(2b)(3b)segmentation results using IFKCN, (1c)(2c)(3c) segmentation results using FKCN in [5].

Fig. 2. (a)The relationship between and iterations in texture A, (b)the relationship between and iterations in texture B, (c) the relationship between and iterations in texture C.

Table 1. Performance comparison about FKCN in [5] and AFKCN in [4] and IFKCN on same initial center value ($\beta = 0.4$)

Texture	Network Type	Iteration	Time consume(s)
	FKCN	82	29.472
Texture A	AFKCN	9	10.251
	IFKCN	8	8.212
	FKCN	27	19.398
Texture B	AFKCN	10	13.941
	IFKCN	10	13.850
	FKCN	25	17.255
Texture C	AFKCN	9	12.341
	IFKCN	9	12.307

reasonable modify the fuzzy factors. From the experimentation, we can see this IFKCN algorithm is a useful method. However, how to choose parameter β is a problem not to be solved in this paper and need to be research future.

References

1. Fu, K.S., Mui, J.K.: A survey on image segmentation. Pattern Recognition, Vol. 14, No. 1 (1981) 3-16
2. Egmont-Petersen, M., Ridder, D,de., and Handels, H.: Image processing with neural networks-a review. Pattern Recognition, Vol. 35, (2002) 2279-2301
3. Tsao, E.C., Bezdek, J.C.: Fuzzy Kohonen clustering networks. Pattern Recognition, Vol.27, No.5, (1994) 757-764
4. Wang, L., Qi, F.H.: Adaptive fuzzy Kohonen clustering network for image segmentation. International Joint Conference on Neural Networks (IJCNN99), Washington, 10-16 July (1999) 2664-2667
5. Tarkov, M.S., Mun, Y.S., Choi, J., etc.: Mapping adaptive fuzzy Kohonen clustering network onto distributed image processing system. Paralle Computing, Vol. 28 (2002) 1239-1256
6. Fan, J.L., Zhen, W.Z., Xie, W.X.: Suppressed fuzzy c-means clustering algorithm. Pattern Recognition Letter, Vol. 24 (2003) 1607-1612

Application of Support Vector Machines in Reciprocating Compressor Valve Fault Diagnosis

Quanmin Ren, Xiaojiang Ma, and Gang Miao

Key Laboratory for Precision and Non-traditional Machining
Technology of Ministry of Education, Dalian University of Technology,
Dalian 116023, P.R. China
renquanmin@163.com

Abstract. Support Vector Machine (SVM) is a very effective method for pattern recognition. In this article, a intelligent diagnosis system based on SVMs is presented to solve the problem that there is not effective method for reciprocating compressor valve fault detection. The Local Wave method was used to decompose vibration signals, which acquired from valves surface, into sub-band signals. Then the higher-order statistics were calculated as the input features of classification system. The experiment results confirm that the classification technique has high flexibility and reliability on valve condition monitoring.

1 Introduction

Machine fault diagnosis is a kind of pattern recognition for machine working conditions. It can increase reliability and decrease possible loss of production due to machine breakdown. The combined suction/discharge valves are the "hearts" of a secondary ethylene compressor that is the key element of the Low Density Polyethylene production plant [1]. Because valve faults are the biggest source of compressor failure, adding up to more than 30 percent of total faults, it is necessary to monitor working conditions of valves online during their lifetime.

The utilization of support vector machine classifiers has gained very popularity in the recent years. SVMs are discriminative classifiers based on Vapnik's structural risk minimization principle [2]. They can implement flexible decision boundaries in high dimensional feature spaces. The implicit regularization of the classifier's complexity avoids overfitting and leads to good generalizations.

In this article, SVMs have been used in automated diagnosis of valves conditions. The input features were extracted from vibration signals by Local Wave and higher-order statistical methods.

2 Support Vector Machines

The objective of SVMs learning is to find an optimal classification function that can classify all the training vectors correctly with high accuracy and good generalization, on the basis of the set of measures $\{x_i, y_i\}$, $i=1,2,\ldots N$, where x_i is an input pattern, and $y_i \in Y=\{+1,-1\}$ is the corresponding target.

In the case of nonlinear condition, the training points are mapped from the input space to a feature space through a nonlinear mapping. Thus, a simple linear hyperplane is used for separating the points in the feature space. Even if mapped in the high-dimensional feature space, it can't always be avoided that there are points misclassified. The SVM allows for some errors but penalizes their cardinality.

Therefore, the above description can be summarized as a CQP. By using the Lagrange multiplier theory, it is written in dual form as fellows:

$$\max_\lambda (\sum_i \lambda_i - \frac{1}{2}\sum_{i,j} \lambda_i \lambda_j y_i y_j K(\mathbf{x}_i, \mathbf{x}_j)) \ . \quad (1)$$

$$\text{subject to } 0 \leq \lambda_i \leq C, \quad i = 1, 2, \ldots, N \ . \quad (2)$$

$$\sum_i \lambda_i y_i = 0 \ . \quad (3)$$

The resulting classifier is

$$f(\mathbf{x}) = sign(\sum_{i=1}^{Ns} \lambda_i y_i K(\mathbf{x}_i, \mathbf{x}) + w_0) \ . \quad (4)$$

where $K(\mathbf{x}_i, \mathbf{x})$ is a kernel function and N_s is the number of support vectors.

3 Fault Detection System

3.1 Vibration Measurements

Vibration signals from valves surface were acquired by accelerometers from three the secondary ethylene compressors as shown in Fig.1 (left). The maximum acquisition frequency was 25.6kHz and the number of sampled data was 16384.

3.2 Feature Extraction

The reciprocating compressor is a very complexity system and the monitored signals are highly nonlinear and non-stationary. Local Wave method is a powerful method for analyzing nonlinear and non-stationary data [3,4]. Here it was used as filters. The signal was firstly decomposed into some 'intrinsic mode functions' (IMFs). Then four frequency sub-band signals were reconstructed according to the energy and frequency distribution of IMFs. They are as fellows: S1 being the IMF1, S2 being the IMF2, S3 being the sum of IMF3-IMF5, and S4 being the sum of others.

Higher-order statistics have been widely used in signal processing and system theory problems. Monitoring moments and cumulants of vibration signals can provide diagnostic information for machines [5]. Here the first four zero-lag cumulants of sub-band signals were used as input features. They were calculated as Fig.1 (right). So there were altogether 16 features that were obtained from sub-band signals. Table 1 shows the statistical parameters of sub-band signals (S1-S4) in healthy and faulty conditions, respectively.

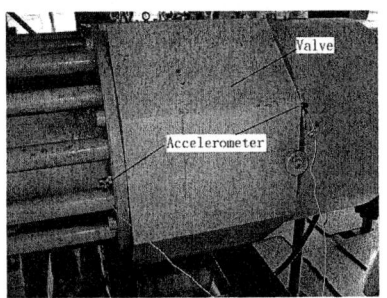 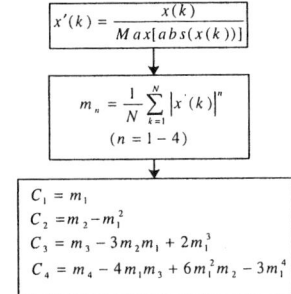

Fig. 1. The picture of acquisition system (left) and calculation of higher-order statistics (right)

Table 1. Statistical parameters of sub-band signals in healthy and faulty conditions

Signal	C1		C2		C3		C4	
	Healthy	Faulty	Healthy	Faulty	Healthy	Faulty	Healthy	Faulty
S1	0.0400	0.0216	0.0052	0.0022	0.0019	9.3188e-004	0.0010	6.2754e-004
S2	0.0423	0.0255	0.0056	0.0026	0.0023	0.0010	0.0015	6.5694e-004
S3	0.0356	0.0195	0.0039	0.0014	0.0015	4.5429e-004	9.6415e-004	2.6668e-004
S4	0.1145	0.0617	0.0090	0.0040	0.0017	0.0013	9.9595e-004	9.3001e-004

3.3 Classification Results

For training and testing, 135 sets of data were used which consist of 90 healthy conditions and 45 faulty conditions. A total 90 sets of data were used for the training (30 data from each compressor) and 45 sets of data were used for the testing (15 data from each compressor).

Here RBF kernel was used as the kernel function of SVMs for its excellent performance for real-world applications. The training of SVMs was carried out using the algorithm proposed by [6]. The RBF kernel width σ was chose by experiments. From Fig. 2, an optimum value for best performance is σ=0.002(C=1000). In this condition, the classification rate is 100% and the number of SVs is 10.Thus these values were selected for the classification system.

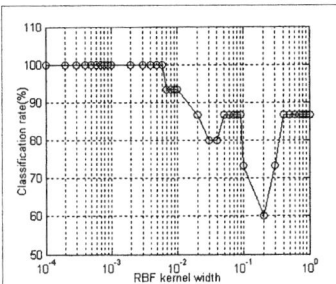 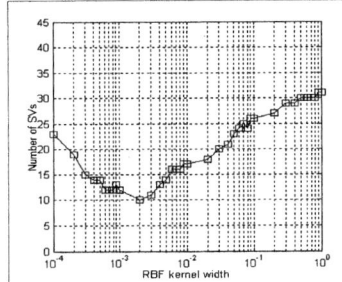

Fig. 2. The influence of RBF kernel width: classification rate (left) and number of SVs (right)

Neural networks were also used in experiments and Probabilistic Neural Networks achieved 100% classification rate. Due to having good performance for small samples, SVMs were finally selected as the classifiers of fault diagnosis system.

4 Conclusions

This paper presents a novel approach to detect faulty condition of combined valves online in the Low Density Polyethylene product lines. The vibration signals acquired from the surface of valves were decomposed into sub-bands by local wave method and the features from them were extracted by statistical method. The classification efficiency is much higher by using SVMs. It can effectively monitor valves working conditions. If other parameters are considered, such as temperature and pressure, this system will be more powerful and can be applied to other kinds of compressors.

Acknowledgement. This research was supported by the National Natural Science Foundation (Grant No. 50475155) of China.

References

1. Paul, C., Hanlon: Compressors Handbook. China Petrochemical Press (2003)
2. Vapnik ,V.N.: The Nature of Statistical Learning Theory. Tsinghua University Press, Beijing (2000)
3. Huang, N.E., Shen, Z., Long, S.R.: The Empirical Mode Decomposition and Hilbert Spectrum for Nonlinear and Non-stationary Time Series Analysis. Proc. Royal Soc. London 454 (1998) 903-985
4. Ma, X.J., Yu, B.: A New method for Time-Frequency—Local Wave Method. J. of Vibration Eng. 13 (2000) 219-224
5. Yang, B.S., Han, T., An, J.L., Kim, H. C.: A Condition Classification System for Reciprocating Compressor. Structural Health Monitoring. 3 (3) (2004) 227-284
6. Osuna, E.,Freund, R.,Girosi, F.: An Improved Training Algorithm for Support Vector Machines. Neural Networks for Signal Processing VII. (1997) 276-285

The Implementation of the Emotion Recognition from Speech and Facial Expression System

Chang-Hyun Park, Kwang-Sub Byun, and Kwee-Bo Sim

School of Electrical and Electronic Engineering, Chung-Ang University, 221,
Heukseok-Dong, Dongjak-Gu, Seoul 156-756, Korea
kbsim@cau.ac.kr

Abstract. In this paper, we introduce a system that recognize emotion by speech and show the facial expression by using 2-dimensional emotion space. 4 emotional states are classified by the work with ANN. The derived features of the signal, pitch, and loudness are quantitatively contributed to the classification of emotions. Firstly we analyze the acoustic elements for using as emotional features and the elements are evaluated by ANN classifier. Secondly, we implement an avatar (simply drawn face) and the facial expressions are changed naturally by using the dynamic emotion space model.

1 Introduction

Emotion related researches have been treated actively in various areas[1][2]. The researches are divided into Emotion recognition and expression. Until now, most researchers studied the subjects separately. However, this paper presents a system that recognize emotion and show the facial expression. In order to recognize the emotion by speech, we used ANN and BL as common researchers did. 1-dimensional emotion space and 2-dimensional emotion circle space have been used as an emotion expression algorithm. The expression extent of those methods were more and less limited, whereas, 2-dimensional dynamic emotion space that we propose has not exactly a separated emotion. That is, it is able to express more delicate emotion than existing methods.

2 Emotion Recognition and Expression System

Emotion recognition and expression system analyzes the incoming sound signal from MIC and extracts the emotional features. We acoustically analyzed the sound to extract the emotional features[3]. As the result of the analysis, we found the parameters such as 'pitch average on a specific part', 'the number of splitting section on the part(this parameter informs us of the rhythm of the speech)','Increasing Rate on the ending part of the sentence','Crossing Rate'and 'Loudness'. So, these parameters were applied to the classifier system (ANN and BL)[4][5]. Firstly, emotion weight, which is the output from emotion recognition, is inputted to the system and an emotion space is constructed by using the weight. After constructing the emotion space, the area each emotion occupies is computed and emotion expression parameters of the avatar are adjusted according to the size of the area.

The dynamic emotion space like fig 1-(3)(b) classifies the emotions by the area each emotion is assigned. That is, the classification of the facial expression depends on the extent of emotion. So the range of expressing the emotion is extended and the system can show the natural facial expression.

3 Results

3.1 Emotion Recognition from Speech

Applying ANN. Emotion recognition and expression system analyzes the incoming sound signal from MIC and extracts the emotional features. The emotions were classified by applying the machine learning algorithms such as ANN and BL. The incoming sound can be formatted to 16bit, mono, 11KHz, 22KHz, and 44KHz and the extracted features can be automatically stored at a DB (MS-ACCESS).

(1),(2) in Fig 1 shows the emotion recognition system and pattern classifier,respectively. Also, the parameters of ANN used for this paper are shown in the Table 1.

The backpropagation neural network was used for this study and it contained 5 input layer nodes, 11 middle (Hidden) layer nodes, and 2 output layer nodes. The output layer node is in the form of 2 binary outputs for each of the 4 emotions that need to be identified.

10 males were asked to speak 500 samples of speech (subjects) with 4 emotions.

The following graph is the test result of applying the training results for 500 speech samples. To verify the usefulness of each feature, 4 feature sets were input to the ANN and tested. Of those sets, Feature2 (Pitch average, Loudness, CR) was the most recognized set.

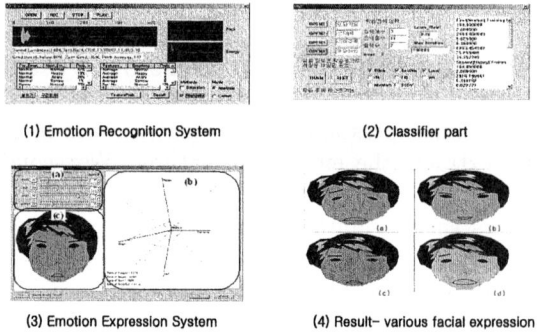

(1) Emotion Recognition System (2) Classifier part

(3) Emotion Expression System (4) Result– various facial expression

Fig. 1. Emotion recognition and expression system

Table 1. Parameters of the ANN for this paper

Parameter	input units	hidden units	output units	learning rate	tolerance	sigmoid function
Values	3~5	11	2	0.003	0.25	$\frac{1}{1+e^{-3x}}$

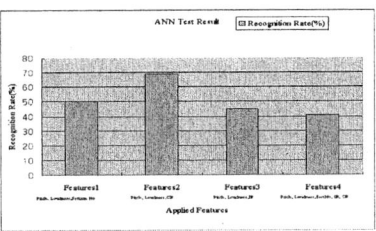

Fig. 2. ANN Test Result

Table 2. BL Experiment Result

	Normal	Happy	Angry	Depress	Average
S1	57%	40%	80%	70%	62%
S2	90%	73%	80%	94%	84%
S3	70%	51%	89%	91%	75%
Average	72%	55%	83%	85%	75%

Applying BL. Bayes theorem provided a way to calculate the probability of a hypothesis based on its prior probability, the probabilities of observing various data given the hypothesis, and the observed data . Therefore, the prior probability about the problem had to be obtained. 500 samples for the prior probability were used. More precisely,we analyzed the 500 samples and observed the relationship between each emotion and the features(Pitch average, Loudness, Section No) obtained from that were used for the bayesian learning.

Table 2 is the result tested on 300 samples (each 100 samples to 3 subjects), which used the previously obtained distributions(prior probability).

According to Table 2 , we can see the recognition rate depended on the subject and emotions because the coincidence rate between the emotion expression pattern of a subject and the expression pattern consisting of the prior probabilities was different. Therefore, the greater the universality of the prior probability is, the better the performance.

3.2 Emotion Expression Experiment Result

Emotion Expression Interface of Avatar. Fig 1-(3) shows the emotion expression interface of using the dynamic emotion space. In Fig 1-(3),(a) part is the control panel which it can control arbitrarily emotion weight value. This part is just for testing facial expression change for various emotions. Emotion recognition part substitutes this part. Fig 1-(3)(b) part is the emotion space and

Fig 1-(3)(c) is the result, which it shows the avatar with facial expression. Of course, the facial expression is the result controlled by the emotion parameters. Hair and nose are fixed because they are nearly independent of the emotion. However, as previously presented, jaw, mouth, eye, eyebrow is changed by the 9 parameters. The interface is implemented for the face color to be also changed by emotion. For deciding the parameter, we initially set an emotion value in the control panel (Fig 1-(3)(a)) to maximum and others are set to minimum. Then, after observing the facial expression of avatar, the parameters are decided.

Various Facial Expression Experiments. Fig 1-(4) shows the resultant facial expression of using the output of emotion recognition. At this time, the format of emotion recognition output is composed of 4 emotion weight values.

4 Conclusions

In order to create machines that directly interact with humans, Some experiments were conducted to implement an emotion recognition system from speech and facial expression system of using 2-dimension dynamic emotion space. As the result of the experiments, we implemented a emotion system.

Acknowledgement. This research was supported by the brain Neuroinformatics research Program by Ministry of Commerce,Industry and Energy.

References

1. R.S.Lazarus and B.N.Lazarus : Passion & Reason. Moonye Publishing, Seoul (1997) 255–256
2. L.S.Chen,H.Tao,T.S. Huang,T.Miyasato and R.Nakatsu: Emotion recognition from audiovisual information,IEEE Second Workshop on Multimedia Signal Processing (1998)
3. J.S.Han: Speech Signal Processing, Seoul, O-Sung-media,(2000) 84–85
4. B.C.J.Moore: Cochlear hearing loss, USA, Academic Press,(2003) 91–93
5. T.M.Mitchell: Machine learning, Singapore, McGRAW-HILL Internatinal Editions, (1997) 81–116

Kernel PCA Based Network Intrusion Feature Extraction and Detection Using SVM

Hai-Hua Gao[1], Hui-Hua Yang[1,2], and Xing-Yu Wang[1,*]

[1] School of Information Science and Engineering,
East China University of Science and Technology, Shanghai 200237, China
hhgao@tom.com, xywang@ecust.edu.cn
[2] Department of Computer Science, Guilin University of Electronic Technology,
Guilin 541004, China
Yang98@gliet.edu.cn

Abstract. This paper proposes a novel intrusion detection approach by applying kernel principal component analysis (KPCA) for intrusion feature extraction and followed by support vector machine (SVM) for classification. The MIT's KDD Cup 99 dataset is used to evaluate these feature extraction methods, and classification performances achieved by SVM with PCA and KPCA feature extraction are compared with those obtained by PCR and KPCR classification methods and by SVM without application of feature extraction. The results clearly demonstrate that feature extraction can greatly reduce the dimension of input space without degrading the classifiers' performance. Among these methods, the best performance is achieved by SVM using only four principal components extracted by KPCA.

1 Introduction

In order to achieve a desired performance in anomaly detection, we need research on two inter-dependent parts. Firstly, we should build a good classifier; secondly, we should seek a good representation of the problem, which is a set of informative features to be fed to the classifier.

For the former, many attempts have been made to model good classifiers, using all the principles available for studying intrusion detection, such as Bayesian parameter estimation [1], data fusion [2] and neural networks [3], etc. Support Vector Machines (SVM) is a newly proposed machine learning approach, owing to its remarkable characteristics such as good generalization performance, the absence of local minimal and the sparse representation of solution, SVM has become a popular research method in anomaly detection, and good results are reported [3].

For the latter, generally, there are two ways to obtain better represented features from the original samples. One is feature selection; the other is feature extraction [4]. Feature extraction constructs new features by means of transforming the original inputs from high dimension to low dimension. Kernel principal component analysis

---

[*] Author for Correspondence. This work was supported by National Science Foundation (No. 69974014) and the Doctorate Foundation of the Education Ministry of China (No.20040251010), China.

(KPCA) [5] is a well-known method for feature extraction. KPCA firstly maps the original inputs into a high-dimensional feature space using the kernel mapping, then calculates PCA in the transformed feature space. Very little work that applies feature extraction to anomaly intrusion has been done. We evaluate this by adopting KPCA for feature extraction and followed by SVM for classification.

The rest of this paper is organized as follows. In section 2 KPCA for feature extraction and classification are described. Section 3 presents the experimental results, followed by the conclusions in the last section.

2 KPCA for Feature Extraction and KPCR for Classification

KPCA firstly map the original input vectors x_i into a high-dimensional feature space $\phi(x_i)$ and then calculate the linear PCA in $\phi(x_i)$.

The PCA problem in a high-dimensional feature space F (with dimension M) can be formulated as the diagonalization of an n-sample estimation of the covariance matrix

$$\hat{C} = \frac{1}{n}\sum_{i=1}^{n}\Phi(x_i)\Phi(x_i)^T \tag{1}$$

where $\Phi(x_i)$ are centered nonlinear mappings of the input variables $\{x_i\}_{i=1}^n \in R^N$. The diagonization leads to following eigenproblem:

$$\lambda v = \hat{C}v \tag{2}$$

where eigenvalues $\lambda \geq 0$ and eigenvectors $v \in F$. Since all solution with $\lambda \neq 0$ lie in the span of mapping $\Phi(x_1),...,\Phi(x_n)$, the equivalent eigenvalue problem was derived

$$n\lambda\alpha = K\alpha, \tag{3}$$

where α denotes the column vector $(\alpha_1,...,\alpha_n)^T$ such that

$$v = \sum_{i=1}^{n}\alpha_i\Phi(x_i), \tag{4}$$

and K is symmetric $n \times n$ Gram matrix with the elements

$$K_{ij} = (\Phi(x_i),\Phi(x_j)) = K(x_i,x_j). \tag{5}$$

Normalizing solutions v^k corresponding to the non-zero eigenvalues $\hat{\lambda}_k = n\lambda_k$ of matrix K, translates into condition $\hat{\lambda}_k(\alpha^k,\alpha^k) = 1$. Finally, we can compute the k-th principal component of x as the projection of $\Phi(x)$ onto the eigenvector v^k:

$$P_k(x) = (v^k,\Phi(x)) = \frac{1}{\sqrt{n\lambda_k}}\sum_{i=1}^{n}\alpha_i^k K(x_i,x) = \hat{\lambda}^{-1/2}\sum_{i=1}^{n}\alpha_i^k K(x_i,x) \tag{6}$$

Denote by V the matrix consisting of the columns created by the eigenvectors $\{v^i\}_{i=1}^{p}$ of $\hat{C}$, let $\hat{V}$ be the matrix consisting of the columns created by the extracted eigenvectors $\{\alpha^i\}_{i=1}^{p}$ of K, and let Λ be a diagonal matrix $diag(\hat{\lambda}_1, \hat{\lambda}_2, ..., \hat{\lambda}_p)$ of the corresponding eigenvalues. Using these notation, for the projection of original (training) data points $\{x_i\}_{i=1}^{n}$, we may rewrite (14) into matrix form

$$P = \Phi V = \Phi \Phi^T \hat{V} \hat{\Lambda}^{-1/2} = K\hat{V} \hat{\Lambda}^{-1/2} = \hat{V} \hat{\Lambda}^{1/2} \tag{7}$$

where we used the fact that $V = \Phi^T \hat{V} \hat{\Lambda}^{-1/2}$. Similarly, for the projection of test data points $\{x_i\}_{i=n+1}^{n+n_t}$, we may write

$$P_t = \Phi_t \Phi^T \hat{V} \hat{\Lambda}^{-1/2} = K_t \hat{V} \hat{\Lambda}^{-1/2} \tag{8}$$

where Φ_t is the $n_t \times M$ matrix of the mapped testing data points $\{\Phi(x_i)\}_{i=n+1}^{n+n_t}$ and K_t is the $n_t \times n$ matrix whose elements are

$$(K_t)_{ij} = (\Phi(x_i), \Phi(x_j)) = K(x_i, x_j) \tag{9}$$

where $\{x_i\}_{i=1}^{n}$ and $\{x_j\}_{j=n+1}^{n+n_t}$ are training and testing points, respectively.

After the training data $X = \{x_i\}_{i=1}^{n}$ has been projected into high-dimensional feature space and extracted the first p principal components, we get the nonlinear principal components P, and then do linear regression

$$Y = PB + \varepsilon \tag{10}$$

where ε is noise, and B is coefficient matrix. The least square solution of B is

$$B = (P^T P)^{-1} P^T Y \tag{11}$$

we get the KPCR classification model

$$Y_t = sgn(P_t B) \tag{12}$$

where P_t are principal components corresponding to test sample $X_t = \{x_i\}_{i=n+1}^{n+n_t}$.

3 Experiments

The KDD Cup 99 dataset consists of a huge collection of samples numbered about 5 million, even a 10% subset of it includes 494,021 records. For our proposed kernel-based feature extraction method, the memory requirement is $O(n^2)$, where n is the size of samples. Due to this limitation, we randomly chose 4,000 unique samples from the 10% sample for our experiment, 2,000 samples are used to train the model and 2,000 to test. The four attack types are merged into one category "Attack", and try to differentiate them from those "Normal" connections. In our sampling, the "Normal" samples and the "Attack" samples are of the same proportion in both the training and

Table 1. Performance comparison of intrusion detection algorithms

Algorithm (Feature number)	Confusion matrix				Accuracy (%)	False alarm rate (%)	Detecting time(ms/sample)
C-SVM(41)	N	A←Predicted as			94.05	5.73	0.66
	943	57	N				
	62	938	A				
PCR(11)	N	A←Predicted as			86.7	6.92	0.02
	941	59	N				
	207	793	A				
PCA-SVM(5)	N	A←Predicted as			94.55	3.15	0.22
	970	30	N				
	79	921	A				
KPCR(5)	N	A←Predicted as			96.05	0.96	2.85
	991	9	N				
	70	930	A				
KPCA-SVM(4)	N	A←Predicted as			97.2	0.42	2.96
	996	4	N				
	52	948	A				

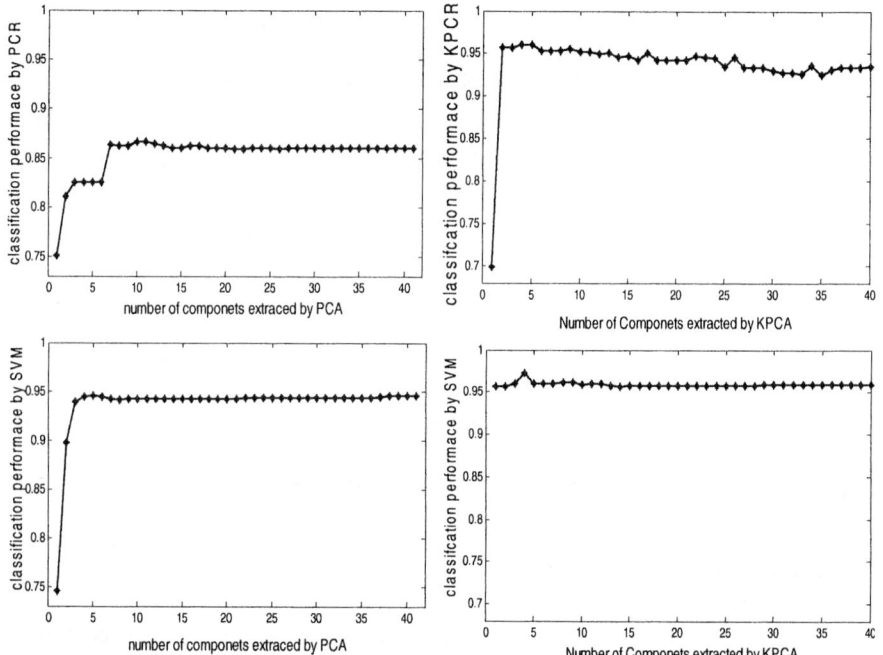

Fig. 1. Comparison of classification performance between PCR and PCA-SVM; between KPCR and KPCA-SVM using extracted features, the x axis asterisks show results achieved by using the selected number of components

testing dataset. In the sampling process, we reduced the portion of easily detected "Probe" attack and included more hard-to-detect attacks such as "U2R" and "R2L", which makes our dataset more challenging for classification.

The network anomaly detection simulation was carried out within a Matlab 7.0 environment, which was running on a PC powered by a Pentium IV 2.5GHz CPU and 256MB RAM.

The experiment results of five approaches with their optimal parameter settings are shown in Table 1, and Fig. 1. Based on those results, we can see that:

1. linear PCR alone doesn't perform well in differentiating the normal from attack;
2. SVM fed with the linear components extracted by PCA performs well and steadily when the number of components is greater than 3;
3. KPCA has a very powerful nonlinear feature extraction capability, and KPCR can achieve better performance than SVM when 2 and above components are extracted;
4. SVM fed with the nonlinear components extracted by KPCA can attain a very good performance even when only one component is available, and its performance increases slightly when more components are extracted.
5. SVM with 4 components extracted by KPCA ranks number one among all the 5 algorithms.

To sum up, the results clearly demonstrate that feature extraction can greatly reduce the dimension of input space without degrading or even boosting the classifiers' performance. We can safely believe that the anomaly detection is an intrinsically nonlinear classification problem, so the linear PCR can't cope with it. All the nonlinear approach can handle it fairy well, SVM works because of its inherent nonlinear kernel mapping, and KPCR acts well for it can extract nonlinear features and then do linear regression. By combining KPCA with SVM, the best detection performance is achieved.

4 Conclusion

In this paper, we proposed a novel approach for anomaly detection from the standpoint of feature extraction. KPCA are applied to extract effective features for SVM. KPCA firstly maps the input data into high dimensional feature space and then calculate PCA, so it can extract nonlinear features. The simulation shows that SVM with KPCA feature extraction can achieve better generalization performance of SVM than that without feature extraction. The experiment also shows that KPCA perform better than PCA, since KPCA utilizes kernel mapping and can explore higher order information of the original inputs than PCA. Thus, through features extraction, the intrusion detection is much more time efficient.

References

1. Cho S. Cha S. SAD: web session anomaly detection based on parameter estimation. Computers & Security, 23 (2004) 312-319
2. Wang Y, Yang HH, Wang XY, et al. Distributed Intrusion Detection System Based on Data Fusion Method. In: The 5th World Congress on Intelligent Control and Automation. New Jersey, IEEE Press, (2004) 4331-4334.

3. Sung AH, Mukkamala S. Identify important features for intrusion detection using support vector machines and neural networks. In: IEEE Proceedings of the 2003 Symposium on Application and the Internet, (2003)209-216.
4. Guyon I, Elisseeff A. An introduction to variable and feature selection. Journal of Machine Learning Research, 3 (2003) 1157-1182.
5. Scholköpf B, Smola A, Muller KR. Nonlinear component analysis as a Kernel eigenvalue problem, Neural Computing. 10(1998):1299-1319
6. LIBSVM, http://www.csie.ntu.edu.tw/~cjlin/libsvm/.
7. KDD Cup 99 Task Description. http://kdd.ics.uci.edu/databases /kddcup99/task.html

Leak Detection in Transport Pipelines Using Enhanced Independent Component Analysis and Support Vector Machines[*]

Zhengwei Zhang, Hao Ye, Guizeng Wang, and Jie Yang

Department of Automation, Tsinghua University, Beijing 100084, P.R. China
zhangzw02@mails.tsinghua.edu.cn

Abstract. Independent component analysis (ICA) is a feature extraction technique for blind source separation. Enhanced independent component analysis (EICA), which has enhanced generalization performance, operates in a reduced principal component analysis (PCA) space. SVM is a powerful supervised learning algorithm, which is rooted in statistical learning theory. SVM has demonstrated high generalization capabilities in many pattern recognition problems. In this paper, we integrate EICA with SVM and apply this new method to the leak detection problem in oil pipelines. In features extraction, EICA produces EICA features of the original pressure images. In classification, SVM classified the EICA features as leak or non-leak. The test results based on real data indicate that the method can detect many leak faults from a pressure curve, and reduce the ratio of false and missing alarm than conventional methods.

1 Introduction

With the development of the transport pipeline industry, leak detection in transport pipelines has drawn intensive attention. For all pipeline leak detection techniques, the negative pressure wave based approach has been widely adopted in real applications.

The basic idea of the negative pressure wave based methods is that, when leak occurs, there is a negative pressure wave propagating from the leak point toward the upstream and downstream ends and so that we can detect leaks by detecting the pressure changes at the both ends [1].

Many approaches have been introduced for leak detection based on negative pressure wave, such as Wavelet Transform [2], Pattern Recognition [3] etc.. However, the performance of these methods is often bound by high false alarm/miss detection rates.

Recent advances in statistical learning theory, especially, the introduction of support vector machines (SVM) has made it possible to get high accuracies for the pattern recognition problem [4]. Enhanced independent component analysis (EICA) is also a very powerful tool for blind signal separation with better generalization performance than Independent component analysis (ICA) [5]. In this paper, we propose a novel Leak Detection method based on EICA/SVM method which integrates EICA with SVM, and apply it to the leak detection problem. The improved performance has been demonstrated by tests based on real data.

---

[*] Supported by the National Natural Science Fund of China (60274015) and the 863 Program of China.

2 Theoretical Background

2.1 Enhanced Independent Component Analysis

ICA, which expands on principal component analysis (PCA) as it considers higher order statistics, is originally developed for blind source separation whose goal is to reduce statistical dependencies and derives a sparse and independent but unknown source signals from their linear mixtures without knowing the mixing coefficients.

Let us assume a linear mixture model

$$X = AS \tag{1}$$

where X denote the linear mixtures, S denote the original source signals whose components are independent and unknown, and A is unknown. The goal of ICA is to estimate the matrix W in the reconstruction model

$$Y = WX \tag{2}$$

A large amount of algorithms have been developed for performing ICA. One of the best methods is the fixed-point-FastICA algorithm proposed by Hyvärinen [6]. FastICA is a method by which the independent components are extracted one after another by using Kurtosis. This method has high-speed convergence.

In order to improve the generalization performance of ICA, Liu et al have proposed a novel EICA method [5]. EICA, whose enhanced retrieval performance and reduced computational complexity are achieved by means of generalization analysis, operates in a reduced PCA space.

Let C denote the covariance matrix of X. We can get the orthogonal eigenvector matrix Ψ and a diagonal eigenvalue matrix Λ with diagonal elements in decreasing order by using PCA. Now let P be a matrix whose column vectors are the first n leading eigenvectors of C,

$$P = [\psi_1, \psi_2, \ldots, \psi_n] \tag{3}$$

where P is the loading matrix, n is determined by balancing two criteria of the PCA procedure: for image feature representation and for ICA generalization [5].

The new random vector Z in this reduced PCA space is defined as

$$Z = P^T X \tag{4}$$

We call the ICA method implemented in this reduced PCA space the EICA method. A more detailed description of the EICA algorithm can be found in [5].

2.2 Support Vector Machines

SVM was originally introduced by Vapnik [4], which is a novel type of learning machine based on Statistical Learning Theory. The SVM aims at minimizing an upper bound of the generalization error through maximizing the margin between the separating hyperplane and the data. Such a scheme is known to be associated with structural risk minimization [4].

Generally, in a SVM classifier, the discriminant function has the following form:

$$f(x) = sgn(\sum_{i=1}^{M} \alpha_i^* y_i K(x_i, x) + b^*) \quad (5)$$

Where the parameters are obtained by maximizing the objective function:

$$Q(\alpha) = \sum_{i=1}^{M} \alpha_i - \frac{1}{2} \sum_{i,j=1}^{M} \alpha_i \alpha_j y_i y_j K(x_i, x_j) \quad (6)$$

$$\text{subject to} \quad \sum_{i=1}^{M} \alpha_i y_i = 0 \quad 0 \le \alpha_i \le C \quad i = 1, \ldots, M$$

By solving the above quadratic programming problem, SVM tries to maximize the margin between data points in the two classes and minimize the training errors simultaneously. For the nonlinear case, the training patterns are mapped onto a high-dimensional space using a kernel function. In this space the decision boundary is linear. The most commonly used kernel functions are polynomials, exponential and sigmoidal functions. Here we choose radial basis function (RBF) kernel function as

$$K(x_i, x_j) = \exp(-\|x_i - x_j\|^2 / N\sigma^2) \quad (7)$$

where N is the number of independent image basis which we extract with EICA.

3 Leak Detection Based on EICA/SVM

In [7], we treated the pressure curve of fixed length as an image and proposed an Eigencurves method based on EICA to detect leaks in oil pipelines. To achieve reduced computational complexity and better classification robustness, in this paper we presents a novel EICA/SVM based method which uses SVM to determine the appropriate class: leak or non-leak. The method includes two steps: (i) EICA based feature extraction; (ii) SVM based classification of EICA features obtained from step (i).

3.1 EICA Based Feature Extraction

Let $\chi \in \Re^{N^2}$ be a vector representing a pressure image with $N \times N$ pixels. The vector is formed by concatenating the rows or the columns of the image. Let the training set of pressure images be $X = \{\chi_1, \chi_2, \cdots, \chi_M\}$, where M is the number of images in the training set.

Since we assume the pressure images are linear combinations of independent image bases in the ICA algorithm, we do not lose information by replacing the original pressure images with their eigenvectors that are linear combinations of the original pressure images [8]. Following this scheme, we firstly compute the loading matrix P [Eq. (3)] of the X, then apply the EICA algorithm as follows:

$$WP^T = Y$$
$$\text{so} \quad P^T = W^{-1} Y \quad (8)$$

where each rows of Y represents an independent image basis [8].

The principal component representation of the set of zero mean images in X^T based on P is defined as $R = X^T P$. A minimum squared error approximation of X^T is obtained by $X^T_{rec} = RP^T$ [8]. From P, a minimum squared error approximation of X^T is obtained by

$$X^T_{rec} = X^T PP^T \qquad (9)$$

From Eq. (8) and (9), we can get,

$$X^T_{rec} = X^T PW^{-1} Y = CY \qquad (10)$$

where PW^{-1} is obtained during the EICA training procedure and each row of C is the EICA feature of corresponding training image. We take PW^{-1} as extraction matrix. For a test image $f \in \Re^{N^2 \times 1}$, we can extract EICA features by project f on PW^{-1}:

$$c = f^T PW^{-1} \qquad (11)$$

3.2 SVM Based Classifier Training

Since we have obtained EICA features matrix $C = [c_1^T, c_2^T, \cdots, c_M^T]^T$ [Eq. (10)], we build the SVM training set $\{C_i, d_i\}_{i=1}^M$, where $d_i = \{\pm 1\}$ is the class type of EICA feature C_i. (+1 means non-leak, -1 means leak)

The support vectors and other parameters in the decision function $f(x)$ [Eq. (5)] are determined through numerical optimization during the classifier training step.

3.3 Online Detection

To realize online detection, this system detects leak by sampling the overlapping M (M=2000) width windows located on the pressure curve which is updated real-timely and classifying them using a trained SVM to determine the appropriate class: leak or non-leak. The window moves on the pressure curve with step of 1000 pressure values and new samples are extracted real-timely.

Applying the thought above, for an unknown pressure curve image f^T, we can get its EICA features c [Eq. (11)]. Then we can decide whether there is any leak in Transport Pipelines by using the nonlinear decision function [Eq. (5)].

4 Experimental Results

4.1 Data Preparation and Sample Set

In this paper, the pressure curve is formed by ordinal connecting 2000 continually sampled pressure data. The sample time is 60 ms. we fragment the original pressure curve image into several 30×30 images and treat them as training and test images set.

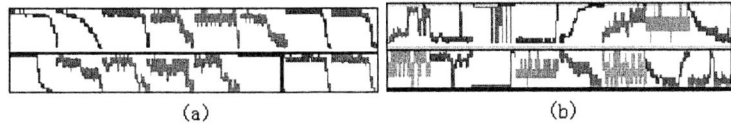

Fig. 1. (a) The negative pressure wave samples. (b) The normal condition samples.

Fig.1 shows some sample images we get by fragmenting one-hour pressure curve obtained from a real oil pipeline.

In this paper, we intercept 5,380 images as sample set in which 1,600 images contain negative pressure wave. We pick 1,500 images (500 images contain negative pressure wave) as training samples and the remnant are used as test images set.

4.2 EICA/SVM Based Negative Pressure Wave Detection

From the training images set, we extract 161 independent basis images with EICA. Fig.2 shows the first 45 learned independent basis images of them.

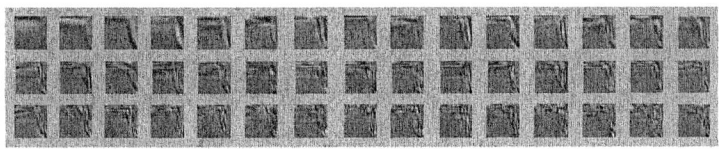

Fig. 2. First 45 learned independent basis images

We can see these independent basis images express more local feature, which suggests that they can lead to more precise representations.

Using the EICA features [Eq. (10)], the SVM is trained for classification. The SVM classifier uses the RBF kernel with $\sigma^2 = 8$ and the upper bound $C = 500$ to obtain a perfect training error. The training result is that there are 109 supports vectors which are about 7.27% of the total number of training images.

4.3 Results

In Table 1 we compared the EICA/SVM training and testing results with direct SVM. It can be seen that the EICA/SVM training achieves fewer support vectors. This suggests EICA/SVM have better generalization capacity. From this table we also see that the EICA/SVM scheme can reduce the false alarm/miss detection rates effectively.

Table 1. Test results

Approach	Support Vectors	Miss Detections	False Detections	Correct %
EICA/SVM	109	72	35	97.24
Direct SVM	341	187	167	91.24

5 Conclusion

In this paper, a new EICA/SVM method to detect the negative pressure wave is proposed. The experiment results show that the EICA/SVM method performs better than direct SVM method. The reason lies in the fact that EICA can explore edge information in the image data. By using EICA feature instead of the original image data, SVM reduced the number of support vectors in training and get lower detection errors.

References

1. Turner, N. C.: Hardware and software techniques for pipeline integrity and leak detection monitoring, Proceedings of Offshore Europe 91, Aberdeen, Scotland (1991)
2. Ye, H., Wang, G. Z., Fang, C. Z.: Application of Wavelet Transform to Leak Detection and Location in Transport Pipelines [J]. Engineering Simulation, Vol.13 (1995)1025-1032
3. Jin, S.J., Wang, L.N., Li, J.: Instantaneous Negative Wave Pattern Recognition Method in Leak Detection of Crude Petroleum Transported Pipeline, Journal of Electronic Measurement and Instrument, Vol.12 (1998) 59-64. (In Chinese)
4. Vapnik, V.: The nature of statistical learning theory, Springer, New York (1995)
5. Liu, C.J.: Enhanced independent component analysis and its application to content based face image retrieval, IEEE Trans. Systems, Man, and Cybernetics-part B: Cybernetics, vol. 34, no. 2 (2004)
6. Hyvärinen, A.: Fast and robust fixed-point algorithm for independent component analysis, IEEE Trans. Neural Networks, vol. 10 (1999) 626-634
7. Zhang, Z. W., Ye, H., Hu, R.: Application of Enhanced Independent Component Analysis to Leak Detection in Transport Pipelines, ISNN (2) (2004) 561-566
8. Bartlett, M.S., Lades, H.M., Sejnowski, T.J.: Independent component representation for face recognition [A], Proceedings SPIE Conference on Human Vision and Electronic Imaging III [C], San Jose, CA, USA (1998) 528-539

Line-Based PCA and LDA Approaches for Face Recognition

Vo Dinh Minh Nhat and Sungyoung Lee

Kyung Hee University – South of Korea
{vdmnhat, sylee}@oslab.khu.ac.kr

Abstract. Principal Component Analysis (PCA) and Linear Discriminant Analysis (LDA) techniques are important and well-developed area of image recognition and to date many linear discrimination methods have been put forward. Despite these efforts, there persist in the traditional PCA and LDA some weaknesses. In this paper, we propose a new Line-based methods called Line-based PCA and Line-based LDA that can outperform the traditional PCA and LDA methods. As opposed to conventional PCA and LDA, those new approaches are based on 2D matrices rather than 1D vectors. That is, we firstly divide the original image into blocks. Then, we transform the image into a vector of blocks. By using row vector to represent each block, we can get the new matrix which is the representation of the image. Finally PCA and LDA can be applied directly on these matrices. In contrast to the covariance matrices of traditional PCA and LDA approaches, the size of the image covariance matrices using new approaches are much smaller. As a result, those new approaches have three important advantages over traditional ones. First, it is easier to evaluate the covariance matrix accurately. Second, less time is required to determine the corresponding eigenvectors. And finally, block size could be changed to get the best results. Experiment results show our method achieves better performance in comparison with the other methods.[1]

1 Introduction

Face recognition research has been started in the late 70s and is one of the active and exciting researches in computer science and information technology areas since 1990 [1]. Eigenfaces approach is one of the earliest appearance-based face recognition methods, which was developed by M. Turk and A. Pentland [2] in 1991. The Fisherface method [4] combines PCA and the Fisher criterion [9] to extract the information that discriminates between the classes of a sample set. It is a most representative method of LDA. However, in the previous PCA and LDA-based face recognition techniques, the 2D face image matrices must be previously transformed into 1D image vectors. In this paper, new approaches called Line-based PCA and

---

[1] This research was supported by the MIC (Ministry of Information and Communication), Korea, under the ITRC(Information Technology Research Center) support program supervised by the IITA (Institute of Information Technology Assessment). Corresponding Authors: Vo Dinh Minh Nhat (vo_dinhminhnhat@yahoo.com), and SungYoung Lee (sylee@oslab.khu.ac.kr).

Line-based LDA are developed for image feature extraction. As opposed to conventional PCA and LDA, Line-based PCA and Line-based LDA is based on 2D matrices rather than 1D vectors. That is, we firstly divide the original image into blocks. Then, we transform the image into a vector of blocks. By using row vector to represent each block, we can get the new matrix which is the representation of the image. Finally PCA and LDA can be applied directly on these matrices.

2 Line-Based PCA and LDA Approaches

In our proposed approaches, we firstly divides the original image into $s = hxw$ size blocks with h, w are the height and width of the block. Then, we transform the image into a vector of blocks. By using row vector r with $r^T \in \mathbb{R}^s$ to represent each block (actually, each block is a line of the raw image, so we call these approaches line-based ones), we can get the matrix $X \in \mathbb{R}^{kxs}$ which is the representation of the image, with k is the number of blocks. See fig. 1 for the process.

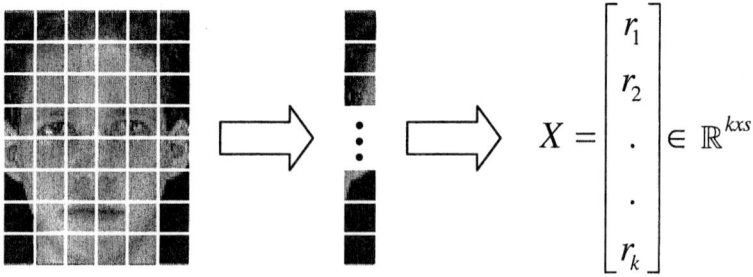

Fig. 1. The process of getting representation of each image

Now, set of N sample images are represented as $\{X_1, X_2,..., X_N\}$ with $X_i \in \mathbb{R}^{kxs}$. Then the between-class scatter matrix S_b is re-defined as

$$S_b = \frac{1}{N}\sum_{i=1}^{c} N_i (\mu_{C_i} - \mu_X)(\mu_{C_i} - \mu_X)^T \quad (1)$$

and the within-class scatter matrix S_w is re-defined as

$$S_w = \frac{1}{N}\sum_{i=1}^{c} \sum_{X_k \in C_i} (X_k - \mu_{C_i})(x_k - \mu_{C_i})^T \quad (2)$$

The total scatter matrix is re-defined as

$$S_T = \frac{1}{N}\sum_{i=1}^{N} (X_i - \mu_X)(X_i - \mu_X)^T \quad (3)$$

with $\mu_X = \sum_{i=1}^{N} X_i \in \mathbb{R}^{kxs}$ is the mean image of all samples and $\mu_{C_i} = \frac{1}{N_i} \sum_{X \in C_i} X$ be the mean of the samples in class C_i.

3 Experimental Results

This section evaluates the performance of our propoped algorithms Line-based PCA and Line-based LDA compared with that of the original PCA and LDA algorithms based on using ORL. Table 1. shows the recognition results of the best recognition accuracy among all the dimension of feature vectors. It means we test on all dimension of feature vectors and choose the best recognition accuracy.

Table 1. The recognition rates on ORL database with different training samples of four methods (PCA, LDA, Line-based PCA – 3x3 block size, Line-based LDA – 3x3 block size)

Training samples	2	3	4	5
PCA (Eigenfaces)	83.4	87.07	89.3	91.5
LDA (Fisherfaces)	78.83	86.9	91.03	93.6
Line-based PCA	85.55	89.05	92.72	95.03
Line-based LDA	86.52	89.12	94.23	95.94

Table 2. The recognition rates with different block sizes of Line-based PCA

	Training samples			
Size of block	2	3	4	5
[2x2]	85.97	89.65	93.60	95.68
[3x3]	85.55	89.05	92.72	95.03
[5x5]	87.31	90.16	94.06	96.04
[10x2]	85.29	89.79	92.70	95.06
[10x10]	82.67	87.54	89.92	92.79

Table 3. The recognition rates with different block sizes of Line-based LDA

	Training samples			
Size of block	2	3	4	5
[2x2]	86.77	90.4	94.23	96.48
[3x3]	86.52	89.12	94.23	95.94
[5x5]	87.88	90.92	94.86	96.89
[10x2]	86.17	90.41	93.6	95.98
[10x10]	83.51	88.52	90.55	93.57

From Table 2&3, it seems to be that the block size 5x5 give the best recognition results among all.

4 Conclusions

New methods for face recognition have been proposed in this paper. That is, we firstly divide the original image into blocks. Then, we transform the image into a vector of blocks. By using row vector to represent each block, we can get the new matrix which is the representation of the image. Finally PCA and LDA can be applied directly on these matrices.

References

1. W. Zhao, R. Chellappa, A. Rosenfeld, J. Phillips: Face Recognition: A Literature Survey. Technical Report, CFAR-TR00-948, Univ. of Maryland, 2000. (Revised 2002)
2. M. Turk, A Pentland: Eigenfaces for recognition. Journal of Cognitive Neuroscience, Vol. 3 (1991) 71-86.
3. W. Zhao, R. Chellappa, P.J. Phillips: Subspace Linear Discriminant Analysis for Face Recognition. Technical Report CAR-TR-914, 1999.
4. P. N. Belhumeur, J. P. Hespanha, D. J. Kriegman: Eigenfaces vs. fisherface: Recognition using class specific linear projection. IEEE Trans. Pattern Anal. Machine Intell., Vol. 19 (1997) 711-720.
5. H. Yu, J. Yang: A direct LDA algorithm for high-dimensional data with application to face recognition. Pattern Recognit., Vol. 34 (2001) 2067-2070.
6. M. Loog, R. P. W. Duin, R. Haeb-Umbach: Multiclass linear dimension reduction by weighted pairwise fisher criteria. IEEE Trans. Pattern Anal. Machine Intell., Vol. 23 (2001) 762-766.
7. A. M. Martinez, A. C. Kak: PCA versus LDA. IEEE Trans. Pattern Anal. Machine Intell., Vol. 23 (2001) 228-233.
8. D. H. Foley, J. W. Sammon: An optimal set of discrimination vectors. IEEE Trans. Comput., Vol. C-24 (1975) 281-289.
9. R. A. Fisher: The use of multiple measurements in taxonomic problems. Ann. Eugenics, Vol. 7 (1936) 178-188.
10. Rui Huang, Qingshan Liu, Hanqing Lu, Songde Ma: Solving the small sample size problem of LDA. Pattern Recognition, 2002. Proceedings. 16th International Conference on , Vol 3 (2002)
11. C. Liu, H. Wechsler: Robust coding scheme for indexing and retrieval from large face databases. IEEE Trans. Image Processing, Vol. 9 (2000) 132-137.
12. Chengjun Liu, Wechsler H.: A shape- and texture-based enhanced Fisher classifier for face recognition. IEEE Trans. Image Processing, Vol. 10(2001) 598-608.
13. L. Chen, H. M. Liao, M. Ko, J. Lin, G. Yu: A new LDA-based face recognition system which can solve the small sample size problem. Pattern Recognit., Vol. 33 (2000) 1713-1726.

Comparative Study on Recognition of Transportation Under Real and UE Status

Jingxin Dong[1], Jianping Wu[2], and Yuanfeng Zhou[1]

[1] School of Traffic and Transportation, Beijing Jiaotong University,
Beijing 100044, China
jingxindong@yahoo.com.cn, zyfbbb@163.com
[2] Transportation Research Group, University of Southampton,
Southampton, SO17 1BJ, UK and Chong Kong Scholar Professor,
Beijing Jiaotong University, Beijing 100044, China
j.wu@soton.ac.uk

Abstract. Transportation system is a complex, large, integrated and open system. It's difficult to recognize the system with analytical methods. So, two neural network models are developed to recognize the system. One is a back propagation neural network to recognize ideal system under equilibrium status, and the other is a counter propagation model to recognize real system with probe vehicle data. By recognizing ideal system, it turn out that neural network can simulate the process of traffic assignment, that is, neural network can simulate mapping relationship between OD matrix and assigned link flows, or link travel times. Similarly, if real-time OD matrix is obtained by probe vehicle technology, and then similarly results like link travel times can be obtained by similarly models. By comparing outputs of two models, difference about real and ideal transportation system can be found.

1 Introduction

The following figure shows the task and work flow of the paper. Two neural network models will be developed to simulate real system base on probe data and ideal system under UE (User Equilibrium) status.

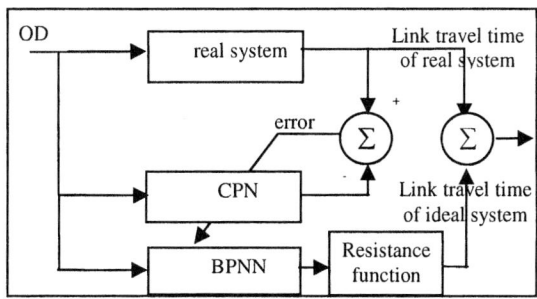

Fig. 1. Work flow

2 Neural Network Model Under User Equilibrium Status

2.1 Concept of User Equilibrium

As we know, an OD pair is generally associated with several parallel routes. These routes can be converted into virtual parallel links on which costs are the sums of cost on all practical links. These virtual networks can then be recognized with neural network in a similar way as shown above. Then, we can similarly deduce equilibrium function for a general transportation network as follows.

$$\begin{cases} t_a(x_a) \cdot \delta_{a,k}^{rs} = T^{rs} & \forall k \\ \sum_k f_k^{rs} = q^{rs} & \forall r,s \\ \sum_r \sum_s \sum_k f_k^{rs} \delta_{a,k}^{rs} = x_a & \forall a \end{cases} \qquad (1)$$

Where, $t_a(x_a)$ denotes costs for link x_a, f_k^{rs} denotes flows on virtual link or route k, T^{rs} denotes costs for OD pair rs, q_{rs} denotes the trips from r to s, $\delta_{a,k}^{rs}$ denotes if link a belongs to the route k connecting r and s, and has values of 1 or 0. In the case, the OD matrix of a traffic network is unknown, as it has been proven that link flows under equilibrium status is the function of OD matrix, we then can have the following Equation:

$$\vec{q} = f(Q) \qquad (2)$$

Where, Q denotes OD matrix of transportation network, $\vec{q}$ denotes the equilibrium flows vector on transportation network.

2.2 Characteristic of Solution Under User Equilibrium Status

Before we use neural network to solve equilibrium function, we have to analyze the convergence of solution, that is, we must judge whether one OD matrix has unique link flows output. The analytical model describing user equilibrium can be constructed as follows:

$$\min Z(x) = \sum_a \int_0^{x_a} t_a(x)$$

$$s.t. \sum_k f_k^{rs} = q_{rs} \quad \forall r,s$$

$$f_k^{rs} \geq 0 \quad \forall k,r,s$$

$$x_a = \sum_r \sum_s \sum_k f_k^{rs} \delta_{a,k}^{rs} \qquad (3)$$

The above formula can explain user equilibrium very well. When number of trips is non-zero, all route resistance of the OD pair are equal to minimum one, and when number of trips is zero, all route resistance of the OD pair is more than or equal to minimum resistance.

Furthermore, when resistances function of link is monotonic increasing function, Hessian matrix of objective function $Z(x)$ is positive definite, that is, objective function is convex function. Otherwise, the constraint function is linear and non-negative. So the problem is convex planning, and assigned link flows are unique for a definite OD matrix.

If we look on OD matrix as system input, and link flows under equilibrium status as output, the above formula has unique solution means that when transportation system is under equilibrium status, there is unique and definite relationship between input and output. So, we can use neural network to simulate transportation system under equilibrium status.

2.3 Structure of Neural Network Model

We choose BPNN to simulate function between OD matrix and link flows under equilibrium status. The network includes input layer, hidden layer and output layer. For a transportation network with n nodes and m links, the number of nodes of input layer is $n^2 - n$, and that of output layer is m, and that of hidden layer is $\sqrt{m(n^2 - n)}$. For simply transportation network, number of nodes of hidden layer should be increased appropriately. Activation function is shown as follows.

$$f(z) = \frac{1}{1 + e^{-z}} \qquad (4)$$

2.4 Training the Neural Network

The data coming from traditional and analytical methods can be one of the training data source. Another training data source comes from traffic planning and management. The model with neural network can easily reflect human's will.

In the course of training, the following rule should be checked frequently to judge whether the training is over

$$SSE = \sqrt{\sum_a (x_a' - x_a)^2 / m} \qquad (5)$$

Where, x_a' ——output of link flows of neural network model.

After training, the output of link flows should be satisfied with characteristic of equilibrium status, that is, any non-zero OD pair has identical resistance on each route. Based on the principle, we deduced the following formula which is recommended to evaluate the performance of the model.

$$\Delta = \frac{\sum_r \sum_s \sqrt{\sum_k (\sum_a t_a(x_a')\delta_{a,k}^{rs} - \frac{1}{k}\sum_k \sum_a t_a(x_a')\delta_{a,k}^{rs})^2}}{n^2 - n} \qquad (6)$$

3 Neural Network Model for Real System

With in-vehicle GPS equipment, OD matrix and link travel times can be obtained with following formula.

$$M_t = \frac{\sum a_{k,t}}{\sum b_{k,t}} \tag{7}$$

$$\mathbf{Q} = \mathbf{q}/M_t^* \tag{8}$$

$$\bar{t}_{link} \approx \bar{t}_{link}^{probe} \tag{9}$$

Where, $a_{k,t}$ denotes total number of probe vehicles that traversed link k and departed during period t; $b_{k,t}$ denotes total number of vehicles observed on link k during period t; M_t denotes the market penetration of probe vehicle. $\mathbf{Q}$ denotes OD matrix of real system, and $\mathbf{q}$ is that of probe vehicle. $\bar{t}_{link}$ denotes link travel times ,and $\bar{t}_{link}^{probe}$ is that of probe vehicles.

Previous research indicates that CPN is better than BP in predicting link travel times, so we suggest using CPN to recognize real system. OD matrix and time is looked as input, and link travel times as output.

4 Comparative Study of Two Models

When we input one matrix into these models, the models will produce ideal and real link travel times. By contrasting two models' result, we can find deviation between ideal and reality, and then find which link is overburden or don't take enough effect. This will give us a direction or clue to find what's wrong with transportation planning or management.

References

1. Haijun Huang: Equilibrium analysis and practice of urban transportation network. People traffic press, Beijing (1994)
2. Sheffi Y.: Urban transportation networks: equilibrium analysis with mathematical programming methods. Prentice-Hall, Englewood Cliffs, New Jersey (1985)
3. Simon Haykin: Neural networks: A comprehensive foundation. Prentice-Hall, Englewood Cliffs, New Jersey (1994)
4. Wenxun Xing and Jinxing Xie: Modern optimal calculation methods. Tsinghua university press, Beijing (1999)
5. Sangjin Han: Dynamic traffic modeling and dynamic stochastic user equilibrium assignment for general road networks. Transportation Research Part B , Vol. 37. Elsevier Science Ltd, London (2003)225-249.

Adaptive Eye Location Using FuzzyART

Jo Nam Jung, Mi Young Nam, and Phill Kyu Rhee

Dept. of Computer Science & Information Engineering, Inha University,
253 Yong-Hyun dong, Incheon, South Korea
jjn10@korea.com, rera@im.inha.ac.kr, pkrhee@inha.ac.kr

Abstract. In this paper we propose a method of locating face and eyes using context-aware binarization. Face detection obtains the face region using neural network and mosaic image representation. Eye location extracts the location of eyes from the detected face region. The proposed method is composed of binarization, connected region segmentation by labeling, eye candidate area extraction by heuristic rules that use geometric information, eye candidate pair detection, and eye area pair determining by ranking method. Binarization plays an important role in this system that converts a source image to a binary image suitable for locating eyes. We consider edge detection based and image segmentation based binarization methods. However, each method alone cannot be used a solution in general environment because these are influenced by the factors such as light direction, contrast, brightness, and spectral composition. We propose a hybrid binarization using the concept of illumination context–awareness that mixes two binarization methods in general environment.

1 Introduction

Face and eyes are considered as a way of communication among people for a long time. For communication between person and computer, many researchers have studied face image processing such as face tracking, face detection, recognizing face and facial expression, lip reading, eye blinking, etc. Therefore, many algorithms and techniques are invented, but it remains a difficult problem yet, [1], [5]. The automatic face processing becomes a significant topic towards developing an effective HCI (Human-Computer Interface) [1], [6], [7]. Eye location with the information of face region consists of largely preprocessing, binarization, connected region segmentation by labeling, detecting of candidates for eye region and eye pair using heuristic rules based on geometric information and determining eye pair by Ranker. Binarization method that converts an original image to a binary image suitable for eye location is considered as edge detection and image segmentation. However, each method is dependent on the environmental factors such as light direction, contrast, brightness, and spectral composition. For solving this problem we propose a new method of mixing two binarization method. We introduce a concept of the context-aware binarization for solving this problem. The changes of illumination environment can be detected by analyzing the input images. We assume that the illumination environment changes continuously. We apply this methodology to face detection and eye location. In section 2, we present binarization. We present face detection in section 3 and locating of eye regions section 4. Finally, we give experimental results and conclusions.

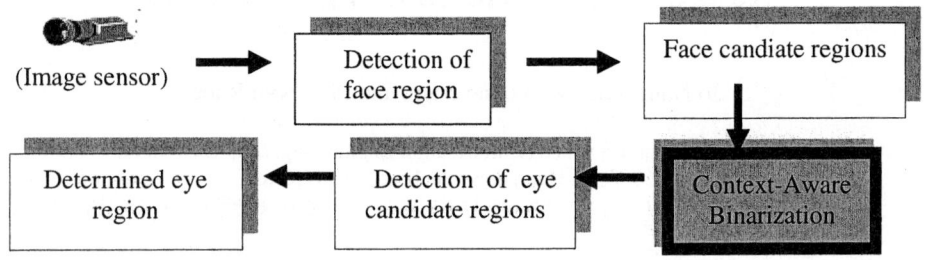

Fig. 1. Block diagram of eye locating process

1.1 Edge Detection

Image edges are defined as local variations of image intensity. This variation is gotten by edge detector operators. The magnitude of image gradient $\nabla f(x, y)$ is given by [3],

$$e(x, y) = |f_x(x, y) + f_y(x, y)| \tag{1}$$

Edge Image is obtained by an edge detector using $e(x,y)$. This image carries information about the edge magnitude. If the edge detector output is large, a local edge is present.

1.2 Image Segmentation

When an image contains an object having homogeneous intensity and a background with a different intensity level, the image can be segmented in two regions using image segmentation by threshold [3]. The following equation is the definition of segmentation adopted in this paper. where T is threshold whose choice can be based on the image histogram. The gray level of facial components such as hair, eyebrow, pupil, nostril, lip, etc. is darker than that of the skin. The threshold T can be obtained

$$E(x, y) = \begin{cases} 1 & \text{if } e(x, y) \geq T \\ 0 & \text{otherwise} \end{cases} \tag{2}$$

nostril, lip, etc. is darker than that of the skin. The threshold T can be obtained using this property. The threshold is used to discriminate pixels belonging to eye region from skin region. Therefore, if we use threshold as a fixed value we cannot obtain a good image because we always experiment in different environments. For solving this problem we experiment a method getting a threshold T using the statistical information of the edge magnitude and the property that the larger the edge magnitude is, the higher possibility of being edge is.

2 Face Detection

The face location algorithm detects a face in an image using mosaic image representation and back-propagation neural network [4]. Because consecutive images obtained from image sensor usually contain a lot of noises, we perform histogram equalization, mosaic image, and normalization as a preprocessing step. When the histogram of some image is biased to one side, histogram equalization can make the histogram distribution uniform. This improves the contrast of image and makes image features more distinguishable. The input image is converted into a low resolution image called mosaic image [5]. The mosaic image representation provides fast noise-insensitive processing. From this mosaic image, all possible 8×8 mosaic called octet faces (the second figure of Fig. 2) are extracted. Each cell of octet is normalized in the $0 \sim 1$ range of a real value. The octet is checked by the back-propagation neural network to extract the most suitable face region. The first figure of Fig. 2 is the original image captured from image sensor, and the second is mosaic image representation. This algorithm returns the coordinates of face region.

(a) Original image (b) Octet face

Fig. 2. The original image and the octet face

Fig. 3 shows examples of the result of face location. Two white rectangles of the second image mean that the number of possible face candidate is two.

Fig. 3. Examples of face detection

3 Locating of Eye Regions

Fig. 4 roughly describes the model that we propose for locating face and eye regions. Eye location begins with inputting each face candidate regions into eye location process given in Fig. 4. However, if image is captured in weak illumination, generally face candidate region becomes a small intensity region, i.e. Face candidate region's image contrast become poor and the subjective image quality become low. For enhancing image quality, histogram equalization that modifies its histogram performs in face candidate regions [4].

We found that binarization processed by edge detection algorithm is efficient when the candidate region is a dark image and binarization by segmentation algorithm is efficient when the candidate region is normal or bright from experiment. Input face candidate region is analyzed using neural network in the context awareness module. The binarization is performed differently according to the analyzed illumination condition. If the image illumination condition is dark, an input face candidate region is binarized by the edge detection method. If the condition is normal or bright, it is done by the segmentation method.

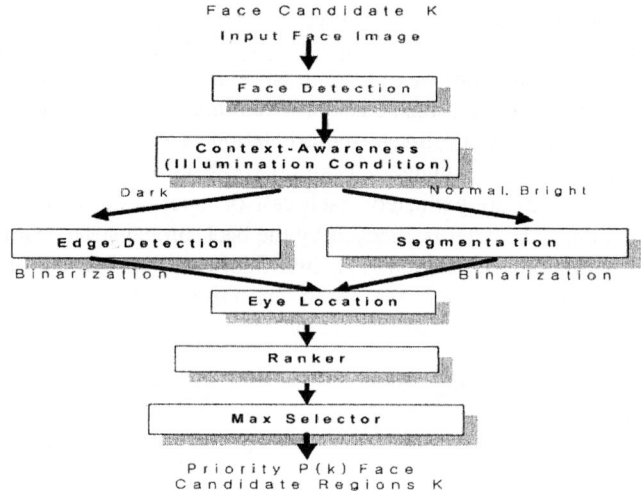

Fig. 4. The block diagram of face and eye location

3.1 Face Candidate Regions

Eye locating is executed in face candidate regions detecting by mosaic and back propagation neural network. However, face candidate region exists more than one. This means that face candidate region is the completely wrong region and whether it can contain a pair of eyes or not.

(a) (b)

Fig. 5. Examples of face candidate regions

3.2 Binarization and Labeling

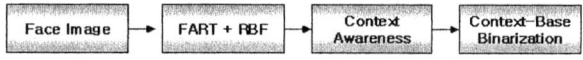

3.2.1 Context Awareness Using FART

In the proposed approach, illumination classification is dealt with as local targets to be detected in an image. We formulate the object detector generator to learn to discriminate object pattern witch can be measured formally, not intuitively as most previous approaches did. The illumination estimator classifies a face pattern into one of the face illuminant set. The facial pose estimation can be used to verify the detection of context-based faces. Gong and colleagues use non-linear support vector regression to estimate facial pose. In this paper, we propose how combined supervised learning and unsupervised learning. The proposed learning based classifier generator has advantages over previous approaches.

3.2.2 Context Awareness by FART+RBF

The RBF networks, just like MLP networks, can therefore be used in classification and/or function approximation problems. In the case of a RBF network, we usually prefer the hybrid approach, described below [10], [11], [12]. The RBFNs, which have a similar architecture to that of MLPs, however, achieve this goal using a different strategy. One cluster center is updated every time an input vector x is chosen by FuzzyART from the input data set. The cluster nearest to x has its position updated using

$$W_{ji}(t+1) = \beta(I \wedge W_{ji}(t)) + (1-\beta)W_{ji}(t) \qquad (3)$$

FuzzyART is a variant of ART system derived from the first generation of ART, namely ART1. It is a synthesis of ART algorithm and Fuzzy operator. ART1 can only accept binary input pattern, but FuzzyART allows both binary and continuous input patterns [9], [13]. The feature space of object instance with multiple viewing angles must be clustered properly so that the location error can be minimized. However, the classification of multiple viewing points is very subjective and ambiguous. Thus, we adopt FuzzyART and RBF methods for achieving an optimal pose classification architecture. Executed step is as following to FuzzyART [9], [13], [14]. In this Paper, Clustering's performance improves by studying repeatedly about done data.

The cluster center is moved closer to x because this equation minimizes the error vector. Each hidden unit calculates the distance of the input vector from the corresponding Gaussian:

$$\phi_j(x) = \exp\left\{-\frac{\|x - \mu_j\|^2}{2\sigma_j^2}\right\} \qquad (4)$$

In this paper, centers are obtained from unsupervised learning (clustering), FuzzyART Algorithm. The weights between the hidden units and the output layer, denoted by w_{kj}, are regular multiplication weights (as in a MLP).

$$y_k(x) = \sum_{j=1}^{M} w_{kj}\phi_j(x) + w_{k0} \qquad (5)$$

Where x is the input vector, m_j is the jth prototype vector, σ_j is the width of the Gaussian of that prototype or cluster centre. There are various approaches for training RBF networks. In this paper, centers are obtained from unsupervised learning (clustering), FuzzyART algorithm. Clustering (FuzzyART algorithm) and LMS are iterative. This is the most commonly used procedure. Typically provides good results. After finding a suitable cluster using clustering algorithm, do laying center on this. The winning node μ_j is what FuzzyART is its best match for the input pattern. Hidden node's center determined by unsupervised learning, FART.

As showed Fig. 6, the idea is to train the network in two separate stages - first, we perform an unsupervised training (FuzzyART) to determine the Gaussians' parameters

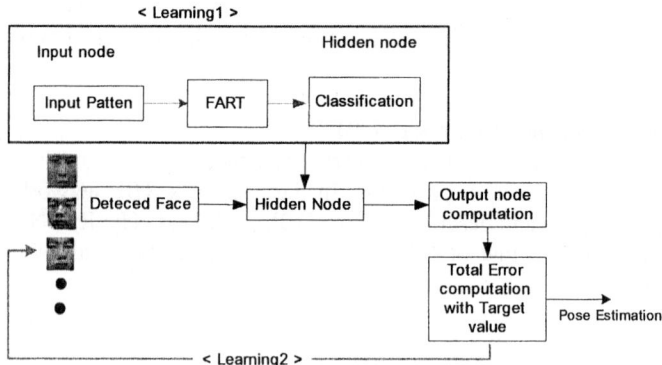

Fig. 6. Training System Architecture

(j, j). In the second stage, the multiplicative weights w_{kj} are trained using the regular supervised approach. Input pattern is vectorized for grayscale image size of 20x20 pixels, input node had mosaic of size of 10x10 pixels. The transformation from the input space to the hidden unit space is non-linear, whereas the transformation from the hidden-unit space to the output-space is linear. RBF classifier expand input vectors into a high dimensional space. RBF network has architecture that of the traditional three-layer back-propagation. In this paper, hidden units is trained using FuzzyART network and basis function used are Gaussians. The proposed network input consists of n normalized and rescaled size of 1/2 face images fed to the network as 1 dimension vector. And input unit has floating value [0, 1]. The vector value is normalized. In case learn by FuzzyART, performance is best in case used picture itself by input node vectorized.

3.2.3 Binarization

The binarization method explained in section 2. The labeling algorithm examines a state of connection between a pixel and its 8-neighborhood pixels, and labels the objects in the image. The labeling algorithm is used to obtain connected and isolated regions [2]. Fig. 7 (a) shows the result of image segmentation by thresholding in a face region. Fig. 7 (b) shows that facial components such as eye, eyebrow, and nose are labeled by the labeling algorithm. The labeled facial components are recorded as eye candidates.

(a) Image segmentation   (b) Labeling

Fig. 7. Example of labeling

3.3 Detection of Candidates of Eye and a Pair of Eyes

Candidates of eye and a pair of eyes are detected by heuristic rules based on eye's geometrical information in face. Eye candidate's width has much correlation with face candidate's height. However, because the height of eye candidate has an extreme changeability on condition of blinking one's eyes, it is difficult to set a correlation between eye candidate's height and face candidate region. Eye detection has a tendency to acquire the boundary of eye. However, image segmentation have a more concern in pupil regions than the boundary of eyes, so the connected regions by labeling have a tendency to become more smaller and more nearer a square than ones obtained by edge detection. Therefore, rules used in eye location differ as to binarization methods. The example of detecting candidates of eye region is shown in Fig. 8.

(a) Connected region segmentation by labeling

(b) Candidates of eye region

Fig. 8. Example of detecting candidates of eye region

Once eye candidate regions are detected, candidates of a pair of eyes are detected. First, because two eyes locate in a similar position by y-axis, eye candidate regions are sorted by y-axis. Candidates of a pair of eyes satisfy the following rules- the gradient of two eyes, comparison between two eye's size and distance between two eyes. These rules also differ as to binarization method similar to the rule of eye candidate regions.

3.4 Ranker

After eye location process, Ranker calculates an energy of each candidate of a pair of eyes detecting in each face region F_k. Each energy obtained by Ranker inputs to *Max* and it selects a max value among those. A candidate of a pair of eyes whose energy is equal to this selected value become a pair of eyes. Fig. 9 shows a template of a pair of eyes that are represented with terms of the size, shape, positional information of eyes, eyebrows and mouth. Using this template, Ranker calculates an energy of a pair of eyes.

Eq (6) is an equation representing a template given in Fig. 8. E_L, E_R, E_M which are the energy, using terms of image intensity, edge magnitude, the region information obtained by connected region segmentation and so forth, calculates in the left eye, right eye, mouth respectively. In addition, E_{LR}, E_{LM} and E_{RM} are the energy between two eyes, the left eye and the mouth, the right eye and the mouth, respectively. Finally, E_{LL} is the energy between the left eye and the left eyebrow, and E_{RR} is the energy between the right eye and the right eyebrow.

$$E = k_1 E_L + k_2 E_R + k_3 E_M + k_4 (E_{LR} + E_{LM} + E_{RM}) + k_5 (E_{LL} + E_{RR}) \qquad (6)$$

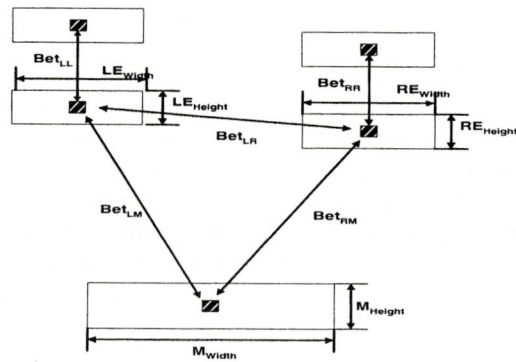

Fig. 9. The template of a pair of eyes

3.5 Determination a Pair of Eyes

There can exist more than one candidate for a pair of eyes obtained in each candidate face region. Now, determined eyes have a maximum value of energy by Ranker. Therefore if there exist m candidates for a pair of eyes obtained in a face candidate region Fi, each candidate for a pair of eyes is expressed as Eye^i_k, $1<=i<=m$ and its energy calculated by Ranker is define as $E(Eye^i_k)$. Therefore, the energy of a determined pair of eyes in face candidate region Fi are defined as below Eq (7),

$$E(k) = \underset{1 \leq i \leq m}{MAX} \left\{ P(Eye^i_k) \right\} \tag{7}$$

and finally, the determined eyes of this facial image should satisfy Eq (8).

$$\underset{1 \leq k \leq m}{MAX} \left\{ E(k) \right\} \tag{8}$$

Fig. 10 shows a process of eye location. Fig. 10 (c) are the results of executing the binarization, connected region segmentation by labeling and conditioning the rule that will be satisfied by a candidate for a pair of eyes. we determine as eye regions because of it having maximum value among them.

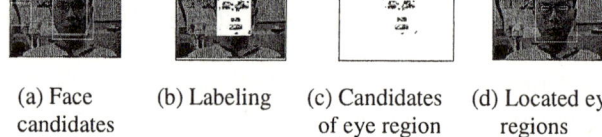

(a) Face candidates   (b) Labeling   (c) Candidates of eye region   (d) Located eye regions

Fig. 10. A process of eye location

4 Experimental Results and Conclusion

Our proposed method of locating eye regions was developed with MFC(Microsoft foundation class) in Pentium IV 2.4GHz CPU PC having Windows XP as operating system. Compiler used was Visual C++ 6.0. Experimental images were captured from image sensor with 320×240 size and 256 gray levels and were collected totally 400 frames from 35 persons(see Table 1).

Table 1. Final results o f different methods of eye location

Glasses	Number of frame	Method of binarization	Total sum	
			Number of Success	Successful rate
Not wearing	247	E	243	98.38%
		S	231	93.52%
		E+S	243	93.38%
Wearing	153	E	116	75.82%
		S	138	90.20%
		E+S	143	93.46%
Total sum	400	E	359	89.75%
		S	369	92.25%
		E+S	386	96.50%

This successful rate of eye locations largely depends on the environmental factors image quality, illumination, glasses and hair of head and so forth. In this experiments, only the factor of glasses was considered and experimental image s were classified by the factor of glasses. These classified images were separately experimented with different methods edge(E), image segmentation (S) and combined method(E+S) and were compared with each result. According to the above result using combined method was superior to single method. In a stable illumination, in case not wearing glasses we could get successful rate using only edge method. However, if glasses were worn, successful rate of edge method was lower than that of segmentation method and at the same time especially in case black glasses worn frame edge method made the rate of success remarkably lowered. Consequently, using a single method is suitable for a particular environment. Nevertheless, because the environment getting images isn't always stable in the real world, if we can't select appropriate method we can't get a good result. So, in this paper we combined two binarization method for locating eye regions and can get a good result in a general environment as well as a particular one. In the future's experiments, we will have experimented on locating eye regions in the more real world's environments an object near eyes and the reflection of a beam of light off a glasses and so forth.

References

1. Lars-Peter Bala., Kay Talmi., and Jin Liu.: Automatic Detection and Tracking of Faces and Facial Features in Video Sequences. Picture Coding Symposium 97, (Sept. 1997) 251-256
2. R. L. Lumina., G. Shapiro., and O. Zuniga.: A New Connected Components Algorithm for Virtual Memory Computers. *Computer Vision, Graphics, and Image Processing.*, Vol. 22 (1983) 287-300
3. I. Pitas, *Digital image processing algorithms.* Prentice Hall (1992)
4. R. Klette., and P.Zamperoni.: *Handbook of image processing operators.* John Wiley&Sons, 1996

5. Zhou ZH., and Geng X.: Projection functions for eye detection. Pattern Recognition 37(5), no.(5) (2004) 1049-1056
6. Bin Chen., Zhi-Qiang Liu., and Xiang-Hua Zhu.: Eye Location In Human Face Images Using Fuzzy Integral. IEEE Trans. On Proceedings of the Second International Conference on` Machine Learning and Cybernetics, Vol.14. no.2-5 (Nov.2003) 2500-2505
7. Li Weijun., Xu jian., and Wang Shoujue.: A Fast Eye Location Algorithm Based on Geometric Complexity. Proceeding of the 5th World Congress in Intelligent Control and Automation, Hangzhou, P.R. China, Vol. 5. no. 6 (2004) 4105-4107
8. Qu Ying-Dong., Cui Cheng-Song., Chen San-Ben and Li Jin-Quan.: A fast subpixel edge detection method using Sobel-Zernike moments operator. Image and Vision Computing, China, Vol. 23. Issue 1, no.1 (Janu. 2005) 11-17
9. T.Kasuba: Simplefied Fuzzy ARTMAP. AI Expert, November (1993) 18-25
10. Shakunaga, T.: An Object Pose Estimation System Using A Single Camera. Proc. of IEEE international conference, Vol.2. (1992) 7~10
11. Paulino, A. Araujo, H.: Pose Estimation for central catadioptric system. An analytic Approach. Proc. Of Pattern recognition (2002) 969-699
12. Huang, J. Shao, X Wechsler, H.: Face Pose discrimination using support vector machanism(SVM). Proc. of Pattern Recognition, Vol.1. (1998) 154-156
13. G.A. Carpenter et al: Fuzzy ARTMAP : A neural network architecture for inceremetal supervised learning of analog multidimensional maps. IEEE Trans. Neural Networks, Vol.3, No. 5. September (1992) 698-712
14. Ramuhalli, P., Polikar, R., Udpa L., Udpa S.: Fuzzy ARTMAP network with evolutionary learning. Proc. of IEEE 25th Int. Conf. On Acoustics, Speech and Signal Processing (ICASSP 2000), Vol. 6. Istanbul, Turkey (2000) 3466-3469

Face Recognition Using Gabor Features and Support Vector Machines

Yunfeng Li, Zongying Ou, and Guoqiang Wang

Key Laboratory for Precision and Non-traditional Machining Technology
of Ministry of Education, Dalian University of Technology, P.R. China
yunfengli2004@tom.com, ouzyg@dlut.edu.cn, wgq2211@163.com

Abstract. This paper presents a face recognition algorithm by using Gabor wavelet transform for facial features extraction and Support Vector Machines (SVM) for face recognition, Gabor wavelets coefficients are used to represent local facial features. The implementations of our algorithm are as follows: Firstly, facial feature points are located roughly by using a set of node templates. Secondly, Gabor wavelet coefficients are extracted at every facial feature point, and all the Gabor wavelet coefficients are catenated to represent a face image. Lastly, SVM classifiers are used for face recognition. The experimental results demonstrate the effectiveness of our face recognition algorithm.

1 Introduction

During the past two decades, several promising approaches have been proposed for face recognition. Among these approaches, elastic graph matching [1] is a representative one that performed best in the FERET test [2], this approach uses Gabor wavelet coefficients to represent local facial features. Facial feature points are located by elastic graph matching which is a two-stage optimization process. The excellent performance of this approach consists in two aspects: one is the use of Gabor features which are biologically inspired [3]; the other is the matching method which can locate facial feature points precisely. Although elastic graph matching is an outstanding face recognition approach, its computation is prohibitive, this usually can not satisfy the practical demands. Support Vector Machines (SVM) [4] provide a powerful tool for machine learning, they have gained successful applications in pattern classification. This paper presents a face recognition algorithm by using Gabor wavelet transform for facial features extraction and SVM for face classification. The implementations of our algorithm are as follows: Firstly, facial feature points are located roughly by using a set of node templates. Secondly, Gabor wavelet coefficients are extracted at every facial feature point, all Gabor wavelet coefficients are catenated to represent a face image. Lastly, SVM classifiers are used for face recognition. The experimental results demonstrate the effectiveness of our face recognition algorithm.

2 Gabor Feature Extraction

2D Gabor wavelet transform is usually used for image representation and analysis. The transform is implemented by the convolutions of a bank of Gabor filters and a given image signal. Usually 40 Gabor filters are employed which are formed by a discrete set of 5 different frequencies and 8 orientations [1]. So 40 complex coefficients can be obtained by Gabor wavelet transform at a given point, in this paper, the 40 magnitudes of the complex coefficients are used to represent local facial features.

Facial feature points can be located by using a priori knowledges: on the one hand, the local facial features are distributed in the same way; one the other hand, the relative distances between two local facial features are different for different individual faces. Based on these knowledges, we can use a set of node templates to obtain the rough positions of facial feature points for geometrically normalized and aligned face images, the node templates can be obtained through clustering from a representative set of face images. In this paper, by using the manually picked eye coordinates of the face images, all the face images are geometrically normalized and aligned, the normalized face images have the same size of 128×128 and the two eyes lie at the uniform positions (52,64) and (76,64) respectively. Totally 42 local facial features are selected for face recognition and 7 representative node templates are used for facial feature points location. For each given face image, all the node templates are put on the face area and the best one are selected, the rough positions of facial feature points are located by the fittest template, some results are shown in Fig.1. After the positions of all facial feature points are obtained, Gabor wavelet coefficients are extracted at every facial feature points, and all Gabor wavelet coefficients are catenated to represent a face image.

Fig. 1. Facial feature points location by the node template

3 Support Vector Machines

SVM perform pattern recognition for two-class problems by finding the decision surface which minimizes the structural risk of the classifier. This is equivalent to determining the separating hyperplane that has maximum distance to the closest samples of the training set. Considering the problem of separating a set of training samples belong to two separable classes, $(x_1, y_1),...,(x_n, y_n)$, where $x_i \in R^d$, $y_i \in \{-1,+1\}$, an optimal hyperplane can be obtained through solving a constrained optimization problem, the decision function can be written as:

$$f(x) = \text{sgn}(\sum_{i=1}^{n} \alpha_i^* y_i k(x_i \cdot x) + b^*) \tag{1}$$

where α_i^* ($i = 1,...,n$) and b^* are the best solutions to the optimization problem, the kernel $k(x, y)$ commonly used include polynomials kernel, radial basis function kernels and sigmoid kernel etc.

The SVM approach was originally developed for binary classification problems. In many practical applications, a multi-class pattern recognition problem has to be solved. Usually there are two strategies [5] to solve multi-class problems by using binary SVM classifiers: The first one is one-against-one, in this method, for each possible pair of classification a binary classifier is calculated, each classifier is trained on a subset of the training set containing only training examples of the two involved classes. If N represents the number of total classes, all $(N-1)N/2$ classifiers are combined through a majority voting scheme to estimate the final classification. The other one is the one-against-rest, in this method N different classifiers are constructed, one for each class. Here the l-th classifier is trained on the whole training data set in order to classify the members of class l against the rest. In the classification stage, the classifier with the maximal output defines the estimated class label of the current input vector. While the former has too many computations, we adopt the latter one for our face recognition task.

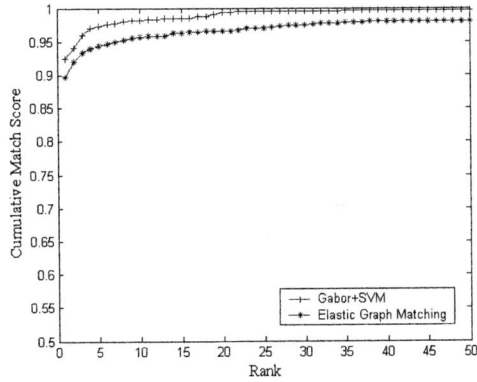

Fig. 2. Cumulative match scores curve of the face recognition results

4 Experimental Results

The experiment is performed on the face database B of the BVC'2004 [6], this face database contains 2000 face images corresponding to 100 distinct subjects. The images were taken at ten different illumination directions, varying facial expressions, diverse background and certain pose changes. We select 10 images from each subject for training, the remaining 10 images are used for testing, and all the face images are geometrically normalized and aligned. This paper selects the polynomials kernel for SVM decision functions, and SMO [7] approach for SVM training. The system was implemented using Visual C++ language on a computer with a Pentium IV(2.4GHz) processor and a 512M EMS memory. Experiment results show an average speed of

0.5 seconds for one face image, which is much faster than 7 seconds of elastic graph matching approach. Fig.2 shows the cumulative match scores curve of the face recognition results. From the figure we can see that the performance of our approach is not worse than the elastic graph matching one.

5 Conclusion

In this paper, a face recognition algorithm has been described, this algorithm uses Gabor wavelet transform for facial features extraction and SVM for face recognition. The implementations of our algorithm are as follows: Firstly, facial feature points are located roughly by using a set of node templates. Secondly, Gabor wavelet coefficients are extracted at every facial feature points, and all the Gabor wavelet coefficients are catenated to represent a face image. Lastly, SVM classifiers are used for face recognition. The experimental results show our approach is not worse than the elastic graph matching one, although our approach only using rough position of each facial feature point, this can be explained in two ways: one is that Gabor features are biologically inspired and insensitive to position, the other is the excellent generalization ability of SVM.

References

1. Wiskott, L., Fellous, J.M., Krüger, N., and von der Malsburg, C.: Face Recognition by Elastic Bunch Graph Matching, Technical Report IR-INI 96-08, Institut für Neuroinformatik, Ruhr-Universität Bochum, D-44780 Bochum, Germany (1996)
2. Phillips, P., J., Moon, H., Rizvi, S., A., et al.: The FERET Evaluation Methodology for Face recognition Algorithms. IEEE Transaction on Pattern Analysis and Machine Intelligence, Vol. 22 (2000) 1090–1104
3. Daugman, J.G.: Two-Dimensional Spectral Analysis of Cortical Receptive Field Profile. Vision Research, Vol. 20 (1980) 847–856
4. Vapnik, V. N.: The Nature of Statistical Learning Theory, Springer-Verlag, New York, (1995)
5. Schwenker, F.: Hierarchical Support Vector Machines for Multi-Class Pattern Recognition. Fourth International conference on Knowledge-Based Intelligent Engineering Systems & Allied Technologies, Brighton, UK, Vol. 2 (2000) 561–565
6. The First Chinese Biometrics Verification Competition. http://www.sinobiometrics.com
7. Platt, J. Sequential Minimal Optimization: A fast algorithm for training support vector machines. Technical Report, MSR-TR-98-14, Microsoft Research, 1998

# Wavelet Method Combining BP Networks and Time Series ARMA Modeling for Data Mining Forecasting

Weimin Tong and Yijun Li

School of Management, Harbin Institute of Technology,
150001 Harbin, China
{tongweimin, yijunli}@hit.edu.cn

Abstract. The business field is one of the important fields where the data mining technology is applied. The study mainly focuses on different attribute object's quantitative prediction and customer structure's qualitative prediction. Aiming at the characteristics of time series in business field, such as near-periodicity, non-stationarity and nonlinearity, the wavelet-neural networks-ARMA method is proposed and its application is examined in this paper. The hidden period and the non-stationarity existed in time series are extracted and separated by wavelet transformation. The characteristic of wavelet decomposition series is applied to BP networks and an autoregressive moving average (ARMA) model. The given example elucidates that the forecasting method mentioned in this paper can be employed to the business field successfully and efficiently.

1 Introduction

The reliable, secure and economical commercial forecasting plays an important role in the business field. Therefore forecasting methods have been studied deeply and can be divided into two categories, namely classical methods and intellectual technologies [1]-[3]. The classical methods mainly include many models based on various statistical theories, whereas intellectual technologies include artificial neural network methods and expert system approaches [4]-[11]. In practice all these methods have been applied in the research of time series to certain degrees. However, because of time series' near-periodicity, non-stationarity and nonlinearity, difficulties do occur when using these methods to solve practical problems [4], [6]. Firstly, Classical time series analysis methods mainly depend on linear time model and linear spectral estimation. Although these methods are based on the simple theories and are convenient to be applied in practice, when forecasting precision needs to be enhanced so as to amplify the model's scale, the forecasting precision becomes lower and the forecasting speed becomes slower due to time series' essence of non-linearity. Secondly, expert system techniques, utilizing the knowledge and analogical reasoning of experienced human operators, have been investigated [12]. Although expert system can synthesize many influencing factors, its knowledge base is very difficult to describe and build and its parameters can't be adjusted flexibly. As a result, in practice, the application of expert system is much limited. In addition, several research groups have studied the use of artificial neural networks (ANN) [13], [14] for ANN techniques are excellent tools to describe nonlinear relation [5]. However when the dependence of ANN learns represents relatively strong nonlinearity, it requires a large numbers of input cells, so the neural network training can often run into local minimum and the convergence speed is extremely low, and finally a great quantity of cyber-resources and times have been consumed. This proves that ANN techniques are inappropriate to solve practical problems [15]-[17]. In this paper, we intend to apply wavelet methods into data mining in the business field, and elucidate in details the procedure and effect of this new method applied in the time series prediction, through analyzing the real data of one supermarket.

2 Wavelet-NN-ARMA Model

Our basic idea is, by utilizing the rule that wavelet transform relies on scale, building various linear or nonlinear models for corresponding transformation types to have a forecasting in different transformation domains, and then applying the wavelet reconstruction technology to synthesize each forecasting at transformation domains for the final forecasting of time series based on data mining. Thus the data processing flow in this paper can be divided into three phases. The first phase is the wavelet decomposition. It aims to attain the wavelet decomposition series and the last approximation series of original time series at each scale domains. The second is modeling and forecasting. Its role is modeling and forecasting for these wavelet decomposition series at each transformation domains by using BP neural net, and for the final scale decomposition series by using ARMA model. The third is the wavelet reconstruction. Here the wavelet reconstructions have been achieved with purpose of synthesizing those forecast series obtained at each transformation domains, to system final forecasting, utilizing the wavelet reconstruction technique.

In figure 1, original system is any time series needs to be analyzed. Wavelet decomposition level 1, wavelet decomposition level 2... wavelet decomposition level M are M wavelet decomposition series of original time series at M levels (decomposition layer) and their notations are d_1, d_2, ..., d_M, respectively. Scale decomposition level M is M^{th} scale decomposition series, its notation is a_M.

As modeling and forecasting at each transformation domains, based on theory of wavelet transform, it is well known that, as the decomposition level increases, the wavelet decomposition series of power short term quarter-hour load time series obtain better stationarity, periodicity and linearity. The last approximation series at the greatest multiresolution layer has very regular stationarity, and it is not only numerically close to original system load series, but also has almost the same variational trend. Thus, at the final scale transformation domain, we will utilize time series ARMA model to modeling and forecasting. At various wavelet transformation domains, we will utilize several BP neutral net models with different input cells to modeling and forecasting.

The final phase of these forecasting models is to synthesize forecasting series at various transformation domains in order to obtain final forecasting series by using wavelet reconstruction technology.

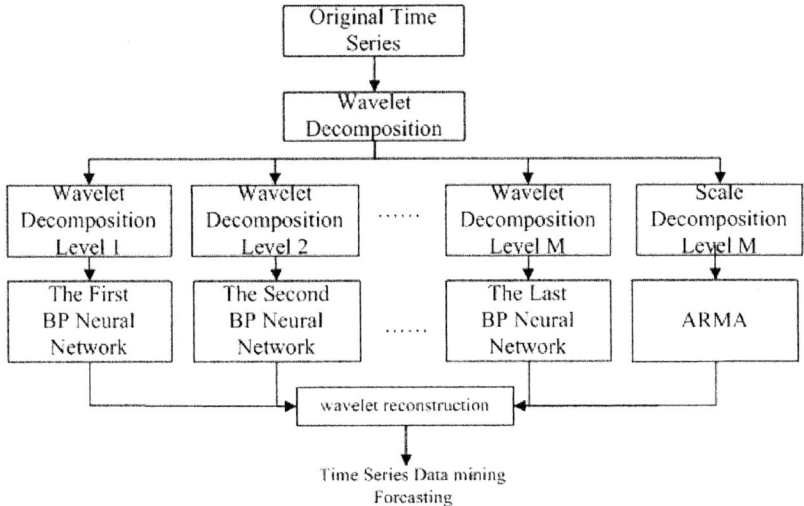

Fig. 1. The architecture of wavelet-neural network-ARMA model

3 Time Series-Based Data Predict

There will be an analysis of 2688 sample datum (4 weeks) of one supermarket, and make forecasting.

3.1 Time Series-Based Wavelet Decompositions

According to the characteristic of the wavelet transformation, the length of decomposition series is decreased doubly with scale increased doubly. Since the scale of the new series is different on each scale, the intervals of samples from neighboring data of series are different too. In order to facilitate modeling, it can make the new series and original series have the same length and sample, and name them as redundant wavelet transformation and redundant scale transformation. The coefficient of Low-pass filter in Biorthogonal wavelets bior(4,4) is (0, 0.0378, -0.0238, -0.1106, 0.3774, 0.8527, 0.3774, -0.1106, -0.0238, 0.0378), the coefficient of High-pass filter is (0, -0.0645, 0.0407, 0.4181, -0.7885, 0.0407, 0.4181, -0.0645, 0, 0), they also have 10 coefficient.

In figure 2, on the top is the primitive time series of 1344 data, its notation is S. In addition to it, from the top to the bottom the scale transformation time series of the 5th scale level is a5. The wavelet transformation time series of 5th, 4th, 3rd, 2nd, 1st scale level is d_5, d_4, d_3, d_2, d_1. By all appearances, there is obvious near-periodicity in series S, a_5 and d_5, and this near- periodicity is one day, it reflects for 96 continuous points in the figure.

As for scale level, in fact 1st scale level corresponds to scale 2, afterwards 4, 8, and 16, 32 in turn. When scale is short, wavelet transformation series express strong change, embodying that the reliance relation of the data is not good, namely, the

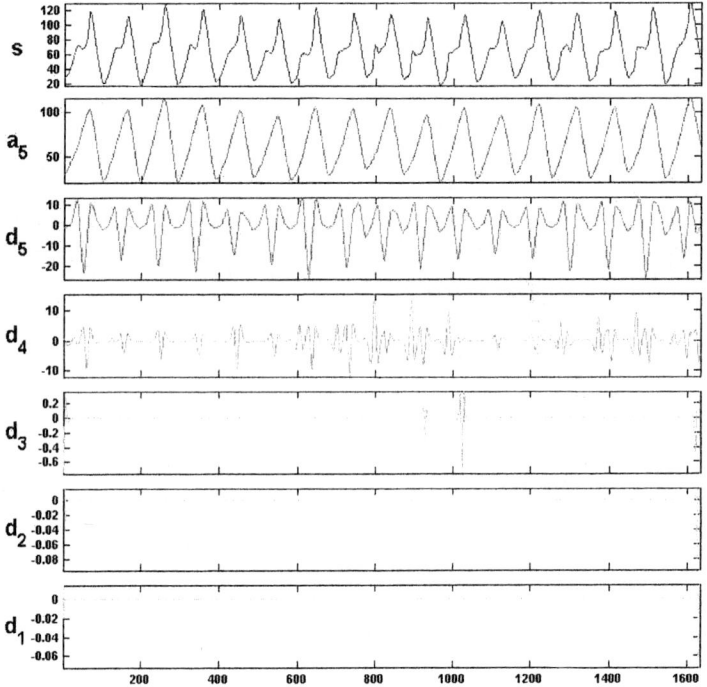

Fig. 2. Time series and its redundant wavelet and scale transforms

reliance time is short, but change scope is little (compared with original data). All these show that this component have no great impact on change trend of original time series, it is just a kind of part influence factor, so the prediction data of this time series has little impact on total predict of original time series. With the increasing scale, wavelet time series becomes more and more smooth. It becomes plainness in the 5th scale, showing that it has stable impact on original time series, and effect time is much longer. In addition, the scale transformations in 5th scale has also become plain and keep the same trend with the original time series, furthermore its value is close to the original time series. This shows that the scale transformation series has the essential impact on original time series. The characters of the time series make wavelet-neural networks-ARMA model available to predict and analysis the original time series.

3.2 Modeling and Forecasting in Scale

When BP neutral nets are built at five wavelet transformation domains, every net model includes three layers, namely, an input layer, a hidden layer and a output layer, and there is only one output cell in every output layer. Design parameters of the five net models are shown in the table 1. In this table, the notation BP_1 is the BP neutral net model, which is built for d_1.

Table 1. Design parameters of BP networks at every scale

Model Parameter	BP_1	BP_2	BP_3	BP_4	BP_5
Input	7	7	7	7	13
Output	14	28	28	56	112

Because the characteristic of these 5 wavelet transformation series is that the range changed is very small relative to original series, and d_5 which range changed is a little greater than other fours has near-periodicity, every input cell of this 5 models is not data on continuous position of time series, but is a vector which contains 96 datum in succession. For example, there are 13 input cells in model BP_5, and $X=\{x_1, x_2 \ldots x_{13}\}$ is the input vector, then x_1 is a vector which consists of the first 96 data of series d_5, and x_2 is a vector which consists of the second 96 data of series d_5, and so on. The forecasting results of this 5 wavelet transformation series are shown in Figure 3.

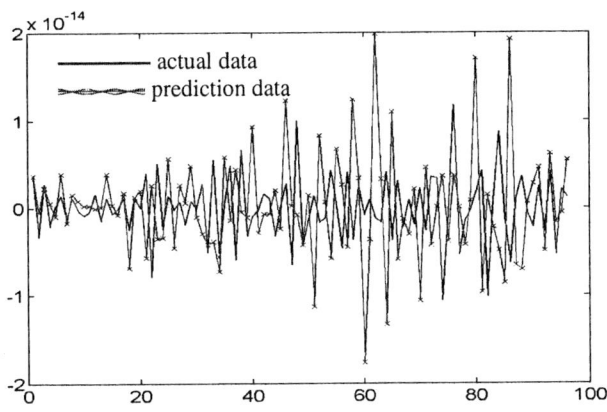

Fig. 3. The comparisons between forecasting and actual sample of d_1

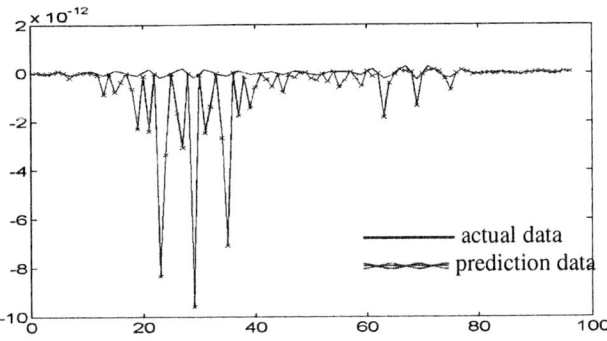

Fig. 4. The comparisons between forecasting and actual sample of d_2

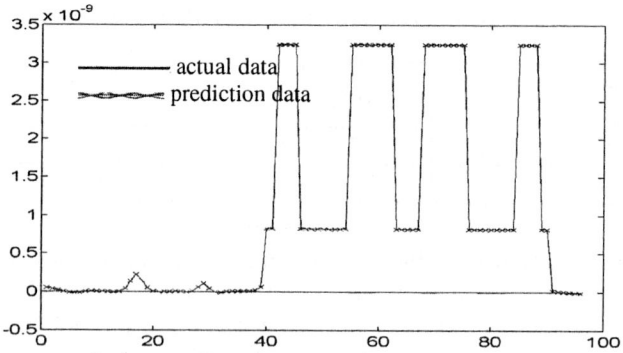

Fig. 5. The comparisons between forecasting and actual sample of d_3

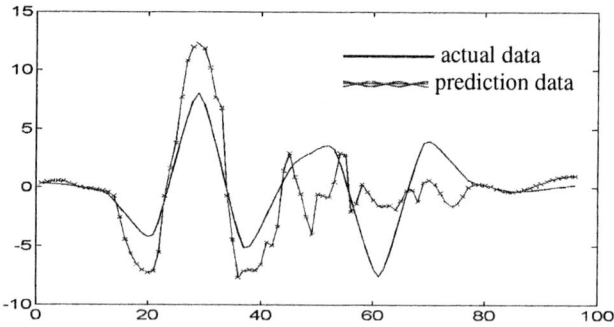

Fig. 6. The comparisons between forecasting and actual sample of d_4

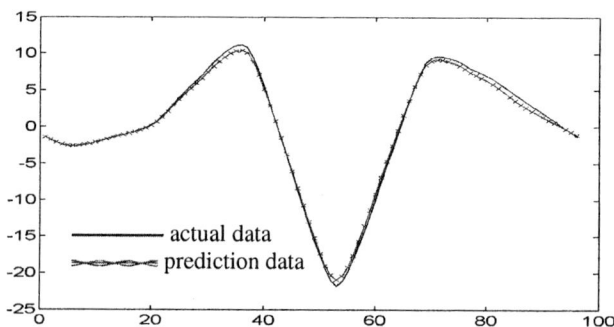

Fig. 7. The comparisons between forecasting and actual sample of d_5

Because the value of this five series is too little, predict has small warp, especially the predict of the top 4, it is only roughly identical with the real data, but because these series are very small to the original time series (the magnitude of d_1 is 10^{-14}), these deviations influence on final result is very little.

Extracted from large scale neural networks relied on hidden time, it is necessary for model building utilizing redundant wavelet transformation to use the data of consecutive position on a long period, therefore large amount input units are essential to make the neural networks complex. However, the special processing method mentioned in above description ensures every BP model to be simpler than other methods. In practice, it is necessary to process five trainings, but each training time of every neural network is short, hence the total duration to accomplish the BP model building is still short comparably, even this BP model building includes five scale levels' wavelet transformation time series.

ARMA model is employed to analyze the 5th scale wavelet transformation. The first thing we need to do is to make this series zero equalization. Namely this series is transformed and every value in this series deducts its mean value, then the mean value of the transformed series is zero.

For conveniently describing, $x_1, x_2...x_n$ represent each value in the processed 5th scale decomposition series a_5 received zero equalization transfers, then the problem of model building for the 5th scale decomposition series a_5 is equal to how to make the series $(x_1, x_2...x_n)$ fit into ARMA (p, q) model, the model is:

$$x_t = \alpha_1 x_{t-1} + \alpha_2 x_{t-2} + \cdots + \alpha_p x_{t-p} + \varepsilon_t - \beta_1 \varepsilon_{t-1} - \beta_2 \varepsilon_{t-2} - \cdots - \beta_q \varepsilon_{t-q}. \quad (1)$$
$$t = p+1, p+2, \cdots, n$$

$\{\varepsilon_t\}$ is white noise series, $E\varepsilon_t^2 = \sigma^2$, $E\varepsilon_t x_s = 0 \ (s < t)$

Firstly the parameter evaluation is processed. The regression approximation method is applied in this paper and consists of two steps. The first step is to make the series $(x_1, x_2...x_n)$ fit the regression model AR (p). And properly large positive integer is empirically selected as order P $(>> p, q)$. Base on the premise that assure precision of evaluation and reduce calculation amount, we select $p = 300$ in this paper. The fitted model is:

$$x_t = \hat{\alpha}_1 x_{t-1} + \hat{\alpha}_2 x_{t-2} + \cdots + \hat{\alpha}_P x_{t-P} + \hat{\varepsilon}_t. \quad (2)$$

The second step is to calculate fitted residual error through the formula (2).

$$\hat{\varepsilon}_t = x_t - \hat{\alpha}_1 x_{t-1} - \hat{\alpha}_2 x_{t-2} - \cdots - \hat{\alpha}_P x_{t-P}. \ t = P+1, P+2, \cdots, n \quad (3)$$

This fitted residual error series, $\hat{\varepsilon}_{P+1}, \hat{\varepsilon}_{P+2}, \cdots, \hat{\varepsilon}_n$, can be seen as the sample values of $\{\varepsilon_t\}$ series in the formula (1). Then, the formula (1) can be near written as

$$x_t = \alpha_1 x_{t-1} + \alpha_2 x_{t-2} + \cdots + \alpha_p x_{t-p} - \beta_1 \hat{\varepsilon}_{t-1} - \beta_2 \hat{\varepsilon}_{t-2} - \cdots - \beta_q \hat{\varepsilon}_{t-q} + \varepsilon_t. \quad (4)$$
$$t = P+1, P+2, \cdots, n$$

Besides $\{\varepsilon_t\}$ in the formula (4), $\{x_t\}$ and $\{\hat{\varepsilon}_t\}$ have sample values or near-sample values in the formula $t = P+1, P+2, \cdots, n$. Thereby the formula (4) has matrix form:

$$x = (X\hat{E})\begin{pmatrix} \alpha \\ -\beta \end{pmatrix} + \varepsilon. \quad (5)$$

Where vector x and ε in the formula (5) are

$$x = \begin{pmatrix} x_{P+q+1} \\ x_{P+q+2} \\ \vdots \\ x_n \end{pmatrix}, \varepsilon = \begin{pmatrix} \varepsilon_{P+q+1} \\ \varepsilon_{P+q+2} \\ \vdots \\ \varepsilon_n \end{pmatrix}.$$

Where sub-matrix X and $\hat{E}$

$$X = \begin{pmatrix} x_{P+q} & x_{P+q-1} & \cdots & x_{P+q-p+1} \\ x_{P+q+1} & x_{P+q} & \cdots & x_{P+q-p+2} \\ \vdots & \vdots & & \vdots \\ x_{n-1} & x_{n-2} & \cdots & x_{n-p} \end{pmatrix}, \hat{E} = \begin{pmatrix} \hat{\varepsilon}_{P+q} & \hat{\varepsilon}_{P+q-1} & \cdots & \hat{\varepsilon}_{P+1} \\ \hat{\varepsilon}_{P+q+1} & \hat{\varepsilon}_{P+q} & \cdots & \hat{\varepsilon}_{P+2} \\ \vdots & \vdots & & \vdots \\ \hat{\varepsilon}_{n-1} & \hat{\varepsilon}_{n-2} & \cdots & \hat{\varepsilon}_{n-q} \end{pmatrix}.$$

The least-squares estimation of parameter α and β is in the formula (6),

$$\begin{pmatrix} \hat{\alpha} \\ -\hat{\beta} \end{pmatrix} = \left\{ \begin{pmatrix} X^\tau \\ \hat{E}^\tau \end{pmatrix} (X\hat{E}) \right\}^{-1} \begin{pmatrix} X^\tau \\ \hat{E}^\tau \end{pmatrix} x$$

$$= \begin{pmatrix} X^\tau X & X^\tau \hat{E} \\ \hat{E}^\tau X & \hat{E}^\tau \hat{E} \end{pmatrix}^{-1} \begin{pmatrix} X^\tau x \\ \hat{E}^\tau x \end{pmatrix}. \tag{6}$$

For conveniently describing, "Zero" is selected as the initial values of $x_0, x_{-1}, \cdots, x_{-q-p}$ and $\varepsilon_0, \varepsilon_{-1}, \cdots, \varepsilon_{-q-p}$. Hence, for given parameters (α, β) at random, the values of $\varepsilon_1, \varepsilon_2, \cdots, \varepsilon_n$ can be calculated by formula (1). These values are depended on the given parameters (α, β),

$$\varepsilon_k = \beta_1 \varepsilon_{k-1} + \beta_2 \varepsilon_{k-2} + \cdots + \beta_q \varepsilon_{k-q} + x_k - \alpha_1 x_{k-1} - \alpha_2 x_{k-2} - \cdots - \alpha_p x_{k-p}$$
$$k = 1, 2, \cdots, n. \tag{7}$$

Although ε_k is relied on the value of parameters α and β, its notation is still ε_k for conveniently written. The function (α, β) is defined as followings:

$$S(\alpha, \beta) = \sum_{k=1}^{n} \varepsilon_k^2. \tag{8}$$

Where corresponding σ^2 estimation is

$$\hat{\sigma}^2 = S(\hat{\alpha}, \hat{\beta}) / (n - P - q). \tag{9}$$

The $\hat{\alpha}$ and $\hat{\beta}$ in the formula (6) are substituted for $\hat{\alpha}$ and $\hat{\beta}$ in this formula.

Due to only value of data series $x_1, x_2...x_n$ are known, the order is also unknown when we fit into ARMA (p, q) model. Therefore it is essential to evaluate the values of p and q when the formula (1) is fitted, AIC order-confirmation criterion is employed to get the ARMA (2, 1) model in this paper. Next this model will forecast the scale transformation series of 5th scale as follows:

Because $p = 2$, $q = 1$, it can be deduced from the formula(7) that

$$\hat{\varepsilon}_k = x_k - \alpha_1 x_{k-1} - \alpha_2 x_{k-2} + \beta_1 \hat{\varepsilon}_{k-1} \quad k = 1, 2, \cdots, n \tag{10}$$

Despite $\hat{\varepsilon}_0$ can be strictly calculated according to the linear least-squares estimation, the calculation amount will be large if that, so this strict calculation method is not applied. In this paper a kind of near-calculation method is used, and the initial value of above formula is $\hat{\varepsilon}_0 = 0$, similarly, $x_k = 0$ $(k \le 0)$. And then other $\hat{\varepsilon}_k$ values can be deduced through this formula, namely,

$$\hat{\varepsilon}_1 = x_1 \quad \hat{\varepsilon}_2 = x_2 - \alpha_1 x_1 + \beta \hat{\varepsilon}_1$$
$$\hat{\varepsilon}_3 = x_3 - \alpha_1 x_2 - \alpha_2 x_1 + \beta \hat{\varepsilon}_2$$
$$\cdots$$
$$\hat{\varepsilon}_n = x_n - \alpha_1 x_{n-1} - \alpha_2 x_{n-2} + \beta \hat{\varepsilon}_{n-1}$$

After $\hat{\varepsilon}_k$ values have been confirmed, each x_{n+k} can be ascertained via confirmation of x_{n+k} conditional expectation, namely

$$\begin{aligned} x_{n+1} &= E(x_{n+1}) \\ &= E(\alpha_1 x_n + \alpha_2 x_{n-1} + \varepsilon_{n+1} - \beta \hat{\varepsilon}_n) \\ &= \alpha_1 x_n + \alpha_2 x_{n-1} - \beta \hat{\varepsilon}_n \end{aligned} \tag{11}$$

When $k>1$, moving average part disappear,

$$x_{n+k} = \alpha_1 x_{n+k-1} + \alpha_2 x_{n+k-2} \tag{12}$$

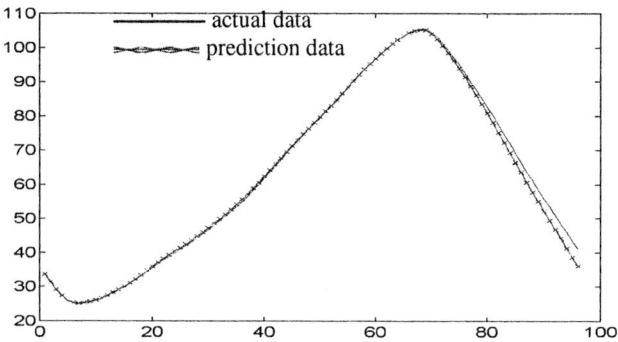

Fig. 8. The comparison between forecasting of a_5 and actual sample

x_{n+k} near-forecasting value can be calculated through formula (11) combined with known $\hat{\varepsilon}_k$, then the forecasting series can be gotten by each value of series $\{x_{n+k}\}$ plus scale transformation series mean value finally. Figure.8 shows us that the comparison between the forecasting and actual 5th scale transformation series data of one day (totally 96 points).

3.3 Short Term Time Series Forecasting

According to the wavelet method, in order to get the systematic short-term forecast of 15- minute interval, wavelet rebuild technology is used to combine the six forecasting series in turn and finally get the prediction data.

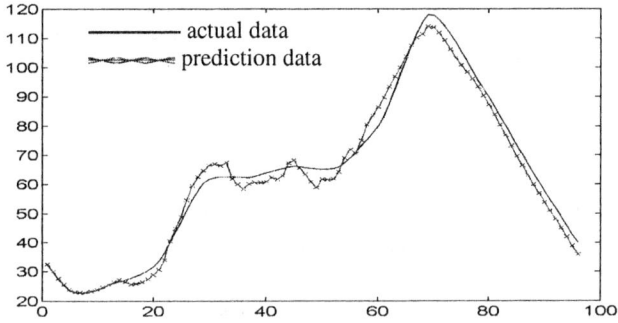

Fig. 9. The comparison between final forecasting and actual sample

In order to compare with other methods (for example, only using BP neural networks or ARMA for model building), $MSE = \sum_{t=1}^{N}(z_t - \hat{z}_t)^2 / N$ is defined and mean square error is used to describe index of forecasting performance. z_t stands for the actual data of time series, and $\hat{z}_t$ stands for the forecasting data. After using 1334 datum of two weeks predicts 96 data in the next day through three different methods, the indexes of forecasting performance of three methods, which are wavelet-NN-ARMA method, BP-NN method and ARMA method, are shown in the table 2. These results prove that the performance of wavelet-NN-ARMA is more ideal than the other two methods'.

Table 2. The comparison of mean-square error of the three methods

	Method of This Paper	BP	ARMA
Forecasting Data	5.6228	115.9997	19.4109

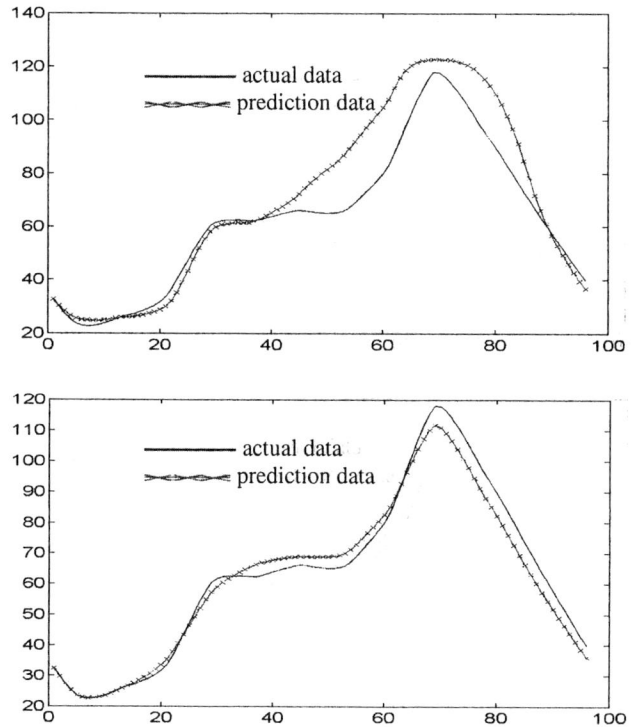

Fig. 10. The forecasting effects of BP network and ARMA

Table 3 shows the absolute errors of the three methods for forecasting performance. In order to show forecasting performance further there are statistic result by relative error in the table 3. According to this comparison, the advantage of wavelet-NN-ARMA method is even apparent.

Table 3. The comparison of absolute error of the three methods

	Method of This Paper	BP	ARMA
Absolute Error	0.97062%	12.323%	1.9004%

4 Conclusions

According to this paper, combining wavelet, ARMA model and neural networks in data mining time series forecast can not only separate all kinds of hidden periods and describe them effectively, but also well depict its essential nonlinearity, thus increase the forecast precision of the data mining time series. The analysis of examples in practice proves that, the forecast method mentioned in this paper can be applied successfully and effectively in the business field.

References

1. C. C. Aggarwal./Yu, P. S.: Data Mining Techniques for Associations, Clustering and Classification. In: Zhong, N./Zhou L. Z., (eds.), Methodologies for Knowledge Discovery and Data Mining, PAKDD-99, Springer, Berlin, 1999, P. 13-23.
2. D. Agrawal and C. C. Aggarwal. On the design and quantification of privacy preserving data mining algorithms. In PODS, pages 247--255, 2001.
3. Christopher J.C. Burges. A Tutorial on Support Vector Machines for Pattern Recognition. Data Mining and Knowledge Discovery,1998.
4. G. P. Nason, and R. V. Sachs. (1999) Wavelets in time- series analysis. Phil. Trans. R. Soc. Lond. A, 357 (1760), 2511-2526.
5. A. J.Campbell and Murtagh, F.(1997) Combining neural networks forecasts on wavelet transformed time series. Connection Sci., vol. 9, 113–121.
6. Wang Jianze, Ran Qiwen, Ji Yaochao, Liu Zhuo(1998) Frequency Domain Analysis of Wavelet Transform in Harmonics Detection. AEPS. 1998, 22(7):40-43
7. S. Rahman and R. Bhatnagar(1988) An expert system based algorithm for short term load forecast. IEEE Trans. Power Systems, 3(2): 392–399.
8. Song Aiguo and Lu Jiren(1998). Evolving Gaussian RBF network for nonlinear time series modelling and prediction. Electro- nics Lett., 34(12): 1241-1243.
9. S. Chen(1995) Nonlinear time series mo- delling and prediction using Gaussian RBF network with enhanced clustering and RLS learning. Electron Lett. 31(2): 117-118.
10. H.T.Yang and C.M.Huang. A new short term load forecasting approach using self organizing fuzzy ARMAX models. IEEE Trans.Power Systems, 1998, 13(1): 217-225.
11. B.Geva. Scale Net-Multiscale neural network architecture for time series prediction. IEEE Trans. Neural Networks, 1998, Vol.9:1471-1482.
12. Moghram and S. Rahman. Analysis and evalua- tion of five short term load forecasting techniques. IEEE Trans.Power Systems,1989, 5(4):1484-1491.
13. A. Campbell and F. Murtagh. Combining neural networks forecasts on wavelet transformed time series. Connection Sci., 1997,vol. 9, pp:113–121.
14. N. Amjady and M. Ehsan. transient stability assessment of power systems by a new estimating neural network. Can. J. Elect. & Comp. Eng., 1997, 22(3): 131–137.
15. Zhao Hongwei, Ren Zhen, Huang Weiying. A Short Load Forecasting Method Based on PAR Model. Proceedings of the CSEE., 1997, 17(5): 348-351
16. S. Rahman. Generalized knowledge-based short- term load forecasting technique. IEEE Trans. Power Systems, 1993, 8(2): 508–514.
17. S. G. Mallat. A theory for multiresolution signal decomposition: the wavelet representation. IEEE Trans. PAMI, 1989, Vol. 11, pp.674–693.

On-line Training of Neural Network for Color Image Segmentation

Yi Fang, Chen Pan, and Li Liu

Key Laboratory of Biomedical Information Engineering of Education Ministry,
Xi'an Jiaotong University, Xi'an 710049, China
fangyi@mail.xjtu.edu.cn

Abstract. This paper addresses implementation of on-line trained neural network for fast color image segmentation. A pre-selecting technique, based on mean shift algorithm and uniform sampling, is utilized as an initialization tool to largely reduce the training set while preserving the most valuable distribution information. Furthermore, we adopt Particle Swarm Optimization (PSO) to train neural network for a faster convergence and escaping from a local optimum. The results obtained from a wide range of color blood cell images show that under the compatible image segmentation performance on the test set, the training set and running time can be reduced significantly, compared with traditional training methods.

1 Introduction

Image segmentation is an essential and critical topic in image processing and computer vision, and many recently studies utilize neural network to segment image to a higher accuracy [1]. Therefore, a method based on neural network is introduced for color image segmentation in this paper. However, suffering from enormous computation in the case of large-scale image samples, neural networks are not virtually practical. There are many efficient methods proposed in [2, 3] to conquer this problem. Although those algorithms have been proved to accelerate the training, the advantages of prior knowledge were not utilized.

Practical experience has shown that training set can be reduced largely through pre-processing the training samples with prior knowledge. In this paper, we present a method based on mean shift algorithm [4] and uniform sampling to initialize training set. A small size of training samples around a proper range of cluster centers are selected for learning. Moreover, PSO-based neural network [5] is used to obtain a better performance. Consequently, the number of training vectors is decreased dramatically, the training period is shortened and less computation is required.

This paper is organized as follows. In section 2, the procedure of constructing training set is presented. Then, experiments and results are observed in section 3. In section 4, we conclude this research.

2 Construction of Training Set

2.1 Selection of Data Around Centers

The data in the same cluster usually exhibit similar characteristic, and samples around the cluster center can represent the cluster samples in a sense. The cluster center selection technique based on mean shift algorithm is described in [4], and the algorithm of selecting data around a proper range of center is given as following:

Let CS be the set of expected samples

Initial $CS \leftarrow \varphi$

For each cluster C_j

    For each data $\mathbf{x}_{i,j}$, where $\mathbf{x}_{i,j} \in C_j$

        If Euclidean distance $(\mathbf{x}_{i,j}, \mathbf{c}_j) < R_j$ where $\mathbf{c}_j$ is the center of C_j, and R_j is a threshold.

        $CS \leftarrow \mathbf{x}_{i,j}$

    end for

end for

Note that the size of threshold R_j is crucial. If the size is too small, we could not obtain enough representative samples, while overlapping of training data occurs if the size is too large. A proper size must be carefully chosen in experiments.

2.2 Uniform Sampling

It is mentioned in [2], the key concern for a classifier is the statistics distribution of training set rather than the size of it. This property would be helpful for reducing the size of training set. Statistics theory has revealed that, through uniform sampling, a subset could be produced to represent the entire data set approximately while preserving the statistical distribution of data in the feature space effectively. Therefore, we can get a smaller training set using the mentioned method.

Let CS (obtained in section 2.1) be a set of samples, which come from the same cluster. We assume the number of samples in CS is N. In this research, the interval of uniform sampling is defined as:

$$\text{interval} = N/n \quad (1)$$

where n is the size of the subset we expect.

The subset of CS with size n can be produced through uniform sampling with this interval. Finally, different subsets coming from different clusters constitute the training set for neural network.

3 Experiments and Results

In the experiments, we compared the performance between our method and the traditional one. In our method, the PSO algorithm was used to train a three-layer neural network ($3 \times 5 \times 1$). The settings of the PSO algorithm are as follows: swarm size was set to 20, c_1 and c_2 were both set to 2, r_1 and r_2 were set at a random number in the range [0, 1], the inertia weight was linearly decreased from 0.9 to 0.4, the number of epochs was limited to a maximum 200, dimension of the optimization problem was 26 according to the weights of neural network (including thresholds). The threshold R (see in section 2.1) was set at 5 according to many R-validation experiments. The traditional training set was constructed by selecting samples that completely describe each class, and the back-propagation (BP) algorithm was employed to train traditional classifier. Simulations were implemented on computer with 256M RAM running Windows 2000.

Table 1. shows the comparative results on the test image Fig. 1. Results indicate that, although our method lowers the accuracy a little (1.9%) compared with the traditional method, it reduces the training set significantly (1/40) and accelerates the training process remarkably. Therefore, the neural network can be trained online and the segmentation algorithm can meet real-time requirement.

Fig. 2 shows the generalization performance of the classifier trained by Fig.1 using our method. The three test images display white blood cells at different growth level. And because of different sample sources, preparation protocols, staining techniques, microscope and camera parameters for the image acquisition, the color of cytoplasm varies. However, the white blood cells in all three images were extracted successfully. The generalization performance of our method is proven to be robust.

Table 1. Comparative Results

Method	Training Set	Training Time (s)	Classification Accuracy
Our method	978	0.5	94.9%
Traditional method	39412	15.5	96.8%

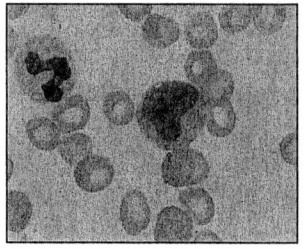

Fig. 1. Training image

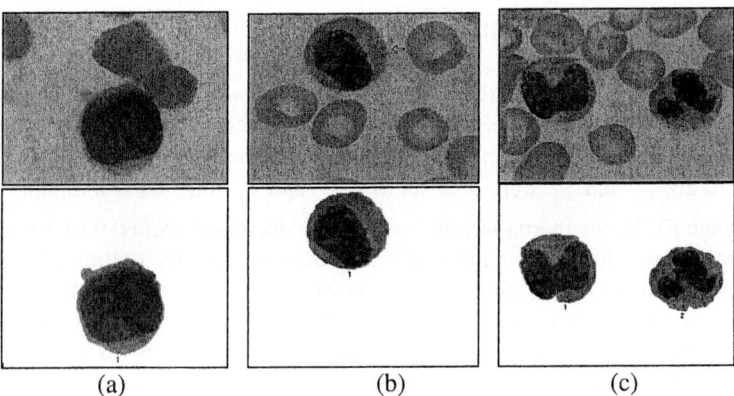

Fig. 2. Color image segmentation. (a) Test image (1) and its segmentation; (b) Test image (2) and its segmentation; (c) Test image (3) and its segmentation.

4 Conclusions

In this paper, we solved the problem of large-scale image data. The training set is reduced largely via a mean shift algorithm based pre-selecting technique. Furthermore, combining PSO algorithm, the neural network could gain a faster convergence and escape from a local optimum.

Experiments were carried out to compare the proposed method with the traditional one that exclusively uses BP neural network, and prove the generalization performance of the trained classifier. Results show that with R properly chosen, training set and time can be remarkably reduced with little accuracy loss.

References

1. Foody, G.M., Mathur, Ajay: Toward intelligent training of supervised image classifications: directing training data acquisition for SVM classification. Remote Sensing of Environment, Vol. 93 (2004) 107-117
2. Kurugollu, F., Sankur, B., Harmanci, A.E.: Color image segmentation using histogram multithresholding and fusion. Image and vision computing, Vol. 19 (2001) 915-928,
3. Morchen, F.: Analysis of Speedup as Function of Block Size and Cluster Size for Parallel Feed-Forward Neural Networks on a Beowulf Cluster Neural Networks. IEEE Transactions on, Vol. 15 (2004) 515-527
4. Chen Pan, Chong-Xun Zheng, Hao-Jun Wang.: Robust color image segmentation based on mean shift and marker-controlled watershed algorithm. International Conference on Machine Learning and Cybernetics, Vol.5 (2003) 2752-2756
5. Da Yi, Xiurun Ge.: An improved PSO-based ANN with simulated annealing technique. Neurocomputing, Vol. 63 (2005) 527-533

Short-Term Prediction on Parameter-Varying Systems by Multiwavelets Neural Network[*]

Fen Xiao, Xieping Gao, Chunhong Cao, and Jun Zhang

Information Engineering College, Xiangtan University, Hunan, China 411105
{xiaof, xpgao}@xtu.edu.cn

Abstract. Numerous studies on time series prediction have been undertaken by a lot of researchers. Most of them relate to the construction of structure-invariable system whose parameter values do not change all the time. In fact, the parameter values of many realistic systems are always changing with time. In this case, the embedding theorems are invalid, predicting the behavior of parameter-varying systems is more difficult. This paper presents a new prediction technique, which is multiwavelets neural network. This technique absorbs the advantage of high resolution of wavelets and the advantages of learning and feed-forward of neural networks. The procedure of using the multiwavelets neural network for predicting is described in detail in this paper. Principal components analysis (PCA) as a statistical technique has been used to simplify the time series analysis in our experiments. The effectiveness of this network is demonstrated by applying it to predict Ikeda time series.

1 Introduction

A Sequence of observed data, $f(1), f(2), \cdots, f(L)$, usually ordered in time, is called a time series, although time may be replaced by any other variable. Real-life time series can be taken from physical science, business, management, social and behavioral science, economics, etc. The goal of time series prediction or forecasting is to find the continuation, $f(L+1), f(L+2), \cdots$, of the observed sequence. Time series prediction is based on the idea that the time series carry within them the potential for predicting their future behavior. Analyzing observed data produced by a system, can give good insight into the system, and knowledge about the laws underlying the data.

Up to now, the studies and the applications of dynamic reconstruction are all based on the assumption that the observed time series is from some chaotic attractor generated by an unknown high-dimensional dynamical system. This underlying dynamical system is always thought of as a structure-invariable system, whose parameter values do not change all the time. However, many realistic systems are naturally structure-variable, which means that the parameter values of these systems

---

[*] This work was supported by the National Science Foundation of China (Grant No.60375021) and the National Science Foundation of Hunan Province (Grant No.00JJY3096 and No.04JJ20010) and the Key Project of Hunan Provincial Education Department (Grant No.04A056).

are always changing with time. Such examples can be found in many biological, ecological, physiological, economic, and some other systems.

Some recent works show that feed-forward neural network, trained with backpropagation and a weight elimination algorithm, outperforms traditional nonlinear statistical approaches in time series prediction. In spite of its numerous advantages, like robustness and ability to learn, neural network sometimes converges to local minimum. At the same time, wavelet analysis has been developed recently as a powerful analytical tool. It has been widely applied to signal analysis and feature extraction due to some excellent properties, for example, in making local analysis. Recently, due to the similarity between wavelet decomposition and one-hidden-layer neural network, the idea of combining both wavelet and neural network has resulted in the formulation of wavelet neural network, which has been used in various fields. They show that, the training and adaptation efficiency of the wavelet neural network is better than other networks. However, according to the traditional single wavelet theory, we cannot construct the wavelets satisfying compact support, orthogonal, symmetric and high order approximating properties at the same time, which limit their application largely. Multiwavelets, which are a generalization of wavelets, overcome above limitations and make a new way of the theory and application study of wavelet theory. And this greatly motivates us to use multiwavelets neural network for predicting time series.

Principal Components Analysis (PCA) is a canonical and widely used method for dimensionality reduction of multivariate data. Applications include the exploratory analysis and visualization of large data sets, as well as the denoising and decorrelation of inputs for algorithms in statistical learning. PCA as a prevalent analysis tool, whose advantages are generally two-fold: the order of uncorrelated principal components is explicitly given in terms of their variances, and the underlying structure of series can be revealed in using the first few principal components.

A main purpose of this article is to present a new model for time series predicting, which is multiwavelets neural network. And the learning algorithm has been described in detail. Time series generated by Ikeda map was chosen to be analyzed. The paper is organized as follows. Section 2 describes the applying the multiwavelets neural network for time series prediction, the network structure and the learning algorithm were presented. Section 3 provides the computer simulations for time series prediction with parameter-varying systems. Finally, in section 4, a conclusion is provided.

2 Multiwavelets Neural Network for Reconstruction of Parameter-Varying Systems

2.1 The Parameter-Varying Dynamical Systems

In many realistic systems, the parameter values are always changing with time. In some such systems especially, we can clearly see the phenomenon of period-doubling bifurcations in time if the parameter values vary relatively slowly. Such bifurcations are obviously different from the usual period-doubling ones.

We consider a parameter-varying dynamical system:

$$X(n+1) = g(X(n), \mu(n)) \tag{1}$$

Where $g: R^m \times R^p \to R^m$ is a continuous smooth function, and $\mu(n)$ is a p-dimensional parameter vector of the system at time n with its components increasing monotonically with n.

Suppose we can only obtain one-dimensional observations from this system. The embedding theorems cannot be applied to this case since the system $X(n+1) = g(X(n), \mu(n))$ has not asymptotic sets. The reason is that each component of $\mu(n)$ increases monotonically with n. Reconstruction of parameter-varying systems will be more difficult because of lacking the related theory. In practice, in a relatively short time interval there should exist a function F such that

$$x_n \approx F(x_{n-d}, x_{n-(d-1)}, \cdots, x_{n-1}) \tag{2}$$

So the problem of forecasting the component x_n reduced to that of estimating the function F. Below, multiwavelets neural network are referred as function approximators.

2.2 The Multiwavelets Neural Network Model

A set of functions $\phi_1, \phi_2, \cdots, \phi_r \in L^2(R)$ are called normalized orthogonal multiwavelets of multiplicity r if $\phi_1(2^j x - k), \cdots, \phi_r(2^j x - k), j, k \in Z$ form a normalized orthogonal basis of $L^2(R)$. Multiwavelets construction is associated with multiresolution analysis (MRA) of multiplicity r. In $L^2(R^d)$, we discuss separable multiwavelets system by tensor product method, and define $\phi^i_{M,k}(x) = 2^{\frac{M}{2}} \phi_i(2^M x - k), M, k \in Z$.

Definition. $\Gamma_d = \{\sigma(d) | \sigma(d) = \sigma_1 \oplus \sigma_2 \oplus \cdots \oplus \sigma_d\}$, where σ_i is any integer from 1 to r, $\oplus$ is connection, for example $2 \oplus 6 = 26$. So we can get a set of normalized orthogonal basis for subspace V_M:

$$\Phi_{M,K}(x_1, x_2, \cdots, x_d) = \left\{ \prod_{p=1}^{d} \phi^{\sigma_p}_{M,k_p}(x_p) \Big| \sigma(d) \in \Gamma_d, M \in Z, k_p \in Z, p = 1(1)d, \right\} \tag{3}$$

From the theory of MRA, we will have $L^2(R^d) \approx V_M$ when M is sufficiently large. For any function $f \in L^2(R^d)$, $d \geq 1$, f can be expanded to a good approximation in the subspace V_M spanned by the scaling functions:

$$f \cong f_M = \sum_{\sigma(d) \in \Gamma_d} \sum_{K \in Z} < f(y_1, \cdots, y_d), \prod_{p=1}^{d} \phi^{\sigma_p}_{M,k_p}(y_p) > \prod_{p=1}^{d} \phi^{\sigma_p}_{M,k_p}(x_p) \tag{4}$$

In this paper the multiwavelets neural network architecture (Fig.1) is made of three layers: the input layer, the hidden layer, and the output layer. The following lemma is available to calculate the size of the hidden layer.

Lemma 1: Suppose the support of $\Phi(x_1, x_2, \cdots, x_d)$ is $[0, u]^d$, normalize the support of the approximated function F to $[0,1]^d$, the number of node in hidden layer must be $r^d * (2^M + u - 1)^d$, and the set of the threshold value should be $J_M = \{-u+1, \cdots, 2^M - 1\}$.

The proof for this lemma can be found in [3].

So, the approximation any $f \in L^2(R^d)$ can be given by:

$$\hat{f}_{M,N}(x_1, x_2, \cdots, x_d) = \sum_{\sigma(d) \in \Gamma_d} \sum_{K \in J_M} \hat{C}_{N,K}^{\sigma(d)} \prod_{p=1}^{d} \phi_{M,k_p}^{\sigma_p}(x_p). \tag{5}$$

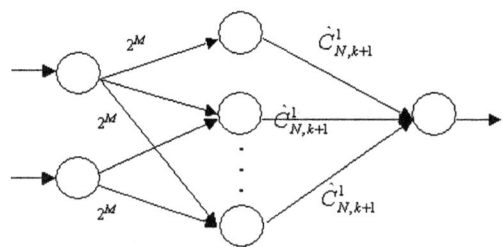

Fig. 1. Multiwavelets neural network structure

2.3 Predicting Algorithm

The basic steps of our algorithm for reconstruction of parameter-varying system by multiwavelets neural network are as follows:

Step 1. Data pre-processing-Input variables are given by the problem definition, for the complex time series, the dimension of input information is often too high. This require us to use an extremely large number of neurons in hidden layer, and large of training examples will be used to ensure that the weights of the network may be properly determined. A preferable strategy is to attempt to reduce the dimension of the input information.

Given training set $T_N = \{(\vec{x}^i, y^i) : y^i = x_{i+d}, \vec{x}^i = (x_i, x_{i+1}, \cdots, x_{i+d-1})\}$, $i = 1, \cdots, N$, where x_i is time series generated by the parameter-varying system. The new "constructed" time series by using PCA on initial inputs are then used as inputs to the prediction algorithm.

Step 2. Select a small integer for M (usually M=0), calculate the size of hidden layer by the lemma 1, at the same time, the threshold value of each hidden nodes and the connection weights between input layer and hidden layer are decided.

Step 3. Initialize $\hat{C}_{N,K}^{\sigma(d)}$ by randomly assigned values between 0 and 1, or by the following equation:

$$\hat{C}_{N,K}^{\sigma(d)} = \frac{1}{N}\sum_{i=1}^{N} y^i \prod_{p=1}^{d} \phi_{M,k_p}^{\sigma_p}(x_p^i) \qquad (6)$$

Step 4. Calculate the actual output of the network using the present values of $\hat{C}_{N,K}^{\sigma(d)}$.

Step 5. Adjust the $\hat{C}_{N,K}^{\sigma(d)}$ to minimize the following square error:

$$E_{M,N} = \sum_{(x^i,y^i)\in T_N} \left\| o^i - y^i \right\|_R^2 = \frac{1}{N}\sum_{k=d+1}^{d+N}(x_k - \hat{f}_{M,N}(x_{k-1},x_{k-2},\cdots,x_{k-d}))^2 \qquad (7)$$

Where o^i and y^i are actual and desired output when the input vector is x^i. By combining gradient descent techniques and delta rule to adjust the connection weights, we have:

$$\Delta \hat{C}_{N,K}^{\sigma(d)^n} = \lambda \frac{\partial E_{M,N}(f,\hat{f}_{M,N})}{\partial \hat{C}_{N,K}^{\sigma(d)}} + \alpha \Delta \hat{C}_{N,K}^{\sigma(d)^{n-1}} \qquad (8)$$

Respectively, where parameters $\lambda, \alpha \in (0,1)$, λ is called learning rate, α is the momemtum.

Step 6: Repeat step 4~5 until the error $E_{M,N}$ is less than a given tolerant value.

3 Simulation Results

In order to investigate the capability of proposed network of forecasting the future state of parameter-varying system, the experiments have been performed on the same chaotic time series using two different network models, which are neural network (NN) and multiwavelets neural network (MWNN) with the same network structure. A time series generated by the Ikeda map [2] with one parameter as a variable was chosen. It is described by the following equations:

$$\begin{cases} x_{n+1} = 1 + \mu_n(x_n \cos(t) - y_n \sin(t)) \\ y_{n+1} = \mu_n(x_n \sin(t) + y_n \cos(t)) \\ \mu_{n+1} = \mu_n + 10^{-4}(1 - 0.5\sin(n)) \end{cases} \qquad (9)$$

Where $t = 0.8 - \dfrac{15}{1+x_n^2+y_n^2}$.

Iterate Eq.9 with initial conditions $x_0 = 0.87$, $y_0 = -0.40$, and $\mu_0 = -0.34$ until μ_n increases to 0.7 (10,400 iterations). We record the x-component value of per iteration and show the time series $x_n, n = 0, 1, 2, \cdots, 10,400$ in **Fig. 2**.

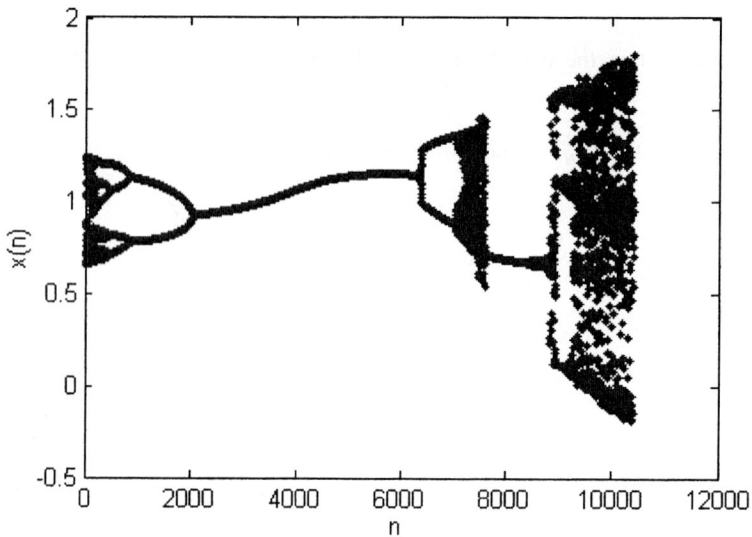

Fig. 2. Time series generated by Ikeda map

The time series were divided in three subsets referred to: the chaotic subset, the training and test subsets. The first 400 points were abandoned for their irregularity. The training set consists of 400 data points $x_{200}, x_{201}, \cdots, x_{799}$, we use the training set to fit F by using the technique of multiwavelets neural network. We make one-step prediction on the next 200 values.

In our experiments, we reduce the input dimension to 2 by PCA. For the training set, we can calculate its covariance matrix R, the eigenvalues and the corresponding eigenvectors. The eigenvalues take the follwing values: $\lambda_1 = 0.1002, \lambda_2 = 0.0053, \lambda_3 = 0.0018$. Obviously, in this case, the first two eigenvectors contains almost all the energy. So the data could be well approximated with a two-dimensional representation.

The activation function of neuron in hidden layer is assumed to be orthonormal balanced multi-scaling functions which are supported on [0,2], **Fig. 3**. So the number of hidden neurons can be calculated from lemma 1. As result the network structure 2-16-1 (ie, the input vector is composed of 2 components, the hidden layer is composed of 16 neurons, and the output layer is composed of 1 neuron) was obtained. The obtained net structure, whose amount of the parameter is quite small if compared to the neural network with the same structure 2-16-1. There are only 17 parameters in the multiwavelets neural network, while neural network has 65 parameters.

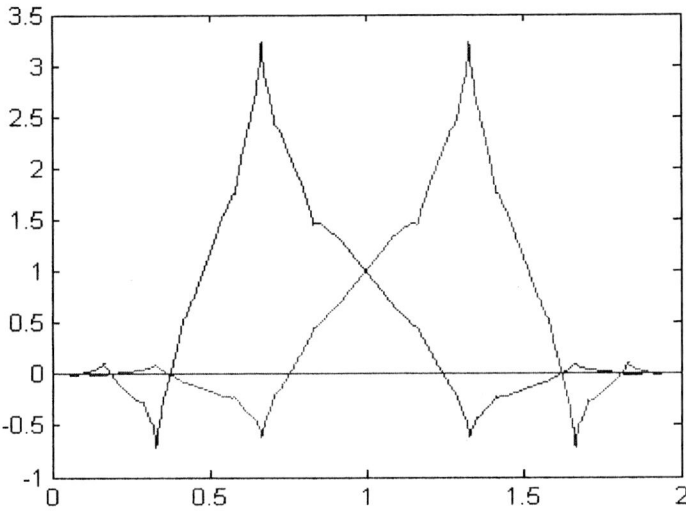

Fig. 3. Multi-scaling functions

In the experiments, in order to compare the capability of predicting the future state of parameter-varying system, some error functions were defined as follows:

$$mse = \frac{1}{l-m}\sum_{i=m}^{l}(y_i - \hat{y}_i)^2$$

$$error1 = \frac{\sqrt{\sum_{i=l}^{k}(y_i - \hat{y}_i)^2}}{k-l} \qquad error2 = \frac{1}{k-l}\sum_{i=l}^{k}\left|\frac{y_i - \hat{y}_i}{y_i}\right|$$

$$error3 = \max_{i=l}^{k}\left(\left|\frac{y_i - \hat{y}_i}{y_i}\right|\right) \qquad error4 = \max_{i=l}^{k}\left(|y_i - \hat{y}_i|\right)$$

Where $m = 400$, $l = 800$, $k = 1000$, y_i is desired output and $\hat{y}_i$ denotes the actual output.

The performance of both networks were lists below:

Table 1. The mean error and the minimum error after 20000 epochs, over 50 simulations

		mse	Error 1	Error 2	Error 3	Error 4
Mean error	MWNN	7.737e-5	6.649e-4	8.779e-3	2.039e-2	1.824e-2
	NN	9.099e-5	8.357e-4	1.111e-2	2.515e-2	2.212e-2
Minimum error	MWNN	2.737e-5	1.641e-4	2.129e-3	4.897e-3	4.693e-3
	NN	2.737e-5	2.211e-4	2.660e-3	9.134e-3	9.731e-3

Table 2. The mean error and the minimum error, over 50 simulations, and the criterion for stop training is the mse smaller than 0.0001

		Training times	Error 1	Error 2	Error 3	Error 4
Mean error	MWNN	1.815e+4	8.698e-4	1.174e-2	2.601e-2	2.431e-2
	NN	1.905+4	9.233e-4	1.205e-2	2.646e-2	2.399e-2
Minimum error	MWNN	3296	3.130e-4	4.010e-3	9.149e-3	1.030e-2
	NN	452	3.052e-4	3.545e-3	1.024e-2	9.290e-3

From Tab.1 and Tab.2, we conclude that the MWNN appear significantly better than the NN on reconstruction of parameter-varying system.

4 Conclusion

In this work a multiwavelets neural network with only one hidden layer is proposed to forecast chaotic time series. The algorithm for predicting the time series has been described in detail. The performance of the multiwavelets neural network was tested in predicting the time series generated by the Ikeda map with one parameter as a variable. The experiments data show that the multiwavelets neural network has better capabilities than the neural network in forecasting the parameter-varying system. In this paper, the dimensionality reduction of input data by PCA accounts for obtaining more precise and reasonable numerical results and the size of hidden layer is lessened.

References

1. Sitharama Lyengar, S., Cho, E.C., Vir Phoha, V.: Foundations of wavelet networks and applications, A CRC Press Company (2002)
2. Ikeda ,K.: Multiple-valued stationary state and its instability of the transmitted light by a ring cavity system, Opt. Commun., 30 (1979) 257-263
3. Xiaolan Li, Xieping Gao: Multiwavelet neural network: A novel model, IEEE International Conference on Systems, Man and Cybernetics, (2003) 2629-2632
4. Dash, P.K., Satpathy, H.P., Liew, A.C., Rahman, S.: A real-time short-term load forecasting system using functional link network, IEEE Transactions on Power System, 12 (1997) 675-680
5. Toulson, D.L., Toulson, S.P.: Use of neural network mixture models for forecasting and application to portfolio management, Sixth International Symposium on forecasting, Istanbul, (1996)
6. Amir B. Geva.: Scale-multiscale neural-network architecture for time series prediction, IEEE Transactions on Neural Networks, 9 (1998), 1471-1998
7. Mallat, S. G. and Zong, S.: Characterization of signal from multiscale edges, IEEE Trans. Pattern. Anal. Machine Intell., 10 (1992) 710-732
8. Jolliffe I.T.: Principal Component Analysis. New york: Springer, (1986)

VICARED: A Neural Network Based System for the Detection of Electrical Disturbances in Real Time

Iñigo Monedero[1], Carlos León[1], Jorge Ropero[1],
José Manuel Elena[1], and Juan C. Montaño[2]

[1] Departamento de Tecnología Electrónica,
University of Seville, Spain
{imonedero, cleon, jmelena}@us.es,
jropero@dte.us.es
[2] Consejo Superior de Investigaciones Científicas,
Seville, Spain
montano@irnase.csic.es

Abstract. The study of the quality of electric power lines is usually known as Power Quality. Power quality problems are increasingly due to a proliferation of equipment that is sensitive and polluting at the same time. The detection and classification of the different disturbances which cause power quality problems is a difficult task which requires a high level of engineering knowledge. Thus, neural networks are usually a good choice for the detection and classification of these disturbances. This paper describes a powerful system for detection of electrical disturbances by means of neural networks.

1 Introduction

Power Quality (PQ) has been a research area of exponential increasing interest particularly in the last two decades [1]. It is defined as the study of the quality of electric power lines and has recently sharpened because of the increased number of loads sensitive to power quality and become tougher as the loads themselves become important causes of the degradation of quality [2].Thus nowadays, customers demand higher levels of PQ to ensure the proper and continued operation of such sensitive equipment.

The poor quality of electrical power is usually attributed to power line disturbances such as waveshape faults, overvoltages, capacitor switching transients, harmonic distortion and impulse transients. Often the greatest damage from these disturbances lies in the loss of credibility of the power utilities on the side of their customers. The classification and identification of each one of the disturbances is usually carried out from standards and recommendations depending on where the utilities operate (IEEE in the United States, UNE in Spain, etc). Our own classification, based on these standards and recommendations, is given in Table 1.

Table 1. Types of disturbances

Type of disturbance	Subtype of disturbance			Time	Range	
					Min. value	Max. value
Frequency	Slight deviation			10 s	49.5 Hz.	50.5 Hz
	Severe deviation				47 Hz.	52 Hz.
Voltage	Average voltage			10 min	0.85 Un	1.1 Un
	Flicker			-	-	7 %
	Sag	Short		10 ms-1s	0.01 U	0.9 U
		Long		1s-1min		
		Long-time disturbance		> 1min		
	Under-voltage	Short		< 3 min	0.01 U	
		Long		> 3 min		
	Swell	Temporary Short		10 ms – 1s	1.1 U	1.5 KV
		Temporary Long		1s - 1min		
		Temporary Long-time disturbance		> 1 min		
		Over-voltage		< 10 ms		6 KV
Harmonics and other information signals	Harmonics			-	THD > 8 %	
	Information signals			-	Included in the other disturbances	

2 Artificial Intelligence on Power Quality

New and powerful tools for the analysis and operation of power systems, as well as for PQ diagnosis are currently available. The new tools of interest are those of artificial intelligence (AI) [1], including expert systems, fuzzy logic and artificial neural networks (ANNs) [3].

For the case of electrical disturbances, all the factors that make ANNs a powerful tool are present. We get information which is massive – electrical signals are constantly received – and distortioned – there is an important noise component.

In addition, the signal must be pre-processed to get a feature extraction by means of wavelet transform and other mathematical techniques which provide a unique characteristic which can represent every single PQ disturbance. It is carried out by means of a different resolutions analysis using the technique called multi-resolution signal decomposition or multi-resolution analysis. In multi-resolution analysis the signal is decomposed in a set of approximation wavelet coefficients and another set of detail wavelet coefficients.

The detail coefficients of the lowest levels store the information from the fastest changes of the signal while the highest ones store the low-frequency information. Thus, with the help of these new mathematic tools the detection of the electrical disturbances has tended to be easy but their classification is still a difficult task in which ANNs play an important role [4-11].

3 Neural Network Real-Time Classifier

We have developed a prototype of a real-time system for the detection and classification of electrical disturbances. The system is a detector of power line disturbances whose detection kernel is based on artificial intelligence techniques (in particular, a first version based on ANNs). The system consists of a PC application which includes the AI kernel and an acquisition card.

A. Environment

The environment of the application shows the information which is acquired and registered by the system. It consists of several windows where the acquired signal is represented by means of the V_{RMS} of the three signal phases, and a neutral. Other windows show the last detected disturbance, a bar diagram that reports the number and the type of detected disturbances and a window with a historic which registers the date and time of the different events.

We also have more options like a bar diagram reporting a temporal graphic view of the disturbances, a more detailed representation of the last detected disturbance or a triphasic diagram and representation of the signal.

The acquisition card obtains 640 samples every 100 milliseconds. These samples are shown on the chart and processed by the AI kernel. When one or more disturbances are detected in the 100 milliseconds, the corresponding registers are updated, changing the corresponding windows for the last disturbance, the bar diagrams and the historic.

B. Kernel

In order to train the ANN, we have to generate the maximum possible number of signals representing patterns of electrical signals which include all the above-mentioned disturbances, so we have designed a signal generator with this aim. In fact, we have generated over 27,000 signals including one-disturbance signals and two-disturbance signals. The detection system uses Wavelet transform of the acquired signal for the generation of signal features [4-10]. The aim of feature extraction by Wavelet transforms is to provide a unique characteristic which can represent every single PQ disturbance.

The input vectors of the ANN are generated carrying out a number of operations on the Wavelet transform. It is known that the Wavelet transform detects better the low-frequency components in the last detail levels and fast variations in first levels. Thus, our solution is based on the concept that the amplitude disturbances would be better detected in the first levels of Wavelet transform while the frequency disturbances would be better detected in the last levels. Therefore, we decided to use parallel neural networks as it is shown on Figure 1.

The signal is pre-processed using the wavelet transform as it has been said above. The result of this are the inputs for all the ANNs. First of all, these inputs are given to the disturbance detector ANN, which output is either 0 - no disturbance - or 1 - disturbance -. If there is a disturbance, the ANN inputs are given to another three

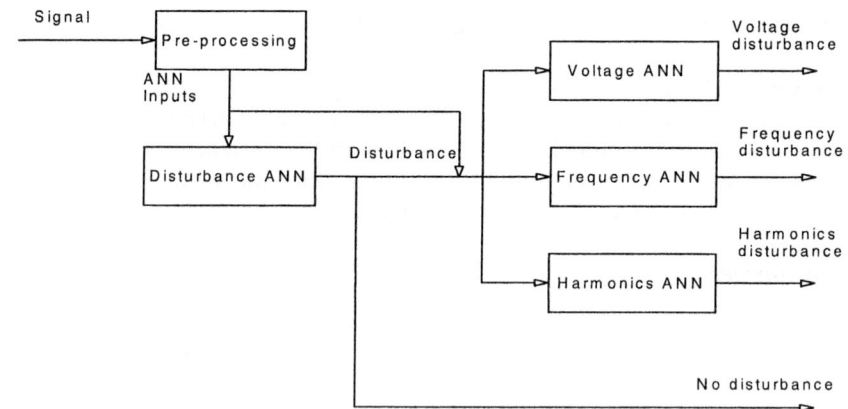

Fig. 1. Block diagram

ANNs, each one specialized in the detection of a different type of disturbance. In the same way, the outputs for these ANNs are 0 or 1, depending on the fact that there is or not that kind of disturbance. These types are, according to Figure 1 above, voltage disturbances – sags, swells, undervoltages and overvoltages -, frequency disturbances – slight and severe deviations – and harmonics disturbances.

The existence of a disturbance detector ANN previous to the other ANNs is due to the greater importance of the detection of disturbances compared with the classification of them. Besides, the disturbance ANN acts as a filter for the next ANNs. Some of the possible mistakes committed by the three parallel specific neural networks are eliminated by the disturbance detector ANN. The reason for using several ANNs and not only one is that a unique ANN with seven outputs – one for every type of disturbance – needs too many neurons to work properly and, consequently, more memory resources.

C. Neural Network building

To be able to train each neural network, firstly we must decide the convenient learning method. There are basically two learning methods mainly used, supervised learning and self-organised learning. The first one gets input data and associates them with a determined output while the second one makes its own input data classification. For our case, we want a different output according to the existence or not of a disturbance or its type, depending on the chosen neural network. That is the reason why a supervised learning works better. Besides, we have to choose a particular type of supervised learning. The best option is the backpropagation (BP) learning method using the multilayer perceptron due to its better rate between simplicity and efficiency.

Important features of the neural networks are the study of the necessary input values, the neural network structures, transfer functions and learning algorithms.

In particular, we have used the following values as input vector of the amplitude neural network: the V_{RMS} of the signal, the integral, the maximum and the V_{RMS} of the detail wavelet coefficients of 1, 2 and 3 level. In order to get a faster convergence and better results these data were scaled so that minimum is -1 and maximum is 1.

The chosen kind of ANN is a multilayer perceptron with 3 hidden layers with different number of neurons, depending on the ANN and its number of outputs. The output functions of the layers have been chosen with a logarithmic sigmoid transfer function for all the layers.

All the inputs, structures, functions and training algorithms have been reached after testing with different ones. The best results until now have been obtained for neural networks shown in Table 2.

Table 2. Neural Network structure

Neural Network type	Number of hidden neurons	Number of outputs	Transfer functions	Training algorithm
Disturbance	20, 14 & 8	1	logarithmic sigmoid	Levenberg-Marquardt
Voltage	12, 9 & 6	4	logarithmic sigmoid	Levenberg-Marquardt
Frequency	16, 12 & 7	2	logarithmic sigmoid	Levenberg-Marquardt
Harmonics	20, 14 & 8	1	logarithmic sigmoid	Levenberg-Marquardt

D. Programming Tasks

For programming tasks we have used the MATLAB tool to test the different possibilities in the pre-processing of the signal and in the structure of the kernel. We used this tool due to the powerful toolboxes with specialized functions contained in it utilizing the signal and the wavelet toolboxes for the pre-processing task and the neural networks toolbox for the design of the kernel [11].

Once we carried out the test and found a good code for the pre-processing and the AI kernel, we programmed them in C++ language in order to optimize the execution time. The tests carried out in execution time about the pre-processing time are around the 0.1 milliseconds for the wavelet transform.

For the design and programming of the tool environment the selected tool has been Borland C++ Builder 5 which is a powerful tool for the development of visual applications as well as a robust C++ compiler.

4 Results

Before embedding the kernel in the classifier tool we selected the best training method for the configuration of ANNs. Thus, for the training of the networks we used 80% of the generated signals as training patterns and 20% as test patterns. On the other hand, thresholds were defined in the ANN outputs in order to distinguish if a particular output value may be considered as a disturbance or not. The defined thresholds were 0.3 and 0.7 and thus, output values above 0.7 were considered as disturbances and below 0.3 ideal signals. Values found between 0.3 and 0.7 were taken as errors in the detection of the input pattern. The distance between the output network and the desired value was defined as a safety coefficient in the detection.

We are going to consider two different kinds of results: the general ones, it is to say, the percentage of success in every ANN – see Table 3 - , and the particular ones, which are more intuitive and consider some particular cases of failure in one of the neural networks. In addition, we have the results for only one disturbance signals and the results for two-disturbance signals which include the one-disturbance signals too.

Table 3. One-disturbance signal results

Type of ANN	Number of outputs	Test signals	Number of errors	Correctly detected %
Disturbance	1	334	1	99.70
Voltage	4	334	20	94.01
Harmonics	1	334	1	99.70
Frequency	2	334	5	98.50

The first conclusion we obtain is that the higher number of ANN outputs we use, the higher number of errors we get. This is due to the higher complexity introduced by the necessity of fixing all the outputs at the same time. The second conclusion is related to the influence of these errors. As said above, the most important ANN is the one which detects disturbances – the existence or not of a disturbance is much more important than its type – so we have focused our efforts on its correct working. On the one hand, we must say that these percentages are referred to all the testing signals but we also have to bear in mind that some of the signals that fail are filtered by the disturbance ANN. On the other hand, we have to analyze what kind of signals tend to fail. To illustrate this point we have considered some of the signals that fail in the voltage ANN –table 4-.

Table 4. Errors in analysis

Real signal	Detected event
Ideal signal with a small 9% sag	Sag
10.8% and 11 ms overvoltage	Swell
99.7% and 35 ms undervoltage	Sag
98% and 10 ms sag	Undervoltage
Ideal signal with a small 8% overvoltage	Overvoltage
80% Swell and 9 ms	Overvoltage
97% and 10 ms sag	Ideal signal

Analogously, results are similar for other signals and other ANNs. We observe that the signals which fail are near the limit of a disturbance, so it is not a big mistake to consider them as the neural network tells us.

In table 5, we have the results obtained for two-disturbance signals, with approximately 27700 signals, about 5500 for the test and the rest for training. Training performance of the disturbance ANN is shown in Figure 5.

Table 5. Two-disturbance signal results

Type of ANN	Number of outputs	Test signals	Number of errors	Correctly detected %
Disturbance	1	5523	70	98.73
Voltage	4	5523	575	89.58
Harmonics	1	5523	57	98.97
Frequency	2	5523	278	94.97

Conclusions are similar to the ones we have achieved for one-disturbance signals. Results are slightly worse due to the greater complexity of the signals.

5 Conclusions

What we have developed is a real-time system for the detection of electrical disturbances based on artificial neural networks. With this system we are capable of detecting the existence or not of disturbances and their type with a very high possibility of success and bearing in mind that most of the mistakes are committed with not very common signals in real life – those in the edge of a disturbance.

The use of C++ language makes it possible to achieve the objective of making our system a real-time one. This may allow electrical companies to detect disturbances with time enough to find possible troubles and take steps to avoid further problems.

Our current work is focused on carrying out tests with the system working in real time in the power line in order to improve our results with real signals. Another line of our investigation is the study of the utilization of different structured parallel networks of the same type using a voting system which will allow us to achieve better results.

References

[1] W.R. Anis Ibrahim and M.M. Morcos, "Artificial Intelligence and Advanced Mathematical Tools for Power Quality Applications: A Survey", 668 IEEE Transactions on Power Delivery, Vol. 17, April 2002.
[2] W.E. Kazibwe and H.M. Sendaula, "Expert Systems Targets. Power Quality Issues", IEEE Comput. Appl. Power, vol. 5, pp 29-33, 1992.
[3] G. Zheng, M.X. Shi, D. Liu, J. Yao, Z.M. Mao, "Power Quality Disturbance Classification Based on Rule-Based and Wavelet-Multi-Resolution Decomposition", Proceedings of the First International Conference on Machine Learning and Cybernetics, Beijing, 4-5 November 2002.
[4] A.Elmitwally, S. Farghal, M.Kandil, S. Abdelkader and M.Elkateb, "Proposed wavelet-neurofuzzy combined system for power quality violations detection and diagnosis", IEEE Proc-Gener. Trans. Distrib. Vol. 148 No 1, pp. 15-20, January 2001.
[5] P. K. Dash, S. K. Panda, A. C. Liew, B. Mishra, and R. K. Jena, "New approach to monitoring electric power quality," Elect. Power Syst. Res. vol. 46, no. 1, pp. 11–20, 1998.

[6] A.K. Ghosh and D. L. Lubkeman, "The classification of power system disturbance waveforms using a neural network approach", IEEE Trans. Power Delivery. Vol. 10. pp. 671-683, July 1990.
[7] J.V. Wijayakulasooriya, G.A. Putrus and P.D. Minns, "Electric power quality disturbance classification using self-adapting artificial neural network", IEEE Proc-Gener. Trans. Distrib. Vol. 149 No. 1, pp. 98-101, January 2002.
[8] R. Daniels, "Power quality monitoring using neural networks," in Proc.1st Int. Forum Applications Neural Networks Power Syst., 1991, pp. 195–197.
[9] S. Santoso, J. P. Edward, W. M. Grady, and A. C. Parsons, "Power quality disturbance waveform recognition using wavelet-based neural classifier - Part 1: Theoretical foundation," IEEE Trans. Power Delivery, vol. 15, pp. 222–228, Feb. 2000.
[10] S. Santoso, J. P. Edward, W. M. Grady, and A. C. Parsons, "Power quality disturbance waveform recognition using wavelet-based neural classifier—Part 2: Application," IEEE Trans. Power Delivery, vol. 15, pp. 229–235, Feb. 2000.
[11] M. Mallini and B. Perunicic, "Neural network based power quality analysis using MATLAB," in Proc. Large Eng. Syst. Conf. Power Eng., Halifax, NS, Canada, 1998, pp. 177–183.

Speech Recognition by Integrating Audio, Visual and Contextual Features Based on Neural Networks[*]

Myung Won Kim, Joung Woo Ryu, and Eun Ju Kim

School of Computing, Soongsil University,
1-1, Sangdo 5-Dong, Dongjak-Gu, Seoul, Korea
mkim@comp.ssu.ac.kr, ryu0914@orgio.net,
blue7786@naver.com

Abstract. Recent researches have been focusing on fusion of audio and visual features for reliable speech recognition in noisy environments. In this paper, we propose a neural network based model of robust speech recognition by integrating audio, visual, and contextual information. Bimodal Neural Network (BMNN) is a multi-layer perceptron of 4 layers, which combines audio and visual features of speech to compensate loss of audio information caused by noise. In order to improve the accuracy of speech recognition in noisy environments, we also propose a post-processing based on contextual information which are sequential patterns of words spoken by a user. Our experimental results show that our model outperforms any single mode models. Particularly, when we use the contextual information, we can obtain over 90% recognition accuracy even in noisy environments, which is a significant improvement compared with the state of art in speech recognition.

1 Introduction

As the technology of mobile devices advances and such devices come into wide use, speech becomes one of important human computer interfaces (HCI). Recently, a study of multi-modal speech recognition is in progress to realize easier and more precise human computer interfaces. Particularly, the bimodal speech recognition has been studied for high recognition rate at environments with background noise. In the bimodal speech recognition if the audio signal is of low quality or ambiguous, visual information, i.e. lip-movements can contribute to the recognition process as well.

In the bimodal speech recognition the most important issues are how well we extract the visual information, as supplementary to the audio signal, and how efficiently we merge these two heterogeneous information. We investigate the second issue which is called the 'information fusion' problem.

The existing fusion methods are divided into the feature fusion and the decision fusion depending on the point of time where the heterogeneous information is fusioned [1].

The feature fusion is a method which fuses the features of information prior to recognition, while the decision fusion is a method which fuses the recognized results and

---

[*] This work was supported by the project of "Super Intelligence Chip and Its Applications" sponsored by the Korea Ministry of Industry and Energy.

executes the final recognition. The HMM(Hidden Markov Model) and the neural networks are models generally used to implement these fusion methods.

[2] proposed a feature fusion method using the HMM. The feature fusion is more difficult to fuse than the decision fusion because the sampling rates of the audio and visual information are different. The low-pass interpolation method is used to extract the sample to solve those synchronization problems, and the new feature was created from the 25msec window where the 10msec is overlapped. However, it is difficult to decide the number of states and the number of Gaussian mixtures which are the learning variables that show a sensitive response to the fusion method using HMM. Moreover, it is especially difficult to apply the generally used CDMM(Continuous Density Hidden Markov Model) because of restriction that its input features satisfy probabilistic independence [3][4].

The TDNN (Time-Delay Neural Network) is a neural network which can recognize phonemes. It has two important properties. 1) Using a 3 layer arrangement of simple computing units, it can represent arbitrary nonlinear decision surfaces. The TDNN learns these decision surfaces automatically using error back-propagation. 2) The time-delay arrangement enables the network to discover acoustic-phonetic features and the temporal relationships between them independent of position in time and hence not blurred by temporal shifts in the input.[5] The MS-TDNN(Multi-State TDNN) is an expanded model of TDNN to recognize continuous words by adding the DTW(Dynamic Time Wrapping) layer[6][7]. Using the MS-TDNN, the bimodal MS-TDNN which fusions audio and visual features was proposed in [8].

The bimodal MS-TDNN is constructed through the two-level learning process. In the first learning process the preprocessed acoustic and visual data are fed into two front-end TDNNs, respectively. Each TDNN consists of an input layer, one hidden layer and the phone-state layer. Back-propagation was applied to train the networks in bootstrapping phase, to fit phoneme targets. Above the two phone-state layers, the Dynamic Time Warping algorithm is applied to find the optimal path of phone-hypotheses for the word models. In the word layer the activation of the phone-state units along the optimal paths are accumulated. The highest score of the word units represents the recognized word. In the second learning process the networks are trained to fit word targets. The error derivatives are back-propagated from the word units through the best path in the DTW layer down to the front-end TDNNs, ensuring that the network is optimized for the actual evaluation task, which is word and not phoneme recognition.

The DTW algorithm is required to solve the time axis variation problem because the bimodal MS-TDNN needs to recognize words from phonemes. Therefore, the MS-TDNN is complex in structure and it still has the problem that its performance is sensitive to noise.

In this paper, we proposes the BMNN(Bimodal Neural Network) which is a neural network model for isolated word recognition, which can efficiently merge heterogeneous information. To improve speech recognition accuracy in noisy environments we also propose the post-processing method using contextual information such as sequential patterns of the words spoken by the user.

This paper is organized as follows. Section 2 describes the methods for extraction of audio features from speech signal and visual features from lip movement images. Section 3 explains our proposed bimodal neural network model, and Section 4 describes the post-processing method using contextual information to improve the speech recognition accuracy. Section 5 discusses the experiments with the proposed method, and finally Section 6 concludes the paper.

2 Audio and Visual Feature Extraction

In this paper we adopt the existing feature extraction methods, the ZCPA(Zero Crossing with Peak Amplitude)[9] method for audio features, and the PCA(Principle Component Analysis) method for visual features. In the following we describe these methods in detail.

2.1 Audio Feature Extraction

The ZCPA models the auditory system to the auditory nerve, which is composed of the cochlear filter bank and a nonlinear transformer connected to the output of each cochlear filter bank. The cochlear filter bank is a modeling of the basilar membrane just like the general auditory model, where the nonlinear transform block is the modeling of the stimulating process of the nerve cell through a mechanical vibration of the basilar membrane, and is connected in series with the linear filters.

The ZCPA is composed of a 16 channels filter bank block, a zero-crossing detection block, a nonlinear transform block, and a feature extraction block. The filter bank is composed of a FIR filter which has the powers-of-two coefficients, and made frequency calculations of high precision possible using bisections recursively. The bisecting method and the binary search method are used in the nonlinear transform block which increases the calculation speed and the memory size. Lastly, the feature vector was extracted for the feature extraction method by accumulating the maximum value which is non-linearized to the corresponding frequency band in the size of the frame of each filter bank.

2.2 Visual Feature Extraction

The most widely used method for visual feature extraction is the PCA, which is a transformation of data based on statistical analysis. The PCA reduces the visual input dimension through statistical analysis, and has the property that it preserves important information even with the reduced dimensions. We extract a basis for representing visual features of an image through the PCA. The given 16x16 sized image of speaker's lips can be represented as a linear combination of those basis as in Fig. 1. Here, $(c_1, c_2, ..., c_n)$ is a feature vector representing the image of a speaker's lips.

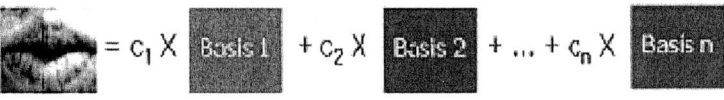

Fig. 1. Lip image representation

When an image stream consists of M frames, M n-dimensional vectors are calculated and represent the visual features of lips movement. However, the extracted features are different between speakers, so it would be better to represent the lips movement by the difference between the feature vector and the average of the feature vectors of the images of M frames as described in equation (1).

$$\bar{u} = \frac{1}{M}\sum_{i=1}^{M} u_i$$
$$v_k = u_k - \bar{u}\ , k=1,2,...,M \qquad (1)$$

where u_k is the feature vector for the k-th frame, and v_k is the extracted feature vector for the k-th frame. In this paper we set the dimension of the feature vector (n) and the number of frames (M) to 16 and 64, respectively. In addition, we use the interpolation method to create the feature vectors for 64 frames because the number of input vectors need to be fixed according to the structure of the recognizer.

3 BMNN (Bimodal Neural Network)

This paper proposes the bimodal speech recognition model that is robust in noisy environments using the neural network. The proposed BMNN structure is as shown in Fig. 2.

The BMNN consists of 4 layers (input layer, hidden layer, combined layer, output layer) and is designed as a feed-forward network with the error back-propagation algorithm as the learning algorithm. Since we deal with isolated word recognition, an overlap zone structure is used which shows high performance for isolated word recognition [10]. The third layer combines audio and visual features of speech to compensate loss of audio information caused by noise.

When the connection structure of the model and the number of frames of each layer is observed, the nodes of the upper layer frame and the corresponding nodes of every frame included in the window are fully connected, and the combined layer is also fully connected to the output layer because no windows are used. Therefore, the number of frames for each layer is automatically determined by equation (2), when the number of lower layer frames, the size of the window, and the size of the overlap zone is determined. This paper set the value of equation (2) to be a constant for the size of the overlap zone, and the number of feature frames of each layer is set so that the number of feature frames of the lower layer is reduced in half each time to it through the experiment. A structure like this can be more efficient compared with the model in [11] because the size of the model and the number of connections reduce.

$$HF = \frac{LF - O}{W - O} \qquad (2)$$

where HF and LF represent the number of frames of the upper layer and the number of frames of the lower layer, respectively, and W is the window size, and O is the overlap zone size.

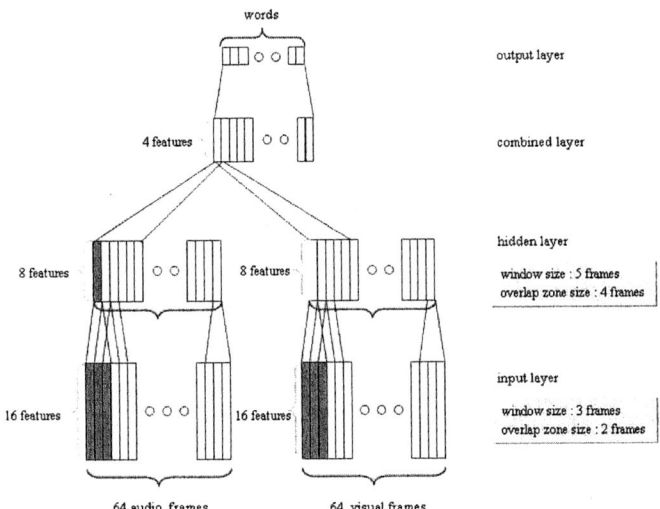

Fig. 2. BMNN architecture

The BMNN recognizes isolated words so we do not have the problem of time axis variation. Therefore, it has the advantage that the learning method and the structure is simpler compared with the bimodal MS-TDNN of phoneme units. We take the advantage of neural network that it allows more efficient fusion of heterogeneous information than the HMM. However, the BMNN with the feature fusion method has the problem that speech and visual information must be synchronized properly. For that reason, the image captured by a camera is stored together the system tick into the visual buffer, and simultaneously the speech signal is input from the microphone, and then the input speech signal is segmented to an isolated word using the endpoint detecting algorithm. At this moment, the tick which indicates the same time as the endpoint detecting time is calculated, and the image which is input at the identical time (starting time ~ finishing time) from the image buffer, is read in from the buffer. Through this process, the extracted images and speech signals are synchronized by extracting feature vectors using the feature extraction method described in section 2.

4 Post-processing of Speech Using Contextual Information

The need of speech recognition that is robust in noisy environments is rising due to the wild use of mobile devices. Therefore, we propose a post-processing method of speech to improve the recognition accuracy using contextual information such as sequential patterns of spoken words of a user.

4.1 Context Recognizer

The context recognizer which recognizes sequential patterns of commands is a multi-layer perceptron of 3 layers. The context recognizer predicts the current command from a sequence of preceding commands. Its input layer represents a sequence of preceding commands while the output layer represents the current command. In this research we adopt local coding in representing data both in the input layer and the output layer, in which each command is represented by a single node. If we take the total number of commands in use and the length of sequences of preceding commands to be n and m, respectively, then we have m blocks of n nodes in the input layer, while we have n nodes in the output layer. A sequence of commands is mapped into geographical positions of input nodes. For example, the first command in a sequence into the left most block of input nodes and the second command into the next left block of nodes and so on.

This structure of neural network is used to capture useful sequential patterns of commands that a user utters. Once the model is trained using the training data, the model learns sequential patterns of commands and can predict the current commands given a sequence of preceding commands.

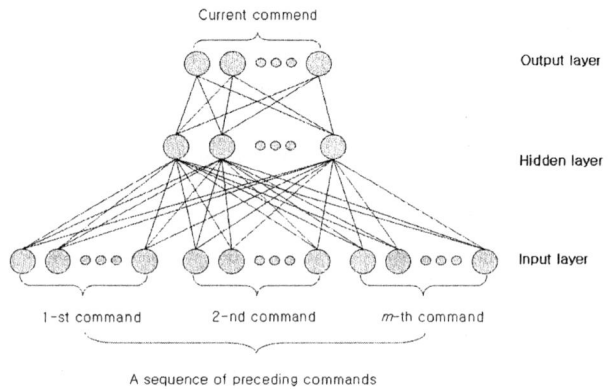

Fig. 3. Context recognizer architecture

4.2 Post-processing Using Word Sequence Patterns

The structure of speech recognition with the post-processing method is shown in Fig. 4. The final recognition result is given by combining the output of the BMNN recognizer and the output of the context recognizer.

To efficiently combine the results of the two recognizers, a sequential combination method is used as shown in Fig. 4. In the method we take the word of the maximum output value of the BMNN if any output value of the BMNN is greater than the given threshold(θ). Else, we take the word of the maximum output value of the context recognizer if any output value of the recognizer is greater than the threshold. Otherwise, we assume that none of the recognition result is reliable and the output values of the two recognizers are multiplied and the word of the largest value is selected to be the final recognition result. The threshold is given by the user and it means the lower margin of the degree that the user can rely on the recognition result.

```
BMNN(Oᵢ): real value of iᵗʰ output node at BMNN
Con(O'ᵢ): real value of iᵗʰ output node at context recognizer
θ : threshold

if (θ < BMNN(Oᵢ))
    i = maxᵢ(BMNN(Oᵢ))           // iᵗʰ word recognition
else if (θ < Con(O'ᵢ))
    i = maxᵢ(Con(O'ᵢ))           // iᵗʰ word recognition
else if ((BMNN(Oᵢ)≤θ) and (Con(O'ᵢ)≤θ))
    i = maxᵢ(BMNN(Oᵢ)·Con(O'ᵢ))  // iᵗʰ word recognition
```

Fig. 4. Sequential combination algorithm

5 Experiments

The speech data used in our experiments is speaker dependent data produced by the ETRI(Electronics and Telecommunications Research Institute). The speech data constitutes of 35 isolated Korean words spoken 27 times. The words are commands which can be used in a mobile device. The noisy data was generated by artificially adding Gaussian noises (20db, 10db, 5db) to simulate speech signal in noisy environment.

The model structure of the BMNN used in this experiment set the number of input frames to 64 (10ms per frame) for isolated word recognition and extracted 16 features from each frame. The window size of the input layer is set to 3 frames of 30ms which is sufficient to represent a phoneme, while the overlap zone size is set to 2 frames. The window size of the hidden layer is set to 5 frames while the overlap zone size is set to 4 frames. Therefore, the number of frames of the hidden layer is 62 and that of the combined layer is 58 on the basis of equation (2).

To verify the efficiency of the BMNN in noisy environments, performance is compared with single mode recognizers using either audio features or visual features only. The single mode recognizers such as the speech recognizer and the image recognizer can be achieved simply by the BMNN with '0' as input for audio features or visual features.

5.1 Speaker Dependent Recognition Without Post-processing

For the speaker dependent recognition we made 350 training data of 35 isolated Korean words spoken 10 times and 595 test data spoken 17 times.

When the SNR is 30db, there is no significant difference between the speech recognizer's performance (94.43%) and the BMNN's performance (95.49%), but when the noise level increases the recognition accuracy decreases by 13.16% for the speech recognizer, while the performance decrease of the BMNN is 8.2%, which is about 3.96% lower. We can notice that the visual features contribute more significantly when there is more noise in the speech.

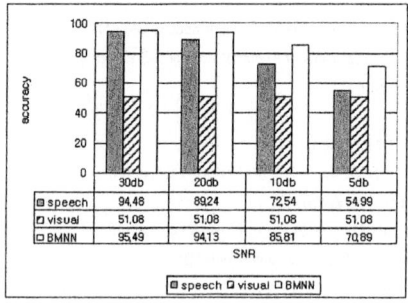

Fig. 5. Performance comparison without post-processing

5.2 Experiment with Post-processing

In this experiment we define sequential command patterns which are used by the user for mobile devices as the contextual information, and we demonstrate the efficiency of the post-processing method in noisy environments.

First of all, it is assumed that the sequential command patterns exist which are used by the user for mobile devices and we create three context recognizers. We generate three training sets for training each context recognizer. Three training sets correspond to the sequential command patterns of the regularities of 70%, 50% and 30%, respectively. For example, for a sequential patterns of regularity 70%, 'start browser, favorite sites, item 5' is uttered as a sequence of commands, and the probability of the 'select' command being followed is 70%, while the probability of a random command followed is 30%. The reason that the training data are created with different regularities is to find out whether the context recognizer performs sensitive to the regularities of patterns.

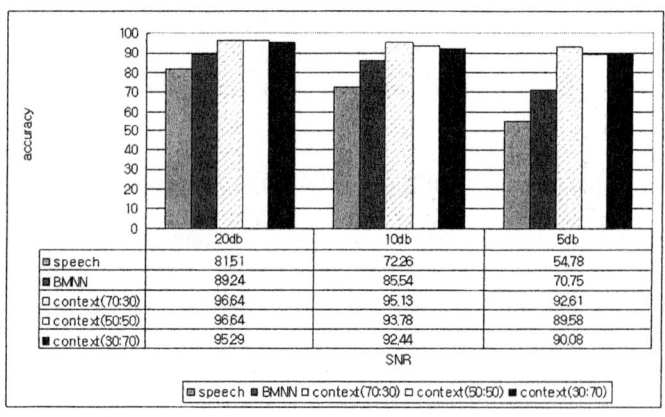

Fig. 6. Experimental result with post-processing

For the context recognizer we set the number of preceding words to 3. Therefore, the number of nodes for each layer is set to 105 for the input layer, 52 for the hidden layer and 35 for the output layer. The input layer has 105 nodes because there are 35 commands to recognize and the number of the preceding commands is 3. The number of nodes for the hidden layer was obtained experimentally.

Fig. 6 shows the result of the post-processing method. We can see that the average performance of the speech recognizer is 69.51% in noisy environments of 20 db, 10 db, and 5 db, and that of the BMNN is 81.84%, while the BMNN with the post-processing shows the best average accuracy, 93.57%. Also, the average reduction of performance was examined as the noise level increases. The speech recognizer shows the average decrease rate of 13.36% and the BMNN shows 9.24%, while the average decrease 2.72% for the post-processing combined. We can see that the BMNN with the post-processing is very little affected by noise. This paper clearly demonstrates the possibility of exploiting contextual information such as sequential patterns of commands of the user for improved speech recognition accuracy, particularly in noisy environments.

6 Conclusion and Future Works

This paper has proposed the BMNN, which can efficiently fusion the audio and visual information for robust speech recognition in noisy environments. BMNN is a multi-layer perceptron of 4 layers, each of which performs a certain level of abstraction of input features. In the BMNN the third layer combines audio and visual features of speech to compensate loss of audio information caused by noise. In order to improve the accuracy of speech recognition in noisy environments, we also proposed a post-processing based on contextual information such as sequential patterns of words spoken by a user. Our experimental results show that our model outperforms any single mode models. Particularly, when we use the contextual information, we can obtain over 90% recognition accuracy even in noisy environments, which is a significant improvement compared with the state of art in speech recognition. Our research demonstrates that other sources of information need to be integrated to improve the accuracy of speech recognition particularly in noisy environments.

For future research, we need to investigate diverse sources of contextual information such as the topics or situation of speech that can be used to improved speech recognition. We will also investigate the more robust integration method for integrating different sources of information in speech recognition.

References

1. Chibelushi, C.C., Deravi, F., Mason, J.S.D.: A Review of Speech-Based Bimodal Recognition. IEEE Transactions on Multimedia, Vol. 4, No. 1 (2002) 23-37
2. Kaynak, M.N., Qi Zhi, Cheok, A.D., Sengupta, K., Ko Chi Chung: Audio-visual modeling for bimodal speech recognition. Proceedings of the IEEE Systems, Man, and Cybernetics Conference, Vol. 1 (2001) 181-186

3. Gemello, R., Albesano, D., Mana, F., Moisa, L.: Multi-source neural networks for speech recognition: a review of recent results. Proceedings of the IEEE-INNS-ENNS International Joint Conference on Neural Networks, Vol.5 (2000) 265-270
4. Xiaozheng Zhang, Merserratt, R.M., Clements, M.: Bimodal fusion in audio-visual speech recognition. International Conference on Image Processing, Vol.1 (2002) 964-967
5. A. Waibel, T. Hanazawa, G. Hinton, K. Shikano, K. J. Lang: Phoneme Recognition Using Time-Delay Neural Networks. IEEE Trans. on Acoustics, Speech and Signal Processing. Vol.37, No.3 (1989) 328-339
6. Haffiner,P., Waibel, A.: Multi-State Time Delay Neural Networks for Continuous Speech Recognition. In Advances in Neural Information Processing Systems 4, Morgan Kaufmann Publishers (1992)
7. Joe Tebelskis: Speech Recognition using Neural Networks. CMU-CS-95-142, School of Computer Science Carnegie Mellon University Pittsburgh (1995)
8. C. Bregler, S. Manke, H. Hild, A. Waibel: Bimodal sensor integration on the example of "speech-reading". Proc. of IEEE Int. Conf. on Neural Networks, San Francisco (1993)
9. Doh-Suk Kim, Soo-Young Lee, Rhee M. Kil: Auditory Processing of Speech Signals for Robust Speech Recognition in Real-World Noisy Environments. IEEE Trans. on Speech and Audio Processing, Vol.7, No.1 (1999) 55-69
10. Mary Jo Creaney-Stockton, Beng., MSc.: Isolated Word Recognition Using Reduced Connectivity Neural Networks With Non-Linear Time Alignment Methods. Dept. of Electrical and Electronic Engineering Univ. of Newcastle-Upon-Tyne (1996)
11. Sang Won Lee, In Jung Park: A Study on Recognition of the Isolated Digits Using Integrated Processing of Speech-Image Information in Noisy Environments. Journal of the Institute of Electronics Engineers of Korea, Vol.38-CI, No.3 (2001) 61-67

A Novel Pattern Classification Method for Multivariate EMG Signals Using Neural Network

Nan Bu, Jun Arita, and Toshio Tsuji

Department of Artificial Complex System Engineering,
Hiroshima University, Higashi-Hiroshima 739-8527, Japan
bu@ieee.org
http://www.bsys.hiroshima-u.ac.jp

Abstract. Feature extraction is an important issue in electromyography (EMG) pattern classification, where feature sets of high dimensionality are always used. This paper proposes a novel classification method to deal with high-dimensional EMG patterns, using a probabilistic neural network, a reduced-dimensional log-linearized Gaussian mixture network (RD-LLGMN) [1]. Since RD-LLGMN merges feature extraction and pattern classification processes into its structure, lower-dimensional feature set consistent with classification purposes can be extracted, so that, better classification performance is possible. To verify feasibility of the proposed method, phoneme classification experiments were conducted using frequency features of EMG signals measured from mimetic and cervical muscles. Filter banks are used to extract frequency features, and dimensionality of the features grows significantly when we increase resolution of frequency. In these experiments, the proposed method achieved considerably high classification rates, and outperformed traditional methods that are based on principle component analysis (PCA).

1 Introduction

Electromyography (EMG) pattern classification has been used to devise elaborate human-machine interfaces for people with physical disabilities [2], [3]. In the recent years, multiple channels of amplitude and/or frequency information of EMG signals have been increasingly used for EMG pattern classification to achieve improved classification performance and to conduct multifunction myoelectric control [3], [4]. Dimensionality of feature grows dramatically when we increase number of electrodes and frequency resolution, and pattern classification is frequently confronted with high-dimensional data. As for high-dimensional pattern classification, feature extraction is usually conducted prior to a classification process, in order to find a compact feature set to avoid exhaustive computation and to reduce statistically redundant/irrelevant attributes to improve classification performance [5], [6].

In feature extraction techniques, original features (d-dimension) are projected into an m-dimensional space, where $m < d$, and the m axes of the reduced feature space are determined according to some optimal criterion. Principal component analysis (PCA) is one of most successful feature extraction techniques, and a reconstruction error is utilized as the optimal criterion [6]. Up to present, PCA has been widely used in pattern classification processes, such as face recognition and text classification [7]. For EMG pattern classification, Du et al. and Englehart et al. have applied PCA to EMG features for dimensionality reduction, and neural networks (NNs) are used as classifiers [3], [4], [8].

Although PCA shows promising characteristics as a feature extractor in pattern classification tasks, it still suffers from some intrinsic limitations. For instance, optimal criterion of PCA is not directly related to training criteria of its counterparts for pattern classification. Since training of the classification part always aims to realize low error probabilities, it may not always be possible for PCA to extract features in a reduced form, containing high discriminant information [9], [10]. On the other hand, it should be noticed that, in the existing methods, training processes for PCA and the classification part are made separately. Optimization of the whole pattern classification process is almost impossible, and it is hard to gain a high performance of classification, especially in practical applications, such as for EMG patterns.

To deal with these problems, Bu and Tsuji have proposed a probabilistic neural network, a reduced-dimensional log-linearized Gaussian mixture network (RD-LLGMN), for high-dimensional pattern classification [1]. RD-LLGMN uses orthogonal transformation to project the original feature space into a lower-dimensional space, and then calculates posterior probabilities with a Gaussian mixture model (GMM) in the projected lower-dimensional space for classification. Also, parameters in the network is trained with a single criterion, i.e., minimizing an error probability, it is expected that such training algorithm may yield better classification performance [1], [9].

In this paper, a novel EMG pattern classification method is proposed based on RD-LLGMN. With RD-LLGMN, it is expected that discriminative features can be extracted from high-dimensional EMG patterns, and an efficient and consistent classification is possible. Moreover, as an application, phoneme classification experiments are presented, in which frequency information of EMG signals is extracted as feature pattern using filter banks. The rest of this paper is organized as follows. Section 2 briefly introduces the conception and network structure of RD-LLGMN. Then, in Section 3, the EMG pattern classification method is proposed. Phoneme classification and experimental results are presented in Section 4. Finally, Section 5 gives a conclusion of this paper.

2 RD-LLGMN [1]

RD-LLGMN provides a novel feature extraction approach to find discriminant features of a reduced size, and calculates posterior probabilities for classification. There are two basic ideas in this NN: 1) orthogonal transformation, which projects the original feature space into a lower-dimensional space, and 2) GMM, which estimates probability distribution of patterns in the projected space. This

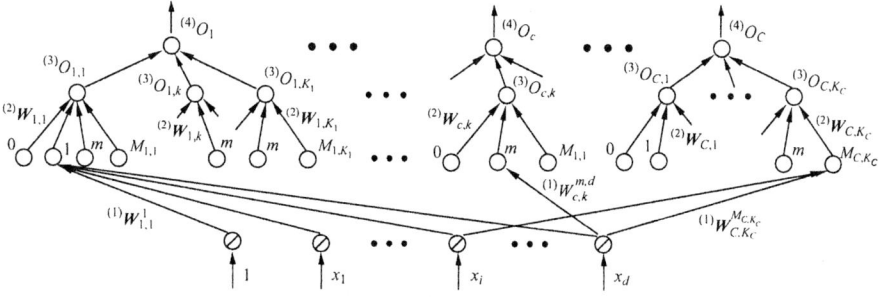

Fig. 1. Structure of RD-LLGMN

network combines the feature extraction process with the classification part, and is trained in a fashion of minimum classification error (MCE) learning [11], which enables the classification part to realize a low error probability.

RD-LLGMN is a four-layer NN, the structure of which is shown in Fig. 1. Given an input vector $\mathbf{x} \in \Re^d$, the first layer consists of $d+1$ units, with one unit has a bias input of 1. Identity function is used for activation of each unit. Let $^{(1)}O_i$ denotes the output of the ith unit in the first layer, we have

$$^{(1)}O_i = \begin{cases} 1, & i = 0 \\ x_i, & i = 1, 2, \cdots, d \end{cases} \quad (1)$$

where x_i ($i = 1, 2, \cdots, d$) is the element of $\mathbf{x}$.

In the second layer, the unit $\{c, k, 0\}$, ($c = 1, \cdots, C$; $k = 1, \ldots, K_c$), is a bias unit, and its output $^{(2)}O_{c,k}^0 = 1$. On the other hand, the unit $\{c, k, m\}$ ($m = 1, \cdots, M_{c,k}$) receives the output of the first layer weighted by $^{(1)}W_{c,k}^m$. The input $^{(2)}I_{c,k}^m$ and the output $^{(2)}O_{c,k}^m$, for ($m \neq 0$), are defined as follows:

$$^{(2)}I_{c,k}^m = \sum_{i=1}^{d} {}^{(1)}O_i \, {}^{(1)}W_{c,k}^{m,i}, \quad (2)$$

$$^{(2)}O_{c,k}^m = ({}^{(2)}I_{c,k}^m)^2, \quad (3)$$

where C is the number of classes under consideration, K_c is the number of components of the Gaussian mixture distribution corresponding to the class c, $M_{c,k}$ is the number of dimension of component k in class c. Through this layer, vector $\mathbf{x} \in \Re^d$ is projected into $M_{c,k}$-dimension spaces, $M_{c,k} < d$.

The unit $\{c, k\}$ in the third layer sums up outputs of the second layer weighted by coefficients $^{(2)}W_{c,k}^m$. The relationships between the input of unit $\{c, k\}$ in the third layer ($^{(3)}I_{c,k}$) and the output ($^{(3)}O_{c,k}$) are defined as

$$^{(3)}I_{c,k} = \sum_{m=0}^{M_{c,k}} {}^{(2)}O_{c,k}^m \, {}^{(2)}W_{c,k}^m, \quad (4)$$

$$^{(3)}O_{c,k} = \frac{\exp[{}^{(3)}I_{c,k}]}{\sum_{c'=1}^{C} \sum_{k'=1}^{K_{c'}} \exp[{}^{(3)}I_{c',k'}]}. \quad (5)$$

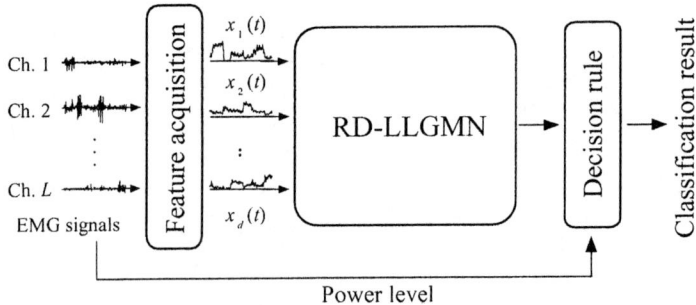

Fig. 2. Schematic view of the proposed method

In the third layer, RD-LLGMN calculates posterior probability of each Gaussian component $\{c, k\}$ using reduced-dimensional features.

The fourth layer consists of C units corresponding to the number of classes. Unit c sums up outputs of K_c components $\{c, k\}$ in the third layer. The function between the input and the output is described as

$$^{(4)}O_c = {}^{(4)}I_c = \sum_{k=1}^{K_c} {}^{(3)}O_{c,k}. \qquad (6)$$

After optimizing the weight coefficients with an MCE-based training algorithm, RD-LLGMN's output, $^{(4)}O_c$, can estimate the posterior probability of class c.

3 EMG Pattern Classification Using RD-LLGMN

The proposed EMG pattern classification method, as shown in Fig. 2, consists of three parts: (1) feature acquisition, (2) RD-LLGMN, and (3) decision rule.

L channels of EMG signals are recorded using surface electrodes attached on muscles. From raw EMG signals, we can calculate amplitude and frequency information to represent EMG features. Suppose that, from each channel, Z features are obtained, the dimensionality of EMG features, d, equals $L \times Z$. Also, normalization method can be applied to decrease variability of EMG features.

For pattern classification, RD-LLGMN described in Section 2 is employed. Using samples labeled with the corresponding motions, RD-LLGMN learns the non-linear mapping between the EMG patterns and the motions. The normalized patterns $\mathbf{x}(t) = [x_1(t), x_2(t), \cdots, x_d(t)]^{\mathrm{T}}$ are used as input to RD-LLGMN.

In this method, we assumed that the amplitude level of EMG signals is changed in proportion to muscle force. A power level is defined as

$$F_{\mathrm{EMG}}(t) = \frac{1}{S} \sum_{s=1}^{S} \frac{E_s(t) - \overline{E}_s^{st}}{E_s^{max} - \overline{E}_s^{st}}, \qquad (7)$$

where S indicates the number of electrodes, $E_s(t)$ is the filtered signal (cut-off frequency: 1 Hz) of rectified raw EMG directly measured from the electrode s

($s = 1, 2, \cdots, S$), $\overline{E}_s^{st}$ is the mean value of $E_s(t)$, which is measured while relaxing the muscles, and E_s^{max} is the mean value of $E_s(t)$ measured under the maximum voluntary contraction (MVC). $F_{\text{EMG}}(t)$ indicates the force information, and is used to recognize whether the motion has really happened or not, by comparing $F_{\text{EMG}}(t)$ with a predefined threshold M_d.

Entropy of RD-LLGMN's output is also calculated to prevent risk of misclassification. The entropy is defined as

$$H(t) = -\sum_{c=1}^{C} {}^{(4)}O_c(t) \log^{(4)} O_c(t). \tag{8}$$

If the entropy $H(t)$ is less than a threshold H_d, the specific motion with the largest probability is determined according to the Bayes' decision rule. If not, the determination is suspended.

4 Experiments

Phoneme classification based on EMG signals was conducted to examine performance of the proposed method. In the experiments, EMG signals measured from mimetic and cervical muscles were used to classify six Japanese phonemes ($C = 6$: /a/, /i/, /u/, /e/, /o/, and /n/). Experiments were held with four subjects (A, B, and C: healthy; D: a patient with cervical spine injury).

4.1 Phoneme Classification Experiments

In this study, cross-talks between EMG signals [12] are used, and a bank of filters is applied to extract frequency features. The EMG signals are measured with monopolar leads, and cross-talk signals can be derived as the difference between potentials of every two electrodes. Three Ag/AgCl electrodes (SEB120, GE marquette Corp.) with conductive paste were attached to muscles (M. Depressor Labii Inferioris (DLI), M. Zygomaticus Major (ZM), and M. Masseer (MA)). EMG signals were recorded with a sampling frequency of 1 kHz. The cross-talk between DLI and ZM was used as input channel one, the cross-talk between DLI and MA as channel two, and the cross-talk between ZM and MA as channel three. Each channel was then fed into a bank of Z band-pass filters (BPF$_i$, $i = 0, \cdots, Z - 1$). Bandwidths of these filters were set as follows:

$$\text{BPF}_i : 20 + \sigma i \ [\text{Hz}] \sim 20 + \sigma(i + 1) \ [\text{Hz}], \ (i = 0, 1, \cdots, Z - 1). \tag{9}$$

Here, $\sigma = U/Z$, and U is the range of spectrum under consideration. In the phoneme classification experiments, U was set as 250 Hz, and the number of band-pass filters Z as 6. After the filter-bank stage, the number of EMG features $d = 18$, and these 18 channels of raw signals are rectified and filtered by a low pass filter (cut-off frequency: 1 Hz). The filtered signals are defined as $EMG_i(t)$ ($i = 1, \cdots, d$), and normalized to make the sum of d channels equal to 1.0.

$$x_i(t) = \frac{EMG_i(t) - \overline{EMG}_i^{st}}{\sum_{i=1}^{d} EMG_i(t) - \overline{EMG}_i^{st}}, \ (i = 1, \cdots, d). \tag{10}$$

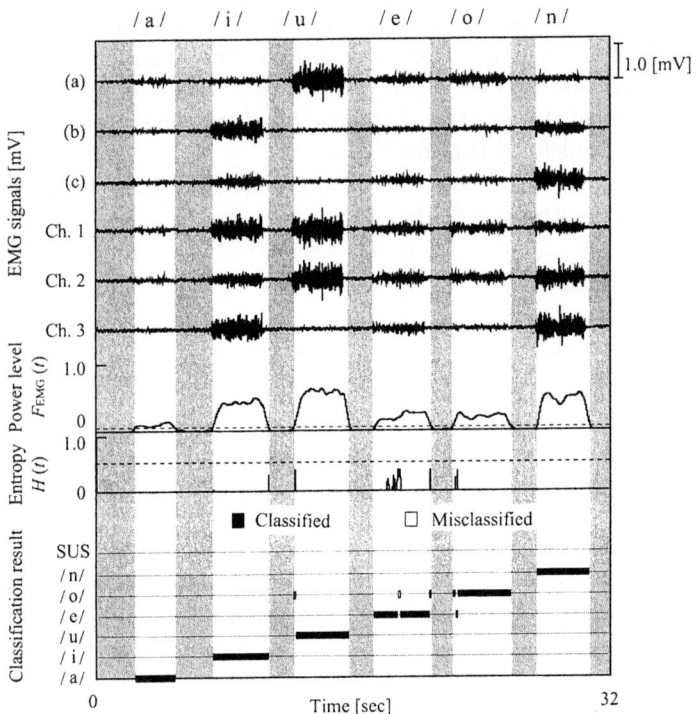

Fig. 3. Examples of the classification results using the proposed method (subject A). (a: M. depressor labii inferioris, b: M. zygomaticus major, c: M. masseter.)

where $\overline{EMG}_i^{st}$ is the mean value of $EMG_i(t)$, which is measured while relaxing the muscles.

Parameters of GMM in RD-LLGMN were set as: $C=6$, $K_c=1$ ($c=1,\cdots,6$). Dimensions of the reduced subspaces $M_{c,k}$, ($c=1,\cdots,C$; $k=1$), were set as $M=9$. In the training phase, 50 EMG patterns were extracted from EMG signals of each phoneme, so that teacher signals consisted of $C \times 50$ patterns. The determination thresholds were set as $M_d = 0.08$, and $H_d = 0.5$.

An example of the classification results (subject A) is shown in Fig. 3. In this figure, three channels of raw EMG signals, three channels of cross-talk EMG signals, the power level $F_{\mathrm{EMG}}(t)$, the entropy $H(t)$, and the classification results are plotted. The gray areas indicate that no utterance was conducted because the power level F_{EMG} was less than M_d. Although misclassification can be found in utterance of /u/, /e/ and /o/, the classification results of RD-LLGMN are relatively stable, and a high classification rate about 96.8% was realized in this experiment. Also, for each misclassified utterance, the corresponding entropy is high. It is believed that misclassification can be reduced using an appropriately modulated threshold H_d.

4.2 Comparison Experiments

Comparison experiments were conducted between the proposed method and traditional pattern classification methods based on PCA with neural classifier schemes. In the PCA part, original features are projected into a lower-dimensional space on directions, which correspond to the M highest eigenvalues of the covariance matrix. Feature vectors extracted with these M directions are then fed into neural classifiers. In this paper, a log-linearized Gaussian mixture network (LLGMN) [13] and a multilayer perceptron (MLP) [14], are used. LLGMN is a feedforward probabilistic NN based on GMM. The number of units in the input layer of LLGMN was set equal to M. Units in the hidden layer corresponded to the Gaussian components in GMM, which was set as one. The output layer had six units, and each unit outputs posterior probability for the input vector. On the other hand, the MLP had four layers. Number of units in the first layer was set as M, in both hidden layers unit numbers were $M \times \frac{10}{3}$ (Here, factor $\frac{10}{3}$ was chosen just for ease of setting the MLP), and in the output layer there is six units. Each output of MLP corresponds to one phoneme, and it was normalized to make the sum of all outputs equal 1.0, so that the normalized outputs can be regarded as posterior probabilities of phonemes. Same values of thresholds, M_d and H_d, were used for three classification method.

In the comparison experiments, classification rates of three methods are evaluated by varying the dimensionality of input EMG features d and an extraction rate (denoted as β), which stands for the ratio of M to d. The dimensionality of input EMG features d varies when we changing the number of filters Z from one to six. Five sets of randomly chosen initial weights were used to train each sample data. The EMG signals for six phonemes used for test were about 30 seconds. Figs. 4–6 depict mean values and standard deviations of the classification rates of subject A for different parameter combinations:

$$d \times \beta : \begin{cases} \beta \in [\frac{1}{3}, \frac{2}{3}, 1] & (d \in [3, 9, 15]) \\ \beta \in [\frac{1}{6}, \frac{2}{6}, \frac{3}{6}, \frac{4}{6}, \frac{5}{6}, 1] & (d \in [6, 12, 18]) \end{cases}. \tag{11}$$

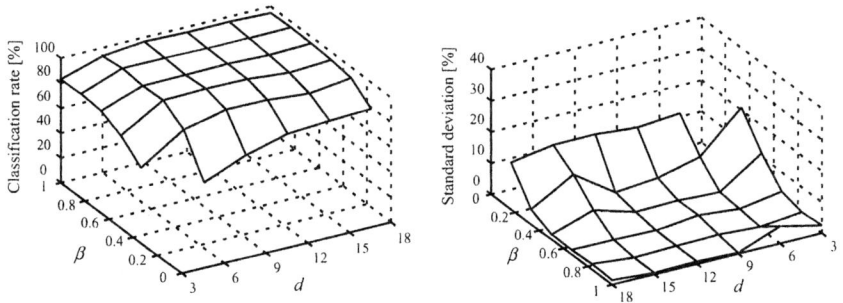

Fig. 4. Classification results using RD-LLGMN (Subject A)

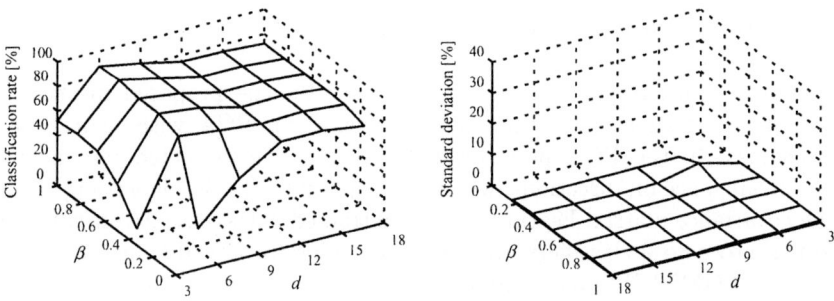

Fig. 5. Classification results using PCA with LLGMN (Subject A)

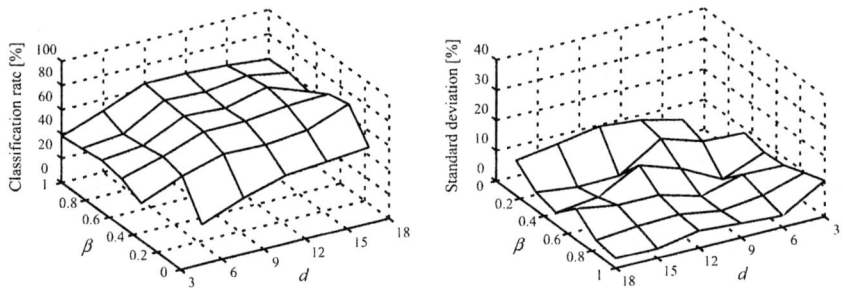

Fig. 6. Classification results using PCA with MLP (Subject A)

Please note that the directions of axes of d and β are reversed in the figures of standard deviations to make them shown clearly. In these figures, it can be found that RD-LLGMN achieved the best classification rates among all methods. Since PCA and the neural classifiers are optimized separately based on different training criteria, the features extracted may not always be consistent with the purpose of classification, and their classification performance was poorer than that of RD-LLGMN. Also, Since RD-LLGMN and LLGMN conduct classification according to probabilistic characteristics of input features, higher classification performance was achieved using RD-LLGMN and PCA with LLGMN than PCA with MLP. Furthermore, we can find that when β increases classification rates of all three method increase slightly. It is due to that more information is used for pattern classification. However, computation complexity and time used for training are significantly increased. On the other hand, when we increase d, similar trend can be observed for RD-LLGMN and PCA with MLP. In contrast, classification rates of PCA with LLGMN method decrease for about 15%. When increasing d, the entropy of LLGMN's output increases at the same time. Since the classification turned more ambiguous, more classification results were suspended, which resulted in decrease in the classification rates of PCA with LLGMN.

Finally, comparison experiments were conducted for four subjects. In these experiments, dimension of the input EMG features (d) was 18, and dimension of

Table 1. Comparison of classification rates for four subjects

Type of methods		PCA with MLP	PCA with LLGMN	RD-LLGMN
Subject A	C.R.	70.0	73.4	88.4
	S.D.	8.1	0.1	8.5
Subject B	C.R.	65.0	31.1	69.6
	S.D.	5.1	0.0	6.2
Subject C	C.R.	49.0	79.8	92.2
	S.D.	4.5	0.8	3.4
Subject D	C.R.	44.3	76.6	90.3
	S.D.	2.8	6.5	5.4

C.R. : Classification rate [%], S.D. : Standard deviation [%]

extracted feature set (M) was set as nine. Five sets of randomly chosen initial weights were used to training of three methods. A summary of classification rates for four subjects using three methods is shown in Table 1.

5 Conclusion

This paper proposes a novel classification method for multivariate EMG patterns. This method uses a probabilistic NN, RD-LLGMN, for high-dimensional pattern classification. With RD-LLGMN, discriminative information benefiting classification can be extracted, and an efficient classification of motions is possible.

To examine the classification capability and the accuracy of the proposed method, phoneme classification experiments have been carried out with five subjects. A bank of filters is applied to acquire frequency features from crosstalk EMG signals, and then the feature vectors are input into RD-LLGMN. In the experiments, the proposed method achieved high classification performance. Furthermore, comparison experiments were carried out between the proposed method and two PCA-based traditional methods, and the proposed method outperforms the other methods.

In Fig. 4, it can be found that standard deviations of the proposed method are larger than that of PCA with LLGMN when β is small. A detailed investigation is worthy to study stability of classification results of the proposed method. Also, in the future research, we would like to improve the pre-processing method for EMG signals, such as modulation of the parameters of filter bank and the low-pass filtering for each raw cross-talk EMG signal. Better classification performance would be available using combination of new pre-processing and RD-LLGMN.

References

1. Bu, N., Tsuji, T.: Multivariate Pattern Classification based on Local Discriminant Component Analisys. Proc. of IEEE International Conference on Robotics and Biomimetics (2004) Paper-ID: 290

2. Fukuda, O., Tsuji, T., Kaneko, M., Ohtsuka, A.: A Human-Assisting Manipulator Teleoperated by EMG Signals and Arm Motions. IEEE Trans. on Robotics and Automation **19** (2003) 210–222
3. Englehart, K., Hudgins, B., Chen, A.D.C.: Continuous Multifunction Myoelectric Control using Pattern Recognition. Technology and Disability **15** (2003) 95–103
4. Du, Y.C., Hu, W.C., Shyu, L.Y.: The Effect of Data Reduction by Independent Component Analysis and Principal Component Analysis in Hand Motion Identification. Proc. of the 26th Annual International Conference of the Engineering in Medicine and Biology Society **1** (2004) 84–86
5. Verikas, A., Bacauskiene, M.: Feature Slection with Neural Networks. Pattern Recognition Letters **23** (2002) 1323–1335
6. Bishop, C.: Neural Networks for Pattern Recognition. New York: Oxford University Press, 1995.
7. Jain, A.K., Duin, R.P.W., Mao, J.C.: Statistical Pattern Recognition: A Review. IEEE Trans. on Pattern Analysis and Machine Intelligence **22** (2000) 4–37
8. Englehart, K., Hudgins, B., Parker, P.A., Stevenson, M.: Classification of the Myoelectric Signal using Time-frequency based Representations. Medical Engineering & Physics **21** (1999) 431–438
9. Lotlikar, R., Kothari, R.: Bayes-Optimality Motivated Linear and Multilayered Perceptron-Based Dimensionality Reduction. IEEE Trans. on Neural Networks **11** (2000) 452–463
10. Tsymbal, A., Puuronen, S., Pechenizkiy, M., Baumgarten, M., Patterson, D.: Eigenvector-based Feature Extraction for Classification. Proc. of International FLAIRS Conference on Artificial Intelligence (2002) 354–358
11. Juang, B-H., Katagiri, S.: Discriminative Learning for Minimum Error Classification. IEEE Trans. on Signal Processing **40** (1992) 3043–3054
12. Ohga, M., Takeda, M., Matsuba, A., Koike, A., Tsuji, T.: Development of A Five-finger Prosthetic Hand using Ultrasonic Motors Controlled by Two EMG Signals. Journal of Robotics and Mechatronics **14** (2002) 565–572
13. Tsuji, T., Fukuda, O., Ichinobe, H., Kaneko, M.: A Log-Linearized Gassian Mixture Network and Its Application to EEG Pattern Classification. IEEE Trans. on Systems, Man, and Cybernetics-Part C: Application and Reviews **29** (1999) 60–72
14. Rumelhart, D.E., McClell, J.L., Williams, R.J.: Learning Internal Representations by Error Propagation. Parallel Distributed Processing **I** (1986) 318–362

Data Fusion for Fault Diagnosis Using Dempster-Shafer Theory Based Multi-class SVMs[1]

Zhonghui Hu, Yunze Cai, Ye Li, Yuangui Li, and Xiaoming Xu

Department of Automation, Shanghai Jiaotong University,
Shanghai 200030, P. R. China
{huhzh, yzcai, liyemail, li_yuangui, xmxu}@sjtu.edu.cn

Abstract. The multi-class probability SVM (MPSVM) is designed by training the sigmoid function to map the output of each binary class SVM into a posterior probability, and then combining these learned binary-class PSVMs using one-against-all strategy. The method of basic probability assignment is proposed according to the probabilistic output and performance of the PSVM. The outputs of all the binary-class PSVMs comprising an MPSVM are represented in the frame of Dempster-Shafer theory. A Dempster-Shafer theory based multi-class SVM (DSMSVM) is constructed by using the combination rule of evidences. To deal with the distributed multi-source multi-class problem, the DSMSVM is trained corresponding to each information source, and then the Dempster-Shafer theory is used to combine these learned DSMSVMs. Our proposed method is applied to fault diagnosis of a diesel engine. The experimental results show that the accuracy and robustness of fault diagnosis can be improved by using our proposed approach.

1 Introduction

It is increasingly important to reduce maintenance costs and prevent unscheduled downtimes for machinery [1]. Shen et al. [2] pointed out that it is difficult to diagnose more than one category of faults and proposed a rough set theory based method that can diagnose more than one category of faults. However, the discretization method has to be used if continuous attributes exist. It is hard to choose an appropriate discretization method, for a prior knowledge about the attribute is difficult to obtain.

The support vector machine (SVM) is derived from statistical learning and VC-dimension theory, and has sound generalization ability [3-7]. In the fault diagnosis field, the fault data are usually difficult to sample and the fault mechanism is very complex. The SVM is a promising method for fault diagnosis. The discrimination between more than two categories is often required. How to extend the SVM for binary classification to solve multi-class problem is a worthwhile research problem. Currently there are two types of approaches for constructing multi-class SVM (MSVM) [8]. One is by constructing and combining several binary SVM classifiers

---

[1] Supported by the National Key Fundamental Research Program (2002cb312200), and partially supported by the National High Technology Research and Development Program (2002AA412010), and the Natural Science Foundation of China (60174038).

while the other is by directly considering all data in one optimization formulation. Hsu and Lin [8] indicated that the first approach is more suitable for practical use.

In general, a posterior probability produced by a classifier is convenient for post-processing. Platt [9] proposed a probability SVM (PSVM) method for fitting a sigmoid function that maps SVM outputs to posterior probabilities. In this paper, we extend the one-against-all MSVM to multi-class probability SVM (MPSVM).

The Dempster-Shafer (D-S) theory is widely used in data fusion field, which is a general extension of Bayesian theory [10]. We extend the SVM to yield an output in the frame of D-S theory. The output of this kind of SVM can directly be combined by using the combination rule of evidences, and a great deal of information for performance evaluation can be obtained. The D-S theory based MSVM (DSMSVM) is constructed by designing the basic probability assignment according to the PSVMs in a MPSVM, and then combining the evidences provided by these PSVMs.

In the data fusion area, the redundant or complementary information from several information sources are used in order to achieve higher classification accuracy and robustness [11, 12]. In general, the MSVM classifiers are combined by using the methods of majority voting, average voting, and so on. In this paper, the combination rule of evidences is applied for combining multiple DSMSVMs in distributed data fusion strategy. Our proposed method is applied to fault diagnosis for a diesel engine.

This paper is organized as below. In Section 2, the MPSVM method is proposed. Section 3 concisely describes the D-S theory. In Section 4, the DSMSVM is proposed and an example is given. In Section 5, the approach of combining multiple DSMSVMs is proposed. In Section 6, our proposed method is applied to fault diagnosis for a diesel engine. Finally, we conclude with a discussion in Section 7.

2 Multi-class Probability Support Vector Machines

In this section, we first introduce the PSVM. Then the standard MSVM is described. Finally, based on the PSVM and standard MSVM, the MPSVM method is proposed.

2.1 Probability Support Vector Machines for Binary Classification

Given the training set $\{(x_i, y_i)\}_{i=1}^{l} \in R^n \times \{+1,-1\}$. SVMs optimize the classification boundary by separating the data with the maximal margin hyperplane [3-5].

For the linearly case, the decision function of SVM in the input space is

$$d(x) = \mathrm{sgn}\left[f(x)\right] = \mathrm{sgn}\left[\sum_{sv} y_i \alpha_i \langle x_i \cdot x \rangle + b\right] \quad (1)$$

For the nonlinearly case, the decision function of SVM in the input space is

$$d(x) = \mathrm{sgn}\left[f(x)\right] = \mathrm{sgn}\left[\sum_{sv} y_i \alpha_i K(x_i, x) + b\right] \quad (2)$$

Platt [9] provided the PSVM method. Let the continuous output of a standard SVM is f. The parametric model as below is given to fit the posterior $P(y=1|f)$.

$$P(y=1|f) = 1/(1+\exp(Af+B)) \quad (3)$$

As long as $A < 0$, the monotonicity of (3) is assured. The parameters A and B are found by minimizing the negative log likelihood of the training data,

$$\min \ -\sum_i t_i \log(p_i) + (1 - t_i)\log(1 - p_i) \quad (4)$$

where

$$p_i = 1/(1 + \exp(Af_i + B)) \quad (5)$$

A new training set (f_i, t_i) is defined by

$$t_i = (y_i + 1)/2 \quad (6)$$

The problem (4) is solved by using a model-trust minimization algorithm for robustness [13]. It can prevent overfitting in training sigmoid to create a model of out-of-sample data [9]. The out-of-sample data is modeled with the same empirical density as the sigmoid training data, but with a finite probability of opposite label.

The probability of correct label can be derived using Bayesian rule. Suppose N_+ positive examples are observed. The maximum a posteriori probability (MAP) for the target probability of positive examples is

$$t_+ = (N_+ + 1)/(N_+ + 2) \quad (7)$$

If N_- negative examples exist, the MAP for the target probability of them is

$$t_- = 1/(N_- + 2) \quad (8)$$

Hence, the modified training set is

$$(f_i, t'_i), \ t'_i = \begin{cases} t_+, & t_i = 1 \\ t_-, & t_i = 0 \end{cases}, \ i = 1, \cdots, l \quad (9)$$

Thus, by training sigmoid using the modified training set, the output of PSVM is

$$p(x) = 1/(1 + \exp(Af(x) + B)) \quad (10)$$

The decision function of PSVM is

$$d(x) = \begin{cases} 1, & p(x) \geq 0.5 \\ -1, & p(x) < 0.5 \end{cases} \quad (11)$$

2.2 Standard Multi-class Support Vector Machines

For a K-class problem, the standard MSVM method is to construct K standard binary SVMs and then combining them [5, 14]. The kth SVM will be trained using all of the instances, among which the instances belonging to kth class are labeled as positive, and all the other instances are labeled as negative. The final decision of standard MSVM is the class that corresponds to the binary SVM with the largest continuous output value. Suppose the output of the kth SVM is $f_k(x)$, the final decision is

$$d(x) = \arg\max\{f_1(x), \cdots, f_K(x)\} \quad (12)$$

2.3 Multi-class Probability Support Vector Machines

Given the training data set $\{(x_i, y_i)\}_{i=1}^{l}$, where $x_i \in R^n$ represents condition attribute and $y_i \in \{1,\cdots,K\}$ is the class attribute. The MPSVM is constructed as below [5, 15].

1) Construct K binary SVMs where $f_k(x)$ ($k=1,\cdots,K$) separates training examples of the class k from the other training examples. The training set used for kth binary SVM is $\{(x_i, y_i')\}_{i=1}^{l}$ ($y_i'=1$, if $y_i = k$; $y_i'=-1$ otherwise).

2) Training the corresponding sigmoid using the modified training set $\{(f_i, t'_i)\}_1^l$, K binary-class PSVMs with outputs $p_k(x)$, $k=1,\cdots,K$ are constructed.

3) Construct the K-class MPSVM by choosing the class corresponding to the PSVM with the maximal value among $p_k(x)$, $k=1,\cdots,K$. Thus, the decision is

$$d(x) = \arg\max\{p_1(x),\cdots,p_K(x)\}. \tag{13}$$

3 The Dempster-Shafer Evidence Theory

D-S theory directly takes into account what remains unknown, and also describes what is known precisely [10, 16, 17].

Let $\Theta = \{h_1, h_2,\cdots,h_n\}$ be a frame of discernment. A function $m: 2^\Theta \to [0, 1]$ is called a basic probability assignment (*bpa*) if it satisfies

$$\sum\nolimits_{X \in 2^\Theta} m(X) = 1,\ m(\varnothing) = 0\ (\varnothing\text{ - empty set}) \tag{14}$$

where the notation 2^Θ is the power set of Θ. Any subset X of the frame of discernment Θ with non-zero mass value is called a focal element and the mass function $m(X)$ represents the exact belief in the proposition depicted by X.

A belief function $bel: 2^\Theta \to [0, 1]$, derived from the mass function, is defined by

$$bel(A) = \sum\nolimits_{X \subseteq A} m(X),\ \text{for all } A \subseteq \Theta \tag{15}$$

It represents the measure of the total belief lying in A and all subsets of A.

A plausibility function $pls: 2^\Theta \to [0,1]$ is defined as

$$pls(A) = 1 - bel(\overline{A}) = \sum\nolimits_{A \cap X \neq \varnothing} m(X),\ \text{for all } X \subseteq \Theta \tag{16}$$

where $pls(A)$ denotes the extent to which we fail to disbelieve A.

For a given subset A, a belief interval represents the information contained in the evidential functions $bel(A)$ and $pls(A)$, that is,

$$[bel(A),\ pls(A)] \tag{17}$$

The residual ignorance is defined by

$$ignorance(A) = pls(A) - bel(A) \tag{18}$$

A method to combine the evidences from N different sources is also provided. The combined mass function $m_1 \oplus m_2 \oplus \cdots \oplus m_N : 2^\Theta \to [0,1]$ is defined by

$$(m_1 \oplus m_2 \oplus \cdots \oplus m_N)(A) = \frac{1}{K_N} \sum_{X_1 \cap X_2 \cap \cdots \cap X_N = A} m_1(X_1) m_2(X_2) \cdots m_N(X_N) \quad (19)$$

where $x_1, x_2, \cdots, x_N$ are focal elements, and the constant $1/K_N$ measures the extent of conflict among these mass functions. The parameter K_N is defined as

$$K_N = \sum_{X_1 \cap X_2 \cap \cdots \cap X_N \neq \varnothing} m_1(X_1) m_2(X_2) \cdots m_N(X_N) \quad (20)$$

4 Dempster-Shafer Theory Based Multi-class SVMs

Suppose there exists a pattern space P containing K mutually exclusive classes, $\Gamma = \{1, 2, \cdots, K\}$ represents a class attribute set, i.e., the frame of discernment Θ. Given training set $\{(x_i, y_i)\}_{i=1}^l$, DSMSVM is constructed by the following procedure.

1) Construct the K-class MPSVM. The ith PSVM is designed to discriminate examples of the ith class from all the other examples. The probability and decision outputs of these PSVMs are p_i and d_i, $i = 1, \cdots, K$, $p_i \in [0,1]$, $d_i \in \Theta$, respectively.

2) Obtain the performance of every PSVM. By applying the K-class MPSVM to a validation set, we can obtain the estimated classification accuracy of K PSVMs, a_i, $i = 1, \cdots, K$, $a_i \in [0,1]$. The accuracy is used to describe the performance of every PSVM. Let the size of validation set be V, the ith PSVM correctly discriminates v_i examples in the validation set. The classification accuracy of the ith PSVM is

$$a_i = v_i / V \quad (21)$$

3) Design the *bpa* for every PSVM. Suppose the classification accuracy of a PSVM is a, which indicates an instance with unknown label will be correctly classified with the probability a. It cannot be determined which class it belongs to with the probability $(1-a)$. The error rate of classification $(1-a)$ is considered as what remains unknown lying in the PSVM. Thus, it is reasonable to set $m(\Theta) = 1-a$. Suppose the probability output, decision output and classification accuracy of the ith PSVM classifier are p_i, d_i and a_i. The *bpa* is defined by

$$m_i(\{k\}) = p_i a_i \quad (22)$$

$$m_i(\{1, 2, \cdots, k-1, k+1, \cdots, K\}) = (1 - p_i) a_i \quad (23)$$

$$m_i(\Theta) = 1 - a_i \quad (24)$$

where $i = 1, 2, \cdots, K$ and $k = i \in \Theta$. Formulas (22)-(24) satisfy the condition (14).

4) Apply the D-S theory to combine evidences from all the individual K PSVMs. All the combined values of mass, belief, plausibility, belief interval and ignorance can be obtained. In this paper, the maximal belief rule is used to obtain the final decision. Because all the non-singletons in focal elements cannot give a decision, only the singletons are compared with each other (A singleton is a subset with only one element). The final decision is the class that corresponds to the singleton with the highest belief value. Therefore, the final decision function is defined as

$$d(x) = \arg\max_{i \in \{1,\cdots,K\}} \{bel(\{1\}), bel(\{2\}), \cdots, bel(\{K\})\} \quad (25)$$

The aforementioned procedure is illustrated in Fig. 1. A simple example is also given to show the usage of DSMSVM.

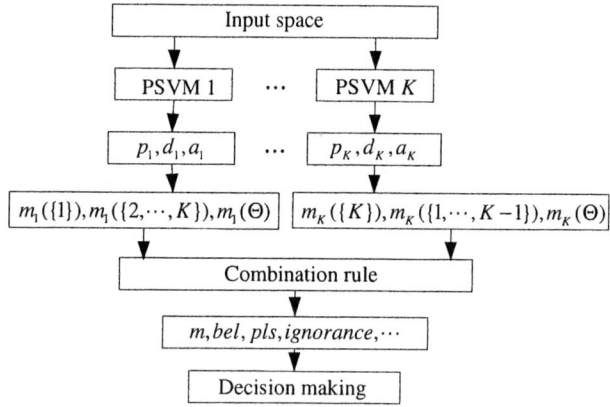

Fig. 1. The method of D-S theory based multi-class SVM

Example: Given a 3-class classification problem, three PSVMs for binary classification are constructed using MPSVM strategy. The accuracy is obtained by using a validation set (Table 1). The probability outputs are also given for an instance with unknown label. Our task is to determine which class the instance belongs to.

According to Formula (11), the decisions of three PSVMs are {2, 3}, {1, 3} and {1, 2}, respectively. None of them can give a definitive decision. We can determine the instance belongs to Class 3 using the MPSVM method (Expression (13)).

Table 1. Outputs and accuracy of three PSVMs in a MPSVM for the instance

Individual classifier	Probability output	Accuracy
PSVM 1	0.37	0.95
PSVM 2	0.34	0.8
PSVM 3	0.38	0.9

Table 2. The values of basic probability assignment for all the focal elements

PSVM 1		PSVM 2		PSVM 3	
Group	Value	Group	Value	Group	Value
{1}	0.3476	{2}	0.2750	{3}	0.3332
{2,3}	0.6024	{1,3}	0.5250	{1,2}	0.5668
Θ	0.0500	Θ	0.2000	Θ	0.1000

Table 3. Combination results of the evidences from three PSVMs

Group	Mass	Belief	Plausibility	Ignorance
{1}	0.3146	0.3146	0.3306	0.0160
{2}	0.3232	0.3232	0.3554	0.0322
{3}	0.3255	0.3255	0.3524	0.0270
{2,3}	0.0207	0.6694	0.6854	0.0160
{1,3}	0.0045	0.6446	0.6768	0.0322
{1,2}	0.0097	0.6476	0.6745	0.0270
Θ	0.0017	1.0000	1.0000	0

The proposed DSMSVM is used to solve this problem as below. Let $\Theta = \{1, 2, 3\}$ be the frame of discernment. The *bpa* is listed in Table 2. The combination results using D-S theory are given in Table 3.

Table 3 shows that the singleton {3} has maximal belief value among all the singletons. Thus, the instance belongs to Class 3. We can find the singleton {2} with maximal ignorance, which is mainly because the lowest accuracy of PSVM 2 results in large classification uncertainty.

5 Combination of DSMSVMs Using Dempster-Shafer Theory

In this section, the approach of combining multiple DSMSVM classifiers using D-S theory is proposed, which is illustrated in Figure 2.

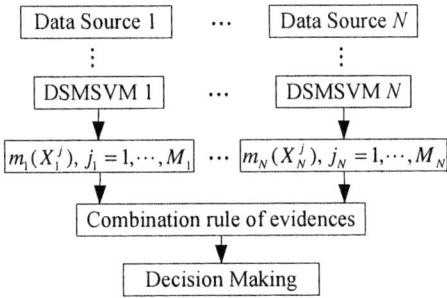

Fig. 2. The combination of multiple DSMSVM classifiers

Suppose there are N data sources and exist exhaustive K patterns (hypotheses) in these data sources. N DSMSVM classifiers, corresponding to the N sources, can be constructed. Set the focal element of the ith DSMSVM is X_i^j, and that the combined mass output is $m_i(X_i^j)$, $i = 1, \cdots, N$, $j = 1, \cdots, M_i$.

The combined mass function $m_1 \oplus m_2 \oplus \cdots \oplus m_N : 2^\Theta \to [0, 1]$ is given by

$$(m_1 \oplus m_2 \oplus \cdots \oplus m_N)(A) = \frac{1}{K_N} \sum_{X_1 \cap X_2 \cap \cdots \cap X_N = A} m_1(X_1) m_2(X_2) \cdots m_N(X_N) \qquad (26)$$

where $X_i \in \{X_i^j \mid j = 1, 2, \cdots, M_i\}$, $i = 1, 2, \cdots, N$. The constant K_N is defined as

$$K_N = \sum_{X_1 \cap X_2 \cap \cdots \cap X_N \neq \varnothing} m_1(X_1) m_2(X_2) \cdots m_N(X_N) \qquad (27)$$

The combined belief value of focal element A is obtained by

$$bel(A) = \sum_{X \subseteq A} m_1 \oplus m_2 \oplus \cdots \oplus m_N(X), \text{ for all } A \subseteq \Theta \qquad (28)$$

The final decision function for classification based on the maximal belief rule is

$$d(x) = \arg\max_{j \in \{1, 2, \cdots, K\}} \{bel(\{1\}), bel(\{2\}), \cdots, bel(\{K\})\} \qquad (29)$$

6 Experimental Results

The dataset given in [2] is used to diagnose the valve fault for a multi-cylinder diesel engine. The whole dataset consists of 37 instances. Four states are researched: Normal state; intake valve clearance is too small; intake valve clearance is too large; exhaust valve clearance is too large. Among these four states, three fault types are simulated in the intake valve and exhaust valve on the second cylinder head. Three sampling points are selected to collect vibration signals. They are the first cylinder head, the second cylinder head and another one at the centre of the piston stroke, on the surface of the cylinder block. The method of extracting features from both the frequency domain and time domain is in detail described by [2]. Thus, each instance in the dataset is composed of 18 condition attributes (six features from each sampling point) and one class attribute (four states). In the distributed schemes, the six features from each sampling point, adding the class attribute, form an individual dataset. Thus, three datasets corresponding to the three sampling points are constructed.

The two-fold cross-validation test is used for showing the effect of rough set theory in fault diagnosis [1]. The classification accuracy excerpted from [1] is listed in Table 4, which shows that the average classification accuracy is 76.32%.

Table 4. Classification accuracy of each part based on the rough set theory (%)

Data set	1st part—training data 2nd part—testing data	2nd part—training data 1st part—testing data
Accuracy	78.95	73.68

Table 5. The experimental comparison of several combination methods (D1, D2, D3: Data sources 1, 2, 3; CF: Centralized fusion; MV: Majority vote) (%)

Scheme	Single data source			CF	MV of MSVM	MV of MPSVM	Our method
	D1	D2	D3				
Average accuracy	88.67	80.50	90.00	93.50	93.67	94.33	96.00
Minimal accuracy	58.33	58.33	50.00	75.00	75.00	75.00	75.00
Standard deviation	0.111	0.128	0.089	0.083	0.076	0.072	0.069

In our experiment, 25 instances are used as training set and the rest are used as testing set. The choice of the kernel and regularizing parameters was determined via performance on a validation set. Eighty percent of the training set is used for training binary SVM classifiers and the rest 20% of the training set is used as validation set. The whole experiment is repeated 50 times, where the training set and test set are randomly selected without replacement every time.

The experimental results of several methods are given in Table 5. In the centralized fusion (CF) scheme, the features extracted from three sampling points are combined to form one input space, and then a DSMSVM classifier is trained (Column CF). In the distributed fusion scheme, three types of MSVM methods, i.e., the standard MSVM, MPSVM and DSMSVM, are trained for each sampling point, respectively. The testing accuracy of three individual DSMSVM classifiers corresponding to the three sampling points is given in D1, D2 and D3 columns. The accuracy of majority vote method for combining three standard MSVMs, and for combining three MPSVMs are respectively given. Table 5 shows the classification accuracy obtained by our proposed methods is satisfactory. The distributed strategy outperforms the centralized one. We also find the robustness of fault diagnosis is also improved by using our proposed methods.

7 Conclusion

The PSVM method can produce a posterior probability for post-processing. Based on PSVM, the MPSVM using one-against-all strategy is proposed.

In this paper, the method of basic probability assignment is designed based on all the probability outputs and performances of MPSVMs. The DSMSVM is constructed by using the D-S theory to combine all the evidences provided by every PSVM comprising the MPSVM, and then applying the maximal belief rule only to the classes corresponding to the singletons. Compared with the standard MSVM and MPSVM, the DSMSVM provides a bulk of useful information for post-processing.

To deal with distributed multi-source multi-class problems, we propose a method of constructing individual DSMSVM for each source and then combining them using evidence theory. The final decision is given by using the maximal belief rule. Our proposed method is applied to fault diagnosis for a diesel engine. This distributed strategy takes full advantages of the DSMSVM method, and obtains better performance than the centralized one.

To sum up, our proposed method improves the accuracy and robustness of fault diagnosis, and enlarges the applicability of SVM based method.

References

1. Tay, F.E.H., Shen, L.: Fault Diagnosis Based on Rough Set Theory. Engineering Application of Artificial Intelligence 16 (2003) 39-43
2. Shen, L., Tay, F.E.H., Qu, L., Shen, Y.: Fault Diagnosis Using Rough Sets Theory. Computers in Industry 43 (2000) 61-72
3. Burges, C.J.C., 1998. A Tutorial on Support Vector Machines for Pattern Recognition. Data Mining and Knowledge Discovery, 2(2), 121-167
4. Cristianini, N., Shawe-Taylor, J.: An Introduction to Support Vector Machines and other Kernel-based Learning Methods. Cambridge, University Press (2000)
5. Vapnik, V.N.: Statistical Learning Theory. Wiley, New York (1998)
6. Kecman, V.: Learning and Soft Computing: Support Vector Machines, Neural Networks, and Fuzzy Logic Models. MIT Press, Cambridge MA (2001)
7. Wang, L.P. (ed.): Support Vector Machines: Theory and Application. Springer, Berlin Heidelberg New York (2005)
8. Hsu, C.-W., Lin, C.-J.: A Comparison of Methods for Multi-class Support Vector Machines. IEEE Transactions on Neural Networks 13(2) (2002) 415-425
9. Platt, J.C.: Probabilistic Outputs for Support Vector Machines and Comparisons to Regularized Likelihood Methods. In: Smola, A.J., Bartlett, P., Scholkopf, B., Schuurmans, D. (eds.): Advances in Large Margin Classifiers. MIT Press (1999)
10. Beynona, M., Coskerb, D., Marshallb, D.: An Expert System for Multi-criteria Decision Making Using Dempster-Shafer Theory. Expert Systems with Applications 20 (2001) 357-367
11. Benediktsson, J.A., Sveinsson, J.R., Ersoy, O.K., Swain, P.H.: Parallel Consensual Neural Networks. IEEE Transactions on Neural Networks 8(1) (1997) 54-64
12. Hall, D.L., Llinas, J.: An Introduction to Multisensor Data Fusion. Proceedings of the IEEE 85(1) (1997) 6-23
13. Gill, P.E., Murray, W., Wright, M.H.: Practical Optimization. Academic Press (1981)
14. Platt, J.C., Cristianini, N., Shawe-Taylor, J.: Large Margin DAG's for Multiclass Classification. In: Advances in Neural Information Processing Systems 12. MIT Press, Cambridge (2000) p.547-553
15. Lee, Y., Lin, Y., Wahba, G.: Multicategory Support Vector Machines: Theory and Application to the Classification of Microarray Data and Satellite Radiance Data. Journal of the American Statistical Association 99(465) (2004) 67-81
16. Guan, J.W., Bell, D.A.: Evidence Theory and its Applications (Vol.1). North-Holland-Amsterdam, New York (1992)
17. Yen, J.: GERTIS: A Dempster-Shafer Approach to Diagnosing Hierarchical Hypotheses. Communications of the ACM 5 32 (1989) 573-585

Modelling of Rolling and Aging Processes in Copper Alloy by Levenberg-Marquardt BP Algorithm

Juanhua Su[1,2], Hejun Li[1], Qiming Dong[2], and Ping Liu[2]

[1] Northwestern Polytechnical University, Xi'an 710072, China
sujh@mail.haust.edu.cn
[2] Henan University of Science and Technology, Luoyang 471003, China

Abstract. Cold rolling is often carried out between the solid solution treatment and aging to assist in the aging hardening of Cu-Cr-Zr lead frame alloys. This paper presents the use of an artificial neural network(ANN) to model the non-linear relationship between parameters of rolling and aging with respect to hardness properties of Cu-Cr-Zr alloy. Based on the Gauss-Newton algorithm, Levenberg-Marquardt algorithm with high stability is deduced. High precision of the model is demonstrated as well as good generalization performance. The results show that the Levenberg-Marquardt(L-M) backpropagation(BP) algorithm of ANN system is effective for predicting and analyzing the hardness properties of Cu-Cr-Zr lead frame alloy.

1 Introduction

As a complex non-linear system, ANN models have been widely employed to map the indeterminate relationship between cause and effect variables in many fields. In the present work a universal ANN program is designed on the basis of improvement upon BP algorithms in fabrication of high performance Cu-Cr-Zr alloy.

The Lead frame Cu-Cr-Zr copper alloys in electronic packaging of integrated circuit provide signals channels and fix devices on circuit boards due to high thermal and electrical conductivity as well as high strength [1]. Cold working is often carried out between the solid solution treatment and aging to assist in the aging hardening by introducing a high density of dislocation. The relationship between cold rolled aging process parameters and properties has so far mainly been studied empirically by trial-and-error method, which is both costly and time consuming. So it is necessary to model the relationship by ANN to simulate the rolled aging processes of the alloy.

2 Topology Design of ANN

The selection of input/output variables is a very important aspect of neural network modeling. Usually this choice is based on the background of a process. In the present work the following is used as input parameters: the reduction ratio of cold rolling (δ), the aging temperature (T) and aging time (t). Output variable is determined by the property acquired: hardness (H).

When designing the topology of ANN a trade-off exists between generalization performance and the complexity of training procedure. In this paper a lot of computational instances show that: two-hidden-layer neural networks are suitable. If the sum of squared error criterion (E) is 0.01, perfect topology {3,3,12,1} of the hardness output is found after many times of trial-and-error computation by the ANN program.

3 Levenberg-Marquardt Algorithm

An error BP network is selected because of its greater capability of association and generalization. The classical error correction rule is the steepest descent algorithm, but the method suffers from the drawback that the rate of convergence is reduced rapidly near the extremum points of the objective function. The method used in this study is the Levenberg-Marquardt (L-M) algorithm that is a kind of quasi-Newton methods. Based on the improved Gauss-Newton algorithm, L-M algorithm is deduced and has high stability [2]. According to the above topology of ANN having two hidden layers {3,3,12,1}, the nonlinearity relationship of ANN can be expressed as:

$$y = f(x, w) \qquad (1)$$

where x_i, y_i (i,1,... ,N_3) are sample data couples, w is weights vector.
  The sum of square error (E) is

$$E(w) = \sum_{i=1}^{N_3}(t_i - y_i)^2 = \sum_{i=1}^{N_3} e_i(w)^2 = e(w)^T e(w) = \|e\|^2 \qquad (2)$$

where e is vector function of w vector. The gradient vector (g) is

$$g = g(w) \equiv \frac{\partial E(w)}{\partial w} = 2\sum_{i=1}^{N_3} e_i(w)\frac{\partial e_i(w)}{\partial w} = 2J^T e \qquad (3)$$

where J is the Jacobian matrix of e with respect to the weights w.
  According to the Thaler transformation, equation (1) can be changed into as following ($i,1,...$, N_3; assuming the number of weights are n, $j,1,...$, n)

$$y_i = f(x_i, w_{now}) + \sum_{j=1}^{n}\left(\frac{\partial f(x_i, w)}{\partial w_j}\bigg|_{w=w_{now}}\right)(w_j - w_{j,now}) \qquad (4)$$

Based on the definition of J

$$J(w - w_{now}) = \left(\frac{\partial f(x_i, w)}{\partial w_j}\bigg|_{w=w_{now}}\right)(w_j - w_{j,now}) \qquad (5)$$

Substituting the equations (4) and (5) into equation (2)

$$E(w) = \|e + J(w - w_{now})\|^2 = (e + J(w - w_{now}))^T (e + J(w - w_{now})) \quad (6)$$

To obtain the minimum $E(w)$,

$$\left.\frac{\partial E(w)}{\partial w}\right|_{w=w_{next}} = \nabla\left[(e + J(w_{next} - w_{now}))^T (e + J(w_{next} - w_{now}))\right] = 0 \quad (7)$$

Because of mathematical principle

$$\nabla[f^T(x)g(x)] = \nabla[g^T(x)f(x)] = J_f^T g + J_g^T f \quad (8)$$

So $$\left.\frac{\partial E(w)}{\partial w}\right|_{w=w_{next}} = 2J_{e+J(w_{next}-w_{now})}^T (e + J(w_{next} - w_{now})) = 0 \quad (9)$$

The Gauss-Newton algorithm can be obtained

$$w_{next} = w_{now} - (J^T J)^{-1} J^T e = w_{now} - 0.5(J^T J)^{-1} g \quad (10)$$

If an adjustable constant λ is put into equation (10), the improved *Gauss-Newton* algorithm can become into L-M algorithm that has high stability. The weights of the neurons are iteratively adjusted by:

$$w_{next} = w_{now} - 0.5(J^T J + \lambda I)^{-1} g \quad (11)$$

where J^T is the transposed matrix of J; I is the identity matrix which has the same dimensions with $J^T J$; λ is a adjustable constant multiplier and when it is down to zero, formula (11) is just approximate *Newton*'s method; when λ is large, it becomes the steepest descent algorithm with a small step size[3].

4 Results and Discussion

The relationship between the predicted values from the trained neural network and the measured data from the experiment are shown in table1. A very good agreement between the predicted values from the trained neural network and the validating data is achieved, which indicates that the trained network takes on optimal generalization performance.

Making full use of the domain knowledge stored in the trained networks, three-dimensional graphs can be drawn. Fig.1 shows that the time to peak hardness decrease with increasing ratio of rolling and the peak hardness increases with increasing ratio of rolling. At 480°C in the 40% and 65% rolled condition the peak hardness is 159.9Hv and 162.9Hv for 3.3h and 1.6h respectively. In fig.2 the variation of hardness with increasing temperature and time at 80% ratio of cold rolling reveals that the time to peak hardness decrease with increasing temperature. At 450°C and 486°C the peak hardness is 157.2Hv and153.6Hv for 3.6h and 2.8h respectively. At the peak hardness the finer precipitates and fuller precipitation are available and the hardening effect is optimum.

Table 1. Predicted values(PV) and measured data (MD)

No.	δ/%	T/℃	t/h	PV /HV	MD /HV	Error/%
1	30	500	1.5	143.2	146.1	1.98
2	30	450	8	146.8	142.8	2.8
3	45	400	0.25	122.1	122.3	0.16
4	45	500	6	144.4	143.9	0.35
5	60	470	0.5	150.6	152.8	1.44
6	60	450	2	163.4	161.2	1.36
7	60	470	1	163.3	162.1	0.74
8	60	600	2	143.3	145.7	1.65
9	60	470	4	152.3	151.8	0.33
10	80	450	3	156.7	158.4	1.07
11	80	600	6	126.1	125.5	0.48

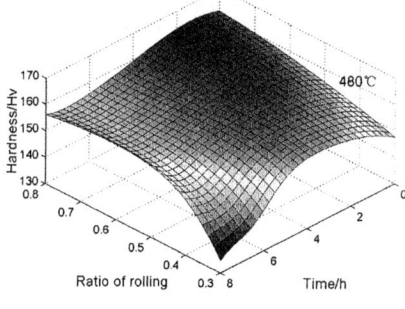

Fig. 1. H as function of T and δ

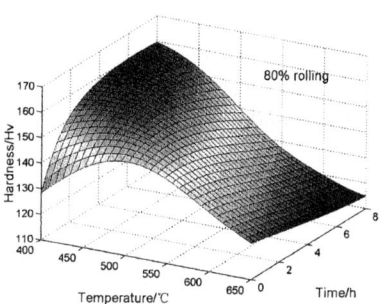

Fig. 2. H as function of T and t

5 Conclusions

(1) A neural network model is proposed for the analysis and prediction of the correlation between rolling and aging processing parameters and mechanical properties in Cu-Cr-Zr lead frame alloy.

(2) The Levenberg- Marquardt training algorithm is deduced from the *Gauss-Newton* algorithm. High precision of the improved model is demonstrated as well as good generalization performance.

Acknowledgements. This work is funded by the Doctorate Foundation of Northwestern Polytechnical University and the Science Research Foundation of Henan University of Science and Technology (2004zy039).

References

1. Ryu H.J., Baik H.K.: Effect of thermomechanical treatment on microstructure and properties of Cu-base lead frame alloy. Journal of Materials Science. 35 (2000) 3641-3646
2. Li A.J.: Modeling of CVI Process in Fabrication of Carbon/Carbon Composites by an Artificial Neural Network. Science in China (Series E). 46 (2003) 173-181
3. Zhang Z.X., Sun C.Z. : Nerve-Fuzziness and Soft Computing (in Chinese). XiAn Jiaotong University Press, Xi'an□(1998)

An Adaptive Control for AC Servo System Using Recurrent Fuzzy Neural Network

Wei Sun and Yaonan Wang

College of Electrical and Information Engineering,
Hunan University, Changsha, P.R. China
david-sun@tom.com
Yaonan@mail.hunu.edu.cn

Abstract. A kind of recurrent fuzzy neural network (RFNN) is constructed by using recurrent neural network (RNN) to realize fuzzy inference. In this kind of RFNN, temporal relations are embedded in the network by adding feedback connections on the first layer of the network. And a RFNN based adaptive control (RFNNBAC) is proposed, in which, two RFNN are used to identify and control plant respectively. Simulation experiments are made by applying proposed RFNNBAC on AC servo control problem to confirm its effectiveness.

1 Introduction

Recently, much research has been done on using neural networks (NN) to identify and control dynamic systems [1]-[3]. NN can be classified as feed forward neural networks and recurrent neural networks. Feed forward neural networks can approximate a continuous function to an arbitrary degree of accuracy. However, feed forward neural network is a static mapping, which can not represent a dynamic mapping well. Although this problem can be solved by using tapped delays, but it requires a large number of neurons to represent dynamical responses in the time domain. On the other hand, recurrent neural networks [4]-[7] are able to represent dynamic mapping very well and store the internal information for updating weights. Recurrent neural network has an internal feedback loop. It captures the dynamical response of a system without external feedback delays. Recurrent neural network is a dynamic mapping and demonstrates good performance in the presence of uncertainties, such as parameter variations, external disturbance, and nonlinear dynamics.

Recurrent fuzzy neural network (RFNN) [8]- [10] is a modified version of recurrent neural network, which use recurrent network to realize fuzzy inference. It is possible to train RFNN using the experience of human operators expressed in term of linguistic rules, and interpret the knowledge acquired from training data in linguistic form. And it is very easy to choose the structure of RFNN and determine the parameters of neurons from linguistic rules. Moreover, with its internal feedback connections, RFNN can temporarily store dynamic information and cope with temporal problems efficiently.

In this paper, a recurrent fuzzy neural network structure is proposed, in which, the temporal relations are embedded by adding feedback connections on the first layer of fuzzy neural network. Back propagation algorithm is used to train the proposed RFNN. For control problem, an adaptive control scheme is proposed, in which two proposed RFNN are used to identify and control plant respectively. Finally, the proposed RFNNBAC is applied on controlling AC servo system, and simulation experiments are made to confirm its effectiveness.

The paper is organized as follows. In section2, RFNN is constructed. RFNNBAC is presented in section 3. In section 4, proposed RFNNBAC is applied on AC servo control and simulation results are given. Finally, some conclusions are drawn in section 5.

2 Construction of RFNN

The structure of the proposed RFNN is shown in Fig.1, which comprises n input variables, m term nodes for each input variable, l rule nodes, and p output nodes. Using u_i^k and O_i^k to denote the input and output of the ith node in the kth layer separately, the operation functions of the nodes in each layer are introduced as follows.

Layer 1 (Input Layer): This layer accepts input variables. Its nodes transmit input values to the next layer. Feedback connections are added in this layer to embed temporal relations in the network. For ith node in this layer, the input and output are represented as

$$u_i^1(k) = x_i^1(k) + w_i^1 O_i^1(k-1), \quad O_i^1(k) = u_i^1(k), \quad i = 1, 2, \ldots, n, \tag{1}$$

where k is the number of iterations, w_i^1 is the recurrent weights. As we know, the inputs of fuzzy inference system always are system error and its variety. By adding feedback connections in input layer of network, only system error needs

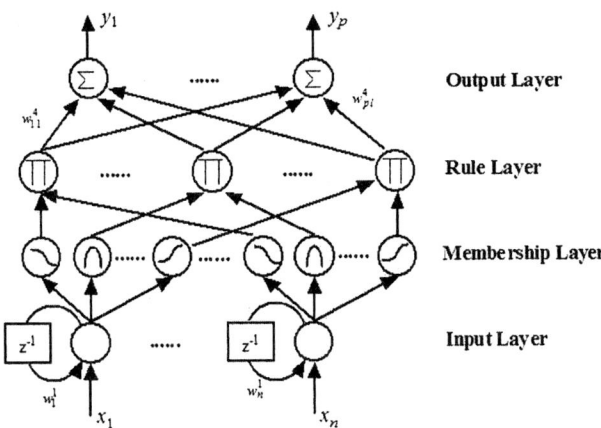

Fig. 1. Structure of four-layer RFNN

to be introduced into network to realize fuzzy inference. This can simplify the network structure and can make the initialization of w_i^1 easy. This is the attribute that distinguishes our RFNN from the others.

Layer 2 (Membership Layer): Nodes in this layer represent the terms of respective linguistic variables. Each node performs a Gaussian membership function.

$$u_{ij}^2 = -\frac{(O_i^1 - a_{ij})^2}{(b_{ij})^2}, \quad O_{ij}^2 = \exp(u_{ij}^2), \tag{2}$$

where $i = 1, 2, \ldots, n, j = 1, 2, \ldots, m$; a_{ij} and b_{ij} are the mean and deviation of the Gaussian membership function; the subscript ij indicates the jth term of the ith input variable.

Layer 3 (Rule Layer): This layer forms the fuzzy rule base and realizes the fuzzy inference. Each node is corresponding to a fuzzy rule. Links before each node represent the preconditions of the corresponding rule, and the node output represents the firing strength of corresponding rule. If the qth fuzzy rule can be described as:

qth rule: if x_1 is $A_1^q, \ldots, x_n$ is A_n^q, then y_1 is $B_1^q, \ldots, y_p$ is B_p^q,

where A_i^q is the term of the ith input in the qth rule; B_j^q is the term of the jth output in the qth rule. Then, the qth node of layer 3 performs the AND operation in qth rule. It multiplies the input signals and output the product.

Using $O_{iq_i}^2$ to denote the membership of x_i to A_i^q, where $q_i \in \{1, 2, \ldots, m\}$, then the input and output of qth node can be described as:

$$u_q^3 = \prod O_{iq_i}^2, \quad O_q^3 = u_q^3, \quad i = 1, 2, \ldots, n; \quad q = 1, 2, \ldots, l. \tag{3}$$

Layer 4 (Output Layer): Nodes in this layer performs the defuzzification operation. The input and output of sth node can be calculated by:

$$u_s^4 = \sum w_{sq}^4 O_q^3, \quad O_s^4 = u_s^4 / \sum O_q^3, \tag{4}$$

where $s = 1, 2, \ldots, p; q = 1, 2, \ldots, l$; w_{sq}^4 is the weight, which represents the output action strength of the sth output associated with the qth rule.

3   RFNNBAC

The block diagram of RFNNBAC is shown in Fig. 2. In this scheme, two RFNNs are used as controller (RFNNC) and identifier (RFNNI) separately. The plant is identified by RFNNI, which provides the model information of the plant to RFNNC. The input of RFNNC is $e(k)$. $e(k)$ is the error between the desired output $r(t)$ and the actual system output $y(k)$. The output of RFNNC is the control signal $u(k)$, which drives the plant such that $e(k)$ is minimized. Since the temporal relations are embedded in RFNN, only $y(k-1)$ and $u(k)$ are need to be fed into RFNNI .

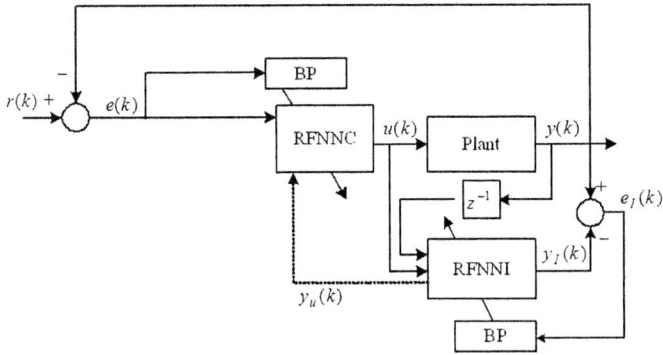

Fig. 2. Structure of RFNNBAC

Both RFNNI and RFNNC are trained by BP algorithm. For training the RFNNI, the cost function is defined as follows:

$$J_I(k) = \frac{1}{2}\sum(e_{Is}(k))^2 = \frac{1}{2}\sum(y_s(k) - y_{Is}(k))^2, \quad (5)$$

where $y_s(k)$ is the sth output of the plant, $y_{Is}(k)$ is the sth output of RFNNI, and $e_{Is}(k)$ is the error between $y_s(k)$ and $y_{Is}(k)$ for each discrete time k.

Then, the parameters of RFNNI can be trained by

$$\theta_I(k+1) = \theta_I(k) - \eta_I \frac{\partial J_I(k)}{\partial \theta_I(k)} = \theta_I(k) + \eta_I \sum e_{Is}(k) \frac{\partial y_{Is}(k)}{\partial \theta_I(k)}, \quad (6)$$

in which, θ_I includes w_{sq}^4, a_{ij}, b_{ij}, and w_i^1 in RFNNI, η_I is the training rate of RFNNI.

For training RFNNC, the cost function is defined as

$$J_C(k) = \frac{1}{2}\sum(e_s(k))^2 = \frac{1}{2}\sum(r_s(k) - y_s(k))^2, \quad (7)$$

where $r_s(k)$ is the sth desired system output, $y_s(k)$ is the sth actual system output and $e_s(k)$ is the error between $r_s(k)$ and $y_s(k)$.

Then, the parameters of RFNNC can be trained by

$$\theta_C(k+1) = \theta_C(k) - \eta_C \frac{\partial J_C(k)}{\partial \theta_C(k)} = \theta_C(k) + \eta_C \sum e_s(k) \frac{\partial y_s(k)}{\partial u_t(k)} \frac{\partial u_t(k)}{\partial \theta_C(k)}, \quad (8)$$

in which, θ_C includes w_{sq}^4, a_{ij}, b_{ij}, and w_i^1 in RFNNC, η_C is the training rate of RFNNC, and u_t is the tth output of RFNNC.

Note that the convergence of the RFNNC cannot be guaranteed until $\frac{\partial y_s(k)}{\partial u_t(k)}$ is known. Obviously, the RFNNI can provide this information to RFNNC.

4 Simulation Experiments

Dynamics of AC servo are highly nonlinear and may contain uncertain elements such as friction and load. Many efforts have been made in developing control

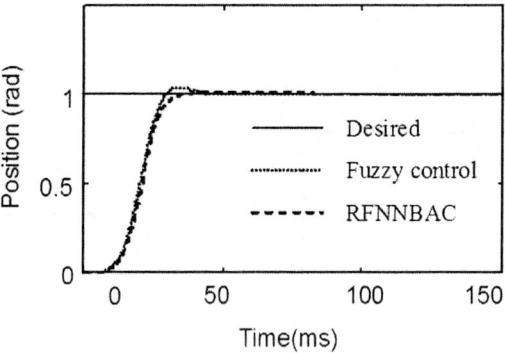

Fig. 3. Step response of system

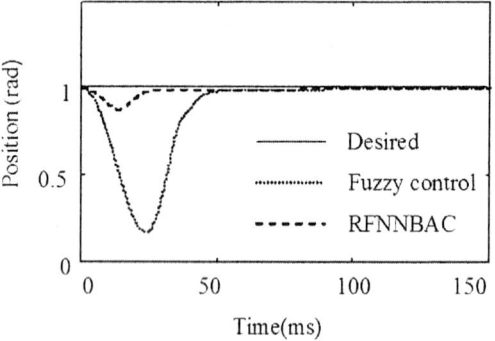

Fig. 4. Disturbance response of system

schemes to achieve the precise servo control of AC motor. In the simulation experiments of this paper, the proposed RFNNBAC is applied on AC servo control to prove its effectiveness. The structure of our AC servo system is just like Fig. 2, the proposed RFNNC is used as position controller. Its input is position error e. Its output is the desired speed of motor. The speed of the motor then is controlled by the speed control subsystem. In our scheme, the speed control subsystem is identified by RFNNI and controlled by RFNNC. The AC motor used for our simulation has following parameters: rated power $P_n = 2.2KW$, rated voltage $U_n = 220V$, rated current $I_n = 5A$, rated rotate speed $n_n = 1440r/min$, resistance of stator $r_s = 2.91\Omega$, resistance of rotor $r_r = 3.04\Omega$, self-induction of stator $l_s = 0.45694H$, self-induction of rotor $l_r = 0.45694H$, mutual inductance between stator and rotor $l_m = 0.44427H$, rated electromagnetic torque $T_{en} = 14N \cdot m$, the number of polar pairs $n_p = 2$, the inertia $J = 0.002276kg \cdot m^2$, rated flux is $\psi_n = 0.96wb$. And the Sampling frequency of the system is 10KHZ.

Simulation results are shown in Fig. 3 and Fig. 4, in which, the proposed RFNNBAC method is compared with common fuzzy control method. Fig. 3

shows the step response of system without load. Fig.4 shows the disturbance response under the condition that motor is added a load of $15N \cdot m$ suddenly when system is stable. From simulation results, it is obvious that the proposed RFNNBAC can control the AC servo system much better than fuzzy control.

5 Conclusions

This paper proposed a RFNN to realize fuzzy inference. The proposed RFNN consists of four layers and the feedback connections are added in first layer. The proposed RFNN can be used for the identification and control of dynamic system. Two RFNN are used to constitute an adaptive control system, one is used as identifier and another is used as controller. The proposed RFNN and adaptive control strategy is used to control an AC servo system and simulation results verified its effectiveness.

References

1. Park, Y. M., Choi, M. S., Lee, K. Y.: An optimal tracking neuro-controller for nonlinear dynamic systems. IEEE Trans. on Neural Networks **7** (1996) 1099–1110
2. Narendra, K. S., Parthasarathy, K.: Identification and control of dynamical systems using neural networks. IEEE Trans. on Neural Networks **1** (1990) 4–27
3. Brdys, M. A., Kulawski, G. J.: Dynamic neural controllers for induction motor. IEEE Trans. on Neural Networks **10** (1999) 340–355
4. Ku, C. C., Lee, K. Y.: Diagonal recurrent neural networks for dynamic systems control. IEEE Trans. on Neural Networks **6** (1995) 144–156
5. Ma, S., Ji, C.: Fast training of recurrent neural networks based on the EM algorithm. IEEE Trans. on Neural Networks **9** (1998) 11–26
6. Sundareshan, M. K., Condarcure, T. A.: Recurrent neural-network training by a learning automaton approach for trajectory learning and control system design. IEEE Trans. on Neural Networks **9** (1998) 354–368
7. Liang, X. B., Wang, J.: A recurrent neural network for nonlinear optimization with a continuously differentiable objective function and bound constraints. IEEE Trans. on Neural Networks **11** (2000) 1251–1262
8. Lee, C. H., Teng,C. C.: Identification and control of dynamic systems using recurrent fuzzy neural networks. IEEE Trans. on Fuzzy Systems **8** (2000) 349–366
9. Lin, C. T., Chang, C. L., Cheng, W. C.: A recurrent fuzzy cellular neural network system with automatic structure and template learning. IEEE Trans. on Circuits and Systems **51** (2004) 1024–1035
10. Lin, C. M., Hsu, C. F.: Supervisory recurrent fuzzy neural network control of wing rock for slender delta wings. IEEE Trans. on Fuzzy Systems **12** (2004) 733–742

PSO-Based Model Predictive Control for Nonlinear Processes[1]

Xihuai Wang and Jianmei Xiao

Department of Electrical and Automation, Shanghai Maritime University,
Shanghai 200135, China
wxh@shmtu.edu.cn, jmxiao@cen.shmtu.edu.cn

Abstract. A novel approach for the implementation of nonlinear model predictive control (MPC) is proposed using neural network and particle swarm optimization (PSO). A three-layered radial basis function neural network is used to generate multi-step predictive outputs of the controlled process. A modified PSO with simulated annealing is used at the optimization process in MPC. The proposed algorithm enhances the convergence and accuracy of the controller optimization. Applications to a discrete time nonlinear process and a thermal power unit load system are studied. The simulation results demonstrate the effectiveness of the proposed algorithm.

1 Introduction

Model predictive control (MPC) refers to a class of algorithms that compute a sequence of manipulated variable adjustments in order to optimize the future behavior of a controlled process [1]. Predictive control seems extremely powerful for processes with dead-time or if the set-point is programmed. Many predictive control technique have been developed, based on the assumption that the plant to be controlled can be regarded as a linear system and that its model is available a priori. Such linear model-based approaches show limited control performance. Naturally several methods involving specific nonlinear modes have also been suggested [2]. Recently, some neural network-based predictive control methods have been found to be effective in controlling a wide class of nonlinear progress [3]. Most previous works are, however, based on the nonlinear programming method [4], which provides local optimum values only and in addition these values depend on the selection of the starting point.

The PSO is known to have more chances of finding an optimal value than descent-based nonlinear programming methods for optimization problems. In this paper, a particle swarm optimization with simulated annealing (SAPSO) technique is adopted to obtain optimal future control inputs in MPC for a discrete time nonlinear process and a thermal power unit load system. The simulation results demonstrate the effectiveness of the proposed algorithm.

---

[1] This work was supported by Key Science Project of Shanghai Education (04FA02).

2 Neural Network-Based Prediction Model

A radial basis function (RBF) neural network has a three-layer architecture with no feedback [5-7]. The hidden layer consists of H hidden neurons (radial basis units), with radial activation functions. A typical choice for this function is the Gaussian function. So, the output of the h-th hidden neuron, z_h, is a radial basis function that defines a spherical receptive field in R^H given by the following equation:

$$z_h = \Phi(\|x - c_k\|) = \exp(-\frac{(x-c_h)^T(x-c_h)}{2\sigma_h^2}), \quad \forall h \tag{1}$$

In other words, each neuron in the hidden layer has a substantial finite spherical activation region, determined by the Euclidean distance between input vector, x, and the center, c_h, of the function z_h normalized with respect to the scaling factor σ_h.

From (1) we can know that each hidden neuron is associated with $H+1$ internal parameters; the H components of vector c_h that represents the H dimensional position of the radial function, and σ_h that determines the receptive field of the neuron. The receptive field is the region of the input space over which the neuron has an appreciable response. The set of hidden neurons is designed so that they cover all the significant regions of the input vector space.

Consider the following general discrete-time nonlinear process:

$$y(k+1) = f(y(k-m_1+1), \cdots, y(k), u(k-m_2+1), \cdots, u(k)) \tag{2}$$

where f(·) is a smooth function with real (m1+m2)arguments. The overall configuration of the prediction model is shown in Fig. 1.

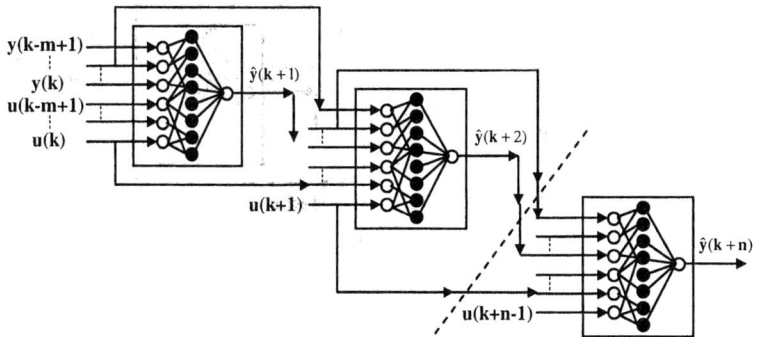

Fig. 1. The structure of predictive model

The prediction output is get by using neural network-based n-step ahead predictor, as follows:

$$y = \sum_{h=1}^{H} w_h z_h \tag{3}$$

The input x of the prediction model is the present and past input data of the plant. Once a predicted output is obtained, the value is used to provide further prediction outputs by taking it as an element of the input vector x.

3 PSO-Based Predictive Control

PSO is a kind of algorithm searching the best answer by simulating the movement and flocking of birds [8-10]. The algorithm initialized the flock of birds randomly over the searching space, every bird is called as a "particle". These "particles" move with a certain law and find the global best result after some iteration. At each iteration, each particle adjusts its velocity vector, based on its momentum and the influence of its best solution (P_{best}) and the best solution of its neighbors (G_{best}), then computes a new point to examine. The original PSO formulae are:

$$v[] = w \cdot v[] + c_1 \cdot rand() \cdot (G_{best}[] - present[])$$
$$+ c_2 \cdot rand()(P_{best} - present[]) \quad (4)$$
$$present[] = present[] + v[]$$

where $v[\ ]$ is the velocity vector, $n \times d$ matrix; n is the number of the particles; d is the number of channels (variables); c_1, c_2 are the acceleration constants and positive constants; $rand$ is a random number between 0 and 1; $present[\ ]$ is the location vector; w is the inertia weight.

PSO has a strong ability finding the most optimistic result. Meanwhile it has a disadvantage of local minimum. SA has a strong ability finding the local optimistic result. And it can avoid the problem of local minimum. But it' ability finding the global optimistic result is weak. Combining PSO and SA, learning from other's strong points to offset one's weaknesses each other, this is the basic idea of the SAPSO.

Similar with the basic PSO algorithm, the SAPSO algorithm's searching process is also started from initializing a group of random particles. First, each particle is simulated annealed independently and a group of new individuals are generated. Then, particles of the new generation are obtained after transforming each particle's velocity and position according to the equation (1). This process repeats time after time until the terminating condition is satisfied.

In the process of simulated annealing, the new individuals are given randomly around the original individuals. Here we set the changing range of original particles as a parameter $r1$, to each particle:

$$present = present + r1 - r1 \cdot 2 \cdot rand(1) \quad (5)$$

where $rand(1)$ is a random number between 0 and 1, the parameter $r1$ here also reduces step by step as the generation increasing just like w.

In the prediction control, an evaluation function in a PSO is replaced by a cost function:

$$J(u) = \frac{1}{2}\sum_{i=1}^{n}\{y_r(k+i) - \hat{y}(k+i)\}^2 \quad (6)$$

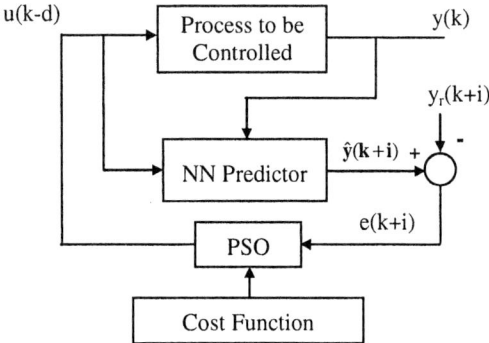

Fig. 2. The diagram of proposed PSO-based MPC

where y is a function of u as given in Eq. 3 and y_r is the reference input. The future control input sequence $u=[u(k), u(k+1), \ldots, u(k+n-1)]^T$ is obtained by minimizing Eq. 6 via a particle swarm optimization.

4 Simulation

To demonstrate the control performance of the PSO-based predictive controller, consider the following two examples:

4.1 Discrete Time Nonlinear Process

$$y(k+1) = -0.3y(k) + 0.5\sin(0.6\pi \cdot u(k)) \cdot u(k) \tag{7}$$

In the simulation, the numbers of input, hidden, and output neurons are $n_i=6$, $n_h=20$ and $n_o=1$, respectively. The parameters of the PSO algorithm are set to pop_size=20,

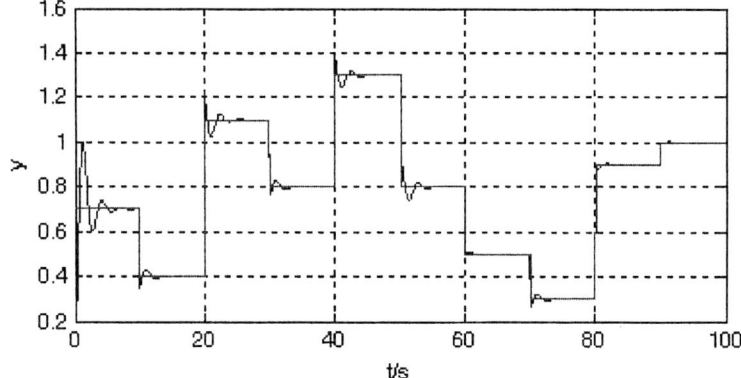

Fig. 3. The output and reference input of system with PSO-based MPC

Table 1. Comparision PSO with GA and quasi-Newton

Predictive horizon	quasi-Newton[4]	GA[4]		PSO	
		pop-size=20	pop-size=50	pop-size=20	pop-size=50
1	0.0505	0.0114	0.0103	0.0102	0.0093
2	0.0204	0.0105	0.0100	0.0081	0.0080

the inertia weight $w=0.25$, acceleration constants $c_1=c_2=1.495$. The range of input is [0 1.5] and the set-point is updated every 10s with a random value selected from $0.3<y_r<1.3$. The initial value of control input u_0 is set to 0.7. Fig. 3 shows the control result obtained by PSO.

As shown in Fig. 3, the plant output shows a good tracking result. The PSO method is compared with the GA method and the quasi-Newton method in terms of squared average tracking error (E_{ave}) as shown in Table 1.

4.2 Thermal Power Unit Load System

The proposed PSO-based predictive controlled is also applied to a power unit load system control problem. Thermal power unit load system is a multi-variable system with 2 inputs and 2 outputs. The object of load system is responding the load requirement rapidly as soon as possible and that the variety of main steam pressure is guaranteed in allowable scope.

In thermal power unit load system, power loop and pressure loop are seriously coupled. Therefore, when adopting boiler-follow mode, the input speed of turbine should be restricted, which will avoid overtopping allowable scope of pressure. And, in order to avoid thermal impulsion to thermal equipments, the input speed should be restricted too. In addition, constraints on the amplitude of inputs are necessary because of limitations of actuators. Fortunately, the presented multi-variable PSO-based MPC is competent for this difficult control problem. Simulation results show that the system adopting the novel algorithm has favorable performance.

The following mathematical model of thermal power unit load system is adopted [11-12].

$$\begin{bmatrix} N_E \\ P_T \end{bmatrix} = \begin{bmatrix} \dfrac{68.81s}{(1+12s)(1+82s)} & \dfrac{1}{(1+83s)^2} \\ -2.194(\dfrac{0.064}{1+3s}+\dfrac{0.936}{1+124s}) & \dfrac{2.194}{(1+80s)^2} \end{bmatrix} \begin{bmatrix} u_T \\ u_B \end{bmatrix} \quad (8)$$

where, u_T, u_B denote governor valve position, the fuel and air flow rate respectively. N_E and P_T represent actual power output and steam pressure.

Sample time takes 5 seconds, the parameters of the PSO algorithm are set to pop_size=100, the inertia weight $w=0.45$, acceleration constants $c_1=c_2=1.495$. Adopting boiler-follow mode, set point of pressure keeps invariable, and load runs up and down at the speed of 3% per minute, the set point trajectories are shown in Fig.4.

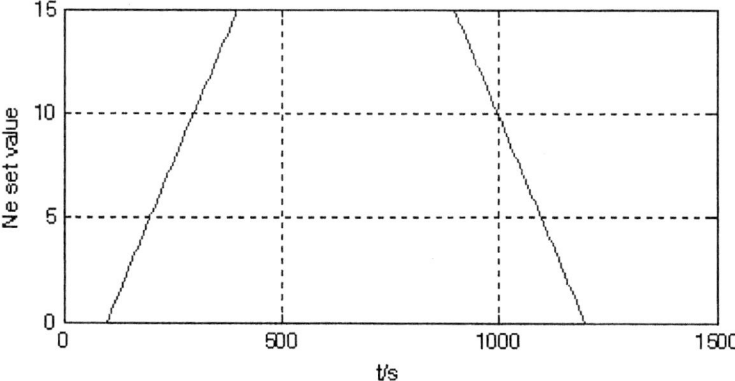

Fig. 4. Power set value curves

The system responses are shown as solid lines in Fig.5. The results show that the system has excellent load tracking ability and superheated steam pressure fluctuates in small scale.

When thermal power unit properties vary from Eq. 8 to the following:

$$\begin{bmatrix} N_E \\ P_T \end{bmatrix} = \begin{bmatrix} \dfrac{68.81s}{(1+10s)(1+100s)} & \dfrac{1}{(1+90s)^2} \\ -2.194(\dfrac{0.064}{1+8s} + \dfrac{0.936}{1+150s}) & \dfrac{2.194}{(1+65s)^2} \end{bmatrix} \begin{bmatrix} u_T \\ u_B \end{bmatrix} \qquad (9)$$

Here, the model is unmatched, and the system responses are shown as dotted lines in Fig.5. The results show that the system has favorable robustness; especially, the change of unit characteristics doesn't weaken the load-tracking ability.

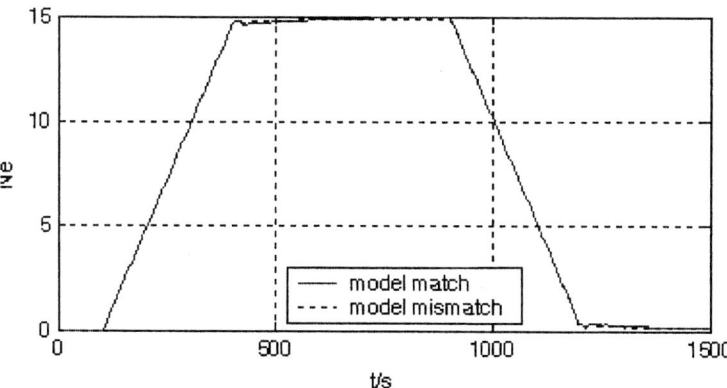

(a) Actual power response curves

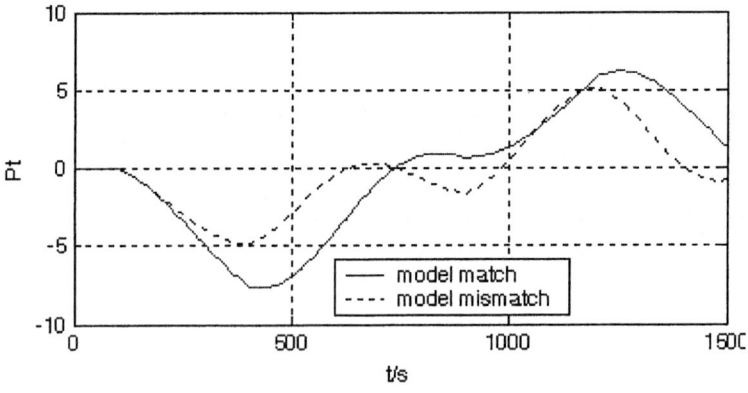

(b) Superheated steam pressure response curves

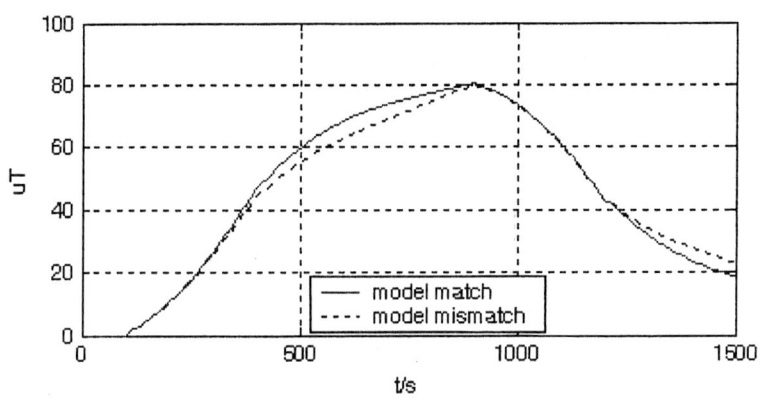

(c) Turbine valve position response curves

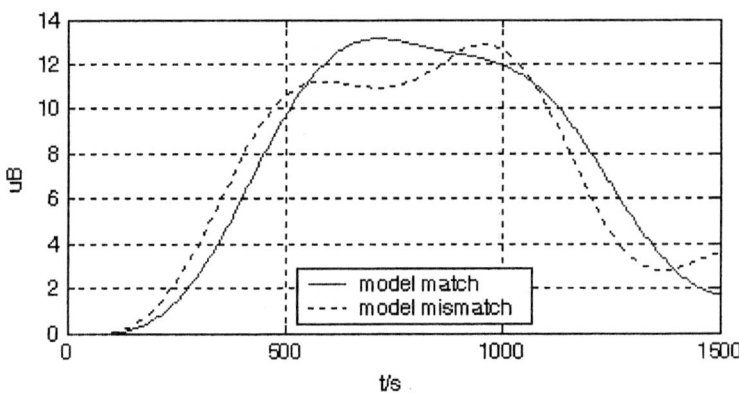

(d) Boiler combustion ratio response curves

Fig. 5. The simulation results of power unit load system with PSO-based MPC

5 Conclusion

It is found from extensive simulation studies that the tracking error of the proposed PSO-based control system is less than that of a GA method and a quasi-Newton method. The PSO-based predictive control method is robust to selection of the control input value and can be used to control a class of nonlinear processes in which control actions can be executed slowly. The proposed multi-variable MPC algorithm is applied to thermal power unit load system, and simulation results show that the system has favorable performance and strong robustness; especially, the variety of unit characteristics doesn't weaken load-tracking ability.

References

1. Richalet J.: Industrial applications of model based predictive control. Automatica, 29 (1993) 1251-1274
2. Li S.Y., Du G.N.: Online parameter tuning of generalized predictive controller based on fuzzy satisfying degree function. Control and Decision, 17 (2002) 852-855
3. Saint-Donat J., Bhat N., McAvoy T.J.: Neural net based model predictive control. Int. J. Control, 54 (1991) 1453-1468
4. Shin S.C., Park S.B.: GA-based predictive control for nonlinear processes. Electronics Letters, 34 (1998) 1980-1981
5. Catelani, M., Fort, A.: Fault diagnosis of electronic analog circuits using a radial basis function network classifier. Measurement. 28 (2000) 147–158
6. Xiao J.M., Wang X.H.: Highway traffic flow model using FCM-RBF neural network. In: F.L.Yin, J. Wang, C. Guo (eds.): Advances in Neural Networks. Lecture Notes in Computer Science, 3174. Springer-Verlag, Berlin Heidelberg New York (2004) 956-961
7. Xiao J.M., Zhang T.F., Wang X.H.: Ship power load prediction based on RST and RBF neural networks. In: J. Wang, X. Liao, and Z. Yi (Eds.): ISNN 2005, Lecture Notes in Computer Science, 3498. Springer-Verlag, Berlin Heidelberg New York (2005) 648-653
8. Eberhart R.C., Kennedy J.: A new optimizer using particles swarm theory. Proceedings of Sixth International Symposium on Micro Machine and Human Science, (1995) 39-43
9. Li J.J., Wang X.H.: A modified particle swarm optimization algorithm. Proceeding of the 5th World Congress on Intelligent Control and Automation, (2004) 354-356
10. Xiao J.M., Li J.J., Wang X.H.: Modified particle swarm optimization algorithm for vehicle routing problem. Computer Integrated Manufacturing Systems, 11 (2004) 577-581
11. Han P., Yu P., Wang G.Y., Wang D.F.: Predictive functional control in thermal power unit load systems. Transactions of China Electro Technical Society, 19 (2004) 47-52
12. Ju G., Wei H.Q.: Multivariable model predictive control for thermal power unit load systems. Proceedings of CSEE, 22 (2002) 144-148

Low Cost Implementation of Artificial Neural Network Based Space Vector Modulation

Tarık Erfidan and Erhan Butun

Kocaeli University, Engineering Faculty,
Electrical Engineering Department,
Veziroglu Campus, Izmit, Kocaeli, Turkey
{tarik, ebutun}@kou.edu.tr

Abstract. This paper presents a neural network based implementation of space vector modulation (SVM) of a voltage-fed inverter that only includes the under-modulation region. SVM has recently grown as a very popular pulse width modulation (PWM) method for voltage-fed converter ac drives because of its superior harmonic quality and extended linear range of operation. However, a difficulty of SVM is that it requires complex on-line computation that usually limits its operation up to several kHz of switching frequency. Switching frequency can be extended by using high-speed digital signal processing (DSP) card and simplifying computations by using look-up tables. In our work a low cost microcontroller was used instead of DSP card. The performances of the drive with artificial neural network (ANN) based sector selected SVM are faster than conventional SVM. The performances of the drive with ANN based SVM are excellent.

1 Introduction

In recent years, ANNs have become very useful tools to develop models which express the interrelationship between the input and the output of complicated systems. Both neural network and PWM principles are basically input-output mapping phenomena. The key benefit of ANNs in the domain of engineering design and group technology is in their ability to store a large set of parameter patterns as memories for the system which can be later recalled. Therefore, theoretically it should be possible to synthesize PWM signals directly with a neural network replacing the conventional SVM algorithm. Once its structure is defined the ANNs must be trained to determine the weights and biases in the network. Switching schemes play the most important role in voltage-source inverters and rectifiers widely applied in high-performance drivers and reactive power compensation systems. Amongst various switching schemes, the SVM technique is popular because of its two excellent features,

    a. Its maximum output voltage 15.5% greater
    b. The number of switching is about 30% less at the same carrier frequency than the one obtained by the sinusoidal PWM method [2, 4].

2 Space-Vector PWM

The main function of the SVM strategy is to determine the pulse-width for active sectors within each sampling interval that contribute fundamental components in the line-to-line voltages. The optimal sequence of the pulse within the sampling interval leads to a superior-performing SVM modulator.

In the vector space as shown in Fig.1, according to the equivalence principle, the following operation rules are obeyed:

$$\vec{U}_1 = -\vec{U}_4 \quad \vec{U}_2 = -\vec{U}_5 \quad \vec{U}_3 = -\vec{U}_6 \quad \vec{U}_1 + \vec{U}_3 + \vec{U}_5 = \vec{0} \tag{1}$$

In one sampling interval, the output voltage vector can be written as

$$\vec{U}(t) = \frac{t_0}{T_s}\vec{U}_0 + \frac{t_1}{T_s}\vec{U}_1 + \ldots + \frac{t_7}{T_s}\vec{U}_7 \tag{2}$$

Where, $t_0, t_1, \ldots, t_7$ is the turn-on time of the vectors $\vec{U}_1, \ldots, \vec{U}_7; t_0, t_1, \ldots, t_7 \geq 0$, $\sum_{i=0}^{7} t_i = T_s$ and T_s is the sampling time.

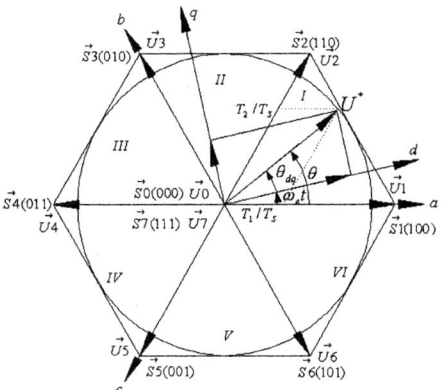

Fig. 1. Voltage vector space

According to equations (1) and (2), the decomposition of $\vec{U}$ into $\vec{U}_1, \vec{U}_2, \ldots, \vec{U}_7$ has infinite ways. However, in order to reduce the number of switching actions and make full use of active turn-on time for space vectors, the vector $\vec{U}$ is commonly split into the two nearest adjacent voltage vectors and zero vectors $\vec{U}_0$ and $\vec{U}_7$ in an arbitrary sector. The switching pattern of the SVM in one sampling interval does affect the number of switching actions. Fewer switching actions lead to less switching loss. All transitions between arbitrary two succeeding space vectors for the optimal switching pattern need only one switching action. The output of the modulator generates the PWM patterns for the inverter switches [3].

The SVM strategy in under-modulation region is based on generating three consecutive switching voltage vectors in sampling period (T_s) such that the average output voltage matches with that of the reference voltage. The equations for effective time of the inverter switching states can be given as

$$t_a = DT_s \sin\left(\frac{\pi}{3} - \theta_r\right) \tag{3}$$

$$t_b = DT_s \sin\theta_r \tag{4}$$

$$t_0 = \frac{T_s - (t_a + t_b)}{2} \tag{5}$$

Where
  t_a = time of switching vector that lags U^*
  t_b = time of switching vector that leads U^*
  t_0 = time of zero switching vector
  T_s = $1/f_s$ = sampling time (f_s = switching frequency)
  θ_r = angle of U^* in a 60 deg. sector, and

$$D = \frac{\sqrt{3}.U^*}{E} \tag{6}$$

The t_a, t_b, t_0 times are distributed to generate symmetrical PWM pulses.

3 Experimental Setup of the System

The block diagram of the implemented circuit is shown in Fig. 2. We used PIC-16F877 as a microcontroller with 33 bit I/O, 6 channels of 8-bit Analog-to-Digital (A/D) converter with 2 additional timers. The IGBT driver shown in Fig. 3 is used to generate switching pulses and to control the inverter. PIC-16F877 microcontroller has a 10 KB program memory, so that an additional memory (EPROM) is needed. The reference wave and carrier wave data are written to EPROM.

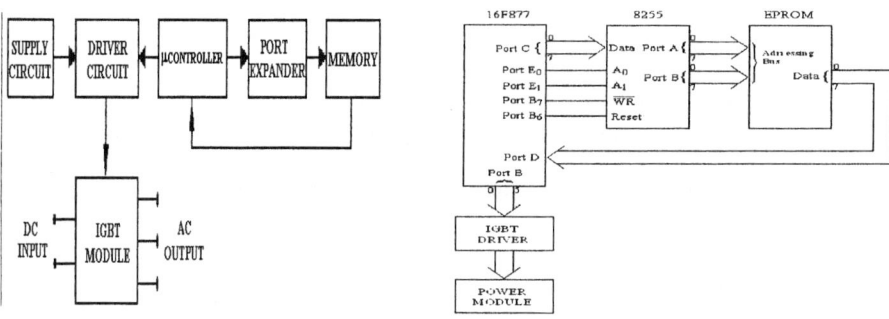

Fig. 2. The block diagram of circuit set-up   **Fig. 3.** Application circuit block diagram

Finally, the IGBT module operates to generate AC on load.

4 Artificial Neural Networks

Artificial neuron is designed for copy to input and output characteristics of biological neuron. Each cell consists of desired number of input and output such as weight, a summation point, a nonlinear activation function and single output in the neural network system. Output of the cell can supply many cells at the same time. Here, each input is multiplied by its weight and the results are sum. The summation is used to define of neuron's activation level as shown Fig. 4.

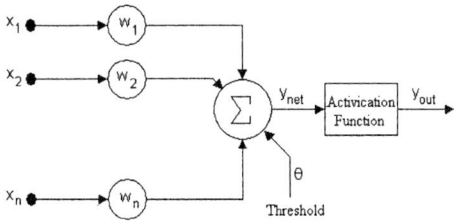

Fig. 4. Model of an ANN

Here x_i, y_{out}, and w_i shows inputs, outputs and weights, respectively. Summation block shows structure of the biological cell. Input vector x (x_1, x_2, ..., x_n) has applied input of the cell and then multiplied by weight vector w (w_1, w_2, ..., w_n). Output vector y_{net} is obtained by;

$$y_{net} = w \cdot x^T \qquad (7)$$

Summation is a function which calculates y_{net} value. It is used for input of the artificial neurons as an input signal. y_{net} is extracted by;

$$y_{net} = \sum_{i=1}^{n} w_i x_i \qquad (8)$$

Output signal (y_{out}) is obtained by application of activation function (f_{ak}) to y_{net}

$$y_{out} = f_{ak}(y_{net}) \qquad (9)$$

Here, activation function (f_{ak}) which calculated output of the artificial neural cell is the most important part of the ANN system.

5 ANN Training

Both neural network and PWM principles are basically input-output mapping phenomena. Therefore, theoretically it should be possible to synthesize PWM signals directly with a neural network replacing the conventional SVM algorithm. Once its structure is defined the ANN must be trained to determine the weights and biases in the network as shown in Fig.5. Two conditions must be satisfied for proper training of the ANN:

1. A set of input – output data representing as wide as possible the operating conditions of the SVM sector selection to be modeled,
2. a numerical algorithm capable of giving accurate and efficient network training.

A multilayer feed forward ANN with back propagation training algorithm is used. To implement of the active sectors selection using ANN, all possible input (position) output (sector) data are logged as ANNs data set. A MATLAB program is written to train the ANNs with the numerical results obtained from the optimal preview controller. The ANNs model is developed using Levenberg-Marquardt approximation algorithm. The accuracy of the neural network models developed in this study has been tested comparing the simulated data obtained from the neural network model with the actual values. The result shows that Levenberg-Marquardt approximation algorithm is the preferred method, although this algorithm reduces the root of the mean sum of the squared (RMS) error to a significantly small value slowly but with minimum iteration number as we need for our 8-bit microcontroller.

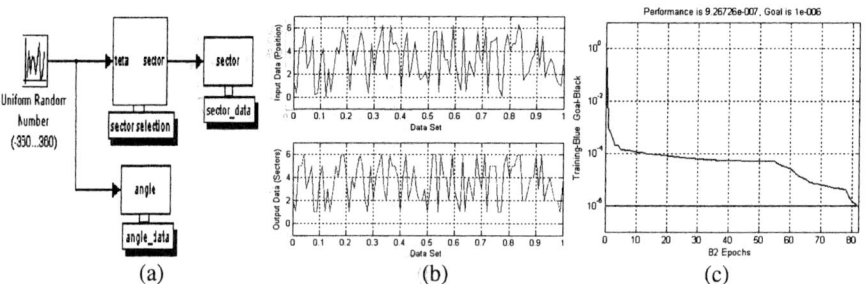

(a)   (b)   (c)

Fig. 5. a. System model, b. data set to obtain data and c. Training process

6 Simulation and Experimental Results

The proposed neural network has the advantages of its simple structure and faster response than conventional active sector computation algorithm. Proposed SVM

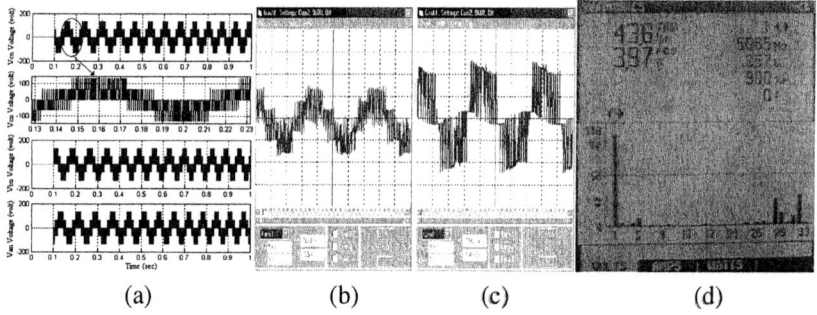

(a)   (b)   (c)   (d)

Fig. 6. Simulation results of (a) Phase voltages, Experimental results of (b) Phase voltages, (c) Phase to phase voltages (d) harmonics of PWM with 1 kHz switching periods

structure is tested on scalar controlled induction machine and simulation results are given below. The agreement between the simulated characteristics in Fig.6 (a) and those measured experimentally in Fig.6 (b) is satisfactory.

7 Conclusions

An ANN based implementation of SVM of a voltage-fed inverter that only includes the under-modulation region was introduced herein. The proposed SVM algorithm gives directly the conduction times of switches to modulate the voltage to be generated without a considerable computational load. The digital words corresponding to turn-on time are generated by the network and then converted to pulse-widths by a single timer. The training data were generated by simulation of a conventional SVM algorithm, and then a back-propagation technique in the MATLAB was used for offline training. But proposed SVM is low-cost according to the SVM structure with DSP and has fewer harmonics than conventional SVM structure. A simple and straightforward algorithm could yield the substantial advantage of a lower CPU load then a possibly higher switching frequency or, conversely, a less powerful and, thus, cheaper microprocessor. The proposed technique points out a very simple structure and it is suitable even for low-cost, standard microcontroller-based inverters. Experimental results have been included to verify the effectiveness of the proposed method. This method is more interesting solution for industrial application thanks to following viable advantages:

1. Simple calculation of switching times,
2. 15% greater DC line voltage,
3. Low harmonic effects and high modulation index
4. 30% less switching number due to conventional method with same frequency.

References

1. J.O.Krah, J,Holtz, "High Performance Current Regulation for Low Inductance Servo Motors", LEEE IAS Annu. Meet. Conf. Rec., (1998), pp. 490-499.
2. J.Holtz, " Pulsewidth Modulation for Electronic Power Conversion", Proc. IEEE. Vol. 82, Annu. (1994), pp. 1194-1214.
3. J.O. Pinto, B.K. Bose, L.E.B. da Silva S.K. Mondal, M.P. Kazmierkowski "A Neural-Network-Based Space-Vector PWM Controller for Voltage-Fed Inverter Induction Induction Motor Drive", IEEE Transactions on Industry Applications, Vol.38, No.3, (2002).
4. J.Holtz, W.Lotzcat, A.Hambadkone, "On Continuous Control of PWM Inverters in the Over Modulation Range Including the Six-Step Mode" in Proc. IEEE IECON'92, (1992), pp. 307-312.

A Novel Multispectral Imaging Analysis Method for White Blood Cell Detection

Hongbo Zhang, Libo Zeng, Hengyu Ke, Hong Zheng, and Qiongshui Wu

School of Electronic Information, Wuhan University,
Wuhan 430072, P.R. China
lbzeng@public.wh.hb.cn

Abstract. This paper presents a novel approach for automatic detection of white blood cells in bone marrow microscopic images. Far more different from traditional color imaging analysis methods, a multispectral imaging techniques for image analysis is introduced. Multispectral image can not only show the spatial features of a cell, but also reveal the unique spectral information of each pixel. The supported vector machine (SVM) classifier is employed to train the spectrum vector of a pixel, and the output of the classifier can indicate the class type of the pixel: nucleus, erythrocytes, cytoplasm and background. Experimental results show that, compared with any other method previously reported, our method is more robust, precise and insensitive to smear staining and illumination condition.

1 Introduction

In this paper, we propose a novel approach for automatic detection of white blood cells in bone marrow microscopic images. Different from traditional grey or color imaging method[1-4], we use multispectral imaging analysis techniques[5][6]. It combines conventional digital imaging with spectroscopy, which can provide us not only common spatial information but also useful spectral information. A mass of experiments are done under the 1000 magnification, and the results show that our segmentation results are highly satisfactory, and it is more robust and precise than conventional color imaging method. The image segmentation approach will be discussed in next section.

2 Methodology

In our approach, the whole image is segmented into four types of regions: nucleus, cytoplasm, erythrocytes and background, which are shown in Fig. 1 (a). For each pixel P(i,j) in a multispectral image, the spectrum shown in Fig. 1 (b) can be expressed as a vector x:

$$x = (w_{\lambda 1}, \cdots, w_{\lambda n})^T \qquad (1)$$

where λ_k is the k th wavelength, $w_{\lambda k}$ is grey intensity at wavelength λ_k, n is the count of wavelength band, here n=30.

A Novel Multispectral Imaging Analysis Method for White Blood Cell Detection

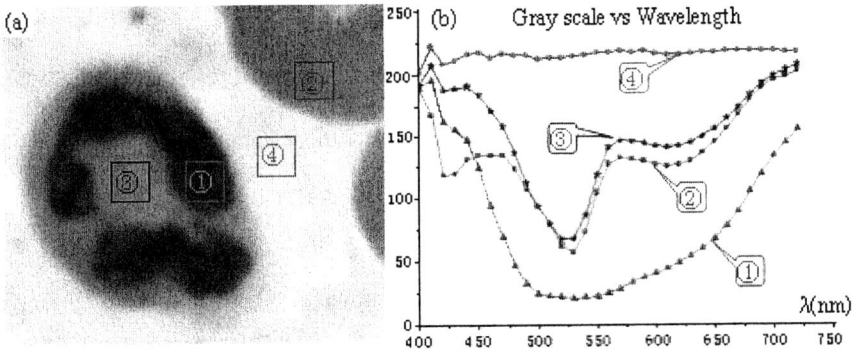

Fig. 1. (a) A typical marrow bone image which consists of a polymorphonuclear leucocyte. ①nucleus ② erythrocytes ③ cytoplasm ④background. (b)Transmitted spectrum of different parts marked in (a). Each rectangle region in (a) is regarded as a point, whose gray scale is the average in the rectangle.

From Fig. 1 (b), we can find that different regions have quite different spectra, though their color may be very similar. So spectra can be used to discriminate different regions, which is the key issue of our segmentation method. Our segmentation is a pixel level classification. And we selected SVM as our classifier. The spectrum of each pixel is used as feature and directly fed into a SVM classifier, and all the pixels are classified into four classes: nucleus, cytoplasm, erythrocytes and background, which are labeled with 1, 2, 3 and 4 respectively as a class type.

The segmentation steps are outlined as follows:

Step 1: Thirty-band multispectral images are manually segmented under the direction of a pathologist.

Step 2: For each image segmented in step 1, manually selected nucleus regions, cytoplasm regions, erythrocytes regions and background regions. Then the spectrum of each pixel in the selected regions is extracted and saved as standard training dataset.

Step 3: All the saved training datasets are fed into a SVM classifier for training and the classification model is obtained.

Step 4: For tested images, the spectrum vector of a pixel is fed into the trained classifier for classification, and the output of the classifier is the class type of the pixel.

For our SVM classifier, we employ C-support Vector Classification(C-SVC)[7]. Since the classification is a multi-class classification, we used the one-against-one approach[8] in which $k(k-1)/2$ classifiers are constructed and each one trains data from two different classes. In classification we propose a voting strategy: each binary classification is considered to be a voting where votes can be cast for all data points. Finally, each point is designated to be in a class with maximum number of votes. A polynomial is selected as the kernel function, and the degree of the polynomial is 3. The program code and more detailed discussion about C-SVC algorithm can be found at Dr. Chih-Jen Lin's Home Page.

Since C-SVC is not very fast, especially if every pixel in a multispectral image is classified with C-SVC, it will be very time-consuming. In order to speed up the classification, background regions are firstly removed by applying a constant threshold value of 200 to the grey image at wavelength 530nm. From Fig. 1(b), it can be easily seen that the difference between background and other regions is very obvious.

3 Experimental Results and Discussions

Eighty multispectral images captured under 1000 magnification were used to evaluate proposed segmentation algorithm. Part of segmentation results are shown in Fig. 2. The segmentation results were evaluated with human eyes. For the nucleus segmentation, the correct rates for acidophilic granulocytes and basophiles are not high due to color variance and lack of training samples, but they are over 94% for other cells. For the cytoplasm segmentation, because the color of cytoplasm is quite similar to erythroblast, the correct rates for orthochromatic normoblasts is up to 87%, but for other cells, it is up to 95%. In general, the experimental results are very satisfactory.

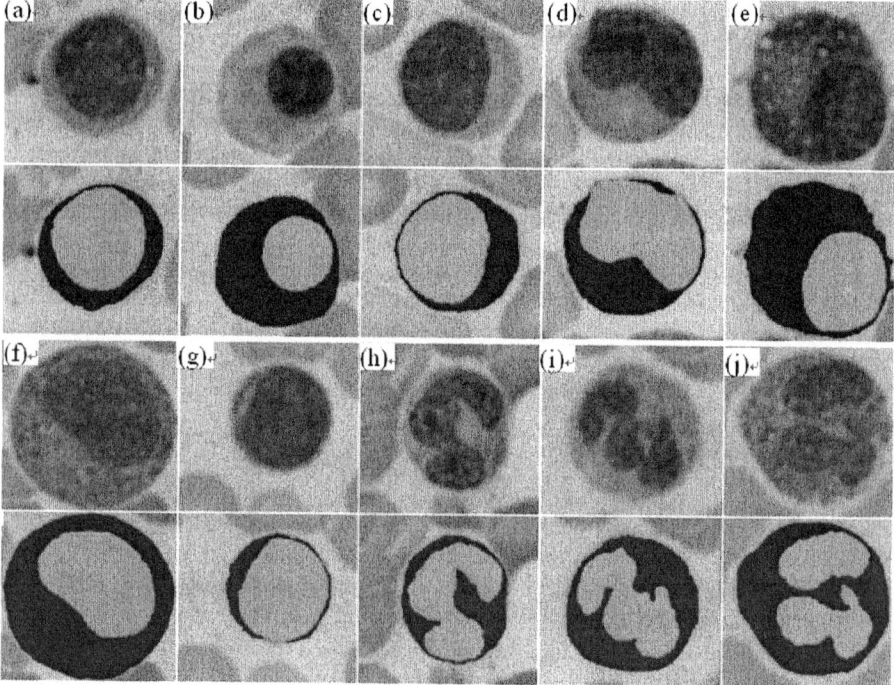

Fig. 2. Segmentation results. (a) early erythroblast (b) orthochromatic normoblast (c) myelocyte (d) monocyte (e) plasmocyte (f) metagranulocyte (g) lymphocyte (h) band-cell (i) polymorphonuclear leucocyte (j) acidophil leukocyte.

4 Conclusions

A multi-spectrum based cell segmentation method is proposed in this paper. It is more robust and precise than conventional color imaging method. Experimental results prove that applying multispectral imaging analysis techniques to the detection of white blood cells is successful. They also prove that SVM-based classifier is a powerful tool in spectrum classification.

References

1. Hengen, H., Spoor, S., Pandit, M.: Analysis of Blood and Bone Marrow Smears Using Digital Image Processing Techniques. Proc. SPIE. Int. Soc. Opt. Eng. (2002) 624-635
2. Park, J.S., Keller, J.M.: Fuzzy Patch Label Relaxation in Bone Marrow Cell Segmentation. Proc. IEEE. Int. Conf. Syst. Man. Cybern. 2 (1997) 1133-1138
3. Sobrevilla, P., Montseny, E., Keller, J.: White Blood Cell Detection in Bone Marrow Images. Annu. Conf. North. Am. Fuzzy. Inf. Process. Soc. NAFIPS. (1999) 403-407
4. Keller, J.M., Gader, P.D., Sohn, S., Caldwell, C.W.: Soft Counting Networks for Bone Marrow Differentials. Proc. IEEE. Int. Conf. Syst. Man. Cybern. 5 (2001) 3425-3428
5. Gat, N.: Imaging Spectroscopy Using Tunable Filters: A Review. Proc. SPIE. Int. Soc. Opt. Eng. (2000) 50-64
6. Levenson, R.M., Hoyt, C.C.: Spectral Imaging and Microscopy. Am. Lab. 32(2000) 26-33
7. Cortes, C., Vapnik, V.: Support-Vector Networks. Mach. Learn. 20 (1995) 273
8. Hsu, C.W., Lin, C.J.: A Simple Decomposition Method for Support Vector Machines. Mach. Learn. 46 (2002) 291-314

Intelligent Optimal Control in Rare-Earth Countercurrent Extraction Process *via* Soft-Sensor[*]

Hui Yang[1], Chunyan Yang[2], Chonghui Song[3], and Tianyou Chai[4]

[1] School of Electrical and Electronics Engineering, East China Jiaotong University,
Nanchang 330013, China
yhshuo@263.net
[2] Mechatronics Research Center, Jiangxi Academy of Science,
Nanchang 330029, China
[3] Department of Information Science and Engineering,
Northeastern University, 110004
[4] Research center of Automation, Northeastern University,
Shenyang 110004, China

Abstract. According to the problems in the on-line measurement and automatic control of component content in rare-earth countercurrent extraction process, soft sensor strategies based on the mechanism modeling of the extraction process and neural network technology are proposed. On this basis, the intelligent optimal control strategy is provided by combining the technologies based on soft sensor and CBR (case-based reasoning) for the extraction process. The application of this system to a HAB yttrium extraction production process is successful and the optimal control, optimal operation and remarkable benefits are realized.

1 Introduction

With the abundant rare earth resources, China has the largest reserves and all kinds of varieties including light, middle and heavy rare earth. In recent years, due to the joint endeavors of the researchers and operators in this field, China have developed advanced rare earth extraction techniques with the largest separation scale and highest capacity output in the world[1]. Efficient and consistent automatic production processes are in desperate need with the emerging of continuous, large-scale and integrated rare earth production. China's automatic facilities in rare earth separation industry are in a generally low level, resting on off-line analysis, manual regulation and empirical control that result in inefficient production, high resource consumption and inconsistent product qualities, which have become the bottleneck of rare earth industry.

In this paper, to provide solution to the problem in the field of on-line measurement and automatic control of component content in rare-earth extraction process, the research begins with the modeling of the mechanism of rare-earth extraction process.

---

[*] The work is supported by the National Natural Science Foundation of China (50474020), the National Tenth Five-Year-Plan of Key Technology (2002BA315A).

By using neural network technology, the soft sensor model of the rare-earth extraction process was established. The structure of optimal pre-setting control system based on Case- Based Reasoning (CBR) technology for rare-earth extraction process was proposed. The industrial application example was given using the strategy in the control of rare-earth extraction process, which proved to be effective.

2 Component Content Soft-Sensor in Rare-Earth Countercurrent Extraction Process

For a specific rare earth extraction process, the first important thing is to select suitable process monitoring points according to characteristics of the production process. After the on-line measurement and control of the component content in the monitoring points, to guarantee product purity in the two outlets. The present chief methods for the element component content on-line measurement in rare earth extraction process include UV-VIS, FIA, LaF_3 ISE, Isotopic XRF etc [2, 3]. Because of high cost of the equipments, low reliability and stability, their usage in industry are generally limited. The soft sensor technology have many advantages such as preciseness, reliability, economy, dynamic fast response, continuous output of the element component content in the extraction process, easy to realize the pre-set control in the outcome product purity etc. The soft sensor method provides a new way to the on-line measurement of component content in rare earth countercurrent extraction process[3, 4].

2.1 Description of Rare-Earth Countercurrent Extraction Process

Fractional extraction processes are generally adopted in industry for the separation of rare earth, because two kinds of high purity, high recovery rate products can be obtained at the same time for the separation of A, B components. The two component A and B extraction process is shown in fig.1.

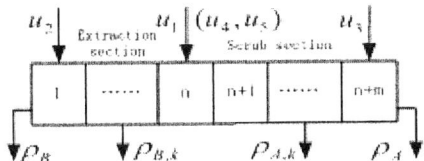

Fig. 1. Rare earth countercurrent extraction process

where u_1 is the flow of rare earth feed, u_2 is the flow of extraction solvent, u_3 is the flow of scrub solvent, u_4 and u_5 are the distribution of A and B in the feed respectively, where $u_4 + u_5 = 1$. ρ_A is organic phase product purity of A at the exit and ρ_B is aqueous phase product purity of B at the exit. $\rho_{A,k}$ is organic phase component content at the specified sampling point in scrub section and $\rho_{B,k}$ is aqueous phase component content at the specified sampling point in extraction section.

Since the whole process is composed from several decades to more than one hundred stages, the flow regulation of extraction solvent, scrub solvent and the feed could influence the product purity at the outlet after several hours (even decade hours) long-time step by step delivery. For this reason, the sampling point is set near the outlet and the outlet product purity (ρ_A, ρ_B) is guaranteed by measuring and control of the component content (ρ_{AK}, ρ_{BK}) at the sampling points. However, because of the complicated industrial process, such as rare earth countercurrent extraction, which has the characteristics of multivariable, strong decoupling, large delay, nonlinearity, and time variance as well as the difficult on-line measure for component content, it is difficult to get optimal control aimed at the outcome product purity.

2.2 Equilibrium Calculation Model for Countercurrent Rare-Earth Extraction

For the rare-earth countercurrent extraction process shown in fig.1, when the component A and B reach the extraction balance at every stage, this state can be described by fig.2.

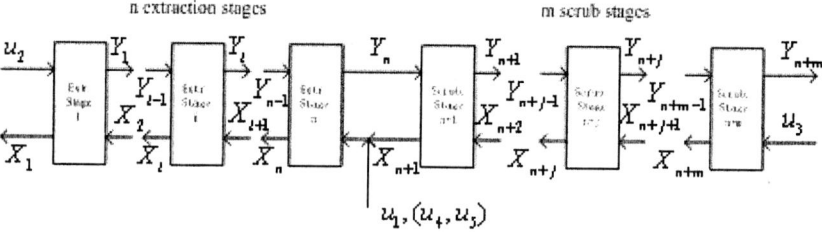

Fig. 2. Balance of rare earth countercurrent extraction process

where $X_k = [x_{A,k}, x_{B,k}]^T$, $Y_k = [y_{A,k}, y_{B,k}]^T$. $x_{A,k}, x_{B,k}, y_{A,k}, y_{B,k}$ ($k = 1,2,...,n+m$) are the corresponding quantity of A and B in the aqueous phase and organic phase at each stage. The A component content $\rho_{A,k}$ in organic phase at the sampling point of scrub section and the B component content $\rho_{B,k}$ in aqueous phase at the sampling point of extraction section can be calculated by equation (1).

$$\begin{cases} \overline{\rho}_{B,k} = x_{B,k}/(x_{A,k} + x_{B,k}) \times 100\%, k = 1,2,...,n \\ \overline{\rho}_{A,k} = y_{A,k}/(y_{A,k} + y_{B,k}) \times 100\%, k = n+1,...,n+m \end{cases} \quad (1)$$

To get the value of $\overline{\rho}_{A,k}$ and $\overline{\rho}_{B,k}$, the $x_{A,k}, x_{B,k}, y_{A,k}, y_{B,k}$ ($k = 1,2,...,n+m$) must be calculated at first.

According to countercurrent extraction principle [1], after the first extraction equilibrium operation, the component A and B satisfied the following extraction equilibrium relationship

$$\beta_k = y_{A,k}(t) \cdot x_{B,k}(t) / y_{B,k}(t) \cdot x_{A,k}(t), \quad k = 1,2,...,n \quad (2)$$

$$y_{A,k}(t) + y_{B,k}(t) = S, \quad k = 1,2,\dots,n \tag{3}$$

$$\begin{aligned} x_{A,k}(t) + y_{A,k}(t) &= M_{A,k}(t) \\ x_{B,k}(t) + y_{B,k}(t) &= M_{B,k}(t) \end{aligned}, \quad k = 1,2,\dots,n+m \tag{4}$$

$$\beta'_k = y_{A,k}(t) \cdot x_{B,k}(t) / y_{B,k}(t) \cdot x_{A,k}(t), \quad k = n+1,\dots,n+m \tag{5}$$

$$x_{A,k}(t) + x_{B,k}(t) = W, \quad k = n+1,\dots,n+m \tag{6}$$

where β_k and β'_k are extraction section average separation coefficient and scrub section average separation coefficient respectively, S, W are corresponding organic extraction quality and aqueous phase scrub quality decided by countercurrent technics. when $u_1 = 1$, t denotes the times of extraction equilibrium operation. $M_{A,k}(t)$ and $M_{B,k}(t)$ are the total quality of component A and B at each stage in the t time extraction equilibrium operation and vary with the two phase distribution data $x_{A,k}(t)$, $x_{B,k}(t)$, $y_{A,k}(t)$ and $y_{B,k}(t)$. At the initial time ($t=1$), it is decided by the fluid filled the tank. Solving equation (2)-(6) can get $x_{A,k}(t)$, $x_{B,k}(t)$, $y_{A,k}(t)$ and $y_{B,k}(t)$ $k = 1,2,\dots,n+m$.

According to the property of extraction process that organic phase and aqueous phase flow countercurrent, two phase flowing into k stage are the organic phase in k-1 stage and the aqueous phase in k+1 stage respectively. Hence the quantity of component A and B at k stage in t+1 time extraction equilibrium operation is

$$\begin{cases} M_{A,k}(t+1) = x_{A,k+1}(t) + y_{A,k-1}(t) \\ M_{B,k}(t+1) = x_{B,k+1}(t) + y_{B,k-1}(t) \end{cases} \tag{7}$$

The procedure to calculate using equation (2)-(7) are summarized as follow

(1) At aqueous phase exit stage, i.e. $k=1$, $y_{A,0}(t) = 0, y_{B,0}(t) = 0$. It means the input organic phase is zero at this stage.

(2) At organic phase exit stage, i.e. $k=n+m$, $x_{A,n+m+1}(t) = 0, x_{B,n+m+1}(t) = 0$. It means the input scrub solvent don't contain the extraction material.

(3) At feed input stage, i.e. $k=n$, right side of equation (7) should add items $u_4(t)$, $u_5(t)$.

(4) Set $t=1$, then use equation (2)-(7) to compute until $\begin{cases} |x_{A,k}(t) - x_{A,k}(t-1)| < \varepsilon_1 \\ |y_{A,k}(t) - y_{A,k}(t-1)| < \varepsilon_2 \end{cases}$,

where ε_1 and ε_2 are specified small positive constant. At this moment. The whole extraction system is considered to reach equilibrium and get the distribution data $x_{A,k}$ $x_{B,k}$ $y_{A,k}$ and $y_{B,k}$ of component A and B at every stage. Then using equation (1) can get $\overline{\rho}_{B,k}$ and $\overline{\rho}_{A,k}$.

2.3 Strategy of Component Content Soft-Sensor in Rare-Earth Extraction Process

The equilibrium calculation model for countercurrent extraction is obtained under the assumption that the mix extraction ratio is constant. Since there are extraction solvent concentration, scrub solvent concentration and feed flow fluctuation, organic phase and aqueous phase flow ratio at each stage are hardly guaranteed constantly. The real extraction production process is not always in the equilibrium state. The above conditions lead to obvious difference between the calculation result using this model and the real measuring result. Hence we propose the soft sensor system described in fig.3, which combines the equilibrium calculation model for multi-component rare earth extraction with the fuzzy system error compensation model to implement the rare earth extraction component content measurement. This system consists of data sampling and pretreatment, extraction equilibrium calculation model, and error compensation model using adaptive neural-fuzzy networks.

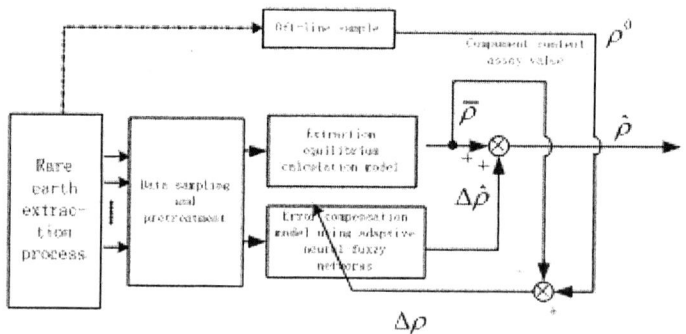

Fig. 3. Framework of rare earth countercurrent extraction component content soft-sensor

Parameter ρ^0 is the component content of off-line assay value, $\bar{\rho}$ is the output of countercurrent extraction equilibrium calculation model, parameter $\Delta\bar{\rho} = \rho^0 - \bar{\rho}$ is the error in modeling, $\Delta\hat{\rho}$ is output of error compensation model. The $\Delta\rho_d = \Delta\bar{\rho} - \Delta\hat{\rho}$ is used to correct the error compensation model. Then the component content of soft sensor measurement in detecting point will be:

$$\hat{\rho} = \bar{\rho} + \Delta\hat{\rho} \qquad (8)$$

The component content error compensation model was established by using Adaptive Neural-Fuzzy Inference Systems (ANFIS)[5,6], as showed in [7].

3 Intelligent Optimal Control Based on CBR

The core of the CBR[8] (Case Based Reasoning) technology lies in that, when you looking for solution to a problem, you can rely on the past find-solution experiences (i.e. cases) in this kind of problem to conduct reasoning. As a kind of problem-find-solution method, CBR has successfully applied in circumstances that short of system model but full of experiences, in fields such as trouble diagnosis, machine translating, design and planning, medical and health, and industry processes, on which experiences are greatly relied [9-11]. However, it is still at the exploring stage for complicated industry processes in modeling and control. Considering the characteristics of rare earth extraction process, the intelligent optimal control strategy is proposed as showed in Fig.4, which combined off-line assay test with soft sensor, optimal setting with close-loop control, and integrated process modeling with control. By conducting optimal setting and feedforward /feedback revision in the flow rate points of extracting solvent, feed solution, and scrubbing solution in rare earth extraction process based on CBR technology, the optimal control of output purity indices in two outlets can be realized.

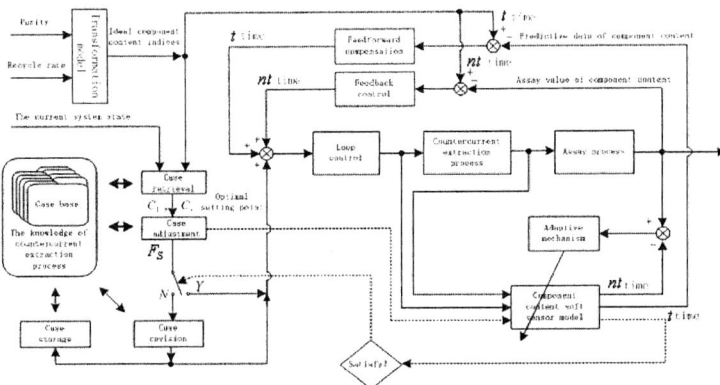

Fig. 4. Case-based reasoning optimal setting control in countercurrent extraction process

Since the optimal control of rare earth extraction is a complicated system, only the loop optimal setting process based on CBR is discussed here. By the acquisition of knowledge from the large number of control data accumulated in the history of rare earth extraction process, the typical operating modes are summarized into case form, and the case base is built. The optimal setting control in rare-earth extraction process is transformed into the process of case adjustment, case revision, and the renewing and addition/reduction of the case base.

3.1 Case Representation and Retrieval

The case base is the memory space for the storage of past cases. The cases should include the succeeded one as well as the failed one. Each case stored in case base should be in certain storage form, and contain the chief factors and environment condition as well as the basic characteristics and main parameters value of the case. There are many factors influencing the separation efficiency of rare earth extraction. Through the analysis of the operation data in the practical rare earth extraction process, the result showed that the variation of processing parameters, such as the component content of A and B in feed (u_4, u_5), rare earth concentration of feed liquid N_F, concentration of extracting solvent N_O, and acidity of scrubbing liquid N_W etc., will significantly influence the extraction process. Therefore, (u_4, u_5, N_F, N_O, N_W) could be selected as the characteristic description of typical operating mode in extraction process, expressed by f_1, f_2, f_3, f_4 and f_5, respectively. The solution of the case are the optimal setting points of flow rate of extracting solvent, feed liquid, and scrubbing liquid in extraction process u_{SO}, u_{SF}, u_{SW}, expressed by fs_1, fs_2 and fs_3, respectively. In case base, each case consists of operating mode characteristics description:

$$F = \{f_1, f_2, f_3, f_4, f_5\} = \{u_4, u_5, N_F, N_O, N_W\}$$

and solution characteristics description:

$$F_S = \{fs_1, fs_2, fs_3\} = \{u_{SO}, u_{SF}, u_{SW}\}$$

The case retrieval and case match are conducted by reasoning system according to the operating mode in extraction process. The distribution variation in rare earth feed is regarded as chief index, because it has big influence on extraction process. While the extracting solvent concentration, feed liquid concentration, and scrubbing liquid acidity are regarded as secondary indexes, for their fluctuation range can be controlled. In the case retrieval process, by using the index structure and calculating similarity function, all the cases which meet the matching threshold value are searched out.

C_{in}, the description of the present operating mode in rare earth extraction process, is defined as $F = (f_1, f_2, f_3, f_4, f_5)$. The solution characteristics description of C_{in} is $F_S = (fs_1, fs_2, fs_3)$. Cases $C_1, C_2, \cdots, C_m$ are in case base, in which the operating mode description of $C_k (k=1,\cdots,m)$ is $F_k = (f_{k,1}, f_{k,2}, f_{k,3}, f_{k,4}, f_{k,5})$. The solution characteristics description of C_k is $F_{Sk} = (fs_{k,1}, fs_{k,2}, fs_{k,3})$.

The similarity function of operating mode characteristics description f_1 and $f_{k,l}$ ($l=1,\ldots,5$) is:

$$S_F(f_l, f_{k,l}) = 1 - \frac{|f_l - f_{k,l}|}{\max(f_l, f_{k,l})}, (k=1,\ldots,m) \quad (9)$$

The similarity function of present operating mode C_{in} and cases in case base C_k ($k=1,\cdots,m$) is [9]:

$$S_C(C_{in}, C_k) = \sum_{l=1}^{5} (\omega_l \cdot S_F(f_l, f_{k,l})) \bigg/ \sum_{l=1}^{5} \omega_l \quad (10)$$

$$S_{\max} = \max_{k \in \{1,\cdots,m\}} (S_C(C_{in}, C_k)) \quad (11)$$

where ω_l is the weighted coefficient of operating mode characteristics description, its value can be decided from experiences. The threshold value of similarity S_{th} is:

$$\text{If } S_{\max} \geq 0.9 \text{ then } S_{th} = 0.9 \text{ else } S_{th} = S_{\max} \quad (12)$$

When similarity is figured out, all the cases in case base which similarity come up to S_{th} (the threshold value of given operating mode) will be searched out as matched cases.

3.2 Case Adjustment

The probability is rather small for using the succeeded cases obtained by case search to get the best solution to the problem. Some adjustment for the case must be made according to the given condition. This adjustment is the adjustment-in-detail based on the succeeded case. The case adjustment does not mean that the original case is not suitable for this condition. The difference is aroused by strategy or technology guidance. The CBR system will carry out the adjustment by using the possessed process knowledge, according to the primary difference between the condition of input operating mode and the restored operating mode searched, to get the best solution for the present operating mode.

Supposing total r matched cases $\{C_1, \cdots, C_r\}$ are searched out in the case base, in which the similarity of C_k ($k=1,\cdots,r$) with the present operating mode is s_k, might as well supposing $S_1 \le S_2 \le \cdots \le S_r \le 1$. The corresponding solution of case is $F_{Sk} = (fs_{k,1}, fs_{k,2}, fs_{k,3})$, ($k=1,\cdots,r$).

Then the solution of the present operating mode is $F_S = (fs_1, fs_2, fs_3)$, where:

$$fs_l = \sum_{k=1}^{r} w_k \times fs_{k,l} \bigg/ \sum_{k=1}^{r} w_k, (l=1,2,3) \tag{13}$$

and w_k ($k=1,\cdots,r$) is decided by the following:

$$\text{If } S_r = 1 \text{ then } w_k = \begin{cases} 1, k=r \\ 0, k \ne r \end{cases}, \text{ else } w_k = S_k, (k=1,2,\cdots,r). \tag{14}$$

3.3 Case Revision

Since there are the succeeded cases as well as the failed cases in the case base, if the cases searched out are the failed cases, it is necessary to revise the cases by using the knowledge in other field. In the revision process, it begins with the analyses of the reason of failures. Then the characteristics parameters and the corresponding rules are revised referring to the reason of failures. The original case is revised based on these rules and the condition of proposed problem.

To inspect the effectiveness of the case after case revision, the evaluation is required. Through the solution of case re-use, the predict value of element component content in detecting points ρ_0 is obtained through the calculation of the component content soft sensor model in rare earth extraction process. This predict value is compared with the target value of component content obtained from the target transform model ρ_m, if $|\rho_0 - \rho_m| \le \delta$ (δ is prearrange index decided from the experiences in process control, usually takes the value 5%~10%). Then the optimal setting value of each flow rate can be downloaded to extraction process. Each flow rate in extraction process is made to steadily follow the optimal setting points by loop feedback control. If

$|\rho_0 - \rho_m| > \delta$, then the case adjustment is required, and the setting points of each flow rate in extraction process are adjusted until they meet the requirement of the target value of component content in detecting points.

Case study is a means of enlargement and renewal of case base. It is also important for CBR system to deal with new operating mode, to ensure long-term, effective, and reliable application.

4 Applications

A company extracted high purity yttrium from ionic rare earth, in which the content of Y_2O_3 is more than 40%, adopting new extraction technique of HAB dual solution. This technique requires the purity of ultimate yttria to be more than 99% and of mixed rare earth containing low purity yttrium to be less than 0.5%. The extraction process consists of sixty stages of mixed extractors. The feed is in the 22th stage. The parameter variation range in the extraction process are $0.4 \leq f_B \leq 0.85$, $0.98 \leq N_F \leq 1.02$, $0.95 \leq N_O \leq 1.05$, $2.95 \leq N_W \leq 3.05$.

Considering the characteristics of HAB extracting yttrium process and combining the experiences of integrated automation system in industry application [12], the control system of HAB extracting yttrium process is built in the company by using the method proposed in this article. Its hardware structure is shown in fig. 5.

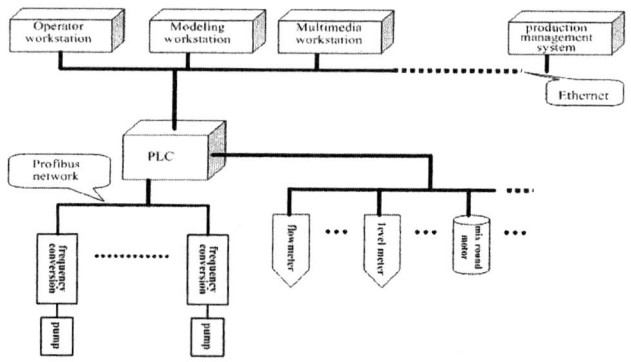

Fig. 5. Hardware structure of integrated automation system in yttrium extraction by HAB

Model computer is to achieve soft sensor and optimal control. Operator monitoring station is used for on-line parameters monitoring and soft manual operation. Multimedia monitoring system is to monitor the key equipments and posts. The connection between each monitoring stations as well as computer and PLC are realized by adopting convenient, fast industrial Ethernet. Hardware of production management system includes PC and server. Database is consisted of real time database and relation database and can integrate information of production management system and process control system by control network (Profibus-DP) and Ethernet. The operators can realize on-line management by management system and real time control by process control system.

Based on this hardware platfom, the componet content soft sensor system and the optimal pre-setting control system software (its structure showed in Fig. 4) in rare earth extraction are developed, to carry out optimal control in HAB extractng Yttrium process. Through the application of process control in rare earth extraction, the yttria purity in the water phase outlet is more than 99.5%. Recycle rate of yttrium rises by 2%, which assures continuous and stable production of high purity and recycle rate, and achieves remarkable benefits.

5 Conclusion

In this article, based on mechanism modeling in countercurrent extraction, neural networks technology, and the technical data in rare earth extraction process, the soft sensor model which can predict component content in rare earth extraction process is established. The optimal pre-setting control system in rare earth extraction process based on CBR is proposed. This system has been applied to a company's rare earth extraction production line successfully, and the optimal control and optimal operation have been achieved.

References

1. Xu G.X.: Rare Earths, Metallurgical Industry Press, Beijing (1995) 612-727
2. Yan C.H., Jia J.T.: Automatic Control System of Countercurrent Rare Earth Extraction Process. Rare Earths, 18 (1997) 37-42
3. Chai T.Y., Yang H.: Situation and Developing Trend of Rare-earth Countercurrent Extraction Processes Control. Journal of Rare Earths, 22 (2004) 590-596
4. Yang H., Chai T.Y.: Neural Networks Based Component Content Soft-sensor in Countercurrent Rare-earth Extraction. Journal of Rare Earth, 21 (2003) 691-696
5. Roger Jang J.S.: ANFIS: Adaptive-Network-based Fuzzy Inference System. IEEE Trans. on System, Man, and Cybernetics, 23 (1993) 665-685
6. Zhang J., Morris A.J.: Recurrent Neuro-fuzzy Networks for Nonlinear Process Modeling. IEEE Trans. on Neural Networks, 10 (1999) 313-325
7. Yang H.: Component Soft Sensor for Rare Earth Countercurrent Extraction Process and Its Applications. Northeastern University, Doctor Dissertation, 2004.
8. Aamodt A., Plaza, E.: Case-based Reasoning: Foundational Issues, Methodological Variations, and System Approaches. AI Communications, 7 (1994) 39-59
9. Rainer S., Stefania M., Riccardo B., et al.: Cased-based Reasoning for Medical Knowledge-Based Systems. International Journal of Medical Informatics, 64 (2001) 355-367
10. Myung K.P., Inbom L., Key M.S.: Using Case Based Reasoning for Problem Solving in A Complex Production Process. Expert Systems with Applications, 15 (1998) 69-75
11. Paul H., Ronan M., Felix C.: Using Case-based Reasoning to Evaluate Supplier Environmental Management Performance. Expert Systems with Applications, 25 (2003) 141-153
12. Chai T.Y., Yang H.: Integrated Automation System for Rare Earth Solvent Extraction Separation Process. Journal of Rare Earth, 22 (2004) 682-688

Three Dimensional Gesture Recognition Using Modified Matching Algorithm

Hwan-Seok Yang[1], Jong-Min Kim[1], and Seoung-Kyu Park[2]

[1] Computer Science and Statistic Graduate School, Chosun University, Korea
[2] Division of Computer Howon University, Korea
mrjjoung@chosun.ac.kr

Abstract. User-friendly Human-Computer interaction becomes more important accordance with rapid development of various information systems. In this paper we describe a three-dimensional gesture recognition algorithm and a system that adopts the algorithm for non-contact human-computer interaction. From sequence of stereo images, five feature regions are extracted with simple color segmentation algorithm and then those are used for three dimensional locus calculation processing. However, the result is not so stable, noisy, that we introduce principal component analysis method to get more robust gesture recognition results. This method can overcome the weakness of conventional algorithms since it directly uses three-dimensional information for human gesture recognition.

1 Introduction

Humans frequently use gestures to communicate information among one other. Considering the fact, it is necessary to develop efficient and fast gesture recognition algorithms for more natural human-computer interaction. In recent years, gesture recognition has become an increasingly important topic in the computer vision field, with the construction of massive video databases, surveillance systems, and highly compressible communication systems. Briefly speaking, gesture recognition means automatically knowing how a human's parts temporally change. However, it is difficult to recognize temporal changes automatically because a human body is a three-dimensional object of a very complex structure [1]. In early works, many researchers tried to measure the configuration of the human body with sensors attached to the joints of limbs and to recognize gesture by analyzing the variation of joint angles. However, this requires the user to wear cumbersome devices such as a data glove and a data suit, and usually long cables connect the device to computers. So, it hinders the ease and natural quality of the user's motion. As a non-tactile method, recently a very accurate gesture recognition method using Moving Light Displays (MLD) was developed. In the MLD method, various bright markers are attached to the joints of a moving articulated body, and the lighting conditions are designed such that only the markers are visible against a black background. However, for this method, it is necessary to arrange the camera in advance and to illuminate the environment, so that it is very expensive and real-time processing is difficult.

Any awkwardness in wearing devices can be dissolved by using video-based *non-contact* recognition techniques. One approach adopts a set of video cameras and computer vision techniques to interpret gestures. We call the method "appearance-based gesture recognition" since only the visual appearance is used in the recognition process. Generally these methods use 2D information. But 2D information is not sufficient for analyzing human's gesture. Recently, in order to solve these problems, many researchers use 3D information for gesture recognition. However, 3D information is hard to extract from human gesture and is not stable.

In this paper, we describe an effective method that can recognize gestures using 3D information estimated with PCA (Principal Component Analysis). And we show an example that can be applied to interactive game system.

2 Overview

Our whole system consists of two modules of recognition and interface as shown in Fig 1. In the recognition module 3D information is captured and it is analyzed into gesture codes with PCA algorithm, then these results are connected to the interface module. The interface module is designed for translating the gesture codes into specific game actions. So, user's gestures are actualized some actions to play a real-time interactive game. First, in recognition module, two stereo images are captured through video cameras. And then five feature points are extracted with simple skin-tone model using YUV color space model and the points are labeled head, both hands, and feet. So we can directly calculate the 3D location of the feature points by utilizing stereo geometry. From the series of location data we can get the feature vector which can express a meaning of human gesture, and by using the feature vector the "Gesture Space" are constructed with PCA. In our method, analysis or recognition of the gesture is to search a feature vector that has minimum distance between gesture models and input feature vector. In the interface module, the results of gesture analysis is convert to a series of action codes for a specific interaction game; Teken3, which is commercialized by NAMCO Inc. Using the system, we can enjoy a playing game in real time.

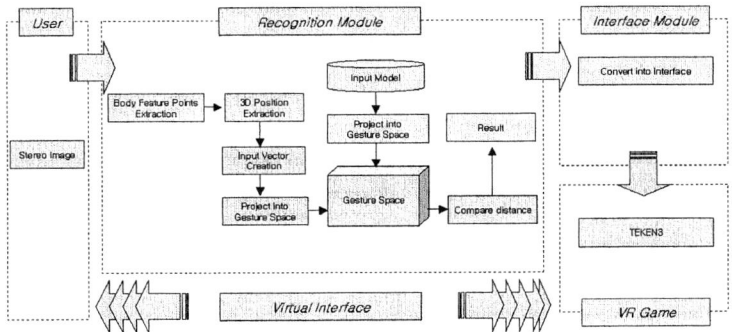

Fig. 1. The whole structure of the 3D gesture recognition system

3 3d LOCATION Estimation

The first step in gesture recognition is to extract five body feature points from stereo images. Those feature points are end point of human body. Whenever human do a gesture, the locations of the feature points are continuously changed over time, so that in general case, meaning of a gesture appears in location variation of these feature points. We define 5 feature points, head, both hands and both feet for recognizing human's gesture as shown in Fig 2.

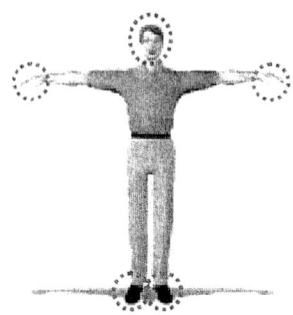

Fig. 2. Define body feature points

3.1 Extract Body Feature Points

In this paper, a head and both hands are segmented with color segmentation method of skin-tone color model. We adopt YUV color model for modeling a skin-tone since YUV color model is more robust than RGB color model in variable illumination condition.

In general, skin-tone has a sharp distribution in small region in YUV color model. Therefore skin-tone area can be extracted by using only simple threshold operation rather than any complex segmentation algorithm. In the process, we employ some assumptions as follows:

1) Images are captured in indoor and under fixed illumination
2) Some influential objects whose color is similar to the skin color should be removed in advance.
3) Background should be uncomplicated like a black screen without any pattern.

Correspondence of detected regions to specific 2D blobs for head, hands and feet must be decided when the system starts up. Since the error recovery process affects computational burden in online system, the feature point decision process should be carefully designed [4]. In this system, blob tracking is accomplished according to the following simple assumption in the case of naturally standing posture of a whole human body.

1) Head is the region of the biggest one among the skin-tone blobs.
2) Right hand is a skin-tone area that is at right side.
3) Left hand is a skin-tone area that is at left side.

Occlusion is a critical problem in motion recognition of articulated object in vision-based systems. Most vision-based system includes process to solve an occlusion problem and many algorithms are presented. For the problem, we adopt the very simple but robust method that utilizes homogeneity of motion. That means current position is predicted from previous position when occlusion is occurred. The predicted position is substituted with median value of current position and previous position as shown in Fig3. However, this method is not adoptable in more complex situation, so we assume the condition of interface for simple interaction game as follows.

1) The motion is not complex.
2) Distinction between left and right is unnecessary.

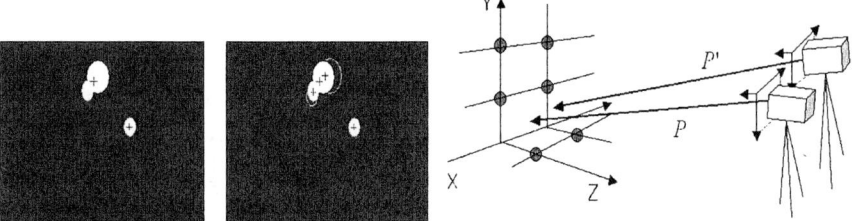

Fig. 3. Median process for occlusion   **Fig. 4.** Camera calibration from a calibration object

3.2 Camera Calibration

After body feature points are extracted, 3D reconstruction is accomplished using stereo geometry. In order to calculate the 3D position, camera projection matrix P should be calculated [5].

In this paper, we adopt a method for estimating the camera projection matrix from corresponding 3D space and image entities. Let's assume that the correspondence between a 3D point X and its image x under the unknown camera mapping. Given 6 correspondences $X_i \leftrightarrow x_i$ the camera matrix P determined as shown in Fig 4.

Projection matrix P is defined as in equation (1) and the new equation (2) is obtained [5].

$$P = \begin{bmatrix} p_{11} & p_{12} & p_{13} & p_{14} \\ p_{21} & p_{22} & p_{23} & p_{24} \\ p_{31} & p_{32} & p_{33} & p_{34} \end{bmatrix} = \begin{bmatrix} p_1^T & p_{14} \\ p_2^T & p_{24} \\ p_3^T & p_{34} \end{bmatrix} \quad (1)$$

$$s\tilde{m} = P\tilde{M} = A[R,t]\tilde{M} \quad (2)$$

where $\tilde{m} = [u,v,1]^T$, $\tilde{M} = [X,Y,Z,1]^T$.

Equation (3) is obtained as in equation (2) and projection matrix P can calculate using equation (3). There are many numerical methods for the eigen vector calculation, but in this paper the SVD (Singular Value Decomposition) algorithm has been used. The SVD provides a series of eigen values and eigen vectors. Equation (3)

generated by each correspondence $X_i \leftrightarrow x_i$. A solution of equation (3) is obtained from unit singular vector of B corresponding to the smallest singular value.

$$BP = 0 \tag{3}$$

where

$$B = \begin{bmatrix} X_1 & Y_1 & Z_1 & 1 & 0 & 0 & 0 & 0 & -u_1X_1 & -u_1Y_1 & -u_1Z_1 & -u_1 \\ 0 & 0 & 0 & 0 & X_1 & Y_1 & Z_1 & 1 & -v_1X_1 & -v_1Y_1 & -v_1Z_1 & -v_1 \\ \vdots & \vdots & \vdots & \vdots & \vdots & \vdots & \vdots & \vdots & \vdots & \vdots & \vdots & \vdots \\ X_6 & Y_6 & Z_6 & 1 & 0 & 0 & 0 & 0 & -u_6X_6 & -u_6Y_6 & -u_6Z_6 & -u_6 \\ 0 & 0 & 0 & 0 & X_6 & Y_6 & Z_6 & 1 & -v_6X_6 & -v_6Y_6 & -v_6Z_6 & -v_6 \end{bmatrix}$$

$$P = [\, p_1^T, p_{14}, p_2^T, p_{24}, p_3^T, p_{34}\,]^T$$

3.3 Calculate 3d Positions

Camera projection matrix has been calculated using camera calibration algorithm. Therefore 3D position of arbitrary points can be calculated based on stereo geometry. Equation (4) is obtained from equation of perspective projection for each camera [5].

$$s\tilde{m} = P\tilde{M} \, , \, s'\tilde{m}' = P'\tilde{M} \tag{4}$$

Where $m = [u, v]^T$, $m' = [u', v']^T$, $\tilde{m}$ is the homogeneous representation of point m and P, P' is a projection matrix for each camera.
And equation (5) is obtained from equation (4).

$$CM = c \tag{5}$$

where,

$$C = \begin{bmatrix} up_{31} - p_{11} & up_{32} - p_{12} & up_{33} - p_{13} \\ up_{31} - p_{21} & up_{32} - p_{22} & up_{33} - p_{23} \\ u'p'_{31} - p'_{11} & u'p'_{32} - p'_{12} & u'p'_{33} - p'_{13} \\ u'p'_{31} - p'_{21} & u'p'_{32} - p'_{22} & u'p'_{33} - p'_{23} \end{bmatrix}$$

$$c = [\, p_{14} - up_{34} \quad p_{24} - vp_{34} \quad p'_{14} - u'p'_{34} \quad p'_{24} - v'p'_{34} \,]^T$$

$$M = [X, Y, Z]^T$$

A solution of simultaneous equation (5) is solved using a method of pseudo-inverse matrix. Pseudo-inverse matrix A^+ is defined as follows [5]:

$$A^+ = (A^T A)^{-1} A^T \tag{6}$$

So solution of equation (5) is obtained as equation (7).

$$M = C^+ c \tag{7}$$

Table 1. 3D reconstruction errors

Axis	Error
X	2.3 Cm
Y	3.9 Cm
Z	4.0 Cm

4 Gesture Analysis

4.1 Define Gestures

In the system, we define 6 gestures that uses in 3D action game TEKEN3 (NAMCO®) as shown in Fig 5.

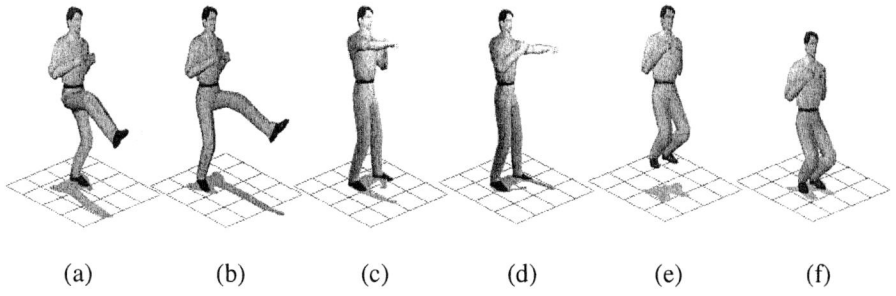

(a)　　　(b)　　　(c)　　　(d)　　　(e)　　　(f)

Fig. 5. Gestures (a) Right kick (b) Left kick (c) Right punch (d) Left punch (e) Jump (f) Squatting position

These gestures are similar in meaning to gesture of character in game and are used to virtual game interface for playing the game. Also these gestures should not be ambiguous to represent numerical. Therefore a good choice of feature vector is an important problem for recognition [3]. In our case, we calculate raw (x, y, z) data from 3D reconstruction as described in section 3, from which we can deduce positions and velocities.

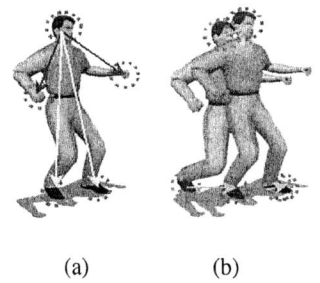

(a)　　　(b)

Fig. 6. Feature vector (a) relative position on the basis of head position (b) difference vector

In this system, feature vector is used as follows:

1) Relative positions of both hands and both feet from the basis of head position.
2) Difference value of head and both feet position.

From the consideration, a 21-dimensional feature vector is constructed from each frame and input gesture can be estimated using these vectors.

4.2 Modeling

As described in section 4.1, we can estimate gestures using input vector without any processing. However, 3D raw data have an error always because 3D data is calculated by numerical. Moreover it is difficult that find a rule of data. So we adopt a PCA (Principal Component Analysis) to analyze a gesture.

Let x_i be the input feature vector in current frame as in equation (8) and let N be the number of the input feature vector used to construct the gesture space.

$$x_i = [P_{LH} \quad P_{RH} \quad P_{LF} \quad P_{RF} \quad V_H \quad V_{LF} \quad V_{RF}]^T \tag{8}$$

By subtracting the average input vector, c, of the all input vector, as in equation (10), the new feature matrix X is obtained, where the size of the matrix is $21 \times N$. The covariance matrix, Q, of input vector can be obtained from equation (11). Then PCA is straightforward requiring only the calculation of the eigen vectors satisfying equation (12).

$$c = (1/N) \sum_{i=1}^{N} x_i \tag{9}$$

$$X \stackrel{\Delta}{=} [x_1 - c, x_2 - c, \ldots, x_N - c]^T \tag{10}$$

$$Q \stackrel{\Delta}{=} X \cdot X^T \tag{11}$$

$$\lambda_i \cdot e_i = Q \cdot e_i \tag{12}$$

There are many numerical methods for the eigen vector calculation, and we use SVD (*Singular Value Decomposition*) algorithm since the algorithm offers stable results. The SVD provides a series of eigen values λ_i (in reducing order of size) and eigen vectors e_i which are orthogonal to each other.

It should be noted that the magnitude of an eigen value corresponds to the importance of that vector in the eigen space. All 21 eigen vectors are needed to represent the feature sets accurately in a gesture space, however, a small number, k ($k \ll N$), of eigenvectors is generally sufficient for capturing the primary appearance characteristics of the gestures [7]. From equation (13), a small number of eigenvectors can be chosen which span the whole space, without any faults. k is selected such that the first eigenvectors of Q capture the important appearance variations in the feature sets.

$$\frac{\sum_{i=1}^{k} \lambda_i}{\sum_{i=1}^{N} \lambda_i} \geq T_1 \tag{13}$$

where , the threshold T_1 is close to, but less than, unity.

Consequently, by using equation (13), a 21-dimensional vector X can be projected to a low k-dimensional eigen space. In our case, only 5-demensional data is used for eigen space. And arbitrary input feature vector, set x, is subtracted from an average vector c, and projected into the eigen space as in equation (14)[7].

$$m_i = [e_1, e_2, \ldots, e_k]^T (x_i - c) \tag{14}$$

Model gesture is projected in this gesture space and then we can estimate an arbitrary input gesture using compare the distance from each model gesture in eigen space. A distribution of model gesture in gesture space is shown as Fig 7.

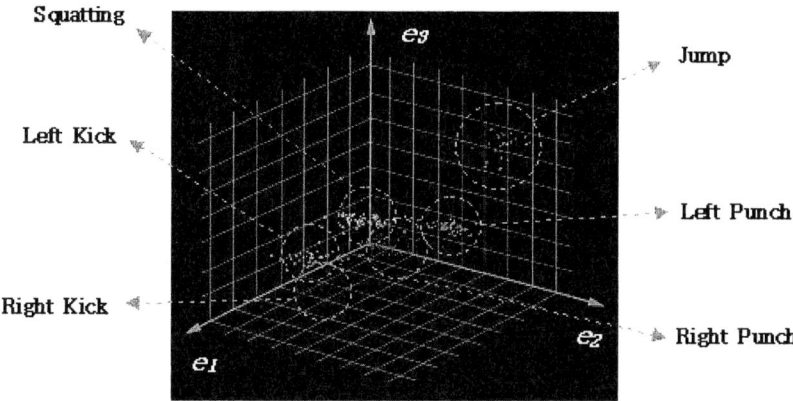

Fig. 7. Model gesture in eigen space (Only 3-demensional for visualization)

4.3 Modified Matching Algorithm

Input gesture is estimated by comparing a distance from each model gesture in gesture space. In general case, the model gesture that has shortest distance from input gesture is decided to output. But systems that adopt this method can recognize only the same gesture as modeled gesture because gesture is estimated using only numerical data. But meaning of gesture is more important than numerical data measured in gesture recognition process. For example, in the case of "Right Kick", considering the heuristics, there exist more important features than others and vice versa. The former is related feature vector with both feet and head and the latter is related feature vector with both hands. Form this consideration, we define important feature vectors for each gesture as shown in Table 2.

Less important feature is substituted with mean value of input vector based on Table 2 and then these modified input vectors are projected in gesture space and compared with model gesture as shown in Fig 8.

Table 2. Important features for each gesture

Gestures	Important Features
Kick	Relative position of feet
Punch	Relative position of hands
Jump	Relative position of feet and Difference vector of feet
Squat	Relative position of feet

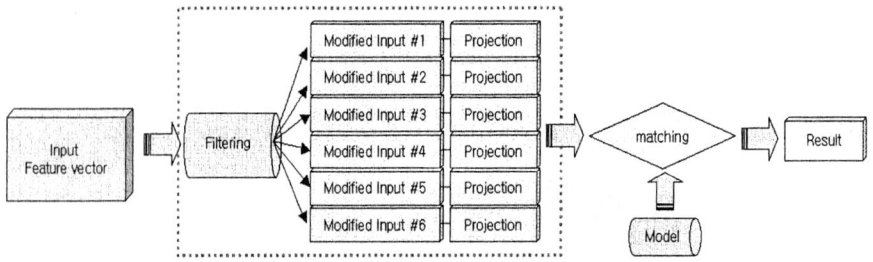

Fig. 8. Modified matching Algorithm

Table 3. Experimental result of modified matching algorithm

RK							
	LP	RP	LK	RK	JP	DN	OUT
Without filtering	59.61	31.04	43.20	41.48	56.07	30.75	N
With filtering	47.25	37.93	36.75	9.00	52.09	18.96	RK
LK							
	LP	RP	LK	RK	JP	DN	OUT
Without filtering	74.88	62.76	45.09	71.10	68.36	55.41	N
With filtering	50.63	47.29	9.24	38.98	56.27	35.26	LK
RP							
	LP	RP	LK	RK	JP	DN	OUT
Without filtering	29.89	12.62	33.49	32.26	36.92	16.03	N
With filtering	24.01	8.50	39.76	36.58	24.62	20.89	RP
LP							
	LP	RP	LK	RK	JP	DN	OUT
Without filtering	18.88	27.82	36.18	43.18	40.14	26.69	N
With filtering	7.39	26.32	38.62	37.07	25.23	20.45	LP
JP							
	LP	RP	LK	RK	JP	DN	OUT
Without filtering	63.25	63.35	62.85	81.42	34.27	59.04	N
With filtering	41.27	33.09	38.40	43.80	15.94	34.63	JP
SQ							
	LP	RP	LK	RK	JP	DN	OUT
Without filtering	46.31	31.08	37.28	48.39	35.94	28.52	N
With filtering	43.55	35.05	34.51	34.28	28.08	15.41	DN

5 Conclusion

In this paper, we have described an algorithm and systems for gesture recognition. The system uses a 3D data using stereo images and adopted a PCA for analysis gestures. And result of gesture recognition is used for virtual reality interface to play a game. And a modified matching algorithm has been proposed that can remove a constraint in gesture. However, there is a problem to be solved. When model is not a normal distribution, the method based on Euclidean distance is not suitable. In the future, we are planning to develop a robust matching algorithm.

References

1. J. Ohya and Y.. Kitamura, etc, "Real-Time Reproduction of 3D Human Images in Virtual Space Teleconferencing" in Proc. of '93 IEEE Virtual Reality Annual Int. Symp. pp.408-414, 1993.
2. Chistopher Wren, Ail Azarbayejani, Trevor Draeerl, and Alex Pentland. Pfinder: Real-time tracking of the human body. In Photonics East, SPIE Proceedings Vol. 2615 Bellingham, WA, 1995. SPIE.
3. Lee W. Campbell, David A. Becker, Ail Azarbayejani, Aaron F. Bobick, Alex Pentland. Invariant features for 3-D gesture recognition. In Second International Workshop on Face and Gesture Recognition, Killington VT Oct., 1996.
4. Daisaku Arita, Satoshi Yonemoto and Rin-ichiro Taniguchi. Real-time Computer Vision on PC-cluster and Its Application to Real-time Motion Capture. 2000 IEEE.
5. Hiroshi Murase and Shree K, Nayar, "Visual Learning and Recogntion 3-D object from appearance", international journal of Computer Vision, Vol,14,1995.
6. William T. Freeman and Michael Roth, "Orientation histograms for hand gesture recognition,"Intl. Workshop on Automatic Face and Gesture Recognition, IEEE Computer Society, pp. 296-301, June 1995, Zurich, Switzerland
7. J. Segen and S. Kumar, "Shadow Gestures: 3D Hand Pose Estimation Using a Single Camera," CVPR99, vol. 1, pp. 479-485, Fort Collins, Colorado, June, 23-25, 1999

Direct Adaptive Control for a Class of Uncertain Nonlinear Systems Using Neural Networks

Tingliang Hu, Jihong Zhu, Chunhua Hu, and Zengqi Sun

State Key Lab of Intelligent Technology and Systems,
Department of Computer Science and Technology,
Tsinghua University, Beijing 100084, China
htl02@mails.tsinghua.edu.cn

Abstract. This paper presents a direct adaptive control scheme based on multilayer neural networks for a class of single-input-single-output (SISO) uncertain nonlinear systems. The on-line updating rules of the neural networks parameters are obtained by Lyapunov stability theory. All signals in the closed-loop system are bounded and the output tracking error converges to a small neighborhood of zero. In this sense the stability of the closed-loop system is guaranteed. The effectiveness of the control scheme is verified by a simulation of inverted pendulum.

1 Introduction

The development of feedback linearization technique is a powerful tool for control of a class of nonlinear systems [1] because it provides the structure information of the dynamic system such as the relative degree and the zero dynamics. If we have exact knowledge of the system, we can transform a nonlinear control problem into a linear control one by using feedback linearization technique. However, in many cases, the plant to be controlled is too complex to find the exact system dynamics, and the operating conditions in dynamic environments may be unexpected. In order to relax some exact dynamics restrictions, several adaptive schemes have been introduced in [2] [3]. In such schemes, it is assumed that an accurate model of the plant is available, and the unknown parameters are assumed to appear linearly with respect to known nonlinear functions. However, this assumption is not sufficient for many practical situations, because it is difficult to describe an unknown nonlinear plant by known nonlinear functions precisely. During the last decade, significant progress has been made in the design of neural network controllers which are able to guarantee the closed-loop stability property for systems with complex and possibly unknown nonlinearities [4] [5] [6] [7] [8] [9]. In such schemes, exploiting the fact of universal approximators, the unknown system nonlinearities may straightforwardly be substituted by a neural network which is of known structure but contains a number of unknown parameters, plus a modeling error term, thus, transforming the original problem into a nonlinear robust adaptive control one, and the stability study is performed by using the Lyapunov synthesis method. Therefore it is not necessary to spend much effort on system modeling which might be very difficult in some cases.

In this paper a neural networks direct adaptive control scheme for a class of SISO uncertain nonlinear systems is proposed. Multi-layer neural networks are used in the controller to cancel the unknown nonlinearities. Using Lyapunov stability theory, the on-line updating rules of the neural networks parameters are obtained, while the stability and the boundedness of all the signals in the closed-loop system are guaranteed and the output tracking error converges to a small neighborhood of zero.

2 Problem Statement

Consider the following SISO system:

$$\dot{x}_i = x_{i+1}, i = 1, \cdots, n-1$$
$$\dot{x}_n = f(x) + g(x)u + d \quad (1)$$
$$y = x_1$$

where $f(x)$ and $g(x)$ are continuous unknown functions, $x = [x_1, x_2, \cdots, x_n] \in R^n$ is the measurable state vector, $u, y \in R$ are the input and output respectively, d is slow changing disturbance with $\|d\| < d_0, \dot{d} \approx 0$.

Define the bounded reference signal vector Y_d and the tracking error vector E as:

$$Y_d = [y_d, \dot{y}_d, \cdots, y_d^{(n-1)}]^T \in R^n \quad (2)$$
$$E = [e, \dot{e}, \cdots, e^{(n-1)}]^T \in R^n \quad (3)$$

where $e = y - y_d \in R$. Then, the control objective is to make the system output follows the given bounded reference signals under the stability constraint and all signals involved in the system must be bounded. In this paper, $\|\cdot\|$ denotes Euclidean norm of vector, $\|\cdot\|_F$ stands for the Frobenius norm of matrix, L_∞ is the bounded continuous function space. For the system (1) we assume that it is controllable, i.e. there exist a constant $b_0 > 0$, such that $\|g(x)\| \geq b_0$.

3 Adaptive Controller

3.1 Controller Structure and the Error Dynamics

The structure of the controller is as follows:

$$u = G(x)(v + F(x) + \delta) \quad (4)$$

where $G(x)$ and $F(x)$ are functions of the state vector x, δ is used to cancel the approximated errors between the nonlinear functions and the neural network approximator with limited neutrons, v is the new control input. Let

$$v = y_d^{(n)} - \lambda^T E \quad (5)$$

choosing $\lambda = [\lambda_0, \lambda_1, \cdots, \lambda_{n-1}]^T \in R^n$ such that $e^{(n)} + \lambda_{n-1} e^{(n-1)} + \cdots + \lambda_0 e = 0$ is Hurwitz.

Applying the controller (4) into the system (1), we obtain

$$y^{(n)} = f(x) + g(x)G(x)v + g(x)G(x)F(x) + g(x)G(x)\delta + d \qquad (6)$$

To guarantee the asymptotic convergence of the output error E, the following relationships should be satisfied:

$$\begin{aligned} g(x)G^*(x) &= 1, \quad d = -g(x)G^*(x)\delta^* \\ f(x) + g(x)G^*(x)F^*(x) &= 0 \end{aligned} \qquad (7)$$

where $G^*(x), F^*(x), \delta^*$ denote the ideal unknown nonlinear functions. Define errors:

$$\begin{aligned} \tilde{G}(x) &= G^*(x) - G(x), \quad \tilde{\psi}(x) = G^{*-1}(x) - G^{-1}(x) \\ \tilde{F}(x) &= F^*(x) - F(x) \quad \tilde{\delta} = \delta^* - \delta \end{aligned} \qquad (8)$$

Substituting (7), (8), (5) into (6), we obtain the error system dynamic and transform it to the state space form

$$\dot{E} = AE + B\Delta \qquad (9)$$

where

$$A = \begin{bmatrix} 0 & 1 & 0 & \cdots & 0 \\ 0 & 0 & 1 & \cdots & 0 \\ \vdots & \vdots & \vdots & \vdots & \vdots \\ 0 & 0 & 0 & \cdots & 1 \\ -\lambda_0 & -\lambda_1 & -\lambda_2 & \cdots & -\lambda_{n-1} \end{bmatrix} \quad B = \begin{bmatrix} 0 \\ 0 \\ \vdots \\ 0 \\ -1 \end{bmatrix}$$

$$\Delta = -\tilde{\psi}(x)u + \tilde{F}(x) + \tilde{\delta}$$

$G^{*-1}(x)$ and $F^*(x)$ are estimated by two single hidden neural networks, the structure of the neural network is shown in Fig.1.

$$G^{*-1}(x) = W_g^{*T}\sigma(V_g^{*T}\bar{x}), \quad F^*(x) = W^{*T}\sigma(V^{*T}\bar{x}) \qquad (10)$$

where $\sigma(z) = [1, \sigma(z_1), \sigma(z_2), \cdots, \sigma(z_N)]$ denotes the output vector of the hidden layer, N is the number of hidden layer neurons, $\bar{x} = [1, \sigma(x_1), \sigma(x_2), \cdots, \sigma(x_n)]$ is the output vector of the input layer, $\sigma(\cdot)$ is the Sigmoid function, W_g^*, V_g^*, W^*, V^* are the ideal bounded weights of the neural networks and $M_{W_g}, M_{V_g}, M_W, M_V$ are their bounds respectively. Assuming

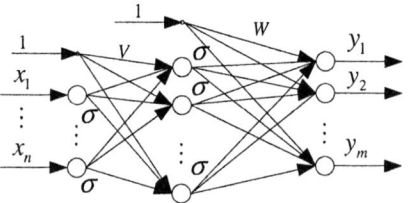

Fig. 1. Single hidden layer neural networks

that the outputs of the neural networks with ideal weights are equal to $G^{*-1}(x)$ and $F^*(x)$, the small bounded approximated error can be merged into δ. Then the outputs of the neural networks can be represented as:

$$G^{-1}(x) = W_g^T \sigma(V_g^T \bar{x}), \quad F = W^T \sigma(V^T \bar{x}) \qquad (11)$$

where W_g, V_g, W, V denote the estimated value of the ideal weight matrices W_g^*, V_g^*, W^*, V^* respectively. Define the following error vectors:

$$\tilde{W} = W^* - W, \tilde{V} = V^* - V, \tilde{W}_g = W_g^* - W_g, \tilde{V}_g = V_g^* - V_g \qquad (12)$$

Using the Taylor series expansion of $\sigma(V^*x)$ about $\sigma(Vx)$, the differences between the true value and the estimated output of the neural networks can be represent as:

$$W^{*T}\sigma(V^{*T}\bar{x}) - W^T\sigma(V^T\bar{x}) = \tilde{W}^T\sigma(V^T\bar{x}) + W^{*T}\left(\sigma(V^{*T}\bar{x}) - \sigma(V^T\bar{x})\right)$$
$$= \tilde{W}^T\left(\sigma(V^T\bar{x}) - \dot{\sigma}V^T\bar{x}\right) + W^T\dot{\sigma}\tilde{V}^T\bar{x} + \tilde{W}^T\dot{\sigma}V^{*T}\bar{x} + W^{*T}O(\tilde{V}^T\bar{x})^2 \qquad (13)$$

where $\sigma(V^T\bar{x}) - \sigma(V^{*T}\bar{x}) = \dot{\sigma}\tilde{V}^T\bar{x} + O(\tilde{V}^T\bar{x})^2$, $\dot{\sigma} = d\sigma(z)/dz|_{z=V^T\bar{x}}$. Since $\sigma, \dot{\sigma}$ and W_g^*, V_g^*, W^*, V^* are bounded, we can obtain the following inequalities:

$$\left\|\tilde{W}^T\dot{\sigma}V^{*T}\bar{x} + W^{*T}O(\tilde{V}^T\bar{x})^2\right\| \le c_1 + c_2\|\tilde{W}\|_F + c_3\|\tilde{V}\|_F \qquad (14)$$

$$\left\|(\tilde{W}_g^T\dot{\sigma}V_g^{*T}\bar{x} + W_g^{*T}O(\tilde{V}_g^T\bar{x})^2)u\right\| \le (d_1 + d_2\|\tilde{W}_g\|_F + d_3\|\tilde{V}_g\|_F)\|u\| \qquad (15)$$

where $c_1, c_2, c_3, d_1, d_2, d_3 > 0$ are positive constants.

3.2 Stability Analysis and Adaptive Rules

Based on the error dynamic equation (9) and Taylor series expansion of ideal output about the estimated value of the neural networks, Theorem of neural networks direct adaptive control is first given as follows:

Theorem: For system (1), the controller structure is (4), where $G^{-1}(x) = W_g^T\sigma(V_g^T\bar{x})$ and $F(x) = W^T\sigma(V^T\bar{x})$, and the parameter adaptive rules are

$$\begin{aligned}
\dot{W} &= \gamma_1\left[\left(\sigma(V^T\bar{x}) - \dot{\sigma}V^T\bar{x}\right)E^TPB - \kappa\|E\|\cdot W\right] \\
\dot{V} &= \gamma_2\left(\bar{x}E^TPBW^T\dot{\sigma} - \kappa\|E\|\cdot V\right) \\
\dot{W}_g &= \gamma_3\left[-\left(\sigma(V_g^T\bar{x}) - \dot{\sigma}V_g^T\bar{x}\right)E^TPB - \kappa_g\|E\|\cdot W_g\right]u \\
\dot{V}_g &= \gamma_4\left(-\bar{x}E^TPBW_g^T\dot{\sigma} - \kappa_g\|E\|\cdot V_g\right)u \\
\dot{\delta} &= \gamma_5 B^TPE
\end{aligned} \qquad (16)$$

where $\gamma_1, \gamma_2, \gamma_3, \gamma_4, \gamma_5, \kappa, \kappa_g > 0$, if the initial value of the neural networks are bounded and $G^{-1}(x) \ne 0$, then the close-loop system is stable, all the signals in the close-loop system is bounded and the output tracking error asymptotically converge to a neighborhood of zero.

Proof: Choosing the Lyapunov function as

$$V = \frac{1}{2}E^TPE + \text{tr}(\tilde{W}^T\tilde{W})/2\gamma_1 + \text{tr}(\tilde{V}^T\tilde{V})/2\gamma_2 \\ + \text{tr}(\tilde{W}_g^T\tilde{W}_g)/2\gamma_3 + \text{tr}(\tilde{V}_g^T\tilde{V}_g)/2\gamma_4 + \tilde{\delta}\tilde{\delta}/2\gamma_5 \qquad (17)$$

where $\gamma_1, \gamma_2, \gamma_3, \gamma_4, \gamma_5$, P is a symmetric positive define matrix which satisfies the Lyapunov equation $A^T P + PA = -Q$, $Q = Q^T > 0$. In terms of (12), we have

$$\dot{\tilde{W}} = -\dot{W}, \dot{\tilde{V}} = -\dot{V}, \dot{\tilde{W}}_g = -\dot{W}_g, \dot{\tilde{V}}_g = -\dot{V}_g \tag{18}$$

In addition, the following inequality is hold

$$\mathrm{tr}(\tilde{Z}^T \tilde{Z}) = \mathrm{tr}\left((Z^{*T} - \tilde{Z}^T)\tilde{Z}\right) \leq \|Z^*\|_F \|\tilde{Z}\|_F - \|\tilde{Z}\|_F^2 \leq Z_M \|\tilde{Z}\|_F - \|\tilde{Z}\|_F^2 \tag{19}$$

where Z represents one of W_g, V_g, W, V.

Differentiate (17) with respect to time and substitute (9), (10), (11), (12), (13), (14), (15), (16), (18) and (19) into it, we have

$$\dot{V} \leq -\frac{1}{2} E^T Q E + \kappa \|E\| \left(M_W \|\tilde{W}\|_F - \|\tilde{W}\|_F^2\right) + \kappa \|E\| \left(M_V \|\tilde{V}\|_F - \|\tilde{V}\|_F^2\right)$$
$$+ \kappa_g \|E\| \left(M_{Wg} \|\tilde{W}_g\|_F - \|\tilde{W}_g\|_F^2\right) \|u\| + \kappa_g \|E\| \left(M_{Vg} \|\tilde{V}_g\|_F - \|\tilde{V}_g\|_F^2\right) \|u\|$$
$$+ \|E\| \cdot \|PB\| \left(c_1 + c_2 \|\tilde{W}\|_F + c_3 \|\tilde{V}\|_F\right) + \|E\| \cdot \|PB\| \left(d_1 + d_2 \|\tilde{W}_g\|_F + d_3 \|\tilde{V}_g\|_F\right) \|u\|$$

For convenience, the products of constant $c_i, d_i, i = 1, \cdots, 3$ and $\|PB\|$ are still denoted by $c_i, d_i, i = 1, \cdots, 3$ respectively, then

$$\dot{V} \leq -\|E\| \cdot \left[\begin{array}{l} \frac{1}{2} \lambda_{Qmin} \|E\| + \kappa \left(\|\tilde{W}\|_F - \frac{1}{2}(\frac{c_2}{\kappa} + M_W)\right)^2 + \kappa \left(\|\tilde{V}\|_F - \frac{1}{2}(\frac{c_3}{\kappa} + M_V)\right)^2 \\ + \kappa_g \|u\| \left(\|\tilde{W}_g\|_F - \frac{1}{2}(\frac{d_2}{\kappa_g} + M_{Wg})\right)^2 + \kappa_g \|u\| \left(\|\tilde{V}_g\|_F - \frac{1}{2}(\frac{d_3}{\kappa_g} + M_{Vg})\right)^2 - \theta \end{array} \right] \tag{20}$$

where

$$\theta = c_1 + \frac{1}{4}\kappa(\frac{c_2}{\kappa} + M_W)^2 + \frac{1}{4}\kappa(\frac{c_3}{\kappa} + M_V)^2$$
$$+ \left(d_1 + \frac{1}{4}\kappa_g(\frac{d_2}{\kappa_g} + M_{Wg})^2 + \frac{1}{4}\kappa_g(\frac{d_3}{\kappa_g} + M_{Vg})^2\right)\|u\|$$

Let

$$\|E\| > \frac{2\theta}{\lambda_{Qmin}} = a_1, \|\tilde{W}\|_F > \sqrt{\frac{\theta}{\kappa}} + \frac{1}{2}(\frac{c_2}{\kappa} + M_W) = a_2, \|\tilde{V}\|_F > \sqrt{\frac{\theta}{\kappa}} + \frac{1}{2}(\frac{c_3}{\kappa} + M_V) = a_3$$
$$\|\tilde{W}_g\|_F > \sqrt{\frac{\theta}{\kappa_g \|u\|}} + \frac{1}{2}(\frac{d_2}{\kappa_g} + M_{Wg}) = a_4, \|\tilde{V}_g\|_F > \sqrt{\frac{\theta}{\kappa_g \|u\|}} + \frac{1}{2}(\frac{d_3}{\kappa_g} + M_{Vg}) = a_5 \tag{21}$$

If $\|u\| \in L_\infty$, then $\theta \in L_\infty$. So long as one of the inequalities in (21) is hold, $\dot{V} < 0$, then the closed-loop system is stable. In the end of this section we give the measure to guarantee the boundedness of input u.

Define error vector and error neighborhood of zero as follows

$$z = \left(\|E\|, \|\tilde{W}\|_F, \|\tilde{V}\|_F, \|\tilde{W}_g\|_F, \|\tilde{V}_g\|_F\right)^T$$
$$\omega = \left\{ z \in \left[\|E\| < a_1 \times \|\tilde{W}\|_F < a_2 \times \|\tilde{V}\|_F < a_3 \times \|\tilde{W}_g\|_F < a_4 \times \|\tilde{V}_g\|_F < a_5\right]\right\}$$

$\bar{\omega}$ is the complementary of ω. If $z \in \bar{\omega}$, then $\|E\| \neq 0$, there exist a constant $\alpha > 0$ such that $\dot{V} = -\alpha\|E\|$, and $\int \dot{V} dt = V(t) - V(0) < e^{-\alpha\|E\|t}$, hence $V(t) < V(0)$, Due to $V(0) \in L_\infty$, $V(t) \in L_\infty$ is hold. From (17), we have $E, \tilde{W}_g, \tilde{V}_g, \tilde{W}, \tilde{V}, \tilde{\delta} \in L_\infty$. Finally we obtain $W_g, V_g, W, V, \delta, x \in L_\infty$ from (3), (8) and (12). Assume that β is the least value of V on the boundary of ω. In terms of the above integral inequality we have $t \leq \ln(V(0) - \beta)/\alpha\|E\|$. Due to $\|E\| \neq 0$, z converges to ω asymptotically in limited time. According to Eq. (21) ω can be reduced by increasing design parameters. If all the inequalities in (21) are not hold, the set comprised by z is a subset of ω, therefore it diminish as ω decreases.

In terms of (4), If the given initial values of neural networks is bounded and $G^{-1}(x) = W_g^T \sigma(V_g^T \bar{x}) \neq 0$, the input u_0 is bounded. Thus according to above theorem, as long as $G^{-1}(x) = W_g^T \sigma(V_g^T \bar{x}) \neq 0$, u is bounded without fail. In light of (7) and (8), let $G^{-1}(x) = b_0 + W_g^T \sigma(V_g^T \bar{x})$, then $\tilde{\psi}(x)$ is unchanged and the above theorem is hold yet. Due to $(a+b)^2 \geq 0$, then $a^2 + b^2 + 2\gamma ab > 0$ where $0 < \gamma < 1$, $a \neq 0$ or $b \neq 0$. Therefore let $G(x) = [b_0 + W_g^T \sigma(V_g^T \bar{x})]/[b_0^2 + (W_g^T \sigma(V_g^T \bar{x}))^2 + 2\gamma b_0 W_g^T \sigma(V_g^T \bar{x})]$, $0 < \gamma < 1$, u is bounded.

4 Simulation Example

An inverted pendulum is utilized in this study to verify the effectiveness of the proposed control scheme. The dynamic model [10] is $y^{(2)} = f(y, \dot{y}) + g(y, \dot{y})u$ where y is the angle of the pole of the inverted pendulum. Let $x_1 = y$, $x_2 = \dot{y}$, we obtain the nonlinear functions of the inverted pendulum.

$$f = \frac{G \sin x_1 - \frac{mlx_2^2 \cos x_1 \sin x_1}{m_c + m}}{l(\frac{4}{3} - \frac{m \cos^2 x_1}{m_c + m})} \qquad g = \frac{\frac{\cos x_1}{m_c + m}}{l(\frac{4}{3} - \frac{m \cos^2 x_1}{m_c + m})}$$

where $G = 9.8$ m/s^2 is the gravitational acceleration, $m_c = 1.0$ kg is the mass of the cart, $l = 0.5$ m and $m = 0.1$ kg is the length and mass of the pole, u is the control input.

The objective is to control the angle of pole to track the output of desired reference model $\dot{y}_m = A_m y_m + B_m r$. The input command is $y_d = (\pi/30)\sin t$. First the tracking response of the nominal model is given. Then the robustness of the control scheme is verified by increasing the mass of pole 0.5Kg and considering external moment disturbance $0.1\sin t$ /N.m at 10s.

The reference model is given as follows

$$\dot{y}_m = A_m y_m + B_m r$$
$$A_m = \begin{bmatrix} 0 & 1 \\ -100 & -20 \end{bmatrix}, \quad B_m = \begin{bmatrix} 0 \\ 100 \end{bmatrix}$$

Adaptive gains $\gamma_1 = \gamma_2 = \gamma_3 = \gamma_4 = 0.01, \gamma_5 = 0, \kappa = 100 \kappa_g = 0.1$, Initial values of the neural networks weights are zero, the number of hidden layer neurons $N = 10$ and $b_0 = 0.1$. Control parameter $\lambda = [-100,-20], Q = 1$ and $x_1 = 2^0, x_2 = 0$ are the initial value of system states. One-order low pass filter with time constant 0.05s serving as the actuator dynamics is added into plant dynamics. Fig 2 is the tracking response of the angle of the pole where solid line represents the actual response and dash line is the desired command. Fig 3 the control input.

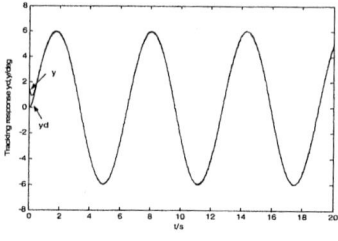

Fig. 2. Tracking response **Fig. 3.** Control input

From the results of simulation, we noticed that the closed system is stable and the output tracking error converge to a desired neighborhood of zero by increasing the control parameters.

5 Conclusion

In this paper, a neural networks direct adaptive control scheme for a class of SISO uncertain nonlinear systems is developed. Single hidden layer neural networks are used to approximate the unknown nonlinear functions. The Lyapunov function-based design of adaptive laws guarantees the global stability of the closed-loop system. The size of the residual set for the tracking error depends solely on design parameters and the initial value of the neural networks, which can be chosen to meet desired upper bounds for the tracking error.

References

1. Isidori A.: Nonlinear control systems II. London: Springer, 1999.
2. Krstic, M. , Kanellakopoulos, I. , Kokotovic, P.: Nonlinear and Adaptive Control Design,Weley Interscience, NewYork, 1995.
3. Slotine, J.E. , Li, W.: Applied Nonlinear Control, Prentice-Hall, Englewood Cliffs, NJ, 1991.
4. Sanner, R.M., Slotine, J.-J. E.: Gaussian networks for direct adaptive control. IEEE Trans. Neural Networks, 3 (1992) 837–863
5. Chen, F.-C., Khalil, H. K.: Adaptive control of a class of nonlinear discrete time systems using neural networks. IEEE Trans. Automat.Contr. 40 (1995) 791–801

6. Sadegh, N.: A perceptron network for functional identification using radial Gaussian networks. IEEE Trans. Neural Networks, 4 (1993) 982–988
7. Ge, S.S., Wang, C.: Adaptive Neural Control of Uncertain MIMO Nonlinear Systems. IEEE Trans. Neural Networks, 15 (2004) 674-692
8. Rovithakis,G.A., Christodulou, M.A.,: neural adaptive regulation of unknown nonlinear dynamical systems. IEEE Trans. Syst., Man, Cybern. B, 27 (1997) 810–822
9. Lewis, F.L., Liu,K., Yesildirek, A.: Neural net robot controller with guaranteed tracking performance. IEEE Trans. Neural Networks, 6 (1995) 703–715
10. Ge, S. S, Hang, C.C., Lee, T. H., et al: Stable adaptive neural network control. Boston : Kluwer Academic, 2002

Neural Network Based Feedback Scheduler for Networked Control System with Flexible Workload

Feng Xia, Shanbin Li, and Youxian Sun

National Laboratory of Industrial Control Technology,
Institute of Modern Control Engineering, Zhejiang University,
Hangzhou 310027, China
{xia, sbli, yxsun}@iipc.zju.edu.cn

Abstract. Most control applications closed over a shared network are suffering from the time-varying characteristics of flexible network workload. This gives rise to non-deterministic availability of communication resources and may significantly impact the control performance. In the context of integrating control and scheduling, a novel feedback scheduler based on neural networks is suggested. With a modular architecture, the proposed feedback scheduler mainly consists of a monitor, a predictor, a regulator and an actuator. An online learning Elman neural network is employed to predict the network conditions, and then the control period is dynamically adjusted in response to estimated available network utilization. A fast algorithm for period regulation is employed. Preliminary simulation results show that the proposed feedback scheduler is effective in managing workload variations and can provide runtime flexibility to networked control applications.

1 Introduction

Today's control systems are representatively closed over a shared network of certain type, e.g. CAN (Controller Area Network), FF (Foundation Fieldbus), and Control-Net. Despite widespread employment in many fields like automotive electronics, process control, and robotics, control networks in real world are always bandwidth limited. The reasons behind may be economical and/or technical. Although the adoption of common-bus instead of point-to-point connections reduces system complexity of installation and maintenance, it also conceives the time-varying property of network workload. For a specific control loop, the availability of communication resources may change unexpectedly [1,2], due to changes in network user demands, or disturbances in the network environments such as the loss of a link. In addition, this may also arise from the alternative use of general-purpose networks like Ethernet for control applications. Consequently, the network QoS (Quality of Service) becomes unexpectedly changeable in such environments that feature workload uncertainty and may not be able to provide QoS requirements to a networked control application as needed. This could considerably impact the networked control systems [3], especially when the available communication resources are scarce.

Although many control techniques have been proposed to attack time delay effects [4], the performance of control applications over a network is still tied with the network conditions regardless of the control algorithm used. It has been recognized that applying these control techniques on existing systems that are extensively being used in industrial plants could be costly, inconvenient, and time consuming. Moreover, as the real-world control applications become more and more complex, only compensating delay effects via controller design could not always guarantee satisfactory performance. While the system may perform unacceptably under overload conditions, certain communication resources may be wasted inadvertently in other cases. That is to say, traditional networked applications lack of flexibility, since they are usually designed regardless of the availability of communication resources.

In this paper, we introduce a novel methodology to address these problems, applying feedback scheduling methodology [5-8] to enable existing networked control applications in the presence of flexible workload. Emerging as a technique that integrates control and scheduling, feedback scheduling maps the methodology of feedback control to scheduling and provides a promising approach to manage uncertainty and enhance runtime flexibility. In this work, the well-established neural network (NN) technology [9] is employed to construct a feedback scheduler that is able to handle the workload variations intelligently. To achieve high efficiency as well as fast computation, we use a modified Elman network to learn from past and current network conditions and predict the future availability of network resources in order that the feedback scheduler can improve its behavior and respond in a pre-active fashion. If the workload abruptly increases, i.e. the QoS requirements cannot be provided as needed, the feedback scheduler will lower the required network utilization of a control loop and use the available network resources to perform the task as best as it can. In other cases when the workload decreases, the control performance will be upgraded to a maximum extent with the help of the feedback scheduler so that the available network resources are maximumly utilized. In this way, the feedback scheduler acts as an intelligent assistant to automate the management of flexible workload in NCSs.

The rest of this paper is structured as follows. Section 2 observes related works associated with our study. The architecture of the neural network based feedback scheduler is given in Section 3. We present the involved algorithms in Section 4. And its performance is evaluated via preliminary simulations in Section 5. Section 6 concludes this paper.

2 Related Works

An area that closely related to network QoS variations is congestion control. In this context, many mechanisms based on feedback methodology have been presented to manage network QoS. Feedback control technologies such as PID and fuzzy logic have been successfully used online to prevent the network from being congested [10]. When the aggregate demand for a bandwidth resource exceeds the available capacity of the network, they attempt to lower communication requirements of certain applications, thereby maintaining good network performance. Others employ neural networks to predict network traffic. Examples can be found in ATM [11], Internet [12] and other networks. However, almost all works in congestion control are not control related. Applications of neural networks can also be found in Internet based control systems, e.g. [13]. In these cases, neural networks are commonly employed for time delay forecast, which is different from the way we utilize them.

Researchers from the control community have made efforts to handle the impact of limited communication on control performance, for example, [14,15]. Most of these works focus on the design of control algorithms, and attempt to improve the system performance such as robustness with respect to uncertain communication delay. The methods used are static, i.e. they cannot provide run time adaptation to control tasks. In addition, these algorithms are often built upon simplified models of the complex characteristics of network workload variations. Instead of controller design, we focus on run time flexibility of control tasks. An interesting approach to providing networked control adaptation for network QoS variations is [1], where Chow and Tipsuwan propose a gain scheduling approach for networked DC motor control systems to compensate for the changes in QoS requirements.

Recent years witness considerable amount of attention on codesign of control and scheduling, both from the control community and the computing community. Several approaches to real-time QoS adaptation and graceful performance degradation in control applications are presented in the literature, e.g. [16,17]. A system' resource allocation is adjusted online in order to maximize the performance in certain respects. Feedback scheduling has been proposed as a promising methodology to increase flexibility and to master uncertainty with respect to resource allocation. Its applications for control purpose include optimal feedback scheduler [18] and its approximation versions [6], intelligent feedback schedulers [8,19] and those for anytime controllers [20,21]. However, these works are dedicated to co-design of control and CPU scheduling, while the main concern of this paper is control over networks with flexible workload.

In order to achieve dynamic integration of control and network scheduling, several methods have been proposed in the context of NCS. For example, Branicky et al [22] propose a co-design approach to the treatment of both network and controlled systems issues, where a set of control loops are optimally scheduled. Park et al [23] present a scheduling method for NCSs to adjust the sampling period as small as possible, allocate the bandwidth of the network for three types of data, and exchange the transmission orders of data for sensors and actuators. In [24], the allocation of bandwidth to control loops is done locally at run time according to the state of each controlled process, and control laws are designed to account for the variations on the assigned bandwidth. The methods employed in these works are reactive in the sense that they will only adjust the communication resource requirements of control applications once the network is already overloaded. We attempt to develop a pre-active approach to flexible quality of control (QoC) management with respect to network workload variations. A more detailed survey with additional references related to real-time scheduling in networked and embedded control systems can be found in [25].

3 Feedback Scheduling Architecture

The system we attempt to deploy the feedback scheduler into is a control loop sharing a network with other communication entities. The workload within the network may vary over time, and hence the available network utilization for this control application is non-deterministic. Generally, a traditional controller is designed offline regardless of workload variations. From the control perspective, the control performance may be degraded, or even destabilized due to the uncertain delays stemming from scarcity of network resources. From the scheduling perspective, the network resources may be under-utilized. To address these problems, both control and scheduling are synthetically considered. Following the methodology of feedback scheduling [5-8], a NN based feedback scheduler (see Fig.1) is proposed to maximize the control performance via maximum use of available network resources.

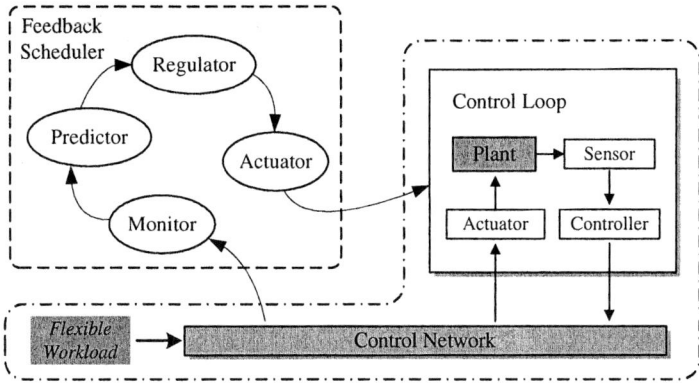

Fig. 1. Architecture of a networked control system equipped with a feedback scheduler

According to real-time scheduling theory, the requested network utilization can be calculated as $U_r = c/h$, where c is the transmission time and h is the transmission period, which is assumed to be equal to the sampling period of the control loop (also called control period). In order to comply with the CPU scheduling theory, we choose c to denote the time needed for transmitting the control loop's data/message in each sampling interval under the condition where total network bandwidth is exclusively dedicated to the considered control application, i.e. no other applications consuming communication bandwidth exist. It is assumed that the size of the data/message to be transmitted remains constant all the time. Therefore, the value of c does not change. For example, for a control network with a data rate of 1 Mb/s, if the data size is 500 bytes, the transmission time $c = 500 \times 8/10^3 = 4$ ms. And then, the requested network utilization U_r will only depend on the control period h. It is well-known in digital control theory that smaller sampling period leads to better control performance. In the case of resource constraints, however, this is not always the fact [3], and the sampling period should be determined properly so that the message is schedulable, i.e. the resource constraints cannot be violated. To reflect the uncertain characteristic of the workload, we use U to denote the available network utilization for the control loop, which is time varying and naturally bounded in the range [0, 1]. As the total bandwidth is fixed, U will be determined directly by current workload. Intuitively, larger U represents light workload while smaller U corresponds to heavy workload. In this way, the workload uncertainty can be reflected by unexpected changes in U.

Then, the problem of managing workload uncertainty can be stated as dynamically adjusting the sampling period with respect to the variations of U so that the tradeoff between control performance and available communication resource is achieved. As shown in Fig.1, the feedback scheduler introduced to address this problem mainly consists of four components: a monitor, a predictor, a regulator, and an actuator. The *monitor* interfaces with the control network and measures the variations in the network condition. It works periodically in time-driven fashion to activate the feedback scheduler. The *predictor* is built using neural networks and responsible for making prediction of the next-to-come value of the available network utilization. This enables the feedback scheduler to work in an intelligent way based on the history knowledge about the workload variations and to act in advance. Furthermore, the online learning capability of neural networks ensures the validity and efficiency of the feedback scheduler even when the characteristic behavior of workload variations changes. The *regulator* makes its decision based on the prediction of the neural predictor. It performs the role of determining a new sampling period to maximize the control performance under the predicted network resource constraint. The *actuator* within the feedback scheduler acts as an interface with the control loop to adjust its sampling period. To reduce sampling period jitters, an invocation condition is introduced in the actuator. The control period will be updated only when the absolute difference between the current value and the newly produced one exceeds a pre-specified deadband/threshold.

From the viewpoint of feedback control, the feedback scheduler can be regarded as a NN prediction based controller. The controlled variable is the network utilization, and the manipulated variable is the control loop's period. With flexible workload, the problem of feedback scheduling is similar to some kind of trajectory tracking issues, which are familiar to control engineers.

4 Algorithms

In this section, we present the algorithms utilized in the feedback scheduler. Particular emphasis is on two major components, the predictor and the regulator.

4.1 Neural Predictor

In the predictor, a neural network is employed to model the complex characteristics of the variations in available network utilization and estimate in real-time the next U value. To meet the timing constraints, we use a modified Elman network [9] (given in Fig.2) because of its simple structure, fast computation, and dynamic memory capability. There are two inputs, the current available network utilization $U(k)$ and its previous value $U(k-1)$, and one output, the predicted value of available network utilization at the next sampling instance, i.e. $\hat{U}(k+1)$, where k denotes sampling instances of the *monitor* within the feedback scheduler. Note that the sampling interval of the monitor is different from that of the control loop. The number of the hidden nodes is chosen to be 3. The squared error between the predicted and actual values, i.e. $\hat{U}(k+1)$ and $U(k+1)$ is chosen as the performance index for the online training operation at the $(k+1)^{th}$ instance.

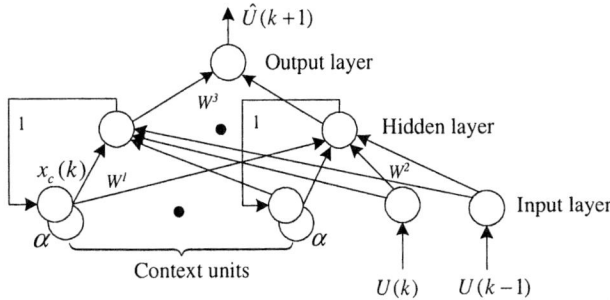

Fig. 2. Neural predictor structure

According to the neural network structure (Fig. 2), it is held that:

$$\hat{U}(k+1) = \sum_{l=1}^{3} W^3{}_l(k) f(\sum_{j=1}^{3} W^1{}_{qj}(k) x_{c,q}(k) + \sum_{i=1}^{2} W^2{}_{ij}(k) I_i(k) - T_{h,j}(k)) - T_o(k) \quad (1)$$

where $x_c(k) = \alpha x_c(k-1) + x(k-1)$, $I_1(k) = U(k)$, $I_2(k) = U(k-1)$, $f(x) = 1/(1+e^{-x})$ is the activation function, T_h and T_o are biases in the hidden layer and the output layer, respectively, and W^1, W^2, W^3 are connection weights.

In this work, the standard BP algorithm is employed for the network training. Thus the weights and biases of the network can be updated at each sampling instance according to:

$$\begin{aligned}\Delta w_j^3 &= \eta \delta^o x_j(k) & j &= 1,2,3 \\ \Delta w_{ij}^2 &= \eta \delta_j^h I_i(k-1) & i &= 1,2 \\ \Delta w_{qj}^1 &= \eta (\delta^o W^3{}_j) \frac{\partial x_j(k)}{\partial w_{qj}^1} & q &= 1,2,3\end{aligned} \quad (2)$$

where $\dfrac{\partial x_j(k)}{\partial w_{qj}^1} = f'{}_j(\cdot) x_q(k-1) + \alpha \dfrac{\partial x_j(k-1)}{\partial w_{qj}^1}$, $\delta^o = (y_d(k) - y(k)) g'(\cdot)$, $g(\cdot)$ is set to be the *purelin* function, $\delta_j^h = (\delta^o w^3{}_j) f'{}_j(\cdot)$, $f'(\cdot)$ and $g'(\cdot)$ are derivatives of $f(\cdot)$ and $g(\cdot)$, respectively.

4.2 Regulator

According to the data/information flow inside the feedback scheduler, the output of the predictor, i.e. the estimated value of the available network utilization $\hat{U}(k+1)$ will be forwarded into the regulator. Based on this input and its internal knowledge about the transmission time of the control loop, the regulator attempts to determine an optimal sampling period. In the newly emerging field of feedback scheduling, it has been revealed [6,18] that a simple rescaling of the sampling period could bring almost optimal solutions in most cases. Therefore, in order to achieve timely responses, we use the following simple and fast calculation to determine the control period:

$$h(k) = \frac{U_0}{\hat{U}(k)} h_0 \qquad (3)$$

where h_0 is the nominal period, and U_0 is the nominal requested network utilization, which satisfies $U_0 = c/h_0$. Let's take a look at the control period $h(k)$ deduced from equation (3) from the viewpoints of both control and scheduling. Firstly, on the behalf of scheduling, the available network resources will be maximumly used, since the requested utilization $U(k) = c/h(k) = h_0U_0/h(k) = \hat{U}(k)$. Given that the available network utilization is accurately predicted, there will be no waste of resources, while the constraints are properly met. Secondly, for control purpose, the minimum control period under current resource constraint is obtained because any h value smaller than the one in (3) will result in a requested utilization more than the network can provide. Therefore, the control performance will be maximized using this *regulator*.

Once produced, the new sampling period $h(k)$ will be put forward to the actuator as its input. And then, it will be decided whether to take an action to update the control period according to the invocation condition inside the actuator.

Obviously, there are two important design parameters within the monitor and the actuator, with one for each. The first one is the sampling interval of the monitor. It is used to determine how often the network condition is sampled. Intuitively, smaller intervals allow high sensitivity while being more resource consuming, and vice versa. The second one is the deadband utilized in the actuator. It is originally employed to avoid too frequent refreshing operations on the control period, which inversely degrades the control performance. Similarly, a smaller deadband leads to more accurate response to workload variations while being more sensitive to noises, and vice versa. Without formal design methodology for these parameters, tradeoffs should be done when implementing the feedback scheduler in practical applications.

5 Performance Evaluation

In this section, we evaluate the performance of the proposed feedback scheduler through considering networked control of a plant over a CAN-bus. The controlled plant is given as $G(s) = 1000/(s^2 + s)$. The transmission time c is assumed to be 4 ms. With nominal network utilization $U_0 = 0.5$ provided, a traditional PID controller is well-designed pre-runtime to control the plant. The nominal control period $h_0 = 8$ ms. During run time, the available network utilization varies as shown in Fig. 3 (dashed magenta line), reflecting characteristic behaviors of flexible workload. The following two cases are simulated.

In Case I, the controller works with a fixed sampling period of 8 ms all along. Therefore, the requested network utilization remains changeless, see dash-dot red line in Fig. 3. In the time interval t = 0 to 1 s, because the available network utilization vibrates around 0.5, the control performance is slightly impacted, as shown in Fig. 4 (dashed red line). Still, the performance is satisfactory. From t = 1 to 2s, the plant performs well thanks to good availability of network resources. However, a lot of network resource is wasted. From time t = 2 s, the control system turns to be unstable because the available network utilization falls below the requested value of 0.5.

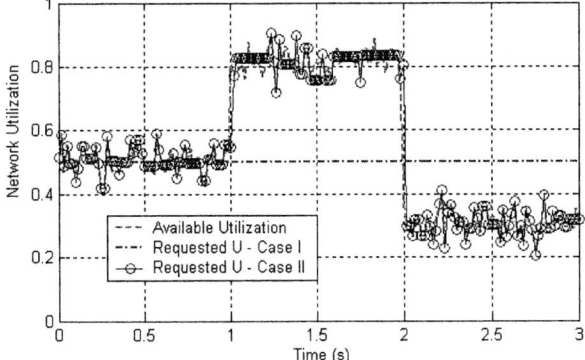

Fig. 3. Network utilization

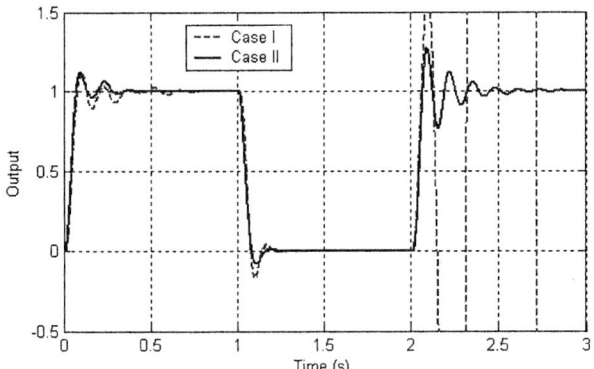

Fig. 4. Transient responses of the plant

In Case II, the NN based feedback scheduler we present is implemented. The sampling interval of the *monitor* is chosen as 15 ms. The deadband in the *actuator* is set to be 0.5 ms. The PID parameters are online updated to compensate jitters of the control period, allowing us to concentrate on the effectiveness of the proposed feedback scheduler. The requested network utilization is illustrated in Fig. 3 (solid blue line with circles). The system response is also plotted in Fig.4 (solid blue line). As we can see, the control performance is improved all along the simulation. This is especially the truth when the available utilization goes below U_0 from t = 2s. With the help of the NN based feedback scheduler, the plant exhibits satisfactory performance even when the network resources become scarce. In response to workload variations, the feedback scheduler attempts to maximize the control performance through maximizing the use of available network resources in an intelligent way all the time, as shown in Fig. 3 and 4. This mainly benefits from the powerful capability of the Elman NN for effectively predicting the network conditions.

6 Conclusions

Control applications built upon a shared control network must meet increasingly demanding requirements to cope with significant degrees of workload uncertainty, especially when the communication resource is limited. These requirements give rise to the integration of feedback control and network scheduling. In this paper, we demonstrate a novel application of neural networks in the newly emerging field of feedback scheduling. In order to handle flexible workload in control networks, we present a feedback scheduler based on a neural predictor. The primary goal is to maximize the quality of control under constraints on the availability of network resources. It is argued that this feedback scheduler allows the control application to be highly flexible with respect to complex workload variations, while improving the control performance to the maximum extent. As a future work in this direction, we will attempt to develop effective control algorithms to compensate the sampling period jitter, which seems to be the main problem in the proposed approach.

References

1. M.-Y. Chow and Y. Tipsuwan: Gain Adaptation of Networked DC Motor Controllers Based on QOS Variations. IEEE Trans. on Industrial Electronics 50:5 (2003) 936-943
2. Feng Xia, Xiaohua Dai, Zhi Wang, and Youxian Sun: Feedback Based Network Scheduling of Networked Control Systems, in Proc. 5th ICCA, Budapest, Hungary (2005)
3. Feng Xia, Zhi Wang, and Youxian Sun: Integrated Computation, Communication and Control: Towards Next Revolution in Information Technology, LNCS, Vol. 3356, Springer-Verlag (2004) 117-125
4. Y. Tipsuwan and M.-Y. Chow: Control methodologies in networked control systems. Control Eng. Practice 11:10 (2003) 1099-1111
5. C. Lu, J. Stankovic, G. Tao, S.H. Son: Feedback control real-time scheduling: framework, modeling, and algorithms, Real-time Systems 23:1/2 (2002) 85-126
6. A. Cervin, J. Eker, B. Bernhardsson, K.-E. Årzén: Feedback-Feedforward Scheduling of Control Tasks, Real-Time Systems 23:1 (2002) 25-53
7. L. Abeni, L. Palopoli, G. Lipari, J. Walpole: Analysis of a Reservation-Based Feedback Scheduler, in Proc. 23rd IEEE RTSS, Austin, Texas (2002) 71-80
8. Feng Xia and Youxian Sun: Neural Network Based Feedback Scheduling of Multitasking Control Systems, to appear in Proc. KES2005, LNCS, Springer-Verlag (2005)
9. Zengyin Sun, Zaixing Zhang, Zhidong Deng: Intelligent Control Theory and Technology, Beijing: Tsinghua University Press (1997) (in Chinese)
10. S. Ryu, C. Rump, C. Qiao: Advances in Internet Congestion Control. IEEE Communications Surveys and Tutorials 5:1 (2003) 28-39
11. Y.-C. Liu, C. Douligeris: Rate Regulation with Feedback Controller in ATM Networks - A Neural Network Approach, IEEE Journal on Selected Area in Communications 15:2 (1997) 200-208
12. A. Bhattacharya, A. Parlos, A. Atiya: Prediction of MPEG-Coded Video Source Traffic Using Recurrent Neural Networks, IEEE Trans. on Signal Processing 51:8 (2003) 2177-2190
13. D. Liu, J. Du, Y. Zhao, N. Song: Study on the Time-Delay of Internet-based Industry Process Control System, in Proc. 5th WCICA, Hangzhou, China, Vol.2 (2004) 1376-1380

14. L. Xiao, M. Johansson, H. Hindi, S. Boyd, A. Goldsmith: Joint Optimization of Communication Rates and Linear Systems, IEEE Trans. on Automatic Control 48:1 (2003) 148-153
15. Shanbin Li, Yong-Yan Cao, Yongqiang Wang, Youxian Sun: Robust H_∞ Control of Uncertain Markovian Jump Systems with Mode-Dependent Time-Delays, in Proc. 16th IFAC World Congress, Prague, Czech Republic (2005)
16. T. Abdelzaher, E. Atkins, and K. Shin: QoS Negotiation in Real-Time Systems and Its Application to Automated Flight Control, IEEE Trans. on Computers 49:11 (2000) 1170-1183
17. G. Beccari, S. Caselli, M. Reggiani, F. Zanichelli: Rate modulation of soft real-time tasks in autonomous robot control systems, in Proc. 11th ECRTS, York, England (1999) 21-28
18. J. Eker, P. Hagander, K.-E. Årzén: A feedback scheduler for real-time controller tasks. Control Engineering Practice 8:12 (2000) 1369-1378
19. Feng Xia, Liping Liu, and Youxian Sun: Flexible Quality-of-Control Management in Embedded Systems Using Fuzzy Feedback Scheduling, to appear in Proc. RSFDGrC, LNCS, Springer-Verlag (2005)
20. Feng Xia and Youxian Sun: Anytime Iterative Optimal Control Using Fuzzy Feedback Scheduler, to appear in Proc. KES2005, LNCS, Springer-Verlag (2005)
21. D. Henriksson, A. Cervin, J. Åkesson, K.-E. Årzén: Feedback Scheduling of Model Predictive Controllers, in Proc. 8th IEEE RTAS, San Jose, CA (2002) 207-216
22. M. Branicky, S. Philips, and W. Zhang: Scheduling and feedback co-design for networked control systems, in Proc. 41st IEEE CDC, Las Vegas (2002) 1211-1217
23. H. Park, Y. Kim, D-S. Kim, W.H. Kwon: A Scheduling Method for Network-based Control Systems, IEEE Trans. on Control System Tech. 10:3 (2002) 318-330
24. M. Velasco, J. Fuertes, C. Lin, P. Marti, S. Brandt: A Control Approach to Bandwidth Management in Networked Control Systems, in Proc. 30th IEEE IECON, Busan, Korea (2004)
25. Feng Xia, Hongxia Yin, Zhi Wang, Youxian Sun: Theory and Practice of Real-time Scheduling in Networked Control Systems, in Proc. 17th Chinese Control and Decision Conference, Harbin, China (2005) (in Chinese)

Humanoid Walking Gait Optimization Using GA-Based Neural Network

Zhe Tang[1,2], Changjiu Zhou[2], and Zengqi Sun[1]

[1] Department of Computer Science and Technology, Tsinghua University,
Beijing 100084, P.R. China
Tangzhe00@mails.tsinghua.edu.cn
[2] School of Electrical and Electronic Engineering, Singapore Polytechnic,
500 Dover Road, Singapore 139651
ZhouCJ@sp.edu.sg
http://www.robo-erectus.org

Abstract. A humanoid walking gait synthesizing approach, which is able to generate gaits in both sagittal and frontal planes, is presented in this paper. To further improve the humanoid walking gait in consideration of both ZMP (Zero Moment Point) and energy consumption constraints, a two-stage optimization method is proposed. At the first stage, real-coded GAs (genetic algorithms) are used to generate a set of near-optimal walking gaits. At the second stage, the near-optimal walking gaits are used as training samples for a GA-based NN (neural network) to further improve the humanoid walking gait. By making use of the global optimization capability of GAs, the GA-based NN can solve the local minima problem. The proposed approach is able to generate near-optimal walking gait at any speed in feasible range. Experiments are conducted to verify the effectiveness of the proposed method.

1 Introduction

Recently intelligent techniques, such as NN (neural network), Fuzzy Logic, GAs (Genetic Algorithms) and hybrid intelligent approaches etc, have found wide applications in advanced control of humanoid robots [1]. The basic strong point of intelligent techniques is the model-free approach for optimization, which requires only feedback from environment to improve performance. Because of the high DOFs (degree-of-freedom) and complex mechanical structure, the precise dynamics model of the humanoid is difficult to obtain. Therefore, intelligent techniques are naturally a good choice in planning and control of humanoid robots.

Any kind of intelligent techniques have their own strong points and drawbacks. To overcome the drawbacks, certain integration and synthesis of hybrid techniques are needed for efficient application in humanoid robotics. Zhou [2] proposed a reinforcement learning-based neuro-fuzzy scheme to synthesize trunk trajectories of the humanoid robot, while all other joint trajectories are prescribed. The proposed gait synthesis can combine the linguistic knowledge of fuzzy logic with the learning strength of NN. Juang [3] presented a fuzzy neural network method to synthesize the humanoid walking gait. The method uses a fuzzy modeling neural network controller with the BTT (back-propagation through time) algorithm. The fuzzy modeling neural network overcomes the uncertainty of network size in the conventional neural network learning scheme. Fukuda, et.al [4] used ZMP as stabilization index, and select the best configuration with recurrent neural network. Recurrent networks are trained by GAs which have the self-adaptive mutation. Nagasaka et.al [5] gave a GA based approach for the motion acquisition problem which treats a real robot with a complicated body and a noisy environment by taking the case of visually guided swing motion by vision-equipped two-armed bipedal robot.

Walking gait synthesis for humanoid has been developed in our previous work [6]. The method decomposed the motion of the humanoid into three planes, sagittal, frontal, and transverse plane. The walking planning was implemented in these three planes independently and the energy optimization was not taken into account for the walking planning. In this paper, we use hybrid intelligent techniques to optimize the humanoid 3D walking gait. The optimization process consists of two stages, at the first stage, real-coded GAs are used to optimize a set of walking gaits, those gaits are walking at different speeds. The optimization objective is to minimize energy consumption and ZMP tracking error. At the second of stage, a GA-based NN is used to generalize the optimal walking gaits set obtained by the first stage. The GAs are used for training NN. After the generalization, the NN is able to give an optimal walking gait at any feasible speeds.

Because of their global search capabilities, EAs (Evolutionary algorithms), such as GAs, ES (evolution strategies), and EP (evolution programming), have been introduced into NN by many researchers [7-13]. The combination of EAs and NN refers to a special class of NN, EANNs (Evolutionary Artificial Neural Networks). The major advantage of EANNs is their adaptability to dynamic environment [9]. Many promising EANNs simulation results have been published. Yao [7, 8, 9] has given a comprehensive reviews on EANNs. However, there are very few pragmatic EANN applications up to now, especially in the robotics field.

This paper is organized as follows. The walking gait synthesis, developed in our previous work, is reviewed in Section 2. In section 3, a two-stage optimization method for humanoid walking gait is proposed. Section 4 gives experiment results. Concluding remarks are given in Section 5.

2 Walking Gait Synthesis

2.1 Humanoid Robot Walking Planning

Humanoid walking is a periodic motion which alternates between the double-support phase and the single-support phase [14]. During the double-support phase, both of the humanoid robot feet are in contact with ground. During the single-support phase, only one foot is in contact with ground to support the humanoid, the other leg swings forward. For one leg, the walking process is composed of a stance phase and swing phase. We define the leg at robot's double support phase as leg's swing phase. The robot's double-support phase is the overlap period of two legs' swing phase.

Fig. 1 gives a walking cycle starting from kth step, where T_c is one walking cycle period, T_d is double support-phase time, and $kT_c + T_m$ corresponds to the point when the foot of swing leg reaches its highest point, where the swing height is H_{ao}, the length relative to the support foot is L_{ao}, D_s is the step length. The motion in the transverse plane gives the desired robot ZMP trajectory.

In order to control a humanoid robot's movement, it is necessary to generate the trajectories of all humanoid joints. The trajectories should have first-order and second-order derivative continuity. First order derivative continuity guarantees the smoothness of joint velocity, while second order is the smoothness requirements of acceleration or torque of joints.

Trajectory generation in Cartesian space for the humanoid robot can be summarized as follows: (the humanoid robot walking model is shown in Fig. 2. This model is a simplified one which neglects the foot and hip, and only considers one leg because the other leg is symmetric.)

1. Defining the position of the ankle position $(x_a(t), y_a(t))$ at the switching points and some other interpolation points to constrain the walking pattern. From these positions, the trajectory is generated using polynomial interpolation.

2. Defining the position of the hip position $(x_h(t), y_h(t))$ at some given via-points, then generating the trajectory of the hip using interpolation by the third-order polynomials. Based on the above positions of hip and ankle, the knee position $(x_k(t), y_k(t))$ is obtained using the geometric equation.1.

$$x_k = x_a + l_2 \cos\left\{\tan^{-1}\left[(y_h - y_a)/(x_h - x_a)\right] - \cos^{-1}\left[(l_2^2 + (x_h - x_a)^2 + (y_h - y_a)^2 - l_1^2)/2l_2\sqrt{(x_h - x_a)^2 + (y_h - y_a)^2}\right]\right\}$$

$$y_k = y_a + l_2 \sin\left\{\tan^{-1}\left[(y_h - y_a)/(x_h - x_a)\right] - \cos^{-1}\left[(l_2^2 + (x_h - x_a)^2 + (y_h - y_a)^2 - l_1^2)/2l_2\sqrt{(x_h - x_a)^2 + (y_h - y_a)^2}\right]\right\} \quad (1)$$

3. From the positions of the joints, the joint angles can be obtained from the inverse kinematics equation.2.

$$\theta_h = -\tan^{-1}\left[(z_k - z_h)/(x_k - x_h)\right] \pm \pi/2$$
$$\theta_a = -(\pi/2 \pm \tan^{-1}\left[(z_k - z_a)/(x_k - x_a)\right]) \quad (2)$$
$$\theta_k = \theta_a + \theta_h$$

Trajectory generation in frontal the plane is relatively simpler than that in the sagittal plane. The objective of the humanoid motion in the frontal plane is to move the ZMP of the robot from one foot to the other alternatively. For one leg of the robot, there are two DOFs to control the robot motion in the frontal plane: on at the hip joint and one at the ankle joint. To simplify the walking planning, two legs always keep parallel, so the angles of the four DOFs are the same. Given the maximum robot swing angle (Q_{max}) in the front plane, the trajectories of the four DOFs can be generated in the joint space.

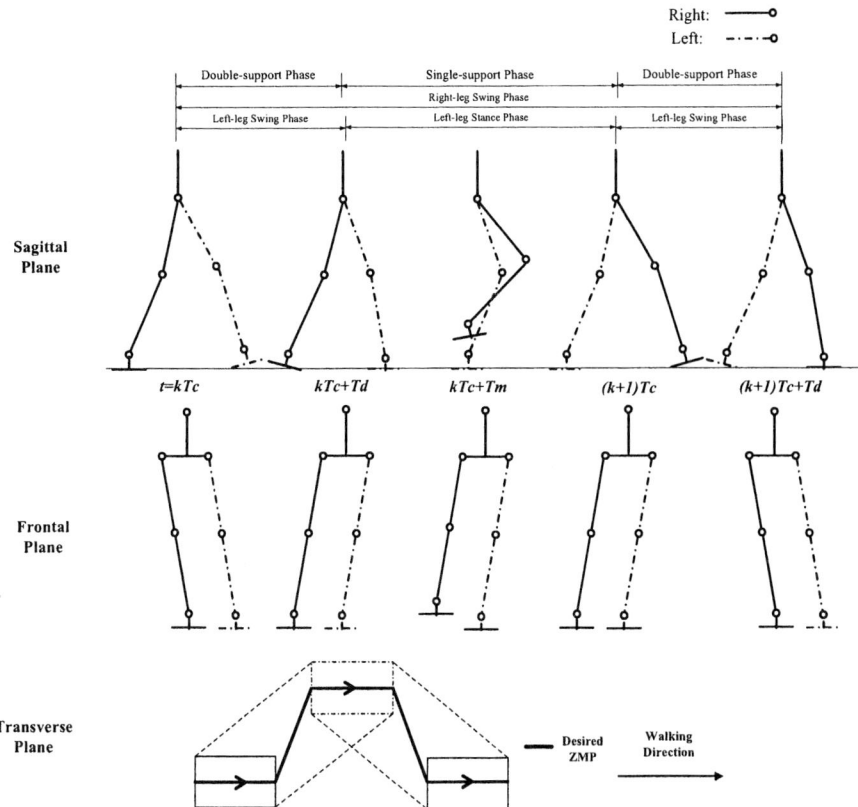

Fig. 1. Walking planning, in the sagittal plane, the robot's double support phase is the overlap of the two legs' swing phase. The four DOFs, which control the humanoid motion in the frontal plane, are assumed to be the same angle. The robot ZMP can be obtained from the transverse plane.

2.2 Problem Identification

From the above walking planning, there are several trial-error procedures: defining many specific interpolation positions of the ankle and the hip to generate joint trajectories. It is difficult to obtain the mathematical relationship between the interpolation points and the ZMP trajectory, so those interpolation points are set only by experiences. This procedure is very time consuming.

There is no unique problem solution for the biped dynamic walking. Any trajectory through the state space (with constrains) that does not result in a failure signal (fall down) is acceptable. To synthesise the biped walking motion, it is required to take a workspace variable p from an initial position p_i at time t_i to a final position p_f at time t_f. The motion trajectory for $p(t)$ can be obtained by solving an optimisation problem. To achieve the dynamic walking, the ZMP is usually used as a criterion, therefore, we can determine the biped motion to minimise the following performance index:

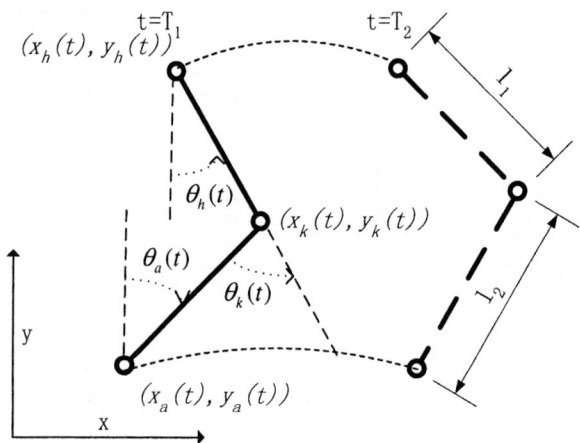

Fig. 2. Simplified walking model of humanoid robot

$$\text{Minimize} \quad \int_{t_i}^{t_f} \left\| P_{zmp}(t) - P_{zmp}^d(t) \right\|^2 dt \quad (3)$$

subject to the boundary conditions of both $p(t)$ and $\dot{p}(t)$ at time t_i and t_f, where P_{zmp} is the actual ZMP, and P_{zmp}^d is the desired ZMP position. The control objective of the gait synthesis for biped dynamic walking can be described as:

$$P_{zmp} = (x_{zmp}, y_{zmp}, 0) \in S \quad (4)$$

where ($x_{zmp}, y_{zmp}, 0$) is the coordinate of the ZMP with respect to O-XYZ. S is the domain of the supporting area.

Apart from the stability region consideration, energy consumption is another crucial evaluation for the biped walking planning. However, the mathematical model, describing the relation between the joint trajectories and the energy consuming is not available either.

3 Optimization of Humanoid Walking Gait

As described in the Section 2, many parameters need to be defined for humanoid walking gait synthesis. However, there is no mathematical model describing the relation between these parameters and walking performance, such as stability region, energy consumption. Tuning these parameters through trial-error is very time-consuming. A two stage optimization method is proposed for the optimal walking gait synthesis. At the first stage, real-coded GAs are used to optimize a set of walking gaits, those gaits are walking at different speed and step length. The optimization objective is to minimize energy consumption and ZMP error. At the second of stage, a

GAs based NN was used to generalize the optimal walking gaits set obtained by the first stage, The GAs are used for training NN. After the generalization, the NN can give an optimal walking gait at any feasible speeds.

To improve walking performance, we first need to identify the key parameters that greatly influence the humanoid walking performance. These key parameters are the maximum lean angle of the robot in the frontal plane (Q_{max}), double support time (T_d), the ankle position (H_{ao}) and hip velocity (H_{vel}) at time (T_m). Q_{max} determines the robot motion in the frontal plane. Increasing the double support time (T_d) means decreasing the single support time when walking cycle is fixed. H_{ao} and H_{vel} determine the motion of swing leg and upper body of robot. These four parameters are used as GAs search space.

Optimal walking gait should possess two characteristics: wide stability region and minimum energy consumption. These characteristics can be described as GAs objective function as follows:

$$J = 1/2(k \int_0^{t_f} \tau^T \tau dt + (1-k) \int_0^{t_f} Edt) \to \min \quad (5)$$

where t_f is walking cycle, τ is the torque vector of robot. E is error of the desired robot ZMP and calculated ZMP, small E value means wide stability region, k is a coefficient, which balances the weight of the two objectives. The detailed procedure of GAs is shown in Fig. 3.

After first stage GAs optimization, a set of optimal walking gaits were obtained for NN training samples. Real-coded GAs are adopted for NN training. To simplify our application, GAs are only for evolution of connection weights, the size of the NN is fixed. A three layer forward NN is used for our experiment.

The input-output relationship of the NN is described by

$$y^d(t) = g(x^d(t)), t = 1, 2, \ldots, n_d \quad (6)$$

Where $x^d(t) = [x_1^d(t) \ x_2^d(t) \ \cdots \ x_l^d(t)]$ and $y^d(t) = [y_1^d(t) \ y_2^d(t) \ \cdots \ y_m^d(t)]$ are given inputs and the desired outputs of an unknown nonlinear function g(.) respectively, l and m are the number of inputs and outputs respectively, n_d denotes the number of input-output data pairs. The fitness function is defined as equations.7,8:

$$Fitness = \frac{1}{err} \quad (7)$$

$$err = \sum_{k=1}^{m} \frac{\sum_{t=1}^{n_d} |y_k^d(t) - y_k(t)|}{n_d} \quad (8)$$

The objective is to maximize the fitness value of equation.7 using GAs. The chromosomes are w_{ij} for all i, j. It can be seen from eqution.7 and equation.8 that a larger fitness value implies a smaller error value.

Step 1: Set up initial condition: walking cycle, step length, robot parameters, GAs parameters, solution space
Step 2: Generate the initial population under constraints, GN=1
Step 3: Obtain the four parameters from the population and walk one cycle through simulation
Step 4: If the walking meets kinematics constraints go to step 6, else go to step 5
Step 5: Adjust the key parameters and go back to step 3.
Step 6: GAs operation, fitness evaluation, apply selection, apply crossover and apply mutation
Step 7: GN=GN+1, if GN<GN_{max} go to step 2 else go to step 8
Step 8: Obtain final parameters and optimal motion set.

Fig. 3. The procedure of the GA optimization

4 Experiment Results

At the first stage of humanoid walking gait optimization, 36 sets of optimal walking gaits are generated through real-coded GAs. The 36 sets of gait are walking at 6 different step lengths and 6different walking cycles. For any set of walking gaits, the four parameters (Q_{max}, T_d, H_{ao}, H_{vel}) are searched by GAs. The objective function is equation.5. The GAs parameters are given in Table.1

Table 1. GA Parameters

Maximum Generations	200
Population Size	10
Crossover Probability	0.6
Mutation Probability	0.1

To demonstrate the effectiveness of the GAs for humanoid walking gait, a set of walking gait results are given. When T_c=3.2 s and D_s=4cm, or velocity = 4/3.2 = 1.25cm/s, Fig. 4 gives the evaluation function value. Fig. 5 shows the improvements of ankle joint torque consumption after optimization. Fig.6 is the ZMP trajectory, it can be seen that the ZMP trajectory is much closer to the desired one after optimization.

After the first stage of optimization, the 36 sets of walking gaits are obtained to train an NN by GAs. There are three layers, two inputs nodes, four output nodes and four hidden nodes for the NN. The GAs parameters, except the maximum generation is set 900, are same with that at the first stage.Fig.7 presents the fitness of the GAs during training the NN. The four key parameters generated by the NN are shown in the Figs.8-11.

5 Conclusions

Humanoid walking gait synthesis is a difficult task, because of high DOFs and variable mechanical structure during walking. This paper proposed a two-stage optimization approach to achieve efficient walking gait for humanoid robot. At the first stage optimization, real-coded GA was adopted to generate a set of near-optimal walking gait in consideration of both energy consumption and ZMP constraints. At the second stage optimization, a GA-based NN was used to generalize the walking gaits. After the GAs training with the optimal gaits obtained in the first stage, the NN is able to give a near-optimal walking gait at any feasible step length and walking cycle. So the two-stage optimization gait synthesis is able to give consecutive actions (near-optimal walking gaits) for higher level decision controller. This is crucial when the robot is operating in a complex environment, which requires the robot dynamically change walking gait in real-time.

Humans have remarkable learning capability to change walking gaits very quickly even in uncertain and unpredictable environments. How to integrate both imitation and reinforcement learning approaches and make use of different kinds of information to further optimize humanoid walking gaits and speed up learning will be our future research focus.

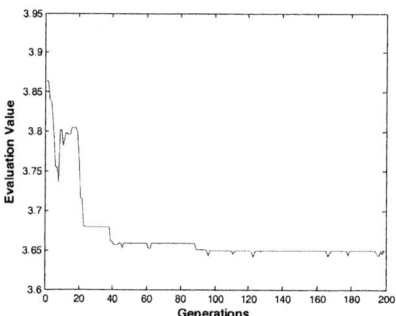

Fig. 4. Evaluation value during GAs training

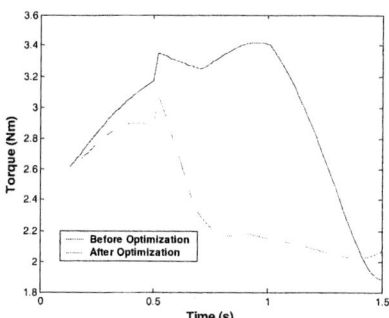

Fig. 5. The torque trajectories of ankle joint

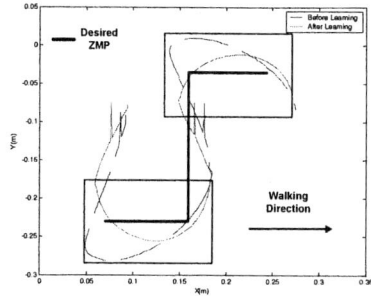

Fig. 6. ZMP trajectories

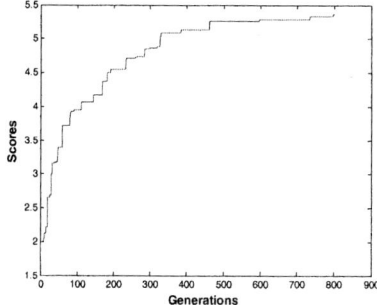

Fig. 7. The fitness value of the GAs based NN during training

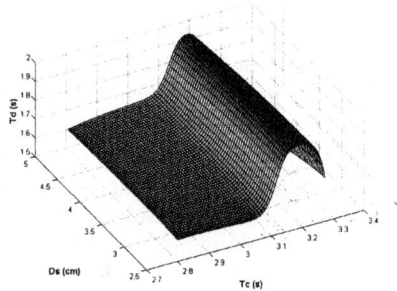

Fig. 8. Double support time (T_d) given by NN

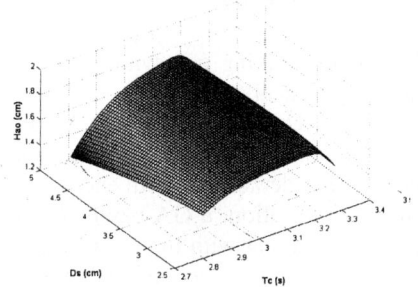

Fig. 9. Ankle maximum swing height (H_{ao}) given by NN

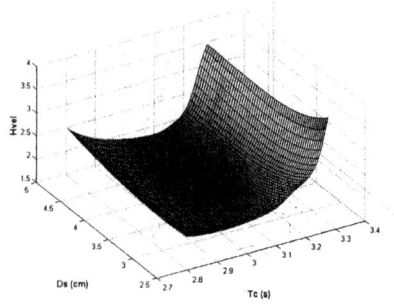

Fig. 10. Hip velocity (H_{vel}) given by NN

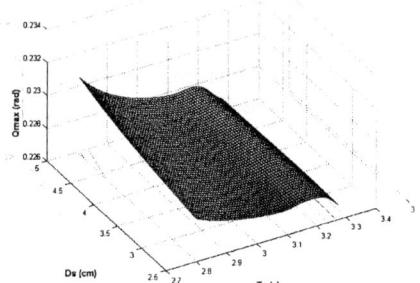

Fig. 11. The Robot maximum lean angle in the frontal plane (Q_{max}) given by NN

References

1. Katic, D., Vukobratovic, M.: Survey of Intelligent Control Techniques for Humanoid Robots. Journal of Intelligent and Robotic Systems, Vol. 37. (2003) 117-141
2. Zhou, C.: Nero-fuzzy gait synthesis with reinforcement learning for a biped walking robot. Soft Computing, Vol. 4. Springer-Verlag, Berlin-Heidelberg, (2000) 238-250
3. Juang, J.-G.: Fuzzy neural network approaches for robotic gait synthesis. IEEE Transactions on Systems, Man and Cybernetics, Part B, Vol. 30. (Aug 2000) 594-601
4. Fukuda, T., Komata, Y., Arakawa, T.: Stabilization Control of Biped Locomotion Robot based learning with GAs having self-adaptive mutation and recurrent neural networks. Proc. Of the International Conference on Robotics & Automation, Albuquerque, New Mexico (April 1997) 217-222
5. Nagasaka, K., Konno, A., Inaba M., Inoue H.: Acquisition of visually guided swing motion based on genetic algorithms and neural networks in two-armed bipedal robot. Proc. Of the International Conference on Robotics & Automation. Albuquerque, New Mexico (April 1997) 2944-2949
6. Tang, Z., Zhou, C., Sun, Z.: Gait Planning for Soccer Playing Humanoid Robots. Lectures Notes in Control and Information Sciences, Vol.299. Springer-Verlag, Berlin Heidelberg New York (2004) 241-262

7. Yao, X.: A review of evolutionary artificial neural networks. Int. J. Intell. Syst., Vol. 8, No. 4, (1993) 539-567
8. Yao, X.: Evolutionary artificial neural networks. Int. J. Neural Syst., Vol. 4, No. 3, (1993) 203-222
9. Yao, X.: Evolving Artificial Neural Networks. Proceedings of the IEEE, 87 (9): (Sep 1999) 1423-1447
10. Richard, K.B., McInerney J., Nicol, N.S.: Evolving Networks: Using the Genetic Algorithm with Connectionist Learning. Proc. Second Conference on Artificial Life, Addison-Wesley. (1991) 511-547
11. Frank, H. F. L., Lam H.K., Ling S.H., Peter, K.S.T: Tuning of the Structure and Parameters of a Neural Network Using an Improved Genetic Algorithm. IEEE Tans. Neural Networks, Vol. 14, No. 1, (Jan 2003) 7988
12. Janson, D.J., Frenzel, J.F.: Application of genetic algorithms to the training of higher order neural networks. Journal of System Engineering, Vol. 2. (1992)272-276
13. Lewis, M.A., Fagg A.H., Solidum, A.: Genetic Programming approach to the construction of a neural network for control of a walking robot. Proc. Of the International Conference on Robotics & Automation, Los Alamitos, CA, Vol. 3, (1992) 2618-1623
14. Vukobratovic, M., Borovac, M., Surla, B., Stokic, D.: Biped Locomotion: Dynamics, Stability, Control and Application, Springer-Verlag, Berlin-Heidelberg New York (1990)

Adaptive Neural Network Internal Model Control for Tilt Rotor Aircraft Platform

Changjie Yu[1,2], Jihong Zhu[1], and Zengqi Sun[1]

[1] State Key Lab of Intelligent Technology and Systems,
Tsinghua University, Beijing 100084, China
[2] Air Defence Command College, Zhengzhou 450052, China
yu-cj03@mails.tsinghua.edu.cn

Abstract. An adaptive neural networks internal model controller is designed for a tilt rotor aircraft platform. The behavior of the research platform, in certain aspects, resembles that of a tilt rotor aircraft. The proposed control architecture can compensate external disturbances and dynamic inversion error. The controller includes an on-line learning neural network of inverse model and an off-line trained neural network of forward model. Lyapunov stability analysis guarantees tracking errors and network parameters are bounded. The performance of the controller is demonstrated using the tilt rotor aircraft platform, including nacelle tilting flight.

1 Introduction

In proposed controller structure of adaptive neural network internal model, the role of the platform forward and inverse models is emphasized. The platform forward and inverse models are used directly as elements within the feedback loop. We propose a two step procedure for using neural networks directly with the internal model control(IMC) structure. The first step involves an off-line training neural network model(NNM) to represent the tilt rotor aircraft platform response. The second step in the procedure is that a neural network controller(NNC) is first trained off-line to emulate the inversion model of NNM directly. During on-line operation, The controller plays a role as a feedforward controller. However, it can cancel the influence due to unmeasured disturbances, which can not be done by a traditional feedforward controller. This approach is performed on the experimental setup of tilt rotor aircraft and it is effective to compensate external disturbances.

Consider for example the costs associated with development of conventional augmentation scheduling techniques, where the control gains are to be scheduled over all the possible flight conditions and configurations of a tilt rotor. The adaptive neural networks model inversion control[1,2,3] and model predictive control[4] result in some progress. Moreover, the idea of using neural networks for nonlinear IMC has been considered by Hunt and Sbarbaro [5]. Fortunately, the combination of adaptive neural networks (ANN) and internal model control can relieve this need for extensive scheduling.

2 Experimental Setup and Controller Architecture

The general appearance picture of our experimental setup is shown in Fig. 1. The tilt rotor aircraft platform is mounted on a base E as shown in Fig. 2. The arm BF can rotate around the center O freely, and ψ and θ are the yaw and the pitch angles, respectively. The wing LR can also rotate freely on the axis BF, and ϕ is the roll angle. The left and right nacelles can tilt around L, R, and the nacelle tilting angle is equal at the same time. n denotes nacelle tilting angle. Thus, the model has four degrees of freedom. The rotors are driven separately by two DC motors, measured by tachogenerators coupled to the points of L, R, respectively. Rotary encoders and accelerometers are mounted on the joint O and L, R to measure the angles ψ, θ, nacelle tilting angle n and corresponding angle acceleration, respectively. The encoder and accelerometer for the roll angle ϕ and roll angle acceleration $\ddot{\phi}$ is mounted on the position F.

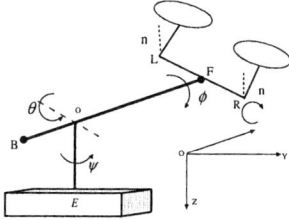

Fig. 1. Experimental setup appearance　　　**Fig. 2.** Tilt rotor aircraft platform scheme

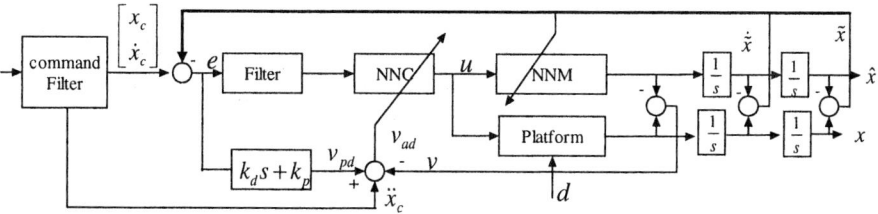

Fig. 3. Adaptive neural networks internal model control architecture of platform

The nonlinear adaptive neural networks internal model control structure is shown in Fig.3. Platform, NNM and NNC represent tilt rotor aircraft platform, the platform neural network model, and neural networks inversion controller, respectively. By suitable design, the Filter can be selected to reduce the gain of the feedback system and project the sign e into the appropriate input space for the NNC. v_{pd} is used to specify the desired tracking error dynamics. u and v denote control input variable, and model output also pseudo control variable respectively. $u = [f_l, f_r, n]^T$, owing to the corresponding connection between DC motor roll velocity and the force f_l, f_r. x_c represents commanded state vector. The state variables are attitude angle and attitude angle rate. The v_{pd} is PD control which is used to shape system response. k_p, k_d are the proportional and derivative control gains. $\ddot{x}_c$ is commanded acceleration which comes from command filter. d is external disturbances.

3 Learning Algorithms and Lyapunov Stability Analysis

Now, consider a representation of the inversion error δ as follows:
$$\ddot{x} = v + \delta \tag{1}$$
the error dynamics become
$$\ddot{\tilde{x}} + k_d \dot{\tilde{x}} + k_p \tilde{x} = v_{ad} - \delta \tag{2}$$
where $\tilde{x} = x_c - (x - \hat{x}) = x_c - x + \hat{x}$, In state-space form,
$$\dot{e} = Ae + b[v_{ad} - \delta] \tag{3}$$
where
$$e = \begin{bmatrix} \tilde{x} \\ \dot{\tilde{x}} \end{bmatrix}, \quad A = \begin{bmatrix} 0 & 1 \\ -k_p & -k_d \end{bmatrix}, \quad B = \begin{bmatrix} 0 \\ 1 \end{bmatrix} \tag{4}$$

Denote the exact weights at any given moment as w^* and define, $\tilde{w} = w - w^*$. The error dynamics as
$$\dot{e} = Ae + B\tilde{w}^T g + B(w^{*T} g - \delta) \tag{5}$$
g is the set of RBF network. To determine the stability characteristics consider a Lya-p unov energy function consisting of the tracking error, e, and the NNC-weights error, $\tilde{w}$,
$$L = \frac{1}{2} e^T P e + \frac{\tilde{w}^T \tilde{w}}{2\eta} \tag{6}$$
where $\eta > 0$ is an adaptation gain. there exists a symmetric definite solution to the Lyapunov equation,
$$A^T P + PA = -Q \tag{7}$$
such that Q is symmetric positive definite. The least conservative and most convenient choice of Q is $Q = I$. The solution for P then becomes,
$$P = \begin{bmatrix} \dfrac{k_p^2 + k_d^2 + k_p}{2k_p k_d} & \dfrac{1}{2k_p} \\ \dfrac{1}{2k_p} & \dfrac{1+k_p}{2k_p k_d} \end{bmatrix} \tag{8}$$
A design of the adaptation law as,
$$\dot{\tilde{w}} = -\eta \begin{bmatrix} \tilde{x} \\ \dot{\tilde{x}} \end{bmatrix} PBg = -\eta e^T PBg \tag{9}$$
$$\dot{L} = -\frac{1}{2} e^T Q e + e^T PB(w^{*T} g - \delta) \leq -\frac{1}{2} \|e\|_2^2 + \delta^* |ePB| \tag{10}$$
$$\dot{L} = \frac{\dot{\tilde{w}} \tilde{w}}{\eta} \tag{11}$$
Thus, the adaptive control signal were represented as follows,
$$v_{ad} = w^T g \tag{12}$$

4 Experiment and Verification

The error signals $[\tilde{x}, \dot{\tilde{x}}]^T$ are used to adjust the NNM weights. Thus the network is forced towards copying the platform dynamics. We choose $k_p = 6.5$, $k_d = 4.2$.
Experiment and simulations are shown by Fig.4-5.

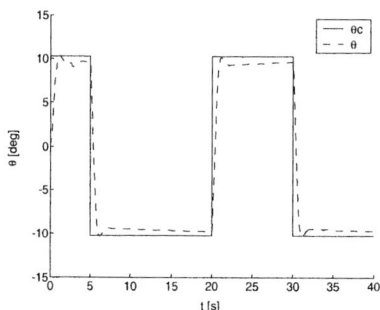

Fig. 4. θ and desired trajectory

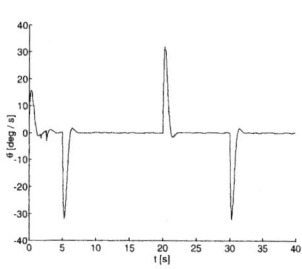

Fig. 5. Pitch velocity $\dot{\theta}$

5 Conclusions

The use of neural networks for nonlinear IMC has been explored. Moreover, we proposed the architectures and algorithm for training networks to represent nonlinear tilt rotor aircraft platform.

A controller architecture, which combines adaptive feedforward neural networks with internal model control, has been outlined and its effectivenesses demonstrated on the tilt rotor aircraft platform. The boundedness of tracking error and control signals is guaranteed by Lyapunov stability analysis. Theoretical and experimental research has shown this approach having outstanding potential for rapid and accurate adaptation. Future work will focus on the robustness of the flight controller.

References

1. Rysdyk, R.T., Calise, A.J.: Adaptive Model Inversion Flight Control for Tiltrotor Aircraft. AIAA Journal of Guidance, Control, and Dynamics (1998)
2. Rysdyk, R.T., Calise, A.J., Chen, R.T.N.: Nonlinear Adaptive Control of Tiltrotor Aircraft Using Neural Networks. AIAA/SAE World Aviation Congress proceedings, Anaheim, CA, October (1997)
3. Kim, B.S., Calise, A.J.: Nonlinear Flight Control Using Neural Networks. AIAA Journal of Guidance, Navigation and Control, Vol. 20, No. 1(1997) 26-31
4. Mehra, R. K., Prasanth, R. K., Bennett, R. L., et al: Model Predictive Control Design for XV-15 Tilt Rotor Flight Control. AIAA Guidance, Navigation, and Control Conference Canada, August (2001)
5. Hunt, K. J., Sbarbaro, D.: Neural Networks for Nonlinear Internal Model control., IEE Proc.-D Vol. 138 No.5 (1991) 431-438

Novel Leaning Feed-Forward Controller for Accurate Robot Trajectory Tracking

D. Bi[1], G.L. Wang[2], J. Zhang[2,*], and Q. Xue[1]

[1] Tianjin University of Science and Technology, Tianjin 300222, P.R. China
50001729@alumni.cityu.edu.hk
[2] Sun Yat-Sen University, GuanZhou 510675, P.R. China
Junzhang@zsu.edu.cn

Abstract. This paper presents a novel learning feed-forward controller design approach for accurate robotics trajectory tracking. Based on the joint nonlinear dynamics characteristics, a model-free learning algorithm based on Support Vector Machine (SVM) is implemented for friction model identification. The experimental results verified that SVM based learning feed-forward controller is a good approach for high performance industrial robot trajectory tracking. It can achieve low tracking error comparing with traditional trajectory tracking control method.

1 Introduction

The industrial robot manipulator is, in general, a highly nonlinear coupled dynamic system and, therefore, achieving high performance in trajectory tracking control is a very challenging task. To be able to track a motion with small errors, a feed-forward controller can be used. The feed-forward controller generates the control signal from the reference (the desired motion). Instead of computing the required feed-forward compensation mathematically, it can also be learnt from the feedback signal using a function approximator. The usually used function approximator is the B-spline neural network [1], which often suffers from curse dimensionality and over fitting problem.

Recently Support Vector Machine (SVM) [2] has aroused research interests in data classification and regression. An SVM for regression, like regularization networks, proves to be a potential tool for constructing the approximation of a function from sparse training data. The approximation of a function using SVM offers some attractive properties. An SVM for regression does not suffer from the over-fitting problem and it has good generalization ability. The feasibility of applying an SVM for learning feed-forward control signals has been investigated in [3], but only with simulation studies. Up to now, using SVM based learning feed-forward control for accurate trajectory tracking has not been exploited much experimentally.

2 SVM Based Learning Feed-Forward Controller

A typical industrial robot trajectory tracking with SVM based learning feed-forward controller is described in [3]. One reason for choosing the feed-forward loop is that,

---

* Author for Correspondence.

for reproducible disturbances such as unmodeled dynamics, feed-forward compensation is principally faster than feedback compensation. In other words, we get the best performance if we try to learn the inverse process in the feed-forward path.

The approximation of a function using SVM offers some attractive properties. For example, it does not suffer from the over-fitting problem and it has good generalization ability. These features suggest that it may be a good candidate for constructing approximations for unknown nonlinear functions needed in learning feed-forward control system designs. So the nonlinear dynamics can be first learned offline by SVM, then model can be implemented in the learning feed-forward control.

3 Support Vector Machines for Model Learning

This section presents SVM [2] for dynamics modeling. The SVM algorithm has its origin in the theory of statistical learning and it has found many applications in pattern recognition [4].

Given l training data (x_i, y_i), where x_i is the input, y_i is the output, SVM based nonlinear dynamics identification algorithm can be derived by preprocessing the training points by a mapping $\phi: x \rightarrow F$ into a very high dimensional feature space F. The dynamics model in high dimensional space F is:

$$f(x) = \pi \cdot \phi(x) + m \qquad (1)$$

With ε-insensitive loss function [2], we have the following convex optimization problem:

Minimize: $\|\pi\|^2 + c \sum_{i=1}^{l} (\zeta_i + \zeta_i^*)$ \qquad (2)

Subject to:

$$\begin{cases} y_i - \langle \pi, \phi(x_i) \rangle - m \leq \varepsilon + \zeta_i \\ \langle \pi, \phi(x_i) \rangle + m - y_i \leq \varepsilon + \zeta_i^* \\ \zeta_i, \zeta_i^* \geq 0 \end{cases} \qquad (3)$$

Where $c \succ 0$ is a constant that determines the tradeoff between the empirical risk minimization (ERM) error and the bound of $\|\pi\|^2$ value.

To solve the convex optimal problem, we need to construct a Lagrange function from both the objective function and the corresponding constraints. It can be shown that this function has a saddle point with respect to the primal and dual variables at the optimal solution [5]. Solving this optimization problem by using kernel property [2], the identified function is:

$$f(x) = \sum_{i=1}^{l} (\alpha_{Fi} - \alpha_{Fi}^*) k(x, x_i) + \overline{m}_F \qquad (4)$$

where $\alpha_{Fi}, \alpha_{Fi}^*, \overline{m}_F$ are constant values obtained by solving the optimization problem.

4 Experimental Results

The learning feed-forward controller designed for one DOF robot can be extended to multi-degree-of-freedom robotics device with no technical difficulty. So in the following, we use a simple one horizontal DOF device to illustrate our SVM based learning feed-forward control strategy. This device consists of a mechanical link driven by a DC motor through a gearbox with a ratio of 1:80.

As the link is horizontal, the gravity torque can be ignored when the robotic device is in motion. So the dynamics of this robotic device can be described by the following equation:

$$\tau_{motor} = \tau_{friction}(\dot{q}) + I\ddot{q} \tag{5}$$

where τ_{motor} is the motor torque, $\tau_{friction}$ is the frictional torque, I is the mass moment of inertia, q is the angular position. According to the dynamics model (equation (5)), the inertia has been designed known, so the unknown nonlinear friction model can be identified through the training data points. As the first step toward off-line learning of the friction model, a number of experiments were performed to obtain the training data sets. The tests included two different directions of motions of the link. The corresponding friction torques were recorded to give two groups of angular velocity-friction torque training data sets for the two cases with the angular velocity $\dot{q} > 0$ and $\dot{q} < 0$ respectively. The zero velocity friction value (at $\dot{q} = 0$) was measured by conducting "break-away" experiments in the two directions, as suggested by Armstrong [6].

After obtain the 54 data points in each data sets with the angular velocity $\dot{q} > 0$ and $\dot{q} < 0$ respectively, the optimal results found for implementing the SVM algorithm were: for $\dot{q} \geq 0$, $C=0.25$, $\varepsilon=0.00025$ with 10 Support Vectors, and for $\dot{q} \leq 0$, $C=0.05$, $\varepsilon=0.0003$ with 9 Support Vectors.

For the evaluation of the performance of the considered controller, the experiments are conducted with reference trajectory tracking as described in Fig. 1. When applying a traditional PD based controller, the proportional parameters $k_p = 5$, the derivate parameters $k_d = 0.01$; when applying the learning feed-forward control, the

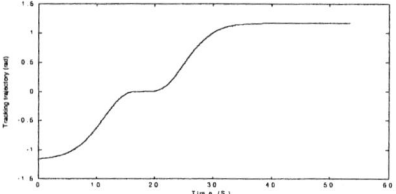

Fig. 1. Reference trajectory

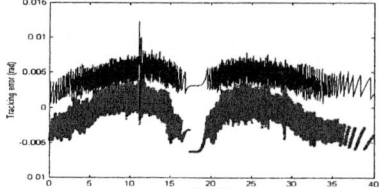

Fig. 2. Tracking error comparison: solid line: PD control; Dotted line: SVM based

proportional parameters $k_p = 5$, the derivate parameters $k_d = 0.01$; Fig.2 shows the trajectory tracking error comparison of these two control methods. We can see that the tracking accuracy of the SVM based learning feed-forward controller has improved compared with that of the traditional PD based controller.

5 Conclusions and Discussion

The experimental results verified that the SVM based learning feed-forward controller is a good approach for high performance industrial robot trajectory tracking. It can achieve low tracking error comparing with traditional trajectory tracking control method. These results suggest that SVM method may be a good candidate for constructing approximations for unknown nonlinear functions needed in learning feed-forward control system designs.

References

1. Ozaki, H., Iwamura K. M., Lin C. J., Shimogawa T.: Improvement of Trajectory Tracking for Industrial Robot Arms by Learning Control with B-Spline. Assembly and Task Planning, Proceedings of the IEEE International Symposium on (2003) 264-269
2. Vapnik V.: Statistical Learning Theory. Wiley, New York, NY (1998)
3. Kruif B. J., de Vries T. J. A.: On Using a Support Vector Machine in Learning Feed-Forward Control. IEEE/ASME International Conference on Advanced Intelligent Mechatronics Proceedings, Como, Italy (2001) 272-277
4. Pontil M., Verri A.: Support Vector Machines for 3D Object Recognition. IEEE Transaction on Pattern Analysis and Machine Intelligence 20 (1998) 637-646
5. Vanderbi R. J., LOQO: An Interior-Point Code for Quadratic Programming. TRSOR-94-15, Statistics and Operations Research, Princeton University (1994)
6. Armstrong H. B.: Control of Machines with Friction. MA: Kluwer Academic, Boston (1991)

# Adaptive Neural Network Control for Multi-fingered Robot Hand Manipulation in the Constrained Environment

Gang Chen, Shuqing Wang, and Jianming Zhang

National Key Laboratory of Industrial Control Technology,
Institute of Advanced Process Control, Zhejiang University,
Hangzhou 310027, P.R. China
gchen@iipc.zju.edu.cn

Abstract. This note presents a robust adaptive neural network (NN) control scheme for multi-fingered robot hand manipulation system in the constrained environment to achieve arbitrarily small motion and force tracking errors. The controllers consist of the model-based controller, the NN controller and the robust controller. The model-based controller deals with the nominal dynamics of the manipulation system. The NN handles the unstructured dynamics and external disturbances. The NN weights are tuned online, without the offline learning phase. The robust controller is introduced to compensate for the effects of residual uncertainties. An adaptive law is developed so that no priori knowledge of the bounds for residual uncertainties is required. Most importantly, the exponential convergence properties for motion and force tracking are achieved.

1 Introduction

In the last decade, intelligent control methodologies have been extensively employed to solve a lot of complicated problems. In particular, many efforts have been made in developing intelligent control schemes to achieve the precise tracking control of robot manipulators [1-7]. Because the fuzzy logic controller has the programming capability of human control behavior, there have been increasing efforts to introduce fuzzy set theory into the control of robot manipulators. Adaptive fuzzy control for cooperative multi-robot systems has been proposed in [1]. Since many parameters are updated online, the computation burden is heavy. NN control is the other popular method used in the control of robot manipulators. For most existing results, the mathematical proof of control system stability was not accomplished. The structure of NN and the adaptive laws have to be found by the trial-and-error method. Some results require a sufficiently high force feedback gain to maintain a specified performance, and/or the persistent excitation condition to assure a zero force tracking error [1], [2]. Furthermore, most results only guarantee the asymptotical convergence of the tracking error to a residual set of the origin. As the size of the uncertain nonlinearities increases, the size of the residual set may also increase. Therefore, these control schemes are not robust to unmodeled dynamics and/or external disturbances. In this note, we will present a new algorithm to solve the aforementioned problems. By combining advantage of NN, robust control and adaptive control, this note proposes an adaptive robust NN control capable of achieving exponential convergence of the position and force tracking error to an arbitrarily small neighborhood of zero.

2 Model-Based Controller

For sparing the space, the complicated derivation of the dynamic model of multi-fingered robot hand manipulation system is omitted here. But interested readers can find it in our recent paper [8]. We directly give the resulting model-based controller

$$u_0 = f_\ell + f_n + f_i, \tag{1}$$

where the three terms f_ℓ, f_n, and f_i can be determined by using the same techniques as in [8]. Finally, we can get the error dynamic model $\dot{e} = De + U(\Delta w - v_R)$, where e denotes the motion and force tracking errors, D and U are known matrices, Δw represents the unstructured uncertainties, v_R denotes the compensation signal.

3 NN Controller

In this note, we consider a two-layer NN [2]. Define W as the collection of NN weights and $\phi(x)$ as the basis functions. Thus, the nonlinear functions Δw can be approximated by a two-layer NN for some constant ideal weights W, i.e., $\Delta w = W^T\phi + \varepsilon$. For the reconstruction error vector ε, we suppose that there exists an unknown constant ρ such that $\|\varepsilon\| \leq \rho$.

Choosing the design parameters such that D is Hurwitz. Thus, for system $\dot{e} = De$ and the real matrix $Q = Q^T > 0$, we can get the real matrix $H = H^T > 0$ by solving the Lyapunov function $D^T H + HD = -Q$. Let $\hat{W}$ and $\hat{\rho}$ denote the estimates of W and ρ, respectively. We choose the controller v_R as

$$v_R = u_1 + u_2, \tag{2}$$

where $u_1 = \hat{W}^T\phi$ is the NN controller, $u_2 = \dfrac{\hat{\rho}^2 U^T He}{\|U^T He\|\hat{\rho} + \varepsilon_1}$ with a small constant $\varepsilon_1 > 0$ is designed to compensate for the residual uncertainties, $\hat{W}$ and $\hat{\rho}$ are adaptively tuned according to

$$\dot{\hat{W}} = L\phi e^T HU - \sigma_1 L\hat{W}, \quad \dot{\hat{\rho}} = h_1\|U^T He\| - \sigma_2\hat{\rho}, \quad \hat{\rho}(0) > 0 \tag{3}$$

where $\sigma_1 > 0$, $\sigma_2 > 0$ and $h_1 > 0$ are design parameters, $L = L^T > 0$.

Theorem 1. Consider the multi-fingered robot hand manipulation system. Let the control input be given by (1), (2) and the adaptive laws provided by (3). Then the motion and force tracking errors exponentially converge to an arbitrarily small ball of the origin.

Proof. Define $\tilde{W} = W - \hat{W}$, $\tilde{\rho} = \rho - \hat{\rho}$, $\lambda_1 = \lambda_{\min}(Q)/2$, where $\lambda_{\min(\max)}(\cdot)$ denotes the operation of taking the minimum(maximum) eigenvalue. Consider the following Lyapunov function candidate

$$V = \frac{1}{2} e^T H e + \frac{1}{2} \text{tr}\left(\tilde{W}^T L^{-1} \tilde{W}\right) + \frac{1}{2h_1} \tilde{\rho}^2. \tag{4}$$

Differentiating (4), we have

$$\dot{V} = -\frac{1}{2} e^T Q e + e^T H U \left(W^T \phi + \varepsilon - v_R\right) - \text{tr}\left(\tilde{W}^T L^{-1} \dot{\hat{W}}\right) - \frac{\tilde{\rho}\dot{\hat{\rho}}}{h_1}$$

$$\leq -\lambda_1 \|e\|^2 + \text{tr}\left(\tilde{W}^T L^{-1}\left(L\phi e^T H U - \dot{\hat{W}}\right)\right) + \frac{\tilde{\rho}}{h_1}\left(h_1\|e^T H U\| - \dot{\hat{\rho}}\right) + \hat{\rho}\|e^T H U\| - \frac{\hat{\rho}^2 \|U^T H e\|^2}{\|U^T H e\|\hat{\rho} + \varepsilon_1}$$

$$\leq -\lambda_1 \|e\|^2 + \sigma_1 \text{tr}\left(\tilde{W}^T \hat{W}\right) + \frac{\sigma_2}{h_1} \tilde{\rho}\hat{\rho} + \varepsilon_1. \tag{5}$$

Using the inequalities $\text{tr}\left(\tilde{W}^T \hat{W}\right) \leq \frac{1}{2}\left(\|W\|_F^2 - \|\tilde{W}\|_F^2\right)$ and $\tilde{\rho}\hat{\rho} \leq \frac{1}{2}\left(\rho^2 - \tilde{\rho}^2\right)$, where $\|\cdot\|_F$ denotes the Frobenius norm, we have

$$\dot{V} \leq -\lambda_2 V + \varepsilon_0 \tag{6}$$

where $\lambda_2 = \min\left\{\frac{2\lambda_1}{\lambda_{\max}(H)}, \frac{\sigma_1}{\lambda_{\max}(L^{-1})}, \sigma_2\right\}$, $\varepsilon_0 = \frac{\sigma_1}{2}\|W\|_F^2 + \frac{\sigma_2}{2h_1}\rho^2 + \varepsilon_1$.

Equation (6) implies $V(t) \leq \left(V(0) - \frac{\varepsilon_0}{\lambda_2}\right)\exp(-\lambda_2 t) + \frac{\varepsilon_0}{\lambda_2}$, $\forall t \geq 0$. By (4), we have

$$\|e\|^2 \leq \frac{1}{\lambda_3}\left(V(0) - \frac{\varepsilon_0}{\lambda_2}\right)\exp(-\lambda_2 t) + \frac{\varepsilon_0}{\lambda_2 \lambda_3} \rightarrow \frac{\varepsilon_0}{\lambda_2 \lambda_3}$$ with $\lambda_3 = \lambda_{\min}(H)/2$. The tracking errors will tend to a ball centered at the origin with radius $\sqrt{\varepsilon_0/\lambda_2 \lambda_3}$, which can be made arbitrarily small by appropriately adjusting the design parameters.

Remark 1. The proposed controller achieves exponential convergence of the motion and force tracking errors to a ball of the origin, instead of asymptotical convergence existing in most NN control schemes. Thus, the proposed algorithm is more robust with respect to unmodeled dynamics and/or external disturbances.

Remark 2. An adaptive approach is introduced to estimate the residual uncertainty bounds. The motivation is as follows. Sometimes, one's knowledge on the residual uncertainties is poor. If one overestimates the bounds of the uncertainties, this will lead to the degradation of the system performance. On the other hand, if the uncertainties are larger than the estimated bounds, no stability or performance are guaranteed.

4 Conclusions

In this note, an adaptive NN control scheme has been proposed for controlling multi-fingered robot hand manipulation system with unstructured uncertainties. The proposed controllers consist of three parts:1)model-based controller;2)adaptive NN controller;3)robust controller. The NN controller copes with the unstructured dynamics of the multi-fingered robot hand and grasped object. Compared with other NN controller, the NN weights here are updated online, without offline learning phase. The robust controller is used to compensate for the residual uncertainties in the manipulation system. The persistent excitation conditions are not required and the exponential convergence properties for motion and force tracking are achieved without needing high-gain feedback.

References

1. Lian, K.Y., Chiu, C.S., Liu, P.: Semi-decentralized Adaptive Fuzzy Control for Cooperative Multirobot Systems with H∞ Motion/Force Tracking Performance. IEEE Trans. Syst. Man, Cybern. 32 (2002) 269-280
2. Kwan, C., Lewis, F.L., Dawson, D.M.: Robust Neural-Network Control of Rid-Link Electrically Driven Robots. IEEE Trans. Neural Networks. 9 (1998) 581-588
3. Yoo, B.K., Ham, W.C.: Adaptive Control of Robot Manipulator Using Fuzzy Compensator. IEEE Trans. Fuzzy Systems. 8 (2000) 186-199
4. Yi, S.Y., Chung, M.J.: A Robust Fuzzy Logic Controller for Robot Manipulators with Uncertainties. IEEE Trans. Syst. Man,Cybern. 27 (1997) 706-713
5. Tascillo, A., Bourbakis, N.: Neural and Fuzzy Robotic Hand Control. IEEE Trans. Syst. Man, Cybern. 29 (1999) 636-642
6. Victor, S., Rafael, K., Miguel, A.L.: Global Asymptotic Stability of a Tracking Sectorial Fuzzy Controller for Robot Manipulator. IEEE Trans. Syst. Man, Cybern. 34 (2004) 710-718
7. Peng, L., Woo, P.Y.: Neural-Fuzzy Control System for Robotic Manipulators. IEEE Contr. Syst. Mag. 22 (2002) 53-63
8. Chen, G., Wang, S.Q.: Robust Control for Multi-fingered Hand Manipulation in the Constrained Environment. Acta Automatica Sinica. (2005) submitted for publication

Control of a Giant Swing Robot Using a Neural Oscillator

Kiyotoshi Matsuoka, Norifumi Ohyama,
Atsushi Watanabe, and Masataka Ooshima

Department of Brain Science and Engineering, Kyushu Institute of Technology,
Hibikino, Wakamatsu, Kitakyushu, Japan
matsuoka@brain.kyutech.ac.jp

Abstract. A neural oscillator model is applied to swing/giant-swing control of an under-actuated double pendulum. The oscillator receives the angle signal of the upper link and provides a relative angle of the lower link. The oscillator tunes itself to the natural dynamics of the pendulum system so as to increase the swing amplitude, and finally the pendulum system enters the phase of giant swing motion. A most remarkable result is that transition from simple swing to giant swing is attained without changing the values of the parameters of the neural oscillator at all.

1 Introduction

Rhythmic movements of animals such as the walking of animals are known to be generated by neural oscillators called the central pattern generators. Although a lot of mathematical models have been proposed for the neural oscillators, the one proposed by one of the authors (Matsuoka [4], [5]) might be a most well-known one. Recently the model has been applied to a lot of robots that perform various rhythmic motions. For example, Taga [8] and Kimura [3] used the model to realize locomotion of bipedal and quadruped robots. Williamson [11] applied the oscillator model to a humanoid robot that performs cranking, sawing, and other rhythmic movements. The control schemes for these robots are similar; some neural oscillators actuate the links of a robot, while the joint angles and other state variables are fed back to the oscillator.

A remarkable aspect of that scheme is that the oscillator is entrained to the natural dynamics of the controlled system and tends to oscillate at a natural frequency of the controlled object. This paper shows an application of the Matsuoka oscillator to swing/giant-swing control of an under-actuated, two-link pendulum (a horizontal bar gymnastic robot). A lot of attempts have been made to realize giant swing motion on a high bar [2], [6], [7], [9, [10]. Some of them devise heuristic control rules and others take some pre-scheduling methods in consideration of mechanical dynamics of the pendulum.

The approach taken in this study is very different; it utilizes the tuning ability of the neural oscillator to the controlled object. If the oscillator and the pendulum are coupled with an appropriate set of parameters, then the swing amplitude will increases rapidly. The tuning to the pendulum dynamics occurs for a considerably wide range of the system parameters. A similar experiment was made by Ferris et al. [1] for a single/double/triple pendulum.

Using the neural oscillator's highly adaptive property, one can easily realize giant swing. The robot changes the motion from suspension state through back-and-forth swing to giant swing without changing the parameters of the oscillator at all. Once the pendulum reaches the upright position, the system enters a completely different phase but the oscillator still adapts to it so as to continue giant swing.

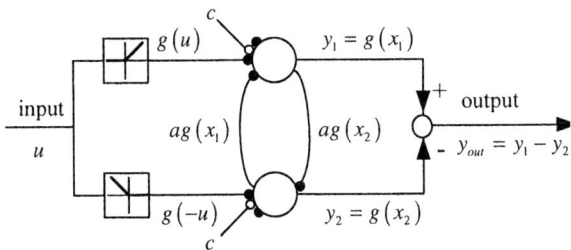

Fig. 1. Scheme of the neural oscillator. The blanked and filled dots represent excitatory and inhibitory synapses.

2 Swing Control by a Neural Oscillator

2.1 The Neural Oscillator

The neural oscillator used here is the one proposed by Matsuoka [4], [5] and Taga [8]. Fig.1 shows the structure of the model. It is composed of two neurons, each of which has a self-inhibitory property. The dynamics is given by

$$\tau \dot{x}_1 = c - x_1 - bv_1 - ay_2 - g(u), \; T\dot{v}_1 = y_1 - v_1,$$
$$\tau \dot{x}_2 = c - x_2 - bv_2 - ay_1 - g(-u), \; T\dot{v}_2 = y_2 - v_2, \qquad (1)$$
$$y_i = g(x_i) \triangleq \max(0, x_i) \; (i=1,2), \; y_{out} = y_1 - y_2.$$

Variables x_i, v_i, and y_i ($i = 1, 2$) are the membrane potential, the self-inhibition, and the output of each neuron. Each neuron i receives an inhibitory input $-g(\pm u)$ from the outside, a mutual inhibition $-y_j = -ag(x_j)$ ($j \neq i$), and an excitatory tonic input c. The input and output of the whole oscillator are represented by u and y_{out}, respectively.

The mutual and self inhibitions of the neurons induce a kind of relaxation oscillation. Parameters a and b represent the strength of mutual and self inhibitions, respectively. Parameter c represents the constant that determines the amplitude of the oscillatory output. Two time constants, τ and T, determine the frequency f_o at which the oscillator produces a periodic oscillation in the absence of the external input (sensory feedback). We call the frequency f_o the "oscillator frequency." If a rhythmic signal is given to the neural oscillator as a sensory feedback signal u, then the output y_{out} of the oscillator comes to lock itself with the oscillatory input.

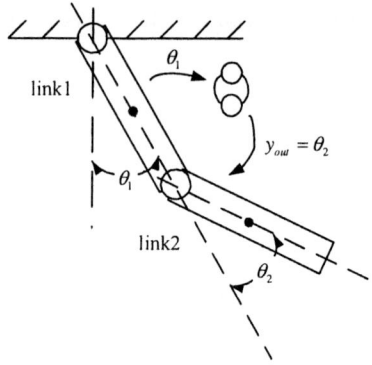

Fig. 2. The under-actuated, two-link pendulum

2.2 Dynamics of the Double Pendulum

The system controlled by the neural oscillator is a two-link, under-actuated pendulum, which is shown in Fig. 2. The upper joint is free and the lower joint is given a forced angle. The angle of the upper link with respect to the vertical line is represented by θ_1, while the relative angle of the lower link with respect to the upper link is represented by θ_2.

Note that the number of the state variables of the system is two because the input to the pendulum system is given as a forced angle, not as a torque. Given the relative angle θ_2 of the lower link, the angle θ_1 of the upper link obeys the following equation of motion:

$$\begin{aligned}&\left(m_1 d_1^2 + I_1\right)\ddot{\theta}_1 \\&+ m_2 \left\{ l_1^2 \ddot{\theta}_1 + d_2^2 \left(\ddot{\theta}_1 + \ddot{\theta}_2\right) - l_1 d_2 \dot{\theta}_2 \left(2\dot{\theta}_1 + \dot{\theta}_2\right) \sin\theta_2 + l_1 d_2 \left(2\ddot{\theta}_1 + \ddot{\theta}_2\right) \right. \\&\left. \cos\theta_2 \right\} + I_2 \left(\ddot{\theta}_1 + \ddot{\theta}_2\right) + m_1 g d_1 \sin\theta_1 + m_2 g \left\{ l_1 \sin\theta_1 + d_2 \sin\left(\theta_1 + \theta_2\right)\right\} \\&= -c\dot{\theta}_1.\end{aligned} \qquad (2)$$

where l_1 and l_2 are the length of the two links, m_1 and m_2 the masses, I_1 and I_2 the moments of inertia, and d_1 and d_2 the distance from the joint to the center of gravity of the links. Term $-c\dot{\theta}_1$ in the right-hand side is a friction force at the upper joint.

If angles θ_1 and θ_2 are sufficiently small, then input-output relation of the system can be represented by the following transfer function:

$$G_p(s) = \frac{A_p s^2 + B_p}{s^2 + 4\pi\zeta f_p s + \left(2\pi f_p\right)^2} \cdot \cdot \quad (3)$$

The values of the parameters for the real robot are $A_p = -0.20$, $B_p = -1.3$ [rad^2/s^2], $\zeta = 0.018$, and $f_p = 0.58$ [Hz]. Henceforth we refer to the natural frequency f_p of the pendulum system as the "pendulum frequency."

2.3 The Coupled System

The pendulum and the oscillator are coupled in the following way. Fig. 3 shows the block diagram of the coupled system. Angel θ_1 sensed by a rotary encoder is sent to the oscillator with feedback gain H. The output of the oscillator is sent to a servomotor attached to the lower joint with output gain h, determining the relative angle θ_2 of the lower link. The whole system was driven at sampling rate of 50 Hz.

Note that the input to the pendulum is given in the form of 'forced' angle. So, the angle should be provided so as to smoothly change with time. Otherwise, the torque or the electrical current of the motor becomes undesirably large. To avoid this problem a low-pass filter is applied to y_{out} to make angle θ_2 smooth. The time constant of this element is set as $T_d = 0.15$[s].

For a set of oscillator parameters the pendulum might only swing back and forth with a relatively small amplitude. The frequency f_r in this situation, which we call the "resonance frequency," will be close to the pendulum's natural frequency.

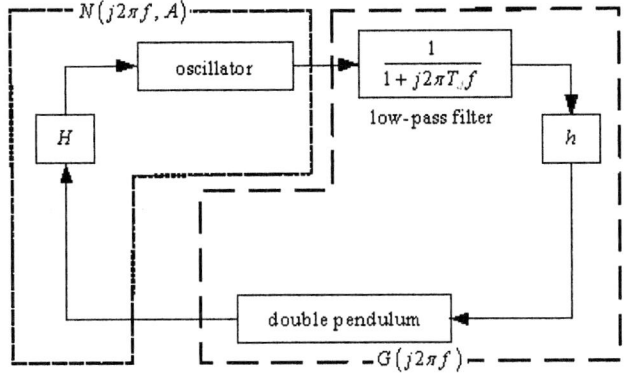

Fig. 3. Block diagram for the coupled system

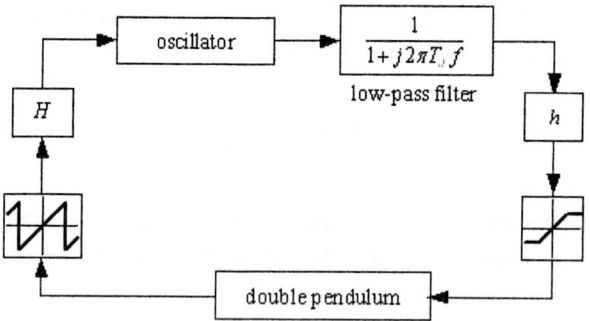

Fig. 4. Block diagram for the coupled system. Two nonlinear elements are added. When θ_1 and θ_2 are small, the systems is virtually equivalent to Fig.3.

On the other hand, in the case of giant swing motion, θ_1 and θ_2 become vary large and therefore two nonlinear elements need to be considered; see Fig.4. The first one is a limiter that is put before the pendulum because the servomotor used in the experiment cannot produce an angle larger than $\pi/2$. Another nonlinearity is essential. In the present experiment the angle is expressed so that it lies always in $[-\pi,\pi]$, not in $[-\infty,\infty]$; it is just the actual output of the absolute-type rotary encoder. This expression is very important in the present control because the input to the oscillator becomes a periodic function during giant motion.

3 Analyses and Experiments

3.1 Describing Function Analysis for Small Swing

In the case of small swing the behavior of the robot can be predicted by the familiar describing function analysis. In Fig.5 the reciprocal of describing function $N(j2\pi f, A)$ of the oscillator and the transfer function $G(j2\pi f)$ ($= hG_p(j2\pi f)/(T_d j2\pi f + 1)$) of the pendulum (with a low-pass filter) are depicted. For the stationary periodic oscillation, the following relation must hold:

$$N(j2\pi f, A)G(j2\pi f) = 1. \tag{4}$$

The frequency f_r and the amplitude A for the limit cycle can be found as a crossing point of $1/N(j2\pi f, A)$ and $G(j2\pi f)$ with the same frequency.

In the analysis of Fig.5 the oscillator frequency is set as $f_o = 0.37$ [Hz] while the pendulum frequency is $f_p = 0.58$ [Hz]. The describing function analysis shows that the resonance frequency becomes $f_r = 0.57$ [Hz], being very close to the pendulum frequency. Fig.6 is the time plot of the swing motion of the real robot. The swing frequency is 0.53[Hz]. It is smaller than the predicted frequency, but much closer to $f_p = 0.58$ [Hz] than to $f_o = 0.37$ [Hz].

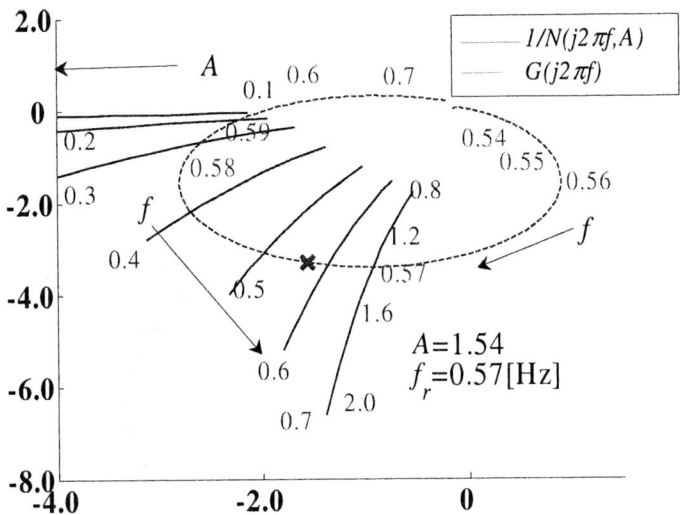

Fig. 5. The plot of the describing function and the transfer function on the complex plane. The parameters are set as $\tau = T/2 = 0.3$ [s] ($f_o = 0.37$ [Hz]), $a = 2.5$, $b = 2.5$, $c = 1.0$, $H = 3.0$ [1/rad], $h = 1.5$ [rad], $\zeta = 0.018$, $f_p = 0.58$ [Hz], $A_p = -0.20$, $B_p = -1.3$ [rad^2/s^2]. Mark "x" indicates a limit cycle solution of the system, where the amplitude and frequency are $A = 1.54$ and $f_r = 0.57$ [Hz], respectively.

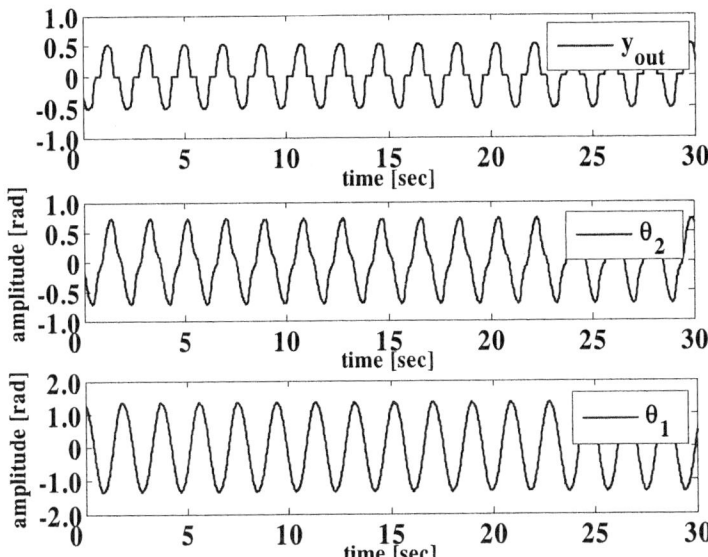

Fig. 6. The output of the oscillator and the angles of the lower and upper links. In this experiment ($f_o = 0.37$ [Hz], $\tau = T/2 = 0.3$ [s]) the system oscillates at $A = 1.36$ and $f_r = 0.53$ [Hz].

3.2 Giant Swing

Here we show that the same oscillator as shown above can produce giant swing motion. Fig.7 is the plots of the input and the output of the oscillator, which correspond roughly to the absolute angle of the upper link and the relative angle of the lower link. The parameters of the oscillator are given as $a = 0.5$, $b = 2.5$, $\tau = T/2 = 0.9$ [s], $c = 5.0$, $h = 3.0$ [rad], and $H = 5.0$ [1/rad]. Initially the pendulum is set in suspension posture.

In some tens of seconds the system reaches a state of stationary swing. The relative angle of the lower link leads by a phase angle of around $\pi/2$ against the angle of the upper link. After 63 seconds have elapsed, the pendulum is temporarily pushed by hand so that it will go over the upright position. Then the pendulum begins giant swing and keeps it. Since the pendulum continues to rotate in one direction, the output of the rotary encoder or the input to the oscillator becomes a saw-tooth wave. The frequency of rotation is twice as high as the swing motion. Also in this state the phase difference between θ_1 and θ_2 are locked at around $\pi/2$. Thus, the system (with this set of parameters) has at least two stable limit cycles. One is swing and the other is giant swing. Which of them actually emerges depends on the initial state of the system.

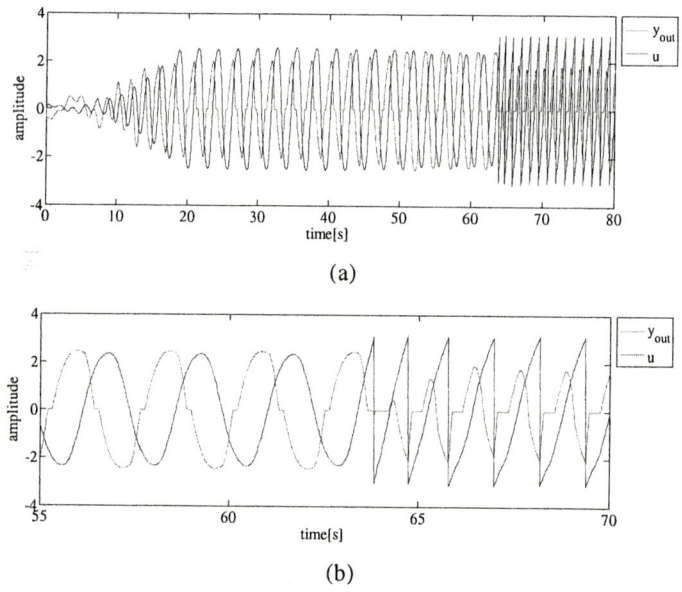

Fig. 7. The oscillator input and output. (a) after 63 seconds of swing the pendulum is pushed temporarily by hand; (b) an enlarged illustration around the time.

The fact that the system inherently has a potential to produce giant swing motion suggests a strategy for realizing a giant swing with an oscillator having fixed parameters. That is, if another set of parameters is chosen so that the small swing limit cycle disappears, then the amplitude will increase until the upright position is attained and then the system state is attracted to a limit cycle of giant swing.

Fig.8 is the plot of the input and the output of the oscillator, where only the time constants are changed compared with the experiment in Fig.7; $\tau = T/2 = 1.1$ [s]. After about 40 seconds of swing, the state enters the giant swing phase. Fig.9 is the skeleton diagram of the robot during the giant swing motion.

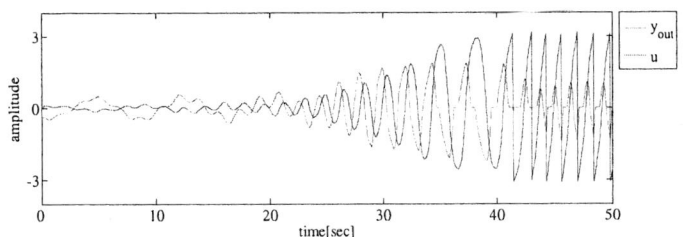

Fig. 8. Automatic transition from suspension to giant swing

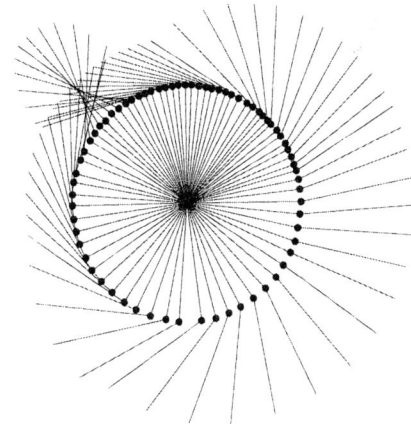

Fig. 9. Skeleton diagram for giant swing of the robot. The pendulum is rotating counterclockwise.

4 Conclusion

In this paper we have described an experiment in which a horizontal bar robot performs swing/giant-swing motion, using the Matsuoka oscillator. An important result is that the system inherently has two stable limit cycles: back-and-forth swing and giant swing. The oscillator 'stubbornly' tries to adapt to the natural dynamics of the pendulum and it enables the robot to perform giant swing easily.

References

1. Ferris, D. P., Viant, T. L., Campbell, R. J.: Artificial neural oscillators as controllers for locomotion simulation and robotic exoskeltons. Fourth World Congress of Biomechanics (2002)
2. Imadu, A., Ono, K.: Optimum trajectory planning method for a system that includes passive joints (proposal of a function approximation method). JSME International Journal, Series C, Vol.42 (1999) 309-315
3. Kimura, H., Sakurama, K., Akiyama, S.: Dynamic walking and running of the quadruped using neural oscillators. Proceedings of IROS '98, Vol.1 (1998) 50-57
4. Matsuoka, K.: Sustained oscillations generated by mutually inhibiting neurons with adaptation. Biological Cybernetics, Vol.52 (1985) 367-376
5. Matsuoka, K.: Mechanisms of frequency and pattern control in the neural rhythm generators. Biological Cybernetics, Vol.56 (1987) 345-353
6. Michitsuji, Y., Sato, H., Yamakita, M.: Giant swing via forward upward circling of the acrobat-robot. American Control Conference 2001, Vol.4 (2001) 3262-3267
7. Ono, K., Yamamoto, K., Imadu, A.: Control of giant swing motion of a two-link horizontal bar gymnastic robot. Advanced Robotics (2001) 449-465
8. Taga, G.: A model of the neuro-musculo-skeletal system for human locomotion, I. Emergence of basic gait. Biological Cybernetics, Vol.73 (1995) 97-111
9. Takashima, S.: Dynamic modeling of a gymnast on a high bar-computer simulation and construction of a gymnast robot. Proceedings of IROS '90, Vol.2 (1990) 955-962
10. Takashima, S.: Control of gymnast on a high bar. Proceedings of IROS '91, Vol.3 (1991) 1424-1429
11. Williamson, M. M.: Robot Arm Control Exploiting Natural Dynamics. PhD thesis, Massachusetts Institute of Technology (1999)

Neural Network Indirect Adaptive Sliding Mode Tracking Control for a Class of Nonlinear Interconnected Systems

Yanxin Zhang[1] and Xiaofan Wang[2]

[1] Institute of Automatic control, School of Electronics and Information Engineering,
Beijing, Jiaotong University, Beijing 100044, P.R. China
zyxhyq@yahoo.com.cn
[2] Institute of Automatic, Shanghai Jiaotong University,
Shanghai 200030, P.R. China
xfwang@sjtu.edu.cn

Abstract. Based on omnipotent approximation principle, a new neural network indirect adaptive sliding mode controller is designed for a class of nonlinear interconnected systems with uncertain dynamics. Different neural networks are adopted to approximate the affection of the uncertain terms in the subsystems and the interconnected terms to the whole system. It uses the mode transformation function to realize the changing between the NN indirect adaptive controller and fuzzy sliding mode controller, which keeps the state of the system changing in a close bounded set. By using Lyapunov method, it is proved that the close-loop system is stable and the tracking errors convergence to a neighborhood of zero. The result of the emulation proofs the validation of the designed controllers.

1 Introduction

In recent years, neural network control has been used successfully in the complex control plant that is ill-defined or has no exact mathematical models ([1]-[7]).NN adaptive control refers to the neural network systems with adaptive learning algorithm. It's usually adopted to maintain certain performance of the systems while there exist uncertainties or unknown factors in the parameters and structure of the controlled objective. It is divided into two cases: indirect one and direct one. The NN indirect adaptive controller means that the neural network system in the controller is used to build models for the control objective but not as a controller itself([1]). Many existed references utilize the approximation property of the fuzzy logic system[2-7] or neural networks[8], and the Lyapunov function syntheses approach to design globally stable adaptive controllers. However, some of them are limited to nonlinear systems with constant control gain; or the convergence of the tracking error depends on the assumption that the error is square integrable; or the control scheme depends on the model-building system to make the parameters matched completely, which may not be easy to check or realize. Many researchers have made some research for the fuzzy sliding mode control, but there's no exact mathematic expression, therefore, it's difficult to analyze the stability of close-loop system. Tong ([5]) and Zhang ([7]) conquered these difficulties and gave out the exact mathematic expression of the fuzzy sliding mode controllers, but the controllers need the information of all states. In [8], a new NN was proposed to approximate the uncertain interconnected terms of large-scale systems. It only need some information of the states and reduces the calculation greatly.

Combining the NN adaptive control algorithm, the NN approximation method and the sliding mode control, a class of nonlinear interconnected systems with more complex models are studied in this paper, in which not only the subsystems have uncertain functions but also the interconnected terms have, too. Obviously, for such high-dimension large-scale systems the decentralized controllers have outstanding advantages without saying for the realizing of the system stability.

2 System Description and Problem Statement

Consider the following nonlinear uncertain dynamic interconnected system:

$$\begin{aligned} \dot{x}_i &= f_i(x_i) + g_i(x_i)[u_i + G_i(\bar{x})] \\ y_i &= h_i(x_i) \end{aligned} \quad i = 1, 2, \cdots, N \quad (1)$$

where $x_i \in R^n, u_i, y_i \in R$ are the state vector, control input and measurable output of the ith subsystem $\sum_i$, respectively. $f_i(x_i), g_i(x_i)$ are the smooth vector field on R^n, $h_i(x_i)$ is smooth function on R^n. They are all uncertain dynamic of subsystem $\sum_i$. $G_i(\bar{x})$ is the interconnected term of the large-scale system and it is also an uncertain smooth function on $R^{N \times n}$. Where $\bar{x} = (x_1, \cdots, x_{i-1}, x_{i+1}, \cdots, x_N)$.

Assumption 1. For the uncertain functions $H_i(x_i) = g_i^{-1}(x_i) f(x_i)$, $g_i(x_i)$ and $G_i(\bar{x})$, suppose that there exist known functions $M_{1i}(x_i)$, $M_{2i}(x_i)$, $M_{3i}(x_i)$ and $M_{4i}(\bar{x})$ such that

(1) $|H_i(x_i)| \le M_{1i}(x_i)$ (2) $|g_i^{-1}(x_i)| \le M_{2i}(x_i)$

(3) $|(g_i^{-1}(x_i))'| \le |\Delta g_i^{-1}(x_i) \dot{x}_i| \le M_{3i}(x_i) \|x_i\|$ (4) $G_i(\bar{x}) \le M_{4i}(\bar{x})$

For the given bounded reference output y_{im}, suppose $y_{im}, \dot{y}_{im}, \cdots, y_{im}^{(r)}$ are measurable and bounded. Let

$$X_{im} = (y_{im}, \dot{y}_{im}, \cdots, y_{im}^{(r-1)}), \ X_{i1} = (y_i, \dot{y}_i, \cdots, y_i^{(r-1)}) \quad (2)$$

Define the tracking errors as:

$$e_i(t) = y_i(t) - y_{im}(t) \quad (3)$$

Control objective: Using the omnipotent approximation property of the neural networks for the bounded continuous functions, design a state feedback NN controller $u_i(x_i | W_i)$ and the adaptive law of parameter W_i such that:

(1) All variables concerned with the close-loop system are uniformly bounded.
(2) Under the constrict condition (3), the tracking error $e_i(t)$ convergences to a small neighborhood of zero.

3 Designing of the NN Indirect Adaptive Controller (NNIAC)

Define the sliding mode plane as

$$s_i(t) = (\frac{d}{dt} + \eta_i)^{(r-1)} e_i \tag{4}$$

Where η_i is nonnegative constant.

If $f_i(x_i)$, $g_i(x_i)$ and $G_i(\bar{x})$ are known, then the controller can be designed as:

$$u_i^* = \frac{1}{g_i(x_i)}[-f_i(x_i) + \lambda_i s_i(t) + \dot{s}_i(t) + y_{im}^{(r)} + e_i^{(r)}] - G_i(\bar{x}) \quad \lambda_i > 0 \tag{5}$$

Substituting (5) into (1) yields:

$$\dot{s}_i(t) + \lambda_i s_i(t) = 0 \tag{6}$$

Thus, it can be deduced that $\lim_{t \to \infty} e_i = 0$. But in the case that $f_i(x_i)$, $g_i(x_i)$ and $G_i(\bar{x})$ are uncertain, u_i^* cannot be obtained. So by utilizing approximation property of neural network system, the NN indirect adaptive controllers can be constructed.

Due to the approximation property of neural network, we construct a simple low-order forward neural network with three levels to approximate the arbitrary continuous function with the ideal weighted value W_g^* and sufficient numbers of the input basis function $\sigma_g(\cdot)$, i.e.,

$$g(x|W_g^*) = (W_g^*)^T \sigma_g(x) + \varepsilon_g(t) \tag{7}$$

Here, we suppose that neural networks for $g(x|W_g)$ can be estimated as follows:

$$\hat{g}(x|\hat{W}_g) = \hat{W}_g^T \sigma_g(x) \tag{8}$$

Then the function estimated error $\tilde{g}$ is as follows:

$$\tilde{g} = (W_g^*)^T \sigma_g(x) - \hat{W}_g^T \sigma_g(x) + \varepsilon_g(t) = \tilde{W}_g^T \sigma_g(x) + \varepsilon_g(t) \tag{9}$$

where $\tilde{W}_g = W_g - \hat{W}_g$

Here we estimated the uncertain subsystem functions $H_i(x_i | W_{1i})$ and $g_i^{-1}(x_i | W_{1i})$ as follows:

$$\hat{H}_i(x_i | \hat{W}_{1i}) = \sum_{l=1}^{p} \hat{W}_{1ij} \xi_{ij}(x_i) = \hat{W}_{1i}^T \xi_i(x_i)$$

$$\hat{g}_i^{-1}(x_i | \hat{W}_{2i}) = \sum_{l=1}^{p} \hat{W}_{2ij} \xi_{ij}(x_i) = \hat{W}_{2i}^T \xi_i(x_i)$$

(10)

Define the bounded close set A_{id}, A_i as follows ([2]):

$$A_{id} = \{x_i \mid \|x_i - x_{i0}\|_{p,\pi_i} \le 1\}, A_i = \{x_i \mid \|x_i - x_{i0}\|_{p,\pi_i} \le 1 + \psi_i\}$$

$$\|x_i\|_{p,\pi_i} = \{\sum_{i=1}^{n} (\frac{|x_{i,n_i}|}{\pi_i})^p\}^{1/p}$$

where $\{\pi_i\}_{i=1}^n$ is a group of strict positive power weight. x_{i0} is a fixed point. ψ_i represents the width of transition field. $\|x_i\|_{p,\pi_i}$ is a kind of P-norm. Then in the close set A_i, by using omnipotent approximation theorem[1], for given $\varepsilon_{1i} \ge 0, \varepsilon_{2i} \ge 0$, there exist the neural network systems with the form as (10) such that the following inequalities hold:

$$|H_i(x_i) - H_i(x_i | W_{1i}^*)| \le \varepsilon_{1i}$$
$$|g_i^{-1}(x_i) - g_i^{-1}(x_i | W_{2i}^*)| \le \varepsilon_{2i}$$

(11)

Furthermore, because of the complex and high dimension of the interconnected terms in the system, we build a model of the nonlinear connection $G_i(\bar{x})$, $i = 1,2,\cdots,N$ through using high-order neural networks. Suppose x be the input of the high-order neural network, y_i be the output, then $y_i = \hat{W}_{3i} s(x')$, i.e.,

$$\hat{G}_i(\bar{x} | \hat{W}_{3i}) = \hat{W}_{3i} s(x')$$

(12)

where $\hat{W}_{3i} \in R^{n \times L}$ is weights matrix, $s_i(x'), i = 1,2,\cdots,L$ is the element of $s(x') \in R^{L \times 1}$, and $s_i(x') = \prod_{k=1}^{N} \prod_{j \in I_i} [s(x_{kj})]^{d_j(i)}$. $\{I_i \mid i = 1,2,\cdots,L\}$ is a collection of L not-ordered subsets of $\{1,2,\cdots,n\}$, $d_j(i)$ is nonnegative integer and $s(x_{kj}) = \frac{\mu_0}{1 + e^{-l_0 x_{kj}}} + \lambda_0$, $j = 1,2,\cdots,n; k = 1,2,\cdots,N$.

For the above models of high-order neural networks, it can be seen that there exists an integer L, a $d_j(i)$ and an optimized matrix W_{3i}^*, such that for any $\varepsilon_{3i} > 0$

$$\left|G_i(\bar{x}) - W_{3i}^* s(x')\right| \leq \varepsilon_{3i} \tag{13}$$

It means if the high-order term is enough large, there exists a weights matrix, such that $W_{3i}^* s(x')$ can approximate $G_i(\bar{x})$ to any degree of accuracy, and W_{3i}^* is bounded, i.e., $\|W_{3i}^*\| \leq M_W$.

Based on reference [2] and [3], design the NNIAC as:

$$u_i = -k_{d_i} s_{i\Delta}(t) - \frac{1}{2} M_{3i} \|x_i\| s_{i\Delta} - (1 - m_i(t)) u_{adi} + m_i(t) k_{1i}(s_i, t) u_{si} \tag{14}$$

where

$$u_{adi} = \hat{H}_i(x_i | \hat{W}_{1i}) + \hat{g}_i^{-1}(x_i | \hat{W}_{2i}) a_{ri} + \hat{G}_i(\bar{x} | \hat{W}_{3i}) + \hat{\varepsilon}_{1i} u_{si} + \hat{\varepsilon}_{2i} |a_{ri}| u_{si} + \hat{\varepsilon}_{3i} u_{si}$$

$$u_{si} = -\operatorname{sgn}(s_i(t))$$

$$a_{ri} = -y_{im}^{(r)} + \sum_{k=1}^{r-1} \binom{r-1}{k} \eta_i^k e_i^{(r-k)} \tag{15}$$

$$s_{i\Delta}(t) = s_i - \varphi_i \operatorname{sat}(s_i / \varphi_i) \quad \varphi_i > 0$$

Where u_{adi} is the adaptive part. u_{si} is the sliding mode controller, $k_{1i}(s_i, t) > 0$. $m_i(t)$ is a mode transformation function, and it realizes the changing between the adaptive control and sliding mode control. The purpose of inducing the mode transformation function $m_i(t)$ is to keep the state in a bounded close set by using the designed NN controllers. $0 \leq m_i(t) \leq 1$, it is defined as:

$$m_i(t) = \max\{0, \operatorname{sat}(\frac{\|x_i - x_{i0}\|_{p, \pi_i - 1}}{\psi_i})\} \tag{16}$$

Where $\operatorname{sat}(\cdot)$ is a saturation function (See reference [7]).

$s_{i\Delta}$ is the distance between the state and the border layer. $\eta_i > 0$ is a constant. $\varphi_i \geq 0$ is the width of the border layer. $s_{i\Delta}$ possess the following properties:

1) if $|s_i| > \varphi_i$, then $|s_{i\Delta}| = |s_i| - \varphi_i$, and $\dot{s}_{i\Delta} = \dot{s}_i$
2) if $|s_i| \leq \varphi_i$, then $\dot{s}_{i\Delta} = \dot{s}_i = 0$

Taking the derivative of $s_i(t)$ yields:

$$\dot{s}_i(t) = e_i^{(r)} + \sum_{k=1}^{r-1} \binom{r-1}{k} \eta_i^k e_i^{(r-k)}$$

$$= f_i(x_i) + g_i(x_i)[u_i + G_i(\bar{x})] - y_{im}^{(r)} + \sum_{k=1}^{r-1} \binom{r-1}{k} \eta_i^k e_i^{(r-k)} \tag{17}$$

From (17), the following can be obtained:

$$g_i^{-1}(x_i)\dot{s}_i(t) = H_i(x_i) + [u_i + G_i(\bar{x})] - g_i^{-1} y_{im}^{(r)} + g_i^{-1} \sum_{k=1}^{r-1} \binom{r-1}{k} \eta_i^k e_i^{(r-k)}$$

$$= H_i(x_i) + g_i^{-1} a_{ri} + G_i(\bar{x}) - k_{d_i} s_{i\Delta} - \frac{1}{2} M_{3i} \|x_i\| s_{i\Delta}$$

$$- (1 - m_i(t))[\hat{H}_i(x_i|\hat{W}_{1i}) + \hat{g}_i^{-1}(x_i|\hat{W}_{2i})a_{ri} + \hat{G}(\bar{x}|\hat{W}_{3i})$$

$$+ \hat{\varepsilon}_{1i} u_{si} + \hat{\varepsilon}_{2i}|a_{ri}|u_{si} + \hat{\varepsilon}_{3i} u_{si}] + m_i(t) k_{1i}(s_i,t) u_{si} \qquad (18)$$

$$= -k_{d_i} s_{i\Delta} - \frac{1}{2} M_{3i} \|x_i\| s_{i\Delta}$$

$$- (1 - m_i(t))[\tilde{W}_{1i}^T \xi_i(x_i) + a_{ri} \tilde{W}_{2i}^T \xi_i(x_i) + \tilde{W}_{3i}^T s_i(x')]$$

$$- (1 - m_i(t))[H_i(x_i|W_{1i}^*) - H_i(x_i) + a_{ri}(g_i^{-1}(x_i|W_{1i}^*) - g_i^{-1}(x_i))$$

$$+ G(\bar{x}|W_{3i}^*)a_{ri} - G_i(\bar{x}) + \hat{\varepsilon}_{1i} u_{si} + \hat{\varepsilon}_{2i}|a_{ri}|u_{si} + \hat{\varepsilon}_{3i} u_{si}]$$

$$+ m_i(t)[H_i(x_i) + g_i^{-1}(x_i)a_{ri} + G_i(\bar{x}) + k_{1i}(s_i,t) u_{fsi}]$$

Where the error $\tilde{W}_{1i}, \tilde{W}_{2i}, \tilde{W}_{3i}$ satisfies $\tilde{W}_{pi} = \hat{W}_{pi} - W_{pi}^*, p = 1,2,3$

Choose the adaptive laws of the parameters and control gains as:

$$\dot{\hat{W}}_{1i} = \begin{cases} \eta_{1i}(1 - m_i(t))\xi_i(x_i) s_{i\Delta} & if |\hat{W}_{1i}| < M_f, or |\hat{W}_{1i}| = M_f and \hat{W}_{1i}^T \xi_i(x_i) s_{i\Delta} \leq 0 \\ P_1\{\eta_{1i}(1 - m_i(t))\xi_i(x_i) s_{i\Delta}\} & if |\hat{W}_{1i}| = M_f and \hat{W}_{1i}^T \xi_i(x_i) s_{i\Delta} > 0 \end{cases}$$

$$\dot{\hat{W}}_{2i} = \begin{cases} \eta_{2i}(1 - m_i(t))a_{ri}\xi_i(x_i) s_{i\Delta} & if |\hat{W}_{2i}| < M_g, or |\hat{W}_{2i}| = M_g \\ & and \hat{W}_{2i}^T \xi_i(x_i) a_{ri} s_{i\Delta} \leq 0 \\ P_2\{\eta_{2i}(1 - m_i(t))a_{ri}\xi_i(x_i) s_{i\Delta}\} & if |\hat{W}_{2i}| = M_g and \hat{W}_{2i}^T \xi_i(x_i) a_{ri} s_{i\Delta} > 0 \end{cases}$$

$$\dot{\hat{W}}_{3i} = \begin{cases} \eta_{3i}(1 - m_i(t))s_i(x') s_{i\Delta} & if |\hat{W}_{3i}| < M_G, or |\hat{W}_{3i}| = M_G and \hat{W}_{3i}^T s_i(x') s_{i\Delta} \leq 0 \\ P_3\{\eta_{3i}(1 - m_i(t))s_i(x') s_{i\Delta}\} & if |\hat{W}_{3i}| = M_G and \hat{W}_{3i}^T s_i(x') s_{i\Delta} > 0 \end{cases} \qquad (19)$$

$$\dot{\hat{\varepsilon}}_{1i} = \eta_{4i}(1 - m_i(t))|s_{i\Delta}|$$

$$\dot{\hat{\varepsilon}}_{2i} = \eta_{5i}(1 - m_i(t))|s_{i\Delta} a_{ri}|$$

$$\dot{\hat{\varepsilon}}_{3i} = \eta_{6i}(1 - m_i(t))|s_{i\Delta}|$$

Where $\eta_{ki} > 0, (k = 1,\cdots,6)$ is the learning ratio. M_f, M_g, M_G are the given positive constants.

$$P_1\{*\} = \eta_{1i}(1-m_i(t))s_{i\Delta}\xi_i(x_i) - \eta_{1i}(1-m_i(t))s_{i\Delta}\frac{\hat{W}_{1i}\hat{W}_{1i}^T\xi_i(x_i)}{|\hat{W}_{1i}|^2}$$

$$P_2\{*\} = \eta_{2i}(1-m_i(t))s_{i\Delta}\xi_i(x_i)a_{ri} - \eta_{2i}(1-m_i(t))s_{i\Delta}a_{ri}\frac{\hat{W}_{2i}\hat{W}_{2i}^T\xi_i(x_i)}{|\hat{W}_{2i}|^2} \quad (20)$$

$$P_3\{*\} = \eta_{3i}(1-m_i(t))s_{i\Delta}s_i(x') - \eta_{3i}(1-m_i(t))s_{i\Delta}\frac{\hat{W}_{2i}\hat{W}_{2i}^T s_i(x')}{|\hat{W}_{2i}|^2}$$

Theorem 1. For system (1), under the assumptions (1),(2),(3), if adopt the NN indirect adaptive sliding mode controller (14)-(15) and adaptive laws (19) and (20), and select

$$k_{1i}(s_i,t) = M_{1i} + M_{2i}|a_{ri}| + M_{4i} \quad (21)$$

then the following properties hold:

(1) $|\hat{W}_{1i}| \le M_f$, $|\hat{W}_{2i}| \le M_g$, $|\hat{W}_{3i}| \le M_G$ $X_{i1}, u_i \in L_\infty$

(2) The tracking error $e_i(t)$ convergences to a neighborhood of zero.

Proof: omitted.

4 Emulation

Example:
Consider the following nonlinear interconnected system with two subsystems:

$\dot{x}_1 = x_2$
$\dot{x}_2 = (x_2^2 + 2x_1)\sin(x_2) + [1 + \exp(-x_1)][u_1 + 0.5\sin(3t)x_3]$
$\dot{x}_3 = x_4$
$\dot{x}_4 = (x_4^2 + 2x_3)\sin(x_4) + [1 + \exp(-x_3)][u_2 + 0.5\sin(3t)x_1]$

The given reference states are

$$x_{1m} = \sin(\frac{\pi}{2}t), \quad x_{2m} = \sin(\frac{\pi}{2}t)$$

We use two different neural networks to approximate the nonlinear terms in the interconnected systems and design the controllers as the form (16) and (20) in the theorem, and choose the initial values as:

$$x_1(0) = 1.5, \quad x_2(0) = 0, \quad x_3(0) = 1.5, \quad x_4(0) = 0$$

The emulation curves are as following Fig. 1:

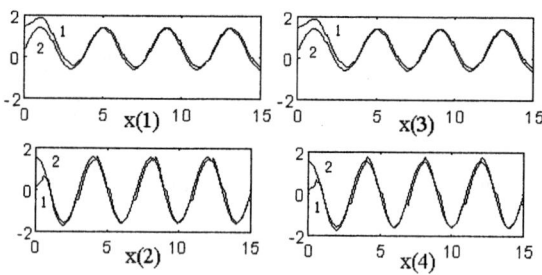

Fig. 1. Curves of the states and the errors (1 is actual state, 2 is reference state)

5 Conclusion

In this paper, a new scheme of NN indirect adaptive control is proposed for the nonlinear interconnected systems with SISO subsystems. It combines the NN adaptive control and sliding mode control. The sliding mode control compensate for the affection of the NN approximation errors on the output tracking errors. It overcomes the defect that the controllers has no mathematical expressions such that it's difficult to analyze the stability of the systems. The scheme adopts sliding mode plane to concentrate the information about errors and error changing ratio. Using the system states information, the mode transformation functions likes a "balance device" to make a decision between the two kinds of controllers (NN indirect adaptive controller and sliding mode controller) that which are more suitable to obtain the tracking objective. There has been some result about the fuzzy indirect adaptive sliding mode control for the interconnected systems[6,7,9]. To compare the virtue and drawback of these two schemes in detailed is our further work.

Acknowledgement

This paper was supported in part by National Natural Science Foundation (79970114) and in part by the National Key Project of China.

References

1. Wang L X.: Adaptive Fuzzy Systems and Control-Design and Stability Analysis. Englewood Cliffs, NJ: Prentice-Hall(1994)
2. Su C.Y., Yury S.: Adaptive Control of a Class of Nonlinear Systems with Fuzzy Logic. IEEE Transition on Fuzzy Systems, 2(2), (1994) 285-294
3. Hajjaji A.E., Rachid A.: Explicit Formulas for Fuzzy Controller. Fuzzy sets and systems, 62(2), (1995) 135-141.
4. Isodori. A.: Nonlinear Control Systems, Spring-Verlag, New York (1989)

5. Tong, S.C.: Fuzzy Indirect Adaptive Output Feedback Control for a Class of Nonlinear System. Acta Automatica Sinica, 25(4), (1999) 553-559
6. Tong S.C., Chai T.Y.: Fuzzy Indirect Adaptive Control for a Class of Decentralized Nonlinear Systems. International Journal of Systems Science, 29(2), (1998) 149-157
7. Zhang T.P.: Fuzzy Adaptive Sliding Mode Decentralized Control for a Class of Large-scale Systems. Acta Automatica Sinica, 24(6), (1998) 747-753 (in Chinese)
8. Zhang Y.W.: Some Control Problem for Similar Interconnected Systems. Doctor Thesis, Shenyang: Northestern University, (2000)
9. Zhang Y.X, Zhang S.Y.: Fuzzy Indirect Adaptive Sliding Mode Tracking Control for a Class of Nonlinear Interconnected Systems. Acta Automatica Sinica, 29(5), (2003) 658-665

Sequential Support Vector Machine Control of Nonlinear Systems via Lyapunov Function Derivative Estimation

Zonghai Sun, Youxian Sun, and Yongqiang Wang

National Laboratory of Industrial Control Technology,
Zhejiang University, Hangzhou 310027, China
zhsun@iipc.zju.edu.cn

Abstract. We introduce the support vector machine adaptive control by Lyapunov function derivative estimation. The support vector machine is trained by Kalman filter. Support vector machine is used to estimate the Lyapunov function derivative for affine nonlinear system, whose nonlinearities are assumed to be unknown. In order to demonstrate the availability of this new method of Lyapunov function derivative estimation, a simple example is given in the form of affine nonlinear system. The result of simulation demonstrates that the sequential training algorithm of support vector machine is effective and support vector machine control can achieve a satisfactory performance.

1 Introduction

Support vector machine (SVM) [1, 2] for pattern classification and regression estimation is an important methodology in the area of neural and nonlinear modeling. In many applications it provides high generalization ability and overcomes the overfitting problem experienced by the other learning technique such as neural network. SVM is a kernel-based approach which allows the use of linear, polynomial and radial basis function and others that satisfy Mercer's condition.

Lyapunov-like techniques have long been used in nonlinear control. But even for completely known nonlinear systems, the construction of Lyapunov function is a challenging task. Obviously the problem becomes intractable for unknown systems. In this paper, we will discuss SVM adaptive control of affine nonlinear systems by Lyapunov function derivative estimation. SVM is used to estimate the derivative of an unknown Lyapunov function. In control the source of data is time-variant; we may adopt a sequential strategy for training SVM. In this paper we focus on SVM, constraining ourselves to sequential training and its application in nonlinear control.

2 The Presentation of State Space for SVM

Given data samples $\{x_i, y_i\}_{i=1}^{N}$, where $x_i \in R^n$, $y_i \in R$, the relation between x_i and y_i is defined as follow

$$y_i = w^T \varphi(x_i) + b, \quad i = 1, \cdots, N \qquad (1)$$

where b denotes the threshold value, and w denotes the weight. In order to estimate the y_i for x_i, we should solve the following optimization problem

$$\min \quad L = \frac{1}{2} w^T w + C \sum_{i=1}^{N} (\xi_i + \xi_i^*) \qquad (2)$$

$$\text{s.t.} \quad \begin{cases} y_i - w^T \varphi(x_i) - b \leq \varepsilon + \xi_i^*, & i = 1, \cdots, N \\ w^T \varphi(x_i) + b - y_i \leq \varepsilon + \xi_i, & i = 1, \cdots, N \\ \xi_i, \xi_i^* \geq 0, & i = 1, \cdots, N \end{cases} \qquad (3)$$

where C denotes balance term, and ξ_i, ξ_i^* denote the slack variables.

By using Lagrangrian optimization method, we may obtain

$$y_i = \sum_{j=1}^{N} (\alpha_j^* - \alpha_j) K(x_i, x_j) + b, \quad i = 1, \cdots, N \qquad (4)$$

with Lagrange factor α_i, α_i^*, $K(x_i, x_j) = \varphi(x_j)^T \varphi(x_i)$ denotes the kernel function. We re-express equation (4) in terms of a moving window over the data and compute the output of SVM each time new data are received:

$$y_{k+1} = \sum_{j=0}^{L} (\alpha_{k+1,k-L+j}^* - \alpha_{k+1,k-L+j}) K(x_{k+1}, x_{k-L+j}) + b_{k+1} \qquad (5)$$

In order to estimate b, $\alpha^* - \alpha$ sequential, we describe (5) by state-space Markovian representation: $\theta_{k+1} = \theta_k + \eta_k$, $y_{k+1} = C_{k+1} \theta_{k+1} + \delta_{k+1}$ with $C_{k+1} = [1 \ K(x_{k+1}, x_{k-L}) \cdots K(x_{k+1}, x_k)]$, $\theta_k = [b_k \ \alpha_{k,0}^* - \alpha_{k,0} \cdots \alpha_{k,L}^* - \alpha_{k,L}]^T$, η_k and δ_{k+1} denote the process and measurement noise respectively.

η_k, δ_{k+1} are assumed to be zero mean Gassian distributed with covariance R, Q respectively. The assumption is motivated by the fact that if we have a linear Gaussian state space model, the optimal solution (minimum variance, maximum a posteriori et al) is given by the Kalman filter [3]. So the parameter θ will be estimated recursively by the Kalman filter.

3 Sequential SVM Control of Nonlinear Systems

We consider an affine nonlinear system [4]

$$\dot{x} = f(x) + G(x)u \qquad (6)$$

where $u \in R^m$ is the control input, the state $x \in R^n$ is assumed completely measurable, and $f(x)$, $G(x)$ are continuous, locally Lipschitz vector fields. The objective is to enable the output x to follow a desired trajectory x_r. For the x_r, we also assume that $\dot{x}_r$ is bounded. We define the tracking error as

$$e = x - x_r \tag{7}$$

According to (6) and (7), we may obtain

$$\dot{e} = f(x) + G(x)u - \dot{x}_r \tag{8}$$

Assumption 1[4]: the solution of system (8) is uniformly ultimately bounded with respect to an arbitrarily small neighborhood of $e = 0$.

From *Assumption 1*, there exits an arbitrarily unbounded Lyapunov function $V(e)$ and a control input such that [4]

$$\dot{V}(e) = \partial V(e)/\partial e \, (f(x) + G(x)u - \dot{x}_r) \leq 0 . \tag{9}$$

Sontag [5] has provided an explicit formula for stabilizing systems of the form (6) whenever V, f, G are known.

In most applications f, G are unknown and the construction of V is a hard problem, which has been solved for special classes of systems. To overcome the highly uncertainty about (6) and provide a valid solution for our problem. The approximation capability of SVM is adopted. Without losing generality, we substitute the unknown term in (9) with $a(x,e) = \partial V(e)/\partial e \, f(x)$, $b(x,e) = \partial V(e)/\partial e \, G(x)$, $c(\dot{x}_r, e) = \partial V(e)/\partial e \, \dot{x}_r$. SVM is used to approximate the unknown functions $a(x,e)$, $b(x,e)$, $c(\dot{x}_r, e)$. In order that output x can track the objective trajectory x_r asymptotically, we have the following lemma to present an ideal control u^*:

Lemma 1. For the system (6) satisfying Assumption 1, if the ideal control is designed as

$$u^* = -(a(x,e) - c(\dot{x}_r, e) + k(t)|e|)/b(x,e) \tag{10}$$

where $k(t) > 0$, for all t, is a design parameter, then tracking error converges to zeros.

4 Numerical Simulations

A simple example is used to illustrate the effectiveness of the proposed SVM control of nonlinear systems by sequential training algorithms. Consider the following scalar system [4]

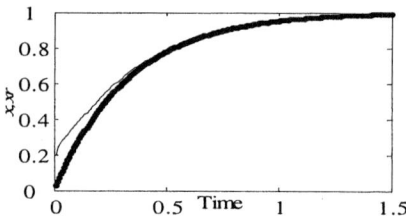 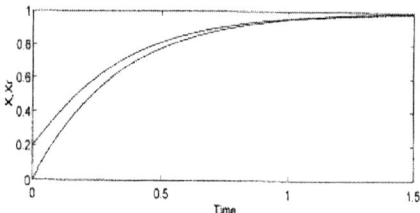

Fig. 1. Tracking performance of SVM adaptive control design

Fig. 2. Closed loop system performance of adaptive neural control design

$$\dot{x} = 2x - x^3 + x^2 u, \quad x(0) = 0.2 \tag{11}$$

The problem is to control (11) to track the desired trajectory $x_r(t) = 1 - e^{-3t}$.

The unknown functions $a(x,e)$, $b(x,e)$, $c(\dot{x}_r,e)$ are estimated by sequential SVM. The kernel function is the Gaussian function. SVM is trained online by Kalman filter with $L = 40$, $k(t) = 10$, $R = 1$, $Q = 2$. Fig.1. shows that the output x tracks the desired trajectory x_r effectively. The dot line denotes desired trajectory x_r, while the solid line denotes the output curve x in fig.1. Fig. 2. is simulation result of [4]. Comparing fig. 1. with fig. 2, we may know that the convergence rate of tracking error of SVM control is bigger than that of adaptive neuro-control. The numerical simulation result above shows good transient performance and the tracking error is small. This demonstrates that the sequential SVM controller can achieve a satisfactory performance.

5 Discussion and Conclusion

In this paper we discussed sequential SVM for regression estimation and sequential SVM control of nonlinear systems via Lyapunov function derivative estimation. Firstly we provided the representation of state-space for SVM. The sequential SVM is realized by Kalman filter. The advantage of the proposed method is that the computational complexity decreases and thus the on-line training and control become feasible. Finally we apply the sequential SVM to estimate the Lyapunov function derivative for nonlinear adaptive control. The simulation result demonstrates that this method is feasible for Lyapunov function derivative estimation.

References

1. V. N. Vapnik: Statistical learning theory. John Wiley and Sons, New York, 1998
2. Sun Zonghai: Study on support vector machine and its application in control. PhD. Thesis. Zhejiang University, Hangzhou, China, 2003
3. J. F. G. de Freitas, M. Niranjan, A. H. Gee, A. Doucet: Sequential monte carlo methods to train neural network models. Neural computation, Vol. 12 (4): 955-993. Apr. 2000
4. George A. Rovithakis: Stable adaptive neuro-control design via Lyapunov function derivative estimation. Automatica, 37(2001): 1213-1221
5. Sontag, E. D. A.: "universal" construction of Artstein's theorem on nonlinear stabilization. Systems Control of Letters, 13: 117-123

An Adaptive Control Using Multiple Neural Networks for the Position Control in Hydraulic Servo System

Yuan Kang, Ming-Hui Chu[a], Yuan-Liang Liu,
Chuan-Wei Chang, and Shu-Yen Chien

Department of Mechanical Engineering,
Chung Yuan Christian University, Chung Li 320, Taiwan, R.O.C
yk@cycu.edu.tw
[a] Department of Automation Engineering,
Tung Nan Institute of Technology, Taipei 222, Taiwan, R.O.C

Abstract. A model following adaptive control based on neural network for the electro-hydraulic servo system (EHSS) subjected to varied load is proposed. This proposed control utilizes multiple neural networks including a neural controller, a neural emulator and a neural tuner. The neural controller with specialized learning architecture utilizes a linear combination of error and the error's derivative to approximate the back propagation error for weights update. The neural tuner is designed to adjust the parameters of the linear combination. The neural emulator is used to approximate the Jacobian of plant. The control of the hydraulic servo actuator is investigated by simulation and experiment, and a favorable model-following characteristic is achieved.

1 Introduction

The electro-hydraulic servo systems are used in aircraft, industrial and precision mechanisms. They are always used for servomechanism to transmit large specific powers with low control current and high precision. The electro-hydraulic servo system (EHSS) consists of hydraulic supply units, actuators and an electro-hydraulic servo valve (EHSV) with its servo driver. The EHSS is inherently nonlinear, time variant and usually operated with load disturbance. It is difficult to determine the parameters of dynamic model for an EHSS. Furthermore, the parameters are varied with temperature, external load and properties of oil etc. Therefore it is reasonable for the EHSS to use a neural network based adaptive control to enhance the adaptability and achieve the specified performance.

Recently, many learning architectures of neural controllers have been presented. The specialized learning architectures are available for motion control system, and easily implemented. There are two strategies to facilitate the specialized learning: the direct control strategy and the indirect control strategy. In the former, the plant can be viewed as an additional but non-modifiable layer of the neural network. The latter, which has been used in many applications, is a two-step process including identification of plant dynamics and control.

In the indirect control strategy, a sub-network (called "emulator") is required to be trained before the control phase. It is used to approximate the plant Jacobian. It is therefore vitally important that the data sets for training the emulator must cover a sufficiently large range of input and output pairs, and it can be improved by training the emulator on-line. This is due to the fact that the connective weights of the emulator can be updated in every sample interval. It can improve the inaccuracy of the emulator induced by the plant parameters variation and off-line training error.

A direct control strategy can be applied when the Jacobian of the plant is available prior. However, it is usually difficult to obtain the plant Jacobian. Zhang etc. [1] presented a direct neural controller for on-line tracking control by using a simple sign function to approximate the Jacobian of a ship. The tracking error will be convergent with their control strategy, but it takes much time for the on-line learning process. It cannot be applied to a high performance motion control system. Lin and Wai [2] proposed the δ adaptation law to increase the on-line learning speed for updating the connective weights. However, no specified method for on-line tuning of the parameters of the δ adaptation law was proposed in their effort. The parameters are only tuned by try and error. It is difficult to obtain the appropriate parameters.

Recently it was proven that a neural network could tune the parameters of a PID controller. Omatu and Yoshioka [3] proposed a PID controller whose parameters are tuned by a neural network for the stable and fast response of an inverted pendulum. Furthermore, Omatu etc. [4] proposed the same method for the stable response of a single-input multi-output control system with double inverted pendulums. In their studies, the PID gains can be tuned by using two neural networks, and their results show that the inverted pendulums can be stabilized.

However the neural based adaptive control for the EHSS has rarely been proposed. Gao and Wu [5] performed stable position control of an EHSS with a specified fuzzy neural control. They could tune the fuzzy membership function on-line by neural networks, and the stability of the position control is proven by experiment. Chu, etc. [6] established the dynamic model of a variable displacement pump, and a model-following adaptive control based on neural network was proposed to control the output flow of a variable displacement pump. They used a linear combination of error and the error's differential to approximate the back propagation error (BPE) for weights update. But no specified method was proposed to determine the parameters of the linear combination.

In this paper, a novel model-following adaptive control, using multiple neural networks, is proposed to control the piston displacement of an EHSS following a reference model. The nonlinear dynamic of the EHSS is emulated by a back propagation neural network (BPNN), which is also defined as a neural emulator and trained priori for approximation of plant Jacobian. The neural controller is a conventional direct neural controller, which uses the linear combination of error and the error's differential to approximate the BPE. And a parameter tuner is designed to on-line tune the parameters of the linear combination.

2 Adaptive Control Using Multiple Neural Networks

The EHSS including hydraulic supply units, EHSV, hydraulic actuator, linear variable differential transformer (LVDT) and load cell is established and shown in Fig. 1. This is viewed as a nonlinear third-order model under specified load condition and defined as

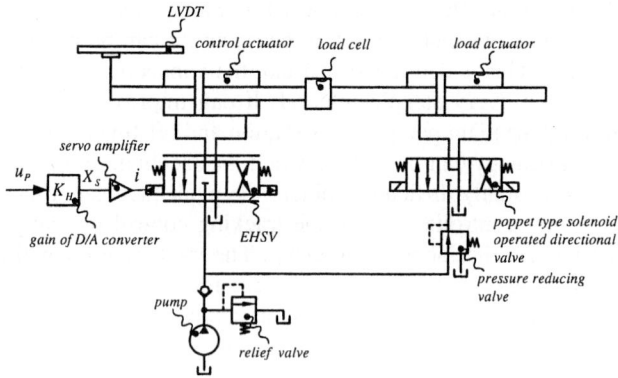

Fig. 1. The schematic drawing of EHSS circuit

$$X_p(n) = f\left(u_p(n-1),\ u_p(n-2), u_p(n-3), X_p(n-1), X_p(n-2), X_p(n-3)\right) \quad (1)$$

where $f(\cdot)$ is a nonlinear function, X_p is the piston displacement for cylinder, u_p is the control input and n represents the n-th sampling interval.

The nonlinear model described by Eq.(1) can be emulated by a BPNN N_2, which is called emulator. The detailed algorithms of N_2 have been presented by Narendra and Parthasarathy [7]. The block diagram of N_2 for off-line training is shown in Fig. 2. The proposed model-following adaptive control system using multiple neural networks (MNNACS) for the position control in EHSS, including a neural controller N_1, neural emulator N_2, and neural tuner N_3, is shown in Fig. 3.

A linear second order transfer function shown in Eq.2 is used to be the reference model. It can perform an ideal output of a well-designed close loop control system.

$$\frac{X_R}{X_r} = \frac{\omega_n^2}{s^2 + 2\varsigma\,\omega_n s + \omega_n^2} \quad (2)$$

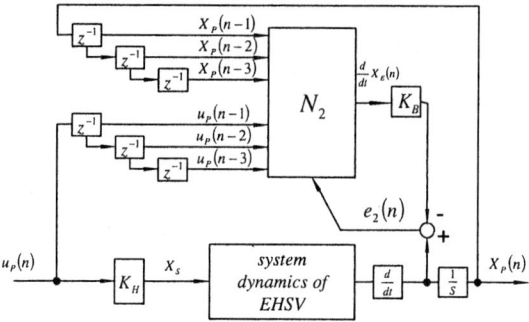

Fig. 2. The block diagram of EHSS emulator for off-line training

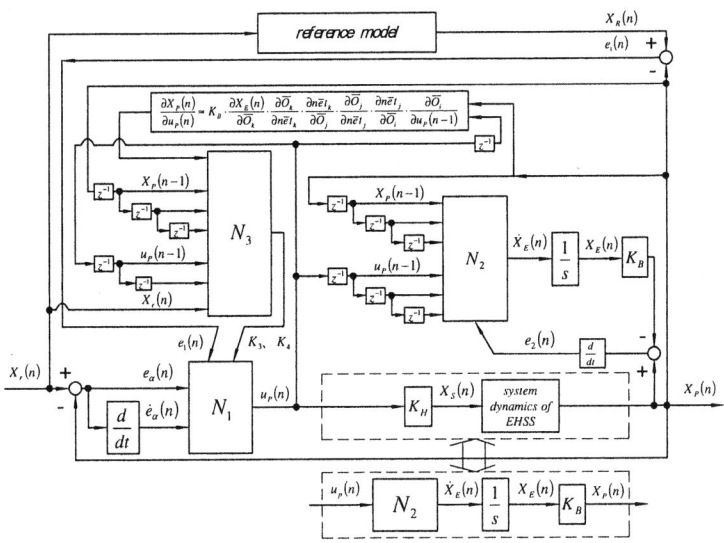

Fig. 3. The block diagram of MNNACS for position control of in EHSS

where X_r and X_R are the input and output of the reference model respectively, s is Laplace operator, ς is damping ratio, ω_n is natural frequency. Both parameters can be determined by the desired performance indexes.

The neural network N_2 is required to be trained priori to describe the inputs and outputs relation of the EHSS. There are 8 hidden neurons, 6 input neurons and 1 output neuron. The random input signals are applied to excite the position displacement in EHSS. The speed responses can be determined and used for off-line training of N_2. The output of N_2 is multiplied by a constant gain K_B to approximate the piston velocity. The well-trained network N_2 can be used as approximation model in the design and simulation of the control system. It also serves as a neural emulator for approximation of Jacobian in the control phase.

Both of the direct neural controller N_1 and neural tuner N_3 has three layers including an input layer (subscripted by "i"), a hidden layer (subscripted by "j") and an output layer (subscripted by "k"). The hyperbolic tangent function is used for both N_1 and N_2 in the hidden and output layers, and the sigmoid function and unity are used for N_3 as the activation for the nodes in the hidden layer and the output layer, respectively. The neural network N_1 has 2 inputs, 1 output and 5 hidden nodes. The 2 inputs are the error e_a and its differential $\dot{e}_a$. The error e_a is the difference between the command X_r and piston displacement X_p. The input signals are well normalized by multiplying K'_1 and K'_2. The output of this neural controller u_p is multiplied by a scaling factor K_H to be the input voltage for the servo amplifier that is used to supply sufficient current to drive the EHSV. The weights of N_I are updated by the BPE, which is approximated by a linear combination of error e_I and its differential $\dot{e}_I$, by multiplying the parameters K_3 and K_4 [2]. The error e_I is the difference between the output of the reference model X_R and piston displacement X_P. Thus, The neural network N_3 has 6 input, 8 hidden and 2 output nodes, and the 2 outputs denoted as the appropriate parameters K_3 and K_4. The 6 inputs are $X_P(n-1)$, $X_P(n-2)$, $X_P(n-3)$, $u_P(n-1)$, $u_P(n-2)$, and $X_r(n)$ with respect to plant output, input and the command signals, which are normalized by multiplying $\hat{K}_1$, $\hat{K}_2$ and $\hat{K}_3$.

3 Weights Updating of BPNN for Neural Networks

Both algorithm of N_1 and N_2 are presented by Narendra and Parthasarathy [7]. N_1 is used as a direct neural controller and N_2 is used as an emulator. However, the algorithm of the neural tuner is not the same as one of the previous networks. The detailed descriptions of the algorithms for N_3 are presented in this study.

The variables and parameters of the three neural networks used in following analysis are denoted by superscript ${}'$, $-$ and $\wedge$ respect to N_1, N_2 and N_3. The weight-update quantities of the neural tuner can be defined by

$$\Delta \hat{W}_{kj}(n) = -\hat{\eta} \cdot \frac{\partial \hat{E}(n)}{\partial \hat{W}_{kj}(n)}, \quad k = 3, 4, \quad j = 1 \sim 8 \tag{3}$$

$$\Delta \hat{W}_{ji}(n) = -\hat{\eta} \cdot \frac{\partial \hat{E}(n)}{\partial \hat{W}_{ji}(n)}, \quad i = 1 \sim 6, \quad j = 1 \sim 8 \tag{4}$$

where the error energy function $\hat{E}(n)$ is defined by

$$\hat{E}(n) = \frac{1}{2}(X_R(n) - X_P(n))^2 = \frac{1}{2}e_I(n)^2 \tag{5}$$

The gradient of $\hat{E}(n)$ with respect to the change of $\hat{W}_{kj}(n)$

$$\frac{\partial \hat{E}(n)}{\partial \hat{W}_{kj}(n)} = \frac{\partial \hat{E}(n)}{\partial n\hat{e}t_k(n)} \cdot \frac{\partial n\hat{e}t_k(n)}{\partial \hat{W}_{kj}(n)} = \hat{\delta}_k(n) \cdot \hat{O}_j(n) = \hat{\delta}_k(n) \cdot f(n\hat{e}t_j), \quad k = 3, 4 \tag{6}$$

where $f(\cdot)$ is the activation function, $\hat{\delta}_k(n)$ is detonated for $\dfrac{\partial \hat{E}(n)}{\partial n\hat{e}t_k(n)}$, thus defined

$$\hat{\delta}_k(n) = \frac{\partial \hat{E}(n)}{\partial n\hat{e}t_k(n)} = \frac{\partial \hat{E}(n)}{\partial X_P(n)} \cdot \frac{\partial X_P(n)}{\partial u_P(n)} \cdot \frac{\partial u_P(n)}{\partial \hat{O}_k(n)} \cdot \frac{\partial \hat{O}_k(n)}{\partial n\hat{e}t_k(n)}$$

$$= -e_I(n) \cdot \frac{\partial X_P(n)}{\partial u_P(n)} \cdot \frac{\partial u_P(n)}{\partial K_k} \cdot 1, \quad k = 3, 4 \tag{7}$$

where $\hat{O}_k(n) = n\hat{e}t_k(n)$. The activation function is unity for output neurons. The Jacobian of EHSV is evaluated by

$$\frac{\partial X_P(n)}{\partial u_P(n)} \approx K_B \cdot \sum_{j=1}^{g} \frac{\partial f(\overline{net}_k(n))}{\partial \overline{net}_k(n)} \cdot \overline{W}_{kj}(n) \cdot \frac{\partial f(\overline{net}_j(n))}{\partial \overline{net}_j(n)} \cdot \overline{W}_{ji}(n) \cdot \overline{K}_I(n) \qquad (8)$$

where K_B is the gain for network N_2, and $\overline{K}_I$ is the gain for the normalization of input for network N_2.

The partial differential of E' with respect to the network output O'_k is defined to be the BPE, can be approximated by a linear combination of the error and its derivative. The $(n-1)$th weights update of the output layer for neural network N_1 is

$$\Delta W'_{kj}(n-1) = \eta' \cdot (K_3 \cdot e_I(n-1) + K_4 \cdot \dot{e}_I(n-1)) \cdot \frac{\partial f(net'_k(n-1))}{\partial net'_k(n-1)} \cdot O'_j(n-1) \qquad (9)$$

where K_3 and K_4 are positive constants.
The derivatives of the n-th weights update with respect to K_3 and K_4 are:

$$\frac{\partial W'_{kj}(n)}{\partial K_3} = \frac{\partial W'_{kj}(n-1)}{\partial K_3} - \eta' \cdot e_I(n-1) \cdot \frac{\partial f(net'_k(n-1))}{\partial net'_k(n-1)} \cdot O'_j(n-1) \qquad (10)$$

$$\frac{\partial W'_{kj}(n)}{\partial K_4} = \frac{\partial W'_{kj}(n-1)}{\partial K_4} - \eta' \cdot \dot{e}_I(n-1) \cdot \frac{\partial f(net'_k(n-1))}{\partial net'_k(n-1)} \cdot O'_j(n-1), \qquad (11)$$

respectively. And the derivatives of plant input with respect to K_3 and K_4 is

$$\frac{\partial u_P(n)}{\partial K_k} = \frac{\partial u_P(n)}{\partial O'_k(n)} \cdot \frac{\partial O'_k(n)}{\partial net'_k(n)} \cdot \frac{\partial net'_k(n)}{\partial W'_{kj}(n)} \cdot \frac{\partial W'_{kj}(n)}{\partial K_k}$$

$$= \frac{\partial f(net'_k(n))}{\partial net'_k(n)} \cdot O'_j(n) \cdot \frac{\partial W'_{kj}(n)}{\partial K_k}, \quad k = 3, 4 \qquad (12)$$

Substituting Eqs. (10) and (11) into Eq. (12) and substituting the result into Eq. (7) will obtain $\hat{\delta}_3$ and $\hat{\delta}_4$, which are then substituted into Eq. (6), and the gradient of $\hat{E}$ with respect to the weights $\hat{W}_{ji}$ of N_3 can be obtained by

$$\frac{\partial \hat{E}(n)}{\partial \hat{W}_{ji}(n)} = \frac{\partial \hat{E}(n)}{\partial n\hat{e}t_j(n)} \cdot \frac{\partial n\hat{e}t_j(n)}{\partial \hat{W}_{ji}(n)} = \hat{\delta}_j(n) \cdot \hat{O}_i(n) \qquad (13)$$

where $\hat{\delta}_j(n)$ is defined by

$$\hat{\delta}_j(n) = \frac{\partial \hat{E}(n)}{\partial n\hat{e}t_j(n)} = \sum_{k=3}^{4} \frac{\partial \hat{E}(n)}{\partial n\hat{e}t_k(n)} \cdot \frac{\partial n\hat{e}t_k(n)}{\partial \hat{O}_j(n)} \cdot \frac{\partial \hat{O}_j(n)}{\partial n\hat{e}t_j(n)}$$

$$= \sum_{k=3}^{4} \hat{\delta}_k(n) \cdot \hat{W}_{kj}(n) \cdot \frac{\partial f(n\hat{e}t_j(n))}{\partial n\hat{e}t_j(n)} \qquad (14)$$

Thus, the weights $\hat{W}_{kj}(n+1)$ and $\hat{W}_{ji}(n+1)$ can be determined. From the time n to $n+1$ by

$$\hat{W}_{kj}(n+1) = \hat{W}_{kj}(n) + \Delta\hat{W}_{kj}(n), \ k = 3, \ 4, \ j = 1 \sim 8 \tag{15}$$

$$\hat{W}_{ji}(n+1) = \hat{W}_{ji}(n) + \Delta\hat{W}_{ji}(n), \ i = 1 \sim 6, \ j = 1 \sim 8 \tag{16}$$

4 Numerical Simulation

An EHSS with a hydraulic double rod cylinder controlled by an EHSV is established for simulation and experiment. The neural network N_2 is established to emulate the inputs and outputs relation. As show in Fig. 2, the step signals $u_p(n)$ with random amplitudes of the interval between 0 and 1 are applied to excite the position responses of EHSS. The position responses $X_p(n)$ of EHSS are measured by LVDT and recorded with the corresponding inputs $u_p(n)$. The speed responses can be obtained by differential of position response $X_p(n)$ for off-line training of N_2. The initial weights of N_2 are chosen between ± 0.5 randomly and updated by $e_2(n)$. The error is difference between the piston velocity and the N_2 outputs multiplied by K_B. All connective weights are defined to be convergent when the MSE is smaller than $0.001 \ m/s$. It needs 150252 iterations. After the training phase, N_2 can describe the input and output relations for EHSS. The linear second-order reference model with $t_s = 0.5 \ sec$, $\varsigma = 1$ and $\omega_n = 8 \ Hz$ is defined by

$$\frac{X_R(z)}{X_r(z)} = \frac{0.000031830681z - 0.000031661319}{z^2 - 1.98406383z + 0.98412732} \tag{17}$$

A conventional direct neural controller N_1 is applied to control the EHSS, and the time responses for piston position are simulated. A tangent hyperbolic function is used as the activation function for N_1, so that the neural network controller output is between ± 1. This is converted to be analog voltage between $\pm 5 \ Volt$ by a D/A converter and amplified in current by a servo amplifier to drive the EHSV. The constants K_3 and K_4 are defined to be the parameters for the linear combination of error (e_1) and its derivative ($\dot{e}_1$), which is used to approximate the BPE for weights update. A simple direct neural controller with $K_3 = 1$, $K_4 = 0$ and 0.6 is applied to control the EHSS, and the time responses for piston positions are simulated. The simulation results shown in Fig.4. Fig. 4(a) reveals that the parameter K_4 will increase the control system stability and convergent speed. Fig. 4(b) shows that the MSE of the $K_4 = 0.6$ condition is less than that of the $K_4 = 0$ condition. It shows that the appropriate constants K_3 and K_4 can improve the system time response and convergence. It is however difficult to evaluate the appropriate K_3 and K_4. The proposed

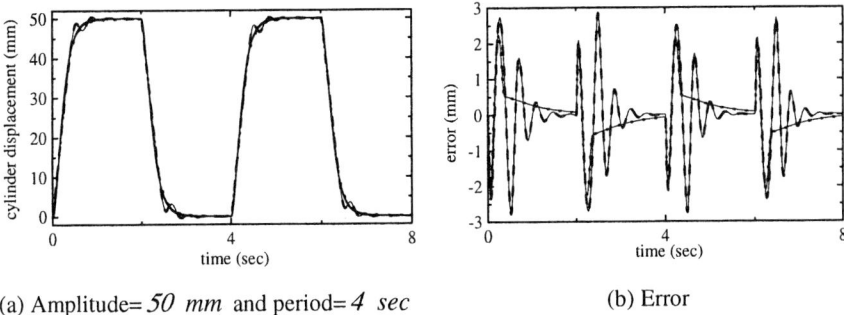

(a) Amplitude= *50 mm* and period= *4 sec*   (b) Error

Fig. 4. The simulation results for DNCS with different parameters K_3, K_4 (reference model: ——————— ; $K_3 = 1$, $K_4 = 0$: — — — — : $K_3 = 1$, $K_4 = 0.6$: •—•—•—•).

MNNACS can evaluate the appropriate K_3 and K_4 with utilizing the neural tuner. All the input signals for the three different neural networks of MNNACS are normalized.

The direct neural control system (DNCS), indirect neural control system (INCS), MNNACS and MNNACS without the emulator N_2 are applied to control the EHSS in the following simulation. The initial weights of N_1 are chosen between ± 0.5 randomly. The square signal with a period of *4 sec* and amplitude of *50 mm* is used as the command input. Fig. 5(a) shows that the position responses of the piston will follow the output responses of the reference model in the four kinds of neural control schemes. However it takes 8 sec for INCS and MNNACS without N_2 to converge the tracking error. Fig. 5(b) shows the tracking errors for EHSS with the four different neural controls and the MNNACS with N_2 has favorable convergent speed.

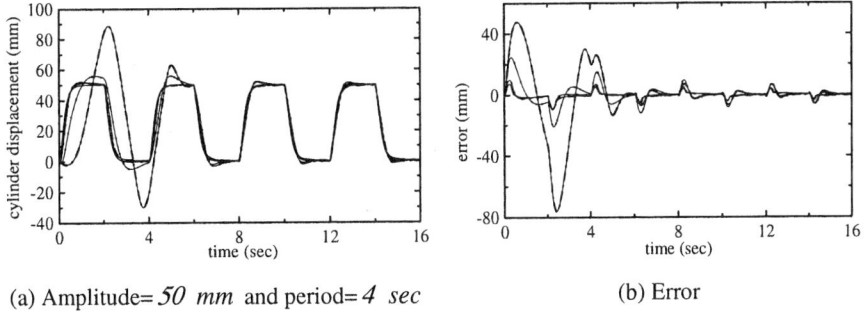

(a) Amplitude= *50 mm* and period= *4 sec*   (b) Error

Fig. 5. Simulation results of position response for four different neural control systems with initial weighting between ± 0.5 and in unloading condition (reference model: ——————— ; DNCS: •—•—•—• ; INCS: — — — — ; MNNACS with N_2: —— —— ; MNNACS without N_2: ••••••••••).

From the simulation results, we can conclude that the proposed MNNACS will have favorable model following characteristics, and it can provide the appropriate parameters to the DNCS.

5 Experiment

The EHSS shown in Fig. 1 is established for our experiment. A hydraulic cylinder with *200 mm* stroke, *20 mm* rod diameter and a *40 mm* cylinder diameter is used as the system actuator. The Atchley JET-PIPE-206 servo valve is applied to control the piston position of hydraulic cylinder.

The output range of the neural controller is between ± 1, and converted to be the analog voltage between ± 5 *Volt* by a *12* bits bipolar DA /AD servo control interface, It is amplified in current by a servo amplifier to drive the EHSV. Two Pentium PCs are applied to real time control and data acquisition. The Labview AT-MIO16E-1 data acquisition interface is used to convert the output voltage of LVDT to numerical digitals for real time control and data acquisition. A crystal oscillation interrupt control interface provides an accurate *0.001 sec* sample rate for real time control.

The DNCS, INCS, MNNACS and MNNACS without N_2 are applied to the experiment. A square signal with amplitude of *50 mm* and period of *4* sec is used as reference input. The learning rates are specified at *0.15* , *0.08* , *0.09* and *0.5* to insure weights convergence. Fig. 6(a) shows INCS and MNNACS without N_2 need more time for weights convergence, and the MNNACS has favorable convergent speed. Fig 6(b) shows the EHSS with external load force *1500 N* will be convergent in the four kinds of neural control schemes, and the MNNACS still has the favorable model following characteristics. Additionally it can provide appropriate parameters K_3 and K_4 for conventional DNCS.

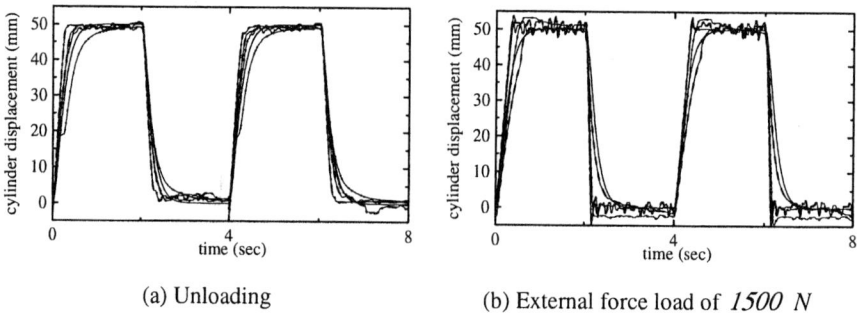

(a) Unloading (b) External force load of *1500 N*

Fig. 6. Experiment results of position responses for four different neural control systems (reference model: ———— ; DNCS: ━•━•━ ; INCS: ━•━•━ ; MNNACS with N_2: ━ ━ ━ ; MNNACS without N_2: ••••••••).

6 Conclusion

The proposed MNNACS is applied to control the piston position of a hydraulic cylinder in an EHSS, and the comparison of time responses for the DNCS, INCS, MNNACS and MNNACS without an emulator is analyzed by simulation and experiment. The results show that the MNNACS has favorable model following characteristic, even under external force load condition. The MNNACS can provide appropriate parameters to DNCS, improve the adaptability and performance of DNCS.

References

1. Zhang, Y., Sen, P. and Hearn, G. E., "An on-line Trained Adaptive Neural Network," IEEE, Control Systems Magazine, Vol. 15, No. 5, (1995) 67-75.
2. Lin, F. J. and Wai, R. J., "Hybrid Controller using a Neural Network for a PM Synchronous Servo-Motor Drive," IEE, Proceedings of Electric Power Applications, Vol. 145, No. 3, (1998) 223-230.
3. Omatu, S. and Yoshioka, M., "Self-tuning neuro-PID control and applications" IEEE, International Conference on Systems, Man, and Cybernetics, Computational Cybernetics and Simulation, Vol. 3, (1997) 1985-1989.
4. Omatu, S., Fujinaka, T. and Yoshioka, M., "Neuro-PID control for inverted single and double pendulums," IEEE, International Conference on Systems, Man, and Cybernetics, Vol. 4, (2000) 2685-2690.
5. Gao, J. C. and Wu, P., "A Fuzzy Neural Network Controller in the Electrohydraulic Position Control System," IEEE, International Conference on Intelligent Processing Systems, Vol. 1, (1997) 58-63.
6. Chu, M. H., Kang, Y., Chang, Y. F., Liu, Y. L. and Chang, C. W., "Model-Following Controller based on Neural Network for Variable Displacement Pump," JSME, International Journal (series C), Vol. 46, No. 1, (2003) 176-187.
7. Narendra, K. S. and Parthasarathy, K., "Identification and control of dynamical systems using neural networks," IEEE, Neural Networks, Vol. 1, No. 1, (1990) 4-27.

Exon Structure Analysis via PCA and ICA of Short-Time Fourier Transform

Changha Hwang[1], David Chiu[2], and Insuk Sohn[3]

[1] Division of Information and Computer Sciences,
Dankook University, Seoul 140 - 714, Korea
chwang@dankook.ac.kr

[2] Department of Computing and Information Science,
University of Guelph, Guelph, Canada N1G 2W1
dchiu@snowhite.cis.uoguelph.ca

[3] Corresponding Author, Department of Statistics,
Korea University, Seoul 136-701, Korea
sis46@korea.ac.kr

Abstract. We use principal component analysis (PCA) to identify exons of a gene and further analyze their internal structures. The PCA is conducted on the short-time Fourier transform (STFT) based on the 64 codon sequences and the 4 nucleotide sequences. By comparing to independent component analysis (ICA), we can differentiate between the exon and intron regions, and how they are correlated in terms of the square magnitudes of STFTs. The experiment is done on the gene F56F11.4 in the chromosome III of C. elegans. For this data, the nucleotide based PCA identifies the exon and intron regions clearly. The codon based PCA reveals a weak internal structure in some exon regions, but not the others. The result of ICA shows that the nucleotides thymine (T) and guanine (G) have almost all the information of the exon and intron regions for this data. We hypothesize the existence of complex exon structures that deserve more detailed analysis.

1 Introduction

Genomic sequence information is at the basic level discrete in nature because there are only a finite number of nucleotides in the DNA alphabets. To capture the recurring characteristics, we may interpret the DNA sequence as a discrete-time sequence that can be studied using techniques from the field of digital signal processing such as short-time Fourier transform (STFT). DNA sequences can be regarded as nonstationary signal whose properties vary with time. However, a single discrete Fourier transform (DFT) estimate is not sufficient to describe such signals. Locating protein coding or exon regions in genomic data has been an important application area of these techniques. See for details Fickett[4], Salzberg[10], Snyder and Stormo [12], Guigo[6], Anastassiou[1] and Vaidyanathan and Yoon[14]. In Anastassiou[1], the protein coding regions have been detected by using a method to maximize the discriminatory capability based on the STFT of the DNA sequence as compared to random sequence.

In this paper, we further analyze the principal component analysis (PCA) in identifying exons in a gene because of their easier interpretations and evaluate their possible internal structures. The PCA is conducted on the short-time Fourier transform (STFT) described in Anastassiou[1]. It is noted that when applying PCA to STFT frequency slices, the principal STFT retains explicit information about the nonstationary spectral content of a sequence, as well as implicit information necessary for the reconstruction of the sequence. Similar to Beyerbach and Nawab[2], we identify exon and intron regions using the first principal component (PC) of the STFTs of the nucleotide sequence. We also use the PCs of STFTs from the codon sequence to investigate whether further internal structures in exons exist. By using independent component analysis (ICA) as described in Bingham and Hyvarinen[3], we identify the nucleotides having information on the exon and intron regions, and how they are correlated in terms of the square magnitudes of the STFTs. These methods are illustrated and analyzed using the gene F56F11.4 in the chromosome III of C. elegans. The rest of this paper is organized as follows. In Section 2, we review the STFT that our analysis of the sequence is based on. In Section 3, we briefly describe the PCA and ICA analysis for complex valued data. In Section 4, the methods are applied to analyzing the gene F56F11.4.

2 STFT of Base Sequence

In this section we briefly illustrate STFT of the nucleotide sequence, wich will be used to locate exon regions in genomic data. For a DNA sequence of length N, assume that we assign the numbers a, t, c, g to the nucleotide characters A, T, C, G, respectively. The resulting numerical sequence is represented as

$$x[n] = au_A[n] + tu_T[n] + cu_C[n] + gu_G[n], \quad n = 0, 1, \ldots, N-1 \quad (1)$$

in which $u_A[n], u_T[n], u_C[n]$ and $u_G[n]$ are the binary indicator sequences, which take the value of either 1 or 0 at location n, depending on whether or not the corresponding character exists at location n. As defined, any three of these four binary indicator sequences are sufficient to determine the DNA character string, since

$$u_A[n] + u_T[n] + u_C[n] + u_G[n] = 1 \text{ for all } n. \quad (2)$$

A proper choice of the values a, t, c and g for a DNA segment can provide potentially useful properties to the numerical sequence $x[n]$.

The main computational tool that we use is the discrete Fourier transform (DFT) of a sequence $x[n]$ of length N. The DFT is itself another sequence $X[k]$ of the same length N, defined as

$$X[k] = \sum_{n=0}^{N-1} x[n] e^{-j\frac{2\pi}{N}kn}, \quad k = 0, 1, \ldots, N-1. \quad (3)$$

The sequence $X[k]$ provides a measure of the frequency content at frequency k, which corresponds to an underlying period of $\frac{N}{k}$ samples. See for details Mitra[9]. From Eqs. (1) and (3) it follows that

$$X[k] = aU_A[k] + tU_T[k] + cU_C[k] + gU_G[k], \quad k = 0, 1, \ldots, N-1 \qquad (4)$$

For DNA character strings based on the raw sequence, the sequences $U_A[k]$, $U_T[k]$, $U_C[k]$ and $U_G[k]$ provide a four-dimensional representation of the frequency spectrum of the character string. From Eqs. (2) and (3), it follows that

$$U_A[k] + U_T[k] + U_C[k] + U_G[k] = \begin{cases} 0, & k \neq 0 \\ N, & k = 0 \end{cases}. \qquad (5)$$

DNA sequence can be viewed as nonstationary signal whose properties vary with time and analyzed from this perspective, as illustrated in Li et al.[8], Silverman and Linsker[11] and Tiwari et al.[13]. A single DFT estimate is not sufficient to describe such signals. As a result, the use of the STFT is proposed, which is defined as follows:

$$X[n, k] = \sum_{m=0}^{L-1} x[n+m]w[m]e^{-j\frac{2\pi}{N}km}, \quad k = 0, 1, \ldots, N-1 \qquad (6)$$

where $w[m]$ is a window sequence. Then $X[n,k]$ is the DFT of the windowed sequence $x[n+m]w[m]$. Here, we suppose that the window has length with samples beginning at $m = 0$. The primary purpose of the window in the STFT is to limit the extent of the sequence to be transformed so that the spectral characteristics are reasonably stationary over the duration of the window. A typical window for spectrum analysis tapers to zero so as to select only a portion of the signal for analysis. Similar to Anastassiou[1], we here use the STFT of a DNA sequence using a Hamming window of given length (of 351). The Hamming window is defined by

$$w[m] = 0.54 + 0.46 \cos\left(\frac{2\pi m}{2L+1}\right), \quad m = 0, 1, \ldots, L. \qquad (7)$$

If the window length L is too long, the signal properties may change too much across the window. If the window is too short, resolution of narrowband components will be sacrificed. This is typical of the trade-off between frequency resolution and time resolution that is required in the analysis of nonstationary signals.

The display of the magnitude of the STFT is called a spectrogram. The frequency $k = \frac{L}{3}$ corresponds to a period of three samples, equal to the length of each codon. Fickett[4] illustrates that the spectrum of protein coding DNA typically has a peak at that frequency Fickett[4]. This property has been used to design a gene prediction algorithm. We define the following normalized DFT coefficients at frequency $k = \frac{L}{3}$:

$$A = \frac{1}{N}U_A[n, \frac{L}{3}], T = \frac{1}{N}U_T[n, \frac{L}{3}], C = \frac{1}{N}U_C[n, \frac{L}{3}], G = \frac{1}{N}U_G[n, \frac{L}{3}]. \qquad (8)$$

Then, from Eq. (4), with $k = \frac{L}{3}$, it follows that

$$W \equiv \frac{1}{N} X[n, \frac{L}{3}] = aA + tT + cC + gG. \tag{9}$$

In other words, for each DNA segment of length (where is a multiple of 3), and for each choice of the parameters a, t, c and g, there corresponds a complex number $W = aA + tT + cC + gG$. As illustrated in Anastassiou[1], for properly chosen values of a, t, c and g, W can be an accurate predictor of a protein coding segment. For each sequence segment, there corresponds a set of complex numbers A, T, C and G which satisfies $A + T + C + G = 0$. The quantity W is a complex random variable and its properties depend on the particular choice of the parameters a, t, c and g. In Anastassiou[1], parameters which maximize the discriminatory capability between exon regions (with corresponding random variables A, T, C and G) and random sequence can be used to find exon regions in a gene. In this paper, we further analyze this capability here using PCA analysis with a more direct interpretation.

3 PCA and ICA of Complex Valued Data

In this section, we briefly describe the PCA used for identifying exons in a selected gene sequence, and for further analyzing their internal structures. The PCA is conducted to the STFTs of the 4 nucleotide sequences and the 64 codon sequences. We also describe the ICA used to differentiate nucleotides having more information in the exon and intron regions in terms of the square magnitude of each STFT. As well known, the data transformed by STFT are complex-valued. Therefore, methods that can be applicable to complex-valued data are used.

Beyerbach and Nawab[2] illustrate that when applying PCA to STFT frequency slices, the principal STFT retains explicit information about the nonstationary spectral content of a sequence, as well as implicit information necessary for reconstruction of the original sequence. Because the STFT is known to be a redundant representation of a signal, various reduced-information versions of the STFT have been investigated. The STFT magnitude is among these. The principal STFT falls into the category of reduced-information STFT representations. The specific method of STFT data reduction employed in the principal STFT is that of principal components, or PC. In this paper, the PCA is applied to the STFTs at the fixed frequency $k = \frac{L}{3}$ of the 4 basic nucleotides and the 64 different codons rather than the STFT frequency slices. These STFT data are complex-valued.

A complex random variable may be represented as $y = u + iv$ where u and v are realvalued random variables. The density of y is denoted as $f(y) = f(u, v) \in R^2$. The expectation of y is $E(y) = E(u) + iE(v)$. Two complex random variables y_1 and y_2 are uncorrelated if $E(y_1 y_2^*) = E(y_1)E(y_2^*)$, where y^* designates the complex conjugate of y. The correlation matrix of a zeromean complex random vector $\mathbf{y} = (y_1, \ldots, y_p)$ is

$$E(\mathbf{y}\mathbf{y}^H) = \begin{bmatrix} C_{11} & \cdots & C_{1p} \\ \vdots & \ddots & \vdots \\ C_{p1} & \cdots & C_{pp} \end{bmatrix} \qquad (10)$$

where $E(\cdot)$ is the expectation, $C_{jk} = E(y_j y_k^*)$ and $\mathbf{y}^H$ stands for the Hermitian of $\mathbf{y}$, that is, $\mathbf{y}$ transposed and conjugated.

Principal component analysis (PCA) in the complex domain follows similar rules as those for PCA in the real domain. Refer to Jollife[7]. The PCA technique seeks linear combinations of the data with maximal variance. Assume that we have a complex data set X composed of a set of zeromean, complex vectors. The correlation matrix is $C_X = E(XX^H)$, where X^H denotes the conjugate transpose of X. Because the correlation matrix of any complex data set is Hermitian, all its eigenvalues are real.

Separation of complex valued signals is a frequently arising problem in signal processing in that frequency-domain implementations involving complex valued signals have advantages over time-domain implementations. Especially in the separation of convolutive mixtures, it is a common practice to transform the signals using Fourier transform, which results in complex valued signals. Therefore we use this algorithm for the separation of complex valued signals based on independent component analysis (ICA) in Bingham and Hyvarinen[3]. Given a high-dimensional dataset, ICA seeks linear projections that are mutually independent. The simplest ICA model assumes that the observed signal $n \times p$ matrix X is a linear mixture of the unobservable independent sources $n \times p$ matrix S with the mixing $n \times n$ matrix A,

$$X = AS$$

ICA methods use the observations to estimate the mixing matrix and the independent components by first specifying a measure of independence, and then providing an algorithm to optimize that measure of independence. There are several different variants of ICA, depending on the independence measure and optimization method. In this paper, we use the complex version of FastICA[3].

The PCA can be considered a special case of ICA where the optimization criteria maximizes the variance, with the constraint that the resulting estimates be orthonormal. Note that for Gaussian signals, orthogonality is equivalent to independence, and ICA only makes sense for non-Gaussian signals. If the physical processes contributing to the overall signal are non-Gaussian, independent, mixed in a linear fashion, then we can expect simple ICA methods to perform better than the PCA in separating the underlying sources.

4 Experiment Using F56F11.4 Gene Sequence Data

Likewise Anastassiou[1], we analyze the F56F11.4 gene sequence from C. elegans, which contains 8,000 nucleotides starting from location 7021 in the chromosome III of C. elegans (accession number AF099922). The gene is known to be divided into five exon regions with intron regions between them. Our goal is to identify these regions from the sequence signals of the STFT transform using PCA and ICA analysis. When these analyses identify these regions, we further evaluate the internal structures of the identified exon regions. Since these methods reflect a meaningful interpretation of these regions, the existence of these internal exon structures can be evaluated. In the experiment, we calculate the STFT at frequency $k = \frac{L}{3}, L = 351$. The relative exon locations are described in Table 1.

Table 1. Locations and reading frames of the five exons of gene F56F11.4

Relative position	Exon length	Reading frame
929 -1135	207	2
2528-2857	330	2
4114-4377	264	1
5465-5644	180	2
7255-7605	351	1

We will here study how well the PCA identifies the exon and intron regions, and then use the analysis to evaluate the internal exon structures. First, we take into consideration the corresponding STFT in Eq. (8) at frequency $k = \frac{L}{3}, L = 351$ for each nucleotide. Second, we put them together so as to make 4-dimensional data at each location. Third, we employ the PCA to these 4-dimensional complex data in order to study how well the PCA identifies the exon and intron regions. Last, we compare this method with the STFT with the choice of the parameters $a = 0.10 + 0.12j, t = -0.30 - 0.20j, c = 0$ and $g = 0.45 - 0.19j$ in Anastassiou[1]. The analysis results are shown in Fig. 1.

We here describe the square magnitudes of STFT and the 4 principal components (PCs). In Fig. 1, the first plot is for $|aA+tT+cC+gG|^2$, and the next four plots are for the square magnitudes of PC1, PC2, PC3 and PC4, respectively.

As seen from Fig. 1, the first PC shows all five exons clearly as the STFT. Therefore, the first PC reflects well in showing clear signal peaks, identifying all the exon and intron regions. Thus the proposed PCA indicates that exon/intron differentiation is largely based on the first principal components of the nucleotide sequence.

The k th cumulative sum of the eigenvalues normalized by the total sum of the eigenvalues defined as $\lambda(k) = \frac{\sum_{j=1}^{k} d_i}{\sum_{i=1}^{p} d_i}$, indicates how much of the variation is explained by the first $k, k \leq p$, components. We get the percent of variation explained for values of k as follows:

$$\lambda(1) = 0.5094, \lambda(2) = 0.8170, \lambda(3) = 1.0000, \lambda(4) = 1.0000$$

Based on values above, the first principal component explains 50.9% of variance. Thus, the first principal component is clearly a very good indicator to show the exon and intron regions for this data set.

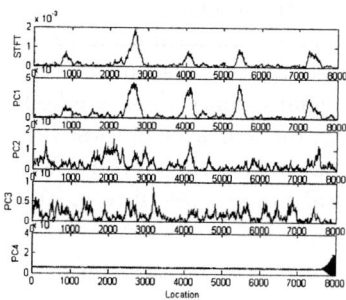

Fig. 1. Square magnitude of the STFT and the 4 PCs

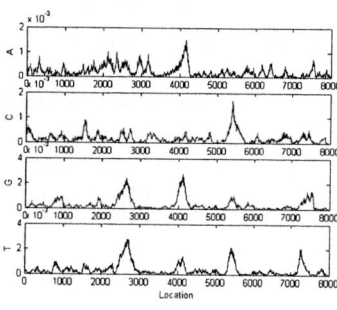

Fig. 2. Square magnitude of the four source signals from A, C, G and T

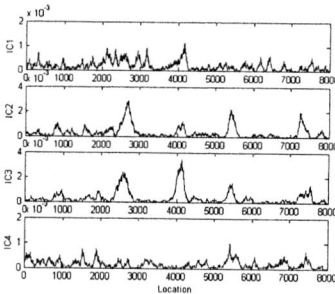

Fig. 3. Square magnitude of the four $IC1, IC2, IC3$ and $IC4$

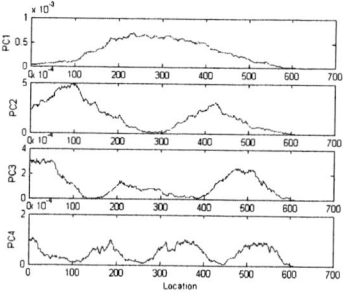

Fig. 4. Square magnitude of the first four PCs of STFTs for the first subsequence

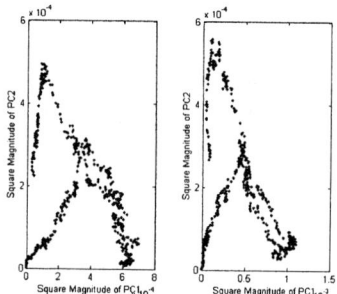

Fig. 5. Scatter plot for the square magnitudes of PC1 and PC2 of STFTs for the first subsequence that includes exon 1(Left), Scatter plot for the square magnitudes of PC1 and PC2 of STFTs for the second subsequence that includes exon 2 (Right)

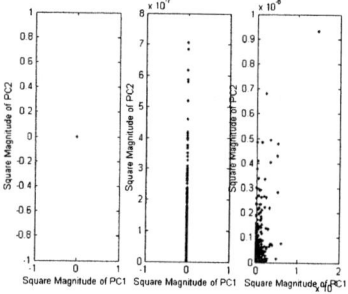

Fig. 6. Scatter plots for the square magnitudes of PC1 and PC2 of STFTs for the third (Left), fourth (Middle) and fifth subsequence (Right) that includes the corresponding exon regions

By using the complex version of ICA, we can further evaluate the various aspects of the exon/intron regions. We will here study which nucleotides in the sequence have more information on exon and intron regions and how they are related to each other. We also investigate which method is better in identifying the exon and intron regions, either PCA alone or ICA used in combination with PCA. To do this, we first take into account the corresponding STFT in Eq. (9) at frequency $k = \frac{L}{3}, L = 351$ for the four nucleotide sequences. Then, we will evaluate the square magnitudes of the STFTs of the four source signals from A, T, C and G which satisfies $A + T + C + G = 0$. The analysis results are shown in Figs. 2 and 3. From Figs. 2 and 3, we observe that signals A, T, G and C are very close to $IC1, IC2, IC3$ and $IC4$, respectively. Although signals from A, T, G and C are correlated complex random vectors, they appear to be mutually independent. We also observe that signals from A and C are likely random noises and that T and G independently have almost all information on the exon and intron regions for this particular data set.

We do not report here the results for the square magnitudes of the first PC obtained by PCA alone and by combining ICA and PCA, respectively. However, we have observed that there is no difference between the two methods for this data set, although the ICA model used in combination with PCA for dimension reduction is in some applications in Fodor and Kamath[5] better than PCA alone. In any case, the first PC is such a good indicator for identifying exon and intron regions for this gene.

The genetic code consists of 64 triplets of nucleotides. These triplets are called codons. Gene sequence can be split into codons. We can then analyze the gene by applying PCA to these codon sequences since the codons may contain more information than the one from the nucleotides. To do this, we partition the 8000 base long sequence into five subsequences. Each subsequence is made by taking all the nucleotides up to the midpoint of the end position of the previous exon and the starting position of the next exon. Therefore, the relative positions of the subsequences are 1-1831, 1832-3485, 3486-4901, 4902-6449 and 6450-8000 in order.

To employ the PCA to codon sequence data, first we make 64 binary indicator sequences for each subsequence, which take the value of either 1 or 0, depending on whether or not the corresponding codon is observed. Second, similar to the nucleotide case, we take into account the STFT for each binary indicator sequences at frequency $k = \frac{L}{3}, L = 351$. Third, we put together the 64-dimensional data at each location. Finally, we employ the PCA to these 64-dimensional complex data.

We have also repeated the whole experiment at several different frequencies with similar results. We report here the plots based on frequency $k = \frac{L}{3}, L = 351$. The results for the first two subsequences are shown indicating internal structure, while the other three subsequences do not show such structure. For the first subsequence, the percent of variation explained for selected values of k are $\lambda(1) = 0.3766, \lambda(2) = 0.6159, \lambda(3) = 0.7573$ and $\lambda(4) = 0.8358$. For the second subsequence, the percent of variation explained for selected values of k are $\lambda(1) = 0.5164, \lambda(2) = 0.7533, \lambda(3) = 0.8387$ and $\lambda(4) = 0.8794$. For these subsequences we show the first four PCs because these PCs explain almost all the variations in the data as illustrated above. As seen from both Figs. 4 and 5, the first PCs show clear signal peaks where they are presumed to be located. The first and second PCs together indicate there are certain internal structures. Fig. 5 shows the scatter plots for the square magnitudes of PC1 and PC2 of the 64 STFTs of codon data for the first and second subsequence that includes the corresponding exon regions, whereas Fig. 6 shows that from the third, fourth and fifth subsequence. Clearly from the differences of the plots, the signals support that coding sequence structures in the first two exons as reflected in the selected subsequences are quite different from those in exons 3-5. In Fig. 5, the shapes of the two scatter plots are strikingly similar if the scale of square magnitude of PC1 is ignored. It reflects the square magnitudes of PC1 and PC2 in both subsequences correspond in similar, but complex way. Comparatively, for the subsequences in Fig. 6, the square magnitude of either PC1 or PC2, or both are approximately zero. The existence of these differences and their reflected internal coding structures of the exons deserve further evaluation from the biological and coding signals point of view. This may be evaluated in future studies.

5 Conclusions

Through experiments on the F56F11.4 gene, we realize that the PCA of STFT derives the satisfying results to differentiate between exons and introns and provides an analytical result for interpretation, including their internal structures. The PCA is conducted to the STFTs of the 4 nucleotide sequences and the 64 codon sequences. By implementing the ICA, we further investigate which nucleotides have the information within their exon and intron regions, and how they are correlated in terms of the square magnitudes of STFTs. We observe that the PCA based on the nucleotides identifies well the exon and intron regions. In particular, the first PC retains most information on the exon and intron regions. The PCA based on the codons reveals evidence of internal structure in some exons but not in others. Even though the signals based on this transform might be weak, its presence in some exons deserves further investigations, especially its biological meaning. The result of the ICA also shows that the nucleotides and have almost all information on exon/intron region differentiation for this particular gene. Does this mean that sometimes only part and not all of the four nucleotides are involved in specifying the exon/intron regions? Or that nucleotides not dominatingly involve in sequence composition can also play in some other ways in sequence functionality? These are important questions that need to be answered when computational sequence analyses are combined with biological analysis.

Acknowledgement

This research was supported by the Research Grants of Catholic University of Daegu in 2003.

References

1. Anastassiou, D. : Frequency-domain analysis of biomolecular sequences. Bioinformatics **16** (2000) 1073-1081
2. Beyerbach, D. and Nawab, H. : Principal components analysis of the short-time Fourier transform, Proc. IEEE ICASSP, (1991), 1725-1728
3. Bingham, E. and Hyvarinen, A. : A fast fixed-point algorithm for independent component analysis of complex-valued signals. Int. J. of Neural Systems, **10**(1) (2000) 1-8
4. Fickett, J. W. : Recognition of protein coding regions in DNA sequences, Nucleic Acids Research **10** (1982) 5303-5318
5. Fodor, I. K. and Kamath, C. : Dimension reduction in the atmospheric sciences, Computing in Science and Engineering special issue on High Dimensional Data, submitted, UCRL-JC-146972, (2002)
6. Guigo, R. : DNA composition, codon usage and exon prediction, Genetic Databases, M.J. Bishop ed., Academic Press, (1999)
7. Jollife, I. T. : Principal component analysis, New York, Springer-Verlag, (2002)
8. Li, W., Marr, T. G. and Kaneko, K. : Understanding long-range correlations in DNA sequences, Physica D, **75** (1994) 392-416
9. Mitra, S. K. : Digital Signal Processing: A Computer-Based Approach, 2nd edn, McGraw-Hill, New York, (2000)
10. Salzberg, S. L. : Locating protein coding regions in human DNA using a decision tree algorithm, Journal of Computational Biology **2**(3) (1995) 473-485
11. Silverman, B. D. and Linsker, R. : A measure of DNA periodicity, J. Theor. Biol. **118** (1986) 295-300
12. Snyder, E. E. and Stormo, G. D. : Identification of protein coding regions in genomic DNA, Journal of Molecular Biology 248 (1995) 1-18.
13. Tiwari, S. , Ramachandran, S., Bhattacharya, A. , Bhattacharya, S. and Ramaswamy, R. : Prediction of probable genes by Fourier analysis of genomic sequences, CABIOS **113** (1997) 263-270
14. Vaidyanathan, P. P. and Yoon, B. : Gene and exon prediction using allpass-based filters. Workshop on Genomic Signal Processing and Statistics (GENSIPS), Raleigh, NC, (2002)

Nonlinear Adaptive Blind Source Separation Based on Kernel Function[*]

Feng Liu[1,4], Cao Zhexin[2], Qiang Zhi[3], Shaoqian Li[4], and Min Liang[3]

[1] National EW laboratory, Chengdu 610036, Sichuan, P.R. China
liufeng@mailst.xjtu.edu.cn
[2] Jinhua College of profession and technology, Jinhua 321000, Zhejiang, P.R. China
[3] China Electronics technology Group Corporation No.29 Research Institute,
Chengdu 610036, Sichuan, P.R.China
[4] University Electronic Science and Technology of China, Chengdu 610054,
Sichuan, P.R. China

Abstract. As the linear method is difficult to recover the sources from the nonlinear mixture signals, in this paper a new nonlinear adaptive blind signal separation algorithm based kernel space is proposed for general invertible nonlinearities. The received mixture signals are mapped from low dimensional space to high dimensional kernel feature space. In the feature space, the received signals form a smaller submanifold, and an orthonormal basis of the submanifold is constructed in this space, as the same time, the mixture signals are parameterized by the basis in the high dimensional kernel space. In the noiseless or noisy situation, the sources are rebuilt online processing by M-EASI and subspace tracking. The results of computer simulations are also presented.

1 Introduction

Blind Source Separation (BSS) is the method that can recover a set of original source signals from instantaneous linear mixtures of these sources in the situation that no information is available about these source signals. The precondition of the separation is to assume that the sources are all statistically independent of one another, the assumption is a compensation for the lack of prior knowledge [1]. In recent years, the BSS has been an active area of signal processing research. It can solve the spatial diversity of a set of sensors, array signal processing [2], sound rebuilding, biomedical data analysis such as electroencephalogram (EEG) [3] ,magnetism encephalogram (MEG)[4] and EMG. Based on independent component analysis (ICA) [5], many algorithms for blind source separation have been proposed on the condition that the mixture matrix is inversed and these source signals are independent of one another. These algorithms are the effective methods that can recover independent source

---

[*] This work is supported by the National EW Laboratory Foundation No.51435010103 DZ0101).

signals from linear mixture of these sources. If the mixture model is nonlinear mixture system, and there is no prior information about the sources and the mixture model to be used or there is no restriction on the sources and the mixture matrix linear methods couldn't recover the source signals from the mixture data generally. Therefore, using nonlinear methods to recover nonlinear mixture signals is the main research way. For instance, kernel canonical correlation analysis [6], nonlinear blind separation using kernels [7], source separation algorithm in post-nonlinear mixture [8], kernel-based nonlinear blind source separation [9]. Anyway, no matter how the sources are mixed, these separation algorithms don't consider the noise is interfused in the mixture model. However, it is inevitable that the noise interfuse in the mixture signals, the noise make the recovery performance of the signal separation algorithms become execrable, even make the algorithm not convergence, especially for the nonlinear mixture signals separation.

In this paper we propose a nonlinear blind source separation algorithm based on kernel function. The algorithm transforms receiving mixture signals into a finite high dimensional kernel feature space, in which the mixture signals form a submanifold, and an orthogonal basis of the submanifold has been constructed at the same time. The mixture signals of the high dimensional space are mapped to the parameter space by the orthogonal basis. In the parameter space, in the noisy situation, the mixture signals are separated online processing by M-EASI and subspace tracking. Furthermore we illustrate the efficiency of the algorithm in different situation.

2 Signal Separation Model

In the nonlinear blind source separation model, it is assumed that n source signals $\mathbf{s}(k) = [s_1(k), s_2(k), \cdots, s_n(k)]^T$ are transmitted from n independent sources at different locations and are spatially independent and obey independence identity density (i.i.d). The m received nonlinear mixture signals are $\mathbf{x}(k) = [x_1(k), x_2(k), \cdots, x_m(k)]^T$ ($m \geq n$). A nonlinear mixture model shown in Fig.1 where the $\mathbf{A}(k)$ is unknown $m \times n$ mixture response matrix and f is a nonlinear function (its inverse function exist), the model is written as

$$\mathbf{x}(k) = f(\mathbf{A}\mathbf{s}(k)) + \mathbf{n}(k) \tag{1}$$

where $\mathbf{n}(k)$ is m column Gaussian white noise vector, and it is assumed that $\mathbf{n}(k)$ is statistic independent with the source signals $\mathbf{s}(k)$.

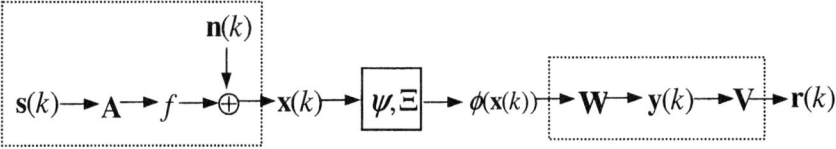

Fig. 1. Nonlinear signals separation model

3 Separation Principle

3.1 Searching Orthogonal Basis

In order to transform nonlinear signals separation problem in the input space into linear problem in feature space, the received signals $\{x(k)\} \in \Re^n$ are mapped to high dimensional feature space Γ by mapping function ψ, which is defined as

$$\psi_x \triangleq [\psi(x(1)), \psi(x(2)), \cdots, \psi(x(T))] \quad (2)$$

To obtain the orthogonal basis of the feature space Γ, we adopt kernel principle component analysis (kernel PCA) method. For simplicity, it is assumed that the signals are unbiased in the feature space. We need to find the eigenvectors and eigenvalues of the covariance matrix of the received signals ψ_x in the feature space via a standard eigendecomposition. That is

$$(\frac{1}{T}\psi_x^H \psi_x) U = U \Lambda \quad (3)$$

where Λ is eigenvalue matrix, $diag(\Lambda) = \{\lambda_1, \lambda_2, \cdots, \lambda_i, \cdots, \lambda_T\}$, and $\lambda_1 \geq \lambda_2 \geq \cdots \lambda_T$. Also, eigenvectors corresponding with the eigenvalues are $U = [u_1, u_2, \cdots, u_T]$.

To multiply Both sides of equation (3) by ψ_x

$$(\frac{1}{T}\psi_x \psi_x^H) \psi_x U = (\psi_x U) \Lambda \quad (4)$$

From the above, it is well known that $\lambda_1 \geq \lambda_2 \geq \cdots \lambda_T$ are the eigenvalues of $\psi_x U$, it is d normalized d eigenvectors as the orthogonal basis of the subspace of the feature space Γ, that is

$$\Xi \triangleq \psi_x U_d (T \Lambda_d)^{-\frac{1}{2}} \quad (5)$$

where $diag(\Lambda_d) = \{\lambda_1, \lambda_2, \cdots, \lambda_d\}$, $U_d = [u_1, u_2, \cdots, u_d]$, and $(T\Lambda_d)^{-\frac{1}{2}}$ ensure that the basis vectors are orthogonal. Then the orthogonal basis U_d can parameterize the signals $\psi(x(k))$ in the feature to d dimension signals

$$\phi(x(k)) = \Xi^H \psi(x(k)) = (T\Lambda_d)^{-\frac{1}{2}} U_d \psi_x^H \psi(x(k)) \quad (6)$$

$$= \frac{1}{\sqrt{T}} \begin{bmatrix} 1/\sqrt{\lambda_1} & \cdots & 0 \\ \vdots & \ddots & \vdots \\ 0 & \cdots & 1/\sqrt{\lambda_d} \end{bmatrix} \begin{bmatrix} u_1 \\ \vdots \\ u_d \end{bmatrix} \begin{bmatrix} k(x(1), x(k)) \\ \vdots \\ k(x(T), x(k)) \end{bmatrix}$$

where kernel function $k(\cdot,\cdot)$ is used to denote inner product of the feature space Γ. '·' denotes function variable. In this algorithm, we adopt radial product kernel function.

3.2 Separation Principle

For the nonlinear mixture model (1), the received signal is mapped into high dimension space and the basis is be parameterized. It can be obtained that

$$\phi(\mathbf{x}(k)) = \Xi^H \psi f(A\mathbf{s}(k)) + \Xi^H \psi \mathbf{n}(k) \tag{7}$$

If mapping function $\psi = f^{-1}$, then

$$\phi(\mathbf{x}(k)) = \Xi^H A\mathbf{s}(k) + \Xi^H \psi \mathbf{n}(k) \tag{8}$$

In the high dimensional space, by separating blind signals we have

$$\begin{aligned}\mathbf{y}(k) &= \mathbf{W}\phi(\mathbf{x}(k)) \\ &= \mathbf{W}\Xi^H A\mathbf{s}(k) + \mathbf{W}\Xi^H \psi \mathbf{n}(k)\end{aligned} \tag{9}$$

If $\mathbf{W} = [\Xi^H A]^\dagger$, and '$\dagger$' denotes pseudo inverse matrix, then

$$\mathbf{y}(k) = \mathbf{s}(k) + \mathbf{W}\Xi^H \psi \mathbf{n}(k) \tag{10}$$

1. In noiseless situation, viz. $\mathbf{n}(k)$ is not existent, we have

$$\mathbf{y}(k) = \mathbf{s}(k) \tag{11}$$

2. In noisy situation, equation (9) exists. According to literature [10], by eigenvalue decomposing the correlation matrix $C = E[\mathbf{y}(k)\mathbf{y}^H(k)]$, we can get the signal space U_s, and can track it, then we can get

$$\hat{\mathbf{s}}(k) = \mathbf{r}(k) = U_s U_s^H \mathbf{y}(k) \tag{12}$$

4 Weight Matrix Iteration and Subspace Tracking

4.1 Weight Matrix Iteration

In the high dimensional space, we can use maximum likelihood algorithm based on relative gradient proposed in literature [11], viz. normalized EASI weight matrix iteration algorithm. The iterative process is as follow

$$\mathbf{W}(k+1) = \mathbf{W}(k) - \lambda \Delta \mathbf{W}(k) \tag{13}$$

where $\Delta = \left[\dfrac{\mathbf{y}(k)\mathbf{y}^H(k)-I}{1+\lambda \mathbf{y}^H(k)\mathbf{y}(k)} + \dfrac{1}{\alpha}\dfrac{(\mathbf{g}(\mathbf{y}(k))\mathbf{y}^H(k)-\mathbf{y}(k)\mathbf{g}(\mathbf{y}^H(k)))}{1+\lambda|\mathbf{y}^H(k)\mathbf{g}(\mathbf{y}(k))|} \right]$, and λ is positive adaptive step size. α is the parameter that is determined by the probability density function of the source signals. $\mathbf{g}(\mathbf{y}(k))=[g_1(y_1(k)),\cdots,g_d(y_d(k))]$, and $g_i(y_i(k))=-q'_i(y_i(k))/q_i(y_i(k))$ denotes the evaluation function of the ith source signal. $q_i(y_i(k))$ is the distributing form obtained by the statistic of the source signals. When the source signals are independent and obey i.i.d and the distributing form is sub-Gaussian distribution, if the probability density function is

$$f(y_i) = k_1 \exp(k_2 |y_i|^{\alpha'}) \tag{14}$$

where $\alpha' > 2$, and k_1, k_2 are normalized constants.

However, for the model in equation (1) in noisy situation, we use normalized M-EASI algorithm, which has stronger robust for noisy interference. The iterative process is as follow

$$\mathbf{W}(k+1) = \mathbf{W}(k) - \lambda \Delta_M \mathbf{W}(k) \tag{15}$$

where

$$\Delta_M = \left[\dfrac{\mathbf{y}(k)sign(\mathbf{y}^H(k))-I}{1+\lambda \mathbf{y}^H(k)sign(\mathbf{y}(k))} + \dfrac{1}{\alpha}\dfrac{\mathbf{g}(\mathbf{y}(k))sign(\mathbf{y}^H(k)) - sign(\mathbf{y}(k))\mathbf{g}(\mathbf{y}^H(k))}{1+\lambda|\mathbf{g}^H(\mathbf{y}(k))\mathbf{y}(k)|} \right]$$

4.2 Subspace Tracking

For the signal model (9) in noisy situation, it can be formulated as

$$\mathbf{y}(k) = \mathbf{B}\mathbf{s}(k) + \mathbf{C}\mathbf{n}(k) \tag{16}$$

First, we must transform the Gaussian color noise into Gaussian white noise in equation (16). According to [12], there is

$$\mathbf{y}(k) = \mathbf{B}'\mathbf{s}'(k) + \mathbf{n}'(k) \tag{17}$$

where the variance of each component in white noises is σ^2.

We can use modified PAST algorithm [10] to track signal subspace. The algorithm will be introduced in detail as follow

In the time interval T', the cost function is can be modified as

$$J'(\mathbf{V}(T')) = \sum_{i=1}^{T'} \beta^{T'-i} \|\mathbf{y}(i) - \mathbf{V}(T')\mathbf{r}(i)\|^2 \tag{18}$$

where the forget factor β must has $0 < \beta \le 1$.

If make the cost function $J'(\mathbf{V}(T'))$ minimum, we have

$$\mathbf{V}(k) = \mathbf{C}_{yr}(k) \cdot \mathbf{C}_{rr}^{-1}(k) \tag{19}$$

where $\mathbf{C}_{yr}(k) = E[\mathbf{y}(k) \cdot \mathbf{r}^H(k)]$, $\mathbf{C}_{rr}(k) = E[\mathbf{r}(k) \cdot \mathbf{r}^H(k)]$.

According to the definition of $\mathbf{C}$, it can be got that

$$\mathbf{C}_{yr}(k) = \sum_{i=1}^{k} \beta^{k-i} \mathbf{y}(k) \mathbf{r}^H(k) = \beta \mathbf{C}_{yr}(k-1) + \mathbf{y}(k) \mathbf{r}^H(k) \tag{20}$$

$$\mathbf{C}_{rr}(k) = \sum_{i=1}^{k} \beta^{k-i} \mathbf{r}(k) \mathbf{r}^H(k) = \beta \mathbf{C}_{rr}(k-1) + \mathbf{r}(k) \mathbf{r}^H(k) \tag{21}$$

5 Computer Simulations

We now explore the performance of the proposed algorithms. The mixture matrix is

$$A = \begin{bmatrix} 0.1 & 0.4 & 0.7 \\ 0.7 & 0.3 & 0.2 \\ 0.3 & 0.5 & 0.4 \end{bmatrix} \tag{22}$$

For nonlinear mixture, f function is

$$f(\mathbf{A}\mathbf{s}(k)) = \exp(\mathbf{A}\mathbf{s}(k)) \cdot \mathbf{A}\mathbf{s}(k) \tag{23}$$

The variance σ^2 of Gaussian noise is 0.16. Because the algorithm maps the received mixture signals $\mathbf{x}(k)$ to high dimensional space by function, the dimension d of the mixture signals $\phi(\mathbf{x}(k))$ is greater than m in high dimensional space. In the processing of subspace tracking, we choose d' eigenvectors corresponding with d' eigenvalues as signal subspace to track. When the number of source signals is $n = m = 3$, we have $d = 20$ and $d' = 10$.

The source signals are sine signals. The number n of the source signals is 3. The frequencies of three users are 40Hz, 100Hz and 200Hz, which are shown in Fig. 2. Because of the expansion of high dimension, 10 separate signals are rebuilt, in which 7 signals have a certain function relation with the source signals [9]. The correlation coefficient of the source signals and 10 rebuilt signals are shown in Table 1.

Table 1. The correlation coefficient of the source signals and the rebuilt signal

	1	2	3	4	5	6	7	8	9	10
40Hz	0.107	0.032	0.176	0.901	0.209	0.258	0.067	0.230	0.128	0.145
100Hz	0.201	0.300	0.097	0.122	0.120	0.153	0.920	0.125	0.201	0.230
200Hz	0.071	0.216	0.111	0.200	0.153	0.143	0.259	0.910	0.136	0.018

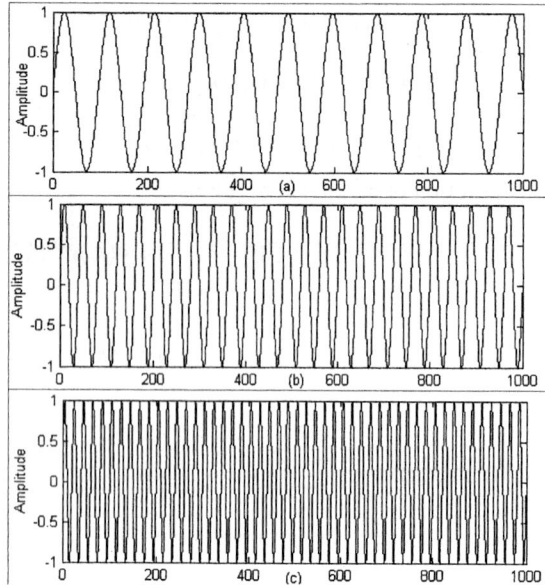

Fig. 2. Three source signals. (a) 40Hz. (b) 100Hz. (c) 200Hz

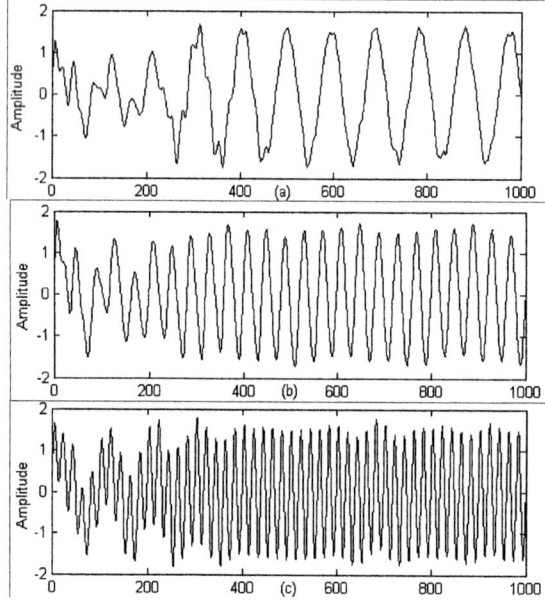

Fig. 3. Three recovered signals. (a) 40Hz. (b) 100Hz. (c) 200Hz

The recovered signals of the source signals are shown in Fig 3. From the recovered signals, we can see that the waveforms of the recovered signals are worse in the first 250 received signal points, but approach the waveforms of the source signals gradually after the 250 received signal points. Because of the effect of the f function, the amplitude of the recovered signals (about -2~2) is greater than the amplitude of the source signals. Aiming at the results, we can adopt the normalized method to resolve it.

6 Conclusion

For the separation problem of nonlinear mixture source signals in noisy situation, the linear methods proposed had some limitation. In this paper a nonlinear adaptive blind signal separation algorithm based kernel space is proposed. The algorithm first maps the received nonlinear mixture signals to a limited high dimensional kernel feature space, in which the mixture signals form a submanifold, and an orthogonal basis is constructed for the submanifold. By the orthogonal basis, the mixture signals are mapped from the high dimensional space to the parameter space. In the noisy situation, the mixture signals are separated online processing by M-EASI and subspace tracking in the parameter space. The results of computer simulation illustrated that the algorithm work as intended.

References

1. Jean-fran, Cardosd C.: Blind Signal Separation: Statistical Principles. IEEE proceedings, Vol. 86. No.10(1998)2099-2125.
2. Kuh A., Xiaohong G.: Independent component analysis for blind multiuser detections. Proc. ISIT, Sorrento, Italy,June(2000).
3. J. Karhunen, Hyvarinen A., Vigario R., Hurri J., and Oja E.: Applications of neural blind separation to signal and image processing. ICASSP, vol. 1(1997).
4. Vigario R.: Extraction ofocular artifacts from EEG using independent component analysis. Electroeneeph, clin. Neurophysiol, vol.3(1997).
5. Common P.: Independent Component Analysis, a new Concept. Signal Processing, Vol. 36.No.3(1994).
6. Fyfe C, Lai P.: ICA Using Kernel Canonical Correlation Analysis. Proc. Int. Workshop on Independent Component Analysis and Blind Signal Separation. Helsinki, Finland: Helsinki University of Technology.
7. Dominque M, Alistair B.: Nonlinear Blind Separation Using Kernels. IEEE Trans on Neural Network, Vol14.No.1(2003).
8. Taleb A, Jutten C.: Source Separation in post-nonlinear mixture. IEEE Trans. on Signal Processing, Vol.47.No,10(1999).
9. Harmeling S, Ziehe A, Kawanable M. : Kernel-Based Nonlinear Blind Source Separation. Neural Computation, Vol15(2003).
10. Yang B. : Projection Approximation Subspace Tracking. IEEE Trans. on Signal Processing, Vol.43.No1(1995).
11. Cardoso J, et al. : Equivariant Adaptive Source Separation. IEEE Trans on Signal Processing, Vol.44.No.12(1996).
12. David F. G.: Maximum-Likelihood Seauence Estimation of Digital Sequences in the Presence of Intersymbol Interference. IEEE Trans. on Information Theory, Vol. IT-18. NO.3(1972).

Hybrid Intelligent Forecasting Model Based on Empirical Mode Decomposition, Support Vector Regression and Adaptive Linear Neural Network

Zhengjia He, Qiao Hu, Yanyang Zi, Zhousuo Zhang, and Xuefeng Chen

The State Key Laboratory for Manufacturing System,
Department of Mechanical Engineering, Xi'an Jiaotong University,
Xi'an 710049, P.R. China
hzj@mail.xjtu.edu.cn, hq@mailst.xjtu.edu.cn

Abstract. In this paper, a novel hybrid intelligent forecasting model based on empirical mode decomposition (EMD), support vector regression (SVR) and adaptive linear neural network (ALNN) is proposed, where these intrinsic mode components (IMCs) are adaptively extracted via EMD from a nonstationary time series according to the intrinsic characteristic time scales. Tendencies of these IMCs are forecasted with SVR respectively, in which kernel functions are appropriately chosen with these different fluctuations of IMCs. These forecasting results of IMCs are combined with ALNN to output the forecasting result of the original time series. The proposed model is applied to the tendency forecasting of the Mackey-Glass benchmark time series and a vibration signal from a machine set. Testing results show that the forecasting performance of this proposed model outperforms that of the single SVR method under single-step ahead forecasting or multi-step ahead forecasting.

1 Introduction

The quick and correct condition trend forecasting system helps to avoid product quality problems and facilitates preventive maintenance for equipment. In fact, due to the fluctuation and complexity of running condition affected by various factors, it is difficult to use the single forecasting methods to accurately describe its moving tendency. Inspired by "divide and conquer" and "neural-wavelet model" [1], we try to simplify the forecasting task by decomposing the time series into separate components and forecasting each component separately. From the methodological point of view, the empirical mode decomposition (EMD) technique is very suitable for decomposing nonlinear and nonstationary signal, which has been reported to work better in depicting the local time scale instantaneous frequencies than wavelet and FFT [2]. After these simple intrinsic mode components (IMCs) are adaptively extracted via EMD from a nonstationary time series, each IMC is predicted by a separate support vector regression (SVR). Then these forecasting results of IMCs are combined with adaptive linear neural network (ALNN) to output the forecasting result of the original time series.

2 Theoretical Background

The section will give the brief theoretical description about EMD, SVR and ALNN.

EMD has recently been pioneered by N.E.Huang *et al.* for adaptively representing nonstationary signals as sums of different simple intrinsic modes of oscillations [2]. With the EMD method, a signal could be decomposed into a number of IMCs, each of which must satisfy the two definition [2]: (1) In the whole data set, the number of extrema and the number of zero-crossings must either equal or differ at most by one. (2) At any point, the mean value of the envelope defined by local maxima and the envelope defined by the local minima is zero.

With a series of sifting, any signal $x(t)$ can be decomposed with EMD as follows:

$$x(t) = \sum_{j=1}^{n} c_j + r_n, \; (t=1,2,\cdots,N). \qquad (1)$$

Thus, one can achieve a decomposition of the signal into n-IMCs and a residue. The IMCs $c_1, c_2, \cdots, c_n$ and residue r_n include different frequency bands ranging from high to low. The EMD techniques provide a multi-scale analysis of the signal as a sum of orthogonal signals corresponding to different time scales.

SVR follows structural risk minimization principle and has an excellent forecasting performance [3]. Its basic idea is to map the data x into a high dimensional feature space via a nonlinear mapping and to perform a linear regression in this feature space. More detailed description of SVR for regression can be found in Ref [3].

ALNN is a single-layer neural network, where the transfer function is linear and the learning rule is based on Widrow-Hoff. The details can be referred to Ref [4].

3 The Architecture of Hybrid Intelligent Forecasting Model

Given the time series $x(t), t=1,2,\cdots,N$, our aim is to predict the l-th sample ahead, $x(t+l)$, of the series. For instance, $l=1$ stands for single-step ahead forecasting and $l=50$ stands for 50-step ahead forecasting. For each value of l we train a separate forecasting architecture.

The proposed scheme is based on the following three steps (see Fig.1):

(1) The time series $x(t), t=1,2,\cdots,N$ is decomposed into n- IMCs $c_1, c_2, \cdots, c_n$ and a residue r_n by EMD.

(2) Each of $c_1, c_2, \cdots, c_n$ and r_n is forecasted by a separate SVR, in which the kernel function is appropriately chosen with these different fluctuations of the IMCs and residue. From a great deal of tests on the practical system by selecting different kernel function, we finally concluded that with the fluctuation decrease the radial-basis function (e.g. c_1), Gaussian function (e.g. c_2, c_3, etc.) and polynomial function (e.g. r_n) was chosen for kernel function, respectively.

(3) These different forecasting results of IMCs are combinated with ALNN to output the forecasting result of the next sample of the original time series.

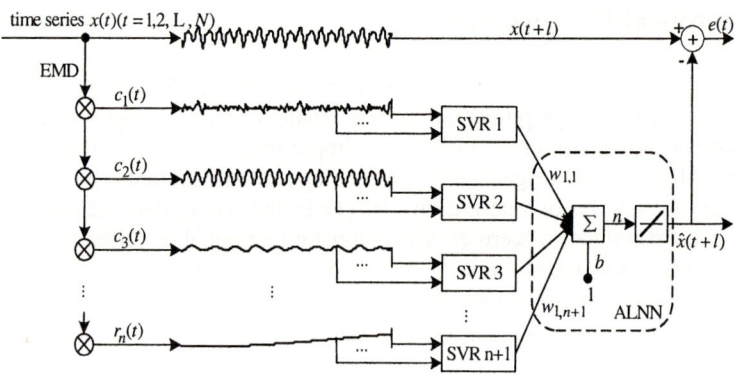

Fig. 1. The architecture of hybrid intelligent forecasting model

4 Experiment and Engineering Application

4.1 Simulation Experiment

To test the learning ability of the proposed model, we take the well-known Mackey-Glass time series for example. We chose the value $\tau = 17$ so that the time series is chaotic. The training data sequence was of length 512, followed by the testing data sequence of length 512 for single-step ahead forecasting and sequence of length 50 for 50-step ahead forecasting. Tests were performed on the proposed model. The five IMCs $c_1 - c_5$ and a residue r_5 after exerting EMD to simulating signal $x(t)$ are obtained. To estimate the performance of the hybrid model, we check the root mean square error (RMSE), the mean absolute error (MAP) and the mean absolute percentage error (MAPE). Table 1 shows the results on regression and forecasting errors using the SVR and the hybrid model.

Table 1. Regression and forecasting errors from the SVR and the hybrid model

Forecasting method		Regression errors			Forecasting errors		
		RMSE	MAE	MAPE(%)	RMSE	MAE	MAPE(%)
Single-step	SVR	0.000752	0.000630	0.0721	0.000758	0.000632	0.0720
	Hybrid	0.000712	0.000581	0.0675	0.000731	0.000597	0.0690
50-step	SVR	0.000098	0.000098	0.0114	0.183196	0.147031	16.7645
	Hybrid	0.000582	0.000442	0.0515	0.101619	0.097294	8.9263

As shown in Table 1, for single-step ahead forecasting, we can see that the two methods have similar regression and forecasting performance with regard to the three performance parameters. For 50-step ahead forecasting, the regression performance of SVR outperforms that of the hybrid model, however, the important forecasting ability of the hybrid model is better than that of the SVR.

4.2 Engineering Application

The hybrid model was applied to forecasting the future running condition of a machine set in an oil refinery. These peak-peak values of vibration signals are picked from a detection-point every other hour, and they form a time series. The training data sequence was of length 120 (5 days), followed by the testing data sequence of length 120 for single-step ahead forecasting and sequence of length 24 (one day) for 24-step ahead forecasting. The six IMCs and one residue are extracted via EMD.

Table 2 shows the results on regression and forecasting errors. It can be obviously seen that not only for the single-step but also for the 24-step ahead forecasting, the forecasting errors of the hybrid model are smaller than the SVR's. Thus we can say that the hybrid model shows better generalization performance than that of the SVR.

Table 2. Regression and forecasting errors from the two methods for peak-peak values

Forecasting method		Regression errors			Forecasting errors		
		RMSE	MAE	MAPE(%)	RMSE	MAE	MAPE(%)
Single-step	SVR	0.009956	0.009914	0.0194	1.593702	1.271893	2.4867
	Hybrid	0.403426	0.256638	0.5040	0.830227	0.629292	1.2318
24-step	SVR	0.000996	0.000992	0.0019	2.039262	7.729737	3.4132
	Hybrid	0.155412	0.119647	0.2353	1.495826	1.195193	2.3944

5 Conclusion

To forecast the future tendencies of nonlinear and nonstationary time series, a hybrid intelligent forecasting model is proposed, which is based on EMD, SVR and ALNN. Testing results of simulation experiment and engineering application show that the hybrid model has an excellent generalization performance and long-term forecasting ability, compared with SVR. The proposed hybrid forecasting model can also be applied to other engineering fields. A more challenging task is to correctly and rapidly forecast the running condition tendency of the machinery online.

Acknowledgements. This work was supported by the key project of National Nature Science Foundation of China (No.50335030), Doctor Program Foundation of University of China (No.20040698026) and Nature Science Foundation of Xi'an Jiaotong University.

References

1. Murtagh, F., Starck, J.L., Renaud, O.: On Neuro-wavelet Modeling. J. of Decision Support System, special issue Data Mining for Financial Decision Making. 37(2004) 475-484
2. Huang, N.E., Shen, Z., Long, S.R.: The Empirical Mode Decomposition and Hilbert Spectrum for Nonlinear and Non-stationary Time Series Analysis. Proc. Royal Soc. London. 454(1998) 903-985
3. Vapnik, V.N.: The Nature of Statistical Learning Theory. Springer, Berlin. 1995
4. Hagan, M.T., Demuth, H.B., Beale, M.H.: Neural Network Design. PWS Publishing Company. 1996

A Real Time Color Gamut Mapping Method Using a Neural Network*

Hak-Sung Lee[1] and Dongil Han[2]

[1] Dept. of Electronics Engineering
hslee@sejong.ac.kr
[2] Dept. of Computer Science, Sejong University 98 Kunja-dong,
Kwangjin-gu, Seoul, 143-747, Korea
dihan@sejong.ac.kr

Abstract. In this paper, a neural network is applied to process the color gamut mapping in real time. Firstly, a neural network is trained to learn the highly nonlinear input and output relationship of the color gamut mapping. And then, the trained neural network is simplified with a look-up table and an address decoder for a fast computation. The proposed method can be easily implemented in high speed and low cost hardware. Simulation result shows the soundness of the proposed method.

1 Introduction

A practical color display device is only capable of producing a limited range of colors which is its *color gamut*. Since each color display device adopts the unique principle of color production mechanism, the color gamut of each device is different from each other. These mismatched color gamut often causes inconsistency of color reproduction between different color display devices. *Color gamut mapping* is a process to correct these mismatches in order to enhance the color production quality of color display devices[1,2]. However, the input and output relationship of the color gamut mapping is very highly nonlinear and it is difficult to process the color gamut mapping in real-time. Using a straightforward implementation of existing color gamut mapping algorithms requires significant computation and they are inadequate for a real time display application such as in digital TV[3].

In this paper, a neural network is applied to the real time gamut mapping method. A neural network is trained to learn the nonlinear input and output relationship of a given color gamut mapping and the trained neural network is utilized for the color gamut mapping. In order to meet the real time requirement of a display application, the computation of the trained neural network is simplified with a look-up table and a fixed-point operation.

---

* This work was supported by the Korea Science and Engineering Foundation under Grant R01-2003-000-10785.

2 Main Results

The conventional color gamut mapping process is usually consists of two device dependent color space conversions and one color gamut mapping algorithm as shown in Fig. 1(a). Since the color space conversion and color gamut mapping algorithm require very highly nonlinear operations, it is very difficult to implement the conventional gamut mapping process in real time.

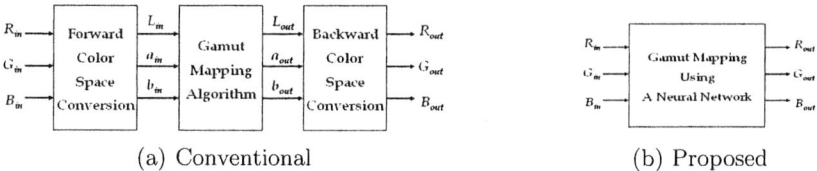

(a) Conventional　　　　　　　　　　(b) Proposed

Fig. 1. Color Gamut Mapping Process

In this paper, a neural network is applied to a color gamut mapping process. A neural network is known to be a good universal approximator of any nonlinear mapping and it has been already successfully applied for various color related engineering[4,5]. Given a set of input-output pairs of a target process or a system, a neural network can be trained to learn the underlying input-output relationship. Based on this learning capability of a neural network, a neural network is to be trained to learn the input-output relationship of the color gamut mapping process. And, as shown in Fig. 1(b), the trained neural network replaces the color gamut mapping process in Fig. 1(a) which consists of three computationally complex nonlinear subprocesses. The design procedure of the neural network for the color gamut mapping process is as follows. Firstly, a gamut mapping algorithm is chosen considering the mapping properties, source and destination color display devices. And then, a color gamut mapping process is conducted for every possible pairs of R_{in}, G_{in}, B_{in} signals of source color display device. And corressponding $R_{out}, G_{out}, B_{out}$ signals for destination color display device are calculated by the color gamut mapping process. As the set of signals of source color display device is presented at the input of a neural network, the neural network is trained to learn the input-output relationship of the given color gamut mapping process. After the neural network is trained, the trained neural network conducts the color gamut mapping process as shown in Fig. 1(b).

Since the sigmoid function in the neural network requires significant computation, the proposed gamut mapping process may be inadequate for display application of moving pictures because of its computational time. In order to cope with this difficulty, the sigmoid function is replaced by an 1-dimensional look-up table where the pre-calculated values of the sigmoid function are stored. Although the sigmoid function is a real valued function and is defined on the whole real value, the look-up table stores the value of the sigmoid function on the interval $[-5,5]$ because the sigmoid function has a saturation property. The value of the sigmoid function is stored in integer format with N bit precision for a fast fixed point operation. This finite precision representation causes a quantization error. But, with the appropriate selection of N, this quantization error has a negligible effect on output values of the neural network because the outputs the neural network are $R_{out}, G_{out}, B_{out}$ signals which also have an 8-bit finite precision.

The proposed computation of the neural network for the real time gamut mapping is illustrated in Fig. 2 where LUT refers to 1-D look-up table for the sigmoid function. In Fig. 2, the computational model of a neuron is simplified with address decoders and look-up tables. The address decoder computes the address of the look-up table based on the weighted summation operation of the neuron. After the weights and bias of neuron are approximated with with a finite precision, the address decoder can be implemented with a "shift and add" operation which is very simple fixed operation[6]. The number of look-up tables is equal to the number of neuron in the neural network.

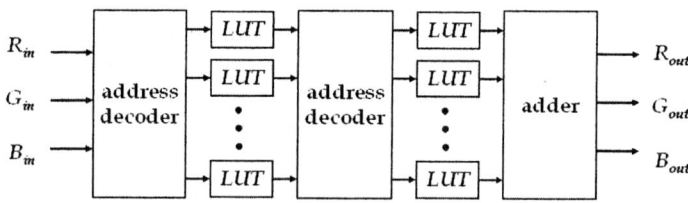

Fig. 2. Proposed Gamut Mapping Process Based on a Neural Network

As an example, the proposed method is applied to a color gamut mapping process between a CRT and a PDP display device. The training data are generated by the conventional color gamut mapping process. A backpropagation neural network is tested and the neural network consists of 2 hidden layers which consist of 20 and 15 neurons respectively. The neural network is trained until the total MSE is below 0.1. And then, the trained neural network is simulated with the proposed computational model in Fig. 2. The size of look-up table is 256×8 bits and the precision of weights is defined as 6 bits. The total number of look-up table is $20+15=35$. Fig. 3 shows the result of the color gamut mapping by the proposed method. As shown in Fig. 3, the reproduced image by the proposed method shows more natural color compared to the original image and little difference is observed compared to the conventionally gamut mapped image.

3 Concluding Remarks

In this paper, a neural network is applied to a real time color gamut mapping process. Usually, the color gamut mapping process shows the very highly nonlinear input and output relationship which causes the difficulty of a real time

(a) Original (b) Conventional (c) Proposed

Fig. 3. A Gamut Mapping Result

implementation. To handle the high nonlinearity of the gamut mapping, a backpropagation neural network is trained to learn the high nonlinear input and output relationship of the color gamut mapping. And then, the trained neural network is simplified with address decoders and look-up tables for a fast computation. By adopting simple "shift and add" operation in the address decoders, it is possible to greatly reduce the overall processing time of the proposed method and the proposed gamut mapping process can be easily implemented in high speed and low cost hardware. Since the proposed method does not depend on the specific color gamut algorithm, arbitrary color gamut mapping process can be easily handled by the proposed method. For a lower cost implementation of the proposed gamut mapping process, the size of look-up table and the precision level for the weights should be optimally chosen based on the resulting image quality.

References

1. Kanamori, K. Kotera, H.: Color Correction Technique for Hard Copies by 4-Neigbors Interpolation Method. Journal of Imaging Science and Technology **36** (1992) 73–80
2. Lee, C.-S., Park, Y.-W., Cho, S.-J., Ha Y.-H.: Gamut Mapping Algorithm Using Lightness Mapping and Multiple Anchor Points for Linear Tone and Maximum Chroma Reproduction. Journal of Imaging Science and Technology **45** (2001) 209–223
3. Han, D.: Real-Time Color Gamut Mapping Method for Digital TV Display Qaulity Enhancement. IEEE tran. on Consumer Electronics. **50** (2004) 691–698
4. Boldrin, E., Schettini, R.: Faithful cross-media color matching using neural networks. Pattern Recogition. **32** (1999) 465–476
5. Campadelli, P., Gangai, C. Schettini, R.: Learning Color-Apprearance Models by Means of Feed-Forward Neural Networks. Color research and application. **50** (1999) 411–421
6. Lee, H.-S., Han, D.: Implementation of Real Time Color Gamut Mapping Using Neural Network. Proc. of 2005 IEEE Mid-Summer Workshop on Soft Computing in Industrial Applications (2005) in press

Adaptive Identification of Chaotic Systems and Its Applications in Chaotic Communications

Jiuchao Feng[1,2,*]

[1] School of Electronic and Information Engineering,
South China University of Technology, Guangzhou 510641, China
[2] Faculty of Electronic and Information Engineering,
Southwest China Normal University, Chongqing 400715, China
fengjc@scut.edu.cn

Abstract. A novel method for identifying a chaotic system with time-varying bifurcation parameters via an observation signal which has been contaminated by additive white Gaussian noise (AWGN) is developed. This method is based on an adaptive algorithm which takes advantage of the good approximation capability of the Radial Basis Function (RBF) neural network and the ability of the Extended Kalman Filter (EKF) for tracking a time-varying dynamical system. It is demonstrated that, provided the bifurcation parameter varies slowly in a time window, a chaotic dynamical system can be tracked and identified continuously, and the time-varying bifurcation parameter can also be retrieved in a sub-window of time via a simple least-square-fit method.

1 The Problem and Objective

We consider the problem of tracking the Henon map which can be represented by the following 2-dim iterative map:

$$x_1(k+1) = 1 - ax_1^2(k) + x_2(k)$$
$$x_2(k+1) = bx_1(k) \qquad (1)$$

where a is a time-varying bifurcation parameter whose variation ensures chaotic motion of the system, and b is fixed at 0.3. The observed signal is $y(k)$, which is essentially $x_1(k)$ with noise added, i.e.,

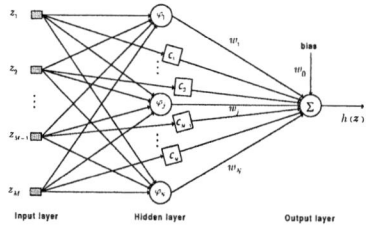

Fig. 1. RBF network configuration

---

* This work was supported in part by the Scientific Research Foundation for the Returned Overseas Chinese Scholars, the Education Ministry of China (Grant No. B7040310); the Research Foundation of Southwest China Normal University (Grant No. 413604); the Natural Science Foundation of Guangdong Province for Research Team (Grant No. 04205783); the Program for New Century Excellent Talents in China University (Grant No. NCET-04-0813); and the Key Project Foundation of the Education Ministry of China (Grant No. 105137).

$$y(k) = x_1(k) + \eta(k) \tag{2}$$

where $\eta(k)$ is the additive white Gaussian noise (AWGN). Our objective is to track and identify x_1 from $y(k)$. It has been demonstrated [1] that for a low dimensional noisy chaotic attractor, noise can be removed or reduced by projecting the chaotic attractor onto a higher dimensional subspace. Because of its ability in modeling any arbitrary nonlinear real-valued map defined on compact real sets [2,3], an RBF neural network whose input space corresponds to the subspace, employed to perform the tracking, which will be assisted by an EKF for coping with the effect of the time-varying parameter.

2 Adaptive Tracking Algorithm

2.1 Review of Radial-Basis-Function Neural Network

The RBF neural network is a three-layer neural network, comprising an input layer, a hidden layer and an output layer, as shown in Fig. 1. The input layer consists of M units, connecting the input vector $\boldsymbol{z}(n)$ which is constructed from the observation $y(k)$ [4]. For brevity we write $\boldsymbol{z}(.)$ as $[z_1, z_2, \cdots, z_M]^T$, which is defined as $\boldsymbol{z}(n) = [y(n(M+1)-1)\ y(n(M+1)-2)\ \cdots\ y(n(M+1)-M)]^T$. The ith input unit is directly connected to the output unit through a gain factor c_i, and the ith hidden unit is connected to the output unit through a weight factor w_i. Effectively, the network performs a nonlinear mapping from the input space $\Re^M$ to the output space $\Re$, which is described by

$$h(\boldsymbol{z}(n)) = w_0 + \sum_{i=1}^{M} c_i z_i + \sum_{i=1}^{N} w_i \varphi_i(\boldsymbol{z}(n)) \tag{3}$$

where w_0 is the bias term. The function $\varphi_i : \Re^M \to \Re$ is called *activation function* and is given generally by

$$\varphi_i(\boldsymbol{z}) = \varphi(\|\boldsymbol{z} - Q_i\|) \tag{4}$$

where $Q_i \in \Re^M$ is known as the RBF center, and $\|\bullet\|$ represents Euclidean distance normal. φ_i is selected as the Gaussian function defined by

$$\varphi_i(\boldsymbol{z}(n)) = \exp\left(-\frac{\|\boldsymbol{z}(n) - Q_i(n)\|^2}{2\sigma_i^2}\right) \tag{5}$$

where σ_i is the width of the Gaussian function of the ith hidden unit.

One complete observation consists of $\boldsymbol{z}(n)$ and $y(n(M+1))$. For brevity we define $(\boldsymbol{z}(n), y(n(M+1)))$ as an observation pair, and the duration for one complete observation as an *observation step*, i.e., the time for reading $(M+1)$ data points. The problem is now reduced to a one-step-ahead prediction which can be formulated as

$$\hat{x}_1(n(M+1)) = h(\boldsymbol{z}(n)) \tag{6}$$

where $\hat{x}_1(n(M+1))$ is the estimate for $x_1(n(M+1))$. In this paper, we assume that the bifurcation parameter a at a time window of T_1 observation steps is constant such that the system can be seen as an autonomous system in the window.

2.2 Network Growth

The network begins with no hidden layer unit. As observation pairs are available, the network grows by creating new hidden units and connecting the received data to the new hidden units. Precisely, given an observation pair $[z(n), y(n(M+1))]$, the criteria for creating a new hidden unit are

$$\|z(n) - Q_{nr}\| > \eta_1 \tag{7}$$

$$\epsilon(n) = y(n(M+1)) - h(z(n)) > \eta_2 \tag{8}$$

$$\epsilon_{rms}^n = \sqrt{\frac{\sum_{i=n-T_2+1}^{n}[y(i(M+1)) - \hat{x}_1(i(M+1))]^2}{T_2}} > \eta_3 \tag{9}$$

where Q_{nr} is the center of the hidden unit which is nearest $z(n)$, T_2 is the number of observation steps of a sliding data window covering a number of latest observations for computing the output error, and η_1, η_2 and η_3 are thresholds. Specifically, $\eta_1 = \max(\eta_{max}\beta^n, \eta_{min})$, where β is a decaying factor, η_{max} and η_{min} are the maximum and minimum of η_1, n's unit is observation step.

The first criterion essentially requires that the input be far away from stored patterns, the second criterion requires that the error signal be significant, and the third criterion specifies that within the sliding data window of T_2 observation steps, the root-mean-square (RMS) error is also significant. Now suppose the $(N+1)$th hidden unit is to be added to the network. The parameters associated with this new unit are assigned as follows:

$$w_{N+1} = \epsilon(n) \tag{10}$$

$$Q_{N+1} = z(n) \tag{11}$$

$$\sigma_{N+1} = \rho\|z(n) - Q_{nr}\| \tag{12}$$

where ρ ($\rho < 1$) is an overlap factor which controls the extent of overlap of the responses of the hidden units for an input.

2.3 Network Update with Extended Kalman Filter

When the observation pair $(z(n), y(n(M+1)))$ does not satisfy the criteria (7) to (9), no hidden unit will be added, and the EKF algorithm [5] is then used to adjust the parameters of the network. These parameters define the state vector, v, of the network,

$$v = [c_1, c_2, \cdots, c_M, w_0, w_1, Q_1^T, \sigma_1, \cdots, w_N, Q_N^T, \sigma_N]^T. \tag{13}$$

Thus, we can write the gradient vector of $h(.)$ with respect to v as $B(z(n)) = \frac{\partial h(.)}{\partial v}|_{z(n)}$. Now, denote the corrected error covariance matrix of v at instant $(n-1)$ by $P(n-1, n-1)$. Then, the current estimate of the error covariance matrix can be found from the following relation:

$$P(n, n-1) = IP(n-1, n-1)I^T = P(n-1, n-1), \tag{14}$$

where I is an identity matrix. Other parameters used in the EKF algorithm are the variance $R(n)$ of y as defined in (2) and the Kalman gain vector $K(n)$, whose propagation equations at instant n satisfy with

$$R(n) = B(\boldsymbol{z}(n))P(n,n-1)B^T(\boldsymbol{z}(n)) + R_D \qquad (15)$$
$$K(n) = P(n,n-1)B^T(\boldsymbol{z}(n))/R(n) , \qquad (16)$$

where R_D is the variance of the measured noise. Having computed $K(n)$, we can then update the state vector according to

$$\boldsymbol{v}(n) = \boldsymbol{v}(n-1) + K(n)\epsilon(n), \qquad (17)$$

where $\boldsymbol{v}(n)$ and $\boldsymbol{v}(n-1)$ are respectively the state vector of the present and previous observation steps. Finally, the error covariance matrix is corrected according to

$$P(n,n) = (I - K(n)B(\boldsymbol{z}(n)))P(n,n-1) + \gamma I , \qquad (18)$$

where γ is a small scaling factor introduced to improve the RBF network's adaptability to future input observations in the case of very rapid convergence of the EKF algorithm [6].

Fig. 2. Lenna image (256×256 pixe

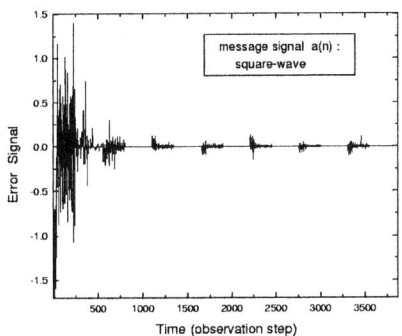

Fig. 3. Error waveform of x_1 for the case of square-wave message

2.4 Pruning of Hidden Units

As the network grows, the number of hidden units increases, and so will the computing complexity. Moreover, some added hidden units may subsequently end up contributing very little to the network output. The network will only benefit from those hidden units in which the input patterns are close to the stored patterns. Thus, pruning redundant units in the hidden layer becomes imperative. We denote the weighted response of the ith hidden unit for input $\boldsymbol{z}(n)$ as

$$u_i(n) = w_i \varphi_i, \quad \text{for } i = 1, 2, \cdots, N . \qquad (19)$$

Suppose the largest absolute output value for the nth input $z(n)$ among all hidden units' weighted outputs is $|u_{\max}(n)|$. Also denote the normalized output of the ith hidden unit for the nth input as

$$\xi_i(n) = \left| \frac{u_i(n)}{u_{\max}(n)} \right|. \tag{20}$$

In order to keep the size of the network small, we need to remove hidden units when they are found non-contributing. Essentially, for each observation, each normalized output value $\xi_i(n)$ is evaluated. If $\xi_i(n)$ is less than a threshold θ for T_2 consecutive observation pairs, then the ith hidden unit should be removed, thereby keeping the network size and the computing complexity to minimal. In the next section, we will test the above algorithm.

2.5 Parameter Estimation

To estimate a, we need to know the type of system. For the Henon map of (1), we have

$$\hat{a}(k)\hat{x}_1^2(k) - 1 = \hat{x}_2(k) - \hat{x}_1(k+1) \tag{21}$$

If $a(k)$ is a constant within a window of T_1 observation steps (i.e., $T_1(M+1)$ time steps), then the Henon map can be seen as an autonomous system in the window, and $\hat{a}$ can be, from (1), estimated by the least-square-fit.

3 Simulation Results

Two different types of signals will be employed as the time-varying parameter to test the proposed algorithm. First we consider a square-wave signal defined by the following piecewise linear function:

$$a(k) = \begin{cases} 1.37, k \in [1, 551] \\ 1.42, k \in [552, 1102] \\ 1.35, k \in [1103, 1653] \\ 1.39, k \in [1654, 2204] \\ 1.32, k \in [2205, 2755] \\ 1.36, k \in [2756, 3306] \\ 1.41, k \in [3307, 3857] \end{cases} \tag{22}$$

Then, we consider an image signal representing of the Lenna image with 256×256 pixels, each pixel having 256 grey levels, as shown in Fig. 2. In this proposed algorithm, $a(k)$ is constant in a time window of T_1 observation steps. For example, each pixel value of the image signal is constant in its T_1 observation steps.

In the simulation, the threshold parameters of the RBF network and the EKF are assigned as follows: $T_1 = 551$, $T_2 = 40$, $M = 5$, $\eta_2 = 0.05$, $\eta_3 = 0.07$, $\eta_{\max} = 2.0$, $\eta_{\min} = 0.02$, $\rho = 0.973$, $p_0 = 15.0$, $\gamma = 0.01$, $\beta = 0.997$, $\theta = 0.001$.

For the square-wave message and an signal to noise ratio (SNR) of 20 dB in y, the error waveform of x_1 is shown in Fig. 3 which shows that in the window of the

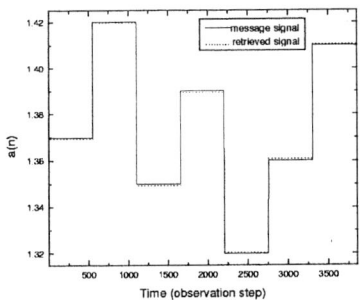

Fig. 4. Square-wave signal (solid line) and retrieved square-wave signal (dotted line, SNR=15 dB)

Fig. 5. Retrieved Lenna image (SNR=15 dB)

first T_1 observation steps, the error is the largest among all subsequent windows of T_1 observation steps. This is because the tracking of the dynamics is mainly done in the first window. In each subsequent window of T_1 observation steps, it is found that the error signal in the sub-window of the first T_4 observation steps ($T_4 = 250$) is larger than that in the rest of the window.

It should be clear that the proposed observer can track the time-varying chaotic system by adaptively adjusting both the number and center positions of the hidden layer units. When SNR of $y(k)$ is 15 dB, the retrieved signals are shown in Figs. 4 and 5, for the cases of the square-wave and the image signal.

4 Conclusion

We have proposed and realized an adaptive approach for identifying a chaotic system with time-varying bifurcation parameter from a noisy observation signal. The essential component of the proposed observer is an RBF neural network which is assisted by an EKF algorithm. Using this observer-based tracking method, message signals in a chaotic modulation system can be retrieved successfully.

References

1. Principe, J., C., Kuo, J., M.: Noise reduction in state space using the focused Gamma neural network. Proc. SPIE **2038** (1993) 326–332
2. Park, J., Sandberg, I., W.: Universal approximation using radial basis function networks. Neural Comp. **3** (1991) 246–257
3. Haykin, S.: Neural Networks: A Comprehensive Foundation. New York: Prentice-Hall (1994)
4. Takens, F.: Detecting strange attractors in turbulence. In: Dynamical Systems and Turbulence, Rand, D., Young I. (Ed.). Berlin: Springer-Verlag (1981)
5. Candy, J., V.: Signal Processing: The Model-based Approach. New pork: McGraw-Hall (1986)
6. Kadirkamanathan, V., Niranjan, M.: A function estimation approach to sequential learning with neural network. Neural Comp. **5** (1993) 954–975

A Time-Series Decomposed Model of Network Traffic

Cheng Guang, Gong Jian, and Ding Wei

Department of Computer Science & Engineering, Southeast University,
Jiangsu Provincial Key Lab of Computer Network Technology, Nanjing 210096
{gcheng, jgong, wding}@njnet.edu.cn

Abstract. Traffic behavior in a large-scale network can be viewed as a complicated non-linear system, so it is very difficult to describe the long-term network traffic behavior in a large-scale network. In this paper, according to the non-linear character of network traffic, the time series of network traffic is decomposed into trend component, period component, mutation component and random component by different mathematical tools. So the complicated traffic can be modeled with these four simpler sub-series tools. In order to check the decomposed model, the long-term traffic behavior of the CERNET backbone network is analyzed by means of the decomposed network traffic. The results are compared with ARIMA model. According to autocorrelation function and predicting error function, compounded model can get higher error precision to describe the long-term traffic behavior.

1 Introduction

The traffic behavior and its tendency have bothered network managers for quite a long time, and is still a not fully understood problem for network management and planning. In order to research network behavior, firstly it is necessary to analysis the measured traffic and to find its statistical laws, such as the work done by Thompson in 1997[1]. Secondly, according to the statistical rules found, some traffic models are built, such as the establishment of self-similar model for Ethernet network traffic in 1994 [2]. If the time-scale of network traffic is considered, the network traffic behavior will be different in different time-scale. Paxson and Floyd [3] showed that the traffic behavior of millisecond-time scale isn't self-similar by the influence of network protocol. Due to the influence of environment, the traffic behavior whose time-scale is larger than ten minutes isn't also self-similar and is a non-linear time-series. Only the traffic behavior in second-time scale is self-similar. In the paper, the traffic behavior model whose time-scale is larger than ten minutes, is concerned.

It is very important to research traffic time-series model in order to describe traffic behavior. The traditional long time-scale traffic model can only model smoothing process and some special non-smoothing process. AR [4] (Auto Regressive) model, MA (Moving Average) model, and ARMA [5] (Auto Regressive Moving Average) model can deal with smoothing process. ARIMA [5] (Auto Regressive Integrated

Moving Average) model and ARIMA seasonal model [6] can describe the uniform non-smoothing process. A large-scale network itself is a complex non-linear system, and is influenced by many environment factors, which is similar with water-volume time series that can be decomposed into mutation item, periodic item, trend item, random item [7]. So network traffic also can be considered to be the combination of periodic item, trend item, random item, and mutation item, which is very difficult to describe these traffic characters with a traditional traffic time-series model.

According to these characters of traffic behavior, in the paper the traffic time-series is decomposed into four simple sub-components: mutation component, trend component, period component, and random component. Firstly, based on the fact that median is the robust estimation of mean, the mutation component of long-term traffic is removed. Secondly, the trend component is separated from the rest traffic components by the GM(1,1) model of gray system theory. Thirdly, the period component is separated from the rest traffic components by the period wave theory. Last, the rest components are modeled on the AR(P) model of time-series theory. So the long-term traffic model can be obtained by combining the theory models of three sub components: trend component, period component, and random component. Finally, in the paper some CERNET traffic data are modeled with the compounded model and the traditional ARIMA seasonal model respectively, and the analyzed results of two kinds of models are compared and analyzed.

2 Traffic Compounded Model

Network user behavior is influenced by environment, so network traffic behavior includes both rule and abnormity. In addition, a large-scale network itself is a non-linear system, so the non-linear long time-scale traffic can behave the characters of mutation, trend, period, and randomness. According to the traffic characters, the network traffic long time-scale time series X(t) can be separated into trend component A(t), period component P(t), mutation component B(t), and random component R(t). So the long-scale time series can be described as

$$X(t)=B(t)+A(t)+P(t)+R(t) \quad (1)$$

In the equation (1), X(t) is the rule traffic time-series. B(t) is effected by exterior environment mutation factors, and A(t) reflects the long term changed trend of network usage or environment factors, and P(t) reflects the periodic movement of traffic phenomena. B(t), A(t), P(t) show the determinate factors of traffic time series change. The random component R(t) can be decomposed into the smoothing random time series component S(t) and simple random component N(t) continuously.

$$R(t)=S(t)+N(t) \quad (2)$$

In the five components, the mutation component and pure random component belong to zero memory components. A(t), P(t), S(t) are the memory components that describe the long term trend, period, and smooth process of network traffic behavior. If the three component models can be modeled as a(t), p(t), and s(t) respectively, then the traffic model x(t) of X(t) can be modeled as

$$x(t)=a(t)+p(t)+s(t) \qquad (3)$$

Therefore, according to equation (1) and (2), the network traffic can be divided into five sub-components with different mathematics tools respectively. Then the trend component, period component, and smoothing random component are modeled separately. The raw traffic time-series model can be obtained by the equation (3).

2.1 Decomposing Mutation Item

The basic idea of decomposed mutation item is to produce a smoothing estimate of curve firstly, then we can obtain a error time-series that is subtracted the smoothing curve from measurements of network traffic. If the error point is larger than the appointed threshold, then that point is considered a mutation point. The method bases on the fact that the median is a robust estimation of mean. The algorithm that the mutation component is removed from traffic time series X(t) is as following.

Step 1. A new time series X'(t) is constructed by traffic time series X(t).

$$X'(t) = \text{middle}(X(t-2), X(t-1), X(t), X(t+1), X(t+2)) \quad t \in [2, n-2] \qquad (4)$$

Where middle() is a function that obtains a median from data in bracket.
Step 2. X''(t) is constructed from X'(t).

$$X''(t) = \text{middle}(X'(t-1), X'(t), X'(t+1)) \quad t \in [3, n-3] \qquad (5)$$

Step 3. X'''(t) is constructed with X''(t).

$$X'''(t) = X''(t-1)/4 + X''(t)/2 + X''(t+1)/4 \quad t \in [4, n-4] \qquad (6)$$

Step 4. If $|X(t) - X'''(t)| > k$, then X(t) is replaced by the linear inner inserted value. Where $t \in [4, n-4]$, k is a predefined value.

Every measuring point in the [4, n-4] aggregate is computed with the fourth step repeatedly, till the mutation item B(t) is separated from the traffic time-series X(t).

2.2 Trend Item Decomposed Model

GM(1,1) is used to separate A(t) from the complex traffic time series X1(t) that includes trend item, period item, and random item. The algorithm is described as following.

Step 1. Accumulated equation is constructed. Traffic series X1(t) is expressed as equation (7).

$$X1^{(0)} = \{X1_0^{(0)}, X1_1^{(0)}, ..., X1_i^{(0)}, ..., X1_n^{(0)}\} \qquad (7)$$

Where X1(0) is equal to X1(t) that doesn't contain the mutation component, and X1i(0) means traffic bandwidth on ith time, and $i \in [0, n]$. The equation (7) is accumulated in turn, and X1(1) is obtained.

$$X1^{(1)} = \{X1_0^{(1)}, X1_1^{(1)}, \cdots, X1_i^{(1)}, \cdots, X1_n^{(1)}\} \qquad (8)$$

Where $X1_i^{(1)} = \sum_{t=0}^{i} X1_t^{(0)} = X1_{i-1}^{(1)} + X1_i^{(0)}$, $i \in [1, n]$, X10(1)=X10(0), X1i(1) is the network traffic throughput from time 0 to time i. Because the distribution of the series X1(1) can be simulated by exponential function, so the smoothing discrete coefficient can be expressed with differential equation. The result is computed by equation (9),

$$X1_t^{(1)} = (X1_0^{(1)} - \frac{b}{a})e^{-at} + \frac{b}{a} \qquad (9)$$

where a and b are the parameters that must be estimated.

Step 2. The parameters a and b are estimated. The evaluation can obtain with the method of least squares,

$$Y = XB \qquad (10)$$

Step 3. If the parameters a and b are estimated, then the A(t) can be extracted from X(t). The model a(t) of A(t) is expressed in equation (8).

$$a(t) = X1_t^{(1)} - X1_{t-1}^{(1)} \; t \in [1, n] \qquad (11)$$

According to the equation (9, 11), the traffic model can be obtained by equation (12).

$$a(t) = (e^{-a} - 1)(X1_0^{(1)} - \frac{b}{a})e^{-a(t-1)} \; t \in [1, n] \qquad (12)$$

Let X2(t) = X1(t) − a(t) = P(t) + R(t) be the rest time-series that B(t) and A(t) be separated from X(t), so X2(t) is a new time series, whose axes is A(t). The advantage of this new time-series is that it emphasizes the effect of P(t).

2.3 Period Item Decomposed Model

X2(t) is considered as the superposition of some different period waves. So firstly some obvious periods are separated from X2(t) in turn, then these periods are accumulated into P(t). Its algorithm is described as following.

Step 1. Lists all possible period in X2(t). Before the period is analyzed, the number of periods contained in the time series is unknown, so each period must be tested separately.

$$K = \left\{\frac{n}{2}\right\} = \begin{cases} \frac{n}{2}, & n \text{ is even} \\ \frac{n+1}{2}, & n \text{ is odd} \end{cases} \qquad (13)$$

where n is the length of X2(t), and K is the maximum possible period number.

Step 2. Computes the square sum of deviating mean, which include the square sum of deviating mean of both inner team (equation 14) and between teams (equation 15).

$$Q_2^2 = \sum_{j=1}^{k} \sum_{i=1}^{m} (y_{ij} - \bar{x}_j)^2, \; \bar{x}_j = \frac{1}{m}\sum_{i=1}^{m} y_{ij} \qquad (14)$$

$$Q_3^2 = \sum_{j=1}^{k} m(\overline{x}_j - \overline{x})^2 \qquad \overline{x} = \frac{1}{m}\sum_{i=1}^{m}\overline{x}_i \qquad (15)$$

where k is the chosen period length, m is the number of a team, yij is the sequence value X2(t) whose freedom degree is f2 = n − k, f3 = n - 1.

Step 3. Compute the variance ratio between different test periods.

$$F = \frac{Q_3^2 / f_3}{Q_2^2 / f_2} \qquad (16)$$

Step 4. Verifies the variance. A confidence limit α is chosen, e.g. α is equal to 0.05. Then the F distribution table [7] is checked to get Fα. If F> Fα, then the test period exists, otherwise the test period does not exist, and skip the step five.

Step 5. Tests k from 2 to K, where K = $\lfloor n/2 \rfloor$ and n is the length of X2(t), until the time series does not have obvious period.

2.4 Random Item Decomposed Model

Let X3(t) = X2(t) − p(t) = R(t) = S(t) + N(t), and a smoothing random item S(t) is expected to be extracted from X3(t).

$$X(t) = x(t) = \beta_{p,1}x(t-1) + \beta_{p,2}x(t-2) + \ldots + \beta_{p,p}x(t-p) \qquad (17)$$

where $\beta_{p,j}$ (j=1,2,…,P) is the auto-regression coefficient, and P is the order number. The algorithm is described as following.

Step 1. Computes the model coefficient.

$$\begin{cases} \beta_{1,1} = \gamma_1 \\ \beta_{k,k} = \dfrac{\gamma_k - \sum_{j=1}^{k-1}\beta_{k-1,k}\gamma_{k-j}}{1 - \sum_{j=1}^{k-1}\beta_{k-1,j}\gamma_j} \quad (k = 2,3,\ldots) \\ \beta_{k,j} = \beta_{k-1,j} - \beta_{k,k}\beta_{k-1,k-j}\ (j=1,2,\ldots,k-1) \end{cases} \qquad (18)$$

where $\beta_{i,j}$ is the auto-regression coefficient, and γ_k is the k order auto-correlation coefficient of X3(t).

Step 2. Computes the order number of model that can be ensured by AIC rule.

$$AIC = \min\left\{ n\ln\frac{\sum(X3(t) - \overline{X3})^2}{n - P - 1} \right\} \qquad (19)$$

where $\overline{X3}$ is the mean of X3(t), n is the length of X3(t).

Step 3. Computes the smooth time-series model s(t). Firstly p values of data in the preceding s(0) are defined, then s(t) is evaluated from X3(t) reversely in order to obtain the data s(-1), s(-2), … , s(-p) before the measuring points, so as to get equation (20).

$$s(t) = \beta_{p,1}s(t-1) + \beta_{p,2}s(t-2) + \ldots + \beta_{p,p}s(t-p) \quad t \in [0, n] \tag{20}$$

Random item of the measuring points can be estimated by means of equation (20).

3 Analysis of Network Traffic

In order to verify the compound model, three different time-scale network traffics are analyzed and modeled. The first group of 11 days data (CERNET01), whose timescale is one hour, comes from one backbone router of CERNET in 2001. The second group of 121 days data (CERNET02), whose time-scale is one day, also comes from CERNET. The third group of data (NSFNET), whose timescale is one week, comes from one national backbone route of NSFNET from Aug. 1, 1988 to Jun. 30, 1993 [8].

3.1 Model Parameters

Table 1. Model Parameters of three Trace. Three kind traffic trace are modeled by the compound model algorithm, and these model parameters are listed in table 1.

Trace			Cernet1	Cernet2	Nsfnet
Model Parameters	A(t)	A	-0.0009	-0.005	-0.018
		B	121.109	149.6	109.0
	P(t)	Period	24	7	26
		A	-0.0056	0.001	-0.406
		B	152.802	50.80	84.47
	S(t)	AR(p)	0.6863	0.684	0.702
			0.0352	0.102	0.008
				-0.009	0.039
				-0.171	-0.144
				0.064	
				0.071	
				-0.001	

3.2 Comparison with ARIMA Seasonal Model

CERNET01 and NSFNET traces are compared with their forecasting result error, which is defined as equation (21). CERNET02 trace is compared with the simulated result SSN, which is defined as equation (22).

$$error = \sqrt{\sum_{i=n+1}^{n+1+r}(X_i - \hat{X}_i)^2 / r} \tag{21}$$

Where n is the time-series length of the model, r is forecasting length. n of CERNET01 trace is 240, and r is 24. In NSFNET trace, n is equal to 253, and r is 52.

$$SSD(m) = \frac{1}{n-1}\sum_{i=1}^{n}(ACF_m(i) - ACF_s(i))^2 \quad (22)$$

Where SSD(m) is the auto-correlation sample variance of model m, and ACFm(i) is the ith order auto-correlation function of model m, ACFs(i) is the ith order auto-correlation function of measuring sample series. The statistical metrics reflects the auto-correlation of the model, the less the value, the better the effect.

The ARIMA seasonal models of three kind traces are as following.

The first forecasting model of CERNET01 trace is ARIMA(2, 0, 2) ×(0, 1, 0) 24, and its parameters are $(\beta_1, \beta_2, \theta_1, \beta_2)$ = (0.1652, -0.676, 0.8705, -1294).

The second forecasting model of NSFNET t race is ARIMA(2, 2, 1)×(2, 2, 0) 52, and its parameters are $(\beta_1, \beta_2, \theta_1, \beta_3, \beta_4)$ = (-0.17682, -0.00068, 0.99389, -0.273511, 0.653531).

The simulated model of CERNET02 trace is ARIMA(7, 0, 0)×(0, 1, 0) 7, its parameters are $(\beta_1, \beta_2, ..., \beta_7)$ = (0.6606, 0.1631, -0.0805, -0.1232, -0.0085, 0.1721, -0.2153).

Table 2. SSD and Forecast Error. The table is the SSD of the decomposed models of CERNET02 trace, and the forecasting error statistics of CERNET 01 trace and NSFNET trace. From the table, we can know that the decomposed model suggested in the paper is very effective.

Model	CER1 error	NSF error	CER2 SSD
Compounded model	6.81	209.31	--
ARIMA Seasonal model	10.26	421.92	0.00547
Decomposed model	--	--	0.00098

4 Conclusion

In the paper, a decomposed model of long time-scale network traffic in a large-scale network is suggested and verified with two groups of CERNET traffic traces and one group of NSFNET trace. The analysis shows that CERNET user behavior has the periodicity of hour, day, and week. The experiment result proved that the prediction precision of the decomposed model is better than the ARIMA seasonal model's.

The decomposed model has three main advantages. Firstly, the decomposed model uses multi-types sub-models to describe traffic behavior, and has more parameters, so it can describe traffic behavior more accurately and perfectly than the traditional ARIMA model. Secondly, the decomposed model is composed of four sub-models that can describe different aspects of the traffic character. Finally, according to the measured traffic behavior, one or multi sub-model can replaced by others sub-model. For example, in order to research self-similar traffic behavior, the random item sub-model can be replaced by FARIMA model or FGN model.

Acknowledgments

The project is supported by the 973 program of China under grant No. 2003CB314803; the Key Project of Chinese Ministry of Education under Grant No.105084; the Foundation of Southeast University of China under Grant No.9209002157; the Natural Science Foundation of Southeast University under Grant No. 9209001348.

References

1. Kevin Thompson, Gregory J. Miller, and Rick Wilder. Wide-Area Internet Traffic Patterns and Characteristics[J].IEEE Network, November / December 1997, 5(6): 10-23.
2. W. E. Leland, M. S. Taqqu, W. Willinger, D. V. Wilson. On the Self-Similar Nature of Ethernet Traffic [J]. IEEE/ACM Transaction on Networking, Feb. 1994, 2(1): 1-15.
3. V. Paxson, S. Flod. Wide-area traffic: The failure of poisson modeling. IEEE/ACM Transactions on Networking [J], June 1995, 3(3):226-244.
4. Rich Wolski. Forecasting Network Performance to Support Dynamic Scheduling Using the Network Weather Service [DB/OL]. UCSD Technical Report, TR-CS96-494(1996). http://citeseer.nj.nec.com/wolski98dynamically.html.
5. S. Basu and A. Mukherjee. Time series models for internet traffic [J]. Proc. IEEE INFOCOM'96, San Francisco, CA., March, 1996, 2: 611-620.
6. N. Groschwitz, G. Polyzos. A Time Series Model of Long-term Traffic on the NSFnet Backbone [j]. In Proceedings of the IEEE International Conference on Communications(ICC'94), New Orleans, LA, May 1994
7. Jing Guangyan, Random Analysis of Hydrology and Water Resource, Press of Chinese Science and Technology, in Beijing, 1992. 5, pp:406-436.
8. K. Claffy, G. C. Polyzos, and H. W. Braun. Traffic Characteristics of The T1 Nsfnet Backbone [J]. proceedings IEEE INFOCOM'93, San Francisco, California, March 28- April 1, 1993: 885-892.

A Novel Wavelet Watermark Algorithm Based on Neural Network Image Scramble

Jian Zhao[1], Qin Zhao[2], Ming-quan Zhou[1], and Jianshou Pan[1]

[1] Electronic Science Department, Northwest University,
Xi'an 710069, P.R. China
zjctec@nwpu.edu.cn
[2] Department of Computer Science, National University of Singapore,
119260, Singapore

Abstract. Image scramble is one of the key technologies in the digital watermarks. In the absence of standardization and specific requirements in Watermark procedures, there are many methods for image scramble. In order to improve robustness, secrecy and exclusion of scrambled image, a method of neural network image scramble for wavelet watermark is proposed in this paper. Because the nonlinear mapping from the original image to its scrambled image is the key for image scramble, the nonlinear feature of neural network can be used to get the scrambled image. Our method embeds watermark into the wavelet descriptors. Watermark scrambled image generated by neural network can be successfully detected even after rotation, translation, scaling. And watermarks of our scheme are good at defending many kind watermark attacks. The experimental results demonstrate that our watermark algorithm is useful and practical.

1 Introduction

With the increasing importance and widespread distribution of digital media, the protection of the intellectual property rights of the media for their owner has become increasingly significant. One type of such media is digital imagery, which can be copied and widely distributed without any significant loss of quality. Protecting the property rights of these images is therefore very important. A straightforward protecting method is to completely encrypt the data, and thereby requires the end user to have the decryption key for the decoding. Another way of protecting the copyright of the data is to apply a digital watermark. Digital Watermark is the process of encoding an image with its owner's watermarks. It can be done in two general approaches. One is to embed the watermark into spatial domain of the original image directly. And the other is to transform the original image into its frequency domain representation and embed the watermark data therein.

In this paper, a robust digital wavelet watermark scheme based on neural network is proposed. The scrambled watermark image is processed by a neural network and spreaded adaptively over the image wavelet domain. The experimental results demonstrate that the watermark is robust to general image processing techniques and geometric distortions. The watermarked image has good visual effect, which demonstrates that this algorithm is feasible.

2 Advantages of Wavelet Image Watermark

Comparing embedding watermark in the spatial domain directly, doing it in the frequency domain has several advantages:

1) people cannot distinguish the distinction between embedded images and original images;
2) the energy of watermark is dispersed to all pixels;
3) computation at the frequency domain matches the international standard (Such as JPEG2000).

In addition, considering the character of a visual system, we can get the effective results in concealment and robustness. The wavelet basis function has closer correlation to the broadband nature of images than the sinusoidal waves used in Discrete Cosine Transform (DCT). The Discrete Wavelet Transform (DWT) is more suitable in HSV than DCT, so it attracts more attention on digital watermark study. The new technologies used in JPEG2000 makes the watermark arithmetic, which is based on DWT, more practicable.

In the wavelet domain, the low frequency band owns much more energy than the high frequency band. That means most energy of image exists in the low frequency, while the energy of the image edge exists at high frequency. If we embed the watermark at the low frequency band, the information of image may be lost. While if we embed it in the high frequency band, some watermark information may disappear after image processing (such as code, compress). So, in the experiment of this paper, the image is disposed by the 3rd DWT function firstly. Then it is divided into the watermark image size, and the sub-images have no any overlapped blocks. After that, we embed watermark to each sub-image. The area of the high frequency is bigger than that of the low frequency, so we get more sub-images at high frequency band. Thus the part of high frequency gets more watermarks while the part of low frequency gets fewer. Through this method, when image with embedded watermark is transformed back to spatial domain, the watermark is widespread to whole image. And the watermark of image is more robust according to the spread-frequency theory.

3 Application of Neural Network at Image Scramble

An artificial neural network is consisted of a great number of parallel processing units called neuron. It has good ability of learning, generalization and nonlinear approximation due to its massively parallel and distributed architecture. The BPNN(Back Propagation Neural Network) is one type of supervised learning neural networks. Through training sample set, it can realize nonlinear map between any dimensions by steepest gradient descent method.

The image hiding and disguise is a very important direction of image study. The image scramble is a pre processing method at image hiding. With the developing of information secrecy, the image scramble transform becomes reversible. Now the algorithm of image scramble can be divided into many categories, such as the methods based on position domain, on color domain and on frequency domain. Here we propose an image scramble algorithm based on neural network at wavelet domain (one kind of frequency domain). From the principal aim of image scramble at watermark, which is to create a nonlinear mapping from original watermark image to scrambled watermark image, we use neural network's nonlinear feature to perform image scramble.

Figure 1 shows the framework of BPNN that realizes nonlinear mapping. The number of neuron in the BPNN's input layer, middle layer, and output layer is 64 respectively. I is the original watermark image, and I_d denotes the scrambled watermark image. We first divided I into blocks with the size of 8*8, and use each block's pixel value as the BPNN input T. And the weight values of BPNN is initialized random value between (0, 1). The BPNN's middle-layer output constitutes the scrambled image I_d. Now we use T as supervised signal to train BPNN's middle-layer and output-layer, and we only adjust weights values between those back two layers. At last, BPNN use input-layer and middle-layer to realize original image I to scrambled image I_d's mapping (image scramble), use middle-layer and output-layer to realize scrambled image I_d to original image I's mapping (restore scramble). The neural network is trained for 1000 epochs or the mean square error is less than 0.00015(the minimum gradient is 0.0001).

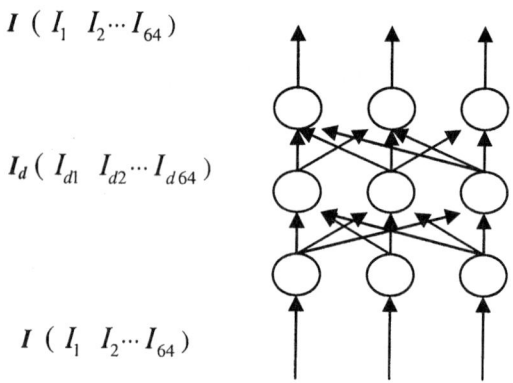

Fig. 1. Nonlinear Mapping

4 The Realization Steps of the Algorithm

Suppose X denotes the original image whose size is $M \times M$, each pixel is s bits, then

$$X = \{x(m,n), 0 \leq m, n \leq M\} \quad (1)$$

Here $x(m,n) \in \{0, 1, \cdots, 2^s - 1\}$ is the value of the point (m, n) at the original image.

Suppose I is the watermark image, which is N×N (N<M), and each pixel is c bits.

$$I = \{I(m,n), 0 \leq m, n \leq N\} \quad (2)$$

Here $I(m,n) \in \{0,1,\cdots,2^c-1\}$ is the value of the point (m, n) at the watermark image.

In general, suppose the size of watermark image is smaller than the size of the original image, and $M = 2^p \cdot N$ (where p is positive integer), then the algorithm process is:

1. Scrambling the watermark image through follow steps.
   1) Read the original image I and divided it into 8*8 blocks, and get the BPNN input T;
   2) Create a 64-64-64 BPNN and initialize the BPNN weights values;
   3) Input T to BPNN, we can get the output of BPNN's middle-layer, which constitutes scrambled image I_d;
   4) Using T as supervised signal to train BPNN, we only adjust weight values between middle-layer and output-layer.

At last, BPNN use input-layer and middle-layer realizing original image I to scrambled image I_d's mapping (image scramble), use middle-layer and output-layer realizing scrambled image I_d to original image I's mapping (restore scramble).

2. Transforming the original image by the 3rd DWT, we get some specifics sub-images X_j^k and an approach sub-image X_3^0 in different respective scale.

$$X_v = DWT(X) = \{X_j^k, j,k = 1,2,3; if \quad k = 0, then \quad j = 3\} \qquad (3)$$

Where X is the wavelet-transformed image.

3. Separating all specifics sub-images to $2^{(p+1)-2(j-1)}$ blocks, which have the same size as the watermark image, and any blocks don't overlap each other.

$$X_b = \text{Block}(X_v) = \{X_j^{k,i}, i = 1,2,\cdots,2^{(p+1)-2(j-1)}\} \qquad (4)$$

4. Computing the data of the watermark image according to formula 3, we'll get the encrypted watermark which processing by step 1.

5. High-frequency part should be embedded repeatly, low frequency should be embedded only once. Embed the encrypted watermark to every subimages with formula:

$$X_{bs}^i = X_b^i + \alpha W_d = \{X_j^{k,i}(m,n) + \alpha w_d(m,n), 0 \leq m,n \leq N\} \qquad (5)$$

Where a means the intensity of the watermark image. We should balance the relation between visibility and robustness of the watermarked image. If the value of a is large, then we'll get high robustness but low quality images, and vice versa.

6. Merging all computed sub-images orderly. We'll get the sub-image X_{bs}, whose size is M×M. Restore the sub-image by reverse DWT, then we'll get the embedded image:

$$X_s = \text{IDWT}(x_{bs}) = \{x_s(m,n), 0 \leq m,n \leq M\} \qquad (6)$$

5 Results and Conclusion

Figure 2 is the performances of the image scramble algorithm, which embeds watermark into Figure 2(a) and generates Figure 2(b). From figures we can tell that there is no much different on visual affection between watermarked image and original image. Figure 3(a) is the original watermark image; figure 3(b) is the scrambled watermark image; figure 3(c) is the restored watermark image from scrambled image. From figures we can see it's the same between original watermark image and restored watermark image from scramble image, so our algorithm lose no information when neural network used. Figure 4 showed the training rate. The neural network is trained for maximal 1000 epochs or the mean square error is less than 0.001, with the minimum gradient of 0.00015, and the setting goal is met by 16 epochs.

A lot of experiments show the algorithm is good at the robustness. The algorithm shows that it can extract watermark from embedded image completely even the image suffers from pepper noise, Gauss noise, or is compressed by JPEG.

As facts show above, we can draw conclusions of the algorithm:

1) Nonlinear mapping. This new image scramble algorithm based on the neural network use the nonlinear character of neural network theory to achieve the scrambled image. Neural network realizes nonlinear mapping from original image to scrambled image.

2) Secrecy. Because original weight and threshold value of neural network is stochastic here, the scramble image is unique. The secrecy of scramble image is strengthened. The illegal user cannot distinguish the original image even if he got the scramble image.

(a) original image   (b) image with watermark

Fig. 2. Watermark performance

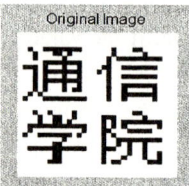  

(a) original image   (b) scrambled image   (c) restored watermark image

Fig. 3. Watermark image

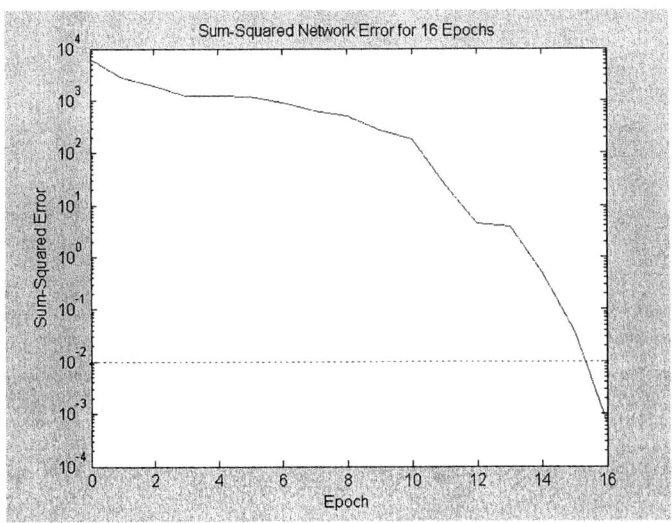

Fig. 4. Training rate of neural network

3) Robustness. The wavelet watermark image scheme has characters of spread spectrum system, which is robust to disturb and noise. Because neural network can get total information from part, we use this character to improve robust here. So our algorithm is more robust than before studied similar algorithm.

4) Watermark invisibility. The embedded digital image is almost the same as original image.

As the mentioned above, this algorithm is valuable and practical. The further study of choosing the chaotic sequence and choosing the key should improve the robustness, exclusivity and credibility.

References

1. Tewfik A H: Digital watermarking. IEEE Signal Processing Magazine, 2000,17(9): 17~88.
2. Nikolaidis A: Asymptotically optimal detection for additive watermarking in the DCT and DWT domains, IEEE Transactions on Image Processing, 2003, 12(5) :563~571
3. Jian Zhao, Ming-quan Zhou, A Novel Wavelet Image Watermarking scheme Combined with Chaos Sequence and Neural Network, Advances in Neural Networks, Lecture Notes in Computer Science, Vol. 3174. Springer-Verlag, Berlin Heidelberg New York (2004), Part II:663-668
4. I. J. Cox, J. Kilian, F. T. Leighton, and T. Shamoon. Secure spread spectrum watermarking for multimedia, IEEE Transactions on Image Processing,1997, 6(12):1673–1687
5. Jian Zhao, Hua Qi, An improved Wavelet Watermarking Scheme Based on Logistic Chaotic Sequences, Acta Photonica Sinica,2004,33(10):1236-1238

A Hybrid Model for Forecasting Aquatic Products Short-Term Price Integrated Wavelet Neural Network with Genetic Algorithm

Tao Hu[1,*], Xiaoshuan Zhang[2], Yunxian Hou[1], Weisong Mu[2], and Zetian Fu[1,2]

[1] College of Economics & Management, China Agricultural University,
P.O. Box 209#, Beijing 100083, People's Republic of China
cauhutao@163.com
[2] College of Engineering, China Agricultural University,
P.O. Box 209#, Beijing 100083, People's Republic of China

Abstract. The technological advances in the production and storage of fishery products have exceeded the development of effective market demand over the past one-decade. As a result, participants within the fishery industry have frequently found themselves facing increased variable and declining prices negatively affected the fishery industry and need to be pro-active instead of reactive to market changes. In this paper, a hybrid model is described, which integrate the Wavelet Neural Network with Genetic Algorithm and can predict the short-term aquatic products price. Then the theory framework and algorithms of the model are discussed. Then an empirical example is described. It shows that the proposed model can predict the short-term aquatic product price with the scale of one day, one week and ten days and the precision of prediction is not the decline trend when the forecasting scale is extended.

1 Introduction

The participant with the fishery industry need to be pro-active instead of reactive to market changes. Fish marketing data, especially price data, are vital for any future aquaculture development project because they can influence potential supply and demand, distribution channels of fish, the economics of aquaculture and the relative importance of wild and cultured fish in rural household consumption (Ker Naret, Sem Viryak, Don Griffiths, 2003). So price forecasting can be expected to reduce the uncertainty and risk in the fish market and can be used to determine the quantity of fish and fish products consumed, lead to improved fish marketing systems and to identify appropriate and sustainable fish culture policy. There is a growing perception that agricultural economists' research on the models and systems of price forecasting (Zhang Zhongping, 1998; Max Nielsen,2000;Xie Liangen, Li Xiaoyong,2000; Zhang Xiaoshuan, FU Zetian,2000). But most of those models are based on the linear

---

* Corresponding Author Tel: +86-10-62736717 Fax: +86-10-62736717
  Email: cauhutao@163.com

regression and can only forecast the long-term aquatic product price, not the short-term aquatic product price.

In this paper we describe the hybrid predication model for Aquatic Products Price, which had Integrated Wavelet Neural Network Model with Genetic Algorithm. This paper is organized as follows. In section 1 describes the theory framework of the hybrid model. Section 2 emphasizes the algorithms adopted by the hybrid model. Section 3 gives an empirical model of aquatic product price. Then the last Section discusses and draws some conclusions.

2 Design of the Architectural Framework of the Model

It is only based on the theory of time series to forecasting the short-term aquatic product price given the the information from the Information Center of Ministry of Agriculture, P.R China is only price time series data. It's difficult to investigate non-linear mapping f between raw data and future data from the mechanism of price time series data $\{x_k\}$. Taking the complex of the prediction into account, the prediction model is structured via the analysis and simulation of time series data of the aquatic products price. Figure 1 shows the theory framework (Li Guoqing, 1995).

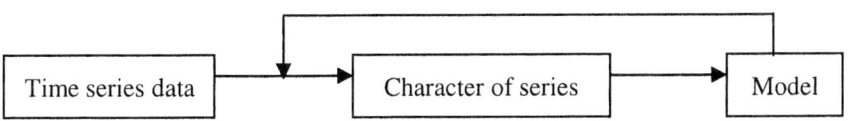

Fig. 1. The framework of prediction theory via time series

(1) extract character of time series data;
(2) build model based on the character;
(3) check up the model, iterate step (1) and (2) if the result is not accurate.

2.1 The Adoption of Wavelet Analysis Technology

The previous works by the authors had shown that the time series data of aquatic product price has the characteristic of non-linear, strong-correlated, multi-fractal and chaos by analyzing carp price time series data (from 1995 to 2003, Xin Fadi wholesale market in BeiJing) (Hu Tao, Fu Zetian, & Zhang Xiaoshuan, 2004).It shows that the main reason of price fluctuation is fluctuation of multi-gene, also called local fractional dimension. If the fluctuation rule of multi-gene can been distinguished and analyzed, we can simulate the price fluctuation regulation and further forecast the price trend (Peters E, 1994; Shu Jianping, 2003).

Due that the wavelet transform can analyze signal in different scales and extract local time-frequency character, we had distilled local fractional dimension of price fluctuation via wavelet analysis. the algorithm is following.

$$W_f(a,b) = \langle f, \psi_{a,b} \rangle = |a|^{\frac{1}{2}} \int_R f(t)\overline{\psi_{a,b}(t)}dt \tag{1}$$

Where, ψ means Mother Wavelet, $\psi_{a,b}(t)$ is named Analyzing Wavelet, a denotes scale, b shows time displacement. Formula(1) means that the definition of Analyzing Wavelet in which the value of a and b are continuous, but in application, especially when it's implemented in computer, Analyzing Wavelet and parameters should be discrete. A convenient mode is binary discrete in which an equals to 2^k, this mode is called Dyadic Wavelet. The algorithm is of the form (2)

$$W_{2^k} f(x) = \frac{1}{2^k} \int_R f(t) \overline{\psi(\frac{x-b}{2^k})} dt \qquad (2)$$

Whereas, in practice, signal $f(t)$ should also be discrete, like $f(k\Delta t), k = 1, 2, \cdots N$; Δt is interval. So form(2) can be transformed of (3):

$$Wf(a,b) = \frac{1}{2^k} \Delta t \sum_{k=1}^{N} f(k\Delta t) \overline{\Psi(\frac{k\Delta t - b}{2^k})}. \qquad (3)$$

2.2 The Adoption of Neural Network Technology

As for the non-linear relation between local fractional dimension (wavelet analysis coefficient) and price future data, we obtained it via neural network. So a wavelet neural network is constructed.

The coupling of Wavelet analysis and neural network in above structure is incompact, firstly original signal is decomposed in different independently frequency channel, in which energy can form a vector, this vector can become input character vector of neural network. And then confirm neural network structure and train it to make certain parameters.

For coupling of wavelet analysis and neural network, there are two main methods (Hiroaki Katsuragi, 2000):

- Using time as benchmark.Using wavelet analysis coefficients of different scales in same time as input character vectors of neural network to predict future data.
- Using scale as benchmark.Using wavelet analysis coefficients of different time in same scale as input character vectors of neural network to predict future data.

Aquatic products price time series data has been proved to present multi-fractal, it means any above method could not reflects and grasps price fluctuation character accurately, so this paper integrates above two methods that input character vectors of neural network comprise not only wavelet analysis coefficients of different scales in same time but also wavelet analysis coefficients of different time in same scale.

Among neural network applications, BP neural network (Back-propagation neural network) is one of the most common and mature model, which is widely used in numerous fields and obtains much success. So we also adopts BP neural network. Kolmogorov theorem assures that a 3 layers neural network can implement any continuous function, Homik (Homik K, Stinchcombe M, &White H, 1990) also proved it. So this paper selects 3 layers BP neural network

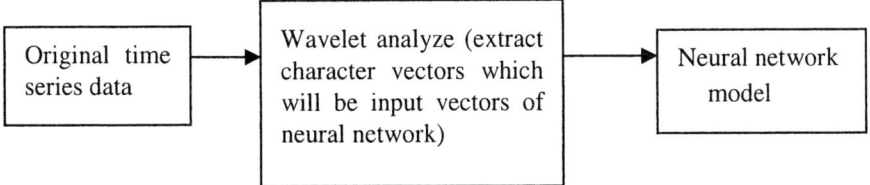

Fig. 2. Wavelet neural network structure

2.3 The Adoption of Genetic Algorithm Technology

It basically uses experience to confirm structure of neural network (Liu jin, 1994). When design a neural network, generally confirm its structure in advance or by the means of increase by degrees or degression. Increase by degrees becomes from a simple network, and make it complex gradually according to needs of problem until discover the best structure. Degression is reverse which start with a complex network, and make it simple gradually until find the best structure. The two methods are also difficult to come across the best structure. In order to solve the above limitation, we adopted genetic algorithm to help search the best Wavelet analysis coefficients and parameters of neural network.

2.4 The Framework of the Hybrid Model

Based on above theory, the whole architectural framework is showed by figure 3.

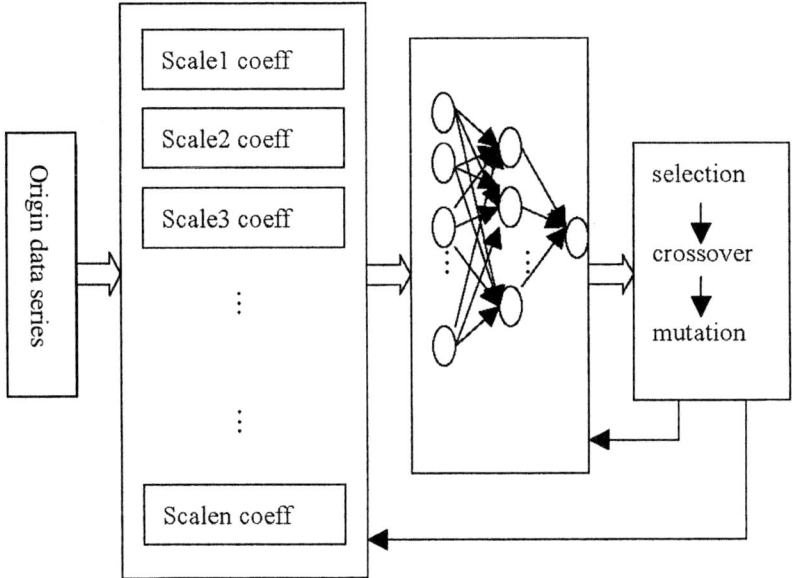

Fig. 3. Structure of the whole framework

3 Algorithm of the Model

3.1 Wavelet Quick Analysis: A TROUS Algorithm

In the methods of Wavelet transformation, the Formula (3) is of direct numerical integral calculation, calculating the Wavelet coefficients dot by dot in the space of (a,b) using the value of $f(t)$ and $\Psi(t)$. However, it is time-consuming. And there also is a sort of Wavelet quick analysis measure, which is simple and prompt without special Wavelet function involved. During this measure, there are two common methods the Mallat algorithm and A Trous algorithm.

The Mallat algorithm requires double extraction, which makes the length of the analysis coefficients to be half. Therefore the method of A Trous is introduced, which cancels the double extraction in the algorithm of Mallat. The formula for the analysis sequence in detail is as follows:

$$C_i(t) = \sum_l h(l) C_{i-1}(t + 2^i l) \tag{4}$$

$$d_i(t) = C_{i-1}(t) - C_i(t) \tag{5}$$

Where, $h(l)$ is discrete lowpass. Suppose the original time series data as $C(t)$ and $C_0(t) = C(t)$, then define the set $W = \{d_1(t), d_2(t), \cdots, d_p(t), C_p(t)\}$ as the Wavelet transformation under the scale of p. The reconstruction formula of the original time series data is as follows:

$$C(t) = C_p(t) + \sum_{i=1}^{p} d_i(t) \tag{6}$$

A Trous algorithm is quick and simple, and its key is to determine the lowpass $h(l)$.

In this paper, $h_3(\frac{1}{16}, \frac{1}{4}, \frac{3}{8}, \frac{1}{4}, \frac{1}{16})$ is adopted.

It can be seen from formula 4 that the problem of boundary prediction arises when the signal $C_i(t)$ of low frequency is calculated. The problem of boundary prediction is that given a limited time series $x(t), t \leq T$, according to Formula

$C_i(t) = \sum_l h(l)C_{i-1}(t+2^i l)$. When the Wavelet coefficient $C_i(\tau)$ is calculated at the time of τ, the data at the time of $\tau + 2^i l$ are required. And when the time of τ is exactly at the boundary or close to the boundary, the calculation of $C_i(\tau)$ will use the data outside the boundary, that is, $x(t)$ with $t \succ T$. As for the Wavelet analysis which takes aim at the prediction, the $x(t)$ with $t \succ T$ is an unknown value to be predicted.

To reduce the effect of the boundary, the measure of Enantiomorphous Delay Development is used, which is the most common in the field of signal processing. That means we suppose $x(N+t)=x(N-t), t=1,2,\cdots,N$, and N is the length of the sequence. This method has been adopted by Aussum Alex (Aussum, 1997) to analyze the effect of the prediction and validate its feasibility. Thereby it is also adopted in this thesis.

3.2 GA Operation

3.2.1 Binary Coding
Binary Coding is a basic one in genetic algorithm, in which only two binary codes 0 and 1 are involved in code symbol set. Therefore the actual gene is of binary symbol type, which is simple to coding and decoding, and genetic operations of crossover and mutation are also made easier. It is also advantageous to go on with the theoretical analysis with the use of the Mode Theorem.

3.2.2 Roulette Wheel Selection
Roulette wheel selection is a ripe one in genetic operation and selection system and easy to deal with. The measure is as follows: calculate the adaptability, selective probability and cumulative probability of each unit, and choose the crossover units by many turns. A random number in the way of [0,1] is produced in every turn. Which is the selecting pointer to select unit.

4 Empirical Model and Result Analysis

All data used in this paper is derived from Chinese agricultural products Value Data Warehouse which is built by information center of MAC (Ministry of Agriculture of People's republic of China). As a large wholesale market in Beijing, Xinfadi wholesale market holds very high market occupancy proportion and especially price time series data of carps from it is complete. So we select its data of carp price to validate the model.

4.1 Wavelet Analysis

A Trous algorithm is taken to decompose the original time serial data in five scales and the wavelet coefficients are showed in Figure 4:

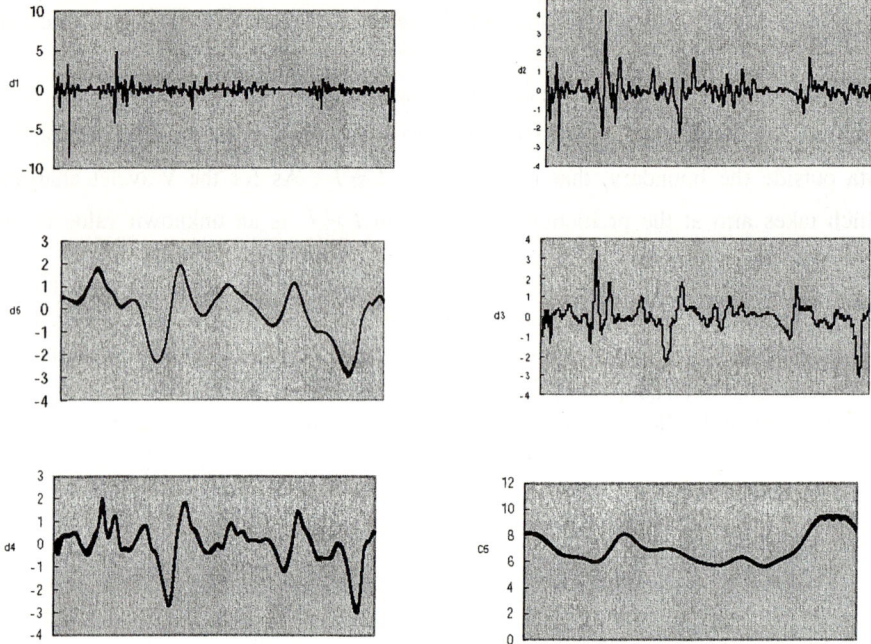

Fig. 4. A Trous wavelet analysis coefficients

Where, d_1, d_2, d_3, d_4, d_5 are high frequency signals (detail signals) in different scales, and c_5 is low frequency (background signals) in the fifth scale

4.2 Confirm Structure of ANN

Instructed as figure 3, initialized a random population, and then ANN is trained via samples to confirm structure of ANN, results are showed in table 1 (Hidden_num is the number of hidden layers).

4.3 Predictions

Table 2 shows precision of 1 day、 7 days and 10 days prediction models, and figure 5 displays comparison of original value and prediction value.

Table 1. Parameters of ANN

Model	Delay of each scale						Hidden_num
	d1	d2	d3	d4	d5	c5	
1 day	8	8	6	6	5	4	28
7 days	10	10	8	6	5	5	25
10 days	10	8	8	8	6	5	32

Table 2. Main Parameters of model structure

Model style	1 day	7 days	10 days
For Training	73.7	73.0	74
For Testing	69.8	70.2	71.5

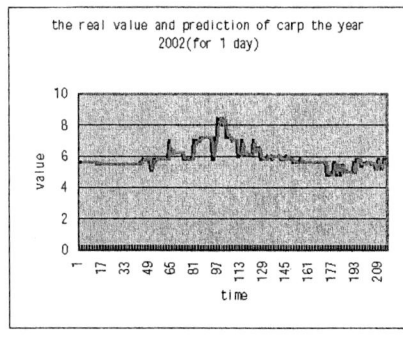
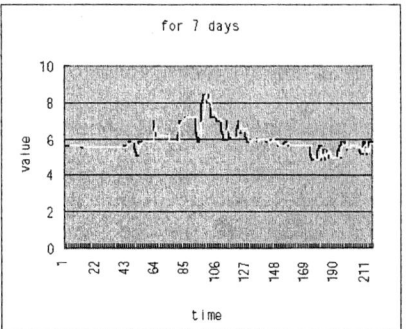

Fig. 5. Comparison of real value and prediction (The period of prediction is 1 day, 7 days)

5 The Conclusion

The training precision of one day, one week and ten days are 73.7, 73, 74, respectively. The testing precision of one day, one week and ten days are 69.8, 70.2, 71.5, respectively. It shows that the proposed model can predict the short-term aquatic product price with the scale of one day, one week and ten days and the precision of prediction is not the decline trend when the forecasting scale is extended.

Acknowledgements

This program is support by NSFC (National Nature Science Foundation of China) under Grant No. 70133001.

References

1. Aussum.et al. Combing neural network forecast on wavelet-transformed series [J]. Connection Science.1997,10 (1):113~121
2. Brummett and Noble, 1995. Aquaculture for African smallholders. ICLARM technical report No. 46, pp. 69
3. Epperson,J.E., Fu,T.T.,Mizzlle,W.O., 1986 .Weekly price forecasting model for Georgia peaches. Hortscince. 1986. 21: 1, 106-107
4. GU hongging(2002).Study on market risk of fishery. Science Fishing, 2001(3):20-21(in Chinese)

5. Hiroaki Katsuragi. Evidence of Multi-affinity in the Japanese Stock market[J]. Physica A, 2000,278:275~281.
6. Homik K, Stinchcombe M, White H. Universal Approximation of an Unknown Mapping and Its Derivatives. Neural Networks,1990,3:551~560
7. Hu Tao, Fu Zetian, & Zhang Xiaoshuan (2004). Fractal Structure of Aquatic Product Wholesale Price and Prediction Based on it. 2004 CIGR International Conference Olympics of Agricultural Engineering.
8. Huntington, D. (2000). Web-based expert systems are on the way: Javabased Web delivery. PC AI Intelligent Solutions for Desktop Computers, 14(6), 34–36.
9. Ker Naret, Sem Viryak, Don Griffiths, 2002. Fish Price Monitoring in Kandal, Prey Veng and Takeo Provinces of Cambodia. IIEFT,2002
10. Li Guoqing, The Application of Time Series Analysis in Power System Transient Stability Prediction. Control and Decision. 1995,10(2).

A Multiple Vector Quantization Approach to Image Compression

Noritaka Shigei[1], Hiromi Miyajima[1], and Michiharu Maeda[2]

[1] Kagoshima University, Kagoshima 890-0065, Japan
shigei@eee.kagoshima-u.ac.jp
[2] Kurume National College of Technology,
Kurume, Fukuoka 830-8555, Japan

Abstract. This paper investigates the effectiveness of a parallelized approach to VQ based image compression. In particular, we consider an image compression method using multiple VQs. The method, called MVQ, generates multiple independent codebooks to compress an image by using a neural network algorithm. In the image restoration, MVQ restores low quality images from the multiple codebooks, and then combines the low quality ones into a high quality one. Further, we present an effective coding scheme for codebook indexes to overcome the in-efficiency of MVQ in compression rate. Our simulation results show that the MVQ method outperforms a conventional single-VQ method when the compression rate is smaller than some values.

1 Introduction

Adaptive Vector Quantization (AVQ) is to find a small set of weight vectors that well approximates a larger set of input vectors[1,4]. Various neural network algorithms for AVQ have been proposed[3,4,5]. AVQ is a useful technique in data compression such as image compression[2,4,5,7,8]. VQ based image compression is a lossy compression technique. The restored image quality greatly depends on the number of weights (codebook size) and the dimension of weights (block size). One of the methods relaxing the trade-off is Multistage Residual VQ (MRVQ)[2], in which multiple quantizers are concatenated in series[2]. In MRVQ, the first stage quantizer operates on the input vectors, and the second stage one operates on the errors between the input vector and the first stage output.

Recently, ensemble learning, such as Boosting and Bagging, has been received considerable attention in the field of machine learning[6]. The basic concept is that a high-accuracy learning machine is built by combining many low-accuracy learning machines, called weak learners. In particular, the typical ensemble learning algorithm trains many weak learners, and constructs a high-accuracy classifier or estimator by a combining technique such as majority vote and averaging. Unlike MRVQ, ensemble learning can be said a parallelized approach, which motivates our work in this paper.

This paper investigates the effectiveness of a parallelized approach to VQ based image compression. In particular, we consider an image compression method using multiple VQs. The method, called MVQ, generates multiple independent codebooks to compress an image by using a neural network AVQ algorithm. In the image restoration, MVQ restores low quality images from multiple codebooks, and then combines the low quality ones into a high quality one. Further, we present an effective coding scheme for codebook indexes to overcome the in-efficiency of MVQ in compression rate. Our simulation results show that the MVQ method outperforms a conventional single-VQ method when the compression rate is smaller than some values.

2   Adaptive Vector Quantization and Learning Algorithms

Vector Quantization (VQ) is to approximate a large set of input vectors $X = \{x_0, x_1, \cdots, x_{\nu-1}\}$ by a smaller set of weight vectors $W = \{w_0, w_1, \cdots, w_{\kappa-1}\}$, where $x_i, w_i \in \mathbf{R}^n$ are n-dimensional Euclidean vectors and X is a random sample from a probability density function (PDF) $p(x)$. In VQ, an input vector $x \in X$ is replaced with a weight vector $w_i \in W$ such that $d(x, w_i) = \min_{w \in W} d(x, w)$, where $d(x, w)$ is the squared error $||x - w||^2$. In other words, VQ divides the input space $\mathbf{R}^n$ into κ sub-spaces $S_0, S_1, \cdots, S_{\kappa-1}$ such that $S_i = \{x \in \mathbf{R}^n | d(x, w_i) \leq d(x, w_j), j \neq i\}$. The approximation accuracy in VQ is evaluated in terms of the following average distortion error:

$$E = \frac{1}{\nu} \sum_{i \in \{0, \cdots, \kappa-1\}} \sum_{x \in S_i} d(x, w_i) \qquad (1)$$

If $p(x)$ is well-known, optimal weight vectors having minimum E can be created directly from $p(x)$. When $p(x)$ is not well-known, an Adaptive Vector Quantization (AVQ) procedure estimates W from X. The estimation can be performed by using neural network algorithms such as competitive learning, neural-gas and Kohonen's self-organizing map[3,4,5].

A fundamental method minimizing Eq. (1) is Competitive Learning (CL), which is based on gradient descent[4]. The CL procedure iterates a simple adaptation step. At t-th iteration, the CL procedure calculates the closest weight (called *winner*) $w_{i_{\text{win}}}$ to a given input vector $x \in X$, and then updates $w_{i_{\text{win}}}$ as follows:

$$w_{i_{\text{win}}} \leftarrow w_{i_{\text{win}}} + \varepsilon(t)(x - w_{i_{\text{win}}}), \qquad (2)$$

where $d(x, w_{i_{\text{win}}}) = \min_{j \in \{0, \cdots, \kappa-1\}} d(x, w_j)$, and $\varepsilon(t)$ is a learning rate decreasing with t. Though CL quickly converges to a local minimum, the resulted W is of very poor accuracy. The achievable accuracy greatly depends on the initial placement of W.

An approach to better accuracy is to introduce a stochastic mechanism like Simulated Annealing (SA). Stochastic relaxation (SR) can enhance the accuracy with a negligible computational overhead[9]. In CL with SR, the input vector is perturbed by a random vector $\xi(t)$ whose average is zero vector and whose variance decreases with learning iteration t. The adaptation rule is as follows:

$$w_{i_{\text{win}}} \leftarrow w_{i_{\text{win}}} + \varepsilon(t)(x + \xi(t) - w_{i_{\text{win}}}), \qquad (3)$$

3 VQ Based Image Compression

We assume G-bit gray-scale images of size N by N pixels. Let $p_{i,j} \in \{0, 1, \cdots 2^G - 1\}$ $(i,j \in \{1, 2, \cdots N\})$ be the gray level of the pixel at coordinates (i,j). Then an image is represented as an $N \times N$ matrix $P = (p_{i,j})$. The typical algorithm of VQ based image compression is as follows.

Step 1. (Input Preparation)
Given an input image P. The $N \times N$ pixels P are divided into N^2/K^2 blocks of size $K \times K$. The blocks are represented as K^2-dimensional vectors $\boldsymbol{x}_0, \boldsymbol{x}_1, \cdots, \boldsymbol{x}_{N^2/K^2-1}$.

Step 2. (Vector Quantization)
The set of weight vectors $W = \{\boldsymbol{w}_0, \boldsymbol{w}_1, \cdots, \boldsymbol{w}_{\kappa-1}\}$, called codebook, is trained by using the set of vectors $X = \{\boldsymbol{x}_0, \boldsymbol{x}_1, \cdots \boldsymbol{x}_{N^2/K^2-1}\}$ as input data. The training is performed by a neural network AVQ algorithm. Through this paper, we use CL with SR whose adaptation rule is defined by Eq.(3) as a neural network AVQ algorithm.

Step 3. (Index Calculation)
For each $i \in \{0, \cdots, N^2/K^2 - 1\}$, the index number l_i is calculated, where $\|\boldsymbol{x}_i - \boldsymbol{w}_{l_i}\| = \min_{j \in \{0,1,\cdots,\kappa-1\}} \|\boldsymbol{x}_i - \boldsymbol{w}_j\|$.

The data of a compressed image are the codebook W and the index sequence $L = (l_0, \cdots, l_{N^2/K^2-1})$. The compression rate is $R(\kappa, N, G, K) = \frac{GK^2N^2}{\kappa G K^2 + \lceil \log_2 \kappa \rceil N^2}$. For example, $R(32, 256, 256, 2) \approx 6.369$.

From W and the index sequence L, an image is restored. In the restored image, each block $\boldsymbol{x}_i \in X$ in the original image is replaced with $\boldsymbol{w}_{l_i}$. The quality of the restored image is evaluated by mean squared error (MSE) as follows:

$$MSE(X, W) = \frac{1}{N^2} \sum_{i \in \{1, \cdots, N^2/K^2\}} \|\boldsymbol{x}_i - \boldsymbol{w}_{l_i}\|^2. \tag{4}$$

The popular choice of K is $2 \sim 4$. In the rest of this paper, $K = 2$ is assumed.

4 Multiple-VQ Based Image Compression

Let us consider to compress an image by using multiple codebooks. Specifically, in the compression phase, C codebooks are generated by performing VQ C times. In the restoration phase, C images are independently restored from the C codebooks and the C index sequences, and a restored image is generated by combining the C restored images, each of which is restored from one of C codebooks. The algorithm is as follows.

Step 1. (Input Preparation)
From the input image P, four input data sets $X^{(0)}$, $X^{(1)}$, $X^{(2)}$ and $X^{(3)}$ are generated as follows:

$$X^{(s)} = \{x_{i,j}^{(s)} | i,j \in \{0, \cdots, N/2 - 1\}\} \text{ for } s \in \{0,1,2,3\}, \qquad (5)$$

$$\begin{aligned}x_{i,j}^{(s)} = (\ &p_{(2i+\phi(s)) \bmod N', (2j+\psi(s)) \bmod N'}, \\ &p_{(2i+\phi(s)+1) \bmod N', (2j+\psi(s)) \bmod N'}, \\ &p_{(2i+\phi(s)) \bmod N', (2j+\psi(s)+1) \bmod N'}, \\ &p_{(2i+\phi(s)+1) \bmod N', (2j+\psi(s)+1) \bmod N'}),\end{aligned} \qquad (6)$$

where $N' = N/2$, $\phi(s) = s \bmod 2$ and $\psi(s) = \lfloor (s+1)/2 \rfloor \bmod 2$. Fig. 1 is a schematic explanation of $x_{i,j}^{(s)}$.

Step 2. (Vector Quantization)
Perform VQ C times to generate C codebooks $W^{(0)}, \cdots, W^{(C-1)}$, where a codebook $W^{(c)}$ ($c \in \{0, \cdots, C-1\}$) is trained by using a data set $X^{(c \bmod 4)}$. The training is performed by a neural network AVQ algorithm. Through this paper, we use CL with SR whose adaptation rule is defined by Eq.(3) as a neural network AVQ algorithm.

Step 3. (Index Calculation)
For each codebook $W^{(c)}$, the index sequence $L^{(c)} = (l_0^{(c)}, \cdots, l_{N^2/4-1}^{(c)})$ is calculated with the data set $X^{(c \bmod 4)}$.

In the restoration restoration, C images $\tilde{P}^{(0)}, \cdots, \tilde{P}^{(C-1)}$ are independently restored from the C codebooks $W^{(0)}, \cdots, W^{(C-1)}$ and the C index sequences $L^{(0)}, \cdots, L^{(C-1)}$, respectively. And then, a restored image $\tilde{P} = (\tilde{p}_{i,j})$ is generated by combining the C restored images as follows:

$$\tilde{p}_{i,j} = \frac{1}{C} \sum_{c=0}^{C-1} \tilde{p}_{i,j}^{(c)}, \qquad (7)$$

where $\tilde{P}^{(c)} = (\tilde{p}_{i,j}^{(c)})$.

In coding, if C index sequences are kept as they are, the compressed data size increases linearly with C, that is the compression rate is $\frac{GK^2N^2}{C(\kappa GK^2 + \lceil \log_2 \kappa \rceil N^2)}$. In order to relax the in-efficiency, we present a coding scheme based on the following observation.

- In any pair of index sequences $L^{(c_1)}$ and $L^{(c_2)}$, for any $\alpha \in \{0, \cdots, \kappa - 1\}$, with high probability, there exists some $\beta \in \{0, \cdots, \kappa - 1\}$ satisfying the following relation:

$$\begin{aligned}&\left|\{i | l_i^{(c_1)} = \alpha, l_i^{(c_2)} = \beta, i \in \{0, \cdots, N^2/4 - 1\}\}\right| \gg \\ &\left|\{i | l_i^{(c_1)} = \alpha, l_i^{(c_2)} \neq \beta, i \in \{0, \cdots, N^2/4 - 1\}\}\right|.\end{aligned} \qquad (8)$$

If $l_i^{(c_1)} = l_i^{(c_2)}$, we may keep only one index for both of $W^{(c_1)}$ and $W^{(c_2)}$. Then, by re-labeling $W^{(c_1)}$ and $W^{(c_2)}$ so as to be $\alpha = \beta$ with the relation of Eq.(8), we

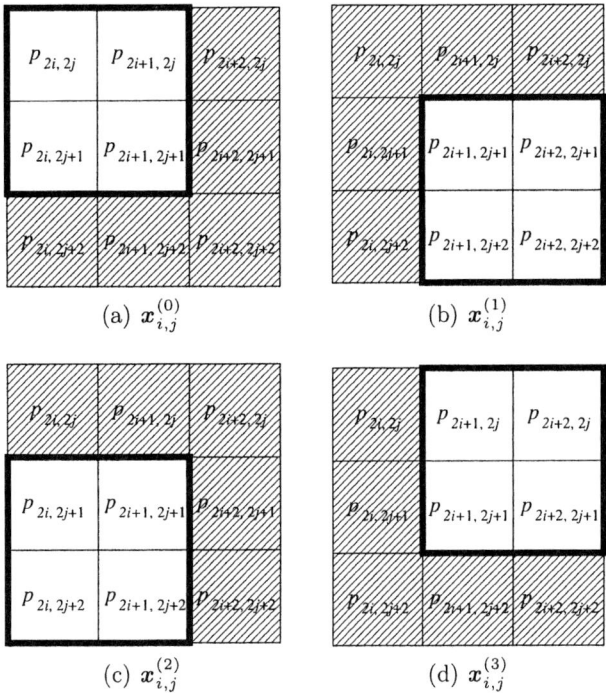

Fig. 1. The structure of $x_{i,j}^{(c)}$

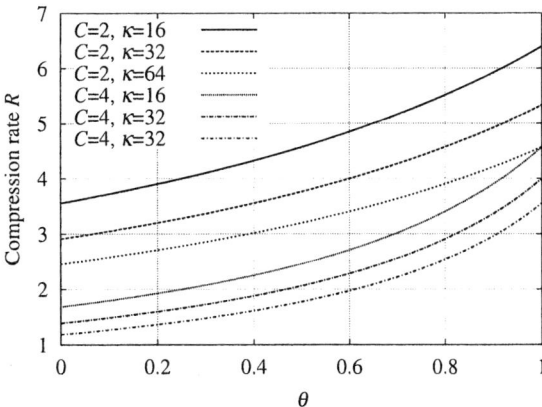

Fig. 2. The compression rate versus a parameter θ ($N = 512$, $G = 8$)

can truncate the large number of the indexes. If the ratio of indexes satisfying $l_i^{(c_1)} = l_i^{(c_2)}$ is θ, the compressed data size is as follows:

$$C \cdot G + (C-1)\frac{N^2}{4} + ((C-1)(1-\theta) + 1)\lceil \log_2 \kappa \rceil \frac{N^2}{4} \quad \text{bits.} \tag{9}$$

(a) Lenna

(b) Peppers

(c) Milkdrop

Fig. 3. Test images

The second term corresponds to one-bit flags, which indicate each index satisfies $l_i^{(c_1)} = l_i^{(c_2)}$ or not. If all the indexes satisfy $l_i^{(c_1)} = l_i^{(c_2)}$, that is $\theta = 1$, the data size is almost the same as the single VQ with codebook size $\kappa + 2^{C-1}$. Fig.2 shows the compression rate versus the parameter θ. We can see that the compression rate increases quadratically with θ.

We perform numerical simulations on MVQ based image compression. In the simulation, we use two test images "Lenna" and "Peppers" shown in Fig.3. Fig.4 shows the simulation results on MSE. In the result, MSE decreases with the number of VQs C, and converges a value, which decreases with the codebook size κ. The maximum decrement of MSE occurs between $C = 1$ and $C = 2$, and the decrement over $C = 2$ is small. For any κ, the MVQ method with $C = 2$ achieves nearly twice better quality than the single VQ one.

Next, we examine the ratio θ of indexes satisfying $l_i^{(c_1)} = l_i^{(c_2)}$. Note that the ratio θ depends on the used re-labeling algorithm. The algorithm used in the simulation is a greedy one as follows:

Step 1: Let $\mathcal{L} = \{(i,j) | i,j \in \{0, \cdots, \kappa - 1\}\}$. Count the appearance frequency $h_{i,j}$ of each index pair $(i,j) \in \mathcal{L}$ in $\{(l_k^{(c_1)}, l_k^{(c_2)}) | k \in \{0, \cdots, N^2/4 - 1\}\}$.
Step 2: Select the highest frequency pair $(i_{\max}, j_{\max}) \in \mathcal{L}$ such that $h_{i_{\max}, j_{\max}} = \max_{(i,j) \in \mathcal{L}} h_{i,j}$.

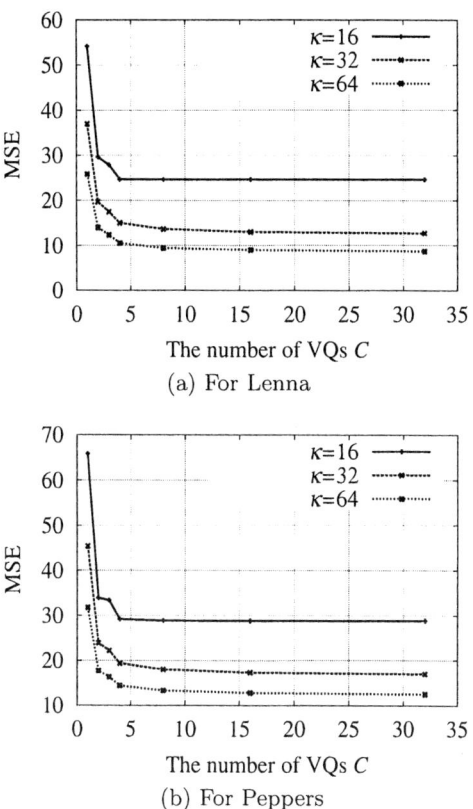

Fig. 4. MSE versus the number of VQs C

Step 3: For each $k \in \{0, \cdots, N^2/4 - 1\}$, re-label $l_k^{(c_2)}$ as follows:

$$l_k^{(c_2)} \leftarrow \begin{cases} i_{\max} & \text{if } l_k^{(c_2)} = j_{\max} \\ j_{\max} & \text{if } l_k^{(c_2)} = i_{\max}. \end{cases} \quad (10)$$

Step 4: $\mathcal{L} \leftarrow \mathcal{L} \setminus \{(i_{\max}, j), (i, j_{\max}) | i, j \in \{0, \cdots, \kappa - 1\}\}$. If $\mathcal{L} = \emptyset$, terminate the algorithm. Otherwise, go to Step 2.

Table 1 shows the simulation result for three test images shown in Fig.3. The ratio θ decreases with the codebook size κ. However, when $\kappa = 16$, nearly one-quarter of the indexes can be truncated.

From the above simulation results, the MVQ method can be considered to be effective when $\kappa = 16$ and $C = 2$. In Fig. 5, MVQ for these parameters is compared with a conventional method using a single VQ. The MVQ method is performed for $\kappa = 16, 32, 64$ and 128. The single VQ method is performed for $\kappa = 16, 32, 64, 128, 256, 512, 1024$ and 2048. For single VQ, although the compression rate gradually increases with κ, its MSE improvement becomes

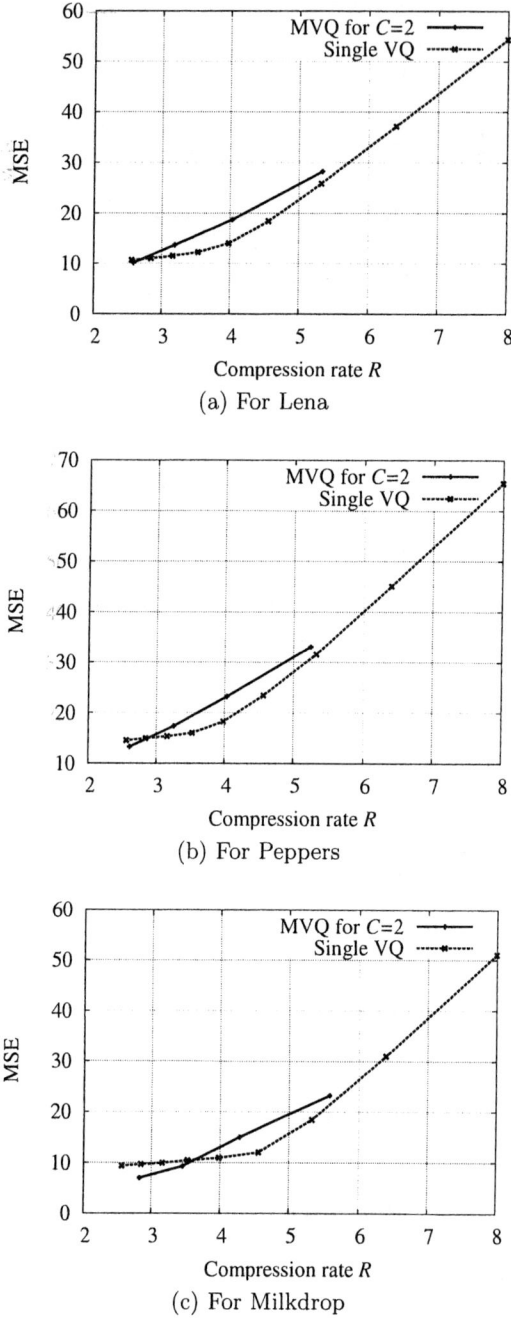

Fig. 5. Compression rate versus MSE

Table 1. The ratio θ of indexes satisfying $l_i^{(c_1)} = l_i^{(c_2)}$ after re-labeling

Image	$\kappa = 16$	$\kappa = 32$	$\kappa = 64$
Lenna	0.74	0.65	0.49
Peppers	0.78	0.61	0.55
Milkdrop	0.82	0.71	0.63

rapidly low with κ. As a result, the MVQ method outperforms the single VQ one when the compress rate is smaller than some values. According to Fig.5, two curves for Lenna, Peppers and Milkdrop are intersecting at $R \approx 2.6$, 2.8 and 3.6, respectively. Therefore, the best result is obtained for Milkdrop. MVQ is considered to be effective against flat images such as Milkdrop.

5 Conclusion

In this paper, we consider a multiple-VQ (MVQ) method that generates multiple independent codebooks to compress an image. We present an effective coding scheme to overcome the in-efficiency of the MVQ method. Our simulation results show that the MVQ method outperforms a conventional single-VQ method when the compression rate is smaller than some values.

We think that the MVQ method can produce a richer diversity of pixels in restored images than the single VQ method. However, in order to make MVQ effective for any compression rate, some more effective coding scheme is needed. This issue is one of our future works.

Acknowledgment

This work is partially supported by the Telecommunications Advancement Foundation in Japan.

References

1. Linde, Y., Buzo, A, Gray, R.M.: An Algorithm for Vector Quantizer Design. IEEE Trans. Commun., **28** (1980) 84–95
2. Gersho, A., Gray, R.M., Vector Quantization and Signal Compression. Kluwer, Boston (1992)
3. Martinetz, T.M., Berkovich, S.G., Schulten, K.J.: Neural Gas Network for Vector Quantization and Its Application to Time-Series Prediction, IEEE Trans. Neural Networks, **4** (1993) 558–569
4. Kohonen, T., Self-Organizing Maps, Springer-Verlag, Berlin Heidelberg New York (1997).
5. Jiang, J.: Image Compression with Neural Networks – A Survey, Signal Processing: Image Comm. **14** (1999) 737–760
6. Dietterich, T.G.: Ensemble Learning, The Handbook of Brain Theory and Neural Networks, 2nd Ed, MIT Press, (2002) 405–408

7. Amerijckx, C., Legat, J.-D., Verleysen, M.: Image Compression Using Self-Organizing Maps, Systems Analysis Modelling Simulation, **43** (2003) 1529–1543
8. Momose, S., Sano, K., Nakamura, T.: Fast Codebook Design for Vector Quantization on Partitioned Space, Procs. of the 2nd International Conference on Information Technology for Application, (2004) 205–210
9. Shigei, N., Miyajima, H., Maeda, M.: Numerical Evaluation of Incremental Vector Quantization Using Stochastic Relaxation, IEICE Trans. Fundamentals, **E87-A** (2004) 2364–2371

Segmentation of SAR Image Using Mixture Multiscale ARMA Network

Haixia Xu[1], Zheng Tian[1,2], and Fan Meng[1]

[1] Department of Applied Mathematics, Northwestern Polytechnical University,
Xi'an 710072, P.R. China
[2] Laboratory of Remote Sensing Information Sciences,
Institute of Remote Sensing Application Chinese Academy of Sciences,
Beijing 100080, P.R. China
xuhaixia_xhx@163.com

Abstract. A mixture multiscale autoregressive moving average (ARMA) network is proposed for unsupervised segmentation of synthetic aperture radar (SAR) image. The network combines the multiscale analysis (MA) method and the feedforward artificial neural network (FANN), thus maintains some of the characteristics of the MA method and the FANN respectively. A corresponding learning algorithm is derived based on the Akaike's information criterion (AIC) and genetic algorithm (GA). Experimental results on SAR images are shown to validate the presented network and learning algorithm.

1 Introduction

The presence of speckle on SAR images not only reduces the interpreter's ability to resolve fine detail, but also makes automatic segmentation of such images difficult, either by gray levels or texture. The conventional prerequisite of SAR image is despeckling. However, the side effect of despeckling is that much of detail information is lost. In order to fully exploit the variations in speckle pattern as image resolution is varied from course to fine, we employ a class of mixture multiscale ARMA model evolving on quadtree. The model provides a powerful semi-parametric framework for describing random fields that evolve in scale. Given parameterized forms for the component densities, the most common technique for developing mixture model is the expectation-maximisation (EM) algorithm [1], so we can use EM algorithm to estimate parameters of mixture multiscale ARMA model and then segment SAR image via Bayesian decision rule. However, the EM algorithm estimates the maximum likelihood (ML) parameters, so may lead to over-fitting problem. Furthermore, due to its use of deterministic gradient descent and batch operation nature, the EM algorithm has a high possibility of being trapped in local optima and is also slow to the convergence [2]. In literature, there have been several works to use FANN as powerful approximator of function in the field of engineering, such as [3]. One key property of FANN is their universal approximation capability: FANN can approximate any reasonable mapping up to any desired accuracy if a sufficient number of neurons are available in the network [4]. The approach has shown advantages over the EM algorithm.

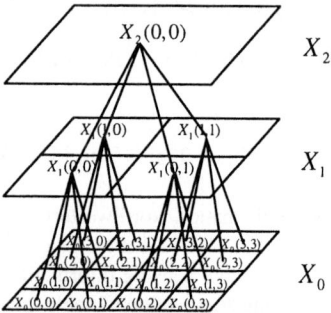

Fig. 1. Sequence of three SAR images mapped onto a quadtree

In this work, we combine the FANN with the mixture multiscale ARMA model of SAR image. The resulting network, namely mixture multiscale ARMA network, not only has advantages of FANN, but also utilizes information of multiscale image. In addition, a learning algorithm is derived based on the AIC and GA.

The organization of this paper is as follows. Upon briefly introducing the quadtree representation of SAR image [5] and the associated mixture multiscale ARMA model, we describe the structure of the mixture multiscale ARMA network and its learning algorithm. Experimental results are then presented in section 4 with conclusions followed in section 5.

2 Mixture Multiscale ARMA Model of SAR Image

The starting point for mixture multiscale ARMA model development is a multiscale sequence X_L, X_{L-1}, ..., X_0 of SAR image, where X_L and X_0 correspond to the coarsest and finest resolution images, respectively. The resolution varies dyadically between images at successive scales. Accordingly, each pixel in image X_m corresponds to four "child" pixels in image X_{m-1}. This indicates that quadtree is natural for the mapping. Each node s on the tree is associated with one of the pixels. As an example, Fig.1 illustrates a multiscale sequence of three SAR images, together with the quadtree mapping. Here the finest-scale SAR image is mapped to the finest level of the tree, and each coarse scale representation is mapped to successively higher levels. We use the notations $X(s)$ and $X(s\bar{\gamma})$ to indicate the pixels mapped to node s and its father.

For SAR image, we define the mixture multiscale ARMA model as

$$f(X(s)\mid \Theta, \Gamma_s) = \sum_{k=1}^{K} \pi_k \varphi\left(\frac{\mu_k(s)}{\sigma_k}\right), \tag{1}$$

where $\Theta = (\pi_1,...,\pi_K, \theta)$, $\theta = (\theta_1,...,\theta_K)$, $\theta_k = (a_{k,0},...,a_{k,p}, b_{k,0},...,b_{k,q}, \sigma_k)$, $\mu_k(s) = X(s) - a_{k,1}X(s\bar{\gamma}) - \cdots - a_{k,p}X(s\bar{\gamma}^p) - b_{k,1}W(s\bar{\gamma}) - \cdots - b_{k,q}W(s\bar{\gamma}^q)$ and $\pi_k > 0$, $\sum_{k=1}^{K}\pi_k = 1$, f is the probability density function. K is the number of classes,

$W(s\bar{\gamma}^i)(i=1,\ldots,q)$ are errors for using $X(s\bar{\gamma}^i)(i=1,\ldots,q)$ to predict $X(s)$, Γ_s is the set of $X(s\bar{\gamma}),\ldots,X(s\bar{\gamma}^p),W(s\bar{\gamma}),\ldots,W(s\bar{\gamma}^q)$, and $\varphi(\cdot)$ be the probability density function of a standard normal distribution.

3 Mixture Multiscale ARMA Network

3.1 Structure of Mixture Multiscale ARMA Network

Based on the mixture multiscale ARMA model (1), the structure of the mixture multiscale ARMA network can be illustrated as in Fig. 2. During the training, SAR image sequence Γ_s is used as the input of the network. The parameters θ_k in hidden layer are the learning weights. The output of a hidden neuron is the conditional density of that component in the mixture. The network output sums the responses of these hidden neurons weighted by the prior probabilities or mixing parameters π_k, which are also the learning weights.

3.2 Learning Algorithm

Suppose that the true density function is $f(x)$, which belongs to a family of distribution $g(x|\beta)$, where $\beta=(\beta_1,\beta_2,\cdots,\beta_l)$ is parameter vector and $f(x)=g(x|\beta^o)$. The Kullbac-Leibler information metric [6] measures the divergence between $g(x|\beta)$ and $f(x)$, and is defined as

$$I(f(\cdot);g(\cdot|\beta)) = -\int f(x)\log\frac{g(x|\beta)}{f(x)}dx. \qquad (2)$$

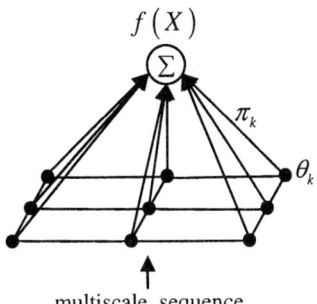

Fig. 2. Structure of mixture multiscale ARMA network

Since the convexity of logarithmic function, $I(f(\cdot);g(\cdot|\beta))\geq 0$, and $I(f(\cdot);g(\cdot|\beta))|_{\beta=\beta^o}=0$. AIC is a powerful method for identification of model in time series analysis, which is derived based on Kullbac-Leibler information metric.

$$\text{AIC} = -2\log\left(\hat{\beta}\right) + 2N, \tag{3}$$

where N is the number of the independent parameters.

When the estimated $\hat{\beta}$ is ML estimation of model, density is modeled as a mixture multiscale ARMA model, i.e., a function of various sub-densities and their parameters. One can seek the optimal estimate of these parameters by minimizing the value of AIC.

As the true SAR image data density is unknown, GA algorithm can be used for stochastic searching. GA is optimization techniques based on the principles of natural evolution, and has been theoretically and empirically demonstrated to provide robust search capabilities in complex spaces, thus offering a valid solution strategy to problems requiring efficient and effective searching [7]. In this study, for the optimization of the mixture multiscale ARMA model, GA uses the serial method of binary type, roulette-wheel used in the selection process, one-point crossover in the crossover operation, and a binary inversion operation in the mutation operator.

4 Experimental Results

To demonstrate the proposed algorithm for SAR image segmentation, we apply it to two SAR images in Fig. 3(a) and (d). From these images, we generate above-mentioned quadtree representation and use 2 order model. Because experiments show that by increasing both the autoregressive order and moving average order to 2, we can achieve a lower probability of misclassification and a good trade-off between

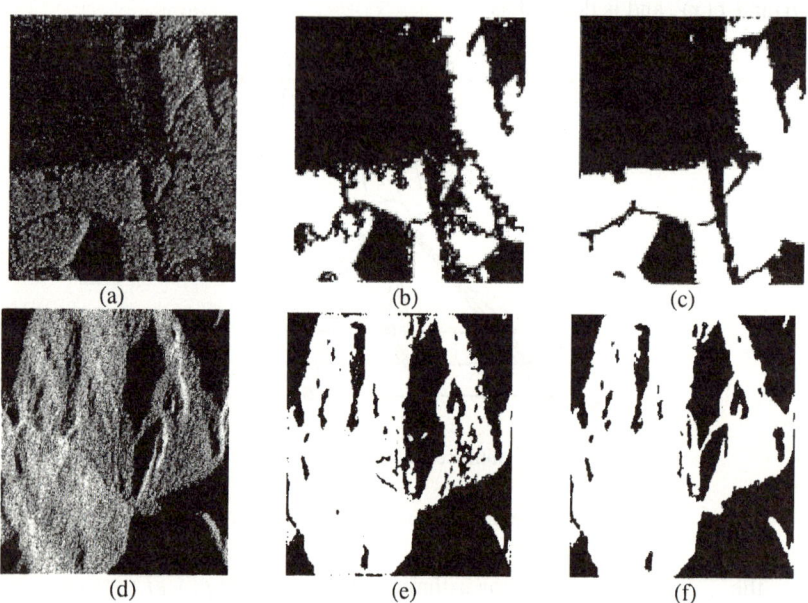

Fig. 3. Results of segmentation: (a) and (d) Original SAR image, (b) and (e) Segmented images based on EM algorithm, (c) and (f) Segmented images based on mixture multiscale ARMA network

modeling accuracy and computational efficiency. The initial values of parameter $a_{ki}, i=1,\cdots,p$, $b_{kj}, i=1,\cdots,q$, the initial weights $\pi_k, k=1,\cdots,K$ and the initial variance $\sigma_k, k=1,\cdots,K$ can be set to small random values, $1/K$ and large value, respectively. In order to improve the efficiency of searching, we take the ML estimation of Θ as the initial value of weighs of the network. When the total 300 iterations are reached, each $X(s)$ is classified into the class k if

$$k(X(s)) = arg\ \{\max_{1\leq j\leq K}[\pi_j \varphi(\mu_j(s)/\sigma_j)]\}\ .\qquad(4)$$

Experimental results of applying mixture multiscale ARMA network to SAR images are given in Fig. 3(c) and (f), as well as results from EM algorithm for comparison. From visual quality, the results of mixture multiscale ARMA network better than the results of EM algorithm.

5 Conclusions

A mixture multiscale ARMA network for unsupervised segmentation of SAR image is proposed. This network not only fully exploits the variations in speckle pattern as the resolution of image changing, but also maintains some advantages of FANN. From experiments it has proved that the presented network is insensitive to speckle and can get better segmented image compared with EM algorithm.

Acknowledgement. This work is supported in part by the National Natural Science Foundation of China (60375003), the Aeronautics and Astronautics Basal Science Foundation of China (03I53059).

References

1. McLachlan, G., Krishnan, T.: The EM Algorithm and Extension. Wiley, New York (1996)
2. Redener, R.A., Walker, H.F.: Mixture densities, maximum likelihood and the EM algorithm. SIAM Rev., Vol. 26. (1984) 195-239
3. Majewski, K.: Heavy traffic approximations of large deviations of feedforward queueing networks. Queueing Systems, Vol. 28. (1998) 125-155
4. Hecht, R.: Kolmogorov's mapping neural network existence theorem. In Proceedings of International Conference on Neural Networks, ICNN (1989) 11-14
5. Irving, W.W., Novak, L.M., Willsky, A.: A Multiresolution Approach to Discrimination in SAR Imagery. IEEE Trans. Aerosp. Electron. Syst., Vol. 33. (1997) 1157-1169
6. Kullback, S., Leibler, R.A.: On information and sufficiency. Ann. Math. Statist., Vol. 22. (1951) 79-86
7. Michalewicz, Z.: Genetic Algorithms + Data Structures = Evolution Programs. 3rd edn. Springer-Verlag, Berlin Heidelberg New York (1996)

Brain Activity Analysis of Rat Based on Electroencephalogram Complexity Under General Anesthesia

Jin Xu[1], Chongxun Zheng[1], Xueliang Liu[1], Xiaomei Pei[1], and Guixia Jing[2]

[1] The Key Laboratory of Biomedical Information Engineering of Ministry of Education, Xi'an Jiaotong University, Xi'an 710049, China
{xujin@mail.xjtu.edu.cn}
[2] The First Hospital of Xi'an Jiaotong University, Xi'an 710061, China

Abstract. In order to estimate the change of brain activity under general anesthesia, the Lempel-Ziv complexity (C(n)) of electroencephalogram (EEG) of SD rat was studied in this paper. The C(n)s of EEG from different channels under different depth of anesthesia were measured and the relationship between C(n) and the depth of anesthesia (DOA) was analyzed. The result shows that the C(n) variations of EEG of different channels with DOA are similar, and predicates that the activities of every part of brain change similarly. Therefore, it is enough to detect DOA by only one channel EEG. The C(n) of EEG will decrease while the depth of anesthesia increasing and vice versa. Two thresholds of C(n) are defined, one distinguishes awake and light anesthesia state, the other distinguishes light and deep anesthesia state. Besides EEG complexity analysis, the complexity variations of four rhythms of EEG (delta, theta, alpha and beta) are also analyzed. The study shows the dynamic change of complexity of delta rhythm leads to that of EEG, so the delta rhythm is the dominant rhythm during anesthesia for rat.

1 Introduction

Anesthesia can make patients losing feeling and consciousness temporarily, and insure the surgical operations to be carried out safely. For a principal action of general anesthetic agents takes place in the brain, it would induce EEG change, and it is reasonable to monitor the brain activity and estimate the depth of anesthesia (DOA) by EEG [1]. EEG signal was used to detect the DOA since 1940[2]. Up to now, numerous efforts have been made to develop and test various EEG-derived parameters in the time-domain, frequency-domain, bispectral-domain et al. [3-4], but none of these methods has been shown to be sufficiently reliable for general use for assessing DOA accurately.

Complexity analysis is a kind of non-linear dynamic methods, which developed quickly in recent years, it is suitable for analyzing nonlinear, non-steady stochastic signals, such as EEG signals which has strong nonlinear and dynamical properties. The idea of complexity was introduced firstly by Kolmogorov in 1965[5]. Abraham Lempel and Jacob Ziv give a definition for complexity in 1976[6], later Kaspar and Schuster presented a program to compute complexity value based on their theory [7]. This method for computing complexity is called Kc (Kolmogorov Complexity), and C(n) is a parameter to quantify complexity. Complexity can show some characteristics of brain activity change induced by physiological, pathological or medicament action. N. Radhakrishnan used C(n) as measure to quantify the regularity of epiletic EEG[8], Xu-Sheng Zhang and Rob J.Roy used C(n) to monitor DOA during general anesthesia[9-10].

In this study, we use C(n) to quantify EEG activity change under different DOA in order to know what influence will be brought to brain by anesthetic during anesthesia.

2   Algorithm of Lempel-Ziv Complexity

Lempel-Ziv complexity analysis is based on a coarse-graining of the measurements, i.e., the signal to be analyzed is transformed into a sequence whose elements are only a few symbols. EEG signal can often be transformed into a binary sequence (0 or 1) by threshold method, and the average value of this EEG signal series can be used as the threshold. If the EEG signal value at some points are larger than the threshold, these points can be transformed to "1", otherwise they are "0". So a new binary sequence is produced, then compute the complexity of the binary sequence. The algorithm is described briefly as bellows [7]:

Let p be a binary sequence: $p = s_1, s_2, s_3, \cdots, s_n$, including n characters. S and Q are defined as subsequence of p respectively, SQ is the concatenation of S and Q, and $SQ\pi$ is derived from SQ after its last character is deleted. Then we judge if Q is a subsequence of p or not. If $Q \notin SQ\pi$, i.e., Q is a subsequence of p, and put a symbol "*" to the end of each different subsequence. If $Q \in SQ\pi$, i.e., Q is not a subsequence of p, S needn't change and now renew Q. Finally the number of different subsequence of p will be got by repeating above procedures from the first character of sequence p to the last one, and this is the complexity counter $c(n)$. The complexity reflects the rate of new patterns arising with the increase of string length n. For example, suppose $p = 01001$,

1) The first character is always a new one, so the first subsequence of p can be showed as 0*.
2) Now, $S = 0$, $Q = 1$, $SQ = 01$, $SQ\pi = 0$, $Q \notin SQ\pi$, Q is the second subsequence, i.e., 0*1*.
3) Renew S, $S = 01$, $Q = 0$, $SQ = 010$, $SQ\pi = 01$, $Q \in SQ\pi$, Q is not a new subsequence, i.e., 0*1*0.
4) S needn't change and now renew Q, $S = 01$, $Q = 00$, $SQ = 0100$, $SQ\pi = 010$, $Q \notin SQ\pi$, Q is the third subsequence, i.e., 0*1*00*.
5) Renew S again, $S = 0100$, $Q = 1$, $SQ = 01001$, $SQ\pi = 0100$, $Q \in SQ\pi$, Q is not a new subsequence, i.e., 0*1*00*1.

By this process, the sequence p is scanned from the first character to the last one, there are four subsequences of sequence p divided by symbol "*", so $c(n) = 4$. In generally, the complexity $c(n)$ of the string tends to the same limit:

$$\lim_{n \to \infty} c(n) = b(n) = \frac{n}{\log_a(n)} \quad (1)$$

Compared with $b(n)$, the normalized complexity measure C(n) is as fellow:

$$C(n) = \frac{c(n)}{b(n)} \quad (2)$$

For a 0-1 sequence, $\alpha = 2$, therefore $b(n) = \frac{n}{\log_2(n)}$.

The degree of complexity can be quantified by C(n). C(n) is usually less than 1, it will tend to be 1 for a full random string and 0 for periodic series.

3 Animal Experiment and EEG Signal Collection

SD rat was chosen as experimental animal, thirty-five anesthesia experiments were done according to the protocol approved by the Ministry of Health People's Republic of China. Rats ranged in weight from 230g to 328g were injected pentobarbital Na (50mg/kg) with intraperitoneal injection (IP) to effect with 30mg/ml diluted only once without maintenance, then EEG signals of rats were recorded during anesthesia. In addition, Electrocardiogram (ECG), respiratory signal and body temperature of SD rats were also recorded at same time. As the level and quality of respiration, heart rate are associated with the DOA, they could be used as the reference indexes to detect the DOA. In our study, the response time of radiate heat evoked tail flick reflex was used to examine the DOA. Body temperature was keeping at about 39°C with an external heat source to prevent the hypothermia. In order to avoid the influence of electromyogram (EMG) artifact, the silver electrodes were placed on the cranium of rat directly. There were four electrodes distributed in the area between coronary suture and lambdoid suture of bone cap of rat, the electrodes were named as R_1, R_2, L_1 and L_2 respectively (see Fig.1). R_1, L_1 and L_2 were used as active electrodes, R_2 was used as reference electrode, the impedance of each electrode was less than 5 kΩ. Three channels were formed as R_1-R_2, L_1-R_2 and L_2-R_2.

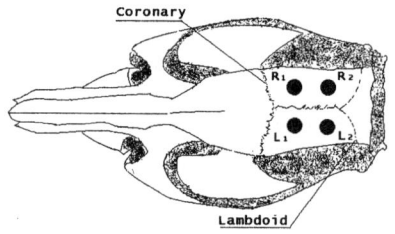

Fig. 1. Position of electrodes

Three channel EEGs were recorded by using Ag electrodes, and the single ECG signal was recorded by needle electrodes. The signals recorded machine is a 32 channels Easy II system made by CADWELL Company. The EEG data were filtered with a high-pass filter at 0.16 Hz and a low-pass filter at 70 Hz, a 50 notch filter was also employed. The sampling rate was 200 Hz, and the A/D conversion resolution was 12-bits.

4 EEG Complexity Analysis

4.1 Reference Index for Detecting DOA

The reaction time of radiate heat evoked tail flick reflex of SD rat was recorded synchronously during anesthesia every 10 minutes, and it can be used as the reference index to detect level of anesthesia. In awake, the reaction time (RT) of radiate heat evoked tail flick reflex is less than 3 seconds. In the deep anesthesia, the RT is more than 8 seconds. When the RT is in the range of 3 to 8 seconds, the rat was regarded in light anesthesia. According to this classification standard, the whole anesthesia process is divided in three states, i.e., awake, light anesthesia, deep anesthesia.

4.2 Three Channels EEG Complexity Analysis

In order to get stable value of C(n), the window length was set as 4000 points, the step length was set as 200 points (the sampling rate is 200 Hz). C(n)s of three EEG channels were computed respectively under different DOA. The result shows that the EEG

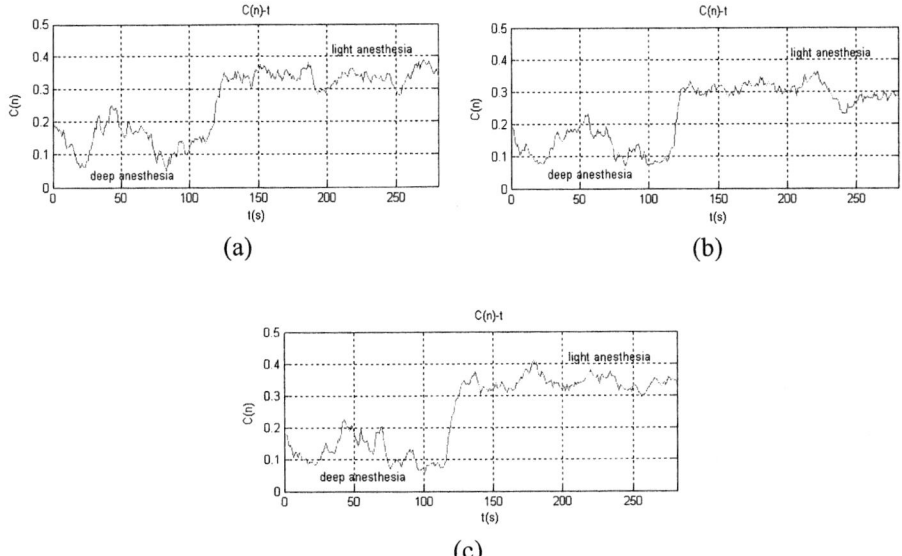

Fig. 2. C(n) changes of different channels when rat was from deep to light anesthesia (a) L_1-R_2 channel (b) L_2-R_2 channel (c) R_1-R_2 channel.

complexity of different channels changing with DOA are similar, Fig.2 shows the C(n) variations of different channels when rat was from deep to light anesthesia.

4.3 EEG Complexity Analysis Under Different DOA

For the EEG complexity of different channels changing with DOA are similar, so it is enough to select one channel EEG to monitor brain activity change by EEG complexity analysis. Now C(n) of R_1-R_2 channel was computed under different DOA (see Fig.3). From Fig.3 we can see that the C(n) decreases while the DOA increases and vice versa. The DOA of whole anesthesia process can be divided in three states according to above classification standard. In awake, C(n) is in range of 0.4-0.5; in deep anesthesia, C(n) is

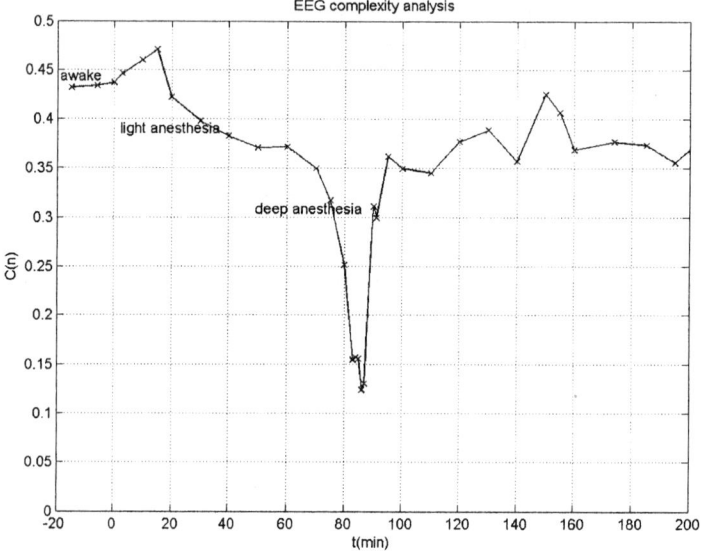

Fig. 3. C(n) change of EEG under different DOA

Table 1. Comparison of C(n), heart rate and the reaction time of radiate heat evoked tail flick reflex under different DOA

	In awake	Light anesthesia	Deep anesthesia
C(n)	0.4-0.5	0.3-0.4	< 0.3
heart rate (bpm)	about 480	360-420	< 360
reaction time of tail flick reflex induced radiate heat (s)	< 3	3-8	> 8

smaller than 0.3; in light anesthesia, C(n) is from 0.3 to 0.4. Therefore, it can be seen that C(n) works very well in tracking a rat's depth and trend of anesthesia.

In Fig.3, the point 0 on time axis stands for the time of injecting anesthetic, the C(n) value increases lasting a short period after injection. This may be a response caused by the injection stimulation, the stimulation made nerve center of rat to produce excitation for a short time, so randomicity of EEG increased.

C(n), the heart rate and the reaction time of radiate heat evoked tail flick reflex of SD rat in these three states are showed in table1.

4.4 Statistical Graph

32 EEG data segments were selected respectively when rat was in awake and deep anesthesia. C(n) of each data segment was computed. Then statistical graphs were made to show the distribution of C(n) under these two different states. The statistical results show that the C(n) is from 0.4 to 0.5 when SD rat is in awake (see Fig.4(a)) and from 0.1 to 0.3 mainly when rat is in deep anesthesia (see Fig. 4(b)). The C(n) in awake is larger than that in deep anesthesia.

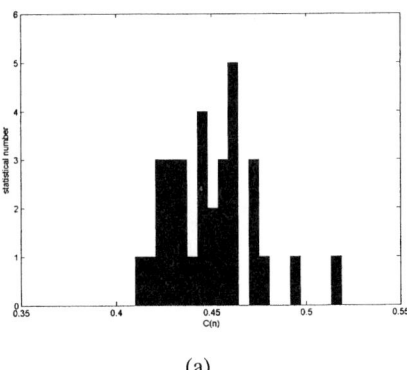
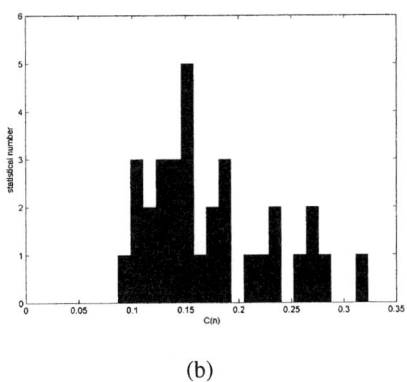

(a)   (b)

Fig. 4. C(n) distributions of 32 EEG data segments (a) when rat is in awake, (b) when rat is in deep anesthesia state.

4.5 Complexity Analysis on Delta, Theta, Alpha and Beta Rhythms of EEG

There are four familiar rhythms in EEG signal, they are delta, theta, alpha and beta pattern. EEG of SD rat recorded in anesthesia experiments (0.16-70Hz) can be decomposed into these four rhythms by wavelet packet decomposition and reconstruction. As the transformation result, four components are got, they are delta (0.16-3.9Hz), theta (3.9-7.8Hz), alpha (7.8-12.5Hz) and beta rhythm (12.5-31.25Hz). Fig.5 shows the transformation results for two segments of EEG of SD rat in awake and deep anesthesia state respectively. Then complexity analysis on EEG and four decomposed components are studied under different DOA. (see Fig.6).

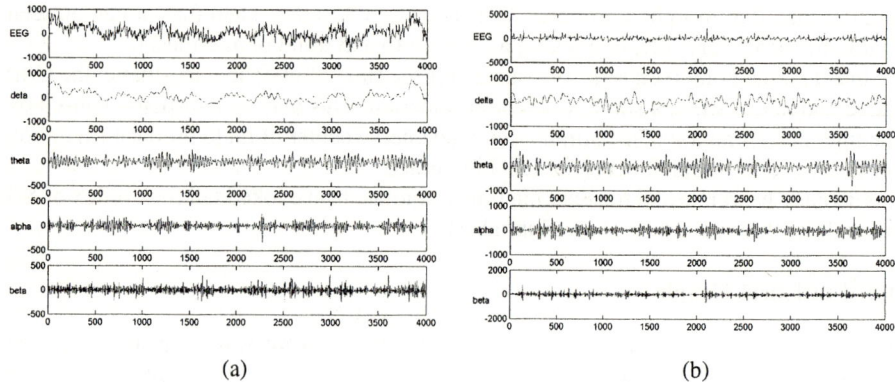

Fig. 5. EEG and four components (delta, theta, alpha, beta) (a) recorded in awake (b) recorded in deep anesthesia.

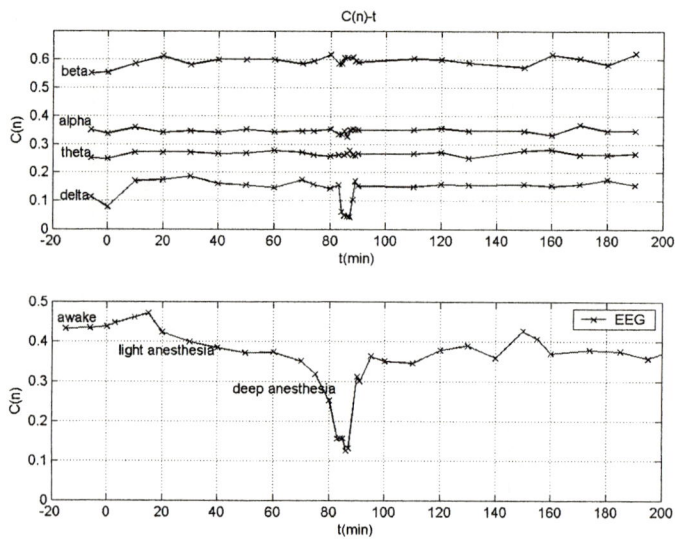

Fig. 6. C(n) change of EEG and four components under different DOA, the point 0 on time axis stands for the time of injecting anesthetic.

From Fig.6, firstly we can see that during anesthesia, C(n) of EEG changes from 0.1 to 0.5, C(n) of delta rhythm shows obvious change, it ranges from 0 to 0.2. C(n) of the other three components(theta, alpha, beta) have few change. Secondly, the C(n) value of four rhythms all increased lasting a short period after injection, which is as same as C(n) of EEG. This phenomenon illuminates that the injection behavior acted as stimulation made all neurons of brain excited, the complex of brain activity increases, and the randomicity of four EEG components increases. Thirdly, for delta component,

C(n) in awake is smaller than it in light anesthesia, which is opposite to that of the EEG. It because that delta component appears seldom in awake, but when rat is getting into light anesthesia state, delta component begins to increase and become dominant gradually, therefore, its complexity rise. C(n) of delta decreases when rat is from light to deep anesthesia, the minimum value is far below 0.1 which is smaller than that in awake. C(n) variation of delta component is similar to that of EEG as rat from light to deep anesthesia or from deep to light anesthesia.

5 Conclusions and Discussions

When rat is in awake, its neurons are excited. At this time the desynchronized EEG occurs, which has high frequency low voltages (see Fig.7(a)). EEG desynchronized is induced by information input which implies a lesser coordination between ongoing processes and more independent neural processes contribute to complex brain dynamics, so the complexity (C(n)) of desynchronized EEG is higher. When rat is in anesthesia state, the synchronized EEG occurs, which has high voltages low frequency (see Fig.7(b)). For the neurons are suppressed, they can be considered to be in an idling state, EEG synchronization implies a more coordination between ongoing processes, so the complexity of synchronized EEG is lower.

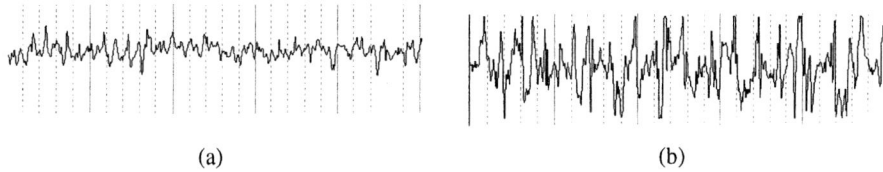

(a)   (b)

Fig.7. EEG patterns (a) desynchronized EEG was recorded in awake, (b) synchronized EEG was recorded during anesthesia.

By studying the complexity change of EEG during anesthesia process, the complexity of different channels changing with DOA are similar (see Fig.2), so we can know that the physiological change in every part of brain of rat are similar during anesthesia, such as the ability of neurons processing information and degree of excitation or suppression of neurons. Furthermore, it is sufficient to monitor DOA with one channel EEG signal analysis for rat, which verifies the results had been got by previous studies [11-12].

It can be seen, EEG complexity (C(n)) increases while decreasing the DOA and decreases while increasing the DOA (see Fig.3), C(n) reflects the dynamic change of brain activity, and do very well in tracking rat's depth and trend of anesthesia. Two thresholds of C(n) are defined according to reference index (the reaction time of radiate heat evoked tail flick reflex) and statistical analysis. One threshold is 0.3 to distinguish light and deep anesthesia, the other is 0.4 to distinguish awake and light anesthesia. In other words, as the C(n) is smaller than 0.3, the rat is in deep anesthesia; as the C(n) is larger than 0.4, the rat is in awake; as the C(n) ranges from 0.3 to 0.4, the rat would be in light anesthesia.

The anesthetic used in our animal experiments is pentobarbital Na, it belongs to short effective barbiturates, the anesthesia time (keep animal in deep anesthesia) is about 15-60 minutes and the sleep time (keep animal in light anesthesia) is about 120-240 minutes for SD rat with intraperitoneal injection (IP). From Fig.3, we can see that the time lasts 20 minutes when $C(n)$ is smaller than 0.3, the period is about 160 minutes when $C(n)$ is from 0.3 to 0.4, in other words, there is about 20 minutes as rat is in deep anesthesia and 160 minutes as rat is in light awake. These results verify the anesthetic efficacy of pentobarbital Na, so these two thresholds are reliable. In the reference [9-10], Xu-Sheng Zhang tried to use complexity as a measure of depth of anesthesia for patients, and give a threshold to distinguish between awake and asleep state. Furthermore, computation algorithm of $C(n)$ is simple, and computation speed is fast, therefore EEG complexity maybe a useful index for real-time monitoring of the depth of anesthesia in clinical practice.

By decomposing EEG into four rhythms (delta, theta, alpha and beta) and studying their complexity changes under different DOA, we can see that the complexity change of delta rhythm is obvious with DOA and the others (theta, alpha and beta rhythm) are not. As it shown in Fig.6, when rat is from light anesthesia to deep, the delta complexity change is as same as EEG's, $C(n)$ of delta rhythm dynamic change leads to the change of EEG mainly. It means that the delta rhythm is the dominant rhythm as rat in anesthesia state.

In reference [13], Feng Zhouyan et al. studied the dynamic change of power spectrum of rat EEG under different DOA, they found the center of gravity of power spectrum shifted to lower frequency as DOA increasing, and the change of delta rhythm leads change of the total power spectrum. Our study provides evidence to confirm the viewpoint proposed by Feng Zhouyan. As well known, the dominant rhythm in the human is different from the lower mammals [14], so the results gained from SD rat is not always suitable for the human.

In this paper, the study shows the complex levels change of brain activity of SD rat under general anesthesia based on complexity analysis of single channel EEG data. Due to different anesthetic agent may produce different effects on the EEG patterns, so more research works are needed to do to further confirm the preliminary results obtained in this study by using different anesthetic agents for different animals.

Acknowledgments

This work is supported by National Natural Science Foundation of China under Grant 30400101 and 30170257.

References

1. I.J.Rampil: A primer for EEG signal processing in anesthesia. Anesthesiology. Vol.89. (1998) 980-1002
2. Rubin MA, Freeman H: Brain potential changes in man during cyclopropane anaesthesia. J Neurophysiol. Vol.3. (1940) 33-42
3. C.E.Thomsen,K. N.Christensen, A.Rosenflack: Computerized monitoring of depth of anesthesia with isoflurane. Br. J. Anesthesia. Vol.63. (1989) 36-43

4. J.C.Drummond, C.A.Brann, etc.: A comparison of median frequency, spectral edge frequency, a frequency band power ratio, total power and dominance shift in the determination of depth of anesthesia. Acta Anaesthesiologica Scandinavica. Vol.35. (1991) 693-699
5. A.N. Kolmogorov: Three approaches to the quantitative definition of information. Probl. Inform. Transmission. (1965) 1-7
6. A.Lempel and J.Ziv: On the Complexity of Finite Sequences. IEEE Trans on Information Theory. Vol.22. (1976) 75-81
7. F. Kaspar, H.G. Schuster: Easily calculable measure for the complexity of spatiotemporal patterns. Physical Review A. Vol.36. (1987) 842-848
8. N. Radhakrishnan, B.N. Gangadhar: Estimating regularity in epileptic seizure time-series data. IEEE Engineering in medicine and Biology. Vol.17. (1998) 89-94
9. Xu-Sheng Zhang, Rob J.Roy: EEG Complexity as a Measure of Depth of Anesthesia for Patients. IEEE Trans on Biomedical Engineering. Vol.48. (2001) 1424-1433
10. Xu-Sheng Zhang, Rob J.Roy: Derived Fuzzy Knowledge Model for Estimating the Depth of Anesthesia. IEEE Trans on Biomedical Engineering. Vol.48. (2001) 312-323
11. Xu-Sheng Zhang, Rob J.Roy: Predicting movement during anesthesia by complexity analysis of the EEG. Medical and Biological Engineering and Computing. Vol.37. (1999) 327-334
12. A. Nayak, R. J. Roy, and A. Sharma: Time-frequency spectral representation of the EEG as aid in the detection of the depth of anesthesia. Ann. Biomed. Eng.. Vol. 22. (1994) 501-513
13. FENG Zhouyan, ZHENG Xiaoxiang: The Dynamic Change of Rat EEG's Complexity and Power Spectrum under Anesthetized Depth. Chinese Journal of Biomedical Engineering. Vol.23. (2004) 87-91
14. Wolfgang Klimesch: EEG alpha and theta oscillations reflect cognitive and memory performance: a review and analysis. Brain Research Review. Vol.29. (1999) 169-195

Post-nonlinear Blind Source Separation Using Wavelet Neural Networks and Particle Swarm Optimization[*]

Ying Gao[1,2] and Shengli Xie[2]

[1] Dept. of Computer Science and Technology, Guangzhou University,
Guangzhou 510405, China
falcongao@21cn.com
[2] College of Electronic & Information Engineering,
South China University of Technology, Guangzhou, 510641, China

Abstract. Blind source separation of post-nonlinear mixtures is discussed. The demixing system of the post-nonlinear mixtures is modeled using a multi-input multi-output wavelet neural network whose parameters can be determined under the criterion of independence of its outputs. A criterion of independence based on higher order moments is used to measure the statistical dependence of the outputs of the demixing system, and the particle swarm optimization technique is utilized to minimized the criterion. Simulation results show that the proposed approach is capable of separating independent sources from their post-nonlinear mixtures.

1 Introduction

The problem of source separation has been intensively studied during the last ten years, mainly in the case of linear instantaneous mixtures, and more recently for nonlinear mixtures. In this paper, post-nonlinear blind source separation[1-4] is discussed. The demixing system of the post-nonlinear mixtures is modeled using a multi-input multi-output wavelet neural network whose parameters can be determined under the criterion of independence of its outputs. A criterion of independence based on higher order moments is used to measure the statistical dependence of the outputs of the demixing system, and the particle swarm optimization technique is utilized to minimized the criterion. The proposed approach for post-nonlinear blind source separation is characterized by high accuracy, robustness, and convergence rate. Simulation results show that the proposed approach is capable of separating independent sources from their post-nonlinear mixtures.

---

[*] The work is supported by the National Natural Science Foundation of China (60325310, 60274006), the Post Doctor Science Foundation of P.R.C. (2003034062), the Natural Science Foundation of Guangdong Province, P.R.C. (04300015) , the Natural Science Foundation of the Education Department of Guangdong Province, the Program for the Development of Science & Technology of Guangzhou, P.R.C.(2004J1-C0323) and the Program for the Development of Science & Technology of Guangzhou Colleges and Universities, P.R.C.(2055).

2 Post-nonlinear Mixtures and Wavelet Neural Networks

The post-nonlinear mixture model for blind source separation can be described as

$$\mathbf{x}(t) = \mathbf{f}(\mathbf{As}(t)) \quad (1)$$

Where A is a mixing matrix, $\mathbf{s}(t)=[s_1(t) \ ... \ s_n(t)]^T$ called the independent source vector, $\mathbf{x}(t)=[x_1(t) \ ... \ x_n(t)]^T$ called vector of observed random variables, $\mathbf{f} = [f_1(\cdot) \ ... \ f_n(\cdot)]^T$. The output of the post-nonlinear separating system can been written as

$$\mathbf{y}(t) = \mathbf{Wg}(\mathbf{x}(t)) \quad (2)$$

Where $\mathbf{g} = [g_1(\cdot) \ ... \ g_n(\cdot)]^T$.

(2) is a multi-input multi-output system, Here a wavelet neural network[5] of Fig.1 is used to approximate the unknown multi-input multi-output system.

Where $\psi(\mathbf{x})$ is an orthonormal wavelet basic function. The outputs of the wavelet neural network showed in Fig.1 can been written as

$$y_i(t) = \sum_{j=1}^{L} \theta_{i,j} \psi(b_{i1} x_1(t) + b_{i2} x_2(t) + \cdots + b_{in} x_n(t) - \tau_j) \quad i=1,2,\cdots,n \quad (3)$$

Where $b_{i,j}(i=1,\cdots,L, j=1,\cdots,n)$ are scale factors, $\tau_j (j=1,\cdots,n)$ are location factors, $\theta_{i,j}(i=1,\cdots,n, j=1,\cdots,L)$ are network weights, L is the number of wavelet neuron. **H** is set of the parameters of wavelet neural network, and it is consists of $b_{i,j}(i=1,\cdots,L, j=1,\cdots,n)$, $\tau_j(j=1,\cdots,n)$ and $\theta_{i,j}(i=1,\cdots,n, j=1,\cdots,L)$.

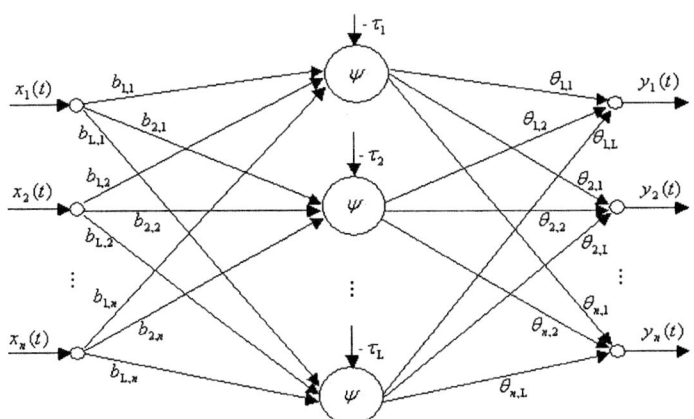

Fig. 1. Wavelet neural network model

3 Dependence Measure and Particle Swarm Optimization

It is possible to recover the source from the post-nonlinear mixture (1) using only the source statistical independence assumption[2]. In order to separate the independent sources from their post nonlinear mixtures, we expect the outputs of the separation system to be mutually statistically independent. For this purpose, we must utilize a measure of independence between random variables. Indeed, if the y_i are independent, one has[6].

$$M(h_1(y_i), h_2(y_j)) = E[h_1(y_i)h_2(y_j)] - E[h_1(y_i)]E[h_2(y_j)] = 0 \quad \forall i \neq j \quad (4)$$

Thus, we define the following cost function for post nonlinear blind sources separation.

$$J(\mathbf{H}) = \sum_{i=1}^{n}\sum_{j \neq i}^{n} [M(h_1(y_i), h_2(y_j))]^2$$

$$= \sum_{i=1}^{n}\sum_{j \neq i}^{n} [E(h_1(y_i)h_2(y_j)) - E(h_1(y_i))E(h_2(y_j))]^2 \quad (5)$$

Where $\mathbf{H}$ is set of the parameters of wavelet neural network.

The minimization of the cost function in (5) can give the correct separation results for post nonlinear mixtures. In this section, we present the PSO(particle swarm optimization) to fulfill the search of the optimal parameter set of the separation model based on the cost functions specified in (5).

PSO was originally designed and developed by Eberhart and Kennedy[7]. In PSO, instead of using genetic operators, each particle (individual) adjusts its "flying" according to its own flying experience and that of its companions. The performance of each particle is measured according to a pre-defined fitness function, which is related to the problem to be solved.

The PSO-based BSS algorithm can be implemented as the following iterative procedure:

1. Set the iteration number T to zero, an initial population $\{\mathbf{H}_i\}_{i=1}^{N}$ and $\{\mathbf{v}_i\}_{i=1}^{N}$ are created from a random initial set of parameters.
2. The fitness for each particle $\{\mathbf{H}_i\}_{i=1}^{N}$ is evaluated using (5),
3. The best previous position (the position giving the best fitness value) of the ith particle is recorded and represented as $\mathbf{p}_i (i = 1,2,\cdots,N)$.
4. The index of the best particle among all the particles in the population is represented as $\mathbf{p}_g$.
5. Change the velocity vector for each particle:

$$\mathbf{v}_i \leftarrow \mathbf{v}_i + c_1 r_1 (\mathbf{p}_i - \hat{\mathbf{H}}_i) + c_2 r_2 (\mathbf{p}_g - \hat{\mathbf{H}}_i)$$

6. Move each particle to its new position: $\hat{\mathbf{H}}_i \leftarrow \hat{\mathbf{H}}_i + \mathbf{v}_i$
7. Let $T = T+1$.
8. Go to step 2), and repeat until convergence.
9. Output the particle $\mathbf{H}$ with the best fitness value and compute the separated signals.

4 Computer Simulation Results

To verify the validity and performance of the proposed algorithm, a computer simulation was conducted to test the PSO-based approach to blind separation of independent sources from their post-nonlinear mixture. Sources signals are shown in Fig.2. The mixing matrix A was randomly generatednonlinear function $f_1(x)=x^3$, $f_2(x)=x^3$. Nonlinear function $h_1(\cdot)$ and $h_2(\cdot)$ in (5) is selected as $h_1(x)=x^3$, $h_2(x) = x - \tanh(x)$. The population size was 20, $c_1=2$, $c_2=2$, $\{\hat{\mathbf{H}}_i\}_{i=1}^{N}$ and $\{\mathbf{v}_i\}_{i=1}^{N}$ are generated from a random initial set of parameters, the maximum generation for PSO process to be 100. Fig.3 are separated signals.

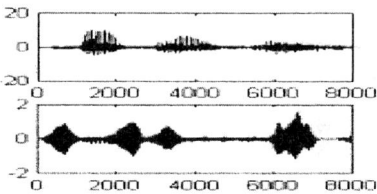

Fig. 2. Source signals

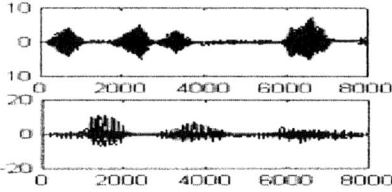

Fig. 3. Separated signals

5 Conclusions

A method to blind source separation in post-nonlinear mixtures is presented. The demixing system of the post-nonlinear mixtures is modeled using a multi-input multi-output parameterized wavelet neural network whose parameters can be determined under the criterion of independence of its outputs. A criterion of independence based on higher order moments is used to measure the statistical dependence of the outputs of the demixing system, and the particle swarm optimization technique is utilized to minimized the criterion. Simulation results show that the proposed approach is capable of separating independent sources from their post-nonlinear mixtures.

References

1. Taleb A., Jutten C. Source separation in post-nonlinear mixtures. IEEE Trans. On Signal Processing, Vol.47, No.10,October 1999. 2807-2820.
2. A.Hyvarinen, P. Pajunen. : Nonlinear independent component analysis: Existence and uniqueness results. Neural Networks 12(1999) 429-439.
3. Y. Tan , J. Wang. : Nonlinear blind source separation using a radial basis function network. IEEE Trans. On Neural Networks. Vol.12, No.1, January 2001, 124-134.
4. Y. Tan , J. Wang. : Nonlinear blind source separation using Higher order statistical and a genetic algorithm. IEEE Trans. On Evolutionary Computation. Vol.5, No.6, December 2001,600-612.

5. Zhang J., Walter G. G., Lee W. N. : Wavelet neural network for function learning. IEEE Trans. On Signal Processing, 1995,43, 1485-1497.
6. Papoulis A. : Probability, Random Variables, and Stochastic Process. 3rd edition. New York: McGraw-Hill, 1991, 190-191.
7. Kennedy J., Eberhart R.: Particle swarm optimization. In: IEEE Int'l Conf. On Neural Networks. Perth, Australia, 1995,1942-1948.

An MRF-ICA Based Algorithm for Image Separation

Sen Jia and Yuntao Qian

College of Computer Science, Zhejiang University,
Hangzhou 310027, P.R. China
zjujiasen@hotmail.com, ytqian@zju.edu.cn

Abstract. Separation of sources from one-dimensional mixture signals such as speech has been largely explored. However, two-dimensional sources (images) separation problem has only been examined to a limited extent. The reason is that ICA is a very general-purpose statistical technique, and it does not take the spatial information into account while separating mixture images. In this paper, we introduce Markov random field model to incorporate the spatial information into ICA. MRF is considered as a powerful tool to model the joint probability distribution of the image pixels in terms of local spatial interactions. An MRF-ICA based algorithm is proposed for image separation. It is successfully demonstrated on artificial and real images.

1 Motivation

Over the past years, Independent component analysis (ICA) [1] has been widely used in many different areas such as audio processing, biomedical signal processing, image processing and econometrics.

As the origination of ICA, separation of sources from one-dimensional mixture signals such as speech has been largely explored [2]. But image separation problem has only been examined to a limited extent. The reason is that ICA is a very general-purpose statistical technique, and it does not think of the spatial information while separating mixture images. In this paper, we introduce Markov random field (MRF) to incorporate the spatial information into ICA. MRF is considered as a powerful stochastic tool to model the joint probability distribution of the image pixels in terms of local spatial interactions [3,4]. Using MRF as the representation of image spatial information has the following advantages. First, MRF is the model of context in the image. Second, the MRF model of prior information need not be an accurate model of the image itself. An MRF-ICA algorithm is proposed for image separation. It is successfully demonstrated on artificial and real images.

The remainder of the paper is organized as follows. Section 2 describes the MRF model. Section 3 develops the MRF-ICA algorithm. Experiments results of applying the MRF-ICA algorithm are reported in Section 4. Section 5 contains our conclusions.

2 MRF Model for Image Separation

MRF models are mainly used in feature extraction and image segmentation. Readers are referred to [3,4] for details.

First we introduce some notations. An image specifies the gray levels for all pixels in a $M \times N$ lattice. Let $F = f$ be the feature vector extracted from a random image $(X = x)$, where F denotes a random variable and f is an instance of F. The image can be represented by the vector random variable $X = (X_1, X_2, \ldots, X_{MN})$. The energy demonstrating MRF can be divided into two components [5,6]: the feature modeling component and the region labeling component. They are described as follows:

$$E_F = \sum_{i=1}^{MN}\left(\frac{1}{2}\ln(\sigma_i^k)^2 + \frac{(x_i - \mu_i^k)^2}{2(\sigma_i^k)}\right) \qquad E_R = \sum_{i=1}^{MN}\sum_{r=1}^{c}\left[\theta_r J(x_i, x_{i:+r})\right] \qquad (1)$$

where μ_i^k and σ_i^k are the mean and standard deviation for the ith pixel in the kth feature component; $J(a,b) = -1$ if $a = b$, 0 if $a \neq b$, c is the number of computing dependence of pixels, and $\{\theta_1, \ldots, \theta_c\}$ are the weighting parameters.

Here, we give an assumption that the standard deviations of feature vector are equal. It not only facilitates the subsequent computation of MRF, but also can be basically satisfied in actual situation without loss of generality. For the convenience of following derivation, Table 1 gives several symbols. And we take two-image separation problem as an example.

Using the assumption, the MRF energy can be expressed in terms of matrix forms:

$$E = \frac{MN}{2}\ln\sigma^2 + \frac{1}{2\sigma^2}\left\{VS^T \cdot VS - 2 \cdot \mu_{VS} \cdot VS + \mu_{VS} \cdot \mu_{VS}^T\right\} + E_R \qquad (2)$$

Substituting $VS = VX \cdot w$ into (2) results in

$$E(w) = \frac{MN}{2}\ln\sigma^2 + \frac{1}{2\sigma^2}\left\{w^T \cdot VX^T \cdot VX \cdot w - 2 \cdot \mu_{VS} \cdot VX \cdot w + \mu_{VS} \cdot \mu_{VS}^T\right\} + E_R \qquad (3)$$

In order to reduce the computational load, we let c be 2 and all parameters θ equal to 1. We only compute the energy of left-right neighbors; the up-down neighbors can be computed in the same way. Here we introduce two matrixes: M_a and M_b to facilitate the representation of the region labeling component.

$$E_{R(Left \& Right)}(w) = \sum_{i=1}^{MN}\sum_{r=1}^{2}\left[J(x_i, x_{i:+r})\right] \approx \left(\sum_{i=1}^{MN+1} J\left[(M_a \cdot VS)_i, (M_b \cdot VS)_i\right]\right) \times 2 \qquad (4)$$

Because the derivative of function J does not exist, we introduce function $H(x) = -e^{-x^2/2}$ to fit it. And Equation (4) can be written as

$$E_{R(Left \& Right)}(w) = \left(\sum_{i=1}^{MN+1} H\left[(M_a - M_b) \cdot VS\right]_i\right) \times 2 \qquad (5)$$

Differentiating (5) with respect to w

$$\frac{\partial E_{R(Left \& Right)}}{\partial w} = \frac{\partial H}{\partial w} \cdot \left[(M_a - M_b) \cdot VX\right] \qquad (6)$$

where $\partial H/\partial w_i = w_i e^{-w_i^2/2}$. The result can be considered to be zero regardless of the value of w_i. So the result of (6) is zero. Similarly, the derivative of energy of up-down neighbors is also zero. That is, $\partial E_R/\partial w = 0$.

Now we use gradient descent methods to obtain the extreme value of MRF model

$$\frac{\partial E(w)}{\partial w} = \frac{1}{2\sigma^2}\left\{\left[VX^T \cdot VX \cdot w + (VX^T \cdot VX)^T \cdot w\right] - 2(\mu_{vs} \cdot VX)^T\right\} = 0 \quad (7)$$

Solving it

$$w = \left(VX^T \cdot VX\right)^{-1} \cdot \left(\mu_{vs} \cdot VX\right)^T \quad (8)$$

This is the solution formula to w.

Table 1. The symbols

Symbol	Explanation	Dimension
VX	The matrix obtained by converting mixtures into vectors	$MN \times 2$
w	Demixing vector that we want to find	2×1
VS	The estimated image-vector	$MN \times 1$
$M_a = \begin{pmatrix} 1 & 0 & 0 \\ 0 & \ddots & 0 \\ 0 & \ddots & 1 \\ 0 & \cdots & 0 \end{pmatrix}$ $M_b = \begin{pmatrix} 0 & 0 & 0 \\ 1 & \ddots & 0 \\ 0 & \ddots & 0 \\ 0 & \cdots & 1 \end{pmatrix}$	The two matrixes are used for dealing with the region labeling component	$(MN+1) \cdot MN$

3 MRF-ICA Algorithm

The algorithm is described as follows:

1. A random vector w is initialized.
2. MRF-ICA step: Transform the image matrixes into vectors, and use FastICA algorithm [7] to estimate w; normalize the obtained w, and then make use of (8) to compute w and normalize it again.
3. Repeat step 2 until a stopping criterion is satisfied, an estimated independent component vector is acquired.
4. Repeat all above steps until all independent components have been acquired.

4 Experimental Results

4.1 Results on Artificial Images

Figure 1(a) shows the source images. Here we take the following mixing matrix:

$$A = \begin{pmatrix} 0.2 & 0.5 \\ 0.6 & 0.3 \end{pmatrix}$$

The mixtures are displayed in Fig. 1(b). The estimates using ICA and MRF-ICA are given in Fig. 1(c) and (d) respectively. It is clear that MRF-ICA algorithm is more effective than FastICA. The color of left figure is reversed, but this has no significance.

Now we consider three-image separation problem. Figure 2(a) and (b) illustrate the source images and the mixtures respectively. The corresponding mixing matrix is:

$$A = \begin{pmatrix} 0.5 & 0.4 & 0.6 \\ 0.6 & 0.5 & 0.4 \\ 0.4 & 0.6 & 0.5 \end{pmatrix}$$

The estimates using ICA and MRF-ICA are given in Fig. 2(c) and (d) respectively. Apparently the estimates of MRF-ICA are better than ICA.

4.2 Results on Real Images

Figure 3(a) and (b) illustrate the real source images and mixtures respectively. Here we still use the two-dimension mixing matrix A mentioned above. The estimates using ICA are given in Fig. 3(c). And the second figure is almost the same as the right of the mixtures. The MRF-ICA estimates are displayed in Fig. 3(d). As can be seen, they are similar to the original source images.

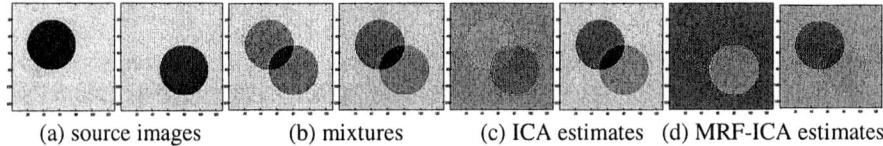

(a) source images   (b) mixtures   (c) ICA estimates   (d) MRF-ICA estimates

Fig. 1. The source images, mixtures, ICA and MRF-ICA estimates of two images

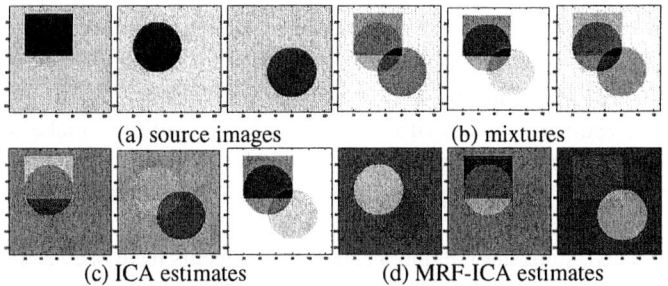

Fig. 2. The source images, mixtures, ICA and MRF-ICA estimates of three images

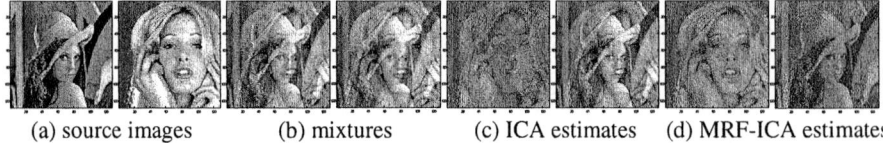

(a) source images   (b) mixtures   (c) ICA estimates   (d) MRF-ICA estimates

Fig. 3. The source images, mixtures, ICA and MRF-ICA estimates of real images

5 Conclusions

By introducing Markov random field (MRF) to incorporate the spatial information into Independent component analysis (ICA), a new MRF-ICA algorithm can be achieved. Experiments demonstrate that the new implementation scheme can obtain more consistent image separation results than ICA. The developed technique can be efficiently applied to artificial and real images.

References

1. Hyvärinen A., Karhunen J., Oja E.: Independent Component Analysis. John Wiley & Sons (2001)
2. Cichocki A., Amari S.: Adaptive Blind Signal and Image Processing: Learning Algorithms and Applications. John Wiley & Sons (2002)
3. Geman S., Geman D.: Stochastic relaxation, gibbs distributions, and the Bayesian restoration of images. IEEE Trans. Pattern Anal. Mach. Intell. 6 (1984) 721-741
4. Li S.Z.: Markov Random Field Modeling in Computer Vision. Springer, New York (2001)
5. Deng H., Clausi D.A.: Unsupervised image segmentation using a simple MRF model with a new implementation scheme. Pattern Recog. 37 (2004) 2323-2335
6. Dubes R.C., Jain A.K., Nadabar S.G., Chen C.C.: MRF model-based algorithms for image segmentation. 10th Int. Conf. Pattern Recog. (1990) 808-814
7. The FastICA MATLAB package. Available at http://www.cis.hut.fi/projects/ica/fastica

Multi-view Face Recognition with Min-Max Modular SVMs

Zhi-Gang Fan and Bao-Liang Lu*

Departmart of Computer Science and Engineering,
Shanghai Jiao Tong University, 1954 Hua Shan Road,
Shanghai 200030, China
zgfan@sjtu.edu.cn, blu@cs.sjtu.edu.cn

Abstract. Through task decomposition and module combination, min-max modular support vector machines (M^3-SVMs) can be successfully used for difficult pattern classification task. M^3-SVMs divide the training data set of the original problem to several sub-sets, and combine them to a series of sub-problems which can be trained more effectively. In this paper, we explore the use of M^3-SVMs in multi-view face recognition. Using M^3-SVMs, we can decompose the whole complicated problem of multi-view face recognition into several simple sub-problems. The experimental results show that M^3-SVMs can be successfully used for multi-view face recognition and make the classification more accurate.

1 Introduction

Support vector machines (SVMs)[1] have been successfully applied to various pattern classification problems. However, SVMs require to solve a quadratic optimization problem and need training time that are at least quadratic to the number of training samples. Therefore, many large-scale problems are too hard to be solved by using traditional SVMs. To solve large-scale multi-class problems, we have proposed a min-max modular support vector machines (M^3-SVMs) in our previous work[3].

In this paper, we explore the use of M^3-SVMs in multi-view face recognition. Multi-view face recognition is a more challenging task than frontal view face recognition. Face recognition techniques have been developed over the past few decades. But many of those existing face recognition techniques, such as Eigenfaces and Fisherfaces [4,5], are only effective for frontal view faces. The difficulties of multi-view face recognition is obvious because of the complicated nonlinear manifolds existing in the data space. Using M^3-SVMs, we can decompose the whole complicated problem of multi-view face recognition into several sub-problems. Every individual sub-problem becomes less complicated than the original problem and it can be solved effectively.

---

* To whome correspondence should be addressed. This work was supported in part by the National Natural Science Foundation of China via the grants NSFC 60375022 and NSFC 60473040.

2 Min-Max Modular Support Vector Machines

Before using M³-SVMs, for a K-class problem, we should divide the K-class problem into $K(K-1)/2$ two-class sub-problems according to one-against-one strategy[2,8]. The work procedure of M³-SVMs consists of three steps: task decomposition, SVMs training and module combination. First, every two-class problem is decomposed into smaller two-class problems. Then, every small two-class SVMs is trained. At last, all trained individual modules are integrated to get a solution to the original problem.

Let $\mathcal{X}^+$ and $\mathcal{X}^-$ be the given positive and negative training data set for a two-class problem $\mathcal{T}$,

$$\mathcal{X}^+ = \{(x_i^+, +1)\}_{i=1}^{l^+}, \quad \mathcal{X}^- = \{(x_i^-, -1)\}_{i=1}^{l^-} \tag{1}$$

where $x_i \in \mathbf{R}^n$ is the input vector, and l^+ and l^- are the total number of positive training data and negative training data of the two-class problem, respectively.

According to [3], $\mathcal{X}^+$ and $\mathcal{X}^-$ can be partitioned into N^+ and N^- subsets respectively,

$$\mathcal{X}_j^+ = \{(x_i^{+j}, +1)\}_{i=1}^{l_j^+}, \quad for\ j = 1, \ldots, N^+ \tag{2}$$

$$\mathcal{X}_j^- = \{(x_i^{-j}, -1)\}_{i=1}^{l_j^-}, \quad for\ j = 1, \ldots, N^- \tag{3}$$

where $\cup_{j=1}^{N^+} \mathcal{X}_j^+ = \mathcal{X}^+$, $1 \leq N^+ \leq l^+$, and $\cup_{j=1}^{N^-} \mathcal{X}_j^- = \mathcal{X}^-$, $1 \leq N^- \leq l^-$.

After decomposing the training data sets $\mathcal{X}^+$ and $\mathcal{X}^-$, the original two-class problem $\mathcal{T}$ is divided into $N^+ \times N^-$ relatively smaller and more balanced two-class sub-problems $\mathcal{T}^{(i,j)}$ as follows:

$$(\mathcal{T}^{(i,j)})^+ = \mathcal{X}_i^+, \quad (\mathcal{T}^{(i,j)})^- = \mathcal{X}_j^- \tag{4}$$

where $(\mathcal{T}^{(i,j)})^+$ and $(\mathcal{T}^{(i,j)})^-$ denote the positive training data set and the negative training data set for subproblem $\mathcal{T}^{(i,j)}$, respectively.

In the learning phase, all the two-class sub-problems are independent from each other and can be efficiently learned in a massively parallel way. After training, all the individual SVMs are integrated into a M³-SVM with MIN and MAX units according to the two combination principles, namely the minimization principle and the maximization principle [2,3].

According to the minimization and maximization principles, the $N^+ \times N^-$ smaller SVMs are integrated into a M³-SVM with N^+ MIN units and one MAX unit as following equations (5, 6). Fig.1 shows the structure of M³-SVMs.

$$\mathrm{M}^i(x) = \min_{j=1}^{N^-} \mathrm{M}^{(i,j)}(x) \quad for\ i = 1, \ldots, N^+ \tag{5}$$

and

$$\mathrm{M}(x) = \max_{i=1}^{N^+} \mathrm{M}^i(x) \tag{6}$$

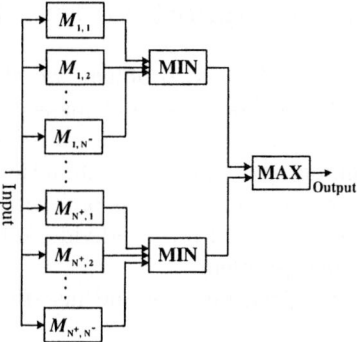

Fig. 1. A M^3-SVM consisting of $N^+ \times N^-$ individual SVMs, N^+ MIN units, and one MAX unit

where $M^{i,j}(x)$ denotes the transfer function of the trained SVM corresponding to the two-class subproblem $T^{(i,j)}$, and $M^i(x)$ denotes the transfer function of a combination of N^- SVMs integrated by the MIN unit.

3 Experiments

We use the UMIST database [6], a multi-view face database consisting of 575 gray-scale images of 20 subjects, each covering a wide range of poses from profile to frontal views. Figure.2 depicts some sample images of one subject in the UMIST database. The overall database is partitioned into two subsets: the training set and test set. The training set is composed of 240 images: 12 images per person are carefully chosen according to face poses. The remaining 335 images are used to form the test set. All input images are of size 112×92. We have used feature selection method to reduce the dimensionality of feature space and the feature selection method we have used is described in detail in [7]. All of the experiments were performed on a 3.0GHz Pentium 4 PC with 1.0 GB RAM.

As shown in Fig.2, using task decomposition principle of M^3-SVMs, we have divided all face images in each face class into 4 subsets according to the face poses. An RBF kernel for SVMs is used. The parameter C is set to 10000 and an optimal σ is used. The experimental results are shown in Table 1 and we can see that M^3-SVMs is more accurate than traditional SVMs.

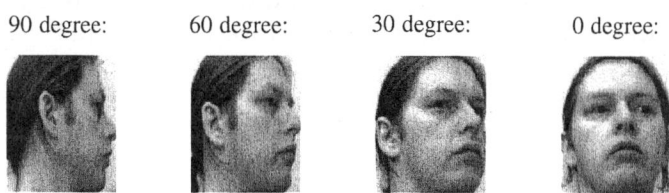

Fig. 2. All images in each class are divided into 4 subsets according to the face poses

Table 1. Test results on UMIST face database

Methods	No. features	σ	Training time (s)		Test time (s)	Correct rate (%)
			Parallel	Serial		
SVMs (rbf kernel)	300	30	0.862	13.588	1.522	92.8358
	200	25	0.748	12.654	0.976	92.2388
	150	25	0.703	11.865	0.757	90.1493
	100	20	0.685	11.269	0.478	82.3881
M³-SVMs (rbf kernel)	300	20	0.531	15.273	1.647	93.1343
	200	15	0.447	13.413	1.215	92.5373
	150	10	0.386	12.587	0.873	91.3433
	100	10	0.359	12.165	0.526	83.8806

4 Conclusion and Future Work

Through task decomposition and module combination, we have applied M^3-SVMs to multi-view face recognition. Comparing to traditional SVMs, our experiments show that M^3-SVMs can improve the accuracy of multi-view face recognition. In the future work, we will enhance the task decomposition method.

References

1. Vapnik, V.N.: The Nature of Statistical Learning Theory. Springer-Verlag, New York (2000)
2. Lu, B.L., Ito, M.: Task decomposition and module combination based on class relations: a modular neural network for pattern classification. IEEE Transactions on Neural Networks, vol.10, (1999) 1244 -1256
3. Lu, B.L., Wang, K.A., Utiyama, M., Isahara, H.: A part-versus-part method for massively parallel training of support vector machines. In: Proceedings of IJCNN'04, Budapest, July 25-29(2004)
4. Turk, M., Pentland, A.: Eigenfaces for Recognition. Journal of Cognitive Neuroscience, vol. 3, no. 1, (1991) 71-86
5. Belhumeur, P., Hespanda, J., Kiregeman, D.: Eigenfaces vs. Fisherfaces: Recognition Using Class Specific Linear Projection. IEEE Trans. Pattern Analysis and Machine Intelligence, vol. 19, no. 7, (1997) 711-720.
6. Graham, D.B., Allinson, N.M.: Characterizing virtual eigensignatures for general purpose face recognition. In: Face Recognition: From Theory to Applications, NATO ASI Series F, Computer and Systems Sciences, vol. 163, (1998) 446-456.
7. Fan, Z.G., Lu, B.L.: Fast Recognition of Multi-view Faces with Feature Selection. submitted to ICCV05, Beijing (2005)
8. Hsu, C., Lin, C.: A Comparison of Methods for Multiclass Support Vector Machines. IEEE Trans. Neural Networks, vol. 13, no.2, (2002) 415-425.

Texture Segmentation Using Neural Networks and Multi-scale Wavelet Features

Tae Hyung Kim[1], Il Kyu Eom[2], and Yoo Shin Kim[3]

[1] Dept. Electronics Engineering, Pusan National University,
30 Jangjeon-dong, Geumjeong-gu, Busan 609-735,
Republic of Korea
[2] Dept. Information and Communications Engineering,
Miryang National University, 50, Cheonghak-ri,
Samnangjin-eup, Miryang-si, Gyeongsangnam-do 627-706, Republic of Korea
[3] Research Institute of Computer, Information and Communication,
Pusan National Univesity, 30 Jangjeon-dong,
Geumjeong-gu, Busan 609-735, Republic of Korea

Abstract. This paper presents a novel texture segmentation method using Bayesian estimation and neural networks. Multi-scale wavelet coefficients and the context information extracted from neighboring wavelet coefficients were used as input for the neural networks. The output was modeled as a posterior probability. The context information was obtained by HMT (Hidden Markov Trees) model. The proposed segmentation method shows performed better than ML (Maximum Likelihood) segmentation using the HMT model.

1 Introduction

Visual texture is expressed as spatial variations or homogeneous patterns of pixel intensities in images, since images of real objects often exhibit variations of intensities with certain repeated structures or patterns. Image texture segmentation is important for many computer-vision and image processes, since real images have textures. According to the size, the structure and the spatial placement of texture primitives, Textures can be roughly categorized into structural textures and statistical textures [1-2]. And textures are segmented by different segmentation methods according to the texture category. In statistical textures the size of texture primitives is small and their structure and spatial placement are not deterministic. Pixels are classified in a win-dow by using statistical moment and entropy: mean, variance, and other typical statistical calculation of pixel intensities [1], [3-4]. In structural textures the size of texture primitives is large and their structure and spatial placement are deterministic or repetitive. Textures are analyzed by extracting texture primitives and determining the regularity of their spatial placement [1-3]. The above-mentioned approaches to performing texture segmentation are analogous to methods for image segmentation. Therefore texture segmentation methods are also classified by region-based and boundary-based methods, which have been used as image model-based segmentation methods [3], [6-7]. MRF(Markov Random Field) is broadly used [10] as a texture model. Fourier [11] or wavelet transform [12] can be used to extract texture image features. The resulting transformed features in multi-scale are efficient for texture image segmentation. Therefore, the HMT model in multi-scale wavelet-domain is used in texture segmentation [12]. And Kohonen neural networks [8] or fuzzy c-means [9] with some features(which are extracted from wavelet transform) are used in texture segmentation. An approach based on support vector machine and neural networks is also investigated for texture segmentation [5]. In this paper, we propose a novel method of texture segmentation using neural networks in a multi-scale wavelet domain and a multi-scale Bayesian image segmentation technique called HMTseg. It is possible to compose neural networks so that their output represents a posteriori when they are trained in supervised training mode [13-14]. It is then possible for Maximum a Posterior (MAP) classification to use the neural networks output. In the proposed method of texture segmentation, the input elements of neural networks consist of multi-scale wavelet coefficients with a quad tree structure, but also include the likelihood probability (evaluated by HMT) of the neighboring wavelet coefficients in one scale as contexts. MAP segmentation by outputs of neural networks performs better than ML segmentation by HMT. The proposed method uses a multi-scale Bayesian image segmentation technique which is called HMTseg to fuse multi-scale MAP segments and finally to improve texture segmentation at the finest scale. This paper is organized as follows. In section 2, after we briefly review wavelet transform of an image and 2-D wavelet-domain HMT model, we explain texture segmentations by HMT in multi-scale and post-processing by HMTseg. In section 3, we explain texture segmentation by the proposed method. In section 4, we evaluate texture segmentation experiments and results.

2 Texture Segmentation by HMT Model

2.1 The Harr Wavelet Transform and the Hidden Markov Tree Model

The multi-level Harr wavelet transform forms a pyramid structure through all scales. Coefficients of Harr wavelets are computed by using four filters as follows:

$$h_{LL} = \frac{1}{2}\begin{pmatrix} 1 & 1 \\ 1 & 1 \end{pmatrix}, g_{LH} = \frac{1}{2}\begin{pmatrix} 1 & 1 \\ -1 & -1 \end{pmatrix}, g_{HL} = \frac{1}{2}\begin{pmatrix} 1 & -1 \\ 1 & -1 \end{pmatrix}, g_{HH} = \frac{1}{2}\begin{pmatrix} 1 & -1 \\ -1 & 1 \end{pmatrix} \quad (1)$$

where h_{LL} is a local smoother, g_{LH} is a horizontal edge detector, g_{HL} is a vertical edge detector, and g_{HH} is a diagonal edge detector. The wavelet transform of a discrete image $x(=u_J)$ forms four subband images: a smoothed image u_{J-1}, a horizontal edge image w_{J-1}^{LH}, a vertical edge image w_{J-1}^{HL}, and a diagonal edge image w_{J-1}^{HH}. The wavelet transform process can now be continued on the image u_{J-1} and the procedure iterated up to J times. Harr wavelet transforms of three levels are shown in figure 1-(a). As shown in figure 1-(a), coefficient

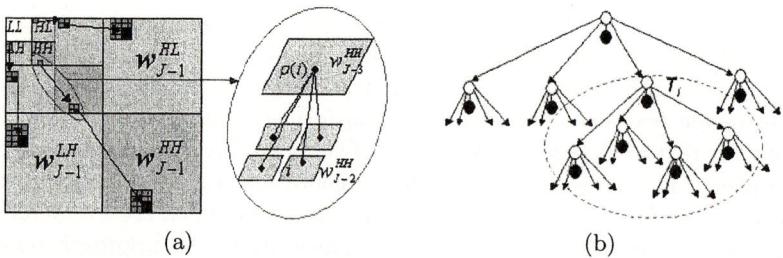

Fig. 1. (a) The Harr wavelet transform and the quad tree structure of wavelet coefficients. (b) The structure of the HMT model for multi-scale wavelet coefficients of one wavelet subband.

w_{J-3}^{HH} in a coarse scale corresponds to four coefficients in the next fine scale and the dependency of these coefficients across scale shows a quad tree structure. The distribution of multi-scale wavelet coefficients is modeled by HMT [17]. The quad tree structure of multi-scale wavelet coefficients for one subband can be represented by HMT as shown in figure 1-(b). In figure 1-(b), a black node represents a wavelet coefficient and a white node represents a state with two hidden states. Wavelet coefficients are composed of a great number of small coefficients and a small number of large coefficients. Therefore the distribution of large coefficients can be represented by a Gaussian probability density function (pdf) with large variance. Similarly the distribution of small coefficients can be represented by a Gaussian pdf with small variance. Hence the distribution of wavelet coefficients is modeled by a Gaussian mixture model with two hidden states. The pdf of wavelet coefficient w_i for node i of a wavelet quad tree is defined as

$$f(w_i) = \sum_{m=S,L} p_{S_i}(m) f(w_i | S_i = m), \quad (2)$$

where a discrete hidden state S_i takes on the values $m = S, L$, signifying the small and large variance, with probability mass function(pmf) $p_{S_i}(m)$, and $p_{S_i}(S) + p_{S_i}(L) = 1$, $f(w_i|S_i = m) \approx N(\mu_{i,m}, \sigma_{i,m}^2)$. In this paper, we will often drop the scale $(J, J-1, ...)$ and the direction (LH, HL, HH), if they are not confused. In the HMT model, the branches between white nodes across scale represent the persistence between the wavelet coefficients across the scale analyzing a common sub-region of the image. The HMT captures the persistence across scale of large/small coefficients using Markov-1 dependencies between the hidden states. As shown in figure 2, state transition probabilities between the hidden states of the white nodes capture the persistence of the wavelet coefficients across the scale. A state transition probability matrix for each white node across the scale is defined as

$$\begin{bmatrix} \varepsilon_{i,S}^{\rho(i),S} & \varepsilon_{i,L}^{\rho(i),S} \\ \varepsilon_{i,S}^{\rho(i),L} & \varepsilon_{i,L}^{\rho(i),L} \end{bmatrix} = \begin{bmatrix} \varepsilon_{i,S}^{\rho(i),S} & 1 - \varepsilon_{i,S}^{\rho(i),S} \\ 1 - \varepsilon_{i,L}^{\rho(i),L} & \varepsilon_{i,L}^{\rho(i),L} \end{bmatrix}, \quad (3)$$

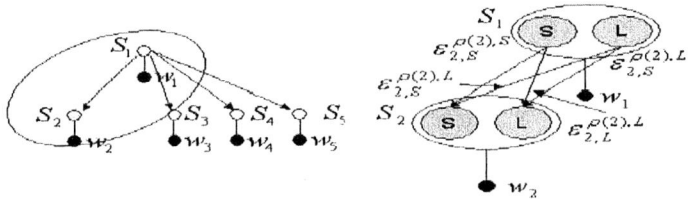

Fig. 2. State transition probabilities capture the persistence of wavelet coefficients across scale

where the state transition probability for states $\{S_{\rho(i)}, S_i\}$ of parent and child nodes is $\varepsilon_{i,m'}^{\rho(i),m}$, $m, m' = S, L$, where $\rho(i)$ is the parent node of node i. So wavelet domain HMT is defined by the mean and variance of the hidden states and the state transition probabilities between the hidden states.

2.2 Texture Segmentation Using HMT Model and Post-processing Using HMTseg Algorithm

An HMT model is trained on $c \in \{1, 2, ..., C\}$ out of C texture classes with iterative EM (Expectation Maximization) algorithm. The likelihood of the coefficients in subtree T_i of figure 1-(b) can be computed as follows:

$$f(T_i|\Theta) = \sum_{m=S,L} \beta_i(m) p(S_i = m|\Theta), \qquad (4)$$

where Θ is the HMT parameters for one subband, and the conditional likelihood $\beta_i(m) = f(T_i|S_i = m, \Theta)$ is obtained by sweeping up the quad-tree from the leaves to node i. The likelihood of wavelet coefficients of all subtrees $\{T_i^{LH}, T_i^{HL}, T_i^{HH}\}$ rooted at node i in wavelet subbands quad-trees is computed as follows:

$$f(d_i|M) = f(T_i^{LH}|\Theta^{LH}) f(T_i^{HL}|\Theta^{HL}) f(T_i^{HH}|\Theta^{HH}), \qquad (5)$$

where $d_i \equiv \{T_i^{LH}, T_i^{HL}, T_i^{HH}\}$ is the wavelet coefficients analyzing a common sub-region of the image in three wavelet subbands and $M \equiv \{\Theta^{LH}, \Theta^{HL}, \Theta^{HH}\}$ is the set of HMT parameters for the three wavelet subbands. The likelihood of multi-scale wavelet coefficients is computed using equation (5). And then texture segmentation is performed using the ML classification from the multi-scale likelihood. ML classification, $\hat{c}_i^{ML}$, of the wavelet coefficients, d_i, is defined as

$$\hat{c}_i^{ML} \equiv \arg \max_{c \in \{1, 2, ..., C\}} f(d_i|M_c), \qquad (6)$$

where M_c is the set of HMT parameters for $c \in \{1, 2, ..., C\}$ class. ML image segmentations in multi-scale have contradictions between reliability and minuteness according to scale. Image segmentation in coarse scale is accurate for large, homogeneous regions but poor along the boundaries between regions. Image segmentation in fine scale is accurate near the boundaries between regions but has poor classification reliability due to the paucity of statistical information. A study shows that image segmentation in the finest scale is improved by using a multi-scale Bayesian image segmentation algorithm called HMTseg that fuses image segmentations in multi-scale and the multi-scale likelihood by HMT [12]. In the HMTseg algorithm, a posterior that considers context is defined and simplified as follows:

$$f(c_i|\boldsymbol{d}_i,\boldsymbol{v}_i) = \frac{f(\boldsymbol{d}_i|c_i)p(c_i|\boldsymbol{v}_i)}{f(\boldsymbol{d}_i|\boldsymbol{v}_i)} \propto f(\boldsymbol{d}_i|c_i)p(c_i|\boldsymbol{v}_i), \tag{7}$$

where c_i is the class of node i in a wavelet quad tree and $\boldsymbol{v}_i$ is the context vector representing the class of the parent (and its neighborhood) node of node i. In equation (7), $f(\boldsymbol{d}_i|c_i)$ is computed by HMT, and $p(c_i|\boldsymbol{v}_i)$ is computed through Bayes rule and $p(\boldsymbol{v}_i|c_i)$. Segmentation is performed by MAP classification and $f(c_i|\boldsymbol{d}_i,\boldsymbol{v}_i)$. Finally after post-processing, the MAP classification, $\hat{c}_i^{MAP}$, of the wavelet coefficients, $\boldsymbol{d}_i$, is

$$\hat{c}_i^{MAP} \equiv arg \max_{c \in \{1,2,...,C\}} f(c_i|\boldsymbol{d}_i,\boldsymbol{v}_i). \tag{8}$$

The HMTseg algorithm fuses the multi-scale MAP segmentation one by one from coarse to fine scale and then finally improves image segmentation at the finest scale. Even if the post-processed segmentation by HMTseg performs better than ML segmentation by HMT, image segmentation by HMTseg relies on the multi-scale likelihood provided by HMT. Therefore, if multi-scale ML segmentations by HMT are not good, post-processed segmentations by HMTseg perform badly. Actually, HMT does not model the distribution of wavelet coefficients in fine scale delicately, and is sensitive to the initial parameters of the HMT training.

3 Texture Segmentation Using Neural Networks

The input and output structures of neural networks can be made so that a posterior is estimated [13-14]. The elements of the input vector of the neural networks were determined by considering the dependency of the wavelet coefficients across scale like HMT. The coefficients of the sub-tree T_i rooted at node i and the pixel intensities of the subimage (analyzed by node i) were used as inputs of the neural networks for node i of a wavelet subband quad-tree. By considering all sub-trees on node i of three wavelet subband quad-trees, the input vector $\boldsymbol{g}_i$ of the neural network is defined as

$$\boldsymbol{g}_i \equiv \{T_i^{LH}, T_i^{HL}, T_i^{HH}, \boldsymbol{p}_i\}, \tag{9}$$

where the $\boldsymbol{p}_i$ is pixel intensities of the sub-image which are analyzed by node i. Let one of the outputs of the neural networks have a value of 1, and let the others have a value of 0. If the output values of K outputs of neural networks sum to 1 and the cost function for the neural networks training is Mean Square Error or cross entropy, then the neural networks can estimate *a posterior* probability.

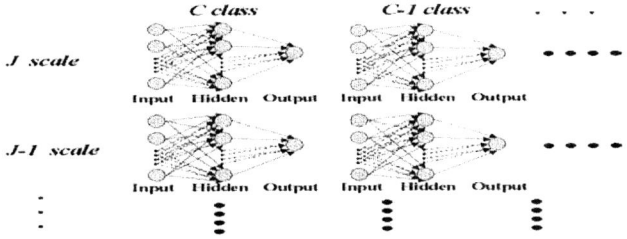

Fig. 3. The structure of input and output layer of the proposed neural networks

To estimate *a posterior* in multi-scale, the proposed system has one multi-layer perceptron(MLP) networks for each wavelet scale. The proposed structure of neural networks is shown in figure 3. In figure 3, there is also one MLP network for each texture class, and the number of output nodes of one MLP network is one. For the MLP network of texture class c_i, target output for training is set up as follows:

$$t_i = \begin{cases} 1, & g_i \in c \\ 0, & g_i \notin c \end{cases}. \tag{10}$$

In this paper, the resilient back-propagation algorithm is used in MLP training [15]. The purpose of the resilient back-propagation training algorithm is to eliminate the faults of the back-propagation algorithm using the magnitudes of the partial derivatives of the cost function. After training the neural networks, the results of the texture segmentation is obtained by the following classification. Texture class, $\hat{c}_i^N$, by MLP is obtained from the MLP outputs.

$$\hat{c}_i^N \equiv \arg \max_{c \in \{1,2,...,C\}} \frac{N(g_i, w_c)}{\sum_{k=1}^{C} N(g_i, w_k)}, \tag{11}$$

where $N(g_i, w_c)$ is the output of the MLP model, which is composed of input vector g_i and weight vector w_c for class c. As using equation (11), a multi-scale texture segmentation is obtained. Multi-scale texture segmentations by equation (11) have contradictions between reliability and minuteness according to scale like the multi-scale ML segmentation by HMT. In the proposed method, multi-scale texture segmentations by equation (11) are post-processed by HMTseg algorithm. To use HMTseg algorithm, we convert equation (7) into equation (12).

$$f(c_i|g_i, v_i) \propto \frac{N(g_i, w_c)}{\sum_{k=1}^{C} N(g_i, w_k)} p(c_i|v_i) \propto N(g_i, w_c) p(c_i|v_i). \tag{12}$$

Post-processed MAP segmentation is obtained by using equation (12) and a Bayes classification like equation (8). If the context information of the image is used to classify the texture for one node of the wavelet quad-tree, then multi-scale texture segmentations are more improved. Coefficients for nodes neighboring the one node of the wavelet quad-tree can be used as context. The eight neighbors and the parent node $\rho(i)$ of the node i, and eight neighbors of the parent node

$\rho(i)$ are considered the context for node i of the wavelet quad-tree. The input vector of MLP is defined as

$$g_i \equiv \{T_i^{LH}, T_i^{HL}, T_i^{HH}, p_i, CV_i\}, \qquad (13)$$

where CV_i is the context vector of node i. And elements of the context CV_i are not composed of wavelet coefficients but the likelihood probabilities of wavelet coefficients by HMT. A posterior $f(c_i|g_i)$ is rewritten as equation (14) by Bayes rule.

$$f(c_i|g_i) = \frac{f(g_i|c_i)p(c_i)}{f(g_i)}. \qquad (14)$$

Equation (14) can be rewritten as equation (15) with a context vector $\{v_{1i}, v_{2i}, ..., v_{Mi}\}$.

$$f(c_i|g_i, v_{1i}, v_{2i}, ..., v_{Mi}) = \frac{f(g_i, v_{1i}, v_{2i}, ..., v_{Mi}|c_i)p(c_i)}{f(g_i, v_{1i}, v_{2i}, ..., v_{Mi})} \qquad (15)$$

$$= \frac{f(g_i|c_i)f(v_{1i}|c_i)f(v_{2i}|c_i)...f(v_{Mi}|c_i)p(c_i)}{f(g_i, v_{1i}, v_{2i}, ..., v_{Mi})}. \qquad (16)$$

In equation (16), the likelihood $f(v_{1i}|c_i), ..., f(v_{Mi}|c_i)$ for the context can be obtained by HMT. In this paper, the likelihood by HMT is used as the elements of the context vector CV_i and inputs for the neural networks.

$$CV_i = \{f(v_{1i}|c_i), ..., f(v_{Mi}|c_i)\} \qquad (17)$$

If context information is not used, the result of texture segmentation is sensitive to local noise and is not good at fine scale. Because the finer scales go, the smaller the size of the classification window becomes and this causes small information for texture classification at fine scale. By using neighboring context information, the effect of local noise can be reduced.

4 Experiments and Results

In this paper, 22 Brodatz texture is used in experiments. From each 640 × 640 Brodatz texture image, we randomly picked ten (overlapping) 64 × 64 blocks. And then the wavelet transform of those blocks are used as training data. The test images for the experiments are shown in figure 4. The results of texture segmentation for each test image are shown in figures 5, 6, and 7. The figures in the left in (a) of figures from 5 to 7 display multi-scale ML segmentation results by HMT(Gaussian mixture model is used in the final pixel domain, scale $j = 6$) and ML classification. The figures in the right in (a) shows MAP segmentation results obtained by applying the HMTseg algorithm to ML segmentation and the multi-scale likelihood in the left of (a). The figures in the left in (b) express multi-scale MAP segmentations by multi-scale a posterior obtained from outputs of MLP for inputs (pixel intensities and multi-scale wavelet coefficients [see equation (9)]) and by equation (11). The figures in the right in (b) shows

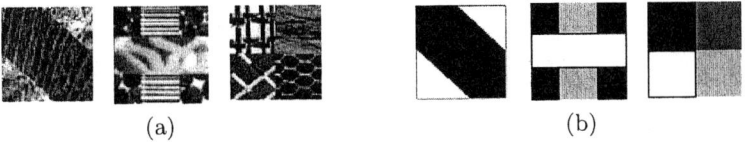

Fig. 4. (a) Test texture images and (b) ideal texture segmentations

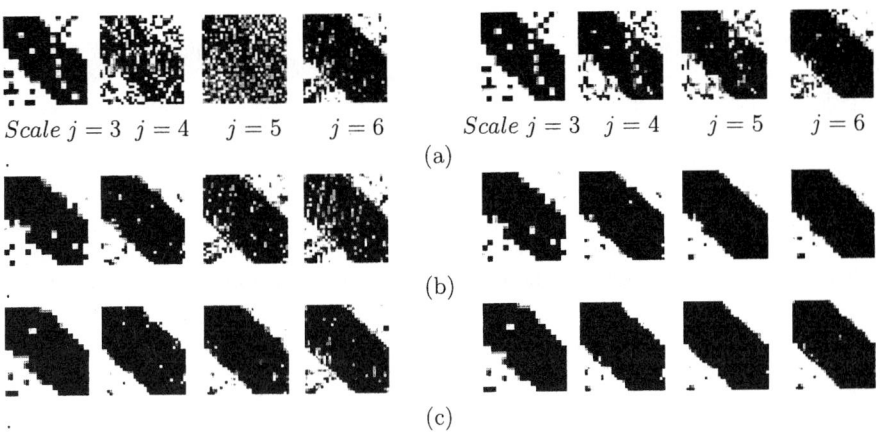

Fig. 5. Results of multi-scale texture image segmentation by each system, (a) left: by HMT, right: by HMT and HMTseg, (b) left: by the proposed method without contexts, right: by the proposed method without contexts and HMTseg, (c) left: by the proposed method with con-texts, right: by the proposed method with contexts and HMTseg.

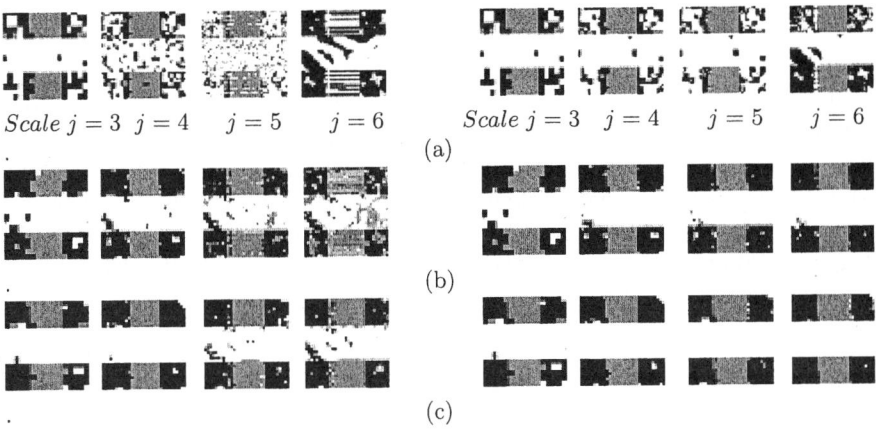

Fig. 6. Results of multi-scale texture image segmentation by each system, (a) left: by HMT, right: by HMT and HMTseg, (b) left: by the proposed method without contexts, right: by the proposed method without contexts and HMTseg, (c) left: by the proposed method with con-texts, right: by the proposed method with contexts and HMTseg.

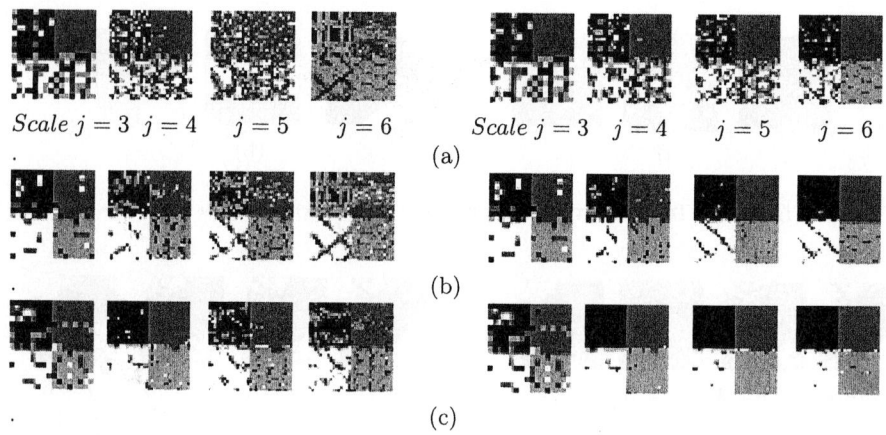

Fig. 7. Results of multi-scale texture image segmentation by each system, (a) left: by HMT, right: by HMT and HMTseg, (b) left: by the proposed method without contexts, right: by the proposed method without contexts and HMTseg, (c) left: by the proposed method with con-texts, right: by the proposed method with contexts and HMTseg.

MAP segmentation results obtained by applying the HMTseg algorithm to MAP segmentation and multi-scale a posterior in the left of (b). Likewise, the figures in the left in (c) show MAP segmentation results by MLP with the inputs of equation (13) and by equation (11). The figures in the right in (c) also show the post-processed results with HMTseg on the left of (c). As the results of the left in (a) and (b) of figures from 5 to 7 shows, the segmentations by MLP are better than those by HMT through all scales. The closer to fine scale, the better the MLP results are than HMT. As shown in the right of (a) and (b), the results by MLP and HMTseg are much better than the results by HMT and HMTseg. This shows that the post-processed segmentation results in the final pixel domain are excellent because multi-scale segmentation results by MLP are outstanding before post-processing. The figures in the left in (c) from 5 to 7 show the effect of considering contexts by the proposed method. Compar-ing (b) and (c), the segmentation results in the left in (c) are less sensitive to local noise at fine scale because of using neighboring context information. Considering context at coarse scale performs better than not considering context, but the effect on considering context at coarse scale is insignificant. The post-processed results in the right of (c) are better than in the right of (b) because the multi-scale texture segmentations in the left of (c) are excellent.

5 Conclusion

In this paper, we proposed a segmentation method using MLP networks, HMT model, and HMTseg algorithm in multi-scale wavelet domain. To compose inputs for MLP, the likelihood obtained from HMT as context information for the image and wavelet coefficients is used. Experiment results show that using context information by the proposed method improves texture segmentations at fine scale more than by only using wavelet coefficients without context information. Comparing the texture segmentation of the proposed method to the texture segmentation of the HMT model and HMTseg algorithm, the proposed method performed better.

References

1. Haralick, R. M.: Statistical and Structural Approaches to Texture. Proc. IEEE 67, no. 5 (May 1979) 786–809
2. Reed, T. R., du Buf, H.J.M.: A Review of Recent Texture segmentation and Feature Extrac-tion Techniques. CVGIP: Image Understanding, vol. 57, no. 3 (1993) 359–372
3. Chen, C. H., Pau, L. F., Wang, P. S. P. (eds.): The Handbook of Pattern Recognition and Computer Vision (2nd Edition). World Scientific Publishing Co. (1998) 207–248
4. Tuceryan, M.: Moment Based Texture Segmentation. In Proc. of 11th international Conf. on Pattern Recognition, The Hague, Netherlands, (August 1992)
5. Kwang In Kim, Keechul Jung, Se Hyun Park, Hang Joon Kim: Support Vector Machine for Texture Classification. IEEE Transactions on Pattern Analysis and Machine Intelligence, Vol. 24, No. 11 (November 2002) 1542–1550
6. Voorhees, H., Poggio, T.: Detecting textons and texture boundaries in natural images. In Proc. of the first international Conf. on Computer Vision, London (1987) 250–258
7. Du Buf, J. M. H., Kardan, M. Spann: Texture Feature Performance for Image Segmentation. Pattern Recgonition, 23 (1990) 291–309
8. Chen, Z., Feng, T.J., Houkes, Z.: Texture segmentation based on wavelet and Kohonen network for remotely sensed images. IEEE International Conf. on Systems, Man, and Cy-bernetics, Tokyo, Japan (1999) 816–821
9. Xiaoyue Jiang, Rongchun Zhao: A new method of Texture segmentation. IEEE Interna-tional Conf. on Neural Networks and Signal Processing, Nanjing, China (December 14–17, 2003) 1083–1086
10. Hu, R., Fahmy, M. M.: Texture Segmentation Based on a Hierarchical Markov Random Field Model. Signal Processing, vol. 26 (1992) 285–305
11. Jain, A. K., Farrokhnia, F.: Unsupervised Texture Segmentation Using Gabor Filters. Pat-tern Recognition, 24 (1991) 1167–1186
12. Hyeokho Choi, Richard G. Baraniuk: Multiscale Image Segmentation Using Wavelet-Domain Hidden Markov Models. IEEE Transaction on image processong, vol. 10, No. 9 (September 2001)
13. Richard, M. D., Lippmann, R. P.: Neural Network Classifiers Estimate Bayesian a posteri-ori Probabilities. Neural Computation, vol. 3 (1991) 461–483
14. Rojas, R.: Short proof of the posterior probability property of classifier neural networks. Neural Computation 8 (1996) 41–43
15. Martin Reidmiller, Heinrich Braun: A direct adaptive method for faster backpropagation learning: the Rprop algorithm. Proceedings of the ICNN, San Francisco (1993)
16. Guoliang Fan, Xiang-Gen Xia: Improved Hidden Markov Models in the Wavelet-Domain. IEEE Transaction on signal processong, vol. 49, No. 1 (January 2001)
17. Guoliang Fan, Xiang-Gen Xia: Wavelet-Based Texture Analysis and Synthesis Using Hidden Markov Models. IEEE Transaction on circuits and systems, vol. 50, No. 1 (January 2003)

An In-depth Comparison on FastICA, CuBICA and IC-FastICA

Bin Wang and Wenkai Lu

State Key Laboratory of Intelligent Technology and Systems,
Department of Automation, Tsinghua University, 100084 Beijing, China

Abstract. FastICA and CuBICA are two remarkable independent component analysis algorithms for dealing with blind signal separation problems. In this paper, we first present a novel ICA estimation algorithm, initialization constrained FastICA (IC-FastICA), through combining the technical merits of these two approaches. Then, a performance comparison study on these three approaches is conducted through the simulations on some standard benchmark data. The experimental results demonstrate that the IC-FastICA achieves higher performances on unmixing error and signal noise ratio while appreciably increasing computation cost.

1 Introduction

Blind Signal Separation (BSS) is an important topic in the research on statistics analysis and signal processing. Due to the wide range of applications in communication technique, speech analysis and other intelligent information processing, BSS has become an active research area in the past decade. Independent Component Analysis (ICA) is an effective method for separating independent sources from the mixed signals. Hyvarinen etc. developed the fixed-point ICA algorithm, which is named as FastICA [1]. The main advantage of the FastICA lies in that the convergence can be obtained fast. Moreover, the so called CuBICA algorithm, which is based on cumulants, achieves good development recently [2]. CuBICA is able to separate the linear mixtures of symmetrically and skew-symmetrically distributed source signal components. Through combining the technical merits of these two classical ICA algorithms, initialization constrained FastICA (IC-FastICA) is proposed for achieving a stable optimization with appreciably increasing the computation cost. A comparison study on these three methods is conducted to validate the efficiency of the IC-FastICA approach.

The remainder of this paper is organized as follows. In section 2, we present IC-FastICA algorithm after a brief introduction of FastICA and CuBICA. The comparison study and analysis are conducted in Section 3, followed by the conclusion in section 4.

2 Algorithms of FastICA, CuBICA and IC-FastICA

Based on the fixed-point iteration scheme for finding a maximum measurement of the non-gaussianity, FastICA algorithm is efficient to achieve the optimization during estimating the blind source signals [1,6]. For a brief introduction, we denote on unit fixed-point algorithm as follows.

$$\mathbf{w}^+ = \mathbf{w} - [\mathbf{E}\{\mathbf{x}g(\mathbf{w}^T\mathbf{x})\} - \beta\mathbf{w}]/[\mathbf{E}\{g'(\mathbf{w}^T\mathbf{x})\} - \beta] \tag{1}$$

From statistic theory, the observation data $\mathbf{x}$ can be described by its cumulants $C^{(\mathbf{x})}$. In fact, ICA is equivalent to finding an unmixing matrix that diagonalizes the cumulant tensors $C^{(\mathbf{x})}$ of the observation data $\mathbf{x}$. Based on this point, Blaschke developed the CuBICA algorithm through simultaneously considering the third- and fourth-order cumulants diagnonalization [2].

The FastICA approach is based on minimization of mutual information while using the negentropy as a measurement of Non-Gaussianity. Although it can reduce the computation, FastICA can not guarantee the global optimization for it is sensitive to the initialization setting. The cumulant based ICA calculations is proved more reliable [2]. But the computation is quite expensive because it requires to calculate the high order statistics for each iteration.

Note that the FastICA does not provide a good estimation of the initialization. We utilize the technique of diagonalization of cumulant tensors in CuBICA to obtain an initialization of source signal separation and use it in the postprocessing procedure by FastICA. Similar with the algorithm in [2], we also defined the contrast function based on third- and fourth-order cumulants as :

$$\Psi(\mathbf{Q}, \mathbf{y}) = \frac{1}{3!}\sum_\alpha (C^{(\mathbf{x})}_{\alpha\alpha\alpha})^2 + \frac{1}{4!}\sum_\alpha (C^{(\mathbf{x})}_{\alpha\alpha\alpha\alpha})^2 \tag{2}$$

$$= \frac{1}{3!}\sum_\alpha (\sum_{\alpha\beta\gamma\delta} \mathbf{Q}_{\alpha\beta}\mathbf{Q}_{\alpha\gamma}\mathbf{Q}_{\alpha\delta} C^{(\mathbf{x})}_{\beta\gamma\delta})^2$$

$$+ \frac{1}{4!}\sum_\alpha (\sum_{\alpha\beta\gamma\delta\epsilon} \mathbf{Q}_{\alpha\beta}\mathbf{Q}_{\alpha\gamma}\mathbf{Q}_{\alpha\delta}\mathbf{Q}_{\alpha\epsilon} C^{(\mathbf{x})}_{\beta\gamma\delta\epsilon})^2$$

where $C^{(\mathbf{x})}$ are the cumulants of the whitened data set $\mathbf{x}$ and $\mathbf{Q}_{..}$ are the elements of the rotation matrix. Eq. 2 is simply the sum of the squared third-order and fourth-order off-diagonal elements. The factors $\frac{1}{3!}$ and $\frac{1}{4!}$ arise from an expansion of the Kullback-Leibler divergence in $\mathbf{x}$ [6].

The problem of selecting proper initialization separating matrix $\mathbf{W}$ is equivalent to an optimization procedure to find the orthogonal matrix $\mathbf{Q}$ which can maximizes Eq. 2. So the initialized value of matrix $\mathbf{W}$ can be denoted as:

$$\mathbf{W}_0 = \arg\max_{\mathbf{Q}} \Psi(\mathbf{Q}, \mathbf{y}) \tag{3}$$

Therefore, we can conduct the IC-FastICA algorithm for estimating the blind source signals in the following steps [6]:

- 1.Calculate the initialization of separating matrix $\mathbf{w}$ from Eq. 3 ;
- 2.Update the vectors of separating matrix by using the simplified form of FastICA: $\mathbf{w}^+ = \mathbf{E}\{\mathbf{x}g(\mathbf{w}^T\mathbf{x})\} - \mathbf{E}\{g'(\mathbf{w}^T\mathbf{x})\}\mathbf{w}$;

- 3.Normalize the vectors of separating matrix : $\mathbf{w} = \mathbf{w}^+/\|\mathbf{w}^+\|$;
- 4.Repeat (2) and (3) until achieve the convergence.

3 Comparison Study

In order to compare these three algorithms, we mainly evaluate the performance in three aspects, unmixing error (PI), signal noise ratio (SNR) and computation time (T). As used in [1,2,6], the unmixing error is defined as:

$$PI = \frac{1}{N^2}(\sum_{i=1}^{N}(\sum_{j=1}^{N}\frac{|P_{ij}|}{max_k |P_{ik}|} - 1) \qquad (4)$$
$$+ \sum_{j=1}^{N}(\sum_{i=1}^{N}\frac{|P_{ij}|}{max_k |P_{kj}|} - 1))$$

Moreover, the performance is also quantitatively measured by the signal noise ratio (SNR), which is calculated as:

$$SNR = 10 \cdot \log \frac{\|\mathbf{s}\|^2}{\|\hat{\mathbf{s}} - \mathbf{s}\|^2} \qquad (5)$$

where $\hat{\mathbf{s}}$ is the estimation of source components $\mathbf{s}$.

Generally speaking, these three criteria can provide enough evaluation of the performance. Five different kinds of public test data, coming from [3, 4, 5] is used in our simulations. The test data cover several kinds of distributions, such as sub-Gaussian and super-Gaussian sources. The summary of these used public benchmarks is given in Table 1. The source data are randomly mixed to generate the observation data.

Table 1. The summary of benchmarks: d denotes the dimensionality of signal, N denotes the length of data.

Benchmark	d	N	Description
1 [3]	4	5000	sounds (speech and music) sources
2 [4]	5	100000	popular songs
3 [3]	7	10000	synthetic signals
4 [3]	10	8000	sounds (speech and music) sources
5 [5]	16	221088	sounds (speech and music) sources

For comparing the performance of FastICA, CuBICA and IC-FastICA, we use the same setting for all the algorithms, such as iteration steps. In Table 2, the simulation results on the test benchmarks are given.

From Table 2, we can conclude a summary on the comparison study. First, about performance evaluated by PI and SNR, FastICA and CuBICA have the

Table 2. The performance comparison of CuBICA, FastICA and IC-FastICA. The performance is evaluated by unmixing error (PI), signal-noise ratio (SNR) and computation time (T).

Test Data	Performance	CuBICA	FastICA	IC-FastICA
Benchmark 1	PI	0.0246	0.0254	0.0179
	SNR	31.3	30.9	32.3
	T	0.24	0.49	0.38
Benchmark 2	PI	0.0269	0.0265	0.0217
	SNR	25.0	30.2	32.6
	T	4.51	4.00	4.68
Benchmark 3	PI	0.0127	0.0084	0.0077
	SNR	34.1	38.8	39.4
	T	1.43	1.16	1.28
Benchmark 4	PI	0.072	0.074	0.057
	SNR	17.6	17.6	20.7
	T	2.71	1.28	2.13
Benchmark 5	PI	0.034	0.040	0.030
	SNR	21.5	21.0	23.2
	T	203.2	47.5	98.7

comparable results. Although CuBICA is claimed to has advantage in dealing with asymmetrically distributed data, most benchmark data and real data do not obey this kind of complicated distributions. However, IC-FastICA obtained better results on all the test data. Second, CuBICA runs even faster than FastICA on low-dimensional data (i.e. benchmark 1, $d = 4$). But its computation cost is dramatically increased as to the increase of data dimensionality. For example, the running time of CuBICA is 4.28 times to that of FastICA (i.e benchmark 5, $d = 16$). The computation cost of our IC-FastICA is between CuBICA and FastICA. For example, during decomposing high-dimensional data such as benchmark 4, the computation cost is increased 66% to FastICA (21.4% faster than CuBICA), while achieving 17.6% gain on SNR and decreasing 30% on PI than FastICA. In general, IC-FastICA usually obtains better performance with acceptable computation increasing.

Here, we give a qualitative explanation on the performance comparison results. As described in Section 2, in order to obtain the optimization of the rotation matrix **Q**, the matrix should be updated for each selected pair of components. We called this one iteration. If the dimensionality of the data is N, there are $\frac{N(N-1)}{2}$ possible pairs of components. In other words, the rotation matrix **Q** can be updated based on all the pair information after $\frac{N(N-1)}{2}$ iterations, which is so called one sweep. For CuBICA the optimization is based on $\lfloor \sqrt{N} \rfloor$ sweeps. When the number samples and dimensionality of data increased, the computation cost will increase dramatically. In fact, the first sweep is most important because it obtains most convergence, which is proved by the experiments in pervious work [2,6]. Motivated by this point, we only execute one sweep on the rotation matrix **Q** and use it as the constrained initialization for FastICA optimization. Our simulation demonstrate that it can utilize the advantage of cumulant diagonalization without increasing too much computation cost. Furthermore, although there is no strictly mathematical proof that IC-FastICA can gurantee the global optimization, IC-FastICA usually obtains a bettern convergence value than FastICA in our experiments. We attribute this merit to the constrained initialization estimation before the first iteration.

4 Conclusion

In this paper, we present a novel ICA estimation method, IC-FastICA. Through simultaneously diagonalizing the third- and fourth- order cumulants, a good initialization of the separating matrix is computed. With this constraint, the approach can obtain a better performance. Note that the high-order statistic only be calculated for one sweep, which only consumes limited computation cost. Moreover, we study the performance comparison on FastICA, CubICA and IC-FastICA through the simulations on some public benchmark data. The experiments demonstrate that CubICA runs much slower than FastICA on high-dimensional data while do not necessarily obtain distinct performance improvement. However, IC-FastICA archives better performance on all our test benchmarks, both low-dimensional and high-dimensional. Although, the computation time of IC-FastICA is correspondingly increased, it is still much faster than CuBICA and acceptable in real applications.

Acknowledgement

This work is supported in part by National Natural Science Foundation of China (No. 40474040, 60390540) and CNPC Innovation Fund.

References

1. Hyvarinen, A.: Fast and robust fixed-point algorithms for independent component analysis. IEEE Trans. on Neural Networks. vol. 10(1999), no. 3. 626-634
2. Blaschke, T., Wiskott, L.: CuBICA: Independent Component Analysis by Simultaneous Third- and Fourth-Order Cumulant Diagonalization. IEEE Trans. on Signal Processing. Volume: 52(2004). Issue: 5 . 1250 - 1256
3. Cichocki, A., Amari, S., Siwek, K. Tanaka, T. et al.: ICALAB Toolboxes. http://www.bsp.brain.riken.jp/ICALAB
4. ICA ' 99 Synthetic Benchmarks. http://sound.media.mit.edu/ica-bench/
5. Pearlmutter, B.: 16 clips sampled from audio CDs. (1996). http://snot.cs.unm.edu/ bap/cICA/clips-wav
6. Bin Wang, Wenkai Lu: A Fixed-Point Independent Component Analysis with Initialization Constraint. the Third International Conference on Communications, Circuits and Systems (ICCCAS'05). 2005

Characteristics of Equinumber Principle for Adaptive Vector Quantization

Michiharu Maeda[1], Noritaka Shigei[2], and Hiromi Miyajima[2]

[1] Kurume National College of Technology,
1-1-1 Komorino, Kurume, Japan
maedami@kurume-nct.ac.jp
[2] Faculty of Engineering, Kagoshima University,
1-21-40 Korimoto, Kagoshima, Japan
{shigei, miya}@eee.kagoshima-u.ac.jp

Abstract. This paper describes characteristics of adaptive vector quantization according to the equinumber principle. Three methods of adaptive vector quantization are presented with the objective of avoiding the initial dependency of reference vectors. The present approaches which have output units without neighboring relations equalize the numbers of inputs in a partition space. The first approach is a creation method which sequentially creates output units to reach a predetermined number of neurons founded on the equinumber principle in the learning process. The second is a reduction method which sequentially deletes output units to reach a prespecified number. The third is an unification method of the creation and reduction methods, which deletes units after creating under the predetermined number. Experimental results show the properties of the present techniques.

1 Introduction

In order to quantize and compress multiple data, vector quantization probabilistically encodes a few vectors. As an useful vector quantization, generally, the Linde-Buzo-Gray algorithm [1] is well known as the batch learning. In the meantime, the adaptive vector quantization is adopted as the on-line learning in competitive learning for neural networks [2],[3]. However the algorithms have a drawback in that the learning results depend on the initial values of reference vectors. For vector quantization in neural networks, variant improvements have been achieved [4]–[7]. The application of competitive learning involves, for example, the combinatorial optimization problem, pattern recognition, image processing, and clustering. Although a number of learning models exist, they differ with respect to the field of application. With respect to the algorithms, asymptotic distributions and quantitative properties for reference vectors are discussed [8]–[11]. For the optimal distribution of reference vectors, it is well known that the average distortion is asymptotically minimized when partition errors are equivalent to each other [12].

In this paper, we describe characteristics of adaptive vector quantization according to the equinumber principle. Three methods of adaptive vector quantization are presented with the objective of avoiding the initial dependency of reference vectors. The present approaches which have output units without neighboring relations equalize the numbers of inputs in a partition space. The first approach is a creation method which sequentially creates output units to reach a predetermined number of neurons founded on the equinumber principle in the learning process. The second is a reduction method which sequentially deletes output units to reach a prespecified number. The third is an unification method of the creation and reduction methods, which deletes units after creating under the predetermined number. The conventional algorithms with high quality in vector quantization are discussed and compared to the present algorithms. Furthermore the present approaches are applied to image data and the validity in employing as an image coding system is examined.

2 Adaptive Vector Quantization

2.1 Fundamental Learning

Kohonen's algorithm suggests that the updating of weights is modified to involve neighboring relations in the output array [13]. In the vector space R^n, the input x which is generated on the probability density function $p(x)$ is defined. Thus x has the components from x_1 to x_n. The output unit y_i is generally arranged in an array of one- or two-dimensional maps, and is completely connected to the inputs by way of w_{ij}.

Let $x(t)$ be an input vector at step t and let $w_i(0)$ be reference vectors at initial values in R^n space. For the given input vector $x(t)$, we calculate the distance between $x(t)$ and $w_i(t)$, and select the reference vector as a winner c minimizing the distance. The process is written as follows:

$$c = \arg \min_i \{\|x - w_i\|\}, \tag{1}$$

where arg(·) gives the index c of the winner.

With the use of the winner c, the reference vector $w_i(t)$ is updated as follows:

$$\Delta w_i = \alpha(t)(x - w_i) \quad (i \in N_c(t)), \tag{2}$$

where $\alpha(t)$ is the learning rate and is a decreasing function of time ($0 < \alpha(t) < 1$). $N_c(t)$ has a set of indexes of topological neighborhoods for the winner c at step t. If $N_c(t)$ only has an index of the winner, the algorithm becomes the standard competitive learning.

2.2 Average Distortion

Generally, the mean quantization error can be represented as follows [6]:

$$H = \sum_{i=1}^{k} \int_{S_i} d(x, w_i) p(x) dx, \tag{3}$$

where k is the number of clustering set represented by the partition space S_i, $d(x, w_i)$ is the square error of the Euclidean distance between the input vector $x = (x_1, x_2, \cdots, x_n)$

and the reference vector $\boldsymbol{w}_i = (w_{1i}, w_{2i}, \cdots, w_{ni})$ (i.e., $d(\boldsymbol{x}, \boldsymbol{w}_i) = \|\boldsymbol{x}-\boldsymbol{w}_i\|^2$), and $p(\boldsymbol{x})$ is the probability density function.

In this study, for the reference vectors obtained from learning results, a distortion error is calculated in the following description. Let D_i and m_i be the i-th partition error and its number of inputs, respectively, as the following equations.

$$D_i = \frac{1}{n} \sum_{\boldsymbol{x} \in S_i} d(\boldsymbol{x}, \boldsymbol{w}_i), \tag{4}$$

and

$$m_i = \mathcal{H}(\boldsymbol{x} \in S_i), \tag{5}$$

where n is the input dimension, $\mathcal{H}$ is a number function, and m_i means the number of input vectors in the partition space S_i.

Continuously, the mean square error E is given as follows:

$$E = \frac{1}{M} \sum_{i=1}^{k} D_i, \tag{6}$$

where,

$$M = \sum_{i=1}^{k} m_i. \tag{7}$$

It is known that Eq. (3) is corresponding to Eq. (6) [14], as the sequence of input vectors $\boldsymbol{x}(t)$ becomes stationary and ergodic [15].

3 Equinumber Principle

In Eq. (6), optimal distributions of reference vectors have been known that the average distortion E yields a minimum when the partition errors D_i ($i = 1, 2, \cdots, k$) are equivalent to each other [12]. In other words, if the equidistortion condition $D_1 = D_2 = \cdots = D_k$ is satisfied, the average distortion E is asymptotically minimized. Here, we assume that the probability density function $p(\boldsymbol{x})$ of the input signal $\boldsymbol{x}$ is sufficiently smooth and the number of reference vectors k is large enough.

Let us now exhibit that the condition $D_1 = D_2 = \cdots = D_k$ is satisfied when the input vector $\boldsymbol{x}$ uniformly distributes and the numbers of inputs in the partition spaces $S_1, S_2, \cdots, S_k$ are mutually same. To begin with, according to Eq. (4), the partition errors are represented as follows.

$$D_1 = \frac{1}{n} \sum_{\boldsymbol{x} \in S_1} d(\boldsymbol{x}, \boldsymbol{w}_1), \quad D_2 = \frac{1}{n} \sum_{\boldsymbol{x} \in S_2} d(\boldsymbol{x}, \boldsymbol{w}_2),$$

$$\cdots, \quad D_k = \frac{1}{n} \sum_{\boldsymbol{x} \in S_k} d(\boldsymbol{x}, \boldsymbol{w}_k). \tag{8}$$

Here we assume that the number of inputs in the partition space S_i ($i = 1, 2, \cdots, k$) becomes m (i.e., $m_1 = m_2 = \cdots = m_k = m$), the partition errors are written as follows.

$$D_1 = \frac{1}{n}\sum_{i=1}^{m} d(\boldsymbol{x}, \boldsymbol{w}_1), \quad D_2 = \frac{1}{n}\sum_{i=m+1}^{2m} d(\boldsymbol{x}, \boldsymbol{w}_2),$$

$$\cdots, \quad D_k = \frac{1}{n}\sum_{i=(k-1)m+1}^{km} d(\boldsymbol{x}, \boldsymbol{w}_k). \qquad (9)$$

As we assumed that the numbers of inputs are mutually equal, when the input vectors are uniformly alloted in the partition spaces $S_1, S_2, \cdots, S_k$, the following equation comes into existence.

$$\sum_{i=1}^{m} d(\boldsymbol{x}, \boldsymbol{w}_1) = \sum_{i=m+1}^{2m} d(\boldsymbol{x}, \boldsymbol{w}_2) = \cdots = \sum_{i=(k-1)m+1}^{km} d(\boldsymbol{x}, \boldsymbol{w}_k), \qquad (10)$$

where $M = km$.

Therefore the following equation holds for the partition error.

$$D_1 = D_2 = \cdots = D_k. \qquad (11)$$

The condition $D_1 = D_2 = \cdots = D_k$ is satisfied when the numbers of inputs in the partition spaces $S_1, S_2, \cdots, S_k$ are mutually equal. Thus, as the partition errors are equivalent to each other, the average distortion is asymptotically minimized. In this paper, we term that the equinumber principle.

4 Adaptive Vector Quantization in Equinumber Principle

A creation method of adaptive vector quantization is presented from the viewpoint of the equinumber principle. To begin with, one output unit is prepared at the initial stage, and a reference vector according to the unit is updated under competitive learning. Then, output units are sequentially created to reach a prespecified number based on the criterion of the equinumber principle, and competitive learning is performed until the termination condition is satisfied. After the number of input vectors in the partition space is calculated, a new neuron is created and its reference vector has the value near the reference vector which has a maximum number of input vectors in the partition space for all the reference vectors. The creation algorithm is presented as follows.

[*Creation algorithm*]

Step C1 Initialization:
Give an initial vector $\boldsymbol{w}_1(0)$, maximum iteration T_{max}, partial iteration u_c, and final number of neurons l. Set $t \leftarrow 0$ and $k \leftarrow 1$.
Step C2 Learning:
(**C2.1**) Choose an input vector x at random among $\{\boldsymbol{x}_1, \boldsymbol{x}_2, \cdots, \boldsymbol{x}_M\}$.
(**C2.2**) Select a winner c according to Eq.(1).
(**C2.3**) Update the winner vector according to Eq. (2).
(**C2.4**) Set $t \leftarrow t + 1$.
(**C2.5**) If $t = u_c \times k$ and $k < l$, then go to Step C3, otherwise go to C4.

Step C3 Creation:
  (C3.1) Create a neuron.
  (C3.2) Set $k \leftarrow k + 1$.
  (C3.3) Calculate m_i according to Eq. (5).
  (C3.4) Give w_k near w_s, where $m_s \geq m_i$ (for all i).
Step C4 Condition:
  If $t = T_{max}$, then terminate, otherwise go to Step C2.

In the algorithm, t is the learning step ($0 \leq t \leq T_{max}$) and k is the number of neurons in the learning process.

For the second approach, a reduction method of adaptive vector quantization is presented according to the equinumber principle as described above. In the first place, many output units are prepared at the initial stage, and reference vectors according to the units are updated under competitive learning. Then, output units are sequentially reduced to reach a predetermined number based on the criterion of the equinumber principle, and competitive learning is performed until the termination condition is satisfied. Here, when a neuron is deleted, its reference vector has a minimum number of inputs after the numbers of inputs in partition space are calculated. The reduction algorithm is presented as follows.

[Reduction algorithm]

Step R1 Initialization:
  Give initial vectors $\{w_1(0), w_2(0), \cdots, w_k(0)\}$, initial number of neurons l_0, final number of neurons l, maximum iteration T_{max}, initial iteration u_0, and partial iteration u_r. Set $t \leftarrow 0$ and $k \leftarrow l_0$.
Step R2 Learning:
  (R2.1) Choose an input vector x at random among $\{x_1, x_2, \cdots, x_M\}$.
  (R2.2) Select a winner c according to Eq.(1).
  (R2.3) Update the winner vector according to Eq. (2).
  (R2.4) Set $t \leftarrow t + 1$.
  (R2.5) If $k > l$ and $t = u_0 + u_r \times q$, then go to Step R3, otherwise go to Step R4, where q is a positive integer.
Step R3 Reduction:
  (R3.1) Delete a neuron.
  (R3.2) Set $k \leftarrow k - 1$.
  (R3.3) Calculate m_i according to Eq. (5).
  (R3.4) Eliminate w_s, where $m_s \leq m_i$ (for all i).
Step R4 Condition:
  If $t = T_{max}$, then terminate, otherwise go to Step R2.

For the third approach, an unification method of adaptive vector quantization is presented according to the equinumber principle. In the first place, the predetermined number of output units is prepared in advance and neurons are generated by the creation method. Next, output units are sequentially reduced to reach a predetermined number by the reduction method. The unification algorithm is presented as follows.

[*Unification algorithm*]

Step U1 Initialization:
Give initial vectors { $w_1(0)$, $w_2(0)$, $\cdots$, $w_k(0)$}, maximum number of neurons l_{max}, final number of neurons l, maximum iteration T_{max}, initial reduction iteration u_0, creation iteration u_c, and reduction iteration u_r. Set $t \leftarrow 0$ and $k \leftarrow l_0$.

Step U2 Learning:
(**U2.1**) Choose an input vector x at random among $\{x_1, x_2, \cdots, x_M\}$.
(**U2.2**) Select a winner c according to Eq.(1).
(**U2.3**) Update the winner vector according to Eq. (2).
(**U2.4**) Set $t \leftarrow t+1$.
(**U2.5**) If $k < l_{max}$ and $t = u_c \times k$, then go to Step U3, otherwise to to Step U5.
(**U2.6**) If $k > l$ and $t = u_0 + u_r \times q$, then go to Step U4, otherwise go to Step U5, where q is a positive integer.

Step U3 Creation:
(**U3.1**) Create a neuron.
(**U3.2**) Set $k \leftarrow k+1$.
(**U3.3**) Calculate m_i according to Eq. (5).
(**U3.4**) Give w_k near w_s, where $m_s \geq m_i$ (for all i).

Step U4 Reduction:
(**U4.1**) Delete a neuron.
(**U4.2**) Set $k \leftarrow k-1$.
(**U4.3**) Calculate m_i according to Eq. (5).
(**U4.4**) Eliminate w_s, where $m_s \leq m_i$ (for all i).

Step U5 Condition:
If $t = T_{max}$, then terminate, otherwise go to Step U2.

5 Experimental Results

In the performance comparison, variant distributions are considered as input patterns as shown in Fig. 1. Input vectors are assigned within [0, 1] on x and y axes, and reference vectors are distributed at random among input vectors. Numerical experiments are performed for each of Kohonen's self-organizing map (SOM), the standard competitive learning (CL), the neural-gas network (NG), the creation algorithm (CA), the reduction algorithm (RA), and the unification algorithm (UA).

In the SOM, N_c has a set of indexes of the winner and its first topological neighborhood for half of all steps as the square array (6×5). For the remaining steps, N_c has the winner index only. The NG has the parameters in Ref. [5]. The parameters are chosen as follows: $M = 5000, l_0 = 60, l = 30, l_{max} = 40, T_{max} = 30000, u_c = T_{max}/4(l+1)$, $u_0 = T_{max}/8, u_r = T_{max}/8(l_0 - l + 1), \alpha(t) = \alpha_0(1 - t/T_{max})$, and $\alpha_0 = 0.1$.

Figure 1 shows the input patterns: (a) and (b) are uniform in the rectangular space, formed by random numbers generated by computer. Table 1 summarizes the mean square error (MSE) and standard deviation of subdistortions (SDS) for each algorithm in the input patterns i and ii, where the subdistortion signifies the partition error D_i. The results are the averages of 1000 trials. Excellent results are shown by the CA, RA, and

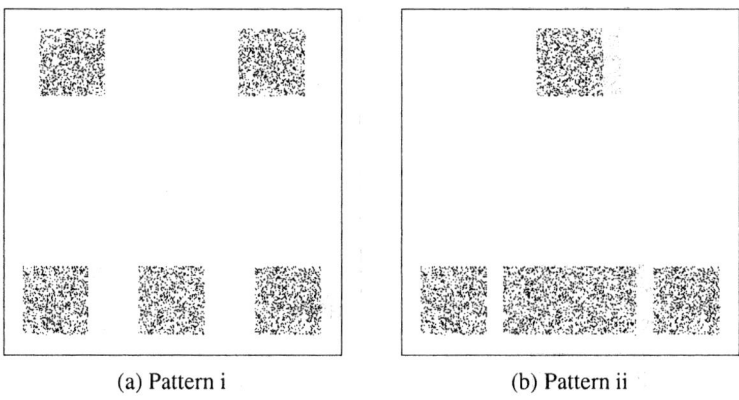

(a) Pattern i (b) Pattern ii

Fig. 1. Variant input patterns. (a) and (b) are uniform in the rectangular spaces.

Table 1. Mean square error (MSE) and standard deviation of subdistortions (SDS) for each algorithm. The results are averages of 1000 trials. (MSE ($\times 10^{-4}$), SDS ($\times 10^{-2}$)).

Algorithm	i		ii	
	MSE	SDS	MSE	SDS
SOM	8.14	22.2	7.12	15.2
CL	7.13	27.2	6.44	15.6
NG	6.20	7.36	6.35	11.5
CA	6.00	5.64	5.97	5.49
RA	6.05	7.35	5.96	6.04
UA	5.99	5.91	5.94	5.51

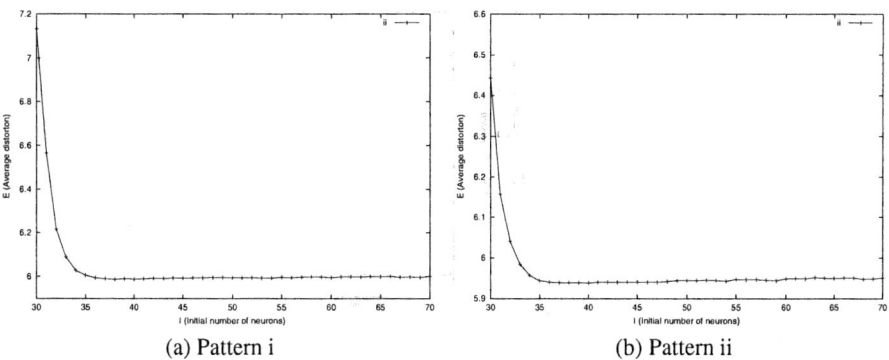

(a) Pattern i (b) Pattern ii

Fig. 2. Relation between average distortion E and maximum number of neurons I for UA

Table 2. Mean square error (MSE) and standard deviation of subsistortions (SDS) for image coding system (SDS ($\times 10^3$))

Algorithm	i		ii	
	MSE	SDS	MSE	SDS
SOM	65.46	2.737	42.11	1.955
CL	65.52	2.777	42.15	1.981
NG	64.20	1.755	41.03	1.096
CA	63.58	1.691	41.34	1.614
RA	64.07	2.070	40.74	1.357
UA	63.70	1.738	40.82	1.358

 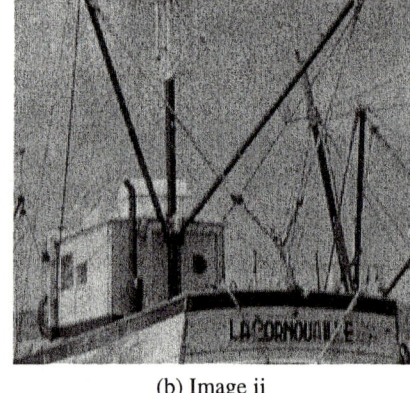

(a) Image i   (b) Image ii

Fig. 3. Original images coded with 8 bits/pixel

UA for all the input patterns. In other words, the three algorithms, CA, RA, and UA, minimize MSE and SDS.

For the UA, the effect of the number of vectors on accuracy in the creation and reduction stage is investigated. In other words, we examine closely the change of the average distortion when the maximum number of neurons varies. Figure 2 shows the relation between the average distortion E and the maximum number of neurons I. The condition for the computation is the same as in the foregoing description. As shown in the figure, the average distortion becomes larger until about $I = 35$. After this, the average distortion scarcely changes when the maximum number of neurons increases.

In the next experiments, we consider an image coding system [16] as an application of the present approaches. In the example for the original 256×256 image, each input vector x_i ($i = 1, 2, \cdots, M$) is constructed as a $2 \times 2 (= n)$ block of pixel, and is replaced to a codebook (reference vector) w_i ($i = 1, 2, \cdots, k$). We assume that the compression rate R [bits/pixel] is prepared in advance, where $R = (\log_2 k)/n$.

Figure 3 illustrates two original images. Numerical experiments are performed for each of Kohonen's self-organizing map (SOM), the standard competitive learning (CL), the neural-gas network (NG), the creation algorithm (CA), the reduction algorithm (RA), and the unification algorithm (UA). Initial values of codebooks are distributed at random among input data. In the SOM, N_c has a set of indexes of the winner and its first topological neighborhood for half of all steps as the square array ($4 \times 2 \times 2 \times 2$). For the remaining steps, N_c has the winner index only. The parameters are chosen as follows: $M = 16384, T_{max} = 98304, l_0 = 64, l = 32$, and $l_{max} = 40$. Here, all the models have the same maximum iterations. The results are averages of 1000 trials.

For the average distortion, the three algorithms, CA, RA, and UA, somewhat yield more optimal results than the other algorithms. The CA, RA, and UA are also effective for the application to the image coding.

6 Conclusions

In this paper, we have described characteristics of adaptive vector quantization according to the equinumber principle. Three methods of adaptive vector quantization was presented with the objective of avoiding the initial dependency of reference vectors. The present approaches which had output units without neighboring relations equalized the numbers of inputs in a partition space. The first approach was a creation method which sequentially creates output units to reach a predetermined number of neurons founded on the equinumber principle in the learning process. The second was a reduction method which sequentially deletes output units to reach a prespecified number. The third was an unification method of the creation and reduction methods, which deletes units after creating under the predetermined number. For the mean square error and the standard deviation of subdistortions, it has been shown that the present methods are more effective than the existing approaches. Finally, for the future works, we will study more effective techniques and practical applications of the present algorithms.

References

1. Linde, Y., Buzo, A., Gray, R.M.: An algorithm for vector quantizer design. IEEE Trans. Commun. **28** (1980) 84–95
2. Grossberg, S.: Adaptive pattern classification and universal recoding: I. Parallel development and coding of neural feature detectors. Biol. Cybern. **23** (1976) 121–134
3. Willshaw, D.J., von der Malsburg, C.: How patterned neural connections can be set up by self-organization. Proc. R. Soc. Lond. B. **194** (1976) 431–445
4. Hertz, J., Krogh, A., Palmer, R.G.: Introduction to the theory of neural computation. Addison-Wesley (1991)
5. Martinetz, T.M., Berkovich, S.G., Schulten, K.J.: "Neural-gas" network for vector quantization and its application to time-series prediction. IEEE Trans. Neural Networks **4** (1993) 558–569
6. Maeda, M., Miyajima, H.: Competitive learning methods with refractory and creative approaches. IEICE Trans. Fundamentals **E82-A** (1999) 1825–1833
7. Maeda, M., Miyajima, H.: Adaptation strength according to neighborhood ranking of self-organizing neural networks. IEICE Trans. Fundamentals **E85-A** (2002) 2078–2082

8. Yamada, Y., Tazaki, S., Gray, R.: Asymptotic performance of block quantizers with difference distortion measures. IEEE Trans. Inform. Theory **26** (1980) 6–14
9. Zador, P.L.: Asymptotic quantization error of continuous signals and the quantization dimension. IEEE Trans. Inform. Theory **28** (1982) 139–149
10. Ritter, H., Schulten, K.: On the stationary state of Kohonen's self-organizing sensory mapping. Biol. Cybern. **54** (1986) 99–106
11. Ritter, H., Schulten, K.: Convergence properties of Kohonen's topology conserving maps: Fluctuations, stability, and dimension selection. Biol. Cybern. **60** (1988) 59–71
12. Gersho, A.: Asymptotically optimal block quantization. IEEE Trans. Inform. Theory **28** (1979) 157–166
13. Kohonen, T.: Self-Organization and associative memory. Springer-Verlag Berlin (1989)
14. Reichl, L.E.: A modern course in statistical physics. University of Texas Press (1980)
15. Imai, H.: Information theory. Shokodo (1984)
16. Gersho, A., Gray, R.M.: Vector quantization and signal compression. Kluwer Academic Publishers (1992)

ANFIS Based Dynamic Model Compensator for Tracking and GPS Navigation Applications*

Dah-Jing Jwo and Zong-Ming Chen

Department of Communications and Guidance Engineering,
National Taiwan Ocean University, 20224 Keelung, Taiwan
djjwo@mail.ntou.edu.tw

Abstract. This paper deals with the design of radar target tracking and GPS (Global Positioning System) navigation based on the ANFIS (adaptive network-based fuzzy inference system) aided adaptive Kalman filtering approach. To achieve good filtering solutions, the Kalman filter designers are required to have good knowledge on both dynamic process and measurement models, in addition to the assumption that both the process and measurement are corrupted by zero-mean Gaussian white sequences. To prevent divergence problem when the Kalman assumptions are violated, the ANFIS is employed as the dynamic model corrector. The performance improvement will be demonstrated and discussed based on the proposed method.

1 Introduction

The Kalman filter (KF) [1] provides optimal (in the viewpoint of minimum mean square error) estimate of the system state vector, is recognised as one of the most powerful state estimation techniques. To achieve good filtering results, the designers are required to have good knowledge on both the dynamic process and measurement models, in addition to the assumption that both the process and measurement are corrupted by zero-mean Gaussian white sequences.

Several researches have been done to combine the learning capability of neural network (NN) [2] and fuzzy reasoning. The scheme is called the fuzzy neural network (FNN) [3-5]. The FNN can be realized as a neural network structure, and the parameters of fuzzy rules can be expressed as the connection weights of the neural network. It is easy to translate the "expert priori knowledge" into the fuzzy if-then rules. The FNN architecture employed in this work is the ANFIS (adaptive network-based fuzzy inference system) [5], in which Sugeno-type fuzzy inference is employed. The ANFIS architecture can construct an input-output mapping based on both human knowledge (in the form of fuzzy if-then rules) and stipulated input-output data pairs. The ANFIS will be employed into the target tracking and navigation systems as a dynamic model corrector, which aids the Kalman filter for real-time identification of nonlinear

---

* This work has been supported by the National Science Council of the Republic of China under grant no. NSC 93-2212-E-019-004.

dynamics errors, especially when the modeling of uncertainty is concerned. By monitoring the measurement residuals, this mechanism will be able to provide real-time error correction for the dynamic modeling errors to prevent divergence of the Kalman filter.

2 The ANFIS Aided Adaptive Kalman Filter

The Kalman filter provides estimation with minimum error variance. The extended Kalman filtering is a nonlinear version of Kalman filtering. Further discussion on the Kalman filter algorithm can be referred to [1].

The ANFIS, in which Takagi and Sugeno's type fuzzy inference is employed, was proposed by Jang in 1993 [5]. As the name implies, the ANFIS is essentially a fuzzy inference system implemented as an adaptive network. It is a multilayer feed-forward network where each node performs a particular node function on incoming signals. Suppose that the fuzzy inference system under consideration has two inputs x and y and one output z. Assume that the rule base contains two fuzzy IF-THEN rules of Takagi and Sugeno's type [5]:

Rule 1: If x is A_1 and y is B_1, then $z = f_1 = a_1 x + b_1 y + c_1$ (1a)

Rule 2: If x is A_2 and y is B_2, then $z = f_2 = a_2 x + b_2 y + c_2$ (1b)

The ANFIS employed in the present work is made of five layers, which has the architecture as shown in Fig. 1. Detailed discussion on the topic can be found in [5].

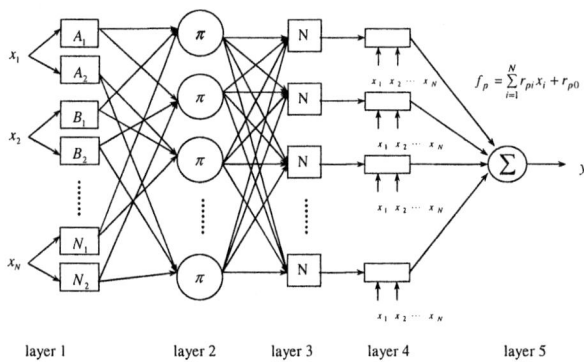

Fig. 1. The ANFIS architecture

The basic idea of this work is to incorporate the well trained ANFIS into the KF so that the ANFIS can realize the mapping from the measurement to the additive correction to the estimation of the KF. The ANFIS is incorporated into the KF in order to compensate the model uncertainties. The ANFIS architecture constructs an input-output mapping based on both human knowledge (in the form of fuzzy IF-THEN rules) and stipulated input-output data pairs. Fig. 2 shows the architecture of the

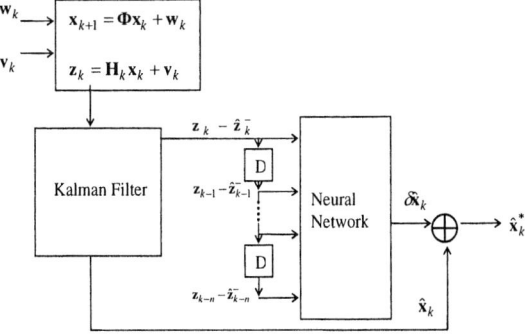

Fig. 2. The ANFIS aided Kalman filter

ANFIS aided Kalman filter. The input parameters of ANFIS are the sequence of correction, i.e., multiplication of innovation sequences $(\mathbf{z}_k - \hat{\mathbf{z}}_k^-)$ and Kalman gain:

$$\mathbf{K}_k(\mathbf{z}_k - \hat{\mathbf{z}}_k^-), \mathbf{K}_{k-1}(\mathbf{z}_{k-1} - \hat{\mathbf{z}}_{k-1}^-) \ldots \mathbf{K}_{k-n}(\mathbf{z}_{k-n} - \hat{\mathbf{z}}_{k-n}^-) \quad (2)$$

and the outputs are the errors between the true and Kalman filtering estimated state, which should be added to the Kalman filtering state estimate for compensating the modeling errors. The notion 'D' denotes the delay.

3 Application to Maneuvering Target Tracking

In actual radar tracking filter designs, there exist the model uncertainties which cannot be expressed by the linear state-space model since the actual target motions are non-linear process. Good performance is derived for the straight portion of the trajectory. Estimation accuracy of the KF is degraded due to the uncertainties which cannot be expressed by the linear state-space model given a priori. Hence, compensating the uncertainties is an important task in the radar tracking filter design. The dynamic process in medium dynamic environment can be represented by the Constant Velocity (CV) model [6], which is used which is computationally less expensive. The inaccuracies in the estimation due to the use of velocity model are corrected by the ANFIS, which is trained off-line to learn the errors in tracking. In the training phase, initially 5 inputs have been used and each input contains 2 bell-shaped membership functions.

The vehicle is assumed to move at a constant velocity of $100 m/s$ with a trajectory represented by the dash line, as shown in Fig. 3(a), while in the testing phase, the vehicle is assumed to move at the same constant velocity with a trajectory as shown in Fig. 3(b). Detailed description of the motion is summarized in Table 1. For both the two scenarios, the user started from the position of North 25.15 degrees, East 121.78 degrees. In Fig. 3(a), the divergence problem by using the standard Kalman filtering is observed, which is shown by the dot line.

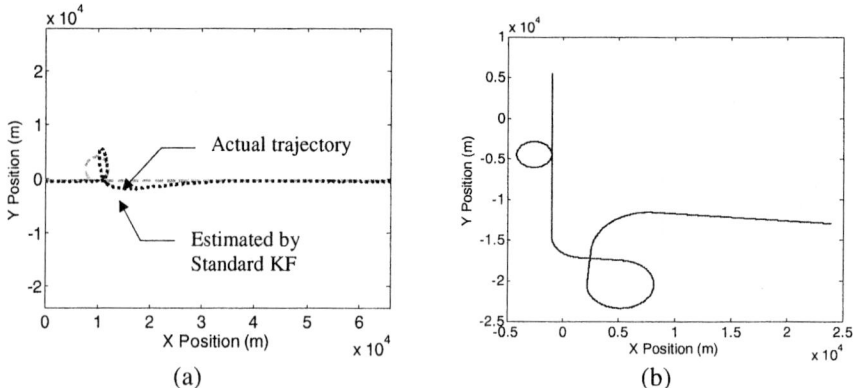

Fig. 3. The vehicle trajectory used for (a) training and (b) testing scenarios

Table 1. Description of vehicle motion in training phase (top) and for testing phase (bottom), respectively

Time interval (sec)	Motion	Description
1-99	Constant velocity	100m/s
100-239	Constant acceleration : Counter-clockwise turn	4.4876m/s²
240-800	Constant velocity	100m/s

Time interval (sec)	Motion	Description
[1-99][200-299][340-379][520-559][640-800]	Constant velocity	100 m/s
100-199	Constant acceleration : Clockwise turn	6.2822 m/s²
300-339	Constant acceleration : Counter-clockwise turn	3.7086 m/s²
380-519	Constant acceleration : Clockwise turn	3.3658 m/s²
560-639	Constant acceleration : Clockwise turn	1.9635 m/s²

The performance improvement gained by incorporation the ANFIS into the KF architecture can be seen from the data provided in Tables 2 and 3, which are obtained based on 100 Monte-Carlo runs. Tracking error statistics obtained when the trained ANFIS is applied to training trajectory (i.e., same trajectories for training and testing phases for algorithm verification) with various velocities using KF and the ANFIS aided KF is summarized in Table 2; error statistics obtained when the trained ANFIS is applied to testing trajectory (i.e., different trajectories for training and testing phases for algorithm generalization) using KF and the ANFIS aided KF is summarized in Table 3. The results clearly indicate that the use of proposed dynamic model compensation scheme can significantly improve tracking accuracy.

Table 2. Tracking errors using ANFIS aided KF for various velocity when the trajectory in the training and testing stage are the same (units: meter; 100 Monte Carlo runs).

		KF		ANFIS aided KF	
		x position	y position	x position	y position
100 m/s	Mean	2.5034	2.5247	0.1911	-0.3078
	Std dev	790.4494	790.6386	11.6222	19.5346
60 m/s	Mean	2.8229	2.9674	3.0018	2.7112
	Std dev	643.5868	643.7824	13.8591	19.3387
150 m/s	Mean	36.2538	36.2275	0.4141	-0.1486
	Std dev	812.6878	812.7122	12.5125	21.8382

Table 3. Tracking errors using ANFIS aided KF when the trajectory in the training and testing stage are different (units: meter; 100 Monte Carlo runs).

	KF		ANFIS aided KF	
	x position	y position	x position	y position
Mean	319.8688	319.8173	12.5502	32.3322
Std dev	1023.8	1023.8	365.9010	401.0242

4 Application to GPS Navigation

The dynamic process of the GPS receiver in medium dynamic environment can be represented by the Position-Velocity (PV) model [1]. In the case that differential GPS (DGPS) mode is used and most of the errors can be removed, but the multipath and receiver thermal noise cannot be eliminated.

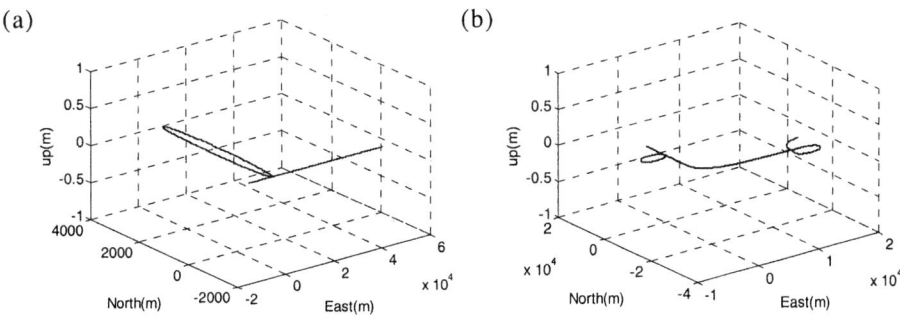

Fig. 4. Scenarios of the vehicle trajectory in (a) training phase and in (b) testing phase

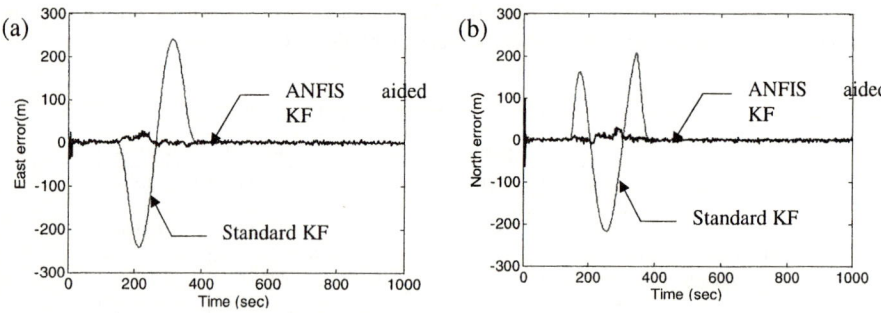

Fig. 5. Positioning errors in the (a) East and (b) North component, respectively, based on the standard KF and ANFIS aided KF.

Table 4. GPS Navigation errors due to standard KF and ANFIS aided KF, when applied to training (top) and testing trajectories (bottom) (units: meter).

	KF		ANFIS aided KF	
	East	North	East	North
Mean	-0.0826	-0.0572	1.3372	1.4915
Std dev	76.7138	66.2228	7.9401	1.8365

	KF		ANFIS aided KF	
	East	North	East	North
Mean	8.6390	10.4667	2.7914	3.5374
Std dev	109.9412	88.2022	10.8966	12.6143

The vehicle is assumed to move at a constant velocity of $100 m/s$ with a trajectory as shown in Fig. 4(a), while in the testing phase, the vehicle is assumed to move at a constant velocity of $70 m/s$ with a trajectory as shown in Fig 4(b). Same as in the case of target tracking, for both the above two scenarios, the user started from the position of North 25.15 degrees, East 121.78 degrees. The performance improvement gained by incorporation the ANFIS into the KF architecture can be seen in Fig. 5. Navigation error statistics when applied to training (i.e., same trajectories for training and testing phases for algorithm verification) and testing (i.e., different trajectories for training and testing phases for algorithm generalization) trajectories, using KF and the ANFIS aided KF is summarized in Table 4, which are also obtained based on 100 Monte-Carlo runs.

5 Conclusions

The ANFIS aided adaptive Kalman filtering approach is presented and applied to radar target tracking and GPS navigation filter designs. The ANFIS is employed as a model nonlinearity identification mechanism for implementing the on-line identification of nonlinear dynamics errors such that the unknown plant is identified and the modeling error can be compensated. The examples on target tracking and GPS navigation filter designs using the proposed approach have demonstrated significant performance improvement in comparison with the standard Kalman filtering method.

References

1. Brown, R. and Hwang, P.: Introduction to Random Signals and Applied Kalman Filtering, John Wiley & Sons, New York (1997)
2. Haykin, S.: Neural networks: a comprehensive foundation, Prentice-Hall (1999)
3. Horikawa, S., Furuhashi, T., Okuma S. and Uchikawa, Y.: Composition Methods of Fuzzy Neural Networks, Proc. IEEE Int. Conf. Industrial Electronics, Control and Instrumentation, (1990) 1253-1258
4. Horikawa, S., Furuhashi, T. Uchikawa, Y.: On Fuzzy Modeling Using Fuzzy Neural Network with the back-propagation algorithm, IEEE Trans. Neural Network, Vol. 3, No. 5, (1992) 801-806
5. Jang, J.-S. R.: ANFIS: Adaptive-Network-Based Fuzzy Inference System, IEEE Transactions on Systems, Man, and Cybernetics, Vol. 23, No. 3, (1993) 665-685
6. Bar-Shalom, Y. and Birmiwal K.: Variable dimensional filter for maneuvering target tracking, IEEE Trans. Aero. Electro Systems. AES-18(5) (1982) 621-628

Dynamic Background Discrimination with a Recurrent Network

Jieyu Zhao

The Research Institute of Computer Science and Technology,
Ningbo University, Ningbo 315211, China
zhao_jieyu@nbu.edu.cn

Abstract. Discrimination between the moving foreground objects and the complex dynamic background is a challenging task. In this paper, we have proposed a probabilistic graphical model – a recurrent stochastic network, which is able to learn the temporal and the spatial correlation from the video input data and make inference with a generalized belief propagation algorithm. Experiments have shown that the proposed recurrent network can model the dynamic backgrounds containing swaying trees, bushes and moving ocean waves. Very promising segmentation results have been obtained.

1 Introduction

Numerous attempts have been made in recent years to develop advanced models for automatic discrimination between the moving foreground objects and the complex dynamic background [1]. Probabilistic approaches, which allow us to handle uncertainties in a systematic way, are widely adopted [5,6,20]. Among those successful ones are Bayesian methods [11] and probabilistic graphical models [10,12,13]. Bayesian methods are able consistently and quantitatively to solve the inference task by the inclusion of a prior. Probabilistic graphical models include Hidden Markov models, Markov random fields, Ising and Potts models and Boltzmann machine etc. The theory of Markov random field (MRF) provides an efficient way of modeling context dependent entities such as pixels and edges in the image. The Markov-Gibbs equivalence theorem points out that the joint distribution of an MRF is a Gibbs distribution, which offers mathematically tractable means for statistical image analysis.

Most research on image segmentation using probabilistic approaches only deals with still images. Work on video image segmentation is less common than still-based image due to the poor video quality, constantly changing background and significant illumination variation. The time-consuming computational process is also a major obstacle for the application of stochastic models. A commonly used approach to extract moving foreground objects from the video clip is the background subtraction method. However, the task becomes difficult when the background contains moving objects such as swaying trees, bushes, ocean waves etc. Some methods have been proposed to model the dynamic background [14,16].

A probabilistic graphical model for video moving object segmentation with a dynamic background is proposed in this paper. The partitioning of the image has been implemented through a belief propagation process on the probabilistic graphical model. The model has an online learning mechanism which captures the temporal and spatial correlation of the video image sequences. Thus it is very adaptive and robust to a changing environment. The detailed introduction of the stochastic model and the related Bayesian interpretation has been presented. Experimental results have shown the successful moving object segmentation on real world video clips with complex backgrounds.

2 Recurrent Network Models

The probabilistic graphical model has a compact representation of joint probability distributions. It provides a natural tool for dealing with the uncertainty and complexity in image processing and computer vision. The nodes in the graph represent random variables, and the arcs represent statistical dependencies between these random variables. Probabilistic graphical models can be either directed or undirected.

Directed graphical models are also known as Bayesian networks, belief networks, generative models, causal models, etc. which is widely used in reasoning and inference. The Bayesian network defines an independency structure where the probability that a node is in one of its states depends directly only on the states of its parents. The conditional probability is associated with each arc in the graph. Hidden Markov model is a particular case of directed graphical model.

Undirected graphical models are more popular in the statistical physics and computer vision communities. Well-known names are Ising and Potts models, Markov Random Fields (MRFs), Boltzmann machines etc. Unlike the Bayesian network, the undirected graphical model does not represent the conditional probability function explicitly. The function associated with each edge in the graph is the compatibility function which reflects the correlation between two connected nodes.

Any undirected graphical model can be practically treated as a Markov Random Field (MRF), which is defined as follows:

A family of random variables $F = \{X_1, X_2, ..., X_n\}$ on set S is defined to be an MRF if and only if the following two conditions are satisfied:

$$P(f) > 0, \quad \text{for all } f$$
$$P(x_i \mid x_{S-\{i\}}) = P(x_i \mid x_{N_i})$$

where N_i is the set of neighbors of vertex i. The second condition states that the assignment of a state to a vertex is conditionally dependent on the assignment to other vertices only through its neighbors. This is a totally local property. The global behavior of a Markov random field is described as a Gibbs distribution, which takes the following form:

$$P(f) = \frac{e^{-E(f)/T}}{\sum_{f \in F} e^{-E(f)/T}}$$

where $E(f)$ is the energy function and T is the temperature. The energy is a sum of clique potentials over all possible cliques C: $E(f) = \sum_{c \in C} Vc(f)$. For the Boltzmann machine, the energy function is simplified as $E = -\frac{1}{2}\sum_{i,j} w_{ij} S_i S_j$.

The Hammersley-Clifford theorem [6] establishes the equivalence of the Markov random field and Gibbs random field (GRF). The theorem states that F is an MRF on S with respect to N if and only if F is a GRF on S with respect to N.

A Bayesian method can be easily adopted to describe the computational process of a probabilistic graphical model. The maximization of the posterior probability in the Bayesian framework is equivalent to minimization of the posterior energy function of a MRF [13].

To successfully apply the above *maximum a posterior* (MAP) approach in image processing, one needs to define a neighborhood structure and derive the posterior energy function to define the MAP solution to an optimization problem, or learn an undirected probabilistic graphical model by the appropriate setting of compatibility function associated with each connection. For the video moving foreground and dynamic background discrimination, the temporal and spatial information are used to find out the correlation between each pair of the nodes.

The inference on a graphical model is to estimate the values of hidden nodes, given the values of the observed nodes. It is usually a NP-hard problem [10]. The exact inference is possible only in restricted circumstance where the graph must be acyclic and the joint distribution over latent variables must be Gaussian. A recent breakthrough is the development of generalized belief propagation algorithm [18] which allows the inference on a graphical model with cycles.

3 Belief Propagation

In general, we assume a set of random variable nodes $X = \{X_1, X_2, ..., X_n\}$ paired with a set of observed nodes $Y = \{Y_1, Y_2, ..., Y_n\}$. The conditional independence of the problem is represented by the neighborhood structure N. There is a connection between two random variable nodes X_i and X_j if they are not conditional independent given the other nodes in the graph. The correlation of the two adjacent nodes is expressed by the compatibility function $\psi_{ij}(x_i, x_j)$, and the observation function (or evidence) is $\phi_i(x_i, y_i) \equiv \phi_i(x_i)$. For pairwise MRFs, the joint probability distribution for random variables X is given by

$$P(X) = \frac{1}{Z} \left(\prod_{(i,j) \in P} \psi_{ij}(x_i, x_j) \right) \left(\prod_i \phi_i(x_i) \right).$$

The belief propagation introduces variables $m_{ij}(x_j)$ which can be intuitively understood as a message from node i to node j about what state node j should be in. The message $m_{ij}(x_j)$ is a vector of the same dimensionality as x_j, with each component being proportional to how likely node i thinks it is that node j will be in the corresponding state. The messages are computed iteratively using the following update rule:

$$m_{ij}(x_j) \leftarrow \sum_{x_i} \left(\phi_i(x_i) \psi_{ij}(x_i, x_j) \prod_{k \in N(i) \setminus j} m_{ki}(x_i) \right).$$

The belief at a node i is proportional to the product of the local evidence and all the messages coming into node i:

$$b_i(x_i) \propto \phi_i(x_i) \prod_{j \in N(i)} m_{ji}(x_i).$$

4 Experimental Setup

We use a large scale recurrent network and generalized belief propagation algorithm to model very noisy and complex backgrounds which include swaying trees, bushes and moving ocean waves. The target is to segment the moving foreground objects (pedestrians, bicycles, cars etc) from these dynamic backgrounds. The model continuously learns from the changing scene and the learned model is used to predict the dynamic background. When the real outcome is significantly different from the predicted values, the corresponding area is regarded as moving foreground targets.

The video clip was in DV format (720x576). The first clip was taken at the front of a running fountain. The second clip involved swaying tree branches, the shadow and a part of ocean view. A pedestrian and a bicycle were the moving foreground objects in these clips.

The recurrent network model we used is a very large size Potts model with limited local connections. It has a simple structure of 720x576 units, arranged on a two dimensional plane and each unit is connected to its four neighbors. Each node in the model represents a discrete random variable with at most 20 different states. This model is equivalent to a pairwise Markov Random Field.

The compatibility function of the network model was continuously learned from the previous 20 successive frames (about 0.8 second) by collecting correlation information between each pair of the units. Since the outdoor background would not have a sudden or a dramatic change, this relatively short range of learning period is sufficient at most of the time.

The generalized Belief Propagation has been used to infer the current background. When the difference between the inferred state of the graphical model and the pixel value of the current input frame is great than a threshold value, the corresponding pixel will be regarded as foreground and shown in red. The final segmentation results are shown in Figure 1 and Figure 2 for these video clips.

It can be seen the dynamic background has been modeled by the probabilistic graphical model very well. The smooth moving of the background has been successfully predicted. The segmentation process took about 3 seconds for each frame on a Pentium IV 2G laptop.

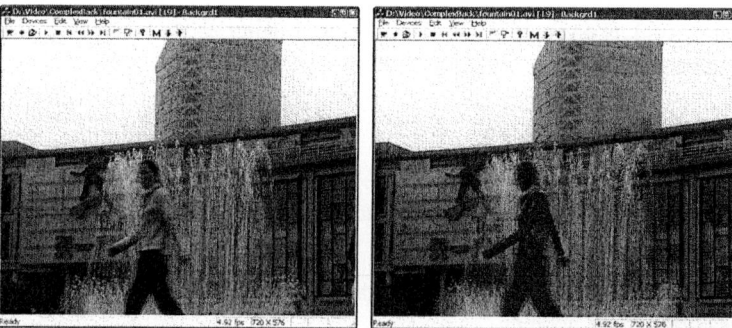

Fig. 1. Original video image (left) and segmentation result (right) of a pedestrian in front of a fountain

Fig. 2. Original video image (left) and segmentation result (right) of a moving bicycle, note the ocean, the wavering tree branches and the shadow

5 Conclusions

A probabilistic graphical model has been proposed to learn and model the complex dynamic backgrounds containing swaying tree branches, bushes and ocean waves etc. To implement high quality video foreground moving object segmentation, the generalized belief propagation algorithm has been used for the inference of the probabilistic graphical model. Excellent experimental results have been obtained for very noisy and complex real world backgrounds.

Future work will be focused on the establishment of a unified framework for video target segmentation, tracking and recognition based on both supervised and unsupervised learning.

Acknowledgements

This research was supported by the National Natural Science Foundation of China, the Natural Science Foundation of Zhejiang Province, the Science and Technology Department of Zhejiang Province, and the Science and Technology Bureau of Ningbo.

References

1. Aggarwal, J. K. and Cai, Q., *Human Motion Analysis: A Review*, Computer Vision and Image Understanding, Vol.73, No.3, (1999) 428–440,.
2. Dougherty, E. R., *Random Process for Image and Signal Processing*, IEEE Press, New York (1999)
3. Fan, J. and Dimitrova, N., Online Face Recognition System For Videos Based On Modified Probabilistic Neural Networks, International Conference on Image Processing (2004)
4. Feng, X., Williams, C., Felderhof, S., Combining Belief Networks and Neural Networks for Scene Segmentation, *IEEE Transactions on Pattern Analysis and Machine Intelligence*, Vol.24, No.4, (2002) 467–482
5. Geman, S and Geman, D., Stochastic relaxation, Gibbs distributions, and the Bayesian restoration of images. *IEEE Transactions on Pattern Analysis and Machine Intelligence*, **6**, (1984) 721–741
6. Hammersley, J. M. and Clifford, P., Markov field on finite graphs and lattices, unpublished (1971)
7. Horn, B. K. P. and Schunck, B. G., *Determining optical flow*, Artificial Intelligence, 17, (1981) 185–203
8. Huang, R., Pavlovic, V., Metaxas, D. N., A Graphical Model Framework for Coupling MRFs and Deformable Models, International Conference on Computer Vision and Pattern Recognition (2004)
9. Ivanovic, A., and Huang, T. S., A Probabilistic Framework For Segmentation and Tracking of Multiple non Rigid Objects for Video Surveillance, International Conference on Image Processing (2004)
10. Jordan, M., *Learning in Graphical Models*. The MIT Press (1998)
11. Lee, T. S. and Mumford, D., Hierarchical Bayesian inference in the visual cortex, *Journal of Optical Society of America, A.* Vol.20, No.7, (2003)1434–1448
12. Li, L., Huang, W. M., Gu, I. Y. H., Tian, Q., Foreground object detection from videos containing complex background. Proc. of ACM Multimedia Conf., USA (2003)
13. Li, S. Z., *Markov Random Field Modeling in Image Analysis*, Springer-Verlag, Tokyo, (2001)
14. Monnet, A., Mittal, A., Paragios, N., Ramesh, V., Background Modeling and Subtraction of Dynamic Scenes, IEEE International Conference on Computer Vision (2003)
15. Rolls, E. T. and Deco, G., *Computational Neuroscience of Vision*, Oxford University Press, New York (2002)
16. Seki, M., Wada, T., Fujiwara, H., Sumi, K., Background Subtraction based on Co-occurrence of Image Variations, Proceedings of the IEEE Computer Society Conference on Computer Vision and Pattern Recognition (2003)
17. Tino, P., Cernansky, M., Benuskova, L., Markovian Architectural Bias of Recurrent Neural Networks, *IEEE Transactions on Neural Networks*, Vol. 15, No. 1 (2004)
18. Yedidia, J. S., Freeman, W. T., Weiss, Y., Understanding Belief Propagation and its Generalizations, Mitsubishi Electric Research Laboratories, Technical Report (2001)
19. Zhao, J., A Recurrent Stochastic Binary Network, *Science in China*, Ser. F, Vol.44, No.5, (2001)
20. Zhu, S. C., Statistical Modeling and Conceptualization of Visual Patterns, *IEEE Trans. on Pattern Analysis and Machine Intelligence*, Vol.25, No.6, (2003) 691–712

Gender Recognition Using a Min-Max Modular Support Vector Machine

Hui-Cheng Lian[1], Bao-Liang Lu[1,*], Erina Takikawa[2], and Satoshi Hosoi[2]

[1] Department of Computer Science and Engineering, Shanghai Jiao Tong University, 1954 Hua Shan Rd., Shanghai 200030, China
[2] Sensing and Control Technology Laboratory, OMRON Corporation
{lianhc, blu}@cs.sjtu.edu.cn, {erinat, hosoi}@ari.ncl.omron.co.jp

Abstract. Considering the fast respond and high generalization accuracy of the min-max modular support vector machine (M^3-SVM), we apply M^3-SVM to solving the gender recognition problem and propose a novel task decomposition method in this paper. Firstly, we extract features from the face images by using a facial point detection and Gabor wavelet transform method. Then we divide the training data set into several subsets with the 'part-versus-part' task decomposition method. The most important advantage of the proposed task decomposition method over existing random method is that the explicit prior knowledge about ages contained in the face images is used in task decomposition. We perform simulations on a real-world gender data set and compare the performance of the traditional SVMs and that of M^3-SVM with the proposed task decomposition method. The experimental results indicate that M^3-SVM with our new method have better performance than traditional SVMs and M^3-SVM with random task decomposition method.

1 Introduction

Gender recognition is one of the most challenging problems for face recognition researchers. Commonly, gray-scale or color pixel vectors, subspace transformed features, wrinkle and complexion, and local facial feature with Gabor wavelet transformation are chosen as features for recognition[4][3][5]. Then classifiers such as k-nearest-neighbor, neural networks and SVMs are often used to gender recognition. Among these classifiers, SVMs seem to be superior to all other classifiers[4]. The advantage of SVMs is to find the optimal linear hyper-plane such that the expected classification error for unseen samples is minimized. However, similar to almost traditional classifiers, SVMs treat all data in one class as a whole in training phase, and will perform coarsely than the method of further dividing the training data set of each class into a number of subsets.

In our previous work, we have proposed a 'part-versus-part' task decomposition method[1] and developed a new modular SVMs, called M^3-SVM, for solving

---

* To whome correspondence should be addressed. This work was supported in part by the National Natural Science Foundation of China via the grants NSFC 60375022 and NSFC 60473040.

large-scale pattern classification problems[2,6]. In this paper, we apply M^3-SVM to solving the gender recognition problem and use a prior knowledge about age information in task decomposition. We perform simulations on a real-world gender data set to compare the generalization accuracy achieved by traditional SVMs and M^3-SVM with our proposed task decomposition method.

2 Feature Extraction for Gender Recognition

The well-performed face feature extraction method that has been developed by Omron Corporation will be used to generate feature vectors for our M^3-SVM classifiers. The main idea of the face feature extraction is to detect the face in an image firstly and then locate the facial points including eyes, nose and mouth. Gabor wavelet transform is then used to extract the facial point characteristics which are combined to form a feature vector[5]. The extracted feature vectors are processed as the input to our recognition system. For more details about this feature extraction method, one can see the paper[5]. Here we will only simply describe the scales of the gallery sets and probe sets for our M^3-SVM gender recognition system in Section 5.

3 Min-Max Modular Support Vector Machine

M^3-SVM is firstly introduced in[2], and our studies show that it have three main advantages over traditional SVMs: (1) Massively parallel training of SVMs can be easily implemented in parallel computing systems; (2) Large-scale pattern classification problems can be solved efficiently; and (3) The generalization accuracy can be obviously improved. Hereto we have succeeded in applying M^3-SVM to several pattern recognition problems such as: large scale text categorization [6] and multi-view face recognition [7].

4 A Task Decomposition Strategy for Gender Recognition

M^3-SVM needs to divide the training data set into several subsets in its first step. So how to divide the training data set effectively is an important issue. Although dividing the data set randomly is a simple and straightforward approach, the geometric relation among the original training data may be damaged[6]. The data belonging to a reasonable cluster may be randomly separated into other clusters. From the viewpoint of SVM, random task decomposition might lead the boundaries of subproblems complex. In this paper, we propose a new task decomposition strategy, called prior knowledge based strategy (PK), for dealing with gender recognition problem.

By using existing random (RAN) task decomposition method [6], we divide training data set into several subsets randomly. Although this is the most simple and straightforward approach and might lead a lower generalization accuracy in most cases than other M^3-SVM with reasonable decomposition strategies. It will still generate better performance than traditional SVMs. Because, despite of not deliberately choosing, M^3-SVM is still 'finer' than SVMs.

In prior knowledge based strategy, we use the age information for gender data decomposition. Considering that we have had the personal age information in each data set for male and female, respectively, we naturally sort the samples using this age information from young to old, and then divide them into different subsets. As an example, we divide the male and female samples into 7 subsets, respectively, which range from 0~9, 10~19, 20~29, 30~39, 40~49, 50~59, and over 60 years old, respectively.

5 Experiments

In this section, we present experimental results on the gender data sets to compare the traditional SVMs with M^3-SVM using our proposed task decomposition method. All SVMs are linear SVM from LibSVM[8] and the parameter C is set to 1.

The gallery sets used for training include 786 male samples and 1,269 female samples, which have the same vector dimension of 1,584, including different age groups respectively. The probe sets used for test include 15 kinds of gender data. These data represent frontal image, various degree view face, face with glasses and different expressions and so on. The number of test samples belonging to these 15 kinds of gender data are 1278, 1066, 820, 819, 816, 805, 805, 805, 813, 814, 815, 805, 819, 816 and 816, respectively.

From Fig. 1 we can see that all M^3-SVM with different task decomposition strategies can improve the classification accuracy by a high degree. For example, M^3-SVM with PK task decomposition strategy achieved 91.53% and 86.03% correct rates on two probe sets, which are better than tranditional SVMs (85.77%

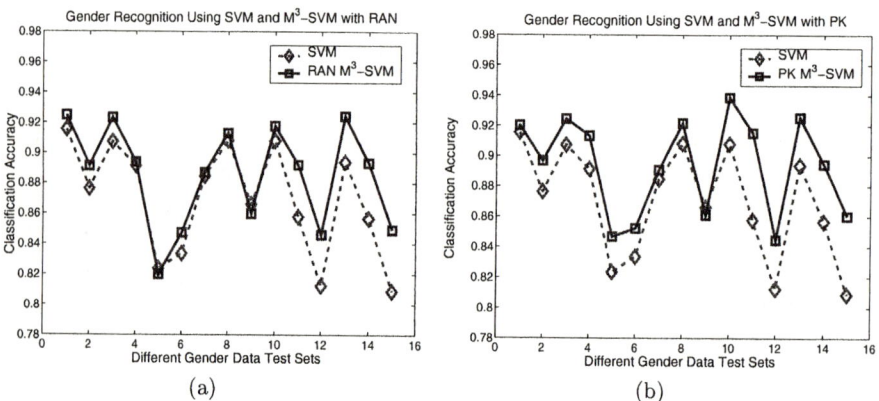

Fig. 1. The comparative results of SVMs with M^3-SVM based on two different decomposition strategies. (a) Results of SVM and M^3-SVM with random strategy; (b) Results of SVM and M^3-SVM with the proposed strategy.

and 80.88%). The reason we consider is that the original complex borders between two classes for SVMs are further simplified by decomposing the complex data sets into relatively simpler subsets, and then the solutions to the subproblems are combined by M^3-SVM without losing generalization, meanwhile its modular structure improves the response speed of the whole system. And as the analysis performed in Section 4, a more reasonable decomposition strategy will perform better than the random one.

6 Conclusions

We have proposed a new task decomposition method using age information for M^3-SVM to deal with gender recognition problem. We have compared our method with the traditional SVMs. From experimental results, we can draw the following conclusions: a) The proposed task decomposition method can help to improve the generalization of M^3-SVM. b) Prior knowledge based task decomposition method could be more efficient than random decomposition method in the aspect of generalization performance. How to choose an optimal task decomposition strategy for M^3-SVM is still an open problem.

References

1. Lu, B.L., Ito, M.: Task Decomposition and Module Combination Based on Class Relations: a Modular Neural Network for Pattern Classification. IEEE Transactions on Neural Networks, **10** (1999) 1244 -1256
2. Lu, B.L., Wang, K.A., Utiyama, M., Isahara, H.: A Part-versus-part Method for Massively Parallel Training of Support Vector Machines. In: Proceedings of IJCNN'04, Budapast, July 25-29(2004) 735-740
3. Koray Balci, LORIA, PCA for Gender Estimation: Which Eigenvectors Contribute? In: 16 th International Conference on Pattern Recognition (ICPR'02) Volume **3** Quebec City, QC, Canada, August 11 - 15, (2002) 363-363
4. Moghaddam B., Yang, M.H.: Gender Classification with Support Vector Machines. In: Proceedings of the Fourth IEEE International Conference on Automatic Face and Gesture Recognition 2000, (2000) 306-311
5. Hosoi, S., Takikawa, E., Kawade, M.: Ethnicity Estimation with Facial Images. In: Sixth IEEE International Conference on Automatic Face and Gesture Recognition May 17-19, Seoul, Korea, (2004) 195-200
6. Wang, K.A., Lu, B.L.: Task Decomposition Using Geometric Relation for Min-Max Modular SVM, Advances in Neural Networks-ISNN 2005, Accepted, 2005
7. Fan, Z.G., Lu, B.L.: Multi-View Face Recognition with Min-Max Modular SVMs, ICNC'05-FSKD'05, Accepted, 2005
8. Chang, C.C., Lin, C.J.: LIBSVM : a library for support vector machines. http://www.csie.ntu.edu.tw/∼ cjlin/papers/libsvm.ps.gz

An Application of Support Vector Regression on Narrow-Band Interference Suppression in Spread Spectrum Systems[*]

Qing Yang and Shengli Xie

Electrical Engineering Department, South China University of Technology,
Guangzhou, P.R. China
ee_qyang@163.com, adshlxie@scut.edu.cn

Abstract. The conventional approaches to suppress the narrow-band interference of spread spectrum systems mostly use the adaptive LMS filter to predict the narrow-band interference and subtract the predicted interfering signal from the polluted received signal before de-spreading. However, since these approaches take no account of complexity control and have no guarantee of global minimum, they often suffer from unsteady performance. In this paper, a novel approach to narrow-band interference suppression is proposed, in which ε − support vector regression method is used to predict the narrow-band interference instead of adaptive LMS filter. With the help of practical parameter selection rules, it is not only effective but also easy to handle. Computer simulations show that it outperforms the conventional approaches in most cases and thus is a desirable choice for narrow-band interference suppression in spread spectrum systems.

1 Introduction

As is well known, the inherent processing gain of spread spectrum (SS) system will, in many cases, provide a sufficient degree of interference suppression capacity. However, when high-power narrow-band interference (NBI) is encountered, sometimes even with the inherent interference suppression capacity of spread spectrum system, communication becomes impossible. An effective solution is to use signal processing techniques to complement the spread spectrum communications, and it is also economic when signal bandwidth is in scarcity.

The main idea of signal processing techniques used in spread spectrum system is based on the different correlation property between the spread signal and the narrow-band interference. Since the spread signal has a nearly flat spectrum, it can hardly be

---

[*] This work was supported by the National Natural Science Foundation of China (Grant 60274006), the Natural Science Key Fund of Guangdong Province, P.R.China (Grant 020826), the National Natural Science Foundation of China for Excellent Youth (Grant 60325310), and the Trans-Century Training Programme Foundation for the Talents by the State Education Ministry.

predicted precisely from its past values [1], while the interference, being narrow-band, can be predicted accurately. Hence, the prediction of received signal based on the previously received samples will, in effect, be the prediction of the interfering signal. By subtracting the estimated narrow-band interference from the polluted received samples, the NBI is effectively suppressed.

Previous work has primarily employed the adaptive filters with least square mean (LMS) algorithm to estimate the NBI, because LMS is convenient to apply. Two most frequently used types of adaptive filters are time-domain nonlinear LMS adaptive filter (TDAF) and frequency-domain adaptive LMS filter (FDAF). However, both of them lack of complexity control and often suffer from local minima, therefore they are sensitive to "noise" ("noise" here is referred to the spread signal and the white noise in the prediction of NBI) and no guaranteed steadily excellent performance. In this paper, support vector regression (SVR) technique, which can overcome these drawbacks, is employed to estimate the NBI in the presence of spread signal and white noise. Experiments show that it outperforms the conventional approaches in most cases.

This paper is organized as follows. In section 2, a mathematical model for received signal is given. In section 3, a basic idea of $\varepsilon-$SVR is briefly described. In section 4, $\varepsilon-$SVR based NBI suppression technique is proposed. In section 5, computer simulations of $\varepsilon-$SVR based NBI suppression technique and conventional techniques are shown and the results are analyzed. Finally, a summary of the work done in this paper and some concluding remarks are given in section 6.

2   A Mathematical Model for the Received Signal in SS Systems

The low pass equivalent of direct-sequence spread spectrum modulation waveform is given by

$$m(t) = \sum_{k=0}^{L-1} c_k q\left(t - k\tau_c\right) \tag{1}$$

Where L is the number of PN chips per message bit, τ_c is the chip interval, c_k is the kth chip of the sequence, and $q(t)$ is a rectangular pulse of duration τ_c.

The total transmitted signal can be expressed as

$$s(t) = \sum_k b_k m\left(t - kT_b\right) \tag{2}$$

where $\{b_k\}$ is the binary information sequence and $T_b = L\tau_c$ is the bit duration.

The received signal has the form

$$z(t) = \alpha s(t - \tau) + n(t) + i(t) \tag{3}$$

where α is an attenuation factor, τ is a delay offset, $n(t)$ is white Gaussian noise, and $i(t)$ is the NBI. For the sake of notational simplicity, it is assumed that τ is zero, and that $\alpha = 1$, since these assumptions do not affect the conclusion drawn from the following analysis.

It is also assumed that the received signal is chip-matched-filtered and sampled at the chip rate of the PN sequence to yield samples

$$z_k = s_k + n_k + i_k \quad (4)$$

where the discrete time sequence $\{s_k\}$, $\{n_k\}$ and $\{i_k\}$ are due to $\{s(t)\}$, $\{n(t)\}$ and $\{i(t)\}$, respectively.

Under the assumption that the PN sequence is truly random, $\{s_k\}$ can be considered as a sequence of independent, identically distributed (i.i.d) random variables taking on values +1 or –1 with equal probability. $\{n_k\}$ is a sequence of i.i.d zero mean Gaussian random variables with variance σ_n^2. The sequence $\{s_k\}$, $\{n_k\}$ and $\{i_k\}$ are assumed to be mutually independent [5]. This is the model of the received signal that will be used in the rest of the paper.

3 The Basic Idea of ε – Support Vector Regression Method

Suppose that we have training data $\{(x_1, y_1), (x_2, y_2), \cdots, (x_N, y_N)\}$, with input $x_i \in R^d$ and target $y_i \in R$. Our goal is to find a function $f(x)$ that deviates least from the training data and is as flat as possible (i.e., $\|w\|$ is as small as possible). As a result, the input x is mapped into a high dimensional feature space by a map Φ, and a linear function $f(x) = \langle w, \Phi(x) \rangle + b$ [1] is constructed in the feature space. Besides, Vapnik's ε – insensitive loss function

$$|y - f(x)| = \begin{cases} 0 & if \ |y - f(x)| \le \varepsilon \\ |y - f(x)| - \varepsilon & otherwise \end{cases} \quad (5)$$

is introduced to measure the deviation from the target with tolerance ε. So far, the regression problem can be interpreted as follows:

$$\textbf{minimize} \ \frac{1}{2}\|w\|^2 + C\sum_{i=1}^{N}(\xi_i + \xi_i^*) \quad (6)$$

$$\text{subject to} \quad \begin{cases} y_i - f(x_i) \le \varepsilon + \xi_i \\ f(x_i) - y_i \le \varepsilon + \xi_i^* \\ \xi_i, \xi_i^* \ge 0 \end{cases} \quad i = 1, 2, \cdots, N$$

where C is a user-defined positive constant.

It was shown in [2], after a series of derivations, (6) could be transformed to the following quadratic programming problem:

---

[1] $\langle *,* \rangle$ denotes inner product calculation.

$$\text{maximize} -\frac{1}{2}\sum_{i,j=1}^{N}(\alpha_i-\alpha_i^*)(\alpha_i-\alpha_i^*)K(x_i,x_j)-\varepsilon\sum_{i=1}^{N}(\alpha_i+\alpha_i^*)+\sum_{i=1}^{N}y_i(\alpha_i-\alpha_i^*) \quad (7)$$

$$\text{subject to } \sum_{i=1}^{N}(\alpha_i-\alpha_i^*)=0, \text{ and } \alpha_i,\alpha_i^* \in [0,C]$$

where $K(x_i,x_j)$ is a kernel function defined in accordance with Mercer's theorem:

$$K(x_i,x_j)=\langle \Phi(x_i),\Phi(x_j)\rangle \quad (8)$$

and the solution is given by

$$f(x)=\sum_{i=1}^{N}(\alpha_i-\alpha_i^*)K(x_i,x)+b. \quad (9)$$

4 SVR-Based NBI Suppression Technique

In NBI suppression application, firstly ε-SVR technique is used to approximate

$$x_n = f(x_{n-1},x_{n-2},...,x_{n-L}) \quad (10)$$

which in effect estimated the predicable NBI from the received signal. Then the estimated NBI is subtracted from the polluted received signal and thus the NBI is effectively suppressed.

To realize a good. ε-SVR generalization performance, first of all, a proper setting of the hyper-parameter selection should be done, namely, parameter C, the trade off between the model complexity and the empirical risk, and parameter ε, the controller of ε-insensitive zone, should be selected carefully.

A popular technique to choose the hyper-parameters is the k-fold cross-validation method, but it is time-consuming and expensive for our application.

For efficiency, a more practical estimate method of hyper-parameters is needed. James T. Kwok and Ivor W. Tsang [3] demonstrated the linear dependence between ε and the input noise. V. Cherkassky and Y. Ma [4] proposed that hyper-parameters choice could be made as follows:

$$C = (|\bar{y}+\sigma_y|,|\bar{y}-\sigma_y|) \quad (11)$$

where $\bar{y}$ and σ_y are the mean and standard deviation of the y values of the training data.

$$\varepsilon = 3\sigma\sqrt{\frac{\ln n}{n}} \quad (12)$$

where n is the number of training data and σ is the standard deviation of the regression noise. In the case of narrow-band interference prediction, simulations showed that better performance was obtained when C is set as equation (7) and ε is fixed at the standard deviation of the regression noise, that is,

$$\varepsilon = \sigma \quad (13)$$

As to kernel selection, in case of narrow-band interference prediction, RBF kernel applied to all three types of interference according to computer simulations, and parameter of RBF kernel, the width σ, is selected by conducting grid search.

5 Experiments

Computer simulations have been carried out to compare the effectiveness to suppress three types of narrow-band interferences between SVR-based NBI suppression technique and that using adaptive filters. Three types of narrow-band interferences include single tone sinusoidal interference having frequency of 0.15 radians with amplitude A and random phase θ, i.e.

$$i_k = A\sin(0.15k + \theta) \tag{14}$$

multiple tone sinusoidal interference having frequency of 0.15 radians, 0.4 radians, 0.65 radians, respectively, with amplitude A and random phase $\theta_1, \theta_2, \theta_3$, i.e.,

$$i_k = A\left(\sin(0.15k + \theta_1) + \sin(0.4k + \theta_2) + \sin(0.65k + \theta_3)\right) \tag{15}$$

and a second-order autoregressive (AR) interference obtained by passing white noise through a second-order IIR filter with both poles at $z = 0.99$, i.e.,

$$i_k = 1.98 i_{k-1} - 0.9801 i_{k-2} + d_k \tag{16}$$

where $\{d_k\}$ is white Gaussian noise.

For all the simulations in this paper, the input SNR is varied by changing the power of the interference. The figures shown are the average performance figures over 10 trials. On each trial the average performance over 4096 data points are computed.

To time-domain adaptive filter, both the structure and algorithm are consistent with those in [5]. The number of taps L is set to 10 and the tuning constant μ is adjusted to have the best performance. To frequency-domain adaptive filter, both the structure and algorithm are consistent with those in [6]. The block size N is fixed to 32 and the tuning constant μ is also chosen to attain the best performance. As to SVR-based suppression technique, for comparison convenience, the dimension of its input data is fixed at 10, that is, $L = 10$ in equation (10). C and ε is calculated as equation (11) and equation (13) on each trial. The first 2048 samples belong to the training data set and all 4096 data points belong to the testing data set.

In the rest of this section, three types of suppression techniques are compared from two aspects, including their power spectral density (PSD) estimates, and signal-to-noise ratio (SNR) improvement, so that we could have a better evaluation of them from varied viewpoints.

5.1 Spectrum Analysis

Since PSD estimate indicates the signal energy distribution in frequency domain, it could act as a vivid illustration of the degree to which various NBIs are suppressed. We computed the PSD estimates, from the unprocessed received signal, and the processed signal shortly after NBI suppression, respectively, on condition that input SNR is set to -20dB. The results are plotted as follows:

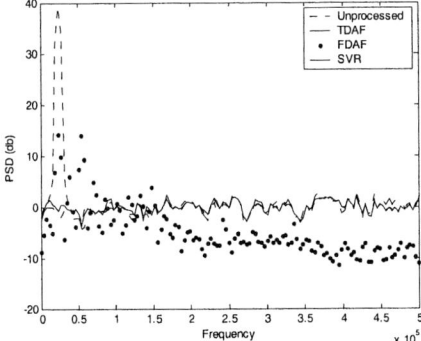

Fig. 1. Single tone sinusoidal interference

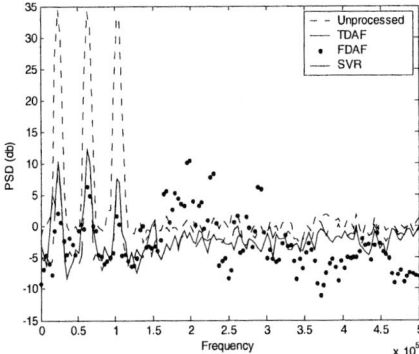

Fig. 2. Multiple tone sinusoidal interference

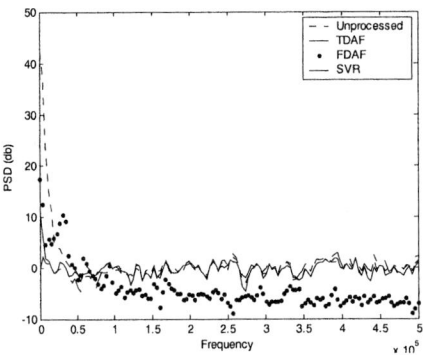

Fig. 3. AR interference

From Fig.1 – Fig.3, we can see that all three types of suppression techniques can suppress different NBI noticeably, especially SVR-based technique and TDAF perform closely and both are better than FDAF. Besides, we also notice that the inherent drawback of frequency-domain adaptive filter, "spectrum leakage", leads to considerable distortion of signal in the neighborhood of NBI.

5.2 SNR Improvement

To give a more objective understanding of the suppression effectiveness of the three techniques, their SNR improvement is calculated and listed in table 1.

The various signal-to-noise ratios (SNR) involved are defined as follows:

$$input \quad SNR \underline{\quad} 10\log \frac{E(s_k^2)}{E(|z_k - s_k|^2)} \quad dB \qquad (17)$$

$$output \quad SNR \underline{\quad} 10\log \frac{E(s_k^2)}{E(|\hat{s}_k - s_k|^2)} \quad dB \qquad (18)$$

$$SNR \quad improvement \underline{\quad} 10\log \frac{E(|z_k - s_k|^2)}{E(|\hat{s}_k - s_k|^2)} \quad dB \qquad (19)$$

Table 1.[2] Single tone sinusoidal interference

Input SNR	SNR Improvement (dB)			
	SVR	GRID	TDAF	FDAF
-20dB	31.7492	32.5184	25.8585	17.2114
-15dB	27.4315	27.4367	20.7992	12.3592
-10dB	21.9835	21.9915	15.3188	7.6741
-5dB	17.0863	17.0963	10.4373	3.3162

Table 2. Multiple tone sinusoidal interference

Input SNR	SNR Improvement (dB)			
	SVR	GRID	TDAF	FDAF
-20dB	18.4967	21.0041	18.8689	17.3395
-15dB	15.1671	16.6454	14.7847	12.5921
-10dB	11.6711	12.2182	11.0683	8.0788
-5dB	7.9991	8.0867	7.6955	4.1764

Table 3. AR interference

Input SNR	SNR Improvement (dB)			
	SVR	GRID	TDAF	FDAF
-20dB	27.1259	27.2084	25.0230	18.3216
-15dB	23.9675	24.2990	20.9187	14.7831
-10dB	26.5164	27.3941	18.2816	12.3620
-5dB	22.5386	25.3572	15.4850	11.0838

---

[2] In Table 1-3, "SVR" denotes SVR-based NBI suppression technique with hyper-parameter selection described in section 3 and "GRID" denotes SVR-based NBI suppression technique with exhaustive grid searching for hyper-parameter.

From Table 1-3, we can see that the SNR improvement of SVR-based suppression technique has the best performance in terms of SNR improvement on average. It outperforms the TDAF and FDAF on all the three types of NBI interference, except multiple tone sinusoidal interference with −20dB input SNR. It is significantly superior to TDAF in single tone sinusoidal interference and AR interference with −15dB and −5dB input SNR, and is superior to FDAF in nearly all levels of the three interferences. On the other hand, performance of both TDAF and FDAF deteriorates with the reduction of input SNR, while it is not the case for SVR-based technique when it deals with the AR interference. The SNR improvement of SVR-based.

5.3 Analysis

From the simulation results shown above, SVR-based suppression technique shows steady and high-quality performance on various narrow-band interferences with changing power levels, it is superior to TDAF and FDAF in most cases even when the input SNR is decreased, namely, the NBI is closer to that of the combination of spread signal and white noise in power and thus harder to predict. These results should not be surprising. The fundamental difference between SVR method and the adaptive filter technique is that the former is based on the structural risk minimization (SRM) induction principle, whose objective function takes into consideration both the complexity control and the approximation accuracy, and is therefore more insensitive to the "noise" (in our case, the "noise" is referred to the combined signal of spread signal and white noise, which acts as an disturbance in the prediction of narrow-band interference); on the other hand, the adaptive filters exclusively aim at minimizing the least mean square of the prediction error, regardless of the complexity control, and hence more vulnerable to "noise".

Another phenomenon we noticed in the course of the simulating is that there were noticeable fluctuations in performance among the different trials of TDAF and FDAF. However, it is not a worriment to SVR-based suppression technique. As a possible explanation, the adaptive filters have no guarantee for global minimum, and more likely, they converged to local minima, which causes unsteadiness in performance. As to SVR-based suppression technique, it ensures the obtaining of the unique global minimum of the objective function and thus ensures the steadiness in performance of the suppressor. Moreover, the SVR-based suppression technique based on the SRM induction principle minimize the upper bound of the generalization error rather than training error, which makes it more advantageous.

Besides, there are other drawbacks that harass TDAF and FDAF, respectively, For example, the slow convergence of TDAF, and the windowing effect and "spectrum leakage" for FDAF. All these lead to unfavorable performance of adaptive filters.

6 Conclusion

In this paper, we propose a novel SVR-based NBI suppression technique in spread spectrum systems. Since SVR method is based on the structural risk minimization induction principle and takes into consideration of the complexity control, it is more insensitive to "noise". Besides, it guarantees global minimum of the objective function, so it overcome the suffering from local minima in conventional approaches and performs more stably. Moreover, by taking advantage of the practical parameter selection method, which is simple but efficient, we circumvent the difficulty of initializing some important constants and variables for adaptive filters without prior knowledge, such as tuning constant, the tap-weights and so on. Computer simulations show that SVR-based NBI suppression technique has more effective and steady performance than conventional approaches in most cases and thus should be a more desirable choice for NBI suppression in SS systems.

References

1. S. Haykin: Adaptive Filter Theory, Third Edition. Prentice-Hall, Inc., 1996
2. A. Smola: Regression estimation with support vector machines. Dec. 1996.
3. James T. Kwok and Ivor W. Tsang: Linear dependency between ε and the input noise in ε-support vector regression. Neural Networks, IEEE Transactions on Volume 14, Issue 3, May 2003 Page(s):544 - 553
4. V. Cherkassky and Y. Ma: Practical selection of SVM parameters and noise estimation for SVM regression. Neural Networks, Vol.7, pp. 113-126, 2004.
5. R. Vijayan and H. V. Poor: Nonlinear techniques for interference suppression in spread-spectrum systems. IEEE Transactions on Communications, Vol.38, pp 1060-1065, Jul. 1990.
6. Y. Hua, Y.Gong, H. Li and Z. Zhou: The realization of narrow-band interferences suppression in derect sequence spread spectrum signal using frequency-domain algorithm. 2002.
7. L. A. Rusch and H. V. Poor: Narrowband interference suppression in CDMA spread spectrum communications. IEEE Transactions on Communications, Vol. 42, pp. 1969-1979, Apr. 1994.
8. E. R. Ferrara: Fast implementation of LMS adaptive filters. IEEE Transactions on Speech and Signal Processing, Vol. ASSP-28, pp. 474-475, Aug. 1980.
9. G. J. Saulnier: Suppression of narrowband jammers in a spread-spectrum receiver using transform-domain adaptive filter. IEEE Journal on Selected Areas in Communications, Vol. 10, pp.742-749, May 1992.
10. L. B. Milstein: Interference rejection techniques in spread spectrum communications. Proceedings of the IEEE, Vol. 76, pp. 657-671, 1988.
11. S. Haykin: Adaptive Filter Theory, Third Edition. Prentice-Hall, Inc., 1996
12. A. Smola and B. Scholkopf: A tutorial on support vector regression. Sept.2003.
13. V. N. Vapnik, S. E. Golowich, and A. J. Smola: Support vector method for function approximation, regression estimation and signal processing. 1996.
14. K. R. Muller, A. Smola, G. Ratsch, B. Scholkopf, J. Kohlmorgen, and V. Vapnik: Predicting time series with support vector machines. Proc. ICANN, 1997.
15. V. N. Vapnik: The Nature of Statistical Learning Theory. Springer Verlag, New York, 1995.
16. S. Haykin: Neural Networks: A Comprehensive Foundation, Second Edition. Prentice-Hall, Inc., 1999.
17. Chih-Chung Chang and Chih-Jen Lin: LIBSVM : a library for support vector machines. 2001. Software available at http://www.csie.ntu.edu.tw/~cjlin/libsvm.

A Natural Modification of Autocorrelation Based Video Watermarking Scheme Using ICA for Better Geometric Attack Robustness[*]

Seong-Whan Kim[1], Hyun Jin Park[2], and HyunSeong Sung[1]

[1] Department of Computer Science, University of Seoul,
Jeon-Nong-Dong, Seoul, Korea
{swkim7, wigman}@uos.ac.kr
[2] Institute for Neural Computation, UC San Diego,
San Diego, 9500 Gilman Drive, La Jolla, CA 92093-0523, USA
hjinpark@ucsd.edu

Abstract. Video watermarking hides information (e.g. ownership, recipient information, etc) into video contents. Video watermarking research is classified into (1) extension of still image watermarking, (2) use of the temporal domain features, and (3) use of video compression formats. In this paper, we propose a watermarking scheme to resist geometric attack (rotation, scaling, translation, and mixed) for H.264 (MPEG-4 Part 10 Advanced Video Coding) compressed video contents. Our scheme is based on auto-correlation method for geometric attack, a video perceptual model for maximal watermark capacity, and watermark detection based on natural image statistics. We experimented with the standard images and video sequences and the result shows that our video watermarking scheme is robust against H.264 video compression (average PSNR = 31 dB) and geometric attacks (rotation with 0-90 degree, scaling with 75-200%, and 50%~75% cropping).

1 Introduction

A digital watermark or watermark in short, is an invisible mark inserted in digital media such as digital images, audio and video so that it can later be detected and used as evidence of copyright infringement. However, insertion of such invisible mark should not alter the perceived quality of the digital media (it is the transparency requirement) while being extremely robust to attack (it is a robust requirement). Basic requirements for video watermarking are geometric attack robustness (intentional attacks) and H.264 video compression (unintentional attacks). There are four major researches for geometric attack robustness, (1) invariant transform, (2) template based, (3) feature point based, and (4) auto-correlation based [1]. Invariant transform approach is to embed the watermark in an invariant domain, like Fourier-Mellin transform [2], whereby geometric transform is still a linear operation. Template approach

---

[*] This work was supported by academic research grant from the University of Seoul (2004).

is to identify the transformation by retrieving artificially embedded references [3]. Feature point based approach is an embedding and detection scheme, where the mark is bound with a content descriptor defined by salient points [1]. Finally, Auto-correlation approach is to insert the mark periodically during the embedding process, and use auto-correlation during the detection process [4, 5].

We designed an auto-correlation based watermark detection scheme for geometric attack robustness, and present a video watermarking scheme, which is robust on geometric attack (scaling, cropping, rotation, and mixed) and H.264 video compression. In autocorrelation based approaches, separation of Gaussian noise components from raw and watermarked images is a crucial function for watermark performance. To improve performance, we applied Gaussian noise filtering method based on statistical model of natural images. The statistic model is based on ICA (independent component analysis) which models image as factorial distribution of super-Gaussian distribution. Since this model is more relevant for natural image than Gaussian distribution model, ICA based de-noising method shows superior performance for filtering (or de-noising) Gaussian noise. We implemented a new watermark insertion and detection scheme based on this method and evaluated performance advantages over conventional Wiener filter approach. Result shows that new watermark scheme is more robust and reliable than Wiener filters approach. Lastly our method considers human perception model for video to achieve maximal watermark capacity. Using this perceptual model we can insure the quality of watermarked videos while achieving maximum watermark robustness.

2 Watermark Embedding and Detection Scheme for INTRA Frame

H.264 is a widely used video compression standard, in which it uses different coding techniques for INTRA (reference) and INTER (motion predicted) frames. We embed the auto-correlated watermark for geometric synchronization in H.264 reference (INTRA) frames, because INTRA frames are used for reference frames of motion predicted (INTER) frames, and they are usually less compressed than INTER frames. In case of geometric attacks for video frames, we can use the watermark in INTRA frames to restore the synchronization misses.

Figure 1 shows the auto-correlation based watermark embedding scheme for INTRA coded frames. We changed the auto-correlation based watermark embedding approach as in [6] with different JND (just noticeable difference) model and different watermark estimation scheme, and also changed the Wiener filter to ICA de-noising based approach. As shown in Figure 1, we embedded the 64*64 block-wise watermarks repeatedly over whole image, thereby we can restore watermark even from 128x128 cropped image blocks.

Watermark embedding for H.264 INTRA frames can be summarized in the following equations. In this equation, I' is watermarked frame, E is ICA de-noised frame, N is the ICA estimated noise, λ is perceptual mask as specified in the previous equation, w_p is payload watermark, and w_s is synchronization watermark. Previous research uses the Wiener filter to compute E and N. For each 64x64 blocks, we adjusted the

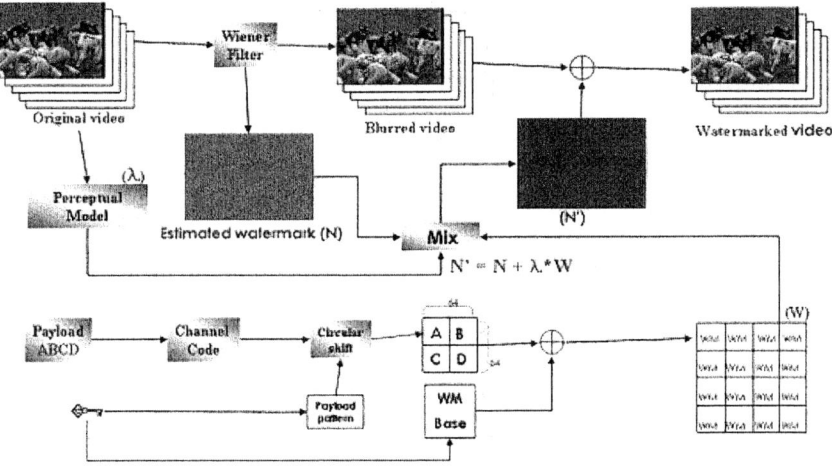

Fig. 1. Watermark Embedding for H.264 INTRA Frame

Embedding	$I' = E + N + \lambda(w_p + w_s)$, where $E = \text{ICADenoise}(I)$, $N = I - E$
Watermark strength	$\lambda * W = \max(\lambda_N W, \lambda_E W)$, where $\lambda_N * W = (1 - NVF) * W * A + NVF * W * B$ $\lambda_E * W = 3.0 * E * W$
NVF model	$NVF = \dfrac{1}{1 + \sigma^2}$
Entropy Masking	$E = \sum_{x \in N(X)} p(x) \cdot \log \dfrac{1}{p(x)}$

watermark strength as image complexity using a mixed perceptual model of NVF (noise visibility function) and entropy masking [7, 8, 9, 10]. We used the following equations for our watermark embedding, and we experimentally set the multiplication factor of entropy model as 3.0. Also the A and B values are set to 5.0 and 1.0.

In the same way, we use ICA de-noising for estimating E' instead of Wiener filter. To detect watermark, we used auto-correlation function to estimate the geometric transform, and used ICA de-noising (modification of Wiener filter box) to estimate the watermark in blind manner as shown in Figure 3. We improved the auto-correlation based watermark detection approach as [6], using ICA de-noising for better watermark estimation than Wiener filter approach. Moreover, to improve the payload detection performance, we used a different payload coding techniques and smaller auto-correlation block size 64x64 than 128x128. Decreasing auto-correlation block size makes multiple auto-correlated blocks to be folded, and it increases the watermark robustness.

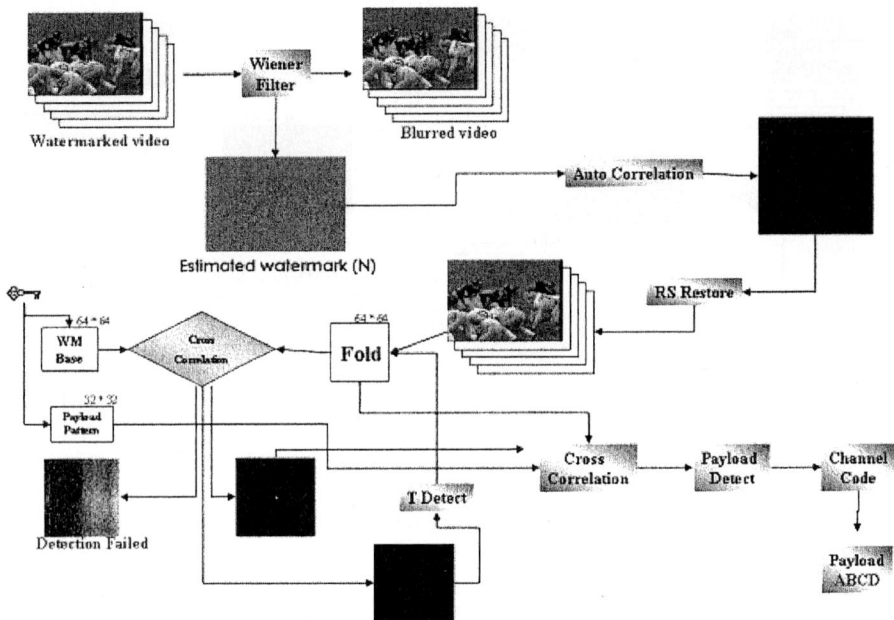

Fig. 2. Watermark Detection for H/264 INTRA Frames

Watermark detection and payload extraction for H.264 INTRA frames can be summarized in the following equations.

Detection	$w_s \cdot w' = w_s \cdot (I'-E')$, where E' = ICADenoise(I') $= w_s \cdot (N' + \lambda w_p + \lambda w_s)$, N' ≈ I' − E'
Payload extraction	$w_p \cdot w' = w_p \cdot (N' + \lambda w_p + \lambda w_s)$

3 Watermark Estimation Using ICA De-noising

We applied Independent Component Analysis (ICA) based Gaussian noise filtering (de-noising) instead of Wiener filter. From the Bayesian viewpoint Wiener filter is an inference method which computes Maximum Likely (ML) estimates of image signal given the noise variance [11, 12, 13]. Wiener filter assumes Gaussian distribution for both original image and noise. But real image statistics are much different from Gaussian distribution and are better modeled by the ICA model. If the ICA model provides better approximation of real image signals, then it can dramatically enhance noise filtering step in Watermark insertion and detection. ICA is an unsupervised learning method which has found wide range of applications in image processing [14]. ICA finds a linear transform W that maps high dimensional data X into maximally independent source signals S. The source signal S are modeled by a factorial probability density function which are usually super-Gaussian distributions like Laplacian distribution. Super-Gaussian distribution is a distribution which has higher peak at 0 and longer trails than Gaussian distribution.

$$S = WX, \quad X = AS \quad (A = W^{-1})$$

$$P(S) = \prod_i^M P(s_i)$$

In [15], it is reported that natural image statistics are well described by such ICA model. Also the linear transform filter W learned by ICA algorithm shows much similarity to simple cell filters [16] in human visual system. The filters learned by ICA algorithm are similar to Gabor filters which are multi-orientation, multi-scale edge filters. ICA models complex statistics of natural image well by factorized independent source distributions. Such independent source distributions are usually modeled as generalized Laplacian distribution which is super-Gaussian and symmetric. This simple PDF can be learned from image data and can be used for Bayesian de-noising of images [17]. Let's assume image patch X that follows ICA model (X=AS) and an independent Gaussian noise n with 0 mean and known variance σ. We assume that ICA source signal S has unit variance. Then we can define noisy image Y as follows.

$$Y = AS + n$$

In Bayesian de-noising the goal is to find $\hat{S}$ s.t.

$$\hat{S} = \underset{S}{argmax} \log P(S \mid Y)$$

$$= \underset{S}{argmax} \left[\log P(Y \mid S) + \log P(S) \right]$$

$$= \underset{S}{argmax} \left[\log N(Y - AS; \sigma) + \log P(S) \right]$$

$$= \underset{S}{argmax} \left[-\frac{|Y - AS|^2}{2\sigma^2} - \sum_i^M \log P(s_i) \right]$$

If we assume unit Laplacian distribution for S and Gaussian noise with signal s, then those equations can be written as.

$$\hat{S} = \underset{S}{argmax} \left[-\frac{|Y - AS|^2}{2\sigma^2} - \sum_i^M |s_i| \right]$$

The objective function of above equation can be further simplified if we assume orthogonal W s.t. $W^T = W^{-1} = A$.

$$-\frac{|Y-AS|^2}{2\sigma^2} - \sum_i |s_i| = -\frac{1}{2\sigma^2}(Y-AS)^T(Y-AS) - \sum_i |s_i|$$

$$= -\frac{1}{2\sigma^2}(Y-AS)^T(W^TW)(Y-AS) - \sum_i |s_i|$$

$$= -\frac{1}{2\sigma^2}(WY-WAS)^T(WY-WAS) - \sum_i |s_i|$$

$$= -\frac{1}{2\sigma^2}(WY-S)^T(WY-S) - \sum_i |s_i|$$

$$= -\frac{1}{2\sigma^2}|WY-S|^2 - \sum_i |s_i| = -\frac{1}{2\sigma_n^2}|S'-S|^2 - \sum_i |s_i|$$

$$= -\sum_i \left(\frac{1}{2\sigma^2}(s'_i - s_i)^2 + |s_i|\right)$$

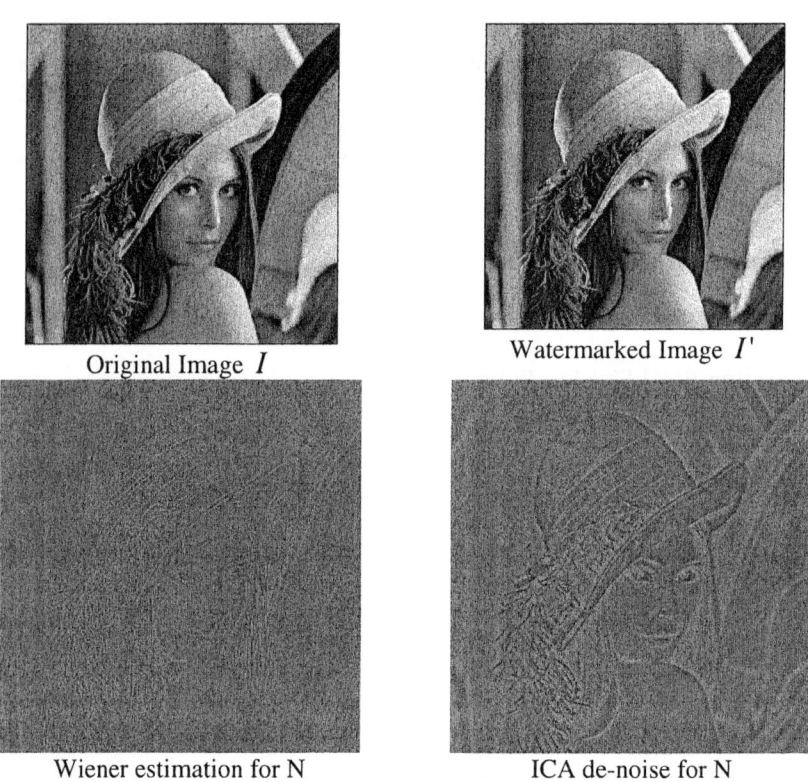

Fig. 3. Noise estimation comparison between Wiener filter and ICA de-noising

As shown, the objective function can be expressed as sum of independent and positive 1D objective functions. So the minimization of the entire objective function is equivalent to minimization of individual source dimensions. The solution to this 1D optimization problem is summarized in [4]. Then using the estimated $\hat{S}$, we can compute de-noised image $\hat{X} = A\hat{S}$ as well as the Gaussian noise $n = Y - \hat{X}$. Figure 3 compares Wiener filter and ICA de-noising for separating Gaussian noise N. ICA de-noising result shows the strong edge-like features, whereas Wiener filtered result shows rather weak edge-like features.

4 Simulation Results

We experimented with the standard test images, and Table 1 shows that we improve the watermark detection performance using ICA de-noising based approach over Wiener approach. We tested our approach over 20 standard test images, and showed that superior detection performance.

Table 1. ICA driven watermark detection improvements over Wiener

	Using Wiener		Using ICA	
	Correlation value	Threshold	Correlation value	Threshold
aerial.bmp	0.252816	0.074945	0.418893	0.246213
airplane.bmp	0.230755	0.046858	0.353133	0.172529
airport.bmp	0.198668	0.037124	0.411544	0.214705
baboon.bmp	0.192640	0.041524	0.362268	0.204293
barbara.bmp	0.203092	0.036492	0.321886	0.154950
boat.bmp	0.236444	0.041021	0.362430	0.158109
couple.bmp	0.230765	0.041714	0.380771	0.171419
elaine.bmp	0.253149	0.044271	0.350184	0.139988
girl.bmp	0.255930	0.052973	0.388574	0.177383
girls.bmp	0.243981	0.038508	0.346012	0.154674
goldhill.bmp	0.228562	0.039083	0.328786	0.144241
house.bmp	0.219754	0.046751	0.328289	0.161131
lake.bmp	0.213744	0.034296	0.302019	0.138336
lena.bmp	0.236769	0.039555	0.352069	0.156090
man.bmp	0.216027	0.035835	0.326558	0.138451
pepper.bmp	0.254798	0.044070	0.361369	0.157697
splash.bmp	0.250747	0.045205	0.351555	0.166243
stream and bridge.bmp	0.186301	0.037753	0.293211	0.159628
toys.bmp	0.222101	0.058213	0.236835	0.160865

We experimented with the standard test image sequence from VQEG (Video Quality Expert Group) as shown in Figure 4 [18]. After INTRA frame watermark embedding, the watermarked images show good subjective quality with the average PSNR

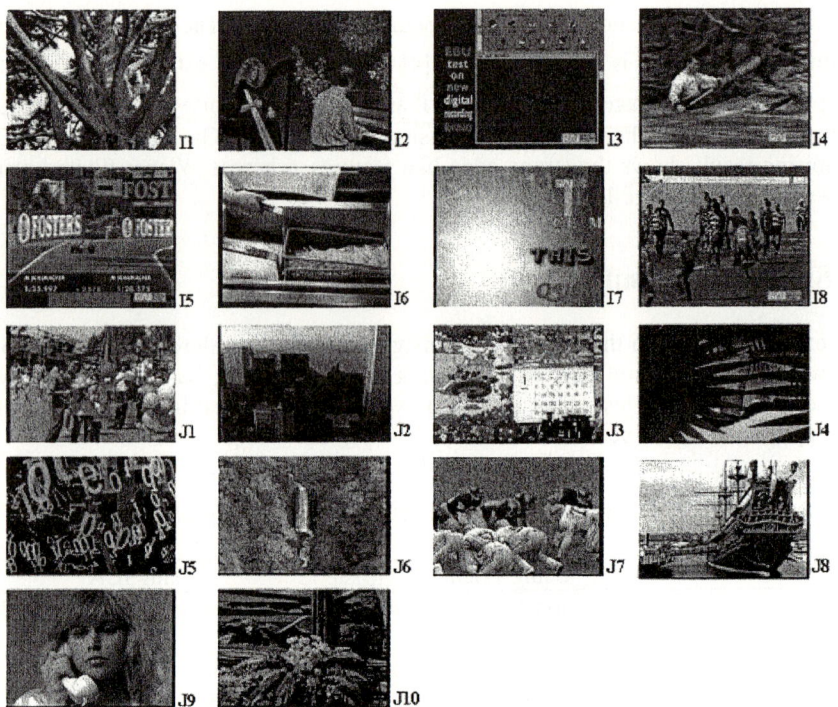

Fig. 4. VQEG Test Sequences

Table 2. Robustness on Geometric Attack for INTRA Frames

	Case 1: Rotation			Case 2: Rotation + Scaling			Case 3: Cropping	
	1	2	5	1	2	5	50	75
I1	O	O	X	X	X	X	O	O
I2	O	O	O	X	O	X	O	O
I3	O	O	X	X	X	O	O	O
I4	O	O	X	O	O	O	O	O
I5	O	O	O	O	O	O	O	O
I6	O	O	O	X	O	X	O	O
I7	O	O	O	X	O	X	O	O
I8	O	O	O	X	O	X	O	O
J1	O	O	X	X	X	O	O	O
J2	O	O	O	X	O	O	O	O
J3	O	O	O	X	X	X	O	O
J4	O	O	X	X	X	O	O	O
J5	O	O	X	X	X	O	O	O
J6	O	O	O	O	O	O	O	O
J7	O	O	O	O	X	O	O	O
J8	O	O	X	X	X	O	O	O
J9	O	O	O	O	O	O	O	O
J10	O	O	X	X	X	O	O	O

for Mobile&Calendar and Football test sequences are 32.03 and 31.80, respectively. To experiment the geometric attack, we used Stirmark 4.0 [19] geometric attack packages for various geometric attacks (rotation with 0-90 degrees, scaling with 75-200%, cropping with 50-75%, and mixed). We experimented with five cases: (case 1) rotation with 1, 2, and 5 degree clockwise; (case 2) case 1 rotation and scaling to fit original image size; (case 3) cropping with 50% and 75% attacks. Table 2 shows robustness result for the various geometric attacks on INTRA frames, and shows successful payload detection results in most geometric attack cases, and shows some misses under combined attack of rotation and scaling.

5 Conclusions

In this paper, we presented a robust video watermarking scheme, which uses autocorrelation based scheme for geometric attack recovery, and uses human visual system characteristics for H.264 compression. For watermark insertion and detection our method uses ICA-based filtering method which better utilizes natural image statistics than conventional Wiener filter. Result shows that the proposed scheme enhances robustness while keeping watermark invisible. Our video watermarking scheme is robust against H.264 video compression (average PSNR = 31 dB) and geometric attacks (rotation with 0-90 degree, scaling with 75-200%, and 50%~75% cropping).

References

1. Bas, P., Chassery, J.M., Macq, B.: Geometrically invariant watermarking using feature points. IEEE Trans. Image Proc. (2002) 1014-1028
2. O'Ruanaidh, J.J., Pun, T,:: Rotation, scale and translation invariant digital image watermarking. IEEE Int. Conf. Image Proc. (1997) 536-539
3. Pereira, S., Pun, T.: Robust template matching for affine resistant image watermarks. IEEE Trans. Image Proc. (2000)
4. Kutter, M.: Watermarking resisting to translation, rotation, and scaling, Proc. SPIE Int. Conf. on Multimedia Systems and Applications, 3528 (1998) 423-431
5. Su, P.C., Kuo, C.C.: Synchronized detection of the block-based watermark with invisible grid embedding. Proc. SPIE Electronic imaging (Security and Watermarking of Multimedia Contents III) (2001)
6. Lee, C.H., Lee, H.K., Suh, Y.H.: Autocorrelation Function-based Watermarking with Side Information. IS&T/SPIE, 15th Annual Symposium Electronic Imaging Science and Technology: Security and Watermarking of Multimedia Contents. (2003)
7. Voloshynovskiy, S., Herrige, A., Baumgaertner, N., Pun, T.: A stochastic approach to content adaptive digital image watermarking. Lecture Notes in Computer Science: Vol. 1768. Springer-Verlag, Berlin Heidelberg New York (1999)
8. Watson, A. B., Borthwick, R., Taylor, M.: Image quality and entropy masking. Proc. SPIE Conf. Human Vision, Visual Processing, and Digital Display VI, (1997)
9. Podilchuk C., Zeng, W., Image adaptive watermarking using visual models, IEEE J. Selected Areas in Communications. 16 (1998)
10. Kim, S.W., Suthaharan, S., Lee, H.K., Rao, K.R.: An image watermarking scheme using visual model and BN distribution. IEE Elect. Letter 35 (1999)

11. Haykin, S.: Neural Networks: A Comprehensive Foundation. Prentice-Hall, New Jersey, 2nd ed. (1999).
12. Rajapakse, J.C., Wang, L.P. (Eds.): Neural Information Processing: Research and Development, Berlin (2004).
13. Tan, Y.P., Yap, K.H. Wang, L.P. (Eds.): Intelligent Multimedia Processing with Soft Computing. Springer-Verlag, Berlin Heidelberg New York (2004).
14. Hinton, G.E., Sejnowski, T.J. Unsupervised Learning: Foundations of Neural Computation (edited), MIT Press, Cambridge, Massachusetts (1999)
15. Bell A.J., Sejnowski, T.J.: The 'Independent Components' of Natural Scenes are Edge Filters, Vision Research 37 (1997) 3327–3338
16. van Hateren, J.H.,van der Schaaf, A.: Independent component filters of natural images compared with simple cells in primary visual cortex, Proc. Royal Soc. London. B. 265:359-336 (1998)
17. Hyvarinen, A., Sparse Code Shrinkage: De-noising of Non-Gaussian Data by Maximum Likelihood Estimation, Neural Computation 11 (1999) 1739-1768
18. http://www.its.bldrdoc.gov/vqeg/
19. http://www.petitcolas.net/fabien/watermarking/stirmark/

Research of Blind Deconvolution Algorithm Based on High-Order Statistics and Quantum Inspired GA

Jun-an Yang[1,2], Bin Zhao[1], and Zhongfu Ye[2]

[1] 702 Research Division of Electronic Engineering Institute,
Hefei, China 230037
yangjunan@ustc.edu, eeizhaobin@163.com
[2] Depart. of Electronic Engineering and Information Science of USTC,
Hefei, China 230036
yezf@ustc.edu.cn

Abstract. This paper analyzes the network structure and algorithm model of Multi-Input and Multi-Output (MIMO) blind deconvolution, proposes a novel blind deconvolution algorithm based on output signals' context information, and puts forward a new optimum method using Quantum Inspired Genetic Algorithm (QIGA). The simulation results demonstrate the effectiveness of the algorithm to the separation of communication signals.

1 Introduction

In communication signal processing, Multi-Input and Multi-Output (MIMO) Blind Source Separation (BSS) is a representative problem. Considering the transmission time delay of the signal, the observed signals should be the convolutive mixture of source signals and channel properties. Blind separation of convoluted signals is called Blind Deconvolution (BD). Compared with the instantaneous mixed BSS [1], BD is more practical and more difficult.

Most of the BD algorithms are the extension of instantaneous mixed BSS algorithms till now, such as Nomura [2] extended H-J algorithm to BD, Lee and Bell [3] transformed Infomax algorithm to frequency domain and used FIR polynomial algebra to solve it, Thi and Jutten [4] used high-order cumulant and high-order moment, and so on. Above algorithms all adopted Newton iteration, gradient or natural gradient algorithm, and it was difficult to acquire global optimum solution. The separated waveforms were quite different with the source waveforms [5]. Genetic algorithm has already widely used in linear and nonlinear BSS and blind identification [6]–[10], and got perfect effects. Quantum-inspired Genetic Algorithm (QGA) is a newly emerging global optimum algorithm. It combines the probabilistic amplitude representation of qubit and the superposition of many states with colony searching property of GA, which can improve the computation efficiency of regular GA effectively [6], [10]. Although QGA has much space to improve its efficiency compared with other 'real time' algorithm, it can acquire perfect effect, so it can be used in no-real time circumstance.

This paper extends high-order mutual cumulant to BD and proposes a BD algorithm based on context information of output signals. This paper also applies

QGA to BD and proposes a new optimum method based on QGA. Simulation results of communication signals indicate its effectiveness.

2 Research of BD Algotithm Based on High-Order Mutual Cumulant

2.1 Network Structure and Algorithm Model of MIMO BD

MIMO model has already widely used in communication system and array signal processing. Considering a discrete MIMO system, there are M inputs and N outputs. The ith output signal at time t is

$$\mathbf{x}_i(t) = \sum_{j=1}^{M} \sum_{k=-\infty}^{\infty} a_{ij}(k) \mathbf{s}_j(t - \tau_{ijk}) \qquad i = 1, 2, \cdots, N \tag{1}$$

Where $\mathbf{s}_j(t - \tau_{ijk})$ represents the jth input signal, τ_{ijk} is unknown time delay of the jth input signal transmitted to the ith sensor. k is an integer, T is unit delay time. $a_{ij}(k)$ is unknown filtering and mixing parameter between the jth signal and the ith sensor. Formula (1) can be expressed as formula (2).

$$\mathbf{x}(t) = \mathbf{A}(z)\mathbf{s}(t) = \sum_{k=-\infty}^{\infty} \mathbf{A}(k)\mathbf{s}(t-k) \tag{2}$$

Where $\mathbf{A}(k) = [a_{ij}(k)]$ is unknown filtering and mixing parameter matrix. Formula (2) indicates that output signal $\mathbf{x}(t)$ is the convolutive mixture of $\mathbf{s}(t)$ with $\mathbf{A}(k)$.

The task of BD is to estimate unknown filtering and mixing parameter through observed signals $\mathbf{x}(t)$, and then to recover source signals. The mathematical model is

$$\mathbf{y}(t) = \sum_{k=-\infty}^{\infty} \mathbf{W}(k)\mathbf{x}(t-k) = \mathbf{W}(z)\mathbf{x}(t) \tag{3}$$

Where $\mathbf{y}(t) = [\mathbf{y}_1(t), \mathbf{y}_2(t), \cdots, \mathbf{y}_N(t)]^T$ is BD output signals, $\mathbf{W}(z) = \sum_{k=-\infty}^{\infty} \mathbf{W}(k) z^{-k}$ is under estimated BD filter matrix. More generally, mixing system and de-mixing system are all unknown LTI system and can be expressed as a finite order's FIR filter.

According to formula (1) and (2), observed signals $\mathbf{x}(t)$ at time t include not only the mixture of source signals $\mathbf{s}(t)$ at the same time through $\mathbf{A}(0)$, but also the mixture of delay source signals $\mathbf{s}(t-k)$ through different matrices $\mathbf{A}(k)$, i.e. the observed signals are related with the current signals and the former signals. So BD is more complex than instantaneous BSS.

2.2 BD Algorithm Based on High-Order Mutual Cumulant

This paper adopts the disappear of high order mutual cumulant of output signals' context as statistical independent criterion. In BD model, the observed signals are related with current and former input signals, so we must take into account output signals' context, i.e. mutual cumulant of two signals at arbitrary time interval.

Theorem 1 [4]: If $y_i(n)$ and $y_j(n)$ are statistical independent, $y_i(n-k)$ and $y_j(n-p)$ are also statistical independent (k and p are arbitrary time delay).

According to theorem 1, we can extend mutual cumulant to different signals at different time, i.e. $y_i(n)$ and $y_j(n-k)$. Then we can get the following definition of fourth-order mutual cumulate.

$$cum_{22}(\mathbf{y}_1(n),\mathbf{y}_2(n-k)) = E\{\mathbf{y}_1^2(n)\mathbf{y}_2^2(n-k)\} - E\{\mathbf{y}_1^2(n)\}E\{\mathbf{y}_2^2(n-k)\} - 2(E\{\mathbf{y}_1(n)\mathbf{y}_2(n-k)\})^2$$

$$cum_{31}(\mathbf{y}_1(n),\mathbf{y}_2(n-k)) = E\{\mathbf{y}_1^3(n)\mathbf{y}_2(n-k)\} - 3E\{\mathbf{y}_1^2(n)\}E\{\mathbf{y}_1(n)\mathbf{y}_2(n-k)\} \quad (4)$$

$$cum_{13}(\mathbf{y}_1(n),\mathbf{y}_2(n-k)) = E\{\mathbf{y}_1(n)\mathbf{y}_2^3(n-k)\} - 3E\{\mathbf{y}_1(n)\mathbf{y}_2(n-k)\}E\{\mathbf{y}_2^2(n-k)\}$$

If source signals' kurtosis has the same sign, we can acquire unique solution using cum_{22}, but not the same contrariwise, as cum_{22} only include square items. Simulation results in [4] indicated that the effect of only using cum_{22} is inferior to using cum_{31} at some circumstance. Using cum_{31} or cum_{13} will avoid such result, but it may generate pseudo signals. It is remarkable that these pseudo signals can be detected by using cum_{22}. So this paper adopts

$$crit(\mathbf{y}_1,\mathbf{y}_2) = \sum_{k=0}^{L}(\text{abs}(cum_{31}(\mathbf{y}_1(n),\mathbf{y}_2(n-k))) + \text{abs}(cum_{22}(\mathbf{y}_1(n),\mathbf{y}_2(n-k)))) \quad (5)$$

as the criterion. Where, L is large than the length of BD filter and less than the length of whole time series. The less $crit(\mathbf{y}_1,\mathbf{y}_2)$ is, the more independent of $\mathbf{y}_1$ and $\mathbf{y}_2$ will be. This criterion can not only use the context of output signals, but also avoid the pseudo signals. Simulation results indicate that the proposed criterion can achieve perfect separation result.

3 Realization of BD Algorithm Based on QGA

The QGA is based on the representation of quantum state vector. It applies the probabilistic amplitude representation of qubit to the encoding of chromosome so that one chromosome can represent the superposition of many states. With the update operation of chromosome by quantum rotation gate, quantum crossover and quantum mutation, it eventually reaches the optimum solution [6], [10].

The key to realize BD based on QGA is: the qubit encoding pattern of chromosome in the solution space, the selection of fitness function, and the chromosome updating mechanism which adopts quantum rotation gate and non-gate.

3.1 Selection of Fitness Function

The reciprocal of $crit(\mathbf{y}_1,\mathbf{y}_2)$ is used as fitness function, i.e.

$$J(y) = 1/\sum_{k=0}^{L}(\text{abs}(cum_{31}(\mathbf{y}_1(n),\mathbf{y}_2(n-k))) + \text{abs}(cum_{22}(\mathbf{y}_1(n),\mathbf{y}_2(n-k)))) \quad (6)$$

Under the constraint of $E\{yy^T\}=I$, to a separating filter matrix $W(z)$, the greater $J(y)$ is, the stronger the independence among y_i will be.

3.2 Qubit Encoding Pattern of the Chromosome

We select 20 initial individuals and adopt multi-qubit to encode the separating filter matrix W(**z**). For example, we want to separate two mixed signals, and the de-mixing matrix is a 2×2 square matrix, so there are 4 deconvolution filters. The order of each filter is set to 10, and there are 40 parameters to be optimized. Each parameter is represent by a 8bit binary number, so the qubit encoding pattern of the chromosome is a 8bit×40=320bit encoding pattern, as shown in Formula (7).

$$q_j^t = \begin{pmatrix} \alpha_{11}^t & \alpha_{12}^t & \cdots & \alpha_{1k}^t & \alpha_{21}^t & \alpha_{22}^t & \cdots & \alpha_{2k}^t & \alpha_{m1}^t & \alpha_{m2}^t & \cdots & \alpha_{mk}^t \\ \beta_{11}^t & \beta_{12}^t & \cdots & \beta_{1k}^t & \beta_{21}^t & \beta_{22}^t & \cdots & \beta_{2k}^t & \beta_{m1}^t & \beta_{m2}^t & \cdots & \beta_{mk}^t \end{pmatrix} \quad (7)$$

where q_j^t represents the t-th generation and the j-th individual chromosome, k is the qubit number of every encoding state, and m is the gene number in each chromosome. (α, β) is two quantum states, satisfies $|\alpha|^2 + |\beta|^2 = 1$.

3.3 Quantum Crossover, Mutation and Quantum Rotation Gate Updating Mechanism [6], [10]

CGA adopts the selection, crossover and mutation to make the colony approach to the global optimum. Because of the random and blind character of the genetic operation, it is essential to have enough individuals and genetic operation to reach the global optimum among each individual. While in QGA, the qubit encoding is probabilistic representation, and each chromosome can represent the superposition of multi-state simultaneously, so it has enough diversity. Quantum rotation gate is employed to search the optimal solution. Quantum crossover is used to utilize all chromosomes' information. Quantum mutation is adopted to avoid the premature convergence and offer local searching ability. So QGA not only possesses rapid convergence, but also has good global search capability.

3.4 Initialization and Restrictions [6], [10]

The prerequisite of adopting mutual cumulant as the criterion of independence is the constraint of zero-mean and $E\{\mathbf{y}\mathbf{y}^T\}=\mathbf{I}$. So it is necessary to centralize and whiten the signals to reach the constraint in every generation.

BD algorithm based on QGA can be realized as:

(1) Read source signals. We select 2 communication signals in this paper.
(2) Centralize and whiten the signals.
(3) Generate n separating filter matrices as initial individuals and encode them with qubit.
(4) Measure the initial colony respectively. The procedure is:
Make $P(t_0)$ by measuring $Q(t_0)$ states; convert $P(t_0)$ to the parameters of separation filter matrices; get the separated signals; centralize and whiten the separated signals; calculate the fitness function; find the optimum individual and its solution as the later evolutionary aim.
(5) Enter the loop.

Measure colony $Q(t)$ once again, get the solution $P(t)$, convert $P(t)$ to the parameters of separation matrices; get the separated signals; centralize and whiten the separated signals; calculate the fitness function; carry out quantum crossover, perform the quantum rotation gate and non-gate as evolutionary method; find the optimum individual and its solution as the next evolutionary aim; go to loop again until reaching the set generation number or the evolutionary aim.

(6) Construct the separating matrix from the best individual. Separate the signals.

4 Simulation Results and Discussion

To verify the effectiveness of the proposed algorithm to communication signals, we perform a great deal of simulations with many type of signals, such as AM, ASK, FSK and noise. The initial population size of QGA is 20, generations is 200. The selection probability of the quantum crossover is 30%. The probability of the quantum mutation is 10% and is increased to 20% after 100 generations.

4.1 Simulation 1

The order of convolution filter is selected as 3, 5 and 7 respectively. The order of deconvolution filter is set as 10. We select two AM signals and acquire perfect separation result. Fig. 1 shows the waveforms when the order of convolution filter is 5. The convolution filter is select randomly as follows:

$$\begin{bmatrix} 0.9+0.5z^{-1}+0.3z^{-2}-0.2z^{-3}+0.1z^{-4} & 0.8+0.4z^{-1}+0.1z^{-2}-0.3z^{-3}-0.2z^{-4} \\ 0.7+0.4z^{-1}+0.3z^{-2}+0.2z^{-3}-0.1z^{-4} & 0.7+0.5z^{-1}+0.1z^{-2}-0.5z^{-3}+0.2z^{-4} \end{bmatrix} \quad (8)$$

4.2 Simulation 2

We select a ASK signal and a FSK signal and also acquire perfect separation result. Fig. 2 shows the waveforms when the order of convolution filter is 5. The convolution filter is the same as simulation 1.

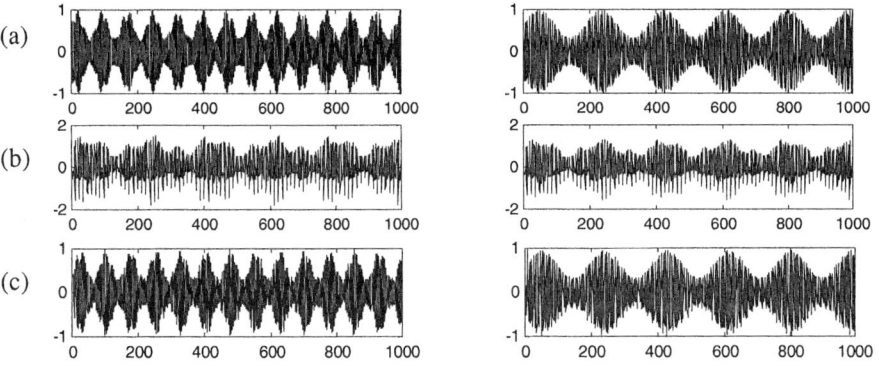

Fig. 1. Separation of two AM signals. (a) source signals, (b) mixed signals, (c) separated signals.

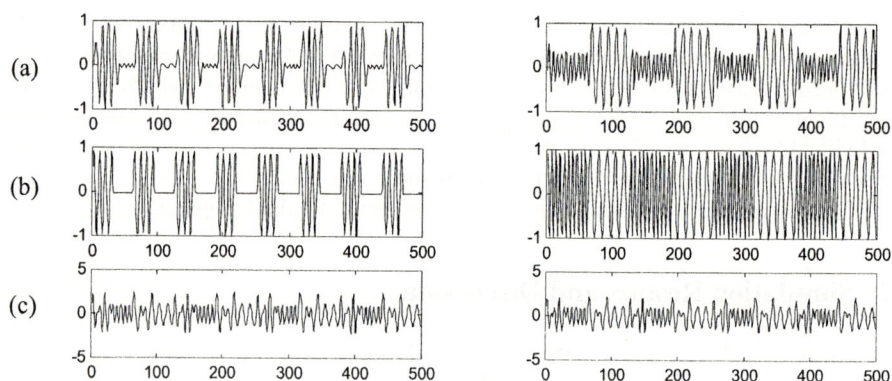

Fig. 2. Separation of ASK and FSK signals. (a) source signals, (b) mixed signals, (c) separated signals.

4.3 Quantitative Analysis

To validate the algorithm quantitatively, we evaluate the algorithm with the SNR as formula (9).

$$SNR(\mathbf{y}_i) = 10\log\frac{E\{|\mathbf{s}_i|^2\}}{E\{|\mathbf{y}_i - \mathbf{s}_i|^2\}} \qquad (9)$$

In simulation1, $SNR(\mathbf{y}_1)$=18.54 dB, $SNR(\mathbf{y}_2)$=19.27 dB. In simulation2, $SNR(\mathbf{y}_1)$=16.25 dB, $SNR(\mathbf{y}_2)$=12.51 dB. The experimental results are superior to that in [11].

5 Conclusion

This paper proposes a novel BD algorithm based on mutual cumulant of observed signals' context and adopts QGA to acquire its optimal solution. Simulation results to communication signals validate the algorithm. Although the cost of computation is large relatively, it can be used in non-real time signal processing effectively.

Acknowledgement

This work is supported by Natural Science Fund of Anhui Province of China (050420101).

References

1. Comon P.: Independent component analysis – a new concept? Signal Processing, 36(3):287-314. 1994
2. Nomura T., Eguchi M., et al.: An Extension of the Herault-Jutten Network to Signal Including Delays for Blind Separation. In: Proceedings of IEEE Workshop on Neural Networks for Signal Processing, P. 443~452, Kyoto, Japan, Sept. 1996

3. Lee T.-W., Bell A.J., Lambert R.: Blind separation of convolved and delayed sources. In: advances in Neural Information Processing Systems 9, P.758~764, 1997, MIT Press
4. Thi H.N., Jutten C.: Blind Source Separation for Convolutive mixtures. Signal Processing, 45(1995), 209~229
5. Yeung K.L., Yau S.F.: A cumulate-based super-exponential algorithm for blind deconvolution of multi-input multi-output systems. Signal Processing, 67(1998), 141~162
6. Yang Jun-an, Zhuang Zhenquan: Research of Quantum Genetic Algorithm and Its Application in Blind Source Separation. Journal of Electronics(China), 2003, 20(1), 62~68
7. Yang Jun-an.: Research & Realization of Image Separation Method Based on Independent Component Analysis & Genetic Algorithm. International Congress on Image and Graph 2002(ICIG2002), Hefei, China, 2002, SPIE Press, 575~582
8. Tan,Y., Wang,J.: Nonlinear blind source separation using higher order statistics and a genetic algorithm. IEEE Trans. Evolutionary Computation, Vol.5, Dec. 2001, 600~612
9. Alkanhal M.A., Alshebeili S.A.: Blind identification of nonminimum phase FIR systems: Cumulates matching via genetic algorithms. Signal Processing, 67(1998), 25~34
10. Yang Jun-an, Zhuang Zhenquan: Research of Blind Source Separation Algorithm based on Quantum Genetic Algorithm. Mini and Micro Computer System, Vol.24, No.8, 1518~1523, 2003 (In Chinese)
11. Tugnait J. K.: Adaptive blind separation of convolutive mixtures of independent linear signals. Signal Processing, 73(1999), 139~152

Differential Demodulation of OFDM Based on SOM

Xuming Li and Lenan Wu

Department of Radio Engineering, Southeast University,
Nanjing, Jiangsu 210096, China
lxm6969@seu.edu.cn

Abstract. In this paper, a novel differential demodulator for OFDM combining traditional differential demodulation with neural computation has been introduced for differential detection. Simulations using a two-path channel model and M-ary differential phase shift keying (MDPSK) modulation have been run to investigate the performance characteristics of the proposed scheme. The results show that it adapts very well to channel conditions with both strong delay and Doppler spread. The new structures are superior when compared to the traditional differential demodulation in frequency selective fast fading channels without any extra computing complexity.

1 Introduction

In wireless communication channels, orthogonal frequency division multiplexing (OFDM) is an effective technique for combating inter symbol interference (ISI) caused by multipath fading and for high-bit-rate transmission [1]. At present OFDM has been adopted for many standards such as digital radio mondiale (DRM) broadcasting systems and digital video broadcasting for terrestrial (DVB-T) [2] [3].

In OFDM, the demodulation techniques can be divided into coherent demodulation, time domain differential demodulation (TDDD) and frequency domain differential demodulation (FDDD). Coherent systems typically outperform differential systems due to the use of pilot symbol with the aid of channel estimation. However, the channel estimation is very difficult at fast fading [4]. In contrast to this, differential demodulation systems are designed to work without channel estimation. Differential demodulation has already been in use for digital audio broadcasting (DAB) [5]. Unfortunately, TDDD and FDDD is sensitive to time-selectivity and frequency-selectivity [6] respectively. Therefore, the performance of both TDDD and FDDD is poor in frequency selective fast fading channels.

In this paper, we suggested a new differential detection structure employing neural computation. In this approach, a neural network algorithms, called a self-organizing map (SOM) algorithm, is connected with traditional differential demodulation. The SOM is a widely used neural network algorithm [7]. The SOM has previously been used to combat unwanted effects such as nonlinear distortions or phase shifts combined with traditional equalizers in single carrier systems [8].

In this paper we will apply SOM to OFDM systems. The new differential detection in the development of neural network architectures includes the effects of time-varying multipah channels. It can obtain the characteristic of interference signal by SOM without knowledge of channels. In our analysis, we assume the ideal synchronization and no ISI. The remainder of this paper is organized as follows. In section 2, transmission systems and channel model are described. Section 3 analyzes the interference of differential demodulation signal in OFDM. In Section 4, the new differential detection scheme based on SOM is proposed. Section 5 presents the results of simulation and concludes this work.

2 Systems and Channel Model

2.1 Channel Model

A two-path Rayleigh fading channel with obvious delay and Doppler spread is considered in this paper. The instantaneous channel impulse response can be written as

$$h(t,\tau) = \sum_{i=1}^{2} \rho_i h_i(t) \delta(\tau - \tau_i). \qquad (1)$$

where ρ_i is path gain of the i-th path; τ_i is the relative delay of the respective path. The $h_i(t)$ is assumed to be uncorrelated complex Gaussian random process. In this paper, we will assume that the $h_i(t)$'s are independent for different i's, but have the same normalized Doppler frequency $f_d T_s$. In addition, we assume that $\rho_i = 1$ $i = 1, 2$ and $\tau_1 = 0$. The channel model employed in this contribution is the bad case operating environment for DRM broadcasting system [2].

2.2 OFDM System

In our analyzed OFDM system, we assume the number of subcarriers N and the duration of each subcarrier symbol T_s and the duration of OFDM symbol $T_u = NT_s$. In addition, we assume the channel bandwidth B of 10 kHz and $B = 1/T_s$.

The serial binary information sequences are mapped to the MDPSK modulation symbols $S_{n,k}$ of the N subcarriers of one OFDM symbol. The subscript n refers to the OFDM symbol time index and k is the subcarrier frequency index. For FDDD, the differential encoding is between two successive modulation symbols $S_{n,k}$ and $S_{n,k-1}$ of the same OFDM symbol. For TDDD, the differential encoding is between the two corresponding identical-frequency subcarriers $S_{n,k}$ and $S_{n-1,k}$ of consecutive OFDM symbols.

The OFDM block is transformed into the time domain by an inverse fast Fourier transform (IFFT). A sufficient guard interval is added as a cyclic prefix, protecting the transmission systems against the ISI. The obtained signal is transmitted over the channel. At the receiver, the guard interval is removed and the signal is transformed into the frequency domain again, yielding the received modulation states $R_{n,k}$, which can be expressed as [1]

$$R_{n,k} = S_{n,k} H_{n,k} + ICI_{n,k} + N_{n,k} .\qquad(2)$$

where

$$ICI_{n,k} = \frac{1}{N}\sum_{\substack{m=0\\m\neq k}}^{N-1}\sum_{l=0}^{N-1} S_{n,m} H_{n,m} e^{j(2\pi/N)(m-k)l} .\qquad(3)$$

$$H_{n,k} = h_1(l) + h_2(l) e^{-j\frac{2\pi}{N}k\tau} .\qquad(4)$$

in which $h_i(l) = h_i(t = lT_s)$, $i = 1, 2$ and $\tau = \tau_2 / T_s$.

In (2), $N_{n,k}$ is complex-valued additive white Gaussian noise (AWGN); $ICI_{n,k}$ is ICI noise caused by Doppler spread; $H_{n,k}$ is the channel frequency response.

3 Analysis of Signal Interference

3.1 FDDD

The received signal after FDDD produces the decision variable

$$D_{n,k}^{fd} = \frac{S_{n,k} H_{n,k} + ICI_{n,k} + N_{n,k}}{S_{n,k-1} H_{n,k-1} + ICI_{n,k-1} + N_{n,k-1}} .\qquad(5)$$

Neglecting the channel and ICI noise, the decision variable is

$$D_{n,k}^{fu} = \frac{S_{n,k}}{S_{n,k-1}} \frac{H_{n,k}}{H_{n,k-1}} .\qquad(6)$$

Using (4) and assuming $h_i(l)$ is nearly constant during one OFDM symbol interval of length T_u, we have

$$\frac{H_{n,k}}{H_{n,k-1}} = \frac{1+e^{-j\frac{2\pi}{N}k\tau}}{1+e^{-j\frac{2\pi}{N}(k-1)\tau}}\qquad(7)$$

$$= \frac{e^{-j\frac{\pi}{N}k\tau}(e^{j\frac{\pi}{N}k\tau}+e^{-j\frac{\pi}{N}k\tau})}{e^{-j\frac{\pi}{N}(k-1)\tau}(e^{j\frac{\pi}{N}(k-1)\tau}+e^{-j\frac{\pi}{N}(k-1)\tau})}.$$

$$= \frac{\cos(\frac{\pi}{N}k\tau)}{\cos\left(\frac{\pi}{N}(k-1)\tau\right)} e^{-j\frac{\pi}{N}\tau}$$

Using (7), we can rewrite (6) as

$$D_{n,k}^{fu} = \frac{S_{n,k}}{S_{n,k-1}} \frac{H_{n,k}}{H_{n,k-1}} \quad (8)$$

$$= \frac{S_{n,k}}{S_{n,k-1}} \frac{\cos(\frac{\pi}{N}k\tau)}{\cos\left(\frac{\pi}{N}(k-1)\tau\right)} e^{-j\frac{\pi}{N}\tau}$$

From (8), we can see that delay spread gives rise to an extra phase rotation of decision symbol, which degrades the performance of FDDD systems. In two-path channels, the phase error is approximately a constant angle ϕ. In addition, the phase error is independent of the subcarrier frequency index k and can be decreased when the number of subcarriers N is increased.

From (5), we can see that the demodulation signal is affected by twice ICI noise. In (3), ICI is modeled as a zero-mean complex Gaussian noise and causes the irreducible error rate at high signal-to-noise ratio (SNR). The system performance is limited by signal-to-ICI ratio (SIR) defined as $\gamma_{SIR} = E_s / \sigma_{ICI}^2$ where E_s is the signal energy per symbol and σ_{ICI}^2 is the power of ICI. The power of ICI resulting from a single fading multi-path component $h_i(t)$ is given by [9]

$$\sigma_{ICI;i}^2 \approx \frac{\pi^2}{3}(f_d(i)NT_s)^2 \quad (9)$$

where $f_d(i)$ is Doppler frequency of the i-th path.

The system performance can be degraded when the normalized Doppler frequency $f_d(i)NT_s$ is increased.

3.2 TDDD

The received signal after TDDD produces the decision variable

$$D_{n,k}^{td} = \frac{S_{n,k}H_{n,k} + \overline{ICI}_{n,k} + N_{n,k}}{S_{n-1,k}H_{n-1,k} + \overline{ICI}_{n-1,k} + N_{n-1,k}} \quad (10)$$

It should be noted that time domain differential encoding is between two OFDM symbols. Thus, TDDD demand the channel being stationary in the duration of length $2NT_s$. In (10), the equivalent ICI can be expressed as

$$\overline{ICI}_{n,k} = \frac{1}{2N}\sum_{\substack{m=0 \\ m \neq k}}^{2N-1}\sum_{l=0}^{2N-1} S_{n,m}H_{n,m}e^{j(2\pi/2N)(m-k)l} \quad (11)$$

The corresponding power of ICI resulting from a single fading multi-path component $h_i(t)$ can be expressed as

$$\overline{\sigma_{ICI;i}^2} \approx \frac{\pi^2}{3}(f_d(i)2NT_s)^2 . \tag{12}$$

In contrast to (9), the ICI power of TDDD is bigger than that of FDDD. Neglecting the channel and assuming that $h_i(l)$ is nearly constant during the interval of length $2T_u$ in (4), we have

$$D_{n,k}^u = \frac{S_{n,k}H_{n,k}}{S_{n-1,k}H_{n-1,k}} = \frac{S_{n,k}}{S_{n-1,k}} . \tag{13}$$

From (13), the performance of TDDD system is not affected by delay spread.

According to the above analysis, we can see that the performance of FDDD is affected by both delay and Doppler spread. The performance of TDDD system is not affected by delay spread. However, TDDD is more vulnerable to time-varying characteristic of channel than FDDD.

4 Improved Differential Demodulation Using SOM

4.1 Basic Idea

Now we know conventional differential demodulation scheme is not adaptable to the channel conditions which exhibit both frequency selectivity and fast fading. To combat fast fading, it is adoptable to select FDDD scheme. In order to improve the performance of FDDD system, the extra phase shift caused by delay spread should be corrective.

The delay spread has two effects on FDDD OFDM systems, as shown in Fig. 1. 4DPSK modulation in each subcarrier and a two-path channel are assumed. First is

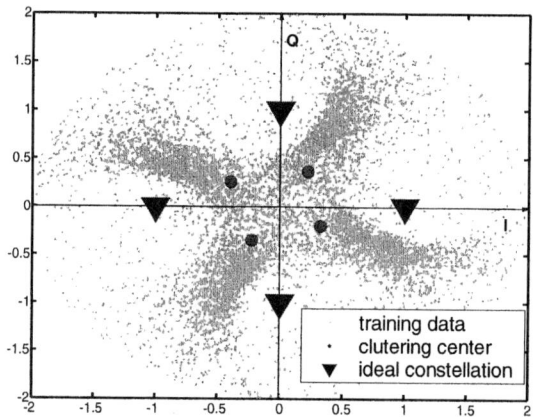

Fig. 1. Signal constellation of 4DPSK (SNR=20dB) after FDDD in a two-path channel

the angular rotation, where the signal constellation after differential demodulation is rotated by a specific angle ϕ. The second is the scattering of the constellation points due to the ICI, where each constellation point after differential detection exhibits some nonlinear distortion. We can think of signal constellation as a two-dimensional coordinate system. Each discrete complex demodulation signal can be regarded as a two-dimensional vector. Hence, the feature of regular rotation of constellation can be extracted by the way of pattern classification. However, the constellation points of interference signal have, in addition to linear phase, other nonlinear distortions. It is well known that the SOM has strong capability of combating nonlinear distortions.

4.2 Phase Shift Correct

In order to improve the performance of FDDD system, an additional rotation of the decision variable $D_{n,k}^{fd}$ by a constant angle $\theta_{n,k}$ is used to compensate for a systematic phase shift. After compensation for de-rotation, we have new decision variable

$$\widehat{D_{n,k}} = D_{n,k}^{fd} e^{j\theta_{n,k}} . \tag{14}$$

In (14), the nature choice for $\theta_{n,k}$ is the negative of argument of $H_{n,k} / H_{n,k-1}$. If we have knowledge of channel, the phase shift $\theta_{n,k}$ can be calculated theoretically as following. Using (7), we have

$$\theta_{n,k} = -\arg(H_{n,k} / H_{n,k-1}) = \frac{\pi}{N}\tau . \tag{15}$$

If we have not the knowledge of channel, we can estimate the phase shift $\theta_{n,k}$ by data clustering based on SOM.

4.3 SOM for Phase Shift

SOM algorithm is able to perform data clustering. Here the training data are the interference FDDD signal in the case of a two-path channel and SNR=20dB as in Fig. 1. Special interest is on finding the centre of interference signals.

The detailed description of the interference estimation is the following

1) When 4DPSK modulation signal is used, the in-phase and quadrature components of signal make up a two-dimensional SOM input vector.
2) The SOM is initialized to a square grid of the same size as DQPSK constellation.
3) Perform training data clustering based on the original SOM algorithm [7].
4) Find the centers of interference signals as shown in Fig. 1.
5) Compare the centers with the ideal signal constellation, and then calculate the phase shift.

5 Simulation Results and Conclusion

The performance characteristics of the new differential demodulation based on SOM described above were evaluated by simulations. We take simulations for 4DPSK/OFDM systems and a rate 1/2 convolution coding, where the Viterbi algorithm is used for soft-decision decoding. Two-path Rayleigh fading channels with delay and Doppler spread are used in our simulations. We choose the number of subcarriers $N = 256$ and the guard interval is enough big.

The performance of differential demodulation systems is investigated in difficult channels. Fig. 2 depicts the BER of differential demodulation systems in channel conditions with strong delay and Doppler spread.

Simulation results shows the new differential demodulator based on SOM can effectively mitigate the effect of delay spread in FDDD systems. The proposed scheme adapts very well to frequency selective fast fading channel conditions, outperforms the conventional differential demodulation without any extra computation complexity.

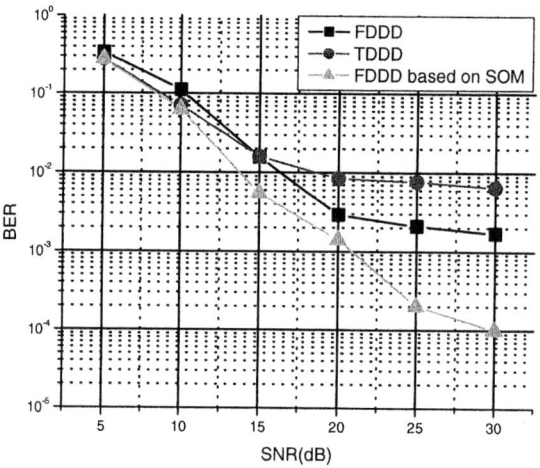

Fig. 2. $f_d T_s = 3 \times 10^{-4}$ $\tau = \tau_2 / T_s = 20$ BER of 4DPSK/OFDM systems in channel conditions with strong delay and Doppler spread

Acknowledgments. This work was supported by the NSF of China under Grant No. 60072013 and No.60472054.

References

1. L. J. Cimini, "Analysis and simulation of a digital mobile channel using orthogonal frequency division multiplexing," IEEE Trans. Commun., vol. COM-33, pp. 665–675, July 1985.
2. ETSI TS 101980: Digital Radio Mondiale; Systems specification (ETSI, 2001). See http://www.etsi.org

3. European standard (telecommunications series), digital video broadcasting (DVB); Framing structure, channel coding and modulation for digital terrestrial television, ETSI EN 300 744 v1.4.1 (2001-01), 2001.
4. S. Chen and T. Yao, "Intercarrier interference suppression and channel estimation for OFDM systems in time-varying frequency-selective fading channels," IEEE Trans. Consumer electronics, Vol. 50, No. 2, pp. 429-435, May 2004.
5. European standard (telecommunications series), radio broadcasting systems; digital audio broadcasting (DAB) to mobile, portable and receivers, ETSI EN 300 401 V 1.3.3 (20001-05), 2001.
6. K. zhong, T. T. Tjhung, F. Adachi, "A general SER formula for an OFDM systems with MDPSK in frequency domain over Rayleigh fading channel," IEEE Trans. Commun., vol. 52, no. 4, pp. 584-594, Apr. 2004.
7. T. Kohonen, "self-orgnized map," Proc. IEEE vol. 78 no. 9 pp. 1464-1480, Sep. 1990.
8. K. Raivio and T. kohonen, "Detection of nonlinearly distorted and two-path propagated signals using SOM based equalizers," in proceeding of the international conference on artificial neural networks, (Sorrento) pp. 1037-1047, May 1994.
9. Y. Li and L. J. Cimini Jr., "Bounds on the Interchannel Interference of OFDM in Time-Varying Impairments," IEEE Trans. Commun., vol. 49, no. 3 pp. 401–404, Mar. 2001.

Efficient Time Series Matching Based on HMTS Algorithm

Min Zhang[1] and Ying Tan[2]

[1] Electronic Engineering Institute, Hefei 230037, China
dyzhangmin@163.com
[2] The Chinese University of Hong Kong, Shatin, Hong Kong
yingtan@ie.cuhk.edu.hk

Abstract. A hierarchical matching of time series(HMTS) algorithm is proposed in this paper. The trend information of the time series is extracted using EMD(empirical mode decomposition) at first, subsequently piecewise linear segmentation is used to represent the trend of the series and the segmental line information is translated into 0-1 character, which substantially reduces the computational amount when comparing to the raw data. Finally the reduced series along with the series' details are matched. As a result, the algorithm significantly improves the efficiency and accuracy of the similarity search, and overcome the difficulties of the direct linear segmentation representation of the raw data. The experimental results illustrate the effectiveness of this algorithm.

1 Introduction

Time series account for much of the data stored in the commerce, the finance, the engineering, the medical data and the social science databases. Recently, there has been much interest in such mining time series data problems as similarity queries, cluster, classification, etc., among which the similarity measure is an important core task. Because of the high dimensionality of most time series, the direct indexing of time series is infeasible in most cases. As a result, dimensionality reduction and efficient matching methods appear to be the most promising method for solving this problem. An abstract representation of time series permits more efficient computation than those by directly using the raw time series data and may allow for a more sophisticated search (or indexing) technique. Up to now, many different representations have been proposed, including Discrete Fourier Transformations[1,2], Wavelet transformation [3,4], and R*-tree [5], etc. All these methods have certain results on the data reduction and efficient matching of time series, but they all have some disadvantages. For instance, they are too sensitive to the noises, bed intuition, and sometimes are required to choose parameters carefully, etc. Keogh proposed an algorithm to match the time series with a piecewise linear representation [6, 7], which has numerous advantages of providing a useful formulation of data compression and noise filtering. Speedup is obtained because the piecewise linear segmentation is a form of abstraction, which makes the searching over these abstract features much more efficient than the searching over the raw data. Therefore the representation is one of the best forms that can handle similar matching of huge dimension data easily and efficiently. The direct piecewise segment representation, however, has some restricted conditions, especially when the time series change quickly, that is, instantaneous frequency of the time series is very high. In this case, the piecewise linear segmentation is hard to represent the raw data precisely, and probably results in wrong matching results.

The paper proposes a hierarchical matching algorithm. After the rough match of the trend series which is suitable for piecewise segment representation, the accuracy series match will be studied with computation decrease and improvement of the matching efficiency. Moreover, it will increase the reliability of the series similarity matching since the trend similarity standard is added to the normal similar standard.

2 Hierarchical Matching of Time Series(HMTS)

One of the human cognitive features is that people can observe and analysis the same problem at different granularity, and obey the law of hierarchy to narrow down the scope of solving problems by utilizing the obtained knowledge until the answer is found. So we use the hierarchy approach for fast and effective time series pattern similar matching.

There are two methods of matching, the whole matching and the subsequence matching. No matter what method is chosen, the reduction data is required to replace the raw data for efficient similarity searching. Piecewise linear segment is one of the effective reduction methods.

2.1 Piecewise Linear Representation

For clarity we will refer to unprocessed temporal data as 'raw' time series, and a piece-wise representation of a time series as a sequence. We will use the following notation throughout this paper. A time series is represented as an uppercase letter like A. The segmented version of A, containing n linear segments sampled at m points for each segment, is denoted as a uppercase letter like A, with $A = \{A_1, A_2, \cdots, A_n\}$.

The ith segment of sequence A_i is represented as $A_i = \{(A_{XLi}, A_{YLi}), (A_{XRi}, A_{YRi})\}$. Fig. 1 illustrates this notation.

One of the advantages of using piecewise linear segments is that distance measure can be calculated approximately k/K times faster than that on the raw data. Speedup is obtained because the piecewise linear segmentation is a form of abstraction, and searching over these abstract features is much more efficient than searching over the raw data. Not all the series, however, are suitable for piecewise linear segments representation. For instance, a time series have abrupt fluctuations in the middle in Fig. 2, but the representations of the series in Fig. 2(a) and 2(b) using the linear segments are different only because a slight back movement of the sample in Fig. 2(b) in contrast with Fig. 2(a). So their piecewise segments are hard to match with each other. Therefore the linear piecewise representation is not suitable for of such time series.

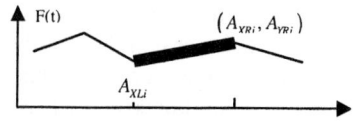

Fig. 1. Piecewise linear representation

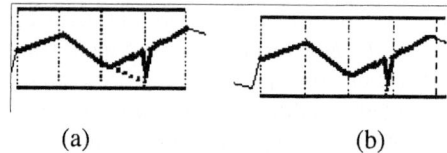

Fig. 2. Piecewise linear representation

When the linear segments representation is approaching to the raw data, the representation is similar to the raw data. With the related theory of signal processing, the higher the sample rate is, the more approaching the segments representation is to the raw data. But the length of the segment is $L = 1/f_s$, that is, the length is decreasing with the increasing sample rate, and the higher the rate is, the shorter the L is, and the lower its reduction ratio is. Therefore, the suitable series for the piecewise linear representation is the low frequency series.

Series signal can be decomposed into trend and detail parts. Because the trend of the series represents the features of the whole part of the signal, has low variation frequency and is hard to be influenced by the noises part, therefore the trend series of the raw data is very fit to be represented by linear segments. So the method of matching the trend series of the raw date is proposed.

2.2 Abstracting the Trend Series and Character Transformation

EMD (empirical mode decomposition) was proposed by N.E.Huang in 1998[8], which decomposes the analyzing signal into a series of narrow band IMF (Intrinsic Mode Function) signals satisfied with Hilbert spectrum analysis.

$$X(t) = \sum_{j=1}^{n} C_j(t) + r_n(t)$$

Here $X(t)$ is signal, $C_j(t)$ is sub-signal in accordance with IMF conditions, and $r_n(t)$ is the needed trend series. It is the best method to abstract the trend of the time series. Fig. 3 shows the trend and details of the time series decomposed by EMD, in which the mixture waveform of the decomposed trend data and raw data are in the first layer, the detail part is in the second layer and the trend data in the third layer. In this paper, EMD is used to abstract the trend part of time series.

A time series consists of sequences of values changing with time. But there are great differences between series data and character strings. Time series data are real value points whereas strings elements are characters, therefore the matching of the

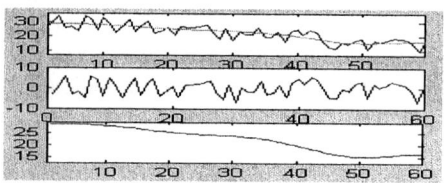

Fig. 3. Signal decomposition by EMD

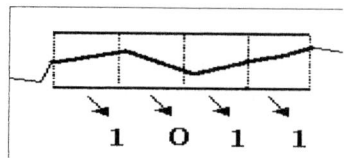

Fig. 4. Segments translating into character strings

former is fuzzy and obtained by comparing the similarity of their values. But the matching of the latter is exact and done by comparing the equivalence of the strings character. So if the time series are changed into character strings, a lot of current effective database techniques such as index technique can be used for fast and efficient similarity search. The concrete procedures are as follows:

Firstly the trend and detail series of the raw data x(t) are obtained by EMD. Suppose that the trend length m×n, it is denoted as: $r_n(t) = (x_1, x_2, \cdots x_m, x_{m+1}, \cdots, x_{m \times n})$.

To build the index we move a fixed-length sliding window across the data sequence. The window contains an equal-spaced grid as illustrated in Fig. 4. The section of the time series which falls within each part of the grid is examined and discretized into two possible classes 'up' or 'not-up' which are represented as one or zero respectively. Then 0-1 character strings $H(x) = (h_1, h_2, \cdots, h_{n-1})$ is obtained with hi=0 on the condition of $A_{YRi} - A_{YRLi} < 0$ and hi=1 on the condition of $A_{YRi} - A_{YRLi} \geq 0$. In this way, the linear segments will be translated into strings, for instance the linear segments in the Fig. 4 will be represented as (1011) characters.

2.3 Similarity Measures of Time Series and HMTS Procedures

In order to measure the similarity of two different time series, criteria of measuring the similarity should be given at first.

Definition 1: Given two time series $\bar{x}, \bar{y}$ of equal length and threshold ε, then the series $\bar{x}, \bar{y}$ is similar on the condition that $D(\bar{x}, \bar{y}) = (\sum_{i=0}^{n-1}(y_i - x_i)^2)^{\frac{1}{2}} \leq \varepsilon$.

Definition 2: Given two time series $\bar{x}, \bar{y}$ of equal length and threshold ε, then the series $\bar{x}, \bar{y}$ is uprightness similar on the condition that
$D_L(\bar{x}, \bar{y}) = (\sum_{i=0}^{n-1}((y_i - x_i) - (\frac{1}{n}\sum_{i=0}^{n-1} y_i - \frac{1}{n}\sum_{i=0}^{n-1} x_i))^2)^{\frac{1}{2}} \leq \varepsilon$.

Since Definition 1 is not suitable in some cases, for instance when the standard of Definition 1 is applied, the time series $f(x)$ and $f(x)+c$ are dissimilar and opposite to the human's judgment, so the definition $D_L(\bar{x}, \bar{y})$ is often used as the series distance. Now we give the series trend similarity in definition 3.

Definition 3: Given two time series $\bar{x}, \bar{y}$ of equal length, the character strings A,B of their trend series transformation and threshold ε, then the series $\bar{x}, \bar{y}$ is trend similar on the condition that $D_S(\bar{x}, \bar{y}) = \sum_i |A_i - B_i| \leq \varepsilon$.

The whole matching series is used to discuss the matching procedures (Note: it is possible to extend subsequence matching to whole matching by sliding a "window" of length n across the series), the HMTS procedures are summarized as follows.

(1) Use EMD to decompose the time series into a set of time series to obtain the trend series.

(2) Roughly estimate the highest frequency of the trend series to choose the length of segment and then represent the time series with linear segment.

(3) Use the method in section2.4 to translate the linear segments of the trend series into character strings.

(4) Search the trend similar series with the standard in Definition 3, which can be used in matching the series roughly.

(5) Match the series in detail among trend similar series according to distance defined in Definition 2.

3 Experiments

The efficient and fast matching of time series by using the linear segment representation of the raw data has been discussed in detail in literatures [6, 7]. One of its advantages is the segment representation reducing of the great amount of computation compared with studying the raw data. Our algorithm bears these advantage factors of the segment representation, so our experiments are not used to prove the advantages of the segment representation, but to show its effectiveness in handling such time series matching issues which general linear segments methods can not process. Since the condition of the trend matching is added, the similar series are much more exact than the usual method.

Experiment 1: Comparing the similarity of the waveforms

The time series similarity is analyzed based on HMTS, whose data are Synthetic Control Chart Time Series obtained from the UCI database. Since the series change acutely with their short length and instability, it is not suitable to use either the direct representation of the linear segment or Discrete Fourier Transformations. The total 600 of 60 dimension raw data are decomposed by EMD method to obtain the 600 trend series. Since the frequency of the trend data is very low, every other 10 dots for each segment of the trend series are sampled with 6 segments for each series. Then character representation of these linear segments is done with 600 of 6 character strings obtained.

Suppose the 490th series whose waveform is shown in Fig. 5(a), the similar series are searched for in the other 599 series. Since the character string of the trend series of 490th is (0,0,0,1,0,0), we choose the best 3 out of the 12 series in the 599 series whose character string is (0,0,0,1,0,0) and show their waveform in Fig. 5(b), 5(c), 5(d). If we choose $\varepsilon = 1$ according to Definition 3 which means one character fault is permitted, then there are 21 trend series similar to one another. Besides 5(b), 5(c), 5(d) in Fig. 5, there are still 2 similar series shown in Fig.5(e), 5(f).

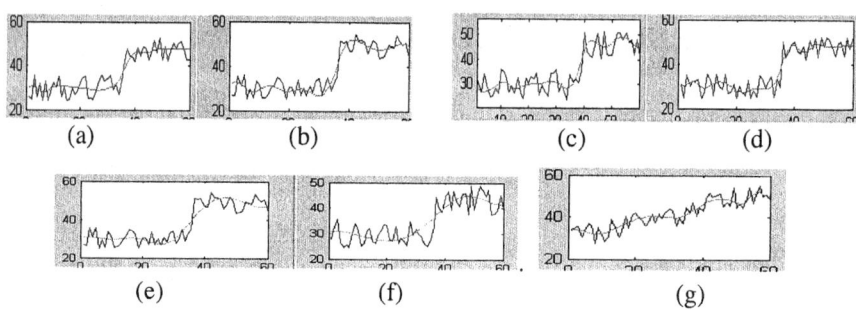

Fig. 5. Waveforms of the time series

If the results are checked with the standard of Definition 2 which compares the distance between the 490th and the other 599 series, the 4 most similar series are the series shown in Fig.5(b),5(c),5(d),5(e) among the series with the permission of one character fault, even though the fifth similar series is the 257th shown in Fig.5(g). Though the 257th is similar in the distance computation, their actual waveforms are not similar because their trend series are different. In the human vision, the series in Fig.5 (f) is much similar to the series 490th compared with in Fig.5(g). Therefore, if the trend series are compared first, the mistake of fake similarity can be avoided.

Experiment 2: Comparing the trend similarity of stocks

The data in Fig. 6 is 5 minutes 180 share index in the Shanghai stock market from 8/7/1996 to 22/1/2003 with 540 days and 25930 dots in all. The data can be divided into 540 series, and each has 48 dimensions. Select any one from the series, for instance, 20/1/2003 series shown in Fig.7(a) for similar pattern matching. The most similar series are the 19/6/2001 and 18/10/2002 series shown in Fig. 7(b) and 7(c). If the series are matched only in distance, then the series of 30/5/2001 shown in Fig. 7(d) are similar to the Fig. 7(a). But it can be seen from the two waveforms that are different and these two series are not similar to each other. The trend similarity is much more important, therefore in the process of the similar pattern matching of the stocks data, the trend similar standard should be combined with the distance standard.

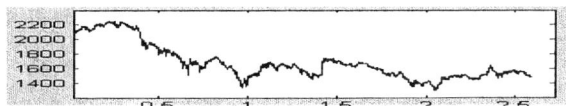

Fig. 6. 5 Minutes180 share Index of Shanghai Stock Market

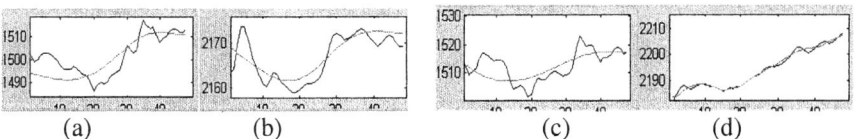

(a)   (b)   (c)   (d)

Fig. 7. 5 Minutes Daily 180 share Index of Shanghai Stock Market

4 Conclusion

A hierarchical matching algorithm based on human cognitive patterns is developed in this paper. The algorithm overcomes the weak points of the direct linear segment representation which is unsuitable for the fast changing series, and can obtain reliable matching pattern compared with direct distance matching method. Experimental results show the effectiveness of the algorithm as well as the worthiness for further research and application.

References

1. Agrawal R, Faloutsos C, & Swami A. Efficient similarity search in sequence databases[A]. Proceedings of the 4th Conference on Foundations of Data Organization and Algorithms. Chicago, USA. 1993. 69~84.

2. Rafiei D, Mendelzon A. Efficient retrieval of similar time semila time sequences using DFT[A]. Proceedings of the 5th International Conference on Foundations of Data Organizations and Algorithms. Kobe, 1998.249~257
3. Das G., Lin K,. Mannila H., Renganathan G., & Smyth P. (1998). Rule discovery from time series[A]. Proceedings of the 4th International Conference of Knowledge Discovery and Data Mining. New York, USA. 1998.16-22.
4. CHAN K, FU W. Efficient time series matching by wavelets [A]. Proceedings of the 15th IEEE International Conference on Data Engineering. Sydney, 1999.126-133.
5. Beckmann N, Kriegel H-P, Schneider R, Seeger B. The R*-tree An efficient and robust access method for points and rectangles[A]. Proceedings of ACM SIFMOD International Conference on Management of Data, New Jersey, USA 1990. 322~331
6. Keogh, E., & Pazzani, M. An enhanced representation of time series which allows fast and accurate classification, clustering and relevance feedback. Proceedings of the 4th International Conference of Knowledge Discovery and Data Mining. AAAI Press. 1998 239-241.
7. Keogh, E,. Chakrabarti, K,. Pazzani, M. & Mehrotra (2000). Dimensionality reduction for fast similarity search in large time series databases. Journal of Knowledge and Information Systems.
8. Huang N.E. Shen Z, Long S R, et al. The empirical mode decomposition and the Hilbert spectrum for nonlinear and non-stationary time series analysis [J].Proceedings of the Royal Society of London, 1998,454:903-995.

3D Polar-Radius Invariant Moments and Structure Moment Invariants

Zongmin Li[1,2,3], Yuanzhen Zhang[1], Kunpeng Hou[1], and Hua Li[2]

[1] School of Computer Science and Communication Engineering,
University of Petroleum, 257061, Shandong, P.R. China
[2] Institute of Computing Technology,
Chinese Academy of Sciences, 100080, Beijing, P.R. China
[3] Graduate School of Chinese Academy of Sciences,
100039, Beijing, P.R. China
{zmli, lihua}@ict.ac.cn
zhangyuanzhen@eyou.com, houkunpeng@163.com

Abstract. A novel moment, called 3D polar-radius-invariant-moment, is proposed for the 3D object recognition and classification. Some properties of these new moments including the invariance on translation, scale and rotation transforms are studied and proved. Then structure moment invariants are given to distinguish complicated similar shapes. Examples are presented to illustrate the performance and invariance of these moments. With the help of these moment invariants, the 3D models are distinguished accurately.

1 Introduction

With the development of computer graphics and related software and hardware technologies, 3D models can be acquired easily and now play an important role in many mainstream applications such as mechanical manufacture, games, biochemistry, medicine, E-business, art, virtual reality, etc. Tools for acquiring and visualizing 3D models have become integral components of data processingAs a result, the need for the ability to retrieve models from large databases has gained prominence and a key concern of shape analysis has shifted to the design of efficient and robust matching algorithms. Shapes are described in a transformation invariant manner, so that any transformation of a shape will be described in the same way, and the best measure of similarity is obtained at any transformation.

In this paper, we present a 3D content based retrieval method relying on 3D polar-radius invariant moments. We define the polar-radius invariant moment and its normalized moment, and the central polar-radius invariant moment and its normalized central moment. The translation, scale and rotation invariance of the normalized moment and normalized central moment are proved theoretically. Then we present structure moment invariants for complicated similar shapes. To support our new theory, an algorithm for object shape recognition is designed based on the new moments and experiments are conducted. Examples are presented to illustrate the performance of these moments. In the comparing experiment of recognition of objects, 3D polar-radius invariant moments give an encouraging high recognition rates. And the complicated similar shapes can be distinguished.

This paper is organized as follows. Firstly, some related works are summarized in Section 2. Then, The 3D polar-radius-invariant-moments representation is presented in Section 3,and the translation, scale and rotation invariance of these moments are proved. In section 4, structure moment invariants are proposed to distinguish complicated similar shapes. Finally, some retrieved examples are presented to analyze the validity of our method in Section 5. We conclude in Section 6 by summarizing our results and discussing topics for future work.

2 Related Works

Up to now, in the area of content-based 3D model retrieval, some original systems investigating theory and algorithm have been implemented, and some systems for general 3D objects retrieval have been introduced. For the latter, the first system was introduced in [1],which was followed by [2].A very present result is presented in[3].The feature of 3D objects extracted in them mainly include shape and color of 3D objects, as well as combination of the bottom level shape feature and semantic feature.

According to the feature description of the 3D objects shape, the shape feature ex-traction consists of:

(1) the shape feature extraction based on the analysis of geometric structure. It was dissertated in the papers [2,4-9].The feature extracted get a better description of information about 3D models structure. But it is applicable to some well required models and need a lot of computation to deal with the coordinates of the model.

(2) the shape feature extraction based on the topological structure. The papers [10,11] introduced MRG (Multiresolution Reeb Graph) to obtain the feature of 3D objects. The MRG can well depicts the topological structure of 3D models and has a good stability to the shape transform of 3D models. But the drawback is much of computation and sensitive to the edge disturbance and noise.

(3) the shape feature extraction based on the image of function. The method gets a detailed depiction in the papers [12-19]. The advantage of it is the simple feature convenient for the similarity matching. The disadvantage is some of important information lost in the course of the functional image.

(4) the shape feature extraction based on the statistical characteristics. The merit of this method is that it is not required to standardize the model coordinate comparing with the above methods, and the feature extracted consists of global shape attribute, such as circularity, eccentricity, algebraic moments etc[20,21]. The feature is simple and can well satisfy the invariance of geometrical transform.The method is also applicable to the incompact and degenerate models and stable for the edge noise. The demerit is that the feature hasn't a sufficient depict of 3D model and is sensitive to the topo-logical structure of 3D models.

3 3D Polar-Radius Invariant Moments

We assume an object is a three-dimensional object represented by a set of vertices and a set of polygonal feces embedded in three dimensions. For object D, the three-dimensional polar-radius invariant moments of order p of a density $f(x,y,z)$ are defined as

$$M_p = \iiint_D r^p dV, \qquad (1)$$

where r is the distance from an arbitrary point of the object to the center of the object, (x_c, y_c, z_c) is center of the object D, and

$$r = \sqrt{(x-x_c)^2 + (y-y_c)^2 + (z-z_c)^2}, \qquad (2)$$

$$x_c = \frac{1}{V}\iiint_D x dV, \; y_c = \frac{1}{V}\iiint_D y dV, \; z_c = \frac{1}{V}\iiint_D z dV. \qquad (3)$$

The central polar-radius invariant moments M_{cp} are defined as

$$M_{cp} = \iiint_D (r-\bar{r})^p dV \qquad (4)$$

where $\bar{r} = \frac{1}{V}\iiint_D r dV$.

The normalized moment of the polar-radius invariant moments and the normalized central moment of the central polar-radius invariant moments are defined as

$$M_{np} = \frac{1}{V}\iiint_D (\frac{r}{\bar{r}})^p dV \qquad (5)$$

$$M_{ncp} = \frac{1}{V}\iiint_D (\frac{r-\bar{r}}{\bar{r}})^p dV \qquad (6)$$

If an analog original object is digitized into its discrete version with its voxels, the integration of (5) must be approximated by summations. It has been a common prescription to replace M_{np} in (5) with its digital version

$$\hat{M}_{np} = \frac{1}{V}\sum_{i=1}^{V}(\frac{r_i}{\bar{r}})^p \qquad (7)$$

$$\hat{M}_{ncp} = \frac{1}{V}\sum_{i=1}^{V}(\frac{r_i-\bar{r}}{\bar{r}})^p \qquad (8)$$

where V is the voxel summation of the object.

The normalized moments M_{np} of the polar-radius invariant moments and the normalized central moments M_{ncp} of the central polar-radius invariant moments are invariants under translation, scale and rotation.

A. Invariants Under Translation

Under translation of coordinates, $x' = x + \alpha$, $y' = y + \beta$, $z' = z + \gamma$, where α, β and γ are constants.

The distance from an arbitrary point of the object to the center of the object don't change, and $\bar{r}$ don't change too, therefore, M_{np} and M_{ncp} are invariants under translation.

B. Invariants Under Scale

D' is the new object of D Under scale transformation, then $r' = \alpha r$, $\bar{r}' = \alpha \bar{r}$, $V' = \alpha^3 V$, $dV' = \alpha^3 dV$ where α is a constant.

Therefore
$M'_{np} = \frac{1}{V'} \int\int\int_{D'} (\frac{r'}{\bar{r}'})^p dV' = \frac{1}{V(\alpha)^3} \int\int\int_D (\frac{\alpha r}{\alpha \bar{r}})^p (\alpha)^3 dV = M_{np}$.
Similarly $(M_{ncp})' = M_{ncp}$.

C. Invariants Under Rotation

Under rotation transformation, the turning of an object by an angle ϕ about the center of the object is equivalent to that first rotate the object about one axis by the angle φ, then rotate the resulting object about another axis by the angle ψ. D' denotes the new object rotate about one axis by the angle φ from D, and V' denotes the volume of D'. D'' denotes the new object rotate about one axis by the angle ψ from D', and V'' denotes the volume of D''. Therefore, $D'' = D' = D$, $V'' = V' = V$, and

$\bar{r}' = \frac{1}{V'} \int\int\int_{D'} r \cdot r dr d(\theta + \varphi) dz = \frac{1}{V} \int\int\int_D r^2 dr d\theta dz = \bar{r}$,

$M'_{np} = \frac{1}{V'} \int\int\int_{D'} (\frac{r}{\bar{r}})^p r dr d(\theta + \varphi) dz = \frac{1}{V} \int\int\int_D (\frac{r}{\bar{r}})^p r dr d\theta dz = M_{np}$.

For D', the above form may be written as
$M'_{np} = \frac{1}{V'} \int\int\int_{D'} (\frac{r'}{\bar{r}'})^p dV'$, where $dV' = r' dr' d\theta' dz'$.

Then
$\bar{r}'' = \frac{1}{V''} \int\int\int_{D''} r' \cdot r' dr' d(\theta' + \psi) dz' = \frac{1}{V'} \int\int\int_{D'} (r')^2 dr' d\theta' dz' = \bar{r}'$,

$M''_{np} = \int\int\int_{D''} (\frac{r'}{\bar{r}''})^p r' dr' d(\theta' + \psi) dz' = \frac{1}{V'} \int\int\int_{D'} (\frac{r'}{\bar{r}'})^p dr' d\theta' dz' = (M_{np})'$.

We have the following expression: $M''_{np} = M_{np}$.
Similarly $M''_{ncp} = M_{ncp}$.

4 Descriptions of Structure Moment Invariants

It is quite difficult to how to distinguish complicated similar shapes. Whether the "structure" of a picture is abundant or not, means that is it sharply or gently of the picture's light intensity when varying with the position. The degree of abundant structure of the 2-D object is consistent with the integral as follows:

$$S_F = \int\int_F I_0^2(x, y) dx dy \qquad (9)$$

That is to say, base on the premise that the total light energy is given definitely in area F, the bigger S_F is, the more abundant the structure of the 2-D object is.

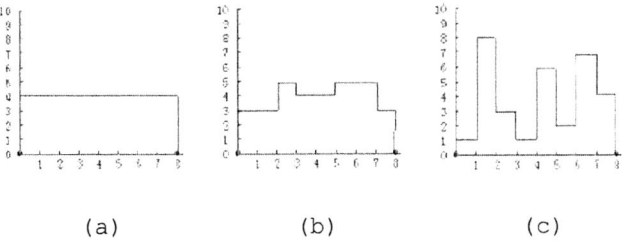

(a)   (b)   (c)

Fig. 1. Examples of the distribution of light intensity

$$\int\int_F I_0^2(x,y)dxdy = const \tag{10}$$

Just like the distribution of light intensity in Fig 1, the total energy of each one is 32. However, the integral value will be different after square of three integrable functions respectively:

Fig 1 (a): $\int I_0^2 dx = 128$
Fig 1 (b): $\int I_0^2 dx = 134$
Fig 1 (c): $\int I_0^2 dx = 180$

Namely the more abundant the structure is, the greater the value is. It is similar in 3D space.

For this reason, in order to achieve the goal of recognition, we mapped the object function $f(x)$ to another transformation space, then we got a new moment and we called it structure moment invariant:

$$\mu_i = <F(f), \psi_i> = \int_\Omega F(f(x)) \cdot \overline{\psi_i(x)} dx \tag{11}$$

Note $F(f)$ is function of f, and we can use the projection of object function $f \in L^2$ on the area of Ω to define the moment μ_i which is used in analysis of object's shape. The function on the area of Ω was defined as $\Psi = \{\psi_i\}$ where $i \in N$.

F can be linear transformation, and can be nonlinear transformation too.

If $g(x) = F(f(x))$, then $v_i = <g(x), \psi_i> = \int_\Omega g(x) \cdot \overline{\psi_i(x)} dx$. The complicated objects will be recognized through the existing pattern recognition methods.

5 Experimentation and Results

Firstly, we test the algorithm with three horse models, a bird model, and a pig model, given in VRML. Fig.a is represented with 3493 points and 6520 patches, Fig.b with 784 points and 1328 patches, Fig.c with 2129 points and 4034 patches, Fig.d with 4203 points and 1928 patches, and Fig.e with 11238 points and 6902 patches.

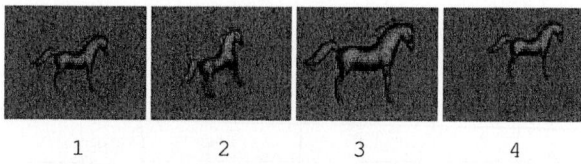

Fig.a Horse1 model: 1.the original, 2.after rotation, 3.after scale, 4.after translation

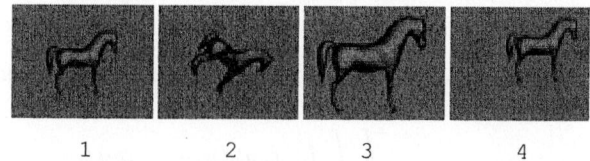

Fig.b Horse2 model: 1.the original, 2.after rotation, 3.after scale, 4.after translation

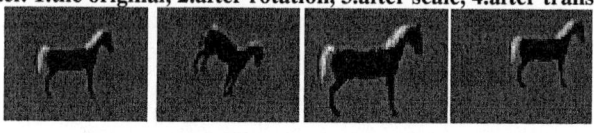

Fig.c Horse3 model: 1.the original, 2.after rotation, 3.after scale, 4.after translation

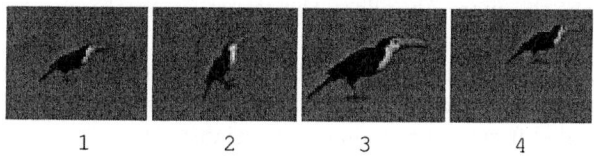

Fig.d Bird model: 1.the original, 2.after rotation, 3.after scale, 4.after translation

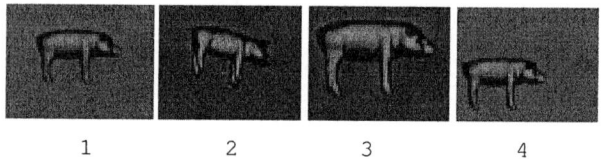

Fig.e Pig model: 1.the original, 2.after rotation, 3.after scale, 4.after translation

In each model, we choose the original object as a pattern. We compute eighteen moments about each object and give some results about fig.(a,b,c) in table 1-3, and the distances between each pattern and models with Minkowski distance method in table 4. Experiments give a high recognition rates. From table 4, the recognition rate is 97% if the threshold is 5.

Then, we find that horse2 is quite similar to horse3. In the horse2 column,fig.b2 is not recognized. we compute the Minkowski distance between horse2 and horse3 with three-dimensional polar-radius invariant moments and structure moment Invariants. From Table 5, the results about structure moment Invariants are better than the ones about three-dimensional polar-radius invariant moments.

Table 1. Normalized moments and normalized central moments for fig.a

	2	3	4	5	6	7	8	9	10
1	1.356	2.247	4.205	8.478	17.94	3.929e+001	8.825e+001	2.023e+002	4.721e+002
2	1.351	2.229	4.158	8.363	17.66	3.860e+001	8.649e+001	1.977e+002	4.595e+002
3	1.349	2.220	4.128	8.285	17.49	3.824e+001	8.588e+001	1.971e+002	4.608e+002
4	1.357	2.248	4.207	8.476	17.92	3.919e+001	8.787e+001	2.011e+002	4.681e+002
Central	2	3	4	5	6	7	8	9	10
1	0.355	0.178	0.353	0.363	0.548	7.202e-001	1.069e+000	1.563e+000	2.401e+000
2	0.351	0.177	0.346	0.356	0.534	6.970e-001	1.023e+000	1.473e+000	2.223e+000
3	0.349	0.172	0.343	0.352	0.535	7.059e-001	1.056e+000	1.554e+000	2.407e+000
4	0.356	0.178	0.352	0.361	0.544	7.108e-001	1.051e+000	1.529e+000	2.341e+000

Table 2. Normalized moments and normalized central moments for fig.b

	2	3	4	5	6	7	8	9	10
1	1.261	1.880	3.149	5.714	10.95	2.182e+001	4.465e+001	9.324e+001	1.977e+002
2	1.263	1.886	3.167	5.762	11.08	2.213e+001	4.545e+001	9.524e+001	2.027e+002
3	1.264	1.890	3.174	5.775	11.09	2.213e+001	4.536e+001	9.482e+001	2.012e+002
4	1.265	1.896	3.197	5.839	11.27	2.257e+001	4.646e+001	9.751e+001	2.077e+002
Central	2	3	4	5	6	7	8	9	10
1	0.261	0.096	0.196	0.157	0.222	2.342e-001	3.043e-001	3.579e-001	4.582e-001
2	0.262	0.097	0.199	0.160	0.228	2.430e-001	3.177e-001	3.776e-001	4.875e-001
3	0.263	0.097	0.199	0.159	0.226	2.388e-001	3.102e-001	3.648e-001	4.668e-001
4	0.265	0.100	0.203	0.165	0.234	2.500e-001	3.256e-001	3.862e-001	4.961e-001

Table 3. Normalized moments and normalized central moments for fig.c

	2	3	4	5	6	7	8	9	10
1	1.251	1.838	3.018	5.356	10.03	1.949e+001	3.894e+001	7.939e+001	1.644e+002
2	1.247	1.824	2.984	5.279	9.863	1.915e+001	3.826e+001	7.807e+001	1.620e+002
3	1.253	1.847	3.047	5.433	10.22	1.997e+001	4.010e+001	8.217e+001	1.710e+002
4	1.252	1.839	3.023	5.368	10.06	1.957e+001	3.913e+001	7.985e+001	1.656e+002
Central	2	3	4	5	6	7	8	9	10
1	0.251	0.084	0.175	0.128	0.181	1.792e-001	2.291e-001	2.565e-001	3.209e-001
2	0.247	0.082	0.171	0.126	0.178	1.779e-001	2.289e-001	2.593e-001	3.275e-001
3	0.253	0.086	0.179	0.134	0.189	1.899e-001	2.437e-001	2.765e-001	3.483e-001
4	0.251	0.084	0.175	0.129	0.183	1.811e-001	2.320e-001	2.607e-001	3.270e-001

Table 4. The distances between each pattern and models

	HORSE 1	HORSE2	HORSE 3	BIRD	PIG
fig. a 1	0	25.088	43.634	85.947	381.636
fig. a 2	4.009	23.912	33.686	92.575	358.754
fig. a 3	3.126	25.064	36.410	88.476	373.436
fig. a 4	3.566	31.048	55.788	92.106	378.349
fig. b 1	25.088	0	7.453	351.668	104.833
fig. b 2	24.472	6.247	18.914	337.567	112.018
fig. b 3	22.965	1.204	10.944	344.392	108.116
fig. b 4	22.841	0.837	8.669	326.948	112.421
fig. c 1	43.634	7.453	0	486.602	78.552
fig. c 2	34.552	3.358	4.838	476.622	78.697
fig. c 3	33.013	2.623	4.256	448.273	83.972
fig. c 4	40.529	6.439	0.463	477.775	78.835
fig. d 1	85.947	351.668	486.602	0	5956.463
fig. d 2	94.761	379.490	522.558	1.786	6470.085
fig. d 3	78.286	324.115	450.404	1.292	5461.081
fig. d 4	85.388	352.403	489.158	0.453	5956.633
fig. e 1	381.636	104.833	78.552	5956.463	0
fig. e 2	315.083	88.940	73.930	4727.385	4.741
fig. e 3	353.968	98.574	76.038	5480.801	1.323
fig. e 4	378.863	104.041	84.843	5974.378	3.456

Table 5. The distances between each of horse2 and horse3

	HORSE2 (THREE DIMENSIONAL POLAR-RADIUS INVARIANT MOMENTS)	HORSE2 (STRUCTURE MOMENT INVARIANTS)	HORSE3 (THREE-DIMENSIONAL POLAR-RADIUS INVARIANT MOMENTS)	HORSE3 (STRUCTURE MOMENT INVARIANTS)
fig. b 1	0	0	7.453	120.8104
fig. b 2	6.247	20.1011	18.914	215.4381
fig. b 3	1.204	19.5362	10.944	197.1861
fig. b 4	0.837	18.1322	8.669	193.6644
fig. c 1	7.453	120.8104	0	0
fig. c 2	3.358	198.2937	4.838	19.7186
fig. c 3	2.623	280.1589	4.256	18.0213
fig. c 4	6.439	132.1127	0.463	17.0269

6 Conclusions and Future Work

We propose a new moment, called 3D polar-radius-invariant-moment, for determining the content-based similarity of three-dimensional objects. Two main issues are considered. The first is the invariance on translation, scale and rotation transform about these new moments. The second issue is the method for distinguishing complicated similar shapes. Experiments exhibit very good results.

Further work is required in order to analyze the computation for these high order moments, and we will propose extensions and improvements. Moreover, we intend to elaborate a new feature vector with the combination of these new moment invariants.

References

1. Paquet E., Rioux M.. A content-based search engine for VRML databases . In Proceedings of IEEE Computer Society Conference on Computer Vision and Pattern Recognition , Santa Barbara, California, USA, 1998, 541-546.
2. Suzuki M., Kato T., Otsu N.. A similarity retrieval of 3d polygon models using rotation invariant shape descriptors. In: Proceedings of IEEE International Conference on Systems , Man, and Cybernetics, Nashville, Tennessee, USA ,2000, 2946-2952.
3. Yang YuBin, Lin Hui, Zhu Qing . Content-Based 3D Model Retrieval: A Survey. In:Chinese Journal Of Computers,China, Vol.27, No.10, Oct.2004.
4. Vranic D., Saupe D.. 3d model retrieval. In: Proceedings of Spring Conference on Computer Graphics ,Budmerice,Slovakia,2000,89-93.
5. Tangelder J., VeltKamp R.. Polyhedral model retrieval using weight point sets. International Journal of Image and Graphics,2003,3(1):1-21.
6. Zhang D., Hebert M.. Harmonic maps and their applications in surface matching. In: Pro-ceedings of IEEE Conference on Computer Vision and Pattern Recognition, Fort Collins, Colorado,USA,1999,2524-2530.
7. Zhang D., Hebert M.. Harmonic shape images: A 3d freeform surface representation and its application in surface matching. In: Proceedings of International Workshop on Energy Minimization Methods in Computer Vision and Pattern Recognition, Sophia Antipo-lis ,France,1999,30-43.
8. Vranic D., Saupe D.. Description of 3d-shape using a complex function on the sphere. In: Proceedings of IEEE International Conference on Multimedia and Expo, Lausanne,Switzerland,2002,177-180.
9. Vranic D., Saupe D.. 3d shape Descriptor based on 3d Fourier transform. In: Proceedings of IEEE EURASIP Conference on Digital Signal Processing for Multimedia Communications and Services, Budapest, Hungary, 2001,271-274.
10. Hilaga M., Shinagawa Y., Kohmura T., Kunii T.. Topology matching for fully automatic similarity estimation of 3d shapes. In: Proceedings of ACM SIGGRAPH, Los Angels, USA, 2001, 203-212.
11. Bardinet E., Vidal S., Arroyo S., Malandain G., Capilla N.. Structural object matching. Department of Computer Science and AI, University of Granada ,Spain: Technical Report DEC-SAI-000303,2000.
12. Funkhouser T., Min P., Kazhdan M. et al.. A search engine for 3d models. ACM Transac-tions on Graphics,2003,22(1):83-105.
13. Cyr C., Kimia B.. 3d object recognition using shape similarity-based aspect graph. In: Pro-ceedings of IEEE International Conference on Computer Vision , Vancouver, Can-ada,2001,254-261.
14. Heczko M., Keim D., Saupe D., Vranic D.. A method for similarity search of 3d objects. In: Proceedings of German Database Conference (BTW),Oldenburg,Germany,2001,384-401.
15. Zhang D., Hebert M.. Harmonic maps and their applications in surface matching. In: Pro-ceedings of IEEE Conference on Computer Vision and Pattern Recognition, Fort Collins, Colorado,USA,1999,2524-2530.
16. Little J., Extended Gaussian images , mixed volumes, shape reconstruction. In: Proceedings of Annual Symposium on Computational Geometry, Baltimore, USA, 1985, 15-23.
17. Delingette H., Hebert H., Ikeuchi K.. A spherical representation for the recognition of curved objects. In: proceedings of IEEE International Conference on Computer Vision, Berlin, Germany, 1993, 103-112.

18. Johnson A., Hebert M.. Using spin-images for efficient multiple model recognition in clut-tered 3d scenes. IEEE Transaction on Pattern Analysis and Machine Intelligence, 1999, 21(5), 433-449.
19. Saupe D., Vranic D.. 3d model retrieval with spherical harmonics and moments. In: Pro-ceedings of Germany DAGM Conference , Munich, Germany, 2001, 392-397.
20. M. Elad, P. Milanfar, and Gene Golub, Shape from Moments - An Estimation Theory Per-spective, the IEEE Trans. on Signal Processing on August 2002, 1814-1829
21. M. Novotni.3D Zernike Descriptors for Content Based Shape Retrieval, proceedings of The 8th ACM Symposium on Solid Modeling and Applications, June 2003,216-225

A Fast Searching Algorithm of Symmetrical Period Modulation Pattern Based on Accumulative Transformation Technique

FuHua Fan[1] and Ying Tan[2]

[1] Electronic Engineering Institute, Hefei, China 230037
davidfaneei@163.com
[2] University of Science and Technology of China, Hefei, China 230027
ytan@ustc.edu.cn

Abstract. A fast search algorithm of periodical and symmetrical modulation pattern is proposed in this paper. The algorithm is effective for the dense pulse deinterleaving of nontraditional radars. Experimental results show that the average accuracy rate of pulse deinterleaving is about 95% and the average missing rate of pulse deinterleaving is about 5% by the algorithm in dense pulse environment.

1 Introduction

It is difficult to deinterleave the traditional radar pulses in dense pulse environment, and even more difficult to deinterleave the dense and nontraditional radar pulses. In recent years, this problem has been seriously treated in the field of radar-counter signal processing. The public algorithms about pulse deinterleaving can be classified as single parameter and multiple-parameter. Generally, the single parameter deinterleaving algorithms are done according to time of arrival (TOA) of pulses. The original versions of these algorithms are CDIF [1] and SDIF [2], which are useful for stable sequences of pulses and low-level staggered pulse trains in non-dense pulse environment. Multiple-parameter deinterleaving algorithms [3 7] previously use pulse parameters such as direction of arrival (DOA), radio frequency (RF), pulse width (PW), or other parameters to sort the pulses into different groups of pulses, and pulse repeat interval (PRI) analysis is accordingly performed on these groups. In these algorithms, the major challenge is to avoid fragmenting pulses from one radar into different groups, or forming excessively large groups. No matter which algorithm above is chosen, TOA is a vital deinterleaving parameter and thus PRI deinterleaving algorithms [4 5 6] play an important role in the whole grouping of radar pulses.

A deinterleaving algorithm in TOA transform in [6] illustrates that the PRI can be calculated by locating the peaks of autocorrelation function of pulses series, but how to determine the threshold for detection of PRIs is its serious drawback. In [7], a synthetically deinterleaving method using a self-organized probabilistic neural network(PNN) is introduced□however the parameters of the PNN is difficult to train. With the development of radar technologies, current design trends are towards radars being capable of greater PRI agility. These pulses will be more difficult to extract. Generally, all the public deinterleaving algorithms are not effective for deinterleaving these nontraditional radar pulses in dense pulse environment. In this paper, a fast searching algorithm is proposed, which is used to deinterleave the nontraditional radar pulses with their PRI modulated by periodical and symmetrical functions in dense pulse environment. Moreover, the proposed algorithm is tolerant to missed pulses.

This paper is organized as follows: In section 2, the basis of accumulative transformation technique is introduced. Section 3 describes the periodicity of accumulative transformation characteristic curve of periodical and symmetric modulation series. In section 4, the searching algorithm is given. Accordingly, the experimental results are presented in section 5. At last, the conclusions are derived.

2 Accumulative Transformations

Each radar can be characterized by a pattern of pulse intervals that repeats from a given start time. TOA is measured at the leading edge of each pulse and is represented by a TOA word, i.e., value 1 at the leading time and otherwise value 0. Supposing that $\{S(t_i) \in \{0,1\}, i = 1 \ldots N\}$ are TOA words of one radar pulse sequence, t_0 is a given receiving time, and t_i would be the receiving time of the ith pulse. The PRI of pulse series, i.e., P(i) is the time span between the adjacent TOA words with "1".

The P(i) can be viewed as a "process of random dots", and we conduct an accumulative transformation similar to shoaling integration on the P(i). Therefore, the accumulative transformation of PRI is written as

$$L_n = \sum_{i=1}^{n} P(i).$$ (1)

The inverse accumulative transformation is expressed as

$$P(n) = L_n - L_{n-1} = \sum_{i=1}^{n} P(i) - \sum_{i=1}^{n-1} P(i).$$ (2)

Obviously, the inverse accumulative transformation uniquely corresponds to the accumulative transformation. Because of merely relating to the operations of "add" and "subtraction", the accumulative transformation is fast.

The sample of pulses to be sorted, stored in TOA words, consists of many interleaved radar pulse sequences taking complex PRI modulation such as symmetrical period pattern. This paper gives an effective method to deinterleave these pulses in dense pulse series.

3 Characteristics of Pulse Sequence with Symmetrical Period PRI

The sine modulation is a typically symmetrical period modulation pattern. Firstly, we discuss the periodicity of accumulative transformation of symmetrical period modulation taking sine accumulation as example. Supposing that $\{P(i), i = 1 \ldots N\}$ is a PRI series modulated by a sine function with modulation mean W' and modulation amplitude P_m, we can decompose the P(i) into Q_i and W' as

$$L_n = \sum_{i=1}^{n} P(i) = \sum_{i=1}^{n} (Q_i + W') = \sum_{i=1}^{n} Q_i + n \cdot W' \qquad (3)$$

$$Q_i = P_m \cdot W' \sin(\tfrac{i-1}{C} \cdot 2\pi + \varphi) \qquad (4)$$

where C is the number of modulated pulses in a modulation period.

All received pulses are map into points in a virtual plane with variable size. This plane is divided into so small square grid that each point can be uniquely identified in one grid. These grids are viewed as the cells of a matrix, defined as plane bitmap matrix (PBM), filling "1" element in the pulse grid and "0" element in no pulse grid. Supposing that the virtual plane is set in a 2-D coordinate where the left lower point is the origin, the coordinate of a point, i.e. a pulse, is the index of the "1" element. It is easily proved that a pulse in series can be uniquely transformed into a "1" element in the plane bitmap matrix. Therefore, the index of these "1" elements are determined by the accumulative transformation of PRI, defined as L(n). And thus an accumulative transformation curve is formed by the "1" elements which correspond to the L(n). When the width of the PBM is W', the accumulative transformation curve is periodical, we can prove it as follows.

The coordinates of a pulse in the PBM with the width of W are written as

$$x_n = round(L_n \bmod W), \quad y_n = \lfloor L_n / W \rfloor . \qquad (5)$$

By substituting W' for W in (5), one can obtain

$$x_n = round(\bmod(\sum_{i=1}^{n} Q_i, W')), \quad y_n = n + \left\lfloor \sum_{i=1}^{n} Q_i \Big/ W' \right\rfloor . \qquad (6)$$

where $\lfloor x \rfloor$ is the operation of $max\{n \mid n \le x,\ integer\ n\}$, and $\lceil x \rceil$ is $min\{n \mid n \ge x,\ integer\ n\}$, and $x \bmod y$ is defined as $x - y \lfloor x/y \rfloor$, and round(x) is $\lfloor x+0.5 \rfloor$.

According to the Euler's formula, we can easily prove that

$$\sum_{i=1}^{k \cdot C} Q_i = 0 . \qquad (7)$$

And one can obtain

$$x_{k \cdot C} = 0, \quad y_{k \cdot C} = k \cdot C . \qquad (8)$$

If the order span between the same pulse train is $k \cdot C$ (k is positive integer), the coordinates of the two pulses in PBM with width of W' are respectively written as

$$x_{n_1} = round(\bmod(\sum_{i=1}^{J} Q_i, W')), \quad y_{n_1} = (k-1) \cdot C + \left\lfloor \sum_{i=1}^{J} Q_i \Big/ W' \right\rfloor . \qquad (9)$$

$$x_{n_2} = round(\bmod(\sum_{i=1}^{J} Q_i, W')), \quad y_{n_2} = k \cdot C + \left\lfloor \sum_{i=1}^{J} Q_i \Big/ W' \right\rfloor . \qquad (10)$$

Thus we obtain a conclusion, i.e., $x_{n_2} = x_{n_1}$, $y_{n_2} = y_{n_1} + C$. \qquad (11)

The expression (8) and (11) show that the accumulative transformation characteristic curve of the PRI sequence modulated by sine function superposed modulation mean W' periodically appears in the PBM with width W'.

Supposing that modulation function f(t) is periodical and symmetrical, i.e. $f(x)=f(x+T)$ and $f(x)=-f(x+T/2)$. By (4), one can obtain

$$\sum_{i=1}^{C} f(\tfrac{i}{C}\cdot T + t_0) = f(t_0) + \cdots + f(\tfrac{\frac{C}{2}-1}{C}\cdot T + t_0) + f(\tfrac{\frac{C}{2}}{C}\cdot T + t_0) + \cdots + f(\tfrac{C-1}{C}\cdot T + t_0) \quad (12)$$

where C is the number of modulated pulses in modulation period T.

Obviously, the expression (12) is zero according to the periodicity and symmetry of the f(t) when C is even and non-negative. However, the expression (12) is not strictly equal to zero when C is odd and non-negative. Another expression of f(t) is

$$f(t) = \sum_{n=1}^{\infty} A_n \sin(n\omega t + \varphi_0), \quad \omega = 2\pi/C . \quad (13)$$

When the harmonic coefficient A_N is less than or equal to ε (ε is positive and close to zero), the expression (13) can be approximately expressed as

$$f(t) = \sum_{n=1}^{N} A_n \sin(n\omega t + \varphi_0), \quad \omega = 2\pi/C . \quad (14)$$

As the number of modulated pulses is $K \cdot N \cdot C$ (K is positive integer), the expression (14) equals zero. Therefore, the period of accumulative transformation characteristic curve is the same as the sine modulation period of PRI of radar pulse sequence.

According to the periodicity of accumulative characteristic curve, a fast searching algorithm is proposed in this paper.

4 A Searching Algorithm of Symmetrical Period Modulation Pattern

The search process of symmetrical and periodical modulation pattern consists of three steps. In step 1, a 2-D plane bitmap matrix (PBM) filled with "0" is built, which the size is limited by searching width and the length of the pulse series. Then the width of the PBM are adjusted from *MeanSt* to *MeanEd* by the step of *Wstep* to search the periodical curve that is formed by "1" elements. According to the periodical PRI modulation pattern gained in step 2, pulse deinterleaving is performed in step 3. The partial key codes of the algorithm are listed here.

Input: *L(n)* is the accumulative transformation of PRI series of a sample of pulses; *MeanSt* and *MeanEd* limit the search range of the virtual plane width; *Wstep* is the search step; *ModExistTh* is the decision threshold, which is adjusted according to the density of the "1" elements in PBM and initially is set to 0.1.

Output: *ModSeries*, i.e., pulse sequence with symmetrical and periodical PRI.

```
program   SearchSPMP(ModSeies)
   const  ModExistTh=0.1; MeanSt, MeanEd: integer;
   var    PlaneW: MeanSt..MeanEd; ModPeriod: integer;
          DetModMat, SeaModMat, ModMat, ModSeies: matrix;
```

```
begin
  PlaneW := MeanSt;
  repeat;
  PlaneMat :=zeros(PlaneW·⌈L(n)/PlaneW⌉);
  MatRow(:,1)  := ⌊mod(L(:,1),PlaneW)⌋;
  MatCol(:,1)  := ⌊L(:,1)/PlaneW⌋;
  set(PlaneMat((MatCol-1)*PlaneW + MatRow)) :=1;
  begin
    ModPeriod :=2;
    repeat;
    DetModMat := copy(PlaneMat, 0, ModPeriod);
    SeaModMat := copy(PlaneMat,
  ModPeriod,2*ModPeriod);
    ModMat :=and(DetModMat, SeaModMat);
    if (sum(ModMat)/sum(DetModMat)>= ModExistTh)
       ModSeries :=Extract(PlaneMat, ModMat);
    end
    ModPeriod := ModPeriod+1;
    until ModPeriod:= size(PlaneMat,1)/4;
  end
  PlaneW := PlaneW+1;
  until PlaneW := MeanEd;
end.
```

The calculation unit of the algorithm is the ratio of the maximum of *L(n)* to the starting search width (*MeanSt*), i.e., $L(n)_{max}$ / *MeanSt*, denoted as *N*. As the time calculation complexity of modulation pattern searching is $O(N^2/2-N)$, and pulse deinterleaving is $O(N/C)$. So the total time calculation complexity is

$$O(N^2/2-N)+O(N/C) \sim O(N^2) \ . \tag{15}$$

As one element is stored in 8 bytes, obviously, space calculation complexity of the algorithm is $8 \cdot L(n)_{max}$.

5 Experimental Results

It is suitable to evaluate the pulse deinterleaving algorithm by accuracy percent (AP) and missing percent (MP). Generally, AP and MP are respectively defined as:

$$AP=(S_R/S) \cdot 100\% \tag{16}$$

$$MP=((S_M-S_R)/S_M) \cdot 100\% \tag{17}$$

where S_R is the number of modulated pulses correctly deinterleaved, and S_M is the number of modulated pulses and S is the number of all the modulated pulses deinterleved by the proposed algorithm. It is certain that pulse density affects AP and MP. In this paper, pulse density, i.e., the density of "1" elements in PBM is given by

$$E_{Den}=(E_1/E) \cdot 100\% \tag{18}$$

where E_1 is the number of "1" elements of the PBM, and E is the number of all elements of the PBM.

Computer simulation using MATLAB is to design complex radar environment, where interleaved radar pulses with PRI modulated by a symmetric and periodical function are inserted in dense random pulses. The density of pulse series emulated varies from 0.5% to 3.0%, and correspondingly the number of pulses increases from 2000 to 12000 at the same time interval. In this pulse series, 400 pulses with PRI modulated by a sine or triangular wave function, i.e., periodical and symmetric in a period, and 31 pulses in a modulation period, is inserted in the dense random pulses series each time. We repeat this experiment 50 times and the experimental results are presented in Fig.1. and Fig.2.

In Fig. 1., the curve denoted by NPM indicates that the searched modulation pulses in a period raises as the pulse density increases, but the APC curve shows that the denser the interleaved pulse series, the lower the accuracy percent of the proposed algorithm. Therefore, the conclusion is derived that in this algorithm the pulse density, i.e., "1" elements must be less than or equal to 3%, which ensure that the valuable pulses from one emitter would be assembled in one group.

Specifically, the curve denoted by MPC in Fig.2 illustrates that the MP of pulse deinterleaving fluctuates with the increment of pulse density. The NMP curve in Fig.1 shows that the number of searched pulses in a modulation period is not 31 in most cases, and rises with increment of pulse density. The reason why MP keeps relatively stable as the pulse density increase is that random pulses barely periodically appear in multi-modulation period. And thus the modulated pulses are easily kicked out in following pulse deinterleaving process. In Fig.2, the ATS curve illustrates that average pattern searching time slightly rises with pulse density.

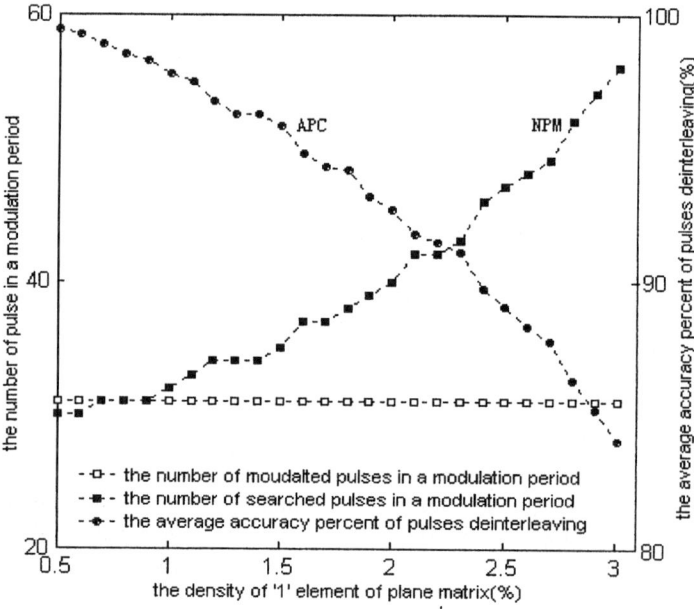

Fig. 1. Evolution of average AP and pulse number searched in a period for pulse density

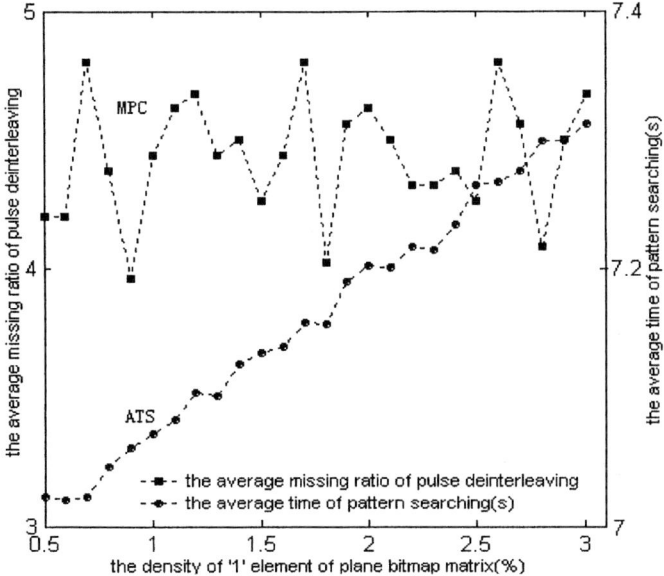

Fig. 2. Evolution of average MP and average pattern searching time for pulse density

6 Conclusions

This paper proposed a fast search algorithm of periodical and symmetrical modulation pattern and its applications in dense and non-traditional pulses deinterleaving, which overcomes the drawbacks of the plane transformation technique [8 9 10] such as slow searching, being ineffective in dense pulse environment, and manual operation, and so on. The modulation pattern searching and the pulse deinterleaving are all automatically preformed, and therefore the algorithm makes great contribution to the increase of complex radar pulse deinterleaving speed, compared with plane transformation technique. Experimental results show that the average accuracy rate and the average missing rate of the pulse deinterleaving fully meet the challenge. As all the experiments are performed on the assumption that pulses are uniformly distributed, the issue on the algorithm self-adapting the density of the pulse series is our research work in future.

Acknowledgement

This paper is supported by Anhui Provincial Distinguished Youth Science Foundation (2002 ~ 2004).

References

1. Mardia H.K.: New techniques for the deinterleaving of repetitive sequences. IEE proceedings. (1989) 136 (4): 149–154
2. Milojevic D.J., Popovic B.M.: Improved algorithm for the deinterleaving of radar pulses. IEE proceedings. (1992) 139 (1): 98–104

3. Mardia,H.K.: Adaptive multidimensional clustering for ESM. IEE Colloquium on signal processing for ESM systems. (1988) 62: 5/1–5/4
4. Nelson D.J.: Special purpose correlation functions for improved signal detection and parameter estimation In Proceedings of International Conference on Acoustics, Speech, and Signal Processing (ICASSP'93). (1993) 73–76
5. Ray, P.S.: A novel pulse TOA analysis technique for radar identification. IEEE transactions on Aerospace and Electronic Systems. (1998) 34(3): 716–721
6. Ken'ichi Nishiguchi, Masaaki Kobayashi: Improved algorithm for estimating pulse repetition intervals. IEEE transactions on Aerospace and Electronic Systems. (2000) 36(4): 407–421
7. Wan Jianwei, et al.: The research of Synthetical Sorting Method for Radar Signal. Acta Electronica Sinica. (1996) 24(9): 91–94
8. Zhao Renjian, et al.: Plane Transformation for Signal Deinterleaving in Dense Signal Environment. Acta Electronica Sinica. (1998) 26(1): 77–82
9. Zhao Renjian, et al.: The Multi-Meaning Analyzing of Plane Transformation in Concentrated Signals Separation. Journal of Sichuan University (Natural Science Edition). (1997) 34(2): 177–182
10. Zhao Renjian, et al.: Separation of Periodic Signals Using Variable Detection Step. Journal of Sichuan University (Natural Science Edition). (1995) 32(5): 527–532

A Granular Analysis Method in Signal Processing[*]

Lunwen Wang[1], Ying Tan[2], and Ling Zhang[3]

[1] 702 Research Division of Electronic Engineering Institute,
Hefei 230037
wanglunwen@163.com
[2] Chinese University of Hong Kong, Shatin, N.T., Hong Kong
yingtan@ie.cuhk.edu.hk
[3] Institute of Artificial intelligence, Anhui University,
Hefei 230039, China
Zling@ahu.edu.cn

Abstract. This paper presents multiple granular descriptions of a signal character and the significance of different granular analyses in signal processing. After given the concepts of granularity, we discuss the relation of different granularity, define the concepts of coarse and fine granularity and propose a granular analysis method (GAM) with which automatically choosing the suitable granularity to analyze a signal. The experimental results of extracting fine characters of a 2FSK signal show the efficiency of the method.

1 Introduction

We often analyze signals in different hierarchies or granularities according to our needs in signal processing. Taking the different characters extracted from a signal for example, the emphases of analysis are different. Some characters can be only extracted through deep and particular analysis, such as the fingerprint character of signals. Some can be extracted easily, such as conventional characters. The reason is that there are different granular descriptions for signals. The Fig. 1 shows an analog signal waveform which different granular spectrums are shown in Fig. 2. Section A of Fig. 2 is the roughest granular description of the signal spectrum, or the frequency resolution is the lowest of the four, section B is the spectrum with 2 times higher frequency resolution than section A. Section C is the spectrum with 4 times, and section D is the spectrum with 8 times.

From the Fig. 2, we can find out that each spectrum diagram reflects the similarity in the spectrum structure. Section A is the roughest description about the spectrum, and hides some details of the signal. Section D is the clearest description, and it reflects the finest spectrum. The different spectrum shows different resolution of the same character. By analyzed and computed, the frequency resolution and the peak value of each section in the Fig. 2 are listed in Table 1.

---

[*] This work was supported by the Natural Science Foundation of China under Grant No.60135010; partially by the National Grand Fundamental Research 973 Program of China under Grant No. G1998030509.

Table 1. Results of granular analysis of the signal in Fig. 1

Sections in the Fig. 2	A (Hz)	B (Hz)	C (Hz)	D (Hz)
Frequency resolution (Analytic granularity)	40	20	10	5
Peak frequency of the signal spectrum	680	680	670	675

From Table 1, we can find that the analytic granularity is proportional to frequency resolution. The higher is the frequency resolution, the finer the analytic granularity is. In addition, the measurement precision of signal is proportional to analytic granularity. With analytic granularity refining, the more precise is the measurement, the nearer is to the real value. The above example shows that the spectrum of the same signal has series of granular descriptions, thus, granular analysis is necessary in signal processing.

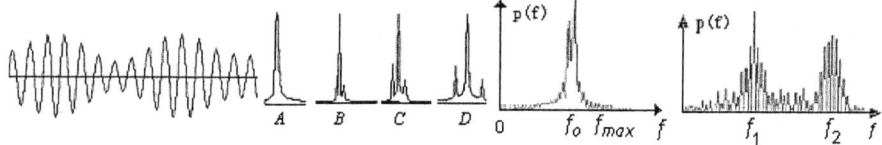

Fig. 1. Signal waveform   **Fig. 2.** Spectrums of different granularities   **Fig. 3.** The original signal spectrum   **Fig. 4.** The spectrum after ZFFT

The idea of using different granularities to analyze a problem has been there for a long time. Many current theories contain the spirit of granular analysis to some different extend, such as the theory of Rough Set [1], Neural Network [2], Fuzzy System [3], Wavelet Transform, Decision Tree etc. Many researchers have carried out deep research in these aspects. In the Ref. 4, the authors considered a hyperbox-based clustering and classification of granular data. In the Ref. 5, the authors explain the application of granular analysis theory in clustering and classifying, and present a new kind of grade classifying method. In Ref. 6, the granular computing is applied to the extraction of correlative rule, which greatly advances the speed of extraction. In Ref. 7, the granularity theory is applied to carry out the data clustering.

However, they have not realized the idea of granular analysis in signal processing domain. There are not reports about deep granular analysis in signal processing. Section 2 introduces the theory of granularity. Section 3 proposes the signal granular analysis method. Section 4 certifies the method through the experiments.

2 Granularity Description of the Problem

A triple form (X, F, Γ) is used to describe granular formalization in Ref. 8, where X, the universe of discourse, is the set of objects; F defines property function, the definition is that $F: X \rightarrow Y$, Y is set of attributes of basic element; Γ denotes the structure of universe, defined as the relation of every elements in the domain. If the problem is solved from a rough view, we should simplify X by viewing the elements in similar property as equivalence and classifying as one kind. In such a way, we can also regard the integer as a new element to form a larger granular description of the problem. Finally we can transform the original problem of (X,F,Γ) into a new problem of $([X],[Y],[\Gamma])$. The relation between granularity and equivalence is very similar. In fact, the above simplification process is the same as the concept of quotient set.

We usually solve the same problem by using different granularity. So it is necessary to study the relation of different granularities. Letting R denote a set constructed by all the equivalent relations of X, we can define the "roughness" and "fineness" of granularity by the equivalent relation.

Definition 1: Let $R_1, R_2 \in R$, for arbitrary $x,y \in X$, $xR_1y \Rightarrow xR_2y$, then R_1 is finer than R_2, denoted by $R_1 \leq R_2$.

Theorem 1: Under the relation "$\leq$" defined above, R forms a completable partial ordered case.

This is a very profound theorem, it reveals the kernel property about granularity, and it is the base of other properties. For details about it, please refer to Ref. 8. Based on the theorem, we can acquire a serial as follow: $R_n \leq R_{n-1} \leq \ldots \leq R_1 \leq R_0$.

Intuitively, the serial acquired above is corresponding with a tree of n layer. Let T denote a tree of n layer, X denote the set of all the leaf nodes, and then the nodes of each layer are corresponding with a division of X. So, there must be an equivalent relation serial corresponding to them.

3 Granular Analysis Method

The purpose of introducing the theory of granular analysis is to solve problems efficiently, the rough granularity analysis is simple but the result is inaccurate, while the result of fine granular analysis is exact, but the analysis time is long. Thus, selecting a suitable analytic granularity is a very important task in signal processing. So, we introduce two equivalent divisions.

Definition 2: Let R_1 and R_2 denote two equivalent relations on universe X, if R is also an equivalent relation in X, where $R_1 < R$ and $R_2 < R$, and there is another R' which satisfies $R_1 < R'$, $R_2 < R'$ and $R < R'$. Then we regard R as the arithmetic product of R_1 and R_2, and denoted by $R = R_1 \otimes R_2$.

Definition 3: Let R_1 and R_2 be two equivalent relations of X, if R is also an equivalent relation in X, where $R_1 < R$ and $R_2 < R$, and there is another R' which satisfies $R' < R_1$, $R' < R_2$ and $R' < R$. Then we regard R as the sum of R_1 and R_2, and denoted by $R = R_1 \oplus R_2$.

From above definitions, we know $R_1 \otimes R_2$ is the roughest equivalent relation that can subdivide R_1 and R_2, and $R_1 \oplus R_2$ is the finest equivalent relation that can be subdivided by R_1 and R_2.

Analyzing a given problem, we divided it with equivalent relation R_1 to obtain a quotient space S_1, then analyze the problem on the base of S_1 and obtain primary results A_1. If the results are rough, we can choose a granularity R_1' according to A_1, let $R_2 = R_1 \otimes R_1'$, then analyze the problem on the base of R_2 and obtain the results A_2. If A_2 is still rough, we can choose a granularity R_2' according to A_2, let $R_3 = R_2 \otimes R_2'$, and analyze the problem on the basis of R_3. The procedure above can be repeated, the more we repeat, the finer granularity we will get.

In contrast, when we divided the problem with equivalent relation R_1 and the result is fine, we choose another equivalent relation R_1', let $R_2 = R_1 \oplus R_1'$, and then analyze the problem on the basis of R_2. If the results are still fine, choose a granularity R_2', let $R_3 = R_2 \oplus R_2'$, and analyze the problem on the basis of R_3. The procedure above can be repeated too, the more we repeat, the rougher granularity we will get.

Definition 4: In order to meet our need, selecting a suitable granularity by automatically using the roughing granularity and fining granularity method to process a signal is called the granular analysis method for the signal.

Now, we take ZFFT for example to illustrate the specific application of GAM. ZFFT can be viewed as a zoom or magnified Fast Fourier Transform (FFT). The purpose is to fine or magnify a narrow section in a wideband spectrum, namely, to analyze the section we concerned by using the fine granularity. Fig. 4 shows the magnified spectrum of the signal in Fig. 3 near the spectrum peak value f_0. The basic flowchart is to shift the sampled signal to the lower side spectrum, perform a low-pass filtering, re-sample to construct equivalent classes, and finally take FFT.

Frequency shifting and low-pass filtering can abandon the unnecessary low and high frequency components. Re-sampling decimates the processed signal at $m-1$ intervals ($m \in N$) and then forms m equivalent classes to construct a quotient space. Performing FFT on an arbitrary equivalent class, consequently, acquires the selected analytic granularity. The procedure shows as follows.

① Frequency shifting $f_0 - f_{max}/2m$ to low side.
② Low-pass filtering, cut-off frequency is $f_0 + f_{max}/2m$, after filtering only the spectrum from band $f_0 - f_{max}/2m$ to $f_0 + f_{max}/2m$ remains, and the bandwidth is f_{max}/m.
③ Re-sampling the data in time domain after filtering at $m-1$ sample period intervals, and forming m equivalent classes to construct a quotient space.
④ Performing FFT, the frequency resolution is, $\triangle f/m$, $\triangle f$ is the original frequency resolution, in fact, the analytic granularity is enhanced m times.
⑤ If the analytic granularity meets our demands, go to end, otherwise, if the granularity is coarse, go to ⑥, if the granularity is fine, go to ⑦.
⑥ $f_{max}' = f_{max}$, let $f_{max} = f_0 + f_{max}'/2\beta$, β ($\beta \in N$) is the multiple of fining at second adjustment.
⑦ Minishing the value of m, go to ①.

In summary, the essential of ZFFT can be comprehended as follows. By regarding frequency shifting, low-pass filtering and re-sampling as an equivalent relation R_1, we can divide several equivalent classes to construct a quotient space S_1, then analyze problems in S_1 and draw a preliminary conclusion A_1. If the analytic granularity is not appropriate, another equivalent relation R_2 is chosen to fine the analytic granularity through the arithmetic product of two equivalent relations or coarsen the analytic granularity through the sum of them. By repeating the procedure of coarsening and fining the granularity, we can acquire a suitable analytic granularity for our problem in signal processing at the end.

Different from the traditional processing methods with a fixed granularity beforehand, our above algorithm can obtain an optimal granularity to solve a problem by automatically repeating adjustments of granularities.

4 The Experimental Results and Analysis

We will use GAM to computer the time of code transitions of a 2FSK signal by wavelet analysis [9] method. A 2FSK signal, which is widely used at present, is frequency shift keying signal using binary digit base-band signal to control the signal carrier. Continuous wavelet transform (WT) of a energy limited signal $f(t)$ is defined as

$$(W_\psi f)(a,b) := \langle f, \psi_{a,b} \rangle = |a|^{-1/2} \int_{-\infty}^{\infty} f(t)\overline{\psi(\tfrac{t-b}{a})}dt \qquad (1)$$

Where $\psi_{a,b}(t) := |a|^{-1/2} \psi(\dfrac{t-b}{a})$ is called as the function of the window [10], a is scale, and b is location parameter. When the scale 'a' is large, open a wide window, the range analyzed is relatively big, and corresponding to rough granular analysis. So scale a is corresponding to the analysis granularity, and the WT analysis method is also a kind of GAM in signal processing.

In the code transition area of 2FSK signal, the signal carrier changes constantly. Because WT analysis can detect the strange points of the signal, and find the carrier change area [10], we can extract time of code transition by using WT analysis. Fig. 5 shows a sampled signal and the maximal norm values of 4 different granular Mallat transform [10] results.

According to Fig. 5, choosing a suitable granular analysis is the key to compute the time of code transition. In Fig. 5, scale 1 is the smallest, and corresponding granularity is the finest. On the contrary, corresponding granularity of scale 4 is the roughest. When the scale is large, analyzed data is big, and the result is inaccurate. However, it can approximately find out the transition area and assist the localization. When the scale is small, analyzed data is littler, some slight changes of transition area is reflected, and the result is accurate. But fine granularity is easy to be influenced by noise such as scale 1 in Fig. 5.

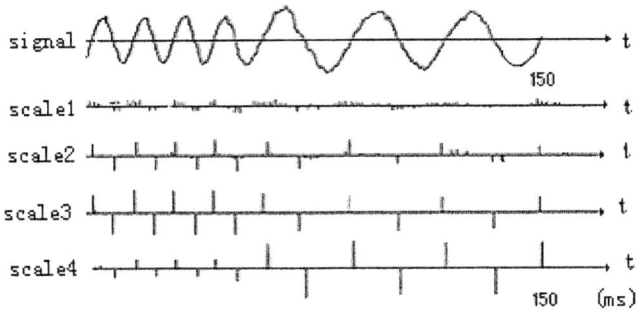

Fig. 5. The signal and results of 4-scale Mallat transform

Traditional analytical methods carry on manifold granularities WT, and compute the time of code transition by artificially selecting granularity, while GAM automatically chooses the suitable granularity analysis according to the definition 4. The results of the two methods are listed in Table 2.

Table 2. Results of code transition time extracted from 2FSK

Analytical methods	Number of WT	Analytical time (second)	Time of code transition (millisecond)
Traditional analytical method	10	30	0.537
GAM	5	0.5	0.537

We can find out from Table 2 that the GAM has the results as accurate as the traditional method, but the analytical time is reduced greatly.

5 Conclusion

The thought of different granular analysis accords with the law of the objective world. While considering and solving problems, people use the concept unconsciously. However, few people formalize it mathematically, especially, in signal processing domain. Applying GAM to signal processing may enrich the theory of signal analysis and reduce the computational complexity. This paper carries on mathematical description of the thought of granular analysis and gives the relationships of different granularities, the basic rule of granular analysis, the method of granular selection, then present an automatic granular analysis method. We take the extraction time of the code transition of 2FSK signal, as an example, to demonstrate the actual efficiency of our granular analysis in signal processing.

References

1. Y.Y. Yao : Stratified Rough Set and Granular Computing. IEEE Computer Society Press, (1999) 800–804
2. Scott Dick, Abraham Kandel : Granular Weights in a Neural Network. IEEE Computer Society Press, (2001) 1708–1713
3. T.Y.Lin: Measure Theoty on Granular Fuzzy Sets. IEEE Computer Society Press, (1999) 809–813
4. Andrzej Bargiela, Witold Pedrycz : Classification and Clustering of Granular Data. IEEE Computer Society Press, (2001) 1696–1701
5. Bu Dongbo, Bai Suo, Li guojie : Principle of Granularity in Clustering and Classification. Chinese J. Computers, Vol.25, No.8, 810~816, 2002
6. T.Y.Lin, Xiaohua Hu, Eric Louie : A Fast Association Rule Algorithm Based On Bitmap and Granular Computing. The IEEE International Conference on Fuzzy, (2003) 678–683

7. Witold Pedrycz, Andrzej Bargiela : Granular Clustering: A Granular Signature of Data. IEEE Transactions on Systems Man and Cybernetics—Part B, CYBERNETICS, VOL. 32, NO. 2, (2002) 212-224
8. Zhang B., Zhang L. : Theory and Application of Problem Solving [M]. Elsevier Science Publishers B.V., 1992
9. Burrus C S etal : Introduction to wavelets and wavelet transforms. New Jersey:Prentice Hall, 1998
10. Daubechies I : The Wavelets transform, time frequency localization and signal analysis [J]. IEEE Trans, 1990,36(5) 961-1005

Adaptive Leakage Suppression Based on Recurrent Wavelet Neural Network

Zhangliang Xiong and Xiangquan Shi

Nanjing University of Science & Technology, Postal code 210094,
200 Xiaolingwei, Nanjing, Jiangsu,
P.R. China
xdz3701@yahoo.com.cn

Abstract. A novel adaptive leakage suppression method based on recurrent wavelet neural network (RWNN) in phase-coded modulation continuous wave (PCM-CW) radar is proposed in this paper. In the proposed model, the orthogonalized received signals do cross multiplication with the orthogonal local reference signals. Based on the characteristics of trigonometric function, the differencing output of the two channels effectively suppresses the leakage from transmitter while retains the interested target echoes. Considering rigorous requirements in military, blind channel equalization based on RWNN is applied to compensate the inequality in the two channels in phase property and amplitude gain to achieve suppression ratio higher than 30dB. The small size and high efficiency of RWNN make it is well suited to be utilized in the real time leakage suppression. The results of theoretical analysis and simulation on the detecting performance of the radar both show the validity and practicability of the proposed method.

1 Introduction

The leakage from transmitter is an unavoidable serious disturbance for PCM-CW radar. It will result in sideband noise, submerge weak target echo, jam the receiver and shorten the radar's detection range. The recent popular approach for leakage suppression is the reflected power canceller (RPC) based on the complicated vector modulator [1] [2]. But unfortunately, the complexity of it make its performance is not satisfactory in harsh military environments. In this paper, we proposed a novel adaptive leakage suppression method based on RWNN for PCM-CW radar. It can obtain LSR higher than 30dB while keep robust in harsh military environments. In the chapter 2, detailed theory analysis on it is given. Chapter 3 gives the results of numeric simulation. At last, the application and development of it are discussed.

2 Theory Analysis

The proposed leakage suppression model is shown in Fig. 1. The transmitted signal and the differencing output are

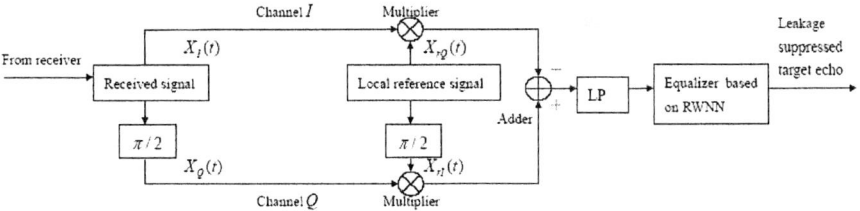

Fig. 1. Adaptive leakage suppression model based on RWNN

$$S_i = PN(t)\cos(\omega_c t + \phi) = \sum_{m=-\infty}^{+\infty}\sum_{i=1}^{N} a_i rect((t - mNT - iT - T/2)/T)\cos(\omega_c t + \phi)$$

$$X_{out}(t) = X_Q(t)X_{rI}(t) - X_I(t)X_{rQ}(t) = X_L(t) + X_{echo}(t) = [R_I \cdot L_Q \cdot PN(t) \cdot \sin(\omega_c t + \phi) \cdot \cos(\omega_c t + \phi)$$
$$- R_Q \cdot L_I \cdot PN(t) \cdot \cos(\omega_c t + \phi) \cdot \sin(\omega_c t + \phi)] + [R_I \cdot K_Q \cdot PN(t - \tau) \cdot \sin(\omega_c t + \omega_d t + \Phi + \phi) \cdot \cos(\omega_c t + \phi) \quad (1)$$
$$- R_Q \cdot K_I \cdot PN(t - \tau) \cdot \cos(\omega_c t + \omega_d t + \Phi + \phi) \cdot \sin(\omega_c t + \phi)],$$

where T is the code element width and $PN(t)$ represents the code series. The proposed method is not sensitive to the code category. τ is the echo delay, L, K and R are the amplitude factors, $\Phi = -(\omega_c + \omega_d)\tau$, ω_d is the Doppler frequency. Limited to the space, we just investigate the single target condition in this paper, which can be generalized to multi-target condition easily. To suppress the leakage, $X_L(t)$ in (1) should be zero. If the channels are ideal, $R_I L_Q = R_Q L_I = A$, $R_I K_Q = R_Q K_I = B$, then

$$X_{out}(t) = A \cdot PN(t) \cdot \sin(\phi - \phi) + B \cdot PN(t - \tau) \cdot \sin(\omega_d t - (\omega_c + \omega_d)\tau + (\phi - \phi)) \quad (2)$$
$$= 0 + B \cdot PN(t - \tau) \cdot \sin(\omega_d t - (\omega_c + \omega_d)\tau) = B \cdot PN(t - \tau) \cdot \sin(\omega_d t - \Phi)$$

From above derivation, one can see the leakage has been suppressed in (2) effectively while the target information is retained. Meanwhile, one can also see the channels' inequality will hinders the further improvement of LSR. If we assume $X_I(t) = X_Q(t)e^{-j(\alpha+\pi/2)}$, $X_{rI}(t) = X_{rQ}(t)e^{-j(\alpha+\pi/2)}$, $\cos\alpha = \cos\beta + \gamma_1$, $\sin\alpha = \sin\beta + \gamma_2$, $R_I L_Q = R_Q L_I + \delta = C + \delta$, $R_I K_Q = R_Q K_I + \lambda = D + \lambda$ in (2), $n_1(t)$ and $n_2(t)$ are the independent Gaussian white noise with zero mean,

$$X_{out}(t) = X_{ideal}(t) + X_{dev}(t) + n_k(t), X_{ideal}(t) = C \cdot 0 + D \cdot \cos\beta \cdot PN(t - \tau) \cdot \sin(\omega_d t - \Phi),$$
$$X_{dev}(t) = \{C \cdot PN(t) \cdot [\gamma_1 \cdot \sin(\omega_c t + \phi) \cdot \cos(\omega_c t + \phi) + \gamma_2 \cdot \cos^2(\omega_c t + \phi)] + \delta \cdot PN(t) \cdot \sin(\omega_c t + \phi + \alpha) \cdot \cos(\omega_c t + \phi)\}$$
$$+ \{D \cdot PN(t - \tau) \cdot \gamma_1 \cdot \sin(\omega_c t + \omega_d t + \Phi + \phi) \cdot \cos(\omega_c t + \phi) + D \cdot PN(t - \tau) \cdot \gamma_2 \cdot \cos(\omega_c t + \omega_d t + \Phi + \phi) \cdot \cos(\omega_c t + \phi) \quad (3)$$
$$+ \lambda \cdot PN(t - \tau) \cdot \sin(\omega_c t + \omega_d t + \Phi + \phi + \alpha) \cdot \cos(\omega_c t + \phi)\}$$
$$n_k(t) = R_{rI} \cdot n_2(t) \cdot \cos(\omega_c t + \phi) - R_{rQ} \cdot n_1(t) \cdot \sin(\omega_c t + \phi + \alpha).$$

In (3), $X_{ideal}(t)$ is the useful output, $X_{dev}(t)$ is the unwished residue results from the channels inequality and $n_k(t)$ is the output noise. According to the conclusion of probability statistics [3], $n_k(t)$ is also a zero mean Gaussian white noise and the pro

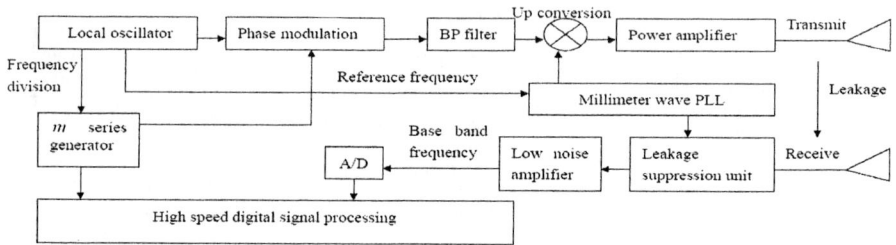

Fig. 2. The block diagram of PCM-CW radar with the proposed leakage suppression unit

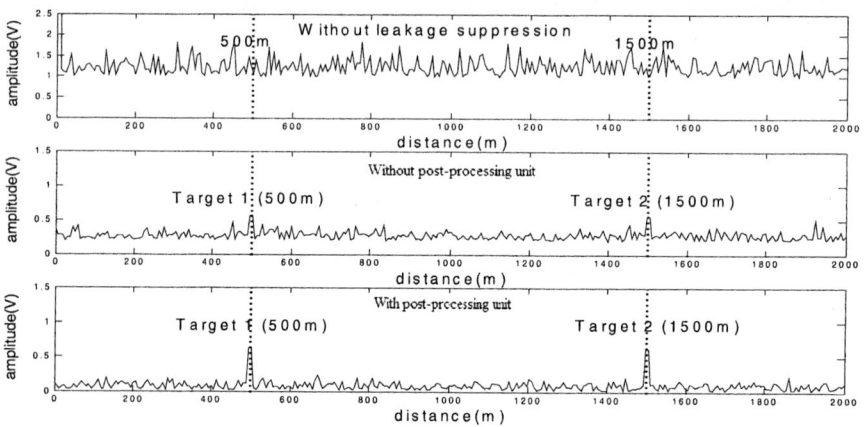

Fig. 3. Comparison of the PCM-CW radar's correlation output

posed method will not worsen the receiver's output SNR no matter what the number of targets is. In essential, the influence of the two channels' inequality on the expected output can be considered as resulting from one equivalent channel's nonlinear characteristics. In the proposed model, we diminish $X_{dev}(t)$ by the post-processing unit based on RWNN. Define the objective function and recursive algorithm are

$$E(k) = \sum_{i=1}^{n} h_i \cdot (E(d_i(k)) - E(\hat{f}_i(X(k-1), R(k-1), p)))^2, p = (\omega, a, b) \quad (4)$$

$$E(\hat{f}_i(X(k), R(k), p)) = ((k-1)E(\hat{f}_i(X(k-1), R(k-1), p)) + \hat{f}_i(X(k), R(k), p))/k.$$

where $d_i(k)$ is the ideal output, $X(k)$ is the input vector, $R(k)$ is the internal state feedback vector, h_i is the constant coefficient and $\hat{f}_i(\cdot)$ is the transfer function. p is the interested parameter to minimize $E(k)$, in which ω is the current weights, a is the translation factor and b is the dilation factor. $E(\hat{f}_i(\cdot))$ in (4) calculated recursively according to the real time recurrent learning algorithm proposed in [4], Then the differential operation of $E(k)$ can be executed recursively [5].

3 Simulation and Discussion

The block diagram of radar with the proposed unit is shown in Fig. 2. In simulation, the code rate is 20MHz, the period of the m series is 63 bit and the carrier frequency is 37.5GHz. The adopted RWNN has three wavelet nodes, single input node and single output node. In (4), $n=3$, $h_1=2, h_2=1$ and $h_1=5$, the mother wavelet is $\Psi(x)=(4-\|x\|^2)\exp(-\|x\|^2/2)/\sqrt{2}$. We construct simulated received signal composed of strong leakage from transmitter, environmental noise and target echo. The input SNR is –6dB. There existing two targets: $V_1=50m/s$, $d_1=500m$; $V_2=150m/s$, $d_2=1500m$. The inequality of the orthogonal signals amplitude is chosen within 20% and the phase offset is within $18°$. The amplitude ratio of the leakage and the target echoes is $A_L:A_1:A_2=100:1:1$. The RWNN is trained in advance. Fig. 3 shows the average correlation output of the radar after 20 times repeated trials. From it, one can see the strong noisy leakage does great harm to the target detection if without the proposed suppression method. The interested targets are completely submerged in the sidelobe of leakage and cannot be detected. With the proposed method while without post-processing unit, the signal detection performance is improved effectively. But because the channels inequality, there are still some unwished disturbance in the radar's output. With the application of the post-processing unit, the performance is further improved and the LSR is higher than 30dB reliably. We also compare the proposed method with the RPC method ($SNR_{in}=-6dB$, $P_f=10^{-5}$), the former can bring about 20% increases in the detection probability.

4 Conclusions

In this paper we developed a novel adaptive leakage suppression method based on RWNN in PCM-CW radar. It can obtain high LSR while keep robust in harsh military environments. With similar structure, we also developed the Doppler tolerance extension (DTE) unit. The further researches on them are absorbing.

References

1. P.D.L. Beasley, A.G. Stove, B.J. Reits etc: Solving the Problems of a Single Antenna Frequency Modulated CW Radar. Proc. IEEE Int. Radar Conf. New York (1990) 391 –395
2. S. Kannangara, M. Faulker: Adaptive Duplexer for Multiband Transceiver. Proc. IEEE Int. Conf. on Radio and Wireless. Boston (2003) 381 –384
3. Yang Fusheng (ed.): Stochastic Signal Analysis. Tsinghua University, Beijing (1990)
4. He Shichu, He Zhenya: Application of Recurrent Wavelet Neural Networks to the Digital Communications Channel Blind Equalization. J. China Institute Commun. 3 (1997) 65-69
5. Wei Wei: Nonlinear Dynamic System Modeling Using Recurrent Wavelet Network. Journal of Electronics. 3 (1999) 193-199

New Multi-server Password Authentication Scheme Using Neural Networks

Eun-Jun Yoon and Kee-Young Yoo*

Department of Computer Engineering, Kyungpook National University,
Daegu 702-701, South Korea
ejyoon@infosec.knu.ac.kr, yook@knu.ac.kr

Abstract. Recently, Li et al. proposed a password authentication scheme based on a neural network in a multi-server environment. The scheme, however, is susceptible to off-line password guessing attacks. Accordingly, this paper will demonstrate the vulnerability of Li et al.'s scheme regarding off-line password guessing attacks, and then present an improvement to isolate such problems. The proposed scheme can withstand off-line password guessing attacks, and also provide mutual authentication.

1 Introduction

Given the distribution nature of computer and network systems, achieving privacy and security have become increasingly important. In the past decade, various kinds of authentication mechanisms have been developed for the purpose of as protecting information or resources from unauthorized users. Among them, the password based authentication scheme is the most acceptable and widely used mechanism because of its low-cost, easy-operation, and simple implementation advantages.

Password based authentication schemes, however, are vulnerable to password guessing attacks [1] since users usually choose easy-to-remember passwords. Ding and Horster [1] divided password guessing attacks into three classes: (1) *Detectable on-line password guessing attacks*: An attacker attempts to use a guessed password in an on-line transaction. He verifies the correctness of his guess by using the response from the server. A failed guess can be detected and logged by the server. (2) *Undetectable on-line password guessing attacks*: Similar to detectable on-line password guessing attacks, an attacker tries to verify a password guess in an on-line transaction. A failed guess, however, can not be detected and logged by the server, as it is not able to distinguish an honest request from a malicious one. (3) *Off-line password guessing attacks*: An attacker guesses a password and verifies his guess off-line. No participation of the server is required, so the server does not notice the attack. We can easily determine that undetectable on-line password guessing attacks and off-line password guessing attacks are the most important consideration in designing a password-based authentication scheme.

---

* Corresponding author: Kee-Young Yoo (yook@knu.ac.kr) Tel.: +82-53-950-5553; Fax: +82-53-957-4846.

Conventional password-based authentication schemes are suited to solve the privacy and security problem for single servers under client/server architecture. The use of computer networks and information technology, however, has grown spectacularly. Many network architectures have become multi-server environments. Recently, Li et al. [2] proposed a password authentication scheme based on a neural network in a multi-server environment. The password authentication system identified the legitimate user in real time by using a pattern classification technique [3,4,5]. In the classification system, the input pattern is the user password and the output is the serviceable server. In Li et al.'s scheme, the users only remember user identity and password numbers in order to log-in to various servers. Furthermore, the users can freely choose their password and the system is not required to maintain a verification table.

Li et al.'s scheme, however, is vulnerable to off-line password guessing attacks. Accordingly, this paper will demonstrate the vulnerability of Li et al.'s scheme against such attacks, and then present an improvement to isolate such problems. The proposed scheme can withstand off-line password guessing attacks, and it can ensure mutual authentication between the remote server and the user so as to enhance the security of the authentication. Mutual authentication between the remote server and the user is an essential issue in password-based authentication schemes. Server spoofing [6] is a well-known attack nowadays. Therefore, protecting the server from other malicious attacks is not sufficient for the authentication scheme. Withstanding the threat of server spoofing needs to be done, in order to, in order to enhance the security of participants during the authentication procedure. Also, the proposed scheme does not have a serious time-synchronization problem unlike Li et al.'s scheme.

The remainder of this paper is organized as follows: Section 2 briefly reviews Li et al.'s scheme, then Section 3 demonstrates an off-line password guessing attack on Li et al.'s scheme. The proposed scheme is presented in Section 4, while Section 5 discusses the security of the proposed scheme. Section 6 offers concluding remarks.

2 Review of Li et al.'s Scheme

This section briefly reviews Li et al.'s remote password authentication scheme for a multi-server environment that utilizes a neural network.

2.1 Notations

Some of the notations used in this paper are defined as follows:

- SA: system administrator.
- $U_1, U_2, ..., U_n$: n users.
- $Ser_1, Ser_2, ..., Ser_m$: m various servers.
- ID_i, PW_i: the user identity and password of U_i.
- k: server's strong secret key.

- p: a large public prime.
- g: a primitive integer number in Galois field $GF(p)$.
- $E_k()/D_k()$: the DES-like encryption/decryption function using a 56-bit secret key k.
- $H(\cdot)$: secure one-way hash function, where H: $\{0,1\}^* \to \{0,1\}^k$.
- $\oplus$: bit-wise XOR operation.

2.2 Li et al.'s Password Authentication Scheme

In the password authentication process, there are three participants: the login users, the various servers, and a system administrator (SA). In the scheme, each legitimate user holds only a user identity and its corresponding password. The system administrator recognizes a user through the neural network. The neural network is trained and the weights are stored in each server. The process can be divided into three phases: (1) the registration phase; (2) the login phase; and (3) the authentication phase. Before logging-in to a server, first a new user must register some information in order to become a legitimate user. The registration phase is performed only once. Each legitimate user obtains a valid user identity and password. Later, the user types his identity and password to login to any one of the servers. In the authentication phase, the servers validate the legitimacy of the remote login user. Figure 1 shows the login and authentication phase of Li et al.'s scheme. Their scheme works as follows:

(1) Registration Phase: The user U_i submits the chosen password PW_i to the SA in a secure manner. The SA then computes the user identity ID_i that satisfies $ID_i = E_k(PW_i)$. Then, SA adds the training pattern of the new user to reconstruct the network. The network architecture consists of three layers: the input layer, the hidden layer and the output layer. The input units are the password characters and the value v. The password characters can be an English word or a numeral. In addition, the value v is related to the expected output. The output represents the serviceable servers. If the system has m servers, the number of output units is m. The training pattern includes the user's password, v and the expected output value. If the user receives the privilege of service from Ser_j, the ith unit of the expected output value denotes one. For example, a system has six servers and a new user can login to Ser_1 and Ser_5. Then, SA collects the entire registered user's training pattern as the training set for the neural network. Once the training process is completed by the SA, the SA sends an ID_i and v to user U_i and stores the networks weights and the secret key k in each server.

(2) Login Phase: If the user U_i wants to login to server Ser_j, U_i obtains a timestamp T and computes $W_i = g^{PW_i^T} \bmod p$. Then, U_i sends ID_i, W_i, v, and T to the login server Ser_j.

(3) Authentication Phase: Upon receiving ID_i, W_i, v, and T at time T^*, first Ser_j checks the correctness of the timestamp. If the time interval between T and

T^* is greater than $\triangle T$, Ser_j rejects the login request. Let $\triangle T$ denote the expected time interval for a transmission delay between the login terminal and the system servers. If the timestamp T is within the valid period, Ser_j decrypts ID_i by using k to obtain $PW_j = D_K(ID_i)$. Then, Ser_j obtains the user password PW_j and Ser_j verifies if the following equation holds: $W_i = g^{PW_j^T} \mod p$. If the verification holds, the server authenticates that ID_i and PW_i are valid. Then, Ser_j authenticates the service privilege. In order to provide the proper service, Ser_j normalizes PW_j and sends these values as an input to derive the output values from the neural network. The outputs obtained represent the privileges that U_i can receive from the allowed servers. In order to transfer the output value into a binary number, Ser_j checks whether v holds. If the jth output unit is the desired output that approaches one, Ser_j accepts U_i for login.

User (U_i)   **Server (Ser_j)**

Generate T
$W_i = g^{PW_i^T} (\mod p)$ $\underrightarrow{ID_i, W_i, v, T}$ Verify T
$PW_j = D_K(ID_i)$
Verify $W_i \stackrel{?}{=} g^{PW_j^T} (\mod p)$

Fig. 1. Li et al.'s login and authentication phase

3 Off-line Password Guessing Attack on Li et al.'s Scheme

This section demonstrates that Li et al.'s scheme is vulnerable to off-line password guessing attacks. An attacker who captured messages exchanged over a network can easily obtain a legitimate user U_i's password PW_i. Suppose that an attacker has eavesdropped on a valid message $m = \{ID_i, W_i, v, T\}$ from an open network. It is easy to obtain the information since they all are exposed over the open network. The off-line password guessing attack can proceed as follows:

(1*) In order to obtain the password PW_i of user U_i, the attacker E makes a guess at the secret password PW_i'.
(2*) E computes $g^{(PW_i')^T} (\mod p)$ and checks if $W_i = g^{(PW_i')^T} (\mod p)$. If the computed value is the same as W_i, then E has guessed the right user U_i's password PW_i. Then, E can freely impersonate the legitimate user U_i by using the guessed password PW_i'. Otherwise, E repeatedly performs it until $W_i = g^{(PW_i')^T} (\mod p)$.

Unlike typical private keys, the password has limited entropy, and is constrained by the memory of the user. For example, one alphanumerical character has 6 bits of entropy. Therefore, the goal of the attacker, which is to obtain a legitimate communication parties' password, could be achieved within reasonable time. Thus, the password guessing attacks on password-based authentication schemes should be considered realistic.

4 Proposed Scheme

This section proposes an enhancement to Li et al.'s scheme that can withstand off-line password guessing attacks. In addition, the proposed scheme provides mutual authentication between a user and a server. The security of the proposed scheme is based on a one-way hash function and a discrete logarithm problem. The process can be divided into three phases: (1) the registration phase; (2) the login phase; and (3) the authentication phase. Figure 2 shows the proposed login and authentication phase.

(1) Registration Phase: The registration phase is the same as in Li et al.'s scheme, which was presented in Section 2.

(2) Login and Mutual Authentication Phase: The proposed login and authentication phase proceeds with the following four steps. For simplicity, we omit mod$p$.

1. If user U_i wants to login to server Ser_j, U_i generates a random number $a \in GF(p)$, and computes $C1 = E_{PW_i}(g^a)$. Then, U_i sends ID_i, $C1$ and v to the login server Ser_j.
2. After receiving U_i's login request, Ser_j decrypts ID_i by using K to obtain $PW_j = D_K(ID_i)$. Ser_j decrypts $C1$ by using PW_j to obtain $g^a = D_{PW_j}(C1)$. Then, Ser_j generates a random number $b \in GF(p)$, and computes $C2 = g^a \oplus g^b$, $SK = g^{ab}$ and $C3 = H(PW_j, SK, g^a)$, and sends $C2$ and $C3$ to U_i.
3. User U_i extracts g^b by computing $C2 \oplus g^a$, and computes $SK^* = g^{ab}$ and $C3^* = H(PW_i, SK^*, g^a)$. Then, U_i compares $C3$ and $C3^*$. If they are equal,

User (U_i)		Server (Ser_j)
Generate $a \in GF(p)$		
$C1 \leftarrow E_{PW_i}(g^a)$	$\xrightarrow{ID_i, C1, v}$	$PW_j \leftarrow D_K(ID_i)$
		$g^a \leftarrow D_{PW_j}(C1)$
		Generate $b \in GF(p)$
		$C2 \leftarrow g^a \oplus g^b$
		$SK \leftarrow g^{ab}$
	$\xleftarrow{C2, C3}$	$C3 \leftarrow H(PW_j, SK, g^a)$
$g^b \leftarrow C2 \oplus g^a$		
$SK^* \leftarrow g^{ab}$		
$C3^* \leftarrow H(PW_i, SK^*, g^a)$		
Abort If $C3 \neq C3^*$		
$C4 \leftarrow H(PW_i, SK^*, g^b)$	$\xrightarrow{C4}$	$C4^* \leftarrow H(PW_j, SK, g^b)$
		Abort If $C4 \neq C4^*$

The session key $SK = SK^* = g^{ab}$

Fig. 2. Proposed login and mutual authentication phase

U_i believes that the responding part is the real server Ser_j, otherwise U_i interrupts the connection. Finally, U_i computes $C4 = H(PW_i, SK^*, g^b)$ and sends this authentication token to Ser_j for mutual authentication and session key agreement.

4. Upon receiving the message $C4$, Ser_j computes $C4^* = H(PW_j, SK, g^b)$ and compares $C4$ and $C4^*$. If they are equal, Ser_j can ensure that U_i is legal, otherwise U_i's login request is rejected. To provide the proper service, Ser_j normalizes the password PW_j and sends these values as an input to derive the output values from the neural network. The outputs obtained represent the privileges that U_i can receive from the allowed servers. To transfer the output value into a binary number, Ser_j checks whether v holds. If the jth output unit is the desired output that approaches one, Ser_j accepts U_i for login.

After mutual authentication and session key agreement between U_i and Ser_j, $SK = SK^* = g^{ab}$ is used as the session key, respectively.

5 Security Analysis

This section provides the security analysis of the proposed scheme. At first, we define the security terms [7] needed for the security analysis of the proposed scheme. This is as follows:

Definition 1. *A weak secret (password) is a value of low entropy $W(k)$, which can be guessed in polynomial time.*

Definition 2. *A secure one-way hash function $y = H(x)$ is one where it is easy to compute y form a given x, but difficult to compute x form a given y.*

Definition 3. *The discrete logarithm problem (DLP) is the following: Given a prime p, a generator g of $GF(p)$, and an element $\beta \in GF(p)$, find the integer α, $0 \leq \alpha \leq p - 2$, such that $g^\alpha \equiv \beta (\bmod p)$.*

Definition 4. *The Diffie-Hellman problem (DHP) is the following: Given a prime p, a generator g of $GF(p)$, and an element g^a and g^b, find $g^{ab}(\bmod p)$.*

Here, four security properties [7]: Passive attack, active attack, known-key attack, and perfect forward secrecy, would be considered for the proposed scheme.

(1) **Passive attack and Active attack:** A secure password authentication scheme should be able to withstand both passive attacks (where an attacker attempts to prevent a scheme from achieving its goals by merely observing honest entities carrying out the scheme) and active attacks (where an attacker additionally subverts communication by injecting, deleting, altering or replaying messages) [8].

(2) **Known-key security:** Known-key security means that each run of a key agreement scheme between the two entities U_i and Ser_j should produce a unique secret session key. A scheme should still achieve its goal in the face of an attacker who has learned some other session keys.

(3) **Perfect forward secrecy:** Perfect forward secrecy means that if the long-term private keys of one or more entities are compromised, the secrecy of previous session keys established by honest entities is not affected.

Under the above definitions, the following theorems are used to analyze the four security properties in the proposed scheme.

Theorem 1. *The proposed scheme can resist a passive attack.*

Proof. If an attacker, called E, who eavesdrops on a successful proposed scheme run can make a guess at the session key by using only information obtainable over a network and a guessed value of PW_i, E could break Diffie-Hellman key exchange [9]. The reason will be clear. Such a problem can be reduced to the computing of keying material g^{ab} from the value $C1$ and $C2$ in Figure 2. Thus, we claim that it is as difficult as to break the Diffie-Hellman problem. Without the ability to compute the keying material g^{ab}, messages $C3$ and $C4$ do not leak any information to the passive off-line attacker. Since U_i and Ser_j do not leak any information either, a passive attacker cannot verify guesses of the user's password. Thus, the proposed scheme can resist passive password guessing attacks.

Theorem 2. *The proposed scheme can resist the active attack.*

Proof. Active attacks can take many different forms, depending on what information is available to the attacker. An attacker who knows U_i's password PW_i can obviously pretend to be U_i and communicate with Ser_j. Similarly, an attacker with PW_i can masquerade as Ser_j when U_i tries to contact him. A man-in-the middle attack, which requires an attacker to fool both sides of a legitimate conversation, cannot be carried out by an attacker who does not know U_i's password. Suppose that attacker E wants to fool Ser_j into thinking he is talking to U_i. First, E can compute $C1' = E_{PW_e}(g^e)$ and send it to Ser_j. Then, Ser_j computes $SK = (D_{PW_j}(C1'))^b$, $C2 = D_{PW_j}(C1') \oplus g^b$ and $C3 = H(PW_j, SK, C2)$, and sends them to E. When E receives $C2$ and $C3$ from Ser_j, E has to make $C4'$ and send it to Ser_j. Since the problem is combined with a discrete logarithm and a secret password, E cannot guess g^b and PW_i. Thus, the proposed scheme can withstand a man-in-the-middle attack.

Theorem 3. *The proposed scheme can resist the known-key attack.*

Proof. If the session key SK is revealed to a passive attacker E, E does not learn any new information from combining SK with publicly-visible information. This is true because message $C3$ or $C4$ do not leak any information to the attacker. We have already established that E cannot make meaningful guesses at the session key SK from guessed passwords. Also, there does not appear to be an easier way for E to carry out off-line password guessing attacks. It means that the attacker, having obtained some past session keys, cannot compromise current or future session keys. Thus, it can resist the known-key attack.

Theorem 4. *The proposed scheme provides perfect forward secrecy.*

Proof. Even if both U_i's password PW_i and Ser_j's secret key k are compromised simultaneously, an attacker E can derive only the fresh session key at this time. Previous fresh session keys cannot be opened because the fresh session key is constructed under the Diffie-Hellman key agreement scheme. That is, it is computationally infeasible to obtain a fresh session key $SK = g^{ab}$ from g^a and g^b by Definition 4. Therefore, the proposed scheme satisfies the property of perfect forward secrecy.

6 Conclusions

The current paper demonstrated the vulnerability of Li et al.'s scheme regarding off-line password guessing attacks, and then presented an improvement to the scheme in order to isolate such problems. The proposed scheme can withstand off-line password guessing attacks, and also it can provide mutual authentication. As a result, the proposed scheme can ensure secure key establishment for secure communication.

Acknowledgements

This research was supported by the MIC (Ministry of Information and Communication), Korea, under the ITRC (Information Technology Research Center) support program supervised by the IITA (Institute of Information Technology Assessment).

References

1. Ding, Y., Horster, P.: Undetectable On-line Password Guessing Attacks. ACM Operating Systems Review. Vol. 29. No. 4. (1995) 77-86
2. Li, L.H., Lin,I.C., Hwang, M.S.: A Remote Password Authentication Scheme for Multiserver Architecture Using Neural Networks. IEEE Trans. Neural Networks. Vol. 12. No. 6. (2001) 1498-1504
3. Bleha, S., Obaidat, M.S.: Dimensionality Reduction and Feature Extraction Applications in Identifying Computer Users. IEEE Trans. Syst. Man Cybern. Vol. 21. (1991) 452-456
4. Obaidat, M.S., Macchiarolo, D.T.: An On-line Neural-network System for Computer Access Security. IEEE Trans. Ind. Electron. Vol. 40. (1993) 235-242
5. Obaidat, M.S., Macchairolo, D.T.: A Multilayer Neural-network System for Computer Access Security. IEEE Trans. Syst. Man Cybern. Vol. 24. No. 5. (1994) 806-812
6. Aoskan, N., Debar, H., Steiner, M., Waidner, M.: Authentication Public Terminals. Computers Networks. Vol. 31. (1999) 861-970
7. Menezes, A.J., Oorschot, P.C., Vanstone, S.A.: Handbook of Applied Cryptograph. CRC Press. New York. (1997)
8. Ryu, E.K., Kim, K.W., Yoo, K.Y.: A Promising Key Agreement Protocol. ISAAC 2003. LNCS 2906. (2003) 655-662
9. Diffie, W., Hellman, M.: New Directions in Cryptography. IEEE Trans. Inf. Theory. Vol. IT-22. No. 6. (1976) 644-654

Time Domain Substructural Post-earthquake Damage Diagnosis Methodology with Neural Networks

Bin Xu[1,2]

[1] School of Civil Engineering, Hunan University,
Changsha, Hunan 410082, P.R. China
[2] Department of Civil, Architectural and Environmental Engineering,
University of Missouri-Rolla, 1870 Miner Circle, Rolla, MO 65409-0030, USA
binxu@umr.edu

Abstract. An emulator neural network (ENN) and a parametric evaluation neural network (PENN) are constructed to facilitate a substructural parametric identification process for post-earthquake damage diagnosis of civil structures by the direct use of dynamic response measurements under base excitations. The rationality of the proposed methodology is explained, and the theory basis for the construction of two neural networks is described according to the discrete time solution of the state space equation of a substructure. An evaluation index called root-mean-square prediction difference vector (RMSPDV) is presented to evaluate the condition of a object substructure. Based on the trained ENN and PENN, the inter-storey stiffness parameters of the object substructure are identified with enough accuracy. The sensibility and the performance of the proposed methodology under different base excitations are examined using a multi-storey shear building structure by numerical simulations.

1 Introduction

Damage diagnosis for vulnerability and safety evaluation of infrastructures following natural or man-made hazards, such as seismic event, flood, hurricane, accidents or terrorism remains a pressing need. Currently, most of the post-event evaluations are carried out by time-consuming visual inspections of experienced experts or engineers under very difficult circumstances for access. Therefore, developing efficient damage diagnosis algorithms is crucial for post-event performance evaluation and crisis management.

Comprehensive literature reviews on system identification methods in civil engineering are available[1,2]. Although having successfully been applied into simple engineering structures, many of the current identification methods inherently involve a complicated optimization process for the parameters identification. Thus, they are often computationally inefficient and even numerically unstable for actual infrastructures that have a significant number of degrees of freedom. Moreover, response measurement for a whole engineering structure is difficult and the accuracy of parameters estimation is rarely reliable. If the object structure is divided to several substructures, measurement and identification may be performed more efficiently. Form such a point of view, several substructural identification algorithms have been proposed in recent years[3].

Instead of the comprehensive search process for identification, pattern matching techniques by neural networks have drawn considerable attention in structural identification and control because of their ability to approximate arbitrary continuous function[4,5]. Modeling dynamic systems by using neural networks has been increasingly recognized as one of the system identification paradigms. Although several neural-network-based strategies are available for qualitative evaluation of damages [6,7], it was not until recently that a quantitative way of detecting damage with neural networks has been proposed. Wu et al. proposed a neural-network-based structural stiffness identification algorithm using macro-strain measurements[8]. Xu et al. proposed strategies for structural stiffness and damping coefficients identification or post-earthquake damage diagnosis using displacement, velocity measurements and excitation information with neural networks[9,10]. For large-scale structures, Yun et al. proposed a substructural identification algorithm using neural networks[11]. Xu et al.[12,13] and Wu et al.[14] also presented decentralized identification and control algorithms. Unlike any conventional system identification technique that involves the inverse analysis with an optimization process, those neural-network-based identification strategies proposed by Xu et al. [13] and Wu et al. [14] with the direct use of dynamic responses can give the identification results in a substantially faster way and thus provide a viable tool for the on-line identification of structural parameters. In this paper, aiming at a substructure of a MDOF structure, a soft substructural parametric identification algorithm with neural networks using dynamics responses under base excitations for post-earthquake damage diagnosis is proposed.

2 Substructural Post-earthquake Damage Diagnosis Strategy

The dynamic responses measurements of substructures under aftershocks following an earthquake are useful and economical information for the diagnosis of damage induced by the earthquake. The motion of a structure modeled as a mass-spring-dashpot system with n degrees of freedom under base excitation can be characterized by the following equation,

$$M\ddot{x} + C\dot{x} + Kx = -MI\ddot{x}_g \qquad (1)$$

where M, C and K = the mass, damping, and stiffness matrices of the structure, $\ddot{x}$, $\dot{x}$ and x = the acceleration, velocity, and displacement vectors, $\ddot{x}_g$ = the acceleration of the base excitation, and I is an unit matrix.

Usually, a multi-degree-of-freedom(MDOF) frame structure may be further divided into several substructures, which are connected with each other through interfaces or boundaries. Consider the object substructure shown in Fig. 1, which includes mass $p+1$ to mass q and interconnected with the upper boundary mass $q+1$ and lower boundary mass p. The lower boundary mass p is selected as a reference point and considered as the nominal ground for the substructure. The vector-matrix equation for the substructure can be written as

$$M_s\ddot{x}_s + C_s\dot{x}_s + K_sx_s = f_s \qquad (2)$$

where

$$M_s = \begin{bmatrix} m_{p+1} & 0 & 0 & 0 & 0 \\ 0 & \cdots & 0 & 0 & 0 \\ 0 & 0 & m_r & 0 & 0 \\ 0 & 0 & 0 & \cdots & 0 \\ 0 & 0 & 0 & 0 & m_q \end{bmatrix}, K_s = \begin{bmatrix} k_{p+1}+k_{p+2} & -k_{p+2} & 0 & 0 & 0 \\ -k_{p+2} & k_{p+2}+k_{p+3} & -k_{p+3} & 0 & 0 \\ 0 & \cdots & \cdots & \cdots & 0 \\ 0 & 0 & -k_{q-1} & k_{q-1}+k_q & -k_q \\ 0 & 0 & 0 & -k_q & k_q+k_{q+1} \end{bmatrix},$$

$$x_s = \begin{Bmatrix} x_{p+1} \\ \vdots \\ x_r \\ \vdots \\ x_q \end{Bmatrix}, \text{ and } f_s = \begin{Bmatrix} -m_{p+1}\ddot{x}_p \\ \vdots \\ -m_r\ddot{x}_p \\ \vdots \\ -m_q\ddot{x}_p + c_{q+1}\dot{x}_{q+1} + k_{q+1}x_{q+1} \end{Bmatrix}. \quad (3a\text{-}3d)$$

Cs is the same form as Ks except using c_r for k_r; x_r, $r=(p+1, q)$ is the relative displacement of each mass with respect to lower boundary of mass p; $\ddot{x}_p$ is the absolute acceleration of mass p. m_r, c_r, k_r, $r=(p+1, q)$ represent mass, damping and stiffness coefficient for mass r.

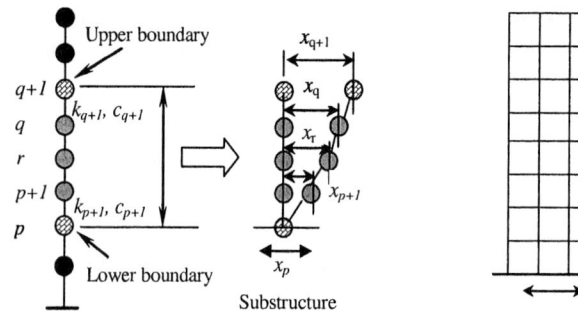
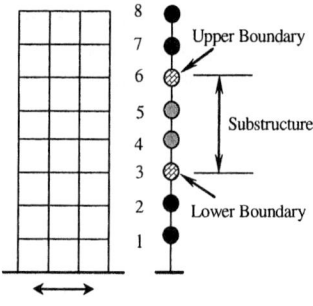

Fig. 1. A substructure in a MDOF system under base excitation

Fig. 2. A substructure in an eight stories frame structure

Equation (2) can be rewritten in state space as the following first-order vector differential equation

$$\dot{Z}_{s,t} = AZ_{s,t} + Bf_{s,t} \quad (4)$$

where the state vector Z_s and the system matrix A and B are defined as

$$Z_{s,t} = \begin{Bmatrix} \dot{x}_{s,t} \\ x_{s,t} \end{Bmatrix}, A = \begin{bmatrix} -M_s^{-1}C_s & -M_s^{-1}K_s \\ I & 0 \end{bmatrix}, \text{ and } B = \begin{bmatrix} M_s^{-1} \\ 0 \end{bmatrix}. \quad (5,6,7)$$

If the time interval t-t_0 in this equation is denoted by kT with T being time interval, the discrete time solution of the state equation can be written as

$$Z_{s,k} = e^{AT}Z_{s,k-1} + f_{s,k-1}\int_0^T e^{A\tau}Bd\tau, \ (k=1,\cdots,K) \quad (8)$$

where $Z_{s,k}$ and $Z_{s,k-1}$ are the state variables at time instants, kT and $(k\text{-}1)T$, respectively.

Consider a linear, viscously-damped eight stories frame structure shown in Fig. 2 whose substructure parameters are to be identified. The middle stories that include mass 4 to 5 and the upper boundary mass 6 and lower boundary mass 3 are considered as an object substructure.

To facilitate the identification process, a reference substructure and a number of associated substructures that have the same overall dimension and topology as the object substructure are created, and an emulator neural network(ENN) and a parameter evaluation neural network(PENN) are established and trained to identify the physical parameters of the object substructure. The basic three-step procedure for substructural post-earthquake damage diagnosis is shown in Fig. 3 and described in detail in the following context.

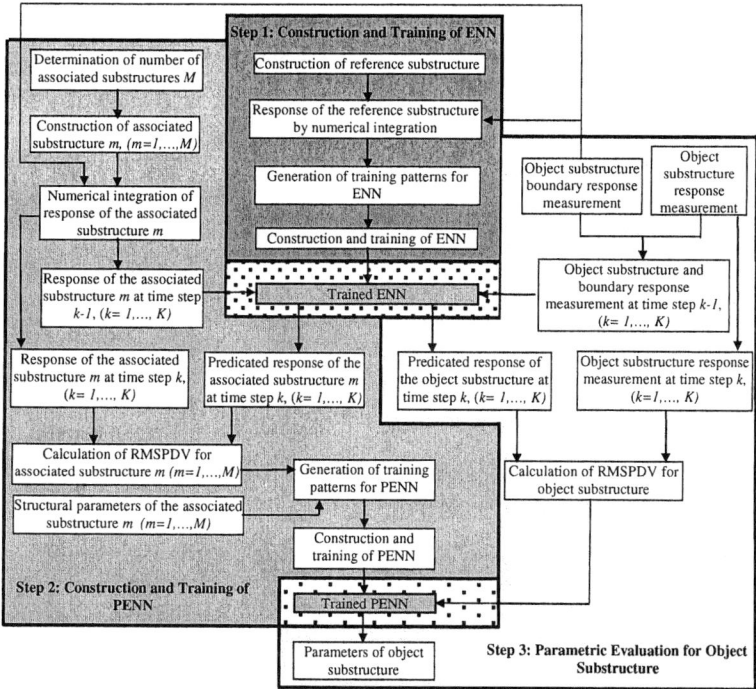

Fig. 3. Substructural post-earthquake damage diagnosis strategy based on neural networks

3 Nonparametric Substructural Identification with ENN

3.1 Rationality and Construction of ENN for the Reference Substructure

For the parametric identification of the structure in Fig.2, an eight stories frame structure with the following known parameters, mass $m_i=185kg$, inter-story stiffness $k_i=5.0*10^5 N/m$ and damping coefficient $c_i=2.0*10^3 N*s/m$ for each storey, is assumed to be the reference structure, which first four natural frequencies are 1.53 Hz, 4.53 Hz, 7.38 Hz and 9.97 Hz.

In Step 1, an ENN is constructed and trained using the responses of the reference substructure under the measured boundary excitations including the acceleration of the lower boundary and the relative displacement and velocity response of the upper boundary as shown in equation (3d). The ENN is treated as a non-parametric model of the reference substructure that acts as a baseline of the parametric identification for the object substructure. The construction of the ENN including the decision and selection the input and output variables and the number of neurons in the hidden layer is crucial. The mapping or function from the input to output should uniquely exist. From equation (8), it is clear that the state vector $Z_{s,k}$ is uniquely and fully determined by the state vector $Z_{s,k-1}$ and $f_{s,k-1}$. So, if the state vector $Z_{s,k}$ is treated as the output of an ENN, and state vector $Z_{s,k-1}$ and $f_{s,k-1}$ are selected as its inputs, the mapping between the inputs and outputs uniquely exists. Using the vibration time series of the reference substructure under the measured boundary excitation form numerical integration, the ENN can be trained until the difference between the state vector $Z_{s,k}$ at time step k and its output reach a very small value. The trained ENN can be used to forecast the structural state vector step by step as described in the following equation,

$$Z_{s,k}^f = ENN(Z_{s,k-1}, f_{s,k-1}), \text{ for } (k = 1,\ldots,K) \qquad (9)$$

where $Z_{s,k}^f$ is the forecast state vector at time step k by the trained ENN.

The architecture of the ENN constructed in this study is shown in Fig. 4. The input layer includes relative displacement and velocity responses of mass 4 to 6, and the absolute acceleration of the lower boundary (mass 3) at time step $k-1$. The number of neurons in hidden layer is twice the number of neurons in the input layer. The neuron in the output layer represents the forecast displacements of mass 4 to 5 at time step k. So the input, hidden and output layer includes 7, 14 and 2 neurons, respectively.

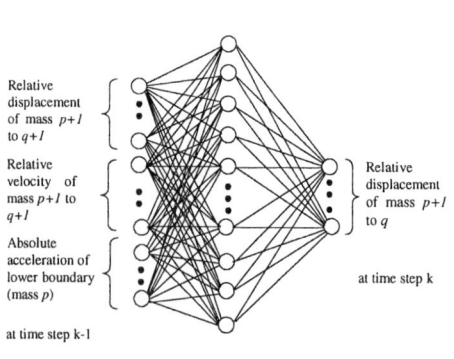

Fig. 4. Architecture of ENN for reference substructure

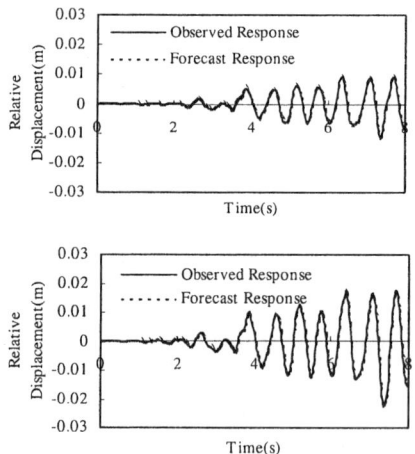

Fig. 5. Compression of relative displacements of the substructure

3.2 Training of ENN and Its Performance for Response Forecasting

As the first example, the Taft earthquake (July 21, 1952, Kern County) scaled with velocity amplitude of 0.30m/s (Case 1) is treated as the base excitation. The data sets for the ENN training are constructed from the numerical integration results under the measured boundary excitations including the acceleration of the lower boundary and the relative displacement and velocity response of the upper boundary. The numerical integration is carried out with integration time step of 0.002 second. The training data sets are performed with the data taken at the intervals of the sampling period of 0.04 second. The data sets used for training the neural networks are the 200 patterns taken from 8 seconds of response of the substructure. Generally, a neural network requires the normalization of the input and output data, because it is difficult to train a neural network without the normalization. In this study, a linear normalization preconditioning for the training data sets is carried out.

Based on the error back-propagation algorithm, the ENN is trained. At the beginning of training the ENN, the weights are initialized with small random values. Fig. 5 gives the comparison between the relative displacement responses determined from the numerical integration (called observed responses) and those forecast by the trained ENN of mass 4 and 5, respectively. It can be seen that the forecast relative displacement responses meet with the numerical integration results.

3.3 Evaluation Index Definition and Its Sensitivity

The difference between the dynamic response measured from a damaged substructure and the output from the trained ENN provides a quantitative measure of the structural physical parameters of the substructure relative to the reference substructure. A root mean square prediction difference vector (RMSPDV), e_s, is defined as an evaluation index for damage diagnosis of damaged substructure. The RMSPDV can be defined as follow:

$$e_s = \{e_1 \quad \cdots \quad e_j \quad \cdots \quad e_n\}, (j=1,\cdots n) \tag{10}$$

$$e_j = \sqrt{\frac{1}{K}\sum_{k=1}^{K}(x_k^f - x_k)^2} \tag{11}$$

where K= the number of sampling data; x_k^f and x_k represent the relative displacement responses forecast by the trained ENN and from the numerical integration of the substructure at time step k, respectively; n is the number of the neurons in the output layer of the ENN.

Let the stiffness of the substructure decrease to 90%, 80%, 70% of the original values of the reference substructure respectively, the components of RMSPDV corresponding to the relative displacement of mass 4 and 5 are shown in Table 1. It is shown that the RMSPDV increases with the degree of damage and is very sensitive to the variation of stiffness of the substructure. Moreover, the root-mean-square(RMS) of the difference between the two relative displacement responses of each mass of the reference structure shown in Fig. 5 can reach a very small value. Nonparametric identification by the trained ENN can be carried out with high accuracy.

Table 1. RMSPDV corresponding to the relative displacements of the substructure

	Components of RMSPDV ($*10^{-4}$ m)		Norm of RMSPDV	Change(%)[a]
	Mass 4	Mass 5		
Reference substructure	6.13	10.22	11.92	-
90% stiffness	9.15	16.29	18.68	56.78
80% stiffness	12.74	23.57	26.79	124.82
70% stiffness	16.12	30.06	34.10	186.22

[a] Change in norm of RMSPDV = 100×(Norm of RMSPDV of the substructure - Norm of RMSPDV of the reference substructure)/Norm of RMSPDV of the reference substructure.

4 Construction and Training of PENN for Substructure Damage Diagnosis

In Step 2, consider M associated substructures that have different structural parameters from the reference substructure in Step 1. On one hand, the relative displacement responses of an associated substructure m at time step k under the same boundary excitation as used in Step 1 for the reference substructure can be calculated with the numerical integration method. On the other hand, the relative displacement responses can be predicted from the ENN trained for the reference substructure. Since the parameters of the associated substructure differ from those of the reference substructure, it is expected that the predicted relative displacement responses are different from those computed by numerical integration.

Corresponding to the associated substructure m, the RMSPDV, $e_{s,m}$, can be determined. It is obvious that the e_m depends on the mass, stiffness and damping matrices of the associated substructure m. Because the mass usually does not change with the occurrence of damage, it is considered as a known constant. And the structural damping coefficients are also supposed to be constant in this study. Therefore, the $e_{s,m}$ is then completely determined by the stiffness parameters of the substructure and can be described by the general functional relation as follow:

$$e_{s,m} = f(K_{s,m}). \qquad (12)$$

If the inverse of the function in equation (12) is known, the structural parameters can be determined according to the e_m. For this purpose, the parametric evaluation neural network (PENN) is constructed and trained to describe the inverse function:

$$K_{s,m} = f^{-1}(e_{s,m}) = PENN(e_{s,m}) \qquad (13)$$

The inputs to the PENN include the components of the RMSPDV and their square of the substructure. The outputs are the stiffness parameters of the corresponding substructure. The architecture of the PENN is shown in Fig. 5. For the substructure shown in Fig. 2, the number of neurons in input, hidden and output layer is 4, 8 and 3 respectively.

For the purpose of training of the PENN, some associated substructures with different degree of damage are assumed, and the RMSPDVs are calculated with the help of the trained ENN. The stiffness of some assumed damaged substructures and the corresponding RMSPDVs are used to train the PENN. Let stiffness of each story of the substructure equals to 1.0, 0.9, and 0.8 times of the original value respectively, therefore, 27 associated substructures are constructed and 27 pairs of training data are determined.

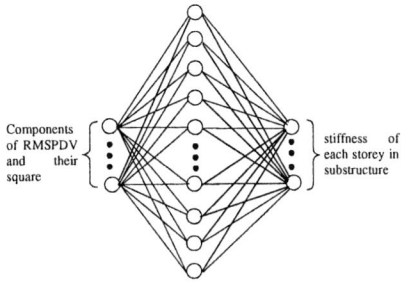

Fig. 5. Architecture of the PENN for substructural parametric identification

5 Substructural Damage Diagnosis with PENN and Adaptability

After the PENN has been successfully trained, it will be applied in Step 3 into the object substructure to forecast the structural parameters with RMSPDV determined from the trained ENN and the relative displacement measurements of the object substructure. Without loss of generality, the damage diagnosis results of three damaged substructures with different degree of stiffness reduction are shown in Table 2. From Table 2, it is clear that the inter-story stiffness parameters of the substructure can be forecasted accurately. The maximum relative errors between the forecasted stiffness and the true value of the selected damage scenarios are within 3%.

Table 2. Damage diagnosis results for substructures

Damaged Structures		Stiffness (10^6 N/m)			Average (%)
		k_4	k_5	k_6	
No. 1	Exact value	0.500	0.500	0.450	-
	Forecast value	0.504	0.491	0.455	-
	Relative error(%)[a]	0.80	1.80	1.11	1.24
No. 2	Exact value	0.450	0.450	0.450	-
	Forecast value	0.463	0.458	0.468	-
	Relative error(%)[a]	3.11	1.78	4.00	2.96
No. 3	Exact value	0.400	0.450	0.500	-
	Forecast value	0.390	0.445	0.483	-
	Relative error(%)[a]	2.50	0.89	3.40	2.26

[a] Relative error = 100×| (Forecast value-Exact value) /Exact value |.

A strong earthquake is usually followed by a number of aftershocks. The performance of the proposed algorithm for different base excitation is investigated. Two base excitations, El Centro earthquake (May 18, 1940, Imperial Valley) and Kobe earthquake (January 17, 1995, Hyogo-ken) scaled with velocity amplitude of 0.30m/s called Case 2 and 3, respectively, are considered.

With the procedure described in Fig. 1, two sets of ENN and PENN are trained for the above two base excitations independently and utilized to identify the damages of the substructure. Table 3 shows the substructural damage diagnosis results for the three assumed damaged structures. It is clear that the proposed algorithm also gives the damage diagnosis results with an average relative error within 5%.

Table 3. Damage diagnosis results for substructures under other base excitations

Damaged structures	Base excitation		Stiffness (10^6 N/m)			Average (%)
			k_4	k_5	k_6	
No. 1		Exact value	0.500	0.500	0.450	-
	Case 2	Forecast value	0.501	0.486	0.456	-
		Relative error(%)[a]	0.12	2.88	1.40	1.47
	Case 3	Forecast value	0.490	0.466	0.462	-
		Relative error(%)[a]	1.94	6.78	2.69	3.80
No. 2		Exact value	0.450	0.450	0.450	-
	Case 2	Forecast value	0.464	0.460	0.468	-
		Relative error(%)[a]	3.11	2.18	3.96	3.08
	Case 3	Forecast value	0.445	0.425	0.478	-
		Relative error(%)[a]	1.13	5.47	6.24	4.28
No. 3		Exact value	0.400	0.450	0.500	-
	Case 2	Forecast value	0.393	0.451	0.483	-
		Relative error(%)[a]	1.83	0.11	3.66	1.87
	Case 3	Forecast value	0.373	0.431	0.493	-
		Relative error(%)[a]	6.75	4.16	1.40	4.10

[a] Relative error = 100×| (Forecast value-Exact value) /Exact value) |.

6 Conclusions

A substructural parametric identification methodology for post-earthquake damage diagnosis with the direct use of dynamic responses by neural networks is proposed.

1. Based on the discrete time solution of the state space equation of a substructure, the rationality of the proposed methodology is explained and the theory basis for the construction of emulator neural network(ENN) and parametric evaluation neural network(PENN) are described.

2. An evaluation index called root-mean-square prediction difference vector (RMSPDV) is presented to evaluate the condition of the object substructure. Numerical simulations show that the RMSPDV is sensitive to the change in structural physical stiffness of the substructure. This characteristic is very beneficial for structural identification and damage diagnosis.

3. Based on the trained ENN and PENN, the inter-storey stiffness parameters of the object substructure are identified with enough accuracy. The adaptability of the proposed algorithm for different base excitation is demonstrated.

The methodology does not require any time-consuming eigenvalues or model extraction form measurement and has the potential of being a practical tool for pose-earthquake damage diagnosis for large-scale civil engineering structures. It is possible to apply this approach to whole structure identification if the required response measurements are available.

Acknowledgment

The author gratefully acknowledges the financial support from the Furong Scholar Program of Hunan provincial government and the "985 project" of the Center for Integrated Protection Research of Engineering Structures (CIPRES) at Hunan University, P.R. China.

References

1. Doebling, S.W., Farrar,C.R., Prime, M.B.: A Summary Review of Vibration-based Damage Identification Methods, Shock and Vibration Digest, 30(2) (1998) 91-105
2. Wu, Z.S., Xu, B. and Harada, T.: Review on Structural Health Monitoring for Infrastructure, Journal of Applied Mechanics, JSCE, 6 (2003) 1043-1054
3. Zhao, Q., Sawada, T., Hirao, K., Nariyuki, Y.: Localized Identification of MDOF Structures in the Frequency Domain, Earthquake Engineering and Structural Dynamics, 24 (1995) 325-338
4. Haykin, S.: Neural Networks: A Comprehensive Foundation. Prentice Hall, New Jersey, 2nd ed. (1999)
5. Rajapakse, J.C., Wang, L.P. (Eds.): Neural Information Processing: Research and Development. Springer, Berlin (2004)
6. Masri, S.F., Smyth, A.W., Chassiakos, A.G., Caughey, T.K., Hunter, N.F.: Application of Neural Networks for Diagnosis of Changes in Nonlinear Systems, Journal of Engineering Me-chanics, ASCE, 126(7) (2000) 666-676
7. Zhao, J., Ivan, John N., Dewolf T.: Structural Health Monitoring Using Artificial Neural Networks, Journal of Infrastructure Systems, 4(3) (1998) 93-101
8. Wu, Z.S., Xu, B.: A Real-time Structural Parametric Identification System Based on Fiber Optic Sensing and Neural Network Algorithms, Smart NDE and Health Monitoring of Structural and Biological Systems, SPIE 5047 (2003) 392-402
9. Xu, B., Wu, Z.S. Chen, G., Yokoyama, K.: Direct Identification of Structural Parameters from Dynamic Responses with Neural Networks, Engineering Applications of Artificial Intelligence, 17(8) (2004) 931-943
10. Xu, B., Wu, Z.S., Yokoyama, K., Harada, T., Chen, G.: A Soft Post-earthquake Damage Identification Methodology Using Vibration Time Series, Smart Materials and Structures, 14(3) (2005) s116-s124
11. Yun C.B., Bahng E.Y.: Substructural Identification Using Neural Networks, Computers and Structures, 77 (2000) 41-52
12. Xu, B., Wu, Z.S., Yokoyama, K.: Neural Networks for Decentralized Control of a Cable-stayed Bridge, Journal of Bridge Engineering, ASCE, 8(4) (2003) 229-236
13. Xu, B., Wu, Z.S., Yokoyama, K.: Decentralized Identification of Large-scale Structure-AMD Coupled System Using Multi-layer Neural Networks, Transactions of the Japan Society for Computational Engineering and Science, 2, (2000) 187-197
14. Wu, Z.S., Xu, B., Yokoyama, K.: Decentralized Parametric Damage Diagnosis Based on Neural Networks, Computer-Aided Civil and Infrastructure Engineering, 17 (2002) 175-184

Conceptual Modeling with Neural Network for Giftedness Identification and Education

Kwang Hyuk Im[1], Tae Hyun Kim[1], SungMin Bae[2], and Sang Chan Park[1]

[1] Department of Industrial Engineering,
Korea Advanced Institute of Science and Technology (KAIST),
373-1, Guseong-dong, Yuseong-gu, Daejeon 305-701, Korea
{gunni, imiss}@major.kaist.ac.kr, sangchanpark@kaist.ac.kr
[2] Department of Industrial & Management Engineering,
HANBAT National University,
SAN 16-1 Duckmyoung-Dong, Yuseong-Gu, Daejeon 305-719, Korea
loveiris@hanbat.ac.kr

Abstract. Today, gifted and talented education becomes an important part of school education. All school staff has increased awareness and knowledge about that. They develop a special program for identification of gifted student and a curriculum for them. In addition, existing gifted education pays too much attention to their curriculum, such as a curriculum compacting, acceleration, and an ability clustering. Currently, the identification of gifted student mainly depends on a simple identification test based on their age. But, the test results could not reveal the "potentially gifted" students. In this paper, we proposed a neural network model for identification of gifted student. With a specially designed questionnaire, we measure implicit capabilities of giftedness and cluster the students with similar characteristics. The neural network and data mining techniques are applied to extract a type of giftedness and their characteristics. To evaluate our model, we apply our model to the science and liberal art filed in Korea to identify gifted student and their type of giftedness.

1 Introduction

Recently, formal education is structured on the assumption of age related development and intellectual homogeneity. [1] It assumes that student's intellectual, emotional and social development depends on age. It denies the real existence of difference in intellectual, social and emotional development of student of similar chronological age. Also, gifted education has not been recognized as important part of the education.

In general, gifted education is only limited to a few "gifted" students because the frequency of its occurrence in the population is very low. Also, the most serious barrier to gifted education is the negative attitudes of teachers, parent of students who are not gifted and the education policy for homogenous education system. But, today, these negative situations have been changed slowly. As we mentioned before, all school staff has increased awareness and knowledge about gifted education and almost parents want to get a special school program for their children.

In this manner, the beginning of gifted education starts the identification of "potentially" gifted students. Traditionally, to identify the gifted students, the paper-based test was taken. The participants of that test should solve difficult and complex problems. For the students' immature of intellectual ability, the "real" gifted students might not pass the test. We lose a big chance.

To avoid this, we develop an easy and simple test for measuring implicit capabilities of giftedness and build a model for distinguishing gifted student from others using a neural network and data mining techniques. In addition, we identify a giftedness feature and classify the type of giftedness. Then, based on these results, we will suggest how to support educational program considering the type of giftedness and the feature of giftedness to the "potential" gifted students.

The paper is organized the following order. In a literature review section, we introduce a short review of gifted education and related researches such as an identification of gifted students and data mining application on educational field. In section 3, we propose a framework of identification of giftedness. After that, we will apply our model to the science and liberal art field in Korea to identify the gifted students. In section 5, we will conclude our paper and present a future research direction.

2 Literature Review

2.1 Gifted Education: A Short Review

In general, gifted education is composed of three parts. The first part is awareness and knowledge, the next is the identification of gifted students, and the third part refers to implementation of gifted programs, a supportive environmental and differentiated curriculum. [1]

To identify gifted students, many researches are divided into two categories: an explicit approach and an implicit approach. [2] In an explicit approach, researchers gather and analyze a number of data from a participant group. They define characteristics of giftedness under assumption that the group has specific characteristics of giftedness. In addition, it measures a degree of giftedness with a number of questions, a student answers correctly. On the other hand, an implicit approach identifies characteristics of giftedness which are not measured from traditional IQ test by investigating and analyzing implicit thinks which general people have. Even if it is difficult for the approach to be used for measuring characteristics of giftedness because of reliability, contents for explaining characteristics of giftedness are easy and simple.

In Queensland at Australia, almost school are using identification procedures which include the UNICORN Model of identification published by Education Queensland. The model uses the "bubble-up" method. The UNICORN model is composed of four stages. [3] But, it needs a teacher's observation of student and the well-designed checklists which are hard to develop. Michael Sayler developed the Gifted and Talented Checklist for Teachers and Parents. It is a recommended identification tool for Australian state schools. [4]

In a gifted education program, five components are considered in common; Thinking, Curriculum compacting, Subject Acceleration, Ability clustering, and Extension activities. [1] Thinking, which is used for curriculum planning, enables differentiation in content and strategies to match the different abilities and learning style of individual students. Curriculum compacting is a process used to streamline the regular curriculum. Subject Acceleration occurs when a student takes a single subject one or two years earlier. Ability clustering is used to build an ability class for specific subject. At last, extension activities include various programs such as individual program, think fest, and so on.

2.2 Data Mining Application on Educational Field

In the age of the Internet, the digital technology is being adapted to humans in education through four ways. [5] The most important trend among them is a shift from mass standardization of education toward mass customization – customizing both education and technology to individual learner needs and preferences. In this manner, almost data mining applications in educational field focus on a personalized education that analyze the learner's behavior and recommend a learning path for individual student.

Ha *et. al* [6] applied a Web mining to the distance education. They analyze a web access history and a user demographic data and recommend individual learning paths and aggregate learning path. Bae *et. al* [7] suggest a web-based distance learning system with a data mining module. The data mining module is used to recommend a new-comer's learning path. In a group learning area, Tang and Chan [8] suggested a novel group forming techniques using a data mining.

3 Identification of Gifted Students: Overall Framework

As we mentioned before, identification of gifted students plays an important role in the gifted education. Existing identification of gifted student only reveals the degree of giftedness. But, today, the degree of giftedness – such as IQ – is not enough. Other measures of giftedness such as EQ are proposed by many pedagogists and psychologists. In this section, as depicted figure 1, we propose a framework of identification of the gifted students based on data mining techniques to classify their type of giftedness and each group's characteristics.

The proposed questionnaire is to measure various implicit capabilities of giftedness such as scientific attitude, leadership, morality, creativity, challenge, and motivation of achievement. In the third step, we compare gifted students' data with average students' data and extract and refine features that distinguish gifted students from average students. The questionnaire and analysis results are stored in the database.

After that, to identify the types of giftedness, we divide group of students into several groups with a similar characteristics such as an interested field and their capabilities. Next, we identify each group's features and patterns of each types of giftedness. When the type of giftedness is decided, we classify extracted features of each group into common and distinct features. With these results, we could define characteristics of each type of giftedness.

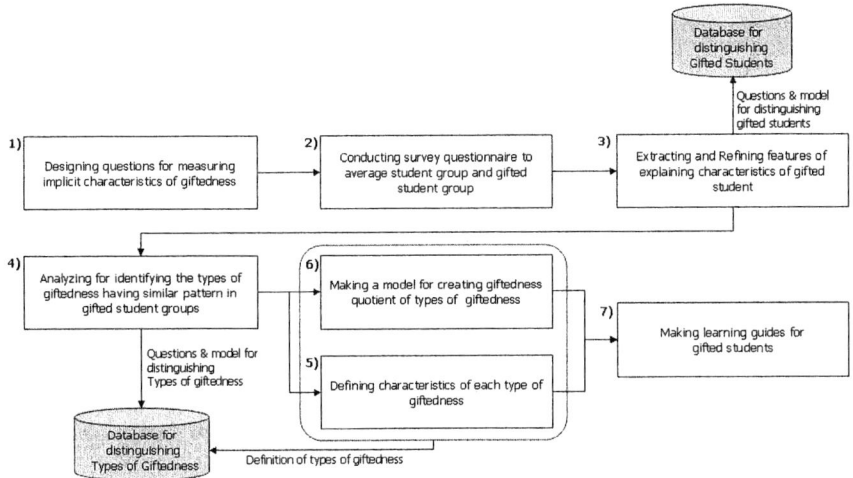

Fig. 1. Identification of Gifted Students: Overall Framework

In the sixth step, we build a model to create a giftedness quotient of type of giftedness. The giftedness quotient should be used to a measurement for evaluating similarity between students' characteristic and students' type of giftedness. In this manner, we could decide student's type of giftedness by comparing each student's giftedness quotients. Finally, we could improve a pertinent learning guide considering their giftedness features for developing capabilities of gifted students.

3.1 Design of Questionnaire

For designing an easy and simple questionnaire for students, we investigate implicit capabilities of giftedness. Implicit capabilities of giftedness are suggested by researchers such as Renzulli, Gardner, and Clark. [9, 10, 11] In the proposed questionnaire, we perform a pilot testing of the questionnaire to measure implicit capabilities of giftedness.

For verifying each question's effectiveness, we randomly select some students in the gifted student's group and average student's group and perform the identification test. With a one-way ANOVA test, we could examine each question's power of discrimination. With this result, the final questionnaire could be refined.

3.2 Clustering and Classification

The next step is a clustering and a classification. We divide the survey data into several clusters using k-means clustering algorithm. K-means clustering algorithm is a method for partition n object into k clusters by measuring cluster similarity. [12]

After that, we identify characteristics of each cluster. In this step, we use a classification tool – C4.5. [15] In general, classification tools are used to identify characteristics of each cluster and to build a model to predict clusters where unclassified data are classified. Decision tree based classification is obtained to a directed graph showing the possible sequences of questions, answers and classification. We can identify features and patterns for distinguishing a giftedness type from the others.

To realize the method, we must examine the most suitable number of type of giftedness as evaluating k value which has a high intra-cluster similarity value and a low inter-cluster similarity value in k-means algorithm. Also, with C4.5, we could select the features that distinguish a type of giftedness from another.

3.3 Creating a Giftedness Quotient Using Neural Network

A giftedness quotient could be a measurement for a similarity between student's characteristics and their type of giftedness. That is, if a student has a high giftedness quotient, we could assume the probability that the student belongs to the specific type of giftedness is high.

Creating a giftedness quotient using a neural network gives us two advantages. The first is that we could evaluate students' type of giftedness and distinguish the excellent students. The second advantage is that we could measure a significant degree of features in the type of giftedness.

As shown as figure 2, we use a back-propagation neural network for creating giftedness quotient. A neural network [12, 13] is a set of connected input and output nodes where each connection has a weight associated with it. We build a neural network model which consists of n input for n questions, one output value between 1 and 100 and one hidden layer which has m hidden node. The hidden layer has $n \times m$ weight vector which connect between each input and hidden node. The number of hidden node is known to double or triple of input node. In our model, sigmoid function is used to threshold activation function and output node's activation function uses a linear function. The following is the procedure for building the neural network model for creating giftedness quotient.

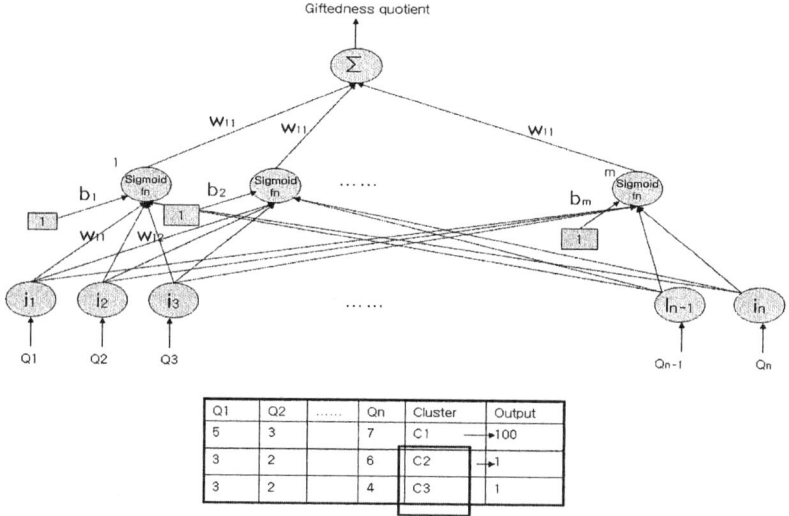

Fig. 2. Neural Network Model for Creating Giftedness Quotient

We choose a specific type of giftedness in interested field such as science, liberal art, and so on. Let's assume that we choose Type X in science filed.

1. We randomly select a part of survey data and give a target output value to 100 if type of giftedness of cluster that selected data belongs to is a Type X, otherwise to 1. In figure 2, target output value of cluster C1 is 100 because type of giftedness of cluster C1 is Type X and that of the others are 1.
2. With a back-propagation algorithm, we revise error of the data between output value evaluated by neural network and its target output value until error is less than termination criteria.
3. When training of neural network is terminated, we can obtain neural network model for creating giftedness quotient. If giftedness quotient of a student is close to 100, we can classify the student to Type C in science field.

Based on our model, we can measure significant degree of the features because we can calculate variation of output value when one question is increased or decreased in input node.

4 Applications

To implement our neural network model, we developed an on-line identification system to distinguish gifted students and to identify their type of giftedness. In figure 3, the identification system has two types of test; a general test of identification and a specific test of identification.

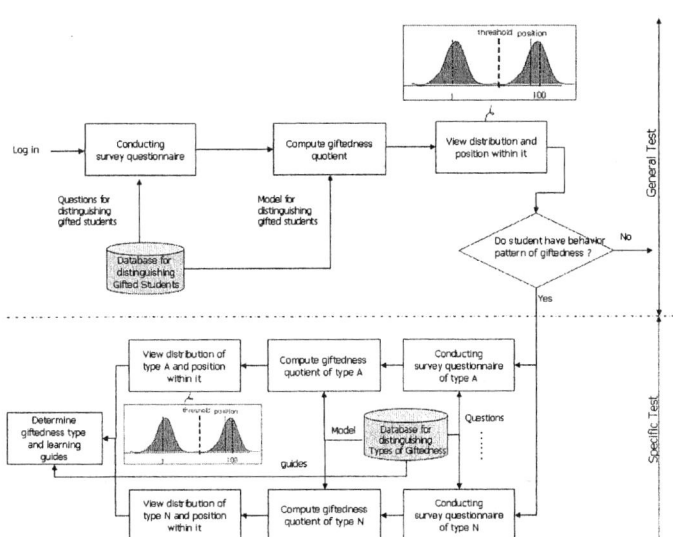

Fig. 3. On-line Identification System is composed of General test and Specific test

When participant logs in the system, a general test of identification begins. Based on his or her answers, we compute a participant's giftedness quotient and view participant's position on distribution. If participant's giftedness quotient is more than a specific threshold value, we decide a participant to a gifted student.

After the general test, it gives various questionnaires retrieved in the database for identifying participant's type of giftedness and computes a giftedness quotient for each giftedness type. Then, it shows characteristics of giftedness type and a learning guide. We applied our identification system to the two giftedness fields, science and liberal art field in Korea.

4.1 General and Specific Test: Identifying of Giftedness and Their Type

To extract the implicit capabilities of giftedness, we organize an advisory committee which consists of scientists, professors, teachers and parents of students. We choose 7 implicit capabilities such as Scientific attitude, Leadership, Motivation of achievement, Morality, Creativity, Challenge and General ability. Based on results, we compose 77 questions for measuring implicit capabilities of giftedness. Then, we conduct the survey to 130 students in high school, 280 students in the science high school (science field) and 183 students in the foreign language high school (liberal art field). We identify features of ordinary type, features and patterns of all giftedness type related in each giftedness field. We obtained four giftedness types for each field and select 34 features which explain giftedness types using clustering and classification techniques. We use k-means as clustering algorithm and C4.5 as classification tool.

We discover eight giftedness types which have similar pattern (features and their values) and select features identifying them. As shown in figure 4, we could present the pattern of giftedness types with 7 feature sets. The ratio of each type means a

Fields	Giftedness Type	Giftedness Pattern	Ratio of each Type to Total
Science	Type A		34.8
	Type B		22.13
	Type C		38.93
	Type D		3.69
Liberal Art	Type E		42.86
	Type F		18.18
	Type G		12.99
	Type H		21.43

Fig. 4. Characteristics and patterns of giftedness type (f1: scientific attitude, f2: leadership, f3: motivation of achievement, f4: morality, f5: creativity, f6: challenge, f7: general ability).

number of gifted students, who belong to each giftedness type, to the total number of gifted students in given field. For example, giftedness type C is the most common type of gifted students in the science field.

We define an eight giftedness type and it has different values of feature sets. For example, type D has high f2 (leadership), f5 (creativity) value and low f1 (scientific attitude), f7 (challenge) values. The others are zero. With this result, we could provide a learning guide that could maximize their creativity and leadership. In addition, we could stimulate them in their scientific attitude and challenge and encourage their motivation of achievement, morality and general ability.

4.2 Evaluating the Result of Identification Test

To evaluate the result of identification test, we compare average students and gifted students in science field distinguished by our model. As shown in Table 1, the test category is composed of four types of capabilities – memorization, cognition, logic, and evaluation.

We perform a significant test to examine the difference between gifted students group and average students group using one-way ANOVA analysis. If a significant test is performed by $\alpha=0.05$ and p-value is less than 0.001, then the null hypothesis is not accepted. That is, we could say that there exists a significant difference between two groups.

Table 1 shows the results of ANOVA analysis for four types of capabilities. Because p-values of four capabilities is less than 0.001, we could confirm that the difference between gifted students group and average stduents group is exist. That is, it shows that gifted students distinguished by our model have more capabilities than average students in fileds of Memorization, Cognition, Logic, Evaluation.

Table 1. Results of ANOVA analysis for four types of Capabilities

	Memorization			Cognition			Evaluation			Logic		
	Mean Square	F	p-value	Mean Square	F	p-value	Mean Square	F	p-value	Mean Square	F	p-value
Between Groups	0.734	52	<0.001	1.371	122	<0.001	3.900	214	<0.001	0.974	67	<0.001
Within Groups	0.014			0.011			0.018			0.015		

5 Conclusions

In this paper, we proposed a neural network model for giftedness identification. We measure the implicit capabilities of giftedness with a specially designed questionnaire and classify the students with their type of giftedness. Data mining techniques such as clustering and classification is applied to extract the type of giftedness and their characteristics. The neural network is used to evaluate the similarity between characteristics of student and type of giftedness. The gifted quotient is gained from the trained neural network.

To evaluate our model's effectiveness, we apply our model to the science and liberal art filed in Korea. The evaluation test's results show that there exist various types of gifted students and they have different characteristics. If we can exactly identify student's type of giftedness, we can support pertinent learning guide for maximizing their strong capabilities and encouraging their weak capabilities. In the future, we could refine our identification model using various data mining techniques and develop an intelligent learning guide system for "potential" gifted students.

References

1. Ken Imison, The acceptance of difference: Report on the review of gifted and talented education in Queenslands state school, Education Queeensland (2001)
2. Renzulli, J. S., Smith, L., Two approaches to identification of gifted students, Exceptional Children, Vol. 43 (1977) 512-518
3. Education Queensland Report, A Model for Curriculum Provisions for Gifted Education and Talent Development, Education Queensland (2000)
4. Dept. of Education and Arts, Framework for Gifted Education, Queensland Government (2004)
5. Hilary McLellan, Being Digital: Implications for Education, Educational Technology, Vol. 36, No. 6 (1996) 5-20
6. Sung Ho Ha, SungMin Bae, Sang Chan Park, Web Mining for distance education, In Proceedings of ICMIT (2000) 715 – 719
7. SungMin Bae, Sung Ho Ha, Sang Chan Park, Web-based distance learning system for Gifted: Applying interactive multimedia, In Proceedings of Asia-Pacific Advanced Network (APAN) Consortium (2000) 1-5
8. Tiffany Y. Tang, Keith C. Chan, Feature Construction for Student Group Forming based on their browsing behaviors in an E-learning system, Lecture Notes in Computer Science, Vol. 2417 (2002) 512-521
9. Renzulli, J. S., The Identification and Development of Giftedness as a Paradigm for School Reform, Journal of Science Education and Technology, Vol. 9 No.2 (2000) 95-114
10. Gardner, H., Intelligence Reframed: Multiple Intelligences for the 21st Century, Basic Books (2000)
11. Clark, B., Growing up gifted: Developing the Potential of Children at Home and at School. 6rd edn. Prentice Hall, New York (2001)
12. Jiawei Han, Micheline Kamber, Data mining – concepts and techniques, Morgan Kaufmann (2001)
13. Haykin, S., Neural Networks – a comprehensive foundation, Prentice Hall (1999)
14. Mitchell, T. M., Machine Learning, McGraw-Hill Companies (1997)
15. Quinlan, J. R., C4.5: Programs for Machine Learning, Morgan Kaufmann (1993)

Online Discovery of Quantitative Model for Web Service Management

Jing Chen[1,2], Xiao-chuan Yin[1], and Shui-ping Zhang[1]

[1] Telecommunication Engineering Institute, Air Force Engineering University,
Xi'an 710077, P.R. China
[2] Institute of Computer System Architecture and Network,
Xian Jiaotong University, Xian 710049, P.R. China
jingchen@263.net

Abstract. Due to the existence of strong correlation between database metrics and response times, an online discovery quantitative models system of web service management with the linear least-squares regression algorithms was proposed. The model used the stepwise linear regression algorithms to choose a particular subset from the numerous metrics as the explanatory variables of the model, so it can be updated continuously in response to the changes made in provider configurations and the evolution of business demands. The simulation experiment for Oracle Universal Database under a TPC-W workload chose three most influential metrics that weight 66% of the variability of response time.The results show that the effectiveness of quantitative model constructing system and model constructing algorithms.

1 Introduction

To ensure the provided quality of web service, the service client jointly with the service provider should define a service level agreement (SLA)[1] as a part of a service contract that can be monitored with web service management by one or both parties. The same service may be offered at different service levels (in terms of responsiveness, availability, throughput) and priced accordingly. So web service management system requires preferably quantitative models that determine if the web service in a safe operating region, early detect SLA violations, and on-going optimize the configurations of performance. This paper presents the online discovery of quantitative models for web service management based on the linear least-squares regression algorithms. The approach can construct the quantitative models real-time without prior knowledge of the managed elements, and it should be generic in that it discovers the explanatory variables to use.

2 Construction of Quantitative Models

Definition of a quantitative model: In service management, for predicting important SLA parameter y, we select several (m) variables ($x_1, x_2, ..., x_m$ in general) from a set of candidate variables $\{x_1, x_2, ..., x_n\}$, and establish the quantitative relation model between y and $x_1, x_2, ..., x_m$. This model is called quantitative model. And the process is called the construction of the quantitative model. We refer y as the response variable and $x_i(1 \leq i \leq m)$ as the explanatory variables and $x_i(1 \leq i \leq n)$ as the candidate variables. Constructing algorithm of the quantitative model is dependent on the modeling techniques employed. Taken Oracle as the resource, [2] has displayed the absolute values of the correlation coefficients between the DB2 Universal Database metrics and the probed client response times. Therefore, this paper employs the linear regression model[3,4], which is widely used to solve real world problems, less computational intensive and more suitable for on-line model operation. The general form of the linear regression model is

$$y = b_0 + b_1 x_1 + b_2 x_2 + \cdots + b_m x_m$$

The model relates the explanatory variables $x_i(1 \leq i \leq m)$ to the response variable y through model parameters $b_i(1 \leq i \leq m)$. For linear regression, knowing explanatory variable $x_i(1 \leq i \leq m)$ and corresponding sample data, it is easy to find the model parameter $b_i(1 \leq i \leq m)$ using least-squares method.

2.1 Construction Algorithm of the Quantitative Models

Our linear quantitative model takes response times as the response variables. The key is how to determine a small number of metrics to use as explanatory variables out of the multitudinous Oracle metrics. Therefore, we employ multiple linear regression analytical method and stepwise regression member choice method as the algorithm of building quantitative models.

There are four ways for member choice in common use, we employ the stepwise regression as our member choice method. This method is formed from improving the choosing forward method. It basically selects the independent variables forward, and at the same time it eliminates the subordinate variables newly discovered. Whenever a new independent variable is selected into the equation, every independent variable will be tested through partial F prominence and those losers would be deleted from the equation, and the equation is re-imitates with the remaining independent variables. The process continues until no more variables in the candidates can be selected or deleted according to the given prominence.

2.2 The Steps of the Stepwise Regression Algorithm

Based on above definition of the quantitative models and the algorithm ideas, we present the idiographic steps below.

Input: The set of candidate independent variables CandidateMetrics. Response variable is ResponseVariable; such as response time ResponseTime.

Output: The set of explanatory variables ExplanatoryVariables; Quantitative models.

1) Initialization.
   (a) Set CandidateMetrics to set of independent variables obtained from the Managed Element.
   (b) Set ResponseVariable to the response variable for the model.
   (c) Set ExplanatoryVariable to null.
2) Find first independent variable that best explain ResponseVariable.
   (a) Compute the cross correlation of each independent variable in set CandidateMetrics with ResponseVariable.
   (b) Set BestMetric to the independent variable with largest absolute value of the cross correlation.
   (c) Remove BestMetric from CandidateMetrics.
   (d) Append BestMetric to ExplanatoryVariable.
   (e) Build the regression model of ResponseVariable on ExplanatoryVariable with least-squares method.
3) Select into new explanatory variables and execute stepwise regression
   (a) Compute the partial F statistic of each independent variable in the set CandidateMetrics.
   (b) Set BestMetric to the independent variable with largest partial F statistic.
   (c) Remove BestMetric from CandidateMetrics.
   (d) If BestMetric does not pass the partial F prominence test, then end.
   (e) Append BestMetric to ExplanatoryVariable.
   (f) Build the regression model of ResponseVariable on ExplanatoryVariable with least-squares method.
   (g) Execute partial F prominence test on each explanatory variable in the set ExplanatoryVariable.
   (h) If the set of explanatory variables that don't pass the partial F prominence test is null, go to k).
   (i) Remove explanatory variables that don't pass the partial F prominence test from ExplanatoryVariable.
   (j) Re-imitate the regression equation of ResponseVariable on ExplanatoryVariable with ExplanatoryVariable.
   (k) If the set CandidateMetrics is null, then end; else go to 3)(a).

The algorithm does not consider all 2^{n-1} possible models (where n is the number of the metrics provided by the managed element), rather, it incrementally selects the best independent variable. This simplifies the computation and makes it suitable for on-line discovery. And, at the same time that it selects a new independent variables into the regression equation, it removes the subordinate variables newly discovered, so that the regression equation imitates data better, and we can use quantitative models to predicting better. Moreover, the set of candidate variables can also include several second powers, third powers or crossers of the independent variables.

3 Simulation Experiment

The managed resource in the simulation experiment is the Oracle9i database management system running on a Windows platform. The response variable is response time measured by an simulation software of JAVA implementation based on TPC-W Benchmark. The software is used as the workload generator through modulating the number of emulated browsers (EB) and also the Oracle9i parameters. The final quantitative model is:

$$ResponseTime(s) = 6.2328 * ApplsExccutingThreadsInDBCurrently - 643.2584 * DBBufferPoolSize(MB) + 6.9944 * 10^4$$

To evaluate data imitation veracity of the regression models, we employ the widely used r^2 [5] metric . We can find that for our model $r^2 = 0.66$, showing that the model established imitates 66% of the variability in the data, that is a fine imitation degree. Since the workload variation is mainly caused by varying the number of emulated browsers, the number of threads executing currently is identified as most important. The other is also relevant because buffer pools impact directly on I/O times for the database files and sort area influences searching efficiency. The relative importance of these metrics is consistent with the expectations of experienced database administrators.

4 Conclusion

Quantitative models have considerable value in distributed service performance management. This paper propose an approach to on-line discovery of quantitative models without prior knowledge to managed elements. A subset of these metrics were selected as the explanatory variables through the linear least-squares regression algorithm then the quantitative model was built. The system taken database system Oracle , which has the most quotient in market, as examples. we demonstrated the approach through estimating the response times with TPC-W workload.

References

1. Chen Jing, Li Zeng-zhi.Research and Implementation of SLA-Driven Distributed Service Management[J].Journal of Beijing University of Posts and Telecommunications, 2004, 27(6): 11-15.
2. Yixin Diao, Frank Eskesen. Generic On-Line Discovery of Quantitative Models for Service Level Management. Proceedings of 2003 IEEE Conference on Integrated Management.
3. Frank E.Harrell.Regression Modeling Strategies:With Applications to Linear Models,Logistic Regression,and Survival Analysis(Springer Series in Statistics).Springer Verlag,2001.
4. Carl Rhodes and Manfred Morari.Determining the model order of nonlinear input.output systems.AIChE Journal,pages 151-163,1998
5. Jing Chen, Zeng-zhi Li.Distributed Service Management Based on Genetic Programming[J].AWIC 2005 Conference LNAI(3528) Proceedings, 2005 : 83-88.

Judgment of Static Life and Death in Computer Go Using String Graph

Hyun-Soo Park[1], Kyung-Woo Kang[2], and Hang-Joon Kim[3]

[1] Department of Computer Information Technology, Kyungdong College of Techno-Information, 224-1, Buho, Hayang, Kyungpook, Korea
hspark@kdtc.ac.kr
[2] Department of Computer and Communication Engineering, Cheonan University, 115, Anseo-dong, Cheonan 330-704, Choongnam, Korea
kwkang@infocom.chonan.ac.kr
[3] Department of Computer Engineering, Kyungpook National University, 1370 Sankyuk-dong, Book-gu, Daegu, Korea
kimhj@kyungpook.ac.kr

Abstract. A String Graph(SG) and Alive String Graph(ASG) were defined to facilitate a static analysis of completed and counted games of Go. For the judgment of life and death, rules are applied to the situation where a stone is included and not included, and these rules are defined as a String Reduction (SR), Empty Reduction (ER), Edge Transform (ET), and Circular Graph (CG) when the stone is not included, and a Dead Enemy String Reduction (DESR) and Same Color String Reduction (SCSR) when the stone is included. Whether an SG is an ASG or not is then determined using these rules. The performance of the proposed method was tested using a problem set of games played by professional players, and all the games had been played to completion and counted. The experiment determined the error on the judgment of life and death. The test was performed on the final positions of the 20 games. The total number of stones was 5,367 and the number of strings was 772. The experimental results produced a very low error ratio for the judgment of static life and death, where the error ratio for the stones was 0.18% and that for the strings was 1.16%.

1 Introduction

Go is a two-person perfect information game played between two players, Black and White, who alternately place a stone of their own color on an empty intersection of a 19 by 19 grid. The goal of the game is to occupy a larger area than the opponent. The determination of life and death for groups are fundamental tasks in Go, and determining whether strings are alive is very important and difficult. The life of strings can be proven by a good static evaluation, which can speed up a search and increase efficiency [3].

David B. Benson [1] previously studied unconditionally alive strings of stones. Such strings can never be captured, not even by an arbitrary number of successive opponent moves. Popma and Allis [4] proposed the notion of an 'X life' – passing X times by the defense, the group can still live. Wolf [5] investigated life and death problems using a tree search. He used a depth first search with an unlimited depth, so there is no evaluation function that terminates the search. As such, a search is only terminated when the position either lives safe or when it is dead. Wolf's program is GoTools that has 35 different heuristics and subroutines, which try to determine whether a position is alive or dead as early as possible. Meanwhile, Muller[2] introduced static rules and methods based on a local search to detect groups of strings that are safe under the usual alternating play, where the defender is allowed to reply to the attacker's moves. Muller defined Benson's Sure Liberty Count as

$$\forall b \in B \sum_{r \in R} SLC_{Benson}(b, r, B) \geq 2. \qquad (1)$$

K. Chen and Z. Chen developed a static life and death analysis for general classes of groups without the involvement of 'ko'.

However, this article describes a static evaluation method using a String Graph that has strings, empty and relational. As such, the intuitional life of strings is presented using a String Graph. In addition, the life and death status of strings and groups is investigated via a static evaluation.

The structure of this paper is as follows. Section 2 describes a String Graph of strings for relationship and Rules, then section 3 presents some experiments and analysis, while section 4 outlines some remaining problems and future work.

2 String Graph (SG) and Rules

A string is the basic unit to be eliminated on the board. A board position is represented by a board graph that has the structure of an $N \times N$ square grid. The board graph $G_B = (V,E)$ defines an undirected graph $G_B \in G_u$. The symmetric binary 'edge' relation $E = \{e_1,...,e_n\}$ with $e_i \in \{\{v, v'\}: v, v' \in V\}$ represents the vertical or horizontal neighborhood between points. G_B is defined following Definition 1.

Definition 1. Let $G_B = (V,E)$ be a graph to represent the state of a Go board. Then,

$V = \{ (i, j) \mid 1 \leq i, j \leq 19 \}$,
$E = \{ ((i, j), (i', j')) \mid (i = i' \land |j - j'| = 1) \lor (|i - i'| = 1 \land j = j') \}$, and
$f : V \rightarrow \{ \text{black, white, empty}\}$

A string of black stones is represented by BS, while a string of white stones is represented by WS, and an empty string is represented by ES. A String Graph $G_{SG} = (V,E)$ consists of two sets: a finite set V of elements called vertices and a finite set E of elements called edges. Each edge is associated with an ordered pair of vertices. The symbols $v_0, v_1, v_2, ...$ are used to represent the vertices, while the symbols $e_0, e_1, e_2,...$ are used to represent the edges of a String Graph.

A String Graph is a directed and undirected graph. As such, an undirected edge e_u is adjacent to two vertices, while a directed edge e_d is included in a relationship between two vertices. A string is then expressed by a directed edge if it is completely surrounded by empty points or another string.

Fig. 1. (a) Example of directed edge. ES1 is surrounded by BS (b) Example of undirected edge. ES1 is adjacent to BS1 and BS2.

Definition 2. Let $e_d = (v_i, v_j)$ be a directed edge if v_i completely surrounds v_j.

BS represents a black string, WS is a white string and ES is an empty string. The left side of Figure 1 (a) shows an example of a directed edge, where ES1 completely surrounds BS1. Meanwhile, the right side of Figure 1 (a) shows a String Graph of the left side.

Definition 3. Let $e_u = (v_i, v_j)$ be an undirected edge if v_i is adjacent to v_j.

An undirected edge exists if a string and an empty point are adjacent to another empty point. The left side of Figure 1 (b) shows an example of an undirected edge, where ES1 is adjacent to BS1. Meanwhile, the right side of Figure 1 (b) shows a String Graph of the left side.

2.1 Stones Not Included

The left side of Figure 2 shows an example of an alive string, where ES1 and ES2 are completely included in BS1. As such, this string is unconditionally alive, and the right side shows a String Graph of the left side. Figure 2 is the prototype of alive. An Alive String Graph(ASG) is defined as having at least two directed edges.

In the directed graph in Figure 2, the initial vertex is BS1 and terminal vertices are ES1 and ES2. The properties of this graph are no self-loop and parallel edges and the initial vertex is always a BS or WS, while the terminal vertex is always an ES. The out degree of the initial vertex is at least 2. This graph means that number and shape of the internal empty points for the terminal vertex do not matter.

Rule (String Reduction). A reduction occurs when an ES exists between the same color vertices, in which case the ES is reduced to a new vertex, denoted by a Link Vertex (LV).

A group can be guaranteed a complete life based on the empty spaces left to share. The example shows that ES1 is included in BS1 and ES4 is included in BS3, yet BS1 is not only alive due to ES1 and BS3 is not only alive due to ES4. As such, ES2 and ES3 also play an important role for the alive group, the black string. In Figure 3 (c), a string reduction occurs, where BS1 and ES2 and BS2 are made into new vertices. A new vertex is denoted by a Link Vertex (LV). LV1 and ES3 and BS3 are then reduced

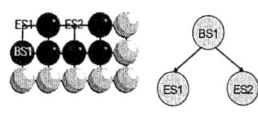

Fig. 2. Prototype of ASG(Alive String Graph). Alive BS1 represented by string

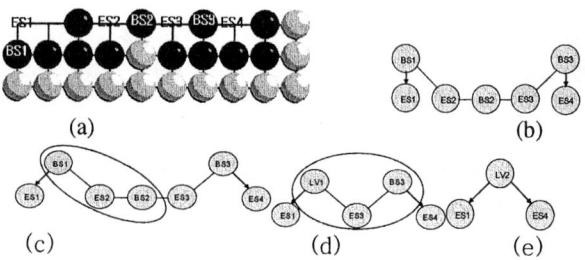

Fig. 3. Example of String Reduction : (a) board graph, (b) String Graph, (c) and (d) the process of String Reduction, and (e) Alive String Graph.

again to LV2 by the string reduction in figure 3 (d). The graph in figure 3 (e) is an ASG(Alive String Graph). Finally, the black group is alive.

Rule (Empty Reduction). The empty vertices resulting from a string reduction are reduced to new empty vertices.

Rule (Edge Transform). Among the resulting reduced empty vertices, if an ES is only adjacent to the same color vertices, then an undirected edge is transformed into a directed edge.

In figures 4 (c) and (d), a string reduction is performed, while in figure (f), an empty reduction occurs, and in figure 4 (g), an edge transform is performed. In figure 4 (h), the graph is an ASG. The empty points(vertices) are reduced to new empty vertices and the undirected edge is transformed into a directed edge.

Rule (Circular Check). If a finite alternating sequence of vertices and undirected edges $v_0, e_1, v_1, e_2, \ldots, v_{k-1}, e_k, v_k$ is a walk and a trail and a closed in a String Graph G_{SG}, it is a circular graph and unconditionally alive.

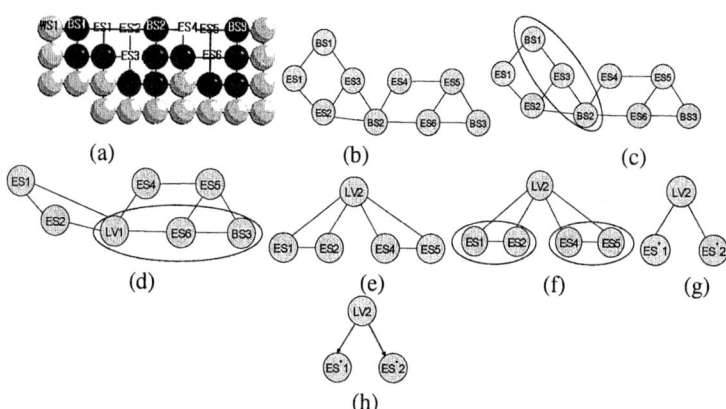

Fig. 4. Example of Empty Reduction and Edge Transform : Board Graph (b) String Graph (c) (d) the process of String Reduction (e) the result of String Reduction (f) the process of Empty Reduction (g) the precess of Edge Transform (h) Alive String Graph.

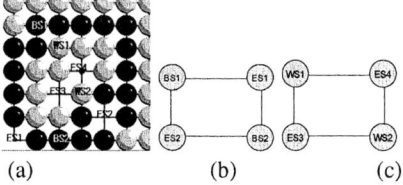

(a) (b) (c)

Fig. 5. Example of Circular Graph : (a) board graph, (b) and (c) Circular Graph

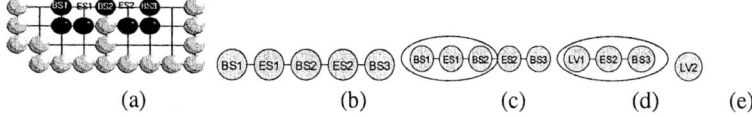

(a) (b) (c) (d) (e)

Fig. 6. No circular and dead (a) Board Graph, (b) String Graph, (c) and (d) The process of String Reduction, and (e) The result of String Reduction.

False eyes are not a real area but rather connect points. In figure 5 (a), BS1 and BS2 is a group with ES1 and ES2. WS1 and WS2 is another group with ES3 and ES4. ES1 and ES2 are false eyes, as the BS group looks like it is not alive, yet the BS and WS groups are both alive, as BS1 and BS2 are circularly linked to ES1 and ES2.

Thus, a finite alternation sequence of vertices and undirected edges, defined as a walk and a tail and a closed, is a circular graph and unconditionally alive.

In Figure 6, since the false eyes, ES1 and ES2, are not circular, ultimately the graph is not an ASG, i.e. not alive. BS1 and BS3 are blocked and the resulting string is in atari and vulnerable to capture by white. Another false eye results in an LV in figure 3, thereby securing the life of the group. An LV and circular false eye are very important for a safe group.

2.2 Included Stones

In figure 7, the black string, BS1, produces an ASG. ES2 and WS1 are included in BS1 and adjacent to each other. ES1 is included in BS1 separately. (b) shows an SG and a dead enemy string reduction is performed in (c) and ES2 and WS1 turn into a new vertex, ES'2. The graph is an ASG in (d).

Rule (Dead Enemy String Reduction). If a dead enemy string is included and adjacent to an included-empty in a string, then it is reduced to a new empty string.

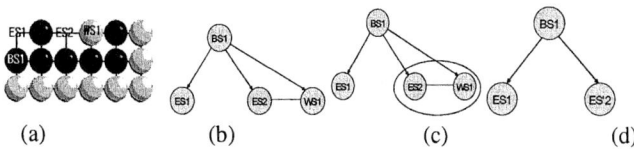

(a) (b) (c) (d)

Fig. 7. Dead Enemy Strings Reduction : (a) Board String, (b) String Graph, (c) the process of Dead Enemy Strings Reduction, and (d) Alive String Graph.

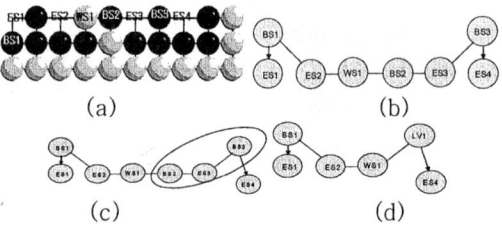

Fig. 8. Example of a Group with enemy String : (a) Board Graph (b) String Graph (c) The process of String Reduction (d) The result of String Reduction.

For another example, in figure 8, BS1 and BS2 are disconnected by WS1 that is adjacent to ES2. ES1 is included in BS1 that has a directed edge. Also, BS3 has a directed edge into ES4. In figure 8 (c), a string reduction is performed to make a new vertex, LV1. Yet, WS1 is not included in BS1 and another reduction is not performed. Eventually, the black group, BS1, BS2, and BS3, is not an ASG and not alive.

In other cases, a string has the same color string and an enemy string. A same color string reduction is performed if the same color string and two more empty strings are included in a string. In figure 9, (b) is an SG and a string reduction is performed in (c). In the end, (d) is completed and ES', BS2, and ES3 are included in BS1 and adjacent to each other. As such, the graph is alive due to a same color string reduction. Although the black string is safe, the area is not territory, because WS1 can still make seki by playing at ES4.

Rule (Same Color String Reduction). If a same color string and more than two empty strings are included in a string, then the string is alive.

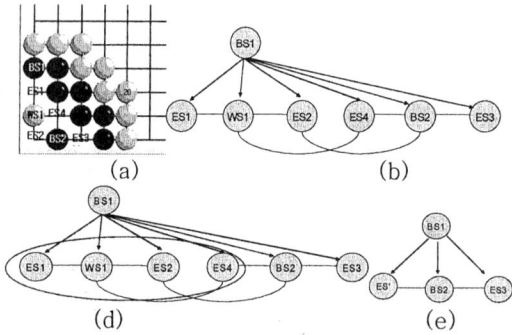

Fig. 9. Example of SCSR(Same Color String Reduction): (a) Board Graph (b) String Graph (c) the process of Dead Enemy Strings Reduction (d) the process of Same Color String Reduction (e) Alive String Graph.

2.3 Articulation Points and Stability Definition

If the internal empties in a string include more than two articulation points[7], a string is unconditionally alive. These points are vital points that make eyes. If an enemy plays at such points, the string is dead. Therefore, articulation points at internal empties in a string are very important. In figure 11, ES2 and ES3 are articulation points, as such, the black string is alive because it has two articulation points.

Rule (APC: Articulation Point Check). If the internal empties in a string have more than two articulation points, a string is alive.

Accordingly, the present method is a heuristic algorithm based on the definition of the stability of strings by Hyun Soo Park [6]. Namely, the basic definition of stability and the present definition are applied to the game.

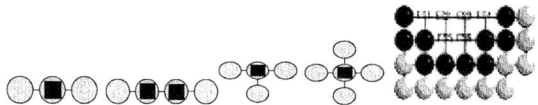

Fig. 10. Example of Articulation Points(ES2 and ES3)

3 Experiments and Analysis

The performance of the proposed method was tested on a problem set of 20 game records from professional games that had been played to completion and counted.

For example, figure 11 shows the result of a static analysis of a semifinal game from the 2nd LG Cup World Baduk Championship. The white player was Myeong Hoon Choi 6P and the black player was Wang Li Cheng 9P. The komi was 5.5 and the last move was 263. Black won by 6.5. All strings were classified correctly by the proposed method. The number of strings was 31, and the life and death of the strings were analyzed perfectly.

In a few cases, the algorithm needed to be improved, for example data 15. This game was held in October, 1947. The black player was Kitani Mino and the white player was Iwamoto Kaoro. The komi was 4.5, and black won by 4.5. Figure 12 shows the problem i.e. one point of black in top-left corner. White gave up a ko, because this was the right of black. Another problem was the thrust on the left of the board. If white had played the position, then two black stones would have been removed. Whereas, if black had played the position, white would have been removed, then the

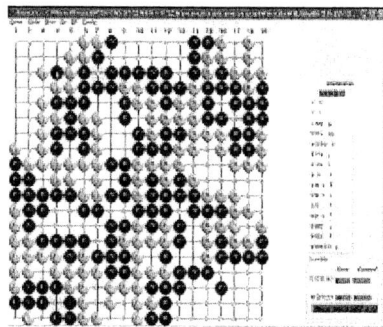

Fig. 11. Example of static analysis of game

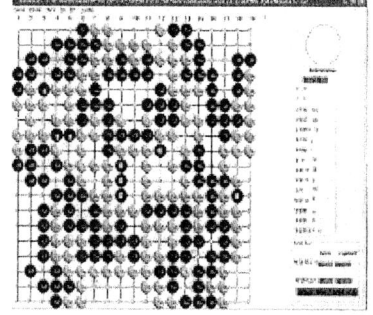

Fig. 13. Example of static analysis of game

black string removed by white. As such, the proposed method was unable to determine the result of the thrust based on a static analysis. The results of the proposed method marked both strings with 'K', meaning killed. Nonetheless, as regards the real counting of the game, black won by 4.5, while the analytic result was that black won by 7.5.

It would appear that these problems require a search-based algorithm. There are also a few more problems that need a search-based algorithm, as the proposed method is essentially a static analysis. These problems include an open-ko, reinforcement of one point, and a thrust. Thus, only a static analysis of the game will not be able to score perfectly. However, an open-ko and reinforcement of one point look ahead two steps. Therefore, it is possible these problems can be evaluated using a static analysis and will be the theme of further research.

The data sets of 20 games were tested. All the games were played to the end and scored. The number of total stones was 5,367 and the number of strings was 772. The results of the experiment produced a very low error ratio for the judgment of static life and death, where the error ratio for the stones was 0.18% and that for the strings was 1.16%. The results of the experiments are shown in Table1.

Table 1. Results of static analyses of games

Data	Points	Strings	Number of life and death errors		Error ratio (Number of errors/ total number)	
			Points	Strings	Points	Strings
1	263	31	0	0	0	0
2	291	36	0	0	0	0
3	256	45	0	0	0	0
4	244	45	0	0	0	0
5	285	34	0	0	0	0
6	256	47	0	0	0	0
7	235	33	0	0	0	0
8	239	51	0	0	0	0
9	295	40	1	1	0.003	0.025
10	240	34	1	1	0.004	0.029
11	245	52	0	0	0	0
12	295	27	0	0	0	0
13	305	37	1	1	0.003	0.027
14	274	36	0	0	0	0
15	283	36	4	3	0.014	0.083
16	237	45	1	1	0.004	0.022
17	307	34	1	1	0.003	0.029
18	275	36	0	0	0	0
19	271	35	1	1	0.003	0.028
20	271	38	0	0	0	0
sum	5,367	772	10	9	0.0018	0.0116

4 Conclusion

A String Graph(SG) and Alive String Graph(ASG) were defined to facilitate a static analysis of completed and counted games of Go. The performance of the proposed method was tested using a problem set of games played by professional players, and all the games had been played to completion and counted. The experiment determined the error on the judgment of life and death. The test was performed on the final positions of the 20 games. The total number of stones was 5,367 and the number of strings was 772. The experimental results produced a very low error ratio for the judgment of static life and death, where the error ratio for the stones was 0.18% and that for the strings was 1.16%.

For the judgment of life and death, rules are applied to the situation where a stone is included and not included, and these rules are defined as a String Reduction (SR), Empty Reduction (ER), Edge Transform (ET), and Circular Graph (CG) when the stone is not included, and a Dead Enemy String Reduction (DESR) and Same Color String Reduction (SCSR) when the stone is included. Whether an SG is an ASG or not is then evaluated using these rules. An Articulation Point Check (APC) rule according to the number of articulation points is also used for a life and death judgment.

As the proposed method is essentially a static evaluation, a search-based algorithm is still required for a few problems, such as an open-ko, the reinforcement of one point, and a thrust. Although just a static analysis cannot score a game perfectly, an open-ko and the reinforcement of one point only look ahead two steps. Thus, the feasibility of evaluating these problems using a static analysis will be the focus of further research.

The proposed method has many important applications in Computer Go. First, it can be applied to count the score if it is necessary to determine which string is safe. Second, it can be applied to end a game. Third, it can be applied to evaluate life and death to minimize the depth of a search.

References

1. Benson, D.B.: Life in the game of Go, Information Sciences, Vol. 10, pp 17-29, ISSN 0020-0255. Reprinted in Computer Games,(Ed. D.N.L.Levy), Vol. II, Springer-Verlag, New York, N.Y. ISBN, (1976) 203-213
2. Muller, M.: Playing it safe: Recognizing secure territories in computer Go by using static rules and search. Game Programming Workshop in Japan '97(Ed. H. Matsubara), Computer Shogi Association, Tokyo, Japan (1997) .80-86
3. Muller, M.: Computer Go. Artificial Intelligence, Vol. 134, Nos. 1-2, ISSN 0004-3702 (2002) 145-179
4. Popma, R. and Allis, L.V.: Life and death refined. Heuristic Programming in Artificial Intelligence 3(Eds. H.J. van den Herik and L.V.Allis), Ellis Horwood Ltd., Chichester, England. ISBN 157-164
5. T.Wolf.: Investigating Tsumego problems with RisiKo, in L D. Levy, D. Beal(Eds,), Heuristic Programming in Artificial Intelligence 2, Ellis Horwood, Chichester (1991) 153-160
6. H. S. Park, D. H. Lee, H. J. Kim.: Static Analysis of String Stability and Group Territory in Computer Go, Journal of the Institute of Electronics Engineers of Korea, Vol. 40CI, No.6, Nov, (2003) 77-86
7. H. S. Park, J. G. Lim, J. C. Lee.: Research On Solving Life-Death Problems Using Heuristic Function in Paduk, Proceedings of 21st KISS Spring Conference, Vol.21, No.1 (1994) 233-236

Research on Artificial Intelligence Character Based Physics Engine in 3D Car Game

Jonghwa Choi[1], Dongkyoo Shin[1], Jinsung Choi[2], and Dongil Shin[1,*]

[1] Department of Computer Science and Engineering, Sejong University,
98 Kunja-Dong Kwangjin-Gu, Seoul, Korea
com97@gce.sejong.ac.kr,
{shindk, dshin}@sejong.ac.kr
[2] Electronics and Telecommunications Research Institute,
161 Gajung-Dong, Yousung-Gu, Taejun, Korea
jin1025@etri.re.kr

Abstract. This paper deals with research on an intelligent game character that judges the game's physics situation and takes intelligent action in the game by applying a physics engine. The algorithm that recognizes the physics situation uses momentum back-propagation neural networks. In the experiment on physics situation recognition, a physics situation recognition algorithm where the number of input layers (number of physical parameters) and output layers (destruction value for the master car) is fixed has shown the best performance when the number of hidden layers is 3 and the learning count number is 30,000. Since we tested with rigid bodies only, we are currently studying efficient physics situation recognition for soft body objects.

1 Introduction

The most important issue for a 3D game is a study of the motion and intelligent action of the game characters. And when a game includes these functions, it must not experience performance problems. The motion of a game character, including-its position and displacement, should be calculated based on physical laws; a physics engine takes charge of this role [1]. A physics engine only expresses realistic motion for a character. Intelligent action by a game character is expressed by the game's artificial intelligence engine. However, many researchers have studied poor characters that act according to limited rules in the game world.

This paper presents research on an intelligent game character that judges the game's physics situation and then takes intelligent action in the game by applying a physics engine. The algorithm that recognizes the physics situation uses momentum back-propagation neural networks [2].

Physics engines are offered as commercial physics engines and open source physics engines. Math Engine [3] and Havok [4], are widely used commercial physics engines. Also, ODE (Open Dynamics Engine) is a well-known open source physics

---
* Correspondence Author.

engine [5]. Research on artificial intelligence for physics situation recognition is incomplete. Research on robot soccer analysis uses a distributed artificial intelligence system and prompted the design of an offline learning method [6]. Naoyuki and Fumio did research on a pet with structured intelligence [7].

2 Component Architecture for Artificial Intelligence Character in 3D Car Game

We applied physics situation recognition in a car collision simulation. This car collision simulation has a master car and an enemy car that attacks the master car. The master car has physical values that change when the player acts. The enemy car recognizes these physical value changes when the master car moves, and judges the moment that can give the most damage when colliding with the master car. Figure 1 shows the master and enemy cars in a car collision simulation.

Figure 2 shows the component architecture for physics situation recognition in the car collision simulation. The physics situation recognition component analyzes the physical values that change when the master and enemy cars move, and predicts the destruction value for the master car when the two cars collide.

Fig. 1. 3D Artificial Intelligence Car Game in Physics Engine

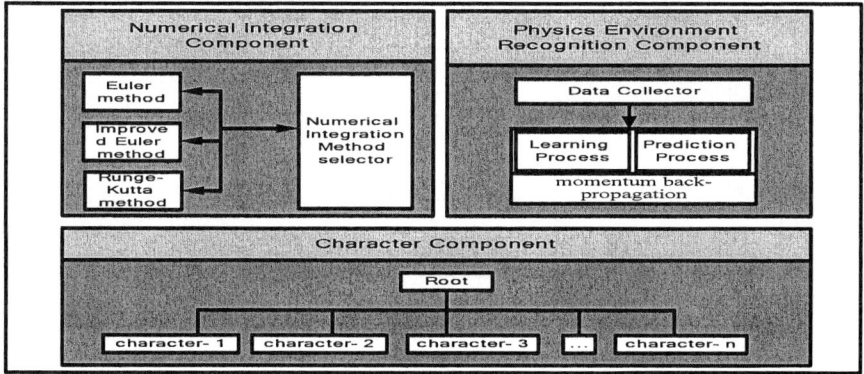

Fig. 2. Component architecture of physics situation recognition system

The 3D game uses an integration method when it calculates a car's motion. When a car moves in the world space of the simulation, a numerical integration component is automatically selected and uses an integration method that displays the optimum performance according to the physics situation of the master and enemy' cars. This numerical integration component analyzes the performance with three integration methods: the euler method, the improved euler method, and the runge-kutta method. The numerical integration component solves the performance problem in a car collision game where the physics situation recognition component is applied.

The character component selects the enemy car in the closest position to the master car from the enemy car list. The selected enemy' car transmits its own physical values to the physics situation recognition component.

In this paper, we use momentum back-propagation neural networks for physics situation recognition. The physical parameters defined in context (car's position, linear velocity, center of mass, car's mass, variable velocity) are used as input values for physics situation recognition.

When a car moves, the physical parameters for the car that change are position, linear velocity, and variable velocity. And when the cars collide, the physical parameters that influence the collision response are the car's mass and center of mass. Position is a sector of the simulation world that is divided into nine sectors. The scope of linear velocity was limited to a range of 0-90 in the experiment and divided into 9 sections. The center of mass is divided into 9 sectors and the maximum values of mass and variable velocity are both 45.

Figure 3 shows the structure of physics situation recognition and its flowchart. If machine learning algorithm is the learn phase, it receives the physical parameters for master and enemy' cars and the destruction value. After the learning process receives all of these physical parameters, it begins learning. If the learning process has started, the weight value of learning process is different.

The prediction process begins after the learning process is completed. The prediction process estimates the destruction value for the master car when two cars collide. According to this prediction result, the enemy car judges whether it will collide with the master car.

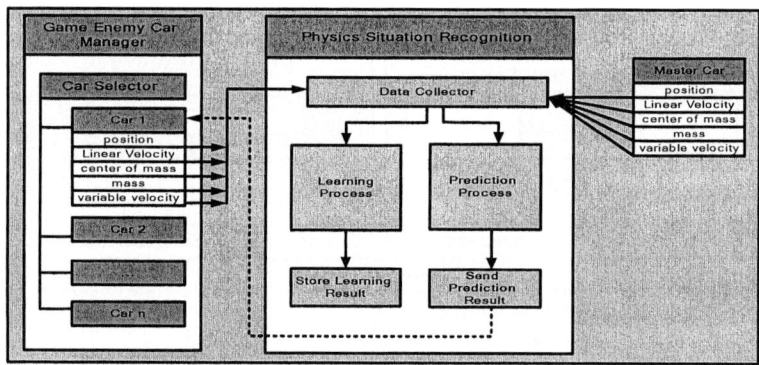

Fig. 3. Structure of Physics Situation Recognition

3 Experiments and Evaluations for Physics Situation Recognition

Experiments in physics situation recognition estimated the accuracy of the algorithm and experimented with two directions. When the master car collides with an enemy car, all of the power of the master car decreases as the destruction value.

Table 1. Algorithm accuracy by modification of hidden layer

Hidden Layer	Success Rate(%)	Cross Validation error signal value by hidden layer	Cross validation error signal value by output layer	Test error signal value by output layer
1	63	31.23532	231.34353	234.12622
3	92	13.23243	164.23213	166.09230
5	84	24.12153	128.64009	130.25030

When hidden layer is 3 classes in table 1, physics situation recognition displays the best performance. Table 2 shows the results of an experiment on the accuracy of the algorithm with variations in the training numbers. When the learning count is 30,000 in table 2, the algorithm displays the best performance.

Table 2. Algorithm accuracy by variation of learning count

Learning Count	Success Rate(%)	Cross Validation error signal value by hidden layer	Cross validation error signal value by output layer	Test error signal value by output layer
10000	71	28.23553	224.23242	225.55020
20000	81	25.25939	130.96954	131.08834
30000	92	13.23243	164.23213	166.09230
40000	85	23.25534	127.94204	128.03253
50000	85	23.25254	127.89042	128.01223

As appeared in an experiment, when the physics situation recognition algorithm has a fixed number of input layers (number of physical parameters) and output layers (destruction value for the master car), it shows the best performance when the number of hidden layers is 3 and the learning count number is 30,000.

4 Conclusions

This paper presented research on an intelligent game character that judges a game's physics situation and takes intelligent action in the game by applying a physics engine. The algorithm that recognizes the physics situation uses momentum backpropagation neural networks. In experiments on physics situation recognition, a physics situation recognition algorithm where the number of input layers (number of physical parameters) and output layers (destruction value for the master car) is fixed has shown the best performance when the number of hidden layers is 3 and the learning count number is 30,000. Since we tested with rigid bodies only, we are currently studying efficient physics situation recognition for soft body objects.

References

[1] Kook, H.J, Novak, G. S., Jr.: Representation of models for solving real world physics problems. Proceedings of the Sixth Conference on Artificial Intelligence for Applications, (1990) 274-280
[2] Chen, Z., An, Y., Jia, K., Sun, C,: Intelligent control of alternative current permanent manage servomotor using neural network. Proceedings of the Fifth International Conference on Electrical Machines and Systems, Volume 2, August (2001) 18-20
[3] Math Engine, http://www.mathengine.com
[4] Havok, http://havok.com
[5] Open Dynamics Engine, http://ode.org
[6] Kubota. N, Kojima. F, Fukuda. T.: IFSA World Congress and 20th NAFIPS International Conference, July (2001) 2786 - 2791
[7] Moller, T., Machiraju, R., Mueller, K., Yagel, R.: Evaluation and design of filters using a Taylor series expansion: IEEE transactions on Visualization and Computer Graphics, Vol.3, No.2, (1997) 184-199

Document Clustering Based on Nonnegative Sparse Matrix Factorization

C.F. Yang, Mao Ye, and Jing Zhao

CI Lab, School of Computer Science and Engineering,
University of Electronic Science and Technology of China,
Chengdu 610054, P.R. China
ycfwsm800@tom.com, maoye@sina100.com

Abstract. A novel algorithm of document clustering based on non-negative sparse analysis is proposed. In contrast to the algorithm based on non-negative matrix factorization, our algorithm can obtain documents topics exactly by controlling the sparseness of the topic matrix and the encoding matrix explicitly. Thus, the clustering accuracy has been improved greatly. In the end, simulation results are employed to further illustrate the accuracy and efficiency of this algorithm.

1 Introduction

For the document data in semantic space, there are three characters: no structure, high dimensions and sparseness. How to make out latent structure in the data explicitly and reduce the dimensionality of the data, so that further computational methods can be applied, are so useful for document clustering. Although there are many document clustering methods, and many methods have been extensively investigated for several decades, such as topic detection and tracking(TDT)[9] and Independent Component Analysis(ICA), however, accurately clustering documents is still a challenging task.

Non-negative matrix factorization(NMF) gives a linear, non-negative and part-based approximate data representation. Compared with ICA, NMF has two useful properties: sparse representation and non-negative constraints of the data. Sparse representation means most of units of a vector taking value close to zero and only few of them take significantly non-zero value. The sparse representation can make encoding easy to interpret in the way of encoding much of the data using few 'active' components. Simultaneously, non-negative constraints make the representation purely additive which is based on the intuition that parts are generally combined additively to form a whole. In a word, these two properties might be useful for learning parts-based representations[3]. Since the document data in the semantic space is sparse, non-negative and part-based(the topics), document clustering based on NMF will achieve better performance than that of other methods, such as singular vector decomposition(SVD) and ICA[9]. However, the sparseness obtained by NMF is somewhat of a side-effect rather than a goal[5], one cannot in anyway control the degree to which the representation is sparse. Thus, NMF cannot obtain the local features exactly. Since the document data in semantic space is very sparse, NMF sometimes cannot obtain the topics exactly.

In this paper, we proposed a novel document clustering algorithm based on the non-negative sparse matrix factorization (SNMF)[5]. In contrast to the algorithm derived by NMF[9], we extend NMF by controlling the sparseness explicitly. Thus, document topics can be obtained exactly, and the clustering accuracy has been improved greatly. Simulation results show that the performance of algorithm SNMF is better than that of algorithms based on NMF.

2 Nonnegative Sparse Matrix Factorization

Given a non-negative matrix V, $V \in R^{n \times m}$, the goal of SNMF is to find non-negative matrices $W \in R^{n \times t}$ and $H \in R^{t \times n}$ to minimize the function[3,5,6,7,8]

$$E(W, H) = \|V - WH\|^2 \qquad (1)$$

with constrains

$$V = WH \qquad (2)$$

and

$$sparseness(w_i) = S_w, \qquad (3)$$

$$sparseness(h_i) = S_h, \qquad (4)$$

where w_i and h_i are the ith column of W and H respectively. And S_w and S_h are the desired sparseness of W and H. For a vector x, the definition of sparseness is the following

$$sparseness(x) = \frac{\sqrt{n} - (\sum |x_i|)/\sqrt{\sum x_i^2}}{\sqrt{n} - 1} \qquad (5)$$

A projected gradient descent algorithm for SNMF is the following[5]:

1. Initialize W and H to random positive matrices and set the sparseness S_w and S_h. If sparseness constraints on W and H apply, then project each column of W and H to be nonnegative
2. Iterate
   - If sparseness constraints on W apply,
     • Set $W = W - \mu_w(WH - V)H^T$
     • Project each column of W to be nonnegative, have unchanged L_2 norm, but L_1 norm set to achieve desired sparseness else take standard steps as NMF
   - If sparseness constraints on H apply,
     • Set $H = H - \mu_h W^T(WH - V)$
     • Project each row of H to be nonnegative, have unit L_2 norm, and L_1 norm set to achieve desired sparseness else take standard steps as NMF

μ_w and μ_h are small positive constants (step sizes) which must be set appropriately for the algorithm to work.

The above algorithm requires a projector, which enforces sparseness of vector x by explicitly setting its L_1 and L_2 norms. The algorithm of this projector is the following[2]:

1. Problem: Given any vector x, find the closest (in the Euclidean sense) nonnegative vector s with a given L_1 norm and a given L_2 norm.
2. Algorithm:
    - Set $s_i = x_i + (L_1 - \sum x_i)/dim(x), \forall i$
    - Set Z={}
    - Iterate
        - Set $m_i = 0$ if $i \in Z$ else $m_i = L_1/(dim(x) - size(A))$
        - Set $s = m + \alpha(s - m)$ where $\alpha \geq 0$ is selected such that the resulting s satisfies the L_2 norm constraint.
        - If all components of s are non-negative, return s, end
        - Set $Z = Z \bigcup \{i; s_i < 0\}$
        - Set $s_i = 0, \forall i \in Z$
        - Calculate $c := (\sum s_i - L_1)/(dim(x) - size(Z))$
        - $s_i = s_i - c, \forall$ i not in Z
        - Goto the first step of the circle.

To the document data in semantic space, every document is expressed with a column in matrix V. Using the SNMF, we can get the topic matrix W and the encoding matrix H. Every column of matrix W is corresponded to a topic of document corpus. Every column of matrix H is corresponded to the encoding a relative column of matrix V. From the matrix H, we can get how a document is encoded by the topics.

3 Document Clustering

Document clustering methods can be mainly categorized into two types: document partitioning (flat clustering) and agglomerative (bottom-up hierarchical) clustering. Generally there are three main steps in document clustering task. They are: modelling and projecting document to semantic space, dimensionality reduction to get topics and encoding matrix, using a clustering algorithm to interim matrix data and evaluating the result.

Since the document data in semantic space is non-negative and sparseness, the clustering method based on the NMF have been studied recently[3,9]. However, the sparseness by NMF is controlled implicitly. So when the data matrix V is too sparse, NMF cannot obtain the correct topics from the matrix V.

In this paper, we use SNMF to obtain the topics of documents by controlling the sparseness of matrix W and H explicitly. The topics of documents are derived from matrix W by sorting the values of every column. Since every document is encoded in semantic space, which is a column of H accordingly, we can perform document clustering by matrix H. Because the matrix H contains valuable values, first, we compute H by algorithm of SNMF, then R partitions of M objects of columns of H is determined by using the algorithm of PAM(Partitioning around Medoids). Our document clustering algorithm is the following:

- **Modelling and projecting document to semantic space:**
  The first step is to get the radix of semantic space. Let $X = \{x_1, x_2, ..., x_n\}$ be the complete vocabulary set of the document corpus after the stop-words removal and words stemming operations. The dimension is n.
  The second step is to model and project every document to the semantic space. The weighted term-frequency vector is used to represent each document. The term-frequency vector V_i of document d_i is defined as

  $$V_i = [v_{1i}, v_{2i}, ..., v_{ni}]^T$$

  and

  $$v_{ij} = f_{ij} \cdot log(cn/qi)$$

  [9] where f_{ij}, qi, cn denote the term frequency of word x_i in document d_j, the number of documents containing the word x_i, and the total number of documents in the corpus,respectively. In addition, V_i is normalized to unit Euclidean length. Using V_i as the i'th column, the $n \times m$ term-document matrix V is constructed.

- **Get the topics matrix W and encoding matrix H:**
  Using the algorithm of SNMF on the matrix V, we can get the topics matrix W which dimension is n by t and the encoding matrix H which dimension is t by m. The parameter t is the number of the topics, n is the dimension of radix in semantic space and m is the number of document in corpus.

- **Using the PAM clustering algorithm on the sparseness matrix H to get the clustering result:**
  The step can be depicted as follows:

  1. arbitrarily choose t columns of the matrix H as the initial medoids(t is the number of the topics abstracted by SNMF);
  2. repeat
  3. assign each remaining column to the cluster with the nearest medoid;
  4. randomly select a nonmedoid column, named $Orandom$;
  5. compute the total cost, S, of swapping O_j with O_{random};
  6. if $S < 0$ then swap O_j with O_{random} to form the new set of R medoids;
  7. until no change;

4 Experiments

The first step is to get the data source. We get about 1000 articles in 10 topics from news groups, Reuters corpus on the net. This document corpora has been among the ideal test sets for document clustering purposes because documents in the corpora have been manually clustered based on their topics and each document has been assigned one or more labels indicating which topic/topics it belongs to. Each topic includes 100 documents.

The second step is to get radix in latent semantic space. We separate every article to words. After removed many stop-words such as 'I, you, he, in, on', and words stemming operations, we get an about 30000 words different words combination as the radix X (the dimension $n = 30000$) of latent semantic space.

The third step is to get the matrix V. Using the method of document clustering in section 3, the matrix V is computed.

We design two experiment with different parameters to compare between SNMF and NMF. At the same time to see the efficiency of SNMF in different parameters.

In the first experiment, parameters are: the number of topic t=3, each topic has 20 documents, so the number of document m=60, the sparseness of W S_w = 0.8, the sparseness of H S_h = 0.9, the number of topic words is 6(by sorting the value of every column of matrix W). Using the method SNMF in section 2 and the method NMF[9], we can get the matrix W and H. Using the method of document clustering in section 3 on the matrix H, we get the clustering result. The result of experiment is in Table 1. From the table 1, it is clear that the topics extracted by SNMF is more correct and clearer than that of NMF. And from Fig.1, we can see that the distribution of SNMF is easier for clustering.

In the second experiment, parameters are: the number of topic t=5, the number of document m=100, the sparseness of W S_w = 0.5, the sparseness of H S_h = 0.8, the number of topic words is 8. Using the same step in the first experiment, we get the clustering result in table 2. From the table 2, we get the same conclusion that the clustering method with SNMF is more correct and clearer than that of NMF. But at the same time, we can see the method SNMF wastes more time than the method NMF. The sparseness is larger, the time is more.

Table 1. Extracted topics and clustering results based on NMF and SNMF of the first experiment

	SNMF			NMF		
topics	space	Israeli	peace	Israel	space	Israeli
	launch	people	boundary	government	people	space
	nasal	government	zone	people	software	Israel
	flight	Armenians	land	Armenians	flight	nasal
	advertise	conflict	Lebanon	space	zone	program
	shuttle	Jews	military	Jews	battery	military
accuracy	0.766			0.678		
time(s)	1460			1130		

Table 2. Extracted topics and clustering results based on NMF and SNMF of the second experiment

	topic					accuracy	time(s)
SNMF	space hit balloon atmosphere game runs land research	runs people Israeli game muslims muslim time software	car article writes cars course Armenian player believe	space launch cost mission program stage advertising shuttle	Israel Israeli government military soldier peace against war	0.712	5010
NMF	stage power cost launch people million articles going	battery software people current car lead reaction Israel	people Israel overhead space car nasal flight player	Israeli Israel space Armenians armenia advertising muslim Jews	space runs game military cost muslims situation land	0.653	2550

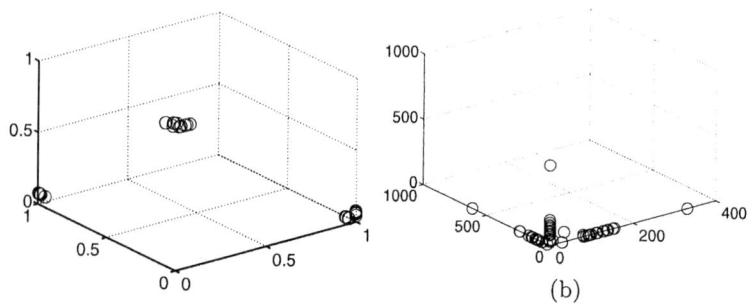

Fig. 1. The performance of SNMF and NMF, the left figure is the distribute of SNMF and the right figure is the distribute of NMF

From the table 1 and table 2 with different parameters, three points can be concluded. The first is that the sparseness of W and H make different accuracy of base topic and different structure of H that infect the easiness of clustering. The second is that with the increasing number of document, the interference among the topics is larger, and clustering accuracy is decreased. In the end, the method based on SNMF has more stabilization than the method based on NMF.

5 Summary and Future Works

From the experiments, it can be concluded that our document clustering algorithm is a rather good clustering method in terms of effectiveness and efficiency. It works because the sparseness is controlled explicitly. However, how to control the sparseness is not clear yet. In the next works, we will derive a method to decide this sparseness.

References

1. Baker L. and McCallum A.: Distributional clustering of words for text classification. Proceedings of ACM SIGIR, Melbourne, Australia (1998) 96-103
2. Ding C., He X., Zha H., Gu M., and Simon H. D.: A min-max cut algorithm for graph partitioning and data clustering. Proceedings of IEEE ICDM (2001) 107-114
3. Lee D.D. and Seung H.S.: Learning the parts of objects by non-negative matrix factorization. Nature 401 (6755) (1999) 788-791
4. Lee D. D. and Seung H. S.: Algorithms for non-negative matrix factorization. Advances in Neural Information Processing Systems 13 (2001) 56-562
5. Patrik O.Hoyer: Nonnegative matrix factorization with sparseness constraints. Journal of Machine Learning Research 5 (2004) 1457-1469
6. Patrik O.Hoyer: Modeling receptive fields with non-negative sparse coding. Neurocomputing 52-54 (2003) 547-552
7. Patrik O.Hoyer: Non-negative sparse coding. Proc. IEEE Workshop on Neural Networks for Signal Processing, Martigny, Switzerland (2002) 557-565
8. Willett P.: Document clustering using an inverted file approach. Journal of Information Science 2 (1990) 223-231
9. Xu Wei, Liu Xin, Gong Yihong: Document Clustering Based On Non-negative Matrix Factorization. Proceedings of ACM SIGIR, Toronto, Canada (2003) 267-273
10. Zha H., Ding C., Gu M., He X., and Simon H.: Spectral relaxation for k-means clustering. Advances in Neural Information Processing Systems 14 (2001) 1057-1064

Prediction Modeling for Ingot Manufacturing Process Utilizing Data Mining Roadmap Including Dynamic Polynomial Neural Network and Bootstrap Method

Hyeon Bae[1], Sungshin Kim[1], and Kwang Bang Woo[2]

[1] School of Electrical and Computer Engineering, Pusan National University,
30 Jangjeon-dong, Geumjeong-gu, 609-735 Busan, Korea
{baehyeon, sskim}@pusan.ac.kr
http://icsl.ee.pusan.ac.kr
[2] Automation Technology Research Institute, Yonsei University,
134 Sinchon-dong, Seodaemun-gu, Seoul 120-749, Korea
kbwoo@yonsei.ac.kr

Abstract. The purpose of this study was to develop a process management system to manage ingot fabrication and the quality of the ingot. The ingot is the first manufactured material of wafers. Trace parameters were collected on-line but measurement parameters were measured by sampling inspection. The quality parameters were applied to evaluate the quality. Therefore, preprocessing was necessary to extract useful information from the quality data. First, statistical methods were used for data generation, and then modeling was performed, using the generated data, to improve the performance of the models. The function of the models is to predict the quality corresponding to control parameters.

1 Introduction

Wafer is an important material in semiconductor industries. In recent years, the size of wafers has been enlarged up to 300 mm, so quality management is fundamentally required and applied. The wafer manufacturing process includes some chemical processes, so there is a time delay that causes difficult measurement and control. Among these processes, ingot fabrication is the most important, because the quality of the ingot will definitely affect the quality of the wafer.

Over decades, many studies have been performed to detect faults and improve yield. An adaptive resonance theory network was used to develop an intelligent system that will recognize defect spatial patterns to aid in the diagnosis of failure causes [1]. A data warehouse approach to the automation of process zone-by-zone defect-limited yield analysis [2], and SOI wafer-specific behavior related to the intrinsic limitations of laser-scattering defect detection were presented [3]. The calculations and results of random defect-limited yield (DLY) using the deterministic yield model was introduced [4], and the spatial defect features and cluster chip locations having similar defect features were extracted through the SOM neural network [5]. An automatic, wafer-scale, defect cluster identifier [6] and Geodesic Active Contours on a wafer-scale image were studied to extract the overall dimensions of the wafer under inspection [7].

The objectives of these studies were focused on detecting faults and adjusting the operational conditions for process optimization and producing wafers having no defects. To detect a fault, data mining tools to analyze input-output data using models are required. However, it is difficult to select a proper method from various data mining methodologies. In this research, a data mining roadmap was made to assist the selection of an appropriate methodology. Based on the roadmap, the selected methodologies were the data model to predict process quality. After selecting the method, data acquisition from the target process is used in data mining, and the collected data should be sufficient in number and clean enough to perform the data mining. The data on the quality of the wafer, prepared for this research, were not sufficient because quality evaluation was performed according to a sampling inspection, not a total inspection. To solve these problems, the bootstrap method, an appropriate data preprocessing method, was used to generate data sufficient for a total inspection. Improvement in model performance was observed from the results.

In Section 2, we describe the target process, which is the ingot fabrication process, and in Section 3, we show one of the important results, the proposed road map for data mining. Section 4 explains the applied data mining techniques, and Section 5 shows the experimental results. Finally, Section 6 concludes the paper.

2 Wafer Fabrication

2.1 Wafer for Semiconductors

Wafers are used in manufacturing memory or non-memory semi-conductor chips. Several circuit masks are mounted on one wafer by UV rays or electron beams in assembly lines. As semiconductor technology has developed, the wafer size has been enlarged to mount more circuits on the wafer. Because semiconductor manufactures want to make larger-memory and non-memory chips, they require larger-diameter wafers and strict quality assessment from wafer manufacturers. To cope with these requirements, optimization of wafer fabrication is essential.

2.2 Ingot Data

Ingot is the first manufactured material in wafer fabrication. In ingot fabrication, some set-points for handling the position or rotation of ingots and control parameters are adjusted for quality management. These operating parameters play an import role in wafer quality and size control. Therefore, they should be properly handled for improvement of productivity and yield. The operating parameters were used as inputs in modeling in this study. The quality parameters consist of five concentration values, and six defect values. Four of these were used for outputs in modeling in this study.

3 Design of Data Mining Roadmap

3.1 Data Mining

Data mining techniques that are well suited to the purpose can improve process performance and product quality. Data mining, a procedure for extracting useful information from data, is composed of data selection, preprocessing, transformation, data mining and interpretation. When collected data is insufficient, a data selection and preprocessing procedure should be considered an important stage. The raw data used in this research were insufficient to train models because most of the data was obtained from sampling inspection. To overcome this problem, a statistical method such as the Monte Carlo/Bootstrap method was used to fill vacancies in the data.

3.2 Data Mining Roadmap

In this study, we proposed the roadmap for data mining. Figure 1 shows the proposed roadmap, which was constructed based on several reference books and papers. We selected the methods and procedures for diagnosis and optimization of the ingot process by referring to the roadmap. The selected methods of this study were data generation (bootstrap method) and prediction modeling (DPNN).

3.3 Application of Data Mining

3.3.1 Data Preprocessing in Reducing Data Effects

The collected data from assembly lines can be missed or limited to specific cases; thus, the quality data are not always uniformly distributed. Insufficient data results in unreliable prediction models in the modeling stage. To solve these problems, data preprocessing is required in order to add data and improve performance. In this study, the Bootstrap method, a type of Monte Carlo method, was applied to compensate leakage data caused by sampling inspection.

3.3.2 Data Modeling in Quality Prediction

In modeling prediction models, inputs of models can affect the performance of the models. Selection of inputs corresponding to data characteristics is necessary to improve model performance, because unnecessary inputs can have a strong influence on prediction results. Therefore, in this study, we selected the principal inputs that greatly influence model accuracy after modeling. For the function, we proposed the dynamic polynomial neural network (DPNN). The DPNN has the advantages that it requires only small computation, so it is very useful in modeling with high-dimension variables and a large amount of data. The other advantage is that this method can select essential inputs through the modeling stages.

3.4 Process Management System in Ingot Fabrication

The designed models and the extracted rules are integrated into the process management system. This system will play important quality management roles in ingot manufacturing. The quality will be predicted by models and the control parameters will be modified by rules on-line. In Fig. 2, the quality predictor is to predict quality of the wafer according to the control parameters and the parameter estimator decides how to adjust the control parameters to improve the quality corresponding to the predicted quality.

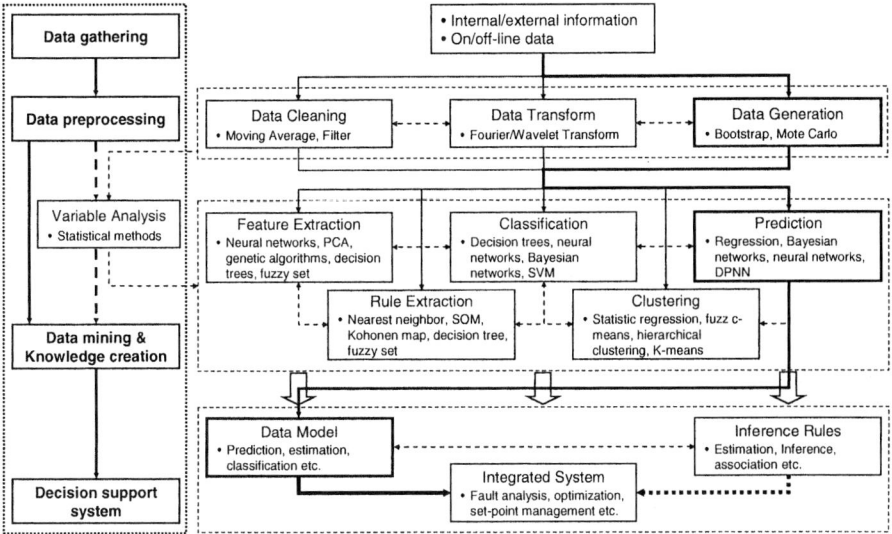

Fig. 1. Data mining roadmap proposed in this research

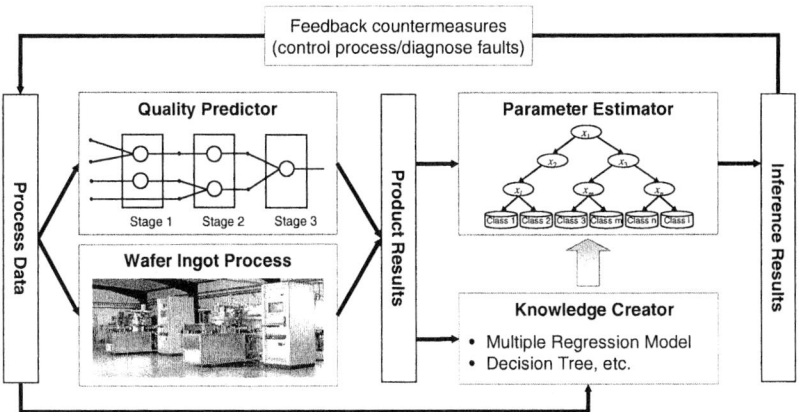

Fig. 2. Structure of the proposed system

4 Applied Data Mining Tools

The process data have limited characteristics. Trace data (control parameters) are collect by real-time measurement, but measurement data (quality parameters) are measured by sampling inspection after manufacturing. Therefore, input and output data cannot be one-to-one correspondent and target data are insufficient. The insufficient data problem results in modeling inadequate performance of the model because the target data are insufficient. To solve this problem, we used the Bootstrap method with data generation. After the data generation, the prediction model was constructed using the DPNN.

4.1 Bootstrap Method

The interested reader is referred to more information on the theory behind the bootstrap. Some studies refer to the re-sampling techniques of the previous section as bootstrap methods. Here, the term *bootstrap* is used to refer to Monte Carlo simulations that treat the original sample as a pseudo-population or as an estimate of the population. The bootstrap is a method of Monte Carlo simulation where no parametric assumptions are made about the underlying population that generated the random sample. Instead, the sample is used as an estimate of the population [8].

4.2 Dynamic Polynomial Neural Network (DPNN)

Polynomial neural network (PNN) based on the GMDH algorithm is a useful method to model the system from many observed data and input variables. It is widely employed for modeling of dynamic systems, prediction, and artificial intelligent control because of its advantages in data handling. Figure 3 includes the recurrent inputs with one-to-n time-delayed output variables [9-11].

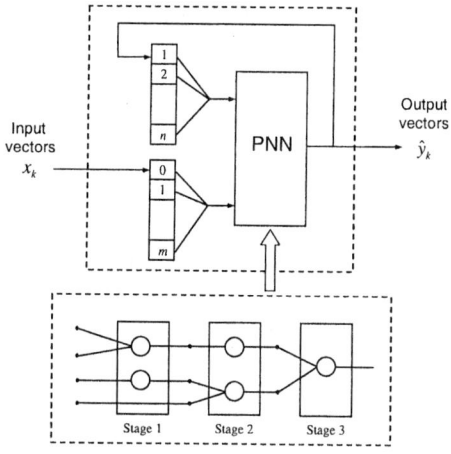

Fig. 3. Basic structure of DPNN

5 Experimental Results

5.1 Trace and Measurement Data of Ingots

Application data were collected from ingot fabrication on the company assembly line. Fourteen trace parameters and 11 measurement parameters that are used for quality analysis were included in the data sets. The trace parameter data are collected on-line.

The measure parameter data are gathered by sampling inspection and used for quality analysis. Forty-eight process parameters are collected by one data set per one minute from a puller.

The measurement parameter data were collected by sampling test, but the trace parameter data were gathered by on-line measurement. Thus, the insufficient data problem exists in modeling stage. The merging data from several pullers can be applied to solve the data insufficient data problem. However, each puller has a unique recipe, so the process features of each are different. Therefore, one puller data set was used with data addition based on data generation at the preprocessing stage. At the preprocessing stage, the number of the target data can be the same as that of the input data. Figure 4 shows the data interpolation.

Trace data (control conditions)											Measure data (product qualities)				
x1	x2	x3	x4	x5	x6	x7	x8	x9	x10	x11	y1	y2	y3	y4	y5
18.00	1.20	0.11	56.20	5.00	204.91	75.55	24.40	18.03	17.97	114.88	15.04	-14.11	10.95	3.30	
17.98	1.04	0.12	56.20	5.00	204.84	77.15	24.40	18.00	17.94	114.90	11.57	-2.79	10.73	2.70	
18.00	1.08	0.12	56.30	5.00	205.25	78.15	24.60	17.97	17.91	114.91			10.71		
18.01	1.21	0.14	56.50	5.00	206.07	80.10	24.20	17.95	17.88	114.82	11.79	-5.85			
18.04	0.82	0.09	56.70	5.00	205.20	82.05	24.20	17.89	17.85	114.80			10.72		
18.03	1.38	0.11	56.70	5.00	206.01	83.45	24.60	17.87	17.82	114.76	•	•	10.69	•	
18.01	1.39	0.16	57.00	5.00	206.34	85.45	24.40	17.84	17.79	114.73	•	•	10.71	•	
18.01	1.45	0.17	57.10	5.00	206.86	87.40	24.20	17.81	17.74	114.70	•	•		•	
18.01	1.30	0.15	57.20	5.00	206.63	89.60	24.80	17.76	17.71	114.65			10.68		
18.01	0.96	0.15	57.50	5.00	206.63	91.55	24.60	17.73	17.68	114.64			10.67		
18.01	1.01	0.12	57.50	5.00	206.77	93.40	24.40	17.68	17.65	114.64			10.7		
18.00	0.98	0.11	57.60	5.00	206.50	94.50	24.60	17.65	17.62	114.61	•	•	10.68	•	
17.99	1.16	0.13	57.70	5.00	206.45	96.10	24.40	17.63	17.59	114.59	•	•		•	
18.00	0.84	0.14	57.90	5.00	206.50	97.95	24.60	17.60	17.56	114.54	•	•	10.69	•	
18.03	0.62	0.06	78.80	5.01	206.70	116.90	24.20	12.88	12.82	111.17			10.25		
18.01	0.62	0.06	78.80	5.03	206.79	116.85	24.20	12.85	12.79	113.12	11.47	-2.71	10.29	1.03	
18.05	0.62	0.06	78.90	5.02	206.83	116.90	24.20	12.82	12.79	113.09					
18.03	0.62	0.06	78.90	5.03	206.86	116.85	24.20	12.82	12.79	113.11			10.2		
18.04	0.62	0.06	79.10	5.04	206.87	116.85	24.20	12.82	12.76	111.30			10.19		

Insert Generated Data

Fig. 4. Data generation for unmeasured quality data

5.2 Quality Prediction and Variable Selection Using DPNN

The process of wafer manufacturing is a chemical process, so the product quality can be measured after fabrication. If the quality is predicted by current control conditions, the manufacturing process can be effectively operated. This section treats modeling stage selection that is based on the roadmap. In this study, we used a DPNN because the DPNN is a useful method for data modeling with many variables and data.

5.2.1 Data Modeling Using One Puller Data (Case 1)

Figures 5 to 6 show the test result using the trained DPNN model with unseen data. The prediction models were designed for quality prediction corresponding to Oxygen, ORG (Oxygen Gradient), RES (Resistivity), and RRG (Resistivity Gradient). In the RES case, the model can be designed by one puller data because the data are sufficient to design a model. And the model performance is also adequate to predict the quality of wafers with RES. However, other three-parameter data are not sufficient to design a good performance model. The model was not trained well with one puller data. Table 1 shows train and test results and selected inputs from modeling using one puller data.

5.2.2 Advanced Proposed Modeling Based on Data Generation (Case 2)

As mentioned above, insufficient data cannot construct a good performance model, so the preprocessing stage was required to compensate for weak points caused by insufficient data before applying the main data mining techniques. In this paper, we used the Bootstrap method to solve the data problem. The Bootstrap method is a type of Monte Carlo simulation. It can generate reasonable data to design data models and improve model performance. Figures 7 to 8 show the improved results that are achieved by data generation. Table 2 shows the prediction results and input selection. As shown in the results, AR gas flow, Chamber press and Heat power were selected.

5.2.3 Comparison of Performance of Prediction Models

Table 3 shows the comparison result for two modeling cases. In Case 1, the models were designed by one puller data that was insufficient in amount, so an overfitting problem occurred. This means that a model trained by insufficient data cannot ensure the good performance of models. However, in Case 2, the model trained stably by data addition using the Bootstrap method showed a good performance. The results provide on indication that statistical data generation can reduce the effect of the insuf-

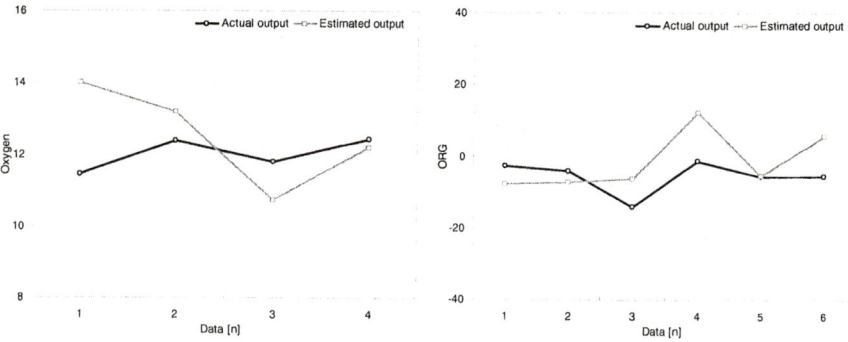

Fig. 5. Prediction result for Oxygen and ORG

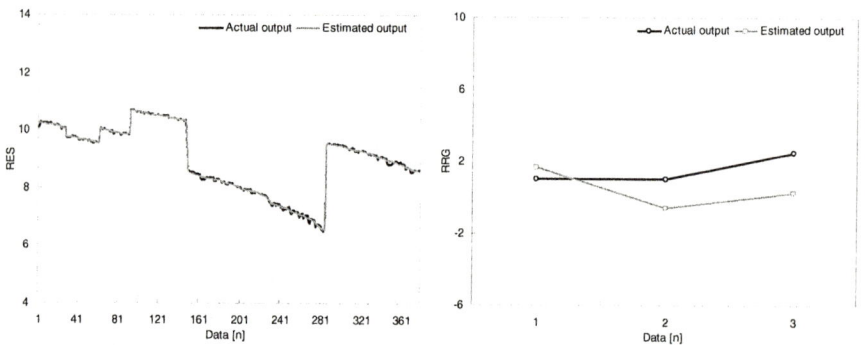

Fig. 6. Prediction result for RES and RRG

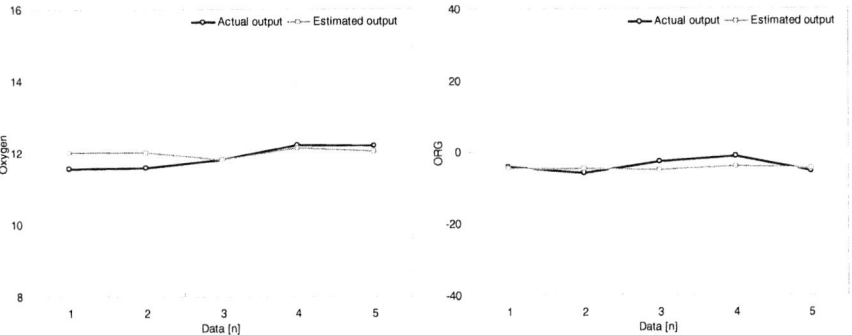

Fig. 7. Prediction result for Oxygen and ORG

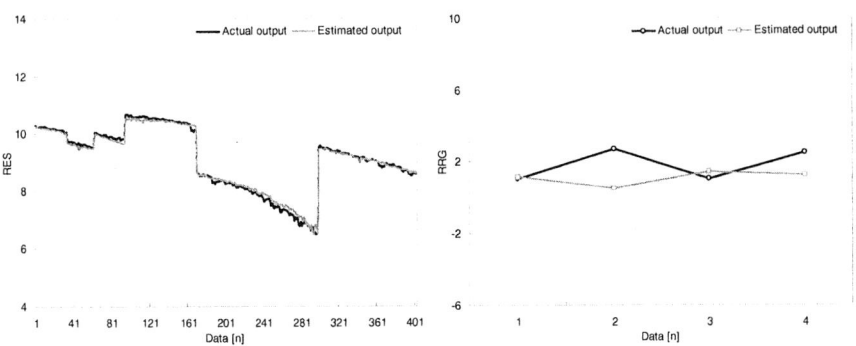

Fig. 8. Prediction result for RES and RRG

ficient data problem. It is difficult to analyze the relationship between inputs and outputs using field data because sometimes field data are insufficient for modeling. Therefore, data preprocessing is required. In this study, an adequately descriptive model was designed by data generation.

Table 1. Modeling results using one puller data including prediction and input selection

Value	Oxygen	ORG	RES	RRG
Learning error	9.7089e-015	4.8174e-014	0.0632	4.5275e-016
Prediction error	1.4422	8.0759	0.043938	1.6293
Selected layer	3	5	3	3
Selected inputs	1 4 5 9 10	2 3 4 5 6 9 10 11	3 4 6 7 9	2 3 4 5 10

Table 2. Modeling results with data generation including prediction and input selection

Value	Oxygen	ORG	RES	RRG
Learning error	0.4550	1.2730	0.3005	0.8512
Prediction error	0.29528	1.8733	0.10423	1.2942
Selected layer	4	4	4	3
Selected inputs	1 2 3 7 8 9 11	1 2 3 5 6 8 11	2 3 4 7 9 11	1 2 6 7 8 9 11

Table 3. Comparison results for three case data sets

Value	Case	Oxygen	ORG	RES	RRG
Learning error	1	9.7089e-015	4.8174e-014	0.0632	4.5275e-016
	2	0.4550	1.2730	0.3005	0.8512
Prediction error	1	1.4422	8.0759	0.043938	1.6293
	2	0.29528	1.8733	0.10423	1.2942
Selected layer	1	3	5	3	3
	2	4	4	4	3

6 Conclusions

In ingot fabrication, quality inspection is accomplished by product sampling testing, and then the control parameter is adjusted by an operator's action corresponding to the quality. Therefore, it is necessary to predict the quality with respect to current control parameters and to handle the parameters effectively.

However, it is difficult to design models using collected data from the field because the data are gathered by sampling inspection. In this study, we proposed data generation using the bootstrap method to solve insufficient data problem. And then we designed prediction models using the DPNN. Through the stages, the performance of the models could be improved and were reasonable. The final goal of this study was to integrate both the diagnosis and the optimization systems of the ingot fabrication process. By using the integrated management system, the quality can be predicted corresponding to the control parameters.

Acknowledgement

This work has been supported by KESRI (R-2004-B-129), which is funded by the Ministry of Commerce, Industry and Energy, in Korea.

References

1. Chen, F. L., Liu, S. F.: A neural-network approach to recognize defect spatial pattern in semiconductor fabrication. IEEE Transactions on Semiconductor Manufacturing **13** (2000) 366-373
2. Iwata, H., Ono, M., Konishi, J., Isogai, S., Furutani, T.: In-line wafer inspection data warehouse for automated defect limited yield analysis. 2000 IEEE/SEMI Advanced Semiconductor Manufacturing Conference and Workshop (2000) 124-129
3. Maleville, C., Neyret, E., Ecarnot, L., Barge, T., Auberton, A. J.: Defect detection on SOI wafers using laser scattering tools. 2001 IEEE International SOI Conference (2001) 19-20
4. Singh, A., Rosin, J.: Random defect limited yield using a deterministic model. 2001 IEEE/SEMI Advanced Semiconductor Manufacturing Conference (2001) 161-165
5. Lee, J. H., Yu, S. J., Part, S. C.: Design of intelligent data sampling methodology based on data mining. IEEE Transactions on Robotics and Automation **17** (2001) 637-649
6. Huang, C. J., Wu, C. F., Wang, C. C.: Image processing techniques for wafer defect cluster identification. IEEE Design & Test of Computers **19** (2002) 44-48
7. Kubota, T., Talekar, P., Sudarshan, T. S., Ma, X., Parker, M., Ma, Y.: An automated defect detection system for silicon carbide wafers. IEEE Southeast Con. (2002) 42-47
8. Zoubir, A. M.: Bootstrap: Theory and Applications. In: Luk, F. T. (ed.): Advanced Signal Processing Algorithms. Architectures and Implementations **2027** (1993) 216-235
9. Kim, S., Vachtsevanos, G. J.: An intelligent approach to integration and control of textile processes. Information Sciences **123** (2000) 181-199
10. Kim, S., Vachtsevanos, G. J.: Polynomial fuzzy neural network for identification and control. NAFIPS'96, North American Fuzzy Information Proc. Society (1996) 5-9
11. Fulcher, G. E., Brown, D. E.: A Polynomial Network for Predicting Temperature Distributions. IEEE Trans. Neural Networks **5** (1994)
12. Graybill, F. A.: Theory and Application of the Linear Model. Duxbury Press, CA (1976)

Implicit Rating – A Case Study[*]

Song Wang[1], Xiu Li[2], and Wenhuang Liu[3]

[1] Department of Automation, Tsinghua University, Beijing, China 10084
Wangsong99@mails.tsinghua.edu.cn
[2] lixiu@tsinghua.edu.cn
[3] Liuwh@sz.tsinghua.edu.cn

Abstract. In this paper, the stable personal browsing patterns shown in Internet surfing are utilized to determine the users' preference on specific content. To be more specific, they are used to calculate the so called implicit ratings. We performed an experiment on all possible combinations of the implicit indicators to pick out the most significant indicators— elements of user browsing patterns. A thorough analysis and comparison are carried out before four indicators are selected as the input of an Artificial Neural Network which is adopted to calculate the implicit ratings. The mechanism of the implicit rating calculation is integrated into an educational resource sharing system as a featured module and works well.

1 Introduction

Seeking for appropriate educational materials in a large Educational Course Sharing System is a vapid job. A technique called Collaborative filtering [1], [2], [3] is then proposed to serve as the underlying recommending mechanism to alleviate such vapidity. Collaborative filtering takes a matrix as its input. Columns of the matrix are users' ratings on a specific course while each row corresponds to a single user. Thus each user is represented by a rating vector with some elements left blank. The vectors can be easily clustered into groups using existing clustering algorithms. Users in the same group generally share common interests. Hence, blank indicators in the rating vectors can be estimated by cross referencing between vectors in the same group.

Note that the input matrix is very sparse -- we should not expect users rate large portion of the courses because explicit rating actions are time consuming and will interrupt normal study processes[9] [10]. Implicit rating is then introduced as compensation.

Several papers have discussed the relative influence of a set of statistical parameters of user behaviors on implicit rating calculation. We examined the problem from another aspect. The contribution of our work is as the following: 1、Our methodology is different, rather than using statistical methods, we did some experiment and reached our conclusion by analyzing the results: 2、We integrated the whole implicit rating scheme into our educational resource sharing system and have got excellent performance.

This paper is organized as following: Section 2 briefly describes current research on implicit rating; In section 3, we give a detailed description about our research; In

---

[*] This work was supported by NSFC 70202008.

section 4, we designed a process to calculate the implicit rating; In section 5, we explained the deployment of the implicit rating in the educational resources sharing system and finally in section 6 we reached our conclusion and pointed out the future work need to do.

2 Related Research

We are directly inspired by the work of Mark Claypool et al. [4] [5]. In their work a browser was developed to record user actions as well as explicit ratings to find the correlation between them [5] [7] [8] [11] [14]. The authors then used Kruskal-Wallis test [6] to examine the degree of independence of the medians among each explicit rating groups for each implicit interest indicator. It is claimed that the higher the independence is, the less valuable an indicator may be for the explicit rating estimation purpose.

But a deeper look into the logic underlying the above reasoning will lead us to a question: from a practical point of view, the probability of the selected indicators not to work in certain circumstances is quite considerable. In another word, the work of Claypool et al. is inspiring and informative, but not very practical. To my knowledge, Kruskal-Wallis test is usually used to check if random numbers in different groups are of identical distribution, while in our case, let us take the time spent on a page for example, if Kruskal-Wallis test rejects the null hypothesis, which means that the distribution of the five ratings values are different, time spent on a page is then recognized as an effective implicit interest indicator. By following such a procedure, a set of indicators are filtered out.

If we choose to use the remaining indicators to predict the implicit rating, we are choosing a way too hard to follow. First we have to keep a trace of everyone's behavior, extracting some statistical features and do a sophisticate comparison to tell which group it should be classified into. We also should notice that such a classification is no longer a personalized one and is not fit for an online prediction.

There is another discrepancy. While calculating the precision of the prediction of the chosen set of indicators, difference between prediction results and explicit rating such '1' and '2' are treated as acceptable. It is quite easy to understand because difference between 1 and 2 or 4 and 5 are not large enough to distinguish user's preference between 'like' and 'dislike'. Here, 1~5 are treated as pure digits, rather than a set of labels, i.e. they are floating-point in the region [0, 5] rather than the set {1, ... , 5}.

Now let us recall the prediction process in which different behavioral patterns are recognized and labeled. 1~5 here are not only digits but labels representing a specific pattern.

Apparently, treating implicit rating as a label of some user's behavioral pattern is inappropriate. Implicit rating should fall into a continuous region and we designed a implicit rating generating system supplying such an requirement.

3 Indicator Selection

Analysis of Claypool et al.'s work gives us some clues about parameter selection. We will employ a more convincing method to avoid the inherent empirical nature of statistical analysis – statistically different parameters may indicate different user preference, but that is not guaranteed in theory.

3.1 Data Preprocessing

Data with explicit rating are effective data. Only effective data (about 80% of the dataset) which are meaningful for our experiment are kept and the other are filtered out. Then we get a dataset containing 1823 items. The ranges of indicators of the

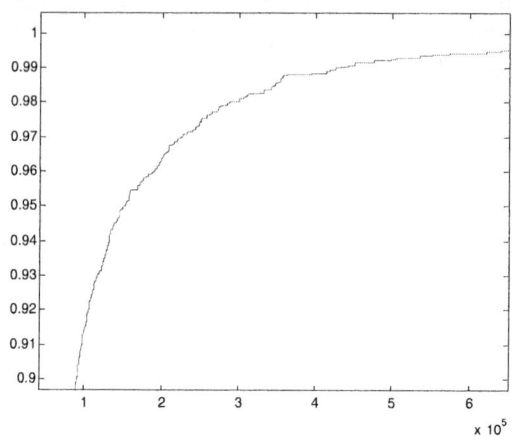

Fig. 1. ECDF of indicator 'time_spent_on_a_page', x-axis stands for the value of 'time_spent_on_a_page', y-axis stands for the ECDF varying with the x-axis value.

And then we plot the histogram:

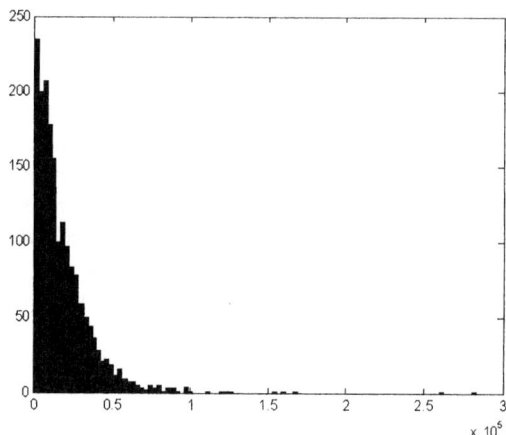

Fig. 2. Histogram of indicator 'time_spent_on_a_page', x- axis stands for the value of 'time_spent_on_a_page', y-axis stands for the histogram value of each bin according to x-axis value.

items are not determined—some may be too large to have a reasonable explanation. Take time_spent_on_a_page for example, its value may reach several hours in the case that a web user went to do something else and forget to close the browser. Such abnormal values are called outliers. We placed a control-boundary on each set of indicators to handle the outliers.

Here is what we do to find the control-boundaries. Again, let us take indicator 'time_spent_on_a_page' for example.

First, we plot the curve of ECDF (Empirical cumulative distribution function) of indicator 'time_spent_on_a_page'.

From the above two figures we can see that less than 2% of value of indicator 'time_spent_on_a_page' are greater than $3*10^5$ milliseconds. So we can safely choose $3*10^5$ milliseconds as the control-boundary of indicator 'time_spent_on_a_page'. Following the same way, we find control-boundaries of the other twelve indicators and listed them as following:

Table 1. Control-boundaries of indicators

Indicator	Control-boundary
1. time_spent_on_a_page	300000 ms
2. time_spent_horizontal_scrolling	45 ms
3. time_spent_vertical_scrolling	50000 ms
4. number_of_scroll_events	10 times
5. time_spent_moving_the_mouse	40000 ms
6. number_of_the_mouse_clicks	20 times
7. '↑'times	10 times
8. '↓'times	30 times
9. '↑'time	1000 ms
10. '↓'time	5000 ms
11. 'page up' time	2000 ms
12. 'page up' times	4 times
13. 'page down' time	2500 ms
14. 'page down' times	5 times

We can also see that, from the histogram, values of indicator 'time_spent_on_a_page' scatters in a very wide range which is a desired property for good indicators. As a comparison, let us take a look at the histogram of indicator 'horizontal_scrolling_time':

Value of indicator 'horizontal_scrolling_time' squeezes in such a narrow region that we can not expect it give us any successful prediction of user's preference.

3.2 Experiment on Indicator Selection

We take matlab as the platform of our experiment. The experiments are carried out as following:

Step one, 'wash the dataset', the preprocessed data are free from unreasonable/odd outliers;

Step two, divide the clean dataset into 5 partitions evenly, four of them will be used as training set and the other is to be used as test set;

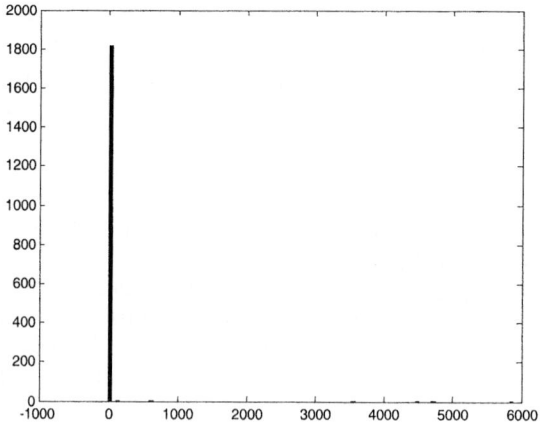

Fig. 3. Histogram of indicator 'horizontal_scrolling_time', x- axis stands for the value of 'horizontal_scrolling_time', y-axis stands for the histogram value of each bin according to x-axis value.

Step three, for every possible combination of the indicators, we train an artificial neural network for it and perform a corresponding test;

Step four, check the prediction performance of each individual indicator；

Step five, verified the obtained good indicators by finding the combination which produces the best prediction.

Now, we will focus on step three and four.

In step three, we are supposed to experiment on all possible combinations of the 14 indicators, that is 214=16384. For convenience, we will denote a specific combination by a binary number with 14 digits. To be clear, we have an example.

The corresponding binary number of 2301 is 00, 1000, 1111, 1101, the combination of indicators denoted by 2301 can then be decided, with indicators 3、 7、 8、 9、 10、 11、 12、 14 selected and others unselected.

The following example is designed to show how prediction performance of each individual indicator is compared in step four.

We will define the complementary of two combinations regarding indicator I before we go on.

Suppose C1 and C2 are binary numbers denoting two different combinations (of the 14 indicators). C1 xor C2 (xor is and operator, we can simply treat it as 'not carry binary adder' here) will produce a third binary, if the corresponding decimal number of this third binary is 215-I, then C1 and C2 are called complementary regarding indicator I.

For example : C1=10,0001,1101,0010, C2=10,0101,1101,0010. C1 xor C2 = 00,0100,0000,0000, so C1 and C2 are complementary regarding indicator 4.

Intuitively, difference between predication performances of complementary combinations regarding indicator I are proportional to the importance of indicator I. So we gather all complementary combinations regarding each indicator and then can find their relative importance. Due to lack of space, we cannot give a detailed description of our experiment, the result is plotted afterwards:

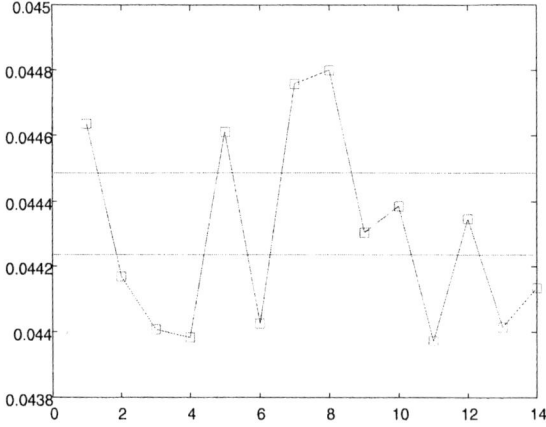

Fig. 4. Importance of indicators, x-axis stands for the indicator NO., y-axis stands for the average error of each indicator in predicting the implicit rating.

As we can see from figure 4, indicator 1, 5, 7, 8, corresponding to time_spent_on_a_page, time_spent_moving_the_mouse, '↑'times and '↓'times respectively, are the most important indicators, which complies with our experience. The 2 red bars partitioned the indicators into 3 parts, the first part, as we pointed out above, has the most satisfying predicting power, the second part has less power while the lowest part; part 3 can only be treated as noise in the predicting process.

4 Calculation of Implicit Ratings

We adopt Artificial Neural Network technique to calculate the implicit rating [8] [15]. From section 3 we know the input number is fixed as 4(the out put is the estimated

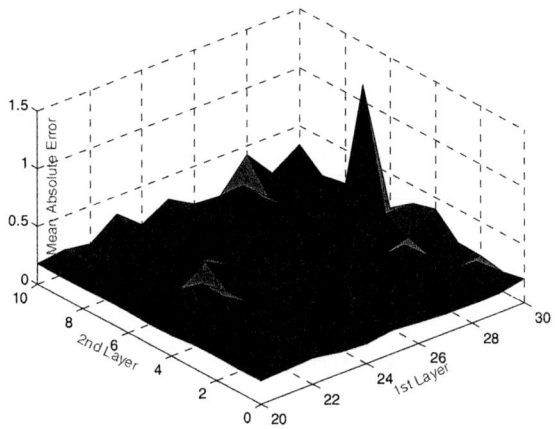

Fig. 5. Error of differently structured ANN

rating value), the work we need to do next is choosing right layer numbers and neuron numbers in each layer. Ref [6] has proved that an ANN can be used to fit any complicated curves in any degree, so we limit the ANN to have no more than 2 layers.

For different neuron numbers in each layer, we do separate experiments, different structure leads to quite different predicting performance.

When training the ANN model, we take mean absolute error as the performance function and use Levenberg-Marquardt back-propagation training algorithm.

To help understand the results better, we plot the result in figure 5.

Clearly, ANN with 30 neurons in the first layer and 7 neurons in the second layer has the least prediction error and that is the best structure we are seeking for.

5 Implementation

The project is supported by the Ministry of Education of P.R. China. The goal of the project is to establish a knowledge management platform for the 1500 nationally approved courses. The courses are open to all those who may need them. To increase the efficiency of the platform, a recommender system is introduced and has shown its power. Figure 6 show the framework of the recommender system.

Notice that implicit rating module stands at a crucial position. To facilitate the calculation of implicit rating, we will keep a set of weights for the ANN of each user, as well as a rating for each user/web page pair and a buffer to maintain the indicators from the latest visit. The whole process is described here:

Step1, the user clicks the 'submit' button to submit his/her indicator values or explicit rating;

Step2, push the indicator values into the buffer and set the flag if explicit rating is given;

Step3, train the ANN for the user/web page pair which has a newly come explicit rating if the CPU has spare time;

Step4, overwrite the old ANN with the learned one;

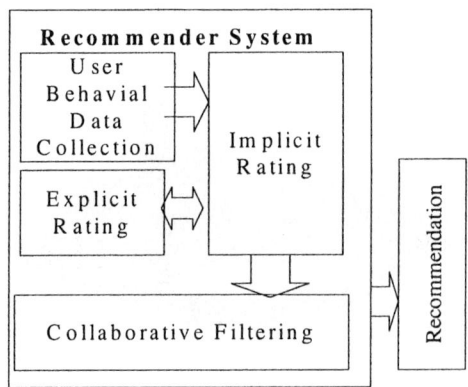

Fig. 6. Framework of the recommender system

Step5, if no explicit rating are given or system are busy to train the ANN, calculate the implicit rating using existed weights in the database and return it to the user as a feedback.

As we have seen, the implicit rating module has two working state: training state and evaluating state.

In the training state, the implicit rating module use indicator values and explicit rating to renew the weights of ANN. This enables the module to trace the browsing pattern and hence sustain/enhance the predicting performance.

In the evaluation state, the module only utilizes the trained ANN to simulate the browsing pattern and approximates the actual rating of the user.

We use a slide bar to collect the explicit rating so that the value we get is continuous rather than discrete numbers. Continuous number has its advantages when training the ANN and making more precise prediction.

Fig. 7. User behavioral data and explicit rating submission

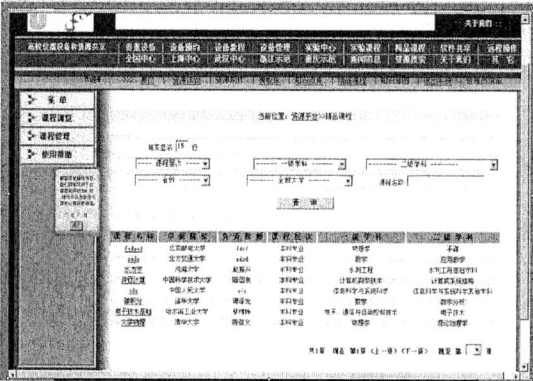

Fig. 8. Feedback of implicit rating

Meanwhile, we calculate the implicit rating and return it to the user. There are two reasons: first of all, to encourage the user to provide information useful to us later on and secondly, to check if our prediction reflects the actual user preference from the user's feedback.

6 Conclusion

The ANN we have introduced into the recommender system for the educational resource system removed the cost of explicit rating input. The sparsity problem facing the Collaborative Filtering has also be solved.

We are now working on the integration of the implicit rating and collaborative filtering. The implementation of collaborative filtering algorithm is also being carried out.

References

1. Badrul Sarwar, George Karypis, Joseph Konstan, and John Riedl: Item-Based Collaborative Filtering Recommendation Algorithms. Proc. of the 10th International World Wide Web Conference (WWW10), Hong Kong, May 2001
2. John S. Breese, David Heckerman, Carl Kadie: Empirical Analysis of Predictive Algorithms for Collaborative Filtering. In Proceedings of the Fourteenth Conference on Uncertainty in Artificial Intelligence, Madison, WI, July, 1998
3. Badrul M. Sarwar, George Karypis, Joseph A. Konstan, John T. Riedl: Application of Dimensionality Reduction in Recommender System -- A Case Study. ACM WebKDD 2000 Web Mining for E-Commerce Workshop 2000
4. Claypool, M., et al.: Implicit interest indicators, in Proceedings of ACM Intelligent User Interfaces Conference (IUI), Santa Fe, New Mexico. 2001, ACM
5. P.Le and M.Waseda: Curious browsers. Major Qualifying Project MQP-DCB-9906, May 2000
6. John A. Rice: Mathematical statistics and data analysis. Beijing: China Machine Press, 2003
7. Liberman, H: Letizia: An Agent that Assists Web Browsing. ZJCAZ-95, pp. 924-929
8. J.Goecks and J.W.Shavlik: Learning users' interests by unobtrusively observing their normal behavior. In proceedings of the ACM Intelligent User Interfaces Conference (IUI), Jan. 2000
9. White, R. W., Ruthven, I., and Jose, J. M.: Finding relevant documents using top ranking sentences: An evaluation of two alternative schemes. In Proceedings of the 24th Annual International Conference on Research and Development in Information Retrieval (SIGIR '02), Finland, 57-64.
10. Rafter, R., and Smyth, B.: Passive Profiling from Server Logs in an Online Recruitment Environment. In Proceedings of the IJCAI Workshop on Intelligent Techniques for Web Personalization (ITWP 2001), USA, 35-41
11. Maglio, P. P., Barrett, R., Campbell, C. S., and Selker, T.: SUITOR: An attentive information system. In Proceedings of the 5th International Conference on Intelligent User Interfaces (IUI '00), USA, 169-176.
12. Kim. J., Oard, D.W., and Romanik, K.: Using implicit feedback for user modeling in internet and intranet searching. University of Maryland CLIS Technical Report 00-01 .

13. Fischer, G., and Stevens, C.: Information access in complex, poorly structured information spaces. In Proceedings of the SIGCHI Conference on Human Factors in Computing Systems (CHI `91), USA, 63-70.
14. Billsus, D., and Pazzani, M. J.: A personal news agent that talks, learns and explains. In Proceedings of the 3' International Conference on Autonomous Agents (AGENTS 99), USA, 268-275
15. Liqun Han: ANN, theory, design and application. Chemical industry press

Application of Grey Majorized Model in Tunnel Surrounding Rock Displacement Forecasting

Xiaohong Li[1], Yu Zhao[1,2], Xiaoguang Jin[1,2], Yiyu Lu[1], and Xinfei Wang[1]

[1] Key Lab. for the Exploitation of South West Resources &
The Environmental Disaster Control Engineering Ministry of Education,
ChongQing 400044, China
[2] College of Civil Engineering, ChongQqing Uuniversity,
ChongQing 400045, China

Abstract. Source grey GM(1,1) model usually be used simulation and prediction of equidistant monitoring data sequnt. But to non-equidistant and high growth data sequnt, had to build the grey GM(1,1) model through equidistant treatment of non-equidistant data or to build directly non-equidistant grey model through complex transfermation, and usually had larger lagging error. In time sequnt [$k,k+1$] interval, in order to majorize and increase accuracy of background value $z^{(1)}(k+1)$, the area of [$k,k+1$] interval and GM(1,1) function curve envelope had been replaced by n small interval trapezoidal area. The GM(1,1) grey majorized model was built based on majorized grey model background value generally be used simulation and prediction of equidistant or non-equidistant and low or high growth data sequnt of surrounding rock displacement in tunnel. Data sequnt characters of Ⅰ, Ⅱ and Ⅲ shape of surrounding rock displacement can be simulated and predicted better by the grey majorized model, and the model had higher simulation and prediction accuracy.

1 Introduction

Grey GM(1,1) model is extensive used in grey forecasting study[1]. Equal interval conception was introduced when set up GM(1,1) model. As a result, premises condition of using GM(1,1) model is modeling sequence must be contented equal interval demand[2]. In geo-mechanics field, non-equidistant monitoring sequence depend time often exist. Some scholars had built the grey GM(1,1) model through equidistant treatment of non- equidistant data and usually had larger error. Others had built directly non-equidistant grey model through complex transfer and usually had more complicated computation ,though the precision is high.

The GM(1,1) grey majorized model was based on grey majorized model background value $Z^{(1)}(k+1)$. The grey majorized model is provided not only with the merits of concise formation and simple calculation but also with the wider application. It can be applied to the simulation and forecasting of equidistant,non-equidistant and high growth data sequnt , which is more accurate in calculating and forecasting the traditional GM(1,1) model.

The forecasting of the tunnel surrounding rock displacement is the important link of the information monitoring construction. It is the key when we want to know about whether the type and parameter of support is reasonable and the safety of the tunnel can be ensured. Now there are so many methods of tunnel surrounding rock displacement forecasting such as linear and non-linear regression prediction, displacement-time curve forecasting, neural networks etc.All of ways have there own features and limitations. Study proves that grey majorized model have general adaptation to underground projects such as tunnel etc.

2 GM(1,1) Modeling Mechanism

Suppose primary accumulating generating (1-AGO) sequence $X^{(1)} = (x^{(1)}(1), x^{(1)}(2), \ldots, x^{(1)}(n))$ of source data sequence $X^{(0)} = (x^{(0)}(1), x^{(0)}(2),\ldots,x^{(0)}(n))$, ($x^{(0)}(k) \geq 0$, k=1, 2,…, n), $X^{(0)}$, $Z^{(1)} = (z^{(1)}(2), z^{(1)}(3),\ldots, z^{(1)}(n))$ are mean generation consecutive neighbors of $X^{(1)}$, $Z^{(1)}(k+1) = 0.5 x^{(1)}(k) + 0.5 x^{(1)}(k+1)$; k=1, 2,…, n-1
Suppose $\hat{a} = (a,b)^T$ are parameter matrix, and

$$B = \begin{bmatrix} -z^{(1)}(2) & 1 \\ -z^{(1)}(3) & 1 \\ \vdots & \\ -z^{(1)}(n) & 1 \end{bmatrix} \quad Y = \begin{bmatrix} x^{(0)}(2) \\ x^{(0)}(3) \\ \vdots \\ x^{(0)}(n) \end{bmatrix} \tag{1}$$

Then GM(1,1) grey differential equation $x^{(0)}(k)+az^{(1)}(k)=b$ smallest second-multiplication estimated should be met with

$$\hat{a} = (B^T B)^{-1} B^T Y \tag{2}$$

The whiten equation is

$$\frac{dx^{(1)}}{dt} + ax^{(1)}(t) = b \tag{3}$$

The time-responding sequence GM(1,1) grey differential equation can be written as:

$$\hat{x}^{(1)}(k+1) = (x^{(0)}(1) - \frac{b}{a})e^{-ak} + \frac{b}{a}, \quad k=1,2\ldots n \tag{4}$$

Then the simulation value of source sequence:

$$\hat{x}^{(0)}(k+1) = x^{(1)}(k+1) - x^{(1)}(k) = (x^{(0)}(1) - \frac{b}{a})(e^{-a} - 1)e^{-a(k-1)} \tag{5}$$

From the above modeling, we can see that accuracy of calculation and prediction is dependent on constant a and b, which is also concerned with the structural style of background value $Z^{(1)}(k+1)$. If average value generates $Z^{(1)}(k+1)$ and constitutes the background value, when time interval is very short and sequence data changes little, the constructed $Z^{(1)}(k+1)$ is suited, and model windage is smaller. But when sequence data changes rapidly, it will generate bigger lagging error, while model windage is bigger[5]. If $-a>1$, we should not use GM(1,1) model[6].

3 Grey Majorized Model

We can find out from Equation.(1) that $z^{(1)}(k+1)$ is the average value of $x^{(1)}(k)$ and $x^{(1)}(k+1)$ which can be regarded as the trapezoidal abcd area of the interval $[k, k+1]$. Because the GM(1,1) model fitting curve is exponential one, the curve area corresponding to exponential curve $x^{(1)}(t)$ is less than the trapezoidal *abcd* area of the interval $[k, k+1]$. The bigger the data sequence change, the bigger the model error ΔS is. So, we can divide the interval $[k, k+1]$ into n small intervals to reduce the speed of variety of the data sequence and replace the real area of curve with n little trapezoidal areas to enhance the precision of background value $z^{(1)}(k+1)$. There should be an optimization value n to make the total areas of n little interval areas approach to actual area corresponding to exponential curve of the interval $[k, k+1]$ theoretically. When $z^{(1)}(k+1)$ is equal to the total areas of n little interval areas, calculated through n corresponding small areas, we can make the deviation of the model minimum and the precision of the simulation and predicting is the highest. The grey majorized model based on $z^{(1)}(k+1)$ can be suitable for the low growth array, can be suitable for the high growth array and has improved the precision and adaptability of the GM(1,1) model. From the grey majorized modeling mechanism, we can indicate that background value $z^{(1)}(k+1)$ is directly correlated with this value n, the change of the value n relates to data sequence. So the grey majorized model value $z^{(1)}(k+1)$ can not be affected by size of data sequence interval or the influence is weak and can be used in the simulation forecasting of non-equidistant tunnel surrounding rock displacement.

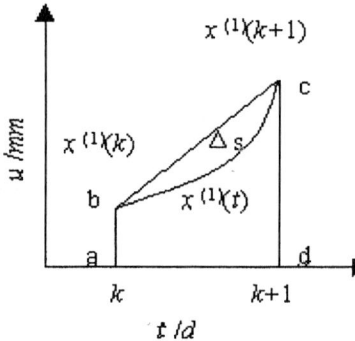

Fig. 1. Schematic diagram of $z^{(1)}(k+1)$

When interval $[k, k+1]$ is divided by n equally, the total areas of n little intervals is:

$$S_n = \frac{1}{2n}[(n+1)x^{(1)}(k) + (n-1)x^{(1)}(k+1)] \tag{6}$$

Define

$$z_n^{(1)}(k+1) = S_n = \frac{1}{2n}[(n+1)x^{(1)}(k) + (n-1)x^{(1)}(k+1)], \quad n=2,\ldots N \tag{7}$$

Then

$$\lim_{n \to \infty} z_n^{(1)}(k+1) = \frac{1}{2}(x^{(1)}(k) + x^{(1)}(k+1)) \tag{8}$$

In the course of procession, the key problem is how to determine the reference points number n. To calculate n, there is an experience formula, the formula is:

$$n = \left(\sum_{i=2}^{N} R_i\right)^{\frac{1}{N-1}} + (N-1) \tag{9}$$

N is the sequence length(the number of original modeling datas)

$$R_i = \frac{x^{(1)}(i)}{x^{(1)}(i-1)}, \quad i=2, 3, \ldots, N \tag{10}$$

Obviously, n is related to both N and 1-AGO sequence $x^{(1)}(k)$.

4 The Type of Tunnel Surrounding Rock Displacement-Time Curves

Both the engineering practice and theory analyse indicate that the type of tunnel surrounding rock displacement-time curves can be classified such three kinds as figure 2 below.

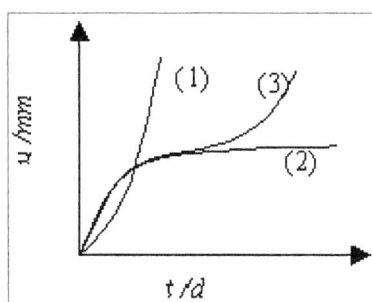

Fig. 2. Curve of u—t

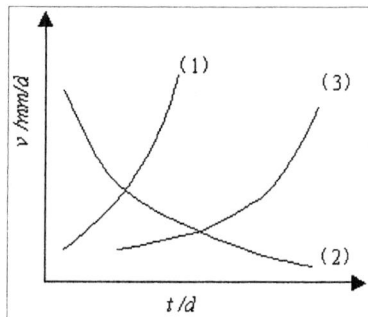

Fig. 3. Curve of v—t

4.1 Model I Displacement-Time Curve

Model I displacement-time curve reflect the part damage character of tunnel surrounding rock ,uncovered and without any treatment. Its characteristic is: the curve is a concave type(Fig2 curve (1)), the speed curve is monotonically increasing(Fig3 curve (1)), the acceleration is greater than zero permanently. Model I displacement-time curve shows that the deformation develops constantly as time goes on, showing the instability of the part or bigger range of rock mass. The time during which it happens is short, if we can't find and take the effective measure in time, it may cause casualties or property loss.

4.2 Model II Displacement-Time Curve

Model II curve often reflect the displacement character of tunnel surrounding rock, already supporteded but the stability is bad. Its characteristic is:the curve is a protruding type(Fig2 curve (2)), the speed curve is monotonically decreasing (Fig3 curve (2)), the acceleration is smaller than zero permanently . The Model II displacement-time curve is the reflection that the surrounding rock is becoming stable gradually.

4.3 Model III Displacement-Time Curve

Model III curve take place in the weak, swelling surrounding rock or long-term creep deformation surrounding rock aroused by bigger stress. Its character is: the curve change from the protruding type into the concave type(Fig2 curve (3)), the speed change monotonically,increasing from the monotonically decreasing, the speed curve have the polar value(Fig3 curve (3)), acceleration a is smaller than zero from beginning, becoming greater than zero later and there is the boundary of equaling zero in the acceleration. Model III curve is the creep instability curve. It's evolution course can be divided into three stages on the whole. The first stage is in increasing displacement state; The second stage is in steady-state creep; The third stage is in accelerating instable -state creep; The starting point at the third stage is a inflexion of the curve. Model III curve is the reflection of surrounding rock creep instability.

Because it is dispersed by the accidental error of field measure, we will not get the right typical curve unless carrying on mathematics disposal and describing them with corresponding formula, but the regression analysis is a better method for measure data. It also prove that the grey majorized model have more general suitability and very high simulation precision. in predicting the deformation character of the rock.

5 Case Analysis

5.1 Model I Displacement-Time Curve Simulation and Prediction

The convergence -time sequence of No 20 III-J2 measure section(in literature[7]) is analyzed. This section lies in fault rupture zone ,belonging to V surrounding rock (II surrounding rock in the highway tunnel). Both the convergency displacement measure

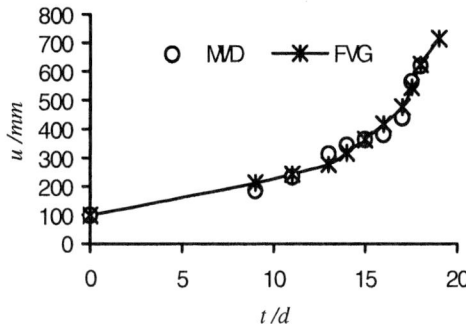

Fig. 4. Results of simulation and prediction of grey majorized model about I shape u-t curve

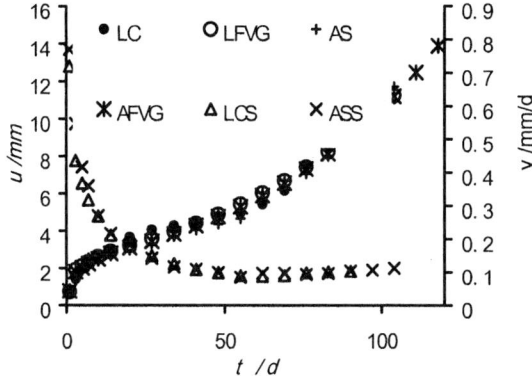

Fig. 5. Results of simulation and prediction of grey majorized model about II shape u-t curve

value and the calculating value of the grey majorized model are showed in Fig4, the results of simulation and prediction is good. The model parameter n=10.340085, a=-0.1352, b=184.031; The simulation prediction formula of GM(1,1) the grey majorized model:

$$\hat{x}^{(0)}(k+1) = 1460.126(e^{0.1352} - 1)e^{0.1352(k-1)}, \; k=1,2,3,\ldots,n \tag{11}$$

Where, MVD=the measured value of displacement; RE=relative error; LFVG=the levelwise convergence forecasting value of GM metabolism majorized model computation; AFVG= the arch settlement forecasting value of neural network model computation;LC= the levelwise convergence;AS= the arch settlement;LCS= the levelwise convergence speed;ASS= the arch settlement speed.

5.2 Model II Displacement-Time Curve Simulation and Prediction

The grey majorized model displacement prediction of model II displacement-time curve is based on the measure datum of the levelwise convergence and arch settlement of the section ZK35 +025 of Huayun mountain tunnel . Section ZK35 +025 locate in the anticline nuclear part of Longwang Hole, the embedded depth is large and the geo-stress is high.At the measure previous stage , the deformation of the surrounding rock is normal, the amount of deformation is relatively small too, about 4 mm. But when fifty days passed , the amount of deformation is still increasing, both the amount of levelwise convergence and arch settlement time sequence curves present obvious up bending trend; When 90 days passed, the deformation is it is not steady, its deformation speed shows a tendency of increasing too. It can be indicated that initial supports can't control the surrounding rock deformation and the deformation is still increasing. In the study of NATM construction monitoring,we make use of the grey majorized model and the result is as Fig. 5 shows.

The model parameter: the levelwise convergence, n=17.2138, a= -0.1044, b=1.7318; the arch settlement, n=19.1946, a= -0.1073, b=1.6284;
The corresponding simulation and prediction formula of GM(1,1) grey majorized model:the levelwise convergence:

$$\hat{x}^{(0)}(k+1) = 17.3088(e^{0.1044} - 1)e^{0.1044(k-1)}; \; k=1,2,3,\ldots,n \tag{12}$$

the arch settlement:

$$\hat{x}^{(0)}(k+1) = 15.9515(e^{0.1073} - 1)e^{0.1073(k-1)}; \; k=1,2,3,\ldots,n \tag{13}$$

It can be indicated that the simulation precision of the grey majorized model is relatively high. According to this tendency of the section displacement-time curve , we have offered information to the construction enterprises in time, the mended strong measure is taken.

5.3 Model III Displacement-Time Curve Simulation and Prediction

The simulation and prediction of Model III displacement-time curve is based on the measure amount of levelwise convergence and the arch settlement of representative Huayun mountain tunnel section. The simulation is analyzed and the precision is predicted.

6 Conclusions

The grey majorized model is provided not only with the merits of concise formation and simple calculation but also with the wider application. It can be applied to the simulation and forecasting of equidistant ,non-equidistant and high growth data sequent , which is more accurate in calculating and forecasting than traditional GM(1, 1) model.Data sequent characters of I, II and III shape of surrounding rock displacement can be simulated and predicted better by the grey majorized model, and the model had higher simulation and prediction accuracy and there are important theory value and practice meaning in the deformation prediction of underground surrounding rock .

References

1. Deng Julong. Grey prediction and decision-making. Wuhan: Huazhong University of Science & Technology Publishing House, 1998.
2. Tan Guanjun. Construction method and application of background value of GM(1,1) model (I). Theory and practice of system engineering, 2000, 20(5): 125~127.
3. Jiang Gang, Lin Lusheng, Liu Zhude etc.Prediction of grey model for slope displacement[J]. Rock and Soil Mechanics,2000,21(3):243~246.
4. Li Wenxou. Study prediction for rockmass instability due to underground excavation under complex topography [J].Chinese Journal of Rock Mechanics and Engineering,2001,20: 1645~1648
5. Liu Sifeng, Guo Tianbang, Dang Yaoguo. Theory and application of grey system (second edition). Beijing: Sciences Press, 1999.
6. Xiong Xiaobo. Research of intelligent prediction and control of deep and large excavation work[D].Tongji University doctor's degree paper,2003
7. Qi Lan, Cui wei, Xiong Kaizhi etc. Application of grey theory to analyse of in-situ stress field[J].Chinese Journal of Rock Mechanics and Engineering,2002,20: 1547~1550.

NN-Based Damage Detection in Multilayer Composites

Zhi Wei[1], Xiaomin Hu[2], Muhui Fan[1],
Jun Zhang[2,*], and D. Bi[3]

[1] School of Mechanical Engineering, Hebei University of Technology,
Tianjin 300130, PR China
[2] Department of Computer Science, Sun Yat-sen University,
Guangzhou 510275, PR China
junzhang@ieee.org
[3] Box 140, Tianjin University of Science and Technology,
Tianjin 300222, PR China

Abstract. The discrete-time system of multilayer composite plate is modeled using neural network (NN) to produce a nonlinear exogenous autoregressive moving-average model (NARMAX). The model is implemented by training a NN with input-output experimental data. Each damaged sample can be modeled by a parameter governed by the propagation behaviors of the NN. A residual signal is evaluated from the difference between the output of the model and that of the real system. A threshold function is used to detect the damaged behavior of the system. The results show that a three-layer neural network can be a general type of and suitable for the nonlinear input-output mapping problems of multilayer composite system.

1 Introduction

Fiber-reinforced multilayer composites are widely used in structures of aerospace, vehicles, architecture and light industrial products. Under aging, chemical corruption and mechanical impact, failure of this kind of components is mostly due to delaminations [1-4].

Damage detection and diagnosis algorithms using mathematical models have been used in a large variety of systems [5-7]. Nevertheless, the reliability of these algorithms deteriorates especially as a result of un-modeled dynamics, poorly known parameters and nonlinearities. Hence it is necessary to develop an adaptive modeling algorithm capable of approximating any nonlinear dynamic behavior and, at the same time, accurately predict detecting system damage [8, 9]. Due to the anisotropy and the complexity of material structure, it is more complicated to carry out dynamic damage detection of composites than that of metals. Especially for nonlinear discrete system, Leontaritis and Billings have proposed the nonlinear, autoregressive, moving average exogenous (NARMAX) structure as a general parametric form for modeling nonlinear system [10, 11]. The function of polynomial type is the most used to the establish-

---

* Corresponding author.

ment of NARMAX model. However, the calculation of term coefficients may be unpractical using the conventional recursive algorithm when the order is as high as more than three [12]. Therefore, this paper focuses on the study of a practical neural network method for modeling of NARMAX model of multilayer composite system, and then, based on this model implements detection and estimation of internal delamination according to experimental signals of both the intact and damaged composite systems.

2 Experiment and Investigation on Nonlinear Nature of Multilayer Composite Plate

2.1 Composite Samples and Experimental Set-Up

Prepared 16-layer carbon fiber-reinforced epoxy plates are used as samples. Each sample has an area of 240×180 mm² in the orientation of $[0/0/90/90/0/0/90/90]_s$. The laminate is fabricated using TC12K33/S-1 prepreg tapes with a thickness of 0.13 mm. Each damaged sample is delaminated at a specified position by inserting Teflon film with a thickness of 0.015 mm. The film is inserted between the forth and fifth layers when the laminate is fabricated. Simply supported boundary condition is adopted during experiment.

For nonlinear nature investigation, both static and dynamic experiments are carried out. The static load-strain test is used to investigate the static behavior of the system. A concentrated compressive load along the opposite of z-direction is applied at the point with coordinates $x=184$ mm and $y=168$ mm on the top surface. The strain ε_x along x-direction is measured at the point with coordinates $x=48$ mm and $y=90$ mm on the top surface.

Periodic signal tests are used to investigate the dynamic nonlinearity of the composite system. Two piezoelectric patches with a thickness of 0.28 mm and a size of 15×25 mm² are bonded on the top and bottom surfaces, respectively as actuators. An accelerometer is used as the transducer and adhered to the point with coordinates $x=184$ mm and $y=168$ mm. Exciting signal is generated by a waveform generator. A power amplifier and a charge amplifier are used to enhance signals from the generator and transducer, respectively. Both the exciting and response signals are recorded and analyzed by an FFT spectrum analyzer.

2.2 Nonlinearity Analysis of Multi-layer Composites

To approximate the nonlinearity of the system, several loads of different amplitudes are applied, and then the nonlinear behavior of the system is determined by the relationship between the values of the inputs and outputs. Fig. 1 shows the nonlinear strain-load relationship of the intact specimen. According to the spectral properties of the signals it is possible to detect and qualify the dynamic behavior of the nonlinearity in a system by examining the additional frequency contributions generated at the system output by nonlinearity [13]. The dynamic results also show the nonlinear nature of the system, because the response of the intact system to a harmonic excitation includes not only main harmonic composition, but also the super- and hypo-harmonic compositions of exciting frequency. The result of root-mean-square (RMS) values of the acceleration response shows that the relationship between the amplitudes of excitation and response is also nonlinear. Thus, a suitable nonlinear model must be established in order to realize damage detection or health monitoring of composite system.

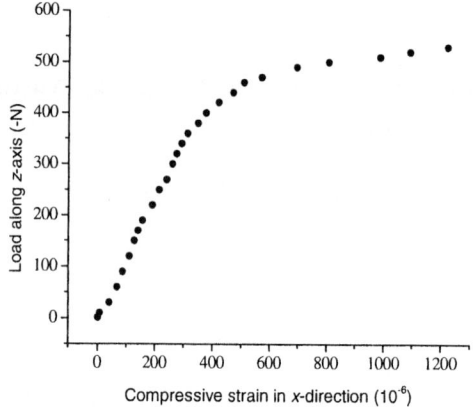

Fig. 1. Strain-load plot obtained by static test for the intact composite plate

3 NN-Based NARMAX Model

3.1 Modeling of Nonlinear System

The identification of system dynamics by means of input-output experimental measurements provides a useful solution for the formulation of a model. A NARMAX model describing the input-output relationship of the nonlinear single-input single-output (SISO) system can be written as

$$y(k) = F(y(k-1),...,y(k-n_y),x(k-d),...,x(k-n_x),e(k-1),...e(k-n_e)) + e(k) \quad (1)$$

In order to establish the NARMAX model of a given system, determination of model structure and terms is the vital stage besides sufficient experimental data. This nonlinear mapping may include a variety of nonlinear terms and polynomial terms are mostly used. However, when the polynomial order is more than three for a high recursive system the possible terms included are too huge to be determined using orthogonal estimation algorithm [12].

3.2 Neural Network Method for NARMAX Model

A network with three layers of weights and sigmoid activation functions can approximate any smooth mapping [14]. Consider a simple three-layer network with two neurons in input and hidden layers, respectively, and one output neuron. The activation functions of neurons for the hidden and output layers are sigmoid and purely linear functions respectively.

The three-layer BPNN topology as show in Fig. 2 is used to build the NARMAX model for composite plates in this study. The three types of layers are: the input layer (with N_p nodes), which receives the measured data of recursive excitation and response; the hidden layer (with N_h nodes) for data processing; the output layer (with only one nodes), which gives the prediction value of the present response. The recursive order and time delay of the excitation and response will be searched, in this study, using the orthogonal estimation algorithm for an ARMAX model [15]. The neuron number N_h of the hidden layer will be selected by training the NN to meet the minimum error.

3.3 The Algorithm for Damage Estimation

The realization of damage detection or prediction relies on the availability of a healthy model of the composite system. This model is obtained by training the BPNN using the experimental data of the intact plate. Once the NN is well trained the response $y(t)$ can be predicted for a certain time step. Using the matrix form the overall BPNN as shown in Fig. 2 can be mathematically defined by

$$y(k) = W_2(\tanh(W_1 p + B_1)) + B_2 \tag{2}$$

where p is the input vector of the input layer and for the intact system

$$p = (y(k-1),...,y(k-n_y), x(k-d),...,x(k-n_x))^T \tag{3}$$

When the plate is damaged the response is assumed to be $y_d(t)=\lambda(t)y(t)$ and the input vector becomes

$$p = (\lambda(k-1)y(k-1),...,\lambda(k-n_y)y(k-n_y), x(k-d),...,x(k-n_x))^T \tag{4}$$

where $\lambda(t)$ represents the response gain due to damage and $\lambda=1$ if the system is intact. Therefore, the parameter $\zeta= 1-\lambda$ is adopted to be the estimation of a delamination severity in the composite plate.

It can be seen that only the parameter λ can affect the system output signals and then the training signals of the neural model. When the plate is intact the training allows an accurate training of the neural model (NARMAX model). However, delamination in the plate would result in an inaccurate model. Therefore, training must be performed during the intact condition only.

If the residual signal is defined as the difference between the measured response and the model output the delamination in a plate will be detected by comparing the residual magnitude against a predefined constant threshold level. It is seen that when the neural network is well trained this difference is very small for the intact system. However, when a delamination occurs in the plate, the actual system output will be different from that of the model, i.e., a large residual can be observed. In this case the damage parameter λ is estimated based on minimization of the following objective function

$$J = \frac{1}{2}(y_m(t) - \lambda(t)y(t))^2 \tag{5}$$

where $y_m(t)$ is the measured response of the system and $y(t)$ is the intact model output.

By defining the error function as

$$e(t) = y_m(t) - \lambda(t)y(t) \quad (\lambda(t)=1 \text{ for the intact system}) \quad (6)$$

the partial derivative is formulated as

$$\frac{\partial J}{\partial \lambda(t)} = -e(t)(\lambda(t)\frac{\partial y(t)}{\partial \lambda(t)} + y(t)) \quad (7)$$

Then, the estimation of damage parameter is

$$\lambda(t+1) = \lambda(t) + \eta e(t)(\lambda(t)W_1 W_2 \frac{dp}{ds}\text{sech}^2(W_1 p + B_1) + y(t)) \quad (8)$$

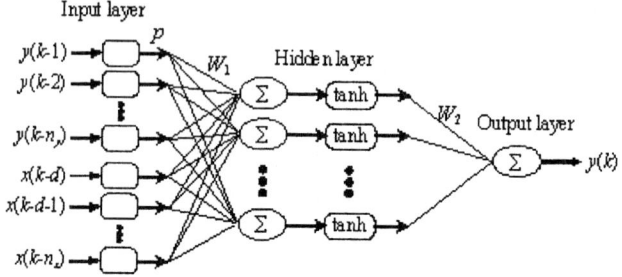

Fig. 2. Three-layer neural network for NARMAX model

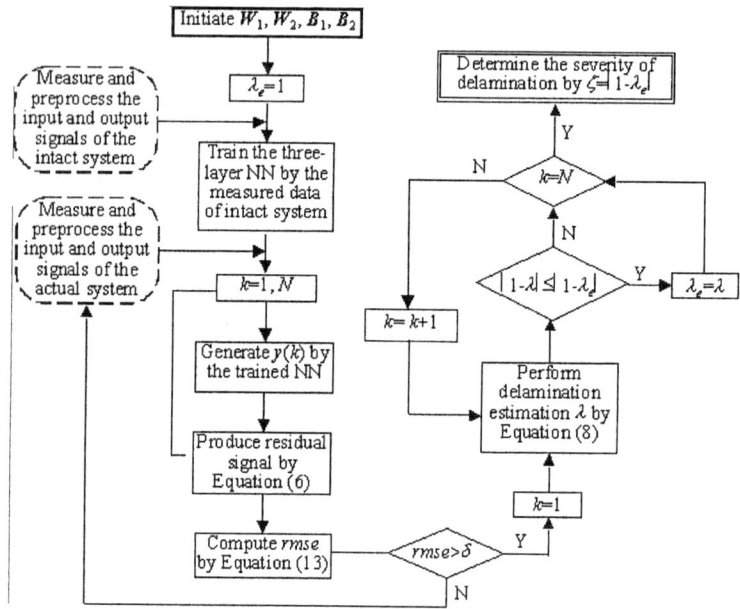

Fig. 3. Flowchart of the delamination estimation algorithm using NN-based NARMAX model

Therefore, Eq. (8) gives a recursive form for delamination estimation in the composite plate. The normalized root-mean-square-error (*rmse*) value defined by

$$rmse = \sqrt{\sum_{k=1}^{N}(y(k)-y_m(k))^2} / \sqrt{\sum_{k=1}^{N}y^2(k)} \qquad (9)$$

is used to represent the residual signals. The overall approach is summarized in Fig. 3, where δ is a constant as the threshold of *rmse*. In order to asymptotically estimate the delamination, the algorithm should remain active until the magnitude of the residual signal of the damaged system closely approaches the magnitude the residual signal of the intact system.

4 Results and Discussions

4.1 Structure Identification of NARMAX Model

The model order (forward or recursive order) is the first unknown encountered in the definition of NARMAX model to describe the dynamics of the composite system. Although tests for the composite system nature indicate that the system is nonlinear identifying initially the best linear model (ARMAX) is always helpful for a suitable choice of n_x, n_y and d in the NARMAX model of Eq. (1) [12].

A white noise signal with width of 1-1600Hz is used as excitation for the intact composite system as described in the second section. For simplicity, the same forward orders of input and output terms are adopted, i.e., $n_x=n_y$. Table 1 lists the computation results of prediction errors for different time delay and forward orders as expressed by

$$\sigma = \sqrt{\frac{1}{N-N_\theta}\sum_{k=1}^{N}(y_m(k)-y(k))^2} \qquad (10)$$

where N_θ represents the total term number of linear form of the NARMAX model as expressed in Eq. (1). It is seen that when the time delay d is 1 σ reaches the minimum for almost all recursive orders and the average is also the minimum for all the time

Table 1. Values of σ for different ARMAX models for the intact system

Recursive order (n_x)	Time delay (d)						Average
	0	1	2	3	4	5	
1	1.02E-2	9.85E-3	9.85E-3	9.85E-3	9.85E-3	9.85E-3	9.90E-3
2	9.99E-3	9.82E-3	9.82E-3	9.82E-3	9.82E-3	9.82E-3	9.84E-3
3	7.45E-3	7.46E-3	7.55E-3	7.83E-3	7.91E-3	7.91E-3	7.72E-3
...	...	...	...	...	...	...	...
11	3.96E-3	3.80E-3	3.96E-3	4.48E-3	4.48E-3	4.77E-3	4.32E-3
12	3.94E-3	3.73E-3	3.94E-3	4.48E-3	4.48E-3	4.78E-3	4.30E-3
13	4.10E-3	3.77E-3	4.12E-3	4.86E-3	4.86E-3	4.88E-3	4.50E-3
14	4.10E-3	3.77E-3	4.12E-3	4.86E-3	4.86E-3	4.88E-3	4.43E-3
15	4.01E-3	3.74E-3	4.07E-3	4.82E-3	4.82E-3	4.98E-3	4.41E-3
Average	6.15E-3	6.01E-3	6.14E-3	6.43E-3	6.48E-3	6.53E-3	

delays. The table also shows that ☐will nearly monotonically decrease with the increase of recursive order until it is 12, and goes up slightly after this order when d=1. The average value is again the minimum when the recursive order is 12. Therefore, the time delay of d=1 will be used to fit the NARMAX model and an appropriate recursive order will be nx= ny =12.

4.2 NARMAX Model Trained by NN

Following the above suggestions of the model structure and the initial values of forward order and time delay, the NARMAX model is estimated by neural method. The input layer of the neural network has N_θ=12+12 neurons fed by the instantaneous values of the variables as

$$p = (y(k-1), y(k-2),..., y(k-12), x(k-1), x(k-2),..., x(k-12))^T \quad (11)$$

and this layer doesn't perform any transformation of their values. During training, the hidden layer is made of a variable number of neurons performing a sigmoid transformation of their inputs. The output layer, with only one neuron, simply transforms its input according to a linear transformation. The optimal dimension of the hidden layer is chosen by increasing, five neurons per time and from five to fifty, the number of hidden neurons in order to determine the neural network with best possible performances. The training set is made of 1000 pattern-target couples (i.e., N=1000). They are the first 1000 record of excitation and response signals of the intact system. In order to ensure fast and efficient convergence the training algorithm follows the Levenberg-Marguardt rule [16], i.e., the matrix of the weights of the network is updated on the base of J, collecting the partial derivatives of the error of the network with respect to the weights. After training, the performance of every possible network is tested by analyzing the normalized error via its autocorrelation function expressed as

$$\phi_e(\tau) \approx \frac{1}{N}\sum_{i=1}^{N}\bar{e}_i(t)\bar{e}_i(t+\tau) \quad (12)$$

where

$$\bar{e}_i(t) = e_i(t)/\sqrt{\sum_{k=1}^{N}e_k^2(t)}, \quad e_i(t) = y_{mi}(t) - y_i(t) \quad (13)$$

When the above function remains inside the range of $\pm 1.96/\sqrt{N}$, the system is then considered accurately modeled [16]. The analysis of the autocorrelation function of the error for increasing hidden neurons pointed out that the best number of hidden neurons to be chosen is N_h=30. Fig. 4 shows the correlation function calculated for the prediction errors of the twelfth-order NARMAX model corresponding to the best possible identification of the dynamics of the intact composite system.

It is seen that the error property can be indeed considered satisfactory, as only occasionally the autocorrelation function slightly exceeds the desired limit (corresponding to $\pm 1.96/\sqrt{N}$ =±0.062). The normalized root-mean-square-error of the trained model is 1.52553×10^{-9}. Fig. 5 shows the comparison between the experimental output and the ahead prediction for the NARMAX model. Therefore, the model is well suited to model the input/output behavior of the multi-layer composite plate dynamics.

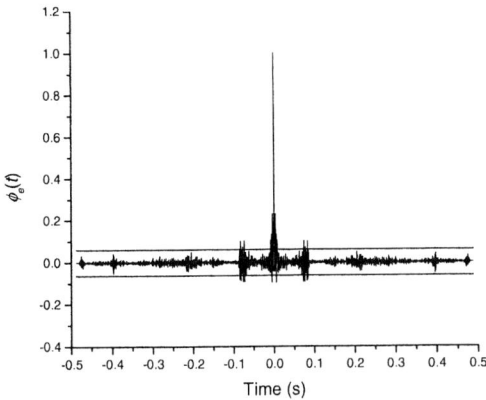

Fig. 4. Autocorrelation function for the prediction errors of the twelfth-order NARMAX model for the intact composite system.

4.3 Delemination Estimation

The damage (delamination) in the composite plate will be detected by comparing the residual magnitude against a predefined constant threshold level, where the residual signal is defined as the difference between the actual system output and the model output. Without delamination the residual is very small for the well-trained NN model of the intact system. However, when delamination occurs the actual output of the system will be different from that of the model, leading to a larger residual magnitude. According to the proposed method four damaged plate systems have been tested. They are all the same as the intact system except with delamination areas of 18×12 mm^2, 36×24 mm^2, 54×36 mm^2 and 72×48 mm^2, respectively.

In order to obtain as identical as possible the response signals for each the measurement, the average of 100 repeated data is used as the final output signal of each

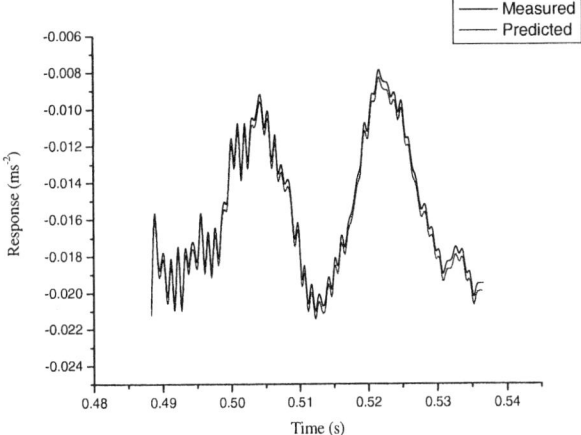

Fig. 5. Response predict of a hundred points ahead by NARMAX model for the intact composite system

dynamic system. During the implement of the damage detecting method, the residual threshold level δ is determined by the maximum *rmse* of 50-time repeated outputs of the NARMAX model for the intact system (i.e., 0.088). Each final estimation of damage severity parameter ζ is obtained by minimizing its value within N (1000) data points and the values are 0.034, 0.052, 0.078 and 0.11 for delamination areas of 18×12 mm^2, 36×24 mm^2, 54×36 mm^2 and 72×48 mm^2, respectively. It is seen that the magnitude of ζ depends on the dimension of delamination area. Therefore, it is practical to detect and estimate delamination in the multilayer composite plates by means of NN-based NARMAX method. If there were enough specimens with different sizes of damage, another NN could be trained by the damage parameters in order to identify a damage as the form of its actual type and size according to the NN output.

5 Conclusions

This paper aims to identify the dynamics of multilayer composite system in order to detect and estimate internal delamination. As the nonlinear nature of the composite system, the identification is performed by means of NARMAX model. The model is implemented by training a three-layer BP neural network with input-output experimental data. Satisfactory agreement between predicted and experimental data is found and results show that the model successfully predict the delamination severity.

The delamination occurred in the composite plates is detected by comparing the difference of outputs between the NARMAX model and the actual system against a predefined constant threshold level. The severity of delamination is estimated according to the weights and biases of the BPNN as representative of the NARMAX model. Result shows that it is reliable to detect and estimate internal delamination in the composite plates. The proposed method consists in the natural ability in modeling nonlinear dynamics in a fast and simple way and in the possibility to address the process to be modeled as an input-output black box, with little or no mathematical information on the system. It can also be used for online or active health monitoring of composite system.

References

1. Tasi SW, Hann HT. Introduction to composite materials. Westport, Connecticut: Technic Publishing Company, 1980.
2. Voyiadjis GZ. Damage in Composite Materials. Amsterdam. New York: Elsevier, 1993.
3. Gadelrab RM. The effect of delamination on the natural frequencies of a laminated composite beam. Journal of Sound and Vibration 1996;197(3):283-292.
4. Osset Y, Roudolff F. Numerical analysis of delamination in multi-layered composite plates. Computational Mechanics 2000;20(1-2):122-126.
5. Frank PM, Fault diagnosis in dynamic systems using analytical and knowledge-based redundancy. Automatica, 1990, 26: 459-474.
6. Isermann R, process fault diagnosis with parameter estimation methods. Proceedings of the IFAC Symposium on Digital Computer Applications to Process Control, Vienna, Austria, 1985, 63-68.
7. Patton RJ, Robust model-based fault diagnosis: the state of the art, Proceedings of the IFAC Symposium SAFEPROCESS'94, Helsinki, Finland, June 1994, 102-110.

8. Zhang J, Roberts PD, Online process fault diagnosis using neural network techniques. Transactions of Institute of Measurement and Control, 1992, 14: 179-188.
9. Wang H, Daley S, An approach to fault detection using nonlinear modeling and estimation. Proceedings of the 11th IFAC World Congress, Sydney, Australia, 1993, 291-294.
10. Leontaritis, I. J., Billings, S. A., 1985, "Input-output parametric models for nonlinear systems," International Journal of Control, 41(2), 303-344.11 Leontaritis IJ, Billings SA, 1985, "Input-output parametric models for nonlinear systems part I: deterministic nonlinear systems," International Journal of Control, 41(2), 303-328.
11. Leontaritis IJ, Billings SA, 1985, "Input-output parametric models for nonlinear systems part II: Stochastic nonlinear systems," International Journal of Control, 41(2), 329-344.
12. Billings, S. A., Tsang, K. M., 1989, "Spectral analysis of nonlinear systems-Part I. Parametric nonlinear spectral analysis," Journal of Mechanical Systems and Signal processing, 3(4), 319-339.
13. Evans, C., Rees, D., Hill, D., 1998, Frequency-domain identification of gas turbine dynamics, IEEE Transactions on Control Systems Technology, 6(5), 651-662.
14. H. Liu, M. Guillot and L. Cheng, Active vibration control of airplane structural elements using neural network, Active-99, Fort Lauderdale, Florida, USA, 2-4 December 1999
15. Boggs P. T., Byrd R. H., Schnabel R. B., A stable and efficient algorithm for nonlinear orthogonal distance regression. SIAM Journal on Scientific Computing, 1987, 8: 1052-1078.
16. Billings SA, Jamaluddin HB, Chen S, Correlation based model validity tests for nonlinear models. International Journal of Control, 1986, 44: 235-244.

Application of Support Vector Machine and Similar Day Method for Load Forecasting

Xunming Li[1], Changyin Sun[1,2,*], and Dengcai Gong[1]

[1] College of Electrical Engineering, Hohai University,
Nanjing 210098, China
[2] Department of Automation, Southeast University,
Nanjing 210096, China
*cysun@ieee.org

Abstract. Support Vector Machine (SVM) is a precise and fast method for the prediction of short-term electrical load and the similar day method is a simple and direct method for load forecasting. This paper tries to combine SVM model and similar day method for next day load forecasting. The proposed method forecasts the load of next day using SVM. Then, the load curve of a similar day is selected to correct the curve forecasted by SVM, which can avoid the appearance of large forecasting error effectively. Corresponding software was developed and used to forecast the next day load in a practical power system, and the final forecasting result is accurate and reliable.

1 Introduction

Load forecasting plays an important role in power system planning and operation. Basic operation functions such as unit commitment, economic dispatch, fuel scheduling and unit maintenance can be performed efficiently with an accurate forecast.

Research on short-term load forecasting has attracted wide attention for many years. Several major methods and techniques have been proposed and developed, including time series models, regression models, Box-Jenkins transfer function, expert system models, neural network models and fuzzy logic [1]. However, load forecasting is a difficult task as the load at a given hour depends not only on the load at the previous hour but also on the load at the same hour on the previous day, and on the load at the same hour on the day with the same denomination in the previous week. Generally, these methods are based on the relationship between load and factors influencing the load. However, the techniques employed for those models use a large number of complex and nonlinear relationships between the load and factors influencing the load. The traditional prediction methods are difficult to estimate these nonlinear relationships. Therefore, some new forecasting models have been recently introduced as expert systems, artificial neural networks (ANN), and fuzzy systems. Among these different techniques of load forecasting, application of ANN technology for electric load forecasting has received much attention in recently years. The main reason of ANN becoming so popular lies in its ability to learn complex and nonlinear relationships that are difficult to model with conventional techniques. However, there are some disadvantages of ANN method such as network structure is hard to determine and training algorithm has the danger of getting stuck into local minima.

Recently, a novel type of learning machine, called support vector machine (SVM), has been receiving increasing attention in areas from its original application in pattern recognition to the extended application of regression estimation [2-3]. This is brought about by the remarkable characteristics of SVM, such as good generalization performance, the absence of local minima and sparse representation of solution. One key characteristic of SVM is that training SVM is equivalent to solving a linearly constrained quadratic programming problem so that the solution of SVM is always unique and globally optimal, unlike ANN' training which is time-consuming and requires nonlinear optimization with the danger of getting stuck into local minima. Recently, there is also a great deal of researches concentrating on applying regression SVM to short-term electrical load forecasting [4-6]. In short-term load forecasting, load of two days that have similar weather condition, same day class (workday or weekend) and several other similar factors are generally very close. From this view, the similar day method [7-8] has been developed. Flowing the idea obtained from the previous work [4], this paper tries to combine SVM theory and similar day method to forecast the next day electrical load. The proposed method uses SVM for next day electric load forecasting. The historical data of some previous days are used as samples data to train SVM. With the trained SVM, the load curve of next day is forecasted. At the same time, a similar day is selected by similar day method. Then, the correction should be done with the forecasted value by SVM when it violates the general rule of load curve of the similar day. This method is used to forecast the next day load of a practical power system in a week. The experimental result shows that the proposed method performs well on both the forecasting accuracy and the computing speed.

The paper is organized as follows. Section 2 gives a brief introduction to SVM in regression estimation and the similar day method. Section 3 presents the proposed method for load forecasting in detail. Section 4 discusses the experimental result and then several error evaluation indexes are engaged. Section 5 concludes the work.

2 The Regression SVM and Similar Day Method

2.1 SVM for Regression Estimation [3]

Given a set of data points $\{(X_i, y_i)\}_i^N$, ($X_i \in R^n$, $y_i \in R$, N is the total number of training sample) randomly and independently generated from an unknown function, SVM approximates the function using the following form:

$$f(X) = <\omega, \varphi(X)> + b \quad (1)$$

where $\varphi(X)$ represents the high-dimensional feature spaces which is nonlinearly mapped from the input space X. The coefficients ω and b are estimated by minimizing the regularized risk function (2):

$$\text{minimize} \quad \frac{1}{2}\|\omega\|^2 + C\sum_{i=1}^{N}\left|y_i - <\omega, \varphi(X_i)> - b\right|_\varepsilon \qquad (2)$$

$$\left|y_i - <\omega, \varphi(X_i)> - b\right|_\varepsilon = \begin{cases} 0 & |y - <\omega, \varphi(X)> - b| < \varepsilon \\ |y - <\omega, \varphi(X)> - b| - \varepsilon & |y - <\omega, \varphi(X)> - b| \geq \varepsilon \end{cases} \qquad (3)$$

The first term $\|\omega\|^2$ is called the regularized term. Minimizing $\|\omega\|^2$ will make a function as flat as possible, thus playing the role of controlling the function capacity. The second term $\sum_{i=1}^{N}\left|y_i - <\omega, \varphi(X_i)> - b\right|_\varepsilon$ is the empirical error measured by the ε-insensitive loss function (3). This loss function provides the advantage of using sparse data points to represent the designed function (1). C is referred to as the regularized constant. ε is called the tube size. They are both user-prescribed parameters and determined empirically.

To get the estimation of ω and b, (2) is transformed to the primal objective function (4) by introducing the positive slack variables $\xi_i^{(*)}$ ((*) denotes variables with and without *)

$$\text{minimize} \quad \frac{1}{2}\|\omega\|^2 + C\sum_{i=1}^{N}(\xi_i + \xi_i^*)$$

subject to

$$y_i - <\omega, \varphi(X_i)> - b \leq \varepsilon + \xi_i$$
$$<\omega, \varphi(X_i)> + b - y_i \leq \varepsilon + \xi_i^* \qquad (4)$$
$$\xi_i^{(*)} \geq 0 \qquad i=1,\ldots,N$$

Final, by introducing Lagrange multiplier and exploiting the optimality constraints, the decision function (1) has the following explicit form:

$$f(X) = \sum_{i=1}^{N}(\alpha_i - \alpha_i^*)K(X_i, X) + b \qquad (5)$$

In function (5), $\alpha_i^{(*)}$ are the so-called Lagrange multipliers. They satisfy the equalities $\alpha_i \times \alpha_i^* = 0, \alpha_i \geq 0$, and $\alpha_i^* \geq 0$ where $i=1\ldots N$, and they are obtained by maximizing the dual function of (4), which has the following form:

$$W(\alpha_i, \alpha_i^*) = \sum_{i=1}^{N} y_i(\alpha_i - \alpha_i^*) - \varepsilon \sum_{i=1}^{N}(\alpha_i - \alpha_i^*)$$
$$-\frac{1}{2}\sum_{i=1}^{N}\sum_{j=1}^{N}(\alpha_i - \alpha_i^*)(\alpha_j - \alpha_j^*)K(X_i, X_j) \qquad (6)$$

Subject to

$$\sum_{i=1}^{N}(\alpha_i - \alpha_i^*) = 0, \qquad 0 \leq \alpha_i, \alpha_i^* \leq C, \quad i=1\ldots N$$

$K(X_i, X_j)$ is defined as the kernel function. The value of the kernel is equal to the inner product of two vectors X_i and X_j in the feature space $\varphi(X_i)$ and $\varphi(X_j)$, that is, $K(X_i, X_j) = <\varphi(X_i), \varphi(X_j)>$. The elegance of using the kernel function that one can deal with feature spaces of arbitrary dimensionality without having to compute the map $\varphi(X)$ explicitly. Any function that satisfies Mercer's condition can be used as the kernel function. Common examples of the kernel function are the polynomial kernel $K(X_i, X_j) = (<X_i, X_j> + 1)^d$ and the Gaussian kernel $K(X_i, X_j) = \exp(-(1/\sigma^2)(X_i - X_j)^2)$, where d and σ are the kernel parameters.

From the implementation point of view, training SVM is equivalent to solving the linearly constrained quadratic programming problem (6) with the number of variables twice as that of the number of training data points. The sequential minimal optimization (SMO) algorithm extended by Scholkopf and Smola is very effective in training SVM for solving the regression estimation problem. In this paper, an improved SMO algorithm [9] is adopted to train SVM.

2.2 The Similar Day Method [7]

In short-term load forecasting, load of two days are generally very close when they have similar weather condition, same day class (workday or weekend) and several other similar factors. Experiential forecaster can find out a similar day and correct the load curve of the similar day to forecast the load curve of the next day.

These central rules should be analyzed at first. In general, the changing of load between two days are influenced by following factors:

(1) Day types are different: loads in weekend are always lower than that in workday, and loads in Monday between midnight and morning are always lower than that in common workdays in that period of time.
(2) Weather conditions are different: weather conditions have a notable influence in electrical load, especially in summer and winter.
(3) Loads structure will change slowly along time. As to two days between a long period of time, even they have the same day type and weather conditions, the loads of two days also exist some differences.

From this view, the similar day method has been developed. The method is composed by two steps: the first is to select the similar day which has the minimal value of a difference estimation function; the second is to correct the load of the similar day according to the parameters of the forecasting day.

The mathematic model is presented in following:

$$\Delta P = P_f - P_h = \phi(\alpha, \beta) \tag{7}$$

$$\|\alpha - \beta\| = [(\alpha_1 - \beta_1)^2 + (\alpha_2 - \beta_2)^2 + \cdots + (\alpha_k - \beta_k)^2]^{\frac{1}{2}} \tag{8}$$

there

ΔP – the variance of load between forecasting day and similar day,

P_f – load of forecasting day,

P_h – load of similar day,

$\alpha_1, \alpha_2, \cdots, \alpha_k$ – the values of factors which influence the load of a previous day,

$\beta_1, \beta_2, \cdots, \beta_k$ – the values of factors which influence the load of forecasting day.

The day with the minima of $\|\alpha - \beta\|$ would be selected as the similar day, and then the load of next day would be forecasted. The advantages of the method are simple, practical and comparatively precise.

3 The Proposed Forecasting Model

In a practical power system, the trend of electrical load can be described by linear changing model, periodic changing model and random model. According to linear changing model, A large part of load is so-called base load which would be not influenced by the change of weather, so in the proposed method, only the part which influenced by weather conditions evidently will be used as target inputs to train SVM. According to periodic model, the historical data in a certain previous period are selected as training samples. Then the SVM will be trained to describe the nonlinear relationship between influencing factors and electrical load.

The specific steps are presented in following:

First, transforming the non-numerical factors into numerical form. Taking sunlight for example: fine is set as 3, cloudy as 2, rain as 1. The maximal and minimal temperature can apply the actual values.

Second, treating disorder samples. Considering the proportion of the load in serial time, it is sure appearing disorder data when the change of load violates the general rule. Checking every point according to this principle to pick out all disorder data and correct them.

Third, for avoiding saturation problems, it is vital to scale input and target input to range of [0,1] as follows

$$X_{Normalization} = \frac{X_{actual} - X_{min}}{1.5 * X_{max} - X_{min}} \tag{9}$$

There X_{max} and X_{min} are maximum and minimum values of training samples. This particular function selected for normalization is chosen based on some tries and errors.

Fourth, training SVM using the normalized samples. Then an effective algorithm SMO is employed there. Taking the influencing factors vector of forecasting day into the trained SVM, the 24 points load of next day will be forecasted.

Five, selecting similar day from previous days. The day with the minimal value of $\|\alpha - \beta\|$ is selected as similar day. The load curve of next day would be forecasted by correcting the load of similar day.

Finally, correcting the result forecasted by SVM. According to random model, the electrical load is influenced by a series of uncertain factors and it is hard to get a satisfy result absolutely using historical data. So, the similar day load curve is used to amend the result forecasted by SVM. When the change of forecasted load violates the regular pattern of result forecasted by similar day method, then this value is insecure usually, which should be corrected or instead by the load forecasted by similar day method. The correction can avoid the appearance of value with comparatively big error effectively.

4 Experimental Results

To evaluate the performance of the proposed load forecasting scheme, the SVM and similar day method were tested with data obtained from a sample study performed on the Henan Province Power System, to predict the daily energy consumption 24-hour ahead. The example data is historical load data in a practical electrical network in October and November in 2003. The data includes the data of weather conditions and the data of 24 points load in every day. The 24 SVM models are trained for 24-hour points. Using the forecasted weather information of next day, 24 load points of next day are forecasted. Our model adopts the improved SMO algorithm to train SVM and RBF kernel function $k(x,\bar{x}) = \exp(-1/\delta^2(x-\bar{x})^2)$ is selected as the kernel function. Corresponding parameters are selected as follows $\delta = 1$, C = 0.1, ε = 0.016.

There are many error evaluation indexes to evaluate the result of daily load forecasting. In this paper, four relative error indexes are selected to evaluate the forecasting result of the proposed method. Table 1 represents the daily load forecasting errors from Nov.15 to Nov.21 in year 2003, and four error indexes of forecasting result are represented here.

Table 1. Relative errors of experimental result

Day	E_{MAPE} /%	E_{MSE} /%	E_{max} /%	E_{min} /%
Monday	1.73	2.06	1.66	1.06
Tuesday	1.98	2.35	1.62	4.07
Wednesday	1.67	2.11	0.38	1.34
Thursday	3.03	3.36	3.89	2.31
Friday	2.73	3.14	1.70	1.53
Saturday	2.15	2.39	1.69	3.85
Sunday	2.16	2.62	2.13	1.96

The content of table 1 indicates that the maximum of the mean average percentage error E_{MAPE} is 3.03% and the minimum is 1.67%. The forecasting result of this new method is accurate and reliable.

Fig. 1 is an example of daily load forecasting for Nov. 17,2003 forecasted by SVM solely. Fig. 2 shows the forecasting result corrected by similar day method. In fig.1, it could be observed that the values in point 9 and point 12 forecasted by SVM violated the general pattern of curve forecasted by similar day method. These values are insecure usually, and should be corrected or instead by the load forecasted by similar day method. There, an abnormal peak occurred in point 9 and the average of values in point 9 and point 11 is used to instead of it. The value in point 12 is lower than the value forecasted by similar day method with a large gap. So, that value is unbelievable and corresponding value in similar day method is used to instead of it. The corrected curve is showed in fig.2. The correction can avoid the appearance of values with comparatively large error, and the mean average percentage error of forecasting result is reduced from 2.23% to 1.73%.

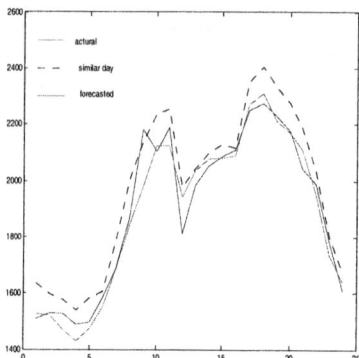

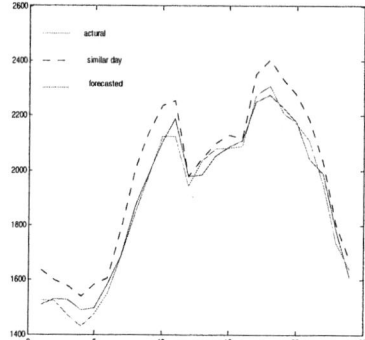

Fig. 1. The forecasting results of SVM

Fig. 2. The curve corrected by similar day method

5 Conclusion

This paper proposed a combined method for next day load forecasting based on SVM model and similar day method. The method used SVM to describe the nonlinear relationship between load and influencing factors, and corrected the forecasted results by the curve of a similar day to avoid the appearance of large forecasting error. This method behaves the advantages of both similar day method and SVM method, i.e. simple, practical, accurate and experience unreliable. Experimental result shows that this method is an effective method of high application value for next day load forecasting.

Acknowledgements

This work was supported by the National Natural Science Foundation of China under Grant 50595412, China Postdoctoral Science Foundation under Grant 2004036124, Jiangsu Planned Projects for Postdoctoral Research Funds and a start-up grant from Hohai University of China.

References

1. Hippert, H.S., Pefreira, C.E., Souza, R.C.: Neural network for short-term load forecasting: a review and evaluation. IEEE Trans. Power Systems, 16 (2001) 44-54
2. Vapnik, V.N., Golowich, S.E., Smola, A.J.: Support vector machine for function approximation, regression estimation and signal procession. Advance in Neural Information Procession System, 9 (1996) 281-287
3. Cao, L.J., Francis, E.H.: Support vector machine with adaptive parameters in financial time series forecasting. IEEE Trans. Neural Networks, 14 (2003) 1506-1518
4. Li, X.M., Gong, D., Li, L., Sun, C.Y.: Next day load forecasting using SVM. Lecture Notes in Computer Science, Springer, Berlin, 3498 (2005) 634-639
5. Yang, J.F, Cheng, H.Z.: Application of SVM to power system short term load forecasting. Electric Power Automation Equipment, 24 (2004) 30-32
6. Li, Y.C, Fang, T.J., Zhang, G.X.: Wavelet support vector machine for short-term load forecasting. Journal of university of science and technology of China, 33 (2003) 726-732
7. Cheng, S.: A new short-term load forecast method based on the similar day. Proceeding of Jiangsu Electrical Engineering Association, 18 (1999) 28-32
8. Ju, P., Jiang, W., Zhao, X.Y.: Ninety-six points short-term load forecasting—theory & applications. Automation of Electric Power Systems, 25 (2001) 32-36
9. Zhang, H.R., Han, Z.Z.: An improved sequential minimal optimization learning algorithm for regression support vector machine, Journal of Software, 14 (2003) 2006-2013

Particle Swarm Optimization Neural Network and Its Application in Soft-Sensing Modeling

Guochu Chen and Jinshou Yu

Research Institute of Automation, East China University of Science and Technology,
Shanghai 200237, China
chgcsh@sohu.com

Abstract. Particle swarm optimization algorithm (PSO) is applied to train artificial neural network (NN) to construct a neural network based on particle swarm optimization algorithm (PSONN). Then, PSONN is employed to construct a practical soft-sensor of gasoline endpoint of main fractionator of fluid catalytic cracking unit (FCCU). The obtained results indicate that soft-sensing model based on PSONN has better performance than soft-sensing model based on BPNN and the new method proposed by this paper is feasible and effective in soft-sensing modeling of gasoline endpoint.

1 Introduction

Soft sensing techniques have been used more frequently as attractive and effective methods of process modeling and a replacement of expensive and ineffective online analytical instrument to some extent [1]. Now, there are two types of models usually used in the soft sensing modeling of the chemical industrial process [1]: mechanistic models (or first principle model, FPM) developed from the underlying physical and chemical knowledge about a process, and empirical models (EM) developed from the operational data of a process. FPM is based on the analysis of the mass, momentum, and energy balance as well as empirical correlation. However, only major characteristics and trends of the process are described by the FPM. Additionally, FPM includes many assumptions, and lacks in considering random disturbances that are present in many real systems. However, the development of FPM for some processes, especially some complex processes, can be too difficult or even not possible. For such processes, empirical models (EM) based on process operational data should be preferred. Many industrial processes exhibit nonlinear dynamic behavior, and nonlinear model should be developed. Artificial neural network (NN) has been shown to be able to approximate any continuous nonlinear functions [2] and is an attractive technique that can be applied to nonlinear process modeling.

Artificial neural network is a representation that attempts to mimic the functionality of the brain. For several decades scientists have being trying to emulate the real neural structure of the brain, believing that the human process of learning might be reproduced by an algorithmic equivalent. Initially the principal motivation behind this research was the desire to achieve the sophisticated level of information processing that could be achieved by the brain. However, it is apparent that present research aims are not directed at emulating the sheer complexity of the brain. Generally, the methodology is used on a more modest scale to develop nonlinear models.

An important issue in NN is the train algorithm. Now back-propagation algorithm (BP) is most commonly used to train NN [2]. BP is a gradient-based method, so some inherent problems are frequently encountered in the use of this algorithm, e.g., very slow convergence speed in training, easily to get stuck in a local minimum, etc. Some techniques are therefore introduced in an attempt to resolve these drawbacks, but all of them are still far from satisfaction [2], so new train algorithm needs developing.

Particle swarm optimization algorithm (PSO) is an evolutionary computation algorithm proposed by Eberhart and Kennedy in 1995 [3-4]. The idea of PSO is based on the simulation of simplified social models, such as bird flocking, fish schooling, and the swarming theory. PSO is a simple algorithm and can be developed over a very simple theoretical framework and can be implemented with a few lines of computer code, requiring only primitive mathematical operators. PSO is computationally inexpensive in terms of both memory requirements and speed. Besides, PSO is indeed a population-based stochastic algorithm. It does not need gradient information, as the gradient-based algorithm does. This allows functions whose gradients are either unavailable or computationally expensive to be solved using the PSO algorithm. It was originally developed for optimization in a continuous space and it has been recently adapted to optimization in binary spaces, presenting good performance also when applied to discontinuous objective functions and is an attractive algorithm in artificial neural network training. Here, PSO is employed to train NN to construct an artificial neural network based on particle swarm optimization algorithm (PSONN). Then PSONN is applied to construct a practical soft-sensor of gasoline endpoint of main fractionator of fluid catalytic cracking unit (FCCU).

2 Particle Swarm Optimization Neural Network (PSONN)

2.1 PSO Algorithm

PSO algorithm uses a population of individual called "particles". Each particle has its own position and velocity to move around the search space. Using the term "particle" may convey finite mass-volume objects, which is not true of the PSO algorithm. These particles are, in fact, points in space. However, since these points have velocity and position, the term "particle" is more suitable than "point". Particles move to trying to find the solution for the problem being solved.

Suppose that the search space is D-dimensional and a particle swarm consists of m particles, then the i-th particle of the swarm can be represented by a D-dimensional vector, $X_i = (x_{i1}, x_{i2}, x_{i3}, \cdots, x_{iD})$, $i = 1, 2, \cdots, m$. The velocity of this particle can be represented by another D-dimensional vector, $V_i = (v_{i1}, v_{i2}, v_{i3}, \cdots, v_{iD})$. The fitness of every particle can be evaluated according to the objective function of optimization problem. The best previously visited position of the i-th particle is denoted as its individual best position, $P_i = (p_{i1}, p_{i2}, p_{i3}, \cdots, p_{iD})$. Define g as the index of the best particle of the whole swarm, the position of the best individual of the whole swarm is denoted as the global best position P_g, and the fitness of the global best position is denoted as the global best fitness F_g. Then the velocity of particle and its new position will be assigned according to the following two equations [3-5]:

$$v_{id} = \chi \cdot (\omega v_{id} + c_1 r_1 (p_{id} - x_{id}) + c_2 r_2 (p_{gd} - x_{id})) \tag{1}$$

$$x_{id} = x_{id} + v_{id} \tag{2}$$

where χ is a constriction factor; ω is called inertia weight; c_1 and c_2 are two positive constants called acceleration coefficients; r_1 and r_2 are two random numbers uniformly from the interval [0, 1].

2.2 The Structure of PSONN

An artificial neural network consists of a system of simple interconnected neurons, or nodes, as illustrated in Fig. 1. It is a model representing a non-linear mapping between input and output vectors. The nodes are connected by weights and output signals, which are a function of the sum of the inputs to the node modified by a simple non-linear transfer function, or activation function. It is the superposition of many simple non-linear transfer functions that enables the neural network to approximate extremely non-linear functions. The output of a node is scaled by the connecting weight and feed forward to be an input to the nodes in the next layer of network. The architecture of a neural network is variable, but, in general, consists of several layers of neurons. The input layer plays no computational role but merely serves to pass the input vector to the network. A neural network may have one or more hidden layers and have only an output layer. The neural network is described as being fully connected to every node in the next and the previous layer.

In Fig. 1, x is the input of NN. net is the sum of the inputs to the node modified by activation function. O is the output of neural node. y is the output of NN. PSONN assumes the weight and threshold of NN as the position of particle of PSO, evaluates the fitness of particle according to objective function of system, then searches for the global best weight and the global best threshold by PSO. If the search is accomplished, the position of the global best particle is the combination of the best weight and the best threshold of PSONN.

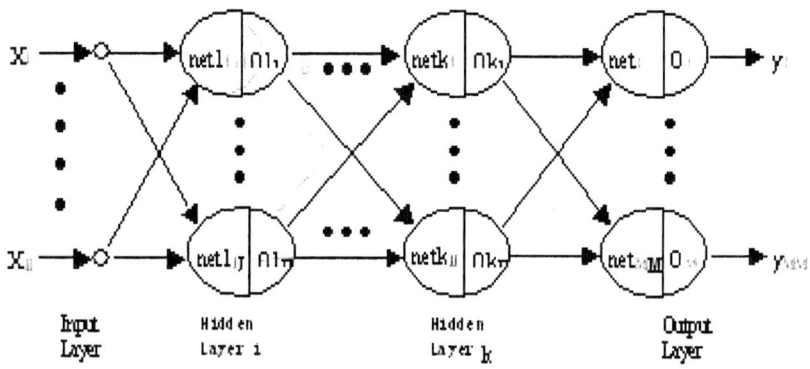

Fig. 1. The structure of PSONN

By selecting a suitable set of weights and transfer functions, it is known that a neural network can approximate any smooth, measurable function between the input and output vectors. The neural network has the ability to learn through training. The training requires a set of training data, i.e., a series of input and associated output vectors. During the training, the neural network is repeatedly presented with the training data and the weights in the network are adjusted from time to time till the desired input–output mapping occurs. If, after the training, the neural network is presented with an input vector, not belonging to the training pairs, it will simulate the system and produce the corresponding output vector. The error between the actual and the predicted function values is an indication of how successful the training is.

2.3 Train Algorithm of PSONN

PSONN train algorithm can be summarized in the following steps:
1. Initialize the structure, activation function and objective function of PSONN.
2. Initialize the algorithm parameters of PSO.
3. Store initial position of each particle. Evaluate and store initial fitness of each particle. Evaluate and store the global best position and global best fitness of the swarm.
4. Update particles' velocities and positions by equation (1) & equation (2), and set a limit to particles' positions and particles' velocities.
5. Update the individual best fitness and the individual best position of each particle; Update the global best fitness and the global best position of the swarm.
6. If the stopping condition is not satisfied, go to step 4. Otherwise, stop iterating and obtain the best weight and the best threshold from the global best position.

3 Practical Application in Soft-Sensing Modeling

3.1 Introduction of Engineering Background

Main fractionator is one of the most important equipment of FCCU, which is a most important unit in refineries [6]. The feed-in material of the tower is get from catalytic cracking reactor. The effluent product of reaction goes to the main fractionator, where the heat is removed in its various pump-around and loops and initial product separation is accomplished, then usable products including gas, gasoline, light diesel oil and heavy diesel oil are produced.

Gasoline endpoint is a most important product quality indicator of main fractionator of FCCU [6]. But gasoline endpoint can't be measured on-line directly. At present, gasoline endpoint is usually acquired mainly by artificial analyzing once every 4 hours. It can cause a long delay in control and the product will be unqualified if the component of the reactor product changes a lot. So it is very important for refineries to acquire gasoline endpoint on-line.

3.2 Soft-Sensing Model of Gasoline Endpoint Based on PSONN

Gasoline endpoint can't be measured directly like temperatures, pressures and flow rates. But it can be estimated by soft-sensor. According to the analysis of system's technological mechanism and the principal component analysis of the practical industrial data, gasoline endpoint is related with these nine variables that can be measured and recorded on-line: the pressure of the top of the tower, the temperature of oil-gas at the top of the tower, the temperature of reflux at the top of the tower, the temperature of the 18-th floor tray, the temperature of the 9-th floor tray, the temperature of the first middle reflux of the tower, the temperature of gasoline of the tower, the flow rate of reflux flow of the first middle reflux and the temperature of the feed oil-gas of main fractionator. In this section, gasoline endpoint is studied. The relationship between gasoline endpoint and the above-mentioned nine variables is complex nonlinear relationship. To estimate gasoline endpoint, we must find the relationship between gasoline endpoint and the nine variables. In this section, a PSONN that has nine input signals that correspond with the above nine variables, a middle layer whose number of node is twenty and an output signal that is gasoline endpoint is employed to find the relationship between gasoline endpoint and the nine variables. The structure of PSONN is 9-20-1. The transfer function of neurons of PSONN takes hyperbolic tangential function. The objective function of the soft-sensing model can be expressed as follow:

$$\min E = \frac{1}{2} \cdot \sum_{kk=1}^{n_p} (t^{kk} - y^{kk})^2 \qquad (3)$$

Where t is the real value of gasoline endpoint, y is the estimated value of gasoline endpoint, kk is the serial number of samples, n_p is the total number of samples.

To evaluate the performance of soft-sensing model conveniently, the mean square error and the mean absolute error are defined as follow:

$$RMSE = \frac{1}{n_p} \sum_{1}^{n_p} (t^{kk} - y^{kk})^2 \qquad (4)$$

$$Meanae = \frac{1}{n_p} \sum_{1}^{n_p} |t^{kk} - y^{kk}| \qquad (5)$$

In searching for the global best weight and threshold of NN by PSO, population of swarm is set to 100; The maximal number of iteration step is set to 20000; Error limit of objective function is 0.2; c_1 and c_2 are set to 2.0; ω is gradually decreased from 1.8 to 0.06; χ is set to 0.8.

In order to compare the result of soft-sensor based on PSONN with the result of soft-sensor based on BPNN that a NN based on BP algorithm, this paper constructs another soft-sensing model of gasoline endpoint based on BPNN. In BPNN, the structure of NN, the transfer function of neurons and the sample data all are the same as that of PSONN. The differences are: the train algorithm is BP algorithm, the learning velocity is 0.016 and the momentum factor is 0.012.

3.3 Discussion of Application Results

There are 127 sets of sample data that consist of nine operating variables in different operating states and one output variable, the real value of gasoline endpoint. 77 pairs of them are used as off-line training data sets and another 50 pairs are used as on-line examining data sets. All the sample data are processed by error-detected, smoothed, filtered and standardized in the intervals [-1, +1] before they are used as input or output of the two soft-sensors.

After the learning and statistical accounting, the errors of 66.2 percent of learning samples are less than ±1℃; The errors of 98.7 percent of learning samples are less than ±2℃; The mean square error of the learning samples is 0.9248℃; The mean absolute error of the learning samples is 0.7671℃ in soft-sensor based on PSONN. However, in soft-sensor based on BPNN, the errors of 64.9 percent of learning samples are less than ±1℃; The errors of 96.1 percent of learning samples are less than ±2℃; The mean square error of the learning samples is 1.0626℃; The mean absolute error of the learning samples is 0.8483℃. Table 1 and Fig. 2 show the comparison between learning result of soft-sensing model based on PSONN and learning result of soft-sensing model based on BPNN. These experiment data, Table 1 and Fig. 2 show that the learning result of soft-sensing model based on PSONN is better than learning result of soft-sensing model based on BPNN. The soft-sensing model based on PSONN has higher learning precision and better learning ability than the soft-sensing model based on BPNN.

Table 1. Comparison of the learning results of the two soft-sensing models

		Avera-value	Mini-value	Maxi-value		|e|	|e|<1	1<|e|<2	|e|>2
Real values (℃)		198.0	192	207	Total		77		
Predictive values	PSONN	197.9	191.6	206.3	Numbers	51	25	1
	BPNN	198.7	192.2	207.0	Numbers	50	24	3
Meanae	PSONN (℃)			0.7671	RMSE	PSONN	0.9248 (℃)		
	BPNN (℃)			0.8483		BPNN	1.0626 (℃)		
the maximum relative error	PSONN			0.01061	the minimum relative error	PSONN	0		
	BPNN			0.01783		BPNN	0.00005		

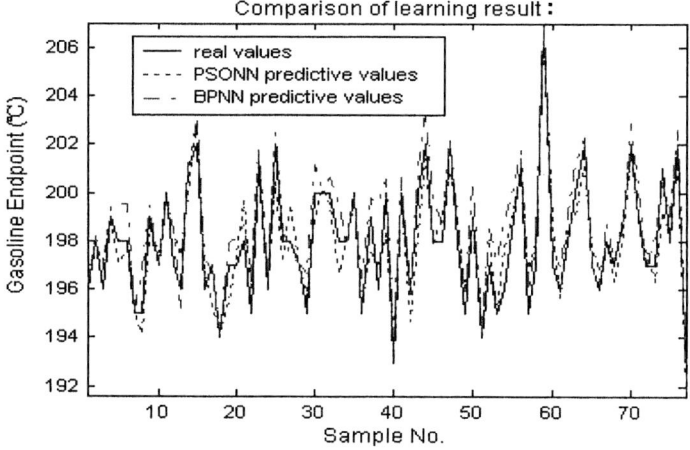

Fig. 2. Comparison of learning result

After the examining and statistical accounting, the errors of 52 percent of examining samples are less than ±1°C; The errors of 88 percent of examining samples are less than ±2°C; The mean square error of the examining samples is 1.3787°C; The mean absolute error of the examining samples is 1.1034°C in soft-sensor based on PSONN. However, in soft-sensor based on BPNN, the errors of 54 percent of examining samples are less than ±1°C; The errors of 86 percent of examining samples are less than ±2°C; The mean square error of the examining samples is 1.4425°C; The mean absolute error of the examining samples is 1.1284°C. Table 2 and Fig. 3 show the comparison between examining result of soft-sensing model based on PSONN and examining result of soft-sensing model based on BPNN. These experiment data, Fig. 3 and Table 2 show that the examining result of soft-sensing model based on PSONN is better than examining result of soft-sensing model based on BPNN. The soft-sensing model based on PSONN has higher examining precision and better generalization ability than the soft-sensing model based on BPNN.

Table 2. Comparison of the examining results of the two soft-sensing models

		Aver-values	Mini-values	Maxi-values		|e|	|e|<1	1<|e|<2	|e|>2
Real values (°C)		197.6	192	205	Total	50		
Predictive values	PSONN	197.9	192.3	204.9	Numbers	26	18	6
	BPNN	198.0	191.2	204.8	Numbers	27	15	8
Meanae	PSONN (°C)			1.1034	RMSE	PSONN	1.3787 (°C)		
	BPNN (°C)			1.1284		BPNN	1.4425 (°C)		
the maximum relative error	PSONN			0.01904	the minimum relative error	PSONN	0.00015		
	BPNN			0.01986		BPNN	0.00018		

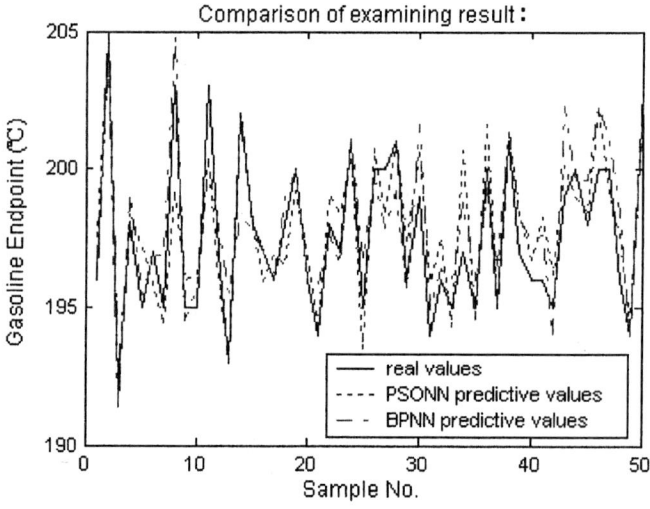

Fig. 3. Comparison of examining result

4 Conclusion

A neural network based on PSO is proposed for soft-sensing modeling of gasoline endpoint of main fractionator of FCCU. The approach takes a novel kind of optimization algorithm, i.e., particle swarm optimization algorithm, to train the neural network. A performance comparison is emphasized on the PSO-based soft-sensing model with the most commonly used BP-based soft-sensing model. The results show that the soft-sensor based on PSONN has better training performance, higher precision and better predicting ability than soft-sensor based on BPNN. It is convenient for refineries to estimate, display, record and analyze gasoline endpoint on-line. It is worth to mention that the current study is very preliminary for the PSO-based neural network approach applied in soft-sensing modeling of gasoline endpoint of main fractionator of FCCU. More researches need to be done, for example, to improve current approach and apply it to other product quality estimate of industrial process or more complex industrial cases.

References

1. Jinshou Yu, Ailun Liu, Kejin Zhang: Soft-senor Technique and Its Applied in Petrochemical Industry Process. Chemical Industry Press, Beijing, China (2000)
2. Licheng Jiao: Theory of Neural Networks System. Xidian University Press, Xi'an, Shanxi, China (1996)
3. Kennedy J, Eberhart R C: Particle Swarm Optimization. Proc. IEEE Int. Conf. on Neural Networks. Perth, WA, Australia (1995) 1942-1948
4. Eberhart R C, Kennedy J: A New Optimizer Using Particle Swarm Theory. Proc. the Sixth Int. Symposium on Micro Machine and Human Science. Nagoya, Japan (1995) 39-43
5. K.E. Parsopoulos, M.N. Vrahatis: Recent Approaches to Global Optimization Problems Through Particle Swarm Optimization. Natural Computing 1 (2002) 235–306
6. Shixiong Lin: Petroleum Processing Engineering. Petroleum Industry Press, Beijing, China (2000)

Solution of the Inverse Electromagnetic Problem of Spontaneous Potential (SP) by Very Fast Simulated Reannealing (VFSR)

Hüseyin Göksu[1], Mehmet Ali Kaya[2], and Ali Kökçe[1]

[1] Süleyman Demirel University, Isparta, Turkey
goksu@sdu.edu.tr, kokce@fef.sdu.edu.tr
[2] Çanakkale Onsekiz Mart University, Çanakkale, Turkey
makaya@comu.edu.tr

Abstract. Very Fast Simulated Reannealing (VFSR) is applied to the solution of an inverse electromagnetic problem. The problem is to model the distribution of dipole current sources in a finitely resistive infinite half space. Modelling is done using the observed electrical potential on the interface between the half space and the free space. This method is known as Spontaneous Potential (SP) and is widely used for geophysical prospecting. Object of the VFSR algorithm is a quadratic error function between measured and synthetic data. Method is tested on a field data.

1 Introduction

Spontaneous Potential (SP) models the polarized underground structures such as active earthquake faults, sulphur mines and hot springs by mapping the surface electrical potential to the distribution of the underground dipole current sources.

Until Abdelrahman et al.'s work [1], studies on the solution of SP problem were only for forward problem by constructing nomogram lines that helped to find a model by visually matching the field data. [7]. These methods can only be used in the presence of a single isolated burried current dipole.

For inverse solution, two consequitive studies [1, 2] attempted solutions by least squares and differential analysis. These studies suffered by being confined to the inverse solution of a single isolated body.

Cooper [4] and Çağlar [5] wrote forward solution programs which seek human help by manual alteration of the parameters until a good match between the forward solution and the measured data is found. However these also did not propose a method for automatic solution. Current study is the first in the literature for automatic inverse solution of models with multiple burried bodies.

2 Very Fast Simulated Reannealing

Monte Carlo (MC) search algorithms do not get caught in local minimas so they are largely used in the inverse solution of multivariate nonlinear problems. However they are computationally expensive because of their use of unweighted random numbers. Two main examples of faster directed MC algorithms are Genetic Algorithms (GA) and Simulated Annealing (SA).

Very Fast Simulated Reannealing (VFSR) is one of the better improved versions of the Simulated Annealing (SA) which imitates the well known statistical mechanical model SA in which a metal is first heated and then cooled down slowly for global stability. Energy is used as analogous to error function of the optimization.

Simulated Annealing, before reaching the VFSR form, has gone through the stages of Boltzmann Annealing (BA) which uses a Boltzmann distribution to guide the heuristics and Fast Simulated Annealing (FSA) which uses Cauchy Annealing [9].

In Very Fast Simulated Reannealing, transition rules are guided by the parameter y_i where a random number u_i is drawn from U[0,1] which is then mapped as:

$$y_i = \text{sgn}(u_i - 1/2)T_i\left[(1+1/T_i)^{|2u_i-1|} - 1\right] \quad (1)$$

VFSR runs on an annealing schedule decreasing exponentially in time k,

$$T = T_0 e^{-ck^{1/D}} \quad (2)$$

This schedule is faster than Fast Cauchy Annealing and much faster than Boltzmann Annealing. Reannealing permits adaptation to sensitivities of the parameters [9]. VFSR was shown to be much faster than Genetic Algorithms (GA) for global optimization of six nonconvex functions [6]. One succesful example of SA in inverse solution of geoscience problems is modelling of Seismic wave forms [8].

3 Inverse Problem

Mapping of the SP electrical potential anomaly to the superposed underground model is a modified version of the single-body expression [3] and is as follows:

$$V_{\text{mod}}(x_i, z, \theta) = \sum_i M \frac{(x_i - D)\cos\theta_i + z_i \sin\theta_i}{\left((x_i - D)^2 + z_i^2\right)^{P_i}} \quad (3)$$

where for each body i, P is the shape factor (P=1.5 for the 3D sphere, P=1 for a 2D horizontal cylinder), x is the horizontal position of the body with respect to the measurement point located at D, z is the depth and θ is the polarization angle of the body. As the model approaches the form of a vertical fault, shape factor goes to zero [2]. Hence, instead of making clear cut distinctions such as sphere, cylinder and plane, it is practical to assume that the shape factor is a measure of the expansion of the body in the third dimension by changing within the (0, 1.5) continuous interval.

After defining a quadratic error function between the calculated and measured data, rest of the inverse problem is to globally optimize it using VFSR. The global minima is expected to correspond to the best possible solution to the problem, however some local minima may be a better solution given the uncertainty from the modelling and measurements. For this reason, VFSR is allowed to run many number of epochs and kept a list of the good local minima as well. This list gave us the option to choose between reasonable underground structures, due to geological knowledge. Number of bodies started with 1 and increased for smaller-error models.

4 Results

Experimental data is from the field work [7]. This data set was used by various researchers for inverse solution attempts [5].

During the solution, as the number of bodies in the model was increased, more realistic parameters and smaller error were found. Figure 1 is a plot of the graph of the best solution and Table 1 shows its parameters.

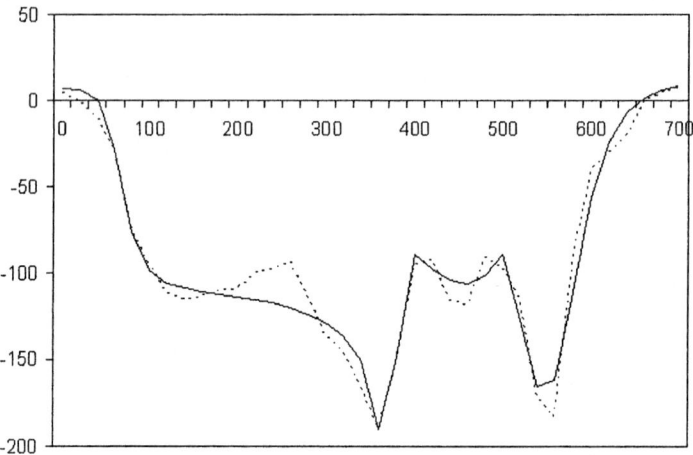

Fig. 1. Electrical Potential (mV) versus Location (m) which corresponds to the best model. (dashed curve is field data and solid curve is inverse solution.)

Table 1. Parameters corresponding to the best model (Number of bodies: 4)

	Body 1	Body 2	Body 3	Body 4
M (mV/m)	109.58	921.01	831.23	544.32
x (m)	65.04	375.86	506.52	568.03
z (m)	26.02	9.91	22.61	40.52
θ (Deg)	259.34	52.02	194.71	43.71
P	0.57	0.92	0.90	0.66

5 Conclusion

Inverse SP problem, which is the modelling of the distribution of dipole current sources inside an infinite half space with finite resistivity, has been studied. Inverse mapping is from the observed electrical potential on the interface between the half space and the free space to underground model parameters. VFSR, which is proven to be fast and effective in global optimization of nonconvex multivariate functions has been used as the solution tool. Object of the algorithm is a quadratic error function between the data from synthetic models and a field data. Calculations started with a model with 1 underground body and incrementally increased. The lowest error and reasonable parameters is obtained at 4 structures. The reason that models with a higher number of bodies have a positive impact on the quality of the solution is that real world models are very complex.

One property of the inverse solution of complex real world problems is that, they can have multiple valid solutions, and also multiple local minima that are equally valuable in each solution. The selection between models has to be done by looking at qualitative constraints, which are geological in this case. The proposed algorithm stores all possible solutions which are close to the global optima and gives the user the option to choose between them. In the future, it might be possible to embed these verbal constraints in the algorithm through knowledge-based methods.

References

1. Abdelrahman, EM, ElAraby, TM, Ammar, AA, Hassanein, HI.: A least-squares approach to shape determination from residual self-potential anomalies. Pure and Applied Geophysics, Vol 150, 1. (1997) 121-128
2. Abdelrahman, ESM, Ammar, AAB, Hassanein, HI, Hafez, MA.: Derivative analysis of SP anomalies. Geophysics, Vol 63, 3. (1998) 890-897
3. Bhattacharya, B.B., Roy, N.: A Note on the use of nomogram for Self Potential Anomalies. Geophys. Prosp., Vol. 29. (1981) 102-107
4. Cooper G.R.J.: Spinv: Self potential data modelling and inversion. Computers and Geosciences, Vol. 23, 10. (1998) 1121-1123
5. Caglar, I.: Visual interpretation of superposed self-potential anomalies in mineral exploration. Computers and Geosciences, Vol. 26, 7. (2000) 847-852
6. Ingber, L., and Rosen, B.: Genetic algorithms and very fast simulated reannealing: A comparison. Mathl. Comput. Modelling, Vol. 16, 11. (1992) 87-100
7. Meiser, P.: A Method of Quantitative Interpretation Self Potential Measurements. Geophysical Prospecting, Vol. 10. (1962) 203-218
8. Rothman D.H.: Nonlinear Inversion, Statistical Mechanics and Residual Statics Estimation. Geophys., Vol. 50. (1985) 2784-2796
9. Ingber, L.: Very Fast Simulated Reannealing. Mathl. Comput. Modeling, Vol. 12, 8. (1989) 967-993

Using SOFM to Improve Web Site Text Content

Sebastián A. Ríos[1], Juan D. Velásquez[2], Eduardo S. Vera[3,4],
Hiroshi Yasuda[1], and Terumasa Aoki[1]

[1] Research Center for Advanced Science and Technology,
University of Tokyo
{srios, yasuda, aoki}@mpeg.rcast.u-tokyo.ac.jp
[2] Department of Industrial Engineering, University of Chile
jvelasqu@dii.uchile.cl
[3] Center for Collaborative Research, University of Tokyo
[4] On leave from Department of Computer Science, University of Chile
esvera@vp.ccr.u-tokyo.ac.jp, esvera@dcc.uchile.cl

Abstract. We introduce a new method to improve web site text content by identifying the most relevant free text in the web pages. In order to understand the variations in web page text, we collect pages during a period. The page text content is then transformed into a feature vector and is used as input of a clustering algorithm (SOFM), which groups the vectors by common text content. In each cluster, a centroid and its neighbor vectors are extracted. Then using a reverse clustering analysis, the pages represented by each vector are reviewed in order to find the similar. Furthermore, the proposed method was tested in a real web site, proving the effectiveness of this approach.

1 Introduction

From the early stages of the web development, designers and web masters have made great efforts to achieve continuous improvements of web site structure and content. This is a non-trivial task, because the site must dynamically change in order to permanently satisfy the visitors' requirements.

To define the correct text content is a complex task, due to the fact that visitors requirements and preferences are continuously changing. Therefore, it is a hard task to figure out which is the best content for a web site [2]. On the other hand, many researchers have proposed several mathematical tools to help improve the web site content. However, it is hard to discover where the changes have to be applied [11,10], or to produce a guide on how to focus the efforts and resources to change the Web Site.

In this paper, we make use of some Web Content Mining (WCM) techniques in order to find the most relevant pages in the whole web site. These are the pages that should be the main focus of attention for the organizations.

2 Related Work

To produce adequate guidelines on how to make web site improvements, we need to find the most relevant text in a particular site. With this purposes in mind, we apply web content mining (WCM) techniques that consist in several sub processes, which are mainly information selection, pre-processing, generalization (automatically discover general patterns), analysis (validation or interpretation of mined patterns) [4].

2.1 Data Selection and Preprocessing

In order to obtain the best possible results, a web site with a relatively high amount of text is needed, and with few images, flash text, videos, audio, etc.

After selecting a web site fulfilling the above requirements, we first filter the non-useful words in order to just apply the clustering algorithm to the most relevant words (for instance, the prepositions, conjunctions and articles are omitted).

We applied later a Porter's stemming algorithm, which allows us to find the root of the words. After applying this two techniques to the selected web site we reduced the universe of different words of the site by about 64%. This allows the next steps to be faster and more precise.

2.2 Using Self Organizing Feature Map

We use SOFM of the Kohonen type to extract significant patterns from the web page text content. But first, we used the Vector Space Model, in order to apply this clustering algorithm. The TFIDF was used to obtain the Web Pages feature vectors.

A toroidal topology is used to maintain the continuity of the space [9]. Then a Gaussian function that depends on the distance from the centroid is used to propagate the learning to the neighbor neurons. This function makes that the centroid neuron learn the pattern shown, and then the effect of the learning is passed to the neighborhood in smaller degree, inversely proportional to the centroid distance.

A very important expression is the Eq.(1), which is use as our similarity measure between the Web Pages and the neurons.

$$pd(p_i, p_j) = \frac{\sum_{k=1}^{W} m_{ki} m_{kj}}{\sum_{k=1}^{W} (m_{ki})^2 \sum_{k=1}^{W} (m_{kj})^2} \quad (1)$$

3 Reverse Clustering Analysis

After finding the clusters, we have the most commonly used words in the whole Web Site, but we know nothing about which are the most relevant web pages.

Moreover, if we study the artificial neural network, we only have a vector of frequencies for all the words that compound the web site. One big challenge that we find in this technique is that such vector is far from a web page, because the network at the beginning is randomly initialized. Therefore, the vectors that the clusters may contain usually do not correspond to a real web site's pages.

That is why a method to find which are the real web pages that the clusters finds relevant is needed. However, as we just mentioned before, it is very hard to find a perfect correspondence between the clusters and real web pages.

Therefore, we apply again the similarity measure between pages eq.1, in order to find the documents which are most similar to our clusters. This way we obtain the most relevant pages in the whole web site.

3.1 Extracting the Clusters and Marking the Real Pages

At this point we need to know which are the cluster's centroids, and associated neurons to perform the reverse clustering analysis. This task is absolutely critic and must be done carefully in order to obtain reliable information. However, there are many ways to do this, so we focus only in two ways.

First we use a very simple circular neighbor function. This consists in taking all the neurons inside the radius r and looking if there is a local maximum in this vicinity.

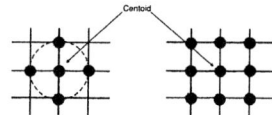

Fig. 1. Square and Circular vicinity for clusters extraction

However, if we use this function the problem is that we can consider more clusters than they really exist, because we do not compare the possible centroid to the vertices of the grid. That is why we take a square vicinity. For instance, if we take $r = 1$ Fig.1 then we only compare the centroid to four neurons, the vertices of the square are outside of the circular vicinity.

The experiments results show that in fact, with an circular vicinity we find more clusters (34 clusters). As we mentioned before, some clusters are not local maximums and must not be considered as clusters we should use the square vicinity instead for find local cluster centroids. Using the square vicinity we only obtain 13 cluster's centroids using the side of the square center in (x_c, y_c) parameter in $a = 2$.

When we have all the clusters and its associated neurons (9 neurons with the square vicinity and $r = 1$), we compare the feature vectors of the centroids's neurons with the real pages. To do so we use the similarity measure, shown in (1), we calculate the minimum for all the pages. In other words, we obtain the most similar page on the web site for each neuron in each cluster. Formally we define the Page Reference Function $PR(n_i, p_j)$ eq.2, where ζ is the set of clusters centroids plus the associated neurons.

$$PR(n_i, p_j) = Min\{pd(n_i, p_j)\} \quad \forall j = 1, \ldots, Q \ \wedge \ i \ \epsilon \ \zeta \qquad (2)$$

Using (2) we obtain the referenced pages's set.

4 A Real Case Application

We applied the process mentioned above to the site of the School of Engineering and Sciences of the University of Chile.[1] This Web Site has 182 web pages. The number of different words in the whole web site is more than 11,000 but after the preparation process (filtering and stemming) only about 4,000 words remain.

The artificial neural network used in the process was set in 100 neurons and applied the examples using 50 epochs. After the application, we found five main clusters, and 13 clusters in total Fig.2. We selected the 13 clusters found for the next process. We did so, because we intended to find few important web pages in the worst case (using all the clusters found).

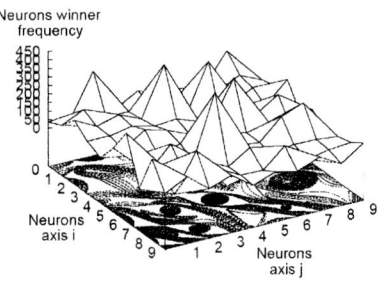

Fig. 2. SOFM for our experiments

After applying the page reference function eq.2 the results were only 8 pages see table 1. This pages are most similar to our clusters based on content, and the real web pages that we could consider as relevant web pages in the whole web site that is composed by 182 pages.

The first page found was the *School's agenda* with 21 cluster references; the second page was *students grades* with 18 references and the third page was the *Engineering Forum* with 9 references.

Table 1. Most representative real pages

Web Page	Cluster References
escuela.ing.uchile.cl/agenda/index.html	21
escuela.ing.uchile.cl/Boletin_Notas/index.html	18
escuela.ing.uchile.cl/foroING/index.html	9
escuela.ing.uchile.cl/departamentos/index.htm	6
escuela.ing.uchile.cl/novedades/novedad_alumnos.php	2
escuela.ing.uchile.cl/sd20a/alumn-sc.php	2
escuela.ing.uchile.cl/sd20a/index.html	1
escuela.ing.uchile.cl/organizaciones/estudiantes.htm	1

---

[1] http://escuela.ing.uchile.cl

5 Conclusions

In this paper we prove that is not sufficient to find the most important words in a Web Site, because this information only helps to know which are the possible key words of the Site. However, in those cases that the management of an organization needs an effective guideline on how to focus its efforts and resources to improve the web site, additional analysis is required.

For the above propose we propose a reverse clustering analysis. In order to do so we extract the cluster's centroids using a circular and a square vicinity. We found out that the square vicinity is much better than the circular vicinity because it is more effective in identifying clusters that really exist.

An important contribution of this work is defining the page reference function as a function which compares the real web page documents with the SOFM neuron's feature vector to obtain relevant web site pages.

Furthermore, these concepts were successfully tested in a real web site where we found a set of only 5% of the web pages of the site.

References

1. Berendt, B., Spiliopoulou, M.: Analysis of navigation behavior in web sites integrating multiple information systems. The VLDB journal. **9**(2001)27–75.
2. Buyukkokten, O., Garcia-Molina, H. & Paepcke, A.: Seeing the whole in parts: text summarization for web browsing on handheld devices. Procs. 10th Int. Conf. on World Wide Web, Hong Kong. (2001) 652–662.
3. Chakrabarti, S.: Data mining for hypertext: A tutorial survey. SIGKDD Explorations: Newsletter of the Special Interest Group (SIG) on Knowledge Discovery & Data Mining. (2000).
4. Kosala, R., Blockeel, H.: Web Mining Research: A Survey. SIGKDD Explorations. **2(1)**(2000)1–15.
5. Loh, S., Wives, L., de Oliveira, J. P. M.: Concept-based Knowledge Discovery in Texts Extracted from the Web. SIGKDD Explorations. **2(1)**(2000) 2(1):29–39.
6. Nielsen, J.: User Interface directions for the web. Communications of ACM **42(1)** (1999) 65–72.
7. Pal, S. K., Talwar, V., Mitra, P.: Web Mining in Soft Computing Framework: Relevance, state of the art and future directions. IEEE Transactions on Neural Networks. **13(5)** (2002)1163–1177.
8. Salton, G., Wong, A., Yang, C. S.: A vector space model for automatic indexing. Communications of the ACM archive. **18(11)** (1975)613–620.
9. Velásquez, J. D., Yasuda, H., Aoki, T., Weber, R., Vera, E.: Using self-organizing feature maps to acquire knowledge about visitor behavior in a web site. Lecture Notes in Artificial Intelligence. **2773(1)**(2003)951–958.
10. Velásquez, J. D., Weber, R., Yasuda, H., Aoki, T.: A Methodology to Find Web Site Keywords. IEEE Int. Conf. on e-Technology, e-Commerce and e-Service Taipei, Taiwan. (2004)285–292.
11. Velásquez, J. D., Ríos, S., Bassi, A., Yasuda, H., Aoki, T.: Towards the identification of keywords in the web site text content: A methodological approach. International Journal of Web Information Systems. **1(1)** (2005)11–15.

Online Support Vector Regression for System Identification

Zhenhua Yu, Xiao Fu, and Yinglu Li

School of Telecommunication Engineering,
Air Force Engineering University, Xi'an 710077, China
zhenhua_yu@163.com

Abstract. Conventional Support Vector Regression (SVR) is not capable of online setting and its training algorithm is inefficient in real-time applications. Through analyzing the possible variation of support vector sets after new samples are added to the training set, and extending the incremental support vector machine for classification, an online learning algorithm for SVR is proposed. To illustrate the favorable performance of the online learning algorithm, a nonlinear system identification experiment is considered. The simulation results indicate that the learning efficiency and prediction accuracy of the online learning algorithm are higher than that of the existing algorithms, and it is more suitable for system identification.

1 Introduction

Support vector machine (SVM) is a new universal learning machine in the framework of Structural Risk Minimization (SRM) [1], which is based on statistical learning theory. SRM has greater generalization ability and is superior to the traditional Empirical Risk Minimization (ERM) principle adopted in many conventional neural networks. In SVM, the results guarantee global minima whereas ERM can only locate local minima. Initially, SVM is designed to solve pattern recognition problems. Recently, SVM has also been successfully applied to regression estimation [2], [8], and the approach is often referred to as the support vector regression (SVR). Conventionally SVR is used for regression estimation of input data that are supplied in batch. In many application problems, such as system identification, time series prediction and signal processing, data are obtained in a sequence and learning has to be done from scratch. Therefore, it is time consuming to achieve the regression using the conventional SVR and it is not possible to apply the SVR for real-time regression problems. Recently several online learning algorithms have been proposed [4], [5], [6]. However, most of these algorithms are only described for classification. In existing online learning algorithms, some algorithms are not suitable for online adjusting due to low efficiency when coping with a large number of support vectors, and others only return approximate solutions for remaining support vectors. In this paper, a novel online learning algorithm for SVR (online SVR) is proposed, which is an extension of the work presented in [3], [7]. Finally, the online SVR is applied to the nonlinear system identification to test the efficiency. Simulation shows the online SVR is adaptive to system identification.

2 Online Learning Algorithm for Support Vector Regression

A more detailed description of SVR can be found in [2]. In SVR, according to dual theory and Lagrangian function, we get the following formulation:

$$L_D = \frac{1}{2}\sum_{i=1}^{l}(\alpha_i - \alpha_i^*)Q_{ij}(\alpha_j - \alpha_j^*) + \varepsilon\sum_{i=1}^{l}(\alpha_i + \alpha_i^*)$$
$$-\sum_{i=1}^{l}y_i(\alpha_i - \alpha_i^*) + \delta\sum_{i=1}^{l}(\alpha_i - \alpha_i^*) \quad (1)$$

with the first order conditions for L_D:

$$g_i = \frac{\partial L_D}{\partial \alpha_i} = \sum_{j=1}^{l}Q_{ij}(\alpha_j - \alpha_j^*) + \varepsilon - y_i + \delta = 0 \quad (2)$$

$$g_i^* = \frac{\partial L_D}{\partial \alpha_i^*} = -\sum_{j=1}^{l}Q_{ij}(\alpha_j - \alpha_j^*) + \varepsilon + y_i - \delta = 0 \quad (3)$$

$$\frac{\partial L_D}{\partial \delta} = \sum_{i=1}^{l}(\alpha_i - \alpha_i^*) = 0 \quad (4)$$

A coefficient θ_i is defined as $\theta_i = \alpha_i - \alpha_i^*$, and θ_i is determined by both α_i and α_i^*. The first order conditions for L_D lead to KKT conditions, which can divide the whole training samples into the following sets: margin support vectors S, error support vectors E, and remaining vectors R. Specifically, centering on g_i, KKT conditions are:

$$\begin{aligned}
2\varepsilon < g_i &\rightarrow g_i^* < 0 \quad \theta_i = -C \quad i \in E \\
g_i = 2\varepsilon &\rightarrow g_i^* = 0 \quad -C < \theta_i < 0 \quad i \in S \\
0 < g_i < 2\varepsilon &\rightarrow 0 < g_i^* < 2\varepsilon \quad \theta_i = 0 \quad i \in R \\
g_i = 0 &\rightarrow g_i^* = 2\varepsilon \quad 0 < \theta_i < C \quad i \in S \\
g_i < 0 &\rightarrow g_i^* > 2\varepsilon \quad \theta_i = C \quad i \in E
\end{aligned} \quad (5)$$

Variations in θ_c of the new sample x_c influence g_i, g_i^*, and θ_i of the other samples in training samples, so the transfer of some vectors from on set S, R, E to another set may be forced. From (5), if one sample remains in S, its g_i does not change. While one sample remains in E and R, its θ_i does not change. The variation in g_i, g_i^* and θ_i are calculated as follows when a new sample with influence θ_c is added.

$$\triangle g_i = Q_{ic}\triangle\theta_c + \sum_{j\in S}Q_{ij}\triangle\theta_j + \triangle b \quad (6)$$

$$\triangle g_i^* = -\triangle g_i \qquad (7)$$

$$\triangle \theta_c + \sum_{j \in S} \triangle \theta_j = 0 \qquad (8)$$

Due to limited space, how the variation in the θ_c of a new sample x_c influences θ_j of samples $j \in S$ or $j \in E \bigcup R$ and the computation of $\triangle \theta_c$ during the migration process can be found in [3]. The online learning algorithm is obtained as follows [7]:

1. Set the coefficient $\theta_c = 0$ of the new sample x_c;
2. if $g_c > 0$ and $g_c^* > 0$, then x_c is added to R and exit;
3. If $g_c < 0$ then increment θ_c, updating θ_i in S and g_i, g_i^* in E, R, until one of the following conditions holds:
   - $g_c = 0$: add x_c to S, update the matrix Q^{-1} and exit;
   - $\theta_c = C$: add x_c to S and exit;
   - samples in S, E or R may migrate and update the matrix Q^{-1};

   Else $g_c^* < 0$ then decrement θ_c, updating θ_i in S and g_i, g_i^* in E, R, until one of the following conditions holds:
   - $g_c^* = 0$: add x_c to S, update the matrix Q^{-1} and exit;
   - $\theta_c = -C$: add x_c to E and exit;
   - samples in S, E or R may migrate and update the matrix Q^{-1};
4. Return to 1.

3 Application of Online SVR to System Identification

Nonlinear system identification is a crucial but complex problem, where data are obtained in a sequence. Therefore, the online learning algorithm for SVR is particularly well suited. Now, we validate the performance of online SVR by simulation experiments and compare its performance to existing SVR algorithms.

Online SVR is applied to nonlinear system identification and compared with the existing incremental algorithm [6] and batch SVR algorithm (LibSVM). In these experiments, the kernel function is Gaussian function $K(x_i, x_j) = exp(-\lambda \|x_i - x_j\|^2)$, $\lambda = 1$, and MSE is used to quantify the performance.

A nonlinear system [9] to be identified is governed by the difference equation

$$y(k+1) = 0.3y(k) + 0.6y(k-1) + f(u(k)) \qquad (9)$$

where $f(u) = 0.6\sin(\pi u) + 0.3\sin(3\pi u) + 0.1\sin(5\pi u)$, and the input $u(k) = \sin(2\pi k/250)$. One takes 1500 points as the training samples, and these samples are sequentially obtained. Table 1. lists the approximation errors and speed using the three algorithms.

From the simulation experiment, one can find the proposed online learning algorithm outperforms the incremental algorithm and batch algorithm. Online algorithm and batch algorithm produce almost the same error, while the accuracy of these algorithms is higher than the incremental algorithm for only providing an approximation solution. As the procedure of online algorithm is iterative, its learning efficiency is higher than the other algorithms; the batch learning algorithm has to be done from scratch when data are obtained in a sequence, so its speed is rather slow.

Table 1. Performance comparison for three algorithms

Learning algorithm	Learning speed(s)	MSE
Online learning	8.46	0.0105
Incremental learning	12.15	0.0332
LibSVM	23.37	0.0109

4 Conclusions

As conventional SVR suffer from the problem of large memory requirement and CPU time when trained in batch mode on large-scale sample sets, this paper presents an online learning algorithm for SVR that have input data supplied in sequence rather than in batch. Online learning algorithm analyzes the possible change of support vectors after new samples are added to training set. Online learning algorithm for SVR is applied to nonlinear system identification. Simulation shows that the online learning algorithm has a much faster convergence and a better generalization performance in comparison with the existing algorithms.

References

1. Wang, L.P.: Support Vector Machines: Theory and Application. Springer-Verlag, Berlin Heidelberg New York (2005)
2. Smola, A.J., Schökopf, B.: A tutorial on support vector regression. NeuralCOLT2 Technical Report Series, No. NC2-TR-98-030. London, Royal Holloway Colledge, University of London (1998)
3. Cauwenberghs, G., Poggio, T.: Incremental and decremental support vector machine learning. In: Dietterich, T.G., Leen, T.K., and Tresp, V. (eds.): Advances in Neural Information Processing Sytems. MIT Press (2001) 409-415
4. Gentile, C.: A new approximate maximal margin classification algorithm. Journal of Machine Learning Research 2 (2001) 213-242
5. Ralaivola, L., d'Alche-Buc, F.: Incremental support vector machine learning: A local approach. Lecture Notes in Computer Science, Vol. 2130. Springer-Verlag, Berlin Heidelberg New York (2001) 322-330
6. Syed, N., Liu, H., Sung, K.K.: Incremental Learning with Support Vector Machines. In Proceedings of the Workshop on Support Vector Machines at the International Joint Conference on Artificial Intelligence. Stockholm, Sweden. (1999)
7. Martin, M.: On-line support vector machine regression. Lecture Notes in Computer Science, Vol. 2430. Springer-Verlag, Berlin Heidelberg New York (2002) 282-294
8. Vapnik, V., Golowich, S., and Smola, A.: Support vector method for function approximation, regression estimation, and signal processing. In: Mozer, M.C., Jordan, M.I., and Petsche, T.: Advances in Neural Information Processing Systems. MIT Press (1997) 281-287
9. Narendra, K., Parthasarathy, K.: Identification and Control of Dynamical Systems Using Neural Networks. IEEE Trans. on Neural Networks 1 (1990) 4-27

Optimization of PTA Crystallization Process Based on Fuzzy GMDH Networks and Differential Evolutionary Algorithm[*]

Wenli Du[**] and Feng Qian

Automation Institute, East China University of Science and Technology,
Shanghai, P.R. China 200237
duwenli.sd@263.net

Abstract. In this paper the optimization of Purified Terephthalic Acid (PTA) crystal crystallizer based on FGMDH networks and Adaptive Differential Evolutionary (ADE) algorithm is discussed in detail. Due to the existence of many by-products and impurity in PTA continuous industry production process, it is very difficult to build mechanism models for this process. Since Artificial Neural networks have been proved to be able to approximate a wide class of functional relationships very well in modeling chemical process, we apply a kind of FGMDH networks to build PTA granularity model, which is incorporated with human experiences. To implement the control of PTA granularity, which is one of the key product quality indexes, a kind of global real-value optimization algorithm----ADE algorithm is proposed for optimizing of PTA crystallization process. The proposed ADE is capable of find the optimal operation conditions effectively and efficiently and suitable for industrial application.

1 Introduction

The control of particle size distribution (PSD) as an end-objective in chemical process control is well motivated in industrial practice, and has been well documented in the literature (Congalidis & Richards, 1998). In PTA continuous industrial production process, PSD is a key product index and should be strictly controlled. To fulfill PSD model-based optimization in PTA unit the challenge is to develop a model satisfying crystal nucleation and growth mechanisms with high fidelity.

Significant work has been devoted to the development of mechanism models of crystallization process especially in emulsion polymerization (Motza S, 2003, Francis J. D, 2003). However, the kinetics describing PTA particle interactions such as crystal nucleation and growth phenomenon are not well understood quantitatively. Here Fuzzy GMDH networks is taken for modeling as can be incorporated with heuristic rules from human experiences.

The commonly used global optimization methods may be classified into the following two categories: deterministic methods and stochastic methods (Törn and

---

[*] The work was support by the National 973-Plan of China (2002CB312200).
[**] Corresponding Author.

Zilînskas,1998, Horst and Pardalos,1995). Deterministic methods can converge fast but have major shortcomings: 1) easily trapped by local optima when feasible region around the global optimum is not well-conditioned; 2) cannot deal with such complex problems as the objective function are not differentiable or when constraints are hard to find ways to transform to appropriate penalty settings. The stochastic methods are famous for global optima search but the convergence speed is relatively slow. Here we employ an adaptive differential evolutionary algorithm, which firstly introduced by Storn R. (1995) to obtain the optimum of PTA crystallization process.

2 Modeling of PTA Granularity

2.1 Fuzzy GMDH Networks

2.1.1 Description of FGMDH Structure

Based on the equivalence of RBF function to certain fuzzy logic system, the structure of FGMDH (see figure 1) is constituted of the fuzzy part and the polynomial part.

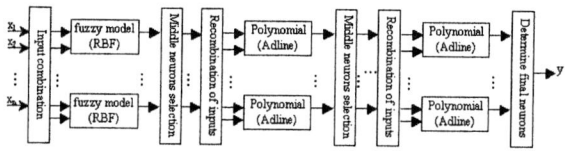

Fig. 1. The structure of fuzzy GMDH network

In the first layer, radial basis function is adopted to express fuzzy basis function, the equivalence between them has been proved by M. Brown and C. Harris (1994). This type of structure takes advantage of RBF good global estimation ability and polynomial fast computing speed.

2.1.2 Learning Algorithm of FGMDH

Fuzzy part learning algorithm: The membership function μ_{ki}, which is the kth rule of the ith input x_i^m in fuzzy inference systems, is described as eq. (1):

$$\mu_{ki}(x_i^m) = \exp\left\{-\frac{(x_i^m - a_{ki}^m)^2}{b_{ki}^m}\right\} . \tag{1}$$

If fuzzy product inference mechanism is adopted here, then the output y^m is:

$$y^m = \sum_{k=1}^{K}[\prod_{i=1}^{2}\mu_{ki}(x_i^m)]w_k^m . \tag{2}$$

First determine the centers c_i of Gaussian function by using clustering algorithm. Suppose there are n classes to be divided, then the t step distance $d_i(t)$ between each center and the input is: $d_i(t) = \|x(t) - c(t-1)\|, 1 \leq i \leq n$; Then locate the subscript of the center who has the nearest distance from x_t, $p = \arg[\min\{a_i(t)\}, 1 \leq i \leq n]$, arg represent the selection of subscript operator. Update the pth center and keep the other centers, $c_i = c_i(t-1)$, $1 \leq i \leq n, i \neq p$, $c_p = c_p(t-1) + \alpha_c(x(t) - c_p(t-1))$; α_c is learning rate, and expressed as $\alpha_c(t) = \dfrac{\alpha_c(t-1)}{sqrt(1 + round[t/n])}$.

Suppose $c_i (i=1,2,\cdots,n)$ is the determined centers, $c_{i_1}, c_{i_2}, \cdots, c_{i_p}$ are the p centers of c_i nearest neighbors, then the width σ_i is:

$$\sigma_i = \frac{1}{p}\sum_{t=1}^{p} \left\| c_i - c_{i_t} \right\| \cdot \qquad (3)$$

Finally, adjust the weight of each node using LMS:

$$e(t) = \hat{y}(t) - y(t) \qquad (4)$$

$$w(t) = w(t-1) + \eta e(t) y(t) \qquad (5)$$

η is training parameter, $\hat{y}$ is target vector, y is network output.

Polynomial part learning algorithm: The Widrow-Hoff learning rule is introduced to determine the coefficient of the binomial. see equation (6)

$$W_{k+1} = W_k + \alpha \frac{X_k}{|X_k|^2}(y_k^d - W_k^T X_k) \qquad (6)$$

2.2 Average Particle Size Model

There are two steps in PTA production: oxidation reaction unit and the refining unit. The refining process is divided for four parts and determines final PTA granularity.

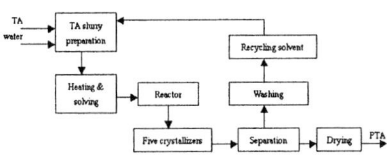

Fig. 2. The schematic representation of PTA refining unit

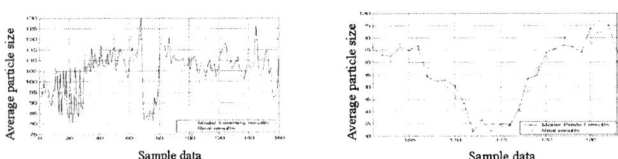

Fig. 3. Learning and generation result of APS model using fuzzy GMDH network

Considering the model complexity and precision, human experience was incorporated into building the PTA granularity model. The Average Particle Size

(APS) model has five inputs. That is [$\Delta T_1, \Delta T_2, \tau_1, \tau_2, APS_{k-1}$], and ΔT_1 is the temperature difference between reactor and the 1st crystallizer, ΔT_2 is the temperature difference between the 1st and 2nd crystallizers, τ_1 is the retention time of the 1st crystallizer, τ_2 is the retention time of the 2nd crystallizer, APS_{k-1} is the last manual analysis value of APS. Fig. 3 shows respectively the learning and generation results.

3 Optimization of PTA Crystallization

Differential evolution (DE) algorithm (Storn, et al. 1995) is put forward as a global-searching method, and successfully applied to solve the optimization and searching problems in the complex real-type space. Here we introduced adaptive idea to automatically change the value of α and CR with objective function, which is first proposed by Srinivas (1994).

For optimization problem:

Minimize $f(x)$, subject to $g_j(x) \geq 0$, $j = 1, 2, \cdots, J$; $h_k(x) = 0$, $k = 1, 2, \cdots, K$

As value of the operators α and CR influence the optimization procedure very much, we introduce the adaptive scheme (7) and (8) to adjust α and CR according to the objective function information.

$$\alpha_{new} = \begin{cases} \alpha_1 - \dfrac{(\alpha_1 - \alpha_2)(f_{max,G} - f(x_{i,G}))}{f_{max,G} - f_{avg,G}} & f(x_{i,G}) \leq f_{avg,G} \\ \alpha_1 & f(x_{i,G}) > f_{avg,G} \end{cases} \quad (7)$$

$$CR_{new} = \begin{cases} CR_1 - \dfrac{(CR_1 - CR_2)(f_{max,G} - f(x_{i,G}))}{f_{max,G} - f_{avg,G}} & f(x_{i,G}) \leq f_{avg,G} \\ CR_1 & f(x_{i,G}) > f_{avg,G} \end{cases} \quad (8)$$

where α_1 is the latest step of difference vector; α_2 is a preset constant of step for the optimal vector of generation G, usually from [0 0.5]; CR_1 is the latest crossover; CR_2 is a preset constant of the optimal vector crossover operator of generation G, usually from [0 0.01];

For the real-time adjustment of PTA granularity, the optimal operating conditions influencing granularity need to be given either when new set point is to be achieved or when disturbances drive the granularity diverge from its target. Thus the optimizing problem is proposed as followed:

$$\text{Min } \|f_{APS}(x_i) - SP_{APS}\|, \quad i = 1 \sim 5. \quad (9)$$

subject to $35 \leq x_1 \leq 42$, $18 \leq x_2 \leq 24$, $0.15 \leq x_3 \leq 0.3$, $0.15 \leq x_4 \leq 0.3$

where f_{APS} is the APS FGMDH network model; SP_{APS} is the granularity target to be achieved; x_i $i = 1 \sim 5$ is the five inputs of APS model; The adjust variants is the pressure and level of both the 1st crystallizer and the 2nd crystallizer.

We employ both the DE and ADE to the optimizing problem of (9). By comparing the offline properties of them, see fig. 4, we found the convergence procedure is speeded with ADE algorithm which helps greatly for industrial optimization applications.

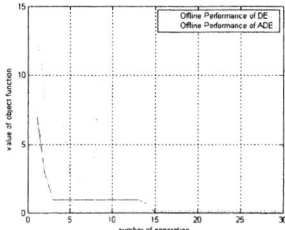

Fig. 4. Comparison of offline properties of DE and ADE

4 Conclusion

In this paper the fuzzy GMDH networks and adaptive differential evolutionary algorithm is applied to the optimization of PTA crystallization process to meet final product quality. As fuzzy neural networks incorporated both the human heuristics and automatically learning character, it is very suitable for the conditions having prior knowledge. The method is applied to build the APS model and satisfactory result is obtained. To improve the convergence performance of the conventional DE, ADE is proposed to adaptively adjust the differential vector step α and the crossover operator CR, and is applied to find the optimum conditions of PTA crystallization process.

References

1. Brown, M., Harris, C.: Neurofuzzy Adaptive Modeling and Control. Prentice Hall, New York, (1994)
2. Ivakheneko, A.G.: Polynominal Theory of Complex System. IEEE Transaction On System, Man and Cybernetics-1 4 (1971) 364-378
3. Rainer Storn, Kenneth Price: Differential Evolution-A Simple and Efficient Adaptive Scheme for Global Optimization over Continuous Spaces, Technical Report TR-95-012.

An Application of Support Vector Machines for Customer Churn Analysis: Credit Card Case

Sun Kim, Kyung-shik Shin, and Kyungdo Park

Ewha Womans University, College of Business Administration,
11-1 Daehyun-Dong, Seodaemun-Gu, Seoul 120-750, Korea
kimsun0122@empal.com, {ksshin, kyungdo}@ewha.ac.kr

Abstract. This study investigates the effectiveness of support vector machines (SVM) approach in detecting the underlying data pattern for the credit card customer churn analysis. This article introduces a relatively new machine learning technique, SVM, to the customer churning problem in attempt to provide a model with better prediction accuracy. To compare the performance of the proposed model, we used a widely adopted and applied Artificial Intelligence (AI) method, back-propagation neural networks (BPN) as a benchmark. The results demonstrate that SVM outperforms BPN. We also examine the effect of the variability in performance with respect to various values of parameters in SVM.

1 Introduction

Increasing the customer retention rate using the customer databases is one of the major concerns among marketing managers. It is widely accepted that the cost of retaining current customers are much cheaper than the cost of obtaining new customers. Due to the high cost of acquiring new customers and considerable benefits of retaining existing ones, building a churn prediction model to facilitate subsequent churn management and customer retention is critical for the success of the firms facing competitive market environment. The economic value of customer retention has been demonstrated in several empirical research applied to financial industry. For example, Reichheld and Sasser (1990) [19] found that a bank is able to increase its profits by 85% due to a 5 % improvement in the retention rate. Similar findings were obtained in Van den Poel and Lariviere (2004) [14], where the financial impacts of one percent increase in customer retention rate were calculated.

This study investigates the effectiveness of support vector machines (SVM) approach in detecting the underlying data pattern for the credit card customer churn analysis. SVM classification exercise finds hyperplanes in the possible space for maximizing the distance from the hyperplane to the data points, which is equivalent to solving a quadratic optimization problem. The solution of strictly convex problems for support vector machines is unique and global. SVM implements the structural risk minimization (SRM) principle that is known to have high generalization performance. As the complexity increases by numbers of support vectors, SVM is constructed through trading off decreasing the number of training errors and increasing the risk of over-fitting the data.

Since SVM captures geometric characteristics of feature space without deriving weights of networks from the training data, it is capable of extracting the optimal solution with the small training set size.

While there are several arguments that support the observed high accuracy of SVM, the preliminary results show that the accuracy and generalization performance of SVM is better than that of the standard back-propagation neural networks. In addition, since choosing an appropriate value for parameters of SVM plays an important role on the performance of SVM, we also investigate the effect of the variability in prediction and generalization performance of SVM with respect to various values of parameters in SVM such as the upper bound C and the bandwidth of the kernel function.

The remainder of this paper is organized as follows. Related studies about credit card research and the business application using support vector machines are provided in section 2. Section 3 provides a brief description of the research methods. In this section we also demonstrate the several superior points of the SVM algorithm compared with BPN. Section 4 describes the research data and experiments. Section 5 summarizes and analyzes empirical results. Section 6 discusses the conclusions and future research issues.

2 Related Studies

Customer churn prediction and management is a concern for many industries, but it is particularly acute in the strongly competitive and now broadly liberalized mobile telecommunications industry. A mobile service provider wishing to retain it's subscribers needs to be able to predict which of them may be at-risk of changing services and will make those subscribers the focus of customer retention efforts [28].

On the contrary, there are relatively few studies on the customer churn analysis of credit card holders. Lee et al. (2001) [15] proposed a fuzzy cognitive map approach to integrate explicit knowledge and tacit knowledge for churn analysis of credit card holders in Korea. Lee et al. (2002) [16] compared the neural network approach with logistic analysis, and C5.0 for churn analysis of credit card holders in Korea.

SVM has shown excellent generalization performance on a wide range of problems including bioinformatics [2] [11] [30], text categorization [12], face detection using image [18], hand written digit recognition [4] [5], medical diagnosis [22], estimating manufacturing yields [21]. These application domains typically involved high-dimensional input space, and the good performance is also related to the fact that SVM's learning ability can be independent of the dimensionality of the feature pace [10].

The SVM approach has been several business applications recently, mainly in the area of time series prediction and classification [9] [13] [17] [23] [24] [25], marketing [1], bankruptcy prediction [20], credit rating analysis [10]. However, there is no research using SVM to credit card customer data. This study is the first attempt of using SVM to credit card customer databases.

3 Support Vector Machines

SVM is a new learning machine method introduced first by Vapnik. The basic SVM deals with two-class problems in which the data are separated by a hyperplane defined by a number of support vectors. It is based on the Structural Risk Minimization (SRM) principle from computational learning theory [26] [27].

The underlying theme of the class of supervised learning method is to learn from observations. SVM produces a binary classifier, the so-called optimal separating hyperplanes, through nonlinear mapping of the input vectors into the high-dimensional feature space. SVM constructs linear model to estimate the decision function using nonlinear class boundaries based on support vectors. If the data is linearly separated, SVM trains linear machines for an optimal hyperplane that separates the data without error and into the maximum distance between the hyperplane and the closest training points. The training points that are closest to the optimal separating hyperplane are called support vectors. All other training examples are irrelevant for determining the binary class boundaries. In general cases where the data is not linearly separated, SVM uses nonlinear machines to find a hyperplane that minimize the number of errors for the training set [20].

Let the labeled training examples as $[x_i, y_i]$, an input vector as $x_i \in R^n$, and the class value as $y_i \in \{-1, 1\}$, for $i = 1,...,l$. For the linearly separable case, the decision rules defined by an optimal hyperplane separating the binary decision classis is given as:

$$Y = sign \left(\sum_{i=1}^{N} y_i a_i (x \cdot x_i) + b \right). \qquad (1)$$

where Y is the outcome, y_i is the class value of the training example x_i, which represents the inner product. The vector $x = (x_1, x_2, \ldots, x_n)$ corresponds to an input and the vectors $x_i, i=1\ldots N$, are the support vectors. In the Equation (1), b and a_i are parameters that determine the hyperplane.

For the nonlinearly separable case, a high-dimensional version of Equation (1) is given as follows:

$$Y = sign \left(\sum_{i=1}^{N} y_i a_i K(x, x_i) + b \right). \qquad (2)$$

In equation (2), the function $K(x, x_i)$ is defined as the kernel function for generating the inner products to construct machines with different types of nonlinear decision surfaces in the input space. For construction the decision rules, three common types of SVM are given as Table 1.

Table 1. Commonly used Kernel functions

Name	Mathematical form*
Polynomial kernel	$K(x, x_i) = (x \cdot x_i + 1)^d$
Radial basis function kernel	$K(x, x_i) = \exp(-\frac{1}{\delta^2 (x - x_i)^2})$
Two-layer neural network kernel	$K(x, x_i) = S[(x \cdot x_i)] = \frac{1}{[1 + \exp\{v(x \cdot x_i) - c\}]}$

* d is the degree of the polynomial kernel.
δ^2 is the bandwidth of the radial basis function kernel.
v and c are parameters of a sigmoid function $S[(x \cdot x_i)]$ satisfying the inequality $c \geq v$.

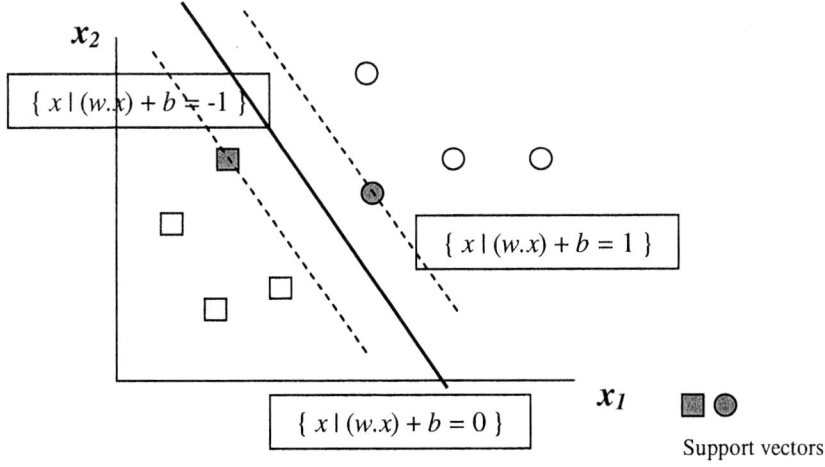

Fig. 1. Classification of data by SVM – Linear case

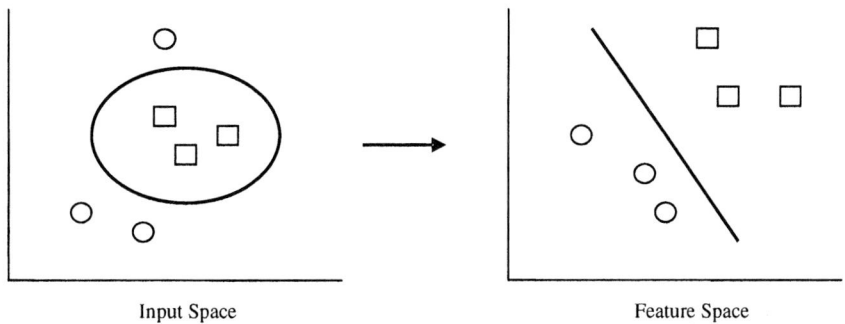

Fig. 2. Non-linear separation of input and feature space

The SVM classification exercise is implemented in solving a linearly constrained quadratic programming (QP) for finding the support vectors and determining the parameters b and a_i. For the separable case, there is a lower bound 0 on the coefficient a_i in Equation (1). For the non-separable case, SVM can be generalized by placing an upper bound C on the coefficients a_i. in addition to the lower bound [29].

In brief, the learning process to construct decision functions of SVM is completely represented by the structure of two layers, which seems to be similar with BPN. However, learning algorithm is different in that SVM is trained with optimization theory that minimizes misclassification based on statistical learning theory. The first layer selects the basis $K(x, x_i)$, $i =1...N$ and the number of support vectors from given set of bases defined be the kernel. The second layer constructs the optimal hyperplane in the corresponding feature space [27]. The scheme of SVM is shown in Figure 3.

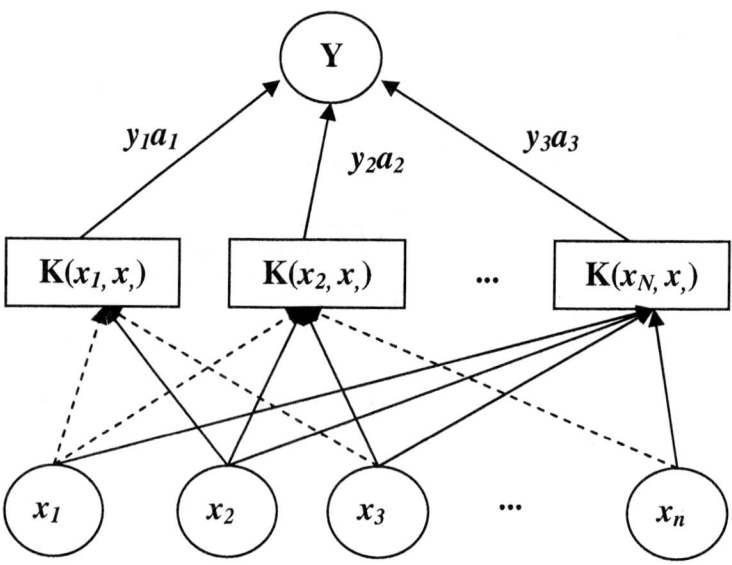

Fig. 3. The scheme of SVM (adapted from [26])

Compared with the limitations of the BPN, the major advantages of SVM are as follows. First, SVM has only two free parameters, namely the upper bound and kernel parameter. On the other hand, because a large number of controlling parameters in BPN such as the number of hidden layers, the number of hidden nodes, the learning rate, the momentum term, epochs, transfer functions and weights initialization methods are selected empirically. Therefore, in BPN, it is a difficult task to obtain an optimal combination of parameters that produces the best prediction performance.

Second, SVM guarantees the existence of unique, optimal and global solution since the training of SVM is equivalent to solving a linearly constrained QP. On the other hand, because the gradient descent algorithm optimizes the weights of BPN in a way that the sum of square error is minimized along the steepest slope the error surface, the result from training may be massively multi modal, leading to non-unique solutions, and be in the danger of getting stuck in a local minima.

Third, SVM implement the structural risk minimization (SRM) principle that is known to have a good generalization performance. SRM is the approach to trading off empirical error with the capacity of the set called VC dimension, which seeks to minimize an upper bound of the generalization error rather than minimize the training error. In order to apply SRM, the hierarchy of hypothesis spaces must be defined before the data is observed. But in SVM, the data is first used to decide which hierarchy to use and then subsequently to find a best hypothesis from each. Therefore the argument that good generalization performance of SVM is attributable to SRM is flawed, since the result of SVM is obtained from a data dependent SRM [3].

Although the other reason why SVM has good generalization performance is suggested [27], there exists no explicitly established theory that shows good generalization performance is guaranteed for SVM. However, it seems plausible that performance of SVM is more general than that of BPN because the two measures in terms of the margin and number of support vectors give information about the relation between the input and target function according to different criteria, either of which is sufficient to indicate good generalization. On the other hand, BPN is based on minimizing a squared error criterion at the network output, and tends to produce a classifier with the only large margin measure. In addition, flexibility caused by choosing training data is likely to occur with weights of BPN model, but the maximum hyperplane of SVM is relatively stable and gives little flexibility in the decision boundary [29].

Finally, SVM is constructed with the small training data set size, since it learns by capturing geometric picture corresponding to the kernel function. Moreover, no matter how large the training size is, SVM is capable of extracting the optimal solution with the small training set size. On the other hand, for the case of BPN containing a single hidden layer and used as a binary classifier, it is provided that the number of training examples, with an error of 10 percent, should be approximately 10 times the number of weights in the network. With 10 input and hidden nodes, the learning algorithm will need more than 1,000 training set size that is sufficient for a good generalization [7]. However, in most practical applications, there can be a huge numerical gap between the actual size of the training set needed and that is available.

Due to utilizing the feature space images by the kernel function, SVM is applicable in such circumstances that have proved difficult or impossible for BPN where data in the plane is randomly scattered and the density of the data's distribution is not even well defined [6].

4 Research Data and Experiments

4.1 Data Description and Variable Selection Procedure

For the purpose of this study, we prepare the data from the credit card company in Korea. We obtain the data about the customers who retain their credit card from April 1997 to October 2000 and the customers who close their account during the same period. The data set covers demographic variables and the variables about credit card usage. After filtering the data with missing values, we select 4,650 samples for each case. The description of the variables for this research is presented in Table 2.

Table 2. Definition of variables

Variable	Definition
x_1 MON2REN	Month to Renewal
x_2 AVG_CLS	Average Line Size (Credit Limit)
x_3 AGE	Age in Years
x_4 GENDER	Male or Female
x_5 AVERAGE	Average Usage Amount
x_6 AGEING	Installment Period
x_7 INTEREST	Average Interest
y STATUS	Holding or not

In this study we limit usage amount and arrear data to 3 months data because we believe a 3-month period would be sufficient time to understand customers' credit status and behavior. That is, credit card companies register a customer that arrears the payment over 3 months into credit defaulter. In this reason the usage amount data we employ is the 3 months average usage amount. We also use the demographic variables such as age and gender (male:0, female:1), categorizing ageing data into 6 installment periods (0, 3, 6, 9, 12, 15). Two status (closing their account: 0, retaining credit card: 1) appear in our data set as a dependent variable. The total sample size is 9,210.

Table 3. The number of sample data

	The Number of Sample Data
Customers that retained credit card	4,605
Customers that closed their account	4,605
Total	9,210

4.2 Experiments

The data set is arbitrarily split into two subsets; about 80% of the data is used for a training set and 20% for a validation set. The training data for SVM is entirely used to construct the model while BPN is divided into 60% training set and 20% test set. We prepare five data sets to conduct the experiment as table 4.

Table 4. Training set and validation set

	SVM		BPN	
	# of Sample	Ratio	# of Sample	Ratio
Training set	800	80%	600	60%
Test set			200	20%
Validation set	200	20%	200	20%
Total	1,000	100%	1,000	100%

In this study, the radial basis function is used as the kernel function of SVM. Since SVM does not have a general guidance for determining the upper bound C and kernel parameter $\gamma (= \frac{1}{\delta^2})$, this study varies the parameters to select optimal values for the best prediction performance. We use the software package Hsu and Lin (2001) [8] provided, BSVM, for our study.

To verify the applicability of SVM, we use BPN as the benchmark with the following controlling parameters. The structure of BPN is a standard three-layer with the same number of input nodes in the hidden layer and the hidden and output nodes use the sigmoid transfer function. For stopping the training of BPN, test set that is not a subset of the training set is used. However the optimum network for the data in the test set is still different to guarantee generalization performance. The neural network algorithms software NeuroShell 2 version 4.0 executes these processes.

5 Results and Analysis

To investigate the effectiveness of the SVM approach on the churn analysis, we conduct the experiment with respect to various kernel parameters and the upper bound C, and compare the prediction performance of SVM with various parameters. Based on the results proposed by Tay and Cao (2001) [23] and Shin, Lee, and Kim (2005) [20], we set an appropriate range of parameters as follows: a range for kernel parameter $\gamma \, (= \frac{1}{\delta^2})$ is between 0.1 and 0.008 and a range for C is between 1 and 100. The results are summarized in Table 5. Each cell of Table 5 contains the accuracy of the classification techniques.

Table 5. Classification accuracies (%) of various parameters in SVM

C	$\gamma=0.1$		$\gamma=0.05$		$\gamma=0.02$		$\gamma=0.01$		$\gamma=0.008$	
	Tr.	Val.	Tr.	Val.	Tr.	Val.	Tr.	Val.	Tr.	Val.
1st										
1	94.3	82.0	94.2	82.0	94.1	82.0	93.2	79.0	93.2	79.5
10	92.2	82.5	95.0	82.0	94.3	80.5	94.5	81.0	94.3	80.5
50	95.7	83.0	95.2	82.5	94.5	79.5	94.5	79.5	94.5	79.5
75	96.1	81.0	95.5	82.5	95.0	81.0	94.5	79.5	94.5	79.0
100	96.1	81.0	95.5	83.0	95.0	81.0	94.5	79.5	94.5	79.0
2nd										
1	95.7	74.0	94.7	76.0	94.5	77.5	94.8	78.5	94.8	78.5
10	96.1	76.5	96.1	77.0	95.8	77.5	95.5	78.0	95.0	78.0
50	96.6	75.5	96.2	77.0	96.1	77.5	96.0	78.0	95.5	78.0
75	96.7	75.5	96.2	76.5	96.0	77.5	96.0	78.0	96.0	78.0
100	96.7	76.0	96.3	76.0	96.0	77.5	96.0	78.0	96.1	77.5
3rd										
1	94.7	83.5	94.6	83.0	95.5	80.5	94.2	83.5	94.0	83.0
10	95.7	81.5	95.0	84.0	95.0	81.0	94.4	84.5	94.3	84.0
50	96.3	79.5	95.7	82.0	95.1	80.5	95.0	84.0	94.5	84.5
75	96.5	79.5	95.7	82.0	95.0	80.0	94.8	83.5	94.5	84.5
100	96.6	79.5	95.7	82.0	95.0	80.0	94.8	83.5	94.8	84.0
4th										
1	95.1	79.0	94.3	80.0	94.0	80.5	93.5	81.5	93.5	81.5
10	95.8	78.0	95.2	80.0	94.8	81.0	94.2	81.5	94.3	81.5
50	96.2	77.5	96.0	79.5	95.5	80.5	94.8	81.0	94.7	81.5
75	96.5	76.5	96.1	78.5	95.5	80.0	94.8	81.5	94.8	81.5
100	96.6	75.5	96.1	78.5	95.5	80.0	95.1	81.5	94.7	81.0
5th										
1	95.5	79.0	95.0	79.0	94.7	80.0	94.6	80.0	94.5	81.0
10	96.5	78.0	96.2	79.0	95.7	79.5	94.8	83.5	94.8	83.5
50	97.2	76.5	96.8	78.0	95.8	80.0	95.5	84.5	95.5	84.5
75	97.0	76.0	96.7	78.5	95.8	80.0	95.5	84.5	95.5	84.5
100	97.2	76.5	96.6	78.5	96.1	78.5	95.7	84.0	95.5	84.5

The experimental results show that the overall prediction performance of SVM is sensitive not only to various data sets but also to various parameters such as the kernel parameter γ and the upper bound C. In Table 5, the results of SVM on the validation set show the best prediction performances when γ is 0.01 on the most data set except 1st set.

The accuracy on the training set increases monotonically as C increases; on the contrary, the accuracy on the validation set shows a tendency to increase slightly. This indicates that a large value for C has an inclination to over-fit the training data and an appropriate value for C plays a leading role on preventing SVM from deterioration in the generalization performance [20]. According to Tay and Cao (2001) [23], a small value for C would under-fit the training data because the weight placed on the training data is too small and leads to small values of prediction accuracy on both the training and validation sets while a large value for C would over-fit the training data. In this study, the prediction performance on the training set increases as C increases while the prediction performance on the validation set maintains an almost constant value as C increases. These results partly support the conclusion of Tay and Cao (2001) [23]. Figure 2 gives the results of SVM on the 2nd data set with various C where γ is fixed at 0.008.

Figure 6 gives the results of SVM on the 5th data set with various γ where C is fixed at 75. The accuracy on the training set of the most data set except 1st set decreases as γ decreases; on the other hand, the accuracy on the validation set shows a tendency to increase with decreasing γ. According to Shin, Lee, and Kim (2005) [20], this indicates that a large value for γ has an inclination to over-fit the training data and an appropriate value for γ also plays an important role on the generalization performance of SVM. These results also support the conclusion of Tay and Cao (2001) [23].

Another focus of this study is on the comparison of prediction accuracies between SVM and BPN. The results of the best SVM model that present the best prediction performance for the validation set from five data sets and average of all sets are compared with those of BPN and are summarized in Table 6. Each cell of the table contains the accuracy of the classification techniques.

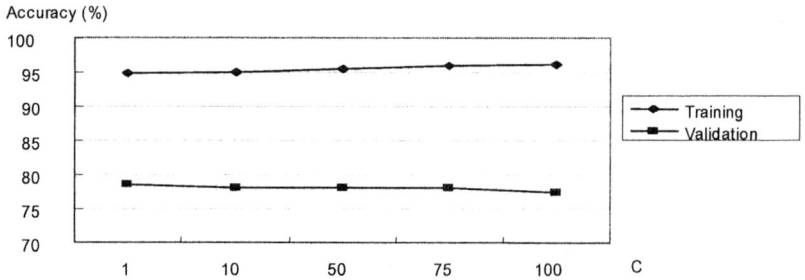

Fig. 5. Results of SVM with various C where γ is fixed at 0.008 on the 2nd set

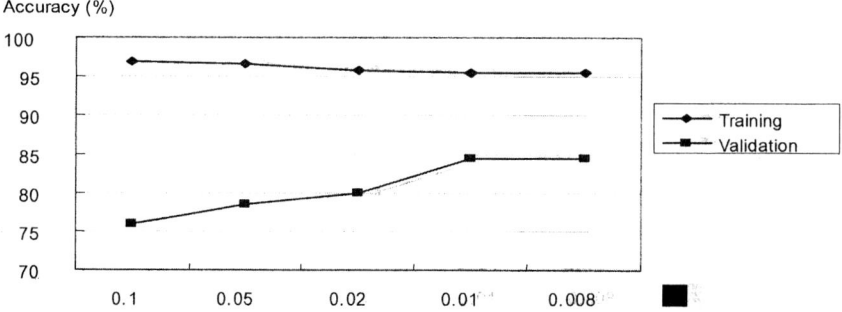

Fig. 6. Results of SVM with various γ where C is fixed at 75 on the 5th set

In Table 6, SVM slightly improved the churning prediction accuracies on all of the data sets and the average. Using SVM, the accuracy (%) on the training set is over 90% and that on the validation set is around 82%. On the other hand, when we use BPN, the accuracy (%) on both of the training and validation set are around 79%. The results show that SVM outperforms BPN in terms of prediction rates

Table 6. Comparison of classification accuracies between the best SVM and BPN

Data set		SVM		BPN	
		Accuracy	%	Accuracy	%
1st set	Training	764	95.5	472	78.7
	Test			159	79.5
	Validation	166	83.0	160	80.0
2nd set	Training	758	94.8	475	79.2
	Test			157	78.5
	Validation	157	78.5	150	75.0
3rd set	Training	755	94.4	484	80.7
	Test			165	82.5
	Validation	169	84.5	163	81.5
4th set	Training	748	93.5	479	79.8
	Test			162	81.0
	Validation	163	81.5	161	80.5
5th set	Training	764	95.5	476	79.3
	Test			161	80.5
	Validation	169	84.5	158	79.0
Total set (Avg. %)	Training	3,789	94.7	2,386	79.5
	Test			804	80.4
	Validation	824	82.4	792	79.2

6 Conclusions

In this study, we applied a newly introduced learning method, support vector machines (SVM), together with a frequently used high performance method, back-propagation neural networks (BPN), to the problem of he credit card customer churn analysis. Although it is the preliminary research, we can draw several conclusions from this experiment. Our results demonstrate that SVM has the higher level of prediction performance than BPN. We also examine the effect of various values of parameters in SVM such as the upper bound C and the bandwidth of the kernel function. We found that the prediction performance is sensitive to the values of these parameters. This result suggests that it is important to optimize the kernel function and various parameters simultaneously because the determination of all these parameter values has critical impacts on the performance of the resulting system. Therefore, developing the structured method of selecting the optimal parameter values for SVM is necessary to obtain the best prediction performance.

References

1. Ben-David, S. and Lindenbaum, M.: Learning distributions by their density levels: A paradigm for learning without a teacher, Vol. 55. Journal of Computer and System Sciences (1997) 171-182
2. Brown, M.P., Grudy W.N., Lin, D., Cristianini, N., Sugnet, C.W., Furey, T.S., Ares, M., Haussler, D.: Knowledge-based analysis of microarray gene expression data by using support vector machines, Vol. 97(1). Proceedings of National Academy of Sciences (2000) 262-267
3. Burges, C.J.C.: A tutorial on support vector machines for pattern recognition, Vol. 2(2). Data Mining and Knowledge Discovery (1998) 955-974
4. Burges, C.J.C., and Scholkopf, B.: Improving the accuracy and speed of support vector machines. In Mozer, M., Jordan, M., and Petche, T., Advances in Neural information processing systems. Cambridge, MA, MIT Press (1997)
5. Cortes, C., and Vapnik, V.N.: Support vector networks, Vol. 20. machine Learning (1995) 273-297
6. Friedman, C.: Credit model technical white paper. Standard and Poor's. New York: McGraw-Hill. (2002)
7. Haykin, S.: Neural networks: A comprehensive foundation. New York: Macmillan (1994)
8. Hsu, C.W. and Lin, C.J.: A comparison of methods for multi-class support vector machines, Technical Report, National Taiwan University, Taiwan, 2001 (2001)
9. Huang, W., Nakamori, Y., Wang, S.Y.: Forecasting stock market movement direction with support vector machine, Computers & Operations Research (2004)
10. Huang, Z., Chen, H., Hsu, C.J., Chen, W.H., Wu, S.: Credit rating analysis with support vector machines and neural networks: a market comparative study, Vol. 37. Decision Support Systems (2004) 543-558
11. Jaakkola, T.S. and Haussler, D.: Esploiting generative models in discriminative classifiers, in: M.S. Kearns, S.A. Solla, D.A. Cohn (Eds.), Advances in Neural Information Processing Systems, MIT Press, Cambridge (1998)
12. Joachims, T.: Learning to classify text using support vector machines, London: Kluwer Academic Publishers (2002)

13. Kim, K.J.: Financial time series forecasting using support vector machines, Vol. 55(1-2). Neurocomputing (2003) 307-319
14. Lariviere, B. and Van den Poel, D.: Investigating the role of product features in preventing customer churn, by using survival analysis and choice modeling: the case of financial services, Vol. 27. Expert Systems with Applications (2004) 277-285
15. Lee, K.C., Chung, N.H., Kim, J.K.: A fuzzy cognitive map approach to integrating explicit knowledge and tacit knowledge: emphasis on the churn analysis of credit card holders, Vol. 11(4). Information Systems Review (2001) 113-133
16. Lee, K.C., Chung, N.H., Shin, K.S.: An artificial intelligence-based data mining approach to extracting strategies for reducing the churning rate in credit card industry, Vol. 8(2). Journal of Intelligent Information Systems (2002) 15-35
17. Mukherjee, S., Osuna, E., and Girosi, F.: Nonlinear prediction of chaotic time series using support vector, Proceedings of the IEEE Workshop on Neural Networks for Signal Processing (1997) 511-520
18. Osuna, E. Freund, R., and Girosi, F.: Training support vector machines: An application to face detection, Proceedings of Computer Vision and Pattern Recognition (1997) 130-136
19. Reichheld, F.F., & Sasser, W.E., Jr.: Zero defections: quality comes to service., Vol. 68(5). Harvard Business Review (1990) 105-111
20. Shin, K.S., Lee, T.S., and Kim, H.J.: An application of support vector machines in bankruptcy prediction model, Vol. 28. Expert Systems with Applications (2005) 127-135
21. Stoneking, D.: Improving the manufacturability of electronic designs, Vol. 36(6). IEEE Spectrum (1999) 70-76
22. Tarassenko, L., Hayton, P., Cerneaz, N., and Brady, M.: Novelty detection for the identification of masses in mammograms, Proceedings Fourth IEEE International Conference on Arificial Neural Networks, Cambridge (1995) 442-447
23. Tay, F.E.H. and Cao, L.: Application of support vector machines in financial time series forecasting, Vol. 29. Omega (2001) 309-317
24. Tay, F.E.H. and Cao, L.J.: Modified support vector machines in financial time series forecasting, Vol. 48. Nerocomputing (2002) 847-861
25. Van Gestel, T. Suykens, J.A.K., Baestaens, D.-E., Lambrachts, A., Lanckriet, G., Vandaele, B. De Moor, B., Vandewalle, J.: Financial time series prediction using least squares support vector machines within the evidence frame work, Vol. 12(4). IEEE Transactions on Neural Networks (2001) 809-821
26. Vapnik, V.N.: The nature of Statistical learning Theory. New York: Springer-Verlag. (1995)
27. Vapnik, V.N.: Statistical learning theory. New York: John Wiley and Sons (1998)
28. Wei, C.P and Chiu, I.T.: Turning telecommunications call details to churn prediction: a data mining approach, Vol. 23. Expert Systems with Applications (2002) 103-112
29. Witten, I.H., and Frank, E.: Data Mining: Practical machine learning tools and techniques with java implementations. San Francisco, CA: Morgan Kaufmann Publishers. (2000)
30. Zien, A., Ratsch, G., Mika, S., Scholkopf, B., Lengauer,T., Muller, K.-R.: Engineering support vector machine kernels that recognize translation initiation sites, Vol. 16(9). Bioinformatics (2000) 799-807

e-NOSE Response Classification of Sewage Odors by Neural Networks and Fuzzy Clustering

Güleda Önkal-Engin[1], Ibrahim Demir[2], and Seref N. Engin[3]

[1] Gebze Institute of Technology,
Department of Environmental Engineering,
Gebze, 41400, Kocaeli, Turkey
guleda@gyte.edu.tr
[2] Environmental Informatics and Control Program,
Warnell School of Forest Resources, University of Georgia,
Athens, GA 30602, USA
ibrahimd@gyte.edu.tr
[3] Department of Electrical Engineering, Yildiz Technical University,
34800 Besiktas, Istanbul, Turkey
nengin@yildiz.edu.tr

Abstract. Each stage of the sewage treatment process emits odor causing compounds and these compounds may vary from one location in a sewage treatment works to another. In order to determine the boundaries of legal standards, reliable and efficient odor measurement methods need to be defined. An electronic NOSE equipped with 12 different polypyrrole sensors is used for the purpose of characterizing sewage odors. Samples collected at different locations of a WWTP were classified using a fuzzy clustering technique and a neural network trained with a back-propagation algorithm.

1 Introduction

A major source of offensive odors is wastewater treatment plants (WWTP) which are open to the atmosphere. The complaints from the public about sewage odor are forcing the water industry to take urgent precautions [1]. There are some odor measurement methods used. The disadvantage of these methods is that these methods measure individual chemicals of a sewage sample introduced, and therefore cannot mimic human response to odors.

It is known that the compounds found in wastewater can vary considerably, and therefore odor variations are expected between sewages of different origins. In this study, an olfactory sensory system (e-NOSE), which is specifically tuned to wastewater odors and which can give an electronic measure of the strength of the combined odor in relation to the way a human nose would detect, was used. The use of electronic noses in water and wastewater odor characterization has been increased within the last decade. Some examples include [2-5].

In this study, sewage samples collected from different locations in a sewage treatment plant was classified using Artificial Neural Networks (ANNs) and fuzzy clustering (FC). These methods have been extensively used in recent years in environmental applications, [3-4].

2 Materials and Methods

An electronic nose, as the name implies, is a simplified form of a human olfactory system. The e-NOSE (Neotronics Olfactory Sensing Equipment Model-D) used in this study was a product of Neotronics Scientific Ltd., Essex, UK. The instrument comprised of 12 conducting polymer (polypyrrole) sensors. Sewage samples were collected from a large plant located near Hatfield, Herts., UK, treating wastewater of domestic and light industrial origin. 1 L grab liquid wastewater samples from the inlet, settlement, biological treatment and outlet units were collected.

The e-nose data was classified with neural networks and fuzzy clustering methods. In the initial stage of Artificial Intelligence (AI) based odor analysis, a feed-forward ANN trained with a back-propagation algorithm was implemented using Qnet v2000 Build 721 software, (Vesta Services, Inc., USA). Fuzzy c-means (FCM) clustering technique (MATLAB, Fuzzy Logic Toolbox v2.1, The MathWorks, Inc., USA) was also applied to the nose data.

ANNs implement algorithms that mimic a neurological way of performance. Neural networks are generally used in two main application areas, function approximation and pattern classification. In function approximation applications, the network is trained to approximate its inputs and outputs. The pattern classification application however, can be regarded as a sub-topic of the function approximation [6]. In this study, a feed-forward ANN trained with a back-propagation algorithm, is built in Qnet computer program.

Cluster analysis is a technique that groups the same kind of points in a multidimensional data space [7]. Clustering is generally used to identify natural groupings of data from a large data set so that the system's behavior can be better interpreted. The aim of FCM is to minimize an objective function that represents the distance from any given data point to a cluster center weighted by that data point's membership grade. Hence, at each iteration, the cluster centers and the membership grades for each data point are updated so that the cluster centers are moved to the "right" location within a data set.

3 Results

The main aim of the study was to see the ability of an e-NOSE to respond to sewage samples. In the first analysis, a back-propagation ANN model was used for the classification of wastewater samples. The network used consisted of one input layer, two hidden layers and one output layer. The input layer had 12 neurons which were corresponding to the 12 sensors located in the e-nose head. Various combinations of networks (different number of hidden layers and neurons) were experimented, and the best results were obtained with two hidden layers having 12 neurons each. The performance of the model were tested with one or three hidden layers, it was observed that the performance was decreased considerably. The sewage locations were represented with one neuron in output layer. All data sets were used for training. In Figure 1, four different sewage classes and network outputs were displayed. As it can be seen, a clear classification was obtained with a correlation of 0.99631 and corresponding to an RMS error of 0.022407. 93.06% of the outputs were classified successfully with an error below 10%. The contribution was in a similar manner, only

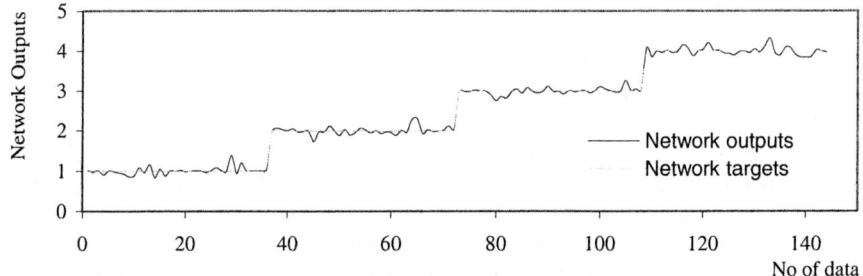

Fig. 1. Network outputs vs. network targets plot

a few of them namely, the 3rd, 7th and 12th neurons have slightly higher values compared to the others.

In the second analysis, FCM technique was employed in order to find the clusters of sewage samples. The technique was employed to the whole set of data by Matlab Fuzzy Toolbox. At the beginning of the analysis, cluster number, exponent for the membership function matrix in fuzzy c-means clustering and minimum amount of improvement were selected as 4, 2 and $1e^{-5}$, respectively.

A successful classification was not achieved for four different clusters which are related to samples taken from four different locations of the treatment plant. This could be due to the complex nature of sewage odor. The influent samples' cluster centers for 12 sensors is separated from the other three clusters considerably. The reason for this could be the change in sewage samples after several treatment processes, such as settlement and aeration processes. For sensors numbered as 2, 3, 5, 6, 7, 9, 10 and 11, an improved classification was observed. Four sensors, namely 2, 3, 5 and 11, were selected randomly for plotting the cluster centers with sensor responses (Figure 2). As indicated above, in these graphs, the cluster (influent samples' centers) in the further top right corner was separated clearly from the other three clusters.

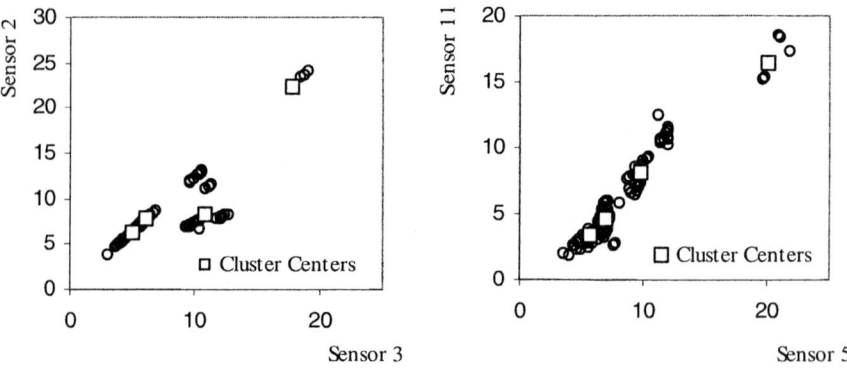

Fig. 2. Cluster centers and sensors' response for different sensor types

In Table 1, distribution percentage of cluster centers for different types of sewage samples was presented. As seen, approximately 69% of the data was in the third cluster for influent samples. For the sewage samples collected from settlement tank, activated sludge and final effluent, it was observed that most of the data were accumulated in the first cluster indicating that a clear classification for these sample types could not be achieved. The reason for this could be that the processes after the first settlement could not give a notable impact on e-NOSE detection of wastewater odors.

Table 1. Percent distribution of 4 cluster centers for different types of sewage samples

	C-1	C-2	C-3	C-4
Influent	0.0	8.3	69.4	22.2
Settlement tank	61.1	0.0	22.2	16.7
Act. Sludge	66.7	8.3	0.0	25.0
Final Effluent	66.7	8.3	0.0	25.0

4 Conclusions

In this study, e-NOSE was used to classify sewage odor samples collected from different locations of a treatment plant. The main problem encountered with sewage samples is that the wastewater odors could vary considerably. There is an additional difficulty with the cluster analysis caused by the complexity of the odor data. The data produced by the e-NOSE needed to be analyzed. For this purpose, clustering analysis was carried out using two techniques, neural networks and fuzzy clustering. Both of these methods are easily applicable and quite rapid compared to other techniques.

Although the number of data used was limited, ANN gave quite satisfactory results for the classification of sewage samples with a correlation of 99%. FCM was not as successful as ANNs for the classification of four different sewage sample types. However, classification is more sensitive and meaningful as a cluster analysis in terms of indicating the degree of closeness of data to a cluster.

References

1. Toogood, S.J.: Odour control for the 1990s – Hit or miss? J. IWEM June (1990) 268-275.
2. Stuetz, R.M., Fenner, R.A., Engin, G.: Characterisation of wastewater using an electronic NOSE. Water Research 33 (1999) 442-452.
3. Bockreis, A., Jager, J.: Odour monitoring by the combination of sensors and neural networks. Environmental Modeling & Software. 14 (1999) 421–426.
4. Gardner, J.W., Shin, H.W., Hines, E.L., Dow, C.S.: An electronic nose system for monitoring the quality of potable water. Sensors and Actuators B. 69 (2000) 336–341.
5. Dewettinck, T., Hege, K.V., Verstraete, W. The e-Nose as a Rapid Sensor for Volatile Compounds in Treated Domestic Wastewater. Water Research 35 (2001) 2475–2483
6. Kosko, B.: A Dynamical Systems Approach to Machine Intelligence. Neural Networks and Fuzzy Systems. Prentice-Hall, Inc, Englewood Cliffs (1992) 449.
7. Sârbu, C., Pop, H.F.: Fuzzy clustering analysis of the first 10 MEIC chemicals Chemosphere 40 (2000) 513-520.

Using a Random Subspace Predictor to Integrate Spatial and Temporal Information for Traffic Flow Forecasting

Shiliang Sun and Changshui Zhang

State Key Laboratory of Intelligent Technology and Systems,
Department of Automation, Tsinghua University, Beijing, China, 100084
sunsl02@mails.tsinghua.edu.cn, zcs@mail.tsinghua.edu.cn

Abstract. Traffic flow forecasting is an important issue for the application of Intelligent Transportation Systems. Due to practical limitations, traffic flow records may be partially missing or substantially contaminated by noise. In this paper, a robust traffic flow predictor, termed random subspace predictor, is developed integrating the entire spatial and temporal information in a transportation network to cope with this case. Experimental results demonstrate the effectiveness and robustness of the random subspace predictor.

1 Introduction

In recent years utilizing signal processing and machine learning techniques for traffic flow forecasting has drawn more and more attention [1][2][3]. In this paper, we concentrate on using the ideology of random subspace to deal with the issue of traffic flow forecasting with incomplete data.

Up to the present, some approaches ranging from simple to complex are proposed for traffic flow forecasting, such as random walk, historical average, time series models, Kalman filter theory, neural network approaches, non-parametric methods, simulation models, fuzzy-neural approach, and Markov chain model [1][4]~[7]. Although these methods have alleviated difficulties in traffic modelling and forecasting to some extent, most of them have not made good use of spatial information from the viewpoint of networks to analyze the trends of the object site. Besides, the existing methods hardly work when data used for forecasting is incomplete, i.e. partially missing or substantially contaminated by noise, while this situation often occurs in practice.

The main contribution of this paper is that we present a robust random subspace predictor to carry out traffic flow forecasting with incomplete data. Encouraging experimental results with real-world data show that our approach is reliable, accurate and robust for traffic flow modelling and forecasting with incomplete data.

2 Random Subspace Predictor

In a transportation network, there are usually a lot of sites (road links) related or informative to the traffic flow forecasting of the current site. However, using all the related links as input variables would involve much irrelevance, redundancy and would be prohibitive for computation. Consequently, a variable selection procedure is of great demand. Up to date many variable selection algorithms include variable ranking as a principal or auxiliary selection mechanism because of its simplicity, scalability, and good empirical success [8].

In this article, we use the norm of Pearson correlation coefficient $|R(i)|$ as a variable ranking criterion [8]. After the variable ranking stage, we can obtain M input variables making up of the input space S which is informative for the prediction of the object flow. However, using the entire high dimensional input space and small training data set to forecast traffic flow directly would arouse over-adaptation. Therefore, we adopt the random subspace ideology [9] and generate K random subspaces $\{S_i\}_{i=1}^{K}$. Every time we randomly select a subspace of m dimensions with replacement from the input space S and use them as an input to forecast the object traffic flow. The dimension m of random subspace is determined by the training set to make the forecasting results stable.

Given the selected input variables and the output variable, we utilize the Gaussian Mixture Model (GMM) to approximate their joint probability distribution whose parameters are estimated through the Competitive Expectation Maximization (CEM) algorithm. Then we can obtain the optimum prediction formulation as an analytic solution under the M.M.S.E. criterion. For details about the GMM, CEM algorithm and the prediction formulation, please refer to our previous articles [2][10]. In succession, we can repeat the above operation K times and would obtain K forecasting results $\{F_k\}_{k=1}^{K}$ for the current object flow. The outputs are combined using the fusion methodology of averaging of them and the average is taken as the final forecasting result $F(S)$ of our random subspace predictor (RSP), i.e. $F(S) = \frac{1}{K} \sum_{k=1}^{K} F_k(S_k)$.

The RSP is very robust and can still work well when the input data are incomplete. If some incomplete data appear in the subspace, we can just remove this subspace and generate a new one till there are no incomplete data involved in the used subspace, and this does not influence the final fusion result much. We will discuss this matter in the following section with a specific instance.

3 Experiments

The field data analyzed is the vehicle flow rates recorded every 15 minutes along many road links by the UTC/SCOOT system in Traffic Management Bureau of Beijing, whose unit is vehicles per hour (veh/hr). We select a representative traffic patch to verify the proposed approach, which is given in Fig. 1. An arrow shows the direction of traffic flow, which reaches the corresponding downstream link from its upstream link. The raw data for use are of 25 days and totally 2400 sample points taken from March, 2002. To validate our approach objectively,

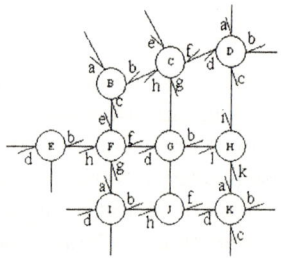
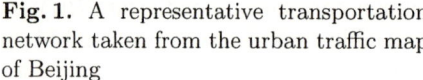
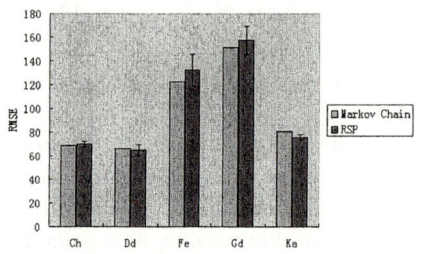

Fig. 1. A representative transportation network taken from the urban traffic map of Beijing

Fig. 2. A performance comparison of two methods for short-term traffic flow forecasting at five different road links

the first 2112 points (training set) of them are employed to learn parameters of GMM and the rest (test set) are employed to test the forecasting performance. To evaluate our presented approach, we utilize the Markov chain method as a base line [6]. The dimension of subspace in our approach is taken as 4 (the same with the Markov chain method in [6]) for each object site. The only difference between our proposed method and the Markov Chain method is that we utilize the whole spatial and temporal information to forecast while the latter only uses the temporal information of the object site.

We take road link Ka as an instance to show our approach. Ka represents the vehicle flow from upstream link H to downstream link K. All the available traffic flows which may be informative to forecast Ka in the analyzed transportation network includes $\{Ba, Bb, Bc, Ce, Cf, Cg, Ch, Da, Db, Dc, Dd, Eb, Ed, Fe, Ff, Fg, Fh, Gb, Gd, Hi, Hk, Hl, Ia, Ib, Id, Jf, Jh, Ka, Kb, Kc, Kd\}$. Considering the time factor, in order to forecasting the traffic flow $Ka(t)$, we might need judge its relevancy from the above sites with different time indices, such as $\{Ba(t-1), Ba(t-2), ..., Ba(t-d)\}$, etc. In this paper, d is taken as 100 empirically. We retain M ($M = 20$ in this article) most correlated traffic flows constructing the entire input space which are selected with the correlation variable ranking criterion with their corresponding correlation coefficients. These correlation coefficients varies from 0.967 for $Hi(t-1)$ to 0.954 for $Eb(t-3)$. With the selected input space, our RSP generates K ($K = 10$ in this article) random subspaces. The joint probability distribution between the random subspace input and the output $Ka(t)$ are approximated with GMM, and thus we can derive the prediction formulation, carry out traffic flow forecasting on the test data set. Finally we combine the K outputs to form one forecasting output. In addition, we also conducted experiments on four other traffic flows Ch, Dd, Fe, Gd. Fig. 2 gives the forecasting results of all the five road links with performances evaluated by Root Mean Square Error (RMSE).

From the experimental results, we can find the effectivity and robustness of our approach which integrates both spatial and temporal information for forecasting. Generally speaking, the RSP has obtained similar accuracy with the Markov chain method. But the PSP can be used in case of incomplete data. In forecasting $Ka(t)$, the Markov chain method would use $Ka(t-1)$, $Ka(t-2), Ka(t-3), Ka(t-4)$ as input. However, if $Ka(t-1)$ is incomplete, then Markov chain method would lose its applicability while the RSP can still work since it can use the other $M-1$ input variables to generate subspace and the final performance would not change much. Further, the RSP can still work stably if multiple input flows are incomplete.

4 Conclusions

In this paper, we propose a robust random subspace predictor integrating the whole spatial and temporal information available in a transportation network to carry out traffic flow forecasting. It is simple, effective and still work well when encountering incomplete data. Experimental results demonstrate the applicability of the random subspace predictor.

Acknowledgements

This work was supported by the National Natural Science Foundation of China under Project 60475001.

References

1. William, B.M.: Modeling and Forecasting Vehicular Traffic Flow as a Seasonal Stochastic Time Series Process. Doctoral Dissertation. University of Virginia, Charlottesville (1999)
2. Sun, S.L., Zhang C.S., Yu G.Q., Lu, N.J., Xiao F.: Bayesian Network Methods for Traffic Flow Forecasting with Incomplete Data. ECML 2004, Lecture Notes in Artificial Intelligence, Vol. 3201. Springer-Verlag, Berlin Heidelberg (2004) 419-428
3. Yang, L.C., Jia, L., Wang, H.: Wavelet Network with Genetic Algorithm and Its Applications for Traffic Flow Forecasting. Proceedings of the Fifth World Congress on Intelligent Control and Automation, Vol. 6 (2004) 5330 - 5333
4. Chrobok, R., Wahle, J., Schreckenberg, M.: Traffic Forecast Using Simulations of Large Scale Networks. Proceedings of IEEE Intelligent Transportation Systems Conference (2001) 434-439
5. Yin, H.B., Wong, S.C., Xu, J.M., Wong, C.K.: Urban Traffic Flow Prediction Using a Fuzzy-Neural Approach. Transportation Research, Part C, Vol. 10 (2002), 85-98
6. Yu, G.Q., Hu, J.M., Zhang, C.S., Zhuang, L.K., Song J.Y.: Short-Term Traffic Flow Forecasting Based on Markov Chain Model. Proceedings of IEEE Intelligent Vehicles Symposium (2003) 208 - 212
7. Sun, S.L., Yu, G.Q., Zhang, C.S.: Short-Term Traffic Flow Forecasting Using Sampling Markov Chain Method with Incomplete Data. Proceedings of IEEE Intelligent Vehicles Symposium (2004) 437 - 441
8. Guyon, I., Elisseeff, A.: An Introduction to Variable and Feature Selection. Journal of Machine Learning Research, Vol. 3 (2003) 1157-1182
9. Ho, T.K.: The Random Subspace Method for Constructing Decision Forests. IEEE Transactions on Pattern Analysis and Machine Intelligence, Vol. 20 (1998) 832-844
10. Zhang, B.B., Zhang, C.S., Yi, X.: Competitive EM Algorithm for Finite Mixture Models. Pattern Recognition, Vol. 37 (2004) 131-144

Boosting Input/Output Hidden Markov Models for Sequence Classification

Ke Chen

School of Informatics, The University of Manchester, United Kingdom
Ke.Chen@manchester.ac.uk

Abstract. Input/output hidden Markov model (IOHMM) has turned out to be effective in sequential data processing via supervised learning. However, there are several difficulties, e.g. model selection, unexpected local optima and high computational complexity, which hinder an IOHMM from yielding the satisfactory performance in sequence classification. Unlike previous efforts, this paper presents an ensemble learning approach to tackle the aforementioned problems of the IOHMM. As a result, simple IOHMMs of different topological structures are used as base learners in our boosting algorithm and thus an ensemble of simple IOHMMs tend to tackle a complicated sequence classification problem without the need of explicit model selection. Simulation results in text-dependent speaker identification demonstrate the effectiveness of boosted IOHMMs for sequence classification.

1 Introduction

Sequence classification is a problem of classifying the data of a sequential structure into a certain category. Such a problem arises in a variety of applications ranging from speech recognition to bioinformatics. Many efforts from different perspectives have been made for sequence classification. In general, the existing methods can be divided into two categories; i.e. generative model and discriminative model. For classification, a generative model, e.g., hidden Markov model (HMM), is built up based on training data belonging to the same class without the consideration of inter-class information. In contrast, a discriminative model, e.g, recurrent neural network, takes into account inter-class information during its creation and therefore is more suitable for sequence classification.

As a modular recurrent neural network, the input/output hidden Markov model (IOHMM) has been proposed for sequence processing [2]. Unlike the traditional HMM that represents only the distribution of output sequences, the IOHMM represents the conditional sequence of output sequences given corresponding input sequences, which leads to a discriminative model for sequence processing. The IOHMM has been applied in different fields [2][3] and turns out to be effective for various sequence processing tasks. However, the IOHMM suffers from several problems especially as is applied to real word problems. First of all, model selection is an open problem that its topological structure, i.e., number of states and admissible transitions between different states in an IOHMM, needs to be determined prior to its training for a sequence classification task. In order to tackle this problem, a common method is cross-validation (for example, see [3]). However, the method suffers from a very high computational burden and demands a considerable amount of training data. In addition, training an IOHMM of a complicated topology often costs considerable amount of time and gets stuck in an unexpected local optimum. These weaknesses of the IOHMM hinder its applications in real world problems.

Boosting is an ensemble learning methodology which uses a set of "weak" learners and allows learners to work on various distributions over the training data. Thus the divide-and-conquer principle is carried out in a transparent way. It has been proved that boosting can remarkably improve the error of any "weak" learner as long as such a "weak" learner consistently yields a performance slightly better than random guessing [8]; i.e., an error rate of a little bit less than 50%. Empirical studies show that the boosting methodology often yields the good generalization for many real world problems.

It is difficult for a classification algorithm to apply to sequential data since there are a huge number of potentially useful contextual features for describing a sequence [11]. It is often difficult to discover useful features explicitly from sequence data. Our earlier work [4][5] uncovers that the salient contextual features may not uniformly distribute in every piece of a sequence and different circumstances demand various kinds of contextual features for sequence classification. Motivated by our earlier work [4][5] and the previous work in static pattern classification with multiple feature subsets (e.g., [1]), we propose an approach to boosting simple IOHMMs of different topological structures for sequence classification. We anticipate that a simple IOHMM of a specific topological structure would capture some useful contextual features for some cases and boosting multiple IOHMMs of various topological structures would be able to eventually exploit all of salient contextual features thoroughly in order to fulfil a sequence classification task. Unlike other work (e.g, [11]), our approach does not have an explicit contextual feature extraction process prior to training of a classifier. Here we would emphasize that our boosting algorithm uses a repository of IOHMMs of different topological structures, which is different from most of the existing boosting algorithms where a learner of a specific architecture is universally applied to various distributions of training data. Thus, IOHMMs in the repository are invoked by our boosting algorithm in an order from simple to complex topological structures, which adheres to the Occam's razor principle [14]. This modified boosting algorithm alleviates the model selection problem of the IOHMM and, therefore, there is no need to explicitly specify a perfect architecture of an IOHMM prior to its training.

The rest of the paper is organized as follows. Sect. 2 reviews the IOHMM model and an EM learning algorithm especially for sequence classification. Sect. 3 presents a modified Adaboost algorithm for the use of IOHMMs in sequence classification. Sect. 4 reports simulation results in speaker identification and Sect. 5 discusses some issues related to our work. The last section draws conclusions.

2 Input/Output Hidden Markov Model

In order to make the paper self-contained, we review the IOHMM architecture [2] and present a specific EM algorithm [6] used for sequence classification.

2.1 IOHMM Architecture

The IOHMM is modeled by a discrete state dynamical system based on the following state space description: $\boldsymbol{y}_t = g(x_t, \boldsymbol{u}_t)$, $x_t = f(x_{t-1}, \boldsymbol{u}_t)$ where $\boldsymbol{u}_t$ is an input vector at time t, $\boldsymbol{y}_t$ is its corresponding output vector and $x_t \in \{1, 2, \cdots, n\}$ is a discrete state. Moreover, admissible state transitions will be specified by a directed graph whose vertexes correspond to the model's states and the set of successors of state j in $\boldsymbol{S}_j$. Bengio and Frasconi model such a system as a recurrent modular neural network architecture [2] as illustrated in Fig. 1.

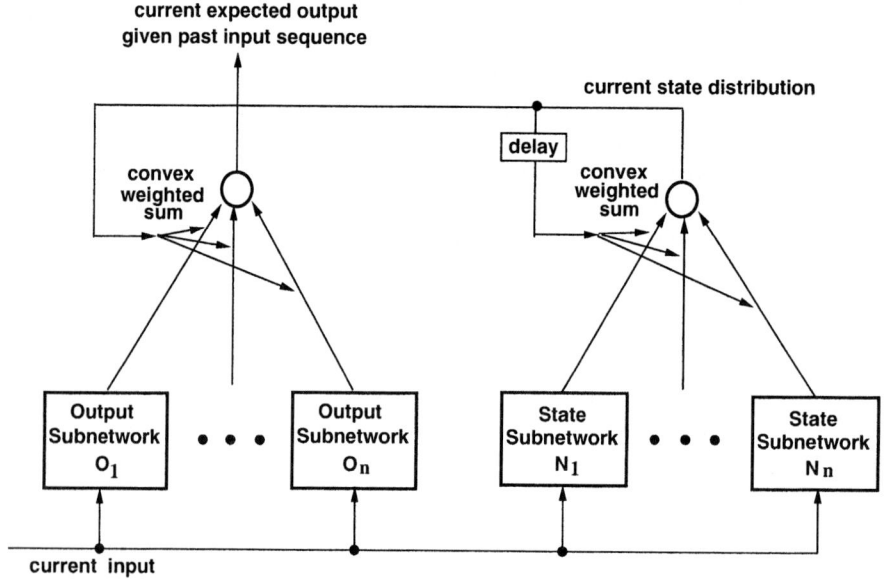

Fig. 1. The input/output HMM architecture

The architecture consists of a set of state networks N_j, $j = 1, \cdots, n$, and a set of output networks O_j, $j = 1, \cdots, n$. Each one of state and output networks is uniquely associated to one of n states, and all networks share the same input $\boldsymbol{u}_t$. Given $x_{t-1} = j$, a state network N_j has the task that predicts the next state distribution based on the current input $\boldsymbol{u}_t$. Similarly, each output network O_j predicts the output of the system given the current state and input. All the subnetworks are assumed to be static. At time t, each output $\varphi_{ij,t}$ of the state subnetwork N_j on the input $\boldsymbol{u}_t$ is associated with one of the successor i of state j as $\varphi_{ij,t} = e^{a_{ij,t}} / \sum_{k \in \boldsymbol{S}_j} e^{a_{kj,t}}$, $j = 1, \cdots, n, i \in \boldsymbol{S}_j$, where $a_{ij,t}$ are intermediate variables specifying activations of the output units of subnetwork N_j. In addition, the condition $\varphi_{ij,t} = 0$ is also imposed for any $i \notin S_j$. In this way, $\sum_{i=1}^{n} \varphi_{ij,t} = 1 \; \forall j, t$. Let vector ζ_t denote the internal state of the model and it can be interpreted as the current state distribution. As a result, $\zeta_t = \sum_{j=1}^{n} \zeta_{j,t-1} \varphi_{j,t}$ where $\varphi_{j,t} = [\varphi_{1j,t}, \cdots, \varphi_{nj,t}]^T$. Output networks compete for predicting the global output of the system η_t on the input u_t so that $\eta_t = \sum_{j=1}^{n} \zeta_{j,t} \eta_{j,t}$ where $\eta_{j,t}$ is the output of subnetwork O_j.

This architecture can be also interpreted as a probability model. For multiple states, the x_t is subject to a multinomial distribution. We initialise ζ_0 to positive numbers summing to one. Thus, an probabilistic interpretation of state subnetwork N_j is as follows:

$$P(x_t = i | u_1^t) = \sum_{j=1}^{n} P(x_t = i | x_{t-1} = j, u_t) P(x_{t-1} = j | u_1^{t-1}), \quad (1)$$

where $P(x_t = i | x_{t-1} = j, u_t) = \varphi_{ij,t}$ and $P(x_{t-1} = j | u_1^{t-1}) = \zeta_{j,t-1}$. Accordingly, the output η_t of this architecture can be interpreted as a "position parameter" for the probability distribution of the output y_t. In additional to being conditional on an input u_t, however, this expectation is also conditional on the state x_t so that $\eta_t = E[y_t | x_t = i, u_t]$. The actual form of the output distribution, denoted $f_Y(y_t; \eta_t)$, will be chosen according to the given task. For sequence classification, in general, $f_Y(y_t; \eta_t)$ is the Bernoulli distribution for binary classification and the multinomial or the generalized Bernoulli distribution for multi-category classification [6].

2.2 EM Algorithm

For the above recurrent architecture, Bengio and Frasconi have proposed an EM algorithm for parameter estimation [2]. Consider the training data are a set of P pairs of input/output sequences of length T_p: $D = \{(u_1^{T_p}, y_1^{T_p})\}$ for $p = 1, \cdots, P$. Let Θ denote the set of all parameters in the architecture. The likelihood function is

$$L(\Theta; D) = \prod_{p=1}^{P} P(y_1^{T_p} | u_1^{T_p}; \Theta) \quad (2)$$

To derive the learning equations with EM algorithm, we define the *complete data* via hidden state paths $\mathcal{X} = \{x_1^{T_p}\}$ for $p = 1, \cdots, P$ as $D_c = \{(u_1^{T_p}, y_1^{T_p}, x_1^{T_p})\}$ for $p = 1, \cdots, P$. The corresponding complete data log-likelihood is

$$L_C(\Theta; D_c) = \sum_{p=1}^{P} \log P(y_1^{T_p}, x_1^{T_p} | u_1^{T_p}; \Theta) \quad (3)$$

Thus, EM algorithm is obtained by introducing the auxiliary function $Q(\Theta, \Theta^{(k)})$ and iterating the following two steps for $k = 1, 2, \cdots$:

E-step: Compute $Q(\Theta, \Theta^{(k)}) = E_{\mathcal{X}}[L_C(\Theta; D_c) | D, \Theta^{(k)}]$
M-step: Update the parameters as $\Theta^{(k+1)} \leftarrow \arg\max_\Theta Q(\Theta, \Theta^{(k)})$

In the E-step, for a sequence of T_p feature vectors, the evaluation of $Q(\Theta, \Theta^{(k)})$ is the equivalent to estimation of a *posteriori* probabilities $h_{ij,t}$:

$$h_{ij,t} = P(x_t = i, x_{t-1} = j | \boldsymbol{y}_1^{T_p}, \boldsymbol{u}_1^{T_p}) = \frac{\beta_{i,t} \alpha_{j,t-1} \varphi_{ij,t}}{\sum_i \alpha_{i,T_p}}$$

where

$$\alpha_{j,t-1} = P(\boldsymbol{y}_1^{t-1}, x_{t-1} = j | \boldsymbol{u}_1^{t-1}) = f_Y(\boldsymbol{y}_{t-1}; \boldsymbol{\eta}_{j,t-1}) \sum_{k \in S_j} \varphi_{jk,t-1} \alpha_{k,t-2},$$

and

$$\beta_{i,t} = P(\boldsymbol{y}_t^T, x_t = i | \boldsymbol{u}_t^T) = f_Y(\boldsymbol{y}_t; \boldsymbol{\eta}_{i,t}) \sum_{k \in S_i} \varphi_{ki,t+1} \beta_{k,t+1}.$$

In the M-step, it can be completed by the *gradient ascent* method [2]. Unfortunately, it suffers from rather slow training. The iterative reweighted least square (IRLS) algorithm is an iterative algorithm for computing the maximum likelihood estimates of the parameters of a generalized linear model (GLM) [13]. Therefore, we can adopt the IRLS algorithm in the M-step since all output and state subnetworks can be modeled as the GLIM [13]. Let $\Theta_i^{(s)}$ and $\Theta_i^{(o)}$, $i = 1, \cdots, n$ denote the parameters of state and output networks, respectively. Thus, the M-step becomes two separate maximization problems

$$\Theta_i^{(s)} = \arg\max_{\Theta_i^{(s)}} \sum_{p=1}^{P} \sum_{t=1}^{T_p} \log(\prod_{i=1}^{n} \prod_{j=1}^{n} \varphi_{ij,t}^{h_{ij,t}}) \quad (4)$$

$$\Theta_i^{(o)} = \arg\max_{\Theta_i^{(o)}} \sum_{p=1}^{P} \sum_{t=1}^{T_p} \sum_{i=1}^{n} \zeta_{i,t} \log f_Y(\boldsymbol{y}_t; \boldsymbol{\eta}_{i,t}) \quad (5)$$

In (4), the multinomial distribution $\prod_{j=1}^{n} \varphi_{ij,t}^{h_{ij,t}}$ in (4) is a member in the exponential family, the IRLS algorithm can be used to solve the problem in (4) as follows:

$$\Delta \Theta_{ir}^{(s)} = [\boldsymbol{U}^T W_{ir}^{(s)} \boldsymbol{U}]^{-1} \boldsymbol{U} \boldsymbol{e}^{(s)}, \quad (6)$$

where $\Theta_{ir}^{(s)}$ denotes the parameter vector related to the rth output node of state network i. The tth component of $\boldsymbol{e}^{(s)}$ is $e_{ir,t}^{(s)} = h_{ir,t} - \varphi_{ir,t}$. $W_{ir}^{(s)}$ is a diagonal matrix whose tth diagonal element is $w_{ir,t}^{(s)} = \varphi_{ir,t}(1 - \varphi_{ir,t})$ [13].

For sequence classification, $f_Y(\boldsymbol{y}_t; \boldsymbol{\eta}_{i,t})$ can be binary or a specific multi-category classification encoded by the *1-of-M* output scheme leading to a special case of the multinomial distribution [6]. We use a *generalized Bernoulli distribution* proposed in [6] as the probabilistic model of output networks. Thus, the unified distribution for classification is $f_Y(\boldsymbol{y}_t; \boldsymbol{\eta}_{i,t}) = \prod_{k=1}^{M} \eta_{ik,t}^{y_{k,t}} (1 - \eta_{ik,t})^{1-y_{k,t}}$ so that $e_{ir,t}^{(o)} = \zeta_{i,t}(y_{r,t} - \eta_{ir,t})$ and $w_{ir,t}^{(o)} = \zeta_{i,t} \eta_{ir,t}(1 - \eta_{ir,t})$. Applying the IRLS algorithm to the problem in (5) yields

$$\Delta \Theta_{ir}^{(o)} = [\boldsymbol{U}^T W_{ir}^{(o)} \boldsymbol{U}]^{-1} \boldsymbol{U} \boldsymbol{e}^{(o)}, \quad (7)$$

where $\Theta_{ir}^{(o)}$ denotes the parameter vector with respect to the rth output node of output network i. The tth component of $e^{(o)}$ is $e_{ir,t}^{(o)} = (y_{r,t} - \eta_{ir,t})/f'(\eta_{ir,t})$ and $f(\cdot)$ is the link function [13] of $f_Y(\boldsymbol{y}_t; \boldsymbol{\eta}_{i,t})$. $\boldsymbol{U}$ is the matrix consisting of all training data. $W_{ir}^{(s)}$ is a diagonal matrix whose tth diagonal element is $w_{ir,t} = [f'(\eta_{ir,t})]^2/Var(y_{r,t})$ and $Var(\cdot)$ is the variance function of $f_Y(\boldsymbol{y}_t; \boldsymbol{\eta}_{i,t})$ [6].

3 Boosting IOHMMs

In this section, we modify Adaboost algorithm [8] to boost IOHMMs for sequence classification.

Adaboost algorithm [8] is a sophisticated boosting method for improving the performance of any "weak" learning system. There are two Adaboost versions; i.e. Adaboost.M1 and Adaboost.M2. Since the IOHMM is a discriminative model, we adopt the Adaboost.M1 as the basis of our boosting algorithm. As a consequence, the modified Adaboost.M1 algorithm is as follows:

Algorithm: Adaboost-IOHMMs

Input: A training set of P examples $\{(\boldsymbol{u}_1^{T_p}, \boldsymbol{y}_p)\}_{p=1}^P$ where $\boldsymbol{y}_p$ is an encoded label of $\boldsymbol{u}_1^{T_p}$ and $\boldsymbol{y}_p \in \{0,1\}^M$ ($M \geq 2$), $\|\boldsymbol{y}_p\| = 1$.
A repository of simple IOHMMs ordered with topological complexity.
A termination condition $\mathcal{T}$ specifying the number of iterations.

Initialize $D_1(p) = 1/P$, for $p = 1, 2, \cdots, P$. (P training examples)

Do for $t = 1, 2, \cdots, \mathcal{T}$;
1. Call an IOHMM in order from the IOHMM repository and provide it with the training set $\{(\boldsymbol{u}_1^{T_p}, \boldsymbol{y}_p)\}_{p=1}^P$ and the distribution $\{D_t(p)\}_{p=1}^P$.
2. Apply the EM algorithm to train the IOHMM to produce a hypothesis h_t.
3. Calculate the error rate of h_t: $\epsilon_t = \sum_{p:C(p) \text{ is true}} D_t(p)$, where $C(p) \equiv \arg\max_{1 \leq m \leq M} h_t(\boldsymbol{u}_1^{T_p}) \neq \arg\max_{1 \leq m \leq M} \boldsymbol{y}_p$ and $h_t(\boldsymbol{u}_1^{T_p})$ is the actual output vector of h_t for the pth input sequence.
4. If $\epsilon_t \leq 0.5$, go to Step 1.
   Otherwise, remove the current IOHMM from the repository. Thus,
   – if there is still at least one IOHMM in the repository, then go back to Step 1,
   – otherwise set $\mathcal{T} = t - 1$ and abort loop.
5. Update distribution $\{D_t(p)\}_{p=1}^P$: $D_{t+1}(p) = \frac{D_t(p)}{Z_t}[\boldsymbol{h}_t(\boldsymbol{u}_1^{T_p}) - \boldsymbol{y}_p]^T[\boldsymbol{h}_t(\boldsymbol{u}_1^{T_p}) - \boldsymbol{y}_p]$
   where Z_t is a normalization constant for the need of being a distribution.

Test For an M-category classification ($M \geq 2$), an unknown sequence $\boldsymbol{u}_1^{T_x}$ is classified by the boosted IOHMMs as $m^* = \arg\max_{1 \leq m \leq M} \sum_{t=1}^{\mathcal{T}} h_t(\boldsymbol{u}_1^{T_x})$.

It is worth stating that there are two critical points in the above algorithm which distinguishes itself from the original Adaboost.M1 algorithm.

Unlike the original algorithm, we introduce a repository of IOHMMs of different topologies to generate hypotheses during boosting. As mentioned in the first section, doing so enables a statistical ensemble to capture various salient contextual features in a divide-and-conquer way for sequence classification. In this paper, we define the topological complexity of an IOHMM based on two factors; i.e. the number of states and the number of admissible transitions between states. If two IOHMMs have different numbers of states, we stipulate that the one of more states has a higher topological complexity. Otherwise the one of more admissible transitions has a higher topological complexity. For example, a four-state IOHMM has a higher topological complexity than the one of three states while an ergodic IOHMM has a higher complexity than a left-to-right IOHMM of the same number of states.

The update of distribution $\{D_t(p)\}_{p=1}^{P}$ plays a crucial role in the Adaboost algorithm, which critically determines the next hypothesis generation. Thanks to the probabilistic nature of the IOHMM and the 1-of-M output encoding scheme for classification, we can apply a confidence-based distribution update rule, which was proposed in our earlier work [12], in Step 5 of the aforementioned algorithm. The basic idea behind the confident-based update rule is that an update takes into account not only misclassified examples by previous hypotheses but also other informative ones located around decision boundaries. The idea was carried out by the Euclidean distance between the actual output and the ideal label based on zero-one loss as follows: $div\left(\boldsymbol{h}_t(\boldsymbol{u}_1^{T_p}), \boldsymbol{y}_p\right) = [\boldsymbol{h}_t(\boldsymbol{u}_1^{T_p})-\boldsymbol{y}_p]^T[\boldsymbol{h}_t(\boldsymbol{u}_1^{T_p})-\boldsymbol{y}_p]$. We can show that $0 \leq div\left(\boldsymbol{h}_t(\boldsymbol{u}_1^{T_p}), \boldsymbol{y}_p\right) \leq 2$ and $div\left(\boldsymbol{h}_t(\boldsymbol{u}_1^{T_p}), \boldsymbol{y}_p\right) \geq 1$ for any sequence misclassified by the current learner. Thus misclassified sequence would be selected to train the learner in the next round while those correctly classified still have chances to be selected, depending on how large the distance between the ideal and the actual outputs. Simulation results [12] showed that our confidence-based distribution turns out to outperform the distribution update rule in the original Adaboost.M1 version [8] for several real world problems.

4 Simulations

Speaker identification is a task that classifies an unlabelled voice token as belonging to one of reference speakers. Text-dependent speaker identification refers to such a task by a given text. It is a typical sequence classification task where an utterance of the specific text consisting of a sequence of short-term frames is associated with its speaker identity. Since a speaker's voice changes over time, it is a hard temporal pattern classification problem where intra-class varieties tend to be large while inter-class varieties are very small. As a consequence, the temporal information or sequential effects must be taken into account during classification.

In this section, we report simulation results of boosted IOHMMs (B-IOHMMs) in text-dependent speaker identification. For a comparison, we also show results by other classical models commonly used for sequence classification, i.e., multi-layered perception (MLP), dynamic time warping (DTW), hidden Markov model (HMM) and input/output HMM (IOHMM), based on our earlier empirical study on the same data set [3]. In our previous work, model selection for MLP, HMM and IOHMM was done by a multi-fold cross validation and the best results are only given here (for details, see [3]).

In our simulations, we adopt an acoustic database consisting of 10 isolated digits from '0' to '9' in Chinese where ten male speakers are registered in the database. In the database, utterances were collected in three different sessions [3]. Like the experimental methodology in [3], we use utterances collected in the first session to be a training set and the remaining two sessions to be test sets named by TEST-1 and TEST-2.

For each digit, we create an ensemble of IOHMMs based on the boosting algorithm in Sect. 3 and the EM algorithm in Sect. 2.2. In our simulations, we use only a repository that contains three different IOHMMs of three states; i.e. a left-to-right model without jumps, a left-to-right model with jumps and the ergodic model which are ordered from simple to complicated topological complexity. In the simulations, the iteration number $\mathcal{T}$ for termination is set to 12 in our boosting algorithm. Furthermore, ten trials on the same training set were done for reliability and only the averaging results are reported here. It is worth mentioning that due to limited space we do not include the standard deviation results in Tables 1 and 2. For your information, no standard deviation in our simulations is greater than 3%. As a result, comparative results are listed in Tables 1 and 2.

Table 1. Identification accuracies (%) of different models on TEST-1

MODEL	'0'	'1'	'2'	'3'	'4'	'5'	'6'	'7'	'8'	'9'	MEAN
MLP	92.5	89.3	89.8	82.1	87.6	85.4	88.9	91.9	79.6	89.5	**87.7**
DTW	92.2	90.1	88.3	83.5	82.8	87.7	86.4	94.7	75.9	89.2	**87.1**
HMM	97.2	95.1	87.3	86.5	86.2	89.4	87.3	99.1	77.1	88.4	**91.4**
IOHMM	97.1	97.1	97.2	94.3	98.6	87.2	97.0	98.6	92.9	94.3	**95.4**
B-IOHMMs	98.1	97.9	97.6	95.1	98.3	90.1	97.6	99.2	93.1	93.8	**96.1**

Table 2. Identification accuracies (%) of different models on TEST-2

MODEL	'0'	'1'	'2'	'3'	'4'	'5'	'6'	'7'	'8'	'9'	MEAN
MLP	88.0	90.0	87.0	85.0	82.0	83.0	84.0	83.0	77.0	89.0	**84.8**
DTW	88.0	90.0	85.0	80.0	83.0	86.0	87.0	87.0	71.0	74.0	**83.1**
HMM	87.0	94.0	87.0	81.0	91.0	88.0	85.0	89.0	67.0	71.0	**83.6**
IOHMM	92.0	98.0	96.0	88.0	90.0	91.0	85.0	89.0	77.0	89.0	**89.5**
B-IOHMMs	94.0	98.0	97.0	92.0	95.0	91.0	90.0	95.0	82.0	90.0	**92.4**

From Tables 1 and 2, it is evident that boosted IOHHMs outperform other models in general. In particular, its results on TEST-2 are remarkably superior to those of others models used for comparison. As pointed out previously, a speaker's voice always changes over time. Utterances collected in TEST-2 have longer time apart from the training data than those in TEST-1, which causes the classification on TEST-2 to be a more difficult problem for a classifier only trained on utterances earlier. The performance of boosted IOHMMs manifests that they capture salient temporal features better than other models used for the comparison in a various environment. In comparison to individual IOHMMs of more states [3], a repository of simple IOHMMs of three states are sufficient to yield the satisfactory performance by using the proposed boosting algorithm. It is also worth mentioning that the ergodic model in the repository is invoked only in last two iterations of the boosting algorithm in our simulations.

5 Discussion

The boosting algorithm in this paper is proposed for sequence classification; i.e., a sequence is treated as a whole and therefore a universal label is assigned to all components of the sequence. The sequential supervised learning [7] is a more general task where components of a sequence are temporally dependant but could be labelled differently, e.g. the part-of speech problem where correlated words in a sentence are often associated with different lexical tags [9]. Since the IOHMM itself is able to cope with this problem, the extension of the proposed boosting algorithm to the sequential supervised learning is straightforward without difficulty although we must use multinomial distribution to model output and state subnetworks in this circumstance [6].

It has been known that the IOHMM suffers from the label bias problem [7], which definitely affects its capabilities to capture contextual information underlying a sequence. In order to remedy this problem, we can replace the IOHMM in our boosting algorithm by an alternative model; i.e., conditional random fields [10]. We anticipate that the use of conditional random fields with different features in our learner repository would better capture different contexts during boosting. Boosting conditional random fields is under our ongoing investigation.

Some topics are left for future researches; e.g, as base learners, how do multiple learners of different architectures affect the final result of sequence classification? Although we argue, based on our preliminary simulation results, that simple IOHMMs of different topological complexity capture salient episodic contexts and the ensemble would eventually capture long-term dependency by combining these simple IOHMMs, it is still unclear that this argument is valid in general. In our going work, we shall systematically look into the effect of temporal models of different architectures used in boosting and the relationship between episodic and long-term contexts for sequence classification.

6 Conclusion

We have presented a boosting algorithm to generate an ensemble of IOHMMs for sequence classification where no explicit model selection is required. Text-dependent speaker identification results reported in the paper demonstrate the effectiveness of our algorithms for sequence classification. We argue that such a boosting approach offers an alternative way to exploit various salient contextual features for sequence classification without the need of an explicit contextual feature extraction process prior to training and, to a great extent, the output of an IOHMM ensemble more likely reaches an expected local optimum. Thus, boosting IOHMMs overcomes several obstacles in applying IOHMM to real world sequence classification tasks.

References

1. S. Bay, "Nearest neighbor classification from multiple feature subsets," *Intelligent Data Analysis*, vol 3., no. 3, 191-209, 1999.
2. Y. Bengio and P. Frasconi, "Input-output HMM's for sequence processing," *IEEE Transactions on Neural Networks*, vol. 7, no. 5, pp. 1231-1249, 1996.
3. K. Chen, D. Xie and H. Chi, "Text-dependent speaker identification based on input/output HMMs: An empirical study," *Neural Processing Letters*, vol. 3, no. 2, pp. 81-89, 1996.
4. K. Chen, D. Xie and H. Chi, "Speaker identification based on time-delay HMEs," *International Journal of Neural Systems*, vol. 7, no. 1, pp. 29-43, 1996.
5. K. Chen, D. Xie and H. Chi, "A modified HME architecture for text-dependent speaker identification," *IEEE Transactions on Neural Networks*, vol. 7, no. 5, pp. 1309-1313, 1996.
6. K. Chen, L. Xu and H. Chi, "Improved learning algorithms for mixture of experts in multiclass classification," *Neural Networks*, vol. 12, no. 9, pp. 1329-1352, 1999.
7. T. Dietterich, "Machine learning for sequential data: A review," In T. Caelli (Ed.) *Structural, Syntactic, and Statistical Pattern Recognition; Lecture Notes in Computer Science,* vol. 2396, pp. 15-30, Springer-Verlag, 2002.
8. Y. Freund and R. Schapie, "A decision-theoretic generalisation of on-line learning and application to boosting," *Journal of Computer and System Sciences*, vol. 55, no. 1, pp. 119-139, 1997.
9. D. Jurafsky and J. Martin, *Speech and Language Processing*, Prentice-Hall, 2000.
10. J. Lafferty, A. McCallum and F. Pereira, "Conditional random fields: Probabilistic models for segmenting and labelling sequence," *Proceedings of International conference on Machine Learning*, Morgan Kaufmann, 2001.
11. N. Lesh, M. Zaki and M. Ogihara, "Mining features for sequence classification," *Proceedings of ACM International Conference on Knowledge Discovery and Data Mining*, ACM Press, pp. 342-346, 1999.
12. D. Luo and K. Chen, "Refine decision boundary of a statistical ensemble by active learning," *Proceedings of IEEE-INNS International Joint Conference on Neural Networks*, IEEE Press, pp. 1523-1528, 2003.
13. P. McCullagh and J. Nelder, *Generalized Linear Models*, Chapman and Hall,1989.
14. T. Mitchell, *Machine Learning*, McGraw Hill, New York, 1997.

Learning Beyond Finite Memory in Recurrent Networks of Spiking Neurons

Peter Tiňo and Ashley Mills

School of Computer Science, University of Birmingham,
Birmingham B15 2TT, UK
{P.Tino, msc57ajm}@cs.bham.ac.uk

Abstract. We investigate possibilities of inducing temporal structures without fading memory in recurrent networks of spiking neurons strictly operating in the pulse-coding regime. We extend the existing gradient-based algorithm for training feed-forward spiking neuron networks (*Spike-Prop* [1]) to recurrent network topologies, so that temporal dependencies in the input stream are taken into account. It is shown that temporal structures with unbounded input memory specified by simple Moore machines (MM) can be induced by recurrent spiking neuron networks (RSNN). The networks are able to discover *pulse-coded* representations of abstract information processing states coding potentially unbounded histories of processed inputs.

1 Introduction

A considerable amount of work has been devoted to studying computations on time series in recurrent neural networks (RNNs). Feedback connections endow RNNs with a form of 'neural memory' that makes them (theoretically) capable of processing time structures over *arbitrarily long* time spans. However, even though RNNs are capable of simulating Turing machines [2], *induction* of non-trivial temporal structures beyond finite memory can be problematic [3]. Finite state machines (FSMs) and automata constitute a simple, yet well established and easy to analyze framework for describing temporal structures that go beyond finite memory relationships. In general, for a finite description of the string mapping realized by an FSM, one needs a notion of an abstract information processing state that can encapsulate histories of processed strings of *arbitrary* finite length. Indeed, FSMs have been a popular benchmark in the recurrent network community and there is a huge amount of literature dealing with empirical and theoretical aspects of learning finite state machines/automata in RNNs (e.g. [4, 5]).

However, the RNNs under consideration have been based on traditional rate-coded artificial neural network models that describe neural activity in terms of *rates* of spikes[1] produced by individual neurons. Several models of spiking neurons, where the input and output information is coded in terms of *exact*

---
[1] Identical electrical pulses also known as action potentials.

timings of individual spikes (*pulse coding*) have been proposed (see e.g. [6]). Learning algorithms for acyclic networks of such (biologically more plausible) artificial neurons have been developed and tested [1, 7].

Maass [8] proved that networks of spiking neurons with feedback connections (recurrent spiking neuron networks – RSNNs) can simulate Turing machines. Yet, virtually no systematic work has been reported on *inducing* deeper temporal structures in such networks. There are recent developments along this direction, e.g. [9, 10]. Such studies, however, usually make a leap in the coding strategy, shifting from the emphasis on spike timings in individual neurons (pulse coding) into more space-rate-based population codings. Even though most of experimental research focuses on characterizations of potential information processing states using temporal statistics of rate properties in spike trains (e.g. [11]) there is some experimental evidence that in certain situations the temporal information may be pulse-coded [12].

In this study we are concerned with possibilities of *inducing* deep temporal structures *without fading memory* in recurrent networks of spiking neurons. We will strictly adhere to *pulse-coding*, e.g. all the input, output and state information is coded in terms of spike trains on subsets of neurons.

2   Recurrent Spiking Neural Network

First, we briefly describe the formal model of spiking neurons, the spike response model [13], employed in this study. Spikes emitted by neuron i are propagated to neuron j through several synaptic channels $k = 1, 2, ..., m$, each of which has an associated synaptic efficacy (weight) w_{ij}^k, and an axonal delay d_{ij}^k. In each synaptic channel k, input spikes get delayed by d_{ij}^k and transformed by a response function ϵ_{ij}^k which models the rate of neurotransmitter diffusion across the synaptic cleft. The response function can be either excitatory, or inhibitory.

Formally, denote the set of all (presynaptic) neurons emitting spikes to neuron j by Γ_j. Let the last spike time of a presynaptic neuron $i \in \Gamma_j$ be t_i^a. The accumulated potential at time t on soma of unit j is:

$$x_j(t) = \sum_{i \in \Gamma_j} \sum_{k=1}^{m} w_{ij}^k \cdot \epsilon_{ij}^k(t - t_i^a - d_{ij}^k), \qquad (1)$$

where the response function ϵ_{ij}^k is modeled as:

$$\epsilon_{ij}^k(t) = \sigma_{ij}^k \cdot (t/\tau) \cdot exp(1 - (t/\tau)) \cdot \mathcal{H}(t - d_{ij}^k). \qquad (2)$$

Here, σ_{ij}^k is 1 and -1 if the synapse k between neurons i, j is concerned with transmitting excitatory and inhibitory, respectively. The decay constant τ governs the rate at which neurotransmitter released from the presynaptic membrane reaches the post synaptic membrane. $\mathcal{H}(t)$ is the Heaviside step function which is 1 for $t > 0$, and is otherwise 0, ensuring that the axonal delay d_{ij}^k is enforced. Neuron j fires a spike (and depolarizes) when the accumulated potential $x_j(t)$ reaches a threshold Θ.

In a feed-forward spiking neuron network (FFSNN), the first neurons to fire a spike are the input units. Spatial spike patterns across input neurons code the information to be processed by the FFSNN, the spikes propagate to subsequent layers, finally resulting in a pattern of spike times across neurons in the output layer. The output spike times represent the response of FFSNN to the current input. The input-to-output propagation of spikes through FFSNN is confined to a simulation interval of length Υ. All neurons can fire at most once within the simulation interval[2]. After the simulation interval has expired, the output spike pattern is read-out and interpreted and a new simulation interval is initialized by presenting a new input spike pattern in the input layer. Given a mechanism for temporal encoding and decoding of the input and output information, respectively, Sander, Bohte and Kok have recently formulated a back-propagation-like supervised learning rule for training FFSNN, called *SpikeProp* [1]. Synaptic efficacies on connections to the output unit j are updated as follows:

$$\Delta w_{ij}^k = -\eta \cdot \epsilon_{ij}^k (t_j^a - t_i^a - d_{ij}^k) \cdot \delta^j, \tag{3}$$

where

$$\delta^j = \frac{(t_j^d - t_j^a)}{\sum_{i \in \Gamma_j} \sum_{k=1}^m w_{ij}^k \cdot \epsilon_{ij}^k (t_j^a - t_i^a - d_{ij}^k) \cdot (1/(t_j^a - t_i^a - d_{ij}^k) - 1/\tau)} \tag{4}$$

and $\eta > 0$ is the learning rate. The numerator is the difference between the desired t_j^d and actual t_j^a firing times of the output neuron j within the simulation interval.

Synaptic efficacies on connections to the hidden unit i are updated analogously:

$$\Delta w_{hi}^k = -\eta \cdot \epsilon_{hi}^k (t_i^a - t_h^a - d_{hi}^k) \cdot \delta^i, \tag{5}$$

where

$$\delta^i = \frac{\sum_{j \in \Gamma^i} (\sum_{k=1}^m w_{ij}^k \cdot \epsilon_{ij}^k (t_j^a - t_i^a - d_{ij}^k) \cdot (1/(t_j^a - t_i^a - d_{ij}^k) - 1/\tau)) \cdot \delta^j}{\sum_{h \in \Gamma_i} \sum_{k=1}^m w_{hi}^k \cdot \epsilon_{hi}^k (t_i^a - t_h^a - d_{hi}^k) \cdot (1/(t_i^a - t_h^a - d_{hi}^k) - 1/\tau)} \tag{6}$$

and Γ^i denotes the set of all (postsynaptic) neurons to which neuron i emits spikes. The numerator pulls in contributions from the layer succeeding that for which δ's are being calculated[3].

Obviously, FFSNN cannot properly deal with temporal structures in the input stream that go beyond finite memory. One possible solution is to turn FFSNN into a recurrent spiking neuron network (RSNN) by extending the feed-forward architecture with feedback connections. In analogy with RNN, we select

---

[2] The period of neuron refractoriness (a neuron is unlikely to fire shortly after producing a spike), is not modeled, and thus to maintain biological plausibility a neuron may only fire once within the simulation interval (see e.g. [1]).

[3] When a neuron does not fire, its contributions are not incorporated into the calculation of δ's for other neurons, neither is a δ calculated for it.

a hidden layer in FFSNN as *the layer responsible for coding (through spike patterns) important information about the history of inputs seen so far (recurrent layer) and feed back its spiking patterns through the delay synaptic channels to an auxiliary layer at the input level, called the context layer.* The input and context layers now collectively form a new 'extended input layer' of the RSNN. The delay feedback connections temporally translate spike patterns in the recurrent layer by the delay constant Δ,

$$\alpha(t) = t + \Delta. \tag{7}$$

Such temporal translation can be achieved using a FFSNN.

The RSNN architecture used in our experiments consists of five layers. The extended input layer (input and context layers, denoted by I and C, respectively) feeds the first auxiliary hidden layer H_1, which in turn feeds the recurrent layer Q. Within each simulation interval, the spike timings of neurons in the input and context layers I and C are stored in the spatial spike train vectors $\mathbf{i}$ and $\mathbf{c}$, respectively. The spatial spike trains of the first hidden and recurrent layers are stored in vectors $\mathbf{h}_1$ and $\mathbf{q}$, respectively. The role of the recurrent layer Q is twofold:

1. The spike train $\mathbf{q}$ codes information about the history of inputs seen so far. This information is passed to the next simulation interval through the delay FFSNN network[4] α, $\mathbf{c} = \alpha(\mathbf{q})$. The delayed spatial spike train $\mathbf{c}$ appears in the context layer. Spike train $(\mathbf{i}, \mathbf{c})$ of the extended input consists of the history-coding spike train $\mathbf{c}$ and a spatial spike train $\mathbf{i}$ coding the external inputs (input symbols).
2. The recurrent layer feeds the second auxiliary hidden layer H_2, which finally feeds the output layer O. The spatial spike trains in the second hidden and output layers are stored in vectors $\mathbf{h}_2$ and $\mathbf{o}$, respectively.

Parameters, such as the length Υ of the simulation interval, feedback delay Δ and spike time encodings of input/output symbols have to be carefully coordinated. The simulation interval for processing of the nth input item starts at

$$t_{start}(n) = (n-1) \cdot \Upsilon.$$

Absolute desired output spike times for the nth input need to be adjusted with the $t_{start}(n)$. The initial context spike pattern, $\mathbf{c}_{start}$, is imposed externally at the beginning of training. The firing times of the recurrent neurons at the end of simulation interval n, $\mathbf{q}(n)$, are translated in time by the delay FFSNN α to give the state (context) inputs $\mathbf{c}(n+1)$ at the start of simulation epoch $(n+1)$. The simulation interval Υ needs to be set so that temporal proximity of $\mathbf{c}(n+1)$ and the input firing times $\mathbf{i}(n+1)$ at the start of simulation epoch $(n+1)$ is achieved.

---

[4] The delay function $\alpha(t)$ is applied to each component of $\mathbf{q}$.

2.1 Training – SpikeProp Through Time

We extended the SpikeProp algorithm [1] for training FFSNN to recurrent models in the spirit of Back Propagation Through Time for rate-based RNN [14], i.e. using the unfolding-in-time methodology. We call this learning algorithm *SpikePropThroughTime*.

Given an input string of length n, n copies of the base RSNN are made, stacked on top of each other, and sequentially simulated, incrementing t_{start} by Υ after each simulation interval. Expanding the base network through time via multiple copies simulates processing of the input stream by the base RSNN.

Adaptation δ's (see equations (4) and (6)) are calculated for each of the network copies. The synaptic efficacies (weights) in the base network are then updated using δ's calculated in each of the copies by adding up, for every weight, the n corresponding weight-update contributions of equations (3) and (5).

In a FFSNN, when calculating the δ's for a hidden layer, the firing times from the preceding and succeeding layers are used. Special attention must be paid when calculating δ's of neurons in the recurrent layer Q. Context spike train $\mathbf{c}(n+1)$ in copy $(n+1)$ is the delayed recurrent spike train $\mathbf{q}(n)$ from the nth copy. The relationship of firing times in $\mathbf{c}(n+1)$ and $\mathbf{h}_1(n+1)$ contains the information that should be incorporated into the calculation of the δ's for recurrent units in copy n. The delay constant Δ is subtracted from the firing times $\mathbf{h}_1(n+1)$ of H_1 and then, when calculating the δ's for recurrent units in copy n, these temporally translated firing times are used as if they were simply another hidden layer succeeding Q in copy n. Denoting by $\Gamma_{2,n}$ the set of neurons in the second auxiliary hidden layer H_2 of the nth copy and by $\Gamma_{1,n+1}$ the set of neurons in the first auxiliary hidden layer H_1 of the copy $(n+1)$, the δ of the ith recurrent unit in the nth copy is calculated as

$$\delta^i = \frac{\sum_{j \in \Gamma_{1,n+1}} (\sum_{k=1}^{m} w_{ij}^k \cdot \epsilon_{ij}^k (t_j^a - \Delta - t_i^a - d_{ij}^k) \cdot (1/(t_j^a - \Delta - t_i^a - d_{ij}^k) - 1/\tau)) \cdot \delta^j}{\sum_{h \in \Gamma_i} \sum_{k=1}^{m} w_{hi}^k \cdot \epsilon_{hi}^k (t_i^a - t_h^a - d_{hi}^k) \cdot (1/(t_i^a - t_h^a - d_{hi}^k) - 1/\tau)}$$
$$+ \frac{\sum_{j \in \Gamma_{2,n}} (\sum_{k=1}^{m} w_{ij}^k \cdot \epsilon_{ij}^k (t_j^a - t_i^a - d_{ij}^k) \cdot (1/(t_j^a - t_i^a - d_{ij}^k) - 1/\tau)) \cdot \delta^j}{\sum_{h \in \Gamma_i} \sum_{k=1}^{m} w_{hi}^k \cdot \epsilon_{hi}^k (t_i^a - t_h^a - d_{hi}^k) \cdot (1/(t_i^a - t_h^a - d_{hi}^k) - 1/\tau)} \quad (8)$$

3 Learning Beyond Finite Memory in RSNN – Inducing Moore Machines

One of the simplest computational models that encapsulates the concept of unbounded input memory is the Moore machine [15]. Formally, an (initial) Moore machine (MM) M is a 6-tuple $M = (U, V, S, \beta, \gamma, s_0)$, where U and V are finite input and output alphabets, respectively, S is a finite set of states, $s_0 \in S$ is the initial state, $\beta : S \times U \to S$ is the state transition function and $\gamma : S \to V$ is the output function. Given an input string $u = u_1 u_2 ... u_n$ of symbols from U ($u_i \in U$, $i = 1, 2, ..., n$), the machine M acts as a transducer by responding with the output string $v = M(u) = v_1 v_2 ... v_n$, $v_i \in V$, computed as follows: first the machine is initialized with the initial state s_0, then for all $i = 1, 2, ..., n$, the new state is recursively determined, $s_i = \beta(s_{i-1}, u_i)$, and the machine emits the output symbol $v_i = \gamma(s_i)$.

Given a target Moore machine M, a set of training examples is constructed by explicitly constructing input strings u over U and then determining the corresponding output string $M(u)$ over V (by traversing edges of the graph of M, starting in the initial state, as prescribed by the input string u). The training set $\mathcal{D}$ consists of N couples of input-output strings,

$$\mathcal{D} = \{(u^1, M(u^1)), (u^2, M(u^2)), ..., (u^N, M(u^N))\}.$$

In this study, we consider binary input and output alphabets $U = V = \{0, 1\}$ and a special end-of-string symbol '2'. We adopt the strategy of *inducing the initial state* in the recurrent network (as opposed to externally imposing it – see [16, 17]). The context layer of the network is initialized with the fixed predefined context spike train $\mathbf{c}(1) = \mathbf{c}_{start}$ only at the beginning of training. From the network's point of view, the training set is a couple $(\tilde{u}, M(\tilde{u}))$ of the long concatenated input sequence

$$\tilde{u} = u^1 2 u^2 2 u^3 2 ... 2 u^{N-1} 2 u^N 2$$

and the corresponding output sequence

$$M(\tilde{u}) = M(u^1)\gamma(s_0)M(u^2)\gamma(s_0)M(u^3)\gamma(s_0)...\gamma(s_0)M(u^{N-1})\gamma(s_0)M(u^N)\gamma(s_0).$$

Input symbol '2' is instrumental in inducing the start state by acting as an end-of-string reset symbol initiating transition from every state of M to the initial state s_0.

The external input spike train $\mathbf{i}$ is partitioned into two disjoint sets of firing patterns: input neurons $\mathbf{i}^s$ coding the current input symbol, and reference neurons $\mathbf{i}^r$ which always fire at the same time relative to t_{start} in any simulation interval. Conversion of input symbols into spike trains $\mathbf{i}^s$ is described in table 1. We convert symbols into binary bitstrings and then encode each binary bit of the bitstring as alternating *high* ($6ms$) and *low* ($0ms$) firing times.

Table 1. Encoding of inputs 0, 1 and 2 in the input spike train $\mathbf{i}^s$

input	Bit1	Bit2
0	0 6	0 6
1	0 6	6 0
2	6 0	0 6

The network is trained using *SpikePropThroughTime* (section 2.1) to minimize the squared error between the desired output spike trains derived from $M(\tilde{u})$ when the RSNN is driven by the input $\tilde{u}$. The RSNN is unfolded and *SpikePropThroughTime* is applied for each training pattern $(u^i, M(u^i))$, $i = 1, 2, ..., N$.

The firing threshold is almost always 50, and the weights are initialized to random values from the interval[5] $(0, 10)$. We use a dynamic learning rate strategy that detects oscillatory behavior and plateaus within the error space. The action to take upon detecting oscillation or plateau, is respectively to decrease the learning rate by multiplying by an 'oscillation-counter-coefficient' (< 1), or increase the learning rate by multiplying by a 'plateau-counter-coefficient' (> 1) (see e.g. [18]).

The network had one output neuron 5 neurons in each of the layers I, C, H_1, Q and H_2 (1 inhibitory neuron and 4 excitatory neurons). Each connection between neurons had $m = 16$ synaptic channels, realizing axonal delays between $1ms$ and $16ms$. with delays $d_{ij}^k = k$, $k = 1, 2, ..., m$. The decay constant τ in response functions ϵ_{ij} was set to $\tau = 3$. The length Υ of the simulation interval was set to 40ms. The delay Δ was 30ms. We used *SpikePropThroughTime* to train RSNN. The training was error-monitored and training was stopped the network had perfectly learned the target (zero thresholded output error). The maximum number of training epochs (sweeps through the training set) was 10000.

First, we experimented with 'cyclic' automata C_p of period $p \geq 2$: $U = \{0\}$; $V = \{0, 1\}$; $S = \{1, 2, ..., p\}$; $s_0 = 1$; for $1 \leq i < p$, $\beta(i, 0) = i+1$ and $\beta(p, 0) = 1$; $\gamma(1) = 0$ and for $1 < i \leq p$, $\gamma(i) = 1$. The RSNN perfectly learned machines C_p, $2 \leq p \leq 5$. The training set had to be incrementally constructed by iteratively training with one presentation of the cycle, then two presentations etc. We examined state information in RSNN coded as *spike trains* in the recurrent layer Q. The abstract information processing states extracted by the network during the training manifested themselves as groupings of normalized spike trains[6] ($\mathbf{q}(n) - t_{start}(n)$). We were able to use the emerging clusters of normalized spike trains to extract abstract knowledge induced in the network in the form of MM, but a detailed account of this issue is beyond the scope of this paper.

Second, we trained RSNN on a two-state machine M_2: $U = V = \{0, 1\}$; $S = \{1, 2\}$; $s_0 = 1$; $\beta(1, 0) = 1$, $\beta(2, 0) = 2$, $\beta(1, 1) = 2$ and $\beta(2, 1) = 1$; $\gamma(1) = 0$ and $\gamma(2) = 1$. Repeated presentation of only 5 carefully selected training patterns of length 4 were sufficient for a perfect induction of this machine. Again, we observed that the two abstract information processing states of M_2 were induced in the network as two clusters of normalized spike trains in the recurrent layer Q.

We stress, that given that the network can only observe the inputs, the above MMs would require an *unbounded input memory buffer*. So no mechanism with vanishing (input) memory can implement string mappings represented by such MMs. After training, the respective RSNN emulated the operation of these

---

[5] The weights must be initialized so that the neurons in subsequent layers are sufficiently excited by those in their previous layer that they fire, otherwise the network would be unusable. There is no equivalent in traditional rate-based neural networks to the non-firing of a neuron in this sense. The setting of initial weights and firing thresholds used in this study follows that of [7].

[6] The spike times $\mathbf{q}(n)$ entering the quantization phase are made relative to the start time $t_{start}(n)$ of the simulation interval.

MM perfectly and apparently indefinitely – the networks had zero test (output-thresholded) error over test sets having length of the order 10^4.

We experimented with more complicated forms of MMs, but did not succeed to train them fully. However, the machines were at least partially induced, and the nature of such partial induction could be understood by the cluster analysis of the normalized recurrent spike trains, but, again, this issue is beyond the scope of this paper.

4 Discussion

We were able to train RSNN to mimic target MMs requiring unbounded input memory on only a relatively simple set of MMs. Spiking neurons used in this paper produce a spike only when the accumulated potential $x_j(t)$ reaches a threshold Θ. This leads to discontinuities in the error-surface. Gradient-based methods for training feed-forward networks of spiking neurons alleviate this problem by resorting to simplifying assumptions on spike patterns within a single simulation interval (see [1]). The situation is much more complicated in the case of RSNN. A small weight perturbation can prevent a recurrent neuron from firing in the shorter time scale of a simulation interval. That in turn can have serious consequences for further long-time-scale processing. Especially so, if such a change in short-term behavior appears at the beginning of presentation of a long input string.

The error surface becomes erratic, as evidenced in Figure 1. We took a RSNN trained to perfectly mimic the cycle-four machine C_4. We studied the influence of perturbing weights $\mathbf{w}_*$ in recurrent part of the RSNN (e.g. between layers I, C, H_1 and Q) on the test error calculated on long test string of length 1000. For each weight perturbation extent ρ, we randomly sampled 100 weight vectors $\mathbf{w}$ from the hyperball of radius ρ centred at $\mathbf{w}_*$. Shown are the mean and standard deviation values of the absolute output error per symbol for $0 < \rho \leq 3$. Clearly, small perturbations of weights lead to large abrupt changes in the test error.

Obviously, gradient-based methods, like our *SpikePropThroughTime* have problems in locating good minima on such error surfaces. We tried

- fast evolutionary strategies (FES) with (recommended) configuration (30,200)-ES[7], employing the Cauchy mutation function (see [19]),
- (extended) Kalman filtering in the parameter space [20], and
- a recent powerful evolutionary method for optimisation on real-valued domains [21]

to find RSNN parameters, but without much success. The abrupt and erratic nature of the error surface makes it hard, even for evolutionary techniques, to locate a good minimum.

We tried RSNNs with varying numbers of neurons in the hidden and recurrent layers. In general, the increased representational capacity of RSNNs with more

---

[7] In each generation 30 parents generate 200 offspring through recombination and mutation.

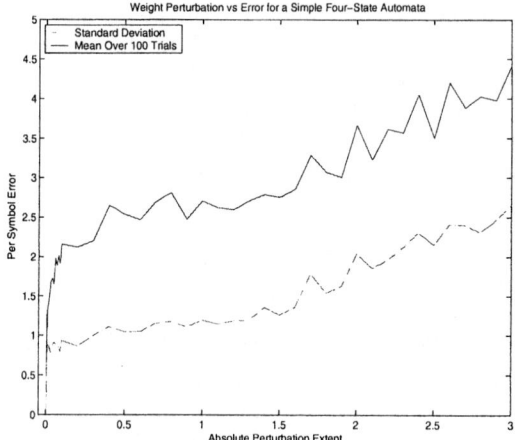

Fig. 1. Maximum radius of weight perturbation vs test error of RSNN trained to mimic the cycle-four machine C_4. For each setting of weight perturbation extent ρ, we randomly sampled 100 weight vectors $\mathbf{w}$ from the hyperball of radius ρ centred at induced RSNN weights $\mathbf{w}_*$. Shown are the mean (solid line) and standard deviation (dashed line) values of the absolute output error per symbol.

neural units could not be utilized because of the problems with finding good weight settings due the erratic nature of the error surface.

We note that the finite memory machines of [9] induced in feed-forward spiking neuron networks with dynamic synapses ([22]) were quite simple (of depth 3). The input memory depth is limited by the feed-forward nature of such networks. As soon as one tries to increase processing capabilities of spiking networks by introducing feedback connections, while insisting on pulse-coding, the induction process becomes complicated. Theoretically, it is perfectly possible to emulate any MM in RSNN. However, weight changes in RSNN lead to complex bifurcation mechanisms, making it hard to induce more complex MM through a guided search in the weight space. It is plausible that in biological systems, long-term dependencies are represented using rate-based codings and/or a Liquid State Machine mechanism [23] with a complex, but non-adaptable, recurrent pulse-coded part.

References

[1] Bohte, S., Kok, J., Poutré, H.L.: Error-backpropagation in temporally encoded networks of spiking neurons. Neurocomputing **48** (2002) 17–37
[2] Siegelmann, H., Sontag, E.: On the computational power of neural nets. Journal of Computer and System Sciences **50** (1995) 132–150
[3] Bengio, Y., Frasconi, P., Simard, P.: The problem of learning long-term dependencies in recurrent networks. In: Proceedings of the 1993 IEEE International Conference on Neural Networks. Volume 3. (1993) 1183–1188

[4] Giles, C., Miller, C., Chen, D., Chen, H., Sun, G., Lee, Y.: Learning and extracting finite state automata with second–order recurrent neural networks. Neural Computation **4** (1992) 393–405
[5] Casey, M.: The dynamics of discrete-time computation, with application to recurrent neural networks and finite state machine extraction. Neural Computation **8** (1996) 1135–1178
[6] Gerstner, W.: Spiking neurons. In Maass, W., Bishop, C., eds.: Pulsed Coupled Neural Networks. MIT Press, Cambridge (1999) 3–54
[7] Moore, S.: Back propagation in spiking neural networks. Master's thesis, The University of Bath (2002)
[8] Maass, W.: Lower bounds for the computational power of networks of spiking neurons. Neural Computation **8** (1996) 1–40
[9] Natschläger, T., Maass, W.: Spiking neurons and the induction of finite state machines. Theoretical Computer Science: Special Issue on Natural Computing **287** (2002) 251–265
[10] Floreano, D., Zufferey, J., Nicoud, J.: From wheels to wings with evolutionary spiking neurons. Artificial Life **11** (2005) 121–138
[11] Martignon, L., Deco, G., Laskey, K.B., Diamond, M., Freiwald, W., Vaadia, E.: Neural coding: Higher-order temporal patterns in the neurostatistics of cell assemblies. Neural Computation **12** (2000) 2621–2653
[12] Nadas, A.: Replay and time compression of recurring spike sequences in the hippocampus. The Journal of Neuroscience, **19** (1999) 9497–9507
[13] Gerstner, W.: Time structure of activity in neural network models. Phys. Rev. E **51** (1995) 738–758
[14] Werbos, P.: Generalization of backpropagation with applications to a recurrent gas market model. Neural Networks **1** (1989) 339–356
[15] Hopcroft, J., Ullman, J.: Introduction to automata theory, languages, and computation. Addison–Wesley, Reading, MA (1979)
[16] Forcada, M., Carrasco, R.: Learning the initial state of a second-order recurrent neural network during regular-language inference. Neural Computation **7** (1995) 923–930
[17] Tiňo, P., Šajda, J.: Learning and extracting initial mealy machines with a modular neural network model. Neural Computation **7** (1995) 822–844
[18] Lawrence, S., Giles, C., Fong, S.: Natural language grammatical inference with recurrent neural networks. IEEE Transactions on Knowledge and Data Engineering **12** (2000) 126–140
[19] Yao, X.: Evolving artificial neural networks. Proceedings of the IEEE **87** (1999) 1423–1447
[20] Puskorius, G., Feldkamp, L.: Recurrent network training with the decoupled extended Kalman filter. In: Proceedings of the 1992 SPIE Conference on the Science of Artificial Neural Networks, Orlando, Florida. (1992)
[21] Rowe, J., Hidovic, D.: An evolution strategy using a continuous version of the gray-code neighbourhood distribution. In et al., K.D., ed.: Proceedings of the Genetic and Evolutionary Computation Conference (GECCO-2004), Lecture Notes in Computer Science, Springer-Verlag (2004) 725–736
[22] Maass, W., Markram, H.: Synapses as dynamic memory buffers. Neural Networks **15** (2002) 155–161
[23] Maass, W., Natschläger, T., Markram, H.: Real-time computing without stable states: A new framework for neural computation based on perturbations. Neural Computation **14** (2002) 2531–2560

On Non-Markovian Topographic Organization of Receptive Fields in Recursive Self-organizing Map

Peter Tiño[1] and Igor Farkaš[2]

[1] School of Computer Science, University of Birmingham,
Birmingham B15 2TT, UK
[2] Faculty of Mathematics, Physics and Informatics, Comenius University,
Mlynská dolina, 842 48 Bratislava, Slovak Republic

Abstract. Recently, there has been an outburst of interest in extending topographic maps of vectorial data to more general data structures, such as sequences or trees. The representational capabilities and internal representations of the models are not well understood. We concentrate on a generalization of the Self-Organizing Map (SOM) for processing sequential data – the Recursive SOM (RecSOM [1]). We argue that contractive fixed-input dynamics of RecSOM is likely to lead to Markovian organizations of receptive fields on the map. We show that Markovian topographic maps of sequential data can be produced using a simple fixed (non-adaptable) dynamic module externally feeding a standard topographic model designed to process static vectorial data of fixed dimensionality (e.g. SOM). We elaborate upon the importance of non-Markovian organizations in topographic maps of sequential data.

1 Introduction

In its original form the self-organizing map (SOM) [2] is a nonlinear projection method that maps a high-dimensional metric vector space onto a two-dimensional regular grid in a topologically ordered fashion. Many modifications of the standard SOM have been proposed in the literature (e.g. [3]). Formation of topographic maps via self-organization constitutes an important paradigm in machine learning with many successful applications e.g. in data and web-mining. Most approaches to topographic map formation operate on the assumption that the data points are members of a finite-dimensional vector space of a fixed dimension. Recently, there has been an outburst of interest in extending topographic maps to more general data structures, such as sequences or trees.

Several modifications of SOM to sequences and/or tree structures have been proposed in the literature ([4] and [5] review most of the approaches). Modified versions of SOM that have enjoyed a great deal of interest equip SOM with *additional feed-back connections* that allow for natural processing of recursive data types. Typical examples of such models are Temporal Kohonen Map [6], recurrent SOM [7], feedback SOM [8], recursive SOM [1], merge SOM [9] and SOM

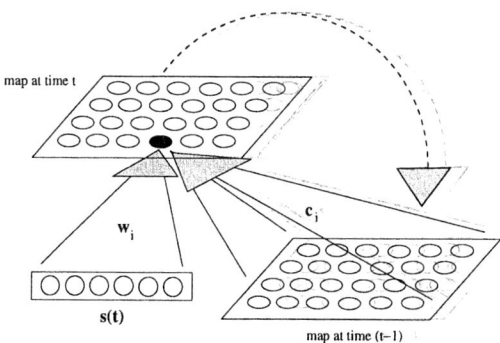

Fig. 1. Recursive SOM architecture. The original SOM algorithm is used for both input vector s(t) and for the context represented as the map activation y(t-1) from the previous time step. Solid lines represent trainable connections, dashed line represents one-to-one copy of the activity vector y. The network learns to associate the current input with previous activity states. This way each neuron responds to a sequence of inputs.

for structured data [10]. However, at present there is still no general consensus as to how best to process sequences with SOMs and this topic remains a very active focus of current neurocomputational research [4,11,12].

In this paper, we view such models as non-autonomous dynamical systems with internal dynamics driven by a stream of external inputs. In the line of our recent research, we study the organization of the non-autonomous dynamics on the basis of dynamics of individual fixed-input maps [13]. We concentrate on the Recursive SOM (RecSOM) [1], because RecSOM transcends the simple local recurrence of leaky integrators of earlier models and it has been demonstrated that it can represent much richer dynamical behavior [12]. The principal question driving this research can be stated as: 'What can be gained by having a trainable recurrent part in RecSOM, i.e. how does RecSOM compare with a much simpler setting of SOM operating on a simple *non-trainable* iterative function system with Markovian state-space organization [14]?"

2 Recursive Self-organizing Map (RecSOM)

The architecture of the RecSOM model [1] is shown in figure 1. Each neuron $i \in \{1, 2, ..., N\}$ in the map has two weight vectors associated with it:

- $\mathbf{w}_i \in \mathbb{R}^n$ – linked with an n-dimensional input $\mathbf{s}(t)$ feeding the network at time t
- $\mathbf{c}_i \in \mathbb{R}^N$ – linked with the context

$$\mathbf{y}(t-1) = (y_1(t-1), y_2(t-1), ..., y_N(t-1))$$

containing map activations $y_i(t-1)$ from the previous time step.

The output of a unit i at time t is computed as

$$y_i(t) = \exp(-d_i(t)), \tag{1}$$

where[1]

$$d_i(t) = \alpha \cdot \|\mathbf{s}(t) - \mathbf{w}_i\|^2 + \beta \cdot \|\mathbf{y}(t-1) - \mathbf{c}_i\|^2. \tag{2}$$

In eq. (2), $\alpha > 0$ and $\beta > 0$ are model parameters that respectively influence the effect of the input and the context upon neuron's profile. Both weight vectors can be updated using the same form of learning rule [1]:

$$\Delta \mathbf{w}_i = \gamma \cdot h_{ik} \cdot (\mathbf{s}(t) - \mathbf{w}_i), \tag{3}$$
$$\Delta \mathbf{c}_i = \gamma \cdot h_{ik} \cdot (\mathbf{y}(t-1) - \mathbf{c}_i), \tag{4}$$

where k is an index of the best matching unit at time t, $k = \mathrm{argmin}_{i \in \{1,2,...,N\}}\ d_i(t)$, and $0 < \gamma < 1$ is the learning rate. Note that the best matching ('winner') unit can be equivalently defined as the unit k of the highest activation $y_k(t)$:

$$k = \underset{i \in \{1,2,...,N\}}{\mathrm{argmax}}\ y_i(t). \tag{5}$$

Neighborhood function h_{ik} is a Gaussian (of width σ) on the distance $d(i,k)$ of units i and k in the map:

$$h_{ik} = e^{-\frac{d(i,k)^2}{\sigma^2}}. \tag{6}$$

The 'neighborhood width' σ decreases in time to allow for forming topographic representation of input sequences.

Under a fixed input vector $\mathbf{s} \in \mathbb{R}^n$, the time evolution (2) becomes

$$d_i(t+1) = \alpha \cdot \|\mathbf{s} - \mathbf{w}_i\|^2 + \beta \cdot \left\| \left(e^{-d_1(t)}, e^{-d_2(t)}, ..., e^{-d_N(t)} \right) - \mathbf{c}_i \right\|^2. \tag{7}$$

After applying a one-to-one coordinate transformation $y_i = e^{-d_i}$, eq. (7) reads

$$y_i(t+1) = e^{-\alpha\|\mathbf{s}-\mathbf{w}_i\|^2} \cdot e^{-\beta\|\mathbf{y}(t)-\mathbf{c}_i\|^2}, \tag{8}$$

or, in the vector form:

$$\mathbf{y}(t+1) = \mathbf{F}_\mathbf{s}(\mathbf{y}(t)). \tag{9}$$

3 IFS Sequence Representations Combined with Standard SOM (IFS+SOM)

Previously, we have shown that a simple affine contractive iterative function system (IFS) [15] can be used to transform temporal structure of symbolic sequences into a spatial structure of points in a metric space [14]. The points represent subsequences in a Markovian manner: Subsequences sharing a common suffix are

---

[1] $\|\cdot\|$ denotes the Euclidean norm.

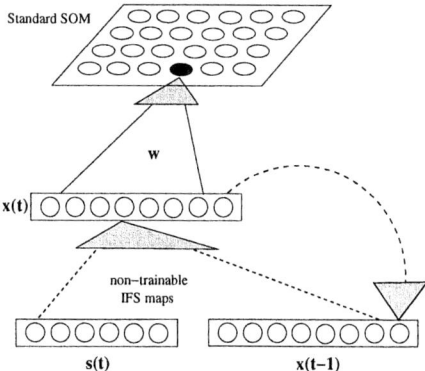

Fig. 2. Standard SOM operating on IFS representations of symbolic streams (IFS+SOM model). Solid lines represent trainable feed-forward connections. No learning takes place in the dynamic IFS part responsible for processing temporal contexts in the input stream.

mapped close to each other. Furthermore, the longer is the shared suffix the closer lie the subsequence representations.

The IFS representing sequences over an alphabet $\mathcal{A}$ of A symbols operates on an m-dimensional unit hypercube $[0,1]^m$, where[2] $m = \lceil \log_2 A \rceil$. With each symbol $s \in \mathcal{A}$ we associate an affine contraction on $[0,1]^m$,

$$s(\mathbf{x}) = k\mathbf{x} + (1-k)\mathbf{t}_s, \quad \mathbf{t}_s \in \{0,1\}^m, \quad \mathbf{t}_s \neq \mathbf{t}_{s'} \text{ for } s \neq s', \quad (10)$$

with contraction coefficient $k \in (0, \frac{1}{2}]$. For a prefix $u = u_1 u_2 ... u_n$ of a string v over $\mathcal{A}$ and a point $\mathbf{x} \in [0,1]^m$, the point

$$u(\mathbf{x}) = u_n(u_{n-1}(...(u_2(u_1(\mathbf{x})))...)) = (u_n \circ u_{n-1} \circ ... \circ u_2 \circ u_1)(\mathbf{x}) \quad (11)$$

constitutes a spatial representation of the prefix u under the IFS (10). Finally, the overall temporal structure of symbols in a (possibly long) sequence v over $\mathcal{A}$ is represented by a collection of the spatial representations $u(\mathbf{x})$ of all its prefixes u, with a convention that $\mathbf{x} = \{\frac{1}{2}\}^m$.

The IFS-based Markovian coding scheme can be used to construct generative probabilistic models on sequences analogous to the variable memory length Markov models [14]. Key element of the construction is a quantization of the spatial IFS representations into clusters that group together subsequences sharing potentially long suffixes (densely populated regions of the suffix-organized IFS subsequence representations).

The Markovian layout of the IFS representations of symbolic sequences can also be used for constructing suffix-based topographic maps of symbolic streams in an unsupervised manner. By applying a standard SOM [16] to the IFS representations one may readily obtain topographic maps of Markovian flavour,

---

[2] for $x \in \mathbb{R}$, $\lceil x \rceil$ is the smallest integer y, such that $y \geq x$.

similar to those obtained by RecSOM. The key difference between RecSOM and IFS+SOM (standard SOM operating on IFS representations) is that the latter approach assumes a fixed non-trainable dynamic part responsible for processing temporal contexts in the input stream. The recursion is not a part of the map itself, but is performed outside the map as a preprocessing step before feeding the standard SOM (see figure 2).

3.1 Relation Between IFS+SOM and Recurrent SOM

There is a connection between the IFS+SOM and recurrent SOM (RSOM) [7] models. Given a sequence $s_1 s_2 ...$ over a finite alphabet $\mathcal{A}$, the RSOM model determines the winner neuron at time t by identifying the neuron i with the minimal norm of

$$\mathbf{d}_i(t) = \nu \, (\mathbf{t}_{s_t} - \mathbf{w}_i) + (1 - \nu) \, \mathbf{d}_i(t-1), \tag{12}$$

where $0 < \nu < 1$ is a parameter determining the rate of 'forgetting the past', $\mathbf{t}_{s_t}$ is the code of symbol s_t presented at RSOM input at time t and $\mathbf{w}_i$ is the weight vector on connections connecting the inputs with neuron i.

Inputs $\mathbf{x}(t)$ feeding standard SOM in the IFS+SOM model evolve with the IFS dynamics (see (10) and (11))

$$\mathbf{x}(t) = k \, \mathbf{x}(t-1) + (1-k) \, \mathbf{t}_{s_t}, \tag{13}$$

where $0 < k < 1$ is the IFS contraction coefficient. Best matching unit in SOM is determined by finding the neuron i with the minimal norm of

$$\mathbf{D}_i(t) = \mathbf{x}(t) - \mathbf{w}_i = k \, \mathbf{x}(t-1) + (1-k) \, \mathbf{t}_{s_t} - \mathbf{w}_i. \tag{14}$$

But $\mathbf{D}_i(t-1) = \mathbf{x}(t-1) - \mathbf{w}_i$, and so

$$\mathbf{D}_i(t) = k \, \mathbf{D}_i(t-1) + (1-k) \, (\mathbf{t}_{s_t} - \mathbf{w}_i), \tag{15}$$

which, after setting $\nu = 1 - k$, leads to

$$\mathbf{D}_i(t) = \nu \, (\mathbf{t}_{s_t} - \mathbf{w}_i) + (1-\nu) \, \mathbf{D}_i(t-1). \tag{16}$$

Provided $\nu = 1 - k$, the equations (12) and (16) are equivalent.

The key difference between RSOM and IFS+SOM models lies in the training process. While in RSOM, the best matching unit i with minimal norm of $\mathbf{d}_i(t)$ is shifted towards the current input $\mathbf{t}_{s_t}$, in IFS+SOM the winner unit i with minimal norm of $\mathbf{D}_i(t)$ is shifted towards the (Markovian) IFS code $\mathbf{x}(t)$ coding the whole history of recently seen inputs.

4 Experiments

We compare RecSOM with standard SOM operating on Markovian suffix-based vector representations of fixed dimensionality (IFS+SOM) on a corpus of written English, the novel "Brave New World" by Aldous Huxley. This data set was used in [1].

In the corpus we removed punctuation symbols, upper-case letters were switched to lower-case and the space between words was transformed into a symbol '-'. The complete data set (after filtering) comprised 356606 symbols. Letters of the Roman alphabet were binary-encoded using 5 bits and presented to the network one at a time. RecSOM with 400 neurons was trained for two epochs using the following parameter settings: $\alpha = 3$, $\beta = 0.7$, $\gamma = 0.1$ and $\sigma : 10 \rightarrow 0.5$. Radius σ reached its final value at the end of the first epoch and then remained constant to allow for fine-tuning of the weights. In the IFS+SOM model, the IFS coefficient was set to $k = 0.3$. Other parameters, such as size of the map, learning rate, and time schedule for reducing the neighborhood width σ were the same as in RecSOM.

We constructed a map of the neurons' receptive fields (RFs) (shown in figure 3). Following [1], RF of a neuron is defined as the common suffix of all sequences for which that neuron becomes the best-matching unit. It is evident that the RFs are topographically ordered with respect to the most recent symbols.

For these RFs, we computed the quantizer depth (according to [1]), which quantifies the amount of memory captured by the map. It is defined as

$$\bar{n} = \sum_{i=1}^{N} p_i n_i, \qquad (17)$$

where p_i is the probability of the RF of neuron i, and n_i is its length. The quantizer depth was $\bar{n} = 1.91$.

The RecSOM model can be considered a nonautonomous dynamical system driven by the external input stream (in this case, sequences over the Roman alphabet $\mathcal{A}$). In order to investigate the fixed-input dynamics (9) of the mappings[3] $\mathbf{F}_s$, we randomly (with uniform distribution) initialized context activations $\mathbf{y}(0)$ in 10,000 different positions within the state space $(0,1]^N$. For each initial condition $\mathbf{y}(0)$, we checked asymptotic dynamics of the fixed input maps $\mathbf{F}_s$ by monitoring L_2-norm of the activation differences $(\mathbf{y}(t) - \mathbf{y}(t-1))$ and recording the limit set (after 1000 iterations). We observed that all autonomous dynamics settle down in the respective unique attractive fixed points $\mathbf{y}_s = \mathbf{F}_s(\mathbf{y}_s)$, $s \in \mathcal{A}$.

It is important to appreciate how the character of the RecSOM fixed-input dynamics (9) for each individual input symbol $s \in \mathcal{A}$ shapes the overall organization of the map. For each input symbol s, the autonomous dynamics $\mathbf{y}(t) = \mathbf{F}_s(\mathbf{y}(t-1))$ induces a dynamics of the winner units on the map:

$$i_s(t) = \underset{i \in \{1,2,\ldots,N\}}{\operatorname{argmax}} \; y_i(t). \qquad (18)$$

The dynamics (18) is illustrated in figure 4 (left). For each of the 10,000 initial conditions $\mathbf{y}(0)$, we first let the system (9) settle down by preiterating it for 1000 iterations and then mark the map position of the winner units $i_s(t)$ for

---

[3] We slightly abuse the mathematical notation here. As arguments of the bounds, we write the actual input symbols, rather than their vector encodings **s**.

n–	n–	h–	ad–	d–	he–	he–	a–	ag	.		in	ig	.	–th	–th	–th	th	ti
an–	u–	–	l–	nd–	e–	re–	–a–	ao	an	ain	in	.	l		t-h	th	.	.
y–	i–	g–	ng–	ed–	f–	–to–	o–		en	un	–in		al	–al		h	wh	ty
ot–	at–	p–	–a–	n–	on–	m–	o–			–an	n	rn	ul	ll	e–l	e–h	gh	x	y
to	t–	es–	as–	er–	er–	mo	o	–to			–on	ion		.	ol	e–m	m	. .	ey
t–	ut–	s–	is–	or–	ero	t–o	o	lo	ho	on	on	oo	.	om	um	im	am	ai	ry
ts	tw	ts–	r–	r–	ro	wo	io	e–o	–o	e–n	on			–m	t–m		si	ai	ri
e–s	he-w	–w	t-w		no	so	tio	–o	ng–o	–o	–n	–l	–h		e–i	di	ei	ni	ui
he-s	e–w	w	nw	ong	no	ak	k	–k	—	–o	.	–l	–h	–i	t–i	–wi	–hi	–li	–thi
ns	rs		ing	ng	nf	e–k	j	e–c	–s		–g	–m	–y		–i	–i	i	li	hi
s	us	uc	e–g	g	if	e–f	e–b	–c	–s	–w	–w	–e	.	–a	–a	n–a	ia	la	ha
is	c	nc		f	of	–f	–f	–b		–u	–u	–d		d–a	t–a	na	da	.	–ha
as	ac	ic	ib	b	.	oc	–v	.	–p	g–t	–t	–d	–e	–q	e–a	a	wa	era	ra
ac		ir	e–r		.	os		–r	–p	–t	s–t		.	ow		sa		ore	re
ar	ar	hr	r	tr	or	op	ov	–v	t–t	d–t	–t	ot	od	.	u	se	we	ere	pe
es	er	her	z	p	e–p	p	av		d–t	n–t	e–t	ot		ou	au	–se	be	ue	me
es	.	her	ter	ap	.	mp	v	st	rt	–st	tt	ut	out	lu	tu	e	e–e	ce	–he
ew		ev	.	q	ea	.	.	at	t	o–t	ent	ont	ind	d	dd	de	te	e	he
the–	e–	e–		em	ec	.		at	–at	ht	–it	nt	–and	rd	e–d		ne	–the	the
he–	e–	eo	.	.	ee	ed	ed	ad	it	it	id	ond	nd	and	ud	ld	le	–the	he

Fig. 3. Receptive fields of RecSOM trained on English text. Dots denote units with empty RFs.

further 100 iterations. If the fixed-input dynamics for $s \in \mathcal{A}$ is dominated by the unique attractive fixed point $\mathbf{y}_s$, the induced dynamics on the map, (18), settles down in neuron i_s, corresponding to the mode of $\mathbf{y}_s$:

$$i_s = \underset{i \in \{1,2,\ldots,N\}}{\operatorname{argmax}} y_{s,i}. \tag{19}$$

The neuron i_s will be most responsive to input subsequences ending with long blocks of symbols s. Such an organization follows from the attractive fixed point behaviour of the individual maps $\mathbf{F}_s$, $s \in \mathcal{A}$, and the unimodal character of their fixed points $\mathbf{y}_s$. As soon as symbol s is seen, the mode of the activation profile $\mathbf{y}$ drifts towards the neuron i_s. The more consecutive symbols s we see, the more dominant the attractive fixed point of $\mathbf{F}_s$ becomes and the closer the winner position is to i_s. This mechanism for creating suffix-based RF organization is reminiscent of the Markovian fractal subsequence representations used in our IFS+SOM model.

We observed a variety of asymptotic regimes of the fixed-input RecSOM dynamics (9). For some symbols, the fixed-input dynamics converges to an attractive fixed point; for other symbols (e.g. symbols 'i', 't', 'a', '-'), the dynamics followed a period-two attractor. Fixed input RecSOM dynamics for symbols 'e' and 'o' followed a complicated a-periodic trajectory.

Dynamics of the winner units on the map induced by the fixed-input dynamics of $\mathbf{F}_s$ are shown in figure 4 (left). For symbols s with dynamics $\mathbf{y}(t) =$

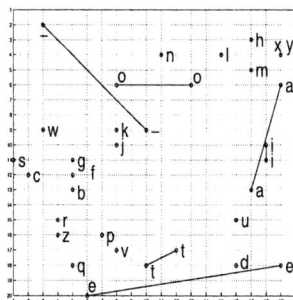 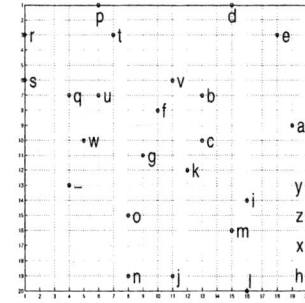

Fig. 4. Dynamics of the winning units on the RecSOM (left) and IFS+SOM (right) maps induced by the fixed-input dynamics. The maps were trained on a corpus of written English ("Brave New World" by Aldous Huxley).

$\mathbf{F}_s(\mathbf{y}(t-1))$ dominated by a single fixed point $\mathbf{y}_s$, the induced dynamics on the map settles down in the mode position of $\mathbf{y}_s$. However, some autonomous dynamics $\mathbf{y}(t) = \mathbf{F}_s(\mathbf{y}(t-1))$ of period two (e.g. $s \in \{n, h, r, p, s\}$) induce a trivial dynamics on the map driven to a single point (grid position). In those cases, the points $\mathbf{y}^1$, $\mathbf{y}^2$ on the periodic orbit ($\mathbf{y}^1 = \mathbf{F}_s(\mathbf{y}^2)$, $\mathbf{y}^2 = \mathbf{F}_s(\mathbf{y}^1)$) lie within the representation region (Voronoi compartment) of the same neuron. Interestingly enough, the complicated dynamics of $\mathbf{F}_o$ and $\mathbf{F}_e$ translates into aperiodic oscillations between just two grid positions. Still, the suffix based organization of RFs in figure 3 is shaped by the underlying collection of the fixed input dynamics of $\mathbf{F}_s$ (illustrated in figure 4 (left)) through the induced dynamics on the map).

The IFS+SOM map ($k = 0.3$) is shown in figure 5 (quantizer depth $\bar{n} = 1.69$). The induced dynamics on the map is illustrated in figure 4 (right). The suffix based organization of RFs is shaped by the underlying collection of autonomous attractive IFS dynamics.

5 Discussion

Periodic (beyond period 1), or aperiodic attractive dynamics of autonomous systems $\mathbf{y}(t) = \mathbf{F}_s(\mathbf{y}(t-1))$ lead to potentially complicated non-Markovian organizations of RFs on the map. By calculating the RF of a neuron i as the common suffix shared by subsequences yielding i as the best matching unit [1], we always create a suffix based map of RFs. Such RF maps are designed to illustrate the temporal structure learned by RecSOM. Periodic or aperiodic dynamics of $\mathbf{F}_s$ can result in a 'broken topography' of RFs: two sequences with the same suffix can be mapped into distinct positions on the map, separated by a region of very different suffix structure. For example, depending on the context, subsequences ending with 'ee' can be mapped either near the lower-left, or near the lower-right corners of the RF map in figure 3. Unlike in contractive RecSOM or IFS+SOM models, such context-dependent RecSOM maps embody a potentially unbounded memory structure, because the current position of the

r	r	tr	r	p	p	p	at	t	t	d	nd	d	ed	d		ne	-e	we	ve
r	r	ur		p	p	t	t	ht	t	d	d	d	d		le	oe	ge	ue	te
r	r	er	r	-vp	t	t	t	t	nt		-d	d		he	le	me	e	ndae	pe
r	ar	er		st	st	ut	-t	-t	ot		d		je	e	e	e	de	tube	re
s	s	s					-t	-t	rot	v	v	b		he	he	ye	fe	be	re
s	s	s		u	u		t	-t		v		b	b			ke	ce	ce	se
s	as	s	q	u	u	u		v	yf	f	issf	b	b	a	a				se
s	s	s		u	-u	u		f	f	f	f	b		a	a	ga	a	la	la
-s	-s	s	w	w	u	u			f	f	c	c		a	sa	a	ma	a	a
			w	-w	w		g	g		c	c	c	c	a	-a	-a	a	a	a
s-	s-	-		-w	w	g	g	g	o			c	c	-a	-a	-a			za
s-	s-	-	h-v-			g	g	so	o	a-tk	k	k		i		a		y	y
s-	-	w-	--	-	g-		o	so	o	rizo	k	-puk	i	i	i	ui	y	y	
y-	k-	o-	o-	n-		-o	-o	o	o	yo		i	i	i	i	i	y	y	
y-	i-	m-	llo-	n-	n-	vo	o	o	o	o		m		i	ii	i	i		z
x-	h-	h-	l-	l-		o	o	o	lo	o		m	m	m		i	bbi	h	wh
a-	a-	d-	d-	d-		po						-m	m	m	yl		h	h	x
e-	u-	d-	d-	d-		n	n	on	kn	n	in	ernm		l	l	l	h	-h	h
e-	e-	e-	d-	t-		n	n	n	n	j	n	l	l	l	dl	l	h	th	h
e-	e-	e-	p-	t-		n	n	an	an	n	l	-l	l	l	l	l	th	th	h

Fig. 5. Receptive fields of a standard SOM with 20 × 20 units trained on IFS outputs, obtained on the English text. Topographic organization is observed with respect to the most recent symbols.

winner neuron is determined by the whole series of processed inputs, and not only by a history of recently seen symbols. Unless we understand the driving mechanism behind such context-sensitive suffix representations, we cannot fully appreciate the meaning of the RF structure of a RecSOM map.

One has to ask what is the principal motivation behind building topographic maps of sequential data? If the motivation is a better understanding of cortical signal representations (e.g. [17]), then a considerable effort should be devoted to mathematical analysis of the scope of potential temporal representations and conditions for their emergence. If, on the other hand, the primary motivation is data exploration or data preprocessing, then we need to strive for a solid understanding of the way temporal contexts get represented on the map and in what way such representations fit the bill of the task we aim to solve.

There will be situations, where finite memory Markovian context representations are quite suitable. In that case, contractive RecSOM models, and indeed IFS+SOM models as well, may be appropriate candidates. But then the question arises of why exactly there needs to be a *trainable* dynamic part in self-organizing maps generalized to handle sequential data. For more complicated data sets, like the English language corpus, RF maps beyond simple Markovian organization may be preferable. Yet, it is crucial to understand exactly what structures that are more powerful than Markovian organization of RFs are desired and why. It is appealing to notice in the RF map of figure 3 the clearly non-Markovian spatial arrangement into distinct regions of RFs ending with the word-separation symbol '-'. Because of the special role of '-' and its high frequency of occurrence, it may indeed be desirable to separate endings of words in distinct islands with more refined structure. However, to go beyond mere commenting on empirical observations, one needs to address issues such as

- what properties of the input stream are likely to induce periodic (or aperiodic) fixed input dynamics leading to context-dependent RF representations in SOMs with feedback structures,
- what periods for which symbols are preferable,
- what is the learning mechanism (e.g. sequence of bifurcations of the fixed input dynamics) of creating more complicated context dependent RF maps.

Those are the challenges for our future work.

References

1. Voegtlin, T.: Recursive self-organizing maps. Neural Networks **15** (2002) 979–992
2. Kohonen, T.: Self-organizing formation of topologically correct feature maps. Biological Cybernetics **43** (1982) 59–69
3. Yin, H.: ViSOM - a novel method for multivariate data projection and structure visualisation. IEEE Transactions on Neural Networks **13** (2002) 237–243
4. de A. Barreto, G., Araújo, A., Kremer, S.: A taxonomy of spatiotemporal connectionist networks revisited: The unsupervised case. Neural Computation **15** (2003) 1255–1320
5. Hammer, B., Micheli, A., Strickert, M., Sperduti, A.: A general framework for unsupervised processing of structured data. Neurocomputing **57** (2004) 3–35
6. Chappell, G., Taylor, J.: The temporal kohonen map. Neural Networks **6** (1993) 441–445
7. Koskela, T., znd J. Heikkonen, M.V., Kaski, K.: Recurrent SOM with local linear models in time series prediction. In: 6th European Symposium on Artificial Neural Networks. (1998) 167–172
8. Horio, K., Yamakawa, T.: Feedback self-organizing map and its application to spatio-temporal pattern classification. International Journal of Computational Intelligence and Applications **1** (2001) 1–18
9. Strickert, M., Hammer, B.: Neural gas for sequences. In: Proceedings of the Workshop on Self-Organizing Maps (WSOM'03). (2003) 53–57
10. Hagenbuchner, M., Sperduti, A., Tsoi, A.: Self-organizing map for adaptive processing of structured data. IEEE Transactions on Neural Networks **14** (2003) 491–505
11. Schulz, R., Reggia, J.: Temporally asymmetric learning supports sequence processing in multi-winner self-organizing maps. Neural Computation **16** (2004) 535–561
12. Hammer, B., Micheli, A., Sperduti, A., Strickert, M.: Recursive self-organizing network models. Neural Networks **17** (2004) 1061–1085
13. Tiňo, P., Čerňanský, M., Beňušková, L.: Markovian architectural bias of recurrent neural networks. IEEE Transactions on Neural Networks **15** (2004) 6–15
14. Tiňo, P., Dorffner, G.: Predicting the future of discrete sequences from fractal representations of the past. Machine Learning **45** (2001) 187–218
15. Barnsley, M.: Fractals everywhere. Academic Press, New York (1988)
16. Kohonen, T.: The self-organizing map. Proceedings of the IEEE **78** (1990) 1464–1479
17. Wiemer, J.: The time-organized map algorithm: Extending the self-organizing map to spatiotemporal signals. Neural Computation **16** (2003) 1143–1171

Quantum Reinforcement Learning

Daoyi Dong, Chunlin Chen, and Zonghai Chen[*]

Department of Automation, University of Science and Technology of China,
Hefei, Anhui 230027, People's Republic of China
{dydong, clchen}@mail.ustc.edu.cn
chenzh@ustc.edu.cn

Abstract. A novel quantum reinforcement learning is proposed through combining quantum theory and reinforcement learning. Inspired by state superposition principle, a framework of state value update algorithm is introduced. The state/action value is represented with quantum state and the probability of action eigenvalue is denoted by probability amplitude, which is updated according to rewards. This approach makes a good tradeoff between exploration and exploitation using probability and can speed up learning. The results of simulated experiment verified its effectiveness and superiority.

1 Introduction

Learning methods are generally classified into supervised, unsupervised and reinforcement learning (RL). Supervised learning requires explicit feedback provided by input-output pairs and gives a map from input to output. And unsupervised learning only processes on the input data. However, RL uses a scalar value named reward to evaluate the input-output pairs and learns by interaction with environment through trial-and-error. Since 1980s, RL has become an important approach to machine intelligence [1-4], and is widely used in artificial intelligence due to its good performance of on-line adaptation and powerful leaning ability of complex nonlinear system [5, 6]. But there are some difficult problems in applications, such as very slow learning speed, especially for the curse of dimensionality problem when the state-action space becomes huge. Although in recent years many researchers have proposed all kinds of methods to speed up learning, few satisfactory successes were achieved.

On the other hand, quantum technology, especially quantum information technology is rapidly developing in recent years. The algorithm integration, which is inspired by quantum characteristics and quantum algorithms, will not only improve the performance of existing algorithms on traditional computers, but also promote the development of relative research areas such as quantum computer and machine learning. Considering the essence of computation and algorithms, we propose a quantum reinforcement learning (QRL) algorithm inspired by the state superposition principle. Section 2 contains the prerequisite and problem description. In section 3, a novel QRL algorithm is proposed. Section 4 describes the simulated experiments and analyzes their results. Conclusion and remarks are given in section 5.

---

[*] corresponding author.

2 Reinforcement Learning (RL)

Standard framework of RL is based on discrete time Markov decision processes [1]. In RL, the agent is to learn a policy $\pi : S \times \cup_{i \in S} A_{(i)} \to [0,1]$, so that expected sum of discounted reward of each state will be maximized:

$$V_{(s)}^{\pi} = E\{r_{t+1} + \gamma r_{t+2} + \gamma^2 r_{t+3} + \cdots | s_t = s, \pi\} = \sum_{a \in A_s} \pi(s,a)[r_s^a + \gamma \sum_{s'} p_{ss'}^a V_{(s')}^{\pi}] \quad (1)$$

$$V_{(s)}^{*} = \max_{a \in As}[r_s^a + \gamma \sum_{s'} p_{ss'}^a V_{(s')}^{*}] \quad (2)$$

$$\pi^* = \arg\max_{\pi} V_{(s)}^{\pi}, \quad \forall s \in S \quad (3)$$

where $\gamma \in [0,1]$ is discounted factor, $\pi(s,a)$ is the probability of selecting action a according to state s under policy π, $p_{ss'}^a = \Pr\{s_{t+1} = s' | s_t = s, a_t = a\}$ is probability for state transition and r_s^a is expected one-step rewards.

As for state-action pair value $Q(s,a)$:

$$Q_{(s,a)}^{*} = r_s^a + \gamma \sum_{s'} p_{ss'}^a \max_{a \in As} Q_{(s',a')}^{*} \quad (4)$$

Let η be the learning rate, and the 1-step update rule of Q-learning is:

$$Q(s_t, a_t) \leftarrow (1-\eta)Q(s_t, a_t) + \eta(r_{t+1} + \gamma \max_{a'} Q(s_{t+1}, a')). \quad (5)$$

3 Quantum Reinforcement Learning (QRL)

In quantum information technology, information unit (qubit) is represented with quantum state and qubit is an arbitrary superposition state of two-state quantum system:

$$|\psi\rangle = \alpha|0\rangle + \beta|1\rangle \quad (6)$$

where α and β are complex coefficients and satisfy $|\alpha|^2 + |\beta|^2 = 1$. $|0\rangle$ and $|1\rangle$ correspond to logic states 0 and 1. $|\alpha|^2$ and $|\beta|^2$ represent the occurrence probabilities of $|0\rangle$ and $|1\rangle$ respectively when this qubit is measured. The value of classical bit is either Boolean value 0 or value 1, but qubit can simultaneously store 0 and 1, which is the main difference between classical and quantum computation.

Let N_s and N_a be the number of states and actions, then choose numbers m and n, which satisfy $N_s \leq 2^m \leq 2N_s$ and $N_a \leq 2^n \leq 2N_a$. And use m and n qubits to represent state set $S = \{s\}$ and action set $A = \{a\}$:

$$s : \begin{bmatrix} a_1 & a_2 & \cdots & a_m \\ b_1 & b_2 & & b_m \end{bmatrix}, \text{ where } |a_i|^2 + |b_i|^2 = 1, \quad i = 1,2,\ldots m$$

$$a:\begin{bmatrix}\alpha_1 & \alpha_2 & \cdots & \alpha_n \\ \beta_1 & \beta_2 & & \beta_n\end{bmatrix}, \text{ where } |\alpha_i|^2+|\beta_i|^2=1,\ i=1,2,\ldots n$$

Thus they may lie in superposition state:

$$|s^{(m)}\rangle = \sum_{s=00\cdots 0}^{11\cdots 1} C_s |s\rangle,\ |a^{(n)}\rangle = \sum_{a=00\cdots 0}^{11\cdots 1} C_a |a\rangle \qquad (7)$$

where C_s and C_a are complex numbers.

The mapping from states to actions is $f(s) = \pi : S \to A$, and we will get:

$$f(s) = |a_s^n\rangle = \sum_{a=00\cdots 0}^{11\cdots 1} C_a |a\rangle \qquad (8)$$

$|C_a|^2$ denotes the occurrence probability of $|a\rangle$ when $|a_s^n\rangle$ is measured.

The procedural form of QRL is described as follows.

Initialize $|s^{(m)}\rangle = \sum_{s=00\cdots 0}^{11\cdots 1} C_s |s\rangle,\ f(s) = |a_s^n\rangle = \sum_{a=00\cdots 0}^{11\cdots 1} C_a |a\rangle$ *and* $V(s)$ *arbitrarily*

Repeat (for each episode)

For all states $|s^{(m)}\rangle = \sum_{s=00\cdots 0}^{11\cdots 1} C_s |s\rangle$:

(1) Observe $f(s)$ and get $|a\rangle$;

(2) Take action $|a\rangle$, observe next state $|s'^{(m)}\rangle$, reward r

Then update: $V(s) \leftarrow V(s) + \alpha(r + \gamma V(s') - V(s))$

$$C_a \leftarrow e^{\lambda(r+V(s'))} C_a$$

Until for all states $|\Delta V(s)| \leq \varepsilon$.

4 Simulation Experiments

To evaluate QRL algorithm in practice, consider the typical rooms with corridor example, gridworld environment of four rooms and surrounding corridors as shown in Fig. 1. From any state the robot (or agent) can perform one of four primary actions: up, down, left and right, and actions that would lead into a blocked cell are not executed. The task is to find an optimal policy which will let the robot move from $S(4,4)$ to $G(8,8)$ in this $13 \times 13 (0 \sim 12)$ grid world with minimized cost. In QRL, the action selecting policy is obviously different from traditional RL algorithms, which is inspired by the collapse theory of quantum measurement. And probability amplitudes $|C_a|^2$ (initialized uniformly) are used to denote the probability of an action.

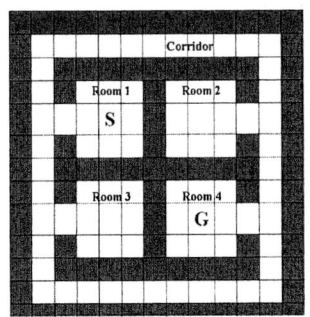 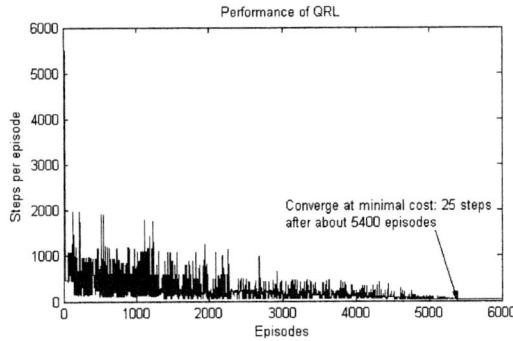

Fig. 1. Rooms with corridor   **Fig. 2.** Performance of QRL

Result and analysis. Learning performance for QRL is plotted in Fig. 2. At the beginning phase this algorithm learns extraordinarily fast, and then steadily converges to the optimal policy that costs 25 steps to the goal G. The results show that QRL algorithm excels other RL algorithms in two main aspects: (1) Action selecting policy makes a good tradeoff between exploration and exploitation. (2) Updating is carried through parallel, which will be much more prominent when practical quantum apparatus comes into use instead of been simulated on traditional computers.

5 Conclusion and Future Work

According to the existing problems in RL algorithms such as tradeoff between exploration and exploitation, low learning rate, QRL is proposed based on the concepts and theories of quantum computation. The results of simulated experiments verified the feasibility of this algorithm and showed its superiority for learning optimal problems with huge state space. With the development of quantum computation theory, the combining of traditional learning algorithms and quantum computation methods will make great change in many aspects such as representation and learning mechanism.

References

1. Sutton, R., Barto, A.G.: Reinforcement Learning: An Introduction. MIT Press, Cambridge, MA (1998)
2. Bertsekas, D.P., Tsitsiklis, J.N.: Neuro-Dynamic Programming. Athena Scientific, Belmont, MA (1996)
3. Sutton, R.: Learning to Predict by the Methods of Temporal Difference. Mach. Learn. 3 (1988) 9-44
4. Watkins, C., Dayan, P.: Q-learning. Mach. Learn. 8 (1992) 279-292
5. Beom, H.R., Cho, H.S.: A Sensor-based Navigation for a Mobile Robot Using Fuzzy Logic and Reinforcement Learning. IEEE Trans. Syst. Man. Cyc. 25 (1995) 464 -477
6. Smart, W.D., Kaelbling, L.P. Effective Reinforcement Learning for Mobile Robots. Proceedings of the IEEE Int. Conf. on Robotic. Autom. (2002)

Characterization of Evaluation Metrics in Topical Web Crawling Based on Genetic Algorithm

Tao Peng, Wanli Zuo, and Yilin Liu

College of Computer Science and Technology, Jilin University, Key Laboratory of Symbol Computation and Knowledge Engineering of the Ministry of Education,
Changchun 130012, China
taopengpt@yahoo.com.cn, wanli@jlu.edu.cn

Abstract. Topical crawlers are becoming important tools to support applications such as specialized Web portals, online searching, and competitive intelligence. A topic driven crawler chooses the best URLs to pursue during web crawling. It is difficult to evaluate what URLs downloaded are the best. This paper presents some important metrics and an evaluation function for ranking URLs about pages relevance. We also discuss an approach to evaluate the function based on GA. GA evolving process can discover the best combination of the metrics' weights. Avoiding misleading the result by a single topic, this paper presents a method which characterization of the metrics' combination be extracted by mining frequent patterns. Extracting features adopts a novel FP-tree structure and FP-growth mining method based on FP-tree without candidate generation. The experiment shows that the performance is exciting, especially about a popular topic.

1 Introduction

A crawler is a program that retrieves web pages for a search engine, which is widely used today. The WWW information is distributed, also the information environments become complex. Because of limited computing resources and limited time, topic driven crawler (also called focused crawler, retrieving web pages relevant a topic) has been developed. Topic driven crawler carefully decides which URLs to scan and in what order to pursue based on previously downloaded pages information. Early, there are breadth first crawlers [1] and depth first crawlers such as Fish Search [2]. And there are some crawling algorithms, such as Shark Search [3], a more aggressive variant of De Bra's Fish Search. There are crawlers whose decisions rely heavily on link-based criteria [4]. InfoSpiders [5] emphasize contextual knowledge for the topic. Some evaluation methods for choosing URLs [4] and several special crawlers, Naive Best-First crawler and DOM crawler [6] do not have satisfying adaptability. In this paper, we present an approach to evaluate a function about pages' relevance based on genetic algorithm (GA). We use GA to evolve some weights of the metrics. GAs are general purpose search algorithms which use principles inspired by natural genetic populations to evolve solutions to problems [7], [8]. And then we extract frequent patterns of the metrics' weights combinations based on FP-growth algorithm. FP-growth algorithm mines frequent patterns using an FP-tree by pattern fragment growth. In our approach, not as usual, an individual is a combination of the real-coded metrics' weight, and it's more natural to represent the optimization problem in the continuous domain.

The rest of the paper is organized as follows. Section 2 introduces the metrics and the evaluation function. Section 3 describes evolving the weights with genetic algorithm. Features extraction of the metrics' combination is illustrated in Section 4. Section 5 reports the results of our experiments. Section 6 draws the conclusion.

2 The Evaluation Function (Metrics)

Not all pages which crawler observed are "relevant" during crawling. For instance, if a crawler builds a specialized database on a particular topic, then pages referring to that topic are more important, and should be visited as early as possible. Similarly, if a page points to lots of authority pages, then the page is a high *hub* score page [9]. If the crawler cannot visit all the pages, then it is better to visit those "important" pages, since this will give the end-user higher-ranking results. We define the evaluation function $I(u)$, u is the URL that the crawler will be pursued, p is the parent page of u. The evaluation function is a weighted combination of followed metrics:

1. *sim(p, q)* (similarity of page p to topic q): A topic q drives the crawling process, and sim(p, q) is defined to be the textual similarity between p and q, this is shown in the work by the authors [10].

$$sim(p,q) = \frac{(\sum_{j=1}^{r} q_j \times l_j \times \omega_j)}{(|\omega'| \times |p|)}. \quad (1)$$

where $\omega' = (\omega_1 \times l_1, \cdots, \omega_r \times l_r)$; ω_j: the weight of the *j*th word; l_j: the inverse document frequency (*idf*) of the *j*th word;

2. *hub(p)* (the evaluation of hubs property): Hub pages are defined to be Web pages which point to lots of "important" pages relevant a topic.

$$hub(p) = \frac{|L_p|}{\frac{\sum_{i=1}^{N} |L_i|}{N}}. \quad (2)$$

where $|L_p|$: the number of out links of page p ;

$\frac{\sum_{i=1}^{N} |L_i|}{N}$: the average number of out-links of the pages that are already downloaded.

3. *bc(p)* (backlink count): the number of links to p

$$bc(p) = \frac{|P_p|}{M}. \quad (3)$$

where M is a parameter provided by user.

4. *uts(u, q)* (similarity of urls text to topic p):

$$uts(u,q) = sim(u,q) + thesaurus(u,q). \quad (4)$$

where *thesaurus(u, q)* is uses the thesaurus dictionary of topic q, this experimentation does not take the metric(the future work I will do).

5. *pagerank(p)* [4]: a page p that is pointed at by pages $t_1, \ldots, t_n$, and c_i is the number of links going out of page t_i. d is a damping factor.

$$pagerank(p) = (1-d) + d(\frac{pagerank(p_1)}{c_1} + \cdots + \frac{pagerank(p_n)}{c_n}). \quad (5)$$

6. *I(u)*: the evaluation function

$$I(u) = \omega_1 \times sim(p,q) + \omega_2 \times hub(p) + \omega_3 \times bc(p) + \omega_4 \times uts(u,q) + \omega_5 \times pagerank(p) \quad (6)$$

where $\sum_{i=1}^{5} \omega_i = 1$. A high $I(u)$ value indicates u links more relevant page to the topic.

3 Evolve the Weights with Genetic Algorithm

The weights of the metrics (6) are evolved with genetic algorithm. The individuals are real-coded, because that the representation of the solution could be very close to the natural formulation of our problem. Since the amount of the weights equals to 1, the weight ω_i is coded into the gene, c_i, and c_i is defined by

$$c_i = \sum_{j=1}^{i} \omega_j, \quad i=1,\ldots,4. \quad (7)$$

Each individual in the population is the combination of $c_1, \ldots, c_4$. Obviously, there must be a restriction of any individual, $x_i \geq x_{i+1}$, to ensure the individual could be decoded into the weights.

The standard fitness proportional model, which is also called roulette wheel selection, is used as the selection method to select the individuals for reproduction. The probability of an individual to be selected is $P_i = f_i / \sum_{j=1}^{n} f_j$, n is the population size[11]. Individuals are crossed using simple crossover method [12]. We can assume that $C_1 = (c_1^1, \ldots, c_5^1)$ and $C_2 = (c_1^2, \ldots, c_5^2)$ are two chromosomes selected for the crossover operator. The single crossing position $j \in \{1, \ldots, 3\}$ is randomly chosen and the two new chromosomes are built as

$$C_1' = (c_1^1, c_2^1, \ldots, c_i^1, c_{i+1}^2, \ldots, c_5^2) \quad C_2' = (c_1^2, c_2^2, \ldots, c_i^2, c_{i+1}^1, \ldots, c_5^1)$$

Of course, due to the restriction of the individual which is referred before, the genes of C_1', C_2' must be sorted according to the sort ascending. If an individual is chosen for the mutation operator, one of the randomly chosen genes c_i will change to

$c_i' \in (c_{i-1}, c_{i+1})$ which is a random value, and we assume that $c_0 = 0$, $c_5 = 1$. Finally, all of the individuals, including new and old ones, are sorted by their fitness, and the best-fit individuals become the new population in the next generation. We set the probability of crossover to be 0.8, and the probability of mutation to be 0.05. After 50 generations, we finish the evolving process, choose the individual with the highest fitness of the population, and decode the genes to the weights as the result.

4 The Characterization of the Metrics

Avoiding misleading the result by a single topic, we present a method which characterization of the metrics' weights combinations be extracted by mining frequent patterns. Characterization of the metrics' weights combinations (also called features extraction) adopts a FP-tree structure and FP-growth [13] mining method based on FP-tree without candidate generation, which optimized from Apriori algorithm. FP-growth just adapt to the system of updating data frequently. Apriori [14] is a basal algorithm of generating frequent patterns. Apriori employs an iterative approach known as a level-wise search, where k-itemsets are used to explore (k+1)-itemsets. Apriori is an influential algorithm for mining frequent itemsets for Boolean association rules. Many association-mining algorithms evolve from it. In many application cases the Apriori behave not as good as expect (i.e., need to repeatedly scan the itemsets, inefficient, consuming abundant resource of CPU). FP-growth is optimized algorithm from Apriori. FP-growth adopts a divide-and-conquer strategy that compresses the database representing frequent items into a frequent-pattern tree (FP-tree), and proceeds to mine the FP-tree. FP-tree is a good compact tree structure, which contains the complete information of the database in relevance to frequent pattern mining, and its size is usually highly compact and much smaller than its original database. The method is highly compressed and frequent itemsets generation is integrated and don't need to repeatedly scan the itemsets. Therefore features extraction adopts FP-growth method.

The main steps of FP-growth method are as follows:

1) Construct conditional pattern base for each node in the FP-tree;
2) Construct conditional FP-tree from each conditional pattern-base;
3) Recursively mine conditional FP-trees and grow frequent patterns obtained so far;
4) If the conditional FP-tree contains a single path, simply enumerate all the patterns.

Let's look at an example of extraction of features. The metrics of the evaluation function $I(u)>0.5$ (in section 2) are the audit data. Audit data must been preprocessed and cleaned (i.e., adds a sign after data items, as 'ω_1' 'ω_2' 'ω_3' 'ω_4' 'ω_5').

Example 1

This example based on preprocessed data of Table 1. Assume the minimum support count is 2. There are five transactions in this database. Fig.1 is the FP-tree constructed from the Table 1. Table 2 is the first scan of the database candidates 1-itemsets and their support counts. Table 3 shows the result.

Table 1. Preprocessed audit data for NTIDS

TID	Items
T100	0.27-ω_1, 0.08-ω_2, 0.23-ω_3, 0.08-ω_4, 0.34-ω_5
T200	0.15-ω_1, 0.10-ω_2, 0.26-ω_3, 0.21-ω_4, 0.28-ω_5
T300	0.27-ω_1, 0.12-ω_2, 0.23-ω_3, 0.12-ω_4, 0.26-ω_5
T400	0.20-ω_1, 0.08-ω_2, 0.17-ω_3, 0.21-ω_4, 0.34-ω_5
T500	0.27-ω_1, 0.12-ω_2, 0.23-ω_3, 0.04-ω_4, 0.34-ω_5

Table 2. Frequent items(1-itemsets) and their support counts generated by scan the database

Itemset	Support count
0.27-ω_1	3
0.23-ω_3	3
0.34-ω_5	3
0.08-ω_2	2
0.12-ω_2	2
0.21-ω_4	2
0.15-ω_1	1
0.20-ω_1	1
0.12-ω_2	1
⋮	⋮
0.28-ω_5	1
0.26-ω_5	1

Table 3. A portion of frequent itemsets generated by mining the FP-tree

TID	Items
0.23-ω_3, 0.12-ω_2	2
0.27-ω_1, 0.23-ω_3	3
0.27-ω_1, 0.34-ω_5	2
⋮	⋮
0.27-ω_1, 0.23-ω_3, 0.34-ω_5	2
0.27-ω_1, 0.23-ω_3, 0.12-ω_2	2

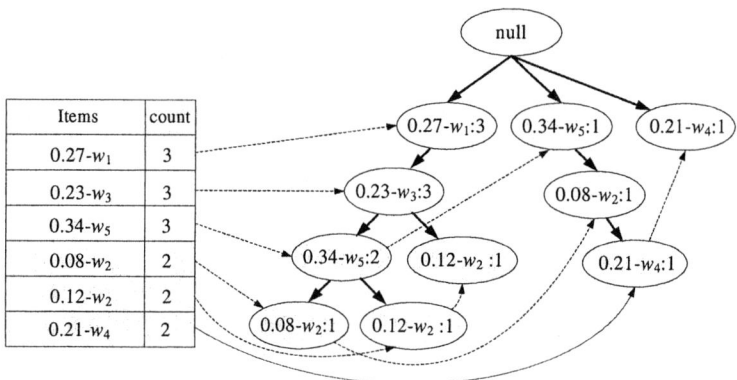

Fig. 1. An FP-tree that registers compressed, frequent pattern information

5 The Experiments and Results

In the experiment, we built a virtual crawler, and crawled the web starting from 200 relevant URLs (Seed URLs) simultaneously. After crawling 18000 pages, all the crawler threads stop. Every crawling 3000 pages, the system will extract the features and adjust the metrics' weights combinations. The minimum support count is 30. We choose the best individual based on the metric of *fitness* function.

$$fitness = \frac{1}{N} \cdot \sum_{i=1}^{N} x_i \quad , \quad x_i = \begin{cases} 1, sim(p_i, q) \geq \theta \\ 0, sim(p_i, q) < \theta \end{cases}. \tag{8}$$

θ is a parameter provided by user, N is the number of crawled pages.

Table 4. The several best weights combinations during the crawling

	ω_1	ω_2	ω_3	ω_4	ω_5
6000 pages	0.22	0.20	0.11	0.25	0.22
12000 pages	0.18	0.21	0.17	0.27	0.17
18000 pages	0.19	0.16	0.18	0.31	0.16

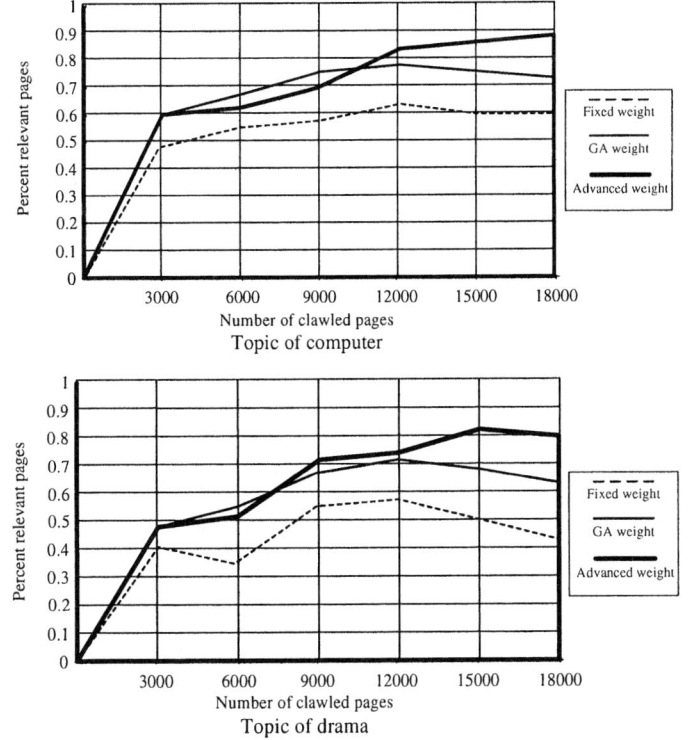

Fig. 2. The percent of the relevant pages (topic of "computer" and "drama")

Table 4 shows the best weights combinations in the topic of computer. Fig. 2 shows the percent of the relevant pages on the topic of "computer" and "drama". The dashed represents every weight ω_i =0.2 fixed. The real line represents the best individual weights based on GA. The bold line represents the best individual weights adjusted based on GA.

6 Conclusions

In this paper, a topic driven crawler based on GA has a good performance during crawling, especially after adjusting the metrics' weights based on FP-growth method. According to the two figures above, popular topic "computer" has a better *fitness* than topic "drama". After GA evolving, the result of above experiment is significant, and this is just what we expected. After crawling the first 3000 pages, the performance of the crawler based on GA is not as good as the one after being adjusted. But after crawling 8000-10000 pages, the performance of the latter is better. We will perfect our work, metrics *thesaurus* (u, q) etc., in future.

Acknowledgment

This work is sponsored by the National Natural Science Foundation of China under grant number 60373099.

References

1. Pinkerton, B.: Finding What People Want:Experiences with the WebCrawler. In Proceedings of the 2nd International World Wide Web Conference, Chicago, IL, USA (1994)
2. De Bra, R. D. J. Post.: Information Retrieval in the World-Wide Web: Making Client-based Searching Feasible. Proceedings of the First International World-Wide Web conference, Geneva (1994)
3. Hersovici, M., M. Jacovi, Y. S. Maarek, D. Pelleg, M. Shtalhaim, and S. Ur: The shark-search algorithm-An application:Tailored Web site mapping. Proc. 7th Intl. World-Wide Web Conference (1998)
4. J. Cho, H. Garcia-Molina, L. Page: Efficient Crawling Through URL Ordering. In Proceedings of 7th World Wide Web Conference (1998)
5. F. Menczer, R. Belew.: Adaptive retrieval agents: internalizing local context and scaling up to the web. Machine Learning 39 (2–3) (2000) 203–242
6. G. Pant and F. Menczer.: Topical Crawling for Business Intelligence. Proc. 7th European Conference on Research and Advanced Technology for Digital Libraries (ECDL) (2003)
7. Holland, J.H.: Adaptation in Natural and Artificial Systems. The University of Michigan Press (1975)
8. Goldberg, D.E.: Genetic Algorithms in Search, Optimization, and Machine Learning. AddisonWesley, New York (1989)
9. J. Johnson, K. Tsioutsiouliklis, C. L. Giles.: Evolving strategies for focused Web crawling. Proceedings of the Twentieth International Conference on Machine Learning (ICML-2003), Washington DC (2003)

10. Xu B W, Zhang W F: Search Engine and Information Retrieval Technology. Tsinghua university press, BeiJing. China (2001) 147–150
11. Zhou C G, Liang Y C.: Computational Intelligence. Jilin university press, Changchun. China (2001)
12. F. Herrera, M. Lozano, J.L. Verdegay.: Tackling Real Coded Genetic Algorithms: Operators and Tools for Behavioural Analysis. Artificial Intelligence Review, @1998 Kluwer Academic Publishers. Printed in the Netherlands (1998) 12: 265–319
13. J. Han, J. Pei, Y. Yin.: Mining Frequent Patterns without Candidate Generation, SIGMOD Conference (2000) 1–12
14. Jiawei Han, Micheline Kamber.: Data Mining:Concepts and Techniques. Higher Education Press (2001)

A Novel Quantum Swarm Evolutionary Algorithm for Solving 0-1 Knapsack Problem

Yan Wang, Xiao-Yue Feng, Yan-Xin Huang, Wen-Gang Zhou,
Yan-Chun Liang, and Chun-Guang Zhou

College of Computer Science and Technology, Jilin University,
Key Laboratory for Symbol Computation and Knowledge Engineering
of the National Education Ministry,
Changchun 130021, China
wy6868@hotmail.com, cgzhou@jlu.edu.cn

Abstract. A novel quantum swarm evolutionary algorithm is presented based on quantum-inspired evolutionary algorithm in this article. The proposed algorithm adopts quantum angle to express Q-bit and improved particle swarm optimization to update automatically. The simulated effectiveness is examined in solving 0-1 knapsack problem.

1 Introduction

Quantum computing was proposed by Benioff and Feynman in the early 1980s [1,2]. Due to its unique computational performance, the quantum computing has attracted extensive attention of researchers [3,4]. In 2002, Han proposed the quantum-inspired evolutionary algorithm (QEA), inspired by the concept of quantum computing, and introduced a Q-gate as a variation operator to promote the optimization of the individuals Q-bit [5]. In 2004, Han applied the QEA to some optimization problems and the performance of the QEA is better than the traditional evolutionary algorithms in many fields [6].

In QEA, the smallest unit of information is called a Q-bit, which is defined as $\begin{bmatrix} \alpha \\ \beta \end{bmatrix}$, where α and β are complex numbers that specify the probability amplitudes of the corresponding states. The moduli $|\alpha|^2$ and $|\beta|^2$ are the probabilities that the Q-bit exists in state "0" and state "1", respectively, which satisfy that $|\alpha|^2 + |\beta|^2 = 1$. And an m-Qbits is defined as $\begin{bmatrix} \alpha_1 | \alpha_2 | ... | \alpha_m \\ \beta_1 | \beta_2 | ... | \beta_m \end{bmatrix}$, where $|\alpha_i|^2 + |\beta_i|^2 = 1$ ($i = 1, 2...m$), m is the number of Q-bits [5].

Quantum gate (Q-gate) $U(t)$ is a variable operator of QEA. It can be chosen according to the problem. A common rotation gate used in QEA is as follows [6]:

$$\begin{bmatrix} \alpha'_i \\ \beta'_i \end{bmatrix} = \begin{bmatrix} \cos(\Delta\theta_i) & -\sin(\Delta\theta_i) \\ \sin(\Delta\theta_i) & \cos(\Delta\theta_i) \end{bmatrix} \begin{bmatrix} \alpha_i \\ \beta_i \end{bmatrix}$$

where $\Delta\theta_i$ represent the rotation angle. Our proposed algorithm, quantum swarm evolutionary algorithm (QSE), is based on an improved quantum rotation gate strategy.

Meanwhile, particle swarm optimization (PSO) demonstrates good performance in many optimization problems [7,8]. Particle swarm optimization (PSO) is a population based optimization strategy introduced by Kennedy & Eberhart (1995) [9]. It is initialized with a group of random particles and then updates theirs velocities and positions with following formulae:

$$v(t+1) = v(t) + c_1 * rand() * (pBest(t) - Present(t)) + c_2 * rand() * (gBest(t) - Present(t))$$
$$Present(t+1) = Present(t) + v(t+1)$$

where $v(t)$ is the particle velocity, $Persent(t)$ is the current particle. $pBest(t)$ and $gBest(t)$ are individual best and global best. $rand()$ is a random number between [0, 1]. c_1, c_2 are learning factors. An improvement of v is utilized in following sections.

In this paper, a novel quantum swarm evolutionary algorithm (QSE) is proposed, which is based on quantum-inspired evolutionary algorithm. A novel quantum bit expression mechanism called quantum angle is employed and the improved particle swarm optimization is adopted to update the Q-bit automatically. The simulated results in solving a 0-1 knapsack problem show that QSE is superior to QEA and many traditional heuristic algorithms.

2 Quantum Angle

Definition 1: A quantum angle is defined as an arbitrary angle θ and a Q-bit is presented as $[\theta]$.

Then $[\theta]$ is equivalent to the original Q-bit as $\begin{bmatrix} \sin(\theta) \\ \cos(\theta) \end{bmatrix}$. It satisfies $|\sin(\theta)|^2 + |\cos(\theta)|^2 = 1$ spontaneously. Then an m-Qbits $\begin{bmatrix} \alpha_1 | \alpha_2 | ... | \alpha_m \\ \beta_1 | \beta_2 | ... | \beta_m \end{bmatrix}$ could be replaced by $[\theta_1 | \theta_2 | ... | \theta_m]$. The common rotation gate

$$\begin{bmatrix} \alpha'_i \\ \beta'_i \end{bmatrix} = \begin{bmatrix} \cos(\Delta\theta_i) & -\sin(\Delta\theta_i) \\ \sin(\Delta\theta_i) & \cos(\Delta\theta_i) \end{bmatrix} \begin{bmatrix} \alpha_i \\ \beta_i \end{bmatrix}$$ is replaced by $[\theta_i'] = [\theta_i + \Delta\theta_i]$.

3 Quantum Swarm Evolutionary Algorithm

Using the concept of swarm intelligence of PSO, we regard all m-Qbits in the population as an intelligence group, named quantum swarm. First, we find the local best quantum angle and the global best value from the local ones. And then according to these values we update quantum angles by Q-gate.

The proposed procedure, called quantum swarm evolutionary algorithm (QSE), based on the procedure of QEA is summarized as follows:

1. Use quantum angle to encode Q-bit, $Q(t) = \{q_1^t, q_2^t ... q_n^t\}$, $q_j^t = [\theta_{j1}^t | \theta_{j2}^t | ... | \theta_{jm}^t]$.
2. Modify the *Update* procedure of QEA to update $Q(t)$ with the following improved PSO formulae:

$$v_{ji}^{t+1} = \chi * (\omega * v_{ji}^t + C_1 * rand() * (\theta_{ji}^t(pBest) - \theta_{ji}^t) + C_2 * Rand() * (\theta_i^t(gBest) - \theta_{ji}^t))$$

$$\theta_{ji}^{t+1} = \theta_{ji}^t + v_{ji}^{t+1}$$

where v_{ji}^t, θ_{ji}^t, $\theta_{ji}^t(pBest)$ and $\theta_i^t(gBest)$ are the velocity, current position, individual best and global best of the ith Q-bit of the jth m-Qbits, respectively. Set $\chi = 0.99$, $W = 0.7298$, $C_1 = 1.42$ and $C_1 = 1.57$, which satisfy the convergence condition of the particles: $W > (C_1 + C_2)/2 - 1$. Since $C_2 > C_1$, the particles will converge faster to the global optimal position of the swarm than the local optimal position of each particle, i.e., the algorithm has global searching property [7].

3. Make each $x_{ji}^t = 0$ or 1 of $P(t)$ by observing the state of $Q(t)$ through $|\cos(\theta_{ji})|^2$ or $|\sin(\theta_{ji})|^2$.

4 Experimental Results

The 0-1 knapsack problem is described as: given a set of items and a knapsack, select a subset of the items so as to maximize the profit $f(X) = \sum_{i=1}^{m} p_i x_i$ subject to $\sum_{i=1}^{m} \omega_i x_i \leq C$, where $X = \{x_1 ... x_m\}$, $x_i = 0$ or 1, ω_i is the weight of ith item, p_i is the profit of ith item, C is the capacity of the knapsack, respectively. $x_i = 1$ if ith item is selected, otherwise $x_i = 0$. In the experiments, we use the similarity data sets in reference [5]. Set random $\omega_i \in [1,10]$, $p_i = \omega_i + l_i$, where the random figure $l_i \in [0,5]$, knapsack capacity is set as $C = \frac{1}{2} \sum_{i=1}^{m} \omega_i$, and three knapsack problems with 100, 250 and 500 items are considered. At the same time, we use the same profit evaluation procedure and add the same repair strategy mentioned in reference [5] based on the structure of QSE proposed.

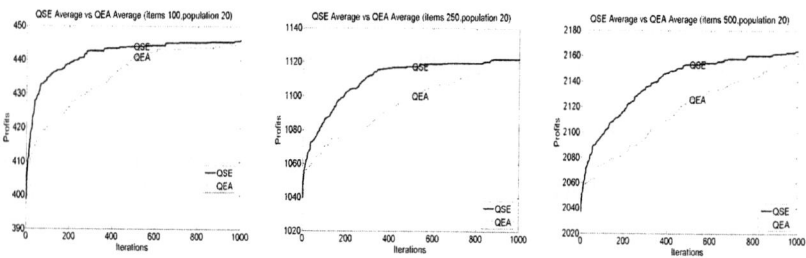

Fig. 1. Comparison of QSE and QEA on the knapsack problems with 100, 250, and 500 items (average of 10 tests, population size 20, Delta 0.01π, iteration times 1000)

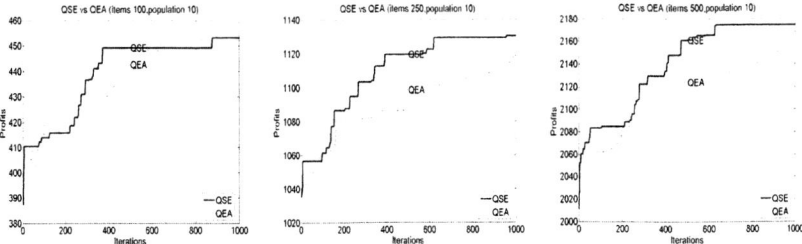

Fig. 2. Comparison of the best single test of QSE and QEA with different items and the same 10 population size (Delta 0.01π, iteration times 1000)

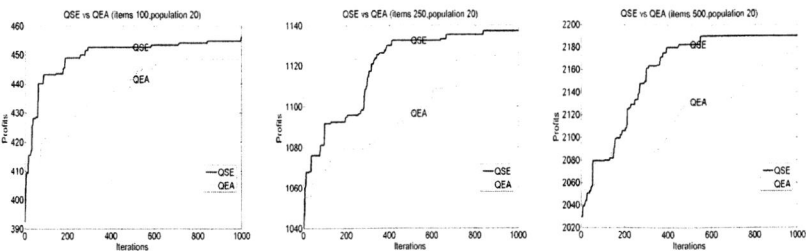

Fig. 3. Comparison of the best single test of QSE and QEA with different items and the same 20 population size (Delta 0.01π, iteration times 1000)

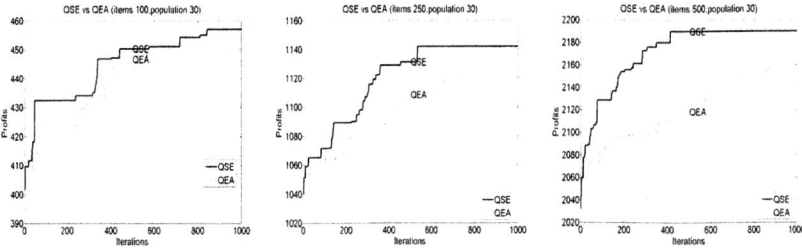

Fig. 4. Comparison of the best single test of QSE and QEA with different items and the same 30 population size (Delta 0.01π, iteration times 1000)

Comparison of QSE and QEA on the knapsack problem with different items and same population size is shown in Fig.1 to Fig.4. QSE is better than QEA in both speed and profits.

From Table 2 and Fig.5, it can be seen that QSE with larger population size obtains faster convergent speed and dominates larger item number, but spends more running time.

From Table 3 and Fig.6, we can see that QSE is better than many traditional heuristic algorithms. The comparison experiment is performed by heuristic algorithm tool kit [10]. It includes several heuristic functions in solving 0-1 knapsack problem, such as the climb hill algorithm (hillks), simulation anneal algorithm (saks) and taboo search algorithm (tabuks). The test environment is P4 2.6G, 512M, Windows XP, Matlab6.5.

Table 2. Results of different population size and iteration times of QSE in knapsack problem*

Item number		100		250		500	
Size	Iteration times	Best profit	time (s)	Best profit	time (s)	Best profit	time (s)
10	100	413.96	1	1079.0	2	2083.5	4
	500	449.11	3	1119.5	8	2161.0	16
	1000	453.18	5	1130.3	14	2174.4	34
20	100	443.12	2	1096.8	3	2122.9	7
	500	452.66	6	1132.4	14	2182.6	33
	1000	455.96	12	1137.2	28	2190.0	67
30	100	445.64	2	1104.5	5	2128.6	10
	500	453.89	8	1132.7	19	2186.9	46
	1000	457.03	16	1141.9	38	2190.0	98

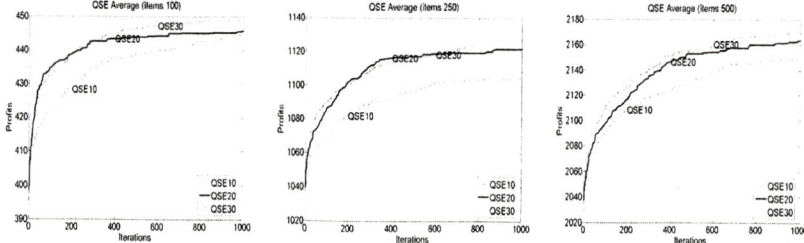

Fig. 5. Comparison of different population size of QSE on the knapsack problems with 100, 250, and 500 items (average of 10 tests, population size 10, 20, 30, iteration times 1000)

Table 3. Results of QSE vs traditional heuristic algorithms in knapsack problem†

Item number	100		250		500	
Method	Best profit	time (s)	Best profit	time (s)	Best profit	time (s)
QSE	455.96	12	1137.2	28	2190	67
HILLKS	412.74	2	1035.9	4	2032.3	7
SAKS	415.27	9	1045.8	27	2048.8	29
TABUKS	429.47	10	1111.8	29	2120.1	77

---

* Running time is the second-round of the average time of 10 tests.
† All parameters are set as same as Fig. 3 and running time is the second-round of the average time of 10 tests.

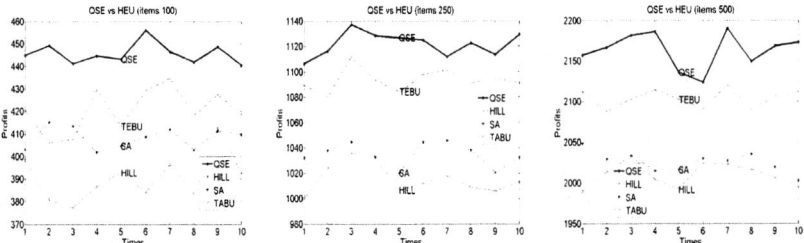

Fig. 6. Comparison of QSE (population size 20) and heuristic algorithms on knapsack problems, includes HILLKS, SAKS (anneal coefficient 0.99, initial temperature 100) and TABUKS (taboo table is 20). Each method tests 10 times and each test iterates 1000 times.

5 Conclusions

In this paper, a novel quantum swarm evolutionary algorithm (QSE) is presented, which is based on the quantum-inspired evolutionary algorithm (QEA). We define quantum angle to express Q-bit and use the particle swarm optimization (PSO) to train them automatically. The results in solving 0-1 knapsack problem show that QSE is superior to QEA and many traditional heuristic algorithms. Future research of this topic is to find a more effective method to choose the parameters according to the information of different problems.

Acknowledgement

This work was supported by the National Natural Science Foundation of China under Grant No. 60175024 and 60433020, and the Key Science-Technology Project of the National Education Ministry of China under Grant No. 02090.

References

1. Benioff P.: The Computer as a Physical System: a Microscopic Quantum Mechanical Hamiltonian Model of Computers as Represented by Turing Machines. J. Stat. Phys., Vol. 22 (1980) 563–591
2. Feynman R.: Simulating Physics with Computers. Internat. J. Theoret. Phys., Vol. 21, No. 6 (1982) 467–488
3. Grover L.K.: Algorithms for Quantum Computation: Discrete Logarithms and Factoring. In Proceedings of the 35th Annual Symposium on Foundations of Computer Science, Piscataway, NJ, IEEE Press (1994) 124-134
4. Shor P.W.: Quantum Computing. Documenta Mathematica, Extra Volume, Proceedings of the International Congress of Mathematicians, Berlin, Germany (1998) 467-486.
5. Han K.H. and Kim J.H.: Quantum-inspired Evolutionary Algorithm for a Class of Combinatorial Optimization. IEEE Transactions on Evolutionary Computation, IEEE Press, Vol. 6, No. 6 (2002) 580-593

6. Han K.H. and Kim J.H.: Quantum-Inspired Evolutionary Algorithms with a New Termination Criterion, HεGate, and Two-Phase Scheme. IEEE Transactions on Evolutionary Computation, IEEE Press, Vol. 8, No. 2 (2004) 156-169
7. Huang Y.X., Zhou C.G., Zou S.X. and Wang Y.: A Fuzzy Neural Network System Based On the Class Cover and Particle Swarm Optimization. Computer Research and Development (in Chinese), Vol. 41, No. 7 (2004) 1053-1061
8. Wang Y., Zhou C.G., Huang Y.X., Feng X.Y.: Training Minimal Uncertainty Neural Networks by Bayesian Theorem and Particle Swarm Optimization. Neural Information Processing: 11th International Conference, ICONIP 2004, Calcutta, India, November, 2004, Lecture Notes in Computer Science, Vol. 3316. Springer-Verlag (2004) 579-584
9. Kennedy J. and Eberhart R.C.: Particle Swarm Optimization. In Proceeding of IEEE International Conference on Neural Networks, Volume IV, Perth, Australia (1995) 1942-1948
10. Heuristic Algorithm Tool Kit: Copyright 2002, Lars Aurdal/Rikshospitalet. [Online] Available: http://www.idi.ntnu.no/~lau/Forelesninger/

An Evolutionary System and Its Application to Automatic Image Segmentation

Yun Wen Chen and Yan Qiu Chen*

Department of Computer Science and Engineering,
School of Information Science and Engineering,
Fudan University, Shanghai 200433, China
chenyq@fudan.edu.cn

Abstract. In this paper, an algorithm built on the notion of evolutionary system is proposed. During the evolution of distributed tribes, the individuals making up the tribes cooperatively effect pixel communication from one agent to the other in order to improve the homogeneity of the ensemble of the image regions that they represent. The proposed Artificial Coevolving Tribes, containing evolution, mature, propagate, and die, is explored in the context of image. Meanwhile, the given image is recognized and segmented. Stability and scale control of the algorithm is maintained. Results obtained on natural scenes are presented with the evolutionary process.

1 Introduction

Artificial life is a growing field of scientific research linking biological science and computer science [1]. With the aid of computers, we can create synthetic processes that emulate the complex behavior of natural life, such as emergence, cooperation, competition and evolution.

Artificial life approaches seem to offer significant advantages in tackling complex problems [2]. One of its engineering applications that is introduced in this paper is image segmented [3]. This approach builds an artificial ecosystem corresponding to the image with each life form being associated with a pixel. After several steps of evolution, different tribes, aiming at minimal intra-tribe variability and maximal inter-tribe variability, will emerge. Finally, the different tribes' demesne represents the parts of segmentation.

2 Artificial Coevolving Tribes

The whole image T is considered as an artificial ecosystem, and each segment T_i associated with a tribe [4]. Every tribe has a set of individuals, and each individual is associated with a pixel. All the individual agents bear similar structures. We denote the agents by an identity characteristic vector $\mathbf{p}_{i,j}^{(t)}$, (i,j is the position

---

* Corresponding author.

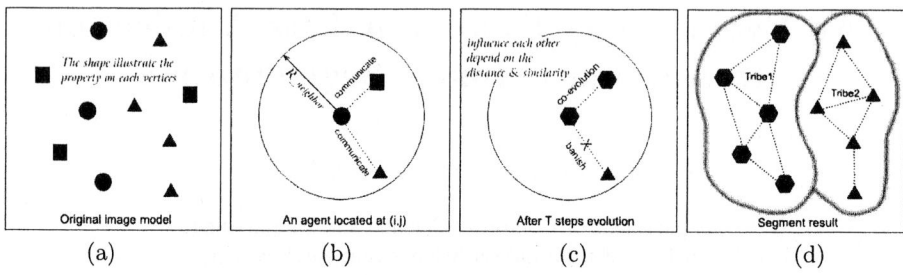

Fig. 1. Artificial Coevolving Tribes

of this agent, t represents the vector after t iterations). This characteristic vector consists of the pixel attributes, such as grey-level, brightness, color, texture, velocity field, etc.

The illustrative image in Fig1(a) shows some agents of different shapes (characteristics). Once the evolution process begins, each agent will communicate with its local neighborhood and exchange identity information, as shown in Fig1(b). The communication weight is based on the principles of: proximity, similarity, common fate, good continuation, surrounding. Each individual tries to influence the others while to adjust its own vector taking into account of the others. Furthermore, those with similar or analogical features will influence each other and finally integrate, as illustrated in Fig1(c). At the same time, those with bigger different characteristics will be excluded, and eventually separated. Finally, all the agents will form stable tribes with specific territory. Thus, we attain the steady segments in Fig1(d). We now describe the proposed method in a more formal way. The presentation starts with the neighborhood definition.

Definition 2.1 (Neighborhood System). *A neighborhood system $\xi(p_{i,j}, r)$ with radius r of a candidate pixel $p_{i,j}$, is the set of all pixels $p_{x,y}$ such as:*

$$\xi(p_{i,j}, r) = \{\ p_{x,y}|\ d(p_{x,y}, p_{i,j}) = r,\ (r \in N)\ \}, \tag{1}$$

where the spatial distance $d(p_{x,y}, p_{i,j}) = |x - i| + |y - j|$, $p_{x,y}$ is the feature vector of the agent at Cartesian coordinates (x, y). The maximum neighbor range is defined by R_{max}, then the number of neighbors at radius r is $K(r) = \|\xi(p_{i,j}, r)\|$, and we have: $K(r) = 4r$.

Definition 2.2 (Communication Weight). *The distance r of a neighbor agent determine the communicate rate between these two agents. We denote the communication weight with $v(r)$. They should satisfy:*

1. $0 \leq v(r) < 1$
2. if $r1 > r2$, $v(r1) < v(r2)$.
3. The whole communication weight: $\sum_{r=1}^{R_{max}} K(r)v(r) = 1$

In the following subsections, we describe how the segments are initially created; how the agents communicate and evolve during the optimization process; and how the process terminates.

2.1 Initialization

For a candidate image T taking dimensions $W * H$, we create N agents, $N = W * H$. Each agent resides on one pixel, and has a feature vector $p_{i,j}^{(t)}$. When agents are created, we have $t = 0$. After creation the evolution process starts.

2.2 Evolution

The evolution process consists of a sequence of epochs. At each epoch t, all agents act parallely and independently. Yet the influence between every neighbor agents is complex and underlying.

Definition 2.3 (Dynamic Influence Factor). *For an arbitrary agent $p_{i,j}$, during each step of evolution, it will communicate with all of its neighbors. Here defined is the dynamic communication weight $w_{x,y}^{(t)}(r)$ at time step t, where $p_{x,y} \in \xi(p_{i,j}, r)$.*

$$w_{x,y}^{(t)}(r) = \begin{cases} \left(1 - \frac{|p_{x,y}^{(t)} - p_{i,j}^{(t)}|}{gap(r)}\right)(1-\varepsilon)v(r) + \varepsilon\, v(r) & : \quad if \ |p_{x,y}^{(t)} - p_{i,j}^{(t)}| \leq gap(r) \\ 0 & : \quad if \ |p_{x,y}^{(t)} - p_{i,j}^{(t)}| > gap(r) \end{cases} \quad (2)$$

where $gap(r)$ is a threshold parameter only when neighbor agent at distance r has less diversity than this threshold, communicate are permitted.

Then for each agent on pixel i, j at time step t, the feature on next time step is:

$$p_{i,j}^{(t+1)} = \sum_{r=1}^{R_{max}} \sum_{p_{x,y} \in \xi(p_{i,j},r)} w_{x,y}^{(t)}(r)\, p_{x,y}^{(t)} + m_{i,j}^{(t)} p_{i,j}^{(t)} \quad (3)$$

$m_{i,j}^{(t)}$ is the mature rate defined as follows:

Definition 2.4 (Mature Rate). *In Eqn3, we define mature rate: $m_{i,j}^{(t)} = 1 - \sum_{r=1}^{R_{max}} \sum_{p_{x,y} \in \xi(p_{i,j},r)} w_{x,y}^{(t)}$*

2.3 Mature or Die

According to the definition, $m_{i,j}^{(t)} \in [0, 1]$ demonstrates the analogical rate between $p_{i,j}^{(t)}$ and its neighbors.

$$p_{i,j}^{(t+1)} = \begin{cases} p_{i,j}^{(t)} & : \quad if \ 0 \leq m_{i,j}^{(t)} \leq \theta_{mature} \\ arg\ min_{p_{x,y} \in \xi(p_{i,j},1)} |p_{x,y}^{(t)} - p_{i,j}^{(t)}| & : \quad if \ 2\theta_{die} - 1 \leq m_{i,j}^{(t)} < \theta_{die} \\ \sum_{r=1}^{R_{max}} \sum_{p_{x,y} \in \xi(p_{i,j},r)} v_{x,y}^{(t)}(r)\, p_{x,y}^{(t)} & : \quad if \ \theta_{die} \leq m_{i,j}^{(t)} \leq 1 \end{cases}$$

(4)

Actually, argument θ_{mature} control the evolution level. When agent reach θ_{mature}, it will be stable. Thereafter, this agent will become inactivated and stop evolution. If it do not have a tribe tag yet, it will form a new tribe T_i. While $\theta_{die} \in [0.5, 1]$ determine the noise sensitivity and robust of this algorithm.

2.4 Propagate and Mark

For each mature agent at (i,j), if any neighbor in $\xi(p_{i,j},1)$ has the analogical characteristic vector which satisfied $\|p_{i,j}^{(t)}-p_{x,y}^{(t)}\| \leq \sigma_{min}$, the tribe will propagate to this pixel by assigning the tribe tag $T(k)$ on it. When all the vertices in the image has been marked and be divided to a certain tribe, we get a set of segments T_i successfully.

3 Experimental Results and Conclusions

The proposed approach works on a 256*256 grey-scale[0,255]image, so the feature vector $p_{i,j}$ at each pixel presents grey-scale[0,255]. We assume that threshold parameters satisfy $\beta = gap(1) = gap(2) = gap(3)$. Here β is an important parameter used to control the segment scale. We set $\beta = 24, \theta_{mature} = 0.001, \theta_{die} = 0.75, R_{max} = 3, \varepsilon = 0.05$, weight parameter $v(1) = 0.08, v(2) = 0.04, v(3) = 0.03$, satisfied Definition(2.2), i.e. $v(1)*K(1)+v(2)*K(2)+v(3)*K(3) = 1$. Fig. 2 shows the evolutionary process on segmenting the house image. The advantage

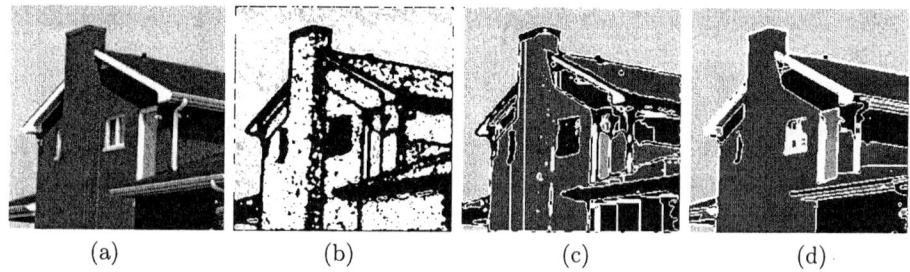

Fig. 2. evolutionary process and the segmentation results of different time steps t, (a) Original input image; (b) step=1; (c) step=5; (d) step=100.

of the Artificial Coevolving Tribes(ACT) model is that it is easy to tune and to optimize. Secondly, the proposed model need not to know a priori information about the image, such as the numbers of segment parts, or the characteristic of the objects and background. In addition, there is little centralized control over the process and consequently, agents evolution along the biological and sociological process and is inherently parallel and autonomous. Finally, as the agents can take various image feature, including texture, color, shape, etc., the proposed method has the capability of incorporating any type of image attribute in any special application, and making this solution both image and application independent.

Acknowledgements

The research work presented in this paper is supported by National Natural Science Foundation of China, project No.60275010; Science and Technology Commission of Shanghai Municipality, project No. 04JC14014; and National Grand Fundamental Research Program of China, project No. 2001CB309401.

References

1. C. G. Langton: Artificial Life: an overview. MIT Press, Cambridge. (1995)
2. Lee MR and Rhee H.: The effect of evolution in artificial life learning behavior. Journal of intelligent & Robotic systems. **30(4)** (2001) 399–414
3. Cufi X. , Munoz X. , Freixenet J.: A review of image segmentation techniques integrating region and boundary information. Advances in Imaging and Electron Physics. **120** (2002) 1–39
4. Hao He and Yan Qiu Chen: Artificial life for Image Segmentation. International Journal of Pattern Recognition and Artificial Intelligence. **15(6)** (2001) 989–1003

Incorporating Web Intelligence into Website Evolution

Jang Hee Lee[1] and Gye Hang Hong[2]

[1] School of Industrial Management, Korea University of Technology and Education,
307 Gajeon-ri, Byeong cheon-myun, Cheonan City,
Choongnam Province 330-708, South Korea
janghlee@kut.ac.kr
[2] Industrial System and Information Engineering, Korea University
kistduck@nate.com

Abstract. Incorporating web intelligence into website is increasingly important, especially in public sector, as the cross-section of user communities is broad. This study presents an intelligent website evolution model of public sector that can continuously provide all the targeted users with different backgrounds with the well-suited web pages to improve their satisfaction, reuse, trust and profits by continuously redesigning the current website. The model can decide what to change next in the website for the improvement of website's outcomes of users using data mining tools and therefore the website evolves.

1 Introduction

Website means the information system of Internet based on web to interactively exchange information and knowledge. In general, it has immense web pages that include countless hyperlinks, however, a small portion of the web pages contain truly relevant or useful information to the website's users. The users have broad and different spectrum of backgrounds, interests, and usage purposes. In particular, the cross-section of user communities in public sector is various, vast and increasingly growing.

Public sector's website provides beneficial public information to these users (e.g., citizens, researchers, public servants in a government agency, other government agency and etc.) and ultimately differs with the private one in its seeking the public benefit and equability. So, public sector's website should be operated for not some users' benefits and their usage elevations but all the users' benefits and their usage elevations. So, it needs to be continuously revised for the users with small benefits/large loss and low usage rates, which we call disadvantaged users.

This study proposes an intelligent evolution model of public sector's website, which can continuously provide all the users including the disadvantaged users with the beneficial information service to improve its outcomes such as their satisfaction, reuse, trust on it and profits to obtain after using its information for their economic behaviors.

It consists of 3 steps: user's current website evaluation based on user satisfaction survey, user segmentation based on user's usage effect and discriminating causal factors identification between user groups, and finally redesigning key web pages in terms of the discriminating causal factors to suit the targeted group's performance improvement. Our model can decide what to change next in the website for the improvement of website's outcome of users through the analysis of user satisfaction survey data using data mining tools. Data mining tools can play an increasingly important role in revising current website and developing the intelligent website.

The research on the website evaluation of public sector has been recently attempted. The technical aspects of Internet such as the connection speed, error rate, number of URL, convenience of use and user's satisfaction in administration service side were proposed as the major criteria of public sector's website evaluation [1]. The research group of cyberspace policy in the university of Arizona proposed 2 evaluation criteria, transparency and accessibility, which focused on the openness of administration [2]. Alesander and Tate proposed 5 evaluation criteria, the information authority, information accuracy, information objectivity, information currency and information coverage of web page [3]. The web support group in New Zealand proposed the evaluation criteria such as scope of content, layout, accessibility, update frequency, extent of feedback, interactivity, site performance, etc [4].

2 Intelligent Website Evolution Using Data Mining Tools

We propose a new intelligent website evolution model using data mining tools for public sector's one, which consists of 3 steps: current website evaluation based on user satisfaction survey, user segmentation based on user's usage effect and discriminating causal factors identification between user groups, and finally redesigning key web pages in terms of the discriminating causal factors to suit the targeted group's performance improvement (refer to Fig. 1).

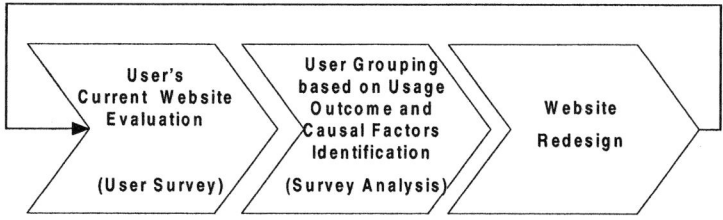

Fig. 1. Intelligent website evolution procedure

2.1 User's Current Website Evaluation

We evaluate the level of user's satisfaction about the current website service, the level of user's reuse intentions, trust on the website and user's usage effects such as profit/loss to obtain after using the website information for user's economic behavior. In this study, we conduct the user satisfaction survey on the website, which asks all the users of website to rate 70 questions addressing website evaluation criteria such as 'Information Content', 'Ease of Use', and user's website usage outcomes such as the level of user's satisfaction, reuse intentions, trust on the website and the level of user's profit/loss, user's demographic information and so on. For the rational survey conduction, we use the major criteria for the website evaluation of federal government of the U.S and NCSI (National Customer Satisfaction Index) model for measuring customer satisfaction, reuse intentions, trust and usage effect in Korea.

'Information Content' and 'Ease of Use' are major criteria for the website evaluation of federal government of the U.S [5]. 'Information content' criteria evaluate the substantive aspects of the website and have 7 sub-criteria, orientation to website, content, currency, bibliographic control, services, accuracy, and privacy. 'Ease of use' criteria evaluate physical movement through the website and have 5 sub-criteria, quality of links, feedback mechanisms, accessibility, design and navigability.

2.2 User Segmentation Based on Usage Outcome and Discriminating Causal Factors Identification Between User Groups

We analyze the user satisfaction survey data and segment all the users based on their levels of satisfaction, reuse intentions, trust on the website and profit/loss. We use SOM (Self-Organizing Map), a special type of neural network using an unsupervised learning scheme, as a clustering tool [6] in order to segment all the users. After SOM using, we obtain several user groups with similar patterns in the satisfaction, reuse intentions, trust and profit/loss.

Among the segmented groups we select the best advantaged group that has the highest level of satisfaction, reuse intentions, trust and profit and then make pairwise comparisons for all two paired user group, the best advantaged group and the other user group among the segmented user groups. In pairwise comparison, we conduct the analysis of survey data using C4.5 [7], a decision tree learning tool, in order to extract the discriminating causal factors in the user satisfaction survey. We choose the nodes appeared in the decision tree generated by C4.5 discriminating causal factors, which can classify the surveyed users into the best advantaged users and the other users with lower ones (i.e., disadvantaged users).

In addition to finding discriminating causal factors, we identify the difference of website usage patterns between the two paired groups by analyzing their web-log data and consequently find the key web pages to be redesigned in the website for the other users' improvement in the level of satisfaction, reuse intentions, trust and profit. We firstly make the summarization table of user, user's total access frequency and connection time of web page during an analyzing time period and the user group to which the user belongs by analyzing user's web-log data. The table describes the access frequency and connection time of all users belonging to the two paired user groups for all possible web pages of current website.

We secondly identify key web pages that can distinguish the best advantaged users from the other users on the basis of website usage patterns by using C 4.5. Like the same way in the identification of discriminating causal factors, we choose the nodes appeared in the decision tree generated by C4.5 key web pages. The generated nodes are the connection time or access frequency of key web pages (e.g., the connection time of web page 38, the access frequency of web page 36) among all possible web pages of current website.

2.3 Redesigning Key Web Pages

For all paired user groups, we differently redesign key web pages in terms of the identified discriminating causal factors for the improvement in the level of satisfaction, reuse intentions, trust and profit of the disadvantaged users. If we provide them with the redesigned key web pages on the basis of discriminating causal factors, their level of satisfaction, reuse intentions, trust and profit can be improved. For the rational evolution of public sector's website, the above described 3 steps are regularly and continuously executed.

3 Conclusion and Further Research

Incorporating web intelligence into website is increasingly important, especially in public sector, as the cross-section of user communities is broad. Our study presents an intelligent website evolution model using data mining tools for web intelligence, which can continuously provide all the targeted users with the lower levels of satisfaction, trust, reuse and benefits with the well-designed information to improve those levels by continuously and suitably redesigning key web pages in the website.

Our evolution model can decide what to change next in the website for the performance improvement of users through the analysis of user satisfaction survey data using data mining tools. We will progress further work about the application of our model to other areas and the supplement of our evaluation model for public sector's website in Usability engineering, requirements engineering, prototyping, and information design.

References

1. Korean National Computerization Agency.: Guide of construction, operation and information resource management of public institution's website. Korean National Computerization Agency. (1999)
2. Research group of cyberspace policy of the university of Arizona.: http://w3.arizona.edu
3. Alesander and Tate.: http://www.widener.edu/wolfgram-memorial-library/inform.htm
4. Web support group of New Zealand.: http://www.theweb.co.nz/govtweb/0115.html
5. Kristin R. E., John C. B., Charles R. M., Steven K. W.: Accessing U.S. Federal Government Websites. Government Information Quarterly. Vol. 14. (1997) 173-189
6. Kohonen, T.: Self-Organization & Associative Memory. 3rd ed. Springer-Verlag, Berlin (1989)
7. Quinlan, J. R.: C4.5: Programs for Machine Learning. Morgan Kaufmann Publishers. San Mateo California (1993)

Evolution of the CPG with Sensory Feedback for Bipedal Locomotion

Sooyol Ok and DuckSool Kim

College of Engineering, TongMyong University of Information Technology,
535 Yongdang-dong, Nam-gu, Busan,
608-711, Rep. of Korea
{sooyol, dskim}@tit.ac.kr

Abstract. This paper shows how the computational model, which simulates the coordinated movements of human-like bipedal locomotion, can be evolutionally generated without the elaboration of manual coding. In the research on bio-mechanical engineering, robotics and neurophysiology, the mechanism of human bipedal walking is of major interest. It can serve as a basis for developing several applications such as computer animation and humanoid robots. Nevertheless, because of the complexity of human's neuronal system that interacts with the body dynamics making the walking movements, much is left unknown about the control mechanism of locomotion, and researchers were looking for the optimal model of the neuronal system by extensive efforts of trial and error. In this work, genetic programming is utilized to induce the model of the neural system automatically and its effectives are shown by simulating a human bipedal gait with the obtained model. The experimental results show some promising evidence for evolutionary generation of the human-like bipedal locomotion.

1 Introduction

Bipedal walking has been extensively studied both in biological science and engineering, but many problems still remain unsolved in designing an optimal controller for bipedal walking to be adopted in diverse applications such as humanoid robotics, computer graphics, and biology.

On the other hand, from basic neuro-physiological experiments, it is now generally accepted that walking of animals is mainly generated at the spinal cord by a combination of a *central pattern generator*(CPG) and reflexes in response to the peripheral stimulus. Also, in a human there is growing evidence that a CPG exists [1][2]. In the study of biomechanical engineering and robotics, CPG with sensory feedback has been formulated as a set of neural oscillators to produce the patterns of oscillations necessary for rhythmic movements such as locomotion and swimming. In the Taga model for bipedal locomotion [10][11], mathematical models of walking were presented based on the theory asserting that the interaction between rhythms generated by the neural system and the musculo-skeletal systems produces autonomous walking movements.

In the Taga system, design of the neural oscillators was carefully hand tuned by the experts to achieve desired movements. Hase [4] applied the idea to human bipedal locomotion, while the method for autonomously determining optimal values of connection coefficients and parameters for neural oscillators was studied using genetic algorithm. However, in their studies a structure of the neural system still had to be predetermined by trial and error, which is quite often the most painful and time-consuming task [14].

This paper describes how a connectionist model of the neural system is constructed to generate bipedal walking without any human interaction, which is validated through experimentation. Since there is no systematic way to determine the structure of the neural system that can generate a described walking movement, the evolutionary approach using *Genetic Programming* (GP) [8][9] is applied to explore the architecture of a connectionist model which determines the muscular activity of a simulated human-like body in interaction with the ground. In this study the creation of sensory feedback pathways as the target to evolve is focused on instead of adopting a handcrafted approach.

In section, the biological model for bipedal locomotion is explained, and then how GP is applied for generating human-like walking patterns is outlined. The details of system implementation and experimental results are then presented and analyzed. The paper ends with a discussion on the results and proposals for future works.

2 Model of Bipedal Locomotion

Neuro-physiological studies on animal locomotion have revealed that the basic rhythm of locomotion is controlled by a rhythm-generation mechanism called the CPG. CPG is a name given to a group of nerve cells in the central nervous system that interacts to produce a coordinated pattern of signals that stimulate muscles to contract in sequence. Taga [10][11] and others applied the idea to human bipedal walking and presented a theory asserting that global entrainment between the neuro-musculo-skeletal system and the environment produces human walking.

The neuronal system autonomously produces rhythmic patterns of neural stimuli and the system of body dynamics generates movements according to the rhythm pattern. Information concerning somatic senses, such as foot-ground contacts and segment angles, is fed back to the neuronal system, and the rhythmic pattern of neural stimuli is regenerated based on this information. This theory holds that the interaction between the neuronal system and the system of body dynamics produces movement. Figure 1 shows a schematic model of the interaction.

Computer simulations have shown that the walking movement generated by this model can adapt to small changes in the environment, such as slopes and mechanical perturbations that occur during walking [15]. A walking model is constructed based on this theory [16].

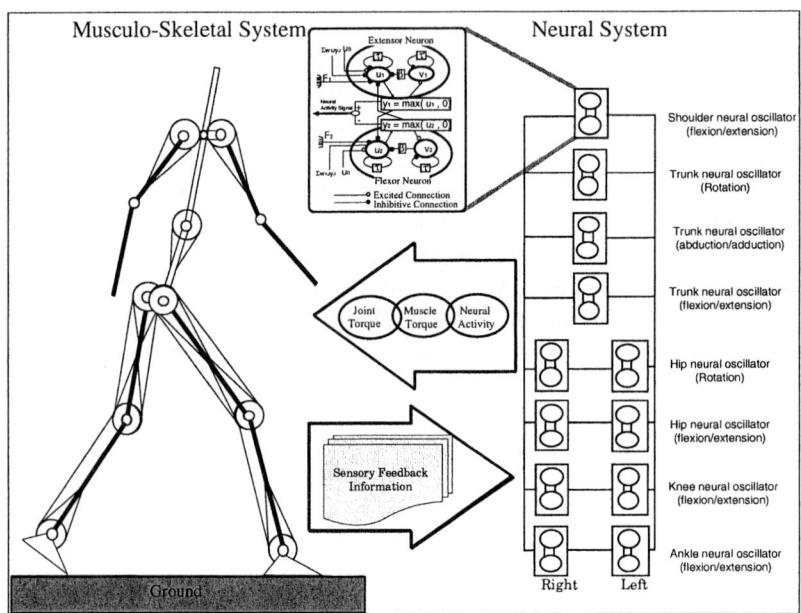

Fig. 1. Overview of 3D autonomous bipedal locomotion system

2.1 3D Model of Body Dynamics

In the present study, the system of body dynamics in bipedal walking is modeled by 12 three-dimensional rigid segments representing feet, shanks, and thighs, lower part of torso, upper part of torso, upper arms, and forearms. A viscoelastic passive moment acts on each joint to represent the influence of soft tissue. The principal 32 muscles involved in movement in the shoulder, waist, and lower extremities were also modeled as shown in Figure 2. Each joint is driven by the moment due to muscular tension and is also affected by the non-linear viscous and elastic moment representing soft tissues such as ligaments. The arrangement of each muscle was represented as a series of line segments, the moment arm of the muscle changes according to joint angle. Each muscle exerts a force in response to stimuli from the neuronal system and drives the body model expressed by the multi rigid-link systems.

The interaction between the foot and the ground is modeled as a combination of spring and damper. Each foot is represented by a triangle of appropriate proportions. The posterior point of the triangle represents the heel where the foot-ground contact is made. The anterior point of the triangle represents the toe where the foot-ground contact ends. The ground reaction forces produced by springs and dampers were assumed to act on four points in each foot: two points in the heel and two points in the toe. This is the most basic model representing the characteristics of human biped walking. The body parameters, such as segment mass, used in the experiments are determined as summarized in Table 1.

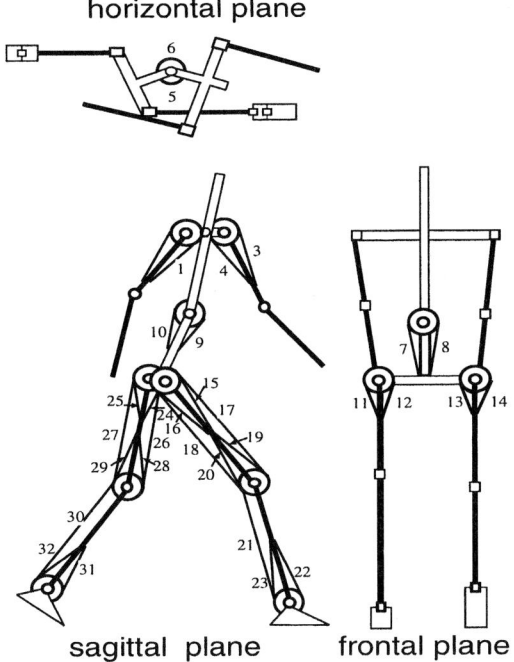

Fig. 2. The three-dimentional body dynamics system with 32 muscles

2.2 Model of Neuronal Controller

The rhythm pattern generator is presented in the Taga model [10] is adopted as a model of the neuronal controller. This neural system represents a rhythm generation mechanism with CPG and is modeled as a network system consisting of a set of neural oscillators. The dynamics of a single neuron can be expressed by the following differential equations:

$$\tau_i \dot{u}_i = -u_i - \sum_j w_{ij} y_j - \beta v_i + u_0 + Feed_i \quad (1)$$

$$\tau'_i \dot{v}_i = -v_i + y_i, \qquad y_i = max(u_i, 0) \quad (2)$$

where, u_i is the inner state of the ith neuron; v_i is the state variable representing the fatigue of the ith neuron; y_i is the output of the ith neuron; u_0 is the constant stimulus; and ; τ, τ' are time constants; and β is the fatigue constant; w_{ij} is a connection weight between neurons in a single neural oscillator which consists of the ith and jth neurons. $Feed_i$ represents the sensory signals fed back from receptors as well as input signals from other neural oscillator. This network is referred to as the feedback network. A feedback network consists of signal information such as sensory signals of inertial angles and angular velocity of joints and the body segments, foot-ground contact data, and the centre of gravity of the entire body. Sensory feedback information modulates and coordinates

Table 1. Body dynamics parameters

Name	Mass (kg)	Moment of inertia (kgm^2) [x, y, z]	Link length (m) [x, y, z]	Center of gravity (m) [x, y, z]
Lower torso	8.5	0.042, 0.041, 0.050	0.00, 0.00, 0.170	0.00, 0.00, 0.085
Upper torso	29.482	1.619, 1.087, 0.378	0.00, 0.00, 0.658	0.00, 0.00, 0.333
Right thigh	6.523	0.113, 0.115, 0.022	0.00, 0.25, 0.405	0.00, 0.00, 0.157
Right calf	2.685	0.039, 0.039, 0.002	0.00, 0.00, 0.415	0.00, 0.00, 0.176
Right foot	0.837	0.003, 0.003, 0.000	0.00, 0.00, 0.150	0.00, 0.00, 0.050
Left thigh	6.523	0.113, 0.115, 0.022	0.00, -0.25, 0.405	0.00, 0.00, 0.157
Left calf	2.685	0.039, 0.039, 0.002	0.00, 0.00, 0.415	0.00, 0.00, 0.176
Left foot	0.837	0.003, 0.003, 0.000	0.00, 0.00, 0.150	0.00, 0.00, 0.050
Right upper arm	1.842	0.013, 0.013, 0.002	0.00, 0.00, 0.282	0.00, 0.00, 0.145
Right forearm	1.513	0.013, 0.013, 0.001	0.00, 0.00, 0.360	0.00, 0.00, 0.120
Left upper arm	1.842	0.013, 0.013, 0.002	0.00, 0.00, 0.282	0.00, 0.00, 0.145
Left forearm	1.513	0.013, 0.013, 0.001	0.00, 0.00, 0.360	0.00, 0.00, 0.120

neuron activity of neural oscillator. In this study, a computational model of the neural system network is constructed based on the following assumptions:

1. A neural oscillator consists of a pair of flexor and extensor neurons and, each neuron produces a signal for either flexion or extension motion of a joint. A neural oscillator exists for each degree of freedom of the joint, and is expressed by the differential equations ((1)-(2)). The neural oscillators are able to generate the basic rhythm of joint movements in walking due to their mutual inhibition. The number of neural oscillators and their inner structure in this study are fixed a priori.
2. Sensory signals of inertial angles, angular velocities, and somatic senses are postulated from sensory receptors.
3. If an output signal of a receptor is connected or fed back to a specific neural oscillator, the same output signal is input to both the flexor and extensor neurons, and this linkage is reciprocal. If one of the connections is inhibitory, then the other connection is excitatory.

There have been many neuro-anatomical and neuro-physiological studies related to reflexes, but no precise mathematical model of the details of the reflex pathways for human gait simulation has been proposed. Therefore, the most difficult problem in constructing the neural system based on the above model is the formulation of a feedback network, which manages the way signals from sensors and other neurons are input to a neuron (i.e., in equation (1)). Although neurons within a single neural oscillator are known to be connected reciprocally to each other, only little is known in the neuro-physiological studies about which receptors and neurons in different neural oscillators are connected and how they are connected. Hence, in developing an artificial neural oscillator system for bipedal locomotion, the feedback networks have been developed by researchers and engineers in a trial and error manner to generate a rhythmic movement that closely matches a human walking pattern.

3 Evolving Neural System

Although the rigid properties of the body and the anatomical properties of the muscle are provided by analyzing body mechanisms, it seems to be extremely difficult to predict or to predetermine the relevancy of sensory feedback pathways in the neural system. As there is no theory about how such a neural system can be constructed, the evolutionary approach is used as a method of choice for building the neural system to control the body dynamics.

Construction of the neural system is modeled as a search process for the structure and parameters of the neural system. Effectiveness of the constructed nervous system is evaluated based on predefined criteria on the walking patterns obtained by simulating interactions among the nervous system, body and environment. It is assumed that the parameters and structures within a single neural oscillator are known and fixed, and attention is focused on the creation of the feedback networks among the neural system and the body dynamics system. This is based on the assumption that each joint (i.e., each neural oscillator) has 2 feedback networks connected to the flexor and extensor neurons. And a feedback network at the joint has a reciprocal value of the other.

In this model of the nervous system, a global feedback network in the neural system is composed of 24 feedback networks. The global feedback network can work consistently only when neural oscillator interact with each other cooperatively through their feedback networks. In this paper, GP is applied with heterogeneous populations to evolve the global feedback network of the nervous system by modeling each feedback network as an independent population of GP individuals.

3.1 Evolutionary Algorithm with Genetic Programming (GP)

GP is an evolutionary search algorithm which searches for a computer program capable of producing the desired solution for a given problem [9]. In a GP population, the individuals represent hierarchical computer programs of various sizes and shapes. In this paper, individuals are s-expressions giving a desired feedback network. A run of GP begins with initial random creation of individuals for the population. Then, on each generation of the run, the fitness of each individual in the population is evaluated, then individuals are selected (probabilistically based on their fitness) to participate in the genetic operations (e.g., reproduction, crossover, mutation). These three steps (fitness evaluation, selection, and genetic operations) are iteratively performed over many generations until the termination criterion for the run is satisfied. Typically, the best single individual obtained during the run is designated as the result of the run.

Of the 12 feedback networks of neural oscillators (i.e., a half of 24 feedback networks due to the reciprocal nature of feedback networks), 8 feedback networks have a symmetric structure because of the left-right symmetry of the human body parts(such as ankles, knees, hip, and waist). Since a human body has a left-right symmetric geometry and walking is left-right alternate movements of the legs, it is safely assumed that the neural oscillators for bipedal locomotion also

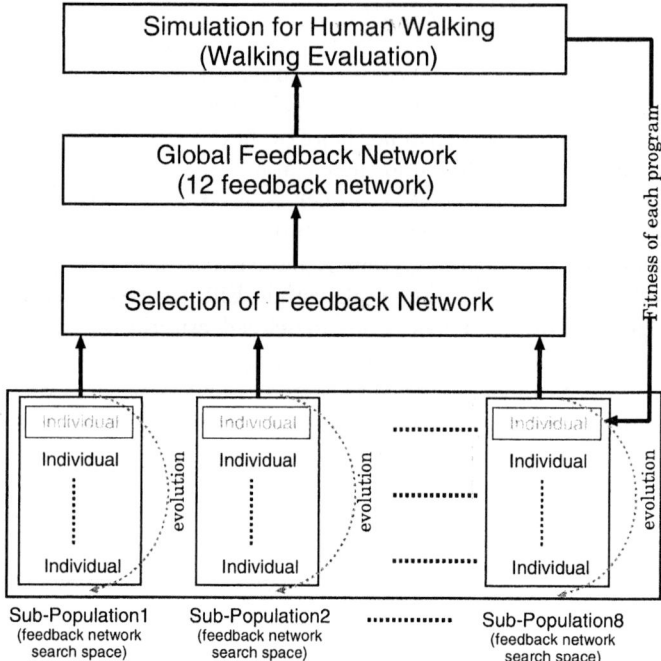

Fig. 3. Evolving feedback network

have left-right symmetric structures. Therefore, in order to construct the neural system for human-like bipedal gait generation, the GP system implemented has 8 distinct sub-populations, each of which corresponds to breeding space for each feedback network. Figure 3 depicts the schematic overview showing how a global feedback network is evolved through the GP system.

Each feedback network can be bred independently within each sub-population of the GP system. The fitness of a feedback network cannot be evaluated separately from the other feedback networks because the fitness should be determined based on the quality of movements that are generated by the interactions among neural oscillators through the global feedback network in the nervous system. Hence, the fitness of a single feedback network must be deduced from the fitness of the entire feedback network.

This is a widely known difficult problem in multi-agent problem solving called *credit assignment*, which is to determine the contribution of each agent when making a solution in cooperation with other agents.

Although there have been many research activities in GP that tackled the problem [5], there is no generic methodology for rational credit assignment. To avoid this problem, groups are formed, each of which representing a global feedback network and consisting of individuals from all sub-populations. The steps in the GP process (selection, evaluation and genetic operation) are executed on the population of groups.

All the individuals in the same group share the same fitness value, thus eliminating credit assignment problem. This is the simplest way of breeding heterogeneous population with GP. In the experiments of generating neural oscillator for bipedal locomotion such an approach has produced some promising results.

4 Implementation

Based on the models of the neuronal system and the musculo-skeletal system described in the previous sections, a system for three dimensional simulation of human-like bipedal locomotion is implemented. For constructing neural oscillators used in the system, GP was used to find appropriate formulation of a feedback network for each neuron, which can cooperatively synthesize human-like bipedal walking movements. Several extended mechanisms of GP for the multi-population learning are proposed in the following:

- Breeding is performed in the same way (selection, and genetic operation) in each subpopulation GP.
- A method applying Automatically Defined Functions Genetic Programming (ADF-GP) is proposed to allow individuals to autonomously learn effectively in order to obtain the feedback networks. By applying the ADF-GP approach, the feedback network can be separated from the actual implementation of each separate sensory module (contact sensory module, angular sensory module, angular velocity sensory module), and both can be simultaneously evolved during the same training run.
- For avoiding physically invalid combinations of terminals in the expressions, several constraints are enforced when creating initial populations randomly.

The developed system consists of a bipedal locomotion dynamics system and evolutionary computation system. The evolutionary computation system utilizes the modified lil-gp system [12] as the platform for GP implementation. Parameters used in the GP system are shown in Table 2. The terminal and function sets used to formulate feedback networks in the simulation are summarized in

Table 2. GP parameters

Maximum generation	500
Reproduction	20%
Mutation	10%
Crossover	70%
Population size	3200
Grow method	FULL
Maximum depth	10
Max mutation depth	5
Selection method	fitness-proportionate greedy overselection
Termination Criterion	After completing 10 walking steps

Table 3. GP Terminals and Functions

		Description	# num
Function set		$+, -, *, \exp, \log$	5
	$H(x) = 1$	(when $x \geq 0$), 0(otherwise)	1
	$Max(x) = x$	(when $x \geq 0$), 0(otherwise)	1
	c_1, c_2, c_3, c_4, c_5	(foot contact phase information)	5
Terminal set	$p_{x,y,z}^{r,l}$	Toe positions in each foot	6
	$\dot{p}_{x,y,z}^{r,l}$	Toe velocities in each foot	6
	a_i^y	Absolute angles at sagittal plane	8
	$\dot{a}_i^y$	Absolute angular velocities at sagittal plane	8
	$cog_{x,y,z}$	Position of center of gravity	3
	$\dot{cog}_{x,y,z}$	Velocity of center of gravity	3
	E_1, E_2, E_3, E_4	Ephemeral random constant	4
	ADF_1	Angle sensory module	1
	ADF_2	Angular velocity sensory module	1
	ADF_3	foot contact phase module	1

Table 3. In the simulation, the differential equations are numerically solved by the improved Euler method with a time step-size of $0.5ms$. The parameters in the equations ((1)-(2)) such as the time constants ((τ, τ')), the fatigue constant(β) were determined a priori so that they could oscillate at a rate of about $1s$ per cycle. A PC cluster machine consisting of 32 CPU's is used for computing the fitness of each GP individual in parallel. Since calculating fitness requires a full simulation of bipedal walking, distribution of the task to many processing elements improved the efficiency of experiments in a nearly linear fashion. All Programs are written in C language on a Linux system.

4.1 Fitness Functions Design of the GP

Fitness of a GP individual is calculated based on the generated walking pattern of human-like 3D model with the evolved neural oscillators. A walking pattern of the simulation was evaluated with a hierarchical hybrid fitness function which is employed as the evaluative criterion for normal walking.

The first criterion combines the distance it could walk before falling down, the number of steps it made while walking, and the horizontal and vertical shakes of the body. After stable walking was achieved, the second criterion is defined with the following considerations from a biomechanical viewpoint: (1) Metabolic energy consumption was calculated from muscular tension. (2) Muscular fatigue was calculated from muscular stress. (3) Load on the skeletal system was calculated from the maximum moment and reaction forces acting on the joints. These three values were normalized by body weight and traveling distance based on a formula for level locomotive efficiency. This criterion is determined so as to minimize energy consumption in the entire body per unit locomotion distance. Fitness functions used in the simulation are shown in Table 4.

Table 4. Fitness functions of the GP

Fitness function1	$a_1 D + a_2 S + a_3 Z + a_4 Y \longrightarrow$ (max) where, $a_{1,...,4}$ are coefficients defining a weight of each criterion in the fitness function1 and their values are decided heuristically as $a_1 = 0.9, a_2 = 0.1, a_3 = -0.05 a_4 = -0.05$; D is the distance it could walk before falling down; S is the number of the steps made during walking; Z is the average of vertical vibrations of the body ; Y is the difference of a horizontal position of its center of the gravity from the initial position to the final position where it fell down
Fitness function2	$$\int (\sum_m \dot{E}_m + \dot{B}) dt / MgD \longrightarrow (min)$$ where, E is the energy consumption rate in the mth muscle; B is the energy consumption rate in regions other than muscles (e.g. ,internal organs);M is the body mass; g is the acceleration due to gravity; D is the traveling distance

5 Simulation and Results

The simulation result of GP run for the desired normal walking pattern is shown in Figure 4, which plots the fitness values with generations. In the simulation, only 10 steps of walking were successfully generated as shown in Figure 5. Figure 6 shows the result of angle and angular velocities of a thigh, a calf and a foot joint in the resultant simulation.

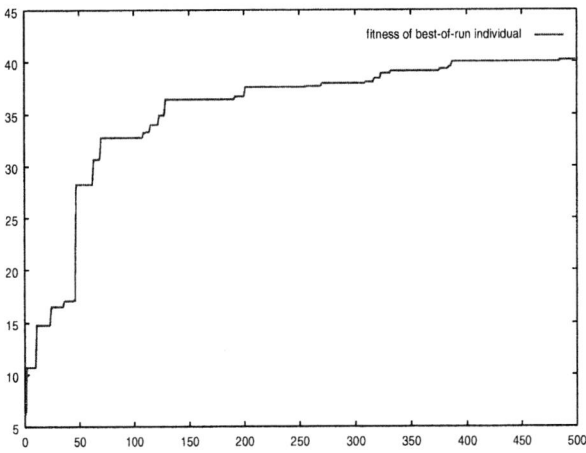

Fig. 4. Fitness transition

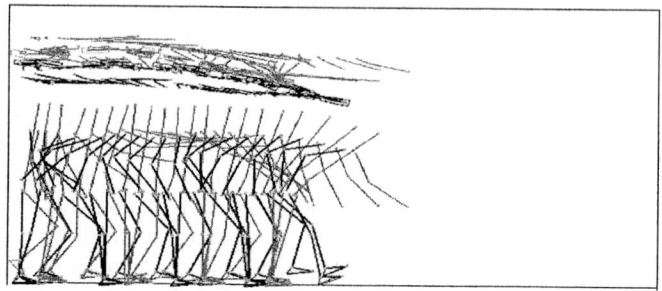

Fig. 5. Emerged walking pattern

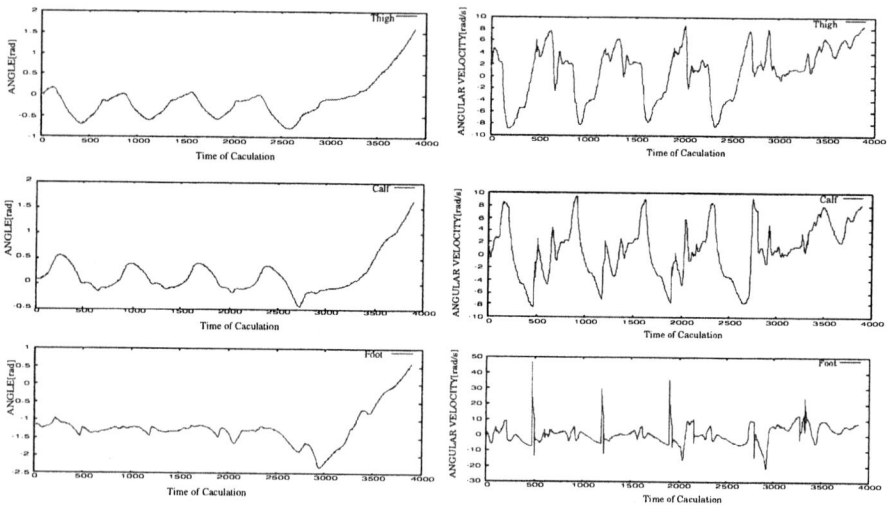

Fig. 6. Angle and angular velocity plots of thigh, calf and foot

From these results, it is clear that those joints have cyclic movements in the simulation. In Figure 7, the phase plots of those joint are presented, where X-axis shows a joint angle and Y-axis shows an angular velocity. This graph shows that the evolved neural oscillator succeeded in generating rhythmical walking movements in the sagittal plane. However, in the simulations the resultant limit cycles are not stable and steady enough for generating locomotion that can walk more than 10 steps before falling down.

The resultant feedback networks are simple enough to be further evolved for generating improved locomotion. Nevertheless, we need to make the evolution process more efficient. For producing better stable feedback networks more sophisticated fitness functions are required. One way of improving is to consider more biomechanical insights on human walking such as smoothness of motion.

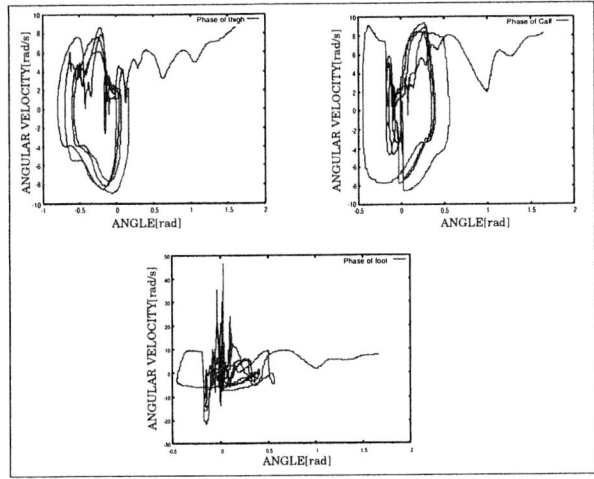

Fig. 7. Phase plots of thigh, calf and foot

By including such factors, the fitness function can direct the GP search process to evolve the desirable bipedal locomotion more efficiently.

6 Conclusion

In this paper, evolutionary creation of an adaptive sensory feedback for a bipedal locomotion is investigated. The proposed evolutionary approach using GP was applied to explore the interactions between neurons, the body and the environment. Using GP for constructing the nervous system model for bipedal walking, the tedious task of searching for appropriate parameter values and network structures of neural oscillators is automated. Comparing with the past research activities which built the neuronal models in a hand-crafted manner, the proposed approach is less dependent on human experts, thus enabling the production of a wide variety of walking patterns for different body configurations efficiently. The approach makes it affordable to utilize a flexible human model for generating locomotion patterns in several practical applications such as humanoid robots and computer animation.

As shown in Table 3, the number of terminals sums up to 41. Since the neuro-physiological study has not clarified the details of the neuronal system that enables bipedal locomotion in the human body, the relevant set of terminals could not be selected exclusively for the desired walking but had to use many terminals as plausible members of the terminal set. Utilizing the adaptive terminal selection method [13] can reduce the GP search space by selecting the relevant nervous attributes for bipedal locomotion, and improve efficiency of the GP process for constructing a model of the neuronal system.

Acknowledgment

This research was supported by the MIC(Ministry of Information and Communication), Korea, under the ITRC(Information Technology Research Center) support program supervised by the IITA(Institute of Information Technology Assessment.

References

1. Dimitrijevic, MR., Gerasimenko, Y., Pinter, MM.: Evidence for a spinal central pattern generator in humans. Annals of the New York Academy of Sciences, **860** (1998) 360–376
2. Duysens, J., Van de Crommert, HWAA.: Neural control of locomotion; part 1. The central pattern generator from cats to humans. Gait Posture, **7** (1998) 131–141
3. Garis, H.: Genetic Programming: building artificial nervous systems using genetically programmed neural networks modules. in Proc of the 7th Internatinal Conference on Machine Learning (1990) 132–139
4. Hase, K., Yamazaki, N.: Computational evolution of human bipedal walking by a neuro-musculo-skeletal model. Artificial Life and Robotics, **3** (1999) 133–138
5. Iba, H.: Evolving multiple agents by genetic programming, Advances in Genetic Programming. MIT Press, Cambridge, Massachusetts, (1999) 447–466
6. Ito, S., Yuasa, H., Luo, Z., Ito, K.: Generation of Locomotion Patterns according to the Energy Consumption. in Proc. of 12th. Annual Conf. of Robotics Society of Japan, (1994) 1159–1160
7. Kimura, H., Sakurama, K. Akiyama, S.: Dynamic Walking and Running of the Quadrupled Using Neural Oscillator. In Proc. of IROS98, (1998) 50–57
8. Koza, J.R., Rice, J.P.: Genetic Generation of Both the Weights and Architecture for a Neural Network. In Proc. of the IEEE International Joint Conference on Neural Networks, **2** (1991) 397–404
9. Koza, J.R.: Genetic Programming: On the Programming of Computers by Means of Natural Selection. MIT Press, Cambridge, Massachusetts, (1992)
10. Taga, G.: A model of the neuro-musculo-skeletal system for human locomotion. I. Emergence of basic gait. Biological Cybernetics, **73** (1995) 97–111
11. Taga, G.: A model of the neuro-musculo-skeletal system for human locomotion. II. Real-time adaptability under various constraints. Biological Cybernetics, **73** (1995) 113–121
12. Zongker, D., Punch, B.: lil-gp 1.0 User's Manual. (1995).
13. Ok. S., Miyashita, K. Nishihara, S.: Improving performance of GP by adaptive terminal selection. In Proc. of PRICAI2000, (2000) 435–445
14. Hase,K., Miyashita, K., Ok, S. Arakawa,Y.: Human gait simulation with a neuromusculoskeletal model and evolutionary computation. Journal of Visualization and Computer Animation, **14(2)** (2003) 73-92
15. Taga, G.: A model of the neuro-musculo-skeletal system for anticipatory adjustment of human locomotion during obstacle avoidance. Biological Cybernetics, **78(1)** (1998) 9–17
16. Inada, H., Ishii, K.: Behavior Generation of Bipedal Robot Using Central Pattern Generator(CPG) (1st Report: CPG Parameters Searching Method by Genetic Algorithm). Proc. of IROS'03, (2003) 2179–2184

Immunity-Based Genetic Algorithm for Classification Rule Discovery

Ziqiang Wang and Dexian Zhang

School of Information Science and Engineering,
Henan University of Technology, Zheng Zhou 450052, P.R. China
wzqagent@xinhuanet.com

Abstract. Immune algorithm is a global optimal algorithms based on the biological immune theory. In this paper, a novel immune algorithm is proposed for classification rule discovery. The idea of immunity is mainly realized through two steps based on reasonably selecting vaccines, i.e., a vaccination and an immune selection. Experimental results show that immune algorithm performs better than RISE with respect to predictive accuracy and rule list mined simplicity.

1 Introduction

Classification rule discovery is one of the important problems in the emerging field of data mining which is aimed at finding a small set of rules from training data set with predetermined targets[1-4].The classification problem becomes very hard when the number of possible different combinations of parameters is so high that algorithms based on exhaustive searches of the parameter space rapidly become computationally infeasible.

The self-adaptability of evolutionary algorithms (EAs)[5] based on population is extremely appealing for the tasks of data mining. Thus it is natural to devote attention to a heuristic approach to find a "good-enough" solution to the classification problem[6-9]. Although GAs have been successfully employed in solving classification rule mining, GAs have the following drawbacks: they make individuals change randomly and indirectly during the whole process, they not only give the individuals the evolutionary chance but also cause certain degeneracy. To overcome the above shortcomings of GA, a novel evolutionary algorithms based on immunity, which are usually simple called immune algorithms(IAs)[10,11], are proposed to this problem. In this paper, the application of IAs in classification rule discovery is introduced, experimental results show that the classification rules discovered by IAs have higher predictive accuracy and much smaller rule list than by the vast majority of data mining systems.

2 Immune Algorithm

In the view of biology, evolution is a process of optimizing population with the selection mechanism. Immunity is the means by which the organism protects itself through the neutralization between antibodies and antigens. If an original genetic algorithm is considered as an organism, then the degeneracy rising inevitably from performing the algorithm can be regarded as an outside antigen. It can be just looked upon as an neutral course that the algorithm utilizes the characteristic information of the pending problem to restrain the above degeneracy through vaccination. The vaccination takes effect of survival of the fittest on the original genetic algorithm, keeps its every operation in the optimal direction, and then realizes the goal of immunity.

The aim of leading immune concepts and methods into GAs is theoretically to utilize the locally characteristic information for seeking the ways and means of finding the optimal solution when dealing with difficult problems. To be exact, it utilizes the local information to intervene in the globally parallel process and restrain or avoid repetitive and useless work during the course, so as to overcome the blindness in action of the crossover and mutation. During the actual operation, IAs refrains the degenerative phenomena arising from the evolutionary process, thus making the fitness of population increase steadily. Because this course is very similar to that of immune phenomenon in nature, the algorithm based on the above idea is named the IAs for the purpose of simplicity and direct-perception. A high-level description of Immune algorithm [10] is shown in Algorithm 1.

Algorithm 1: A high-level description of the immune algorithm
Step1: Create initial random population A_1.
Step2: Abstract vaccines according to the prior knowledge.
Step3: IF the current population contains the optimal individual, THEN the course halts; Or ELSE, continues.
Step4: Perform crossover on the kth parent A_k and obtain the results B_k.
Step5: Perform mutation on B_k and obtain C_k.
Step6: Perform vaccination on C_k and obtain D_k.
Step7: Perform immune selection on D_k and obtain the next parent A_{k+1}, and then go to Step3.

To be more exact, the idea of immunity is mainly realized through two steps based on reasonably selecting vaccines, i.e., a vaccination and an immune selection, of which the former is used for raising fitness and the latter is for preventing the deterioration.

3 Immune Algorithm for Classification Rule Discovery

3.1 Individual Representation

In IA, The genome of an individual (antibody) consists of a conjunction of conditions composing the antecedent (IF part) of the rule. Each antibody represents a conjunction of conditions composing a given rule antecedent. Each condition is an attribute-value pair. The consequent (THEN part) of the rule, which specifies the predicted class, is not represented in the genome. The rule antecedent contains a variable number of rule conditions. In our IA the maximum number of conditions, n. To represent a variable-length rule antecedent (phenotype) we use a fixed-length genome, for the sake of simplicity. For a given IA run, the genome of an individual consists of n genes, where $n = m - k$, m is the total number of predictor attributes in the data set and k is the number of ancestor nodes of the decision tree leaf node identifying the small disjunct in question. Hence, the genome of a IA individual contains only the attributes that were not used to label any ancestor of the leaf node defining that small disjunct.

The overall structure of the genome of an individual is illustrated in Figure 1. Each gene represents a rule condition of the form $A_i OP_i V_{ij}$, where the subscript i identifies the rule condition, $i = 1, 2, \cdots, n$; A_i is the ith attribute; V_{ij} is the jth value of the domain of A_i; and OP_i is a logical/relational operator compatible with attribute A_i. Each gene consists of four elements as follows:

1) Identification of a given predictor attribute, $i = 1, 2, \cdots, n$.

2) Identification of a logical/relational operator OP_i. For categorical (nominal) attributes, OP_i is "in". For continuous (real-valued) attributes, OP_i is either " $\geq$ " or " $\leq$ ". We have considered four types of possible condition operations: $(1) A_i \in [k_1, k_2]$, $(2) A_i \leq k_1$, $(3) A_i \geq k_2$, $(4) A_i \leq k_1 \, or \, A_i \geq k_2$, where k_1 and k_2 are numerical constants.

3) Identification of a set of attribute values $\{V_{i1}, V_{i2}, \cdots, V_{ik}\}$.

4) A flag, called the active bit F_i, which takes on 1 or 0 to indicate whether or not, respectively, the ith condition is presented in the rule antecedent.

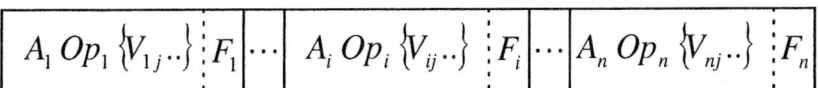

Fig. 1. Structure of an individual (antibody)

3.2 Fitness Function

To evaluate the goodness of an individual an appropriate fitness function is to be considered. Taking in mind that most data mining systems rely on Ockham's razor("the simpler a description, the more likely it is that it describes some really existing relationships in the database "), we have decide to yield a more discriminating fitness function. In particular we have considered two quantities which take into account in some way the simplicity and the compactness of the description.

The concept of simplicity is incorporated in the function f_1, and it is related to the number of conditions. Its definition is as follows:

$$f_1 = 1 - \frac{n_c}{n} \qquad (1)$$

where n_c is the number of the conditions present in the actual description, and n is the maximum number of conditions that in our encoding corresponds to the number of attributes.

The compactness is considered in the function f_2. For each condition in the current rule the ratio between the range of the corresponding attribute and the range of the domain of the attribute is evaluated. The function f_2 is given by the sum of all these ratios divided by n_c. This factor varies in $(0.0, 1.0)$ and it gives an indication on the strength of the conditions present in the rule. The definition of function f_2 is as follows:

$$f_2 = 1 - \frac{1}{n_c} \sum_{i=1}^{n_c} \frac{\chi_i}{\Delta_i} \qquad (2)$$

where $\Delta_i = (max_i - min_i)$ is the range of the domain of the ith attribute and χ_i is given by the following equation:

$$\chi_i = \begin{cases} k_2 - k_1 : & if A_i \in [k_1, k_2] \\ k_1 - min_i : & if A_i \leq k_1 \\ max_i - k_2 : & if A_i \geq k_2 \\ \Delta_i - (k_2 - k_1) : & if A_i \leq k_1 \, or \, A_i \geq k_2 \end{cases} \qquad (3)$$

where k_1 and k_2 are defined as above.

Then, our fitness function f is defined as follows:

$$f = \frac{1}{\omega_1 + \omega_2}(\omega_1 f_1 + \omega_2 f_2) \qquad (4)$$

where ω_1 and ω_2 are weights, their values are range $(0.0, 1.0)$ in order not to affect too much the evaluation of the description.

3.3 Adaptive Mutation Operator

Tradition bit inversion is used on mutation. However, Experiments show that many examples will not be matched if we keep number of 1's and 0's approximately equivalent in an individual. The learning process will become a majority guess if there are too many unmated example. Therefore, we propose a strategy of a adaptive mutation in which the inversion probability from 1 to 0(from 0 to 1) is self-adaptive during the process of run. The adaptive mutation biases the population toward generating rules with more coverage on training examples. The self-adaptation of inversion probability makes the optimal mutation parameter be automatically adjusted. The process of self-adaptive mutation is described as follows:

1) An individual inversion probability is set. Use this probability on mutation to produce a new generation. Calculate the average fitness of this generation.

2) Randomly select the direction of changing this probability (e.g., decrease or increase). Modify the probability along that direction with a small amount. Use the new probability to produce the next generation and calculate the average fitness of the new generation.

3) If the fitness is better (value is larger), continue on this direction and the amount of change is:

$$\Delta f = max\{0.05, (\frac{f_{new}}{f_{old}} - 1) \times 0.15\} \qquad (5)$$

If the fitness is worse (value is smaller), reverse this direction and the amount of change is:

$$\Delta f = max\{0.05, (1 - \frac{f_{new}}{f_{old}}) \times 0.1\} \quad (6)$$

Use the new probability to produce the next generation.

3.4 Immune Operators

In fact, the idea of immunity is mainly realized through two steps based on reasonably selecting vaccines[10], i.e., a vaccination and an immune selection, of which the former is used for raising fitness and the latter is for preventing the deterioration. Now they are explained as follows.

1) The Vaccination: Given an individual x, a vaccination means modifying the genes on some bits in accordance with priori knowledge so as to gain higher fitness with greater probability. This operation must satisfy the following two conditions. Firstly, if the information on each gene bit of an individual y is wrong, i.e., each bit of it is different from that of the optimal one, then the probability of transforming from x to y is 0. Secondly, if the information on each gene bit of is right, i.e., is the optimal one, then the probability of transforming from x to x is 1. Suppose a population is $c = (x_1, x_2, \cdots, x_{n_p})$, then the vaccination on c means the operation carried out on $n_p = \alpha n$ individuals which are selected from c in proportion as α. A vaccine is abstracted from the prior knowledge of the pending problem, whose information amount and validity play an important role in the performance of the algorithm.

2) The Immune Selection: This operation is accomplished by the following two steps. The first one is the immune test, i.e., testing the antibodies. If the fitness is smaller than that of the parent, which means serious degeneration must have happened in the process of crossover or mutation, then instead of the individual the parent will participate in the next competition; the second one is the annealing selection[12], i.e., selecting an individual x_i in the present offspring $E_k = (x_1, x_2, \cdots, x_{n_p})$ to join in the new parents with the probability as follows:

$$P(x_i) = \frac{e^{\frac{f(x_i)}{T_k}}}{\sum_{i=1}^{n_p} e^{\frac{f(x_i)}{T_k}}} \quad (7)$$

where $f(x_i)$ is the fitness of the individual x_i, $\{T_k\}$ is the temperature-controlled series approaching 0, i.e.,

$$T_k = \ln(\frac{T_0}{k} + 1) \quad (8)$$

4 Computational Results

To evaluate performance of our proposed immune algorithm for classification rule discovery, we have conducted experiment with it on a number of datasets taken from the UCI repository[13]. The main characteristics of the data sets used in our experiment are summarized in Table 1. The first column of this table gives the data set name, while the other columns indicate, respectively, the number of cases, the number of categorical attributes, the number of continuous attributes, and the number of classes of the data set. We have evaluated the performance of immune algorithm(IA) by comparing it with RISE[14], a well-known classification-rule discovery algorithm. All the results of the comparison were obtained using a Pentium 4 PC with clock rate of 2.2G MHz and 256 MB of main memory.

Table 1. Data Sets Used in Experiments

Data set	#Cases	#Categ. Attrib.	#Contin. Attrib.	#Classes
Ljubljana Cancer	282	9	-	2
Wisconsin Cancer	683	-	9	2
Tic-tac-toe	958	9	-	2
Dermatology	366	33	1	6
Hepatitis	155	13	6	2
Cleveland Disease	303	8	5	5

The comparison was carried out across two criteria, namely, the predictive accuracy of the discovered rule lists and their simplicity. Predictive accuracy was measured by a well-known ten-fold cross-validation procedure [15]. In essence, each data set is divided into ten mutually exclusive and exhaustive partitions and the algorithm is run once for each partition. Each time, a different partition is used as the test set and the other nine partitions are grouped together and used as the training set. The predictive accuracies (on the test set) of the ten runs are then averaged and reported as the predictive accuracy of the discovered rule list.

The results comparing the predictive accuracy of immune algorithm and RISE are reported in Table 2, where the " $\pm$ " symbol denotes the standard deviation of the corresponding predictive accuracies rates. It can be seen that predictive accuracy of immune algorithm is higher than that of RISE. As shown in this table, immune algorithm discovered rules with a better predictive accuracy than RISE in all data sets.

Table 2. Predictive Accuracy Comparison

Data set	Immune Algorithm(%)	RISE(%)
Ljubljana Cancer	76.36 $\pm$ 0.49	68.58 $\pm$ 0.64
Wisconsin Cancer	96.18 $\pm$ 0.71	94.69 $\pm$ 0.72
Tic-tac-toe	97.84 $\pm$ 0.43	96.56 $\pm$ 0.45
Dermatology	93.28 $\pm$ 0.63	90.78 $\pm$ 0.83
Hepatitis	92.57 $\pm$ 0.29	91.14 $\pm$ 0.57
Cleveland Disease	58.85 $\pm$ 0.51	57.59 $\pm$ 0.85

We also compare the results concerning the simplicity of the discovered rule list, measured, as usual in the literature, by the number of discovered rules and the average number of terms (conditions) per rule. The results comparing the simplicity of the rule lists discovered by immune algorithm(IA) and by RISE are reported in Table 3.

Table 3. Simplicity of Discovered Rule List Comparison

Data set	Immune Algorithm(%)	RISE(%)
Ljubljana Cancer	9.24 ± 0.17	25.38 ± 0.87
Wisconsin Cancer	8.63 ± 0.48	12.57 ± 0.63
Tic-tac-toe	10.14 ± 0.36	26.61 ± 0.43
Dermatology	7.63 ± 0.37	14.43 ± 0.51
Hepatitis	5.67 ± 0.19	6.43 ± 0.31
Cleveland Disease	11.28 ± 0.31	32.37 ± 0.67

A disadvantage of our immune algorithm is that it is much more computationally expensive than the use of RISE alone. This point is left for future research.

5 Conclusions

A novel evolutionary algorithm based on biological immune theory, called immune algorithm, is proposed to mine classification rule in this paper. The idea of immunity is mainly realized through two steps based on reasonably selecting vaccines, i.e., a vaccination and an immune selection, of which the former is used for raising fitness and the latter is for preventing the deterioration. We have compared the performance of immune algorithm and RISE in public domain data sets. Experimental results show that immune algorithm has a higher predictive accuracy and much smaller rule list than RISE.

References

1. Fayyad,U.M.,Piatetsky-Shapiro,G.,Smyth,P.: From data mining to knowledge discovery: an overview. In Advances in Knowledge Discovery and Data Mining.AAAI Press(1996)1–34
2. Quinlan,J.R.:Induction of decision trees. Machine Learning.1(1986)81-106
3. Ziarko,W.:Rough Sets, Fuzzy Set and Knowledge Discovery.Springer-Verlag(1994)
4. Lu,H.,Setiono,R.,Liu,H.:NeuroRule: a connectionist approach to data mining. In Proc. of the 21st International Conference on Very large Data Bases,Zurich, Switzerland(1995)478–489
5. Fogel,B.: Evolutionary Computation: Toward a New Philosophy of Machine Intelligence.IEEE Press(1994)
6. Goldberg,D.E.:Genetic Algorithms in Search, Optimization, and Machine Learning. Addison-Wesley(1989)

7. Yang,L.,Widyantoro,D.H.,Ioerger,T.,Yen,J.:An entropy-based adaptive genetic algorithm for learning classification rules.In IEEE Proceedings of the 2001 Congress on Evolutionary Computation,Seoul,Korea(2001)790–796
8. Carvalho,D.R.,Freitas,A.A.:A genetic-algorithm for discovering small-disjunct rules in data mining.Applied Soft Computing.2(2002)75–88
9. Falco,I.D.,Iazzetta,A.,Tarantino,E.,Cioppa,A.D.:An evolutionary system for automatic explicit rule extraction.IEEE Proceedings of the 2000 Congress on Evolutionary Computation. 1(2000)450–457
10. Jiao,L.C.,Wang L.:A novel genetic algorithm based on Immunity. IEEE Transactions on Systems,Man,And Cybernetics-Part A:System and Humans.30(2000)552–561
11. Wang,L.,Jiao,L.C.:Immune Evolutionary Algorithms.In Proceedings of 5th International Conference on Signal Processing,Beijing,China(2000)21–25
12. Zhang,J.S.,Xu,Z.B.,Liang Y.:The whole annealing genetic algorithms and their sufficient and necessary conditions of convergence. Science in China. 27(1997)154–164
13. Hettich,S.,Bay,S.D.:The UCI KDD Archive, URL:http://kdd.ics.uci.edu,1999
14. Domingos P.:Unifying instance-based and rule-based induction. Machine Learning. 24(1996)141–168
15. Weiss,S.M.,Kulikowski,C.A.:Computer Systems that Learn. Morgan Kaufmann (1991)

Dynamical Proportion Portfolio Insurance with Genetic Programming

Jiah-Shing Chen and Chia-Lan Chang

Department of Information Management,
National Central University,
Jungli, Taniwan 320
{jschen, lans}@mgt.ncu.edu.tw

Abstract. This paper proposes a dynamic proportion portfolio insurance (DPPI) strategy based on the popular constant proportion portfolio insurance (CPPI) strategy. The constant multiplier in CPPI is generally regarded as the risk multiplier. Since the market changes constantly, we think that the risk multiplier should change accordingly. This research identifies factors relating to market volatility. These factors are built into equation trees by genetic programming. Experimental results show that our DPPI strategy is more profitable than traditional CPPI strategy.

1 Introduction

Constant proportion portfolio insurance (CPPI) is a simple strategy based on an investor's preference of risk to calculate the amounts invested in risky assets. The rest of capital is invested in risk-free assets or just keep in hand. The purpose of CPPI is to help investors gain the opportunity to capture the upside potential of the equity market while maintaining a floor for the portfolio.

Because the risk multiplier in the CPPI is predetermined by the investors, incorrect expectations of the market will result in loss [8]. When the market becomes more volatile, the protection level error with the large multiple will increase substantially. Thus, a new dynamic hedging model is needed to be developed [29]. Although the concept of CPPI originally requires no volatility estimation for its implementation, choosing multiple and floor according to market volatility is necessary and performance of strategy is mostly affected by market trends. Investors should adjust the multiple in CPPI to adapt to the changing circumstances [5, 2].

As a result, this paper proposes a new trading strategy, named dynamic proportion portfolio insurance (DPPI), based on the market volatility factors which are built into equation trees for risk multiplier by genetic programming. The performance of DPPI is evaluated to compare with traditional CPPI.

The rest of this paper is organized as follows. Section 2 introduces the background about the researches on traditional CPPI, risk multiplier, market volatility factors, and technical indicators. A review of genetic programming, the experimental tool used in this paper, is given in Section 3. Section 4 describes our proposed approach of dynamic proportion portfolio insurance (DPPI). The experiment results will be presented in Section 5. The concluding remarks and discussion of future research are stated in Section 6.

2 Background

2.1 Constant Proportion Portfolio Insurance

Constant proportion portfolio insurance (CPPI) is introduced by Black and Jones in 1987 [2]. The portfolio contains an active asset and a reserved asset, such as a risk-free asset. The active asset has higher expected return than the reserved asset. For example, the active asset is stock while the reserved asset might be bills. The theory can be explained by the following formula:

$$E = M \times (A - F), \qquad (1)$$

where "E" is the exposure, i.e., the positions invested in the active assets; "A" is the asset, i.e., the value of investor's portfolio; and "F" is the floor, i.e., the lowest acceptable value of the portfolio. The difference between asset and floor computes the cushion as the excess of the portfolio value over the floor. In addition, "M" is the risk multiplier, i.e., the ratio of the initial exposure to the initial cushion. When the market trend goes up or down, the initial portfolio value will change and the cushion is also different from its initial value. The variable cushion multiplies the constant risk multiplier, which is predetermined by investors, to get the new value of exposure.

This simple formula is easily understood by investors and helps them design their own strategy to meet their preference level for risk. However, setting the best risk multiplier is a difficult task.

2.2 Deciding the Risk Multiplier in CPPI

Genetic algorithms (GA) have been used to optimize the risk multiplier in CPPI instead of the investor's experiences. By using the Sharpe ratio as fitness function, GA can pick the best risk multiplier from historical data [4].

Investors can use this method to optimize the risk multiplier in the CPPI formula, but the risk multiplier is still a constant and does not adapt to the changing market conditions.

2.3 The Market Volatility Factors

The factors affecting market volatility have been researched for years. Schwert used standard deviation of stock returns to estimate the market volatility [24]. Furthermore, the standard deviation of stock returns will decrease while investment duration increases [12]. The book-to-market ratio helps much explain the average stock returns. The two have strong positive relationship [9]. When the average beta of portfolio is greater than 1, there exists a positive autocorrelation between market volatility and portfolio [23]. The beta of portfolio is the sum of individual assets' betas multiplied by their weights. Since the betas are not usually changeable, this paper uses buy price, sell price, risk-free rate, and market factor as volatility factors instead of betas according to the Capital Asset Pricing Model (CAPM). Besides, the exchange rate has negative correlation with market volatility [6]. Lastly, trading volume turnover rate of stock market can explain the short-term volatility [10, 22], and the trading volume turnover rates of individual stocks are also considered.

2.4 Technical Indicators

As for technical indicators, Levy pointed out that technical analysis is able to predict the stock price variability [17]. The concept behind the stock price variability is a part of phenomenon representing market volatility. Thus, the technical indicators are also used in this paper to evaluate the risk multiplier. The technical indicators used in several academic papers are listed in Table 1. The 5 frequently used technical indicators in the Table I are adopted in this paper with the moving average (MA) replaced by disparity index since the MA represents the absolute value while the disparity index represents the divergence of price from moving average [21]. In sum, disparity index, relative strength index (RSI), stochastic oscillator (STO), William's %R, and money flow index (MFI) are used in this paper.

Table 1. Technical indicators used in academic papers

Technical indicators Source	MA	RSI	STO	%R	MFI	CVI
Levy (1967) [18]		X				
Pruitt & White (1988) [20]	X	X				X
Brock et al. (1992) [3]	X					
Tsaih et al. (1998) [28]		X	X			
Carroll et al. (1998) [1]		X			X	
Kim & Han (2000) [13]		X	X	X		
Suraphan et al.(2003) [26]	X	X	X	X	X	

3 Genetic Programming

Genetic Programming [14] is a recent development which extends classical genetic algorithms [16] to process non-linear problem structure. This optimization technique is based on the principles of natural evolution, which consists of several genetic operators: selection of the fittest, crossover, and mutation. The major difference between genetic programming and genetic algorithms is the representation of the solution candidates. A hierarchical tree structure represents the solution candidates in genetic programming while a string of characters with a fixed length, called chromosome, represents the solution candidates in genetic algorithms. The genetic programming framework consists of the following elements: node definitions, initialization, fitness evaluation, selection, reproduction and crossover, mutation, and termination condition.

- *Node Definitions*: The nodes in the tree structure of genetic programming can be classified into two types. One of them is the terminal set which corresponds to the inputs of the program. It is determined according to the domain of problems and the elements can be constants or variables. Another one is the function set which may be standard arithmetic operations, standard programming operations, standard mathematical functions, logical functions, or domain-specific functions. The terminal set and the function set are used to construct expression trees which are solutions to the problem.
- *Initialization*: Genetic programming starts with an initial population which is a set of randomly generated expression trees.
- *Fitness Evaluation*: The evolutionary process is driven by a fitness that evaluates how well each individual performs in the problem environment.
- *Selection*: The selection method determines how to select individuals from the population to be parents for crossover. Parents with better quality are usually selected with the hope that they can produce better offsprings with larger chance.
- *Reproduction and Crossover*: The reproduction operation involves making a copy of the selected expression trees from the current population based on their fitness without any modification. The crossover operation creates new offspring expression trees from two selected parents by exchanging their subtrees.
- *Mutation*: A mutation operator randomly changes the offspring generated from crossover. When mutation operation starts, the subtree under the root which has been selected as mutation node will be replaced by another randomly generated subtree.
- *Termination Condition*: The termination conditions for genetic programming usually include considering the convergence level of evolution generations, the operation time or the fitness measure.

4 Proposed Approach

Since the constant risk multiplier in CPPI cannot adapt to the changing market considtions, this paper develops a new dynamical proportion portfolio insurance (DPPI) strategy whose risk multiplier is a function of the market volatility factors generated by genetic programming.

The new trading strategy has the same formula as in CPPI: $E = M \times (A - F)$, but the M here is an expression tree established by genetic programming. Therefore, the new trading model becomes:

$$E = GPtree \times (A - F). \qquad (2)$$

The terminal set of our genetic programming consists of the market volatility factors described in Sections 2.3 and 2.4. They include investment duration, book-to-market ratio, risk-free rate, market factor, exchange rate, trading volume turnovers of the stock market and the individual stock, disparity index, relative strength index, stochastic oscillator, William's %R, and money flow index.

The arithmetic operators usually used in academic researches are listed in Table 2. This paper adopts the 4 commonly used operators in Table 2: +, -, ×, ÷.

Table 2. Arithmetic operators used in GP researches

Source	Function nodes
Neely et al. (1996) [19]	+, -, ×, ÷
Lensberg (1999) [27]	+, -, ×, ÷
Fyfe et al. (1999) [7]	+, -, ×, ÷
KaBoudan (2000) [11]	+, -, ×, ÷, %, exp, sqrt, ln
Yeh (2001) [26]	+, -, ×, ÷, exp, sqrt, log
Potvin et al. (2004) [15]	+, -, ×, ÷

The fitness measure of our GP is (rate of return+1) / (standard deviation+1). The addition of 1 to the rate of return is to avoid negative fitness and the addition of 1 to the standard deviation is to avoid zero denominator.

To avoid transaction costs due to frequent minor adjustments, we readjust the portfolio according to the theoretical DPPI exposure only when the difference between the current exposure and the theoretical exposure is larger than 5%. Figure 1 presents the algorithm of our trading rule.

```
Procedure Trading () {
  for (each trading day) {
    Calculate the risk multiplier and exposure
    if (the difference between current and theoretical exposure > 5%) {
      Reallocate capital in risky asset according to theoretical exposure
    }
  }
}
```

Fig. 1. The algorithm of our trading rule

5 Experimental Results

To show the effectiveness of our DPPI, we compare it with the traditional CPPI strategy with its constant risk multiplier optimized be a genetic algorithm. Therefore, the DPPI by genetic programming is the experiment groups and the traditional CPPI by genetic algorithm is the control groups in this study. Then t-test is used to evaluate the fitness obtained from the experiment and control groups.

5.1 Data

In this study, five American company stocks and six periods from July 1, 2001 to December 31, 2004 are selected for experimentation. The training and testing periods are both half a year. The five stocks symbols are IBM, Lee, Mot, UPS, and Xom. The trading rules produced by genetic programming on the training period were then evaluated on the testing period. The experiment and control groups are tested in the same periods.

Table 3. Experimental periods in this study

Training Periods	Testing Periods
2001.07 ~ 2001.12	2002.01 ~ 2002.06
2002.01 ~ 2002.06	2002.07 ~ 2002.12
2002.07 ~ 2002.12	2003.01 ~ 2003.06
2003.01 ~ 2003.06	2003.07 ~2 003.12
2003.07 ~ 2003.12	2004.01 ~ 2004.06
2004.01 ~ 2004.06	2004.06 ~ 2004.12

The terminal sets of genetic programming are corresponding to market volatility factors mentioned in Section 4. The exact targets for the unspecified factors are described in Table 4.

Table 4. The targets of the unspecified market volatility factors

Market volatility factors	Target
Risk-free	30-day T-bill
Market factor	NYSE Index
Exchange rate	U.S Dollars to European Euros
Disparity index	5 days, 10 days, and 20 days
Relative strength index	6 days and 12 days

5.2 Parameter Settings

The parameters used in this study are listed in Table 5. The common settings between experiment and control groups are set to the same values.

Table 5. Parameter settings

Population size	500
Number of generations	200
Maximum depth of programs	8
Selection method	Roulette Wheel
Crossover method	Random single point
Crossover rate	100%~15% (Reduced in generations)
Mutation method	Random subtree replacement
Mutation rate	1%

5.3 Numerical Results

Because the performance on the testing periods is the most concerned results, Table 6 just reports the fitness on testing periods. Then the null and alternative hypothesis is established and t-test is used to evaluate under the assumption of underlying normality in the sampled population. The result of t-test is described in Figure 2.

Table 6. Numerical results

Testing periods	Symbol	Control groups (CPPI) Fitness	No. of adj.	Exp. groups (DPPI) Fitness	No. of adj.
2002.01~2002.06	IBM	0.8608	111	0.9257	33
	Lee	0.8011	29	0.9470	35
	Mot	0.8647	88	1.0005	1
	UPS	0.8474	87	0.9057	12
	Xom	0.7926	36	1.0183	2
2002.07~2002.12	IBM	0.8511	93	0.9452	48
	Lee	0.8419	79	0.9471	92
	Mot	0.8410	98	0.9348	97
	UPS	0.5995	1	0.9930	7
	Xom	0.8363	113	0.9069	11
2003.01~2003.06	IBM	0.6293	3	0.9119	16
	Lee	0.8223	57	1.0113	3
	Mot	0.8636	84	0.9405	46
	UPS	0.8434	61	0.9443	61
	Xom	0.7554	21	0.9465	18
2003.07~2003.12	IBM	0.5997	1	1.0003	1
	Lee	N/A	N/A	0.9982	5
	Mot	0.6602	5	0.9821	8
	UPS	0.8189	54	0.9994	13
	Xom	0.7825	31	0.9945	31
2004.01~2004.06	IBM	0.7531	20	0.9276	12
	Lee	0.6003	1	0.9726	7
	Mot	0.6072	1	0.9908	6
	UPS	0.8087	36	0.9872	25
	Xom	0.5997	1	0.9628	18
2004.07~2004.12	IBM	0.8139	36	1.0075	3
	Lee	0.7464	16	0.9524	11
	Mot	0.8426	94	0.9980	3
	UPS	0.8201	55	0.9935	55
	Xom	0.5996	1	1.0085	4
Average	Total	0.7622	45.28	0.9685	22.2
Deviation	Total	0.012		0.0015	

$H_0: \mu_A \leq \mu_B$
$H_1: \mu_A > \mu_B$ (A: Experiment groups; B: Control Groups; $\alpha=0.05$)

t = 10.8692 > 1.6716, So reject H_0.

Fig. 2. The t-test result

According to the t-test result, DPPI definitely outperforms traditional CPPI. Furthermore, the fitness values of experiment groups are all better than that of control groups. It reveals that the dynamically adjusted risk multiplier according to market volatility factors really works better than the constant risk multiplier determined by genetic algorithms or investors' experiences.

6 Conclusion

This paper proposes a dynamic proportion portfolio insurance (DPPI) trading strategy which generalizes the well-known CPPI strategy by making the constant risk multiplier in CPPI an expression tree. It allocates capital in the risky asset by dynamically adjusting the risk multiplier according to market volatility factors. The experimental results reveal that our DPPI outperforms the traditional CPPI.

Future works include finding more market volatility factors and using automated defined function in genetic programming to simplify the equation trees. Extending our DPPI for portfolios is another interesting direction.

References

1. Aby, Jr., C. D., Simpson, Jr., C. L., and Simpson, P. M.: Common stock selection with an emphasis on mispriced assets: Some evidence from technical analysis. Journal of Pension Planning & Compliance 23 (1998)
2. Black, F. and Jones, R.: Simplifying portfolio insurance. Journal of Portfolio Management (1987)
3. Brock, W., Lakonishok, J., and LeBaron, B.: Simple Technical Trading Rules and the Stochastic Properties of Stock Returns. Journal of Finance 47 (1992)
4. Huang, C.-K.: Apply Genetic Model to Strategy Operation of Dynamic Portfolio Insurance. Master Thesis, Institute of Information Management, National Chiao-Tung University (2001)
5. Chiu, Y.-M.: Portfolio Insurance Strategy: Taiwan Evidence. Master Thesis, Institute of Money and Banking at National Chengchi University (2000)
6. Hung, C.: An Empirical Test of the Components of the Aggregate Volatility. Master Thesis, Institute of Business Administration at National Cheng Kung University (2002)
7. Fyfe, C., and Marney, J. P.: Technical Analysis versus Market Efficiency--A Genetic Programming Approach. Applied Financial Economics 9 (1999) 183-191
8. Hakanoglu, E., Kopprasch, R., and Roman, E.: Constant Proportion Portfolio Insurance for Fixed-Income Investment. Journal of Portfolio Management (1989)
9. Fama, E. F., and French, K. R.: The Cross-Section of Expected Stock Returns. Journal of Finance 47 (1992)
10. Hsu, W. C.: An Assessment of Stock Market Volatility: the Case of Taiwan. Master Thesis, Institute of Finance at National Sun Yat-Sen University (1996)
11. Kaboudan, M.A.: Genetic Programming Prediction of Stock Prices. Computational Economics 16 (2000) 207-36
12. Kenneth, R., French, G., Schwert, W., and Stambaugh, R. F.: Expected stock returns and volatility. Journal of Financial Economics 19 (1987)

13. Kim, K.J., and Han, I.: Genetic algorithms approach to feature discretization in artificial neural networks for the prediction of stock price index. Expert Systems with Applications 19 (2000) 125-132
14. Koza, J. R.: Genetic programming: on the programming of computers by means of natural selection. Cambridge, MA: MIT Press (1992)
15. Potvina, J.-Y., Soriano, P., and Vallee, M.: Generating trading rules on the stock markets with genetic programming. Computers & Operations Research 31 (2004) 1033–1047
16. Holland, J. H.: Adaptation in Natural and Artificial Systems: An Introductory Analysis with Applications to Biology, Control, and Artificial Intelligence. MIT Press (1992)
17. Levy, R.A.: Conceptual Foundation of Technical Analysis. Financial Analysis Journal (1966)
18. Levy, R.A.: Random Walks: Reality or Myth. Financial Analysts Journal 23 (1967)
19. Neely, C., J., Weller, P., and Dittmar, R.: Is Technical Analysis in the Foreign Exchange Market Profitable? A Genetic Programming Approach. Centre for Economic Policy Research, Discussion Paper (1996) 1480.
20. Pruitt, S. W., and White, R. E.: The CRISMA Trading System: Who Says Technical Analysis Can't Beat the Market? Journal of Portfolio Management (1988)
21. Nison, S.: Beyond Candlesticks: New Japanese Charting Techniques Revealed. Wiley (1994)
22. Schwert, G. W.: Stock Market Volatility. Financial Analysts Journal 46 (1990)
23. Schwert, G. W., and Seguin, P. J.: Heteroskedasticity in Stock Returns. Journal of Finance 45 (1990)
24. Schwert, G. W.: Why Does Stock Market Volatility Change Over Time? Journal of Finance 44 (1989)
25. Chen, S.-H., and Yeh, C.-H.: Evolving traders and the business school with genetic programming: A new architecture of the agent-based artificial stock market. Journal of Economic Dynamics & Control 25 (2001) 363-393
26. Thawornwong, S., Enke, D., and Dagli, C.: Neural Networks as a Decision Maker for Stock Trading: A Technical Analysis Approach. International Journal of Smart Engineering System Design 5 (2003) 313–325
27. Lensberg, T.: Investment behavior under Knightian uncertainty--an evolutionary approach. Journal of Economic Dynamics & Control 23 (1999) 1587-1604
28. Tsaih, R., Hsu, Y., and Lai, C. C.: Forecasting S&P 500 stock index futures with a hybrid AI system. Decision Support Systems 23 (1998) 161-174
29. Zhu, Y., and Kavee, R. C.: Performance of Portfolio Insurance Strategies. Journal of Portfolio Management (1988)

Evolution of Reactive Rules in Multi Player Computer Games Based on Imitation

Steffen Priesterjahn[1], Oliver Kramer[2],
Alexander Weimer[1], and Andreas Goebels[2]

[1] Department of Computer Science
[2] International Graduate School on Dynamic Intelligent Systems,
University of Paderborn, 33098 Paderborn, Germany
swarmgroup@upb.de

Abstract. Observing purely reactive situations in modern computer games, one can see that in many cases few, simple rules are sufficient to perform well in the game. In spite of this, the programming of an artificial opponent is still a hard and time consuming task in the way it is done for the most games today. In this paper we propose a system in which no direct programming of the behaviour of the opponents is necessary. Instead, rules are gained by observing human players and then evaluated and optimised by an evolutionary algorithm to optimise the behaviour. We will show that only little learning effort is required to be competitive in reactive situations. In the course of our experiments our system proved to generate better artificial players than the original ones supplied with the game.

1 Introduction

Modern computer games have become much more complex and dynamic than their ancestors. With this increase of complexity, the demands for the design of artificial game players have also become higher and higher. On the other hand A.I. routines are not allowed to consume much computing time, since most of this is reserved for the graphics and the user interface. So, programming A.I. routines for modern computer games is very hard, time consuming, and therefore expensive.

We think that much of this programming is unnecessary, since many situations in computer games (e.g. combat) can be handled very well by reactive rules. This is especially the case in so called "first person shooter" (FPS) games in which the player is running through three-dimensional environments (maps) and has to defend himself against other artificial or human players.

In this paper, we propose a system for learning such reactive rules for combat situations by observing the behaviour of human players. Based on this data evolutionary algorithms are used to select the best and most important rules and to optimise the behaviour of the artificial player. The modelling of these rules is presented in section 3. Section 4 gives information about the evolutionary algorithm which was used to optimise the rule sets. Finally, section 5 presents the results we gained from our experiments and in which our agents eventually were able to defeat the artificial players provided by the game.

2 Related Work

Using computer games for artificial intelligence research has become more common in recent years. Games can be used very well as a testbed for different A.I. techniques. Especially three-dimensional action games are frequently used in current research.

An interesting approach for a learning agent has been proposed by Laird et al. in [6]. Their agents try to anticipate the actions of the other players by evaluating what they would do, if they were in the position of the other player. In a later version reinforcement learning was added to their approach [9]. Hawes [4] uses planning techniques for an agent. It uses times of low activity to plan extensive behaviours and generates only short plans if no time is available. Nareyek [7,8] has also implemented an agent which uses planning and local search. Another interesting approach has been applied by Norling [10], in which a BDI-model (Belief-Desire-Intention) is used to model a human-like agent.

The research of Thurau et al. [13,14,15] has much in common with the approach presented in this paper, because it also relies on imitation. [13] emphasises the imitational aspect of their approach. However, the used representation and learning techniques are different. In [14] and [15], neural nets which are trained on data gained from human players and neural gas to represent the structure of the environment are used to learn gaming behaviour. Our approach is oriented to evolution strategies as described in [2] and [12].

Since this paper is focussed on the training of single agents, we will just give some short examples on the research of teams of game agents. Bakkes et al. [1] use evolutionary algorithms to evolve team strategies for the "capture the flag" game. In [5], Kaminka et al. use arbitration to negotiate team strategies. Priesterjahn et al. [11] have developed a system which enables the agents to avoid dangerous areas in the environment based on the past experience of the team. The concept of stigmergy[1] is used to accomplish such behaviour.

3 Basic Modelling

In this section the modelling of the rules and the environment of the player is described. Since it is common to call artificial players in a computer game *bots* or *agents*, we will also use these denotations. We have chosen the game Quake3 (see figure 1) as the basis of our research, because it allows fundamental modifications to the game. Quake3 is a first person shooter game and is focussed on multi player gaming. This means that several human players are competing

---

[1] Stigmergy denotes that information is not exchanged directly but through the environment.

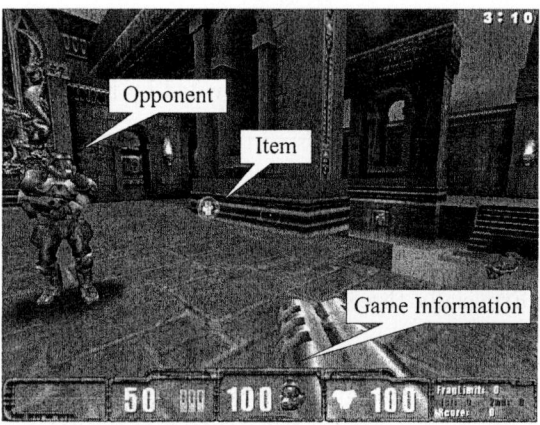

Fig. 1. A scene from Quake3

in a highly dynamic environment. Therefore, a bot has to be able to compete with the human players, because its purpose is to substitute one of them. For our first experiments, we have modified the game so that jumping or ducking is not allowed. We also use a map which does not have several ground levels. So, looking up and down is not needed.

3.1 The Rules

We use reactive rules to describe the agent behaviour. Each rule is defined by an input and an adequate output. For the input, we compress the incoming information, to reduce the search space. The input does not need to hold every possible information. For example, only the vicinity of the bot is important. Furthermore, though Quake3 runs in a three-dimensional environment, the game is mostly played in two dimensions, because the players can only walk on the ground. Therefore, we chose to use a two-dimensional representation for the input in the form of a matrix. This matrix is constructed as follows.

The environment of an agent is segmented into a grid of quadratic regions lying on the floor (see figure 2). Every grid field corresponds to a position in the matrix. The bot is positioned at the centre of the grid. The alignment of the grid is always relative to the bot. So, if the bot moves, the grid will be rotated and shifted to fit these movements. Every grid field is always placed at the same relative position to the agent. The size of the grid is limited to the size of the matrix. So, it only covers the vicinity of a bot.

In each acting frame of the agent, it "traces" to the center of every grid field on the floor of the environment. This can be compared to using a laser sensor. In each trace a ray is sent from the head of the bot. If this ray reaches the center of the grid field it was sent to, the corresponding value of the matrix is set to a value which indicates that this field is empty. Otherwise, the field is indicated as filled. If a field is occupied by an opponent, a corresponding value will be written into the matrix. The central field is always regarded as empty and can

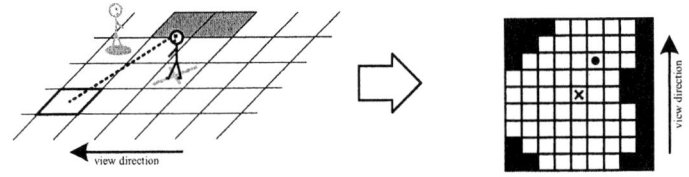

Fig. 2. Obtaining the grid from the player (x - player, • - opponent)

not be changed. In the following, we will also use the term *grid* for this matrix. A detailed and formal description of this grid is given in the following definition.

Definition 1 (Grid)
A grid G is a matrix $G = (g_{i,j})_{1 \leq i,j \leq n} \in \mathbb{N}_0^{n \times n}$, $n \in \mathbb{N}$ with $n \equiv 1 \mod 2$ and

$$g_{i,j} = \begin{cases} 0, & \text{if the field is occupied} \\ 1, & \text{if the field is empty} \\ 50, & \text{if the field contains an opponent.}^2 \end{cases}$$

$\mathcal{G}$ *denotes the set of all grids.*

The output of a rule represents a *command* which is executed by the bot and is defined as follows.

Definition 2 (Command, Rule)
A command C is a 4-tuple $C = (f, r, \varphi, a)$ with $f, r \in \{-1, 0, 1\}$, $a \in \{0, 1\}$ and $\varphi \in [-180°, 180°]$. The interpretation of these variables is as follows.

$$f = \begin{cases} 1, & \text{move forward} \\ 0, & \text{no movement} \\ -1, & \text{move backward} \end{cases} \qquad r = \begin{cases} 1, & \text{move to the right} \\ 0, & \text{no movement} \\ -1, & \text{move to the left} \end{cases}$$

$$a = \begin{cases} 0, & \text{do not attack} \\ 1, & \text{attack} \end{cases} \qquad \varphi = \text{alteration of the yaw angle}$$

$\mathcal{C}$ *denotes the set of all Commands.*

A rule $R : \mathcal{G} \to \mathcal{C}$ maps a grid to a command. $\mathcal{R}$ denotes the set of all rules.

3.2 Creating the Rule Base

Though we already have reduced the complexity of the problem, the search space is still very large. [3]. Therefore, we chose to generate a basic rule set by recording

---

[2] A value of 50 has been chosen to emphasise the position of an opponent.
[3] At least $3^{n \cdot n}$ for a $n \times n$ grid.

human players. This is simply done by letting them play against each other and by recording their grid-to-command matches for every frame of the game. So, rules which are executed very often, are put more often into our rule base.

In the first step, certain behaviours of the players will then be imitated by our bots. Then the selection of the appropriate rules from the rule base and the performance of the agents is optimised by an evolutionary algorithm. This approach has the advantage that certain behaviours can be presented to the bot, from which it learns to use the best in relation to its fitness function. In this way an agent can be trained to have a certain behaviour without programming it manually.

3.3 Rule Comparison

Each bot owns an individual set of rules from which it chooses the best one for its current situation. For this selection process, it has to be able to compare different grids to find the rule with the grid which fits best to its current input. Therefore, a distance measure between two grids has to be introduced. We chose to use the euclidean distance.

Definition 3 (Euclidean Distance)
The euclidean distance between two $n \times n$-grids G and G' is defined by

$$\text{dist}(G, G') = \sum_{1 \le i,j \le n} (g_{i,j} - g'_{i,j})^2.$$

However, this distance does not take into account the rough similarity of two grids. For example the following matrices A, B and C have the same euclidean distance, though A and B are more similar to each other.

A	B	C	A'	B'	C'
1 0 0	0 1 0	0 0 0	1 0.5 0	0.5 1 0.5	0 0 0
0 0 0	0 0 0	0 0 0	0.5 0.2 0	0.2 0.5 0.2	0 0.2 0.5
0 0 0	0 0 0	0 0 1	0 0 0	0 0 0	0 0.5 1

If A, B and C are smoothed with a smoothing operator, matrices like A', B' and C' will result. Now the euclidean distance between A' and B' is smaller as between A' and C' or B' and C'. Therefore, we convolve the grid with the Gaussian smoothing filter. This operator is commonly used in image processing and its filter matrix $F = (f_{i,j})_{-r \le i,j \le r}$ is defined as

$$f_{i,j} = e^{-\frac{i^2+j^2}{r^2}},$$

where r is the radius of the filter. For further information about convolution, see [3]. We define the *euclidean gauss distance* as follows.

Definition 4 (Gaussian Grid, Euclidean Gauss Distance)
Let G be a $n \times n$-grid. Then, $G_g = (g^g_{i,j})_{1 \le i,j \le n} \in \mathbb{R}^{n \times n}_{\ge 0}$ denotes the result of a convolution of G with a Gaussian filter of radius $r \in \mathbb{R}_{\ge 0}$. The euclidean gauss distance dist_g between two grids G and G' is defined as

$$\text{dist}_g(G, G') = \text{dist}(G_g, G'_g).$$

We used a radius of $r = 5$ for our Gaussian filter, which results in a 5×5 filter matrix.

4 Rule Evolution

During the optimisation phase of our approach the rule base is optimised with an evolutionary algorithm (EA). Every bot has a rule set $\{R_1, ..., R_k\} \in \mathcal{R}^k$ with a fixed size $k \in \mathbb{N}$. At the beginning the first individuals are initialised with randomly chosen rules from the rule base, which is created as described in section 3.2. Then crossover and mutation are used to select the best rules and to gain further optimisation of the performance of the bots.

Population and Structure:
Concerning the population structure and the selection scheme of our evolutionary algorithm we use a (μ, λ)-EA oriented to evolution strategies. The size of the parental population is $\mu \in \mathbb{N}$. In each generation $\lambda \in \mathbb{N}$ offspring individuals are produced applying the variation operators crossover and mutation.

Crossover:
For the crossover, two parents are chosen randomly with uniform distribution from the parental population. Let $\{R_1, ..., R_k\} \in \mathcal{R}^k$ and $\{R'_1, ..., R'_k\} \in \mathcal{R}^k$ be the rule sets of the parents. Then, for the rule set of the offspring $\{O_1, ..., O_k\} \in \mathcal{R}^k$, rule O_i is randomly chosen from $\{R_i, R'_i\}$ with uniform distribution. So, crossover effects the structure of the rule sets.

Mutation:
In contrast to crossover, the mutation operator effects the structure of the rules itself. All changes are made with the same probability p_m and uniform distribution. For the grid, a grid field can be changed from empty to full or vice versa. The position of an opponent on the grid can be changed to one of the neighbouring grid fields, though it can not be moved beyond the grid borders. For the command (f, r, a, φ) of a rule, f, r and a can be set to another value. The alteration of the view angle φ can be changed by adding a random angle $\Delta\varphi \in [-5°, 5°]$.

Simulation and Fitness Calculation:
The fitness of each bot is evaluated by letting it play and apply its rule set for a simulation period of n_{sim} seconds. The summed health loss of the opponents $h_{\text{opp}} \in \mathbb{N}_0$ and the health loss of the bot $h_{\text{own}} \in \mathbb{N}_0$ is counted and integrated into the fitness function

$$f = w_{\text{opp}} h_{\text{opp}} - w_{\text{own}} h_{\text{own}}.$$

Health loss of the opponent increases, own health loss decreases the fitness of the agent.

Selection:
We use the plus-selection scheme. The parental population $P_p(t+1)$ for generation $t+1 \in \mathbb{N}$ consists of the μ best individuals of the current offspring $P_o(t)$ and the last parental population $P_p(t)$. In this selection scheme parents with superior fitness values can survive as long as their fitness belongs to the μ best ones.

5 Results

A series of experiments showed that our agents succeed in imitating the behaviour of the base players and that they are able to improve their behaviour beyond their basis. The selection of the following parameters is a result of our initial experiments.

5.1 Experimental Setup

We used an evaluation timespan of 45 seconds for each individual, which was just long enough to provide reliable results. For a population of 40 individuals, this results in an evaluation timespan of 30 minutes for each generation.

To have a constant opponent for our experiments, we used an original Quake3-bot for the training. We also used the behaviour of the Quake3-bot to generate the rule base. This was accomplished by letting it play against itself. We also chose the Quake3-bot as the basis, because we wanted to find out if our bot would be able to surpass its basis and to generate new behaviour. We made experiments with a dense grid of 25×25 fields and a coarse grid of 15×15 fields, which were both sized to represent approximately 15×15 metres in Quake3.

The size of the rule set of an agent was set to 50 rules and 400 rules in different experiments, to study the influence of this parameter on the behaviour of the agent. On the one hand it was interesting to see how much rules are necessary to gain competitive behaviour. On the other hand we wanted to find out if more complex behaviour can be gained by using large rule sets.

As it was already indicated above we chose a population of 40 individuals for each generation, consisting of $\mu = 10$ parents and $\lambda = 30$ offspring individuals. We used these values because they are small enough to allow a relatively fast evolution and big enough to retain diversity.

The last parameter we had to choose was the mutation probability p_m. In early experiments we found out that using a mutation probability that is too high can destroy good behaviours that have already been learned. So, we decided to use a relatively small mutation probability of $p_m = 0.005$. This results in an algorithm that is mainly focussed on selecting the best rules and not on learning new behaviour. However, we also conducted experiments with $p_m = 0.1$. To avoid the destruction of important rules in these experiments, we chose to apply the mutation only to the command part of a rule and not to the grid. Thus, the rule inputs remained untouched. This approach implies the assumption that all important states are already included into the rule base.

We decided to stop the evolution after a fixed number of steps, which was based on our initial experiments. Table 1 gives an overview of the conducted experiments.

Table 1. Experimental setup

exp #	grid density	rule set	grid mutation	p_m
1	25 × 25	50	yes	0.005
2	25 × 25	400	yes	0.005
3	15 × 15	50	yes	0.005
4	15 × 15	400	yes	0.005
5	25 × 25	50	no	0.1
6	25 × 25	400	no	0.1

5.2 Equally Weighted Fitness

In our first series of experiments we calculated the fitness by $f = 1 \cdot h_{\text{opp}} - 1 \cdot h_{\text{own}}$. If our bot has caused more damage to its opponent than it has received from it, the fitness will be greater than zero.

We obtained several interesting results. First of all, our agents performed well and the best of them were able to defeat the Quake3-bot already after 5 generations. After 20 to 30 generations the bots reached satisfiable and competitive behaviour in almost all experiments. Figure 3 shows the fitness progression of the best fitness of each generation for these experiments. We smoothed the plots with a Bezier curve to improve readability.

Figure 4 shows the fitness progression of the best experiment (exp1). The best, worst and average fitness of each generation is displayed. These plots are

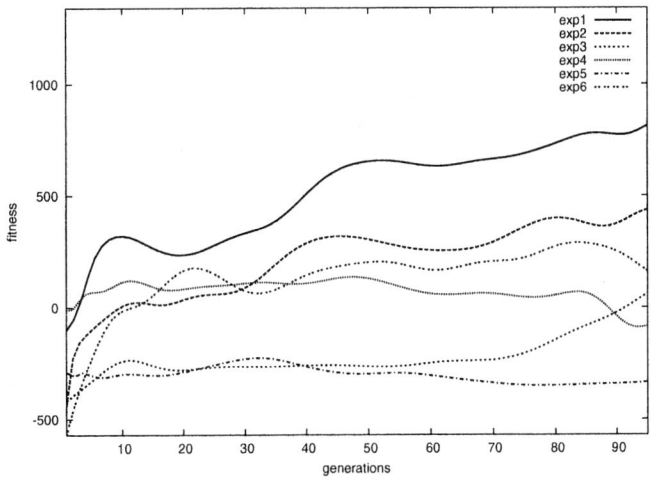

Fig. 3. Smoothed plots of the fitness progression ($w_{\text{opp}} = w_{\text{own}} = 1$)

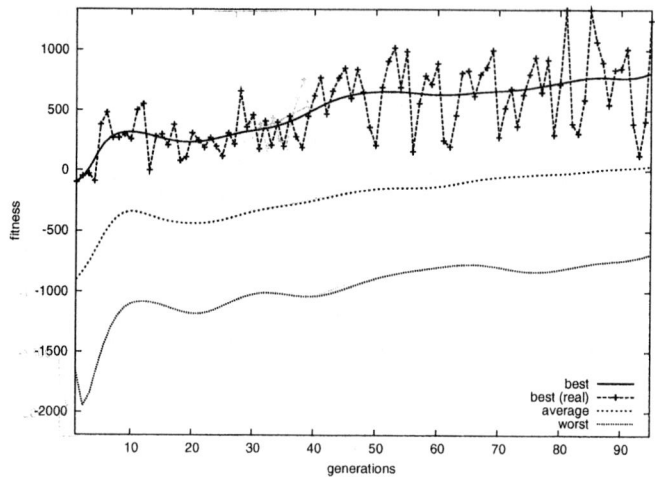

Fig. 4. Performance of the best experiment ($w_{\text{opp}} = w_{\text{own}} = 1$)

again smoothed with a Bezier curve. Furthermore, the real data for the best fitness of each generation is displayed for comparison. It should be noted that even the average fitness grew above zero in this experiment.

At the beginning the agents imitated some behaviours of the Quake3-bot closely. However, there were individuals which ran into corners and could not get out of them. These ones were sorted out by the EA after few generations. In the course of the evolution the agents even developed new behaviour. For example the best ones began to take cover behind a column. This behaviour is not implemented in the Quake3-bot. In the experiments with the higher mutation probability the bots took more freedom in their movements. However, their performance never got as good as the performance of the agents with grid mutation. The usage of a more dense grid resulted in an improvement of the performance.

Concerning the number of used rules, we made further experiments with a trained agent and a rule set of 400 rules by letting it play for one hour. It used more than 300 of its rules. However, experiments 1 and 2 show, that limiting the number of rules to 50 can be advantageous. Observing the behaviour of the agents, the ones with 50 rules also behaved more efficiently and flawlessly. An exception is experiment 5 in which the algorithm got stuck in a local maximum. In this setting the agents learned to run away from their opponent, thus applying only little damage to it.

5.3 Aggressive Fitness

To investigate the influence of the fitness function on the behaviour of the agents we conducted a second series of experiments. We chose $f = 2 \cdot h_{\text{opp}} - 1 \cdot h_{\text{own}}$ as the fitness function, to suppress the tendency to run away. So, neither the fitness values of these experiments can be directly compared to the ones obtained above,

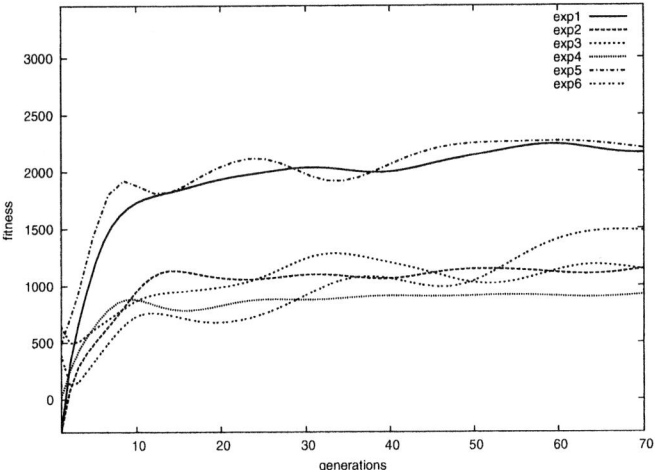

Fig. 5. Smoothed plots of the fitness progression ($w_{\text{opp}} = 2, w_{\text{own}} = 1$)

nor a comparison with the Quake3-bot based on the fitness values is possible in a direct way. Another series of experiments with the same parameter sets as above was conducted.

Figure 5 again shows the smoothed progression of the best fitness of each generation. Again experiment 1 provided good results. However, this time experiment 5 also delivers good results. The experiments without grid mutation showed no disadvantage in this setup. Concerning the rule set size, the agents using the smaller sets performed better than the ones using a large set. Again, the coarse grid produced inferior results. There were some agents which were able to defeat the Quake3-bots in all experiments. Though, after longer[4] evolution the bots tended to act very aggressively and to disregard their own health. So, the fitness function can be used to learn certain aspects of the behaviour. The overall convergence in these experiments was better than in the equally weighted setting.

6 Conclusion and Future Work

In the experiments, our agents were able to behave in the same way as the original players already after few generations. They also were able to improve their performance beyond their basis and to develop new behaviour. We have presented a system which uses evolutionary algorithms to learn rules for successful reactive behaviour in multi player games based on imitation. This approach can be used to train certain aspects of the behaviour of an artificial opponent based on the imitation of other players and to emphasise desired behaviours. Our approach has also turned out to prevent disadvantageous behaviour, because such

---

[4] About 50 generations.

behaviour, e.g. getting stuck in corners or standing still, has been eliminated in all experiments after at most 20 to 30 generations.

In the future we will conduct further experiments to find out more about the parameter dependency of our approach and to get statistically more significant data. Other representations will also be studied. We will also apply preprocessing steps to our rule base, like data mining and clustering techniques, to find out important states in our data and to improve the imitation. Furthermore, we want to use reinforcement learning for a more complex, preprocessed representation to learn more complex behaviour.

References

1. S. Bakkes, P. Spronck, and E. Postma. TEAM: The Team-Oriented Evolutionary Adaptability Mechanism. In *Proceedings of the ICEC*, pages 273–282, 2004.
2. H.-G. Beyer and H.-P. Schwefel. Evolution strategies – A comprehensive introduction. *Natural Computing*, 1:3–52, 2002.
3. R. C. Gonzalez and P. A. Wintz. *Digital Image Processing*. Addison Wesley, 1992.
4. N. Hawes. An Anytime Planning Agent For Computer Game Worlds. In *Proceedings of the Workshop on Agents in Computer Games at The 3rd International Conference on Computers and Games*, pages 1–14, 2002.
5. G. Kaminka, J. Go, and T. Vu. Context-dependent joint-decision arbitration for computer games, 2002.
6. J. Laird. It Knows What You're Going to Do: Adding Anticipation to a Quakebot. In *AAAI 2000 Spring Symposium Series: Artificial Intelligence and Interactive Entertainment: AAAI Technical Report SS-00-02*, 2000.
7. A. Nareyek. A Planning Model for Agents in Dynamic and Uncertain Real-Time Environments. In *Proceedings of the Workshop on Integrating Planning, Scheduling and Execution in Dynamic and Uncertain Environments at the Fourth International Conference on Artificial Intelligence Planning Systems*, pages 7–14. AAAI Press, 1998.
8. A. Nareyek. Constraint-Based Agents - An Architecture for Constraint-Based Modeling and Local-Search-Based Reasoning for Planning and Scheduling in Open and Dynamic Worlds. In *Künstliche Intelligenz 2*, pages 51–53, 2002.
9. S. Nason and J. Laird. Soar-RL: Integrating Reinforcement Learning with Soar. In *International Conference on Cognitive Modelling*, 2004.
10. E. Norling. Capturing the Quake Player: Using a BDI Agent to Model Human Behaviour. In *Proceedings of the Second International Joint Conference on Autonomous Agents and Multiagent Systems*, pages 1080–1081, 2003.
11. S. Priesterjahn, A. Goebels, and A. Weimer. Stigmergetic Communication for Cooperative Agent Routing in Virtual Environments. In *Proceedings of the International Conference on Artificial Intelligence and the Simulation of Behaviour*, Apr. 2005.
12. H.-P. Schwefel. *Evolution and Optimum Seeking*. Sixth-Generation Computer Technology. Wiley Interscience, New York, 1995.
13. C. Thurau, C. Bauckhage, and G. Sagerer. Imitation learning at all levels of game-AI. In *Proceedings of the International Conference on Computer Games, Artificial Intelligence,Design and Education*, pages 402–408, 2004.

14. C. Thurau, C. Bauckhage, and G. Sagerer. Learning Human-Like Movement Behavior for Computer Games. In *Proceedings of the 8th International Conference on the Simulation of Adaptive Behavior (SAB'04)*, 2004.
15. C. Thurau, C. Bauckhauge, and G. Sagerer. Combining Self Organizing Maps and Multilayer Perceptrons to Learn Bot-Behavior for a Commercial Game. In *Proceedings of the GAME-ON'03 Conference*, pages 119–123, 2003.

Combining Classifiers with Particle Swarms[*]

Li-ying Yang[1] and Zheng Qin[1,2]

[1] Department of Computer Science and Technology, Xi'an Jiaotong University,
Xi'an 710049, China
yangliying1208@163.com
[2] School of Software, Tsinghua University, Beijing 100084, China
qingzh@mail.tsinghua.edu.cn

Abstract. Multiple classifier systems have shown a significant potential gain in comparison to the performance of an individual best classifier. In this paper, a weighted combination model of multiple classifier systems was presented, which took sum rule and majority vote as special cases. Particle swarm optimization (PSO), a new population-based evolutionary computation technique, was used to optimize the model. We referred the optimized model as PSO-WCM. An experimental investigation was performed on UCI data sets and encouraging results were obtained. PSO-WCM proposed in this paper is superior to other combination rules given larger data sets. It is also shown that rejection of weak classifier in the ensemble can improve classification performance further.

1 Introduction

The ultimate goal of designing pattern recognition systems is to achieve the best possible classification performance for the task at hand. This led to the overproducing of pattern recognition algorithms for given problem and the traditional approach to supervised learning problem, i.e. evaluation and selection, which evaluates a set of different algorithms against a representative validation set and selects the best one. It is now recognized that the key to recognition problems does not lie wholly in any particular solution which has been vigorously advocated by one or another group. No single model exists for all pattern recognition problems and no single technique is applicable to all problems. Rather what we have is a bag of tools and a bag of problems. Furthermore, the sets of patterns misclassified by the different algorithms would not necessarily overlap, which suggested that different algorithms potentially offered complementary information. Therefore, to solve really hard problems, we'll have to use different models [1]. Multiple classifier systems (MCS) are to integrate several models for the same problem. MCS came alive in the 90's of last century, and almost immediately produced promising results [2]. From this beginning, research in this domain has increased and grown tremendously, partly as a result of the coincident

---

[*] This work is supported by the Major State Basic Research Development Program of China (973 Program), No.2004CB719401.

advances in the technology itself. These technological developments include the production of very fast and low cost computers that have made many complex pattern recognition algorithms practicable [3].

Research on MCS follows two parallel lines of study. One is decision optimization and the other coverage optimization [4]. Assuming a given, fixed set of carefully designed and highly specialized classifiers, decision optimization attempts to find an optimal combination of their decisions. Assuming a fixed decision combination function, coverage optimization generates a set of mutually complementary, generic classifiers that can be combined to achieve optimal accuracy. We focused on decision optimization in this work. Majority vote is the simplest combination method and has been a much-studied subject among mathematicians and social scientists. In majority vote, each individual has the same importance. A natural extension to majority vote is to assign weight to different individual. Thus weighted combination algorithm was obtained. Since under most circumstances, there is difference between individuals, weighted combination algorithm provides a more appropriate solution. The key to weighted combination algorithm is the weights. In this paper, a weighted combination model based on particle swarm optimization (PSO-WCM) is proposed. To the best of our knowledge, former evolution-based research on MCS concentrated on classifier selection rather than weights optimization [5].

The rest of this paper is organized as follows. In section 2, Particle Swarm Optimization is presented: origin, principle and development. Detailed algorithm for PSO-WCM is proposed in section 3. Experiments and discussion are given in section 4. Conclusion is drawn in section 5.

2 Particle Swarm Optimization

Inspired by simulating social behavior (such as bird flocking), Everhart and Kennedy introduced Particle Swarm Optimization (PSO) in 1995, which is a population-based evolutionary computation technique [6][7]. In PSO, candidate solutions are denoted by particles. Each particle is a point in the search space and has two attribute values: fitness determined by the problem and velocity to decide the flying. Particles adjust their flying toward a promising area according to their own experience and the social information in the swarm. Thus they will at last reach the destination through continuous adjustment in the iteration. Given a D-dimension search space, m particles constitute the swarm. The i-th particle is denoted by $x_i = (x_{i1}, x_{i2}, ..., x_{iD}), i = 1, 2, ..., m$. Taking x_i into the objective function, the fitness for the i-th particle can be work out, which could tell the quality of current particle, i.e. the current solution. The current velocity and the best previous solution for the i-th particle are represented by $v_i = (v_{i1}, v_{i2}, ..., v_{iD})$ and $p_i = (p_{i1}, p_{i2}, ..., p_{iD})$. The best solution achieved by the whole swarm so far is denoted by $p_g = (p_{g1}, p_{g2}, ..., p_{gD})$. In Everhart and Kennedy's original version, particles are manipulated according to the following equations:

$$v_{id} = v_{id} + c_1 r_1 (p_{id} - x_{id}) + c_2 r_2 (p_{gd} - x_{id}) \qquad (1)$$

$$x_{id} = x_{id} + v_{id} \qquad (2)$$

where $i = 1,...,m$; $d = 1,...,D$; c_1 and c_2 are two positive constants called cognitive learning rate and social learning rate respectively; r_1 and r_2 are random numbers in the range [0,1]. The velocity v_{id} is limited in $[-v_{max}, v_{max}]$ with v_{max} a constant determined by specific problem. The original version of PSO lacks velocity control mechanism, so it has a poor ability to search at a fine grain [8]. Many researchers devoted to overcoming this disadvantage. Shi and Eberhart introduced a time decreasing inertia factor to equation (1) [9]:

$$v_{id} = w v_{id} + c_1 r_1 (p_{id} - x_{id}) + c_2 r_2 (p_{gd} - x_{id}) \qquad (3)$$

where w is inertia factor which balances the global wide-range exploitation and the local nearby exploration abilities of the swarm. Clerc introduced a constriction factor a into equation (2) to constrain and control velocities magnitude [10]:

$$x_{id} = x_{id} + a v_{id} \qquad (4)$$

The above equations (3) and (4) are called classical PSO, which is much efficient and precise than the original one by adaptively adjusting global variables.

3 Weighted Combination Algorithm Based on PSO

3.1 Weighted Combination Model

Weighted Combination Model (WCM) is an extension of simple majority vote. Consider a pattern recognition problem with M classes $(C_1, C_2, ..., C_M)$ and K classifiers $(R_1, R_2, ..., R_K)$. For a given sample x, $R_i(i=1,...,K)$ outputs $M_{R_i} = (m_i(1),...,m_i(M))$, where $m_i(j)(j=1,...,M)$ denotes the probability that x is from class j according to R_i. The weight vector for classifier ensemble is represented as $\varphi = (\varphi_1,...,\varphi_K)$ with $\sum_{k=1}^{K} \varphi_k = 1$. Let $M = (M_{R_1},...,M_{R_K})$. WCM under such circumstance is shown in Fig. 1. The sample x is classified into the class with maximum posteriori probability and the decision rule is:

$$x \rightarrow C_j, \text{ If } \sum_{i=1}^{R} \varphi_i m_i(j) = \max_{k=1}^{M} (\sum_{i=1}^{R} \varphi_i m_i(k)) \qquad (5)$$

In formula (5), if $\varphi_i = \dfrac{1}{K}$, then: majority vote is obtained when classifiers output at abstract level, and sum rule is obtained when classifiers output at measurement level. If there is only one "1" in the weight vector and the other elements are all "0", the combination model is equal to the individual classifier whose weight is "1".

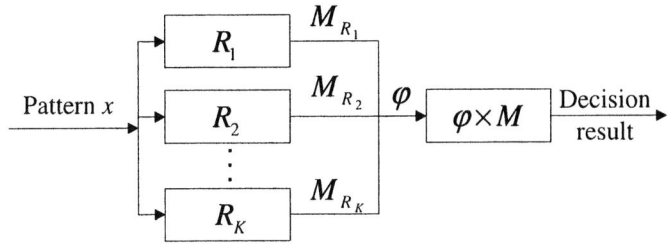

Fig. 1. Weighted combination model for multiple classifier systems

3.2 PSO-WCM

There are two methods for acquiring the weights in WCM. One set fixed weights to each classifier according to experience or something else. The other obtains weights by training. Training methods gain better performance at the cost of computation. It has two steps: (1) training individual classifiers on training set; (2) determining the weights based on validation set. In the second step, traditional approach set the weights in directly proportional to classifiers' accuracy on validation set [11]. We proposed to determine the weights based on PSO, that is, PSO-WCM. Optimal weights are achieved by searching in K-dimension space. A solution is a particle in PSO and coded into one K-dimension vector $\varphi = (\varphi_1, ..., \varphi_K)$. Fitness function is computed as combination model's error rate on validation set using the weights. Thus the task is converted into an optimization problem for minimum.

4 Experiments

Five classifiers used in this work are: (1) LDC, Linear Discriminant Classifier; (2) QDC, Quadratic Discriminant Classifier; (3) KNNC, K-Nearest Neighbor Classifier with K=3; (4) TREEC, a decision tree classifier; (5) BPXNC, a neural network classifier based on MATHWORK's trainbpx with 1 hidden layer and 5 neurons in this hidden layer. Six combination rules were included in our experiments for the sake of comparison and they are majority vote rule, max rule, min rule, mean rule, median rule and product rule [12].

4.1 Data Sets Used in the Study

The weighted combination model based on PSO (PSO-WCM) was applied to eight real world problems from the UCI repository: Letter, Vehicle, Glass, Waveform,

Satimage, Iris, Ann and Wine [13]. In PSO-WCM, for each dataset, 2/3 examples were used as training data, 1/6 validation data and 1/6 test data. In other combination rules or individual classifiers, 2/3 examples were used as training data and 1/3 test data. All experiments were repeated for 10 runs and averages were computed as the final results. Note that all subsets were kept the same class probabilities distribution as original data sets. The characteristics of these data sets are shown in Table 1.

Table 1. Data sets used in the study

	#Samples	#Inputs	#Outputs
Ann	7200	21	3
Glass	214	9	7
Iris	150	4	3
Letter	20000	16	26
Satimage	4435	36	6
Vehicle	846	18	4
Waveform	5000	21	3
Wine	178	13	3

4.2 Results and Discussion

Since there are 5 classifiers, the number of weights is 5. A particle in PSO was coded into one 4-dimension vector $\varphi = (\varphi_1, \varphi_2, \varphi_3, \varphi_4)$. The fifth weight φ_5 was computed according to $\sum_{k=1}^{5} \varphi_k = 1$. Classical PSO was adopted in PSO-WCM. Parameters were set as following: size of the swarm =10; inertia factor w linearly decreases from 0.9 to 0.4; $c_1 = c_2 = 2$; constriction factor $a =1$; for i-th particle, each dimension in position vector x_i and velocity vector v_i were initialized as random number in the range [0,1] and [-1,1]; max iteration = 1000.

The performance of individual classifiers was list in Table 2. It shown that different classifier achieved different performance for the same task. But no classifier is superior for all problems. The combination performance of 5 classifiers by majority

Table 2. Error rate of individual classifiers

Data sets	LDC	QDC	KNNC	TREEC	BPXNC
Ann	0.0609	0.9583	0.0734	0.0033	0.0734
Glass	0	0.0417	0.0417	0.1250	0.0833
Iris	0.3529	0.6176	0.3824	0.2941	0.3824
Letter	0.3079	0.1182	0.0592	0.3458	0.9633
Satimage	0.1591	0.1457	0.1104	0.1797	0.3268
Vehicle	0.2357	0.1714	0.2929	0.2571	0.1786
Waveform	0.1433	0.1489	0.1892	0.2953	0.1322
Wine	0.0033	0.0267	0.3367	0.0833	0.0067

Table 3. Error rate comparison of combination algorithms

Data sets	Majority vote	Max rule	Min rule	Mean rule	Median rule	Product rule	PSO-WCM
Ann	0.0584	0.1685	0.8866	0.0601	0.0601	0.1334	0.0050
Glass	0.3235	0.5294	0.5588	0.3529	0.3529	0.6176	0.3529
Iris	0.0417	0	0	0.0417	0.0417	0.0417	0
Letter	0.1066	0.6144	0.9209	0.3877	0.1125	0.9175	0.0499
Satimage	0.1179	0.2088	0.3018	0.1336	0.1146	0.2904	0.1080
Vehicle	0.1429	0.1786	0.2429	0.2000	0.2000	0.1929	0.1786
Waveform	0.1379	0.1597	0.1816	0.1444	0.1382	0.1499	0.1351
Wine	0.0067	0.0067	0.0100	0.0033	0.0033	0.0033	0.0033

vote, max rule, min rule, mean rule, median rule, product rule and PSO-WCM, were given in Table 3. It is shown that PSO-WCM outperforms all comparison combination rules and the best individual classifier on data sets Ann, Letter, Satimage and Waveform. These data sets have a common characteristic, that is, the sample size is large. Therefore, the optimal weights obtained on validation set are also representative on test set. The same thing is not true on smaller data sets (such as Glass, Iris, Vehicle and Wine) for the obvious reason that overfitting tends to occur. Optimal weights might appear in initial process, so the succedent optimization makes no sense.

It is also found that, the more accurate the classifier is, the larger weight it is assigned. This is in agreement with one's intuition. Considering that some classifiers perform even poorly on some data sets, we delete the weakest classifier from the ensemble. This was done on data sets Ann and Letter in the experiments. Weakest classifiers on the two data sets, i.e., QDC and BPXNC were deleted respectively. Then PSO-WCM and 6 comparison combination rules were used to combine four classifiers, and the results were presented in Table 4. The error rates on two data sets before and after rejection of the weakest classifier were plotted in Fig. 2.

Table 4. Error rate after the weak classifier was rejected

Data sets	Majority vote	Max rule	Min rule	Mean rule	Median rule	Product rule	PSO-WCM
Ann	0.0534	0.0550	0.0517	0.0575	0.0559	0.0601	0.0058
Letter	0.1037	0.3034	0.1846	0.1025	0.1025	0.1816	0.0493

From Fig. 2, it was seen that rejection of the weakest classifier benefits the combination rules. This demonstrates that the size of the ensemble is worth investigating, which is the focus of coverage optimization. The effect of rejection is much significant on max rule, min rule and product rule, while it is not so obvious on majority vote, mean rule, median rule and PSO-WCM. For combination rules based on Bayes theory (such as max rule, min rule and product rule), final decision was obtained by combining the probabilities that a sample belonged to one class. When this probability is very high for the weakest classifier, error would occur. On the contrary, rejection could not produce much effect on the majority, mean and median. In PSO-WCM, the weight for the weakest classifier is minor, so its absence didn't give rise to much difference.

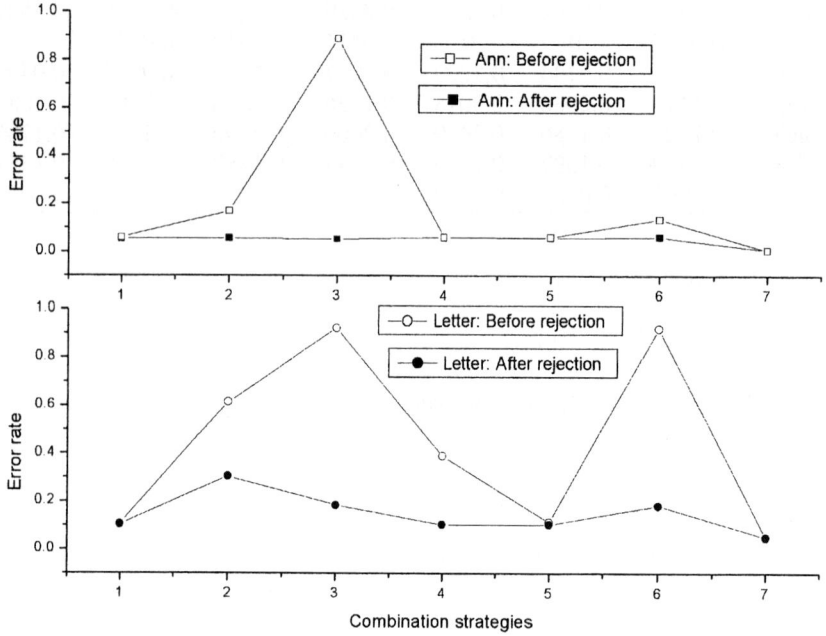

Fig. 2. Error rates on two data sets before and after rejection of the weak classifier in ensemble. 1-7 in X-coordinate denotes majority voting, max rule, min rule, mean rule, median rule, product rule and PSO-WCM respectively.

5 Conclusion

PSO-WCM was proposed in this paper. Experiments were carried out on eight real world problems from the UCI repository. It is shown that PSO-WCM performs better than the best base learner and the comparison combination rules (majority voting, max rule, min rule, mean rule, median rule and product rule) when the data set is large enough. It is also indicated that the rejection of weak classifier in the ensemble could improve classification performance. This effect is much more significant on Bayes-theory-based combination methods than on PSO-WCM.

References

1. Ghosh, J.: Multiclassifier systems: back to the future. In: Roli, F., Kittler, J. (eds.): Multiple Classifier Systems. Lecture Notes in Computer Science, Vol. 2364. Springer-Verlag, Berlin Heidelberg (2002) 1–15

2. Suen, C.Y., Nadal, C., Mai, T.A., Legault, R., Lam, L.: Recognition of totally unconstrained handwriting numerals based on the concept of multiple experts. In: Suen, C.Y. (eds.): Frontiers in Handwriting Recognition, in Proc. Int. Workshop on Frontiers in Handwriting Recognition, Montreal, Canada (1990) 131-143
3. Suen, C.Y., Lam, L.: Multiple classifier combination methodologies for different output levels. In: Kittler, J., Roli, F. (eds.): Multiple Classifier Systems. Lecture Notes in Computer Science, Vol. 1857. Springer-Verlag, Berlin Heidelberg (2000) 52–66
4. Ho, T.K.: Complexity of classification problems and comparative advantages of combined classifiers. In: Kittler, J., Roli, F. (eds.): Multiple Classifier Systems. Lecture Notes in Computer Science, Vol. 1857, Springer-Verlag (2000) 97-106
5. Ruta, D., Gabrys, B.: Application of the evolutionary algorithms for classifier selection in multiple classifier systems with majority voting. In: Kittler, J., Roli, F. (eds.): Multiple Classifier Systems. Lecture Notes in Computer Science, Vol. 2096, Springer-Verlag (2001) 399-408
6. Kennedy, J., Eberhart, R.: Particle Swarm Optimization. IEEE International Conference on Neural Networks, vol. 4, Perth, Australia (1995) 1942–1948
7. Eberhart, R., Kennedy, J.: A New Optimizer Using Particle Swarm Theory. Proceeding of the Sixth International Symposium on Micro Machine and Human Science, Nagoya, Japan (1995) 39–43
8. Angeline, P.J.: Ebulutionary optimization versus particle swarm optimization: philosophy and performance differences. Evolutionary programming □: Proceedings of the seventh annual conference on evolutionary programming (1998)
9. Shi, Y., Eberhart, R.: A modified particle swarm optimizer. IEEE World Congress on Computational Intelligence, (1998) 69–73
10. Clerc, M.: The Swarm and the Queen: Towards a Deterministic and Adaptive Particle Swarm Optimization. Proceeding of the Congress of Evolutionary Computation, vol.3, (1999) 1951-1957
11. Baykut, A., Ercil, A.: Towards automated classifier combination for pattern recognition. In: Windeatt, T., Roli, F. (eds.): Multiple Classifier Systems. Lecture Notes in Computer Science, Vol. 2709, Springer-Verlag (2003) 94-105
12. Kittler, J., Hatef, M., Duin, R.P.W., Matas, J.: On combining classifiers. IEEE Transactions On Pattern Analysis and Machine Intelligence, 3 (1998) 226-239
13. Blake, C., Keogh, E., Merz, C.J.: UCI Repository of Machine Learning Databases, 1998. www.ics.uci.edu/~mlearn/MLRepository.html

Adaptive Normalization Based Highly Efficient Face Recognition Under Uneven Environments

Phill Kyu Rhee, InJa Jeon, and EunSung Jeong

Dept. Of Computer Science & Engineering, Inha Univ.,
253 Yong-Hyun Dong Nam-Gu, Incheon, South Korea
pkrhee@inha.ac.kr, {juninja, eunsung}@im.inha.ac.kr

Abstract. We present an adaptive normalization method based robust face recognition which is sufficiently insensitive to such illumination variations. The proposed method takes advantage of the concept of situation-aware construction and classifier fusion. Most previous face recognition schemes define their system structures at their design phases, and the structures are not adaptive during run-time. The proposed scheme can adapt itself to changing environment illumination by situational awareness. It processes the adaptive local histogram equalization, generates an adaptive feature vectors for constructing multiple classifiers in accordance with the identified illumination condition. The superiority of the proposed system is shown using 'Yale dataset B', IT Lab., FERET fafb database, where face images are exposed to wide range of illumination variation.

1 Introduction

Many face recognition methods are proposed such as PCA, FLD, ICA, and Gabor based approaches [1, 3, 5, 6, 10, 21]. Even though many algorithms and techniques are invented, face recognition still remains a difficult and unsolved problem in general. Existing technologies are not sufficiently reliable, especially under changing lighting conditions [7]. The performance of most current face recognition systems are heavily depending on lighting conditions [22, 23]. Liu and Wechsler have introduced EP (Evolutionary Persuit) for face image encoding, and have shown its successful application [24]. However, EP needs too large search space, i.e. time-consuming, to be employed in a real world application. The illumination cone for sample pose space is approximated by a linear subspace [25]. The illumination cone approach, however, assumes the pose of face images is fixed. In practical situation, face location may not be accurate enough, and the illumination cone approach leads to dramatic corruption of its performance due to the landmark mismatches. Recently, Liu et. al. proposed the idea of MMI(Multi-Method Integration) for detecting face automatically and tracking face in real time [26].

There are three major approaches for solving this problem: variation normalization, variation modeling, and invariant representation. The variation normalization methods are canonical approaches, and try to normalize the variations in face appearance. The most commonly used histogram equalization is in this category. Some examples can be found in [22, 23]. The variation modeling approaches is based on learning the model of the variation using sufficiently large examples [18, 19, 20]. Sometimes, the lack of sufficient learning samples has been resolved by image synthesis. The approaches of invariant features attempt to take advantage of invariant features are not sensitive under changing environment [19]. Quotient image, intensity derivation, and edge map are in this category. The performances of most traditional face recognitions are very much sensitive to the amount of variations observed in images. Proper treatment of illumination variations is a major requirement for robust face recognition algorithms. The proposed normalization method focuses on solving the brittleness problem of recognition systems under varying lighting conditions.

In this paper, we devise a framework of systematic solution to alleviate the effect of varying illumination conditions. Image contrast enhancement using local or sub-block histogram equalization can be found in the literature [2].

We employed similar strategy for improving the recognition accuracy of shaded face images adaptively. The adaptive capability of the proposed scheme is achieved by adopting the concept of the situation-aware evolution and classifier fusion. We start developing our approach by first considering the problem of recognition of frontal face under varying lighting condition. Adaptive local histogram equalization in the normalization stage is tested for efficient face recognition under varying illumination.

In the section 2, we present the proposed an adaptive normalization. In the section 3, we discuss about adaptive classifier fusion based situation-awareness. In the section 4, we discuss about adaptive normalization based classifier fusion for face recognition. Finally, we give the experimental results and the concluding remarks in the section 5 and 6, respectively.

2 Adaptive Normalization Using Situation-Awareness

The block diagram of the proposed face recognition scheme adopting the situation-awareness classifier fusion method with adaptive local histogram equalization is depicted in Figure 1. The architecture implements the searching strategy for optimal local histogram and Gabor transformed vector in the space of plausible solutions.

The determines the illumination category of each image by identifying a illumination situation. The situation awareness module (SAM) is implemented by MLP. The 1 × s input vector of the MLP is generated by resizing the n x m input

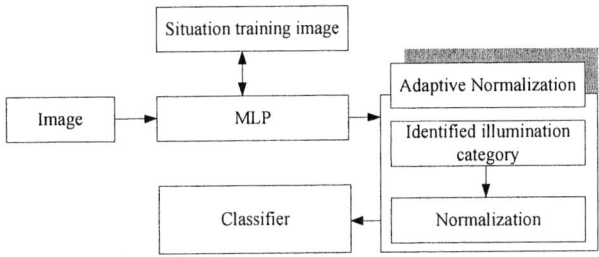

Fig. 1. The face recognition architecture using adaptive local histogram and evolutionary Gabor transform

image at time, where $s \ll n \times m$. We uses $n \times m$ pixels as the situation information, i.e., $C_I = <t, c_1, c_2, \ldots, c_{n \times m}>$. Then, the derived situation tuples DCI are described as $<t, d_1, d_2, \ldots, d_s>$, where d_i is a mosaic cell generated from the input image.

We devise an adaptive partitioning of face image for each identified lighting condition by employing the genetic algorithm. The control module searches for the best image partitioning method from the situation knowledge base, and activates local histogram equalization accordingly. The proposed adaptive local histogram equalization in the normalization stage is summarized as follows.

Step 1. At time t, the derived situation information, $DCI = <t, d_1, d_2, \ldots, d_s>$, is derived from an situation information, i.e. input image here, where di is a cell of the mosaic image.

Step 2. The situation Information, illumination category here, is decided by MLP from the derived situation information DCI.

Step 3. The control module finds a matched image partitioning method for normalization in the situation knowledge base, and triggers the matched action.

Fig. 2 shows some examples of nine categories determined by MLP.

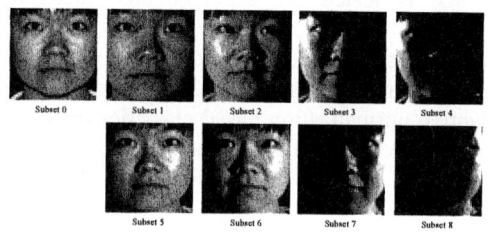

Fig. 2. Example images of nine categories from Yale face database B

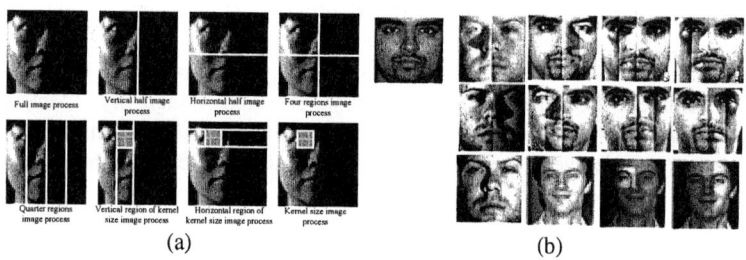

Fig. 3. (a) The partitioning methods of various local histogram methods (b) Adaptive classifier fusion based on situation-awareness.

Figure 3 (a) describes the partitioning methods of various local histogram methods. Fig. 3 (b) shows the results of applying various local histogram methods.

Figure 3 (b) was image applies the quarter partition based local histogram equalization. It uses the image where the preprocessing is applied and it accomplishes recognition. The image uses feature point and it recognizes. The feature point it searches it used the genetic algorithm.

3 Adaptive Normalization Based Classifier Fusion Scheme

3.1 Classifier Fusion Using Situation-Awareness

In this section, we introduce a novel classifier fusion scheme with the capability of situation-awareness, called situation-aware classifier fusion scheme. The situation-aware classifier fusion scheme applied to the preprocessing and feature representation of our face recognition scheme will be discussed in the next section. Classifier fusion is to combine a set of classifier or classifier components to configure an efficient classifier. The combination can be represented by as follows [4].

$$\text{CFS}(x) = F(C_1(x), C_2(x), \ldots, C_k(x)) \tag{1}$$

CFS is a classifier fusion scheme, and x denotes input image vector. F denotes classifier fusion operation, i.e., an aggregation of the K individual classifiers. C_i denotes i-th classifier or classifier component to be combined. Situation-aware classifier fusion is to select and/or to combine a subset of classifiers or classifier components. The subset is decided by the situation-awareness.

$$\text{SA-CFS}(x) = F \{ CA (C_1(x), C_2(x), \ldots, C_k(x)) \} \tag{2}$$

SA-CFS is a situation-aware classifier fusion scheme, and *CA* is a situation-aware operator. C_i is an i-th classifier or classifier component. The main difference of the proposed situation-aware fusion scheme from traditional classifier fusion schemes is that it can select a subset of classifiers or classifier components in accordance with an identified situation. Hence, the proposed SA-CFS can adapt under dynamically varying situation or environment in real-time while traditional CFS can hardly be employed under such a dynamic situation or a dynamic environment.

3.2 The Proposed Adaptive Normalization Based Classifier Fusion Scheme

The proposed SA-CFS can be implemented by the situation-awareness module(SAM), the control module(CM), the action module(AM), the genetic algorithm module(GAM) and the situation knowledge base(SKB) (see Figure 5). The AM consists of image preprocessing & normalization methods and two or more

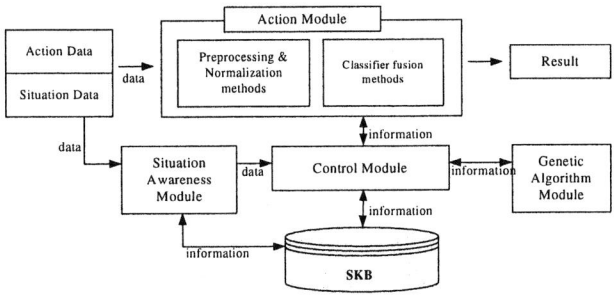

Fig. 5. The conceptual diagram is the proposed SA-CFS for efficient face recognition under varying illumination

classifiers components. Image preprocessing can image enhancement processed that is image filtering processing algorithm. The classifier can be heterogeneous, homogeneous, or hybrid ones. The components of normalization are feature representation, class decision, and post-processing ones. The CM searches for a best combining structure of classifiers or classifier components for each identified situation during the learning phase. The structures of optimal combination of classifiers/classifier components and parameter values are stored in the SKB corresponding situation expression. The SAM identifies a situation/context or an environment using situation information and their analysis.

Situation can be various configurations, computing resource availability, dynamic task requirement, application condition, environmental condition, etc [9]. Situation/context is defined as any observable and relevant attributes, its interaction with other entities and/or surrounding environment at an instance of time. Context information is denoted by a context tuples as follows.

$$CI = <t, c_1, c_2, \ldots, c_s>$$

t is the time stamp and $c_1, c_2, \ldots, c_s$ are a set of situation attributes. Derived situation information is generated from the context tuples, and represented as follows.

$$DCI = <t, d_1, d_2, \ldots, d_t>$$

di is a preprocessed attribute from a subset of situation information. Situation is expressed by a situation attributes as follows.

$$SE = <t, s_1, s_2, \ldots, s_u>$$

t is the time when the situation is identified and $s_1, s_2, \ldots,$ and s_u are a set of situation attributes representing the situation. They can be module configuration, parameter values, thresholds, parameter types, threshold types, etc.

Initially, the system accumulates the knowledge of the SKB that guarantees optimal performance for each identified situation. The SKB stores the expressions of identifiable situations and their matched actions that will be performed by the AM. The matched action can be decided by either experimental trial-and-error or some automating procedures. In the operation time, the situation expression is determined from the derived situation information, where the derived situation information is decided from the situation information. The CM searches the matched action in the SKB, and the AM performs the action.

4 Adaptive Normalization Based Classifier Fusion for Face Recognition

The block diagram of the proposed face recognition scheme adopting the situation-aware classifier fusion method with adaptive local histogram equalization is depicted in Figure 5 at section 3. The architecture implements the searching strategy for optimal local histogram and Gabor transformed vector in the space of plausible solutions.

Varying illumination is modeled as situation information, is observed and categorized by the SAM. The SAM is implemented by a MLP. The proper action of the AM to each illumination condition is predefined and stored in the SKB. The AM consists of the preprocessing and normalization, the feature extraction, and the class decision modules. The CM searches the SKB for a proper action of each identified situation, i.e. a current identified lighting condition. Finally, the face class is decided by the class decision module. The class decision module performs the task of face recognition using k-NN algorithm. In this way, the proposed system can achieve the optimal performance in dynamically changing lighting condition. The details will be discussed in the following.

4.1 Gabor Wavelet and Feature Space

The feature spaces of the proposed face recognition system by the Gabor wavelet transform. It is a simulation or approximation to the experimental filter response profiles in visual neurons [15]. The Gabor transform shows desirable characteristics of spatial locality, frequency and orientation selectivity similar to those of the Gabor kernels. The convolution coefficient for kernels of different frequencies and orientations starting at a particular fiducial point is calculated. Gabor wavelet is usually used at five different frequencies, $v = 0, \ldots, 4$, and eight orientations, $\mu = 0, \ldots, 7$ [9, 14]. The Gabor wavelet transformation of an image is defined by the convolution of the sub-area of image using a family of Gabor kernels as defined by [14].

4.2 Evolution of the Gabor Feature Space Using Genetic Algorithm

We adopt the Genetic algorithm to search an optimal type of local histogram equalization and an optimal representation of Gabor feature vector. Each combination of local histogram equalization and Gabor feature vector is encoded by a chromosome. This process is repeated until a best feature vector is reached with an optimal type of local histogram equalization, or a generation exceeds a desired criterion value. The chromosome represents the all possible combination of fiducial points and their Gabor feature vectors for all types of local histogram. The optimality of the chromosome is defined by classification accuracy and generalization capability. The total Gabor feature vector for all fiducial point V, is evolved from a larger vector set. The contribution of fiducial point is in n-dimensional space by a set of weights in the range of (0.0, 1.0). If the weights are discrete with sufficiently small steps, we use the GA to search this discrete space. The control module derives the classifier being balanced between successful recognition and generalization capabilities. The fitness function can be defined as follows:

$$\mu(V) = \lambda_1 \eta_s(V) + \lambda_2 \eta_g(V) \tag{7}$$

Where $\eta_s(V)$ the term for the system correctness, i.e., successful recognition is rate and $\eta_g(V)$ is the term for class generalization. λ_1 and λ_2 are positive parameters that indicate the weight of each term, respectively.

4.3 The Situation-Aware Face Recognition Using the Adaptive Normalization

Traditional classifier fusion schemes can not be applicable in dynamically changing situations since they usually require too much computation resources to be used in real time application. The situation-aware classifier fusion method can be applied to the preprocessing and the feature representation for real time robust face recognition.

The SKB stores the expressions of identifiable situations and their matched actions performed by the AM in the form of chromosomes. The detail of constructing the SKB is given in the following.

1. Identify an illumination category for an input image data.
2. Select a type of local histogram equalization, and perform the local histogram equalization.
3. Derive the Gabor feature $F(x_i)$ for each fiducial point, and normalize it. Concatenate the Gabor vectors for fiducial points to generate the entire Gabor feature space.
4. Begin the Gabor feature representation optimization until a criterion is met.
   1) Generate a new Gabor feature representation population.
   2) Evaluate the fitness function $\mu(V) = \lambda_1 \eta_s(V) + \lambda_2 \eta_g(V)$ of the classifiers using the newly derived Gabor feature representation population. If the criterion is met, go to Step 5.
   3) Search for the Gabor feature representation in the Gabor feature space population that maximizes the fitness function and keep those as the best chromosomes.
   4) Applying GA's genetic operators to generate new population of Gabor feature space. Go to step 4.2).
5. Steps 2 - 4 are repeated until a best feature vector is reached with a proper type of local histogram equalization, or a generation exceeds a desired criterion value.
6. Update the SKB for the identified illumination category as the chromosome of the selected local histogram equalization and reconstructed Gabor feature space.

Enrollment data use to learning data in 'Yale Face Database B' and total 810 face data, to 10 frontal face data in 90 face data by one. Extract 32 feature points in enrolling face data and formative Gabor vector, so is enrolled formation value. The recognition task is performed by constructing multiple classifiers using the generated SKB as follows:

1) Identify the illumination situation using the SAM.
2) Search a chromosome representing optimal preprocessing and Gabor feature representation for the identified illumination situation.
3) Perform the preprocessing and restructuring Gabor representation (multiple classifier) using the matched chromosome.
4) Derive the Gabor feature $F(x_i)$ for each fiducial point of the enhanced image, and normalize it.
5) Concatenate the Gabor features for fiducial points to generate total Gabor feature space.
6) Perform the task of recognition using the restructured Gabor feature vector.

5 Experimental Results

The feasibility of the proposed face recognition scheme has been tested using Yale database. 810 face images of the Yale database has been used as training data. The input node is composed of 121 items. The output node is composed of 9 items. We used 0.95 as Momentum constant, 0.45 as learning constant and 0.1 as error rate.

Five methods are devised based on the inclusion of situation-awareness, the partitioning method of local histogram, and the adoption of GA based feature optimization as shown in Table 2. The test was accomplished in order to confirm the effect the union against the method of a local histogram equalization and histogram equalization, selection of feature extraction against an illumination situation.

The recognition rate most was highly measured from the method5 which uses the situation-awareness, local histogram equalization with quarter partitioning, effective

Table 2. Experimental methods

	Illumination situation-awareness	Partitioning method for histogram equalization	GA based feature optimization
Method 1	X	Full image	X
Method 2	O	Vertical half partition	O
Method 3	O	Horizontal half partition	O
Method 4	O	Quarter partition	X
Method 5	O	Quarter partition	O
Method 6	O	Four regions partition	O
Method 7	O	kernel size region partition	O
Method 8	O	Partition of vertical region in kernel size	O
Method 9	O	Partition of Horizontal region in kernel size	O

Table 3. Recognition rate for Yale face database B, FERET fafb dataset

	Method 1	Method 2	Method 3	Method 4	Method 5	Method 6	Method 7	Method 8	Method 9
Image set of situation 1	91.75%	90.47%	76.65%	82.69%	80.95%	90.47%	91.75%	91.38%	91.57%
Image set of situation 2	90.93%	84.33%	64.93%	81.14%	79.58%	84.33%	90.93%	91.29%	91.48%
Image set of situation 3	88.27%	61.23%	47.89%	76.56%	76.83%	61.23%	88.27%	89.73%	90.28%
Image set of situation 4	74.89%	19.80%	19.14%	62.00%	66.39%	19.80%	74.89%	86.16%	86.98%
Image set of situation 5	91.93%	91.29%	77.84%	81.96%	81.50%	90.10%	91.93%	91.48%	91.29%
Image set of situation 6	80.93%	90.74%	67.86%	79.58%	79.85%	80.93%	89.83%	90.74%	90.74%
Image set of situation 7	54.81%	90.19%	49.63%	76.01%	77.20%	54.81%	87.81%	89.28%	90.19%
Image set of situation 8	19.16%	87.44%	19.23%	63.00%	69.78%	19.16%	74.06%	86.16%	87.44%
Average rate	74.08%	76.94%	52.90%	75.37%	76.51%	62.60%	86.18%	89.53%	90.99%

feature space GA based on in Table 2. It uses the image where the preprocessing is applied and it accomplishes recognition. The image uses feature point and it recognizes. The feature point it searches it used the genetic algorithm. We can conclude that the SA-CFS method can acquire a high successful recognition rate. We used 11×11 rescaled images for illumination situation-awareness since the rescaled image provides the highest accuracy. Table 3 shows the experimental results in which are exposed high illumination variation in 9 methods. As expected, the method 9 has achieved highest accuracy in face recognition in 'Yale Face Database B' total 810's data, FERET fafb dataset and IT Lab. dataset.

6 Concluding Remarks

In this paper, we propose a novel adaptive normalization technique combining situation-awareness and classifier fusion for robust face recognition. The object recognition technology does not provide sufficiently reliable performance under the variations of illumination. The proposed method adopts the concept of situation-aware construction and classifier fusion. The proposed scheme can adapt itself to changing environment illumination by situational awareness. It processes the adaptive local histogram equalization, generates an adaptive feature vector for constructing multiple classifiers in accordance with the identified illumination situation. The superiority of the proposed system is shown using 'Yale dataset B', IT Lab., FERET fafb database, where face images are exposed to wide range of illumination variation.

References

1. K. I. Diamantaras, S.Y. Kung, Principle Component Neural Networks: Theory and Application, Johj Wiley and Sons (1996)
2. Caselles, V, Lisani, J.-L, Morel, J.-M, Sapiro, G., "Shape preserving local histogram modification," Image Processing, IEEE Transactions on, Vol.8, Issue.2, Feb. 1999, pp.220-230.
3. D. Swets and J. Weng, "Using discriminant eigenfeatures for image retrieval," IEEE Trans. on PAMI, Vol.18, Issue.8, (1996)831-836
4. Ludmila I. Kuncheva, James C. Bezdek, Robert P.W. Duin, "Decision Templates for Multiple Classier Fusion: An Experimental Comparison," Pattern Recognition, Vol.34, Issue.2, (2001) 299~314
5. G. Donato, M. Bartlett, J. Hager, P. Ekman, Sejnowski, "Classifying facial actions," IEEE Trans. on PAMI, Vol.21, Issue.10 (1999) 974-989
6. M. Potzsch, N. Kruger, C. Von der Malsburg, "Improving Object recognition by Transforming Gabor Filter reponses," Network: Computation in Neural Systems, Vol.7, No.2, 341-347
7. A. S. Georghiades, P. N. Belhumeur, D. J. Kriegman, "From Few to Many: Illumination COne Models for face recognition under Variable Lighting and Pose", IEEE Trans. on PAMI, vol. 23 no. 6, (2001) 643-660
8. A. Georghiades and D. Kriegman,Peter N. Belhumeur, "Illumination Cones for Recognition Under Variable Lighting: Faces," Proc. IEEE Conf. CVPR, (1998) 52-58

9. H. Liu et. al., "Illumination Compensation and Feedback of Illumination Feature in Face Detection", Proc. International Conferences on Information-technology and Information-net, Beijing, vol. 3, (2001) 444-449
10. Bossmaier T.R.J, "Efficient image representation by Gabor functions - an information theory approach," in J.J. Kulikowsji, C.M. Dicknson, and I.J. Murray(Eds.), Pergamon Press, Oxford, U.K., 698-704
11. J. H. Holland, Adaptation in Natural and Artificial Systems, University of Michigan Press, (1975)
12. D. Goldberg, Genetic Algorithm in Search, Optimization, and Machine Learning, Addison-Wesley (1989)
13. R. C. Gonzalez, R. E. Woods, Digital Image Processing, Addison-Wesley Publishing Company (1993)
14. D. Field, "Relations between the statistics of natural images and the response properties of cortical cells," J. Opt. Soc. Amer. A, 4(12) (1987) 2379-2394.
15. J. Faugman, "Uncertainty relation for resolution in space, spatial frequency, and orientation optimization by two-dimensional cortical filters," Journal Opt. Soc. Amer. 2(7) (1985) 675-676
16. W.Zhao, R.Chellappa, "Robust Image-Based 3D Face Recognition," CAR-TR-932, N00014-95-1-0521, CS-TR- 4091, Center for Auto Research, UMD (2000)
17. W.Gao, S.Shan, X.Chai, X.Fu, "Virtual Face Image Generation For Illumination And Pose Insensitive Face Recognition," Proc. of ICASSP2003, Vol.IV, pp776-779, HongKong, (2003)
18. H.Murase, S.Nayar, Visual Learning and recognition of 3D object from appearance, IJCV, 14 (1995) 5-24
19. A.Shashua and T.Riklin-Raviv, "The Quotient Image: Class-Based Re-Rendering And Recognition With Varying Illuminations", IEEE Trans. on PAMI, (2001) 129-139
20. A.S.Georghiades, P.N.Belhumeur and D.J.Kriegman, "From Few to Many: Illumination Cone Models for Face Recognition under Differing Pose And Lighting", IEEE TPAMI, Vol.23, No.6, (2001) 643-660
21. Jianwei Yang, Lifeng Liu,Tianzi Jiang, Yong Fan,:"A modified Gabor filter design method for fingerprint image enhancement", Pattern Recognition Letters archive, Volume 24 , Issue 12, ISSN:0167-8655 (2003) 1805-1817
22. Shiguang Shan, Wen Gao, Bo Cao, Debin Zhao,: "Illumination normalization for robust face recognition against varying lighting conditions", Analysis and Modeling of Faces and Gestures, 2003. AMFG 2003 IEEE International Workshop on, (2003) 157-164
23. Toshiaki Kondo,Hong Yan, "Automatic human face detection and recognition under non-uniform illumination", Pattern Recognition, Volume 32, Issue 10 (1999) 1707-1718
24. C. Liu, and H. Wechsler, "Evolutionary persuit and its application to face recognition", IEEE Trans. on PAMI, Vol. 22, No. 6, (2000) 570-582

A New Detector Set Generating Algorithm in the Negative Selection Model

Xinhua Ren[1], Xiufeng Zhang[1], and Yuanyuan Li[2]

[1] Network Center of Taiyuan Univ of Tech, Taiyuan, Shanxi, China 030024
{renxh, zhangxiufeng}@tyut.edu.cn
[2] College of Computer Science and technology & Software of Taiyuan Univ of Tech,
Taiyuan, Shanxi, China 030024
li_yy2008@hotmail.com

Abstract. In order to improve the generating efficiency of the detector set, a new detection rule called edit distance rule is presented in this paper, based on the negative selection model of Artificial Immune System (AIS). Under this rule, edit distance is adopted to measure the similarity between self strings and randomly generated strings. Then a new detector generating algorithm used the new rule is discussed. It is necessary to use the Trie data structure to store the strings in the self set in this new algorithm. Finally, the advantages of the algorithm are given through the theoretical analysis.

1 Introduction

Recently, computer immunology has become the hotspot in the computer science field. It simulates the mechanism of body immune system (BIS) and has been applied widely on intrusion detection, machine learning, and information processing and so on.

At present, there have a few immune models used to interpret immune phenomena. In these models, the negative selection model presented by Forrest et al. of New Mexico University is the most frequently used one [1]. The model simulates the life process of T cell in BIS. During biosome generates the T cell, gene recombination is proceeded randomly at first and then negative selection will be proceeded for all of the T cells. If the receptor on T cell surface responses to the biosome genes, the T cell will be deleted. Only those T cells not sensible to self cell can leave thymus to exert immune function. The negative selection model adopts the work mechanism similar to that one mentioned above: First, it generates detector set randomly and deletes those detectors sensible to the self cell during the negative selection. Thus the detectors are left which only responses to the nonself cells.

The detector set generation is of important in the negative selection model and directly relates to the detection rule adopted by the system. Therefore, a good detection rule can improve the performance of the detector set generation and further of the system.

This paper presents a new detector set generation algorithm based on a new detection rule which is based on edit distance.

2 Problem Definition

It usually uses the binary string to represent cell types in AIS, including self cells, detector cells and nonself cells. In this paper self and detector are defined as binary string of length l on alphabet $\sum : \{0,1\}$. Fig.1 indicates the relationship between each binary string set.

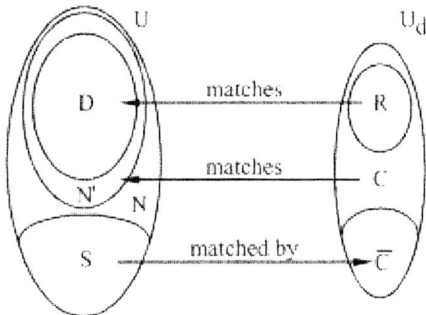

Fig. 1. The relationship between each binary string set. The symbols are defined as following: U : binary string universal; U_d : detector universal; D : nonself subset has been detected out; N' : nonself subset can be detected; N : nonself set; S : self set; R : detector set; C : candidate detector set; $\bar{C}$: detector set has been deleted; obviously, $S \bigcap N = \emptyset, S \bigcup N = U$. And generally, $N - N'$ is called detector hole.

In Fig.1, match means pattern recognition based on some specific detection rule. The binary strings in S and N stand for self pattern, nonself pattern respectively.

3 Edit Distance Detection Rule

Detection rule is the criterion for distinguishing self and nonself pattern and also for generating detector set. Given R as a detection rule, $\forall s \in S, d \in U_d$, if sRd, then we call s matches d, denote $Match(s,d) = True$. And d will be deleted during negative selection. Otherwise it will be preserved to become mature detector.

3.1 Edit Distance Definition

Edit distance is also called Levenshtein distance which was presented by Levenshtein researching error correction code in 1966 [2]. Levenshtein pointed out that there were three types of errors taken place as following:

(1) Inversion: i.e. $0 \rightarrow 1$ or $1 \rightarrow 0$;
(2) Deletion: i.e. $0 \rightarrow \Lambda$ or $1 \rightarrow \Lambda$;
(3) Insertion: i.e. $\Lambda \rightarrow 1$ or $\Lambda \rightarrow 0$.

Here, Λ stands for the lost of bit.

Definition 1: the edit distance between two binary strings b and b' is the minimal edit operator (Inversion, Deletion, Insertion) number to change b into b'.

For example, the edit distance between 10010 and 1001 is 1, because it only need delete the last bit of 10010 to change itself into 1001.

In 1974, Wagner and Fischer presented a dynamic programming algorithm to compute edit distance [3].

3.2 The Computing of Edit Distance

For two binary strings: $b = b_1 b_2 \cdots b_m$, $b' = b'_1 b'_2 \cdots b'_n$, a $(m+1)(n+1)$ order matrix $M[\cdot, \cdot]$ is defined. Here, $M[i, j]$ stands for the minimal edit operator number to change $b_1 b_2 \cdots b_i$, one of the substrings of b, into $b'_1 b'_2 \cdots b'_j$, one of the substrings of b', and $0 \leq i \leq m, 0 \leq j \leq n$. And we have [4]:

(1) $M[0, j] = j$;
(2) $M[i, 0] = i$;
(3) For $i, j \geq 1$,
$$M[i,j] = min\{M[i-1,j]+1, M[i,j-1]+1, M[i,j]+change(b_i, b'_j)\}$$
Here,
$$change(b_i, b'_j) = \begin{cases} 0 & b_i = b'_j; \\ 1 & b_i \neq b'_j \end{cases}$$

Then, $M[m,n]$ is the edit distance between b and b', denote $ed(b, b') = M[m,n]$.

3.3 Edit Distance Detection Rule

Now we present a new detection rule on the basis of previous two sections as following: Given s and d are two binary string of length l, $s \in S, d \in U_d$. And k is a given integer, $1 \leq k \leq l$. if $ed(s, d) \leq k$, then we call s match d, i.e. $Match(s, d) = True$ and detector d will be deleted according to the negative selection model.

The detection rule stated above is called edit distance detection rule, in which k is called threshold of the rule, and $l - ed(s, d)$ is called similarity between s and d. Obviously, the smaller the edit distance is, the bigger similarity is, and vice versa.

4 Detector Set Generating Algorithm

According to the negative selection model, it generates randomly candidate detector set firstly and then deletes those detectors sensible to self set during the negative selection and finally gets the detector set. Obviously, for any detection rule, the directive detector generating method is exhaust algorithm. However, due to the very low efficiency of exhaust algorithm, its time complexity and space complexity are increase exponentially with the self set scale increasing. Therefore, it is necessary to look for more efficient generating algorithm against to a specific detection rule.

The following section gives a more efficient detector set generating algorithm based on the Trie data structure [5].

4.1 Storing Self Set Using Trie Data Structure

Trie is a tree data structure which is also called key tree. It is a tree whose nodes are greater than 1. And every node in it does not include one or a few keys, but includes the characters which consist of key [6]. The Trie tree is used to store a great deal of strings and its advantage lies in saving the storing space efficiently.

It can use Trie structure directly to store self set. Own to the elements in self set being binary string, the Trie tree storing the self set is a binary tree essentially. For example, if $l = 4$ and $S = \{0000, 0010, 1100, 1110, 1111\}$, then the Trie tree storing self set is shown as Fig.2.

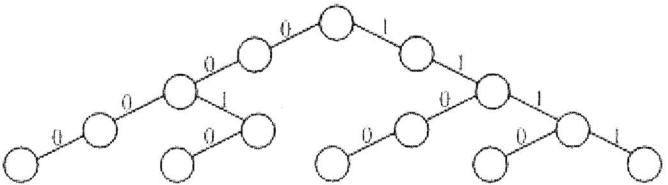

Fig. 2. Trie tree example

4.2 Detector Set Generating Algorithm Based on Edit Distance Detection Rule

In Fig.2, given $s_1 = 0000$, $s_2 = 0010$, and $d = 0101$ is a candidate detector binary string. According to section 3.2, the following two matrixes can be obtained:

$$M[s_1, d] = \begin{pmatrix} 0 & 1 & 2 & 3 & 4 \\ 1 & 0 & 1 & 2 & 3 \\ 2 & 1 & 1 & 1 & 2 \\ 3 & 2 & 1 & 2 & 1 \\ 4 & 3 & 2 & 1 & 2 \end{pmatrix} \quad M[s_2, d] = \begin{pmatrix} 0 & 1 & 2 & 3 & 4 \\ 1 & 0 & 1 & 2 & 3 \\ 2 & 1 & 1 & 1 & 2 \\ 3 & 2 & 1 & 2 & 1 \\ 4 & 3 & 2 & 2 & 2 \end{pmatrix}$$

It is obvious that the first three columns of the above matrixes are exactly same. That is to say, when computing $ed(s_1, d)$, we can copy the first three columns to the matrix of $M[s_2, d]$ while computing $ed(s_2, d)$. Thus, it can get the edit distance between the prefix string of each node and the candidate detector string and put the computing result into a uniform table while traveling the whole Trie tree. The binary strings which have the same prefix string can share the result computed previously. So it reduces the computing amount efficiently by this way.

In addition, for the given threshold k and the distance matrix M, if $\exists i, 0 \leq i \leq l$, there has $M[i,j] > k, j = 0, 1, \cdots, l$, and then the distance between the candidate detector binary string and the binary string which has the preceding string $s_1 s_2 \cdots s_i$ is greater than k. Under this condition, the algorithm will be terminated and the detector d is a valid detector which will be added into detector set. Thus, it narrows the compare domain and improves the performance of the algorithm.

On the basis of the two features stated above, a new detector set generating algorithm against to the edit distance can be designed which includes two sections as following:

The first is the recurrence procedure TrieTreval traveling the Trie tree. In the procedure, there probably exists a node that the distance between itself and the candidate detector is greater than the given threshold and at this time the algorithm is terminated. And the current detector string will be preserved as a valid detector. If the algorithm is still active after travel all of the nodes, then this detector string is not a valid detector which will be deleted.

The second is the function named as EditDist computing the edit distance. According to the discussion in section 3.2, it just need compare the current bit to the candidate detector string. And associating with the computing results previously, the values of all of the elements of the current column will be computed out immediately.

Here is the detail description of the algorithm:

(1) Input the candidate detector string d.

(2) Traveling the Trie tree begins with the root node of itself. For the top level, it begins with its left child node and can get the similarity classified two cases below:

(a) The edit distance is greater than the given threshold. In this case, the distance between the candidate detector string and the self string preceded with the string from the root node to the current node is also greater than the given threshold. So, $\exists s \in S$, and there has $Match(s, d) = False$. Thus, the candidate detector string is a valid detector and the algorithm is terminated.

(b) The distance is no greater than the given threshold. Then repeat the step.

(3) If all of the nodes have been travelled, then $\forall s \in S$, there must have has $Match(s, d) = True$. In this case, the candidate detector string is not a valid detector and will be deleted. And the algorithm will end normally.

4.3 Complexity Analysis

Supposing the radix of the self set $|S| = N_S$, then the node number in the Trie tree $N_T < 2^l$ and the time complexity and the space complexity are both less than $O(2^l)$. In addition, the space complexity of EditDist function is less than $O(l \cdot 2^l)$. Because there just process single bit during the traveling, the time complexity of EditDist function is $O(1)$. Thus, the total time complexity and the space complexity of the algorithm are less than $O(2^l)$ and $O((l+1) \cdot 2^l)$ respectively. Because in the actual applications, there has $l << N_S$ generally, the performance of the new algorithm is better than exhaust algorithm.

5 Conclusions

This paper presents a detection rule based on edit distance. And a new more efficient detector set generating algorithm is presented on the basis of the new detection rule. The new algorithm requests using Trie data structure to store the self set so that it saves the storing space of self set greatly. Finally, this paper analyses the complexity of the new algorithm and concludes that it is prior to exhaust algorithm.

References

1. S Forrest,A S Perelson ,L Allen R ,et al.: Self-onself Discrimination in a Computer [C]. Proceedings of the 1994 IEEE Symposium on Research in Security and Privacy Los Alamitos. CA: IEEE Computer Society Press ,1994.
2. V.I. Levenshtein: Binary codes capable of correcting deletions, insertions, and reversals. Soviet Physics Doklady. 10 (1966) 707–710
3. Kenneth Sörensen: Distance measures based on the edit distance for permutation-type representations. In GECCO 2003: Proceedings of the Bird of a Feather Workshops. Genetic and Evolutionary Computation Conference. (2003) 15–21
4. http://www.cs.berkeley.edu/ luca/cs170/notes/lecture13.pdf
5. Wang Yi: Match algorithm of approximate string with wildcard based on Trie data structure. Computer Application. 10 (2004) 121–124 (in Chinese)
6. Yan Weimin, Wu Weimin: Data structure (C language version). Tsinghua University Press. (1997) 247-250 (in Chinese)

Intrusion Detection Based on ART and Artificial Immune Network Clustering

Fang Liu, Lin Bai, and Licheng Jiao

School of Computer Science and Engineering,
Xidian University, Xi'an 710071
f63liu@163.com

Abstract. Intrusion Detection based on Adaptive Resonance Theory and Artificial Immune Network Clustering (ID-ARTAINC) is proposed in this paper. First the mass data for intrusion detection are pretreated by Adaptive Resonance Theory (ART) network to form glancing description of the data and to get vaccine. The outputs of ART network are considered as initial antibodies to train an Immune Network, Last Minimal Spanning Tree is employed to perform clustering analysis and obtain characterization of normal data and abnormal data. ID-ARTAINC can deal with mass unlabeled data to distinguish between normal and anomaly and to detect unknown attacks. The computer simulations on the KDD CUP99 dataset show that ID-ARTAINC achieves higher detection rate and lower false positive rate.

1 Introduction

Security is the guarantee of applications in network environment. Traditional intrusion detection systems (IDS) can not find unknown intrusion effectively. Some traditional systems (such as MADAM/ID [1]) employ supervisory learning algorithm and purely normal data for training, which are hard to put to use.

Clustering is a typical embranchment of unsupervised learning method. Some clustering procedures have been applied to intrusion detection [2] [3]. The methods introduced by Luo and Wang [2] and Portnoy [3] require predetermined parameters, in which values significantly affect the algorithms' results. Leandro proposed an evolutionary artificial immune network for clustering according to Jerne's theory of immune network [4] [5]. ART [6] fit unsupervised clustering and can adjust the cluster number adaptively. A combination of ART and immune network can reduce the complexity of the immune network and offer a priori knowledge to the immune network in order to concentrate the data effectively.

2 Intrusion Detection Based on ART and Artificial Immune Network Clustering (ID-ARTAINC)

Intrusion detection data are pretreated by ART network, then the outputs of ART are considered as the initial antibodies of immune network instead of producing initial antibodies randomly to improve the convergence speed and decrease the computational amount of immune network. ART learning algorithm is in [6]. Learning algorithm based on AiNet [4] is described as follows.

Step 1. $i=1$, generate initial network C: the network nodes that is to say antibodies y_j ($j=1,2,...,N_C$) are p-dimensional vectors, matrix $C(N_C * p)$ is used to represent the network.

Step 2. For each input antigen x_i ($i=1,2,...,n$), do:

Step 2.1. Calculate Ab-Ag affinity: $f(x_i, y_j) = \dfrac{1}{1+(x_i - y_j)^T(x_i - y_j)}$

Step 2.2. Select k antibodies ($y_{r_1}, y_{r_2},..., y_{r_k}$). We confirm clonal scale q_m according to the principle that the higher the affinity, the bigger the clonal scale. $T_c^C(y_{r_m}) = I_m \times y_{r_m}$ ($m = 1,2,..., k$), and $q_m = Int(n_c * \dfrac{f(x_i, y_{rm})}{\sum_{b=1}^{k} f(x_i, y_{rm})})$ $m = 1,..., k$,

where I_m is a q_m-dimensional row vector and all elements are 1. $Int(x)$ represents a function that returns the minimum integer larger than x, n_c is a predetermined clonal scale

Step 2.3. Mutation: mutate the antibody y_j^* which have been run Clonal operation in order to improve the antibody y_j^* and antigen x_i affinities: $C = C - \alpha(C - X)$, where α is the mutation rate. The higher the affinity, the smaller the α.

Step 2.4. Calculate Ab-Ag affinities, re-select $t\%$ antibodies whose affinities are higher and create a memory cell matrix M_p

Step 2.5. Eliminate the cells in M_p whose affinities are inferior to threshold ω

Step 2.6. Calculate Ab-Ab avidity in M_p: $s_{ij} = \|y_i^* - y_j^*\|$, eliminate the cells whose avidities are inferior to σ

Step 2.7. Concatenate C and M_p: $C \leftarrow [C; M_p]$, $i=i+1$, if $i \leq n$, go to *Step 2.1*

Step 3. Network compression: Calculate all antibody- antibody avidities in the network C and eliminate those cells whose affinities are less than threshold σ

Step 4. Network output: replace the eliminated antibodies by some novel ones and put them into the network C to get a novel network

Step 5. If the iterative number process arrive the pre-defined iteration steps, stop. Else go to *Step 2*.

In order to obtain the network structure which can reflect the distribution of original data, we will analyze its output with minimal spanning tree [7] and lead to some clusters. The dataset is divided into h subsets H_c ($1 \leq c \leq h$) after clustering. The subsets generated should be labeling normal or anomaly in the IDS. If the tota sample number rate of sample number in a cluster is no less than r ($0 \leq r \leq 1$), this cluster is considered as a normal cluster. Each abnormal cluster can be determined according to the inner distance of cluster and field knowledge. For dataset X, calculate the distances between x_i ($0 \leq i \leq n$) and immune network cells y_j: $d(x_i, y_j)$. Find the nearest distance $d(x_i, y_{min})$ ($1 \leq min \leq N_C$), $y_{min} \in H_c$, then associate x_i with cluster c and label this cluster as x_i. If $d(x_i, y_{min}) \geq \zeta$, x_i is considered as an attack of unknown type.

3 Simulations and Results

The dataset employed is the KDD CUP99 data [8]. ART1 network is used in this paper. So the data must be discrete. Equal-width-intervals algorithm [9] is employed here. Because the original dataset is too mass to operate, so we select 200,000 records randomly from 10% KDD CUP99 for training, 2000 attacks included in them. Since the training set comprises 22 attack types while the testing set contains 37 ones in all. In order to test the detection of unknown attacks using ID-ARTAINC, two testing sets are set with 100,000 records which are selected from KDD CUP99 test set respectively. Each of them contains 1000 intrusion (37 attack types). The algorithms have operated 50 times. Under the average condition, the number of clustering over training dataset equals 6 by ID-ARTAINC, where AiNet is 6 and [2] is 7. For the clustering results, an algorithm performs well when the distances among clusters are large and the inner distances of each cluster are small. ID-ARTAINC accords with this standard and is superior to other two algorithms (as shown in Table 1 and Table 2). Inner distance of cluster: $D_c = \frac{1}{n(n-1)}\sum_{i=1}^{n}\sum_{j=1}^{n}d(x_i,x_j)$ $c\in[1,r]$, where r is the cluster number. Cluster-to-cluster distance: $D(C_i,C_j) = \frac{1}{n_i n_j}\sum_{p\in C_i}\sum_{q\in C_j}d(p,q)$, where n is the number of objects in each cluster.

Table 1. The inner distance of cluster result of each method

Cluster	1	2	3	4	5	6	7
ID-ARTAINC	0.96	1.03	1.81	0.69	2.17	0.77	\
AiNet algorithm	1.61	1.57	2.93	1.33	2.78	0.97	\
Method in [2]	2.93	2.85	4.05	1.82	3.71	1.53	2.78

Table 2. The cluster-to-cluster distance results of three algorithms

Algorithm	cluster	2	3	4	5	6	7
ID-ARTAINC	1	12.68	20.36	21.51	19.23	22.56	\
	2	\	20.83	23.01	18.58	21.28	\
	3	\	\	18.63	17.75	17.93	\
	4	\	\	\	16.95	17.56	\
	5	\	\	\	\	15.81	\
AiNet algorithm	1	12.71	17.55	20.13	16.37	19.18	\
	2	\	15.35	16.61	18.15	16.63	\
	3	\	\	13.21	16.72	13.96	\
	4	\	\	\	14.38	11.12	\
	5	\	\	\	\	14.55	\
Method in [2]	1	12.51	16.17	16.29	15.73	13.88	11.93
	2	\	14.46	17.16	18.58	14.71	9.61
	3	\	\	11.88	14.75	11.91	15.12
	4	\	\	\	11.02	10.03	15.73
	5	\	\	\	\	10.11	16.33
	6	\	\	\	\	\	14.56

To evaluate the IDS, there are two major indications of performance: the Detection Rate (DR) is defined as the number of intrusion samples detected by the system divided by the total number of intrusion samples presented in the test set, the False Positive Rate (FPR) is defined as the total number of normal samples that were incorrectly classified as intrusions divided by the total number of normal samples. The training dataset is divided into 6 clusters using ID-ARTAINC. The average result of detection by operating each algorithm 30 times is given in Table 3. ID-ARTAINC meets the standards of clustering [10]. The results indicate that the intrusion detection based on ARTAINC has more superior detection rate and lower false positive rate.

Table 3. The result of each algorithm

Dataset	Algorithm	DR of know (%)	DR of un-known (%)	FPR (%)
	ID-ARTAINC	**93.16**	**81.02**	**3.88**
Test 1	AiNet	82.53	71.72	7.61
	Method in [2]	59.76	49.53	7.85
	ID-ARTAINC	**93.53**	**80.67**	**4.03**
Test 2	AiNet	81.88	72.33	7.12
	Method in [2]	61.28	49.17	7.52

Acknowledgements. This work is supported by the National Natural Science Foundation of China under Grant No.60372045 and No.60133010, and the National Grand Fundamental Research 973 Program of China under Grant No.2001CB309403.

References

1. Lee, W., Stolfo, S.J., Mok, K.: Data Mining Work Flow Environments Experiences in Intrusion Detection. In Proceedings of the 1999 Conference on Knowledge Discovery and Data Mining. (1999)
2. Luo, M., Wwang L.N.: An Unsupervised Clustering-Based Intrusion Detection Method. Acta Eelctronica Sinica. 30(2003): 1713-1716
3. Leonid Portnoy: Intrusion Detection with Unlabeled Data using Clustering. Undergraduate Thesis. Columbia University, (2000)
4. de Castro, L.N., Fernando J. Von Zuben: An Evolutionary Immune Network for Data Clustering. In: Proc. of IEEE SBRN. Rio de Janeiro, (2000) 84-89
5. de Castro, L.N., Timmis, J.: Hierarchy and Convergence of Immune Networks: Basic Ideas and Preliminary Results. In: I International Conference on Artificial Immune Systems. Canterbury, Kent. (2002)
6. Jiao L.C.: Neural Network System Theory. Xidian University Press. 12 (1990)
7. Everitt, B.: Cluster Analysis. Heinemann Educational Books Ltd.. (1974)
8. kdd cup99 dataset: http://kdd.ics.uci.edu/databases/kdd cup99/kdd cup99.html. (1999)
9. Catlett, J.: On Changing Continuous Attributes into Ordered Discrete Attributes. In Proceedings of the European working session on learning on Machine learning. (1991): 164-178
10. Han J.W.: Data Mining Concepts and Techniques. China Machine Press. (2001)

Nature-Inspired Computations Using an Evolving Multi-set of Agents

E.V. Krishnamurthy[1] and V.K. Murthy[2]

[1] Computer Sciences Laboratory,
Australian National University, Canberra, ACT 0200, Australia
abk@discus.anu.edu.au
[2] School of Business Information Technology,
RMIT University, Melbourne 3000, Victoria, Australia
kris.murthy@rmit.edu.au

Abstract. A multiset of agents can mimic the evolution of the nature-inspired computations, e.g., genetic, self-organized criticality and active walker (swarm and ant intelligence) models. Since the reaction rules are inherently parallel, any number of actions can be performed cooperatively or competitively among the subsets of the agents, so that the system evolve reaches an equilibrium, a chaotic or a self-organized emergent state. Examples of natural evolution, including wasp nest construction through a probabilistic shape-grammar are provided.

1 Introduction

This paper describes the application of a multi-set of agents for nature-inspired computational schemes. These include all **conventional algorithms, Evolutionary algorithms, Genetic algorithms,** Michalewicz and Fogel [13], **Genetic Programming,** Koza[12], **Immunocomputing** [20], **Self-organized criticality**[18], and **Active Walker models** (ants with scent or multiwalker-paradigm where each walker can influence (repel or attract) the other through a shared landscape based on probabilistic selection, Bonabeau et al.[3], Chu et al.[5], Dorigo et al.[6], Kennedy and Eberhart [11], **Biomimicry,** Pacino [16], Bio-inspired robotics, Bar-Cohen and Breazeal [1] and Brownian Agents , Ebeling and Schweitzer [7].

Principal Features

The multiset of agents paradigm (MAP) consists of the following features [24]:

(i) A multiset M that contains evolving agents (called the agent-space) whose information is structured in an appropriate way to suit the problem at hand. Conventionally the elements of the multiset are passive datastructures, Murthy and Krishnamurthy [14] . Here each element of the multiset is an agent. Thus apart from the advantages resulting from the use of intelligent agents as elements, we have a strong theoretical background from the abstract rewriting systems on multisets Suzuki et al.[21].

(ii) A set of interaction rules that prescribes the context for the applicability of the rules to the agents. Each rule consists of a left-hand side (a pattern or property or attribute) describing the conditions under which the agents can communicate and interact, and a right hand side describes the actions to be performed by the agents, if the rule becomes applicable, based on deterministic, fuzzy or probabilistic criteria, Murthy and Krishnamurthy[14].

(iii) A control strategy that specifies the manner in which the agents will be chosen and interaction rules will be applied, the kinetics of the rule- interference (inhibition, activation, diffusion, chemotaxis) and a way of resolving conflicts that may arise when several rules match at once.

(iv) A coordinating agent or an agent by itself evaluates the performance of each agent to determine the effectiveness (fitness) of rule application.

(v) Interaction -Based: The computations are interpreted as the outcome of interacting agents to produce new agents (or same agents with modified attributes) according to specific rules. Hence the intrinsic (genotype) and acquired properties due to interaction (phenotype) can both be incorporated in the agent space. Since the interaction rules are inherently parallel, any number of actions can be performed *cooperatively or competitively* among the subsets of agents, so that the new agents evolve toward an equilibrium or unstable or chaotic state.

(vi) Content-based activation of rules: The next set of rules to be invoked is determined solely by the contents of the agent-space, as in the context of chemical reactions.

(vii) Pattern matching: Search takes place to bind the variables in such a way to satisfy the left hand side of the rule. It is this characteristic of pattern (or attribute) matching that gives the agent-based paradigm its distinctive capabilities for nature-inspired computing.

(viii) Choice of objects, and actions:

We can several types of objects, as the basic elements of computation to perform suitable actions on them by defining a suitable topology, geometry or a metric space.

The rest of this paper is organized as follows: In Sections 2 and 3, general properties and of rule based paradigms are developed. In Section 4 examples of nature-inspired computations realised by MAP. Section 5 deals with some simulation tools currently available. Section 6 contains the conclusion.

2 Multi-set of Agents Based Programming Paradigm

The multiset-agent system consists of several single agent-systems, Fig.1, [24]. Thus if N agents are involved $i = 1, 2, \ldots, N$, each of the agents will be denoted with a label (i).

(1) Worldly states or environment U:
Those states which completely describe the universe containing all the agents.

(2) Percept: Depending upon the sensory capabilities (input interface to the universe or environment) an agent can receive from U an input T (a standard set of messages), using a sensory function Perception (PERCEPT): PERCEPT : $U \rightarrow T$.

PERCEPT can involve various types of perception: see, read, hear, smell. The messages are assumed to be of standard types based on an interaction language that is interpreted identically by all agents. Since U includes both the environment and other agents the input can be either from the agents directly or from the environment that has been modified by other agents. This assumption permits us to deal with agents that can communicate directly, as well as, indirectly through the environment as in active walker model; this is called "stigmergy" in Ant colony where one ant can modify its environment and affect the behaviour of another ant (see also EFFECT).

(3) Mind M:

The agent has a mind M (essentially a problem domain knowledge consisting of an internal database D for the problem domain data and a set of problem domain rules P) that can be clearly understood by the agent without involving any sensory function. Here, D is a set of beliefs about objects, their attributes and relationships stored as an internal database and P is a set of rules expressed as preconditions and consequences (conditions and actions). When T is input, if the conditions given in the left-hand side of P match T, the elements that correspond to the right-hand side are taken from D, and suitable actions are carried out locally (in M) as well as on the environment.

The nature of internal production rules P, their mode of application and the action set determines whether an agent is deterministic, nondeterministic, probabilistic or fuzzy. Rule application policy in a production system P can be modified by:

(1) Assigning probabilities/fuzziness for applying the rule
(2) Assigning strength to each rule by using a measure of its past success
(3) Introducing a support for each rule by using a measure of its likely relevance to the current situation.

The above three factors provide for competition and cooperation among the different rules. Such a model is useful for many applications, e.g., Active -walker, Self-organization and swarm models, Chemotaxis. Accordingly, we assume that each agent can carry out other basic computations, such as having memory, simple addition capability, comparison, simple control rules and the generation of random numbers, Pacino [16]. These mechanisms enable us to simulate tumbling, as well as running of organisms for foraging.

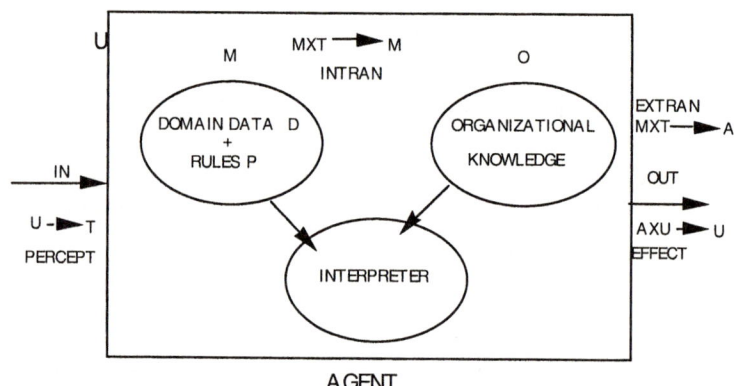

Fig. 1.

(4) Organizational Knowledge (O): Since each agent needs to communicate with the external world or other agents, we assume that O contains all the information about the relationships among the different agents, e.g., the connectivity relationship for communication, the data dependencies between agents, interference among agents with respect to rules and information about the location of different domain rules.

(5) INTRAN:
On the receipt of T, the action in the agent M is suitably revised or updated by the function called Internal transaction (INTRAN).

Revision: Revision means acquisition of new information about the environment, that requires a change in the rule system P. This may result in changes in the database D. In a more general sense, revision may be called "mutation' of the agent since the agent exhibits a mutation in behaviour due to change of rules or code.

Example: The inclusion of a new tax-rule in the Tax system.

Update: Update means adding new entries to the database D; the rules P **are not changed**. In a more general sense, the update may be called "Reconfiguration" since the agent's behaviour is altered to accommodate a change in the data.

Example: Inclusion of a new tax-payer in the Tax system. Both revision and update can be denoted in set-theoretic notation by:

$$\text{INTRAN: M} \times \text{T} \rightarrow \text{M(D,P)}$$

Both mutation and reconfiguration play important roles in Nature-inspired computing. These are achieved in our model by introducing changes in D and P as required. This can be interpreted as updating or revising a set of database instances. Hence, if one or several interaction conditions hold for several non-disjoint subsets of objects in the agent at the same time, the choice made among them can be nondeterministic or probabilistic. This leads to *competitive parallelism*. The actions on the chosen subset are executed atomically and committed. In other words, the chosen subset undergoes an 'asynchronous atomic update'. This ensures that the process of matching and the follow-up actions satisfy the four important ACID properties: Atomicity (indivisibility and either all or no actions or carried out), Consistency (before and after the execution of a transaction), Isolation (no interference among the actions), Durability (no failure). Once all the actions are carried out and committed the next set of conditions are considered.

As a result of the actions followed by commitment, we may revise or update and obtain a new database for each agent; this may satisfy new conditions of the text and the actions are repeated by initiating a new set of transactions. These set of transformations halt when there are no more transactions executable or the databases does not undergo a change for two consecutive steps indicating a new consistent state of the databases.

However, if the interaction condition holds for several disjoint subsets of elements in the database at the same time, the actions can take place independently and simultaneously. This leads to *cooperative parallelism*; e.g. vector parallelism, pipeline parallelism.

(6) EXTRAN: External action is defined as an external transaction (EXTRAN) that maps a state of mind and a partition from an external state into an action performed by the agent. That is: EXTRAN: M X T $\rightarrow$ A. That is, the current state of mind and a new input activates an external action from the action set A.

(7) EFFECT: The agent also can affect U by performing an action from a set of actions A (ask, tell, hear, read, write, speak, send, smell, taste, receive, silent), or more complex actions. Such actions are carried out according to a particular agent's role and governed by an etiquette called protocols. The effect of these actions is defined by a function EFFECT that modifies the world states through the actions of an agent: EFFECT: A X U $\rightarrow$ U; EFFECT can involve additions, deletions and modifications to U. Thus an agent is defined by a set of nine entities, a 9-tuple: (U,T, M(P,D),O,A,PERCEPT,INTRAN,EXTRAN,EFFECT).

Operational Aspects of Multiagent System

A multi-agent system is realised as a loosely coupled network of single agents shown in Figure 1; they interact among themselves and through the environment to solve a problem. Operationally, the multiagent system uses certain protocols having the following features or its variants:

1. There is a seeding agent who initiates the solution process.
2. Each agent can be active or inactive.
3. An active agent can do local computation, send and receive messages (through message-passing or shared memory) and can spontaneously become inactive.
4. An inactive agent becomes active if and only if it receives a message
5. Each agent may retain its current belief or revise its belief as a result of receiving a new message by performing a local computation. If it revises its belief, it communicates its revised state of belief to other concerned agents; else it does not revise its solution and remains silent.

3 Kinetics of the Multi-agent System

In order to speed up the use of the multi-agent paradigm we need to consider how to permit multiple agent execution concurrently. This offers the possibility of carrying out parts or all of computations in parallel on distinct processors or performing multiple-simulations simultaneously in a grid or cluster computing environment. Such possibilities would require the analysis as to how the rules interfere with each other. These interference rules are similar to those enunciated by Turing [22] to describe the development of shape, form and pattern in organisms (chemical morphogenesis rules). Such interferences can take place in four ways.

1. Enabling dependence (ED): Agents $A(i)$ and $A(j)$ are called enable dependent (or dataflow dependent) through $A(k)$ if the messages from A (i) creates the required precondition in $A(k)$ and results in a message to $A(j)$ and creates the required precondition in $A(j)$ to act (fire).

2. Inhibit dependence (ID): Agents A (i) and A (j) are called inhibit dependent, if the actions of A (i) do not create the required precondition in A(k) needed by A (j) and prevents it from executing any action.

3. Opposition dependence (OD): Agents A (i) and A (j) are opposition dependent (also called data-output dependent) through A(k)), if the order in which A (i) and A (j) enable A(k) and update A(k) produce different results in A(k); that is the objects A(i) and A (j) perform conflicting operations on A(k) and not interleavable. Hence, the local serializability in A(k) is not ensured, if the actions are carried out in different order.

4. Data Antidependence (AD): Agents A (i) and A(j) are data antidependent through A(k) if A(i) enables A(k) and receives the data from A(k) subsequently, the firing of another object A(j) enables A(k) and results in updates of the same set of elements.

Concurrency and Conflicts

Traditionally, we require that the following two conditions are satisfied for global serialization in distributed computing and transaction processing:

1. At each agent the actions in local actions are performed in the non-conflicting order (**Local serializability**).

2. At each agent the serialization order of the tasks dictated by every other agent is not violated. That is, for each pair of conflicting actions among transactions p and q, an action of p precedes an action of q in any local schedule, if and only if, the preconditions required for p do not conflict with those preconditions required for execution of the action q in the required ordering of **all tasks in all agents** (**Global serializability**).

The above two conditions require that the preconditions for actions in different agents A(i) and A(j) do not interfere or cause conflicts. These conditions are necessary for the stabilization of the multi-agent systems that the computations are locally and globally consistent.

Termination: For the termination of agent –based program, the interaction among the agents must come to a halt. When the entire set of agents halt we have an equilibrium state (or a fixed point) also called stability while dealing with exact computation in a deterministic system.

Non–termination, instability, chaos: These cases arise when the agents continue to interact indefinitely as in chemical oscillations. Then the multiagent-space reaches a non-equilibrium state. It is also possible that the evolution of the agent system leads to instability, chaos and self-organization.

4 Nature-Inspired Computations

MAP can simulate nature-inspired computations- chemical oscillatory behaviour, swarm dynamics and self-organized criticality.

(i) Swarm and Ant Colony Paradigm
A swarm consisting of birds, ants, cellular automata ,Wolfram[23], Ilachinski [10], is a population of interacting agents that is able to optimize some global objective through cooperative search of space, Kennedy and Eberhart [11],Bonabeau et al.[3].

Here, individual agents are points in space, and change over time is represented as movement of points, representing particles with velocities and the system dynamics is formulated in MAP using the rules:

(1) **Stepping rule:**
The state of each individual agent is updated or revised in many dimensions, in parallel, so that the new state reflects each agent's previous best success; e.g. the position and momentum (velocity) of each particle.

(2) **Landscaping rule:**
Each agent assumes a new best value of its state that depends on its past best value and a suitable function of the best values of its interacting neighbours, with a suitably defined neighbourhood topology and geometry.

The first rule reflects the betterment of the individual, while the second rule reflects the betterment of the collection of the individuals in the neighbourhood as a whole, by evaluating the relevance of each individual and providing support for its activity.

These two rules permit us to model self-avoiding, self-repelling and active random-walker models. This can result in a system whose global non-linear dynamics emerges from local rules, and interesting new properties may show up- bifurcations and chaos and various kinds of attractors with fractal dimensions presenting a swarm -like, flock-like appearances depending upon the Jacobian of the mapping, Wolfram [23], Ilachinski [10].

In the agent model, shared landscape can be simulated through a blackboard and self-avoiding walks can be simulated using a table that stores the locations visited earlier.

Also MAP can handle Parallel ant colony system simulation suggested by Chu et al. [5], Blackwell and Branke[2].If many different equally likely independent modes m are to be searched for, it is more efficient to choose a multiset with m sets, each with k agents so that $mk = N$ where N is the total number of agents; i.e., the agents are partitioned into distinct groups each with their own speciality.

(ii) Bistability in Perception
In visual perception, as for example, in the Necker cube illusion, the attention is switched between two images. This switching is chaotic and corresponds to two different chaotic attractor, Hoppensteadt and Izhikevich [9]. Also we can simulate multistable perception arising due to deterministic chaos, in which many ambiguous interpretation of the image alternate spontaneously, Nishimura et al. [15].

(iii) Comb Pattern in honey-bee colonies
Agents supported by blackboard facility can realise the probabilistic rule-based generation , Camazine et al.[4], of the honey-comb pattern in bee colonies. The comb pattern is generated by certain simple rules of production (Deposition) and consumption (Removal) of eggs, honey and pollen, as stated below :

Rule 1: The queen (agent) lays an egg every minute 24 hours in a vacant cell not more than at a distance of 4 cells from a brood.

Rule 2: The eggs hatch at the end of 21 days and the cell becomes vacant.

Rule 3: The honey and pollen arte deposited by agents (bees) at empty cells close to the brood.

Rule 4: The honey is removed at the rate 0. 6 and pollen is removed at the rate 0.95 from cells near to the brood.

Using a blackboard marked as cells the above system can be simulated as an agent – based Monte Carlo to obtain the desired honey comb pattern.

(iv) Wasp Nest Evolution: Use of GP and Shape Grammar

The nest construction rules used by wasps, Camazine et al. 2001, can be simulated through Multiset of agent based Genetic programming. It seems that the insects and animals use their perceptive skill to evaluate the compactness of the resulting construction by using the Isoperimetric Quotient(IQ) to measure the fitness of their construction, Sankar and Krishnamurthy [17]. In self-organization the nests are evalauted locally and that should ensure that it is globally fit. IQ tells us how to maximize surface area for a given perimeter in a 2-d object and how to maximize the volume in a 3-d object given the surface area. For a 2- dimensional object, the IQ is given by $4 \pi A/P^2$, where A is the area and P is the perimeter (number of sides for a regular polygon). This ratio is a maximum equal to unity for the circle and its near approximants [17]. Here we omit the constants and compute the reciprocal of IQ, namely, the square of the perimeter divided by area of the hexagon (assumed to be unity), which we call Quality Index (QI).

For a 3- dimensional object the IQ = $6 V \pi^{1/2} / S^{3/2}$ where V is the volume and S is the surface area. This is a maximum equal to unity for the sphere or closer or its closer approximants. This measure is useful when dealing with polyhedral grammars (termite mounds [4]).

In self- organization, a global pattern emerges solely from the interactions among the lower level components of the system. The rules specifying the interactions among the components use only local information without reference to the global pattern.

In the following wasp-nest rules, we denote an assembly of hexagons by (p,q) where p is the number of sides in the assembly (perimeter), and q is the number of hexagons (area), $QI = p^2/q$. The graph isomorphic variants of these rules are omitted.

Rule 0: (Probability 1)   (6,1),QI= 36

NULL

Rule 1:Probability 1
(6,1),QI=36   (10,2),QI=50

Rule 2a: (10,2), QI=50   (12,3),QI= 48
Probability >> 0.5

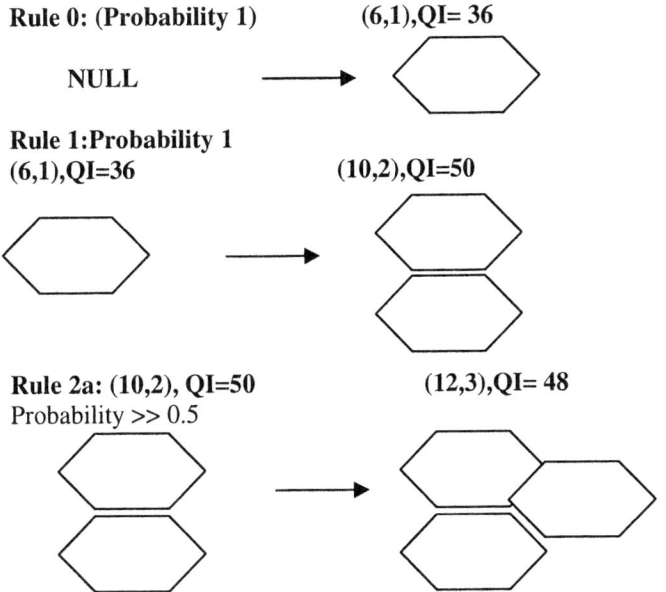

Rule 2b: (10,2),QI=50 (14,3),QI=65
Probability < < 0.5

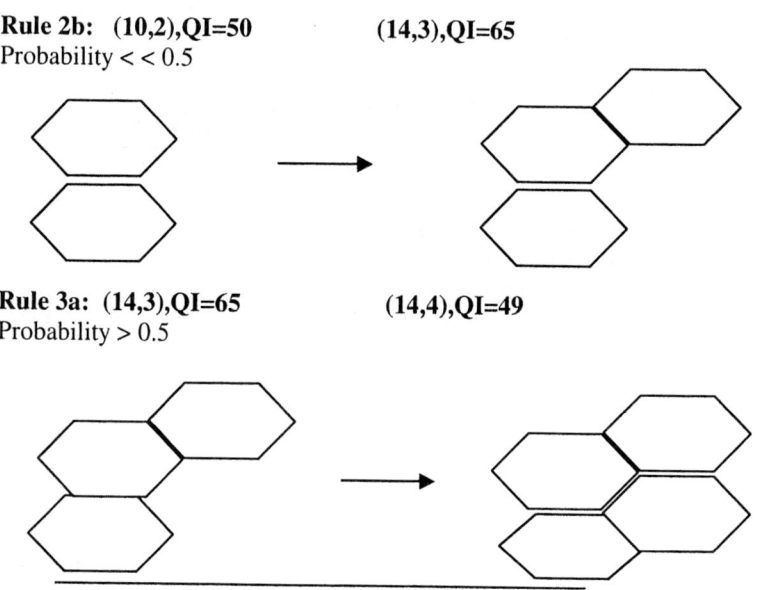

Rule 3a: (14,3),QI=65 (14,4),QI=49
Probability > 0.5

Rule 3a is similar to Rule 2a omitting the left lowermost hexagon

Rule 3b:(12,3),QI=48 (14,4),QI= 49
Probability > 0.5

Since the rules are based on local information, it is sufficient to consider sharing of 1,2, 3 edges among the hexagons. This is because each time a wasp leaves the best possible configuration with the least QI.; it will not leave an open configuration with 4 unfilled sides with perimeter 18 , QI= 81 or 5 unfilled sides with perimeter 22 with QI = 96. Another wasp would have completed the earlier configuration having a lower QI ,since evolution prefers the higher probability rules 2 a, 3a and 3b .

5 Multi-agent Toolkits

Gorton et al. [8] have evaluated agent architectures: Adaptive Agent architecture (AAA), Aglets developed by IBM, and the Java based architecture Cougaar. The paradigm described here is well-suited for implementing in Cougaar, a Java based agent architecture, since Cougaar is based on human reasoning. A Cougaar agent consists of a blackboard that facilitates communication and operational modules called plug-in that communicate with one another through the blackboard and contain the logic for the agent's operations. The use of blackboard and direct communication are useful for simulating the problems described in Section 4.

Shakshuki et al.[19], evaluate multiagent tool kits,such as:Java Agent development framework (JADE), Zeus Agent building toolkit (Zeus) and JACK Intelligent Systems. They consider Java support, and performance evaluation. The number of agents they consider is of the order of 32. For implementing the paradigm described here, major developments are needed in Agent technology, since we need a very large number of agents to simulate many real-life scientific applications.

6 Conclusion

This paper, described a multi-set agent paradigm (MAP) for nature -inspired soft computation; here we allow the possibility of error, randomness, and nonterminating computation to model features that are inherent in problems arising in Nature. The introduction of probabilistic choices in a this model enables us to study the evolutionary biological, chemical and physical systems based on intermittent feedback from the environment.

References

1. Bar-Cohen, Y., and Breazeal, C: Biologically-Inspired Intelligent Robotics, S.P.I.E. Press, Bellingham, Washington, U.S.A.(2003).
2. Blackwell, T and Branke,J: Multi-swarm Optimization in Dynamic environments, Lecture Notes in Computer Science,3005, Springer Verlag, New York (2004)489-500,.
3. Bonabeau, E., Dorigo,M., and Theraulaz, G., Swarm Intelligence :From natural to artificial systems, Oxford University Press, London U.K.(1999)
4. Camazine, S. et al.: Self-organization in Biological Systems, Princeton University Press, Princeton (2001)
5. Chu, S et al., Parallel Ant colony Systems, Lecture Notes In Artificial Intelligence, 2871, Springer Verlag, New York (2003)279-284
6. Dorigo, M.,Caro ,G.D., and Sampels, M.: Ant Algorithms, Lecture Notes in Computer Science, Vol.2463, Springer Verlag, New York (2002)
7. Ebeling,W and Schweitzer, F: Self-organization, Active Brownian Dynamics and biological Applications, Nova Acta Lepoldina,88,332 (2003)169-188.
8. Gorton,I, et al :Evaluating agent Architectures: Cougaar, Aglets and AAA, Lecture Notes in Computer Science,2940,Springer Verlag, New York (2004)264-274
9. Hoppen steadt ,F.C, and Izhikevich, E.M.: Weakly Connected Neural Networks, Springer, New York (1997)
10. Ilachinski A.: Cellular Automata, World Scientific, Singapore (2001)
11. Kennedy,J. and Eberhart,R.C.:Swarm Intelligence, Morgan Kauffman. London (2001)
12. Koza, J.R.:Genetic programming III, Morgan Kaufmann, San Francisco (1999)
13. Michalewicz, Z., and Fogel, D.B.: How to Solve it: Modern Heuristics, Springer Verlag, New York (2000)
14. Murthy, V.K and E.V. Krishnamurthy.: Probabilistic Parallel Programming based on multiset transformation , Future generation Computer systems 11(1995) 283-293.

15. Nishimura, H et al.:Neural chaos scheme for perceptual conflicts, Lecture Notes In Artificial Intelligence, 2773, Springer Verlag, New York (2003) 170-196
16. Pacino,K.M.:Biomimicry of bacterial foraging for distributed optimisation and control, IEEE Control System Magazine,22(3)(2002)52-68
17. Sankar,P.V and Krishnamurthy,E.V: On the compactness of subsets of digital pictures, Computer Graphics and image Processing, 8(1978) 136-143
18. Serugendo,.D.M, et al.: Self Organization : Paradigms and Applications, Lecture notes in Artificial Intelligence, 2977, Springer Verlag, New York(2004)1-19
19. Shakshuki,E and Jun,Y.: Multi-agent development toolkits: An Evaluation, Lecture Notes in Artficial intelligence, 3029, Springer Verlag, New York(2004)209-218
20. Stepney,S et al.: Artificial Immune System and the grand challenges for non-classical computation, Lecture notes in Computer Science,2787, Springer Verlag, New York (2003)204-216
21. Suzuki,Y et al.:Artificial Life applications of a class of P systems: Abstract rewriting systems on Multisets, Lecture notes in computer science,2235, Springer Verlag, New York(2001)299-346.
22. Turing, A.M.:The chemical basis for morphogenesis, Phil.Trans.Roy.Soc. London, 237 (1952)37-79
23. Wolfram, S.:A New kind of Science, Wolfram Media Inc., Champaign, Ill (2002)
24. Woolridge,M: Introduction to Multi-Agent systems, John Wiley, New York(2002)

Adaptive Immune Algorithm for Solving Job-Shop Scheduling Problem[*]

Xinli Xu, Wanliang Wang, and Qiu Guan

Information Engineering Institute, Zhejiang University of Technology,
Hangzhou 310014, P.R. China
{xxl,wwl,gq}@zjut.edu.cn

Abstract. Based on the information processing mechanism of immune system in biotic science, the process of the vaccination was analyzed. Then a new approach of immune algorithm problems for job-shop scheduling was proposed. This method can make self-adjustment of the immune responses along with the cultivation period of antibodies, and accelerate or suppress the generation of antibodies. Furthermore, it can gradually enhance recovery ability of the system, and find the optimal solution with more efficiency. Simulation results show that it is an effective approach.

1 Introduction

Job-shop Scheduling Problem (JSP) [1] is a resource allocation problem subject to allocation and sequencing constraints. As a ubiquitous and general production problem in manufacturing, JSP is very complicated and challenging. It has been researched for several decades and many approaches for solving the optimization problems are proposed. However, systemic approaches and theory have been not formed so far [2].

As an intelligence approach newly put forward, immune algorithm [3-6] (IA) has some advantages different from the other optimization methods such as genetic algorithm[7]. For example, it is capable of diversity in the generation of antibodies, self-adjusting mechanism and immune memory function [3,4]. Based on the vaccination, IA can use the transcendent knowledge of the problem to quicken the convergence of the solutions. An approach of injecting bacterin in the immune system is proposed in literature [6]. Because the transcendent knowledge of many actual problems is lacking and unreliable, it is difficult to distill bacterin in the course of the vaccination. Generally, it can result in the mistaken search and the low efficiency of solving. In this paper, adaptive immune algorithm (AIA) is proposed to solve JSP. Based on self-learning and self-recognition, the effective bacterin is generated to suppress the objective produced by the antigen. Namely, the objective value can approach automatically to the optimal solution of scheduling.

---

[*] Foundation item: this research is supported by the National Natural Science Foundation of China (NSFC Grant No.60374056 and 60405009).

2 Job-Shop Scheduling Problem

For m-machines and n-jobs JSP, it is known as follow: (1) a set of machines is $M = \{M_i \mid 1 \leq i \leq m\}$ and M_i is the i-th number of machine, (2) a set of jobs is $J = \{J_i \mid 1 \leq i \leq n\}$ and J_i is the i-th job, (3) a set of operations is $O = \{O_i \mid 1 \leq i \leq n\}$ where $O_i = \{o_{ij} \mid 1 \leq i \leq n, 1 \leq j \leq m\}$, and o_{ij} is the machine where the j-th operation of the i-th job is processed, and (4) the processing times matrix is $T = \{T_{ij} \mid 1 \leq i \leq n, 1 \leq j \leq m\}$ and T_{ij} is the processing time of the j-th operation of J_i.

JSP is satisfied with some conditions: (1) only one operation can be processed once on one machine, and (2) one operation is not suspended by another operation in the course of being processed until it is completed on the same machine.

The objective of scheduling is to decide a set of sequences $\{P_1, P_2, ..., P_n\}$ of all jobs on each machine in order to minimize the total operating costs. Generally, the objective is to minimize the maximum among completion-dates (the time at which the last operation of a job is completed), namely, $\min f(\{P_i\}) = \min(\{F_i \mid 1 \leq i \leq n\})$. Where F_i is the complete time of the i-th job.

3 Job-Shop Scheduling Method with Adaptive Immune

For JSP, the antigen is described as $\{m/n/M/J/O/T/\min F_{max}\}$. Where m, n, M, J, O and T are defined as Section 2, and $\min F_{max}$ is the objective to minimize the max complete time.

An antibody is defined as a schedule scheme. The format of decimal numbers is applied into the coding of an antibody. It can be expressed as $A = \{A_{ij} \mid 1 \leq i \leq m, 1 \leq j \leq n\}$ and A_{ij} is the j-th job processed on the i-th machine.

The affinity $Ag(x)$ between the antigen and the antibody x is defined as follow:

$$Ag(x) = (f_{max} - f(x))/(f_{max} - f_{min}) . \quad (1)$$

Where $f(x)$ is the value of the objective function corresponding to the antibody x, and f_{max} and f_{min} are the maximum and minimum respectively.

In this paper, there are 9 steps in the job-shop scheduling algorithm with adaptive immune as follow:

Step 1 (Recognition of Antigen). Input the job-shop scheduling problem, which is regarded as the antigen of adaptive immune algorithm. Based on the characters of the problem, the system is judged whether the kind of problem has been solved.

Step 2 (Generation of Initial Antibodies Based on Working Procedure). If the kind of problem has been solved then the antibodies (namely better solutions) found in the memory cell are decided as the initial antibodies. Or else initial antibodies based on operations are generated stochastically in the space of solutions.

Step 3 (Computation of Affinity [3,4]**).** By identifying the gene types, diverse antibodies are generated in the immune system. The similarity between the antibody x_1 and x_2 is described as the affinity $Ab(x_1, x_2)$. Because there are n antibodies and every antibody consists of m genes in the immune system. Based on the theory of information entropy, the j-th allelic entropy $H_j(x_1, x_2, ..., x_n)$ is defined as

$$H_j(x_1, x_2, ..., x_n) = \sum_{i=1}^{n} -p_{ij} \log p_{ij} \ . \tag{2}$$

Where p_{ij} is the allele derived from the probability of the j-th gene.

For l random antibodies, the sum $H(x_1, x_2, ..., x_l)$ of all allelic entropies is

$$H(x_1, x_2, ..., x_l) = \sum_{j=1}^{m} H_j(x_1, x_2, ..., x_l) \ . \tag{3}$$

Then the affinity $Ab(x_1, x_2)$ between the antibody x_1 and x_2 is decided as

$$Ab(x_1, x_2) = 1/(1 + (H(x_1 + x_2))) \ . \tag{4}$$

From Eq. (4), it is known that $Ab(x_1, x_2) \in [0, 1]$.

Step 4 (Update of Memory Cell). Among n_A antibodies, $\alpha n_A (\alpha \in (0,1))$ antibodies whose high affinities between the antigen and those are selected and sent into the memory cell. Because of the capacity C_s of the memory cell is limited, the new antibody is substituted for the old antibody whose affinity between the new antibody and that is highest.

Step 5 (Pick-up of Bacterin). The pattern of gene is identified in the gene chain of every antibody and its probability is computed statistically. So bacterin is not an individual but the characteristic of some gene bits. Assume that there are l ($0 < l \leq C_s$) antibodies $x_{i1}, x_{i2}, ..., x_{il}$ in the i-th iterative period and the j-th allele of those has the common pattern v. Namely, it is satisfied with

$$H_j(x_{i1}, x_{i2}, ..., x_{il}) = 0 \ . \tag{5}$$

The inoculable probability of the pattern v is set as

$$P_v(j) = \frac{1}{l}[A_g(x_{i1}) + A_g(x_{i2}) + ... + A_g(x_{il})] \ . \tag{6}$$

Where $j = 1, 2, ..., m$. Assume that there are M_j patterns distilled from the j-th allele, and then the total patterns are distilled from n antibodies as follow

$$M = \sum_{j=1}^{m} M_j \ . \tag{7}$$

Step 6 (Vaccination). Among the antibodies not sent into the memory cell, $\beta \cdot (1-\alpha) \cdot n_A$ antibodies are stochastically selected and inoculated bacterin based on the idea of the rotating bet wheel. Where $\beta \in (0,1)$. Rotate the wheel once and then the corresponding bacterin pattern is selected from every gene bit of those antibodies in term of the inoculable probability of Eq. (6).

Step 7 (Mutation and Crossover). In order to maintain the diversity of antibodies and prevent from the assimilation of those, the antibodies which are not sent into the memory cell and also not inoculated the bacterin are executed the mutation and crossover operation. Firstly, stochastically select the two antibodies and their gene bits according to the mutation probability P_m, and then mutate the gene bits. Secondly, randomly select one row from the antibody matrixes respectively, and then exchange them. Finally, the antibodies generated by the mutation and crossover operations are tested whether they are satisfied with the restrictions of working procedure so that they are all feasible solutions.

Step 8 (Accelerating and Suppression to Generate Antibodies). Compute the desired value E_i of the antibody x_i as follow

$$E_i = A_g(x_i)/d_i .\tag{8}$$

Where d_i is the density (number) of the antibody x_i.

Step 9 (Termination Conditions). When the termination conditions (the max iterative times N_1 or the max times N_2 of continuous appearances of the invariable optimal) are fulfilled, the optimization process is finished.

4 Experiments and Results

AIA is applied to solve the 8-jobs and 4-machines JSP. The set of operations is given as

$O = \{\{1,3,2,4\},\{3,1,2,4\},\{1,4,3,2\},\{3,2,1,4\},\{4,2,3,1\},\{2,4,1,3\},\{2,3,4,1\},\{4,1,2,3\}\}$, and the matrix of processing time of jobs is also given as

$T = \{\{4,4,7,3\},\{3,4,4,2\},\{3,4,6,3\},\{2,6,4,3\},\{4,5,5,3\},\{4,6,5,4\},\{2,4,5,5\},\{3,3,2,5\}\}$.

Fig.1 (a) shows that the optimal objective value and the average objective value in the memory cell vary with the iterative process. The Gantt charts of the optimal are shown in Fig.2. It is shown that the max completing time of the problem is 35.

In order to compare with the ability of searching the optimal, AIA and IA [3,4] are applied to independently solve the above problem for 100 times with the same parameters, respectively. Fig.1 (b) shows the curves of the optimal objective value for the two algorithms every time. Obviously, the optimal gained every time in AIA is superior to that in IA [3,4].

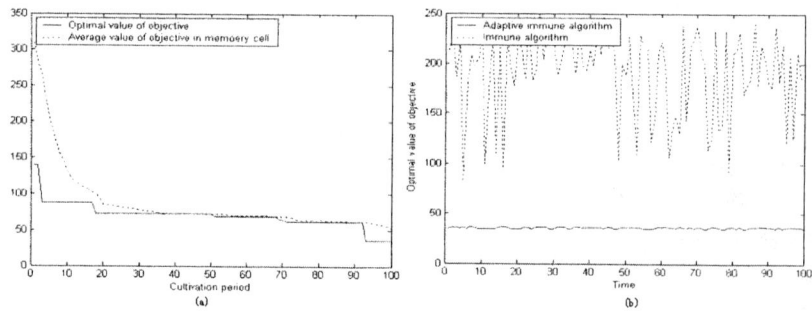

Fig. 1. Here, the max iterative steps $N_1 = 100$, the number of antibodies $n_A = 100$, the capacity of memory cell $C_s = 20$, the mutation probability of antibodies $P_m = 0.3$, the proportion of antibodies sent into memory cell $\alpha = 0.2$, and the proportion of vaccination $\beta = 0.5$.

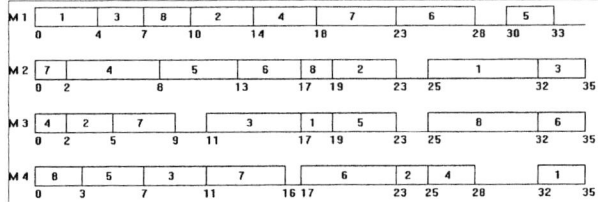

Fig. 2. M_i is the i-th machine and the number in the grid is described as the number of job

5 Conclusions

In this paper, the mechanism of vaccination is analyzed in the immune system and AIA for JSP is presented. The adaptive process of vaccination with the automatic pattern recognition can not only quicken the convergence of the algorithm but also overcome some deficiencies in distilling manually the transcendent knowledge of the problem. The proposed method can reserve the advantage of vaccination and it is independent of the initial antibodies.

References

1. Conway R. W., Maxwell W. L.: Theory of Scheduling. Addison-Weslet, Reading, Mass. (1997)
2. Wu Cheng : The Theoretical Background of Contemporary Integrated Manufacturing Systems: One Type of Complexity Problems and Its Solution . Computer Integrated Manufacturing Systems,Vol.7, No.3. (2001) 1-7
3. Chen J-S, Chi D-H, Kim M K, et al.: A Study on Comparison between Immune Algorithm and the Other Algorithms in Motor Design. Proc. ISAP'97 Int. Conf. on Intelligent System Application to Power Systems. Seoul, South Korea (1997) 588-592
4. Hu Zhao-yang, Wen Fu-shuan: A Study on Comparison between Immune Algorithm and the Other Algorithms in Motor Design. Information on electric Power, No.1 (1998) 61-63, 73
5. Dasgupta D: Artificial Immune Systems and Their Application. Nerlin: Springer-Verlag (1999)
6. Wang Lei, Pan Jin, Jiao Li-cheng: The Immune Algorithm. Acta Electronica Sinica, Vol.28, No.7 (2000) 74-78
7. Cheng R, Gen M, Tsujimura Y: A Tutorial Survey of Job-shop Scheduling Problems Using Genetic Algorithms – I. Representation. Computers & Industrial Engineering, Vol.30, No.4 (1996) 983-997

A Weather Forecast System Based on Artificial Immune System

Chunlin Xu, Tao Li, Xuemei Huang, and Yaping Jiang

Department of Computer Science, Sichuan University,
Chengdu, China
scu_xcl@yahoo.com.cn, litao@scu.edu.cn

Abstract. Inspired by the learning mechanism of the biological immune system, the paper presents a method for weather forecast. Expressions of antigen and B-cell are defined. An immune-based supervised learning algorithm is described in detail. A weather forecast system based on immune theory has thus been presented. The experimental results show that the proposed method has higher forecast accuracy rate than neural network based weather forecast technique.

1 Introduction

Over the last few years, some methods based on artificial neural network(ANN) for weather forecast have been proposed [1][2]. These methods have the disadvantage of lower efficiency, less accuracy etc.

The artificial immune system (AIS) and ANN are both inspired by biology [3]. Like ANN, AIS can also be applied to complicated problems in the engineering fields [3]. Recently, many immune-inspired models such as aiNet[4], RAIN [5] and AIRS [6][7] are proposed. There appears very good performance when these models are applied to the classification for datasets and filtration analysis [7]. It shows that immune system may be an excellent machine learning method [8].

In this paper, we propose an immune-inspired supervised learning method for weather forecast. The expressions of antigen and B-cell are given out. The immune learning algorithm is realized and the weather forecast system based on AIS is built. The simulation experimental results show that the proposed system has more forecast accuracy compared with the system based on ANN.

2 The Weather Forecast System Based on AIS

There are three primary stages in the system. The first stage is the process of antigenic presentation, which encodes the actual weather data to form antigens data set, defines antigen expression and calculates average affinity value. The second stage is to design and implement the immune learning algorithm. In this stage, each item in the antigens set will go through clonal selection process and dynamic evolution process, and then the evolved memory cells are available for weather forecast. The final stage is to output actual weather forecast results by using of memory cells and weather data.

2.1 The Process of Antigen Presentation

In the paper, antigens are the actual weather data. The antigenic determinant, which is the feature vectors of the antigen, can be extracted from the weather data. This process is similar to the antigen-presentation process in a biological immune system.

Let $\Omega = \bigcup_{i=1}^{\infty}\{0,1\}^i$ represent the set of binary strings.

Define antigens set Ag: $Ag=\{<a,c>|a \in D_1 \wedge c \in D_2 \wedge |a|=l \wedge |c|=3\}$, Where $D_1=\{0,1\}^l$, l is a constant, and a is antigenic determinant, which is extracted from weather data and mainly composed of the value of absolute atmospheric pressure, the difference in atmospheric pressure, the sign of the difference and the wind. $|a|$ is the length of string a. $D_2=\{0,1\}^3$ and c represents the class of a given antigen. Actually, according to actual weather data, c consists of the weather of today, tomorrow and the day after tomorrow. $|c|$ is the length of string c.

Define B-cells set: $B=\{<d,c,stim,res>|d \in D_1 \wedge c \in D_2 \wedge |d|=l \wedge |c|=3 \wedge 0 \leq stim \leq 1 \wedge res \in R\}$, where d is antibody gene, c is the class of d, $stim$ is the stimulation value between d and ag, res is resources number held by d and R is real number set.

Denote M as the set of the memory cells, $M \subset B$. Initialize the B and M to empty.

Function $f_{stim}(x,y)$ is defined as $f_{stim}(x,y) = 1 - f_{affinity}(x,y)$, which is used for calculating stimulation value between two cells, where $f_{affinity}(x,y)$ is used for calculating affinity value between two cells, which is calculated as the *Euclidean* distance and defined as $f_{affinity}(x,y) = \sqrt{(x.d_1 - y.a_1)^2 + (x.d_2 - y.a_2)^2 + ... + (x.d_i - y.a_i)^2}$, where $x \in B$, $y \in Ag$, $i=l$. All elements in the Ag will be normalized such that the *Euclidean* distance between two elements is in the range of [0,1].

Now the average affinity value (named as δ) over all antigens is calculated as:

$$\delta = \sum_{i=1}^{n-1}\sum_{j=i+1}^{n} f_{affinity}(ag_i, ag_j) \Big/ n(n-1)/2$$, where n is the number of antigens, ag_i and ag_j are the ith and the jth antigen in Ag.

2.2 The Process of Immune Learning

The process of immune learning is the key stage of the paper. The system is trained by each element in the antigens set. There are three steps involved in this process.

2.2.1 The Procedure of Clonal Selection

The first step is to let a given antigen go through a clonal selection procedure. Given an antigen, ag ($ag \in Ag$), and find the memory cell from M set, mc_{clone}, that is of the same classification as ag and whose stimulation value with ag is maximum. If such a cell is not found in M, then $ag \rightarrow mc_{clone}$ and add mc_{clone} to M.

Now clone mc_{clone} and the clonal number $f_{clonal\_num}(mc_{clone}) = \alpha * f_{stim}(mc_{clone}, ag)$, where α is clonal_ rate, which is a integer defined by system. For each new clonal cell, its feature vectors and classification will be mutated based on probability denoted as β ($0<\beta<1$). Add new cells which have undergone mutation and mc_{clone} to B set.

2.2.2 The Procedure of Dynamic Evolution

In this step, a concept named limited resources [6][7] is introduced. The number of resources in the system is a fixed value. Each element in B is allocated a number of resources. The principle of resources allocation is that a B-cell which is highly stimulated by the given *ag* can own more resources, and the total resources which are allocated to B-cells can not exceed the number of resource in the system. This competitive allocation of resources will result in some B-cells owning the least resources died. Only those B-cells owning more resources can be alive. The goal is to control the number of B-cells.

Some cells are randomly selected from *B* set to undergo the procedure of clonal selection again, and then a new *B* set is produced. Calculate the average stimulation values between the *ag* and each class of *B*. These values are denoted as s_i ($0<i<cn$), where *cn* is the number of classes in *B*. The method of calculating s_i is described as below:

$$b.stim = f_{stim}(b, Ag) \qquad b \in B, \qquad s_i = \sum_{j=1}^{|B_i|} b_j.stim \Big/ |B_i|, b_j \in B_i, i \in D_2 .$$

Where B_i is the *i*th subset of B, $|B_i|$ represents the number of all elements in B_i.

At this point, the stopping criterion is examined. The stopping criterion is reached iff existing certain $s_i >= stimulation\_threshold$ named θ ($0<\theta<1$). If the stopping criterion is met, the procedure of dynamic evolution is stopped, otherwise repeated.

2.2.3 Producing Memory Cells

In this step, find the cell from *B*, mc_{cand}, that is of the same classification as *ag* and whose stimulation value with *ag* is maximum, and add it to *M*. The affinity value between mc_{cand} and mc_{clone} is calculated. If this value is less than the average affinity value (i.e. δ), mc_{clone} is removed from *M*. Now the training on given antigen *ag* is completed. The next antigen in the set is selected to undergo these steps. The whole training process is ended until all antigens have been presented to the system.

2.3 Output of Forecast Results

Input actual weather data into the system, and forecast results are determined by using a majority vote of the outputs of the *k* most stimulated memory cells.

3 Simulations and Experimental Results

In order to assess the forecast performance of the system, the experiments are carried out. At the same time, in order to draw a convictive conclusion, another weather forecast system[2] based on traditional ANN is built for comparing performance.

The parameters used in the system are set as below: *l* is 12, clonal_rate α is 10, mutation probability β is 0.2, the total number of resources in the system is 500, stimulation threshold θ is 0.8, *k* value is 3. The weather data of April and May are coded[2] to form antigens set and presented to train the system.

After training has completed, the weather data of April and May are presented to the system to forecast weather. The weather data of June which were not used for training the system are presented to the system too. The forecast results include the weather of today, tomorrow, the day after tomorrow. Table 1 shows the results.

Table 1. Comparison of experimental results. Percentum represents the forecast accuracy rate. The symbol 1 represents today's weather. The symbol 2 represents tomorrow's weather. The symbol 3 represents the day after tomorrow's weather.

The Forecast System	Weather of Apr. and May			Weather of June		
	1	2	3	1	2	3
based on ANN[2]	86.4%	76.3%	88.1%	71.4%	64.3%	64.3%
based on AIS	95.1%	92.3%	91.4%	87.2%	82.3%	81.1%

4 Conclusion

The experimental results show that the proposed system based on AIS has higher forecast accuracy rate when compared with the weather forecast system based on ANN. Because the system is trained by the weather data of April and May, The forecast accuracy rate of April and May is higher than that of June. The system is more stimulated by weather data of April and May.

Although the forecast results are rough, the proposed system provides a new solution for weather forecast. The realization of the system shows that a practical forecast system based on AIS can be built.

References

1. Jin, L., Luo, Y., Li, Y.H.: Study on Mixed Prediction Model of Artificial Neural Network for Long-range Weather. Journal of Systems Engineering (2003) 331-336
2. Wang, H.B., Li, T.: Intelligent Neural Networks and It's Application in Weather forecasting System. Computer Engineering and Design (1999) 42-44
3. Li, T.: Computer Immunology. 1st edition. Publishing House of Electronics Industry Beijing (2004)
4. De Castro, L. N., Von Zuben, F. J.: aiNet: An Artificial Immune Network for Data Analysis. USA:Idea Group Publishing (2001) 231-259
5. Timmis, J., Neal, M.: A Resource Limited Artificial Immune System for Data Analysis. Knowledge Based Systems, vol. 14 (2001) 121-130
6. Watkins, A., Timmis, J., Boggess, L.: Artificial Immune Recognition System (AIRS): An Immune Inspired Supervised Machine Learning Algorithm. Genetic Programming and Evolvable Machines, vol. 5 (2004) 291-317
7. Watkins, A., Timmis, J.: Artificial Immune Recognition System(AIRS): Revisions and Refinements. In Proc. of 1st ICARIS (2002) 173-181
8. Watkins, A., Boggess, L.: A New Classifier Based on Resource Limited Artificial Immune Systems. In Proc. of CEC2002 (2002) 1546-1551

A New Model of Immune-Based Network Surveillance and Dynamic Computer Forensics

Tao Li, Juling Ding, Xiaojie Liu, and Pin Yang

Sichuan University, Chengdu, China
litao@scu.edu.cn, beathann@hotmail.com

Abstract. Dynamically evolutive models and recursive equations for self, antigen, dynamic computer forensics, immune tolerance, mature-lymphocyte lifecycle and immune memory are presented. Following that, a new model, referred to as *Insdcf*, for computer network surveillance and dynamic computer forensics is proposed. Simulation results show that the proposed model has the features of real-time processing, self-learning, self-adaptivity, and diversity, thus providing a good solution for computer network surveillance and dynamic computer forensics.

1 Introduction

Network surveillance and computer forensics have been listed and received substantial attention on *FIRST* (Forum of Incident Response and Security Teams) since year 2001. However, current solutions for computer forensics are mostly static methods[1]-[6], which are only used to collect, analyze and extract evidences after intrusions. Other more important evidences can't be preserved.

We believe that if the techniques of computer forensic are tightly combined with network surveillance, the complete process of intrusion can be recorded. Forensic tools can be started immediately. This kind of dynamic computer forensics has more advantages regarding the forensic time, place, system environment etc. However, to the best of knowledge, research on this kind of dynamic computer forensics has not been reported yet.

There is actually a direct analogy between the problem of computer security and that of biological immune system[7]. In most immune-based network intrusion detection systems(e.g., [7,14-16]), the concepts of self/nonself allow little change after defined. It is necessary to update the definitions of self/nonself from time to time. The dynamic clonal selection algorithm [14-16] attempted to solve this. However, it lacks comprehensive and quantitative descriptions and, therefore, has its limitation.

In this paper, dynamic evolution models and the corresponding recursive equations for self, antigen, dynamic computer forensics, immune tolerance, mature- lymphocyte lifecycle, and immune memory are introduced. A new model, which is called *Insdcf* for computer network surveillance and dynamic computer forensics, is developed. Our experiment results show that it is a good solution for computer network surveillance and dynamic computer forensics.

2 Proposed Theoretical Models

Let $\Omega = \bigcup_{i=1}^{\infty}\{0,1\}^i$ be a set of binary strings. Given $\Psi \subset \Omega$, where Ψ is the set of network IP packets. Let $\Re = \{<a,b> | a \in D \wedge |a| = l \wedge b \in \Psi\}$, where $D = \{0,1\}^l$, l is a fixed natural number, and $|a|$ is the length of a. Given antigen set $Ag \subset \Re$, for $\forall x \in Ag$, $x.b$ is the original IP packets, $x.a$ is the antigenic determinant, which is the character of $x.b$ and composed of source and destination IP, port number etc. Ag contains Self and Nonself, $Self \cup Nonself = Ag$, $Self \cap Nonself = \Phi$. In an NIDS, Nonself represents network intrusions, while Self are normal network transactions.

Define the lymphocyte set: $B = \{<d, age, count> | d \in D, age \in N, count \in N\}$, where d is antibody, age is the age of antibody, $count$ (affinity) is the antigen number matched by antibody d, and N is the set of natural numbers. B contains two subsets: mature lymphocyte set: $T_b = \{x | x \in B, x.count < \beta, \forall y \in Self < x.d, y > \notin Match\}$) and the memory one: $M_b = \{x | x \in B, x.count \geq \beta, \forall y \in Self < x.d, y > \notin Match\}$), where β is the activation threshold, and $Match = \{<x, y> | x, y \in D, f_{match}(x,y) = 1\}$ is the matching relation within D, and the value of $f_{match}(x,y)$ depends on the affinity between x and y: it equals 1 if the affinity is greater than certain given threshold, or 0 otherwise. The affinity may be evaluated by rules such as r-contiguous bits matching rule, Hamming Distance etc. Define the immature lymphocyte set: $I_b = \{<d, age> | d \in D, age \in N\}$.

Let $\Gamma \subset \{<t, x, y, s> | t \in N, x \in Ag, y \in \Omega, s \in \Omega\}$ represent the digital evidences, where t is the evidence collecting time; x is the captured IP packets, $x.b$ is the original evidence (original IP packets), and $x.a$ is the evidence extracted from $x.b$; y depicts the network environment in the host at time t, s denotes the digital signature of the evidence: $s = E_{k_{private}}(H(t + x + y))$, where E is the signature algorithm (e.g., RSA), $k_{private}$ is a private key, H is a hash function (e.g., SHA-1), '+' is the operator for string connection. For $\forall \tau \in \Gamma$, equation (1) can verify evidence τ:

$$f_{verify}(\tau) = \begin{cases} 1 & D_{k\,public}(\tau.s) = H(\tau.t + \tau.x + \tau.y) \\ 0 & otherwise \end{cases} \quad (1)$$

where $D_{k\,public}(\tau.s)$ denotes decryption computing with the public key k_{public} and the corresponding public key algorithm E, thus the original hash value h is returned. However, $H(\tau.t + \tau.x + \tau.y)$ is to recompute the hash value h' with the same method shown in signature equation. If $h=h'$, then the evidence τ is integrity and valid, otherwise, τ is destroyed or altered, and unbelievable.

Insdcf monitors the network activities and classifies an input set (Ag) into Self and Nonself by the lymphocytes within δ (>0) steps. When finding an intrusion, the corresponding evidences will be collected immediately. The following shows the dynamic evolution models for self, antigen, dynamic computer forensics, immune tolerance, mature- lymphocyte lifecycle, and immune memory.

2.1 Dynamic Evolution of Self

In a real-network environment, some ever forbidden network activities, are permitted now. So a dynamic model for the normal network activities (*Self*) is needed to depict the evolution of *Self*:

$$Self(t) = \begin{cases} \{x_1, x_2, ..., x_n\} & t = 0 \\ Self(t-1) - Self_{variation}(t) \cup Self_{new}(t) & t \geq 1 \end{cases} \quad (2)$$

$$Self_{variation}(t) = \{x \mid x \in Self(t-1) \land \exists y \in B(t-1) \\ (f_{check}(y,x) = 2 \land f_{costimulaton}(x) = 0)\} \quad (3)$$

$$f_{check}(y,x) = \begin{cases} 2 & f_{match}(y,x) = 1 \land x.a \in Self(t-1) \\ 1 & f_{match}(y,x) = 1 \land x.a \notin Self(t-1) \\ 0 & otherwise \end{cases} \quad (4)$$

where $Self_{new}(t) = \{y \mid y$ is the new self element collected at time $t\}$ .Equation (2) stimulates the dynamic evolution of self-antigens, where $x_i \in \Re(i \geq 1, i \in N)$ is the initial self element defined. $Self_{new}$ is the set of newly defined elements at time t, and $Self_{variation}$ is the set of mutated elements. $f_{check}(y,x)$ is used to classify antigens as either self or nonself: if x is a self-antigen, return 0; if x is a nonself one, return 1; if x is detected as nonself but was detected as a self-antigen before, then it may be a nonself antigen (needs to be confirmed), and return 2. $f_{costimulation}(x)(x \in Ag)$ simulates the co-stimulation in a biological immune system and indicates whether x is a self-antigen by an external signal. If x is confirmed self, return 1, otherwise, return 0. It is usually from the administrator.

There are two crucial points in this model. 1) *Self immune surveillance*: The model deletes mutated self-antigens (*Self*$_{variation}$) in time through surveillance.The false-negative error is reduced. 2) *The dynamic growth of Self*: The model can extend the depiction scope of self through adding new self-antigens (*Self*$_{new}$) into *Self*. Therefore, the false-positive error is prevented.

2.2 Dynamic Evolution of Antigen

The Equation (5)-(6) shows the dynamic model of antigens:

$$Ag(t) = \begin{cases} Self(0) & t = 0 \\ Ag(t-1) - Ag_{nonself}(t) & t > 0, t \bmod \delta \neq 0 \\ Ag_{new}(t) & t > 0, t \bmod \delta = 0 \end{cases} \quad (5)$$

$$Ag_{nonself}(t) = \{x \mid x \in sAg(t-1) \land \exists y \in B(t-1)((f_{check}(y,x) = 2 \\ \land f_{costimulation}(x) = 0) \lor f_{check}(y,x) = 1)\} \quad (6)$$

where $sAg(t) \subset Ag(t)$, $|sAg(t)| = \eta * |Ag(t)|$, $t \geq 0$, i.e. sAg is selected from Ag randomly in the proportion of η (detective coefficient, $0<\eta\leq1$). $Ag_{nonself}$ is the set of nonself antigens detected by lymphocytes at time t, where $Ag(0) = Self(0)$ indicates that is try to do the job of self tolerance for the new generated immature lymphocytes and produce new mature cells (see Section 2.4 "*Marrow Model*"). δ is called antigen update period, indicating that Ag is replaced by the new antigen set (Ag_{new}) every δ steps. In each antigen update period, the detected nonself antigens are deleted from Ag.

2.3 Dynamic Computer Forensic

$$\Gamma(t) = \begin{cases} \phi & t = 0 \\ \Gamma(t-1) \cup \Gamma_{new}(t) & t > 0 \end{cases} \quad (7)$$

$$\Gamma_{new}(t) = \{\tau \mid \tau \in \Gamma \wedge (\tau.t = t, \tau.x = x, \tau.y = y', \tau.s = s', \\ s' = E_{k\ private}(H(\tau.t + \tau.x + \tau.y)), x \in Ag_{nonself}(t))\} \quad (8)$$

where $\Gamma_{new}(t)$ denotes the new evidences caught at time $t(t>0)$, x is the intrusion *IP* packets caught by lymphocytes including two parts: $x.b$, the original evidence (the original *IP* packets), and $x.a$, the evidence extracted from $x.b$; y' depicts the snapshot of the environment in the host machine at time t, including the status of network, *CPU*, memory, and processes in the system etc.; and s' denotes the digital signature of the evidence, insuring its integrality, originality and authority.

To ensure the security and integrity of computer evidences, we have to obey the following rules when extracting evidences:

1) The tools used to collect and analyze evidences should be safe.
2) The evidences should not be damaged by machines, electromagnetism etc.
3) The original evidences cannot be analyzed directly. Evidences should be digital signed before analysis.
4) The analysis results of the evidences should be digital signed to ensure the continuity of evidences.
5) Each time after being analyzed, the evidences should be backuped.
6) The evidence server, which is a highly safe and reliable host machine, is used to store the evidences collected from *Insdcf*. It should be connected with the network by secure transfer way (e.g. VPN) [6]. It must ensure its security, reliability, integrity and authority.

2.4 Marrow Model (Self Tolerance Model)

$$I_b(t) = \begin{cases} \{x_1, x_2, ..., x_\xi\} & t = 0 \\ I_{tolerance}(t) - I_{maturation}(t) \cup I_{new}(t) & t \geq 1 \end{cases} \quad (9)$$

$$I_{tolerance}(t) = \{y \mid y \in I_b(y.d = x.d, y.age = x.age + 1, x \in (I_b(t-1) - \\ \{x \mid x \in I_b(t-1), \exists y \in sAg(t-1)(f_{match}(x,y) = 1)\}))\} \quad (10)$$

$$Tself(t) = \begin{cases} sAg(t) & t = 0 \vee t \bmod \delta \neq 0 \\ sAg(t-1) & t > 0 \wedge t \bmod \delta = 0 \end{cases} \quad (11)$$

where $I_{new}(t) = \{y_1, y_2, ..., y_\xi\}$, $I_{maturation}(t) = \{x \mid x \in I_{tolerance}(t) \wedge x.age > \alpha\}$. Equation (9) stimulates the growth of lymphocytes in marrow [7], x_i=<d,0> ($d \in D, 1 \le i \le \xi$) is an immature lymphocyte generated randomly. $I_{tolerance}$ is the set of surviving immature cells in $I_b(t$-1) after one step of tolerance process [11][17][18]. Immature cells need undergo α ($\ge$1, tolerance period) steps of tolerance processes and then evolve into mature ones. $I_{maturation}$ is the set of immature cells which have undergone α steps of tolerance processes at time t. I_{new} is the set of new immature cells generated randomly at time t. $Tself$ is the set of surviving immature cells in sAg, which has been detected by mature cells and memory cells, and thus is taken as self-antigens used in tolerance process for immature cells.

2.5 Mature-Immunocyte Lifecycle

$$T_b(t) = \begin{cases} \phi & t = 0 \\ T_b'(t) \cup T_{new}(t) - T_{memory}(t) - T_{dead}(t) & t \ge 1 \end{cases} \quad (12)$$

$$T_b'(t) = T_b''(t) - P(t) \cup T_{clone}(t) \quad (13)$$

$$T_b''(t) = \{y \mid y.d = x.d, y.age = x.age + 1, y.count = x.count, x \in T_b(t-1)\} \quad (14)$$

$$P(t) = \{x \mid x \in T_b''(t), \exists y \in sAg(t-1)(f_{check}(x,y) = 1 \\ \vee (f_{check}(x,y) = 2 \wedge f_{costimulaton}(y) = 0))\} \quad (15)$$

$$T_{clone}(t) = \{y \mid y.d = x.d, y.age = x.age, y.count = x.count + 1, x \in P(t)\} \quad (16)$$

$$T_{new}(t) = \{y \mid y.d = x.d, y.age = 0, y.count = 0, x \in I_{maturation}(t)\} \quad (17)$$

$$T_{dead}(t) = \{x \mid x \in T_b'(t)(x.age > \lambda \wedge x.count < \beta)\} \cup \{x \mid x \in T_b''(t), \\ \exists y \in Ag(t-1)(f_{check}(x,y) = 2 \wedge f_{costimulation}(y) = 1)\} \quad (18)$$

where $T_{memory}(t) = \{x \mid x \in T_b'(t), x.count \ge \beta\}$. Equation (12) depicts the lifecycle (λ) of mature lymphocytes. If a mature lymphocyte matches enough antigens ($\ge\beta$) in its lifecycle, it will evolve into a memory one (T_{memory}). Lymphocytes will be killed and replaced by new ones (T_{new}), if they do not match enough antigens. T_{dead} is the set of lymphocytes that have not match enough antigens ($\le\beta$) in lifecycle or classify self-antigens as nonself at time t. T_b' simulates the mature cells undergoing one step of evolution. T_b'' indicates the mature cells getting older. P depicts the mature lymphocytes set whose antibody matches nonself antigens. T_{clone} depicts the clone process of mature lymphocytes, which is simplified by adding matching count by 1.

2.6 Dynamic Immune Memory

$$M_b(t) = \begin{cases} \phi & t = 0 \\ M_b(t-1) - M_{dead}(t) \cup T_{memory}(t) & t \geq 1 \end{cases} \quad (19)$$

$$\begin{aligned} M_{dead}(t) = \{x \mid x \in M_b(t-1) \wedge \exists y \in Ag(t-1) \\ (f_{check}(x, y, t) = 2 \wedge f_{costimulation}(y) = 1)\} \end{aligned} \quad (20)$$

Equation (19) depicts the dynamic evolution of immune memory, where T_{memory} is the set of new generated memory lymphocytes. A memory cell will be deleted if it matches a known self-antigen (M_{dead}, i.e., false-positive error).

The above dynamic model of immune memory reduce both false-positive error rate and false-negative error rate in contrast to the traditional NIDS techniques, and have thus enhanced the ability of self-adaptation for the system.

3 Simulations and Experiment Results

The experiments are carried out in the Laboratory of Computer Network and Information Security at Sichuan University. 40 computers in a network are under surveillance. In the experiment, 20 kinds of attacks carry out, such as *syn flood, land, smurf*, etc. According to *Insdcf*, an antigen is defined as a fixed length binary string (l=256) composed of the source/destination *IP*, port number and type, *IP* flags, *IP* overall packet length, TCP/UDP/ICMP fields, MAC address etc. The task is aimed at the detection of network attacks. We use *r-contiguous* bits matching rule (r=8) for computing the affinity, n=40 (the size of initial self set), and ξ =4 (the number of new generated immature cells), therefore, a total of 40 self elements can be protected very well [10]. Given the detective coefficient η =0.8. Let TP (true positive rate) denote the nonself detection probability, and FP (false positive rate) indicate the probability in which the self-antigen is found out by mistake.

Fig.1~4 illustrate the effects of the activation threshold β of mature cells, the tolerance period α of immature cells, the mature-lymphocyte lifecycle λ, and the antigen update period δ. Fig.5 is a satisfied result obtained in the experiments, where $\delta = \alpha$ =50, β =5, λ =40.

Given $\delta = \alpha$ =50, β =5 and λ =40, we have used the dynamic computer forensic model to collect evidences for the 20 kinds of attacks in the experiment. Take a DDoS attack[6], e.g., *syn flood*, as an example, where the IP addresses of the target server and the attack machine are, respectively, 192.168.0.17, and 222.18.5.199. Table 1 shows a portion of the evidences extracted by *Insdcf* in real time.

In contrast to the earlier research works on computer forensics, we have used The Coroner's Toolkit (TCT) 1.15 [19], which is a static forensic tool and widely used in

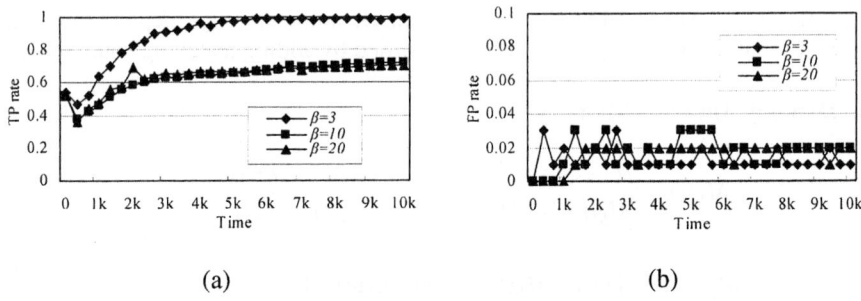

Fig. 1. Effect of activation threshold β, (a) TP rate, (b) FP rate

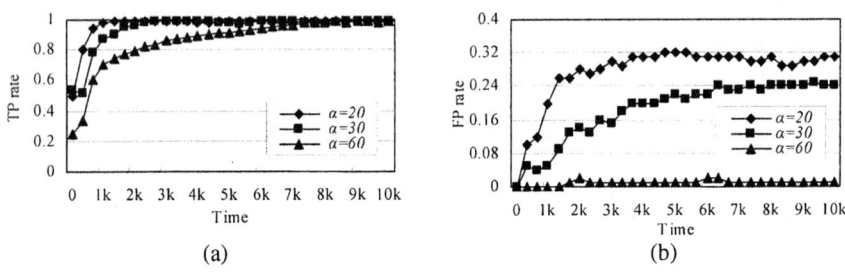

Fig. 2. Effect of tolerance period α, (a) TP rate, (b) FP rate

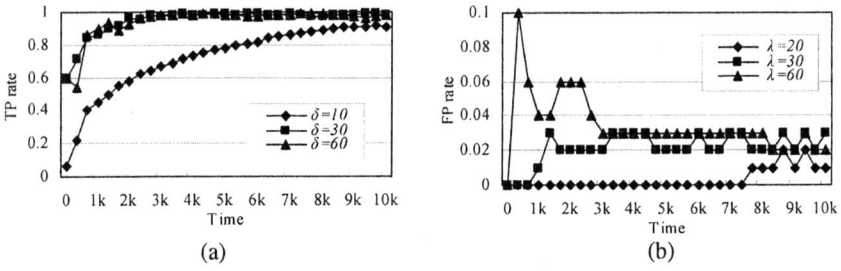

Fig. 3. Effect of lifecycle λ, (a) TP rate, (b) FP rate

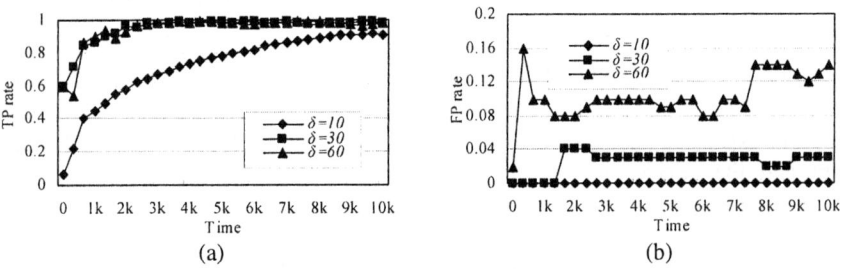

Fig. 4. Effect of antigen updating period δ, (a) TP rate, (b) FP rate

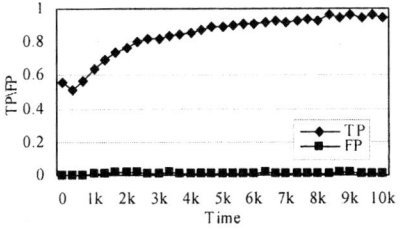

Fig. 5. A satisfied TP and FP, where $\delta = \alpha =50$, $\beta =5$ and $\lambda =40$

Table 1. Portion of Evidences collected by *Insdcf* for *syn flood*

Attack time	Sep 13 20:22:17 2004
Essential character of original IP packets	222.18.5.199 192.168.0.17 TCP df 20 12261 21...S.. 00:20:ed:66:22:b7
	222.18.5.199 192.168.0.17 TCP df 20 1281 21 ...S... 00:20:ed:66:22:b7
	......
Network connection status	tcp 192.168.0.17:21 192.168.0.12:2927 ESTABLISHED 967/vsftpd
	tcp 192.168.0.17:ftp 222.18.5.199:7448 SYN_RECV
	......
	notes☐SYN_RECV connection number is 837
Network connection number	32
Network flux	73171 packets/second
CPU status	0.1% user, 95.1% system, 0.0% nice, 4.6% idle
System performance	lower 90.3%
Login users	root, djl, ftp, wangyl,..., the total number is 16
Running processes	httpd,vsftpd, smbd, forensic, nmbd, login, portmap, syslogd ..., the total number is 50
Swap status	265064K av, 544K used, 264520K free, 96000K cached
Memory status	125104K av, 119208K used, 5896K free, 2920K buff
......	......

Table 2. Portion of Evidences for *syn flood* collected with TCT 1.15 and Analyzed by Forensic Analyzer

Sep13 20:22:18 targetserver kernel: TCP: drop open request from 222.18.5.199/44681
Sep13 20:22:18 targetserver kernel: TCP: drop open request from 222.18.5.199/37109
Sep13 20:22:18 targetserver kernel:TCP:drop open request from 222.18.5.199/61058
Sep 13 20:22:18 targetserver kernel: NET: 352530 messages suppressed.

the world. TCT 1.15 is a collection of tools that are either oriented towards gathering or analyzing forensic data on a Unix system [20]. When attack happens, since *syn flood* is to try to force the target server to get into a paralysis state but not directly destroy it, there are few evidences left after the attacks. In the experiment, we found effective evidences that can be directly collected by TCT 1.15 are almost nothing for *syn flood*. Only a few evidences, shown in table 2, are found from the system log file after a long time analysis of the file system in the target server.

The evidences shown in table 1 indicate, clearly, the network attack situation: The attack happened at 20:22:17 on Sep.13 2004. Host 222.18.5.199 (attack machine) sent lots of requests to port 21(ftp service) in host 192.168.0.17 (target). A large number of SYN_RECV half-connection were established between these two machines. The target server was providing the services of ftp, samba, etc. The current network connections were 32, while the network flux reached 73171 packets/s. The *CPU* of the target server was greatly occupied by system processes. And the performance of the target server was decreased by 90.3%. During the attack, a total of 50 processes such as vsftp, httpd, smbd, forensic, nmbd, login, and so on were running, while 16 users, e.g., root, djl, ftp, etc., were working in the system. The resource of the host was almost exhausted. Specifically, about 120Mb were being occupied in a total of 125Mb memory (the system has a total of 128Mb RAM, of which 3Mb is used for kernel and shell etc.). All these evidences definitely show the attack is *syn flood*.

In contrast, Table 2 only shows that the target server rejected a lot of network requests from 222.18.5.199 at 20:22:18 on Sep 13 2004, while the server suffered from a great deal of network connection requests. Lacking detailed connection information, we only know that the host may be attacked. We do not know what kind of attacks it suffered from. Furthermore, there is little information about the network status, the system information etc. There is also no description of the attack aftereffect.

The experiment shows that the usefulness of static computer forensic methods depends on the ability of the forensic practitioners. It is impossible, or very hard, to use them to collect detailed information related to the attacks. On the other hand, our *Insdcf* can collect evidences of attack accurately and in a timely fashion. Therefore, *Insdcf* provides more useful information for the reconstruction of the attack scene.

4 Conclusion

In this paper, we have quantitatively depicted the dynamic evolutions of self, antigens, immune-tolerance, lymphocyte lifecycle and the immune memory. With that, we have developed a dynamic computer forensic model, referred to as *Insdcf*. Our model can provide effective surveillance on large-scale network activities in real time and dynamically collect evidences of the intrusions. Being an active network security technique, *Insdcf* has desirable features such as self-adaption, diversity, self-learning, and real-time processing.

References

1. Moan, J.: Computer Forensics in a Global Company. in Proc. of 16th FIRST Conf. Computer Security Incident Handling & Response, Budapest (2004)
2. Yoon, A.: Network Monitoring and Web Portal Site Project in AP Region. in Proc. of 16th FIRST Conf. Computer Security Incident Handling & Response, Budapest (2004)

3. Bashaw, C.: Computer Forensics in Today's Investigative Process. in Proc. of 15th FIRST Conf. Computer Security Incident Handling & Response, Ottawa (2003)
4. Lidz. E. L: Network Forensics. in Proc. of 15th FIRST Conf. Computer Security Incident Handling & Response, Ottawa (2003)
5. Reis, M. A., Geus, P. L.: Standardization of Computer Forensic Protocols and Procedures. in Proc. of 14th FIRST Conf. Computer Security Incident Handling & Response, Hawaii, vol. 1(2002) 15-20
6. Li, T.: An Introduction to Computer Network Security. Publishing House of Electronics Industry, Beijing (2004)
7. Li, T.: Computer Immunology. Publishing House of Electronics Industry, Beijing (2004)
8. Chao, D. L., Forrest, S.: Information Immune Systems. in Conf. 1st International Conf. AIS, Canterbury(2002) 132-140
9. Hofmeyr, S., Forrest, S.: Architecture for an Artificial Immune System. Evolutionary Computation, vol. 7(1) (2000) 443-473
10. Harmer, P. K., Williams, P. D., Gunsch, G. H., Lamont, G. B.: An Artificial Immune System Architecture for Computer Security Applications. IEEE Trans. Evolutionary Computation, vol. 6, no. 3(2002) 252-280
11. Forrest, S., Perelson, A. S.: Self-Nonself Discrimination in a Computer. in Proc. of IEEE Symposium on Security and Privacy, Oakland (1994) 202-213
12. Nasaroui, O., Gonzalez, F., Cardona, C., Dasgupta, D.: A Scalable Artificial Immune System Model for Dynamic Unsupervised Learning. in Proc. of Genetic and Evolutionary Computation Conf., Chicago (2003) 219-230
13. De Castro, L. N., Timmis, J. I.: Artificial Immune Systems as a Novel Soft Computing Paradigm. Soft Computing Journal, vol. 7(8) (2003) 526-544
14. Kim, J., Bentley, P. J.: Towards an Artificial Immune System for Network Intrusion Detection: An investigation of Dynamic Clonal Selection. in Proc. of the Congress on Evolutionary Computation, Honolulu (2002)1015 - 1020
15. Kim, J., Bentley, P. J.: Immune Memory in the Dynamic Clonal Selection Algorithm. in Proc. of 1st International Conf. Artificial Immune System, Canterbury (2002) 57-65
16. Kim, J., Bentley, P. J.: A Model of Gene Library Evolution in the Dynamic Clonal Selection Algorithm. in Proc. 1st International Conf. AIS, Canterbury (2002) 175-182
17. Miller, J.: Immune Self-tolerance Mechanisms. Transplantation, vol.72(8)(2001) S5-9
18. Ayara, M., Timmis, J., de Lemos, R., de Castro, L. N., Duncan, R.: Negative Selection: How to Generate Detectors. in Proc. 1st International Conf. AIS, Canterbury (2002) 89-98
19. Top 75 Security Tools (2004, August). Available: http://www.insecure.org/tools.html
20. The Coroner's Toolkit (2004, August). Available: http://www.fish.com/tct

A Two-Phase Clustering Algorithm Based on Artificial Immune Network

Jiang Zhong, Zhong-Fu Wu, Kai-Gui Wu, Ling Ou,
Zheng-Zhou Zhu, and Ying Zhou

College of Computer Science and Engineering, ChongQing University,
ChongQing 400044, China
{zjstud,wzf, kaiguiwu, ouling, zzz, z_ying}@cqu.edu.cn

Abstract. This paper proposes a novel dynamic clustering algorithm called DCBAIN, which based on the artificial immune network and immune optimization algorithm. The algorithm includes two phases, it begins by running artificial immune network to find a clustering feasible solution (CFS), then it employs antibody clone algorithm (ACA) to get the optimal cluster number and cluster centers on the CFS. Some experimental results show that new algorithm has satisfied convergent probability and convergent speed.

1 Introduction

Clustering is an important problem that must often be solved as a part of more complicated tasks in pattern recognition, image analysis and other fields of science and engineering. Given a data set of n objects and k, the number of clusters to form, a partitioning algorithm organizes the objects into k partitions, where each partition represents a cluster. Clustering aims at answering two main questions: how many clusters there are in the data set and where they are located. We denote the problem here as static clustering if the number of clusters (k) is known beforehand, and as dynamic clustering if the number of clusters must also be solved[1].

Static clustering problem can be solved by methods such as the k-means clustering algorithm, which is one of the most widely used. However, it may trap in the local minima. In [2,3], the author presented a tabu search (TS) method for solving the clustering problem. In [4,5] the authors applied genetic algorithm to avoid local minima. In [6] authors employed artificial immune network for clustering. Although these methods are satisfied to solve the static clustering problem, they are not suitable for solving the dynamic clustering problem because of time consuming.

In this paper, we propose an efficient approach called dynamic clustering based on artificial immune network (DCBAIN), which combine artificial immune network and antibody clone algorithm. It optimizes the number and locations of the clusters at the same time.

2 Clustering Feasible Solution

Definition 1. Ideal Clustering Centers Set (ICCS): let V^* be a p-dimension objects set and $J(W,V)$ be the validation function, if $J(W,V^*) = \min_{V \neq V^*}(J(W,V))$, we say V^* is the Ideal Clustering Centers Set of the data set.

Definition 2. Partition-Clusterable Data set: If a data set X can be clustered by partitional clustering methods such as k-means clustering algorithm then we say that X is a Partition-Clusterable Data set.

Definition 3. Cluster Center Area (CA): if v_i is the center of the cluster i, we call the p dimension set $Ca(i,r) = \{x \in R^p \mid \| x - v_i \| < r, r > 0\}$ is a Center Area of the cluster i, and r is the radius of the area.

Definition 4. Cluster Center Areas Set (CAS): We call the set $S = \{Ai \mid Ai \text{ is } CA, 1 \leq i \leq k\}$ is a CAS of the data set.

Definition 5. Convergent Cluster Center Areas Set (CCAS): Let $C^* = \{c_1, c_2, ..., c_k\} \subset R^p$, elements are selected from a CAS's areas respectively and arbitrarily, let C* be the initial cluster centers of the K-means clustering algorithm, if we get the ideal cluster centers, we say that the CAS is a Convergent Cluster Center Areas Set (CCAS) of the data set. We say that the minimum radius of the areas in the CCAS is Convergent radius of CCAS, denoted as r_c.

Definition 6. Degree of Partitionability (ρ): we say that the maximum convergent radius of all the CCAS of the Data set is the degree of partitionability of the data set, denoted as $\rho = \max_{Ca \in all\ CCAS} (r_c(Ca))$.

It is clear that the greater ρ of data set, the fewer difficulties to be clustered. If ρ equals to zero, it means that we can't get the optimal result unless we know one of the clustering center beforehand. Therefore, we call such data set is not a partition-clusterable data set.

Definition 7. Clustering Feasible Solution (CFS): let Cs be a CCAS of the data set, if a set R is satisfied $\forall A_i \mid A_i \in Cs \to R \cap A_i \neq \varphi$, we say R is a clustering feasible solution of the data set.

According to the above definitions, if we get a CFS including few objects, we could cluster the data set quickly based on CFS more than based on original data set. We will introduce an algorithm for CFS based on artificial immune network in the next part.

3 Applying Artificial Immune Network for CFS

A powerful paradigm to improve the efficiency a given data analysis task is to reduce the size of data set (often called data reduction), while keeping the accuracy loss as small as possible[7]. The data reduction techniques include data sampling, SOFM. In this paper we employ the artificial immune network (AIN) algorithm to reduce the size of data set.

The immune network theory, as originally proposed by Jerne, hypothesized a novel viewpoint of lymphocyte activities, natural antibody production, pre-immune repertoire selection, tolerance, self/nonself discrimination, memory and the evolution of the immune system[8]. All of these ideas provide inspiration for developing an artificial immune System (AIS) that is capable of performing effective data analysis. In literature [9] the authors have employed AIN for clustering problem. Although the algorithm is difficult to determine the correct number of and location of the clusters, it reduces the data set size greatly and could get the outline of data set. Accordingly, improvement has been made in this algorithm to be applied for the CFS of the data set.

Algorithm 1. algorithm for CFS
Input : data set X and the threshold value of immune suppression ts
Output : R, a CFS of data set,
Step1: Random initialize the network cells (antibodies) set Abs and let M ={ } ;
Step2:Select an object from data set X as Ag do:
  2.1: Determine its affinity to all the cells in Abs according to a distance metric;
  2.2: Select the c highest affinity cells from Abs;
  2.3: Reproduce (clone) the selected cells and add these cells into a temporary antibodies set, $tmpM$;
  2.4: apply clone mutation to the $tmpM$;
  2.5: apply immune suppression to the $tmpM$;
  2.6: add Ag to M in tail position;
  2.7: add $tmpM$ into M in tail position;
  2.8: apply immune suppression to M;
Step3: Test the stopping criterion, if it not stops, then let Abs = M , M ={ } , and go to Step2; otherwise let R = M and stop.

This algorithm has two main differences to the original algorithm which is presented in [9]:

1) It adds step2.6, so every antigen has a chance to enter into immune network M during the iterations. This step helps the algorithm avoid losing information in sparse data areas.

2) In the immune suppression procedure, if there are two antibodies M_i and M_j included in M , and $i < j , \| M_i - M_j \| \leq ts$, then M_j will be removed from M . Although this requirement is not necessary, it makes the algorithm analyzing easier.

Because the algorithm is an evolutional procedure, it's difficult to give the necessary conditions for acquiring a CFS through this method. A sufficient condition is presented in this section.

Lemma 1: If a data item of X is included in $CA(v_i, ts)$, the output of algorithm1 must contain one antibody in $CA(v_i, 2*ts)$ at least.

Proof: Let x_i be the data point in $CA(v_i, ts)$, there exist two states when the algorithm select x_i in the last iteration at step2, one is that there is already a antibody in M and within $CA(v_i, 2*ts)$, another is that all the antibodies in M are not in $CA(v_i, 2*ts)$.

For the first condition, the antibody will be held until the end of algorithm;
For the second condition, an antibody same as x_i will be added into M after step2.6. Since the distances between x_i and the other antibodies are greater then ts , the

antibody will be held in step2.8 according to property of the immune suppression procedure. Also it will be held until the end of algorithm.
The end.

Theorem 1: A sufficient condition for that the algorithm1 could get a CFS of data set X is $\rho \geq 2*ts$ and $\forall i \mid CA(v_i, ts) \cap X \neq \phi$.

Proof: Let R be the output of algorithm1.
According to the Lemma 1, $\forall i \mid CA(v_i, ts) \cap X \neq \phi$ means that R satisfies $\forall i \mid CA(v_i, 2*ts) \cap R \neq \phi$.

Let the radius of a CCAS is equal to ρ. If $\rho \geq 2*ts$, then $\forall i \mid CA(v_i, 2*ts) \subseteq CA(v_i, \rho)$ and $\forall i \mid CA(v_i, \rho) \cap R \neq \phi$. Thus, by definition 6, R is a CFS of data set.
The end.

Let $P_{1,ts,i}$ be the probability of that there is at least one object in $CA(v_i, ts)$, and R is the output of algorithm 1. If $\rho \geq 2*ts$ and k is the number of clusters, the probability of that R is CFS is not less than $\prod_{i=1}^{k} P_{1,ts,i}$ according to theorem 1.

Suppose the data set is composed of Gaussian clusters, n_i is the number of data items in the ith cluster, and p is the probability of each object in $CA(v_i, ts)$, According to the property of Gauss distribution, $\lim_{n_i \to \infty} P_{1,ts,i} = 1 - \lim_{n_i \to \infty} \prod_{i=1}^{n_i}(1-p) = 1$. Hence, it can be concluded that the convergence probability of the algorithm is high for Gaussian data set.

4 Dynamic Clustering Based on CFS

Let C be the initial cluster centers of the k-Means clustering algorithm and $f(C)$ be the evaluation of the clustering result. If we get a CFS of the data set, the question to find the 'optimal' cluster count and center locations will be equaled to find a subset C^* from CFS (R) and $f(C^*) = \min_{\forall C \subset R}(f(C))$. Thus, the dynamic clustering problem is formulated as a nonconvex optimization problem. A lot of optimization techniques have been suggested by a crowd of researchers of different fields, such as genetic algorithm (GA), tabu search (TS). Recently, some researchers find antibody clone algorithm (AGA) can be used to solve the optimization problem, and the results of AGA may be better than GA[11].

Just like the chromosome in GA, the antibody is represented by a string of m bits, and a_i denotes an antibody. The antibody population is denoted by $A = \{a_1, a_2 ... a_n\}$. $s(a_i, R)$ is the function of selecting objects from R accroding a_i. For example, let a_i =001100, $C=s(a_i, R)$ indicates that there are six objects in R and the third and the fourth object are selected into C.

In this paper we employ *Davies-Bouldin* function ($DB_{q,t}$) as clustering evaluation[10], and smaller the value of $DB_{q,t}$, the better clustering quality. Let R be a CFS of the data set, the stimulation of each antibody is calculated by $1/f(s(a_i,R))$. In this algorithm, we use the antibody clonal operators defined in [11], such as antibody clone, clonal mutation and clonal selection operator.

Algorithm 2. Dynamic clustering based ACA
Input : data set X and the CFS of data set R
Output : the cluster centers set V
  Step1: nitial the antibody population randomly, let it=0;
  Step2: alculate the stimulation of each antibody in the population;
  Step3: pplying antibody Clone to the population according to the stimulation;
  Step4: pplying clonal mutation to the population;
  Step5: pplying clonal selection to the population and generate the new generation population;
  Step6: est the stopping criterion, if it not satisfied the stopping criterion, let it=it+1 and go to step 2, else output the best clustering result V.

5 Algorithm DCBAIN

Now, we give the complete description of the DCBAIN (*Dynamic Clustering Algorithm Based on Artificial Immune Network*). This algorithm includes two phases: firstly, it employs algorithm 1 to get a CFS, then it use ACA to get the 'optimal' cluster centers number and locations.

Algorithm 3. Algorithm DCBAIN
Input : data set X
Output : the cluster centers set V
Step1: applying Algorithm1 to find a CFS of the data set X, denoted by R;
Step2: employ Algorithm 2 to calculate cluster centers number and locations.
Step3: output result, stop.

6 Experimental Results

In this section we present several experimental results to demonstrate that this algorithm is a fast and effective method to dynamic clustering problem. In order to show the clustering result, we firstly use two synthetic Gauss distribution data set. Data1 is a two dimensions data set, Data2 is a three dimensions data set, and each cluster contains 100 data items. Data1 consists of nine spaced clusters, and data2 consists of five clusters. Lastly, we apply this algorithm to the well-known Anderson's IRIS data set.

If d_{mean} denotes the average distance of all pairs of points in the data set, let $t_s = 0.3 * d_{mean}$. The iteration number of ACA is *itMax=20*, and the antibody population size is *N=20*.

6.1 Results of the Synthetic Data Set

Over 50 trials of Algorithm 3, we have seen that the algorithm get the optimal number and center location of clusters every time. The results indicate that the convergent probability of new algorithm is high.

The average size of the CFS of data1 and data2 are *37* and *21* respectively, thus it reduce the data size greatly. In the Fig1, it shows that the CFS almost covers all of the data space, and it could represent the structure of the data set.

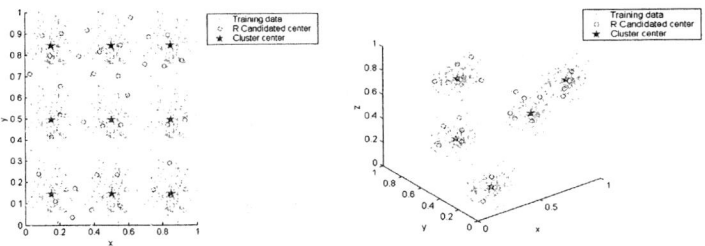

Fig. 1. Results of the two synthetic datasets. It shows that the CFS covers all of the data space, and it could represent the structure of the dataset. Also the algorithm gets the right cluster centers for these synthetic datasets.

6.2 Results of IRIS

Although Iris contains observations from three physical classes, classes 2 and 3 are known to overlap in their numeric representations, while the 50 points from class 1 are very well separated from the remaining 100. Geometrically, the primary structure in Iris is probably $k=2$ but the physical labels insist that $k=3$. Consequently, the best value for k is debatable [10].

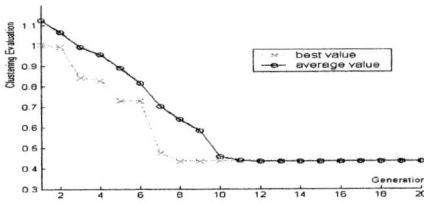

Fig. 2. Clustering evaluation with generation. The algorithm get the best result after 8 times iterations. It shows that the convergence speed of this algorithm is high.

Since clusters are defined by mathematical properties, within models that depend on data representations that agree with the model, we take $k=2$ as the correct choice for Iris, because what matters to an algorithm is how much cluster information is captured by the numeric representation of objects.

The results is convergent within 10 iterations every time, the number of clusters is $k=2$ and the clustering quality is $v_{DB,22}=0.44$, which better then the value (0.46) reported in [10]. Fig2 shows that the best values and average values in every generation in an experiment.

6.3 Performance Comparison

According to the basic tasks of dynamic clustering, we measure the performance of algorithms by the flowing three factors: V_{best}, the best evaluation of cluster result; T_k, the times achieving the right number of clusters; T_b, the times achieving the best evaluation.

Here, GA[5], aiNet[8] and DCBAIN have been tested on Iris data set 50 times ($T_A=50$). The generation in GA and DCBAIN is equal to 40. The results of BHCM are taken from [9].

Table 1. Performance Comparison (N/A: not provided)

Algorithms	T_A	V_{best}	T_k	T_b
GA[5]	50	0.44	22	17
aiNet[8]	50	0.44	50	20
DCBAIN	50	0.44	50	50
BHCM[9]	N/A	0.46	N/A	N/A

From the results in Table1, it can be concluded that new algorithm not only avoid the local optima and is robust to initialization, but also increase the convergence speed.

7 Conclusions and Future Work

This paper proposes an efficient dynamic clustering algorithm based artificial immune algorithm. Usually, it is very difficult to know the number of clusters beforehand, Consequently, there are many application fields to this new algorithm, such as network intrusion detection, data mining. However it is necessary to point out that there is also a lot of work to do on selecting the parameter *ts*, which is very important parameter concerning the convergent probability and convergent speed of this algorithm.

References

1. Karkkainen,I.; Franti, P.: Dynamic local search for clustering with unknown number of clusters, IEEE 16th International Conference on Pattern Recognition, Quebec CANADA, pp.240 –243, August 2002.
2. Hong-Bing Xu: Fuzzy tabu search method for the clustering problem, IEEE Proceeding of the first International Conference on Machine Learning and Cyberneteics, Beijing, pp. 876-880, November 2002

3. K.S AL-Sultan: A tabu search approach to the clustering problem, Pattern Recongnization, Vol 28, No.2 pp.1443 –1445, November 1995.
4. Krovi,R: Genetic algorithms for clustering:a preliminary investigation, IEEE Proceedings of the Twenty-Fifth Hawaii International Conference on System Sciences, pp.540 –544, January 1992.
5. Hall,L.O.;Ozyurt, I.B.: Clustering with a genetically optimized approach, IEEE Transactions on Evolutionary Computation , Vol 3 , No.2,pp 103 –112, July 1999.
6. Xing Xiao Shuai□Pan Jin□Jiao Li-Cheng: A Novel K-means Clustering Based on the Immune Programming Algorithm, Chinese Journal of computers, Vol 26,No. 5, pp.605 – 610, May 2003.
7. George Kollios: Efficient Biased Sampling for Approximate Clustering and Outlier Detection in Large Data Sets, IEEE Transactions on knowledge and data engineering, Vol.15, No.5, pp.1170-1186, September/ October 2003.
8. Timmis: Artificial immune system: an novel data analysis technique inspired by immune network theory [doctor thesis], Wales university, 2001.
9. Leandro Nunes de Castro: An Evolutionary Immune Network for Data Clustering, IEEE SBRN (Brazilian Symposium on Artificial Neural Networks), Brazilian, pp.84-89, November 2000.
10. Bezdek, J.C.; Pal, N.R: Some new indexes of cluster validity, IEEE Transactions on Systems, Man and Cybernetics, Part B, Vol 28 ,No.3,pp.301 –315, June 1998.
11. Hai-Fen DU,LI-cheng Jiao: Clonal operator and antibody clone algorithm, Proceeding of ICMLC2002 Conference Beijing, pp. 506-510, November 2002.

Immune Algorithm for Qos Multicast Routing

Ziqiang Wang and Dexian Zhang

School of Information Science and Engineering,
Henan University of Technology, Zheng Zhou 450052, P.R. China
wzqagent@xinhuanet.com

Abstract. A novel immunity-based genetic algorithm is proposed to resolve Qos multicast routing effectively and efficiently in this paper. The idea of immunity is mainly realized through two steps based on reasonably selecting vaccines, i.e., a vaccination and an immune selection. Experimental results show that this algorithm can find optimal solution quickly and has a good scalability.

1 Introduction

Over the past decades, many works have done to solve multicast routing problems using conventional algorithm, such as exhaustive search routing and greedy routing. But due to the high degree of complexity, it is not practical to use these algorithms in real-time multicast routing. Recently, some nature-based heuristic algorithms have been proposed[1,2]. In this paper, a novel evolutionary algorithms based on immunity, which are usually simple called immune algorithms(IAs)[3], are proposed to tackle Qos Multicast Routing problem. Experimental results show that this algorithm can find optimal solution quickly and has a good scalability.

2 Qos Multicast Routing Model

Communication network can be modeled as an undirected graph $G = <V, E>$, where V is a finite set of vertices (network nodes) and E is the set of edges (network links) representing connection of these vertices. Each link in G has three weights $(B(x,y), D(x,y), C(x,y))$ associated with it, in which positive real values $B(x,y), D(x,y), C(x,y)$, denote the available bandwidth, the delay and the cost of the link respectively. Given a path $P(x,y)$ connected any two nodes x, y in G, it can be presumed that:1)The delay of a path is the sum of the delays of the links $(a,b) \in P(x,y)$:$Delay(P(x,y)) = \sum D(a,b)$;2)The available bandwidth of $(a,b) \in P(x,y)$ is considered as the bottle neck bandwidth of $P(x,y)$:$Width(P(x,y)) = min(B(a,b))$.

In Qos transmission of real time multimedia service, the optimal cost routing problem with delay and bandwidth constrained can be described as follows.Given $G = <V, E>$, a source node s, and a multicast member set $M \subseteq V - \{s\}$,the problem is to find the multicast tree $T = (V_T, V_E)$ from source s to all destinations $v \in M$ and T must satisfy the following conditions:

$$Cost(T) = min(\sum_{(x,y)\in(E_T)} C(x,y)) \tag{1}$$

$$\sum_{(x,y)\in(E_T)} C(x,y) \leq D_{max}, \forall v \in M \tag{2}$$

$$Width(P_T(s,v)) \geq W_{min}, \forall v \in M \tag{3}$$

where $P_T(s,v)$ is the set of links in the path from source nodes s to destination v in the multicast tree.

3 Immune Algorithm for Qos Multicast Routing

3.1 Pre-processing of Algorithm and Coding of Chromosome

Before starting the genetic algorithm, we can remove all the links which their bandwidth are less than the minimum of all required thresholds W_{min}. If in the refined graph, the source node and all the destination nodes are not in a connected sub-graph, the source should negotiate with the related application to relax the bandwidth bound.

we choose the tree structure coding method, in which a chromosome represents a multicast tree. For a given source node s and a destination set $M = \{m_1, m_2, \cdots, m_n\}$, a chromosome can be presented by a string of integers with length k. A gene g_i of the chromosome is an integer in $\{1, 2 \cdots, R\}$ which represents a possible route between s and $m_i \in M$.

3.2 Fitness Function

The construction of the initial population is based on a modified randomized depth-first search algorithm. The fitness function definition is based on penalty technique, the fitness function definition of each individual, i.e., the tree $T(s, M)$, is as follows:

$$F(T) = \frac{\prod_{m\in M} \phi(Delay(P(s,m)) - D_{max})) \times \prod_{m\in M} \phi(W_{min} - Width(P(s,m)))}{\sum_{e\in T} cost(e)} \tag{4}$$

$$\phi(x) = \begin{cases} 1 : x \leq 0 \\ \gamma : x > 0 \end{cases} \tag{5}$$

where $\phi(x)$ is the penalty function, the value of γ determine the degree of penalty.

3.3 Evolutionary Operator Design

Our selection procedure is based on the well-known tournament selection[5], with tournament size of 2. Furthermore, we use elitism with an elitist factor of 1.

We use a simple one-point crossover operator, with a fixed probability p_c. The constructed offspring do not necessarily represent Steiner trees. Then, we connect the separate sub-trees to a multicast tree according to tree recovery and check algorithms of Ref.[6].

The mutation procedure randomly selects a subset of nodes and breaks the multicast tree into some separate sub-trees by removing all the links that are incident to the selected nodes. Then, it re-connects those separate sub-trees into a new multicast tree by randomly selecting the least-delay or the maximal-bandwidth paths between them.

The idea of immunity is mainly realized through two steps based on reasonably selecting vaccines, i.e., a vaccination and an immune selection.Now they are explained as follows:1)The Vaccination: Given an individual m, a vaccination means modifying the genes on some bits in accordance with constraint conditions so as to gain higher fitness with greater probability.2)The Immune Selection: This operation is accomplished by the following two steps. The first one is the immune test, i.e., testing the antibodies. If the fitness is smaller than that of the parent, which means serious degeneration must have happened in the process of crossover or mutation, then instead of the individual the parent will participate in the next competition; the second one is the annealing selection [7].

4 Experimental Results

We have performed simulation to investigate the performances of multicast routing algorithms based on immune algorithm. A random generator developed by Salama[8] is used to create links interconnecting the nodes. The random graphs are generated using the above graph generator with an average degree 4,which have the appearance roughly resembling that of geographical maps of major nodes in the Internet . For the same multicast routing, we made 300 simulations by immune algorithm against Hopfield Neural Networks(HNN) and GA. The computation results are shown in Table 1.

Table 1. Predictive Accuracy Comparison

Algorithm	Optimal Solutions	Sub-optimal Solutions	Invalid Solutions
Hopfield Neural Networks	75.6%	21.5%	2.9%
Genetic Algorithm	78.4%	19.4%	2.2%
Immune Algorithm	81.2%	17.3%	1.5%

From Table 1, we can find that immune algorithm performances better than HNN and GA. So our proposed algorithm has good performance.

5 Conclusions

In this paper, we studied the bandwidth-delay-constrained least-cost multicast routing problem, and presented an immune algorithm to solve the problem. The experimental results show that this algorithm is an efficient algorithm.

References

1. Chotipat,P.,Goutam,C.,Norio S.:Neural network approach to multicast routing algorithms for real-time communication on high-speed networks.IEEE Journal on Selected Areas in Communications.15(1997)332–345
2. Wang,Z.,Shi,B.:Solution to Qos multicast routing problem based on heuristic genetic algorithm. Journal of Computer.24(2001)55–61
3. Jiao,L.C.,Wang L.:A novel genetic algorithm based on Immunity. IEEE Transactions on Systems,Man,And Cybernetics-Part A:System and Humans.30(2000)552–561
4. Tarjan,R.:Finding optimum branchings. Networks.7(1977)25–35
5. Goldberg,D.E.:Genetic Algorithms in Search, Optimization, and Machine Learning. Addison-Wesley(1989)
6. Zhang,Q.,Lenug, Y.W.:An orthogonal genetic algorithm for multimedia multicast routing. IEEE Transactions on Evolutionary Computation.3(1999)53–62
7. Zhang,J.S.,Xu,Z.B.,Liang Y.:The whole annealing genetic algorithms and their sufficient and necessary conditions of convergence. Science in China. 27(1997)154–164
8. Salama,H.F.,Reeves,D.S.,Viniotis, Y.:Evaluation of multicast routing algorithms for real-time communication on high-speed networks. IEEE Journal on Selected Areas in Communications. 15(1997)332–345

IFCPA: Immune Forgetting Clonal Programming Algorithm for Large Parameter Optimization Problems

Maoguo Gong[1], Licheng Jiao[1], Haifeng Du[1,2], Bin Lu[1], and Wentao Huang[1]

[1] Institute of Intelligent Information Processing, P.O. Box 224, Xidian University,
Xi'an 710071, P.R. China
maoguo_gong@hotmail.com
[2] School of Mechanical Engineering, Xi'an Jiaotong University,
Xi'an 710049, P.R. China

Abstract. A novel artificial immune system algorithm, Immune Forgetting Clonal Programming Algorithm (IFCPA), is put forward. The essential of the clonal selection inspired operations is producing a variation population around the antibodies according to their affinities, and then the searching area is enlarged by uniting the global and local search. With the help of immune forgetting inspired operations, the new algorithm abstract certain antibodies to a forgetting unit, and the antibodies of clonal forgetting unit do not participate in the successive immune operations. Decimal coding with limited digits makes IFCPA more convenient than other binary-coded clonal selection algorithms in large parameter optimization problems. Special mutation and recombination methods are adopted in the antibody population's evolution process of IFCPA in order to reflect the process of biological antibody gene operations more vividly. Compared with some other Evolutionary Programming algorithms such as Breeder Genetic Algorithm, IFCPA is shown to be an evolutionary strategy which has the ability for solving complex large parameter optimization problems, such as high-dimensional Function Optimizations, and has a higher convergence speed.

1 Introduction

Artificial immune systems provides the evolutionary learning mechanism like noise enduring, non-teacher learning, self-organization, and memory, and combine with some advantages of other systems like classifier, neural network and machine reasoning, so its research production refers to many fields like control, data processing, optimization learning and fault detection, and it has been a research hotspot after the neural network, fuzzy logic and evolutionary computation [1, 2, 3, 4].

2 Presentation of the Algorithm

Inspired by Antibody Clonal Selection Theory of the Immunology, we proposed a Clonal Selection Operator (CSO) for AIS, which implements Clone Operation, Immune Genic Operation, Clonal Selection Operation on the antibody population $A(k)$. The major steps are presented as follows.

Operation 1: Clonal Selection Operator(CSO)
   Step1: Clone Operation for antibody population $A(k)$,
          $Y(k) = T_c^C(A(k))$;
   Step2: Immune Genic Operation, $Z(k) = T_m^C \circ T_r^C(Y(k))$;
   Step3: Clonal Selection Operation, $A(k+1) = T_s^C(Z(k) \tilde{\cup} A(k))$.

In IFCPA, we simulate the antibody clonal deletion through the operation in the following

Operation 2: Clonal death in IFCPA
   Step1: Sort the antibody population $A(k)$ as the
          Affinity, named by $A'(k) = \{a_1'(k), a_2'(k), \cdots, a_n'(k)\}$,
          where $f(a_i'(k)) \le f(a_{i+1}'(k))$ $i = 1, 2, \cdots, n-1$;
   Step2: Calculate the clonal death ratio $T\%$,
          $j + l = n$ and $l = \text{fix}(T\% \times n)$;
   Step3: Antibody population updating:
          $A(k) = \{a_1'(k), a_2'(k), \cdots, a_j'(k), a_1'(k), a_2'(k), \cdots, a_l'(k)\}$

Where $\text{fix}(\bullet)$ is the floor function and $\text{fix}(x)$ returns the largest integer no more than x. The update of clonal forgetting unit can be implemented as follows:

Operation 3: The update of the clonal forgetting unit
   Step1: $k=0$, $M(0) = \Phi$;
   Step2: $k=1$, $M(1) = a_{best}^1$;
   Step3: $k = k \bullet 1$
      Step3.1: Randomly select $m(k-1) \in M(k-1)$;
      Step3.2: Calculate $\varepsilon = \|a_{best}^k - m(k-1)\|$;
      Step3.3: If $\varepsilon > \delta_g$, and $f(a_{best}^k) > f(m(k-1))$, then
               let $m(k-1) = a_{best}^k$, $M(k) = M(k-1)$;
      Step3.4: If $\forall m(k-1) \in M(k-1)$, $\varepsilon > \delta_c$ is right,
               $M(k) = M(k-1) \cup \{a_{best}^k\}$;
      Step3.5: If $|M(k)| > n_m$, then compress the unit.

The activation of the clonal forgetting unit needs to match the gene model (namely, the distance) between all the antibodies and the antibodies in the clonal forgetting unit. If the antibody $a_i(k)$ and antibody $m_j(k)$ in the clonal forgetting unit have more than δ_s gene bits are matched, where δ_s is a constant, then we compare their affinity. If the affinity of $a_i(k)$ is worse than $m_j(k)$, then $m_j(k)$ is activated, and we replace $a_i(k)$ by $m_j(k)$; Otherwise $m_j(k)$ is not activated.

In this paper, the algorithm integrating clonal selection, clonal death, clonal forgetting is named the Immune Forgetting Clonal Programming Algorithm, and its flow is described as follows:

Algorithm 1: The Immune Forgetting Clonal Programming Algorithm (IFCPA)
Step1: Give the termination criterion, and set the mutation probability p_m, recombination probability p_c, clonal size n_c, twisting probability p_i, the antibody death proportion $T\%$, threshold value δ_c, δ_g and δ_s. Randomly generate the initial antibody population $A(0)=\{a_1(0),a_2(0),\cdots a_n(0)\}\in I^n$ in the domain [0, 1], set initial clonal forgetting unit $M(0)=\Phi$;
Step2: Calculate $X=e^{-1}(A)$ and the affinity of antibody population, $F^A(0):\{f(\vec{X}(0))\}=\{f(X_1(0)),f(X_2(0)),\cdots f(X_n(0))\}$; k=1, $M(1)=a_{best}^1$;
Step3: While there is no satisfied candidate solution in $A(k)$, do
  Step3.1: Update $A(k)$ by Clonal Death;
  Step3.2: Implement Genic Twisting Operation with p_i on $A(k)$: $A'(k)=T_T^G(A(k))$;
  Step3.3: Get $A(k+1)$ by implementing Clonal Selection Operator on $A'(k)$;
  Step3.4: Get the new clonal forgetting unit $M(k+1)$ by updating the clonal forgetting unit $M(k)$;
  Step3.5: Activate the clonal forgetting unit and update $A(k+1)$;
$k=k+1$

3 Validation of IECPA's Effectiveness

Here we take Rastrigin's function, Schwefel's function, Griewangk's function, and Ackley's function [7] to compare the performance. The experiment results of IFCPA, MCA[7], AEA[6] and BGA[5] to optimize the functions are shown in Table 1 and Table 2. In the tables, the data are the statistical results obtained from 10 times of random running. It can be seen that the ability of IFCPA to optimize the high-dimensional function is much better than that of MCA, BGA and AEA. In the tables, "/" denotes that the algorithm fails in the experiment.

Table 1. Performance comparison of IFCPA, MCA, AEA and BGA

N	Rastrigin's function (ε=0.1)				N	Schwefel's function (ε=10^{-2})			
	number of function evaluations					number of function evaluations			
	IFCPA	MCA	AEA	BGA		IFCPA	MCA	AEA	BGA
20	693	1469	1247	3608	20	1197	3939	1603	16100
100	2453	4988	4798	25040	100	3789	11896	5106	92000
200	3877	5747	10370	52948	200	6990	16085	8158	248000
400	6455	12563	23588	112634	400	11722	26072	13822	699803
1000	11592	24408	46024	337570	1000	22375	60720	23687	/

Table 2. Performance comparison of IFCPA, MCA, AEA and BGA

N	Griewangk's function ($\varepsilon=10^{-4}$)				N	Ackley's function ($\varepsilon=10^{-3}$)			
	number of function evaluations					number of function evaluations			
	IFCPA	MCA	AEA	BGA		IFCPA	MCA	AEA	BGA
20	1035	2421	3581	40023	20	803	1776	7040	197420
100	3181	6713	17228	307625	100	2943	5784	22710	53860
200	5037	8460	36760	707855	200	4859	9728	43527	107800
400	8564	15365	61975	1600920	400	6092	13915	78216	220820
1000	15138	30906	97600	/	1000	13362	26787	160940	548306

4 Concluding Remarks

Known as an important mechanism of immune system, some characteristics of clonal selection theory such as memory, study and evolution are paid more and more attention by the artificial intelligence researchers. In this paper we propose a novel artificial immune system algorithm, named the Immune Forgetting Clonal Programming Algorithm. Although it is inspired by the evolutionary theory which is similar to EA, their idea is different from the existing evolutionary algorithms. In fact, the corresponding immune system algorithm does not aim at improving the deficiency of evolutionary algorithms, and it has its own biologic foundation which is different from EA. The simulation results for typical large parameter optimization problems show that compared with evolutionary algorithms, IFCPA converges faster, has less computation complexity, and can be used to solve difficult problems.

References

1. Dasgupta, D., Forrest, S.: Artificial Immune Systems in Industrial Applications. In: Proceedings of the Second International Conference on Intelligent Processing and Manufacturing of Materials (IPMM), Vol. 1. Honolulu (1999) 257–267
2. Gasper, A., Collard, P.: From GAs to artificial immune systems: improving adaptation in time dependent ptimization. In: Proceedings of the Congress on EvolutionaryComputation (CEC 99). IEEE press (1999) 1859–1866
3. de Castro, L. N., Von Zuben, F. J.: Learning and Optimization Using the Clonal Selection Principle. IEEE Transactions on Evolutionary Computation, Special Issue on Artificial Immune Systems, 6(3)(2002) 239–251
4. Kim, J. W.: Integrating Artificial Immune Algorithms for Intrusion Detection. PhD Thesis, Department of Computer Science, University College London (2002)
5. Mühlenbein, H., Schlierkamp-Voosen, D.: Predictive Models for the Breeder Genetic Algorithm. Evolutionary Computation, 1(1) (1993) 25–49
6. Pan, Z., Kang, L. and Chen, Y.: Evolution Computation (in Chinese). Beijing: Tsinghua University Press, Guangxi: Guangxi Science Technology Press (1998)
7. Du. H. F., Gong, M. G., Jiao L. C., Liu, R. C.: A novel artificial immune system algorithm for high-dimensional function numerical optimization. Progress in Nature Science, 8(2004) 925–933
8. Gong, M.G., Du, H.F., Jiao, L.C., Wang, L.: Immune Clonal Selection Algorithm for Multiuser Detection in DS-CDMA Systems. Springer-Verlag, LNCS 3339, 2004. 1219-1225

A New Classification Method for Breast Cancer Diagnosis: Feature Selection Artificial Immune Recognition System (FS-AIRS)

Kemal Polat[1], Seral Sahan[1], Halife Kodaz[2], and Salih Güneş[1]

[1] Selcuk University, Eng.-Arch. Fac. Electrical & Electronics Eng.,
42075-Konya, Turkey
{kpolat, seral, sgunes}@selcuk.edu.tr
[2] Selcuk University, Eng.-Arch. Fac. Computer Eng.
42075-Konya, Turkey
hkodaz@selcuk.edu.tr

Abstract. In this study, diagnosis of breast cancer, the second type of the most widespread cancer in women, was performed with a new approach, FS-AIRS (Feature Selection Artificial Immune Recognition System) algorithm that has an important place in classification systems and was developed depending on the Artificial Immune Systems. With this purpose, 683 data in the Wisconsin breast cancer dataset (WBCD) was used. In this study, differently from the studies in the literature related to this concept, firstly, the feature number of each data was reduced to 6 from 9 in the feature selection sub-program by means of forming rules related to the breast cancer data with the C4.5 decision tree algorithm. After separating the 683 data set with reduced feature number into training and test sets by 10 fold cross validation method in the second stage, the data set was classified in the third stage with AIRS and a quite satisfying result was obtained with respect to the classification accuracy compared to the other methods used for this classification problem.

1 Introduction

Cancer begins with uncontrolled division of one cell and results in a visible mass named Tumour. Tumour can be benign or malignant. Malignant Tumour grows rapidly and invades its surrounding tissues causing their damage. Breast cancer, the second type of widespread cancer in women, is a malignant tissue beginning to grow in the breast. The abnormalities like existence of a breast mass, change in shape and dimension of breast, differences in the colour of breast skin, breast aches,...etc are the symptoms of breast cancer. Cancer diagnosis is performed based on the non-molecular criterions like tissue type, pathological properties and clinical location [1].

As for the other clinical diagnosis problems, classification systems have been used for breast cancer diagnosis problem, too. When the studies in the literature related with this classification application are examined, it can be seen that a great variety of methods were used which reached high classification accuracies. Among these, Quinlan reached 94.74% classification accuracy using 10 fold cross validation with C4.5 decision tree method [2]. Hamilton et al., obtained 94.99% accuracy with RIAC method [3] while Ster and Dobnikar obtained 96.8% with linear discreet analysis (LDA) method [4]. The accuracy obtained by Bennett and Blue who used Support Vector Machine (SVM) (5xCV) method was 97.2% [5] while by Nauck and Kruse was 95.06% with neuro-fuzzy techniques [6] and by Pena-Reyes and Sipper was 97.36% using Fuzzy-GA method [7]. Moreover, Setiono was reached 98.1% by using neuro-rule method [8]. Goodman et al. applied three different methods to the problem which were resulted with the following accuracies: Optimized-LVQ method's performance was 96.7%, big-LVQ method reached 96.8% and the last method, AIRS which he proposed depending on the Artificial Immune System, obtained 97.2% classification accuracy [9]. Nevertheless, Abonyi and Szeifert applied Supervised Fuzzy Clustering (SFC) technique and obtained 95.57% accuracy [10].

In this study, the feature number of each data in the Winconsin breast cancer dataset (WBCD) was reduced to 6 from 9 with the use of C4.5 decision tree algorithm. This was done through forming rules for data set in a feature selection subprogram. After feature selection process as a first stage of the applied method, the dataset consisting of 683 data was separated into training and test sets using 10 fold cross validation scheme and this constitutes the second stage. In the third and last stage of the method, the training of AIRS was performed using training set and 98.51% classification accuracy was reached with the test data.

The rest of the paper is organized as follows. Breast cancer diagnosis problem and data pre-processing method are explained in the following second section. Third section covers the mechanism and structure of the immune system. AIRS classification algorithm is mentioned with information about the Artificial Immune Systems (AISs) in the fourth section. The performance of the applied method is given comparatively with related conducted studies in the literature in fifth section, which is followed by the last section that involves the discussion of performance results with future works.

2 The Wisconsin Breast Cancer Dataset (WBCD) Classification Problem and Feature Extraction

2.1 The WBCD Classification Problem

Breast cancer is a common disease and a frequent cause of death in women in the 35-55 year age group. The presence of a breast mass is an alert sign, but is does not always indicate a malignant cancer. Fine needle aspiration of breast masses is a cost-effective, non-traumatic, and mostly non-invasive diagnostic test that obtains information needed to evaluate malignancy. [7]. The data set consist of 683 samples that were collected by Dr. W.H. Wolberg at the University of Wisconsin-Madison Hospitals taken from needle aspirates from human breast cancer tissue [11]. The WBCD consists of nine features obtained from fine needle aspirates, each of which is ultimately represented as an integer value between 1 and 10. The measured variables are as follows: (1) Clump Thickness (x_1); (2) Uniformity of Cell Size (x_2); (3) Uniformity of Cell Shape (x_3); (4) Marginal Adhesion (x_4); (5) Single Epithelial Cell Size (x_5), (6) Bare Nuclei (x_6); (7) Bland Chromatin (x_7); (8) Normal Nucleoli (x_8); and (9) Mitosis (x_9). 444 of the data set with 683 samples belong to benign, and remaining 239 data is of malignant.

2.2 Feature Extraction

The number of features (attributes) and number of instances in the raw dataset can be enormously large. This enormity may cause serious problems to many data mining systems. Feature selection is one of the long existing methods that deal with these problems. Its objective is to select a minimal subset of features according to some reasonable criteria so that the original task can be achieved equally well, if not better. By choosing a minimal subset of features, irrelevant and redundant features are removed according to the criterion. Simpler data can lead to more concise results and their better comprehensibility. Since feature selection can only deal with discrete features (attributes), you need to run Discretion first if there are continuous features in the dataset. C4.5 decision tree algorithm cannot directly use a data file with continuous attributes in mining. To solve this problem, a discrimination system has to be used. You might pass your data file with continuous attributes to this system, which will discrete the continuous attributes and output a file that contains the discredited data. Upon return, discredited data can then be used in the mining.

Feature extraction (FE) was done according to the feature distributions over the data set. After it was detected for classes in clump thickness, bland chromatin and normal nucleoli features distributions to be mixed, it was concluded with the consultations of medical experts that these features were not critical in diagnosis. So the number of features was reduced to 6 by removing these features with the use of C4.5 decision tree algorithm. Block diagram of FE is shown in Fig. 1.

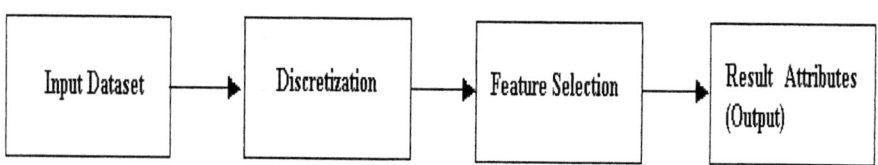

Fig. 1. Block diagram of FE

3 Immune System

Natural immune system is a layered and distributed defence mechanism against foreign elements named as Antigen (Ag) like microbes, bacteria, viruses...etc. Immune system works through distinguishing these invaders from the cells of body resulting with immune response. Although the immune system consists of a great variety of units, the most active ones in immune response are B and T Lymphocytes (cells), which have receptors providing them to bind other cells including Antigens. The receptor of T cells are called TCR (T-cell receptor) while the one of the B cells are named as Antibody (Ab), the most common modelled unit of immune system in Artificial Immune Systems [12], [19].

The simplified working procedure of our immune system is illustrated in Fig. 2. Specialized Antigen Presenting Cells ($APCs$) called Macrophages circulates through the body and if they encounter an Antigen, they ingest and fragment them into antigenic peptides (I). The pieces of these peptides are displayed on the cell surface by *MHC* (Major Histocompatibility Complex) molecules existing in the digesting *APC*. The presented *MHC-peptide* combination on the cell surface is recognised by the *T*-cells causing them to be activated (II). Activated *T* cells secrete some chemicals as alert signals to other units in response to this recognition. *B* cells, one of the units that take these signals from the *T* cells become activated with the recognition of Antigen by their Antibodies occurred in the same time (IV). When activated, *B* cells turn into plasma cells that secrete bound Antibodies on their surfaces (V). Secreted Antibodies bind the existing Antigens and neutralize them signalling other components of immune system to destruct the Antigen-Antibody complex (VI) [13], [19].

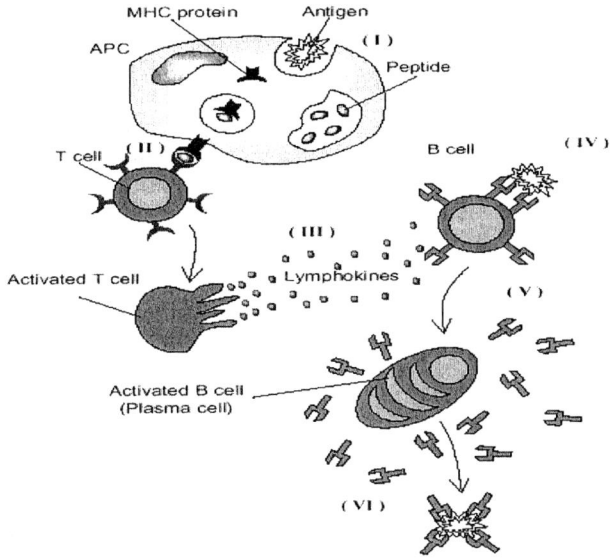

Fig. 2. General immune response to invaders[13]

4 Artificial Immune Systems and Artificial Immune Recognition System (AIRS)

Artificial Immune System (AIS) can be defined as a computational system based upon metaphors of biological immune system [13]. The topics involved in the definition and development of Artificial Immune Systems cover mainly: hybrid structures and algorithms that take into account immune-like mechanisms; computational algorithms based on immunological principles, like distributed processing, clonal selection algorithms, and immune network theory; immune based optimization, learning, self-organization, artificial life, cognitive models, multi-agent systems, design and scheduling, pattern recognition and anomaly detection and lastly immune engineering tools [13], [14].

In unsupervised learning branch of AISs, there are lots of works conducted by researchers De Castro, Timmis, Watkins, Dasgupta, ...etc [14], [15], [16]. There are only two studies in supervised AISs. First of these was performed by Carter [17]. The other work is AIRS (Artificial Immune Recognition System), proposed by A.Watkins which is a supervised learning algorithm inspired from the immune system [18].

The used immune metaphors used in AIRS are: antibody-antigen binding, affinity maturation, clonal selection process, resource competition and memory acquisition. AIRS learning algorithm consists of four stages: initialisation, memory cell recognition, resource competition and revision of resulted memory cells.

4.1 AIRS Algorithm

The AIRS algorithm is as follows:

1. *Initialization:* Create a random base called the memory pool (M) and the pool (P).
2. *Antigenic Presentation:* for each antigenic pattern do:
   a) *Clonal Expansion:* For each element of M determines their affinity to the antigenic pattern, which resides in the same class. Select highest affinity memory cell (mc) and clone mc in the proportion to its antigenic affinity to add to set of ARBs (P).
   b) *Affinity Maturation:* Mutation each ARB descendant of this highest affinity mc. Place each mutated ARB into P.
   c) *Metadynamics of ARBs:* Process each ARB through the resource allocation mechanism. This will result in some ARB death, and ultimately controls the population. Calculate the average stimulation for each ARB, and check for termination condition.
   d) *Clonal Expansion and Affinity Maturation:* Clone and mutate a randomly selected subset of the ARBs left in P based in proportion to their stimulation level.
   e) *Cycle:* While the average stimulation value of each ARB class group is less than a given stimulation threshold repeat from step 2.c.
   f) *Metadynamics of Memory Cells:* Select the highest affinity ARB of the same class as the antigenic from the last antigenic interaction. If the affinity of this ARB with the antigenic pattern is better than that of the previously identified best memory cell mc then add the candidate (mc-candidate) to memory set M. Additionally, if the affinity of

mc and mc-candidate below the affinity threshold, then remove mc from M.
3. *Cycle:* Repeat step 2 until all antigenic patterns have been presented.

5 FS-AIRS System

Fig. 3 shows the block diagram of developed Feature Selection Artificial Immune Recognition System (FS-AIRS). Parameters of FS-AIRS were taken as in Table 1. The obtained classification performance was evaluated using 10 fold cross validation method. By this method, data set was divided 10 clusters each having similar cases with similar class distributions. Training and test processes were repeated for three runs by taking one of the clusters as test set and remaining 9 clusters as training set. This was performed for all clusters and the average training and test accuracies were taken as resulted training and test accuracies. In test process, k-nearest neighbour method was used to determine the class of given data.

Classification performance of proposed system for test sets is tabulated in Table 2 and comparatively given with the studies in the literature.

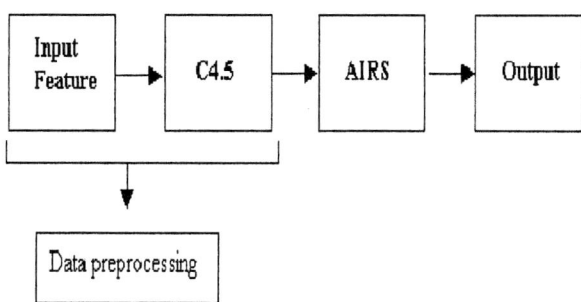

Fig. 3. Block diagram of FS-AIRS

Table 1. Used parameter values in FS-AIRS for the problem

Parameter	Value
Mutation rate	0.15
ATS (Affinity Threshold Scalar)	0.1
Stimulation Threshold	0.91
Clonal Rate	10
Hyper Clonal Rate	2.0
Number of resources	250
Iteration Number	10000
K value for nearest neighbour	1

Table 2. FS-AIRS classification performance for the problem with classification accuracies obtained by other methods in literature

Author(Year)	Method	Accuracy (%)
Quinlan(1996)	C4.5 (10xCV)	94.74
Hamilton et al. (1996)	RIAC (10xCV)	94.99
Ster and Dobnikar (1996)	LDA (10xCV)	96.80
Bennett and Blue (1997)	SVM (5xCV)	97.20
Nauck and Kruse (1999)	NEFCLASS (10xCV)	95.06
Pena-Reyes and Sipper (1999)	Fuzzy-GA1 (train : 75%- test: 25%)	97.36
Setiono (2000)	Neuro-Rule 2a (train : 50%- test: 50%)	98.10
Goodman et al. (2002)	Optimized- LVQ (10xCV)	96.70
Goodman et al. (2002)	Big- LVQ (10xCV)	96.80
Goodman et al. (2002)	AIRS (10xCV)	97.20
Abonyi and Szeifert (2003)	SFC (10xCV)	95.57
Our study (2005)	**FS-AIRS (10xCV)**	**98.51**

6 Conclusions

In this study WBCD was applied to AIRS after being presented to a feature selection process by using C4.5 decision tree algorithm to eliminate useless features in determining malignancy. In C4.5 algorithm, 9-featured WBCD was represented by 43 rules that were used to reduce the number of features to 6. 98.51% classification accuracy was reached with proposed FS-AIRS algorithm. With this result it can be said that higher classification accuracy than the preceding methods was obtained.

Although the main purpose of this study is to get higher classification accuracy in breast cancer diagnosis problem, the importance of proposed system is beyond this application. AIRS is an attractive algorithm as well as being a new method in supervised AISs. For its higher classification accuracies among the proposed AIS algorithms for classification, it is more appropriate to start with this system in supervised AISs branch as have being done. So, the feature selection process in this study can be conceived as a modification in the algorithm and can be improved for a much more efficient system. For example, the adaptation property can be added to the feature selection block and this part can be used in a combined manner with AIRS without the need of data pre-processing. Moreover, the feature selection process can be done with other mechanisms or with more effective methods to be proposed causing the system to have a considerably high performance for a great variety of data types. Besides, the performance of proposed method can be improved with the development of hybrid systems like Neuro-AIRS, Fuzzy-AIRS, Genetic-AIRS or combination of all. Certainly, it will be closer to human modelled in technological innovations by this hybrid models and it won't be take a long time to see artificial human model in the literature.

Acknowledgements

This work is supported by the Coordinatorship of Selçuk University's Scientific Research Projects Grant.

References

1. Du, X.L., Key, C.R., Osborne, C., Mahnken, J.D., Goodwin, J.S.: Discrepancy Between Consensus Recommendations and Actual Community Use of Adjuvant Chemotherapy in Women with Breast Cancer, Annals of Internal Medicine, Vol. 138, (2003) 90-97
2. Quinlan, J.R.: Improved use of continuous attributes in C4.5, Journal of Artificial Intelligence Research, Vol. 4, (1996) 77-90
3. Hamilton, H.J., Shan, N. and Cercone, N.: RIAC: A Rule Induction Algorithm Based on Approximate Classification, Tech. Rep. CS 96-06, Regina University (1996)
4. Ster, B. and Dobnikar, A.: Neural Networks in Medical Diagnosis: Comparison With Other Methods, Proceedings of the International Conference EANN '96, (1996) 427-430
5. Bennett, K.P. and Blue, J.A.: A Support Vector Machine Approach to Decision Trees, Rensselaer Polytechnic Institute, Math Report (1997) 97-100
6. Nauck, D. and Kruse, R.: Obtaining Interpretable Fuzzy Classification Rules From Medical Data, Artificial Intelligence in Medicine. Vol. 16, (1999) 149-169
7. Pena-Reyes, A.C., Sipper, M.: A Fuzzy-Genetic Approach to Breast Cancer Diagnosis, Artificial Intelligence in Medicine. Vol. 17, (1999) 131-155
8. Setiono, R.: Generating Concise and Accurate Classification Rules for Breast Cancer Diagnosis, Artificial Intelligence in Medicine. Vol. 18 (2000) 205-219
9. Goodman, E.D., Boggess, C.L., Watkins, A.: Artificial Immune System Classification of Multiple-Class Problems, In Intelligent Engineering Systems through Artificial Neural Networks: Smart Engineering System Design: Neural Networks, Fuzzy Logic, Evolutionary Programming, Complex Systems and Artificial Life, Vol. 12, (2002) 179-184
10. Abonyi, J., Szeifert, F.: Supervised Fuzzy Clustering for The Identification of Fuzzy Classifiers, Pattern Recognition Letters. Vol. 24, (2003) 2195-2207
11. Blake, C.L., and Merz, C.J.: UJI Repository of Machine Learning Databases, ftp://ftp.ics.uci.edu/pub/machine-learning-databases (last accessed: 7 April 2005)
12. Nasaroui, O.F., Gonzalez, F., Dasgupta, D.: The Fuzzy Artificial Immune System: Motivation, Basic Concepts, and Application to Clustering and Web Profiling, International Joint Conference on Fuzzy Systems, (2002) 711-717
13. De Castro, L.N., Timmis, J.: Artificial Immune Systems: A New Computational Intelligence Approach, Springer-Verlag Press (2002)
14. Knight, T., and Timmis, J.: Assessing The Performance of The Resource Limited Artificial Immune System AINE, Computing Laboratory, University of Kent at Canterbury, Technical Report (2001)
15. Watkins, A., and Timmis, J.: Artificial Immune Recognition System (AIRS): Revisions and Refinements, Proc. Int. Conf. on Artificial Immune Systems (ICARIS), (2002) 99-106
16. Dasgupta, D.: Artificial Immune Systems and Their Applications, Springer-Verlag Press, Germany (1999)

17. Carter, J. H.: The Immune System as a Model for Pattern Recognition and Classification, Journal of the American Medical Informatics Assocation, Vol. 7(3), (2000) 28-41
18. Watkins, A.: AIRS: A Resource Limited Artificial Immune Classifier, A Thesis Submitted to the Faculty of Mississippi State University (2001)
19. Şahan, S., Kodaz, H., Güneş, S., Polat, K.: A New Classifier Based on Attribute Weighted Artificial Immune System , Lecture Notes in Computer Science (LNSC 3280), (2004) 11-20

Artificial Immune Strategies Improve the Security of Data Storage*

Lei Wang[1], Yinling Nie[1], Weike Nie[2], and Licheng Jiao[2]

[1] School of Computer Science and Engineering, Xi'an University of Technology,
710048 Xi'an, China
{leiwang, yinlingnie}@xaut.edu.cn
[2] School of Electronic Engineering, Xidian University,
710071 Xi'an, China
{wknie, lchjiao}@mail.xidian.edu.cn

Abstract. A novel artificial immune strategies based data storage model, called AIS-DS, is proposed for dealing with the problem of resources sharing in a storage area network (SAN). Especially for the multi-user's tasks, this technology has some essential features for ensuring the security and privacy of information and/or data, because a SAN here can be regarded exclusive for each user with its own vaccines (a kind of special codes assigned for this user), and on the other hand, damage or interference to the disk or type to some extent in a local area of SAN, will not destroy the integrity of the saved data. Furthermore, with AIS-DS, the privacy of user's coded/decoded data is guaranteed even if the disk is physically handed by some other unwanted users.

1 Introduction

As we know, with rapid development of computer networks, we have entered into the times full of information, which makes the security and privacy of data become more and more important. For saving or protecting our rapidly growing data, we have to employ a large number of disks and some access control techniques, which costs us not only money, but also time. Aiming at such kind of problems, some available technologies of data storage, for examples, consolidated disk storage, storage area network based disk array sharing, and so on, make cost saving to a certain extent and system uptime improved. However, most of them increase the complex of application, for example, they need higher scalability of the size of data before usage, and are required to deal with the problems of clustering limitation, uneasy for tape backup, etc. Based on this consideration, it is still necessary to develop some techniques that are competent for data integrity, and improve the methods of management and system availability at the same time. Fortunately, with the development of biology, we are provided with plentiful inspirations from natural information processing mechanisms, especially the immune systems. Some researchers are trying to design and/or develop a model with the ability of imitating natural immune functions [1].

---

* This research is supported by National Science Foundation of China under grant n°60372045.

Natural immune system, usually we use NIS as the abbreviation, consists of many interacting components adapting to a changing environment, which can be regarded as a paradigm for designing a complex adaptive system [2]. On the other hand, NIS offers an inspiration for mathematical modeling and computer simulation, which leads to the creation of a new research field of computer science called "artificial immune systems", and AIS for short [3]. From this perspective, NIS is a compelling example of an adaptive information processing system that may provide new insights into the development of artificial systems exhibiting properties such as robustness, adaptation, and autonomy. One of these applications is the development of the computer immune systems [4].

In the following, several basic concepts of biological immune systems are introduced in Section 2, which is helpful for learning how this kind of natural intelligent mechanism works, and from which we may find some inspiration for designing our artificial intelligent systems. Then Section 3 describes a structure of a data storage system. Here, the code division multiple access technology is employed for data processing, which is called vaccination. The purpose of such process is to decrease the information intensity during data storage so as to make it available that the interference from other users or damages to the data is weaken greatly. In Section 4, some results of a simple simulation on data storage are provided, and finally, a brief summary is made and some ideas about future research are also proposed.

2 Brief Presentation to Artificial Immune System

Immunity in biology normally means: 1, protection against infectious disease by either specific or non-specific mechanisms, and 2, pertaining to the immune system or immune response [5]. The immune system contains a large number of interacting molecules, cells, and organs whose complex interactions form an efficient system that is able to protect an individual from both outside invaders and its own altered internal cells that may lead to disease (pathogens) [6].

2.1 Vaccination and Immunity

The practice of vaccination against disease began in 1796 by Edward Jenner, who used the pus of blisters from cowpox to vaccinate people against smallpox [7]. Vaccines are suspensions of infectious agents used to artificially induce immunity against specific diseases. The aim of vaccination is to mimic the process of naturally occurring infection through artificial means. Therefore, vaccination can be regarded as a main approach of artificially improving our innate specific immunity.

2.2 Artificial Immune System

As mentioned in introduction, research on natural immune systems offers an inspiration for mathematical modeling and computer simulation [8], which leads to the creation of a new research area in computer science, i.e., artificial immune systems-AIS. AIS provides a novel tool of classification and data analysis that belongs to the emerging field of artificial intelligence and computer science. Due to many good performances, such as massive distribution, wide parallelism, high self-adaptability and intelligent functions of computational and biological reasoning, AIS is being paid more and more attention in more and more applications, especially in computer security systems design.

3 Immune Mechanism Based Data Storage and Protection

Usually, the data's storage and protection concern three domains, that are respectively data confidentiality, which aims at fighting against the exposition of data; data integrity, i.e. to keep from tempering with data; and data availability, for preventing the denial of data's normal access. For dealing with the above problems, on one hand, we usually set up some kinds of access passwords (with different limits of authority) to the database where data are saved. On the other hand, we have to backup our data periodically in case of possible damage to the data, and/or copy some segments of data for special usage, in order to keep data's integrity and availability.

3.1 Architecture of Industry-Wide Disk Storage

Some special users, such as bank, stockjobber, etc, employ a large number of disks or types to save and backup their data for subsequent handling. Nowadays, for the technologies of data storage, no matter the distributed storage architecture or the consolidated external disk arrays, aim to be benefit from moveable, over time and resources sharing in a storage area network (SAN). Besides, for the methods of data protection, they can be differentiated as online and offline, the two kinds of techniques. In which, the online data protection consist of RAID, namely a storage system of redundant array of inexpensive disks, *snapshot*, a point-in-time static copy of a disk volume or file system, and *replication*, that means to copy date to another storage subsystem, either as the same location or at a remote site. For the offline data protection, it suggests that data is backed up to tape and the tapes are then stored locally (called on site), or into a remote and more secure location (namely off site).

In recent years, in order to achieve economies of scale, a method called consolidated disk storage was proposed [9], which supports cache management, load balancing across drives and other performance-enhancing technologies. A sketch map of such kind of technology is shown as Fig.1, in which large and external enterprise disk arrays are employed to which each host is directly connected by some kinds of communication protocols, such as SCSI or IEEE 1394. Except for improved system uptime, the outstanding advantage of such structure is that the purchase cost saving may be achieved, as well as reduced management, maintenance and so on. Resource sharing is a primary benefit of a SAN-based storage architecture, for example the space division based consolidated disk storage as shown in Fig.2. Due to supporting for enterprise clustering, improving system uptime and making cost savings available from flexibility, this storage architecture is currently used widely.

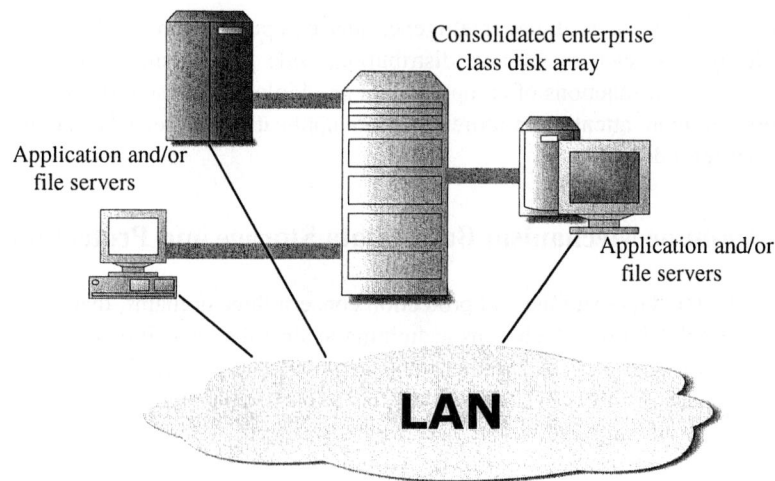

Fig. 1. The architecture of consolidated disk storage proposed by ENSTOR®

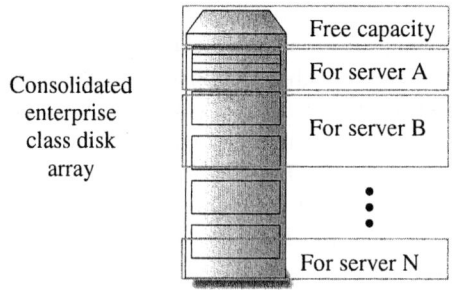

Fig. 2. Space division based consolidated disk storage

However, this capability of a disk or a tape is always limited, even if it is quite large. Therefore, the disk for data storage must be monitored online and replaced periodically in case of data overflow. On the other hand, any damage to the disk or tape may destroy data's integrity, so several duplications are needed for some important data, which makes cost increasing. Are there any other methods for multi-user's data storage? or is the space division based method the best/only choice for consolidated disk storage? This kind of questions lead to our new model called AIS-DS, which will be introduced in the next section.

3.2 Artificial Immune Strategies Based Data Storage Model (AIS-DS)

The idea of code division based consolidated disk storage aims to deal with the problem if multi-user's data can be stored in the same space at the same time. For such purpose, each user is assigned a code, which is a kind of special pseudo-noise (PN) sequence. With this code, each user accesses his data under vaccination (a process of user's data multiplying his assigned PN sequence when writing information) or devaccination (a similar process of user's stored data multiplying his assigned PN sequence when reading).

As illustrated in Fig.3, before a user's information is written into the disk, at first, it is processed by a special pseudo noise sequence, and similarly before reading, the same code of sequence is needed to devaccinate the data. Although this idea is more complicated than normal data access methods, it makes available that multi users can access the same disk at the same time. The principle concerned is analyzed as follows.

$$v_K(i) = \sum_{n=0}^{N-1} a_n g(i - nD_b) \qquad (1)$$

where, $\{a_n = \pm 1\}$, and $g(i)$ is a rectangle pulse with the width of D_b. $PN_K(i)$ is the PN sequence for modulating User$_K$'s data sequence, as shown in Fig.4(b), namely:

$$PN_K(i) = \sum_{n=0}^{N-1} c_n p(i - nD_c) \qquad (2)$$

where $\{c_n\}$ denotes a binary PN sequence with the value of ± 1, and $p(i)$ is a rectangle pulse with the width of D_c that is set as $D_c = 1/B_c$.

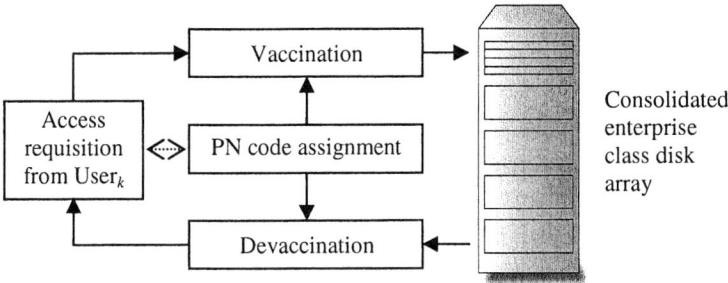

Fig. 3. Vaccination/devaccination (with pseudo-noise code division) based consolidated disk storage model (AIS-DS)

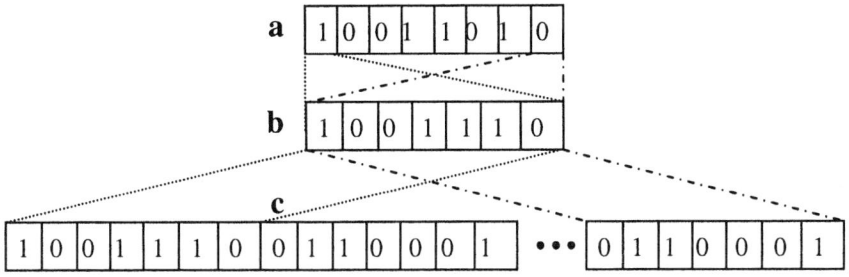

Fig. 4. Data of user$_K$ vaccinated with a PN sequence, in which, a. v_K, a type of User$_K$'s data sequence to be saved; b. PN$_K$, the PN sequence for modulating User$_K$'s data sequence; and c. $S_K = v_K \otimes PN_K$, a type of User$_K$'s data sequence to be saved in the disk.

If the interference or damage caused accidentally or by man-made factors is $I(i)$, with the information intensity A_J, the final sequence $S(i)$ of one type that sums up all users' data is given by:

$$S(i) = \sum_{j=1}^{N_{Users}} v_j(i) PN_j(i) + I(i) \tag{3}$$

Then for User$_K$, the $S(i)$ devaccinated by its PN sequence PN_K is given by:

$$S(i)PN_K(i) = v_K(i)PN_K^2(i) + \sum_{j=1, j \neq K}^{N_{Users}} \left(v_j(i) PN_j(i) PN_K(i) \right) + I(i) PN_K(i) \tag{4}$$

Due to the properties of PN sequence, it holds that. By definition, a PN sequence is approximatively orthogonal to each other, which means the scalar product $PN_j(t) \cdot PN_K(t)$, $j \neq K$, is near to zero. Therefore, for the above equation, the sum of the second item can be ignored, and that is to say the effect from the other users has been eliminated by PN_K. For the interference $I(i)$, multiplied by $PN_K(i)$, it becomes a long byte-length interference with the information density:

$$J_0 = \frac{P_J}{W} \tag{5}$$

where $P_J = A_J^2/2$ is the average information intensity of the disturbance data. Therefore, the total disturbance from data devaccinated is:

$$J_0 B_L = \frac{P_J B_L}{W} = \frac{P_J}{W/B_L} = \frac{P_J}{L_c} \tag{6}$$

where $L_c = W/B_L$ is the controlled information intensity of modulating process to disturbance/damage. Suppose W is the type-length of disk/type, and also let B_L be far less than W (so L_c is a quite large positive number), therefore, the information intensity of disturbance/damage will be weakened by L_c times through devaccination.

From the above analysis it follows that if the data are obtained by other users or business spies, it is very difficult to recoded them out without the corresponding PN code. It also concludes that if the data stored are destroyed to some extent, they could be easily restored. The later can be derived as the following:

If Δv_K is the destroyed part during User$_k$'s data storage, and v'_K is his data sequence obtained from disk finally, namely,

$$v'_K(i) = v_K(i) PN_K(i) - \Delta v_K(i) \tag{7}$$

then Equ(4) can be rewritten as:

$$S(i)PN_K(i) = v'_K(i) PN_K(i) + \sum_{j=1, j \neq K}^{N_{Users}} \left(v_j(i) PN_j(i) PN_K(i) \right) + I(i) PN_K(i) \tag{8}$$

$$= (v_K(i)PN_K(i) - \Delta v_K(i))PN_K(i)$$
$$+ \sum_{j=1, j \neq K}^{N_{Users}} (v_j(i)PN_j(i)PN_K(i)) + I(i)PN_K(i)$$
$$= v_K(i)PN_K^2(i) + \sum_{j=1, j \neq K}^{N_{Users}} (v_j(i)PN_j(i)PN_K(i))$$
$$+ (I(i) - \Delta v_K(i))PN_K(i)$$

From the above equation, it concludes that Δv_K can be regarded as a part of interference, so its effect will also be eliminated with devaccination.

It is interesting to note that the above detail process is similar to code division multiple access (CDMA) communications, but it still has its own features. For example, firstly, the length of PN code is not very long, or else, the storage efficiency falls down greatly. Secondly, although data from different users can be stored simultaneously on a same disk, the management of whole system gives priority to time-sharing. Finally, due to the characteristics of data backup, at the stage of data recoding, the technique for data processing is quite easier than that in CDMA communications.

4 Simulations

In this section, a simple simulation is designed for exposing how the method proposed in this paper protects user's data against occasional damage or man-made interference.

Suppose there are 8 users who share a same disk at a same time, therefore, we set $L_c = 31$ in accordance with the properties of PN sequence. That also means we must use two 5-level m-sequences for constructing PN sequence generator, which are shown as follows:

Sequence 1 = [1 0 1 0 0]
Sequence 2 = [1 1 1 0 1]

According to the above two m-sequences, the structure of PN sequence generator is designed as illustrated by Fig.5.

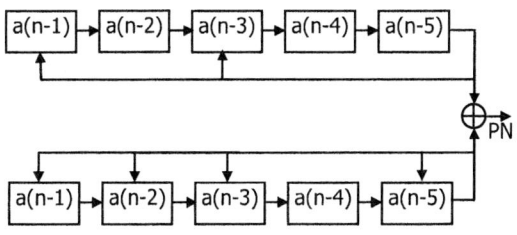

Fig. 5. PN sequence generator used in this test

In Fig.6, the following items are shown: the data of $User_K$ to be saved (Fig.6-a), the real data to be saved with all users' information together (Fig.6-b), the interference to data (Fig.6-c), the data interfered (Fig.6-d) and the recovered data for $User_K$ (Fig.6-e).

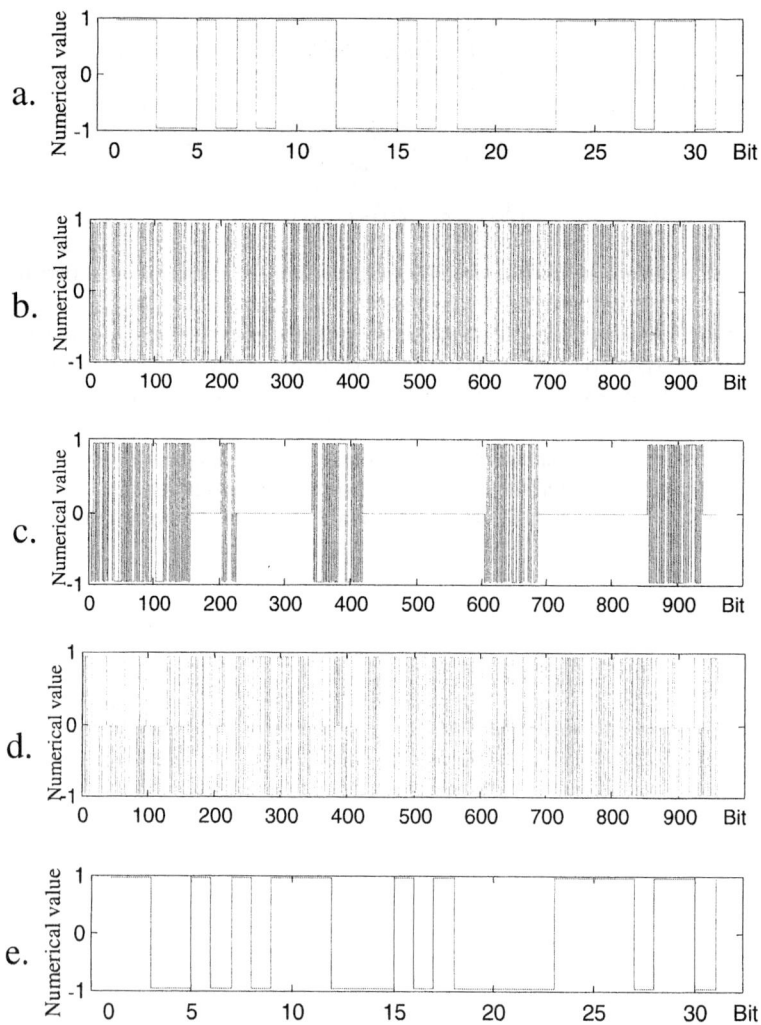

Fig. 6. The process of data modulation and demodulation, in which, a. Data of $user_k$ to be saved, v_K; b. Real data saved to be saved from all users' data,; c. Interference to saved data $I(i)$ with the average intensity of 18%; d. Data interfered, $S(i)$; and e. Data of $User_k$ restored, v'_K.

The above test has been made 10'000 times for every 8 users, and if the average information intensity of interference is less than about 18% of that of data saved, no error bits have been found, as shown in Fig.7. With the increase of interference intensity from 18% to about 40%, data of most users can be recovered, however one or two users' data cannot be used normally. Starting from about 40%, error bit ratio (EBR) begins to rise very quickly.

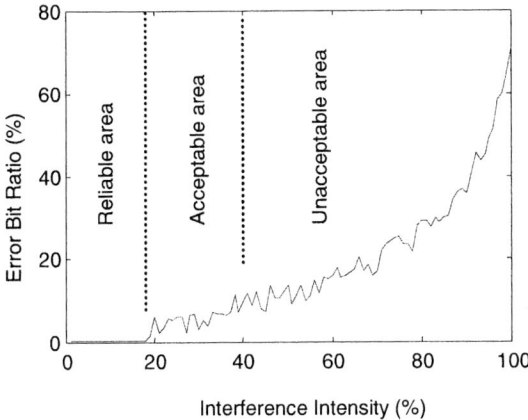

Fig. 7. Variation of the error bit ratio with the intensity of interference

5 Conclusion and Discussion

With regard to the problems of multi-user's information storage and protection in SAN, a novel data storage method is proposed. Different with ordinary methods such as space or time division multiple access, this technology has some essential features for ensuring the security and privacy of user's information and/or data. Through decreasing the information intensity by multi times during user's data storage and then recovering it normal when scan, the method makes the interference from other users or damages to the data weaken enormously. Therefore, damage to some extent in some local area of SAN will not destroy the integrity of saved data. On the other hand, because a SAN here can be regarded exclusive for each user with its own special code, the data management could be simplified. Due to coded when data storage and/or backup and decoded when scan, the probability of user's data leakage is also very low even if the disk is physically handed by some other users.

Although some simulation results have been performed, there still exist a lot of works necessary for practical applications, for example, the further theoretical analysis on the relationship between data's security and interference/damage intensity, the detailed technique requirements under currently applied protocols, and the physical system development for data management and maintenance. Another remaining problem we can forecast is, comparing with the ordinary methods, although we could take the advantage of better convenience of data maintenance, the cost should be paid is that an accessorial workload is required for encoding/decoding user's data as they are written into or read out from the disk/type, which increases the difficulties of the operating system. Therefore, how to bring them into balance and to make this system compatible to what we are now use is the key for its application and further development.

References

1. Klarreich, E.: Inspired by Immunity. Nature, Vol.415 No.1 (2002) 468-470
2. Esponda, F., Forrest, S., Helman. P.: A formal framework for positive and negative detection. IEEE Transactions on Systems, Man, and Cybernetics –Part B: Cybernetics, Vol. 34 No.1 (2004) 357-373
3. De Castro, L. N., Von Zuben, F. J.: Learning and Optimization Using the Clonal Selection Principle. IEEE Transactions on Evolutionary Computation, Special Issue on Artificial Immune Systems, Vol.6, No.3 (2002) 239-251
4. Dasgupta, D., Gonzalez, F.: An Immunity-Based Technique to Characterize Intrusions in Computer Networks. IEEE Transactions on Evolutionary Computation, Vol. 6, No. 3 (2002) 102-119
5. Wassung, K. W.: Challenging the theory of artificial immunity. http://www.atlaschiro.com/artificial-immunity.htm
6. Janssen, M. A.: An immune system perspective on ecosystem management. Conservation Ecology, Vol.5 No.1 (2001) 13-15
7. New York Hall of Science website: http://www.nyhallsci.org/whataboutaids/whatis/immune/frame.html
8. ENSTOR® website: Optimized storage systems. http://www.enstor.com.au/sol_store_data/cons_disk.html
9. John, P. G.: Digital Communications. New York, McGraw Hill (1995)

Artificial Immune System for Associative Classification

Tien Dung Do, Siu Cheung Hui, and Alvis C.M. Fong

School of Computer Engineering, Nanyang Technological University,
Nanyang Avenue, Singapore
{pa0001852a, asschui, ascmfong}@ntu.edu.sg

Abstract. Artificial Immune Systems (AIS), which are inspired from nature immune system, have recently been investigated for many information processing applications, such as feature extraction, pattern recognition, machine learning and data mining. In this paper, we investigate AIS, and in particular the clonal selection algorithm for Associative Classification (AC). To implement associative classification effectively, we need to tackle the problems on the very large search space of candidate rules during the rule mining process. This paper proposes a new approach known as AIS-AC for mining association rules effectively for classification. In AIS-AC, we treat the rule mining process as an optimization problem of finding an optimal set of association rules according to some predefined constraints. The proposed AIS-AC approach is efficient in dealing with the complexity problem on the large search space of rules. It avoids searching greedily for all possible association rules, and is able to find an effective set of associative rules for classification.

1 Introduction

Artificial Immune Systems (AIS) [1,2] are inspired from nature immune systems. The powerful information processing capabilities of the immune system, such as feature extraction, pattern recognition, learning and its distributive nature provide rich metaphors for its artificial counterpart. Specifically, three immunological principles [1] are primarily used in AIS methods. These include the immune network theory, the mechanisms of negative selection, and the clonal selection principles. In this paper, we focus only on investigating the clonal selection principles [2] for data classification. The clonal selection algorithm follows the population-based search model of evolutionary algorithms that have the capability of dealing with complex search space.

In this paper, artificial immune system, and in particular the clonal selection algorithm is investigated for mining association rules for associative classification. Associative classification (AC) [3,4] takes the advantage from association rule mining in extracting high quality rules that can accurately generalize the training dataset. However, the problem of AC, which is also the problem of association rule mining [5,6], is the very large search space of rules. The greedy search of association rules from the huge search space of possible rules is very computationally expensive. To tackle this problem, we first formulate a set of constraints, which can be used to determine an effective set of association rules for classification. As such, the rule mining process becomes an optimization problem of searching for a set of association rules based on the constraints. The proposed approach is known as AIS-AC which avoids searching greedily for all possible association rules, and is able to find an effective set of associative rules for classification.

2 Artificial Immune Systems

Immune systems are seen as a complex of cells, molecules and organs that protect organisms against infections. One of the fundamental roles of an immune system is to recognize and eliminate disease-causing agents known as *pathogens*. An immune system recognizes pathogens indirectly via molecules called *antigens*, a small portion of the pathogen. *B-cells*, which are a kind of immune cells, depend on its protein molecules called *antibodies* to recognize antigens. A B-cell recognizes the antigen when its antibodies come into contact with an antigen of complementary shape [1]. The B-cell is also said, in other words, to stimulate the antigen.

For a given antigen, there are some B-cells that are sufficiently stimulated through high affinity. These B-cells then rapidly produce *clones* with *mutations* at particular sites in the gene. The mutations help to produce higher affinity cells, and the proliferation matches better for the antigen with successive generations. Some B-cells of high affinity to the antigen mature into *memory* cells, which retain the immunological memory of the stimulating antigen. This brings the immune system the capability of producing high affinity antibodies, pre-selected for the specific antigen that has stimulated the primary response [7].

2.1 Clonal Selection Algorithm

Artificial immune systems are developed based on metaphors from the immune system. The current AISs observe and adopt immune functions, principles and models, and apply them to solve problems in computing, engineering and other research areas [1,8]. In [2,7], an algorithm called CLONALG that focuses on the clonal selection principle and affinity maturation process of adaptive immune response was proposed. CLONALG with population-based search is characterized as an evolutionary-like algorithm. Basically, it follows the principle of natural evolution [9] in which (i) the fitter individuals survive longer and reproduce more children than the others; and (ii) when individuals reproduce, their genetic information is passed on to the children.

However, there are some important differences between CLONALG, which is developed with the inspiration from the immune system, and the typical evolutionary algorithm, the genetic algorithm (GA), which is based on the theory of evolution. Firstly, the computation and operators are different. CLONALG performs only mutation operator and there is no crossover. Secondly, CLONALG is more diverse in comparison with GA [2]. Thirdly, in CLONALG, the solution is usually extracted from the memory pool constituted during the whole evolutionary process. In standard GA, the final solution is usually gathered from the population of the last generation of evolution.

2.2 AIS-Based Data Classification

Artificial immune systems have recently been introduced into data mining applications including the classification problem [10,11]. In [10], the Resource Limited Artificial Immune Classifier was proposed. Given a dataset, the classifier would produce a set of limited resources that can generalize the dataset. The classification can then be carried out based on this set of limited resources, which may be significantly smaller than the original dataset.

Potter and De Jong [11] proposed an immune-based approach for the binary classification problem. In the proposed approach, a binary scheme was used to represent antibodies. The antibodies, with this representation, can match with a wide range of antigens. Thus, an antibody or its B-cell may be present for a group of antigens or data samples, thereby enabling data generalization. The approach can also evolve with a co-evolutionary genetic algorithm to maintain the diversity of cells [11].

3 Rule Mining for Associative Classification

Associative classification (AC) [3] uses association rules for classification. It has achieved high accuracy in comparison with other classification approaches such as C4.5 [3,4]. In AC, the association rules are mined in the form of $iset \Rightarrow c$ where $iset$ is an itemset and c is a class. These association rules are referred to as *class association rules* (CARs) [3]. Rules with small values of support and confidence, which are not appropriate for AC, can be eliminated using appropriate support and confidence *thresholds*. The major problem of AC, which is also the problem of association rule mining, is the very large search space of rules. The greedy search of association rules from the huge search space of possible rules is very computationally expensive [12]. In our proposed approach, to avoid massively searching the rule space, only a subset of rules satisfying the support and confidence thresholds is gathered. It is, therefore, important that the generated subset should contain most accurate rules (i.e. highest confidence rules [3]) so that the classification accuracy is comparable to the conventional AC. As such, we need to increase the confidence threshold as high as possible.

In addition to the support and confidence measures, another factor that affects the accuracy of an associative classifier is the proportion of data samples from a dataset that can be classified by the set of rules. The *coverage* measure (denoted as $cover(CARs, D)$) of a set of classification association rules (or CARs) for a dataset D is defined as the percentage of the data samples in D, in which there is at least one rule in CARs matching with each data sample. Here, the coverage measure can be considered as the support measure for a set of rules. The support measure is used for specifying if a rule is observed frequent enough in a dataset, whereas coverage is used for determining how large a set of rules covers the dataset so it can be used to classify the dataset. As such, three factors, namely support, confidence and coverage can affect the quality of association rules mined for associative classification. They can be considered as constraints for mining a set of CARs for AC with a training dataset D.

Problem statement. Given the support and coverage threshold values *minSupport* and *minCoverage*, determine the maximal confidence threshold *minConfidence* and a set of association rules *CARs* such that *CARs* satisfy the following constraints:

$\text{supp}(R, D) \geq \text{minSupport}$ for every $R \in \text{CARs}$
$\text{conf}(R, D) \geq \text{minConfidence}$ for every $R \in \text{CARs}$
$\text{cover}(\text{CARs}, D) \geq \text{minCoverage}$

4 Rule Mining with Artificial Immune System

In our proposed approach, the problem of mining a set of association rules for AC defined in the previous section will be considered as an optimization process for searching a set of association rules *CARs* and the confidence threshold *minConfidence*. The optimization process searches for association rules in an evolutionary manner based on artificial immune system, and in particular, the clonal selection principle. For mining association rules with AIS, association rules are considered as immune cells. The population in each generation is then a set of association rules. The resultant association rules will be extracted from the memory pool. The CLONALG model can be used to search for association rules with the following adaptations:

- *Affinity calculation.* Our target is to search for rules with the highest confidence values. Thus, the confidence measure plays the role of affinity in artificial immune systems so that cells with high affinity are considered as good cells in the system. The *minSupport* threshold can be used to filter out specific rules from the population before the rule selection and reselection processes.
- *Memory selection.* As the optimal value of confidence threshold *minConfidence* may vary depending on the dataset, there is no fixed value for the optimal *minConfidence* that can be used to select rules from the population into the memory pool. In our approach, the threshold *minConfidence* initially set to a high value. After a certain number of generations, if the coverage value increases too little, *minConfidence* is reduced by a specific rate.
- *Termination condition.* The coverage of the memory set will be increased during the evolutionary process as more rules are inserted into the memory pool after each generation. The search is completed when the coverage value reaches the minimum coverage threshold *minCoverage*, or in other words, the coverage constraint can be considered as the termination condition of the evolutionary process.

4.1 CLONALG vs. GA

We elaborate the differences between CLONALG and GA for association rule mining for AC as follows:

- *Operators.* In conventional association rule mining algorithms, the support with anti-monotone property is used efficiently to search for association rules in the popular generate-and-count framework [5]. In evolutionary search, this property can be used as follows. Suppose *iset* is a frequent itemset and a rule *iset* $\Rightarrow c$ satisfies the support and confidence constraints. We can imply that if an itemset *iset_sub* is a subset of *iset* (*iset_sub* $\subset$ *iset*) then *iset_sub* is a frequent itemset.

We can also imply that if itemset *iset_sup* is a superset of *iset* (*iset* ⊂ *iset_sup*) then *iset_sup* is potentially a frequent itemset as it contains frequent subset *iset*. Besides, as *iset_sub* and *iset_sup* have many items in common with *iset* (in the AIS-AC approach presented later, *iset_sub* and *iset_sup* are only 1-item different from *iset*), the implications *iset_sub* ⇒ *c* and *iset_sup* ⇒ *c* are probably similar to the implication *iset* ⇒ *c*. Thus, we may consider *iset_sub* ⇒ *c* and *iset_sup* ⇒ *c* as candidate rules and test for the support and confidence constraints. We may also observe that *iset_sub* and *iset_sup* may be obtained when we impose mutation operator on *iset*[1]. Thus, the mutation (or maturation) operator is appropriate for candidate expansion in evolutionary search. On the other hand, the crossover operation between two rules having many different items may produce offspring that probably have many items different from either parent. This means that the crossover operator may not be suitable for searching itemsets using the *apriori* principle.

- *Rule diversity.* The diversification feature of an immune system enables the mining of a set of rules with high coverage values. The diversity of rules means the diversity of itemsets of rules, which in turn implies a higher number of data samples that the set of rules has matched.
- *Rule collection.* In standard GA, the solution (set of rules) is usually obtained from the last generation of evolution. If a good rule occurs during the evolutionary process, it may either disappear due to the crossover or mutation operations, or occupy the room of new generated rules. In AIS, the rule will then be put into the memory pool. The resultant memory pool then includes best rules from all generations of evolution.

As shown from the above discussion, GA is not particularly suitable for searching a set of association rules for AC in comparison with CLONALG.

4.2 AIS-AC Approach

The AIS-AC approach is implemented as follows. Firstly, in each generation, the support constraint is used to filter out specific rules from the population. Next, the confidence values of the rules are used for affinity selection. The population is then cloned, mutated and diversified. Finally, the best rules in the population are moved to the memory based on the confidence constraint. The process will be terminated when the coverage constraint is satisfied or the number of generations reaches a predefined maximum number of generations. The proposed AIS-AC approach, which is given in Figure 1, is discussed as follows.

---

[1] Let's consider one of the simplest representations of itemsets - the binary presentation. An itemset *iset* is represented by a binary string of N bits where N is the number of the set of items. For i = 1 to N, if i[th] bit of iset is set to 1, then the ith item is included in *iset*; otherwise the ith item is not included in *iset*. For example, let {1,2,3,4} be the set of items. The string "0101" then represents itemset {2,4}. Now, consider a mutation operation on "0101". When the operator turns a bit "0" into "1" we have a superset of {2,4} such as {1,2,4} (i.e. "1101") or {2,3,4} (i.e. "0111"). In contrast, when the operator turns a bit "1" into "0", we have a subset of {2,4} such as {2} (i.e. "0100") or {4} (i.e. "0001").

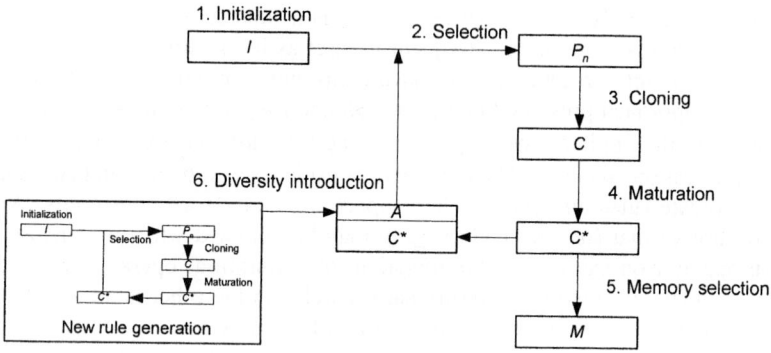

Fig. 1. The proposed AIS-AC approach

1. *Initialization.* Similar to the approach described in [3], AIS-AC will mine association rules for each class separately (i.e. all the rules with $iset \Rightarrow c$ that have the same consequence c). The population P is first initialized by the set I of all 1-itemset rules (i.e. $\{item\} \Rightarrow c$).
2. *Selection.* The selection process firstly filters specific rules with support values below the support threshold. The actual affinity selection is carried out by retaining n highest confidence rules (i.e. $n = |P_n|$) from the population. This will move the population towards containing higher affinity rules. The parameter n is used to control the approximately equal number of populations for generations during the evolutionary process.
3. *Cloning.* The cloning process is simply the reproduction of cells which will then mutate in the maturation process. In CLONALG, the clonal rate of a cell is directly proportional to the affinity of the cell so that more offspring will be produced for higher affinity cells. In AIS-AC, we have selected a single *clonalRrate* for every cell, to produce the same number of offspring (i.e. $|C| = n \times clonalRate$). This may slow down a bit on the process moving towards local optimal cells, but it helps to keep the population more diversify.
4. *Maturation.* In the CLONALG, the mutation rate of a cell is inversely proportional to the affinity of the cell. It gives the chance for low infinity cells to mutate more in order to improve its affinity. In AIS-AC, the mutation rate is equal to "one item" for every rule. That is, when a rule is mutated, the newly produced rules in C^* will differ from the parent rule in C only by one item. The reason is that cells are rules with relatively small number of items (mostly 2, 3 or 4). Two rules with two or more different numbers of items may mean different implications or have no relation at all.
5. *Diversity introduction.* To maintain diversity, AIS-AC updates the population by adding new cells (i.e. set A in the figure) into it. For the very large search space of possible rules, if we generate new rules arbitrarily, the quality of the rules (support and confidence) would be very low. In AIS-AC, to gather better new rules, we have a separate process executing the selection, cloning and maturation steps of AIS-AC to generate them. This separate process synchronizes with the main AIS-AC process and aims to generate new rules after a specified number of

generations (say 3 generations) from the initial 1-item rules. This mechanism brings much higher confidence values for new generated rules.

6. *Memory selection.* The memory selection process adds high confidence rules into the memory pool using the minimum confidence threshold *minConfidence*. Here we recalculate *minConfidence* after each k continuous generations. After k generations, if the coverage value of the memory set does not increase by *CoverIncr*, then *minConfidence* is reduced by *ConfDecr*. The parameters *CoverIncr* and *ConfDecr* are calculated as follows. Assume that *Cmax* (e.g. 100%) and *Cmin* (e.g. 50%) are the maximum and minimum values set for *minConfidence*, and N is the maximum number of generations. The number of times recalculating the coverage is about N/k. Thus, after k generations, the coverage value is supposed to increase by *CoverIncr* = 100% / (N/k) = $100*k/N$ %. With N/k times recalculated, *minConfidence* may decrease from *Cmax* to *Cmin*, that *ConfDecr* = (*Cmax*-*Cmin*) / (N/k) = $100*(Cmax-Cmin)*k/N$ %.

5 Performance Evaluation

We have conducted an experiment on a 1.4GHz Pentium PC with 400MB of memory to measure the performance of the proposed AIS-AC approach. The datasets used in the experiment are obtained from the UCI Machine Learning Repository [13]. In this experiment, we have selected large datasets from the repository for testing. Apart from measuring the accuracy of AC, this also aims to measure the scalability of the algorithms when mining the association rules. As such, we have chosen four datasets, namely *Adult*, *Digit*, *Letter* and *Nursery*, with each consisting of more than 10,000 transactions. In addition, the use of larger dataset size in performance measurement will also make the evaluation more credible and reliable. The discretization process, which discretizes continuous data into intervals and then maps them into items, is performed using the Entropy method from the MLC++ machine learning library [14]. Table 1 lists the properties of the four datasets. The *Adult* and *Digit* datasets have already been separated into training and test sets in the repository. For the *Letter* and *Nursery* datasets, we classify the data from the datasets randomly into training and test sets, in which the training set is about twice the size of the test set.

In this experiment, we have implemented the AIS-AC approach and the conventional associative classification algorithm (AC) [3] for comparison. In the implementation of the AIS-AC approach, the clonal rate is set to 20 and the population is set to 200. The number of new rules for diversity introduction and the maximum number of generations are both set to 40. The coverage threshold is set to 100% and the minimum confidence threshold is recalculated after each 4 generations. Figure 2 shows the performance results, based on accuracy (in bar chart) and runtime (in line chart), of the experiment on the two approaches using the four datasets. The experiment is conducted with minimal support thresholds ranging from 0.3% to 10%. The performance of AIS-AC is obtained from 10 runs for each dataset with different support thresholds.

Table 1. Datasets used in the experiment

Dataset	No. of attributes	No. of items	No. of classes	No. of samples
Adult	14	147	2	48842
Digit	12	151	10	10992
Letter	16	256	26	20000
Nursery	8	27	5	12960

From the performance results, while the runtime of AIS-AC is quite steady and consistent, the runtime of AC is increased exponentially when the support threshold is decreased. It is because the number of frequent itemsets satisfying the support constraint has increased exponentially. For illustration, Table 2 shows the number of frequent itemsets found with different support thresholds for the *Adult* dataset. However, this does not apply to the *Nursery* dataset. The reason is that the *Nursery* dataset contains only 27 items compared with more than a hundred items in other datasets. As such, the number of combinations of items using different attributes is relatively small.

Further, the performance of AC with small support values does not shown in Figure 2. This is because we are unable to obtain the performance results for the corresponding support values. This may be due to the reasons that the runtime is too

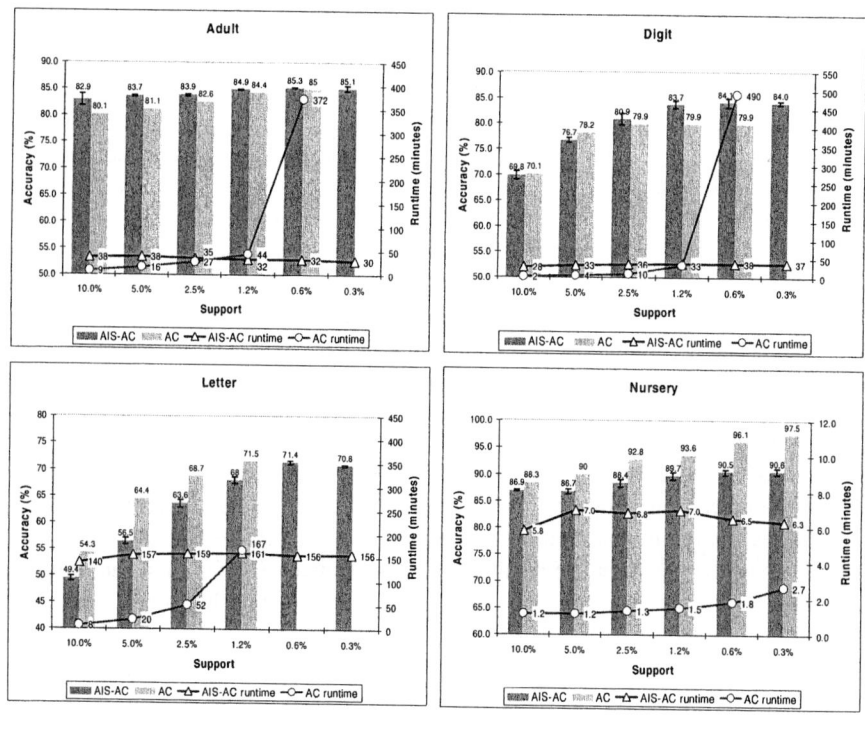

Fig. 2. Performance results

long or the number of possible rules is too large that the system has run out of memory during the rule mining process. The ability of mining rules with small support values gives AIS-AC an advantage in dealing with very large datasets. In addition, from Table 2, we have also observed that the number of rules used for classification in AIS-AC is much smaller than that in the AC approach. This also means that the classification process of AIS-AC is much simpler than that of AC.

Table 2. Number of rules and frequent itemsets for the Adult dataset

Support threshold	AIS-AC No. of rules	AC No. of frequent sets	AC No. of rules
10.0%	138	10794	174
5.0%	227	34344	575
2.5%	202	102722	1333
1.2%	290	280452	2689
0.6%	384	663276	4690
0.3%	327	1462940	7737

Let us look at the performance on accuracy for both classifiers. In principle, the AC algorithm has obtained the complete set of association rules (with the constraints on support and confidence). Therefore, it should be more accurate than AIS-AC with the same support threshold value. However, the performance results from the *Adult* and *Digit* datasets have shown that AIS-AC has surprisingly outperformed AC with most of the threshold values. One of the possible reasons is that the coverage constraint helps to obtain a balance of rules for each class which can consequently lead to accurate classification results. In the dataset *Letter*, the best performance of AIS-AC is with the support value of 0.6%, and in AC, it is 1.2%. The accuracy is similar (71.4% vs. 71.5%) while the runtime of AIS-AC is faster. In the dataset *Nursery*, the AC approach performs better than AIS-AC. The reason is that the small search space of association rules in this dataset, in which the AIS-AC approach loses its advantages.

6 Conclusion

In this paper, we have proposed a new approach known as AIS-AC for mining association rules for AC. The proposed approach aims to mine a candidate set of association rules that is suitable for effective AC. The searching of rules is carried out using the artificial immune system model based on the clonal selection theory. The advantage of this approach is that it can avoid the need for massively searching for association rules as in the conventional AC approach. The proposed AIS-AC approach, therefore, can be used to classify large datasets associatively, from which the conventional approach may have difficulties in mining the association rules.

In the current implementation, only the confidence threshold is refined over generations to gather rules with optimal confidence values. However, the evolutionary approach enables adjustment for the other parameters as well. For example, the support threshold should be reduced and/or the number of population should be increased if there are too few rules added into the memory after a given number of continuous generations. With the capability of parameter adaptation, the search becomes non-deterministic and more dynamic that is adjustable according to the data.

However, there is still a problem faced by the proposed AIS-AC approach in that it requires multiple scans of the dataset (as many as the number of generations is required). This will slow down the mining process as well as limit the number of generations in the evolutionary process. One of the possible solutions is to use the FP-growth approach [6] for counting the support and confidence. When the dataset is compressed into the FP-tree structure, the counting process for each generation can be much simpler and faster. This may also help increase the accuracy of the classification task as we can increase the number of generations, which will lead to a better set of association rules for associative classification.

References

1. de Castro, L.N., Von Zuben, F.J.: Artificial Immune Systems: Part I – Basic Theory and Applications. Technical Report – RT DCA (1999)
2. de Castro, L.N., Von Zuben, F.J.: The Clonal Selection Algorithm with Engineering Applications. In Proc. of GECCO'00. Workshop on Artificial Immune Systems and Their Applications (2000) 36-37
3. Liu, B., Hsu, W., Ma, Y.: Integrating classification and association rule mining. In Proc. of the Fourth International Conference on Knowledge Discovery and Data Mining. New York (1998) 80-86
4. Li, W., Han, J., Pei, J.: CMAR: Accurate and efficient classification based on multiple class-association rules. In Proc. of ICDM (2001)
5. Agrawal, R., Srikant, R.: Fast algorithms for mining association rules. In Proc. of the 20th Int'l Conf. on Very Large Databases (VLDB '94). Santiago, Chile (1994) 487-499
6. Han, J., Pei, J., Yin, Y.: Mining frequent patterns without candidate generation. In Proc. of the 2000ACM-SIGMOD International Conference on Management of Data. Dallas, Texas, USA (2000)
7. de Castro, L.N., Von Zuben, F. J.: Learning and Optimization Using the Clonal Selection Principle. IEEE Transactions on Evolutionary Computation, Special Issue on Artificial Immune Systems, Vol 6, No 3 (2002) 239-251
8. de Castro, L.N., Timmis, J. I.: Artificial Immune Systems as a Novel Soft Computing Paradigm. Soft Computing, Vol 7, No 8 (2003) 526-544
9. Goldberg, D.E.: Genetic Algorithms in Search, Optimization and Machine Learning. Addison-Wesley (1989)
10. Watkins, A.B., Boggess, L.C.: A Resource Limited Artificial Immune Classifier. In Proc. of Congress on Evolutionary Computation, Part of the 2002 IEEE World Congress on Computational Intelligence. Honolulu, USA (2002) 926-931
11. Potter, M., De Jong, K.: The coevolution of antibodies for concept learning. In Proc. of Parallel Problem Solving From Nature - PPSN V (1988) 530-540
12. Hegland, M.: Algorithms for association rules. Advanced lectures on machine learning, Springer-Verlag, New York (2003)
13. UCI Machine Learning Repository. Available online at <http://www.ics.uci.edu/~mlearn/MLRepository.html>
14. Kohavi, R., John, G., Long, R., Manley, D., Pfleger, K.: MLC++: A machine learning library in C++. In Tools with Artificial Intelligence (1994) 740-743

Artificial Immune Algorithm Based Obstacle Avoiding Path Planning of Mobile Robots

Yen-Nien Wang, Hao-Hsuan Hsu, and Chun-Cheng Lin

Lunghwa University of Science and Technology, Electronic Engineering,
No.300, Sec. 1, Wanshou Rd., Guishan Shiang, Taoyuan County 333, Taiwan
ynwang@mail.lhu.edu.tw

Abstract. This investigation studies the applicability of using mobile robots with artificial immune algorithm (AIA) based obstacle-avoiding path planning inside a specified environment in real time. Path planning is an important problem in robotics. AIA is applied to determine the position and the angle between a mobile robot, an obstacle and the goal in a limited field. The method seeks to find the optimal path. The objectives are to minimize the length of the path and the number of turns. The results of the real-time experiments present the effectiveness of the proposed method.

1 Introduction

Over recent years, artificially intelligent systems have been developed for robots. Every class of robot is applied in industry and society. Neural networks, genetic algorithms [1] [2], fuzzy control [3], and robust control are important to AI. These methods have been developed and some have exhibited excellent planning performance.

The modern industry applies an effective method to optimize the performance. In fact, it is an optimization planning problem. This artificial immune algorithm was developed based on a biological immune system. The biological immune system incorporates three functions - the defense of the body, the maintenance of the homeostasis of the body and surveillance. The biological immune system exhibits a high degree of specificity and the remarkable characteristic of remarkable memory. The biological immune system incorporates various cells, such as T-cytotoxic cells, T-helper cells, B cells and others. Fig. 1 shows that the main cellular agents of the artificial immune algorithm including the B cells, the antibody, the antigen, the idiotope and the paratope, according to N. K. Jerne, who created the idiotypic network hypothesis [4] [5]. The relationship between the antigen and the antibody is like that between a key and a lock.

The investigation proposes an AIA method to be applied to mobile robot behaviors. This investigation compares Dongbing Gu's method [6] with the proposed method. Section II introduces the artificial immune algorithm. III describes the mobile robot's sensor and the learning and settings for this method. Section IV compares results.

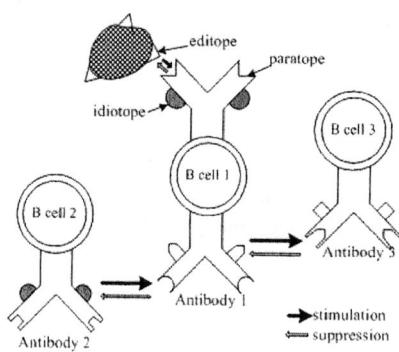

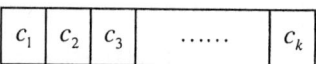

Fig. 2. One antibody

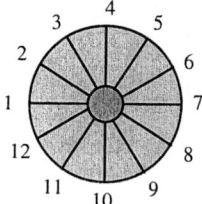

Fig. 1. Jerne's idiotypic network hypothesis

Fig. 3. Construction of Mobile Robot

2 Introduction of Artificial Immune Algorithm (AIA)

In this investigation, a behavior is viewed as an artificial immune algorithm. The running of the robot using AIA is evaluated. The artificial immune algorithm specifies rules. Therefore, fig. 2 defines one antibody again.
The operations of the AIA include the following:

1. Initialization: The first antibody is initialized randomly. Each antibody is uniformly selected from the AIA singletons.
2. Detect antigen: The first antigen is recognized simply because every B cell can recognize a particular antigen.
3. Individual immune network: The antigen combines with the antibody. In the adaptive mechanism, the lymph hormone simulates and activates the division of the B cell, or antibodies suppress the B-cell.
4. Antibody concentration: The antibody concentration closely relates to the relationships among crossover, mutation and artificial immune network function.
5. Eliminate antigen: When the antigen enters a human body, the B-cell triggers the antibody production until the antigen is eliminated.

3 Mobile Robots That Use the Artificial Immune Algorithm (AIA)

The mobile robot is used 12 sensors to detect the distance and angle between the robot and the obstacles or the goal. Every included angle of the robot is 30°. Fig. 2 shows the construction of the mobile robot. The environment of the mobile robots is a playing field with an area of 90cm². In this simulation, the mobile robot must move across numerous obstacles and arrive at a goal, which is a limited area. Then, the mobile robot associates with several selected angles when the obstacles are detected behind the mobile robot.

The immune networks are divided into two groups. One part is between the mobile robot and the obstacle in the immune network a_i^o. The other is between the mobile robot and the goal of the immune network a_i^g. The antibody α_i is defined as follows:

$$a_i = (1-\gamma_i) \cdot a_i^o + \gamma_i \cdot a_i^g \quad (1)$$

where γ_i is the ratio between antibody a_i^o and antibody a_i^g. The antibody with the highest α_i is selected. γ_i is:

$d_o > d_g$	$d_o < d_g$	only d_g
$\dfrac{d_o}{d_o + d_g}$	$\dfrac{d_g}{d_o + d_g}$	1	(2)

where d_o and d_g are the distance the obstacles to the mobile robot and the goal to the mobile robot. When d_o exceeds d_g, the numerator is d_o. Otherwise, the numerator is d_g. If the robot is detected only at the goal, then γ_i equals 1. The obstacle antibody a_i^o and the goal antibody a_i^g in an immune network are calculated as:

Obstacle	Goal
$a_i^o = \left\{ \dfrac{\sum_{j=1}^{n} m_{ji}^o \cdot a_i^o}{n} - \dfrac{\sum_{i=1}^{n} m_{ji}^o \cdot a_i^o}{n} + m_i^o - k_i^o \right\} \cdot a_i^o$	$a_i^g = \left\{ \dfrac{\sum_{j=1}^{n} m_{ji}^g \cdot a_i^g}{n} - \dfrac{\sum_{i=1}^{n} m_{ji}^g \cdot a_i^g}{n} + m_i^g - k_i^g \right\} \cdot a_i^g$	(3)

where n is the number of antibodies in the first term and second term. The first term on the right hand represents the degree of stimulation by other antibodies. The second term represents the degree of suppression by other antibodies. The third term represents the external input from the antigens. The fourth term is the natural death ratio. a_i^o and a_i^g can be calculated using similarly method. m_{ji}^o and m_{ji}^g are the obstacle matching ratio and the goal matching ratio between the antibody and the antibody. m_i^o and m_i^g are antibody and antigen matching ratios.

Obstacle ($\alpha_o = \dfrac{D-d_o}{D}$)	Goal ($\alpha_g = \dfrac{D-d_g}{D}$)
$m_{ji}^o = \dfrac{m_{ji}^o}{1-\alpha_o} \quad d_o > d_{set}$	$m_{ji}^g = \dfrac{m_{ji}^g}{1-\alpha_o} \quad d_g > d_o$	(4)
$m_{ji}^o = \dfrac{m_{ji}^o}{\alpha_o} \quad d_o < d_{set}$	$m_{ji}^g = \dfrac{m_{ji}^g}{\alpha_o} \quad d_g < d_o$

The matching ratio of the obstacle was calculated before α_o. D was the maximum size of the limited area. d_o is the distance between the robot and the obstacle. d_{set} is the radius of the robot required to avoid the obstacle. When d_o exceeds d_{set}, the denominator is $1-\alpha_o$. When d_o is less than d_{set}, the denominator is α_o. d_g is the distance between the robot and the goal. When d_g less than d_o, the denominator is $1-\alpha_g$. The other way round, d_g exceeds d_o, the denominator is α_o.

4 Experimental Results

This section presents simulation results that validate the proposed method. This investigation compares two methods. Fig. 4 shows the simulation results when the artificial immune algorithm and Dongbing Gu's genetic algorithm are used.

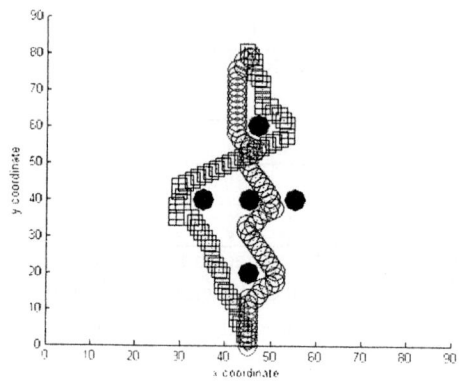

Fig. 4. Obstacle avoiding path planning of mobile robot. ("○" :the proposed method, "□" : Dongbing Gu's method.)

The solid circles refer to the obstacle. The other circles refer to the proposed method. The squares refer to Dongbing Gu's method. The fork represents the position of the goal. The total step is 59 in the artificial immune algorithm and 66 in Dongbing Gu's genetic algorithm. Fig.4 shows that the proposed method resulting in the selection of more actions. The proposed method is clearer when compared with the other method because the robot moves among obstacles toward the goal.

5 Conclusion

In this investigation, the presented method is the artificial immune algorithm controlling the mobile robot for decreasing the distance to prevent the obstacle from arriving the goal position. The robot was controlled by calculating only a few parameters. This focuses on the external environment for robot's sensors and learning methods in different conditions. Experiments were performed to elucidate the artificial immune algorithm control rules as the length of the antibody in the immune network were adjusted using this method.

References

1. Shuhua Liu, Yantao Tian, Jinfang Liu: Multi mobile robot path planning based on genetic algorithm. IEEE Trans. on Intelligent Control and Automation, Vol. 5. (2004) 4706-4709
2. Ying Zhang, Cheng-Dong Wu, Meng-Xin Li: Rough set and genetic algorithm in path planning of robot. IEEE Trans. on Machine Learning and Cybernetics, Vol. 2, (2003)698-701
3. Kawanaka H., Yoshikawa, T., Tsuruoka S.: Acquisition of Fuzzy Control Rules for a Mobile Robot Using Genetic Algorithm. IEEE Trans on Advanced Motion Control, (2000)507-512
4. N.K.Jerne: The immune system. Scientific American, Vol. 229, No. 1, (1973)52-60
5. N.K.Jerne: Idiotypic networks and other preconceived ideas. Immunological Rev., Vol.79, (1984)5-24
6. Dongbing Gu, Huosheng Hu, Jeff Reynolds, Edward Tsang: GA-based Learning in Behaviour Based Robotics. IEEE Trans. on Computational Intelligence in Robotics and Automation, Vol. 3, (2003)1521-1526

An Adaptive Hybrid Immune Genetic Algorithm for Maximum Cut Problem*

Hong Song[1], Dan Zhang[2], and Ji Liu[2]

[1] School of Mechanical Engineering, Xi'an Shiyou University,
Xi'an Shaanxi 710065, China
[2] School of Electronics & Information Engineering, Xi'an Jiaotong University,
Xi'an Shaanxi 710049, China
danzhang@mailst.xjtu.edu.cn

Abstract. The goal of maximum cut problem is to partition the vertex set of an undirected graph into two parts in order to maximize the cardinality of the set of edges cut by the partition. This paper proposes an Adaptive Hybrid Immune Genetic Algorithm, which includes key techniques such as vaccine abstraction, vaccination and affinity-based selection. A large number of instances have been simulated, and the results show that proposed algorithm is superior to existing algorithms.

1 Introduction

The maximum cut problem (MCP) is a well-known NP-hard problem [1]. Let $G = (V, E)$ be an edge-weighted undirected graph, where V is the set of vertices and E is the set of edges. The edge from vertex v_i to vertex v_j is represented by $e_{ij} \in E$. $w_{ij} = w_{ji}$ defines non-negative weights on edges whose endpoints are vertex v_i to vertex v_j. The goal of the MCP of $G = (V, E)$ is to find a partition of V into two disjoint vertex sets S_0 and S_1 such that the cut size is maximized. In this paper, we propose an adaptive hybrid immune genetic algorithm (AHIGA) for MCP. Based on the theory of immunity in biology, AHIGA is a hybrid of two immune techniques, which one is vaccination and another is affinity-based selection in antibody production. The simulation results are superior to those found by the algorithm of Hsu [2] and Lee et al [3].

2 AHIGA for Maximum Cut Problem

It is well known that GA [4] pertains to searching algorithms with an iteration of generation-and-test by crossover and mutation. Because the crossover and mutation operations make individuals change randomly and indirectly during the whole process, they not only make the individuals evolve better but also cause certain degeneracy. On the other hand, GA lacks the capability of meeting an actual situation to utilize basic and obvious characteristics or knowledge of the

---
* Supported by the Nation Science Foundation of China (No.60173059).

pending problem. In addition, the real immune system can retain diversity with self-adjustment mechanism by promotion and suppression of production of antibodies. The proposed Adaptive Hybrid Immune Genetic Algorithm (AHIGA) is a hybrid of two immune techniques [5] [6]. The AHIGA is defined as follows.

1) Create initial random population A_1.
2) Abstract vaccines according to the prior knowledge.
3) Evaluate fitness values of current population, if the finish condition (maximum iterations) is satisfied, exit and gain the optimal solutions; or else, continues.
4) Perform crossover on the kth parent A_k and obtain the results B_k.
5) Perform mutation on B_k and obtain C_k.
6) Perform vaccination on C_k and obtain D_k.
7) Perform affinity-based selection on D_k and obtain the next parent A_{k+1}, and then go to 3).

Definition 1. *For the S_0 and S_1 sub-graphs, the antibody B is defined as a binary string of length n. A gene (bit) denotes whether a vertex belong to S_0 or S_1 sub-graphs $(0 \rightarrow S_0, 1 \rightarrow S_1)$. $B = (b_1, \ldots, b_n), b_i \in \{0, 1\}, n = |V|$*

Definition 2. *For an antibody B, the fitness $f(B)$ is computed according to equation (1), which denotes the cut size in the case of sub-graphs partition of B.*

$$f(B) = \frac{\sum_{i=1}^{n}\sum_{j=1}^{i-1}\left(w_{ij} \times (b_i\ XOR\ b_j)\right)}{\sum_{i=1}^{n}\sum_{j=1}^{i-1} w_{ij}}; 1 \leq i, j \leq n; b_i, b_j \in B \qquad (1)$$

XOR: exclusive or operator.

A. Vaccine Abstraction

Vaccine contains some basic characteristics of problem, while antibodies are potential solutions. In other words, a vaccine can be regarded as an estimation on some genes of the optimal antibody. For MCP, some gene fragments are generated as vaccines. A vaccine is a local maximum spanning tree (MST). Two nodes connected by a tree edge can be simply assigned to different sub-graphs because the tree found by MST does not form a cycle. MST ensures that we can assign nodes connected via an edge with heavy weight, which implies that the sub-graph partition we get would be local optimal.

B. Vaccination

Vaccination operation is to modify some gene-bits according to a vaccine's scheme, which goal is that antibodies have higher probabilities to get higher fitness [5]. For an antibody, the vaccination operation is performed with each vaccine according to its vaccination probability P_v. The whole vaccination process is performed according to immunity probability P_i to each antibody.

C. Affinity-Based Selection

To guarantee the diversity, The affinity-based selection is to select antibodies according to the similarity between antibodies. The ones with high similarity degree to others are assigned low selection probabilities, and vice versa. Hence, it can control excessive production of the similar antibodies fit to the antigen. The affinity is defined by using the information entropy theory.

Definition 3. *Diversity: Population contains N antibodies having M genes. Each gene has S alleles. The information entropy $H_j(N)$ of jth gene is*

$$H_j(N) = \sum_{i=1}^{S} -p_{ij} \log p_{ij} \quad (2)$$

$p_{ij} = \frac{1}{N} \sum_{k=1}^{N} \left(\begin{cases} 1, & \text{i-th allele appear at j-th gene in antibody k;} \\ 0, & \text{elsewise.} \end{cases} \right)$

So, the average information entropy $H(N)$ of diversity is defined,

$$H(N) = \frac{1}{M} \sum_{j=1}^{M} H_j(N) \quad (3)$$

Definition 4. *Affinity: The affinity between the antibody x and y is defined,*

$$Affinity_{xy} = 1/(1 + H(2)) \quad (4)$$

$H(2)$ is the information entropy of antibody x and y only and has the value between 0 and 1. All affinity values constitute a $n \times n$ triangle matrix.

Definition 5. *Density: The density of the antibody x is defined,*

$$Density_x = \frac{1}{N-1} \sum_{y=1, y \neq x}^{N} Affinity_{xy} \quad (5)$$

Definition 6. *Affinity-based selection probability: The selection weight of the antibody x is defined,*

$$W_{sele_x} = \frac{1 - Density_x}{\sum_{y=1}^{N}(1 - Density_y)} \quad (6)$$

Then, the selection weight is normalized to compute selection probability.

$$P_{sele_x} = W_{sele_x} / \sum_{y=1}^{N} W_{sele_y} \quad (7)$$

3 Experimental Results and Analysis

To evaluate the efficiency of the proposed algorithm, we have implemented it in C++ on AMD Athlon XP1700+ 512M. The parameters are as follows: population-size = 20, maximum iteration = 500, $P_i = 0.3$, T (vaccine size) = 2.

Table 1 shows the comparison of the solution quality among AHIGA, Hsu (Greedy Search) [2] and Lee (Maximum Neural Network) [3] for unweighted random graphs, where the 5%, 15% and 20% density graph problems with up to 100 vertices have been examined. Table 1 shows that AHIGA can find better solutions than GS and MNN. Table 2 shows the comparison among GS, MNN and AHIGA for weighted random graphs and the results of AHIGA is superior to GS and MNN.

Table 1. The results of GS, MNN and AHIGA for unweighted graph

Node	5% GS	5% MNN	5% AHI	15% GS	15% MNN	15% AHI	20% GS	20% MNN	20% AHI
10	2	2	2	6	6	6	6	6	7
20	8	8	9	24	25	25	26	28	31
30	19	20	20	49	50	52	52	56	66
40	36	36	36	90	90	90	96	99	112
50	50	53	54	128	135	136	143	149	172
60	78	80	80	191	195	196	210	218	239
70	102	107	109	246	254	254	282	282	320
80	125	132	133	311	330	332	363	367	411
90	158	162	164	390	405	408	445	459	513
100	185	195	198	478	494	499	553	564	634

Table 2. The results of GS, MNN and AHIGA for weighted graph

Node	GS	MNN	AHIGA
100	136781	136876	136982
200	534669	534726	535357
300	1184563	1188594	1192183

4 Conclusions

This paper has proposed an adaptive hybrid immune genetic algorithm (AHIGA) for maximum cut problem. Based on the immunity theory in biology, AHIGA is a hybrid of two immune techniques - vaccination and affinity-based selection. The simulation results shows that AHIGA is superior to existing algorithms, e.g. GS and MNN, for both weighted and un-weighted graph.

References

1. Garey, M.R., Johnson, D.S. In: Computers and intractability. Freeman, San Francisco (1979)
2. Hsu, C.P.: Minimum-via topological routing. IEEE Trans. on Computer-Aided Design **2** (1983) 235–246
3. Lee, K.C., Funabiki, N., Takefuji, Y.: A parallel improvement algorithm for the bipartite subgraph problem. IEEE Trans. on Neural Networks **3** (1992) 139–145
4. Goldberg, D.E. In: Genetic Algorithms in Search, Optimization, and Machine Learning. Addison-Wesley, Mass. (1989)
5. Jiao, L.C., Wang, L.: A novel genetic algorithm based on immunity. IEEE Trans. on Systems, Man and Cybernetics, Part A **30** (2000) 552–561
6. Chun, J.S., et al.: Shape optimization of electromagnetic devices using immune algorithm. IEEE Trans. on Magnetic **33** (1997) 1976–1879

Algorithms of Non-self Detector by Negative Selection Principle in Artificial Immune System[*]

Ying Tan and Zhenhe Guo

School of Information Science and Technology,
University of Science and Technology of China,
Hefei 230027, P.R. China
ytan@ustc.edu.cn

Abstract. According to the principles of non-self detection and negative selection in natural immune system, two generating algorithms of detector are proposed in this paper after reviewing current detector generating algorithms used in artificial immune systems. We call them as Bit Mutation Growth Detector Generating Algorithm (BMGDGA) and Arithmetical-compliment Growth Detector Generating Algorithm (AGDGA) based on their operational features. The principle and work procedure of the two detector generating algorithms are elaborated in details in the paper. For evaluation of the proposed algorithms, they are tested and verified by using different datasets, and compared to Exhaustive Detector Generating Algorithm (EDGA). It turns out that the proposed two algorithms are superior to EDGA in detection performance and computational complexities.

1 Introduction

The immune system defends the body against harmful diseases and infections and plays very important adjustment functions in the whole lifetime of biological creatures. It has many features that are desirable for information security research and problem solving of complex problems encountered in many engineering fields. Based on natural immune principles, many algorithms and architectures are proposed [1]-[7] in many engineering fields. Among them, the non-self recognition interests greatly IT and computer researchers and stimulates a lot of artificial immune systems (AIS) for change detection and pattern recognition. Forrest, et.al., [7] proposed the well-known negative selection algorithm (NSA) as a detector generating algorithm by simulating the negative selection process of T cells generating in thymus. This paper studies the detector-generating algorithm carefully, and proposes two-detector generating algorithms based-on non-self detection and negative selection principles from the perspective of optimizing detector generation. Two algorithms are elaborately described in

---

[*] This work was supported by the Natural Science Foundation of China with Grant No. 60273100.

theory and implementation and completely compared with Exhaustive Detector Generating Algorithm (EDGA).

2 Negative Selection Principle and Related Algorithms

2.1 Negative Selection Principle and Algorithm

Negative selection is one of important phases of generation and maturation of T cells in thymus. T-cells with essentially random receptors are generated in thymus. Before they are released to the rest of body, those T-cells that match self are deleted. This process is called negative selection process based on which a number of detector generating algorithms are created in many artificial immune systems (AIS). In 1994, Forrest, et.al, proposed so-called negative selection algorithm (NSA) inspired by negative selection principle (NSP) [7]. NSA consists of two stages of *censoring* and *monitoring*. The censoring phase caters for the generation of change-detectors. Subsequently, the system being protected is monitored for changes using the detector set generated in the censoring stage.

2.2 Current Detector Generating Algorithms

There are a number of detector-generating algorithms with different matching rules applied for 'self' and 'non-self' matching methods. Currently, for binary code, there are mainly three kinds of matching rules, which are perfect matching, r-contiguous bits matching [2] and Hamming distance matching. Exhaustive detector generating algorithm (EDGA) is suitable for three matching rules and is used to repeat the NSP till the number of detectors meets a preset demand or candidate set is vanished. However, negative selection algorithm with mutation [9] has different evaluating rules in the negative selection process from EDGA. With r-contiguous bits matching rule, the related algorithms mainly include Liner Time Detector Generating Algorithm and Greedy Detectors Generating Algorithm [9][10].

3 Bit Mutation and Arithmetic-Compliment Growth Algorithms

3.1 Growth Algorithm

The main difference between growth algorithm and NSA is the generating method of candidate detectors. For NSA, each detector candidate in EDGA is randomly selected from whole candidate space. Thus, after the number of detector candidate space N_{r0} is determined, EDGA randomly selects N_{r0} detectors to construct the detector candidate set R_0. Then, the algorithm generates detector set R through negative selection process. On the other hand, growth algorithm does not need to maintain a huge detector candidate set R_0. It directly generates the detector set R by utilizing detector mutation or growth in whole shape space and combining with negative selection process. Its flow chart is shown in Fig.1.

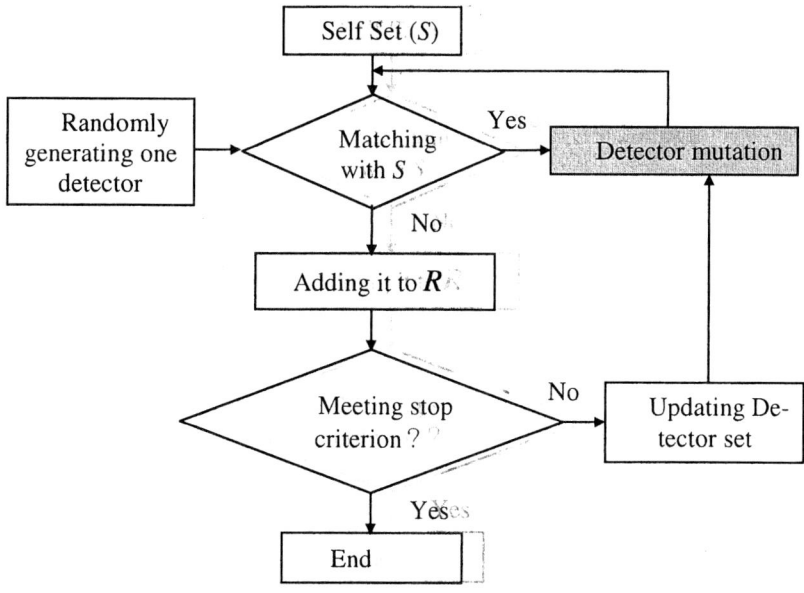

Fig. 1. Flow chart of detector generation growth algorithm

Growth Algorithm
Step 1. Generating self set S with its number N_s.
Step 2. Generating one detector generating seed which is randomly selected from the whole shape space.
Step 3. Matching the new detector candidate with S.
Step 4. Experiencing a negative selection process. If the candidate is not matched with S, then a new one is generated and added into R.
Step 5. If the stop criterion is met, then exit.
Step 6. Mutating the candidate and going to step 3.

3.2 Bit Mutation and Arithmetical-Compliment Growth Methods

Here, we design two detector mutation methods of bit mutation and arithmetical-compliment growth according to different detector mutation rules.

3.2.1 Bits Mutation

This method is similar to bit mutation of Genetic Algorithm. But this algorithm mutates multiple bits of detector candidate, not only one bit. If we let the string length be l and the maximum number of mutation bits be N_m ($N_m = m$), then, at one time, the mutated bits of detector candidate is less than or equal to m.

Bit Mutation Algorithm

Step 1. Set the maximum number of mutation bits N_m.
Step 2. Input detector DetectorM to be mutated.

Step 3. Generate mutation seed MutationBits (its length is same as detector): N_m bits of MutationBits are randomly generated at range of 1 and l and set to 1, and others are set to zero.

Setp 4. Detector mutation: an exclusive OR operation performed on the corresponding bits of arrays DetectorM and MutationBits.

Pascal language description of bits mutation algorithm:

```
Program Bits_Mutation(DetectorM, Nm )
        var
          MutationBits    : Longword;        //Mutation seed
          MutationBit     : array[1.. Nm ] of Byte;
        begin
           MutationBits := 0;
           For i := 1 to Nm  do              //Generating mutation seed
           begin
                MutationBit[i] := Random( l );
                MutationBits := (1 shl MutationBit[i]) or MutationBits;
           end;
           DetectorM:= DetectorM xor MutationBits; //Detector mutation
  end;
```

3.2.2 Arithmetic-Compliment Growth Algorithm

This mutation method consists of two phases. Phase 1 is used to generate mutation seed and phase 2 is to mutate the detector candidate. The process of generating mutation seed in phase 1 is same as bit mutation method described above except that the sum of arithmetic-compliment of mutation seed and detector mutation is used as the detector candidate.

Pascal language description of Arithmetic-compliment growth algorithm:

```
Program Arithmetical-compliment_growth(DetectorM, Nam )
         var
           MutationO     :Longword;            //Mutation seed
           MutationBit   :array[1.. Nam ] of Byte;
         begin
           MutationO := 0;
           for i := 1 to Nam  do               //Generating mutation seed
           begin
           MutationBit[i] := Random( l );
           MutationO := (1 shl MutationBit[i]) or MutationO;
           end;
           DetectorM := MutationO + DetectorM;
             If DetectorM >= 2^l  then DetectorM := DetectorM - 2^l ;
         end;
```

3.3 BMDGA and AGDGA

Once the proposed two mutation methods are separately applied to the detector mutation part of the growth algorithm in Fig.1, we can obtain two kinds of detector generating algorithms which are called as bit mutation algorithm (BMDGA) and arithmetical-complement growth algorithm (AGDGA), respectively.

4 Experiments

4.1 Experimental Goals

There are three main goals for our experiments. They are:

- Validating algorithms' quality of generated detector set by using detection rate P_c.
- Comparing the algorithm's complexity to EDGA.
- Setting parameters including N_m and N_{am}, according to algorithms' performance.

4.2 Selection of Experimental Parameters

We set two kinds of experiments. One chooses random dataset with string length 8, 16 and 24 bits, respectively. Another experiment is to detect the changes of static files.

4.3 Random Dataset Experiments

4.3.1 8-Bit Dataset Experiments

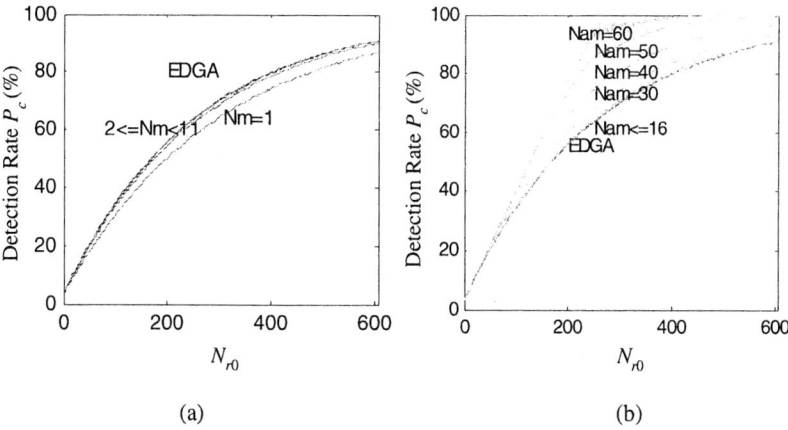

Fig. 2. Experimental results of Detection rate P_c versus N_{r0} when N_s is constant, where N_s =8, N_{r0} increases from 1 to 604, size of test set is 256, and 1000 runs. (a) Curves of P_c versus N_{r0} for EDGA and BMGDGA, (b) Curves of P_c versus N_{r0} for EDGA and AGDGA.

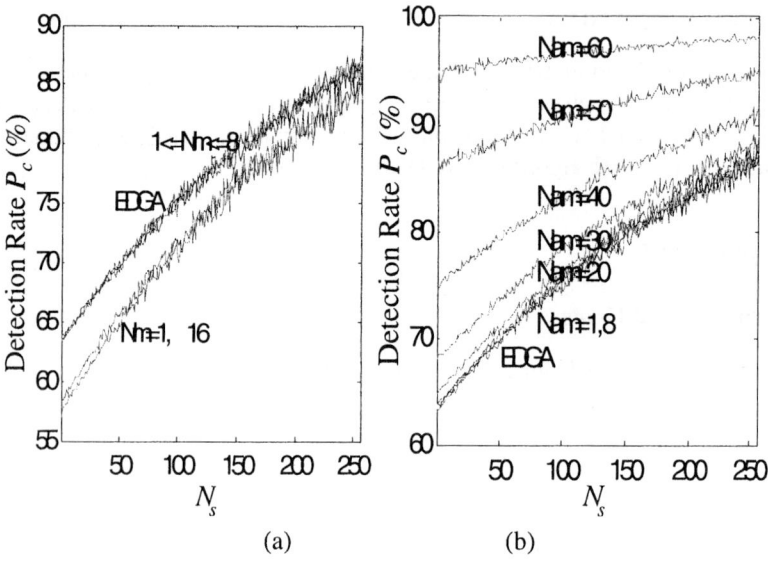

Fig. 3. Experimental results when N_{r0} is constant and N_s changing from 1 to 256. (a) When N_{r0} =256, the experimental result comparison of EDGA to BMGDGA, (b) When N_{r0} =256, the experimental result comparison of EDGA to AGDGA.

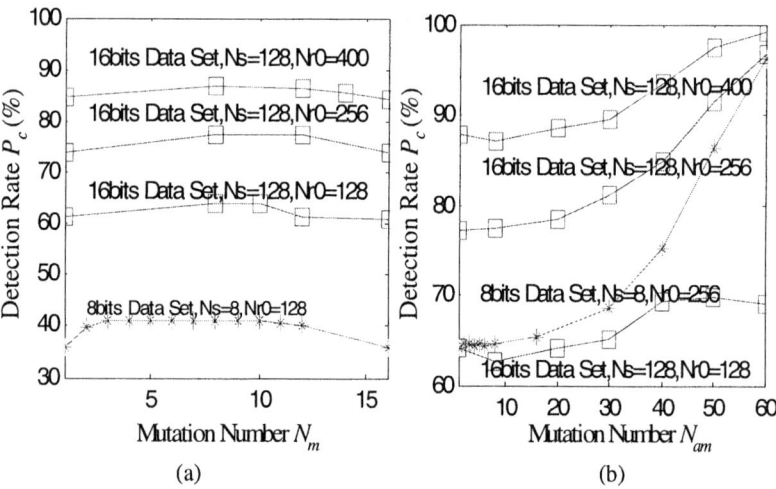

Fig. 4. Experimental results of detection rate versus mutation number, where N_s, N_{r0} are constants. To different datasets, N_m is increasing from 1 to 16, and N_{am} is increasing from 1 to 64. (a) Curve of P_c vs. N_m, (b) Curves of P_c vs. N_{am}.

4.3.2 16-Bit and 24-Bit Dataset Experiments

a. 16-bit dataset experiment

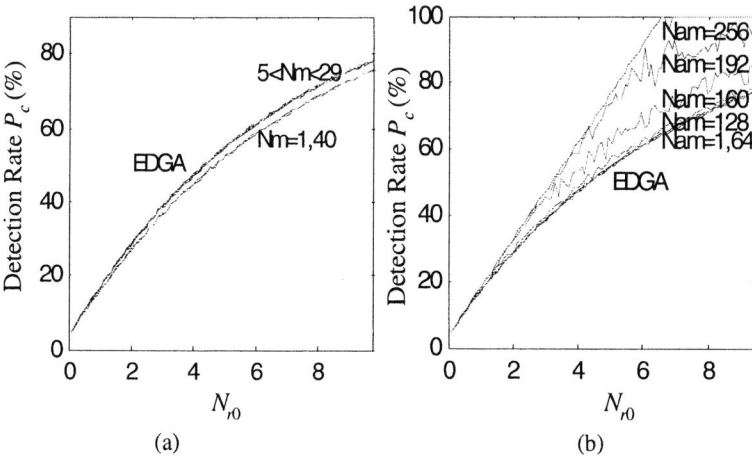

Fig. 5. 16-bit dataset experimental results when N_s is constant. (a) Experimental results of BMGDGA and EDGA, (b) Experimental results of AGDGA and EDGA.

Table 1. Computational complexity comparison for 16-bit dataset

Algorithm	Parameters setting			Computational time (ms)	Note
EDGA	N_{r0} =65536,	N_S =2048		730	
BMGDGA	N_{r0} =65536,	N_S =2048	N_m =8	594.5	10 runs
	N_{r0} =65536,	N_S =2048	N_m =4	585	10 runs
AGDGA	N_{r0} =65536,	N_S =2048	N_{am} =4	584.5	10 runs
	N_{r0} =65536,	N_S =2048	N_{am} =200	909.5	10 runs

Notice: experimental platform: Intel Pentium 993M CPU, 256M memory and Windows Me.

b. 24-bit dataset experiment

Table 2. Computational complexity comparison for 24-bit dataset

Algorithm	Parameters setting			Detection rate	Computational time (ms)
EDGA	N_S =2048, N_{r0} =65536, N_t =65536			0.3787231445	731.5
BMGDGA	N_S =2048		N_m =1	0.3834533691	534.2
	N_{r0} =65536		N_m =16	0.3952026367	538
	N_t =65536		N_m =24	0.4139709472	547
AGDGA	N_S =2048		N_{am} =1	0.4036712646	534
	N_{r0} =65536		N_{am} =256	0.3980255126	899.1
	N_t =65536		N_{am} =512	0.4000701904	1252.66

4.3.3 Discussions

To BMGDGA, the detection rate P_c is not lower than EDGA's under all circumstances, and when $N_m = l/2$, the detection rate reaches the best. Its computational complexity is also superior to EDGA's, with almost same memory space. So the overall performance of proposed BMGDGA is better than EDGA.

To AGDGA, when $N_{am} \in [1, l^2]$, its detection rate P_c is all, superior to EDGA's. With the increasing of N_{am}, P_c and computational complexity are increasing. When N_{am} is less than l, its computational complexity is less than EDGA's. With the increasing of N_{am}, the computational complexity slowly exceeds EDGA's a bit. However, their space complexities are almost same. Therefore the overall performance of proposed AGDGA is also better than EDGA.

4.4 Change Detection of Static Files

We conduct three experiments with two algorithms to validate their detection abilities for the change of static files, and compare to EDGA. First of all, we compare two different files by using the algorithms. We select two files of 'FTP.exe' and 'Ping.exe' and define 'Ping.exe' as self (S). The experimental results of anomaly number are listed in the first sub-column of Anomaly number column of Table 3. Secondly, they are used to detect the change of programs. Here the protected program files are compiled in Delphi environment and some simple functions are added into the program files to form the changed program. The experimental results of anomaly number are listed in the second sub-column of Anomaly number column of Table 3. The third is anomaly detection of the file infected by a virus, where we define a benign file '*.exe' as protected file and detect its changing when infected by Fun Love virus. The experimental results of anomaly number are listed in the third sub-column of Anomaly number column of Table 3. Experimental results are all compared to EDGA and listed in Table 3 for convenience.

Table 3. Experimental results of anomaly numbers for file comparison (first sub-column of last column), program change detection (second sub-column of last column), and anomaly detection of file (third sub-column of last column).

Algorithms	Parameters setting		Anomaly number		
EDGA	Detector length l =16bits		3775.2	4138.5	469.3
BMGDGA	Detector length l =16bits	N_m =1	3389.5	4018.3	455.2
		N_m =10	3724.8	4551.8	467.1
		N_m =16	3709.6	4229.2	466.7
AGDGA	Detector length l =16bits	N_{am} =1	3718.2	4281.1	473.1
		N_{am} =128	4073.7	4429.5	483.4
		N_{am} =256	4540.8	5512.8	555.7

It can be seen from the experimental results that we can obtain the same results as random dataset experiments. To BMGDGA, when $N_m=1$, the quality of detector set generated by this algorithm is worst. When $N_m = l/2 \sim l$, the performance of BMGDGA is almost same to EDGA. To AGDGA, when $N_{am}=1$, its performance reaches EDGA. As N_{am} increases, the detection performance is also increasing. It turns out from our experiments that it is possible to detect the changes of static files with these two algorithms.

5 Conclusions

This paper proposes two novel detector-generating algorithms based on negative selection principle of immune system. Extensive experimental results show that they all have better performances than current EDGA. Under all circumstances, the AGDGA's detection rate is always higher than EDGA. As the increase of the number of mutation bits, the detection rate P_c increases and the computational complexity also increases. In summary, the proposed algorithms outperform EDGA in both detection performance and computational complexity.

References

1. D'haeseleer, P.: An Immunological Approach to Change Detection: Theoretical Results. Proceedings of the 9th IEEE Computer Security Foundations Workshop, IEEE Computer Society Press (1996).
2. D'haeseleer, P., Forrest, S., Helman, P.: An Immunological Approach to Change Detection: Algorithms, Analysis and Implications. Proceedings of the IEEE Symposium on Security and Privacy, IEEE Computer Society Press (1996).
3. D'haeseleer, P.: A Change Detection Method Inspired by the Immune System: Theory, Algorithms and Techniques. Technical Report CS95-06, The University of New Mexico, Albuquerque, NM, 1995.
4. D'haeseleer, P.: Further Efficient Algorithms for Generating Antibody Strings. Technical Report CS95-03, The University of New Mexico, Albuquerque, NM, (1995).
5. Somayaji A., Hofmeyr S., Forrest S.: Principles of a Computer Immune System. 1997 New Security Paradigms Workshop (1998) 75-82.
6. Forrest S., Hofmeyr S., Somayaji A., Longstaff T.A.: A Sense of Self for Unix Processes. In Proceedings of 1996 IEEE Symposium on Computer Security and Privacy (1996).
7. Forrest S., Perelson A.S., Allen L., Cherukuri R.: Self-Nonself Discrimination in a Computer. In Proceedings of the 1994 IEEE Symposium on Research in Security and Privacy, Los Alamitos, CA: (1994).
8. Kim J., Bentley P.: Immune Memory in the Dynamic Clonal Selection Algorithm. In Proceedings of ICARIS'02, (2002).
9. Ayara M., Timmis J., de Lemos R., de Castro L., Duncan R.: Negative Selection: How to Generate Detectors. In Proceedings of ICARIS'02, (2002).
10. Singh S.: Anomaly Detection Using Negative Selection Based on the r-contiguous Matching Rule. In Proceedings of ICARIS'02, (2002).

An Algorithm Based on Antibody Immunodominance for TSP

Chong Hou[1], Haifeng Du[1,2], and Licheng Jiao[1]

[1] Institute of Intelligent Information Processing, Xidian University,
710071 Xi'an, China
houchong79@126.com
[2] Industry Training Center, Xi'an Jiaotong University,
710049 Xi'an, China

Abstract. A new algorithm based on antibody immunodominance (AIDA) for TSP is explored. The main content of this paper is to explore how to produce the set of immunodominance and the superior antibodies. The experience proves that the algorithm has higher convergence speed and better solution compared with the corresponding genetic algorithm and is fit to solving complex problems.

1 Introduction

The traveling salesman problem (TSP) can be stated very simply: A salesman visits n cities (or nodes) cyclically. In one tour he visits each city just once, and finishes up where he started. In what order should he visit them to minimize the distance traveled? It is one of the typical and most widely-studied problems [1]. Immunity algorithm is a novel algorithm based on the theory of biological system [2] [3], and is more effective than GAs in some cases.

This paper proposed an immunity algorithm based on antibody immunodominance. First, an immunodominance set is formed based on the basic knowledge of the problem; the antibodies those gain the immunodominance by this set become superior ones. Second, strengthen these superior antibodies. Gradually, the algorithm will converge to the optimal answer (or satisfactory answer).

2 Algorithm Based on Antibody Immunodominance

2.1 Immunodominance

By the theory of immunology [4], there are many epistasises on an antigen, but only one epistasis works when the immunity respond takes place. This phenomenon is called immunodominance. Immunodominance was the product of the operation between antibody and antigen. Its produce and operation are both dynamic processes.

This work denotes the different significance of every section of the code of antibody by the definition of the immunodominance. So the principle of the antibody immunodominance is determining some section of the antibody to decrease the range of the search, moreover, developing the performance of the algorithm. An antibody immunodominance operator for TSP (TSP-AIDO) is proposed in the following.

2.2 Antibody Immunodominance Operator

Commonly, in immunity algorithm for TSP an antibody expresses an answer:

$$a = \pi(X = \{v_1, v_2, \cdots, v_n\}) \tag{1}$$

Antigen corresponds to the object function and the affinity between antibody and antigen is determined by the distance of the corresponding path.

$ID = \{(d_i, v_i, v_j)\}$ is defined as the basic immunodominance set, $v_i \in e_1 \subset a$, $v_j \in e_2 \subset a$, e_1, e_2 are the two subset of a, usually, $e_1 \cap e_2 = \Phi$, d_i, v_i, v_j satisfies the require:

$$d_i = \min(d(v_i, v_j)) \quad v_i \in e_1, v_j \in e_2 \tag{2}$$

v_i, v_j are called the immunodominance sections of the antibody. On the assumption that $a \in A$, $i = 1, 2, \cdots, m$ is an antibody, if the kth position is to be changed, it must follow the basic immunodominance rules in certain way; this process is called immunodominance obtainment. The immunodominance operator is illustrated as Fig 1.

TSP Antibody Immunodominance Operator (TSP-AIDO)
Begin:
    while($e_1 \neq \Phi$)do
        { $ID = \{(d_i, v_i, v_j)\}$, $d_i = \min(d(v_i, v_j))$, $v_i \in e_1, v_j \in e_2$;
        Put v_i behind v_j;
        Remove v_i from e_1;}

Fig. 1. Immunodominance Operator

TSP Antibody Immunodominance Algorithm(TSP-AIDA)
Begin:
  Initialize population p;
  Estimate the affinity between antibody and antigen;
  While(**not** termination condition)do
  {Form immunodominance set ID based on the knowledge of the problem;
    Get immunodominance to produce qt;
    Immunity selection: if affinity $_{qt}$ > affinity $_{p_{(min)}}$ ($p_{(min)}$ express the antibody
    with minimal affinity);
    { qt substitute for $p_{(min)}$;}
    inverse operator; }   // local search

Fig. 2. Process of the algorithm

2.3 Process of the Algorithm

The process of TSP antibody immunodominance algorithm (TSP-AIDA) is illustrated in Fig 2.The affinity between antibody and antigen is corresponding to the fitness in GA The code method and inverse operator are as same as those in GA.

The TSP-AIDO is similar to the crossover operator in GA, but there are essential differences between them. TSP-AIDO is not simply exchanging the section of the antibodies as the crossover operator in GA but forming and obtaining immunodominance based on the different significant of every position of the antibody.

3 Validity of TSP-AIDA's Effectiveness

In order to test the performance of the algorithm, gridding, circle problems and benchmark problems [5] were tested in this paper. The method was implemented on a Pentium IV 2.4 GHz personal computer with a single processor and 1 GB RAM.

TSP-AIDA is compared to an improved GA which is called NGA in this paper. The crossover operator of NGA is "similar OX" that is said to be better than conventional ones in reference [6].

In the first part, the known optimal solutions are found by TSP-AIDA every time of 10-time independent test. The results is illustrated in table 2, in which, n expresses the number of the "cities" and S_0 expresses the known optimal solution.

Table 2. Test result 1

Problem	n	S_0	algorithm	time spent on getting the optimum (CPU time) (s)		The minimal distance	
				Min	Mean	Min	Mean
Gridding TSP*	36	6.0000	NGA	/	/	6.1381	6.1934
			TSP-AIDA	433.5	769.7	6.0000	6.0000
Circle TSP*	100	62.8215	NGA	/	/	69.0863	70.3446
			TSP-AIDA	1032.7	1189.7	62.8215	62.8215
Pa561	561	19330.8	NGA	20.4	23.0	16558.14	16674.70
			TSP-AIDA	12.5	14.4	15739.69	16146.23
Gr666	666	3952.54	NGA	25.4	32.5	3321.1	3416.7
			TSP-AIDA	8.5	11.0	3200.6	3275.3

Note: 1.the problems those are marked with * are tested with the programming language MATLAB6.5 and the others with VC++6.0

2. In terms of some problems, NGA can't find the optimal solutions of them every time, so the time is unable to be measured; they are expressed by / in the table.

In the second part, TSP-AIDA can't find the known optimal solutions every time, but it is still superior to the corresponding NGA. The test results are shown in table 3.

Table 4. Test result 2

problem	n	S_0	algorithm	The minimal distance		σ (%)
				min	mean	
Pcb442	442	5078.35	NGA	5657.77	5705.79	12.36
			TSP-AIDA	5184.49	5278.40	3.94
Pr1002	1002	259068	NGA	286740	288010	11.17
			TSP-AIDA	269343	269355	3.97
Pr2392	2392	378063	NGA	427515	431036	14.01
			TSP-AIDA	409779	415130	9.80

Note: 1.all the problems are tested with programming language VC++6.0

2. $\sigma = \sum_{i=1}^{10}(S_{Ti} - S_0)/10 S_0 \times 100\%$ S_{Ti} expresses the minimal distance gotten in the first part test.

4 Conclusions

In this paper, we proposed a novel immunity algorithm for TSP, which is named TSP-AIDA. TSP is a NP-hard problem, with the augment of the number of the "cities", the amount of the local optimal solutions has an exponential increase, TSP-AIDA can't find the optimal solution of some problems(n>1000,usually) every time, although it is better than the corresponding GA. One hand, it is because the common currency of the algorithm is considered in this paper, another hand, the performance of the algorithm is related to the parameters, the size of the population, for example. Improving the algorithm's performance and extending it to other optimization problems are our future work.

References

1. Cheng Guoliang, Wang Xufa, Zhuang Zhenquan.: Genetic algorithm and its application. People's Post and Telecom Publishing Company, Beijing (1996)
2. Dasgupta, D., Forrest, S. Artificial Immune Systems in Industrial Applications. In Proceedings of the Second International Conference on Intelligent Processing and Manufacturing of Materials (IPMM).Vol.1 (1999) 257 –267.
3. Licheng, J., Lei, W.: A Novel Genetic Algorithm based on Immunity. IEEE Trans. Systems, Man and Cybernetics, Part A. Vol.30, No.5 (2000) 552–561
4. Zhou Guangyan.: Principles of Immunology. Shang Hai Technology Literature Publishing Company, Shanghai (2000)
5. G Reinelt: TSPLIB—A traveling salesman problem library. ORSA Journal of Computer, No.3 (1991) 376–384
6. LiangYanchun, FengDapeng, ZhouChunguang.: Order Preserving of Gene Section for Solving Traveling Salesman Prob- lems Using Genetic Algorithms. Theory and Practice of Systems Engineering, No.4 (2000) 7–12

Flow Shop Scheduling Problems Under Uncertainty Based on Fuzzy Cut-Set*

Zhenhao Xu and Xingsheng Gu

Research Institute of Automation, East China University of Science and Technology,
Shanghai 200237, China
lyshxzh@sina.com, xsgu@ecust.edu.cn

Abstract. Production scheduling is an important part in the factories, and there are various uncertainties in the production scheduling of industrial processes. A scheduling mathematical model for flow shop problems with uncertain processing time has been established based on fuzzy programming theory. And in this paper, the fuzzy model can be translated into two mathematical models about the characteristic of scheduling problems. Furthermore, a fuzzy immune scheduling algorithm combined with the feature of the Immune Algorithm is proposed, which prevents the possibility of stagnation in the iteration process and achieves fast convergence for global optimization. The effectiveness and efficiency of the fuzzy scheduling model and the proposed algorithm are demonstrated by simulation results.

1 Introduction

Production scheduling plays an important role in practice industries, which deals with the allocation of limited resources for tasks. There exists a broad literature on the subject, which presents various algorithms for various types of problems. But, in practice, there can be uncertainty in a number of factors such as processing times and costs. For this reason, it is important to be able to take the imprecision into account in the modeling of the problems itself, so that the algorithms are run on the basis of the information about the problem we really possess.

The prevalent approach to the treatment of these uncertainties is through the use of probabilistic models that describe the uncertain parameters in terms of probability distributions [1]. Li Mingqie et al [2] applied stochastic variables to describing the uncertainties of scheduling problems, in which the mathematical model is changed to the Stochastic Programming problems. However, the evaluation and optimization of these models are computationally expensive. Furthermore, the use of probabilistic models is realistic only when these descriptions of the uncertain parameters are available. When such data is not available, we don't have enough information for inferring or deriving the probabilistic models [3].

Among several theories developed to account for uncertainty, fuzzy set theory is more and more frequently used, because of its simplicity and similarity to human

---

* This work was supported by the National Natural Science Foundation of China (Grant No.60474043) and The Key Technologies Program of Shanghai Municipal Science and Technology Commission (Grant No. 04dz11008).

reasoning [4]. When fuzzy numbers are most often understood as imprecise or approximate concepts, they may also convey preferences and therefore, in some sense, they may represent flexibilities. So, in this work, we draw upon concepts from fuzzy set theory to describe the imprecision and uncertainties in the durations of batch processing tasks. McCahon and Lee [5] were the first to illustrate the application of fuzzy set theory as a means of analyzing performance characteristics for a flow shop system.

Computational methods based on analogy of biological system have been paid much attention in recent years, such as the Immune Algorithm, which imitates the defending process of an immune system against its invaders in a biological body. In this paper, a new fuzzy scheduling algorithm is proposed based on the Immune Algorithm to solve flow shop problems. The study is organized as follows. In Section 2, the definition and mathematical model of the problems that we intend to treat are given. The proposed fuzzy method is introduced and described in Section 3. In Section 4, the computation procedures and the simulation results are discussed. Conclusions from this work are drawn in Section 5.

2 Problems Statement

One kind of scheduling problem that frequently occurs in real world application environments is the flow shop problem. In a flow shop, different products can be made up in diverse equipments, and all products follow essentially the same processing steps.

2.1 Problem Definition

Flow shop problems can be described as: there are N products, which need to be processed, and the number of processing units is M. The processing time of products i in unit j is $\tilde{T}_{ij}$, which includes the transfer time, the set-up time and the clean-up time, etc. Because it is mutative and uncertain, it is represented by the fuzzy number.

Every product has the same processing sequence in all units, $\tilde{S}_{ij}$ and $\tilde{C}_{ij}$ respectively represents the starting time and the finishing time of product i in unit j. As for the uncertainty of the processing time, the starting time and the finishing time are also uncertain. Accordingly, $\tilde{S}_{ie}$ and $\tilde{T}_{ie}$ mean the starting time and the finishing time of the last operation of product i. In the paper, the scheduling criterion is makespan, that is, the last job should be completed as soon as possible.

2.2 Mathematical Model

The definition and assumptions can be represented by the following model:

$$\min \ \{ \tilde{Z} = \max \ (\tilde{S}_{ie} + \tilde{T}_{ie}) \}$$

$$\text{s.t.} \quad \tilde{S}_{ij} \geq \tilde{S}_{i(j-1)} + \tilde{T}_{i(j-1)} \tag{1}$$

$$\tilde{S}_{ij} \geq \tilde{S}_{(i-1)j} + \tilde{T}_{(i-1)j} \quad i \in N, \ j \in M \quad (2)$$

$$\tilde{S}_{ij} \geq 0 \quad (3)$$

Eq. (1) is the sequence constraint of products, which represents that product i can not start in unit j until its completion in the previous unit.

Eq. (2) is the resource constraint, which means product i can not be processed until completing the product $i-1$ by unit j.

Eq. (3) represents each product may be started at time zero, i.e. the starting time of each one must more than or equal to zero.

2.3 Description of the Solution

In the section, we discuss the flow shop scheduling with fuzzy processing time. Let us assume that the processing time of each job in each unit is given as a triangular fuzzy number. A triangular fuzzy number $\tilde{A}$ is denoted by its three parameters as follows.

$$\tilde{A} = (\ A_L, \ A_C, \ A_U\ )$$

Where, A_L is the lower limit, A_C means the center value, and A_U is the upper limit.

There are many approaches to solving the fuzzy mathematical model based on fuzzy theory. We use the concept of fuzzy α-cuts solution in this paper.

α is also called the level of probability. Since the α-cut of a fuzzy number is a closed and convex subset, it can be written a closed interval with $A_\alpha = \left[a_\alpha^L, a_\alpha^R \right]$. As for $\alpha \in [0,1]$, the higher the value of α, the smaller the scope of the feasible solution, and vice versa.

Then, the initial scheduling model can be transformed into the following two programming problems based on the concept of the fuzzy α-level theory.

The optimal programming model of α-level:

$$\min \ \{\ Z_\alpha^L = \max \ \left(S_{ie\alpha}^L + T_{ie\alpha}^L \right) \} \quad (4)$$

$$\text{s.t.} \quad S_{ij\alpha}^L \geq S_{i(j-1)\alpha}^L + T_{i(j-1)\alpha}^L$$

$$S_{ij\alpha}^L \geq S_{(i-1)j\alpha}^L + T_{(i-1)j\alpha}^L \quad i \in N, \ j \in M$$

$$S_{ij\alpha}^L \geq 0$$

The worst programming model of α-level:

$$\min \{ Z_\alpha^R = \max (S_{ie\alpha}^R + T_{ie\alpha}^R) \} \tag{5}$$

$$\text{s.t.} \quad S_{ij\alpha}^R \geq S_{i(j-1)\alpha}^R + T_{i(j-1)\alpha}^R$$

$$S_{ij\alpha}^R \geq S_{(i-1)j\alpha}^R + T_{(i-1)j\alpha}^R \quad i \in N, \ j \in M$$

$$S_{ij\alpha}^R \geq 0$$

By solving the two programming problems, we can get the interval $[(z^*)_\alpha^L, (z^*)_\alpha^R]$ about the α-level set of the optimal objective Z^* for the initial fuzzy problem. This can help managers gain the variation range of the optimal objective function under a certain possible extent.

According to the fuzzy theory, the fuzzy addition and maximum operations have the resolvability. Thus, the details of solution can be described as follows:

If $i=1, \ j=1$

$$\begin{aligned} S_{ij\alpha}^L &= 0, & C_{ij\alpha}^L &= S_{ij\alpha}^L + T_{ij\alpha}^L = T_{ij\alpha}^L \\ S_{ij\alpha}^R &= 0, & C_{ij\alpha}^R &= S_{ij\alpha}^R + T_{ij\alpha}^R = T_{ij\alpha}^R \end{aligned} \tag{6}$$

If $i=1, \ j>1$

$$\begin{aligned} S_{ij\alpha}^L &= C_{i(j-1)\alpha}^L, & C_{ij\alpha}^L &= S_{ij\alpha}^L + T_{ij\alpha}^L = C_{i(j-1)\alpha}^L + T_{ij\alpha}^L \\ S_{ij\alpha}^R &= C_{i(j-1)\alpha}^R, & C_{ij\alpha}^R &= S_{ij\alpha}^R + T_{ij\alpha}^R = C_{i(j-1)\alpha}^R + T_{ij\alpha}^R \end{aligned} \tag{7}$$

If $i>1, \ j=1$

$$\begin{aligned} S_{ij\alpha}^L &= C_{(i-1)j\alpha}^L, & C_{ij\alpha}^L &= S_{ij\alpha}^L + T_{ij\alpha}^L = C_{(i-1)j\alpha}^L + T_{ij\alpha}^L \\ S_{ij\alpha}^R &= C_{(i-1)j\alpha}^R, & C_{ij\alpha}^R &= S_{ij\alpha}^R + T_{ij\alpha}^R = C_{(i-1)j\alpha}^R + T_{ij\alpha}^R \end{aligned} \tag{8}$$

If $i>1, \ j>1$

$$\begin{aligned} S_{ij\alpha}^L &= \max(C_{(i-1)j\alpha}^L, C_{i(j-1)\alpha}^L), & C_{ij\alpha}^L &= S_{ij\alpha}^L + T_{ij\alpha}^L \\ S_{ij\alpha}^R &= \max(C_{(i-1)j\alpha}^R, C_{i(j-1)\alpha}^R), & C_{ij\alpha}^R &= S_{ij\alpha}^R + T_{ij\alpha}^R \end{aligned} \tag{9}$$

The function objective at the α-level:

$$\begin{aligned} \min \{ Z_\alpha^L &= \max (S_{ie\alpha}^L + T_{ie\alpha}^L) \} \\ \min \{ Z_\alpha^R &= \max (S_{ie\alpha}^R + T_{ie\alpha}^R) \} \end{aligned} \tag{10}$$

Then, the scope of the optimal objective under α-level can be represented by the interval $\left[Z_\alpha^L, Z_\alpha^R \right]$. The following is the optimization strategy of the fuzzy scheduling algorithm.

3 The Fuzzy Scheduling Algorithm Based on the IA

The Immune Algorithm is inspired by the characteristic of the natural immune system. One of its most outstanding features is a self-organizing memory which is dynamically maintained and which allows items of information to be forgotten. And it promotes diversification. It does not attempt to focus on local optima; Furthermore, the algorithm operation on the memory cell will achieve very fast convergence during the search process. So, these features make it widely used in many fields, such as Intelligent Control, Pattern Recognition and Optimization Design [6-7].

Because the scheduling problem is a sequence operation, the objective function has much to do with not only the value of the optimal solution but also the position in the coding strings. Character coding technique is adapted for the representations of those antibodies in the Immune Algorithm. That is, according to the characteristic of scheduling problems, each character represents a processing job. The order of the character in the strings is the processing sequence of jobs.

The computation steps are discussed below.

Step1: Initial antibody population formulation.

In the initial step, the antibodies are generated randomly in the feasible space. A population pool comprises these antibodies. And a group of genes form an antibody. Each antibody represents a possible solution to a schedule of flow shop.

Step 2: Affinity calculation.

Two affinity calculation forms are calculated. One is the affinity ax_v between the antigen and antibody v, the other is the affinity ay_{vw} between antibody v and w, and the expected propagation proportion of each antibody E_v is also computed. These will provide a useful reference in the following evaluation process.

Step 3: Evaluation and selection.

Based on the results of the computation procedure mentioned earlier, the antibody that has high affinities with the antigen is added to the new memory cell. As most selected antibodies exhibit higher affinities with the antigen, the averaged affinity of the new population pool will be higher than that of the original pool. Therefore, a new antibody chosen from the pool comes with a higher affinity with the antigen. The average affinity of a new antibody pool chosen from this new memory cell is higher than that of the old antibody pool.

Step 4: Boost or restriction of antibody generations.

According to the expected propagation proportion, the antibodies in the population pool will be sequenced. The antibody with lower expectation will be restricted. It can be inferred that the antibody with a high affinity and low density will be the most possible candidate. This indeed is a critical role that controls excessive production as for the boost of antibodies with higher affinities and the restriction of antibodies with the higher density.

Step 5: Crossover and mutation

Based on the new antibodies selected from the memory cell, the crossover and mutation of the new antibodies are performed. Crossover is a random process of recombination of strings. With the probability of crossover, a partial exchange of characters between two strings is performed. With the crossover operation, the proposed algorithm is able to acquire more information with the generated individuals. The search space is thus extended and more complete. Mutation is the occasional random alteration of the bits in the string. The mutation operator helps reproduce some individuals that may be vital to the performance.

Step 6: Decisions.

All the antibodies in each generation must be evaluated. The antibodies with higher affinity are tracked to the memory cell for each generation. If the termination criterion is satisfied or no further improvement in relative affinity can be obtained, the optimal search will end. And genes of the antibody can be decoded to be solutions of the scheduling problem. Otherwise, the procedure must turns to step 2.

4 Computational Experience

Consider the following example where ten products have to be processed in five units. The fuzzy processing time data for the example can be found in Table 1. The fuzzy processing times are specified by three parameters, which represent the lower bound, the most likely value and the upper bound on the processing time.

Table 1. The fuzzy processing times of products

	Machine 1	Machine 2	Machine 3	Machine 4	Machine 5
Job 1	(23 25 31)	(11 15 21)	(10 12 14)	(34 40 46)	(6 10 12)
Job 2	(6 7 11)	(37 41 47)	(21 22 24)	(28 36 40)	(6 8 10)
Job 3	(38 41 45)	(137 155 167)	(27 33 37)	(111 121 141)	(145 160 188)
Job 4	(64 74 90)	(8 12 16)	(16 24 30)	(40 48 58)	(66 78 86)
Job 5	(6 7 9)	(69 95 107)	(51 72 84)	(51 52 56)	(148 153 179)
Job 6	(10 12 16)	(8 14 16)	(26 62 74)	(26 32 38)	(140 162 190)
Job 7	(9 11 17)	(5 7 12)	(20 31 35)	(20 26 30)	(26 32 38)
Job 8	(25 31 39)	(35 39 43)	(135 141 175)	(4 6 10)	(15 19 23)
Job 9	(24 32 34)	(84 92 98)	(10 12 14)	(8 14 18)	(84 102 122)
Job 10	(19 27 31)	(109 114 128)	(17 21 23)	(78 90 102)	(44 52 66)

In the algorithm, the population size is 40, the size of memory cell is 20 and the number of iteration is 150. The scheduling algorithm has been executed many times. Figure.1 and 2 are the evolution curves of the algorithm when α is 0.3.

Fig.1 and 2 illustrate the evolution curve of the model. In each chart, the above curve is the reciprocal value of the mean objective, which means the reciprocal of the average value of the affinities between the antigen and antibodies of populations in evolution; The middle curve is the mean value of the objective of antibodies in

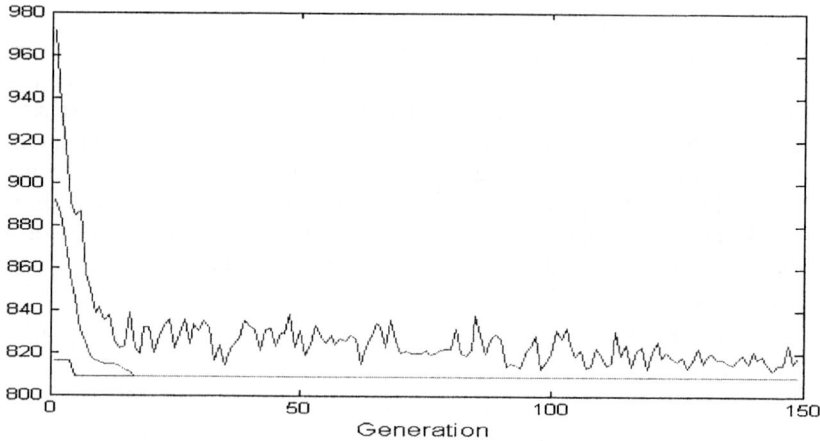

Fig. 1. The evolution curve of the optimal programming model ($\alpha = 0.3$)

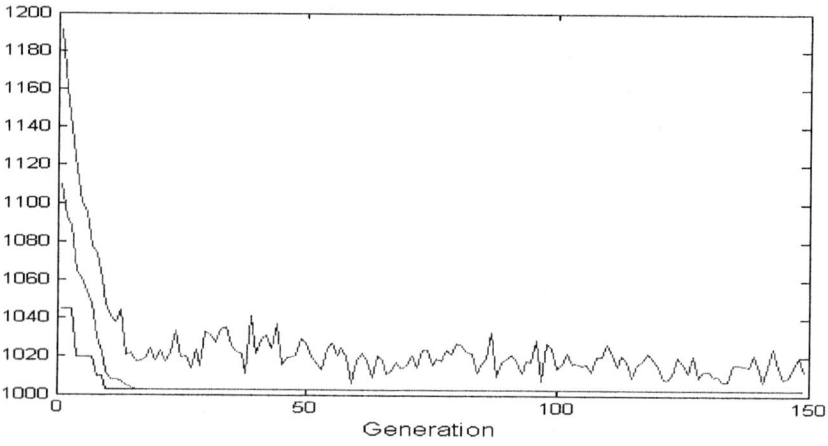

Fig. 2. The evolution curve of the worst programming model ($\alpha = 0.3$)

memory cell, which represents the average objective of all individuals in memory cell; and the nether one is the optimal curve, which means the optimal objective of each generation in iteration. Along with the evolution process, the average curve and the optimal curve have not changed intensively, which indicates the convergence of the method.

Let $\alpha = 0$, step size is 0.1, the detail results at the various a-levels are shown in Table 2.

If α increases constantly, the objective tends to converging to the smaller feasible region. That is, the interval of the function objective is getting smaller and smaller, and will converge to the most possible value. As for the same objective, two different

Table 2. The scheduling results at different α-levels

α	The optimal programming model		The worst programming model	
	Job sequence	Functional objective	Job sequence	Functional objective
0	7 6 5 3 1 4 8 9 2 10	775	7 6 9 5 3 2 4 1 8 10	1052
0.1	7 6 5 3 4 8 10 2 1 9	786.2	7 6 4 5 8 9 3 1 10 2	1035.5
0.2	7 6 5 9 1 3 8 2 10 4	797.4	7 6 8 9 2 1 4 5 3 10	1019
0.3	7 6 1 5 2 8 4 9 3 10	808.6	7 6 8 9 4 5 1 3 2 10	1002.5
0.4	7 6 9 5 2 1 4 8 3 10	819.8	7 6 9 1 5 4 10 3 2 8	986
0.5	7 6 9 5 4 3 2 10 8 1	831	7 6 5 3 2 9 10 1 4 8	969.5
0.6	7 6 5 3 9 2 1 4 10 8	842.2	7 6 4 9 5 3 10 2 8 1	953
0.7	7 6 2 9 5 4 1 3 8 10	853.4	7 6 5 9 4 2 3 8 1 10	936.5
0.8	7 4 5 3 2 1 8 10 9 4	864.6	7 6 5 4 3 2 9 1 8 10	920
0.9	7 6 10 1 9 4 5 3 2 8	875.8	7 6 2 9 5 4 1 8 3 10	903.5
1	7 6 5 3 2 4 9 8 1 10	887	7 6 5 1 2 9 4 3 10 8	887

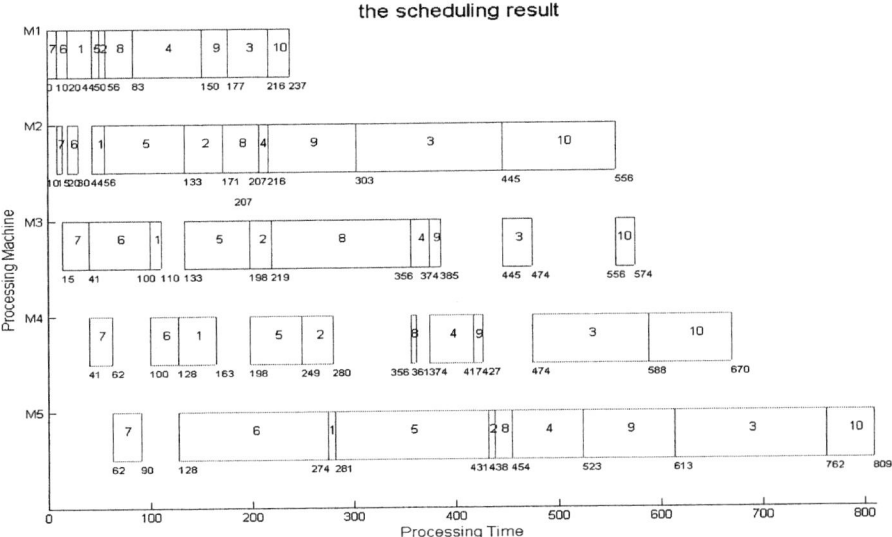

Fig. 3. The Gantt chart of the schedule (the optimal model $\alpha = 0.3$)

job sequences may be obtained. Thus can help managers gain a broader overall view of scheduling and make the proper decision.

When α is 0.3, the Gantt chart of the job sequences of the optimal model and the worst model are respectively shown in Fig.3 and Fig.4. Then, the optimal objective of the example is 808.6, and the worst objective is 1002.5.

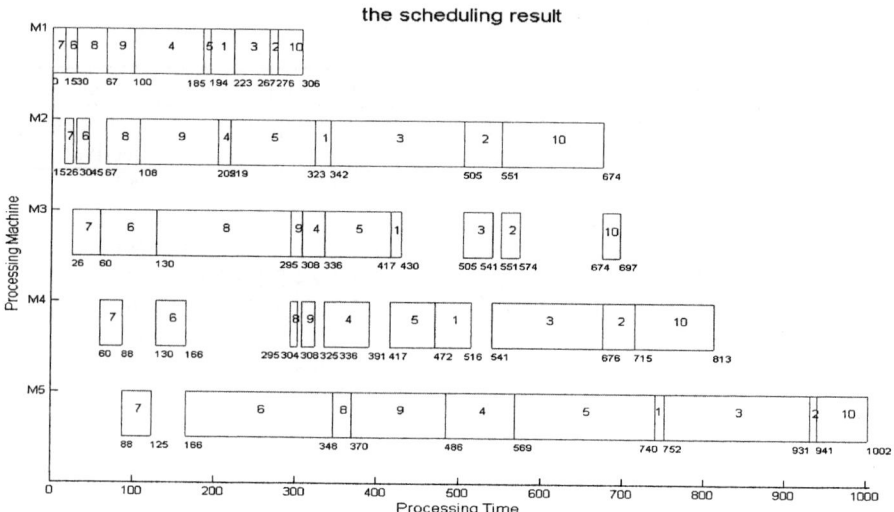

Fig. 4. The Gantt chart of the schedule (the worst model $\alpha = 0.3$)

5 Conclusions

Flow shop scheduling problems under uncertainty are discussed in this paper. As for the uncertainty of processing time, the fuzzy mathematical model is proposed based on the fuzzy cut-set theory. And integrated with the characteristic of the Immune Algorithm, a fuzzy scheduling algorithm is presented to solve the problems. By the results obtained from both simulated and experimental data, it is proven that the feasibility and effectiveness of the scheduling model and the fuzzy scheduling algorithm. And the results can help managers have a broader view of problems and to make the proper decision.

References

1. Gu, X.S.: The Robust Scheduling for Flow shop Problem under Uncertainty. Proceedings of the 3-rd Asian Control Conference, 2000, Shanghai, 361-366.
2. Li, M.Q. and Gu, X.S.: Robust Scheduling Research of Job shop Problem with Processing Time under Uncertainty. Journal of Zhejiang University (Natural Science), 1998, 32(2), Supplement, 711-719.
3. Schmidt, C.W. and Grossmann, I.E.: The Exact Overall Time Distribution of a Project with Uncertain Task Durations. European Journal of Operational Research, 2000, 126(3), 614-636.
4. Kamdel, A.: Fuzzy Expert Systems, CRC Press, Boca Raton, 1992, 8-19.
5. McCahon, C.S. and Lee, E.S.: Fuzzy Job Sequencing for a Flow Shop. European Journal of Operational Research, 1992, v62, 294-305.

6. John, E.H. and Denise, E.C.: Learning Using an Artificial Immune System. Journal of Network and Computer Applications, 1996, 19: 189-212.
7. Shao, X., Chen, Z.,and Lin, X.: Resolution of Multicomponent Overlapping Chromatogram Using an Immune Algorithm and Genetic Algorithm. Chemometrics and Intelligent Laboratory Systems, 2000, 50: 91-99.

An Optimization Method Based on Chaotic Immune Evolutionary Algorithm

Yong Chen[1] and Xiyue Huang[2]

[1] Navigation & Guidance Lab, Automation College,
Chongqing University, 400030 Chongqing, China
chensaiyang@tom.com
[2] Navigation & Guidance Lab, Automation College,
Chongqing University, 400030 Chongqing, China
xyhuang@equ.edu.cn

Abstract. Immune Evolutionary Algorithm (IEA) is proposed on the shortages of evolution algorithm and biological immune mechanism. According to the characteristics of chaos, a novel Chaotic Immune Evolutionary Algorithm (CIEA) is presented which introduces chaos to IEA. The algorithm has the merits of chaos, immunity and evolutionary algorithm. It can ensure the ability of global search and local search and enhance the performances of the algorithm. At last, we analyze the efficiency of the algorithm with two typical optimization problems. The analysis result shows that CIEA converges quickly and effectively avoids the inherent problem that the evolution algorithm traps in immature convergence, so CIEA is an effective way to solve complex optimization problem.

1 Introduction

At present, evolution algorithm simulates the evolution phenomenon of biological colony and can solve some complicated optimization problems. According to the operating mechanism of evolution algorithm, it is based on the existing individuals of the previous generation and searches at random without guidance. In addition, under the action of selection operator, the colony tends converge ultimately by reserving optimum individuals. Moreover, crossover operator and mutation operator are both calculated according to an invariable probability. Therefore, evolution algorithm appears to be immature in convergence, bad in ability of local search, and low in convergence rate. The optimization process of practical problems by evolutionary algorithm is quite similar to the immune mechanism of biology.

Immune algorithm, on the one hand, it makes full use of the information of the optimum individuals in each generation .On the other hand, combining with evolution algorithm, it can combine random search with deterministic change. Hence, it reduces the effect of random factors and overcomes immature convergence fairly well. However, immune evolution algorithm adjusts global search and local search by standard deviation. The search is guided by some probability and will diminish the scope of the search. Chaos is a specific motive form in nonlinear mechanical system.

Chaotic variables seem to be a random change process, but in fact it implies internal rules. Optimization search can be carried out by the randomization, ergodicity and rule of chaotic variables. A chaotic optimization method first change optimized variables into chaotic variables, and examines each point in the entire solution space by change rule of chaotic variables, accepts the better point as the present optimum solution. Then, it takes the present optimum solution as the kernel and goes on searching the optimum solution by affixing a perturbation until the requirements are met.

In this paper, the proposed CIEA combines the merits of chaotic optimization method, immune mechanism and evolution algorithm. Its basic idea is to introduce chaotic optimization method to immune evolution algorithm, improving the search pattern of algorithm and enhancing the convergence rate of algorithm.

2 CIEA

CIEA inherits the characteristics of chaotic optimization algorithm and immune evolution algorithm.

2.1 Immune Evolutionary Algorithm [1]

The natural defense mechanism which biological immune system puts up is obvious and effective. If we consider algorithm as immune system, we can specifically design algorithm according to the characteristics of biological immunity system. Map the external invasive antigen and the antibody generated by immune system to the objective function and the solution of the practical problem respectively. The process revising parameters according to bacterin is vaccination, the purpose of which is eliminating the negative effect of antigen on some parameters.

Due to the action of cell division and differentiation, immune system can produce a large number of antibodies to resist various antigens. Once a cell appears to be deformed, unhealthy or degenerative, immune system will eliminate it immediately. Economy immunocyte has different reactions to different kinds of microbe. Such is the main idea of immune evolution that once the optimum individual is found in the process of evolution, analogous individuals will be reproduced with considering the diversity of the colony. The optimum individual in immune evolutionary algorithm is the feasible solution with the highest affinity degree in each generation. Referring to biologic immune mechanism, the generating mode of the offspring individuals in the immune evolutionary algorithm is [2]

$$\left. \begin{array}{l} X(t+1) = X_{best}(t) + \sigma(t)N(0,1) \\ \sigma(t+1) = \sigma(t)\exp(\frac{Bt}{T}) \end{array} \right\} \quad (1)$$

$X(t+1)$ ---feasible solution of offspring individuals, $X_{best}(t)$ ---optimum individual in parents generation, $\sigma(t+1)$ ---standard deviation of offspring population, $\sigma(t)$ ---standard deviation of parents colony, B--- dynamic adjustment coefficient of standard deviation, T---total evolution algebra, $N(0,1)$ ---generated random number submitted to standard normal distribution, t --evolution algebra, where $B \in [1,10]$ and $\sigma(0) \in [1,3]$.

2.2 Chaotic Optimization Method [3]

The fine search mode in the chaotic optimization method is

$$R' = R + \delta \beta_k \tag{2}$$

Where, $R = (r_1,...,r_n)$ is disturbed solution, δ is adjustment constant, and $\beta_k = (\beta_{k1},...,\beta_{kn})$ is the present chaotic vector. Chaotic vector is based on larval population model which is familiar to us, i.e. Logisic mapping:

$$\beta_{ki} = \lambda \beta_{(k-1)i}(1 - \beta_{(k-1)i}) \tag{3}$$

Where, $i = 1,...,m$, $k = 1,2,...$, $\lambda \in [0,4]$ are control parameters and Logisic mapping is irreversible mapping in[0, 1]. We can prove that when $\lambda = 4$, the system is in chaos.

We need to deal with R' out-of-range:

$$\beta'_k = (1-\delta)\beta + \delta \beta_k \tag{4}$$

Where, $0 < \delta < 1$. β is the vector which is produced after each disturbed component mapped to the interval [0,1]. Formula (4) restraints the value of each component of β'_k to the interval [0,1]. Then, Formula (5) maps β'_k to optimum variables by way of carrier.

$$R' = c + d\beta'_k \tag{5}$$

Where, c and d are constant vectors.

2.3 CIEA

From Formula (1) we can see the nature of immune evolutionary algorithm. It makes full use of the information of optimum individual and substitutes the evolution of the optimum individual for that of the colony. In the early and medium phase, the generated colony enhances the solution space round the optimum individual by dynamic adjustment of standard deviation. Random numbers are generated according to standard normal distribution. Now, we introduce chaotic optimization algorithm. Let N(0,1) change according the chaotic rule denoted by Formula (5), which makes the generation mode of random number and the search mode become diverse, so this method outperforms existent methods.

Now, we study the typical optimization problem.

iii. Estimation of newly differentiated lymphocytes carrying low-affinity antigenic receptors.

2.2 Improved Immune Algorithm

In the implementation of the proposed algorithm, the Ag's and Ab's represent the optimization problems and their candidate solutions respectively. While the fitness functions of the candidate solutions are regarded as the antigenic affinities of the Ab's. The algorithm comprises the following five operators, clonal selection, cell clone, hypermutation, receptor editing and elitist preserving.

Firstly, the clonal selection operation selects the B cells with the highest-affinity Ab receptors to be the B memory cells. Secondly, the cell clone process proliferates the clonal selected B cells in a small neighborhood to produce the Ab's with high affinity, which can improve the local search capabilities of the algorithm and obtain better optimal solution. Thirdly, the hypermutation process is performed dependent on receptor affinity. Cells with low-affinity receptors may be further mutated and, as a rule, die if they do not improve their clone size or antigenic affinity. In cells with high-affinity Ab receptors, however, hypermutation may become inactive, generally in a gradual manner. Unlike the CSA, the IIA undergoes hypermutation in a relatively large neighborhood to realize the global exploration, which may rescue the solving stuck on unsatisfactory local optima. Then, to improve the diversity of the population and escape from local optima ulteriorly, receptor editing is performed. Those B cells undergone receptor editing delete their low-affinity receptors and developed entirely new ones in the feasible region randomly. Finally, the elitist preserving strategy is adapted to maintain the convergence of the algorithm in each iteration processing. [7]

The procedure of the IIA can be described as follows. For the convenience of description, no distinction is made between a B cell and its receptor, known as an Ab.

Step 1: Parameters definition: the radius of the cell clone r, the radius of the hypermutation R, the number of the populations, the maximum generation Gen_{max}, the initial population A_t, that composed by M random initial Ab's, $t=0$.
Step 2: $t=t+1$.
Step 3: Clonal selection: Select N ($N \leq M$) highest affinity Ab's from A_t to compose a new set B_t of memory Ab's. This paper defines $N=int\ (\alpha*M)$, where α is selection probability, and $0<\alpha<1$.
Step 4: Cell clone: IIA generates randomly (M-N) new sets of memory Ab's B_t' in a relative small neighborhood around the Ab's in B_t. Suppose $x_{i,t}$ is an Ab in B_t. Then, the new Ab generated randomly is:

$$x'_{i,t} = \begin{cases} x_{i,min} & x_{i,t} * rand(1-r, 1+r) < x_{i,min} \\ x_{i,max} & x_{i,t} * rand(1-r, 1+r) > x_{i,max} \\ x_{i,t} * rand(1-r, 1+r) & otherwise \end{cases} \quad (1)$$

where r is the radius of cell clone, and $r \in [0,1]$; $[x_{i,min}, x_{i,max}]$ is the space of feasible region; $rand(1-r, 1+r)$ is a random number between $1-r$ and $1+r$.

As shown above, the number of clones is proportional to the antigenic affinity. Then, a selecting method is proposed based on the "roulette wheel" strategy in this paper. Suppose the antigenic affinities of the N Ab's in B_t is $f(1),f(2),\ldots,f(N)$ respectively, then the probability of a new Ab generated for each of the Ab's in B_t is:

$$p(k) = \frac{f(k)}{\sum_{i=1}^{N} f(i)}; \qquad k = 1, 2, \ldots, N. \tag{2}$$

Define $S(0) = 0$, then

$$S(k) = \sum_{i=0}^{k} p(k); \qquad k = 1, 2, \ldots, N. \tag{3}$$

Generate (M-N) random numbers evenly distributed between 0 and 1, $\xi s \in U(0, 1)$, $s = 1,2,\ldots,M$-N. If $S(k-1) < \xi s < S(k)$, then select Ab k as a new Ab generated randomly in the neighborhood around the "mother Ab", whose radius is r. According to this method, generate M-N new Ab's. So, the higher the antigenic affinity, the higher the number of clones generated for each of the selected Ab's, which means the algorithm has more chance to explore new Ab with higher affinity in a small neighborhood of the elitist. In a word, the cell clone is a process to search for the local optimum.

Step 5: Hypermutation: Cell clone is merely a process to search for the local optimum. However, to prevent from unexpected local optima, and meanwhile, to obtain the ability to search for the global optimum, IIA undergoes the process of hypermutation, in which random genetic changes are introduced into each of the Ab's in a large neighborhood. Suppose $x_{i,t}$ is an Ab in B_t, Then, the new Ab after mutation is:

$$\overset{\cdot}{x}_{i,t} = \begin{cases} x_{i,\min} & x_{i,t} * rand(1-R, 1+R) < x_{i,\min} \\ x_{i,\max} & x_{i,t} * rand(1-R, 1+R) > x_{i,\max}, \\ x_{i,t} * rand(1-R, 1+R) & \text{otherwise} \end{cases} \tag{4}$$

where R is the radius of cell clone, generally. R is larger than the radius of cell clone r; $rand(1-R, 1+R)$ is a random number between $1-R$ and $1+R$. The process of hypermutation generates a set B_t'' composed of N new Ab's.

Step 6: Compose a new C_t of the new Abs generated by the cell clone and hypermutation processes. Then $C_t = B_t' \cup B_t''$, and M is the number of the new Abs.

Step 7: Receptor editing: To improve the diversity of the population and escape from local optima ulteriorly, receptor editing is performed in IIA. Those B cells replace the d lowest affinity Ab's from C_t by the d new Ab's in set D_t. Where $d=int\ (\mu*M)$; μ is the editing probability, and $0<\mu<1$.

Step 8: Elitist preserving: The B cells replace the lowest affinity Ab's from D_t by the Ab's with the highest affinity in set A_t, and form a new set A_{t+1} of Ab's. The algorithm maintains its convergence based on elitist preserving.

Step 9: If the termination condition is satisfied, then the iteration processing stops, else, go to step 2.

2.3 Parameters Setting

Studies of IIA for function optimization have indicted that good performance requires proper values of the parameters. A low probability of selection may result in convergence to local optima. On the contrary, a high probability of selection may result in poor speed of convergence. Typical values of selection probability are in the range 0.4~0.5. The value of the editing probability can not be too large either. Although a high probability of selection may improve the diversity of the algorithm, it can decrease the efficiency of convergence. Based on the experience, typical values for selection probability are in the range 0.1~0.2.

The radius of hypermutation R and the values of the radius of clone selection r determine the ability to converge in the global solving space and explore the optimum in the local neighborhood. They are both set according to the optimization problems. Generally, R is ten to fifty times of r. The value of r decreases linearly as follows:

$$r = r_{max} - \frac{r_{max} - r_{min}}{Gen_{max}} \times Gen , \qquad (5)$$

where Gen_{max} is the maximum generation set in IIA, and Gen is the current generation.

On the early stage of the searching process, the value of r is set to be relatively large to maintain the global search capability. Then, on the latter stage, the solutions gradually move close to the optimum, therefore, small value of r is needed to realize local searching. This method to determine the value of r does improve the performance of the IIA.

3 Evaluation Criterion of Optimization Efficiency

In order to evaluate IIA's convergence speed and degree of instability, this paper presents two indices, "Average truncated generation" and "Distribution entropy of truncated generation". Thereafter, they are unified as a monolithic criterion.

Definition 1: Truncated generation
A global numerical optimization can be formulated as solving the following objective function:

$$\max f(x_i), \quad i=1,2,...,n, \quad st. a_i \le x_i \le b_i . \qquad (6)$$

Based on one of the possible strategies (such as different mutation probability and selection probability), when the computing accuracy ε ($\varepsilon = f_{max} - f$) is reached. The final generation is defined as the truncated generation. If the computing accuracy would not be reached until the predefined maximum generation Gen_{max}, then the truncated generation is defined as Gen_{max}.

Definition 2: Average truncated generation
Assume that the algorithm is performed for L runs, and T_i is defined as the truncated generation of the i th run, then the set T is composed of the T_i as follows:

$$T = \{T_i | 0 < T_i \le Gen_{max}, \ T_i \in Z^+, \ i=1,2,...,L\}.$$

Arranging the elements in the set T according to their magnitudes, then a new set $T' = \{T_i' | T_i' < T_{i+1}', i=1,2,..,K-1, K \leq L\}$ can be derived. Given $C = \{C_i | 0 < C_i \leq L, C_i \in Z^+, i=1,2,..,K\}$ and $P = \{P_i | P_i = \frac{C_i}{L}, \Sigma P_i = 1, i=1,2,..,K\}$, when the algorithm reaches its computing accuracy ε ($\varepsilon = f_{max} - f$) under the guidance of strategy S, the average truncated generation is defined as follows:

$$T(S,\varepsilon) = \sum_{i=1}^{K} T_i' P_i, \qquad (7)$$

Definition 3: Distribution entropy of truncated generation
The distribution entropy of truncated generation can be defined as follows:

$$H(S,\varepsilon) = \frac{-\sum_{i=1}^{K} T_i' \ln(P_i)}{\ln(K)}, \qquad (8)$$

when the algorithm reaches its computing accuracy ε ($\varepsilon = f_{max} - f$) based on strategy S. The definition of K and P_i is same as that defined in definition 2. The distribution entropy of truncated generation represents the measure of uniformity that the distribution of the truncated generation have and the stability of the algorithm.

According to the above definitions, the average truncated generation is used to evaluate the average convergence speed of the optimization algorithm for several independent runs. The distribution entropy of truncated generation is used to evaluate whether the convergence of the algorithm is stable. The lower its degree, the more stable the convergence of the algorithm. This paper unified the two indices as a monolithic criterion on the plane (T, H) to evaluate the optimization efficiency of the proposed algorithm based on different strategies [8]. Then on the plane (T, H), the closer point to the origin represents the higher the optimization efficiency.

4 Experiment Results

In this paper, four benchmark functions are given as follows, which are widely used to test the efficiency of the optimization algorithms.

$$F_1 = 0.5 + \frac{\sin^2\sqrt{x_1^2 + x_2^2} - 0.5}{\left[1.0 + 0.001\left(x_1^2 + x_2^2\right)\right]^2}, \qquad |x_i| \leq 100$$

$$F_2 = 100\left(x_1^2 - x_2\right)^2 + \left(1 - x_1\right)^2, \qquad |x_i| \leq 2.048$$

$$F_3 = \left(x_1^2 + x_2^2\right)^{0.25}\left[\sin^2\left(50\left(x_1^2 + x_2^2\right)^{0.1}\right) + 1.0\right], \qquad |x_i| \leq 10$$

$$F_4 = \frac{1}{4000}\sum_{i=1}^{30} x_i^2 - \prod_{i=1}^{30}\cos\left(\frac{x_i}{\sqrt{i}}\right) + 1, \qquad |x_i| \leq 600.$$

To demonstrate the superiority of the proposed IIA approach, simulation results for the above benchmark functions have been compared with various techniques available in literature, namely, standard genetic algorithm (SGA), clonal selection algorithm (CSA) and particle swarm optimization algorithm (PSO).

The maximal generation is set to $Gen_{max}=100$ for all four algorithms and the population size is set to be 100. The computing accuracy is set to be 10^{-5}. To avoid any hazardous interpretation of optimization results, related to the choice of particular initial population, we performed the simulation 200 times for each function, starting from different populations randomly generated in the search space. The rest running parameters of the algorithms are chosen to be those by which the best performance could be obtained.

Figure 1 shows convergence characteristic of F_1 obtained using the four optimization algorithms respectively. The 'fitness' shown in the Figure are the average values of the optimal individual in each generation during the 200 runs of each algorithm. It is clear for the figure that the solution obtained by IIA converges to higher quality solutions at earlier iterations (about 15 iterations) rather than the other three algorithms. Similar results can be obtained for F_2 to F_4.

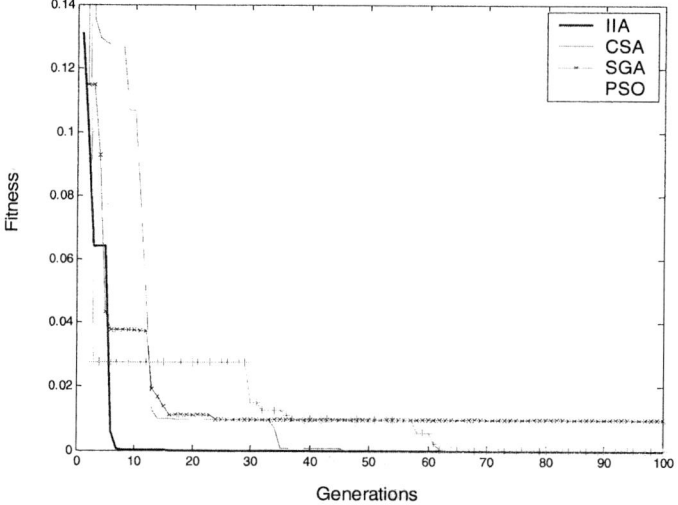

Fig. 1. Optimization procedure with four algorithms

Table 1. Comparison of optimal results for different methods

func	IIA		CSA		SGA		PSO	
	Best	Average	Best	Average	Best	Average	Best	Average
F_1	0	0	0	2.62e-10	0	1.11e-2	9.97e-10	3.90e-3
F_2	5.57e-9	9.21e-5	1.50e-6	8.05e-4	2.57e-7	3.25e-3	2.61e-8	6.45e-4
F_3	0	6.23e-21	0	2.90e-3	1.37e-4	1.26e-2	3.78e-6	5.15e-4
F_4	0	0	0.58	1.26	0.79	2.65	0.57	0.94

Table 2. Comparison of iteration for different methods

func	IIA		CSA		SGA		PSO	
	Best	Average	Best	Average	Best	Average	Best	Average
F_1	11	15	23	58	41	92	59	96
F_2	13	48	18	94	79	97	32	57
F_3	50	61	27	82	100	100	100	100
F_4	45	52	100	100	100	100	100	100

Table I and II summarizes the optimal results and convergence iterations of the best and average solutions as obtained by different methods when applying to the all four benchmark functions over 200 runs. These results show that the optimal solutions determined by the IIA lead to lower optimal value than that found by other methods, which confirms that the IIA is well capable of determining the global or near-global optimum solution. It can also be seen that IIA performs better than other methods in convergence speed.

The phenomenon sufficiently incarnates the characteristics of IIA as follows:

i. Clonal selection and elitist preserving operations both preserve the high-affinity Ab's. This feature makes IIA maintain its convergence.
ii. IIA select high-affinity Ab's to undergo cell clone operation in small neighborhoods, by which the fine search around a local minimum is performed.
iii. Hypermutation are operated in a large neighborhood. Therefore, IIA can improve its global search capabilities.

5 Evaluation of IIA's Optimization Efficiency

This paper performs the F_1 optimization task to evaluate the optimization efficiency of IIA based on a monolithic criterion defined in section 4, which is combined by the two proposed indices "Average truncated generations" and "Distribution entropy of truncated generations". The results are compared with that of CSA.

Meanwhile, the effects of parameters r and R on the optimization efficiency are also evaluated in the following descriptions.

The population size of each algorithm is set to be 100. The IIA and CSA are both processed for 100 generations ($Gen_{max}=100$) and repeated for 200 runs. The computing accuracy is 10^{-5}. During IIA operation, the radius of cell clone is set to be $r_{max}=0.1$, $r_{min}=0.05$, and the radius of hypermutation is $R=20$, $r_{min}=1$.

5.1 Selection Probability α

To evaluate the optimization efficiency in relation to α, we fix $\mu=0.2$. And α is assumed as the following values {0.1, 0.2, 0.3, 0.4, 0.5, 0.6, 0.7, 0.8, 0.9} respectively. On the plane (T, H) shown in Fig.2, each point represents the result obtained by the optimization algorithm when taking corresponding parameter pair (α, μ).

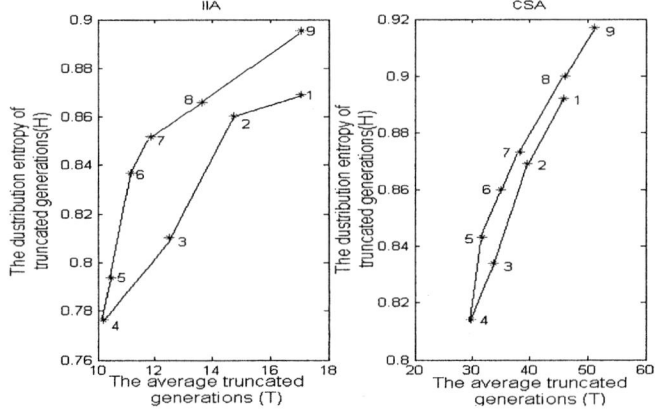

Fig. 2. Optimization efficiencies with various selection operators

From Fig.2, we can see that with the increase of α, the optimization efficiency rises gradually to the maximum when $\alpha=0.4$, and then decreases.

5.2 Editing Probability μ

In order to study how μ effects on the optimization efficiency, α is fixed to be 0.4, while μ takes various values {0.05, 0.1, 0.15, 0.2, 0.25, 0.3, 0.35, 0.4, 0.45} respectively.

Fig.3 shows the similar results to those in Fig.2: The optimization efficiency rises gradually to the maximum when $\mu=0.2$, and then decreases, with the increase of μ.

Moreover, both in Fig.2 and Fig.3, each point in the left plane (T, H) is closer to the origin than the corresponding one in the right plane, which demonstrate that with the proper parameters, the proposed algorithm have higher optimization efficiency than CSA.

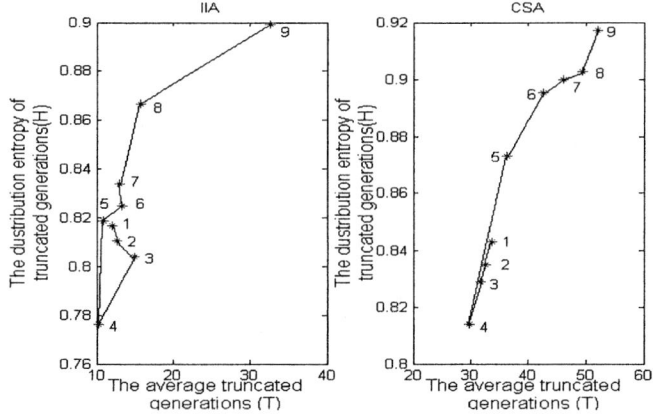

Fig. 3. Optimization efficiencies with various editing operators

6 Conclusions

This paper proposes an improved immune algorithm based on clone selection principle. IIA contributes mainly to introducing two new operators, cell clone and elitist preserving, meanwhile, modifying the hypermutation operator. Therefore, the parallel global and local searching capabilities can be obtained. Simulation results for some benchmark functions show that IIA greatly outperforms the algorithms SGA, PSO and CSA.

Acknowledgements

This work is supported by the Outstanding Young Scholars Fund (No. 60225006) and Innovative Research Group Fund of Natural Science Foundation of China.

References

1. Li, T.: Computer Immunology. Beijing: Publishing House of Electronics Industry (2004)
2. Jiao, L. C., Du, H. F.: Development and Prospect of the Artificial Immune System. Acta Electronica Sinica. 31 (2003) 1540-1548
3. Cao, X. B., Liu, K. S., Wang, X. F.: Solving Packing Problem Using an Immune Genetic Algorithm. Mini-Micro System. 21 (2000) 361-363
4. Gao, J.: The Application of the Immune Algorithm for Power Network Planning. System Engineering – Theory & Practice. 21 (2001) 119-123
5. Timmis, J., Neal, M., Hunt, J.: Data Analysis Using Artificial Immune Systems, Cluster Analysis and Kohonen Networks: Some Comparisons. Proc. IEEE SMC '99 Conference (1999) 922-927.
6. De Castro, L. N., Von Zuben, F. J.: Learning and Optimization Using Clonal Selection Principle. IEEE Trans. Evol. Comput. 6 (2002) 239-251
7. Zuo, X. Q., Li, S. Y.: Adaptive Immune Evolutionary Algorithm. Control and Decision. 19 (2004) 252-256.
8. Sun, R. X., Qiu, L. S.: Quantitative Evaluation of Optimization Efficiency for Genetic Algorithms. Acta Automatica Sinica. 26 (2000) 552-553

Simultaneous Feature Selection and Parameters Optimization for SVM by Immune Clonal Algorithm

Xiangrong Zhang and Licheng Jiao

National Key Lab for Radar Signal Processing, Institute of Intelligent
Information Processing, Xidian University, 710071 Xi'an, China
{xrzhang, lchjiao}@mail.xidian.edu.cn

Abstract. The problems of feature selection and automatically tuning parameters for SVM are considered at the same time. It is reasonable because the parameters of SVM are influenced by the given feature subset. Both of the problems can be considered as combination optimization problems. Immune clonal algorithm offers natural and potential way to solve the task because of its characteristic of rapid convergence to global optimal solution. In the evolution, the suitable feature subset and optimal parameters are got simultaneously by minimizing the existing bound on the generalization error for SVM. The results of experiments on sonar data set show the effectiveness of the method.

1 Introduction

The ability to identify the important inputs and redundant inputs for a classifier leads directly to reduced size, faster training and possibly more accurate results. For example, for a radial basis function (RBF) neural network, the number of hidden units will be too large and require heavy computation due to high input dimension [1]. Therefore, it is critical to be able to identify the important features of data to achieve maximal performance. Though support vector machine (SVM) [2] has excellent ability for the processing of multi-dimension data, it does not offer automatic detection of internal relevance of data. Irrelevant and redundant information usually contaminate the performance of machine learning algorithm. The removal of it, namely feature selection or dimension reduction, is essential for improving the performance of the classifiers.

On the other hand, the kernel parameters optimization of SVM is also important for improving the generalization performance. The idea of finding the parameters is to minimize the generalization error of SVM. According to the estimation of generalization error, there exist two techniques for parameters setting. It can be estimated by testing on some data which has not been used for learning through hold-out testing or k-fold cross validation techniques. In addition, the existing bounds for generalization error [3] can be used.

It is obvious that the kernel parameters are influenced by the input data. And the input data are described by different features in feature selection step. Therefore, it is reasonable that feature selection and parameters optimization are performed at the same time. In this paper, the existing theoretical bounds on the generalization error for SVM are used for the estimation of generalization error to perform feature selection and parameters optimization. This is much computationally faster than k-fold cross-validation since we train just once on each feature subset instead of k-times.

Moreover, both feature selection and parameters optimization can be usually considered as optimization problems. Genetic algorithm (GA) is widely used in feature selection [4] [5] [6]. However, the optimal solution cannot be got in limited evolutionary generation by GA because of its low convergence speed. In this paper, we propose to apply Immune Clonal Algorithm (ICA) [7] [8] to search the optimal feature subset and the optimal kernel parameters simultaneously considering that ICA has the global search capacity and can converge to the global optimal solution rapidly.

2 A Brief Review of Support Vector Machine

As a member of many kernel methods, SVM is a promising classification and regression technique proposed by Vapnik and his group at AT&T Bell Laboratories [2], which can be non-linearly mapped to a higher-order feature space by replacing the dot product operation in the input space with a kernel function $K(\cdot,\cdot)$. The method is to find the best decision hyperplane that separates the positive examples and negative examples with maximum margin [9]. By defining the hyperplane this way, SVM can be generalized to unknown instances effectively, which has been proved by varies applications. In a word, SVM learns a separating hyperplane to maximize the margin and to produce good generalization ability. In successful applications, one of the main attractions of SVM is that it is capable of learning in sparse, high-dimensional spaces with few training samples.

Suppose training samples $\{(x_1, y_1), \cdots (x_l, y_l)\}$, in which $x \in R^N$, $y \in \{-1,1\}$ and R^N denotes the input space. Then original input space is projected to high dimension feature space Ω by kernel projection, which ensures that the patterns can be recognized linearly in feature space. For pattern recognition problem, SVM training turns to a programming question as following.

$$\max Q(x) = \sum_{i=1}^{l} \alpha_i - \frac{1}{2} \sum_{i,j=1}^{l} \alpha_i \alpha_j y_i y_j K(x_i, x_j). \quad (1)$$

$$\text{subject to } \begin{array}{l} \sum_{i=1}^{l} \alpha_i y_i = 0 \\ 0 \leq \alpha_i \leq C, i = 1, \ldots, l \end{array}. \quad (2)$$

The decision function provided by SVM is $sign(f(x))$, where function $f(x)$ is given by:

$$f(x) = w^T \phi(x) + b = \sum_{i=1}^{l} y_i \alpha_i^* K(x \cdot x_i) + b. \quad (3)$$

The mapping $\phi(\cdot)$ is performed by a kernel function $K(\cdot,\cdot)$. Different mapping $x \mapsto \phi(x)$ construct different SVMs. There are some commonly used kernels:

Gaussian RBF: $K(x, x_i) = \exp(-\frac{\|x - x_i\|^2}{2\sigma^2})(\sigma \neq 0 \in R)$

Polynomial of degree d: $K(x, x_i) = (1 + x \cdot x_i)^d$.

From the above, it is clear that the performance of SVM algorithm usually depends on several parameters. One of them, denoted by C, is a constant penalizing the training errors and controls the tradeoff between margin maximization and error minimization. In addition, other parameter appears in the kernel function such as the width of RBF kernel σ or the degree of polynomial d. For convenience, C is considered as a kernel parameter in the following sections. Then, all the kernel parameters can be treated in a unified framework and optimized simultaneously with the feature selection.

3 Feature Selection and Parameters Optimization for SVM by Means of ICA

3.1 Estimating the Performance of SVM

For the estimation of the generalization performance for SVM, besides statistical general methods, such as cross-validation, there exist theoretical bounds on the leave-one-out error [3]. Among these bounds existed, Vapnik and Chapelle [10] derived an estimate using the concept of the span of support vectors in particular.

Theorem 1. Let α_p^0 be the tuple of Langragian multipliers which are obtained by maximizing functional (1). Suppose we have a SVM without threshold. Under the assumption that the set of support vectors does not change when removing example p we have

$$EP_{err}^{n-1} \le \frac{1}{n} E\left\{ \sum_{p=1}^{n} \psi\left(\frac{\alpha_p^0}{(K_{SV}^{-1})_{pp}} - 1 \right) \right\}, \tag{4}$$

where $\psi : \mathbb{R} \to \{0,1\}$ is the step function $\psi(v) = \begin{cases} 0 : v \le 0 \\ 1 : otherwise \end{cases}$, K_{SV} is the matrix of dot products between support vectors in feature space, P_{err}^{n-1} is the probability of test error for the machine trained on a sample of size $n-1$ and the expectations are taken over the random choice of the samples.

As the computation of the inverse of the matrix K_{SV} is rather expensive, one can upper bound $(K_{SV}^{-1})_{pp}$ by $\frac{1}{K(x_p, x_p)}$ [3]. Thus one recovers the Jaakkola-Haussler bound:

$$EP_{err}^{n-1} \le \frac{1}{n} E\left\{ \sum_{p=1}^{n} \psi\left(\alpha_p^0 k(x_p, x_p) - 1 \right) \right\}. \tag{5}$$

For the computation of the bound, SVM has to train just once for the feature subset considered with certain kernel parameters. In the multi-class case one can compute one of the bounds pair wise for classes c and c' and sum it up. Then the task to improve the generalization performance of SVM is reduced to find a feature subset and the corresponding optimal kernel parameters simultaneously to minimize the bound in equation (4).

3.2 ICA for Feature Selection and Optimization of Kernel Parameters

It is rational that ICA is introduced to the feature selection because the encoding of a feature subset into an antigen is straightforward and the function that is optimized does not need to be smooth and can directly be the generalization error. In addition, because of the global search capacity, it overcomes the disadvantages of GA, torpid convergence and local optimum. For parameter optimization, it is easy to concatenate representations of parameters to existing antigen (coding of total features) and run ICA. Then the tasks of feature selection and the choice of parameters for the given feature subset are carried out by evolution at the same time.

3.2.1 Immune Clonal Algorithm

Derived from traditional evolutionary algorithm, ICA [11] [12] introduces the mechanisms of affinity maturation, clone and memorization. Rapid convergence and good global search capability characterize the performance of the corresponding operators. The property of rapid convergence to global optimum of ICA is made use of to speed up the searching of the most suitable feature subset and corresponding kernel parameters for SVM.

The clonal selection theory is used by the immune system to describe the basic features of an immune response to an antigenic stimulus; it establishes the idea that the cells are selected when they recognize the antigens and proliferate. When exposed to antigens, immune cells that may recognize and eliminate the antigens can be selected in the body and mount an effective response against them during the course of the clonal selection. The clonal operator is an antibody random map induced by the affinity including three steps: clone, clonal mutation and clonal selection. The state transfer of antibody population is denoted as follows:

$$C_{MA}: A(k) \xrightarrow{clone} A'(k) \xrightarrow{mutation} A''(k) \xrightarrow{selection} A(k+1) \tag{6}$$

According to the affinity function f, a point $a_i = \{x_1, x_2, \cdots, x_m\}$, $a_i(k) \in A(k)$ in the solution space will be divided into q_i same points $a_i'(k) \in A'(k)$ by using clonal operator. A new antibody population is produced after the clonal mutation and clonal selection are performed. The fundamental steps of ICA are summarized in Fig. 1.

---

1. $k = 0$; Initial the antibody population $A(0)$, set the parameters, calculate the affinity of the initial population;
2. According to the affinity and the clonal size set of the antibody, perform operations of clone T_c^C, clonal mutation T_g^C and clonal selection T_s^C, then obtain the new antibody population $A(k)$;
3. Calculate the affinity of $A(k)$;
4. $k = k+1$; If satisfying the iterative termination condition, stop the iteration, otherwise, return to 2.

Fig. 1. Immune Clonal Algorithm

3.2.2 Simultaneous Feature Selection and Parameters Optimization for SVM

For the task of both feature selection and parameters optimization, the existing bound of generalization error can be used as the evaluation function. Then the purpose of ICA is to find a suitable feature subset and the corresponding kernel parameters for SVM with which a minimum of the estimation of generalization error, as shown in equation (4), can be obtained. The details of ICA for simultaneous feature selection and parameters optimization for SVM must be mentioned here, including population initialization, decoding strategy, clone operator and so on. The RBF kernel is used. Then C and the width of RBF kernel σ are optimized. In feature selection, scaling factor for each input feature is optimized. If one of the input features is useless for the classification, its scaling factor is likely to become small and if a scaling factor becomes small enough, it means that it is possible to remove it without sacrificing the performance of the classification algorithm. The idea leads to the following coding scheme.

Population Initialization

The initial antibody population $A(0)$ is generated randomly at between 0 and 1. And each one of N_p (population size) antibodies comprises three parts, the scaling factors of all features (the number of features D determines the length of this part), the codes of kernel parameters C and σ respectively. Then the total length of an antibody is $D+2$ decimal bits. Let $(a_{v_1}, a_{v_2}, \cdots, a_{v_D}, a_{v_{D+1}}, a_{v_{D+2}})$ denotes an antibody, where a_{v_i} denotes locus, $a_{v_1}, \ldots, a_{v_D}$ denote the scaling factors of associated features, $a_{v_{D+1}}$ denotes C and $a_{v_{D+2}}$ denotes σ.

Decoding

$a_{v_1}, \ldots, a_{v_D}$ denote the importance of each feature for classification. Features with large scaling factors are kept to constitute a suitable feature subset. And optimizing scaling factors naturally leads to feature selection.

The second part is C. Usually it is not necessary to consider any arbitrary value of C, but only certain discrete values, e.g. 0.001, 0.01, ..., 10000 respectively $10^{-3}, \ldots, 10^4$. With a decimal coding bit, the value of C can be obtained by the following decoding method: $c(k) = round(bd + (bu - bd)a_{v_{D+1}}(k))$ where $bu=4$ and $bd=-3$ are upper limit and lower limit of $a_{v_{D+1}}(k)$ respectively, $round(a)$ is a function by which a is rounded to an integer. Then $C_j(k) = 10^{c_j(k)}$ and $C_j(k) = 10^{-3}, \ldots, 10^4$.

For σ, any tiny change may influence the generalization performance. In order to get a more stable optimization, $\log \sigma$ is used in coding. Then the value of σ can be obtained by: $\sigma_j(k) = \exp(d(k))$, where $d(k) = bd + (bu - bd)a_{v_{D+2}}(k)$ in which $bu=5$ and $bd=-4$ are upper limit and lower limit of the variable $a_{v_{D+2}}(k)$ respectively. Then, $\sigma_j(k) \in [\exp(-4), \exp(5)]$.

Clone
Implement the clonal operator on current parent population $A(k)$, then $A(k)' = \{A(k), A_1'(k), A_2'(k), \cdots, A_{N_p}'(k)\}$. The clonal size N_c of each individual can be determined proportionally by the affinity between antibody and antigen or be a constant integer for convenience.

Clonal Mutation
The clonal mutation operator is implemented on $A'(k)$ cloned with the mutation probability $p_m = 1/(D+2)$, and then $A''(k)$ is achieved.

Clonal Selection
In subpopulation, if mutated antibody $b = \max\{f(a_{ij}) | j = 2,3,\cdots,q_i - 1\}$ exists so as to $f(a_i) < f(b)$, $a_i \in A(k)$, b replaces the antibody a_i and is added to the new parent population, namely, the antibodies are selected proportionally as the new population of next generation $A(k+1)$ based on the affinity. It is a map $I^{N_c(k)+n} \to I^n$, which realizes population compressing through selecting local optimum.

Iterative Termination Condition
The termination condition can be a threshold obtained by the affinity such as the minimum of the estimation of the generalization error or be the maximal evolution generation. If it holds, the iteration stops and then the optimal antibody in current population is the final solution. In our method, the latter is the preferred.

4 Experiment Results and Discussion

To evaluate the performance of the proposed method, sonar data from UCI machine learning repository [13] are used. Sonar data are described by 60 attributes and comprise two classes, one class is labeled Mine with 111 data, the other is Rock with 97 data. In our experience, the available samples are randomly divided into two equal data sets: training set and test set. In comparison with the proposed method, we perform the experiments in three cases: simultaneous feature selection and parameter optimization with GA, parameters optimization with ICA without feature selection and simultaneous feature selection and parameter optimization with ICA. For each case, we carry out the experiments 10 runs. The experimental results including the optimal classification error rate in 10 runs and the corresponding optimal kernel parameters, average error rate of 10 runs and the average dimension of selected features are listed in table 1.

Another fact must be mentioned that the threshold of scaling factors affects the results of feature selection seriously. In order to get a comparably stable dimension of feature subset, in our method, all the optimized scaling factors $a_{v_i}, i = 1,2,\cdots,D$ are normalized first and let $\sum_{i=1}^{D} a_{v_i} = 1$. Then, the threshold is set to be $1/D$. The features whose scaling factors are lower than the threshold are discarded from the feature subset considered.

In ICA, the size of the antibody population is 10 and the length of each antibody is the number of features plus 2. The maximal number of evolutionary generation is 50 and the clonal size is 5. In GA, the size of the initial population is 10, the crossover probability 0.8 and the mutation probability 0.01. The termination criterion is triggered whenever the maximum number of generations 50 is attained also.

Table 1. Comparison of test results of feature selection and parameters optimization for SVM

	Average error rate (%) and standard deviation	Minimal error rate (%)	Optimal kernel parameters	Average num. of used features
Parameters optimization by ICA	13.64 ± 3.69	9.62	$C=10000$ $\sigma=0.4879$	60
Feature selection and parameter optimization by GA	13.75 ± 3.12	11.54	$C=10$ $\sigma=0.3524$	30.3
Feature selection and parameter optimization by ICA	13.06 ± 3.38	10.58	$C=10$ $\sigma=1.1974$	29.2

It is shown in table 1 that the proposed method has better classification performance than the method based on GA. And in the limited number of evolution generations, the method based on ICA can get more satisfied solution than GA. In addition, the method with simultaneous feature selection and parameters optimization by ICA outperforms the one with parameters optimization only. And the dimension of the selected feature subset is approximately a half of the number of the total features.

5 Conclusion

In this paper, we proposed a new method based on Immune Clonal Algorithm in which feature selection and automatically tuning parameters for SVM are performed at the same time. It is reasonable because the parameters of SVM are influenced by the given feature subset. Both of the problems can be considered as combination optimization problems. The characteristic of rapid convergence of ICA, which putts both the global and local searching into consideration, ensures that the suitable feature subset and the optimal kernel parameters for the selected subset are got simultaneously. The existing bound on the generalization error for SVM is used as the evaluation function in the evolution. The experimental results on sonar data set show the effectiveness of the method. Certainly, we just get some primary results and the implementation of the method on the territory classification in remote sensing images is our focus of further study.

Acknowledgements. This work is supported by grants from the Key Program of National Natural Science Foundation of P.R.China (No. 60133010) and the National "863" Program (No. 2002AA 135080).

References

1. Fu, X.J., Wang, L.P.: Data Dimensionality Reduction with Application to Simplifying RBF Network Structure and Improving Classification Performance. IEEE Trans. System, Man, Cybernetics, Part B: Cybernetics. 33 (2003) 399–409
2. Vapnik, V.: The Nature of Statistical Learning Theory. Springer-Verlag, Berlin Heidelberg New York (1999)
3. Chapelle, O., Vapnik, V., Bousqet, O., Mukherjee, S.: Choosing Multiple Parameters for Support Vector Machines. Machine Learning. 46 (2002) 131–159
4. Frohlich, H., Chapelle, O., Scholkopf, B.: Feature Selection for Support Vector Machines by Means of Genetic Algorithms. In: Proceedings of the 15th IEEE International Conference on Tools with Artificial Intelligence. Sacramento, USA. (2003) 142–148
5. Raymer, M.L., Punch, W.F., Goodman, E.D., Kuhn, L.A., Jain, A.K.: Dimensionality Reduction Using Genetic Algorithms. IEEE Trans. Evolutionary Computation. 4 (2000) 164–171
6. Oh, I.S., Lee, J.S., Moon, B.R.: Hybrid Genetic Algorithms for Feature Selection. IEEE Trans. Pattern Analysis and Machine Intelligence. 26 (2004) 1424–1437
7. Jiao, L.C., Du, H.F.: Development and Prospect of the Artificial Immune System. Acta Electronica Sinica. 31 (2003) 73–80
8. Zhang, X.R., Wang, S., Tan, S., Jiao, L.C.: Selective SVMs Ensemble Driven by Immune Clonal Algorithm. In: Proceeding of the 7th European Workshop on Evolutionary Computation in Image Analysis and Signal Processing. Lausanne, Switzerland. Lecture Notes in Computer Science, Springer-Verlag. 3 (2005): 325–333
9. Wang, L.P. (Ed.): Support Vector Machines: Theory and Application. Springer, Berlin Heidelberg New York (2005)
10. Vapnik, V., Chapelle, O.: Bounds on Error Expectation for Support Vector Machines. Neural Computation, 12 (2000) 2013–2036
11. Du, H.F., Jiao, L.C., Gong M.G., Liu R.C.: Adaptive Dynamic Clone Selection Algorithms. In: Pawlak, Z., Zadeh, L. (eds): In: Proceedings of the Fourth International Conference on Rough Sets and Current Trends in Computing. Uppsala, Sweden. (2004) 768–773
12. Du, H.F., Jiao, L.C., Wang S.A.: Clonal Operator and Antibody Clone Algorithms. In: Proceedings of the First International Conference on Machine Learning and Cybernetics. Beijing. (2002) 506–510
13. Blake, C.L., Merz, C.J.: UCI Repository of Machine Learning Databases [http://www.ics.uci.edu/~mlearn/MLRepository.html]. Irvine, CA: University of California, Department of Information and Computer Science. (1998)

Optimizing the Distributed Network Monitoring Model with Bounded Bandwidth and Delay Constraints by Genetic Algorithm

Xianghui Liu[1], Jianping Yin[1], Zhiping Cai[1], Xueyuan Huang[2], and Shiming Chen[2]

[1] School of Computer Science, National University of Defense Technology,
Changsha City, Hunan Province, 410073, PRC
LiuXH@tom.com
[2] Ende Technology, Changsha City, Hunan Province, 410073, PRC

Abstract. Designing optimal measurement infrastructure is a key step for network management. In this work the goal of the optimization is to identify a minimum aggregating nodes set subject to bandwidth and delay constraints on the aggregating procedure. The problem is NP-hard. In this paper, we describe the way of using Genetic Algorithm for finding aggregating nodes set. The simulation indicates that Genetic Algorithm can produce much better result than the current method of randomly picking aggregating nodes.

1 Introduction

The explosive growth of Internet has emerged a massive need for monitoring technology that will support this growth by providing IP network managers with effective tools for monitoring network utilization and performance[1][2]. Monitoring of the network-wide state is usually achieved through the use of the Simple Network Management Protocol (SNMP) with two kinds of entities: one management center and some monitoring nodes. The management center sends SNMP commands to the monitoring nodes to obtain information about the network and this function is performed by a centralized component responsible for aggregating all monitoring nodes [3]. Yet such processing queries have some inherent weaknesses. Firstly it can adversely impact router performance and result in significant volumes of additional network traffic. Secondly aggregating procedure is its time dependency. The support of knowledge of the up-to-date performance information requires the establishment of reliable, low delay and low cost aggregating routes [4] [5].

In above traditional centralized monitoring system, although the center provides a network-wide view but has some inherent weaknesses as being pointed out and not suitable for large scale network. Taking into account the issues of scalability and network-wide view for large service provider networks, an ideal monitoring architecture is a hierarchical system which implied that there is a management center but the resource intensive nodes such as polling are distributed. Between the management center and the monitoring nodes, there exists a set of aggregating nodes.

The aggregating nodes are distributed and each node is responsible for an aggregating domain consisting of a subset of the network nodes. Information gathered from the individual monitoring nodes is then aggregated. Such a hierarchical architecture overcomes the weaknesses while still maintaining a network-wide view [4] [5].

In particular, the most recently works addresses the problem of minimizing the number of aggregating nodes while keeping the aggregating bandwidth or delay within predefined limits individually [4] [5]. And all these problems are NP-Hard with solutions to this problem by using heuristics based on the aggregating load and the maximum assignment of monitoring nodes. The difficulties of using heuristics for optimal distributed network monitoring model is that after a possible aggregating node is picked, the algorithm tries to assign the maximum number of un-assigned monitoring nodes to the it without violating bandwidth and delay constraints. Unfortunately the general problem that assigns the maximum number of un-assigned monitoring nodes without violating constraints is also NP-Hard and all the heuristics only consider some special situation now[4] [5].

As the idea of using Genetic Algorithm to provide solutions to difficult NP-Hard optimization problems has been pursued for over a decade and have some significant results. There are no polynomial-time algorithms (yet) that solve NP-Complete problems, finding approximate solutions for these problems is usually made more efficient when we use the GA concept. (Although a main drawback is that we are not guaranteed to be given an optimal solution, even if we spend a large amount of time running this genetic process.)

1. GA provides approximate solutions to several problems.
2. GA is a valid approach, since we are often times willing to settle for approximate solutions.
3. GA allows one to spend as much time as is allowed to find a solution, while providing the "best" solution so far, if terminated.

In this paper, we consider optimizing distributed monitoring modal with bounded bandwidth and delay constraints problem by Genetic Algorithm [6] [7] [8].

2 Problem Formulation

We represent the whole monitoring domain of our model as an undirected graph $G(V, E)$, where $V = \{v_1, v_2, \cdots v_n\}$ is the set of all nodes or routers that are in the monitoring domain and. $E \subseteq V \times V$ represents the set of edges. The node set $S_m (S_m \subseteq V \wedge S_m \neq \Phi)$ represents the monitoring nodes in the monitoring domain. Each node $v (v \in S_m)$ generates an aggregating traffic of w_i bps. This aggregating traffic is destined to the relative aggregating node which has been assigned to. We define function $L: E \to R^+$ and $B: E \to R^+$ which assign a non-negative weight to each link in the network and represent the actual aggregating bandwidth used and the amount of link bandwidth allocated for aggregating traffic for each of the edges. And we also define edge-delay function $D: E \to R^+$ which assigns a non-negative weight to each of the edges. The value $D(e)$ associated with edge $e \in E$ is a measure (estimate) of total delay that packets experience on the link. Let the set $E(Path(u,v))=\{e_1,e_2,\cdots,e_m\}$ represents the links in the path between node u and v.

The optimal aggregating node location and monitoring node assignment problem can therefore be stated as follows: Given a network $G(V,E)$, determine (1) a minimum subset of nodes $S_a(S_a \subseteq V)$ on which to place aggregating node such that the bandwidth constraint on each and every link $L(e) \leq B(e)$ is satisfied (where $B(e)$ is the maximum bandwidth that can be used for aggregating on link e) and the delay constraint on every node $v(v \in S_m)$ satisfy $Delay(Path(v,w)) \leq \delta$ (where δ is the maximum delay that can be used for aggregating by a node defined as w). (2) A mapping λ which maps a monitoring node to its aggregating node. That is, for any node $v(v \in S_m)$, if $\lambda(v)=w$, then node v is assigned to the aggregating node w. Note in some situation, we can use additional constraints to decide whether the monitoring node v can be aggregated by itself.

Now we define some variable to describe the integer program formulation about the problem. The binary variable x_{ij} indicates whether monitoring node v_i is aggregated by node v_j, where $v_i \in S_m$ and $v_j \in V$. The binary variable b_e^{ij} indicates whether edge e belongs to the $Path(v_i,v_j)$ between node v_i and v_j. The binary variable y_j indicates whether node v_j is an aggregating node or not. The problem minimizing the number of aggregating nodes in a given network subject to delay constraints can naturally expressed as an integer programming formulation:

The objective is: $Minimize \sum_{j=1}^{|V|} y_j$ and the constraints are below:

$$\sum_{j=1}^{|V|} x_{ij} = 1 (\forall v_i \in S_m) \quad (1)$$

$$x_{ij} \leq y_j (\forall v_i \in S_m, \forall v_j \in V) \quad (2)$$

$$\sum_i \sum_j b_e^{ij} L(v_i) x_{ij} \leq B(e)(\forall v_i \in S_m, \forall v_j \in V, e \in E) \quad (3)$$

$$\sum_{e \in E} b_e^{ij} D(e) x_{ij} \leq \delta(\forall v_i \in S_m, \forall v_j \in V) \quad (4)$$

$$x_{ij} \in \{0,1\}(\forall v_i \in S_m, \forall v_j \in V) \quad (5)$$

$$y_j \in \{0,1\}(\forall v_j \in V) \quad (6)$$

The first constraint makes sure that each monitoring node v_i is aggregated by exactly one aggregating node. The second constraint guarantees that a node v_j must be an aggregating node if some other monitoring node v_i is assigned to (aggregated by) it. The third constraint ensures the aggregating traffic on every link e not exceed the predefined bandwidth limits $B(e)$. The fourth constraint ensures that delay during aggregating procedure not exceeds the delay constraint on the path between each monitoring node and its aggregating node.

It is well-known that the integer programming formulation has an exponential running time in the worst case. In the previous work the greedy algorithm normally consists of two steps. In the first step the algorithm calculate out the maximum number of monitoring nodes satisfying the bandwidth or delay constraint when they are assigned to an aggregating node, and the set of these monitoring nodes is called candidate monitoring set of the relative node. In the second step algorithm greedily repeatedly picks an additional aggregating node (based on the greedy selection criteria) if there are any monitoring nodes still present in the network that does not have an aggregating node assigned to it. After an aggregating node is picked, the algorithm assigns candidate monitoring set to it without violating bandwidth or delay constraint. The repeat will interrupt when all monitoring nodes have been assigned, and the approximate aggregating node set includes all pickup additional aggregating nodes. Unfortunately the general problem that assigns the maximum number of un-assigned monitoring nodes without violating constraints is also NP-Hard and all the heuristic algorithm only consider some special situation. So the below we consider using Genetic Algorithm to solve the problem.

3 Evolution and Genetic Algorithm

Evolutionary algorithms are optimisation and search procedures inspired by genetics and the process of natural selection. This form of search evolves throughout generations improving the features of potential solutions by means of biologically inspired operations. On the ground of the structures undergoing optimisation the reproduction strategies, the genetic operators' adopted, evolutionary algorithms can be grouped in: evolutionary programming, evolution strategies, classifier systems, genetic algorithms and genetic programming.

The genetic algorithms behave much like biological genetics [8]. The genetic algorithms are an attractive class of computational models that mimic natural evaluation to solve problems in a wide variety of domains [9] [10]. A genetic algorithm comprises a set of individual elements (the population size) and a set of biologically inspired operators defined over the population itself etc. Genetic algorithms manipulate a population of potential solutions to an optimisation (or search) problem and use probabilistic transition rules. According to evolutionary theories, only the most suited elements in a population are likely to survive and generate offspring thus transmitting their biological heredity to new generations. A genetic algorithm maps a problem onto a set of strings (the chromosomes) and each string representing a potential solution. The three most important aspects of using genetic algorithms are: (1) definition of the objective function, (2) definition and implementation of the genetic representation, and (3) definition and implementation of the genetic operators.

There are a lot of list heuristic methods which are used to scheduling nodes onto parallel processors. Most of them give a good solution problem. Example, each node graph is assigned a priority, and then added to a list of waiting nodes in order of decreasing priority. As processors become available the node with the highest priority is selected from the list and assigned to the most suited processor. If more than one node has the same priority a node is selected randomly.

Initialisation - an initial population of the search nodes is randomly generated. The strings encoding mechanism should map each solution to a unique string. The encoding mechanism depends on the nature of the problem variables and it use for representing the optimisation problem's variables. The representation is unique. In some cases the variables assume continuous values, while in other cases the variables are binary. It can be integer parameters, real-valued parameters, vectors of parameters, Gray code, dynamic parameter encoding etc. The fitness values of each node are calculated according to the fitness function (objective function). The fitness function provides the mechanism for evaluating each chromosome in the problem domain. It is always positive. Three operators are needed to achieve this selection, crossover and mutation. The selection criterion is that string with higher fitness value should have a higher chance of surviving to the next generation. A quality measure for the solutions (fitness function) of the problem is known. Fitter solutions survive, while weaker ones perish. There are many different models of selection. The most popular selection in genetic algorithms is fitness proportionate selection, rank selection, tournament selection and elitist selection. After selection comes crossover.

The crossover operator takes two chromosomes (parents) and swaps part of their genetic information to produce new chromosomes (child). The offspring (child) keep some of the characteristics of the parents. One point crossover involves cutting the chromosomes of the parents at a randomly chosen common point and exchanging the right - hand – side sub-chromosomes. In two – point crossover chromosomes are thought of as rings with the last and the first gene connected. The rings are cut in two sites and the resulting sub-parts are exchanged. In uniform crossover each gene of the offspring is selected randomly from the corresponding genes of the parents. Crossover is applied to the individuals of a population with a constant probability, usually from 0.5 to 0.95.

Mutation consists of making (usually small) alterations to the values of one or more genes in a chromosome. In genetic algorithms, mutation is considered a method to recover lost genetic material. When we have the network topology graph, we need use topological sorting. Topological sorting consists of finding some global aggregating node set with these local constraints.

4 Proposed Algorithm

Now, we will consider initialisation, crossover, and mutation and evaluation algorithm.

With initialisation we will make population of solutions. Let be N population size and Z will be number of node in network topology graph. Randomly we choose the one of processors from set of [1,P] where P is total number of processors and then add the node from the list of node sortie by indexes on increasing order.

The chromosome is consisting from P sorted arrays. Example, let be P=3 and Z=10. One example of string looking as:

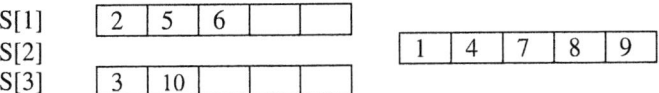

Fig. 1. Example of string (work with indexes (sorted by width) of nodes)

This is only chromosome (string) but not scheduling. On that way and with number of iterations we have defined algorithm of initialisation.

The crossover operator use two strings randomly choose (choose one at random node) T_i from one of two sets and put on the new string. Precedence relation must be kept and whole time we work with indexes of nodes (getting by topological sorting). If T_i element the same set at both parents then T_i is coping on the same place for new string (child). If we randomly choose two same parents (strings A=B) and if one of parents e.g. A the best string we use operator mutation on the second B string. It is elitism. Else, we mutate the first set and child generate randomly.

This algorithm performs the crossover operation on two strings (A and B) and generates new string.

```
Crossover (A; B) {
  If (A==B) {//elimination duplicate
    If (A is the best string) mutation (B);
    Else mutation (A);
    Random generate child;
    Return
  }
  For (i=1;i<=Z;i++){
    If (Tᵢ∈P on both parents)
      Tᵢ copy on the same place on the child
    Else
      Tᵢ below one from sets of parents (randomly);
  }
}
```

Increasing order indexes of the nodes must be kept.
Before crossover operation:

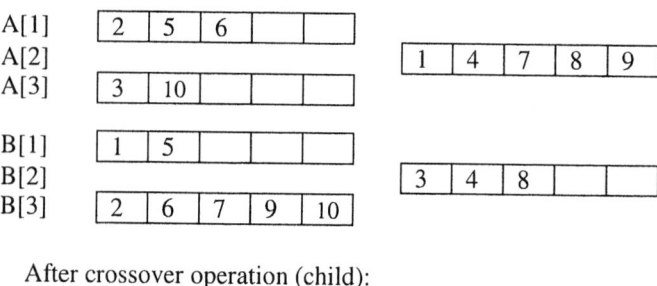

Fig. 2. Example of crossover operator

Next, what we must to do is define the mutation operator. We first generate two randomly chosen numbers r i q from the sets *[1,P]*. The condition for that is that: a) r ≠ q, and b) set r aren't empty.

After that from set r, choose one node at random and remove him in the set q. We must take in the account that the node which we move, must be put on the place that indexes of node be ordered by increasing.

Let be r=1 and q=2 and randomly choose the node has the index 5.
Before mutation:

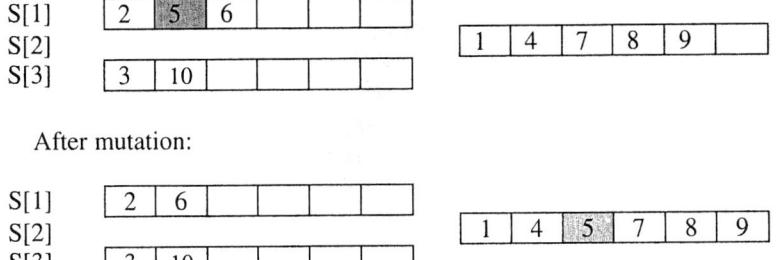

Fig. 3. Example of mutation operator

The below is the evaluation algorithm.

```
Evaluation () {
   For (i=1;i<=P;i++) FTP[i]=0;// reset FTP for all processors
   For (i=1;i<=Z;i++){
// T_i∈{sets of nodes processor p}, p∈[1,P]
      FTP[p] += duration (T_i);
      For (j=1;j<=P;j++){
         If (j == p) continue;
         // the precedence relations are maintained in this line
         If (((T_x∈j)<T_i ) && (FTP[j]>pom))
         /* x is the biggest index of nodes set p (nodes which execution onto processor p), and that content the condition x<j.*/
            FTP[p] = FTP[j] + T_i;
      }
   }
   FT = max_{i∈[1,P]}{FTP[i]};
}
```

The fitness function for the multiprocessor scheduling problem in our genetic algorithms is finishing time a besides it can be also throughput and processor utilization. Finishing time of a schedule is defined as follows: $FT=max_{i\in[1,P]}\{FTP[i]\}$ where $FTP[i]$ is the finishing time for the last node in processor i.

5 Simulation

In this section, we evaluate the performance of proposed algorithm with the heuristic algorithm on several different topologies and parameter settings. For simplicity, we make the reasonable assumption of shortest path routing.

The network graph used in this study is the Waxman model. We generate different network topologies by varying the Waxman parameter β for a fixed parameter $\alpha = 0.2$. The varying β gives topologies with degrees of connectivity ranging from 4 to 8 for a given number of nodes in the network. Each link allocates a certain fraction of their bandwidth for aggregating traffic based on the capacity constraint imposed for the link. In our simulation, the fraction is the same for all links and the value is 5% and 10% respectively. The delay for every link changes from 0.1 to 2.0 with a fix delay tolerance parameter $\delta = 10$. Simulation results presented here are averaged over 5 different topologies. Our performance metrics are (1) total number of aggregating nodes required, and (2) fraction of total bandwidth consumed for aggregating.

Random Picking of Aggregator: the heuristic is to pick a possible aggregating node from V randomly. This heuristic serves as a base-line comparison for the neural network algorithm proposed in the paper. Once we select an aggregating node, we need to determine the set of monitoring nodes to be assigned to that it. Ideally, we would like to assign maximum number of unassigned monitoring nodes to a new aggregating node. The algorithm is present in paper [4].

The simulation shows the Hopfield network have more better result than the randomly method.

Nodes	Algorithm	Link Fraction	β			
			0.05	0.10	0.15	0.20
200	Random Picking	5%	13.973%	9.257%	7.193%	5.067%
		10%	17.157%	14.928%	13.016%	9.942%
	GA	5%	11.265%	8.364%	6.327%	3.985%
		10%	12.943%	11.406%	9.158%	9.043%
400	Random Picking	5%	18.278%	14.487%	11.975%	10.013%
		10%	21.345%	19.857%	15.475%	13.976%
	GA	5%	15.433%	12.587%	10.247%	8.083%
		10%	19.164%	16.169%	14.724%	12.867%

Fig. 4. The result for simulation

6 Conclusion

The primary motivation for work to design good measurement infrastructure it is necessary to have a scalable system at a reduced cost of deployment. As the model is NP-Hard and the current heuristics algorithm is that after a possible aggregating node is picked, the algorithm tries to assign the maximum number of un-assigned monitoring nodes to it without violating bandwidth and delay constraints. Unfortunately the general problem that assigns the maximum number of un-assigned monitoring nodes without violating constraints is also NP-Hard.

In this paper, we have demonstrated that Genetic Algorithms techniques can compete effectively with more traditional heuristic solutions to practical combinatorial optimization problems, but they are not guaranteed to perfectly solve a problem (esp. in polynomial time).

References

[1] A. Asgari, P. Trimintzios, M. Irons, G. Pavlou, and S. V. den BergheR. Egan.: A Scalable Real-Time Monitoring System for Supporting Traffic Engineering. In: Proceedings of IEEE Workshop on IP Operations and Management, IEEE, New York (2002)
[2] Y. Breitbart, C. Y. Chan, M. Garofalakis, R. Rastogi, and A. Silberschatz.: Efficiently Monitoring Bandwidth and Latency in IP Networks. In: Proceedings of IEEE Infocom 2002, IEEE, New York (2002)
[3] D. Breitgand, D. Raz, and Y. Shavitt.: SNMP GetPrev: An efficient way to access data in large MIB tables. In: IEEE Journal of Selected Areas in Communication, Volume 20, No 4, IEEE, New York , (2002), 656–667,
[4] L. Li, M. Thottan, B. Yao, S. Paul.: Distributed Network Monitoring with Bounded Link Utilization in IP Networks. In: Proceedings. of IEEE Infocom 2003, IEEE, San Francisco (2003)
[5] Liu, Xiang-Hui; Yin, Jian-Ping; Lu, Xi-Cheng; Cai, Zhi-Ping; Zhao, Jian-Min.: Distributed network monitoring model with bounded delay constraints. In: Wuhan University Journal of Natural Sciences, Volume 9,No 4, (2004) 429-434
[6] Ricardo C. Correa, Afonso Ferreira, Pascal Rebreyend.: Scheduling Multiprocessor Node with Genetic Algorithm. In: IEEE Transactions on Parallel and Distributed systems. Volume 10, No 8, IEEE, New York (1999)
[7] Albert Y. Zomaya, Chris Ward, Ben Macey.: Genetic Scheduling for Parallel Processor Systems: Comparative studies and Performance Issues. In: IEEE Transactions on Parallel and Distributed systems. Volume 10, No 8, IEEE, New York (1999)
[8] G.N. Srinivasa Prasanna , B.R. Musicus.: Generalized Multiprocessor Scheduling and Applications to Matrix Computations. In: IEEE Transactions on Parallel and Distributed systems, Volume 7, No 6, IEEE, New York (1996)
[9] C.W. Ahn and R. S. Ramakrishna.: A Genetic Algorithm for Shortest Path Routing Problem and the Sizing of Populations. IEEE Transactions on Evolutionary Computation, Volume 6, Issue 6, IEEE, New York (2002), 566–579
[10] D.E. Goldberg. Genetic Algorithms in Search.: *Optimization, and Machine Learning*. Addison-Wesley, Reading, MA, (1989)

Modeling and Optimal for Vacuum Annealing Furnace Based on Wavelet Neural Networks with Adaptive Immune Genetic Algorithm

Xiaobin Li and Ding Liu

Control and Information Center, Xian University of Technology,
Xian 710048, China
lixiaobinauto@163.com

Abstract. The accurate control of the work pieces temperature is a nonlinear, large time-delay, and cross-coupling complicated control problem in vacuum annealing furnace. In order to control the temperature of work pieces accurately. The optimization model for accurate work pieces temperature control has been proposed by the data gathered from the scene. The model was set up with Wavelet Neural Networks (WNN). Adaptive Immune Genetic Algorithm (AIGA) optimized the WNN structure and parameters (weights, dilation and translation). Simulation and experiment results show that the model in this paper is better than the model established with NN and optimizing the weights of NN by GA. And, it improves the training rate of Networks and obtains a system with good steady state precision, real timeliness and robustness.

1 Introduction

The high vacuum annealing furnace is primarily used to process the vacuum annealing of metal pieces that desire higher precision for the characteristics of pieces in aerospace and national defense. In the aspect of common metallurgy heat treatment, people have done much work on modeling and optimizing of metallurgy annealing that takes temperature of heat zones as the control target[1][2][3][4], and there are also some paper on the modeling and optimizing of ordinary heating furnace that takes the heat state of work pieces temperature as the target have been reported[5][6]. But these methods can't satisfy the requirement of high accuracy annealing at all.

This paper will use Wavelet Neural Networks with many data of heat zones and work pieces which were gathered from the production to set up a model. The model will adopt the compound coding adaptive immune genetic algorithm in which has strong ability to search for optimum construction to optimize the weights, dilation and translation parameters of WNN. It has overcome many weak points of BP algorithm which difficult to search for the best, and the early maturity of GA which easy to fall into local optimization and slow-rate convergence[7]. An optimization model for accurate control work pieces temperature is acquired. Through comparing with the model was based on NN and optimizing the weights and bias of NN that based on genetic algorithm in simulation and experiment. The model based on the method in this paper improves the training rate of Networks and steady state precision of system. It makes system obtain much better characteristics in real-time and robustness.

2 Determination of Model

According to wavelet transform theory and document[8]. We have known to assume $\psi(x)$ is a mother function, and $\psi(x) \in L^2(R)$. Then a group of wavelet functions can be expressed as formula (1) by dilation and translation:

$$\psi_{a,b}(x) = |a|^{-\frac{1}{2}} \psi\left(\frac{x-b}{a}\right) \tag{1}$$

where a, b are respectively dilation and translation parameters.

The satisfactory condition of $\psi(x)$ is:

$$\int_{-\infty}^{+\infty} \psi(x) dx = 0 \tag{2}$$

i.e.: $$\int_{-\infty}^{+\infty} |\psi(x)| dx < \infty \tag{3}$$

The compatible condition satisfied is:

$$2\pi \int_{-\infty}^{+\infty} \frac{|\psi(\omega)|^2}{|\omega|} d\omega < +\infty \tag{4}$$

where $\psi(\omega)$ is the Fourier transform of $\psi(x)$.

From this, an unknown function $f(x)$ may be approximated as by a group of $\psi(x)$:

$$\hat{f}(x) = \sum_{k=1}^{M} W_k \Psi_k\left(\frac{x-b_k}{a_k}\right) \tag{5}$$

where $\hat{f}(x)$ is the synthesized function of $f(x)$. Weights are W_k. Dilation parameters are a_k. Translation parameters are b_k. M is the wavelet number.

The least average square error energy function is expressed as:

$$E = \frac{1}{2} \sum_{j=1}^{P} \left[\hat{f}(x) - f(x)\right]^2 \tag{6}$$

where p is sample number.

For MIMO system formula (5) can be expressed as:

$$\hat{f}_j(x) = \sum_{k=1}^{M} W_{jk} \Psi_k \left(\frac{\sum_{i=1}^{N} W_{ki} x_i - b_k}{a_k} \right) \tag{7}$$

where $\hat{f}_j(x)$ is the Number j output of system. M is wavelet number. Input variable number of system is N. Formula (6) can be expressed as:

$$E = \frac{1}{2} \sum_{j=1}^{P} \left[\hat{f}_j(x) - f_j(x) \right]^2 \tag{8}$$

In this paper we select radical wavelet function as:

$$\Psi(x) = \cos(1.75 x) \exp\left(-\frac{x^2}{2}\right) \tag{9}$$

2.1 The Construction of Wavelet Neural Networks

An internal heating type of vacuum annealing furnace is discussed in this paper. In order to heat work pieces evenly. The heating wires and thermocouples are installed at the top, side and bottom of the furnace. Thermocouple of work pieces is installed at the middle of work pieces. During the annealing process, vacuum degree is maintained between 10^{-4}-10^{-3}Pa. According to thermodynamics theory. The primary transmission form is heat release in which the electric heating wires generate energy is transmitted to work pieces. Simultaneously another transmission form is heat conduction in which the remnant part of energy is transmitted to the external. The heat release is a typical nonlinear process. There is time delay in the heating device. It exists cross-coincidence between heating devices. Because of it exists the difference characteristics for the devices and space distribution. So vacuum annealing furnace is a typical nonlinear time delay inertia cross coincidence complicated control object.

Three layers NN construction is adopted in this paper. The first is input layer. The second is hidden layer. The third is output layer. Input neural unit number and output layers are 4 and 1 respectively. Neural number of hidden layer M can be obtained by optimization using AIGA. WNN construction is shown as Fig.1:

The relationship between input and output of the first layer neural units (input layer) is expressed as:

$$v_i = x_i \quad (i=1, 2, 3, 4) \tag{10}$$

where: v_i is neural unit output of number i. x_i is neural unit input of number i.

The relationship between input and output of the second layer neural units is expressed as:

$$s_k = \sum_{i=1}^{N} W_{ki} v_i \tag{11}$$

($N = 4$ is the neural unit number of the first layer neural Networks)

$$h_k = \Psi(\frac{s_k - b_k}{a_k}) \quad (12)$$

where: v_i is the number i neural unit input. h_k is the number k neural unit output. W_{ki} are the weights between input layer and output layer which are optimized by AIGA. $\Psi(\bullet)$ is transform function. Where is radical wavelet function. a_k are the dilation parameters of radical wavelet function. b_k are the translation parameters of radical wavelet function.

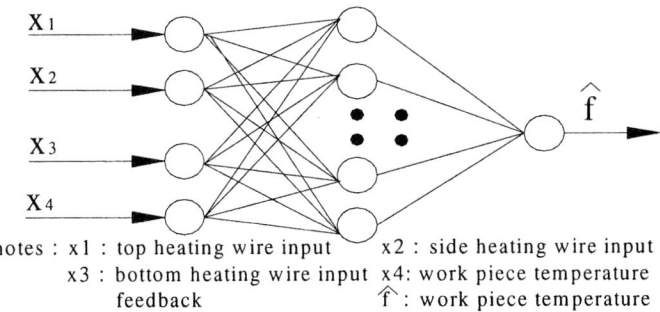

notes: x1: top heating wire input   x2: side heating wire input
x3: bottom heating wire input   x4: work piece temperature
feedback $\hat{f}$: work piece temperature

Fig. 1. The component frame chart of Neural Networks

The relationship between input and output of the third (output layer) is expressed as:

$$\hat{f} = \sum_{k=1}^{M} W_k h_k \text{ (M is the hidden neural unit number)} \quad (13)$$

where $\hat{f}$ is the output Neural Networks. W_k are the weights between hidden layer and output layer. h_k is the Number k output of hidden layer.

2.2 Optimization of the Weights of NN and Dilation Parameters Translation Parameters and the Number of Wavelet Function

The AIGA is an improving algorithm in order to avoid the immature convergence and to improve the population diversity. It is used to optimize the weights of NN and dilation parameters translation parameters and the number of radical wavelet function. This algorithm includes such three kinds of basic operations. They are selection extension and mutation[7]. The concrete optimization procedures are described in the following:

(1) Process initialization: in this operation. The main work is determined the range of each parameter in searching for optimization. Accordingly, the parameter range should be appropriate medium. Therefore, too small range is bound not to obtain the optimal solution. But too large range is bound to prolong the process of searching for optimization and to affect real timeliness. It is here that we should be first on the site

to select the relative optimal parameters of several groups. Then fix the range of searching for optimization in the vicinity of these parameters. It is just here that we will fix the weights w. Dilation parameters a_k. Translation parameters b_k of the wavelet Networks range as $[-2,2]$ and the number of the wavelet function maximal number as 15.

(2) Population initialization: the parameters and structure of the wavelet Networks are coded firstly when optimizing the wavelet Networks based on the AIGA. The compound coding system combines the advantages of decimal system and binary system that usually is used to code the initial population. It is selected to code the initial population. An individual is composed of 4 parts. The part 1 to 3 coded by decimal system denote the weights, dilation and translation parameters of wavelet Networks. The part 4 coded by binary system denotes the structure of the wavelet Networks (here 0 denotes invalid and 1 denotes valid). The larger number of the population is the wider. It is representation that the larger possibility of obtaining optimal solution. But it is inevitable to cause an increase in calculation time. In general, the number p of the population is to select 20 to 100. It is here that the number of population is fixed as $p = 26$.

(3) Calculation of evaluation value of individuals: the E value of optimal objective functions should be worked out. E is used to obtain the evaluation function value fit. $fit = \dfrac{1}{E+1}$. In here, the denominator of the evaluation function formula. We can be expressed as $E+1$. It is to prevent the occurrence of calculation overflow when the optimal objective function value tends to become zero. The optimal objective function E is calculated from formula (8).

(4) It is necessary to judge whether the evaluation function value reaches the requirement of optimization or not. If the requirements are met with the most optimal values of structure and parameters of WNN can be obtained so that the process of searching for the optimization should be exited. Otherwise continue operations as following.

(5) Selective operation: It is here that the q pieces of individuals with the highest evaluation values can form the population $pop1$. Here $p=integer\ (\beta \times p)$ The selective probability β can be obtained by the calculation with formula (16). The β value taking range here is (0,1).

(6) Extension operation: Each individual in new population $pop1$ formed through selective operation should have the extension probability calculated through formula (14)

$$pr_l = \dfrac{fit_l}{\sum_{s=1}^{q} fit_s} \qquad (14)$$

And then, the roulette wheel method is used to determine the number of new individual extended from each individual. And then, the corresponding number of new individuals is selected at random in the adjacent field to obtain new population *pop2*. The adjacent field is selected with the *l* pieces of individual as the center. The section space with r_1 as the radius, and r_1 selection is obtained through the calculation with formula (17). The r_1 value taking section space can be *(-d, d)*, and *d* is the minimum value of the two ends distance from the *l* pieces of individuals to the tracking zone of searching for the optimization.

(7) Mutation operation: The mutation operation is conducted for the poorest $p-q$ pieces of individuals in population *pop2*. Whose mutation can be any individual in the adjacent field. The adjacent field selection is the same as the method used in the (6) step. The radius r_2 here can be obtained through the calculation with formula (18).

In the process of optimizing parameters the adaptive adjustment of the immune genetic algorithm is realized mainly via such three parameters as β, r_1 and r_2. Once the searching for the optimization starts. It is expected to have a larger selective probability and a smaller extension and mutation radius. When searching for the optimization is carried out to a certain extent, and particularly nearing convergence. The diversity of the population becomes small so that it is just at this time. It is expected to have a smaller selective probability and a larger extension and mutation radius. In order to judge the population diversity and be able to have the adaptive adjustment of such three parameters as β, r_1 and r_2. The method set in literature[7]can be borrowed to introduce the function of determining population diversity in the following:

$$V = \frac{1}{p}\sum_{s=1}^{p-1} \|gen(s) - gen(s+1)\| \quad (15)$$

where, V is the judgment function. p is the number of the population. gen(s) is the s pieces of individual. If β, r_1 and r_2 variable range can be (c_0, d_0), (c_1, d_1), (c_2, d_2) respectively. The adaptive adjustment of algorithm parameters should be as follows:

$$\beta = c_0 + \frac{(c_0 - d_0)V}{1+V} \quad (16)$$

$$r_1 = c_1 + \frac{c_1 - d_1}{1+V} \quad (17)$$

$$r_2 = c_2 + \frac{c_2 - d_2}{1+V} \quad (18)$$

3 The Simulation and Test Results

3.1 Simulation Test

It is here that takes a Φ2100×2100 high vacuum annealing furnaces as a research object. The simulation model is carried out through the method in this article. It is based on the amount of data gathered from the production scene. It takes the temperature of annealing work pieces as a target temperature parameter. In order to proved the availability of the model set up with the method in this article. One of group data is recorded in table1:

Table 1. The data gathered from scene

Time(M)	0	15	30	45	60	75	90	105
Top heating current(A)	0	120	420	280	300	400	400	400
Side heating current (A)	0	100	300	420	420	420	420	420
Bottom heating current (A)	0	100	700	300	400	640	700	760
Workpieces temperature (℃)	0	24	70	139	220	287	375	461

Time(M)	120	135	150	165	180	195	210
Top heating current(A)	400	400	400	380	320	320	300
Side heating current (A)	420	420	420	400	380	240	260
Bottom heating current (A)	680	700	700	700	700	700	700
Workpieces temperature (℃)	529	576	600	609	615	616	616

Test: A simulation is carried out through the MATLAB program language with the data in table1, and the compare between the simulate result and the real output is shown in Fig.2 and Fig.3

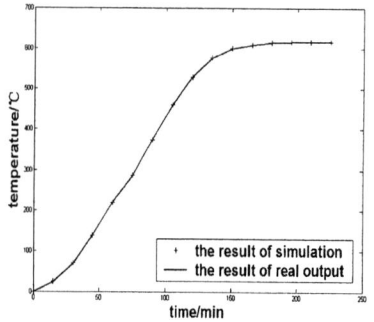

Fig. 2. Simulate result and real output compare

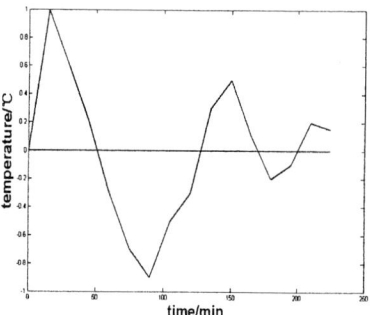

Fig. 3. Simulation error compare

It can be seen from Fig.2 and Fig.3 that the deviation between the simulate result and the real output can stabilize in ±1 ℃. So it is a satisfied precision requirement completely.

3.2 Control Test

The control component frame chart was shown in Fig. 4. It is used to test annealing system. The model as a predictive model is used to adjust on line so as to get an optimal approach between the predictive model and real vacuum annealing furnace model. Transfer unit give an input signal into heating wires and NN model as the same time that the last time vacuum annealing furnace output is put into NN model. The output of NN is used as a predictive temperature value $\hat{f}$ in which realizes the adjustment to the controller. It was optimised which the construction, weights, dilation and translation parameters of wavelet Networks. At the same time the AIGA is used to adjust the deviation of output as learning guide signal.

It is here that takes a kind of work pieces whose technology requirement is: vacuum degree as $2\times10^{-3}Pa \sim 5\times10^{-4}Pa$ and the deviation of work pieces temperature as $\leq \pm 5°C$ as an example. The results compare of control though the model set up in this article and the model set up by NN based on GA is shown in Fig. 5.

It can be seen from Fig.5.The control system based on the model in this article has a small deviation and can track the set value well in the control process. It only has $\pm 1°C$ control deviation. But that based on the model by NN has a temperature deviation as $\leq \pm 2°C$. A conclusion can be obtained to prove this method is available.

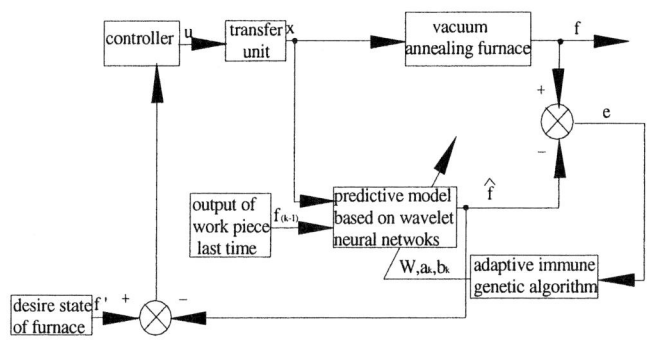

Fig. 4. The component frame chart of control

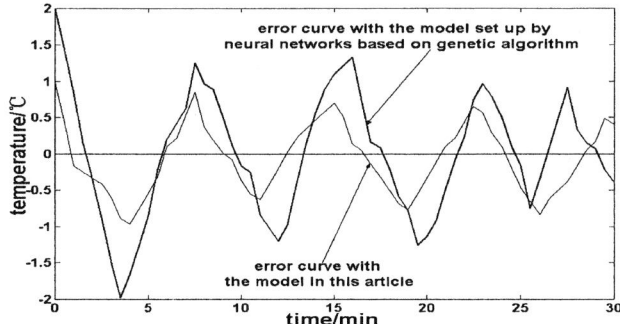

Fig. 5. Control error curve compare

4 Conclusion

As of the heating behaviors in the frontier industrial production process as well as special requirements of process control. It use of high vacuum annealing furnace used in precise machinery manufacturing, aerospace, national defense, etc. A kind of optimal model of vacuum annealing furnace is advanced in this paper. The model set up in this paper is applied to practice and realizes the combination of modeling and control, and the rolling optimization for different kinds of work pieces on line. And a good control result is realized though the model in this paper.

Acknowledgements

Li Xiaobin (born in 1966 -) male, associate Prof. Ph.D, majors in the comprehensive automation and intelligent control system in industrial production process as the research direction.

Liu Ding (born in 1957 -) Ph..D, Prof. Ph.D tutor, has been for long engaged in researches on industrial automation, intelligent control theory and applications, and published over 300 thesis and won 4 rewards of national, provincial and ministerial sci-tech progress.

References

1. Gerard Bloch ,Franck Sirou and Philippe Fatrez.: Neural intelligent control for a steel plant, vol.8. IEEE Transactions on neural Networks(1997)910-918.
2. Naoharu yoshitani and Akihiko Hasegawa.: Model-based control of strip temperature for the heating furnace in continuous annealing, vol.6. IEEE Transactions on control systems technology(1998)146-156.
3. Young C.Cho , Wook hyun kwon and Christos G. Cassandras.: Optimal control for steel annealing processes as hybrid systems. Proceedings of the 39th IEEE conference on decision and control. Sydney,Australia(2000)540-545.
4. Wang Xiong, Yu Zhaohui, Xu Yongmao.: An optimal control system on line for the continuous annealing furnace, vol.16. Computer Simulation, China(1999) 61-67.
5. Lu Yongzai and William TJ.: Modeling Estimation and Control of the Soaking Pit. New York: Instrument Society of America(1983).
6. Wang Rengrong, Shi Yinwei, Wang Wenhai, Sun Youxian :A New Method to Optimize the Control of Reheating Furnaces, vol.18. Control Theory & Applications, China(2001)145-148.
7. Zuo Xingquan, Li Shiyong.: A Kind of Adaptive Immune Algorithm Used in Optimal Algorithm, vol.20. Computer Engineering and Applications, China(2003) 68-70.
8. Q.Zhang, A.Benveniste.: Wavelet Networks, vol.6. IEEE Transactions on neural Networks(1992)889-898.

Lamarckian Polyclonal Programming Algorithm for Global Numerical Optimization

Wuhong He, Haifeng Du, Licheng Jiao, and Jing Li

Institute of Intelligent Information Processing and
National Key Lab of Radar Signal Processing, Xidian University,
710071 Xi'an, China
hewuhong@163.com

Abstract. In this paper, Immune Clonal Selection theory and Lamarckism are integrated to form a new algorithm, Lamarckian Polyclonal Programming Algorithm (LPPA), for solving the global numerical optimization problem. The idea that Lamarckian evolution described how organism can evolve through learning, namely the point of "Gain and Convey" is applied, then this kind of learning mechanism is introduced into Adaptive Polyclonal Programming Algorithm (APPA). In the experiments, ten benchmark functions are used to test the performance of LPPA, and the scalability of LPPA along the problem dimension is studied with great care. The results show that LPPA achieves a good performance when the dimensions are increased from 20-10,000. Moreover, even when the dimensions are increased to as high as 10,000, LPPA still can find high quality solutions at a low computation cost. Therefore, LPPA has good scalability and is a competent algorithm for solving high dimensional optimization problems.

1 Introduction

In recent years, evolutionary algorithm (EA) has been widely used for numerical optimization, combinatorial optimization, classifier systems, and many other engineering problems [1][2]. Global numerical optimization problems arise in almost every field of science, engineering, and business. Since many of these problems can't be solved analytically, EA has become one of the popular methods to address them. But the major problem of EA is that they may be trapped in the local optima of the objective function.

Clonal selection theory is very important for the immunology. Clone means reproduction or asexual propagation. A group of genetically identical cells descended from a single common ancestor, such as a bacterial colony whose members arose from a single original cell as a result of binary fission.

Learning mechanism, namely Lamarckism [3], is introduced into Adaptive Polyclonal Programming Algorithm (APPA) [4], and Lamarckian Polyclonal Programming Algorithm (LPPA) is presented in this paper. Based on the idea "gain and convey" of Lamarckian evolution, LPPA makes full use of the experiences gained during the learning process to enhance the information communication among individuals, and improve the performance of algorithm. Relative function optimization experimental results shows that compared with APPA and other evolutionary algorithms, LPPA has better performance in global search and computing efficiency.

The rest of this paper is organized as follow. Section 2 describes LPPA and analyzes its convergence. Section 3 discusses the experimental studies on the problems of global numerical optimization, and the scalability of LPPA along the multimodal functions dimension is analyzed. Finally, Section 4 concludes the paper with a short summary.

2 Lamarckian Polyclonal Programming Algorithm

2.1 Two Operators in LPPA

In our society, there are many "Heroes" directing the progress of human being's society, meanwhile, some of Non-Heroes can learn from Heroes then become parts of Heroes. And the others in Non-Heroes can also go into Heroes by individuals' efforts. Then, based on this concept, we present the skeleton of LPPA below.

According to the fitness distribution in population, several subpopulations are formed in Fig. 1. In general, the whole candidate population is divided into two parts: high-fitness subpopulation Heroes and low-fitness subpopulation Non-Heroes. Furthermore, Non-Heroes can be divided into Employees evolving by conveying the Heroes' Experiences (HE) and Civilians evolving by themselves. After iterations, some individuals in Employees can go into Heroes, which are called Successful Employees (SE), while the others are named Unsuccessful Employees (USE). In the same naming way, Civilians can be divided into Successful Civilians (SC) and Unsuccessful Civilians (USC), and USC can get Successful Civilians Experiences (SCE) from SC.

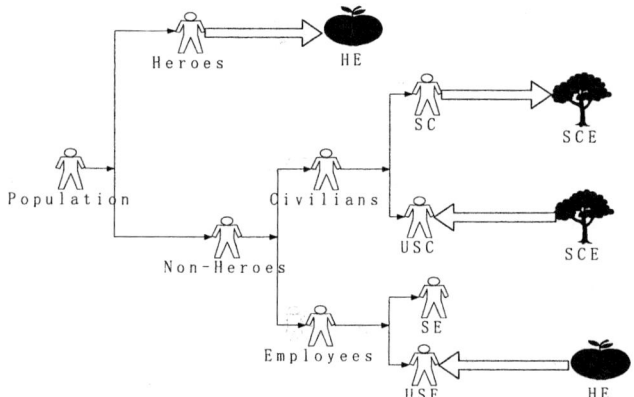

Fig. 1. Several subpopulations are formed according to the fitness distribution in population

In order to use clonal selection mechanism and Lamarckism, two main operator – Adaptive Polyclonal Operator [4] and Lamarckian Learning Operator are proposed in this paper.

Lamarckian Learning Operator

Divide the population T_d^C :

The population is divided as $[H(k), C(k), E(k)]^T = T_d^C(A(k))$, where, $H(k)$, $C(k)$ and $E(k)$ denote Heroes, Civilians and Employees respectively, whose population size are h_n, c_n and e_n, moreover,

$$h_n + c_n + e_n = n \tag{1}$$

Get Heroes' Experiences (HE) T_{HE}^C : $H_E = T_{HE}^C [H(k)]^T$.

Where, $H_E = s_r \times H_{h_i}(k)$ $1 \le h_i \le h_n$, and s_r is a randomly generated binary string with the length l:

$$s_r = \{r_1, r_2, L, r_l\} \quad \text{and} \quad r_i \in \{0,1\} \quad 1 \le i \le l \tag{2}$$

Gain the Successful Civilians' Experience (SCE) T_{SCE}^C : $C_{SE} = T_{SCE}^C [C_S(k)]^T$.

Through generation of Adaptive Polyclonal Operator, some individuals in $C(k)$ and $E(k)$ can go into Heroes, which are called Successful Civilians (SC) $C_s(k)$ and Successful Employees (SE) $E_s(k)$ relatively. Others are named Unsuccessful Civilians (USC) $C_{US}(k)$ and Unsuccessful Employees (USE) $E_{US}(k)$.

s'_r is a randomly generated bit string constructed by 0 and 1:

$$s'_r = \{r_1', r_2', L, r_l'\} \quad \text{and} \quad r_i' \in \{0,1\} \quad 1 \le i \le l \tag{3}$$

then $C_{SE} = s'_r \times C_{MS}(k)$, and $C_{MS}(k) = \max(f(C_S(k)))$.

Conveying HE and SCE T_T^C : Convey HE and SCE to $E_{US}(k)$ and $C_{US}(k)$ respectively.

2.2 Implementation of LPPA

$f : R^m \to R$ is the optimized object function, without loss of generality, we consider the maximum of affinity function the affinity $\Phi : I \to R$ where $I = R^m$ is the individual space, n is the population size, m is the number of optimized variable, namely, $a = \{x_1, x_2, \cdots, x_m\}$. The details of the overall algorithms are implemented as follow.

k=0

Initial: Set the mutation probability p_m, recombination probability p_c, clonal size N_c, inversion probability p_i. And give the termination criterion. Randomly generate the original antibody population $A(0) = \{a_1(0), a_2(0), \cdots, a_n(0)\} \in I^n$ with the size n in the domain [0,1].

Calculate the affinity.
While the Termination Criterion can't be met, do

Inversion: Select some antibodies from $A(k)$ to inverse with p_i. Under the two point p and q (suppose $p<q$) randomly chosen in the antibody $a_i = \{x_{i1}, x_{i2}, \cdots, x_{ip}, \cdots, x_{iq}, \cdots, x_{im}\}$, the offspring of antibody a_i will be,

$$a_i = \{x_{i1}, x_{i2}, \cdots x_{iq}, x_{iq-1} \cdots, x_{ip+1}, x_{ip}, \cdots, x_{im}\} \tag{4}$$

Adaptive Polyclonal Clone: Generate the provisional new antibody population $A'(k+1)$ by adaptive Polyclonal clone operator.

Lamarckian Learning Operator: Generate the new antibody population $A(k+1)$ by Lamarckian Learning operator.
$k=k+1$;
end

2.3 Convergence of LPPA

Define the global optima set of problem P as:

$$B^* \equiv \{A \in I : f(A) = f^* \equiv \max(f(A') : A' \in I)\} \tag{5}$$

For antibody population A, $\vartheta(A) \equiv |A \cap B^*|$ denotes the number of optima in A.

Definition 1. I^* is called the optimal antibody population space, which is expressed as $I^* = \{A \in I^* | \vartheta(A) \geq 1\}$.

It is shown from the definition that there is at least one best antibody in the optimal antibody population space. Furthermore, $\bar{I}^* = I^n - I^*$ is called the common antibody population space. Additionally, define $I^{N_c(k)}$ resulting from cloning operating as the clone antibody population space, which is a variable space, where $N_c(k) = \sum q_i(k)$.

Definition 2. For the randomly initialized state A_0, if there is always:

$$\lim_{k \to \infty} P\{A(k) \cap B^* \neq \Phi | A(0) = A_0\} = \lim_{k \to \infty} P\{A(k) \in I^* | A(0) = A_0\} = 1 \tag{6}$$

namely,

$$\lim_{k \to \infty} P\{\vartheta(A(k)) \geq 1 | A(0) = A_0\} = 1 \tag{7}$$

Then it is indicated that the algorithm converges to the optimal population set with probability 1.

It is suggested from Definition 2 that algorithm convergence means the probability with which population has the best individual is close to 1 after adequate iterations.

Theorem 1. LPPA converges with probability 1.
Proof:
Define $P_0(k) = P\{\vartheta(A(k)) = 0\} = P\{A(k) \cap B^* = \varnothing\}$, according to Bayesian probability formula, then there is:

$$P_0(k+1) = P\{\vartheta(A(k+1)) = 0\}$$

$$= P\{\vartheta(A(k+1) = 0) | \vartheta(A(k) \neq 0)\} \times P\{\vartheta(A(k) \neq 0)\}$$

$$+ P\{\vartheta(A(k+1) = 0) | \vartheta(A(k) = 0)\} \times P\{\vartheta(A(k) = 0)\}$$

It is known from the characters described in section 2 that $P\{\vartheta(A(k+1) = 0) | \vartheta(A(k) \neq 0)\} = 0$, so

$$P_0(k+1) = P\{\vartheta(A(k+1) = 0) | \vartheta(A(k) = 0)\} \times P_0(k) \tag{8}$$

Moreover,

$$P\{\vartheta(A(k+1) = 0) | \vartheta(A(k) = 0)\} = P_I + P_{II} > 0 \tag{9}$$

namely, the probability with which antibody population gain the best solution consists of two parts, one part is $P_I(k)$ due to evolving population, and the other part is $P_{II}(k)$ caused by learning.

Define $\zeta = \min_k P_I(k) \quad k = 0,1,2\cdots$

The way to convey the experience shows that $P_{II}(k) > 0$;
In addition, $P_I(k) \geq 0$ (It can be proved that the equal sign is not correct) therefore,

$$P\{\vartheta(A(k+1) = 0) | \vartheta(A(k) = 0)\} \geq \zeta > 0 \tag{10}$$

Then

$$P\{\vartheta(A(k+1) = 0) | \vartheta(A(k) = 0)\} = 1 - P\{\vartheta(A(k+1) \neq 0) | \vartheta(A(k) = 0)\}$$

$$= 1 - P\{\vartheta(A(k+1) \geq 1) | \vartheta(A(k) = 0)\}$$

$$\leq 1 - P\{\vartheta(A(k+1) = 1) | \vartheta(A(k) = 0)\} \leq 1 - \zeta < 1$$

And

$$0 \leq P_0(k+1) \leq (1-\zeta) \times P_0(k) \leq (1-\zeta)^2 \times P_0(k-1) \cdots \leq (1-\zeta)^{k+1} \times P_0(0) \tag{11}$$

Because $\lim_{k \to \infty} (1-\zeta)^{k+1} = 0$, $1 \geq P_0(0) \geq 0$

$$0 \leq \lim_{k \to \infty} P_0(k) \leq \lim_{k \to \infty} (1-\zeta)^{k+1} P_0(0) = 0 \tag{12}$$

then $\lim_{k \to \infty} P_0(k) = 0$

and $\lim_{k \to \infty} P\{A(k) \cap B^* \neq \Phi | A(0) = A_0\} = 1 - \lim_{k \to \infty} P_0(k) = 1$

namely $\lim_{k \to \infty} P\{A(k) \in I^* | A(0) = A_0\} = 1$.

3 Experimental Studies on Global Numerical Optimization

3.1 Test Functions

In order to test the performance of LPPA, ten benchmark functions have been used

$$f_1(x) = \sum_{i=1}^{N} x_i^2 \quad -100 \leq x_i \leq 100 \tag{13}$$

$$f_2(x) = \sum_{i=1}^{N} |x_i| + \prod_{i=1}^{N} |x_i| \quad -10 \leq x_i \leq 10 \tag{14}$$

$$f_3(x) = \sum_{i=1}^{N} (\sum_{j=1}^{i} x_j)^2 \quad -100 \leq x_i \leq 100 \tag{15}$$

$$f_4(x) = \sum_{i=1}^{N} (\lfloor x_i + 0.5 \rfloor)^2 \quad -100 \leq x_i \leq 100 \tag{16}$$

$$f_5(x) = \sum_{i=1}^{N} i x_i^4 + random[0,1) \quad -1.28 \leq x_i \leq 1.28 \tag{17}$$

$$f_6(x) = \frac{1}{N} \sum_{i=1}^{N} (x_i^4 - 16 x_i^2 + 5 x_i) \quad -5 \leq x_i \leq 5 \tag{18}$$

$$f_7(x) = \sum_{i=1}^{N} (x_i^2 - 10\cos(2\pi x_i) + 10) \quad -5.12 \leq x_i \leq 5.12 \tag{19}$$

$$f_8(x) = -\sum_{i=1}^{N} x_i \sin(\sqrt{|x_i|}) \quad -500 \leq x_i \leq 500 \tag{20}$$

$$f_9(x) = \sum_{i=1}^{N} \frac{x_i^2}{4000} - \prod_{i=1}^{N} \cos(\frac{x_i}{\sqrt{i}}) + 1 \quad -600 \leq x_i \leq 600 \tag{21}$$

$$f_{10} = -20\exp\left(-0.2\sqrt{\frac{1}{N}\sum_{i=1}^{N} x_i^2}\right) - \exp\left(\frac{1}{N}\sum_{i=1}^{N} \cos(2\pi x_i)\right) + 20 + e \quad -30 \leq x_i \leq 30 \tag{22}$$

f_1-f_5 are unimodal functions, and f_6-f_{10} are multimodal functions where the number of local minima increases with the problem dimension. For example, the number of local minima of f_7 is about $10N$ in the given search space. Some parameters must be assigned to before LPPA is used to solve problems. In LPPA, $n \times N_c$ is equivalent to the population size in traditional GAs, so n can be chosen from 5 to 40, and N_c can be chosen from 2 to 10. In the following experiments, the parameters settings in LPPA are: $n = 20$, $N_c = 10$, $p_c = 0.85$, $p_m = 0.3$, $p_i = 0.3$.

3.2 Results and Comparison

A) Comparison between LPPA, APPA and OGA/Q on functions

OGA/Q[5] has good performances on numerical optimization problems. The termination criterion of LPPA, APPA and OGA/Q is to run 150 generations for each function. The results averaged over 50 trials are shown in Table 1, where $N=30$, except for f_6 with 100.

As can be seen, the mean number of evaluations of LPPA is the least, namely the computational cost is smaller than that of OGA/Q, although its mean function values and standard deviation of function values is worse than APPA[4] and OGA/Q. In all, LPPA is competent for the numerical optimization problems.

Table 1. Comparison between LPPA, APPA and OGA/Q on functions with 30 dimensions except for f_6 with 100

f	f_{min}	Mean number of function evaluations			Mean function value (Standard deviation of function value)		
		LPPA	APPA	OGA/Q	LPPA	APPA	OGA/Q
f_1	0	2,863	5,117	112,559	1.553×10^{-7} (3.232×10^{-12})	2.809×10^{-7} (2.969×10^{-7})	0 (0)
f_2	0	2,670	4,220	112,612	2.738×10^{-9} (5.164×10^{-16})	3.579×10^{-9} (3.362×10^{-9})	0 (0)
f_3	0	31,506	47,406	112,576	4.5776×10^{-11} (6.895×10^{-20})	3.826×10^{-10} (4.340×10^{-10})	0 (0)
f_4	0	1,455	1,534	62,687	0 (0)	0 (0)	0 (0)
f_5	0	14,025	24,261	112,652	5.450×10^{-4} (3.390×10^{-6})	4.808×10^{-4} (3.298×10^{-4})	6.301×10^{-3} (4.069×10^{-4})
f_6	-78.33236	5,034	11,541	245,930	-78.323 (1.525×10^{-4})	-78.33009 (8.381×10^{-4})	-78.3000296 (6.288×10^{-3})
f_7	0	1,995	4,657	224,710	0.02836 (0.059296)	1.106457×10^{-10} (1.359×10^{-10})	0 (0)
f_8	-12569.5	3,258	9,499	302,166	-12569 (0.041479)	-12569.49 (1.253×10^{-5})	-12569.4537 (6.447×10^{-4})
f_9	0	2,914	8,280	134,000	2.9712×10^{-5} (6.084×10^{-8})	5.129230×10^{-15} (3.463×10^{-15})	0 (0)
f_{10}	0	2,540	8,970	112,421	2.4974×10^{-4} (5.190×10^{-6})	1.953993×10^{-15} (2.398×10^{-15})	4.440×10^{-16} (3.989×10^{-17})

B) Performance of LPPA on multimodal functions with 20 ~ 1000 dimensions

Because the size of the search space and the number of local minima increase with the problem dimension, the higher the dimension is, the more difficult the problem is.

Therefore, this experiment studies the performance of LPPA on functions with 20 ~ 1000 dimension. Table 2 gives the mean number of function evaluations of LPPA averaged over 20 trials, and the required precision for test function is given in the Table 2 too.

APPA [4], AEA [6] and BGA [7] are also tested on f_7-f_{10} with 20, 100, 200, 400, 1000 dimensions. The comparison is made between LPPA, APPA, AEA and BGA, which is shown in Table 2 and 3. In the table, "/ " denotes that the algorithm did not do the experiment.

As can be seen, the number of evaluations of LPPA is slightly smaller than that of APPA, and much smaller than that of BGA for all the four functions. For f_7, when $n \leq 100$, the number of evaluations of LPPA is slightly greater than that of AEA, while $200 \leq n \leq 1000$, it is slightly smaller than that of AEA. For f_8, the number of evaluations of LPPA is greater than that of AEA at all dimensions. For both f_9 and f_{10}, the number of evaluations of LPPA is smaller than that of AEA at all dimensions. In general, LPPA obtains better solutions at a lower computational cost than BGA, AEA and APPA, and displays a good performance in solving high dimensional problems.

Table 2. Mean number of function evaluations of LPPA, APPA, AEA and BGA on $f_7 \sim f_8$ with 20 ~ 1000 dimensions

N	f_7 (1e-1)				f_8 (1e-1)			
	LPPA	APPA	AEA	BGA	LPPA	APPA	AEA	BGA
20	1,680	2,777	1,247	3,608	2,355	6,063	1,603	16,100
100	4,864	7,221	4,798	25,040	6,299	20,978	5,106	92,000
200	8,071	13,354	10,370	52,948	11,989	34,728	8,158	248,000
400	12,131	15,475	23,588	112,634	17,444	68,556	13,822	699,803
1000	20,293	37,250	46,024	337,570	29,629	116,120	23,687	/

Table 3. Mean number of function evaluations of LPPA, APPA, AEA and BGA on $f_9 \sim f_{10}$ with 20 ~ 1000 dimensions

N	f_9 (1e-4)				f_{10} (1e-3)			
	LPPA	APPA	AEA	BGA	LPPA	APPA	AEA	BGA
20	2,132	2,967	3,581	40,023	1,718	1,899	7,040	197,420
100	5,971	6,510	17,228	307,625	5,478	6,237	22,710	53,860
200	9,404	9,522	36,760	707,855	8,700	9,447	43,527	107,800
400	15,041	16,233	61,975	1600,920	13,274	15,407	78,216	220,820
1000	28,294	31,363	97,600	/	24,479	30,242	160,940	548,306

C) Performance of LPPA on multimodal functions with 100 ~ 10000 dimensions

In order to study the scalability of LPPA along the problem dimension further, in this experiment, LPPA is used to optimize $f_7 - f_{10}$ with higher dimensions. The problem dimension is increased from 100 to 10000.

In order to study the complexity of LPPA further, comparison between LPPA and APPA in the mean number of function evaluations for multimodal functions with 10000 dimensions is made, and the results averaged over 10 trials are shown in Table 4 and Fig 2.

As can be seen, the number of evaluations of APPA dramatically increases with the dimensions, and much greater than that of LPPA. In LPPA, for f_7, f_8, f_9 and f_{10}, the number of evaluations increases with the dimension, they are only 89,065, 199,116, 11,6130 and 120,450 respectively, even when dimensions increase to 10000. It can be considered that the number of evaluations of LPPA increases less than 20 with 1 dimension increasing of functions.

Table 4. Mean number of function evaluations of LPPA and APPA on $f_8 \sim f_{10}$ with 2000 ~ 10000 dimensions

N	f_7 (1e-1)		f_8 (1e-1)		f_9 (1e-4)		f_{10} (1e-3)	
	LPPA	APPA	LPPA	APPA	LPPA	APPA	LPPA	APPA
2000	**35,164**	43,956	**51,415**	157,200	**36,849**	56,306	**42,180**	45,896
5000	**52,690**	84,224	**110,560**	314,578	**77,844**	100,694	**67,469**	104,194
10000	**89,065**	150,580	**199,116**	/	**116,130**	147,044	**120,450**	146,930

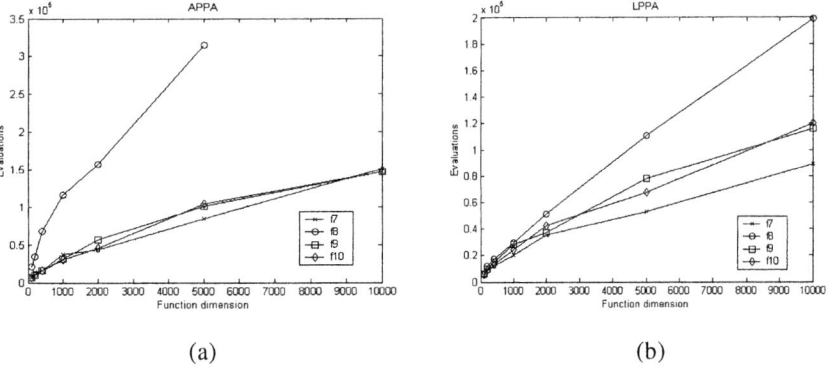

(a) (b)

Fig. 2. Comparison between LPPA and APPA on $f_7 - f_{10}$ with 100 ~ 10000 dimensions

In addition, it is indicated that the bigger clonal size can improve the diversity furthermore, as a result, the prematurity can be avoided effectively, but the number of function evaluations will be increased.

4 Conclusion

Based on immune clonal selection and Lamarckism, a new numerical optimization algorithm, LPPA, has been proposed in this paper. In Section 3, LPPA was tested on 10 benchmark functions and compared with 4 famous algorithms, APPA[4],

OGA/Q[5], AEA[6] and BGA[7]. The experiments on functions with 30 dimensions and 20-1000 dimensions indicated that LPPA outperforms the four algorithm. In order to study the scalability of LPPA along the problem dimension, LPPA was used to optimize the 10 functions with 100 ~ 10000 dimensions. The results indicated that LPPA can obtain high quality solutions at a low computation cost even for the functions with 10000 dimensions. For example, LPPA only used less than 100000 evaluations to optimize f_7.

To summarize, LPPA obtains a good performance function optimization. This benefits mainly from the model of Lamarckian Learning Operator, which means "Gain and Convey", and integrates the learning and evolution effectively.

Acknowledgment

The work was sponsored by the National Natural Science Foundation of China (No: 60133010) grants and the Natural Science Foundation of Shaanxi (No: 2004F29).

References

1. Goldberg, E.: Genetic Algorithms in Search Optimization & Machine Learning. Reading, MA: Addison – Wesley, 1989
2. Michalewicz, Z.: Genetic Algorithms + Data Structures = Evolution Programs. Berlin, Germany: Springer – Verlag, 1994
3. Dawkins, R.: The Blind Watchmaker. Norton, 1996
4. Du, H. F. Jiao, L. C. and Liu, R. C.: Adaptive Polyclonal Programming Algorithm with application. ICCIMA (2003) 350 – 355
5. Leung, Y.W. and Wang, Y. P.: An orthogonal genetic algorithm with quantization for global numerical optimization. IEEE Trans. Evol. Comput., vol.5, No.2 (2001) 41 -53
6. Pan, Z. J. and Kang, L. S.: The Adaptive Evolutionary Algorithms for Numerical Optimization. Proc. of Simulated Evolution and Learning (SEAL '96), Taejon, Korea, (1996) 53 – 60
7. Muhlenbein, H. and Schlierkamp– Vose, D.: Predictive models for the breeder genetic algorithm. Evol. Computat., vol. 1, No.1 (1993) 25 – 49

Coevolutionary Genetic Algorithms to Simulate the Immune System's Gene Libraries Evolution

Grazziela P. Figueredo[1], Luis A.V. de Carvalho[1], and Helio J.C. Barbosa[2]

[1] COPPE/UFRJ, Rio de Janeiro, RJ, Brazil
[2] LNCC/MCT, Petropolis RJ, Brazil

Abstract. Two binary-encoded models describing some aspects of the coevolution between an artificial immune system and a set of antigens have been proposed and analyzed. The first model has focused on the coevolution between antibodies generating gene libraries and antigens. In the second model, the coevolution involves a new population of self molecules whose function was to establish restrictions in the evolution of libraries' population. A coevolutionary genetic algorithm (CGA) was used to form adaptive niching inspired in the Coevolutionary Shared Niching strategy. Numerical experiments and conclusions are presented.

1 Introduction

This work proposes simulations of the dynamics between antigens and antibodies' library genes, inside artificial organisms, along the evolution of a species. Coevolutionary Computation has been chosen to implement the models studied. In gene libraries populations, a genetic algorithm (GA) was used to form adaptive niching based on the ideas of Goldberg and Wang [1]. Two models are described in Sections 2 and 3, respectively, which also present numerical experiments. The paper ends with Section 4 which discusses the results of our ongoing work.

2 The First Model

2.1 The Libraries Population's GA

Each individual in this first GA's population represents a simplified library which contains only three binary encoded segment groups V, D and J. Initially, the libraries have only one segment of each group and their initialization is entirely random. One example of an individual is shown in Figure 1. The junction between one segment of each group forms the genetic code for producing an antibody.

Decoding an individual here means to produce all of its potential antibodies repertory. This is done by making recombination between the individual library segments of V, D and J kind, in this order, as shown in Figure 2. The libraries recombination operator used was a crossover in which one of the segment groups

V: 000 001 110 111

D: 100 011 000 101 111 110 010

J: 111 110 010 011 100

Fig. 1. A library individual

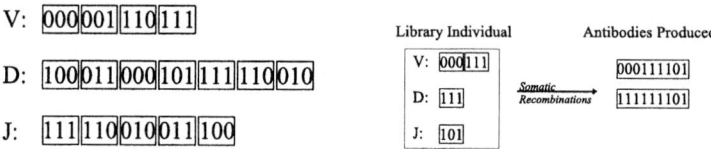

Fig. 2. Antibodies generation

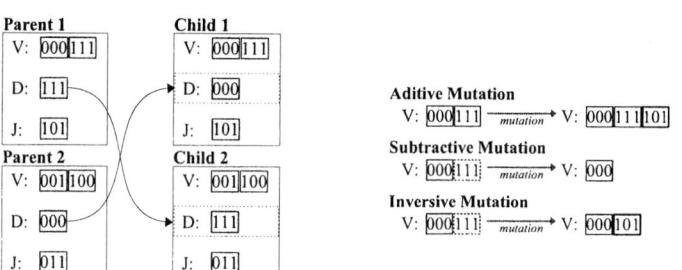

Fig. 3. Crossover operator

Fig. 4. Mutation operators

V, D, or J, is randomly chosen and exchanged between the parents, as shown in Figure 3. There are three kinds of mutation in the libraries GA. These mechanisms are illustrated in Figure 4.

The fitness of each library is given by its capacity of producing an antibody potential repertory capable of maximizing the neutralization of the antigens population. To neutralize an antigen, the antibody's paratope needs to bind an antigenic determinant in the pathogen's molecule. In the model, the antibody is constituted only by the paratope. The antigen can be larger than the antibody. Thus, there might be more than one region in the antigenic molecule where a set of antibodies could bind. An example is shown in Figure 5.

The capability of an antibody to neutralize an antigen is measured by means of a computational distance, known as matching function. Chromosomes are compared bitwise, and the matching value is determined by the longest complementary chain between them [2], as it can be seen in Figure 5. In the example of Figure 5, it was established that the necessary matching to consider a bind was of 100%.

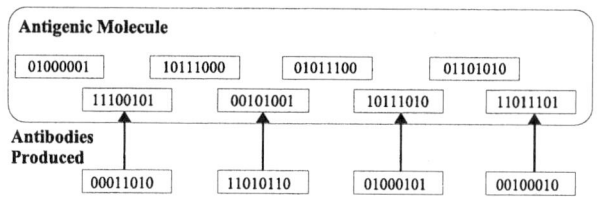

Fig. 5. An antigenic molecule and the correspondent binding antibodies

As more than one antibody could match a certain antigenic molecule, the pathogen can be seen as the owner of its complementary antibodies niche. In terms of the CSN, antigens and antibodies play the roles of the businessmen and clients, respectively. Each antibody is compared to an antigen, in order to establish which antigen is best neutralized and, consequently, which niche the antibody will belong to. The fitness of a library is measured by summing fitness from all of its produced antibodies.

2.2 The Antigens Population's GA

The GA operates in the antigens' population by making mutations on the individual's chromosome. If the mutation increases the antigen fitness, this change on the genetic material is kept. The antigen fitness is given by its capacity of aggression inside the organism. A mutation in the antigen's chromosome is made by randomly selecting and inverting a bit. The fitness calculation is similar to the one done for libraries. The difference is that the antibodies have to maximize matching in the niche, while antigens need to minimize it.

In our experiment, the parameters used for the libraries population GA were: 120 generations per epoch, 10 individuals in the population, elitism of 1 individual, 4 bits per gene segment and 85% of probability of crossover and mutation. The probabilities of application assigned to the additive, subtractive, and inversive mutations were, respectively, 20%, 10%, and 70%. The group of segments V, D, and J had the same chances of selection for mutation. The antigens GA used 400 generations, 200 individuals, 64 bits per chromosome and 85% of mutation probability. The number of recognized antigens along the generations is shown in the graphic of Figure 6.

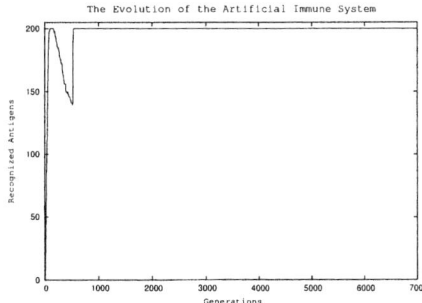
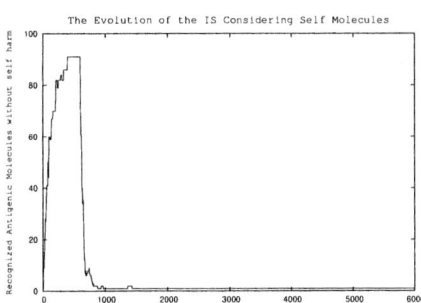

Fig. 6. First Model: The evolution of the IS

Fig. 7. Second Model: The evolution of the IS

3 The Second Model

This second model simulates IS tolerance by adding a new population representing self. Now, the libraries' population has to evolve maximizing the coverage of the antigens population and minimizing the attack of self molecules. To implement this new requirement, a penalization for those individuals that produce self-reactive antibodies is introduced. Such penalization is computed by dividing the antibodies fitness sum by the number of self molecules attacked. For the experiment, the libraries' GA used 600 generations per epoch. The other parameters assumed the same values used in the first model. The antigens' GA used 1500 generations per epoch, 100 individuals with chromosomes of 120 bits and mutation probability of 85%. The self population had size 50 and its molecules were represented by chromosomes of 12 bits. The results can be seen in Figure 7.

4 Conclusions

This paper has proposed two models describing some aspects of the evolution in an artificial immune system with some characteristics similar to the real biological systems. The first model has focused on the coevolution between an antibodies producing gene libraries population and a set of antigens. Results of this experiment showed that, as evolution proceeded, antibodies became much more adapted to the environment presented, being able to recognize any new mutated antigen that would appear in the population. Also, the real immune systems coverage stability was reached and an artificial system able to adapt and recognize any given binary segment has been created. In addition, the necessity and ability of a fast changing genetic mechanism to provide robustness to a biological species antibodies' genotype has been demonstrated. The improvement of the first model produced a second one with characteristics more similar to real immune systems. Now the evolution has involved a new group of strings that represented molecules belonging to the organism and against who the immune system could not activate defense mechanisms. The results obtained have shown that the antigens' evolution proceeded towards imitating self molecules bits sequences. As a result, antigens became invisible to the antibodies defense mechanisms pointing to the necessity of other means of protection. In real immune systems, these other means are constituted by T-cells.

References

1. David E. Goldberg and Liwei Wang: Adaptive Niching via Coevolutionary Sharing. Genetic Algorithms and Evolution Strategy in Engineering and Computer Science, John Wiley and Sons, Chichester. Ed. D. Quagliarella and J. Périaux and C. Poloni and G. Winter, 21-38, 1998.
2. S. Forrest, B. Javornik, R.E. Smith, and A.S. Perelson: Using genetic algorithms to explore pattern recognition in the immune system. Evolutionary Computation, Vol. 1, No. 3 (1993), pp.191-211

Clone Mind Evolution Algorithm[*]

Gang Xie, Xinying Xu, Keming Xie, and Zehua Chen

College of Information Engineering, Taiyuan University of Technology,
030024 Taiyuan, Shanxi, P.R. China
xiegangtut@yahoo.com.cn

Abstract. A new algorithm of evolutionary computing, which combines clone selective algorithm involved in artificial immunity system theory and mind evolution algorithm (MEA) proposed in reference [4], is presented in this paper. Based on similartaxis which is the one of MEA operators, some operators borne by the new algorithm including such as clone mutation, clone crossover, clone selection are also introduced. Then the clone mind evolution algorithm (CMEA) is developed by using the diversity principle of antigen-antibody. Not only can CMEA converge to globally optimal solution, but also it solve premature convergence problem efficiently. The simulating results of the representative evaluation function show that the problem of degeneration phenomenon existing in GA and MEA can be perfectly solved, and the rapidity of convergence is evidently improved by CMEA studied in the paper. In the example of the solution to the numerical problem, the search range of solution is expanded and the possibility of finding the optimal solution is increased.

1 Introduction

Artificial immune system (AIS) is an other research focus subsequently following cranial nerves (e.g. neural network) and evolutionary computing (e.g. GA), which is inspired by the biological immune system (BIS). BIS mechanics based research on computing model is concentrated on two main aspects: network model of AIS and immune learning algorithm. The former aims to construct various computing model, based on the clone selective theory of Bernet[1] and the unique network adjusting theory of Jernet[2], to imitate or explain immune phenomena by simulation experiments. The latter is focused on computing methods with stronger intentness or implement strategies based on existed system models. Clonal selection algorithm [3] that is presented by Castro, Kim, Du, etc. is one of outstanding achievement. The characteristics of memory, learning and evolution are utilized to implement the task such as machine learning or pattern recognition. Mind evolution algorithm (MEA)[4] that is a kind of evolution computing method has been applied in the field of intelligent control[5]. In this paper, how to utilize practicable clone selective behavior to design suitable clone selective optimal method in order to improving the optimal result of MEA is studied.

---

[*] Financed by Visiting Scholar Foundation of Shanxi Province, P. R. C. (2004-18) and Youth Science Foundations of Shanxi Province, P.R.C. (20041015).

2 Philosophy of MEA

MEA is a evolutionary method of learning by iterative computing, its main principles are as follows:

2.1 Population and Group

The set of all individuals is called a population. The population is divided into several groups, and there are two main classes of groups: the winner groups and the temporary groups.

2.2 Billboard

The billboards, which record the information of the individuals or the groups including thiers serial number, operation and score, provide the environment of information communication among the individuals or the groups. There are two kinds of billboards: one is the local billboard which is used to record information of individuals in each group; another is the global billboard which is used to record information of each group in the whole population.

2.3 Similartaxis and Dissimilation

Similartaxis means that some individuals of each group learn the information of superior individual in the same group, and each other compete until a winner individual comes forth. Along with the operation of similartaxis, some individuals produce several temporary groups in course of searching the whole solution space. If the scores of any temporary group are higher than of any mature winner group, the temporary group would replace the winner group and become a new winner group. This operation is called dissimilation.

2.4 Convergence

It can be proved by means of Markov chains that population of discrete state executed by similartaxis operator is convergent at the global optimal state with total probability. But because of localness of similartaxis, there is little probability that the local optimal state transfers to the global optimal state. In order to this transfer probability, it is necessary to introduce dissimilation operator [6].

3 Mechanism of Clone Selection Algorithm

Nowadays, most of researches on the intelligent systems revolve around the mechanism of inspiring and learning of person brain. But in the artificial intelligent methods, another kind of intelligent system-the biological immunity system, which is not obviously related to the manner in which brain behaves, is neglected. The clou of reference [7] is that antibody in cell surface as offspring of natural exists in the form of receptor, and can selectively react to antigen. The reaction, which takes place between antigen and receptor, can cause to clonal breeding of cell. So the great numbers of clonal cell own the identical specificity of antibody. Some of these clonal cells in which some cells differentiate to a generation of antibody cell, and others form immunity memory cell so as to attend the second immunity reaction later. Clone selective theory acts as an important enlightenment role for improving the performance of MEA, because of the clone selective course of antibody possesses learning, memory development, diversity of antibody, self-adaptive adjustment and such performance, so as to prevent the phenomenon of "prematurity" well, efficiently improve the rapidity of optimization and advance the quality of optimization result.

4 Clone Mind Evolutionary Algorithm

In general, the following steps of CMEA are made up of 6 key steps illustrated in figure 1.

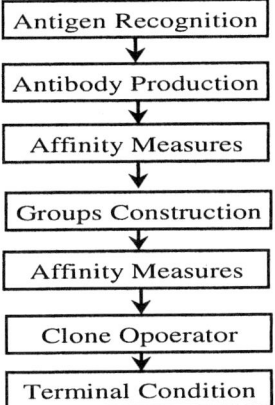

Fig. 1. Diagram of CMEA

It is well known that antigen, antibodies, affinity of antigen-antibody is respectively corresponded to the object function, optimal solution, and match degree of solution to the object function.

Step 1: Antigen recognition. Choose the target function and various constraints as the antigen of CMEA, then the immune system confirms that the antigen invades;

Step 2: Initial antibody production. While iterating at the first time, the antibody is produced at random in the whole solution space, or by means of activating memory cells. At the same time, the foregone antigen is removed, and M individuals from the database including the optimal antibody (optimal solution) are chosen to produce initial antibody groups;

Step 3: Affinity calculation. Separately calculate the affinity between antigen and antibody, and the affinity between antibody and antibody;

Step 4: Groups' construction. N individuals with supreme affinity are arranged in an order. For every individual with supreme affinity, k-1 individuals are randomly chosen among the remaining individuals, and are constructed to a group (the size of group is k). Thus N groups are produced by the identical operation to the N individual of supreme affinity;

Step 5: Calculate every individual affinity in each group again;

Step 6: According to clone operators, produce new group with the following steps:

1) **Clone:** choose A (m) individuals that own higher antibody-antigen affinity and lower antibody- antibody affinity, then regard them as cloned individuals and add clonal results to new groups.

2) **Clone mutation:** carry out clone mutation operation on the groups after completing clone operator. In order to reserve the original information of antibody population, do not operate mutation to A (m) individuals.

3) **Clone crossover:** choose A (n) individuals that have higher antibody-antibody affinity and lower antigen-antibody affinity, and uniformly code them. Then, execute crossover operator.

4) **Clone selection:** select M new individuals owning the highest affinity to form a new generation of population in order to keep the number of individuals. Meanwhile, other rejected individuals are deleted from groups.

Step 7: Terminal condition repeat step5 and step6, until satisfy termination condition (convergence criterion), optimal course end. In this paper, limited iteration times is adopted as termination condition. Choose the optimal individual as the result of algorithm.

5 Research Example

In order to verify the preceding analysis, numerical experimentation employing MEA, CMEA and GA are studied by the following classical testing functions.

1) $fit_1 = \sum_{i=1}^{3} x_i^2 \quad x_i \in [-5,5]$

The function is adopted for testing rapidity of convergence, the global minimum $f(0,0,0) = 0$.

2) $fit_2 = 100(x_1^2 - x_2)^2 + (1 - x_1)^2 \quad x_i \in [-5,5]$

The minimum point (0, 0) of this function locates at curved surface with a long and narrow paraboloid, so it is difficult to find the minimum. The function is used to test immaturity convergence.

3) $fit_3 = 0.5 + [\sin^2(x_1^2 + x_2^2)^{1/2} - 0.5]/[1 + 0.001(x_1^2 + x_2^2)]^2$

Minimum of this function is $fit_3(0,0)=0$. Within scope of 3.14 around (0, 0), there are many protuberant department that is the global suboptimal points. The function characteristic that is properties of strong oscillation and the global optimal point surrounded by the suboptimal global points make it is very difficult to find the global optimal solution.

In experiments, let $M=200$, there kinds of algorithms are respectively examined 100 times with evaluation function. But if the optimal solution is not improved within 10 times, then the calculating is terminal in advance. In every operation cycle, if the value of fitness is smaller than the threshold 0.0001, the algorithm is regarded as success, otherwise failure. The number of successful optimization is denoted as N_{TS}, and the number of failure is denoted as N_{TF}, where $N_{TS}+N_{TF}=100$. The sum of all successful iteration times divided by the successes times is the mean successful iteration times denoted as N_{MIS}. Table 1 shows test data.

Table 1. Optimization Result

evaluation function	algorithm	threshold	N_{TS}	N_{TF}	N_{MIS}	optimal evaluation value
fit_1	MEA		100	0	20.24	5.252053e-5
	CMEA		100	0	19.27	2.225179e-14
	GA		99	1	69.20	6.628564e-6
fit_2	MEA		84	16	79.37	1.864154e-4
	CMEA	0.0001	100	0	8.11	1.272805e-7
	GA		100	0	98.75	3.464789e-5
fit_3	MEA		4	96	77	9.172560e-5
	CMEA		100	0	11.86	2.947642e-14
	GA		82	18	42.63	1.096471e-6

Showed from experiment results, the searching and optimization ability of CMEA is greater than of MEA and GA. Especially, when the extreme point is surrounded by the local sub-extreme points, more embody the superiority of CMEA. Function fit_3 optimization result shows, in 100 times operations, MEA succeeds four only, and CMEA have 100% rate of success. The optimization result of CMEA is 10e-9 times more accurate than that of MEA.

6 Conclusions

Both CMEA and MEA belong to group search strategy, and emphasize the information exchanging among the individuals of population. So there are similarities between CMEA and MEA.

Both of them circularly proceed with a course that is "initial population production → dividing into smaller groups → calculating evaluation function → exchanging information among individuals of groups → producing a new generation of population". Population is divided into several groups to prevent information exchange among groups. So it is helpful for the population differentiation, for the maintenance of diversity and for the prevention of prematurely, eventually the optimal solution is obtained with greater probability.

Both of them inhere parallelism in essence so as to make it difficult to fall into the local minimum in searching process.

On the other hand, due to the introduced operators such as antigen recognition, clone, clone mutation, clone crossover, and clone selection etc., there are some difference between them as follows:

(1) Clone mutation operator does not affect on the optimal solution which is held in memory units. Thus it ensures to converge fast the global optimal solution;

(2) The considerable calculation is caused by affinity measure, including the affinity of the antibody-antigen and the affinity of antibody-antibody. But it does not influence the rapidity of convergence;

(3) By promoting or restraining the antibody production, the function of self-regulation is achieved, and the diversity of individuals is guaranteed. Considering both the local and global search ability, it is especially suitable to optimize the multimodal function;

(4) Mutation operator of MEA is replaced by clone crossover and clone mutation, thus it is sure to extend the search region and to ensure the convergence to the global optimal solution.

References

1. Burnet F M: The Clonal Selection Theory of Acquired Immunity. Cambridge University Press (1958)
2. Jerne N K: The immune system. Scientific American (1973), 229(1) 52–60
3. Castro L. N. D., Zuben F. J. V.: An evolutionary immune system for data clustering. Proceedings of Sixth Brazlilian Symulation on Neural Network (2000) 84-89
4. Sun C. Y., Xie K. M., Cheng M.Q.: Mind-Evolution-Based Machine Learning Framework and New Development. Journal of Taiyuan University of Technology (1999), 30(5): 453–457
5. Xie K. M., Du Y.G., Sun C. Y.: Application of the mind-evolution-based machine learning in mixture-ratio calculation of raw materials cement. Proceedings of the World Congress on Intelligent Control and Automation (WCICA) (2000). 132–134
6. Wang C. L., Xie K. M., Sun C. Y.: A Study of convergence of mind evolution based machine learning. Journal of computer research & development. (2000).37(7): 838–842
7. Zhou G.Y.: Principles of Immunology. Shanghai Press of Science and Technology Literature. (2000)

The Application of IMEA in Nonlinearity Correction of VCO Frequency Modulation[*]

Gaowei Yan, Jun Xie, and Keming Xie

College of Information Engineering, Taiyuan University of Technology,
Taiyuan, Shanxi, P.R. China 030024
yangaowei@tyut.edu.cn

Abstract. In this paper, Immune Mind Evolutionary Algorithm (IMEA) is introduced to correct the nonlinearity of frequency modulation (FM) of voltage controlled oscillator (VCO) in linear frequency modulation continuous wave (LFMCW) radar level gauge. Firstly, the FM voltage is divided into several subsections, then by using fast Fourier transform (FFT) for the beat frequency signals, the characteristic of the spectrum is distilled, and furthermore an evaluation function is constructed. IMEA is applied to optimize the endpoint coordinates of the subsections to get nonlinear curve of FM voltage so as to compensate for the nonlinearity of VCO. Experiments show that the proposed method has good correction performance with no requirement for additional hardware, and it can complete correction in a relative short time.

1 Introduction

Mind evolutionary algorithm (MEA) is a new type of evolution computing method which simulates evolution process of human's thoughts. Memory function and directional study mechanism are introduced so that the intelligence of the algorithm is improved. It has now been successfully applied in engineering areas[1,2]. However, it is still convergent to local optimal solutions in case of multi-peak problems.

Artificial immune algorithm is a new kind of intelligent computing method, which takes advantage of immune system of biology. Its significant features lie in the: diversity of antibody, adjustment mechanism of antibody concentration, immune memory characteristics, self-recognition ability of the antibody, and self-organization, self-learning ability[3,4]. The combination of the immune system with the MEA may greatly improve the performance of the traditional MEA, and the new algorithm in this paper is shortly called immune mind evolutionary algorithm (IMEA).

The nonlinearity of the frequency modulation (FM) of voltage controlled oscillator (VCO) is a headache problem in the design, manufacture and application of the linear frequency modulation continuous wave (LFMCW) radar level gauge. The beat frequency signal is no longer the idea single frequency signal, the spectrum width will be broadened, then the resolution of the LFMCW radar will be decreased, and so does the S/N ratio. Thus the computation accuracy will also be affected[5]. In this paper, IMEA is adopted to correct linearity of the frequency modulation of the VCO in the LFMCW radar.

---

[*] Supported by Shanxi Province Tackle Projects in Science and Technology (001043),Visiting Scholar Foundations Project (2004-18) of Shanxi Province, P.R. China.

2 Basic Thoughts of the FM Nonlinearity Correction of VCO

The LFMCW radar adopts periodic modulated voltage to control VCO so as to generate continuous wave signal $s(t)$ with bandwidth B. Suppose the initial control voltage $V(t)$ is a sawtooth wave $V(t)=V_0+V_m t/T$, which varies periodically within $[V_0, V_0+V_m]$, and T is the period. The relation of the output frequency signal of VCO and the stimulated voltage in a period can be expressed as follows:

$$f(t) = F[V(t)] = F_0 + KV_0 + \frac{KV_m t}{T} + E[V(t)] \stackrel{\Delta}{=} f_0 + Bt/T + e(t) \qquad (1)$$

Where $e(t)=E[V(t)]$ is the error function of frequency characteristic. It is a nonlinear frequency modulation (FM) when $e(t)\neq 0$. Literature[6] analyzes the approximate relation of the FM linearity and the distance resolution, and adopts the variation of spectrum bins to express the influence of the nonlinear FM on the broadened spectrum.

To eliminate $e(t)$ from equation (1), a nonlinear FM voltage can be used to compensate for the nonlinearity of VCO. The FM voltage curve can be divided into M subsections; there are $M+1$ ends—original spot, terminal spot and $M-1$ mid spots. Whereas the original and terminal spots are invariable, the mid ones are changeable. And the ends of each subsection vary in a limited area. Thereby the problem of correction is transformed to the optimization of the coordinates of these ends. Then, the curve of optimal nonlinear voltage is gained by joining each endpoint. By constructing proper fitness function, IMEA is adopted to optimize the changeable endpoints of the FM curve, so as to realize the linear correction.

3 Immune Mind Evolution Algorithm

The evolution groups of IMEA include: N_S superior subpopulation, N_T temporary subpopulation and a global billboard. Each subpopulation is composed of S_G individuals and a local billboard. Local billboard and the global billboard together realize memory function of the IMEA. There are two main advantages of IMEA: firstly, the winner in MEA is selected only by its higher score, however IMEA also considers diversity of the individuals. Secondly, common MEA in global competition in dissimilation process is also stimulated by individual score, which will cause local convergence, but IMEA in this stage will keep the diversity of the population by adopt concentration adjustment mechanism, which will help finding the global optimal value. The basic steps of the algorithm are listed below:

Step 1: Initialization. Take objective function and all kinds of restraint conditions as the antigen of the IMEA.

Step 2: Generate initial antibody. In the 1st generation, randomly scatter and evaluate each initial antibody in the solution space.

Step 3: Dissimilation process. Global competition. Compute affinity of the antibody and antigen of the winners recorded in the global billboard, the concentration of superior antibody. Select N_S-k antibodies from the winners by adopt concentration adjustment mechanism (accordingly, k is less than 3). Randomly scatter k individuals in the solution space, form N_S antibodies; and around each antibody, generate N_S subpopulations by normally distributed S_G antibodies with variance $\sigma_d = (H_d - L_d) / \theta$ (where, H_d, L_d are respectively upper and lower limit of the dth dimension variable, θ is a constant).

Step 4: Similartaxis process. Compete in subpopulation. Firstly, evaluate each antibody, then compute affinity of each antibody and antigen, and the concentration of each antibody. According to concentration adjustment mechanism, select a certain proportion superior antibodies from S_G individuals in each subpopulation, other antibodies will learn from the winners by MEA, Gaussian mutation is occurred to all antibodies after learning is finished, until the subpopulation is matured.

Step 5: Stop condition. Judge whether the stop condition is satisfied, if yes then stop, otherwise repeat step 3 to 5.

Setp 6: Output result, end.

4 The Nonlinear Correction of VCO Based on the IMEA

4.1 Nonlinear Correction Scheme

The center frequency of the Radar Gauge used in this paper is 9.5GHz, FM bandwidth is 0.7GHz, FM period is 0.7ms. TMS320VC5509 Digital Processor (DSP) is adopted, and system clock frequency is 120MHz. The FM voltage is divided into 6 segments, shown as Fig.3, there are 5 changeable endpoints, that means there are 10 variables need to be optimized. In the experiment, a metal slab is laid 2.5 meters away from the radar gauge, and the beat frequency signal is processed by fast Fourier transform (FFT). Compute fitness function which represent the system performance, and then look it as the antigen, the optimized changeable endpoints are the antibodies, thus the best coordinates of FM voltage curve are those antibodies who have the biggest affinity with the antigens.

Float encoding is used for individuals, each antibody is corresponding to a group of changeable endpoints in a FM voltage curve, 10 variables in 5 changeable endpoints are encoded and then they form an antibody string. To each antibody in the evolution computing, it can be changed into the coordinate (x_i, y_i) of the changeable endpoint after decoding, then link the coordinates of the start point, the changeable endpoints and endpoint, the FM voltage curve is obtained. After D/A converter, it will control VCO and then generate FM microwave signal. Homodyne beat frequency signal will be turned into digital series after A/D converter, and then its spectrum will be analyzed by DSP, later, the fitness function is computed, and thus the evaluation for the antibody is finished.

4.2 The Design of Fitness Function

The purpose of this paper is to reduce the extended spectrum brought by FM nonlinearities of VCO and restrain the fake peaks arose by nonlinearity and phase noise. Accordingly, the fitness function employed in this paper has the form of:

$$Fit = \alpha Fit_1 + \beta Fit_2$$

$$Fit_1 = \begin{cases} L_{initial} - l_n & L_{initial} \geq l_n \\ 0 & L_{initial} < l_n \end{cases} \quad (2)$$

$$Fit_2 = \frac{P_{max}}{P_1} + \frac{P_{max}}{P_2}$$

Where α and β are evaluating coefficients. Fit_1 denotes the evaluation to spectral spread. As limited with the dashed square in Fig.1, the number of the spectrum bins over 1/2 peak magnitude is used to evaluate the extended spectrum, $L_{initial}$ is the number before corrected. l_n is the number during the evolution. Considering some changeable ends randomly generated in initial stages of evolution might worsen the linearity, let $Fit_1=0$ when $L_{initial}<l_n$.

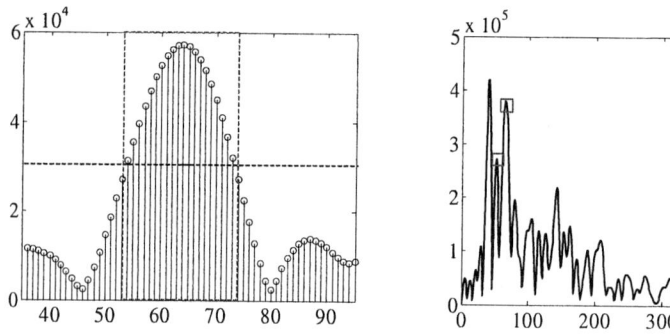
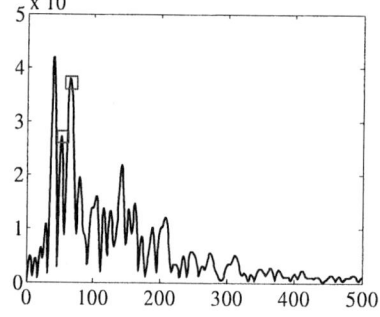

Fig. 1. Schema of the evaluation function Fit_1 **Fig. 2.** Schema of the evaluation function Fit_2

Fit_2 evaluates the restraint effect on the fake peaks beside the main peak. P_{max} is the magnitude value of the main peak after spectrum analysis. P_1 and P_2 respectively denotes the magnitude values of the two fake peaks closest to the main peak which is marked in square in Fig.2.

4.3 Experiment Results

The FM voltage curve after correction is shown in Fig.3, obviously, the curve is no longer a straight line. Fig.4(a) is the spectrum of beat frequency signal before correction, Fig.4(b) is that after correction. Fig.5(a), Fig.5(b) are the detailed part of main peak in Fig.4(a) and Fig.4(b). It can be seen from the figures that the spectrum extended by the FM nonlinearity of VCO is narrowed, the magnitude value of the main peak is strikingly improved, and the fake peaks along the main peak is effectively restrained, all of these prove the efficiency of the proposed method.

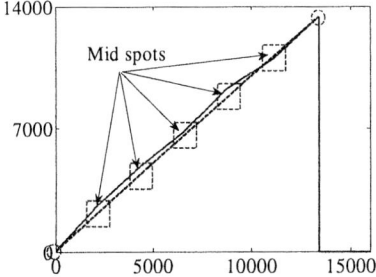

Fig. 3. FM voltage curve after nonlinearity correction. Dashed line is the line of linear FM voltage, solid curve is the result by the proposed method.

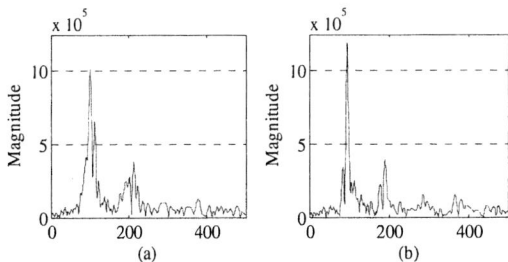

Fig. 4. The spectrum variation: (a) is before correction and (b) is after correction

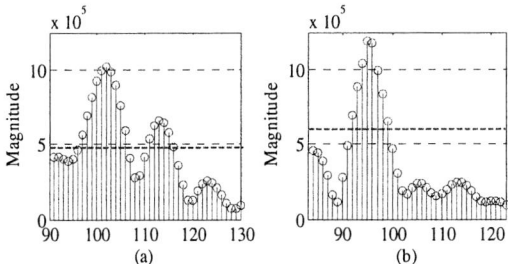

Fig. 5. The spectrum bins variation: (a) is before correction and (b) is after correction

To test the efficiency of the proposed method, some comparisons are done among genetic algorithm (GA), MEA, and IMEA. The time cost in the correction process is used to evaluate their performance, which is shown in Table 1. It can be seen from Table 1 that IMEA is better than the traditional GA and MEA no matter in shortest time or average time in repetitious corrections.

Table 1. The comparison of GA, MEA and IMEA

Algorithm	Correction time	Shortest time(s)	Average time(s)
GA	20	168	287
MEA	20	95	162
IMEA	20	65	156

5 Conclusion

The concentration mechanism and diversity of individuals in immune system are introduced into MEA, which help preserve the diversity of the population and overcome the premature of the MEA. By distilling the feature of the spectrum, and by constructing nonlinear evaluation function, IMEA is used to find the optimal nonlinear FM voltage curve to compensate the nonlinearity of the VCO of the LFMCW radar level gauge. The experiments results show that the proposed method can greatly improve the FM linearity of the VCO, effectively narrow the extended spectrum, and decrease the influence of phase noise on the distance resolution without any extra hardware circuit and any added measurement for the high frequency microwave. The proposed method is of low cost, and convenient for further applications.

References

1. Xie, K.M., Mou, C.H., Xie, G.: The multi-parameter combination mind-evolutionary-based machine learning and its application. Proceedings of 2000 IEEE International Conference on Systems, Man, and Cybernetics (SMC2000) (2000) 183-187
2. Xie, K.M., Du, Y.G., Sun, C.Y.: Application of the mind-evolution-based machine learning in mixture-ratio calculation of raw materials cement. Proceedings of the World Congress on Intelligent Control and Automation (2000) Vol.1:132-134
3. Dasgupta, D., Forrest, S.: Artificial Immune Systems in Industrial Applications. Proceedings of the Second International Conference on Intelligent Processing and Manufacturing of Materials (IPMM) (1999) 257-267
4. Dasgupta, D.: Artificial immune systems and their applications. Berlin: Springer-Verlag (1999)
5. Piper, S.O.: Homodyne FMCW Radar Range Resolution Effects with Sinusiodal Nonlinearity in the Frequency Sweep. IEEE International Radar Conference (1995) 563-567
6. Zhang, L.Z., Wang, X.G., Xiang, J.C.: The Relationship Between FM linearity and Range Resolution in FMCW Radar. Signal Processing (1999) Vol.15:93-97

A Quick Optimizing Multi-variables Method with Complex Target Function Based on the Principle of Artificial Immunology[*]

Gang Zhang, Keming Xie, Hongbo Guo, and Zhefeng Zhao

College of Information Engineering of Taiyuan University of technology,
P.R. China 030024

Abstract. Choice of ADPCM's step-size updating factors M has a sea capacity of computing that optimizes multi-variables with complex target function. There is the effective scheme such as GA or MEA but its convergence rate becomes too slowly in the neighborhood of peak value of multi-peak function to come away from local optimization. The Clone Mind Evolution Algorithm (CMEA) that introduces the clone operator to reserve the strong component of the weak individual to next iterativeness, which effect is very obvious with testing the typical function, comes into the MEA's similartaxis operator and is used to optimize ADPCM's 8 step-size updating factors. The experiment result shows that the CMEA's SNR has been reformed average 1.03dB every generation, which is exceeding MEA's by 0.4dB, in beginning five of iterativeness and overrun the MEA's from generation 5. Furthermore, the MEA's quantity of computing is equal to CMEA's by 1.67 times and the latter is of anti-prematurely.

1 Introduction

In researching speech or image signal processing, it is often dealt with that system is optimized in order to reform Signal Noise Ratio (SNR), which relation between the target function and any variable adjusted is too complex to describe it as linear or nonlinear or other any expression. Resolving this kind problem can depend on nothing of conventional optimization method besides trying repeatedly with human experience, which calculation quantity becomes very hugeness with the more number of variables or higher need of computing precision, upon a way that is said as the evolutionary computing GA or Mind Evolution Algorithm MEA [1]. However, the evolutionary computing only insists on keeping the best and discarding the weaker, and ignores that there is ability of becoming strong and anti-ebbing away in any individual itself which implies the information on the optimal solution and is highly closed to each other in the cost value of target function order after computing some generation of iterative. It is obviously unsuited to judge an individual either strong or weaker so as to keep back or away it only according to the result of the taxis, which always

---

[*] Financed by Chinese National Natural Science Foundations (60372058, 60374029) and Visiting Scholar Foundation of Shanxi Province P.R.China (2004-18) and Shanxi Province Natural Science Foundations (20041046).

results in taking a lot of invalid computing for similar individuals. It is a reason why the GA or MEA can speedily approximate the optimal solution in the beginning but its convergence rate becomes too slowly in the neighborhood of the peak value of multi-peak function to come away from local optimization. The literature [2] proposed The Clone Mind Evolution Algorithm (CMEA) that is composed of operators of clone mutation and clone crossover, in which the antigen, antibody, affinity of antigen-antibody are respectively corresponded to the target function, optimal solution, match degree of solution to the target function, by combining the MEA's similartaxis operator with the clone selective course based on the principle of artificial immunology. Testing it with the typical function, it is shown that the CMEA can overcome the degeneration phenomena appearing in GA and MEA while its convergence rate and precision are remarkably improved. In paper, it is handled with the CMEA to optimize ADPCM's 8 step-size updating factors in improved algorithm of G.728's gain quantifiedor[3][4]. The same result has been obtained. Next section is expression of the based elements; the section 3 describes how designs a gain quantifiedor of G.728 improved algorithm; the section 4 is experiment result and conclusion.

2 Clone Mind Evolutionary Algorithm

In general, the steps of CMEA are made up of 6 key steps as following:

Step1: antigen recognition Choose the target function and various constraints as the antigen of CMEA, then the immune system confirms itself invaded by the antigen;

Step2: initial antibody generation Beginning iteration, the antibodies are produced in random from the solution space, or activation of memory cells. While the foregone antigen is removed, and M individuals from the database including the optimal antibody (optimal solution) are picked up to produce initial antibody group;

Step3: affinity calculation Calculation of the affinity between antigen and antibody, and between antibody and antibody, separately;

Step4: groups construction N individuals with supreme affinity are arranged in an order. For every individual with supreme affinity, k-1 individuals are randomly produced among the remaining individuals, and are constructed to a group (the size of the group is k). Thus N groups are produced by the identical operation from the N individuals of supreme affinity;

Step5: According to clone operators, produce new group with the following steps:

1. *clone mutation*: Choose m individuals $A(m)$ that owns the affinity of higher antibody-antigen and lower antibody-antibody, carrying out n times of clone mutation operation for any A(m) then produces m groups $A(m,n)$.
2. *clone crossover*: Choose n individuals $A(n)$ that have the affinity of higher antibody-antibody and lower antigen-antibody, and uniformly code them. Then, execute crossover operator.

Step6: Terminal condition Repeat *step5* until the terminal condition (convergence criterion) is satisfied, optimal course end. In this paper, the limited times of iteration is adopted as terminal condition.

From *sept5*, it is found that criticizes the affinity of not only antigen-antibody (the match degree of a solution to the target function) but also antibody-antibody (the similarity of a solution to each other, which can be denoted as any distance) in the CMEA. A simple effective way is that discards some individuals owning the higher affinity of antigen-antibody as useless to get antibody saturation low. The affinity of the antibody-antibody indicates the difference between an individual and other, which is made reference to mutation or crossover. It is key point that distinguishes the CMEA from the MEA.

3 Optimizing Multi-variables with Complex Target Function

3.1 G.728's Exciting Gain

According to the formula (3-1), G.728 performs a process to search codebook.

$$D_{min} = \sigma^2(n) \| \hat{x}(n) - g_i H(n) y_j \|^2 \quad (3\text{-}1)$$

Where, $\sigma(n)$ is the estimation value of exciting gain, $\hat{x}(n)$ is the target vector adjusted by $\sigma(n)$, $H(n)$ is the unit impulse respond of short-term predictor, g_i is gain codeword y_j is shape codevector. Therefore, the minimum of the formula (3-1) equals the maximum follow

$$\hat{D}_{max} = 2 g_i P^T(n) y_j - g_i^2 E_j \quad (3\text{-}2)$$

Where, $P(n) = H^T \hat{x}(n)$, $E_j = \|Hy_j\|^2$. In formula (3-2), let $\partial \hat{D}_{max} / \partial g_j = 0$, we have

$$g_j = [P^T(n) y_j] / E_j \quad (3\text{-}3)$$

That is the exact value of gain codeword. To understand easy, let y_j is normalized unit power. Then (3-1) can be

$$D_{min} = \| x(n) - G_j(n) H(n) y_j(n) \|^2 \quad (3\text{-}4)$$

Where, $x(n) = \sigma(n)\hat{x}(n)$ and $G_j(n) = \sigma(n) g_j(n)$ are the target vector and the exact value of exciting gain not adjusted by gain, respectively. Let $\hat{G}_j(n)$ denote the value of quantified $G_j(n)$[4]. Let $g_j(n) = G_j(n)/\sigma(n)$, then gain prediction residual error in logarithm domain is

$$\log_2 g_j(n) = \log_2 G_j(n) - \log_2 \sigma(n) \quad (3\text{-}5)$$

Use $Q\{\bullet\}$ to denote the quantified value of the signal $\{\bullet\}$, then

$$\log_2 \hat{G}_j(n) = Q\{\log_2 g_j(n)\} + \log_2 \sigma(n) \quad (3\text{-}6)$$

3.2 Gain Adaptive Quantization (GAQ)

Fig.1 is the GAQ block scheme. The 4-bits index $I(n)$ obtained by quantifying $\log_2 g_j(n)$ will be sent to decoder. At the same time, $I(n)$ is decoded in local to obtain the quantified difference signal $\log_2 \hat{g}_j(n)$ which is added with the gain estimation value $\log_2 \sigma(n)$ to obtain the local rebuild signal $\log_2 \hat{G}_j(n)$.

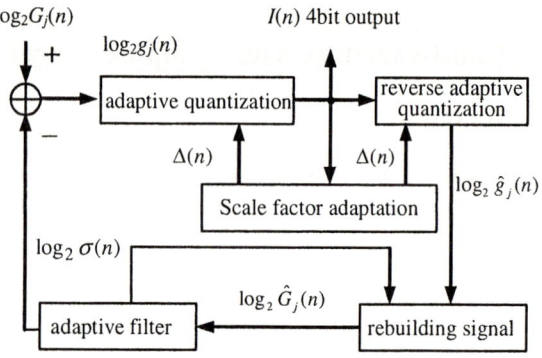

Fig. 1. Encoder block scheme

The adaptive predictor is a 12 order AR model and the quantization step $\Delta(n)$ is controlled adaptively by the input signal. The adaptive robust multiplying algorithm of quantization step can be described as: $\Delta(n) = M[I(n-1)]\Delta^{\beta}(n-1)$. Where $0 < \beta < 1$ is the attenuation factor increasing the robustness of quantifiedor. The step-size updating factors M is the function of last index $I(n-1)$[5]. The smaller the signal probability density is the bigger M is. For getting stable SNR as high as possible when signal energy is kept invariable, updating factors should satisfy $\prod_{i=0}^{7} M_i^{p_i} = 1$, where p_i ($i=0,...,7$) is occupancy probability of the leve-i. The parameters $W[I(k)]$ can be gotten with $W[I(k)] = 2^5 \log_2 M[I(k-1)]$. Then optimum factors M_i are selected according to the average segment SNR of quantization gain. The relation between M_i and SNR is too complex to describe it as linear or nonlinear or other any expression. Resolving this kind problem can depend on nothing of conventional optimization method besides trying repeatedly with human experience. There are 8 levels besides the sign with 4 bit of quantization, which means 8 of M_i variables shall been optimized. There are 10^4 different choices by controlling three efficient digitals of precision to a variable and as much as 10^{32} to 8 variables. For any choice, millions of speech samples shall be computed quantified SNR, which is so a sea capacity of operation as to nothing of efficiently optimization of M_i be found out until now. This paper, the trying calculation again and again by the seasoned computing engineer for 6 month, obtains 19.12dB of the quantified SNR.

4 Experiment and Conclusion

4.1 Optimizing M_i Scheme of the CMEA

It is step5 that distinguishes optimizing M_i scheme of the CMEA from it of the MEA. Choose 10 individuals (testing schemes) that owns the affinity (SNR) of higher antibody-antigen perform clone operation from the all individuals.

1. *clone mutation*: From 10 individuals ahead of other in the taxis, pick up 5 odd number of the individuals in which neighborhood 16 new individuals are produced in random with the normal distribution, totaling 85 individuals.
2. *clone crossover*: For N individuals of 8 variables, the coding algorithm of the clone crossover is expressed as:

The individual i is denoted $m_i=\{ m_{i,0},.., m_{i,j},.., m_{i,7} \}$ $i=0,1,.., N-1$, there $m_{i,j}$ is the value of the variable j of individual m_i. There are N^8 difference new schemes (new individuals) generated by clone crossover. A new individual corresponds only to a N-notation number of 8 digitals k ($0 \leq k \leq N^8-1$), and k is said as the code of new individual by the clone crossover. Writing $k=\{k_0,.., k_j,.., k_7\}$, there $0 \leq k_j \leq N-1$, then the new individual corresponds to a code k is:

$$\{ m_{k_0,0}, m_{k_1,1}, ..., m_{k_j,j}, ..., m_{k_7,7} \} \tag{4-1}$$

In this paper, get $N=2$ run clone crossover, there are $2^8 = 256$ difference new individuals generated by individual 2 and 4. Them are incorporated 85 individuals of clone mutation, totaling 341 individuals, as the members of next iterative.

The MEA algorithm has also been tested with same speech data. Leave 10 individuals ahead of other in the taxis among which every one of 8 individuals of the forepart are performed with the similartaxis operator and 64 new individuals are produced, totaling 522 individuals, as the members of next iterative.

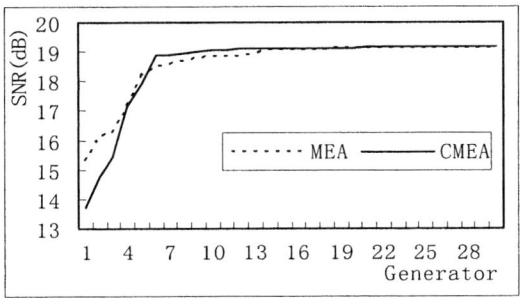

Fig. 2. Convergence curves between CME and MEA

Table 1. The Portion of The Iterative Results

Scheme	0s	1s	3s	5s	18s	19s	20s	30s
MEA	15.31	16.15	17.12	18.49	19.119	19.119	19.119	19.119
CMEA	13.72	14.76	17.12	18.89	19.123	19.123	19.15	19.15

4.2 The Results and Conclusion

With 1.1 million of gain signals produced from 5.5 million of speech samples about 11.5 minutes of vocal material by the half of male's and female's, the MEA and the CMEA has been respectively executed for 30 generations by getting primal individuals in random. The Fig.2 and Tab.1 are their convergence curves and the portion of the iterative results, separately. It can be seen from Tab.1 that the CMEA's SNR has being overrun the MEA's from generation 5. In beginning 5 generations of iterativeness, the rise of the CMEA's SNR and the MEA's are 5.169dB and 3.1736dB, which are averagely reformed 1.03dB and 0.63dB every generation, respectively. So the CMEA's initial convergence is better than the MEA's. After 20 generations of iterativeness, the CMEA's SNR is steady of 19.1462dB, higher than the result of human calculation and the MEA's is steady of 19.1185dB ahead of 2 generations, lower than it. Furthermore, there respectively is 522 and 341 individuals deal with every iterativeness, so the MEA's quantity of computing is equal to CMEA's by 1.67 times and the latter is of anti-prematurely.

References

1. Xie, K.M., Du. Y.G., Sun. C.Y.: Application of the mind-evolution-based machine learning in mixture-ratio calculation of raw materials cement. Proceedings of WCICA, Vol.1. (2000) 132–134
2. Gang, X., Xu., X. Y.,: Clone Mind Evolution Algorithm. The First International Conference on Natural Computation (ICNC'05), Changsha, China.
3. Huangfu, L.Y.: Improvement on G.728 Recommendation and Research on Low Rate LD-CELP Algorithm. Taiyuan University of Technology Master's Dissertation, (2002)
4. Zhang, G., Xie, K.M., Zhang, X.Y., Huangfu, L.Y.: Optimizing Gain Codebook of LD-CELP. Proceeding of ICASSP, Vol.2. (2003)149-152
5. Jayant, N.S.: Adaptive Quantization with a One-word memory. Bell Syst.Tech.J, Vol.52. (1973)1119-1144

Operator Dynamics in Molecular Biology

Tsuyoshi Kato

Department of Mathematics, Faculty of Science,
Kyoto University, Kyoto 606-8502, Japan

Abstract. In this paper we propose one way of mathematical formulation of structure of molecular activity from operator algebraic view points.

1 Introduction

Recent develpment of molecular biology revealed some mathematical nature of the structure of genes. Basic elements of genes are DNA, which are (double helixed) sequences consisted by four bases, $X = \{A, T, G, C\}$. A primary structure of genes is just a finite sequence of X. There are higher structures, at least until fourth ones. These are related to folding of proteins, which reflects some phisical force.

One way to represent molecular biology is a mathematical formulation of molecular activity of life. Here we will use algebra A as a box which contains all informations in the formulation. Multiplication of elements of A corresponds to composition of functions of genes. Here one will use involutive algebras, in particular C^* ones, and will represent phisical states by vectors in A.

Frist we will fix a set $X = \{X_1, \ldots, X_n, \ldots\} \subset A$, whose elements will consist of *primary structure*. A primary structure is just a sequence of finite length by elements of X:
$$V = v_1 v_2 \ldots v_l, \quad v_i \in X.$$

Then we will express higher structure of V by elements $a_1, \ldots, a_{l+1} \in A$ where we will force *shift relation* as:

$$a_i a_{i+1}^* = v_i, \quad i = 1, 2, \ldots, l.$$

Combining these, we will express total structure as:

$$V = a_1[v_1]a_2[v_2] \ldots a_l[v_l]a_{l+1}.$$

We will call this as a *m-dna sequence*. The sequence $(a_1, \ldots, a_{l+1})$ will be called as a *state set* which should represent higher structures. State sets will be more flexible than the primary sets. For example folding of proteins can change by phisical force, like catalyzing as ensymes. The energy of the state at v_i is defined as:
$$\text{trace } a_i a_i^* \in \mathbf{R} \cup \infty.$$

Thanks to functions of replication of genes, molecular lives are very active during its total life. Here we will introduce *infinitely many reflectivity* on m-dna sequences which represents possibility of replication. There are sufficiently many common operations which are shared among all lives. The aim here is, first to formulate these operations whose results are also required to be infinitely many reflective.

One of the main aim of this direction is to study structures of systems of families of these sequences. Along the direction in this paper, we have formulated metabolisms in [K1], and reconstructed some basic structures of Glycolysis, using particular choice of X, consisted by shift operators and projections. A fundamental problem will be to seek for primitive elements (metabolism) which can grow to Glycolysis.

This study arose from a question how to express functions of ensymes systematically, which is very close to a question how to represent shapes of proteins. Functions of proteins make sense only inside interaction systems where they live. For furthur developments, one may try to understand how systems grow up when one is given families of operatros randomly. One of the basic questions in molecular biology will be how to understand pattern formation in macro scale from micro level. A related problem is to study stability of systems under deformations of operators. One direction will be to construct some functionals over operators which correspond to some entropies.

In this paper 2×2 matrices will appear, and we will denote diagnonal matrices $A = (a_{i,j})$ by diag (a,b). For anti-diagonal matrices, we will denote antidiag (a,b) where $a = a_{2,1}$ and $b = a_{1,2}$.

This work is essentially a half part of [K1] which was done during his stay at IHES, where he would be very thankful for their hospitality. In particular he would like to express his gratitude to Professor Misha Gromov for encouragement, from whom he has received many stimulation and to the organizers of stimulating seminars on mathematical aspects of molecular biology held at the institut Henri Poincar'e.

2 M-DNA Sequences and Mutation

Let A be a (non commutative) algebra with involution $*$. Let us choose subsets:
  (1) $I = \{s_1, \ldots, s_m\} \subset A$ and
  (2) $X = \{X_1, \ldots, X_n, \ldots\} \subset A$. We say that I is the initial sets and X is the primary sets. We will say that (A, I, X) as a *m-dna data*.

A *m-dna sequence* is a finite length string $V = X_1 X_2 \ldots X_l$, where X_i are in X with extra structures described below. Both sides of each X_i are assigned with elements a_i and a_{i+1} in A and $a_1 \in I$ which satisfy the *shift relation*:

$$X_1 = a_1 a_2^*, \quad \ldots \quad X_i = a_i a_{i+1}^*, \quad \ldots$$

We will denote these data as:

$$V = a_1[X_1]a_2[X_2]\ldots a_l[X_l]a_{l+1}.$$

Usually one assumes $I = \{id\}$.

Let $W = X_1 \ldots X_l$ be a string which are assigned with only a sequence of primary sets. Then one can assign m-dna sequences $V = a_1[X_1]a_2[X_2]\ldots a_l[X_l]a_{l+1}$ if there exists a family $\{a_i\}_i$ satisfying the shift relation. We will denote the set of m-dna sequences with respect to W as:

$$V(W, A) = \{V = a_1[X_1]a_2[X_2]\ldots a_l[X_l]a_{l+1} : m - \text{dna sequence }\}.$$

We will say $W = X_1 \ldots X_l$ is a *primary sequence* with respect to V.

Example 1. Let $V = a_1|X_1|a_2|\ldots|X_l|a_{l+1}$ be a m-dna sequence. Then $V^* \equiv a_{l+1}|X_l^*|a_l|\ldots a_2|X_1^*|a_1$ is also a m-dna sequence. We call this assignment $V \to V^*$ as an *involution*. We will say that V is *palindrome*, if $V = V^*$.

2.A Point Mutation: Let $V = a_1|X_1|a_2\ldots a_l|X_l|a_{l+1}$ be a m-dna sequence. A *point mutation* of V is another m-dna sequence:

$$V' = a_1'|X_1\ldots a_{k-1}'|a_k'|X_k'|a_{k+1}'|X_{k+1}\ldots a_{l+1}'$$

(V' differs from V in primary sequences only by replacing X_k by another X_k').

Example 2. Let P and P' be projections on a Hilbert space where the equality $PP' = P'$ holds. Then $V = id[id]id[P]P$ is a m-dna sequence. $V' = id[id]id[P']P'$ is a mutation of V.

2.B Intron: Let V be a m-dna sequence. Supose the string splits into three parts:

$$V = V_1 \cup V_2 \cup V_3 \tag{1}$$
$$= a_1|X_1|a_2|X_2\ldots a_{l_1}|X_{l_1}|a_{l_1+1} \cup a_{l_1+1}|X_{l_1+1}|a_{l_1+2}|X_{l_1+2}\ldots \tag{2}$$
$$a_{l_2}|X_{l_2}|a_{l_2+1} \cup a_{l_2+1}|X_{l_2+1}|a_{l_2+2}|X_{l_2+2}\ldots a_l|X_l|a_{l+1}. \tag{3}$$

An *elimination* of V_2 from V consists of another m-dna sequence:

$$V_1 \cup V_3 = a_1'|X_1|a_2'|X_2\ldots a_{l_1}'|X_{l_1}X_{l_2+1}|a_{l_2+2}'|X_{l_2+2}\ldots a_l'|X_l|a_{l+1}'.$$

Let us say that for a m-dna sequence V, V_2 is a *pre-intron*, if $V_1 \cup V_3$ exists. $V_1 \cup V_3$ is called as a *spliced m-dna sequence*.

2.C Amplification: Let us take m-dna sequences $V = a_1|X_1|a_2\ldots a_{l-1}|X_{l-1}|a_l$ and $V' = b_1[Y_1]b_2[Y_2]\ldots[Y_k]b_{k+1}$. Suppose that there is a primary element Y such that:

$$V[Y]V' = a_1'[X_1]a_2'\ldots a_{l-1}'[X_{l-1}]a_l'[Y]b_1'[Y_1]b_2\ldots b_{k-1}'[Y_{k-1}]b_k'$$

consists of also a m-dna sequence. We will say that $V[Y]V'$ is an *amplification* and Y is a *connecting element*.

Let us take two m-dna sequences V and V'. Suppose there is connecting element Y which makes an amplification $V|Y|V'$. We will say that this mutation is *non commutative*, if $V'|Y|V$ does not admit any m-dna sequence.

Example 3. Let P, P', P'' be projections satisfying $PP' = P'$ and $P'P'' = P''$. Let us consider:

$$V = id|P|P, \quad V' = id|P''|P'', \quad Y = id|P'|P', \tag{4}$$
$$V|Y|V' = id[P]P[P']P'[P'']P'', \quad V'|Y'|V = id[P'']P''[P']P'[P]P. \tag{5}$$

$V|Y|V'$ satisfies shift relation, but $V'|Y'|V$ does not when $P'' \neq P'$.

2.D Frame Shift: Let $V = a_1|X_1|a_2|\ldots a_l|X_l|a_{l+1}$ be a m-dna sequence, and $u \in A$ be a unitary, $uu^* = $ id. Then $V(u) = a_2u|X_1|a_3u|\ldots|a_lu|X_{l-1}|a_{l+1}u$ is also a m-dna sequence, and we will say that V' is a *frame shift* of V.

Example 4. Let $V = a_1|X_1|a_2|\ldots a_l|X_l|a_{l+1}$ be a m-dna sequence, and take a unitary $\sigma \in A$ with $\sigma^3 = $ id. Then one considers another m-dna sequence:

$$\tilde{V} = \text{diag }(\sigma, a_1)[\text{diag }(\sigma^*, X_1)]\text{diag }(\sigma^2, a_2)[\text{diag }(\sigma^*, X_2)]\text{diag }(1, a_3) \tag{6}$$
$$[\text{diag }(\sigma^*, X_3)]\text{diag }(\sigma, a_4)[\text{diag }(\sigma^*, X_4)]\text{diag }(\sigma^2, a_5)[\text{diag }(\sigma^*, X_5)]\ldots \tag{7}$$

Now let us choose $u = \text{diag }(\sigma, 1)$. Then $\tilde{V}(u)$ expresses frame shift on *codon correspondence* between DNA (RNA) and amino-acids.

2.E Inequal Crossing Over: Let $V = V_1V_2$ and $V' = V_1'V_2'$ be two m-dna sequences with primary sequences as $(X_1('),\ldots,X_{l(')}('),Y_1('),\ldots,Y_{k(')}('))$ respectively. If both of another primary sequences $V_1V_2' = (X_1,\ldots,X_l,Y_1',\ldots,Y_{k'}')$ and $V_1'V_2 = (X_1',\ldots,X_{l'}',Y_1,\ldots,Y_k)$ also admit m-dna sequences U and U' respectively, then we will say that U and U' as *inequal crossing over* of V and V'.

2.F System of Mutations: A system of mutation is a finite set **S** where any element $s \in \mathbf{S}$ represents some operation described from 2.A to 2.E. Let $\bar{V}$ be a set of m-dna sequences. Then $\mathbf{S}(\bar{V})$ gives another set of m-dna sequences. One may iterate this process as:

$$\bar{V} \subset \mathbf{S}(\bar{V}) \subset \mathbf{S}^2(\bar{V}) \subset \mathbf{S}^3(\bar{V}) \subset \ldots$$

This will represent a simple model of *evolution*.

Example 5. Let $M_n(\mathbf{C})$ be the set of $n \times n$ complex matrices, and put $M_\infty(\mathbf{C}) = \lim_n M_n(\mathbf{C})$. Suppose the primary sets $X = \{X_1,\ldots,X_n,\ldots\} \subset M_\infty(\mathbf{C})$. Then we will call X as a *finite type*. Any set $\bar{V}$ whose primary sets consistes of finite type will be also called as finite type.

Let **S** be the set of $2.A, 2.B, 2.C, 2.E$. Then N-th stage of evolution of $\bar{V}$ is also of finite type for any $N \geq 0$.

3 Replication

3.A Replication: Suppose the algebra A is a closed $*$ subalgebra of $B(H)$, where H is a separable Hilbert space. Let us say that an operator $a \in A$ is replicable, if there is a unitary operator $U : H \cong H \oplus H$ satisfying:

$$UaU^* = \text{diag}\,(a', a'').$$

We will say that a'' is a *reflective element*. Reflective elements are not unique. Let $X = \{X_1, \ldots, X_l, \ldots\}$ be the primary set. In the following, we will assume that X is *closed* under replication, in the sense that any X_i has a unitary U satisfying $UX_iU^* = \text{diag}(X_j, X_k)$ for some j, k.

Let us take a m-dna data (A, I, X) where A is as above, and I and X are both consisted by replicable elements. Let us denote by Y_i as reflective elements of X_i. Let us take a m-dna sequence $V = a_1|X_1|a_2|X_2 \ldots a_l|X_l|a_{l+1}$. A *replication* of V is another m-dna sequence $b_1|Y_1|b_2|\ldots b_l|Y_l|b_{l+1}$ where each Y_i is a reflective element of X_i, using the same unitary U for all i.

Remark 3.1: (1) Suppose there are no invariant subspace for $a \in A$, and so no non trivial splitting as above. In this case, one replaces a by $\text{diag}(a, a, \ldots)$ acting on $H \oplus H \oplus \ldots$ Then the latter splits as $\text{diag}(a, a, \ldots) \oplus \text{diag}(a, a, \ldots)$. Then even though $\text{diag}(a, a, \ldots)$ contains the same information as a, this allows to make replication. (but the algebra A becomes much larger). In later examples, one assumes when a primary sequence $(X_1, \ldots, X_l)$ admits a m-dna sequence, then it always can make replication.

(2) Here one will only consider single sequences, even though in practice when genes make replication, the *double helix structure* plays an important role.

Example 6. (1) Let us take an orthonormal basis $H = \{v_0, v_1, v_2, \ldots\}$ and an unitary $U_0(v_{2i}) = v_i + 0, U_0(v_{2i+1}) = 0 + v_i \in H \oplus H$. Then $R: v_i \to v_{i+2}$ is replicable.

(2) Let us modify U_0 above slightly, and define $U_0(2i, 0)$ by the following:

$$U_0(2i, 0)(v_k) : \{v_{2i} + 0 \;,\; k = 2i, \quad v_i + 0, \; k = 4i, \tag{8}$$
$$v_j + 0, \; 2j, j \neq i, 2i, \quad 0 + v_j, \; k = 2j+1\}. \tag{9}$$

Then $U_0(2i, 0)$ are all unitary and satisfy $U_0(2i, 0)(v_{2i}) = v_{2i}$. Let $P(2i, 0)$ be the projection to v_{2i}, $P(2i, 0)(v_{2i}) = v_{2i}$. Then clearly $P(2i, 0)$ are all replicable. One can obtain $P(i, j)$ similarly.

(3) Let us take a Hilbert space H and its basis $\{\ldots, v_{-l}, \ldots, v_0, v_1, v_2, \ldots\}$. Let us put shift operators as follows:

$$Q: \{v_{2i+1} \mapsto v_{2i+3} \quad v_{2i} \mapsto v_{2i+4}\}, \tag{10}$$
$$P: v_i \mapsto v_{i+1}, \quad R = P^2: v_i \mapsto v_{i+2}. \tag{11}$$

Let us consider two m-dna sequences:

(1) $id[P^*]P[Q]Q'$, (2) $id[R^*]R[Q]R'$.

Using U_0 above, these have replications as follows:

(1) diag $(1,1)$[antidiag $(P^*, 1)$]antidiag $(1, P)$[diag (R, P)]antidiag (P^*, P^*).

Thus (1) is not reflective. For (2), we have a splitting:

(2) diag $(1,1)$[diag (P^*, P^*)]diag (P, P)[diag (R, P)]diag $(P^*, 1)$.

Thus the reflective element is $id[P^*]P[P]id$ (parindrome) which also consists of a m-dna sequence. The second stage of replication is as follows:

(2)′ diag $(1,1)$[antidiag $(P^*,1)$]antidiag $(1,P)$[antidiag $(1,P)$]diag $(1,1)$.

Thus the above reflective element is not secondary reflective. Thus the sequence (1) cannot replicate. (2) can do only once.

3.B Iterated Replication: Let $X' = (X_1, \ldots, X_l)$ be a primary sequence. Let us choose an isomorphism $U : H \cong H \oplus H$ with $UX_iU^* = \text{diag}(X_i(1)', X_i(1))$. If one can find another unitary U_1 as above with a decomposition $U_1 X_i(1)(U_1)^* = \text{diag}(X_i(2)', X_i(2))$, we say that $X_i(2)$ is a *secondary reflection element*. One may iterate this process, and find seccesively $U_2, U_3, \ldots$ and $X_i(2), X_i(3), \ldots$

Recall $V(X', A)$ in section 1. Let $V = a_1|X_1|a_2 \ldots a_l|X_l|a_{l+1}$ be a m-dna sequence. Then V is *infinitely many reflective*, if $V((X_1(i), \ldots, X_l(i)), A)$ are non empty for all i.

Example 7. Let us choose arbitrarilry a family $\{X_0, X_1, \ldots\} \subset X$, choose any isomorphism $H \cong \text{closure } \oplus_{i=0}^{\infty} H_i$ where H_i are all the same Hilbert spaces. Passing through this, one obtains an operator $X' = \text{diag}(X_0, X_1, \ldots)$ acting on H. Then one naturally gets a reflective element $X_1' \equiv \text{diag}(X_1, X_2, \ldots)$. As a secondary reflective element, one gets $X_2' \equiv \text{diag}(X_2, X_3, \ldots)$. Iterating one obtains n-th reflective element $X_n' \equiv \text{diag}(X_n, X_{n+1}, \ldots)$. Thus the realizing problem of reflective elements has a trivial solution.

Similarly choose any family $\{\ldots, X_{-l}, \ldots, X_0, X_1, \ldots\}$ and an isomorphism $H \cong \text{closure } \oplus_{i=-\infty}^{\infty} H_i$. In the both sides case also, the realizing problem has a trivial solution, from an operator $X'' = \text{diag}(\ldots, X_0, X_1, \ldots)$.

Let us take a unitary $U : H \cong H = \text{closure } \oplus H_i$, and choose any vectors $v_i \in H_i$ and $v_j \in H_j$, $i < j$. Then we will say that U *preserves the order* on (v_i, v_j), if there is a pair $i' < j'$ with $U(v_i) \in H_{i'}$ and $U(v_j) \in H_{j'}$.

Now let $\{\ldots, X_{-l}, \ldots, X_0, X_1, \ldots\}$ be as above, and consider one side and both sides sequences:

$$X' = (X_{i_0}, X_{i_1}, \ldots) \in B(H) = B(\text{closure } \oplus_{i=0}^{\infty} H_i), \qquad (12)$$
$$X'' = (\ldots, X_{i_{-l}}, \ldots, X_{i_0}, X_{i_1}, \ldots) \in B(H) = B(\text{closure } \oplus_{i=-\infty}^{\infty} H_i). \qquad (13)$$

where the indices $I' = \{i_0, i_1 \ldots\}, I'' = \{\ldots, i_{-l}, \ldots, i_0, i_1, \ldots\} \subset \{0, 1, 2, \ldots\}$ satisfy the followings:

(1) each $l \in \{0, 1, 2, \ldots\}$ appears infinitely many times in both of I' and I'' in the positive direction, and
(2) for a sufficiently large j_0, $i = 0$ for all $i \leq -j_0$ in I''.

Let us consider a problem to seek for a unitary $U : H \cong H$ satisfying the following:

(1) $U^* X' U = \text{diag}(X_0', X_1')$ where X_0 does not appear in X_1',
(2) $X_0' = X'$, and

(3) for any i_l, i_k in X'_m component, U preserves the order between H_{i_l} and H_{i_k} for $m = 0, 1$ respectively.

We will call such an operator as an *order preserving separating unitary*. Notice that once a family $\{X_i\}_i$ is fixed, then X' and X'' are expressed as one side or both sides sequences by $\{0, 1, \ldots\}$ respectively.

An unexpected answer is that (1) in one side case, there are always no order preserving separating unitary, and (2) in both sides case, it always exists. In terms of an expression of numbers, this is the following lemma:

Lemma 1. *Let $X' = (x_0, x_1, \ldots)$ be a one side sequence in $\{0, 1, \ldots\}$. Then there are no division of X' into two sequences $X' = Y \cup Z$ ($Y = (x_{m(l)})$ and $Z = (x_{n(l)})$ with $\mathbf{N} = \{m(l)\}_l \cup \{n(l)\}_l$) such that*

(1) both of Y and Z consist of infinite sequences and they are order preserving,

(2) $Y = X'$ as sequences and (3) Z does not contain 0.

Let X'' be a both side sequence. Then there is a division of X'' into two sequences satisfying (1), (2) and (3) above.

Proof: This can be seen from the next two examples. Let us consider $X'' = (\ldots, 0, 0, 0, 1, 0, 1, 2, 0, 1, 2, 3, \ldots)$. Then one can divide as:

$$X'' = (\ldots, 0, 0, 1, 0, 1, 2, 0, 1, 2, 3, \ldots) \cup (1, 2, 3, \ldots).$$

In the case $X' = (0, 0, 1, 0, 1, 2, 0, 1, 2, 3, \ldots)$, there are no such division.

Notice that automorphism groups of one or two sides subshift of finite types have mutually very different structures ([Ki]).

4 Ensyme

Ensymes play roles to activate or disactivate functions of genes. They can find particular genes to which they catalyze. Then a particular domain of ensymes (activating domain) attaches to domains of genes. For this, higher dimensional structures of genes are very important.

Let us take two m-dna sequences $V = a_1|X_1|a_2|\ldots a_l|X_l|a_{l+1}$ and $W = b_1|Y_1|b_2|\ldots b_k|Y_k|b_{k+1}$. Let us say that W *catalyzes* (as an *ensyme*) on V (m-dna sequence) at (i, j), if the primary sequence:

$$V[W] \equiv (X_1, \ldots\ldots X_{i-1}, X_iY_j, X_{i+1}, \ldots X_l)$$

posesses another m-dna sequence. Namely there is $(a'_1, \ldots, a'_{l+1})$ with:

$$a'_1|X_1|\ldots a'_{l-1}|X_{l-1}|a'_l|X_iY_j|a'_{i+1}|X_{i+1}|\ldots |a'_l|X_l|a'_{l+1}$$

consists of a m-dna sequence.

4.A Inversible Ensymes: Let V and V' be two m-dna sequences. If there are ensymes W and W' with the equalities:

$$V[W] = V', \quad V'[W'] = V$$

then we will say that W and W' are mutually *inverse* ensymes w.r.t. (V, V').

Example 8. Let $H = \{v_0, v_1, \ldots\}$ be a Hilbert space. Let us take S, the standard shift $S : v_i \mapsto v_{i+1}$ and P, the projection as $P(v_i) = v_i$, $i \neq 0, 1$ and $P(v_0) = P(v_1) = 0$. Let us take two m-dna sequences:

$$V = id[PS](PS)^*, \quad V' = id[S^2](S^2)^*.$$

Notice the equality $PS^2 = S^2$. Then one can find:

$$W = id[S]S, \quad W' : \{v_0 \to 0v_i \to v_{i-1}, \quad i \geq 1.$$

These give mutually inversible ensymes.

Notice that the primary structure of $V[W]$ also differs from that of V. After W has stopped catalyzing, $V[W]$ will return to the original V. So in practice catalyzing should be inversible.

4.B Promotor: Let $V_0 = a_0|X_0|a_1|X_1|a_2|\ldots|a_{l-1}|X_{l-1}|a_l$ be a sequence whose primary sequence does not admit any m-dna sequences. Let $W = id|Y|Y^*$ be a m-dna sequence so that the primary sequence $(X_0Y, X_1, \ldots, X_{l-1})$ has m-dna sequences. Thus V_0 cannot replicate by itself. After catalyzed by W, $V = V_0[W]$ becomes a m-dna sequence and begins replicating. One will call V_0 as a *pre m-dna sequence*. X_0 is called a *promotor*.

Example 9. Let $H = \{\ldots, v_{-l}, \ldots, v_0, \ldots, v_l, \ldots\}$ be a Hilbert space, $Q(i)$ and $Q(i,j)$ be the projections on $\{v_i\}$ and $\{v_i, v_j\}$ respectively. $P(i) \equiv id - Q(i)$.

Let us consider a pre m-dna sequence $V_0 = id[id]id[Q(1)]Q(1)[Q(1,2)]Q(1,2)$ and take $W = id[P(2)]P(2)$. Then the primary sequence $(P(2), Q(1), Q(1,2))$ has a m-dna sequence $id[P(2)]P(2)[Q(1)]Q(1,2)[Q(1,2)]id$.

4.C Mutually Exclusive Promotors: Let $V = a_1|X_1|a_2|\ldots a_l|X_l|a_{l+1}$ be a pre m-dna sequence. Suppose V posseses two promotors at X_i and X_j such that two ensymes Y_i and Y_j catalyze on these regions respectively.

If the following conditions are satisfied, then these two promotors are said to be *mutually exclusive*;

(1) both of $V[Y_i]$ and $V[Y_j]$ are infinitely many reflective,
(2) $V[Y_i][Y_j]$ is only finitely many reflective.

Example 10. Let $P(i_1, \ldots, i_N)$ be the corank N projection by:

$$P(i_1, \ldots, i_N)(v_l) = \{0 \ l = i_j, \quad v_l \text{ others }\}.$$

One puts $Q(i_1, \ldots, i_N) = 1 - P(i_1, \ldots, i_N)$. Moreover let S be the shift by $v_i \mapsto v_{i+1}$. Then one considers the primary sequence:

$$X = (P(1), P(0,1), P(-1,1)).$$

$V(X, A)$ is empty. Let us choose $Y_1 = Y_2 = S$. Then one has three primary sequences:

$$X_1 = (P(1)S, P(0,1), P(-1,1)), \quad X_2 = (P(1), P(0,1)S, P(-1,1)), \quad (14)$$
$$X_3 = (P(1)S, P(0,1)S, P(-1,1)). \quad (15)$$

$V(X_1, A)$ and $V(X_2, A)$ are both non empty, on the other hand $V(X_3, A)$ is empty as shown below:

$$id[P(1)S]S^{-1}P(1)[P(0,1)]S^{-1}P(2)[P(-1,1)]S^{-1}P(0) \in V(X_1, A), \quad (16)$$
$$id[P(1)]P(1)[P(0,1)S]S^{-1}P(0)[P(-1,1)]S^{-1}P(2) \in V(X_2, A), \quad (17)$$
$$id[P(1)S]S^{-1}P(1)[P(0,1)S]S^{-2}P(2)[P(-1,1)] *. \quad (18)$$

One can see there are no a with $S^{-2}P(2)a = P(-1,1)$ which is equivalent to $P(2)a = S^2P(-1,1)$, since the r.h.s. contains non zero v_2 component in the image, on the other hand the l.h.s. does not for any a.

In practice, many mutually exclusive promotors are found, e.g., the switching of grobin genes.

4.D Succesive Ensymes: Let $V = a_1|X_1|a_2|\ldots a_l|X_l|a_{l+1}$ be a m-dna sequence, and consider the primary sequence $(X_1, \ldots, X_l)$. Suppose there are two states Y_i and Y_j catalyzing on V respectively.

If the following conditions are satisfied, then these two catalyzing processes are said to be *succesive*;

(1) $V[Y_1]$ and $V[Y_j]$ are only finitely many reflective, and
(2) $V[Y_i][Y_j]$ is infinitely many reflective.

Example 11. Let $P(i_1, \ldots, i_N)$ and $Q(i_1, \ldots, i_N)$ be as before. First one considers a simple case. Let us consider a m-dna sequence:

$$V = id[id]id[P(2)]P(2)[Q(1)]Q(1).$$

Then one chooses two ensymes:

$$Y_1 = P(1), \quad Y_2 = P(1).$$

When these catalyze on V, then the corresponding primary sequences become as:

$$V[Y_1] = (P(1), P(2), Q(1)), \quad V[Y_2] = (id, P(1,2), Q(1)), \quad (19)$$
$$V[Y_1][Y_2] = (P(1), P(1,2), Q(1)). \quad (20)$$

Let (a_1, a_2, a_3, a_4) be a sequence with $a_1 = id$. Let us try to find m-dna sequences $V = a_1|P(1)|a_2|P(2)|a_3|Q(1)|a_4$, $V' = a_1|id|a_2|P(1,2)|a_3|Q(1)|a_4$ and $V'' = a_1|P(1)|a_2|P(1,2)|a_3|Q(1)|a_4$. V'' has a solution by:

$$V'' = id|P(1)|P(1)|P(1,2)|P(2)|Q(1)|Q(1)$$

One has partial solutions for:

$$V = id|P(1)|P(1)|P(2)|*, \quad V' = id|id|id|P(1,2)|P(1,2)|Q(1)|*.$$

Here it is impossible to find $*$ to satisfy the shift relation.

4.D Extension: Let us take a Hilbert space $H' = H_1 \oplus H_2 \oplus H_3$ where each H_i is also an infinite dimensional Hilbert space. Let $P(i)$, $i = 1,2,3$, be the projections to H_i. Let us take another projection P and a primary sequence $X = (P, 0, P(1))$, where the first two states are promotors as above. Then there is a m-dna sequence with this primary sequence, if and only if $PP(1) = P(1)$.

Notice that any projection with infinite dimensional kernel and range are all unitary equivalent. Thus there is a unitary U satisfying:

$$U^*P(1)U = \text{diag}\,(P(1), P(1)).$$

Let us take a family of unitaries U_i, $i = 1, 2, \ldots$ so that one gets inductively equations $U_i^* P_i U_i = \text{diag}(P_i, P_{i+1})$, $P_1 = P$. Let $(a_1^i, a_2^i, a_3^i, a_4^i)$ be a sequence with $a_1^i = id$, and try to judge whether V_1 is infinitely many reflective, i.e., to find a family of m-dna sequences:

$$V_i = a_1^i | P_i | a_2^i | 0 | a_3^i | P(1) | a_4^i.$$

Then the following can be seen; V_1 is infinitely many reflective, if and only if $P(1) \subset\subset P_i$ are satisfied for all $i = 1, 2, \ldots$

4.E Switching, Special Cases: Let PV be a pre m-dna sequence where two different ensymes W and W' at i and (i,j), acts on the promotor P which are mutually exclusive. Let us denote $PV(1) = PV[W]$ and $PV(2) = PV[W']$. Here one considers a special case of functions of (PV, W) as follows:

(1) W catalyzes on P and produces $PV(1)$.
(2) $W' = PV(1)$ catalyzes on P, and produces $PV[W'] = PV(2)$.

Thus when $PV(1)$ has been produced too much, then $PV(2)$ also increases.

Example 12. Let $P(i_1, \ldots, i_N)$ and $Q(i_1, \ldots, i_N)$ be in 4.C. Then one considers a pre m-dna sequence $PV = id[id]id[Q(1)]Q(1)[Q(1,2)]Q(1,2)$ and an ensyme $W = id[P(2)]P(2)$. Then:

$$W' = id[P(2)]P(2)[Q(1)]Q(1,2)[Q(1,2)]id$$

catalyzes on P and produces

$$PV[W'] = id[idQ(1)]Q(1)[Q(1)Q(1,2)]Q(1,2)[Q(1,2)]id \qquad (21)$$
$$= id[Q(1)]Q(1)[Q(1)]Q(1,2)[Q(1,2)]id. \qquad (22)$$

4.F Switching: Let us take a pre m-dna sequence V, and ensymes W, W', U, U' with a diagram:

$$W - [U] \to W' - [U'] \to W, \qquad (23)$$
$$W' \to V. \qquad (24)$$

Thus U, U' are ensymes which act on W and W' as mutual inverses. W' can catalyze on V and W cannot.

4.G Relation with Inequally Crossing over: Let us take two m-dna sequences $V = V_0 V_1$ and $U = U_0 U_1$. Suppose the inequally crossing over occurs:

$$(V, U) \mapsto (V_0 U_1, V_1 U_0).$$

This will produce new ensymes.

4.H Inactivating: Let us take a m-dna sequence V, and ensymes W and U, U'. suppose both of U and U' catalyze on W satisfying:

(1) $W[U]$ can catalyze on V,
(2) $W[U']$ cannot do it.

The ensyme U' is said to be *inactivating*.

4.I Indirect Ensymes: Let us take two m-dna sequences V and W. Suppose there is a cycle of catalyzing system:

$$W - [V] \to W[V] \equiv W', \quad V - [W'] \to V[W'] \equiv V'.$$

Then we will say that W is an *indirect ensyme* for this catalyzing system $V \to V'$.

4.J Rigidity: Let us fix a primary sequence $X = \{X_1, \ldots, X_l\}$. Recall $V(X, A)$ in section 1. We will say that X is *rigid* if there is exactly only one $V \in L(X, A)$ with $a_1 \in I$ and $V = a_1 | X_1 | a_2 \ldots | a_l | X_l | a_{l+1}$.

In many of the examples here, the primary sets are rigid with $I = \{id\}$.

Let us take a m-dna sequence $V = a_1 | X_1 | a_2 | X_2 \ldots$ and an ensyme $W = b_1 | Y | b_2$. We will say that V is *projectively rigid*, if the following is satisfied; suppose W catalyzes on V at i. If $V[W]$ consists of a m-dna sequence, then one has the equality $X_i = X_i Y$

Example 13. Let us put $H = H_1 \oplus H_2$ and put P_i as the projections on H_i. Let us take a m-dna sequence $V = id[P_1]P_1[P_1]id[id]id$. Let us take another projection X. Let us put $W = id[X]X$ and catalyze W on $id[P_1]P_1$ factor in V. Then one has $V[W] = id[P_1 X]P_1 X[P_1]id[id]id$. Thus by the definition, if $V[W]$ consists of a m-dna sequence, then the equality $P_1 X = P_1$ holds.

4.K Amplification: Let PV be a m-dna sequence. Let us consider a pre m-dna sequence PVV.

Suppose that V and VV catalyze on P as ensyme. If the following two conditions are satisfied, then the amplification PVV will be called *self controlling*:

(1) $PV[V]$ is infinitely many reflective,
(2) $PVV[VV]$ is only finitely many reflective.

If the converse holds:

(1) $PV[V]$ is only finitely many reflective,
(2) $PVV[VV]$ is infinitely many reflective,

then PVV will be called *self amplification*.

Example 14. Let us take a Hilbert space $H = H_1 \oplus H_2$ and put the projections on H_i by P_i. Let us consider m-dna sequences:

$$P = id|id|id|id|id, \quad V = id|P_1|P_1.$$

Then the followings show that PVV is self amplification:

$$PV = id[id]id[id]id[P_1]P_1, \quad PVV[VV] = id[P_1]P_1[P_1]P_1[P_1]P_1[P_1]P_1, \quad (25)$$
$$PVV = id[id]id[id]id[P_1]P_1[P_1]P_1, \quad PV[V] = id[P_1]P_1[id]id[P_1]P_1. \quad (26)$$

5 Selective Splicing

Let $V = PV_1V_2$ be a (pre) m-dna sequence. If there is an ensyme W so that $V[W]$ has a maximal sequence V_1 of infinitely many reflection, then the procedure $V \to V[W] \to V_1$ is called *splicing*.

Example 15. Let us put $H = H_1 \oplus H_2 \oplus H_3$ where H_i are infinite dimensional Hilbert spaces. Let us denote by P and P' as the projections on $H_1 \oplus H_2$ and on H_1 respectively. Let $V = P_1V_1P_2V_2$ be a m-dna sequence, where:

$$P_1 = id|P|P, \quad V_1 = P|P|id, \quad P_2 = id|id|id, \quad V_2 = id|id|id.$$

Let us take an ensyme $W = id|P'|P'$ and catalyze it on P_2. Then as a maximal sequence, one gets the following:

$$V' = id[P]P[P]id[P']P'.$$

5.A Splicing Systems: Let $V = PV_1 \ldots V_l$ be a (pre) m-dna sequence. Suppose there are subindices $\{m_1, \ldots, m_k\} \subset \{1, \ldots, l\}$ so that each V_{m_j} is also infinitely many reflective. We will say that a family of ensymes $\{W_1, \ldots, W_k\}$ splices $\{V_{m_j}\}_j$, if each W_j splices V_{m_j}.

Let $V = PV_1V_1'V_2V_2' \ldots V_lV_l'$ be a m-dna sequence. A *succesive splicing* on V is a system of splicing as follows; there is an ensyme W catalyzing on P, and replicating V_1. Then V_1 again catalyzing on P, and replicating V_2. One can continue this process until replicating V_l.

5.B Self Splicing Systems: Let $V = a_1|X_1|a_2 \ldots$ be a (pre) m-dna sequence. Suppose an ensyme W catalyzes on V, $V_1 = V[W]$ and it produces W_1 by splicing. Next let us catalyze W_1 on V_1 catalyzing as an ensyme, and produces W_2. Similarly let us catalyze W_2 on V_2 and produce W_3. Succesively one may obtain (V_l, W_l), $l = 1, 2, \ldots$ This process will be called as a *self splicing system*.

Example 16. Let us define shifts $S(n)$ and projections $P(n)$ as follows:

$$S(n): \{v_{2^n k} \to v_{2^{n+1} k} \quad v_i \to v_i, \quad i \neq 2^n k\}, \quad (27)$$
$$P(n): \{v_{2^n k} \to 0 \quad v_i \to v_i, \quad i \neq 2^n k, \quad k = 0, 1, 2, \ldots\}. \quad (28)$$

Notice the relations:

$$S(n)P(n) = P(n), \quad P(n)S(n-1) = P(n-1), \tag{29}$$
$$P(n-1)P(n) = P(n)P(n-1) = P(n-1). \tag{30}$$

Let us consider a primary sequence:

$$(S(1), S(2), \ldots, S(n)).$$

This admits a m-dna sequence $V = a_1[S(1)]a_2[S(2)]\ldots[S(n)]a_{n+1}$ with $a_1 = id$. For example one determines $a_2, a_3, \ldots$ as:

$$a_2^* = S(1), \tag{31}$$
$$a_3^* : \{v_{4k} \to v_{16k}, \quad v_{4k+2} \to v_{2(4k+2)}, \quad v_{2k+1} \to v_{2k+1} \quad (k = 0, 1, \ldots)\}, \tag{32}$$
$$a_4^* : \{v_{8k} \to v_{16(4k)}, \quad v_{8k+4} \to v_{4(8k+4)}, \quad v_{4k+2} \to v_{2(4k+2)}, \quad v_{2k+1} \to v_{2k+1}\}, \tag{33}$$
$$\ldots \tag{34}$$

Thus $V^* = a_{n+1}[S(n)^*]a_n[S(n-1)^*]\ldots[S(1)^*]a_1$ also consists of a m-dna sequence. Now let us consider a primary sequence:

$$S = (S(n)^*, S(n-1)^*, \ldots, S(1)^*).$$

Take an ensyme $W = id[P(n+1)]P(n+1)$ and catalyze it on V^* as follows:

$$V_1 = V^*[W] = a_{n+1}[S(n)^*P(n+1)]a_nP(n)[S(n-1)^*]a_{n-1}[S(n-2)^*]a_{n-2}\ldots \tag{35}$$
$$= a_{n+1}[P(n)]a_nP(n)[S(n-1)^*]a_{n-1}[S(n-2)^*]a_{n-2}\ldots \tag{36}$$

Then by splicing, V_1 produces $W_1 = id[P(n)]P(n)$. Next let us catalyze W_1 on V_1 as follows:

$$V_2 = V_1[W_1] = a_{n+1}[P(n)]a_nP(n)[S(n-1)^*P(n)]a_{n-1}P(n)[S(n-2)^*]a_{n-2}\ldots \tag{37}$$
$$= a_{n+1}[P(n)]a_nP(n)[P(n-1)]a_{n-1}P(n)[S(n-2)^*]a_{n-2}\ldots \tag{38}$$

Again by splicing, V_2 produces $W_2 = id[P(n)]P(n)[P(n-1)]P(n-1)$. One can iterate this process until obtaining W_n.

6 Convergence and Divergence

Let V and V' be two infinitely many reflective m-dna sequences. Given a system of mutations **S**. Let us denote by $V_n = a_1(n)|X_1(n)|\ldots a_{l(n)}(n)$ ($V_n' = a_1'(n)|X_1'(n)|\ldots a_{l(n)'}(n)$) as n-th generations of V (V') w.r.t. **S**. We will say that V and V' have *convergent evolution* w.r.t. **S**, if there is n_0 so that for all $n \geq n_0$, $l(n) = l(n)'$ and $X_j(n) = X_j'(n)$ for all j.

Let us take two systems of mutations **S** and **S'**. Let us denote by V_n and V_n' as n-th generations of V w.r.t. **S** and **S'**. We will say that V have *divergent evolution* w.r.t. **S** and **S**, if there is n_0 so that for all $n \geq n_0$, $l(n) \neq l(n)'$ or $l(n) = l(n)'$ and $X_j(n) \neq X_j'(n)$ for some j.

Example 17. Let $H = H_1 \oplus H_2 \oplus H_3$ where H_i are infinite dimensional Hilbert spaces. Let us put the projections on H_i by P_i and $Q_i = id - P_i$. Let us take a m-dna sequence $V = id[Q_3]Q_3[Q_3]id[Q_2]Q_2$. Suppose V accepts two point mutations as:

$$\nearrow V_1 = id[Q_3]Q_3[P_1]Q_2[Q_2]id, \qquad (39)$$
$$V \qquad\qquad\qquad\qquad\qquad\qquad\qquad (40)$$
$$\searrow V_2 = id[Q_3]Q_3[Q_3]id[P_2]P_2. \qquad (41)$$

Let us take two ensymes $W_1 = id|P_1|P_1$ and $W_2 = id|P_2|P_2$ acting on V_i as follows:

$$V_1[W_1] = id[P_1]P_1[P_1]id[Q_2]Q_2, \quad V_2[W_2] = id[Q_3]Q_3[P_2]P_2[P_2]id, \quad (42)$$
$$V_1[W_2] = id[Q_3]Q_3[0]P_3[Q_2]*, \quad V_2[W_1] = id[P_1]P_1[Q_3]*. \quad (43)$$

Both of $V_i[W_i]$ are m-dna sequences, and both of $V_1[W_2]$ and $V_2[W_1]$ are not.

7 Loop Structure

Let $V = WV_1W'V_2W''$ be a m-dna sequence with a structure:

$$V_1 = a_1|X_1|a_2\ldots a_l|X_l|a_{l+1}, \qquad (44)$$
$$V_2 = a_{l'+1}|X_{l'+1}|a_{l'+2}|\ldots|a_{l+l'}|X_{l+l'}|a_{l+l'+1} \qquad (45)$$
$$\equiv b_{l+1}|Y_l|b_l|\ldots b_2|Y_1|b_1. \qquad (46)$$

Suppose there exists a family of primary elements $\{Z_1, \ldots, Z_l\}$ so that the shift relation is satisfied, $a_i b_i^* = Z_i$, $i = 1, \ldots, l$. Then the structure:

$$a_1|X_1| \; a_2|X_2| \; a_3|\ldots \; a_l|X_l|a_{l+1}\ldots \qquad (47)$$
$$- \quad - \quad - \quad - \quad - \qquad (48)$$
$$Z_1 \quad Z_2 \quad Z_3 \quad Z_l \quad Z_{l+1} \qquad (49)$$
$$- \quad - \quad - \quad - \quad - \qquad (50)$$
$$b_1 \; |Y_1| \; b_2 \; |Y_2| \; b_3 \;|\ldots \; b_l \; |Y_l| \; b_{l+1}\ldots \qquad (51)$$

is called *loop structure*.

7.A Parindrome: Let $V = a_1|X_1|\ldots a_{2l-1}|X_{2l-1}|a_{2l}$ be a m-dna sequence with parindrome. Let us rewrite V as $a_1|X_1|\ldots a_l|X_l|a_{l+1}|X_l|\ldots|X_1^*|a_1$. Then one obtains a loop structure by:

$$a_1| \; X_1 \; |a_2| \; X_2 \; |a_3| \; \ldots \; | \; a_j \; | \; X_j \; | \; a_{j+1} \; |\ldots \qquad (52)$$
$$X_1^* \qquad X_2^* \quad \ldots X_{j-1}^* \qquad X_j^* \qquad (53)$$
$$a_1 \; |X_1| \; a_2 \; |\ldots \; |a_{j-1}|X_{j-1}|a_j|\ldots \qquad (54)$$

References

[CG] A. CARBONE AND M. GROMOV, *Mathematical slices of molecular biology*, Gaz. Math. vol 88 suppl (2001).
[CGP] ED. A.CARBONE, M.GROMOV AND P.PRUSINKIEWICZ, *Pattern formation in biology, vision and dynamics*, World Scientific (2000).
[K1] T.KATO, *Operator dynamics in molecular biology*, IHES preprint (2001).
[K2] T.KATO, *Interacting maps, symbolic dynamics and automorphisms in microscopic scale*, to appear in International Journal of Pure and Applied Mathematics.
[Ki] B.P.KITCHENS, *Symbolic dynamics*, Springer, (1998).

Analysis of Complete Convergence for Genetic Algorithm with Immune Memory

Shiqin Zheng[1], Kongyu Yang[2], and Xiufeng Wang[3]

[1,3] College of Information Technology and Science, Nankai University,
Tianjin 300071, China
shiqin_zheng@sohu.com,
[2] College of Information & Electrical Engineering,
Shandong Institute of Architecture & Engineering,
Jinan 250101, China
yangkongyu@tsinghua.org.cn

Abstract. A new Immune Memory Genetic Algorithm (IMGA) based on the mechanism of immune memory and immune network is proposed in this article . Using Markov chains theory, we proven that NGA(Niche Genetic Algorithms) can't not be complete convergence but IMGA can. The contrast simulation experiments between NGA and IMGA are performed. The experiments results validate the theoretical analysis and testify that IMGA has availability on solving multi-modal optimization problems, with quickly convergence ability and wonderful stability.

1 Introduction

Niche Genetic Algorithms(NGA) as introduced in [1,2] is often used to tackle multi-modul optimization problems of the type.

Definition 1.

$$B = \{b|b \subseteq B \text{ and f(b) is the max of f()}\} \quad (1)$$

where $f()$ is a multi-model function and assuming that $0 < f(b) < \infty$ for all $b \in IB^l = \{0,1\}^l$ and $f(b) \neq const$.

Although empirical indicates that NGA has some multi-modul searching capability, but it can't implement the complete convergence which is defined below:

Definition 2. assume that $f()$ has m peaks (i.e. maxes)in the definition scope, signed as $\phi_1, \phi_2, ..., \phi_m, Z(t)$ is the population of t generation. If and only if

$$\lim_{t \to \infty} \prod_{i=1}^{m} P(\phi_i \in Z(t)) = 1 \quad (2)$$

We call the genetic algorithm is complete convergence.

Inspired by the biology immune system, this paper proposes an immune memory genetic algorithm (IMGA) in part 2. And it proves that NGA can't implement complete converge but IMGA can using Markov chain in part3. Contrast simulation experiments to validate the theoretical analysis is in part 4.

2 Immune Memory Genetic Algorithm

2.1 Biology Immune Mechanism

1. Immune Memory
When an antigen invades the body at the first time, the immune system produce antibodies in response to eliminate it. Some antibody cells with high fitness will differentiate into memory cells which will remain in the immune system for a long periods of time and will promote faster and more effective response to the same antigentic challenge.[3]

2. Immune Network Regulation
The immune network theory is based on the premise that an antibody can be recognized by other free antibodies and it also can recognize other antibodies. This recognizing and being recognized action will result in an activation or suppression of this kind of antibody. And the connected antibodies form a network. Those capabilities endow the immune system with an intrinsic dynamic behavior and the diversity of antibodies.[3]

2.2 Immune Memory Genetic Algorithm

Inspired by the immune memory and immune network regulation mechanism, we design a memory calculator and add to the Niche Genetic Algorithm(NGA). In the memory calculator, restrain calculator and gradient calculator can ensure the algorithm finds all peaks.

1. Memory Calculator. If the affinity of an individual exceeds the memory threshold, it is moved into the memory sub-population for special cultivation and deleted from the original population. If the new population size is smaller than that of the original population after memory, new individuals are generated randomly to complement.

2. Restrain Calculator. The restrain calculator simulates the immune network that the resemble antibodies restrain each other. If $D_{ij} \leq \delta_r$, where D_{ij} is the distance between i, j, and δ_r is a threshold, the individual with higher affinity will be reserved.

3. Gradient Calculator. The actual optimization algorithms have a common problem: the searching result is often near the real optimization, but cannot reach the optimization accurately. So a gradient calculator is imported. When a new individual comes into the memory subpopulation, the gradient calculator will lead it to its peak.[5, $p303$]

4. Describe of Immune Memory Genetic Algorithm
The algorithm can be sketched as follows:

generate an initial population
determine the affinity of each individual
perform selection
repeat

perform each step of NGA
perform memory calculator
perform gradient calculator   ♯ just in memory subpopulation
perform restrain calculator   ♯ just in memory subpopulation
Until some stopping criterion applies

3 Complete Convergence Analysis of IMGA

Markov chain is good tools to analysis the convergence of standard genetic algorithm. Analogously, we use Markov chain to prove that the conventional NGA can't be complete convergence and IMGA can.

3.1 The Complete Convergence Analysis of NGA

In reference 6, the author defined a Canonical Genetic Algorithm,[6,p96], from this point of view,NGA is a kind to CGA. So we use can results of convergence analysis of CGA in that article in our proof.

Theorem 1. *NGA can't implement complete convergence.*

Proof. Suppose that $i \in \Phi$ satisfies $\prod_{k=1}^{m} P(\phi_k \in i) = 1$, $j \in \Phi$ satisfies $\prod_{k=1}^{m} P(\phi_k \in j) < 1$. We call i is a globe peak state. Because the Markov chain of the NGA is ergodic [6,p98,corollary1], $P_{i,j} > 0$. This indicates that state i can't stay in the globe peak state i.e. $\lim_{t \to \infty} \prod_{i=1}^{m} P(\phi_i \in Z(t)) < 1$ this can't satisfy the definition 2.so the NGA is't complete converge. Theorem1 is proved.

3.2 Complete Convergence Prove of IMGA

Lemma 1. *Let P be a reducible stochastic matrix,where $C : m \times m$ is a primitive stochastic matrix and $R, T \neq 0$, then*

$$P^\infty = \lim_{k \to \infty} \begin{pmatrix} C^k & 0 \\ \sum_{i=0}^{k-1} T^i R C^{k-i-1} & T^k \end{pmatrix} = \begin{pmatrix} C^\infty & 0 \\ R^\infty & 0 \end{pmatrix} \quad (3)$$

is a stable stochastic matrix[6,p.97].

Theorem 2. *The NGA with immune memory can implement complete convergence.*

Proof. All the individuals in the sub-population is regarded as a state. Assumed that the size of population is bigger than the number of peaks, the size of sub-population is not more than the size of original population. Obviously, the state space is finite. The dimension of state space is $|\Phi| = \sum_{i=0}^{n} 2^{li} = \frac{2^{nl}-1}{2^l-1}$ The states are sorted from big to small according to the number of peak individuals (the individual corresponding to the local max). If the number of the peak individuals is equal, the states are sorted from small to big according to the number of individuals in the memory population .For any two states whose peak individual numbers are different $i, j \in \Phi$, suppose that the number of peak individuals of state i is less than that of state j. According to the principle of memory operation, the state with less peak individuals can transfer to the state with more peak individuals, the contrary propositions isn't right i.e. $p_{ij} > 0$ but $p_{ji} = 0$. For the individuals whose the number of peak individuals is equal but the size of sub-population is different, according to the gradient evolution principle ,the state with bigger memory sub-population size can reach the state with smaller size, the contrary propositions isn't right. So the state at top left corner just which includes m peak individuals corresponding to m peaks is the global peak state. This state forms a closed class. The state transition matrix can be express as $P = \begin{pmatrix} 1 & 0 \\ T & U \end{pmatrix}$ The lemma 1 can ensure that the genetic algorithm stays in the state of the top left corner, i.e. the memory sub-population only includes the individuals corresponding to the peaks,so $\lim_{t \to \infty} \prod_{i=1}^{m} P(\phi_i \in Z(t)) = 1$,Thus the theorem 2 is proved.

4 Simulation Experiment of Algorithm Convergence

4.1 Experiment Scheme

Four functions are chosen to do experiments. We use NGA and IMGA to search the function peaks at the same experimental condition and compare the searching results and the algorithm stability.

The functions are list below ,$f_1(x), f_2(x), f_3(x)$,where $x \in [0, 1]$, have 5 peaks and $f_4(x)$ has 4. Each algorithm performs 50 times for each function, and experiment parameters are list in table 1.

$$f_1(x) = \sin^6(5\pi x) \qquad (4)$$
$$f_2(x) = f_1(x) \times e^{-2\ln 2 \times (x-0.0667)^2} \qquad (5)$$
$$f_3(x) = \sin^6(5\pi x^{0.75}) \times e^{-2\ln 2 \times (x-0.0667)^2} \qquad (6)$$
$$f_4(x) = x_1 \cdot \sin(x_1^2) + x_2 \cdot \sin(x_2^2) \ .x_1, x_2 \in [2, 4] \qquad (7)$$

Table 1. Parameters setting for algorithm experiment

parameter	parameter value	operate method
population size (n)	20	real number code
crossover probability (p_c)	0.3	restrained crossover
mutation probability (p_m)	0.02	random mutation
mate share (δ_{share})	0.15	proportional select on share mechanism
max generation $(MaxGen)$	200	t=200

4.2 Test Results and Contrast Analysis

Test result is list in table 2, From the table2,we can see, NGA can't steadily converge to all peaks, but IMGA can. Furthermore, the evolution generations of IMGA can be decreased more.

Table 2. Simulation experiment results compare table

test function	algorithm	peaks number and reached times				
		1	2	3	4	5
$f_1(x)$	NGA	30	26	31	28	35
	IMGA	50	50	50	50	50
$f_2(x)$	NGA	44	35	16	3	2
	IMGA	50	50	50	50	50
$f_3(x)$	NGA	48	35	0	3	0
	IMGA	50	50	50	50	50
$f_4(x)$	NGA	32	41	26	30	null
	IMGA	50	50	50	50	null

5 Conclusion

Inspired by the biology immune system, we propose an immune memory genetic algorithm(IMGA) in this article. We prove the complete convergence of IMGA in theory and validate the theoretical conclusion through simulation experiments.

References

1. Holland J H.: Adaptation in natural and artificial systemAn Introduction Analysis with Applications to Biology, Control, and Artificial Intelligence. USA The University of Michigan Press(1975).
2. Goldberg D. E., Richardson. J.: Genetic algorithms with sharing for multi-modal function optimization. Proceedings of the second International Conference on Genetic Algorithms: July 28-31,1987 at the Massachusetts Institute of Technology, Cambridge, MA: 41-49.
3. Leandro N. de Castro and Jonathan Timmis: Aritificial immune systems: A New Computational Intelligence Approach. Springer Press(2002).pp.13-15,30-33
4. YUN Weijun,Xi Yug-geng: Globe convergence and compute efficiency analysis of genetic algorithm,CONTROL THEORY AND APPLICATIONS,13(4)(1996)455-460
5. LIU Hong-jue,WANG Xiu-feng: Adaptive genetic algorithm for multi-peak searching:Control Theory & Applications,(21)2(2004):302-304310
6. G.Rudolph: Convergence Analysis of Canonical Genetic Algorithms . IEEE Trans. on Neural Networks. 5(1)(1994):96-101

New Operators for Faster Convergence and Better Solution Quality in Modified Genetic Algorithm

Pei-Chann Chang, Yen-Wen Wang, and Chen-Hao Liu

Dept. of Industrial Engineering and Management, Yuan Ze University,
Chung-Li, Taiwan 32026
iepchang@saturn.yzu.edu.tw

Abstract. The aim of this paper is to study two new forms of genetic operators: duplication and fabrication. Duplication is a reproduce procedure that will reproduce the best fit chromosome from the elite base. The introduction of duplication operator into the modified GA will speed up the convergence rate of the algorithm however the trap into local optimality can be avoided. Fabrication is an artificial procedure used to produce one or several chromosomes by mining gene structures from the elite chromosome base. Statistical inference by job assignment procedure will be applied to produce artificial chromosomes and these artificial chromosomes provides new search directions and new solution spaces for the modified GA to explore. As a result, better solution quality can be achieved when applying this modified GA. Different set of problems will be tested using modified GA by including these two new operators in the procedure. Experimental results show that the new operators are very informative in searching the state space for higher quality of solutions.

1 Introduction

Since Holland proposed the genetic algorithm back in 1975, this adaptive system, which is biologically motivated, has been successfully applied to solve different application problems. In the standard GA, the population diversity is obtained and maintained using the genetic operators of crossover and mutation, which allow the GA to find more promising solutions and avoid premature convergence to a local maximum (Goldberg 1989). However, the use of the genetic operators has been the object of study of many researchers. Some important work related with crossover and mutation can be found in (Davis 1989; De Jong et al. 1992; Schaffer et al. 1991).

In addition to the traditional genetic operators, many researchers have presented new genetic domain-dependent operators, for instance, (D'Haeseleer 1993; Mathias et al. 1992). Nevertheless, no new biologically inspired genetic operators have been widely adopted since the advent of GAs. Mitchell et al. (1994) point out the importance of studying new genetic operators. Mitchell et al. (1994) and Mitchell (1996) state that it would be interesting to analyze if any of these biological mechanisms, incorporated in a GA, could lead to any significant advantages. Banzhaf et al. (1998) share the same opinion and they highlight the significance of implementing evolutionary approaches using mechanisms such as conjugation, transduction or transposition.

This paper tries to develop two new operators, which can be embedded in the original GA procedure. They are duplication operator and fabrication operator. Duplication operator just like a general biological cloning technology, it clones the chromosome from the parent to breed the offspring. Fabrication operator attempts to extract the superior gene structure from the chromosome, and will generate the new offspring. These two new operators will either duplicate or fabricate new chromosomes from the chromosome base. With these new duplicated or artificial chromosomes, the convergence rate and solution quality of the GA searching procedure will be improved greatly.

The rest of the paper is divided in five sections. Section 2 introduces the modified GA. The following section describes two new operators: duplication and fabrication and gives detailed procedure of these two operators. Section 4 is the experimental tests conducted to test the quality of solution generated by using these two new operators. Finally, conclusion is made and future direction of the research is provided.

2 The Modified GA

The evolution procedure of modified GA as shown in Figure 1 is pretty similar to the procedure in general GA except that two new operators are included in the procedure, i.e., duplication and fabrication operators. The modified GA starts with a randomly initialized population of candidate solutions and then assigns fitness value to each individual in the population. Individuals with highest fitness value will be extracted into the elite chromosome base for storage. Then roulette wheel selection procedure will be applied to select N pairs of parents for reproduction. Later on, the modified GA associates each individual candidate in the population with a fitness, which measures the quality of a solution. Selection chooses individuals probabilistically, according to their fitness. The higher the fitness, the more likely it is for an individual to be selected. Next, duplication operator will duplicate d% of best fit individual into the next generation population. Duplication operator is similar to Elitism, but duplication operator clones the elitist repeatedly and Elitism does not.

While fabrication operator will produce f% of individuals from the elite chromosome base by assigning job into the position using statistical inference. These individuals are called artificial chromosomes. After that, regular crossover and mutation operator will be applied again to generate new individual for the next generation population. Crossover and mutation produce new individuals: the first operator exchanges genetic information between two selected parents; mutation randomly changes one gene value to the generated offspring. The modified GA searches through an iterative process: the process of one generation involving selection, duplication, fabrication, crossover and mutation is called one cycle of iteration and is repeated until convergence is reached or the number of generations achieves the established limit.

New Operators for Faster Convergence and Better Solution Quality in Modified GA   985

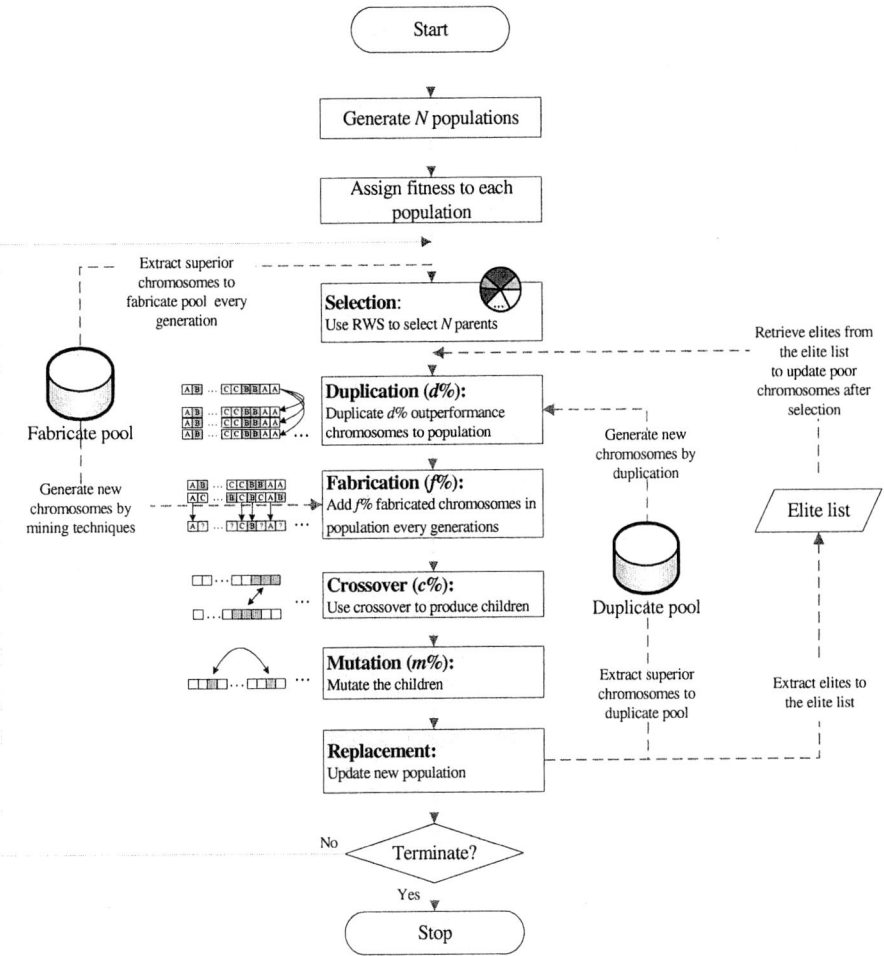

Fig. 1. The Modified Genetic Algorithm

3 New Operators

The cloning of "dolly" in 1997 is the first example in real life that duplication can be applied to copy an existing chromosome to retain the quality of solution in the next generation. Duplication is a very easy and fast computational procedure. However, the duplication operator can be applied to intelligently evolve population and fine-tune the solution quality that is the merits of this research try to achieve. Fabrication is also a new operator to be dealt with. Duplication is a reproducing procedure of a chromosome but fabrication is to make up a new chromosome with the help of statistical information from the elite chromosome base. With the advance of the data mining technology, more sophisticated chromosome can be produced through the fabrication procedure. Detailed explanations of these two new operators are given in the following two sections.

3.1 Duplication

Duplication is a very simple procedure in the modified GA and it makes a single copy of the best fit chromosome, similarity to Elitism. The difference of duplication and Elitism is that, Elitism only retains the best fit chromosome in the next generation, but duplication involves multiple copies of the best fit chromosome in the next generation. However, questions such as the particular individual to be copied? Or how many copies to be made during the evolution process? How does duplication affect the convergence rate of the GA searching procedure? They are interesting questions to be answered later on in this research.

Actually, duplication may increase convergence rate by introducing more elite chromosome into the population, however, there is a chance that the searching procedure might be trapped into local optimality. The percentage of duplication should be controlled within certain limit in order to keep diversity of the searching procedure in the population.

The modified GA by including duplicate operator is described as follows:

1. Following the general GA's procedure, first generate initial populations, and calculate their fitness. Then, using the selection operator (i.e., the RWS) to produce candidate chromosomes for next generation.
2. To apply the "duplicate" operator, we will extract the best chromosome from the Duplicate Pool and then reproduce it N times (N is determined by the rate of duplicate, i.e., d %).
3. After that, we substitute the worst N chromosomes in the original populations by the duplicated chromosomes.
4. And then, just like the general GA's procedure, crossover, mutation, replacement.
5. During the replacement, we will update the "Duplicate Pool", i.e., the best chromosome will be retracted and recorded in Duplicate Pool.
6. Terminate or not? If not, go to 2. Else, 7.
7. Stop the GA and output the best solution.

3.2 Fabrication

Fabrication is the procedure to make up a set of new chromosome based on the elite chromosome base. There is a lot of gene information left in the elite chromosome base; however general GA searching procedure just reuses only 20% of the chromosomes generated. Fabrication will follow the sequence structure of each chromosome in the elite chromosome base, and according to the votes from the elite chromosome base; a job-position matrix M_{ij} can be formed, i.e., a dominance matrix describing the number of times job shown up in each position will be recorded in this matrix. For each chromosome, the gene represents the job and the sequence the position each job is assigned. We will count the number of times job showing up in each different positions and recorded in the matrix. Thus a dominance matrix generated from the chromosome base is formed. Next we will mine this matrix according to the votes from each elite chromosome, and fabricate an artificial chromosome.

The algorithm for fabricate operator is described as follows:

Let A : the set of cities have to be assigned

A' : the set of assigned-cities

B' : the set of weed-out cities

$|V_l|$: the highest number of vote of the $l-th$ sequence = $MAX(V_{kl})$, $\forall k$

$|C_l|$: the city with the highest number of vote of the $l-th$ sequence

Processes of generate fabricated chromosomes:

Step 1. For all l in A, find l, where $|V_l|$ is the maximum

If there is any other l' where $|V_{l'}| = |V_l|$, go to step 3; otherwise, go to step 2.

Step 2. Remove city $|C_l|$ from A to A', and let it to hold the $l-th$ sequence in fabricated chromosomes. Then, go to step 4.

Step 3. Remove cities $|C_l|$ and $|C_{l'}|$ from A to B'. Then, go to step 4.

Step 4. If $A = \phi$, then, go to step 5; otherwise, go back to step 1.

Step 5. Random assign the cities in B' to the unassigned sequences in fabricated chromosomes.

In the following is a simple example for our fabricate operator:

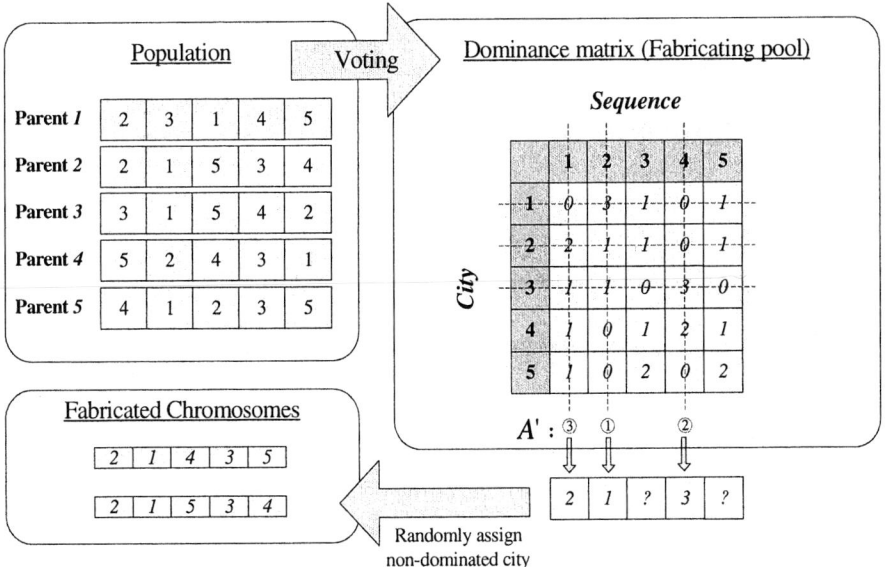

Fig. 2. The Diagram of Fabrication

4 The Test Functions and Results

First, we will analyze the duplication and fabrication results individually, explaining how the duplicating and fabricating operators can influence the performance of the GA. Empirical results show how we can choose the appropriate size for the duplicating sequences, depending on the size of population.

4.1 Experimental Test for Parameter Setup

We setup the parameters using three different levels for duplication and fabrication and they are 10%, 30% and 50%.

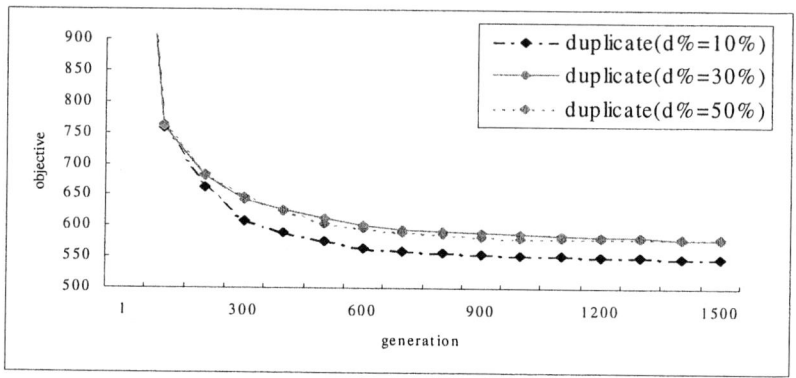

Fig. 3. Test for duplication percentage: d%

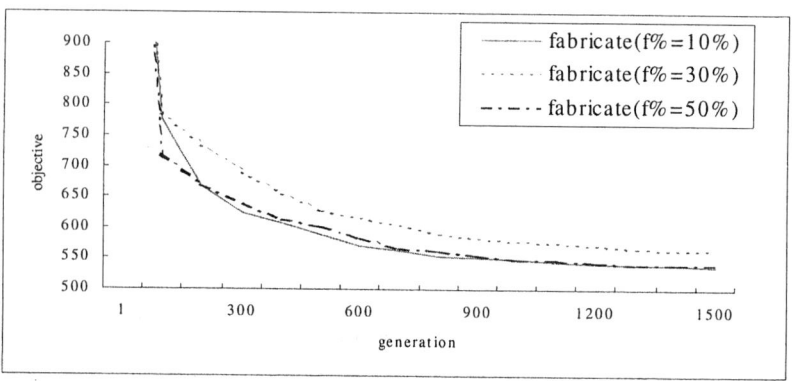

Fig. 4. Test for fabrication percentage: f%

The final result of this testing can be shown in the figures above. The duplication and fabrication operator can further improve the convergence of the algorithm however the duplicating rate and fabricating rate should be controlled at 10%. That is when increasing duplicating rate and fabricate rate over 10% there is a chance for the algorithm to be trapped into local optimality.

4.2 Testing for TSP Problem

The benchmark problem of 51-cities Traveling Salesman Problem from TSPLIB is applied to examine the performance of duplicate and fabricate operators..

Table 1. The mean and std. of final results

	$MEAN(f_{min})$	$STD(f_{min})$
Pure GA	515.3	17.47
GA-Duplicate	484.08	18.16
GA-Fabricate	479.78	9.55

From the results above, the modified GA obtains an improvement in terms of efficiency and solution quality when compared to general GA. Both mean objective values from GA-duplication and GA-fabrication are much less than those of pure GA. This implies that duplication and fabrication operators can further improve the quality of solution and rate of convergence. In addition, the standard deviation of GA-fabrication is much less than that of GA-duplication. This indicates that the fabrication operator seems posses a better robust performance during the searching procedure.

4.3 Testing for Continuous Function

The evolutionary parameters for our modified GA are designed as follows:

Table 2. Evolutionary parameters used for testing

Number	Items	Values
1	The scale of the population	50
2	The maximum number of iteration times	200
3	Crossover rate	0.85
4	Mutation rate	0.1
5	Number of calculation times	10
6	Length of binary code of each variance	8
7	Percentage of duplicate (d%)	10%
8	Percentage of artificial (f%)	10%

The five benchmark functions are chosen and tested in our numeric experiments and they are listed in the followings:

Example 1: GP (Goldstein-Price function)

$$f(x_1, x_2) = [1 + (x_1 + x_2 + 1)^2 (19 - 14x_1 + 3x_1^2 + 6x_1 x_2 + 3x_2^2)] \\ \times [30 + (2x_1 - 3x_2)^2 \times (18 - 32x_1 + 12x_1^2 + 48x_2 - 36x_1 x_2 + 27x_2^2)] \quad (1)$$

Where $-2 < x_i < 2$, $i = 1, 2$, min $f(x_1, x_2) = 3$

Example 2: BR (Branin)

$$f(x_1, x_2) = a(x_2 - bx_1^2 + cx_1 - d)^2 + e(1 - f)\cos(x_1) + e \quad (2)$$

Where $a = 1$, $b = 5.1/(4\pi^2)$, $c = 5/\pi$, $d = 6$, $e = 10$, $f = 1/(8\pi)$, $-5 \le x_1 \le 10$, $0 \le x_2 \le 15$, min $f(x_1, x_2) = 5/(4\pi)$

Example 3: RO (Rosenbrock function)

$$f(x_1, x_2) = (1 - x_1)^2 + 105(x_2 - x_1^2)^2 \quad (3)$$

Where $-2 < x_i < 2$, $i = 1, 2$, min $f(x_1, x_2) = 0$

Example 4: RA (Rastrigin function)

$$f(x_1, x_2) = x_1^2 + x_2^2 - \cos(18x_1) - \cos(18x_2) \quad (4)$$

Where $-1 \le x_i \le 1$, $i = 1, 2$, min $f(x_1, x_2) = -2$

Example 5: SH (Shubert function)

$$f(x_1, x_2) = \left\{ \sum_{i=1}^{5} i \cos((i+1)x_1 + i) \right\} \left\{ \sum_{i=1}^{5} i \cos((i+1)x_2 + i) \right\} \quad (5)$$

Where $-10 \le x_i \le 10$, $i = 1, 2$, min $f(x_1, x_2) = -186.7309$

From table 5, it is found that in most of continuous benchmark problems, our modified GA outperforms the general GA in solution quality and convergence rate except for the RO. problem. But when we observe the convergence charts, it is clearly to know that, the modified GA still has achieved a higher rate of convergence.

Table 3. Comparison of the final results

Continuous Problem	The average generation times when the f_{max} is reached for the first time	
	Pure GA	Duplicate & Fabricate GA
1. GP.	228	51
2. BR.	>300	178
3. RO.	158	256
4. RA.	>300	20
5. SH.	>300	271

5 Conclusions

This research develops two new operators: Duplication and Fabrication. Duplication is a very useful operator that can speed up the convergence rate after a series of experimental tests including TSP and Continuous test problem sets. The modified GA-duplication can have a faster convergence rate and produces near optimal solution within 100 generations when compared with traditional GA&Ellite. Fabrication is another new operator that deserves our attention. With the advanced in data mining technique, we can introduce more sophisticated chromosome into the GA procedure. One interesting phenomena we observe that Fabrication operator can further improve the quality of the solution by almost 10% if properly adjusted in the GA-fabrication procedure. Furthermore, duplication and fabrication performance depend essentially on two factors: the percentage of them and when to use them. We would like to explore more application of these two operators in the future.

References

1. Banzhaf, W., Nordin, P., Keller, R.E., Francone, F.D.: Genetic Programming – An Introduction – On the Automatic Evolution of Computer Programs and its Applications. CA: Morgan Kaufmann (1998).
2. Davis, L.: Adapting Operator Probabilities in Genetic Algorithms. In J. D. Schaffer (ed.), Proceedings of the Third International Conference on Genetic Algorithms, CA: Morgan Kaufmann (1989) 61-69.
3. Jong, K. A. D., Spears , W. M.: A Formal Analysis of the Role of Multi-Point Crossover in Genetic Algorithms. Annals of Mathematics and Artificial Intelligence, Vol. 5, No. 1, (1992) 1-26.
4. D'Haeseleer, P.: Context Preserving Crossover in Genetic Programming. In Proceedings of the 1994 IEEE World Congress on Computational Intelligence, Vol. 1, (1993) 256-261.
5. Goldberg, D. E.: Genetic Algorithms in Search, Optimization and Machine Learning. Addison-Wesley Publishing Company, Inc. (1989).
6. Mathias, K., Whitley, D.: Genetic Operators, the Fitness Landscape and the Traveling Salesman Problem. In R. Männer and B. Manderick (eds.), Proceedings of Parallel Problem Solving from Nature Vol. 2, (1992) 219-228.
7. Mitchell, M., Forrest, S.: Genetic Algorithms and Artificial Life. Artificial Life, Vol. 1, No. 3 (1994) 267-289.
8. Mitchell, M.: An Introduction to Genetic Algorithms. MIT Press (1996).
9. Schaffer, J. D., Eshelman, L. J.: On Crossover asan Evolutionarily Viable Strategy. In R. K. Belew, L. B. Booker (eds.), Proceedings of the Fourth International Conference on Genetic Algorithms, (1991) 61-68.

Fuzzy Programming for Multiobjective Fuzzy Job Shop Scheduling with Alternative Machines Through Genetic Algorithms[*]

Fu-ming Li[1,2,**], Yun-long Zhu[1], Chao-wan Yin[1], and Xiao-yu Song[1,2]

[1] Shenyang Institute of Automation of the Chinese Academy of Sciences,
110016 Shenyang, China
Tel: +86-24-2397-0681
[2] Graduate school of the Chinese Academy of Sciences,
100039 Beijing, China

Abstract. The optimization of Job Shop scheduling is very important because of its theoretical and practical significance. Much research about it has been reported in recent years. But most of them were about classical Job Shop scheduling. The existence of a gap between scheduling theory and practice has been reported in literature. This work presents a robust procedure to solve multiobjective fuzzy Job Shop scheduling problems with some more realistic constraints such as fuzzy processing time, fuzzy duedate and alternative machine constraints for jobs. On the basis of the agreement index of fuzzy duedate and fuzzy completion time, multiobjective fuzzy Job Shop scheduling problems have been formulated as three-objective ones which not only maximize the minimum agreement index but also maximize the average agreement index and minimize the maximum fuzzy completion time. By adopting two-chromosome representation, an extended G&T algorithm which is suitable for solving the fuzzy Job Shop scheduling with alternative machines has been proposed. Finally, numerical examples are given to illustrate the effectiveness of our proposed method that provides a new way to study planning and scheduling problems in fuzzy circumstances.

1 Introduction

During the last decade, numerous works on the Job Shop scheduling problems concentrated on the deterministic problems. Naturally, in these Job Shop scheduling problems, not only various factors, such as processing time, duedate and so forth , have precisely been fixed at some crisp values, but also a series of machines are specified, on which a given number of operations of each job are processed.

However , when formulating Job Shop scheduling problems which closely describe and represent the real-world problems, various factors involved in the problems are often only imprecisely or ambiguously known to the analyst. In fact, since it is often

---

[*] Foundation item: Project supported by the National Natural Science Foundation, China (No. 70171043), the National Natural Science Foundation, China (No. 70431003) and the National Basic Research Program, China (2002CB312200).
[**] Corresponding author. E-mail: lfm@sia.cn

encountered with uncertainties during the procedure in production, we can only obtain an assumable processing time or its bounds. In the mean time, owing to the fact that the duedate and the grade of satisfaction of a customer are closely interconnected, the different customer has the different requirement for duedate. Thus, not all duedate is strict immobility but is a time-window associated with the grade of satisfaction of a customer, that is duedate is stochastic and fuzzy. During real processing in the workshop, in order to increase the flexibility to manufacturing a wide range of products in a short time, the machine is alternative, on which a certain operation of each job is processed. In such conditions, it may be more appropriate to consider fuzzy processing time due to various factors, fuzzy duedate tolerating a certain amount of earliness or tardiness and alternative machines processing a certain operation of each job. For such kind of Job Shop scheduling, we formulate it as fuzzy Job Shop scheduling with alternative machines.

One of the earlier attempts to approach fuzzy Job Shop scheduling problems considering both fuzzy processing time and fuzzy duedate through the application of genetic algorithms(GA) can be seen in the research of Masatoshi Sakawa, Tetsuya Mori [1-3]. On the basis of the achievement obtained by Masatoshi Sakawa and Tetsuya Mori, this paper will study fuzzy Job Shop scheduling with alternative machines considering not only fuzzy processing time and fuzzy duedate but also alternative machines processing a certain operation of each job. For reflecting real-world situations more adequately, we formulate multiobjective fuzzy Job Shop scheduling with alternative machines as three-objective ones which not only maximize the minimum grade of satisfaction of a customer but also maximize the average grade of satisfaction of a customer and minimize the maximum fuzzy completion time. Then by incorporating the fuzzy theory into the GA, a fuzzy GA which is suitable for solving the formulated problems is proposed. These will provide a kind of effective mean and practice way for studying fuzzy Job Shop scheduling with alternative machines.

2 Formulation and Models of Problems

2.1 Formulation of Problems

Fuzzy Job Shop scheduling with alternative machines may be formulated as follows. Let n jobs be processed on m machines, and each job consists of a set of operations as well as a fuzzy duedate associated with the grade of satisfaction of a customer. Each job must be processed in a given order. Each operation is characterized by specifying both the alternative machine constraints and the fuzzy processing time. Several constraints on jobs and machines, which are listed as follows:

(1) Each operation may be processed on multi-machine.
(2) Each operation consists of a set of fuzzy processing time that involves all possible fuzzy processing time belonged to the multi-machine processing this operation.
(3) Each job must pass through each machine once and only once.
(4) Each machine can only handle at most one operation at a time.
(5) Each operation must be executed uninterrupted on a given machine.
(6) The machine orders between different jobs are unconfined.

The problem is to find a feasible schedule to determine the operation sequences as well as the fuzzy commencing time on the machines under the constraints of the technology sequence.

During the procedure in production, some unexpected events may occur, resulting in small changes to the processing time of each job. Therefore, in many situations, the processing time of which a certain operation l of job i is processed on some machine k or other can only be estimated as being within a certain interval. Let O_{ilk} expresses the l th operation of job i processed on machine k, so the fuzzy processing time of operation O_{ilk} is represented by a triangular fuzzy number (TFN) $\tilde{p}_{ilk}$ and denoted by a triplet ($p_{ilk}^1, p_{ilk}^2, p_{ilk}^3$), that is the most likelihood value of the fuzzy processing time will be p_{ilk}^2, the optimism value will be p_{ilk}^1, the pessimism value will be p_{ilk}^3. The possibility measure of fuzzy processing time is represented by the membership function $\mu_i(x)$ whose possibility distribute function is defined as

$$\mu_i(x) = \begin{cases} (x - P_{ilk}^1)/(P_{ilk}^2 - P_{ilk}^1) & x \in [P_{ilk}^1, P_{ilk}^2] \\ (P_{ilk}^3 - x)/(p_{ilk}^3 - P_{ilk}^2) & x \in [P_{ilk}^2, P_{ilk}^3] \\ 0 & x < P_{ilk}^1, x > P_{ilk}^3 \end{cases} \quad (1)$$

Notation x: the likelihood value of fuzzy processing time.

Owing to the fact that the duedate and the grade of satisfaction of a customer are closely interconnected, the different customer has the different requirement for duedate. Thus, not all duedate is strict immobility but is a time-window associated with the grade of satisfaction of a customer, that is duedate is stochastic and fuzzy. In this paper, the fuzzy duedate is represented by the grade of satisfaction with respect to the job completion time and denoted by a trapezoid fuzzy number $\tilde{D}_i(d_i^c, d_i^a, d_i^b, d_i^d)$. In other words, it will be desired when the value of fuzzy duedate belongs to the interval $[d_i^a, d_i^b]$, whereas it should be avoid when the value belongs to the interval $[d_i^c, d_i^a]$ and $[d_i^b, d_i^d]$ respectively, because the former will result in increasing the work-in-process and the latter will delay the process schedule of the back closely job. The possibility measure of fuzzy completion time is represented by the membership function $\mu_i(c)$ of the trapezoid fuzzy number whose possibility distribute function is defined as

$$\mu_i(c) = \begin{cases} 1 & c \in [d_i^a, d_i^b] \\ (c - d_i^c)/(d_i^a - d_i^c) & c \in [d_i^c, d_i^a] \\ (d_i^d - c)/(d_i^d - d_i^b) & c \in [d_i^b, d_i^d] \\ 0 & c < d_i^c, c > d_i^d \end{cases} \quad (2)$$

Notation c: the likelihood value of fuzzy duedate.

2.2 Models of Problems

When considering fuzzy processing time and fuzzy duedate simultaneously, we can't adopt conventional agreement index to construct performance index because of both processing time and duedate are fuzzy variables. The literature[1] adopted maximize the minimum grade of satisfaction of a customer as performance index. Under the condition of considering not only fuzzy processing time and fuzzy duedate but also alternative machine constraints, the scheduling problem in this paper is still related to the grade of satisfaction whether the jobs delivery will be in time. Consequently it is reasonable and feasible to adopt the grade of satisfaction of a customer as performance index in this paper. The grade of satisfaction of a customer, or the agreement index AI, is defined as value of the area ▲ of membership function intersection(shown in fig. 1) divided by the area △ of the fuzzy completion time $\tilde{C}_i$ membership function with respect to that of the fuzzy duedate $\tilde{D}_i$ membership function. To be more explicit, AI can be expressed as follow.

$$AI = (\text{area } \tilde{C}_i \cap \tilde{D}_i)/(\text{area } \tilde{C}_i) \tag{3}$$

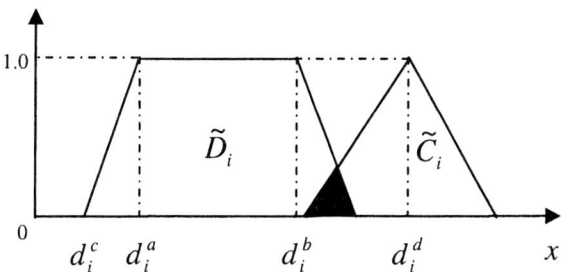

Fig. 1. Customer satisfaction

Notation $\tilde{C}_i$: the fuzzy completion time of the job

$\tilde{D}_i$: the fuzzy duedate of the job

Analyzing the fig. 1, we can come to a conclusion that the grade of satisfaction of a customer defined by formula (3) may be occur such extreme instance as to be zero resulting from no intersection between $\tilde{C}_i$ and $\tilde{D}_i$. In fact, the duedate of each job, which neither defers the delivery of job scheduled in time nor exceeds the existing throughput, has always been holding some grade of satisfaction as a result of being negotiated well between the producer and the customer. The scheduling problem described in this paper is just about such case that the duedate of each job always holds some grade of satisfaction.

Given is a set of n jobs to be scheduled for processing by m machines. Each job consists of s operations. It is requirement that each job has to meet the duedate with some grade of satisfaction. So, giving the priority to the grade of satisfaction of a customer, the multiobjective fuzzy job shop scheduling with alternative machines can be formulated as three-objective ones which not only maximize the minimum agreement index AI but also maximize the average agreement index AI and minimize the maximum fuzzy completion time. To be more explicit, the formulated problems are to

$$\max\{\min_i AI_i\} \quad (4)$$

$$\max\{\frac{1}{n}\sum_{i=1}^{n} AI_i\} \quad (5)$$

$$\min\{\max \tilde{C}_i\} \quad (6)$$

S.t $\tilde{c}_{ilk} - \tilde{p}_{ilk} + M_1(1-a_{ihk}) + M_1(1-f_{ilk}) + M_1(1-f_{igh}) \geq \tilde{c}_{igh}$ (7)

$i=1,2,\ldots,n;\ l,g=1,2,\ldots,s;\ h,k=1,2,\ldots,m$

$\tilde{c}_{jlk} - \tilde{p}_{igk} + M_1(1-x_{ijk}) + M_1(1-f_{jlk}) + M_1(1-f_{igk}) \geq \tilde{p}_{jlh}$ (8)

$i,j=1,2,\ldots,n;\ l,g=1,2,\ldots,s;\ k=1,2,\ldots,m$

$\tilde{c}_{ilk} \geq 0,\quad i=1,2,\ldots,n;\ l=1,2,\ldots,s;\ k=1,2,\ldots,m$

$M_2(1-f_{ilk}) = \tilde{p}_{ilk}, i=1,2,\ldots,n;\ l=1,2,\ldots,s;\ k=1,2,\ldots,m,\ M_2 \ll M_1$

$x_{ijk}=0$ or $1,\ i,j=1,2,\ldots,n;\ k=1,2,\ldots,m$

$a_{ijk}=0$ or $1,\ i,j=1,2,\ldots,n;\ k=1,2,\ldots,m$

$f_{ilk}=0$ or $1,\ i=1,2,\ldots,n;\ l=1,2,\ldots,s;\ k=1,2,\ldots,m$

It should be emphasized here that these objective functions (4), (5), (6) respectively denote maximize the minimum agreement index AI, maximize the average agreement index AI and minimize the maximum fuzzy completion time.

Notation Formula (7): the technological sequence of the job operation under the costraints of the technics,

Formula (8): machines order for processing the jobs,

$\tilde{c}_{ilk}$: fuzzy completion time of operation l of job i processed on some machine k

$\tilde{p}_{ilk}$: fuzzy processing time of operation l of job i processed on some machine k

M_1, M_2 : a positive constant of extremely large value,

$$a_{ihk} = \begin{cases} 1, & \text{processing on machine } h \text{ precedes on machine } k \text{ for job } i \\ 0, & \text{otherwise} \end{cases}$$

$$x_{ijk} = \begin{cases} 1, & \text{if job } i \text{ precedes job } j \text{ on machine } k \\ 0, & \text{otherwise} \end{cases}$$

$$f_{ilk} = \begin{cases} 1, & \text{if operation } l \text{ of job } i \text{ is processed on machine } k \\ 0, & \text{otherwise} \end{cases}$$

3 Design of Algorithm

In this paper, we apply genetic algorithms to fuzzy Job Shop scheduling with alternative machines and introduce some fuzzy number and interrelated fuzzy operators as well as the method for ranking triangular fuzzy number to construct algorithm when we deal with the fitness function of genetic algorithms. For notational convenience, we adopt two-chromosome representation [4-6] to represent the solution under the condition of alternative machine constraints.

3.1 Operations on Fuzzy Number

Among the application of fuzzy genetic algorithms, fuzzy number operations are the linchpin of evaluating the fitness of genetic algorithms. These operations involve the operation sum and the operation max as well as the method for ranking triangular fuzzy number.

Denote a triangular fuzzy number $\tilde{r}$ by a triplet (p, r, q). Then, as is well-known, the addition of two triangular fuzzy numbers $\tilde{r} = (p, r, q)$ and $\tilde{t} = (u, t, v)$ is shown by the following formula:

$$\tilde{r} + \tilde{t} = (p + u, r + t, q + v)$$

The addition is used when calculating the fuzzy completion time of each operation. For simplicity, we approximate the max operation with the following formula:

$$\widetilde{\max}(\tilde{r}, \tilde{t}) = (p, r, q) \vee (u, t, v) \cong (p \vee u, r \vee t, q \vee v)$$

Such max operation is used when calculating the fuzzy starting time for each operation.

Since fuzzy completion times are calculated as the sum of fuzzy processing times, they become TFNs. Hence, when considering to minimize the maximum fuzzy completion time as an objective function, some ranking methods become necessary for ranking the fuzzy completion times. In this ranking method, the criterion for dominance is one of the following three in the order given below.

Criterion 1. $C_1(\tilde{r}) = \dfrac{p + 2r + q}{4}$. The greatest associate ordinary number is used as a first criterion for ranking the two TFNs.

Criterion 2. $C_2(\tilde{r}) = r$. If C_1 does not rank the two TFNs, those which have the best maximal presumption will be chosen as a second criterion.

Criterion 3. $C_3(\tilde{r}) = q - p$. If C_1 and C_2 do not rank the TFNs, the difference of the spreads will be used as a third criterion.

3.2 Design of Genetic Algorithms

(1) Representation design

For fuzzy Job Shop scheduling with alternative machines, in this paper, we adopt two-chromosome representation to construct a dual matrices to coding. In such scheduling problem involving m jobs and n operations, the first line of the matrices represents $m \times n$ array of all operations. For the sake of simplicity, let $m = 3$, $n = 3$, the genes of the first line are represented as [1 2 3 1 1 3 2 2 3]. We assign same symbols for the operations of same job. Here, 1 denotes the job j_1, 2 denotes the job j_2 and 3 denotes the job j_3. Since each job consists of three operations, the symbol of each job will appear three times in the chromosome and the processing order of the operations are corresponding to the position order of the job in the chromosome.

The second line of the matrices represents on which machines the corresponding operations of the first line are processed. Each element of the second line being as the complementary information of the first line is an accessional information of that of the second line. Each column of dual matrices represents a gene of chromosome. Thus is achieved the design of chromosome representation on fuzzy Job Shop scheduling with alternative machines.

(2) Initial solutions generating algorithm

It is known in Job Shop scheduling problems of which the scheduling index is normal that an optimal schedule exists within the set of active schedules. Although the multiobjective fuzzy Job Shop scheduling with alternative machines incorporating not only fuzzy processing time and fuzzy duedate but also alternative machines, since the schedule indexes are still normal in this problem, we can expect an optimal schedule to exist within the set of active schedules. Therefore, in this paper, we use the set of active schedules as the search space.

The Giffler and Thompsom algorithm (G&T algorithm) is well-known as the procedure for generating active schedules. To deal with the multiobjective fuzzy Job Shop scheduling with alternative machines, this algorithm can be extended to generate the initial solutions in the following way.

Step 1. Find the set C of all the earliest operations in technological sequence among the operations which are not yet scheduled. If the earliest operation of a certain job can be processed on alternative machines, the alternative operations will belong to the set C.

Step 2. Calculate the fuzzy completion time for each operation and denote the obtained fuzzy completion time of each operation by (EC_{ilk}^1, EC_{ilk}^2, EC_{ilk}^3).

Step 3. According to the criterions of ranking the fuzzy completion time, find the operation $O_{i^*l^*k^*}$ that has a minimum fuzzy completion time in the set C.

Find the set G of operations which consists of the operations $O_{ilk^*} \in C$ sharing the same machine k^*. Since the operations in G overlap in time, G is called the conflict set.

Step 4. Randomly select one operation $O_{i_s j_s k^*}$ among the conflict set G. Taking the select operation as a standard, update EC_{ilk}^1, EC_{ilk}^2, EC_{ilk}^3 by adding the fuzzy processing time to the fuzzy operation starting time determined by the max of the selected operation as the precedent on of the same job among the jobs including the operations with conflicts. Remove the selected operation $O_{i_s j_s k^*}$ from the set C (if exist corresponding alternative operations with respect to the selected operation $O_{i_s j_s k^*}$, remove the alternative operations together.). Add the back closely operation (including the alternative operations) of $O_{i_s j_s k^*}$ to the set C and calculate the fuzzy completion time.

Step 5: Repeat Steps 3 to 5, until all operations are scheduled.

Step 6: Verify whether the grades of satisfaction of the jobs are less than the preestablished value. If it is true, then the chromosome will be quit and be regenerated.

In this way, an initial population can be obtained and the constraints subjected to the individuals can be met automatically. Step 6 is a heuristic rule. It contributes to avoid such bug as the grade of satisfaction of a certain job is equal to zero among the chromosome and ensure that an initial solution of better quality can be obtained.

(3) Selection operator

In this paper, the values of the objective function are directly served as that of the fitness function. We adopt roulette wheel selection as a selection method. It is a direct ratio selection strategy and can select a new population according to the direct ratio with respect to fitness values.

Step 1. Calculate the fitness values $eval(v_k)$ of each chromosome v_k.

$$eval(v_k) = f(AI_k); \quad k = 1, 2, \ldots, N \ (N : \text{the number of the population})$$

Step 2. Calculate the sum of fitness values of all chromosomes among the population.

$$F = \sum_{k=1}^{N} eval(v_k)$$

Step 3. Calculate the select ratio of p_k of each chromosome v_k.

$$p_k = \frac{eval(v_k)}{F}; \quad k = 1, 2, \ldots, N$$

Step 4. Calculate the cumulate ratio of q_k of each chromosome v_k.

$$q_k = \sum_{j=1}^{k} p_j; \quad k = 1, 2, \ldots, N$$

Step 5. Give the random number $r \in [0, 1]$ at the interval $[0, 1]$.

Step 6. If $r \leq q_1$, then select the first chromosome v_1, or else select the k th chromosome v_k ($2 \leq k \leq N$) and make $q_{k-1} \leq r \leq q_k$ hold.

Step 7. Repeat Steps 5 to 6 up to N times, until new population is selected.

In order to prevent the optimal solution from being destroyed by crossover and mutation operations, we also use the elitist way on the basis of roulette wheel selection, which can accelerate the searching speed. In other words, the individual with the greatest fitness value among the current population can't participate in the operations of crossover and mutation but is preserved to the next generation to substitute for the individual with the worst fitness value.

(4) Crossover operator and mutation operator

For ensuring that the child individual is still active schedule after the operations of crossover and mutation between two parent individuals, we adopt the generating algorithms for crossover and mutation based on the essential of the G&T algorithm. Comparing the crossover algorithm with the G&T algorithms, there is the difference of Step 4 between them. Step 4 of the G&T algorithm is to randomly select an operation form the conflict set G, and that of the crossover algorithm is to select an operation according to the occurring order in two parent individuals. The process is described as the following.

Step 1. Find the set C of all the earliest operations in technological sequence among the operations which are not yet scheduled. If the earliest operation of a certain job can be processed on alternative machines, the alternative operations will belong to the set C.

Step 2. Calculate the fuzzy completion time for each operation and denote the obtained fuzzy completion time of each operation by (EC_{ilk}^1, EC_{ilk}^2, EC_{ilk}^3).

Step 3. According to the criterions of ranking the fuzzy completion time, find the operation $O_{i^*l^*k^*}$ that has a minimum fuzzy completion time in the set C.

Find the set G of operations which consists of the operations $O_{ilk^*} \in C$ sharing the same machine k^*.

Step 4. Select an operation from the conflict set G.

1) Give a random number $\varepsilon \in [0, 1]$, and compare it with mutation ratio of p_m. If $\varepsilon < p_m$, randomly select an operation O_{il}^* from the conflict set G.

2) Otherwise, select one of two parent individuals with the same ratio, denoted by p_s. Find an operation O_{il}^* among all operations of the set G, which is scheduled at the earliest in the p_s.

3) Schedule the operation O_{il}^* according to the earliest completion time of l operation of job i among the next generation chromosome.

Step 5. Update the set C.

1) Remove the operation O_{il}^* (if exist the corresponding alternative operations, remove them together) from the set C.

2) Add the back closely operation (including the alternative operations) of O_{il}^* to the set C, and calculate the fuzzy completion time.

Step 6. Repeat Steps 3 to 5, until all operations are scheduled.

Here, the process conflict is settled by randomly selecting the operation in the substep 1) of Step 4 and that is settled by according priority to the operation scheduled at the earliest among the parent individuals with conflict operation in the substep 2) of Step 4.

(5) Termination criterion

The termination condition of the algorithm is the preestablished number N_{max} of maximal generation.

The above algorithm is constructed on the basis of the G&T algorithm. The G&T algorithm is regarded as the element of all heuristic algorithms based on priority rules and possesses the attribute of performing easily and less time complexity [7]. In this paper, the time complexity of the algorithm adopting two-chromosome representation can not exceed twice as that of the sing-chromosome representation (based on G&T algorithm). So the algorithm proposed in our paper also possesses the merit of performing easily and less time complexity and is suitable for solving a larger scale scheduling problems.

4 Analysis of Numerical Examples

As illustrative of the algorithm proposed in this paper, we apply the algorithm to the multiobjective fuzzy Job Shop scheduling with alternative machines and adopt such machine constraints (shown in table 1) as were in the numerical example [6] of 6 jobs and 6 operations on 10 machines (6/6/10-example). For example, the 3rd operation of job J_3 can be processed on either machine M_6 or machine M_8 (shown in table 1). However, in the numerical example proposed by Christoph S, the processing time and duedate are both crisp. This paper uses the machine constraints proposed by Christoph S for reference, the fuzzy processing time and fuzzy duedate of each job are shown in table 2.

The proposed algorithms have been coded with VC++ and run on an Intel-compatible PC with PIV 1.6 GHz processor under Windows professional 2000. The parameter values of GA are given as following: population number N =60, crossover ratio of p_c =0.90, mutation ratio of p_m =0.03, the maximal generation N_{max} =80.

Table 1. The alternative machines and the machine constraints

Jobs	Machine constraints (M_i/M_j)					
J_1	3/10	1	2	4/7	6/8	3
J_2	2	3	5/8	6/7	1	4/10
J_3	3/9	4/7	6/8	1	2/10	5
J_4	4	1/9	3/7	2/8	5	6
J_5	5	2/7	3/10	6/9	1	4/8
J_6	2	4/7	6/9	1	5/8	3

Table 2. The fuzzy processing time and fuzzy duedate of each job

	Fuzzy processing time					
	J_1	J_2	J_3	J_4	J_5	J_6
1	(1, 3, 4)/ (4, 5, 6)	(4, 6, 8)	(1, 1, 2)/ (3, 4, 6)	(5, 7, 9)	(5, 6, 7)	(2, 3, 4)
2	(8, 10, 12)	(7, 8, 9)	(4, 5, 7)/ (6, 7, 8)	(3, 4, 5)/ (1, 3, 5)	(8, 10, 12)/ (10, 12, 15)	(9, 10, 12)/ (9, 11, 13)
3	(7, 9, 11)	(1, 1, 2)/ (3, 4, 5)	(3, 5, 6)/ (4, 6, 8)	(3, 4, 5)/ (4, 6, 8)	(6, 7, 8)/ (7, 9, 12)	(7, 8, 10)/ (5, 7, 9)
4	(3, 5, 6)/ (3, 4, 6)	(4, 5, 6)/ (4, 6, 7)	(4, 5, 6)	(1, 3, 4)/ (4, 5, 7)	(6, 8, 10)/ (7, 8, 9)	(8, 9, 10)
5	(2, 3, 4)/ (2, 3, 4)	(2, 3, 5)	(7, 9, 11)/ (9, 11, 13)	(1, 1, 2)	(3, 5, 6)	(3, 4, 6)/ (3, 5, 7)
6	(8, 10, 12)	(2, 3, 4)/ (1, 3, 4)	(1, 1, 2)	(2, 3, 5)	(2, 4, 6)/ (6, 7, 8)	(8, 9, 10)
Fuzzy duedate	D_1 (25, 31, 43, 55), D_2 (24, 28, 35, 45), D_3 (21, 25, 32, 45), D_4 (25, 29, 36, 47), D_5 (32, 37, 43, 53), D_6 (34, 38, 43, 54)					

For the three different agreement indexes (formula (4), formula (5) and formula (6)) of 6/6/10 multiobjective fuzzy Job Shop scheduling with alternative machines, the optimal scheduling results of jobs are shown respectively as following.

The optimal scheduling with $\max\{\min_i AI_i\}$:

$$\begin{pmatrix} 361563261322134544251636134245245156 \\ 323547261835214797634110865215910 61543 \end{pmatrix}$$

The optimal scheduling with $\max\{\frac{1}{n}\sum_{i=1}^{n} AI_i\}$:

$$\begin{pmatrix} 3 & 6 & 1 & 5 & 6 & 3 & 2 & 3 & 1 & 2 & 2 & 3 & 1 & 4 & 6 & 5 & 2 & 4 & 6 & 4 & 5 & 1 & 3 & 6 & 1 & 3 & 4 & 2 & 4 & 2 & 5 & 4 & 5 & 6 & 1 & 5 \\ 3 & 2 & 3 & 5 & 4 & 7 & 2 & 6 & 1 & 3 & 5 & 1 & 2 & 4 & 9 & 7 & 6 & 9 & 1 & 7 & 3 & 4 & 1 & 0 & 8 & 6 & 5 & 2 & 1 & 5 & 1 & 0 & 9 & 6 & 1 & 3 & 5 & 4 \end{pmatrix}$$

The optimal scheduling with $\min\{\max \tilde{C}_i\}$:

$$\begin{pmatrix} 3 & 6 & 1 & 5 & 6 & 3 & 2 & 6 & 1 & 3 & 2 & 2 & 1 & 3 & 4 & 5 & 4 & 4 & 2 & 5 & 1 & 6 & 3 & 6 & 1 & 3 & 4 & 2 & 4 & 5 & 2 & 4 & 5 & 1 & 5 & 6 \\ 3 & 2 & 3 & 5 & 4 & 7 & 2 & 6 & 1 & 8 & 3 & 5 & 2 & 1 & 4 & 7 & 9 & 7 & 6 & 3 & 4 & 1 & 1 & 0 & 8 & 6 & 5 & 2 & 1 & 5 & 9 & 1 & 0 & 6 & 1 & 5 & 4 & 3 \end{pmatrix}$$

The grade of satisfaction of a customer and the fuzzy completion time of each job with respect to three agreement index are shown respectively as following.

Table 3. The grade of satisfaction of a customer and the fuzzy completion time of each job

Job	J_1	J_2	J_3	J_4	J_5	J_6
I	0.894545	0.881177	1.000000	0.916190	0.837507	0.912222
II	0.916522	0.909091	1.000000	0.924577	0.893775	0.984367
III	(34, 44, 57)	(29, 36, 47)	(25, 31, 39)	(28, 36, 49)	(38, 45, 57)	(39, 46, 57)

I — The grade of satisfaction($\max\{\min_i AI_i\}$);

II — The grade of satisfaction($\max\{\frac{1}{n}\sum_{i=1}^{n} AI_i\}$)

III — Fuzzy completion time($\min\{\max \tilde{C}_i\}$)

The obtained results show that the customer requirement for duedate of each job can be met with a certain grade of satisfaction. So the scheduling results are practical and feasible. These indicate that the algorithm proposed in this paper is effective to solve the fuzzy Job Shop scheduling with alternative machines.

From the optimal scheduling, it is easy to make a conclusion that the agreement indexes, or $\max\{\min_i AI_i\}$ and $\min\{\max \tilde{C}_i\}$, are equivalent, namely, the same optimal scheduling results can be obtained with respect to the equivalent agreement index.

5 Concluding Remarks

This paper made a deep study of fuzzy Job Shop scheduling problems. Fuzzy set theory is adopted to formulate models of fuzzy Job Shop scheduling with alternative machines which consider not only fuzzy processing time and fuzzy duedate but also alternative machine constraints. On the basis of the agreement index of fuzzy duedate and fuzzy completion time, multiobjective fuzzy Job Shop scheduling problems have been formulated as three-objective ones which not only maximize the minimum agreement index but also maximize the average agreement index and minimize the maximum fuzzy completion time. By adopting two-chromosome representation, an extended G&T algorithm which is suitable for solving the fuzzy Job Shop scheduling with alternative machines has been proposed. Finally, numerical examples are given to illustrate the effectiveness of our proposed method that provides a new way to study planning and scheduling problems in fuzzy circumstances.

References

1. Masatoshi Sakawa, Tetsuya Mori. An efficient genetic algorithm for Job-Shop scheduling problems with fuzzy processing time and fuzzy duedate . Computers &Industrial Engineering, 36(2)(1999): 325 – 341.
2. Masatoshi Sakawa, Ryo Kubota. Fuzzy programming for multiobjective Job Shop scheduling with fuzzy processing time and fuzzy duedate through genetic algorithms . European Journal of Operational Research, 120(2)(2000): 393-407.
3. Masatoshi Sakawa, Ryo Kubota. Two-objective fuzzy Job Shop scheduling through genetic algorithm . Electronics and Communications in Japan, Part 3, 84(4)(2001): 60-67.
4. Nabil. Nasr, Elsayed E A. Job Shop scheduling with alternative machines . International Journal of Production Research, 28(9)(1990): 1595-1609.
5. J.Christopher Beck, Mark S. Fox, Constraint-directed techniques for scheduling alternative activities . Artificial Intelligence, 121(2)(2000): 211-250.
6. Christoph S. Thomalla. Job shop scheduling with alternative process plans . International Journal of Production Economics., 74(1)(2001): 125-134..
7. Storer, R. , S. Wu, and R. Vaccari, New Search Spaces for Sequencing Problems with Application to Job Shop Scheduling[J].Management Science, 38(10)(1992): 1495-1510.

The Study of Special Encoding in Genetic Algorithms and a Sufficient Convergence Condition of GAs[*]

Bo Yin[1], Zhiqiang Wei[1], and Qingchun Meng[1,2]

[1] Computer Department of Ocean University of China,
Postfach 26 60 71, Qingdao, China
{ybfirst, weizhiqiang, mengqc}@ouc.edu.cn
[2] State Key Lab. of Intelligent Technology & Systems Tsinghua University,
Postfach 10 00 84, Beijing, China
Mengqc@ouc.edu.cn

Abstract. In this paper, the encoding techniques of Genetic Algorithms are studied and a sufficient convergence condition on genetic encoding is presented. Some new categories of codes are defined, such as Uniform code, Bias code, Tri-sector code and Symmetric codes etc. Meanwhile, some new definitions on genetic encoding as well as some operations are presented, so that a sufficient convergence condition of GAs is inducted. Based on this study, a new genetic strategy, GASC(Genetic Algorithm with Symmetric Codes), is developed and applied in robot dynamic control and path planning. The experimental results show that the special genetic encoding techniques enhance the performance of Genetic Algorithms. The convergence speed of GASC is much faster than that of some traditional genetic algorithms. That is very significant for finding more application of GAs, as, in many cases, Genetic Algorithms' applications are limited by their convergence speed.

1 Introduction

The study of Genetic Algorithms(GAs) and their applications have fascinated a great number of researchers during last decades. GAs have enjoyed wide recognition in a large range of domains [1],[2]. A number of experimental studies show that GAs exhibit impressive efficiency in practice and consistently outperform both gradient techniques and various forms of random search on many complex problems. But with the increasing of the problem complexity, classical GAs usually can't solve the problem efficiently. Therefore, it is necessary to improve the performance of GAs and bring some good properties to them, so that they can solve complex problems with higher efficiency[3],[4].

In this paper, the problems of encoding and algorithm convergence in GAs will be studied. Some new encoding techniques are developed. Meanwhile, some definitions in genetic encoding as well as some operations are presented, so that a sufficient convergence condition of GAs could be inducted. Following these studies, some new genetic strategies are proposed, such as Genetic Algorithms with Symmetric Codes, etc. These genetic strategies have been successfully applied to solve the problem of robot dynamic control and path planning [5],[6].

---

[*] This research is supported by the National Natural Science Foundation of China(60374031).

2 The Influence of Encoding on the Performance of GAs

It is known that encoding is the first step of GAs. GAs encode the parameters of a problem and produce the initial population. From the initial population, GAs begin to search for the problem's solution. If the initial population is an ill distribution due to the encoding deficiency, i.e. it can not reflect the possible distribution of the optimal solution, it will take a long time to get the optimal solution, or even the solution can't be obtained sometimes. Therefore, encoding can affect the GAs' performance, especially their convergence.

However, the research of the encoding problem has not got enough attention so far. Bethke[7] and Holland[8] analyzed the properties of the binary code string from the concept of Building Block. But they didn't systematically analyze the influence of encoding on the performance of GAs from the aspect of the population members' distribution in the solution space.

In the following section, we will focus our study on some special encoding techniques.

3 Some Special Encoding Techniques in GAs

Encoding determines whether GAs can represent a problem effectively. In order to guarantee GAs' performance, some special genetic codes and encoding techniques have been developed. These typical encoding techniques are introduced as follows.

3.1 Some Traditional Special Encoding Techniques

3.1.1 Bias Encoding
Bias encoding is to encode the problem solution space in different member densities. In a sub-spaces, in which there exists bigger possibility of solution, more members should be encoded.

3.1.2 Uniform Encoding
Uniform encoding will distribute the population members in a manner of uniform possibilities.

3.1.3 Tri-sector Encoding
Tri-sector code is a special kind of Bias Code. According to its definition, the population will be encoded in three sectors, and in each sector the values of members are biased to some values.

3.2 Symmetric Encoding

In this section, the Symmetric Encoding is proposed to improve the performance of GAs. Symmetric codes include Horizontal Symmetric Code, Vertical Symmetric Code, General Horizontal Symmetric Code and General Vertical Symmetric Code.

Definition 1. Horizontal Symmetric Code String: HSCS

(1) If a code string S_i satisfies the following constraint:

$$\sum_{k=1}^{K} Sb_{ik} = 0 . \tag{1}$$

Then, it is called a horizontal symmetric code string, denoted by HSCS.

(2) The encoding of the string S_i is called Horizontal Symmetric Encoding (or Horizontal Symmetric Code), denoted by HSC. And $S_i \in$ HSC.

(3) If a sub-code string of S_i satisfies the following constraint:

$$\sum_{j=J1}^{J} Sb_{ij} = 0, J \in [2, K] \quad and \quad J - J1 + 1 \geq 2 . \tag{2}$$

then the sub-code string $(Sb_{iJ1}, Sb_{iJ1+1}, \cdots, Sb_{iJ})$ is called a sub-horizontal symmetric code string, denoted by $(J-J1)d$-SHSCS.

(4) If $J-J1=2$, this sub-horizontal symmetric code string is called 2-distance sub-horizontal symmetric code string, abbreviated as $2d$-SHSCS. Analogically, $(J-J1)d$-SHSCS can be defined. Its corresponding sub-code string is called sub-horizontal symmetric code string.

Definition 2. Vertical Symmetric Code String: VSCS

Suppose there are n horizontal symmetric code strings with the same length K:

$$\begin{aligned}
S_1 &= (Sb_{11}, Sb_{12}, \cdots\cdots, Sb_{1K}) \\
S_2 &= (Sb_{21}, Sb_{22}, \cdots\cdots, Sb_{2K}) \\
&\vdots \\
S_n &= (Sb_{n1}, Sb_{n2}, \cdots\cdots, Sb_{nK})
\end{aligned} \tag{3}$$

(1) If there are two code strings l and i, which have the following relation:

$$\sum_{k=1}^{K} (Sb_{ik} - Sb_{lk}) = 0 \quad j \neq l \text{ and } l, i \in n . \tag{4}$$

then the code strings S_l and S_i are called vertical symmetric code strings, denoted by VSCS.

(2) The encoding of VSCS are called Vertical Symmetric Encoding, denoted by VSC, or abbreviated as Vertical Symmetric Codes, which is expressed by $(S_i, S_l) \in$ VSC.

According to definition 1, we can define $(J-J1)$ distance sub-vertical symmetric code strings $(J-J1)d$-SVSCS. In the operation of GAs, a sub-symmetric code string can generate new symmetric code strings.

Definition 3. General Horizontal Symmetric Code: GHSC
If a symmetric code string S_i satisfies:

$$\sum_{k=0}^{K} Sb_{ik} = C_2 - C_1 . \quad (5)$$

Then the code string S_i is called a General Horizontal Symmetric Code String, denoted by GHSCS, i.e. $S_i \in$ GHSC. C_1 and C_2 are two constants. According to Definition 1, sub-General Horizontal Symmetric Code ($J-J1)d$ –GHSCS) can be defined.

Definition 4. General Vertical Symmetric Code : GVSC
If two general horizontal symmetric code strings satisfy:

$$\sum_{k=1}^{K} (Sb_{ik} - Sb_{jk}) = C_2 - C_1 . \quad (6)$$

Then the code strings S_i and S_j are called General Vertical Symmetric Code Strings, denoted by VGSCS, $(S_i, S_j) \in$ GVSC. C_1 and C_2 are constants. According to Definition 2, sub-General Vertical Symmetric Code (SGVSC) can be defined.

Based on these special codes, some new genetic strategies are developed, such as Genetic Strategy with Gate Change Function and Genetic Algorithm with Symmetric Codes [5],[6].

4 Some Definitions for the Study of Genetic Algorithm Convergence

The former study[5]shows that the influence of genetic encoding on GAs' performance is significant. Based on the encoding techniques, some new and powerful genetic strategies may be developed, so as to deal with more complex engineering problems. In practice, it is obvious that GAs must be modified when they are applied to solve some complex problems. Therefore, it is necessary to study more genetic encoding and GAs' convergence problems.

In this section, some new definitions and member operations are proposed to describe the encoding problem and encoding mechanism.

Supposing that a population *P-space* has m members and each member has n binary bits complying with the requirement of GAs coding, i.e.

$$P-space = (S_1, S_2, \cdots, S_m)^T = (C_1, C_2, \cdots, C_n) \\ = [a_{ij}]_{i=1,\cdots,m, j=1,\cdots,n} . \quad (7)$$

Here, a_{ij} is a binary bit '0' or '1'. $C_1, C_2, \cdots, C_n$ represent n columns in *P-space*. $S_1, S_2, \cdots, S_m$ represent m rows.

Definition 1. (Link)
A column C_i of a population P-space is called as a Link, so there are n Links in the population P-space.

Definition 2. (Dead-block)
In a P-space, if there exists one or several sub-matrix blocks in which all its elements can not be changed when a cross-over operation is proceeded, it is called as a Dead-block. In another word, in Dead-block, all the elements are of same value.

Definition 3. (Living-block)
In a P-space, if there exists one or several sub-matrix blocks in which all its elements can be changed when a cross-over operation is proceeded, it is called as a Living-block. In the same way, Living-population (Definition 4) and Dead-population (Definition 5) can be defined.

Definition 4. (Fix-link)
If all the elements in a Link C_i of a population are of same values '0' or '1', it is called as a Fix-link.

Definition 5. (Unfix-link)
If in the m elements of a Link C_i, there is at least one element which has different value from those of the others, this link is called as an Unfix-link.

Definition 6. (Bit-exchange position)
When a cross-over operation is conducted between two members S_l and S_k at the ith bit position, this bit is called as Bit-exchange position P_{ci}.

Definition 7. (Bit-transformation)
A cross-over operation between two members at P_{ci} is called as genetic transformation noted as T_i.

Definition 8. (Bit-transposition)
An operation between two consecutive Bit-transpositions T_i and T_{i+1} is known as a Bit-transposition operation, noted as TP_i.

Definition 9. (Bit-and operation)
If an operation, conducted between two bits b_i of member S_k and b_j of member S_l, satisfies the following law:

$$\begin{aligned} &\text{if } b_i = b_j && \text{then } b_i \otimes b_j = b_i. \\ &\text{if } b_i \neq b_j && \text{then } b_i \otimes b_j = *. \\ &\text{if } b_i \text{ or } b_j = * && \text{then } b_i \otimes b_j = *. \\ &i, j = 1, 2, \cdots, n, \ b_i \in S_k, \ b_j \in S_l. \end{aligned} \quad (8)$$

Here, the symbol * represents a Don't Care Bit [12]. This operation is called as Bit-and operation. Based on this operation, Member-and (Definition 12) and Population-and operation (Definition 13) can be defined in the same way.

As it is known, a population, $P\text{-}space = (C_1, C_2, \ldots C_n)$, in which a member has n elements, will have 2^n possible members. Therefore, in general a Genetic Algorithm should be able to generate any one of the 2^n possible members. According to the above definitions, we can get the sufficient convergence condition of GAs.

5 The Sufficient Convergence Condition on Encoding of GAs

Based on the above definitions on population and genetic operations, some conclusions will be discussed in the following lemmas and theorems.

Lemma 1. In a population with m members and n Links, if all of its n Links are Unfix-links, then an Unfix-member will be generated after a population-and operation.

Lemma 2. In a Living-population with m members and each member with n elements, any of the n elements in a member may be changed by limited times of transposition operations.

Lemma 2 means that, in a Living population, any of the 2^n possible members in solution space may be obtained by limited times of transposition operations.

Theorem 1. In a population with m members and each member with n bits, only if the result of its Population-and operation is a Don't Care member, it is possible to generate any of the possible 2^n members in the population by limited times of Transposition or Transformation operations. In another word, each Link in the population is required to be Unfixed Link.

Theorem 1 means that only if every link in a population is Unfixed Link, it is possible for Genetic Algorithm to generate any of 2^n possible members of the population by limited numbers of genetic operation. Otherwise GAs will run the risk of being unable to generate some members.

Theorem 2. Supposed that an optimization problem has a solution space that is covered by a Living-population of GAs, and the population has m members and each member has n bits. If the condition in Theorem 1 is satisfied, then in GAs the problem's solution or solutions may be got by limited genetic Transposition or Transformation operations.

Theorem 2 presents a sufficient condition on the convergence of GAs. This sufficient condition will help us to take a better encoding requirement, so that a GA can get its convergence, i.e. this condition can guarantee a GA to avoid the risk of missing some solutions during the solution procedure.

6 The Application of GASC in Robot Optimal Control and Path Planning

The problem of robot dynamic control and path planning has been studied for decades. This problem has very high algorithm complexity, as there are multiple variables and solutions. In order to solve this problem using GAs, some measures must be taken so as to improve the efficiency of GAs. In this paper, the special genetic strategy-GASC is employed to solve this problem.

From literature[5], it is known that the robot has a linear dynamic model (the relation between controls C_1, C_2 and linear velocity and angular velocity; the final velocities: $v(T) = w(T) = 0$, there T is the time in which robot finishes one trajectory). According to the definition of Symmetric Codes, we can know that the population in GASC can automatically satisfy the robot linear speed and angular speed constraints at the final point of a trajectory. This property will make the problem easier to solve. That is why we develop GASC. The following two theorems can express the advantages of the application of Symmetric Codes to the robot problem.

Theorem 1. If and only if two controls C_1 and C_2 (the members of a population) are Horizontal Symmetric Code: HSC, then linear velocity at the final point of trajectory v(T) is zero. Or in the following expression:

$$v(T)=0 \Leftrightarrow (C_1, C_2) \in HSC. \tag{9}$$

Theorem 2. If and only if two controls C_1 and C_2 are Vertical Symmetric Code: VSC, then angular velocity at the final point of trajectory w(T) is zero. Or in the following expression:

$$w(T)=0 \Leftrightarrow (C_1, C_2) \in VSC. \tag{10}$$

The above theorems are derived under the condition of linear robot dynamic model and zero final velocity. They can be extended to general final velocity conditions.

From the above two theorems, it is clear that if the population (C_1 and C_2) of GA is encoded in Symmetric Codes, the robot's linear and angular final velocities' constraints will be automatically satisfied.

7 Experimental Results

From the previous section, we can see that the robot optimal dynamic control and path planning problem can be mathematically formulated into an optimization problem. GAs are applied to solve this problem. Since GAs have learning abilities, they can search and improve the solution generation by generation.

In the application of GASC, the robot energy consumed is considered as a criterion. The optimization function is formatted according to the principle of external penalty method for dealing with the constraints. The main algorithm parameters are: Popsize= 50; Pc=1; Pm=0.02. Two kinds of Genetic Algorithms are used in the experiment:(1) Simple Genetic Algorithms; (2) GASC.

7.1 Experimental Results of Simple Genetic Algorithms

In this phase several simple genetic techniques are used. We have practiced two kinds of codes and three "mutation—crossover" methods:

1. Code 1: uniform code. The robot torques C_1 and C_2 are uniformly coded from -0.10 to 0.10.

    Code 2: 3--sector code. In this code, C_1 and C_2 are divided into 3 sectors (T1, T2, T3). T1=15, T2=20, T3=15.

    During T1 stage, roughly 70% of C_1, C_2 have values from .04 to .10, 20% from 0 to .04 and 10% from -0.10 to 0.

    During T2 stage, approximately 60% of C_1, C_2 have values from -0.02 to 0.02, 20% from 0.02 to 0.10 and 20% from -0.10 to -0.02.

During T3 stage, roughly 70% of C_1, C_2 have values from -0.10 to -0.04, 20% from -0.04 to 0 and 10% from 0 to 0.10.
2. Random 10-point cross-over technique. In every member of a generation, 10 points are chosen randomly, and cross-over occurs between two strings chosen randomly.
3. 1-point cross-over technique. In every generation, we choose two members randomly and a cross-over is performed at the point at which robot meet an obstacle.
4. 10-point--1-point cross-over technique. During the operation of the first half number of generations given, 10-point crossover technique is introduced in, and the second half, 1-point method is used.

The results obtained by simple GAs are listed in Table 1. Meanwhile, Fig.1 is the trajectory obtained by the simple GAs. From Fig.1, we can see that the trajectory is not satisfactory. Even if the simulation is allowed to proceed to 100000 generations, there is not any string which arrived at the final point X(20,20). This is comprehensible, since simple GAs often break the hopeful strings and destroy the previous search work unreasonably.

Table 1. The list of the results obtained by simple Gas

Tests	Codes	GN	K_{j1}	K_{j2}	Q_o	BP(x,y)
P1T1	1	2000	0.4	4.0	0.8	8.7/9.8
P1T2	1	2000	0.6	6.0	0.8	10/0.3
P1T3	2	2000	0.6	6.0	0.8	10.8/0.3
P1T4	2	10000	1.2	0.6	1.0	16.1/9.5
P1T5	1	10000	1.2	0.6	1.0	15.3/10.9

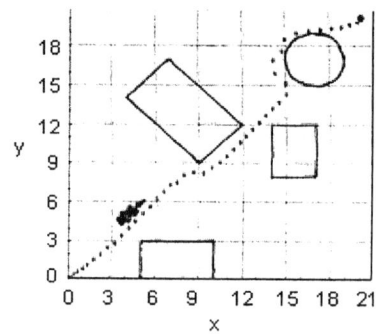

Fig. 1. The trajectory obtained by Simple Genetic Algorithms

Where, GN is the generation number of GAs. K_{j1} and K_{j2} are the weights assigned for the code strings of the control parameters. Q_o is the initial angle of the robot. $BP(x,y)$ represents the best position the robot arrives at when the algorithm is over. P1T1--P1T5 represent the cases with different parameters in the simulation experiment.

7.2 Experimental Results of GASC

In this experiment, GASC is employed to solve the optimization function. Meanwhile, some special genetic tactics are also introduced, such as "Hopeful Member Immigrating", "Good member Protection", etc. These techniques also have an important influence on the performance of GASC[5]. The trajectory obtained by GASC is shown in Fig.2. From the result, we can see that GASC outperforms simple GAs, as the quality of the trajectory is much better than the one in Fig.1.

8 Conclusion

Our study shows that genetic encoding techniques have significant influence on GAs' performance in solving problems with high algorithm complexity. In such problems, some special codes must be taken, otherwise the algorithms may not be able to get convergence or the solution obtained is poor. The experiments show that the proposed Genetic Algorithms with the symmetric codes can find solutions with better quality in shorter time than some classical GAs.

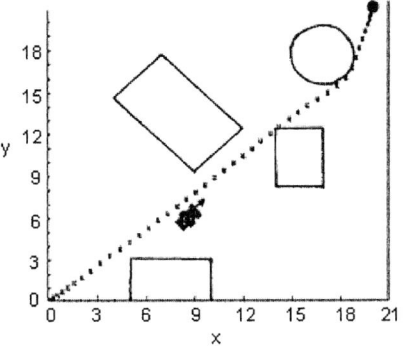

Fig. 2. The trajectory obtained by GASC

In this paper, the genetic encoding problem and a sufficient convergence condition of GAs are studied. Some new categories of genetic codes are defined, and they are applied into robotic problem successfully. Meanwhile, some new definitions on genetic encoding as well as some operations are presented, so that a sufficient convergence condition of GAs is inducted. This condition can help encoding the population so as to ensure the convergence of a GAs. It is proved that this condition is necessary for GAs.

References

1. Gautam Garai, Chaudhuri B.B.: A novel genetic algorithm for automatic clustering. Pattern Recognition Letters. 25(2004) 173-187
2. Barrie M.Baker, M.A. Ayechew: A genetic algorithm for the vehicle routing problem. Computers & Operations Research. 30(2003) 787-800
3. Chi-bin Cheng, C.J.Cheng, E.s.Lee: Neuro-Fuzzy and Genetic Algorithm in Multiple Response Optimization. Computers and Mathematics with Applications. 44(2002) 1503-1514
4. Yas Abbas Alsultanny, Musbah M. Aqel: Pattern recognition using multiplayer neural-gentic algorithm. Neurocomputing. 51(2003) 237-247
5. Qingchun Meng, Hongbo Ji, Hao Dong: Application of a new Genetic strategy to robot control. In Proc. of Intl. Conf.IEEE, ICIPS'97. Beijing (1997) 568-570
6. Qingchun Meng, Changjiu Zhou, et al: Genetic Algorithm with Symmetric Code and Its Application to Dynamic System. ACTA ELECTRONICA SINICA. 27(1999) 59-63
7. Bethke A.D.: Genetic algorithm as function optimizers. Ph. D. Thesis, Dept. Computer and Communication Sciences, University of Michigan(1981)
8. Holland J. H: Adaptation in natural and artificial systems. University of Michigan press. Ann Ardor, Michigan(1975)

The Convergence of a Multi-objective Evolutionary Algorithm Based on Grids

Yuren Zhou[1] and Jun He[2]

[1] School of Computer Science and Engineering,
South China University of Technology,
Guangzhou 510640, China
zhouyuren@hotmail.com
[2] School of Computer Science, The University of Birmingham,
Birmingham B15 2TT, UK

Abstract. Evolutionary algorithms are especially suited for multi-objective optimization problems. Many evolutionary algorithms have been successfully applied to various multi-objective optimization problems. However, theoretical studies on multi-objective evolutionary algorithms are relatively scarce. This paper analyzes the convergence properties of a simple pragmatic (μ+1)-MOEA. The convergence of MOEAs is defined and the general convergence conditions are studied. Under these conditions, it is proven that the proposed (μ+1)-MOEA converges almost surely to the Pareto-optimal front.

1 Introduction

Evolutionary algorithms (EAs), which adopt a population-based search, are especially suited for multi-objective optimization problems with several conflicting objectives [1-2]. EAs can search multiple objectives simultaneously and always keep the better solutions to next generation. Multi-Objective Evolutionary Algorithms (MOEAs) have been studied for more than ten years. It is generally recognized that Schaffer [3] was the first researcher to use EAs to handle vector optimization problems. Today various MOEAs, e.g., NSGA [4], SPEA [5], PAES [6] and NSGA-II [7], have been proposed and applied in many practical fields. Compared with a great amount of theoretical study on single-objective evolutionary algorithms [8-11], rigorous analysis of MOEAs is still in its infant phase, and attracts little attention from researchers [12-16]. Up to today only a few theoretical results on MOEAs have been obtained. Rudolph and Agapie [13] analyzed and proved MOEAs' convergence using Markov chain. Hanne [14] proposed a convergence theorem of function MOEAs with probability 1 under strict condition of "efficiency preserving", a requirement that some current pragmatic MOEAs do not meet. Laumanns [15] established a MOEA model which have both properties of converging to the Pareto-optimal front and maintaining a spread among obtained solutions, but he failed to rigorously define the convergence of MOEAs and prove that the MOEA model converges to the Pareto optimal sets. Recently Laumanns [16] presented the running time analysis of multi-objective EAs on pseudo-Boolean model problems.

This paper aims to discuss convergence of function MOEAs. We will introduce the rigorous definition of strong and weak convergences of MOEAs and discuss general conditions that guarantee the convergence of MOEAs. Under these conditions, we show that the proposed MOEA converges almost surely to the Pareto optimal set.

The remainder of this paper is arranged as follows: Section 2 describes the $(\mu+1)$ MOEA and introduces some basic definitions and terms; Section 3 analyzes the proposed MOEA's convergence; Section 4 concludes the paper.

2 Definitions and Algorithm Description

Without loss of generality, consider following multi-objective optimization problem with n decision variables and m objectives:

(MOP)   Maximize $\mathbf{y} = \mathbf{f}(\mathbf{x}) = (f_1(x_1,...,x_n),\ ...,\ f_m(x_1,...,x_n))$ (1)

Subject to $g_i(\mathbf{x}) \leq 0$, $i=1,...,q$.

Where $\mathbf{x}=(x_1, ..., x_n) \in X \subset R^n$, $\mathbf{y}=(y_1,...,y_m) \in Y \subset R^m$, $\mathbf{x}$ is the decision (parameter) vector, X is the decision space, $\mathbf{y}$ is the objective vector and Y is the objective space, $g(\mathbf{x})$ is the constraint condition. This paper deals with non-constraint problems only.

2.1 Dominance Relation

Different from fully ordered scalar search spaces, multidimensional search spaces are only partially ordered, i.e., two different solutions are related to each other in two possible ways: either one dominates the other or none of them is dominated. Firstly let's introduce two basic definitions used in MOEAs: dominance relation and Pareto set.

Definition 1: Let $\mathbf{f}, \mathbf{g} \in R^m$, vector $\mathbf{f}$ is said to dominate vector $\mathbf{g}$ (written as $\mathbf{f} \succ \mathbf{g}$) if and only if

1) $\forall\ i \in \{1,...,m\}: f_i \geq g_i$;
2) $\exists\ j \in \{1,...,m\}: f_i > g_i$

if $\mathbf{f} \succ \mathbf{g}$, it also means that $\mathbf{g}$ is dominated by $\mathbf{f}$, denoted as $\mathbf{g} \prec \mathbf{f}$.

Definition 2: Let $F \subset R^m$ be a vector set, the set of vectors in F that are not dominated by any vector in F is called Pareto set of F, denoted as $P(F)$, i.e., $P(F) := \{\mathbf{g} \in F | \neg \exists \mathbf{f} \in F : \mathbf{f} \succ \mathbf{g}\}$.

Based on the above notation, now we define Pareto-optimal front, Pareto-optimal solution and Pareto-optimal set as follows.

Definition 3: Let R_f be the range of function $\mathbf{f}$ in MOP (1), the Pareto set of R_f is called Pareto-optimal front. That is $P(R_f) = \{\mathbf{y} \in R_f | \neg \exists \mathbf{y}' \in R_f : \mathbf{y}' \succ \mathbf{y}\}$.

Definition 4: Let $P(R_f)$ be the Pareto-optimal front of MOP (1), the image source of $P(R_f)$ under mapping $\mathbf{f}$ is said to be Pareto-optimal set, denoted as $P(\mathbf{f}(\mathbf{x}))$, i.e. $P(\mathbf{f}(\mathbf{x})) := \{\mathbf{x} \in X | \neg \exists \mathbf{x}' \in X : \mathbf{f}(\mathbf{x}') \succ \mathbf{f}(\mathbf{x})\}$.

The vector in P(**f**(**x**)) is called Pareto-optimal solution.

The concept of ε-neighborhood, which is useful in discussing convergence of MOEA, is defined as follows.

Definition 5: Let $\mathbf{f}=(f_1, f_2, \ldots, f_m) \in R^m$, $\varepsilon > 0$, the ε-neighborhood $N_\varepsilon(\mathbf{f})$ of **f** is defined as follows:

$$N_\varepsilon(\mathbf{f}) := \{ \mathbf{y} \in R^m \mid \mathbf{y}=(y_1, y_2, \ldots, y_m), y_i \in (f_i - \varepsilon, f_i + \varepsilon), i=1,\ldots,m \}$$

In fact, $N_\varepsilon(\mathbf{f})$ is an m-dimension hyper-box centered on **f** in R^m.

Let $F \subset R^m$, the union of the vectors' ε-neighborhood in F is said to be F's ε-neighborhood, denoted as $N_\varepsilon(F)$, i.e.,

$$N_\varepsilon(F) = \bigcup_{\mathbf{f} \in F} N_\varepsilon(\mathbf{f}).$$

2.2 (μ+1)-MOEA

Since there are more than one objectives to be optimized simultaneously in multi-objective optimization, the solution is no longer a single optimal point, rather a whole set of possible solutions with equivalent quality, i.e., Pareto-optimal set. This determines that the task faced by MOEAs is also two-objective:

To guide the search towards the Pareto-optimal set;

To maintain a diverse population in order to achieve a well distributed trade-off front.

Researchers have developed several MOEAs to implement the above tasks. One of them is the MOEA based on grids, developed mainly by Knowles [6] and Laumanns [15]. Based on ε-dominance concept (or grid), Deb [17] proposed a steady-state MOEA that had a good compromise in terms of convergence near to Pareto-optimal front, diversity of solutions and computational time. The basic idea of this MOEA is to divide the search space into a number of grids (or hyper-boxes) and to maintain the diversity by ensuring that a hyper-box can be occupied by only one solution. Many MOEAs (including the algorithm developed in [17]) make use of two co-evolving populations: an EA population and an archive population. This kind of MOEA is more difficult to analyze and we don't discuss it in this paper.

In this paper we only discuss a simple (μ+1) MOEA for MOP(1) based on grids introduced in [15][6]. This (μ+1) MOEA is composed of algorithm 1-3 where the details of Algorithm 1, Algorithm 3 and the notations can be found in [15]. It is similar to (μ+1) evolution strategy [18] and uses only one population.

The (μ+1) MOEA is described as follows:

Algorithm 1: Iterative search algorithm
t := 0
$A^{(0)} := \emptyset$
while terminate ($A^{(t)}$, t) = false **do**
  t := t+1

$\mathbf{f}^{(t)} := \text{generate}(A^{(t-1)})$
$A^{(t)} := \text{update}(A^{(t-1)}, \mathbf{f}^{(t)})$
end while
Output: $A^{(t)}$

Algorithm 1 is the general framework of iterative searching algorithm. The integer t denotes the evolution generation. The set $A^{(t)}$ is the population of objective space at generation t with a dynamic size. The vector $\mathbf{f}^{(t)}$ in objective space is the new individual yielded by using "generate" function. "Update" function is used to produce the next population from current population and new individual.

Algorithm 2: "generate" function
Input: $A^{(t-1)} = \{\mathbf{a}_1, \mathbf{a}_2, ..., \mathbf{a}_\mu\}$
$(A^{(t-1)})^{-1} := \{\mathbf{f}^{-1}(\mathbf{a}_1), \mathbf{f}^{-1}(\mathbf{a}_2), ..., \mathbf{f}^{-1}(\mathbf{a}_\mu)\}$
$:= \{\mathbf{x}_1, \mathbf{x}_2, ..., \mathbf{x}_\mu\}$
$\mathbf{x}_i := \text{Random}\{\mathbf{x}_1, \mathbf{x}_2, ..., \mathbf{x}_\mu\}$
$\mathbf{x}' := \text{mutate } \mathbf{x}_i$
$\mathbf{f}^{(t)} := f(\mathbf{x}')$
Output: $\mathbf{f}^{(t)}$

The purpose of algorithm 2 is to generate a new individual. The process works in a simple way: a individual is randomly selected from a population and then variation is conducted to generate a new individual.

Algorithm 3: "update" function
Input: A, **f**
$D := \{\mathbf{f}' \in A | \text{box}(\mathbf{f}) \succ \text{box}(\mathbf{f}')\}$
if $D \neq \emptyset$ **then**
  $A' := A \cup \{\mathbf{f}\} \setminus D$
else if $\exists \mathbf{f}' : (\text{box}(\mathbf{f}') = \text{box}(\mathbf{f}) \wedge \mathbf{f} \succ \mathbf{f}')$ **then**
  $A' := A \cup \{\mathbf{f}\} \setminus \{\mathbf{f}'\}$
else if $\neg \exists \mathbf{f}' : \text{box}(\mathbf{f}') = \text{box}(\mathbf{f}) \vee \text{box}(\mathbf{f}') \succ \text{box}(\mathbf{f})$ **then**
  $A' := A \cup \{\mathbf{f}\}$
else
  $A' := A$
end if
Output: A'

Algorithm 3 is the "update" function. Let the objective space Y be $\{(f_1, f_2, ..., f_m) \mid a_i \leq f_i \leq b_i \ (i=1,...,m)\}$, $\delta_1, \delta_2, ..., \delta_m$ be previously given positive real vector (the smaller the number δ_i (i=1,...,m), the higher precision of the algorithm). Firstly, the objective space is divided into a number of m-dimension hyper-boxes, each having δ_i size in the i-th objective. The number of hyper-boxes in objective space Y is less than or equal to $\prod_{i=1}^{m}([\frac{b_i - a_i}{\delta_i}]+1)$. The box dominance relation can be easily generalized from the vector dominance relation. The algorithm allows at most one solution to be present in each hyper-box and always maintains a set of non-dominated boxes. Thus it maintains the diversity in the population and forces the population to converge to Pareto-optimal front. It is an elitist approach and its population size μ changes dynamically.

3 Convergence Analysis of (μ +1) MOEA

Unlike the single objective optimization problem where its optimal value is a real number, Pareto-optimal front in MOPs is a set of points in R^m. It is necessary to give the rigorous definition of convergence of MOEAs. Recall the definition of convergence for random variable sequence { X_n, $n \geq 1$}, there are definitions such as convergence almost surely, convergence in probability and convergence in mean [19].

Definition 6: Let $\{X, X_n$ (n=1, 2, ...) $\}$ be random variables on a probability space (Ω, F, P), the random variable sequence X_n is said to converge almost surely to random variable X, if

$$P\{\lim_{n \to \infty} X_n = X\} = 1;$$

converge in probability to X, if

$$\lim_{n \to \infty} P\{|X_n - X| \leq \epsilon\} = 1, \forall \epsilon > 0;$$

converge in mean to X, if

$$\lim_{n \to \infty} P\{|X_n - X|\} = 0.$$

Both convergence almost surely and convergence in mean implies convergence in probability whereas the converse is wrong in general.

Lemma 1: The following statements are equivalent
Random variable sequence X_n converge almost surely to random variable X;

$\forall \epsilon > 0$, $\lim_{m \to \infty} P\{|X_n - X| < \epsilon$, for all $n \geq m\} = 1$;

$\forall \epsilon > 0$, $\lim_{m \to \infty} P\{|X_n - X| \geq \epsilon$, for some $n \geq m \} = 0$;

$\forall \varepsilon > 0$, P{$|X_n - X| \geq \varepsilon$ appears infinite times} = 0;

$\forall \varepsilon > 0$, P$\{\bigcap_{m=1}^{\infty} \bigcup_{n=m}^{\infty} (|X_n - X| \geq \varepsilon)\} = 0$.

Proof: see [19].

With the equivalent definitions in Lemma 1 we can define the convergence of (μ +1)-MOEA as follows.

Definition 7: Let $A^{(n)}$ (n=1,2,...) be the sequence of populations generated by (μ +1)-MOEA. Objective space is divided into m-dimension hyper-boxes. Let B_i (i=1,...,s) denote the hyper-boxes that contain the Pareto front of MOP(1), and F_i (i=1,...,s) the Pareto-optimal front in B_i. F_i's ε-neighborhood is denoted as $N_\varepsilon(F_i)$ (see Definition 5).

The (μ +1)-MOEA is said to converge almost surely to the front of MOP(1) if
$\forall \varepsilon > 0$, $\lim_{m \to \infty}$ P{ $A^{(n)} \cap N_\varepsilon(F_i) \neq \emptyset$ for all $n \geq m$ } = 1, $1 \leq i \leq s$;

The (μ +1)-MOEA is said to converge in probability to the front of MOP(1) if
$\forall \varepsilon > 0$, $\lim_{n \to \infty}$ P{ $A^{(n)} \cap N_\varepsilon(F_i) \neq \emptyset$ } = 1, $1 \leq i \leq s$.

Similar to Lemma 1, we have the equivalent definition as follows.

Lemma 2: The following statements are equivalent
The (μ +1)-MOEA converge almost surely to the front of MOP(1);
$\forall \varepsilon > 0$, $\lim_{m \to \infty}$ P{ $A^{(n)} \cap N_\varepsilon(F_i) = \emptyset$ for some $n \geq m$ } = 0 ($1 \leq i \leq s$);

$\forall \varepsilon > 0$, P{ $A^{(n)} \cap N_\varepsilon(F_i) = \emptyset$ appears infinite times} = 0 ($1 \leq i \leq s$);

$\forall \varepsilon > 0$, P$\{\bigcap_{m=1}^{\infty} \bigcup_{n=m}^{\infty} (A^{(n)} \cap N_\varepsilon(F_i) = \emptyset)\} = 0$ ($1 \leq i \leq s$).

Lemma 3: (Borel-Cantelli) Let { X_n, n=1,2,...} be event sequence, then

$\sum_{n=1}^{\infty} P(X_n) < \infty \Rightarrow P\{\bigcap_{m=1}^{\infty} \bigcup_{n=m}^{\infty} X_n\} = 0$.

Proof: See [19].

Based on above definitions and lemmas, we give the main MOEA convergence theorems as follows.

Theorem 1: Let $A^{(n)}$ (n=1,2,...) be the sequence of populations generated by (μ +1)-MOEA. $N_\varepsilon(F_i)$ (i=1,...,s) is the ε-neighborhood as specified in definition 7. Let

$\alpha_n^i := $ P{ $A^{(n+1)} \cap N_\varepsilon(F_i) = \emptyset | A^{(n)} \cap N_\varepsilon(F_i) \neq \emptyset$ }, $n \geq 1$, i=1,...,s;

$\beta_n^i := P\{ A^{(n+1)} \cap N_\varepsilon(F_i) = \emptyset \mid A^{(n)} \cap N_\varepsilon(F_i) = \emptyset \}$, $n \geq 1$, $i=1,\ldots,s$;

$\gamma_n^i := \beta_1 \times \beta_2 \ldots \times \beta_n$, $n \geq 1$, $i=1,\ldots,s$.

Then

(1) If $\forall \varepsilon > 0$, $\lim_{n\to\infty} \gamma_n^i = 0$ ($i=1, \ldots, s$), then ($\mu+1$)-MOEA converges in probability to the Pareto-optimal front;

(2) If $\sum_{n=1}^{\infty} \gamma_n^i < \infty$ ($i=1, \ldots, s$), then ($\mu+1$)-MOEA converges almost surely to Pareto-optimal front.

Proof: Firstly note that $\alpha_n^i = 0$ ($n \geq 1$, $i=1, \ldots, s$) because ($\mu+1$)-MOEA uses an elitist preserving approach.

(1) Given $i \in \{1,2,\ldots s\}$, let
$P^{(i)}(n) = P\{ A^{(n)} \cap N_\varepsilon(F_i) = \emptyset \}$.

According to Bayesian formula, we obtain

$P^{(i)}(n+1) = P\{ A^{(n+1)} \cap N_\varepsilon(F_i) = \emptyset \}$

$= P\{ A^{(n+1)} \cap N_\varepsilon(F_i) = \emptyset \mid A^{(n)} \cap N_\varepsilon(F_i) \neq \emptyset \} P\{ A^{(n)} \cap N_\varepsilon(F_i) \neq \emptyset \}$

$+ P\{ A^{(n+1)} \cap N_\varepsilon(F_i) = \emptyset \mid A^{(n)} \cap N_\varepsilon(F_i) = \emptyset \} P\{ A^{(n)} \cap N_\varepsilon(F_i) = \emptyset \}$

$= \alpha_n^i P\{ A^{(n)} \cap N_\varepsilon(F_i) \neq \emptyset \} + \beta_n^i P(n)$

$= \beta_n^i \ldots \beta_1^i P(1)$

$= \gamma_n^i P(1)$

Because $\lim_{n\to\infty} \gamma_n^i = 0$, we get $\lim_{n\to\infty} P^{(i)}(n+1) = 0$.

Hence, according to Definition 6(2), ($\mu+1$)-MOEA converges in probability to Pareto-optimal front.

(2) From $P^{(i)}(n+1) = \gamma_n^i P(1)$, $\sum_{n=1}^{\infty} \gamma_n^i < \infty$ and Lemma 3, we know that the ($\mu+1$)-MOEA converges almost surely to Pareto-optimal front. □

Theorem 2: Let the ($\mu+1$)-MOEA be used to solve Problem MOP(1). Assume that the decision space X in MOP(1) is a compact set in R^n, the objective function $\mathbf{f}(x)$ is continuous on X, and the variation in Algorithm 2 of the ($\mu+1$)-MOEA is a Gaussian variation. Then ($\mu+1$)-MOEA converges almost surely to the Pareto-optimal front of MOP(1).

Proof: Given $i \in \{1, 2, \ldots, s\}$, $\forall \varepsilon > 0$, according to Theorem 1(2), it is sufficient to show that there exists a constant $c \in (0,1)$, $\beta_n^i \leq c$ ($n=1, 2, \ldots$).

The Gaussian variation of the (μ+1)-MOEA is denoted as $\mathbf{x}' := \mathbf{x}+\mathbf{Z}$, where $\mathbf{Z} \sim N(0, \sigma^2 I_n)$ is a normally distributed random vector and I_n denotes the n-dimension unit matrix.

Let $\mathbf{y}_0$ be a point on Pareto front in B_i, where $\mathbf{y}_0 = f(\mathbf{x}_0)$, $\mathbf{x}_0 = (x_0^1, x_0^2, \ldots x_0^n) \in X$.

Because $f(\mathbf{x})$ is continuous on X, there exists a positive $r>0$ such that when $\mathbf{x}$ satisfies $\|\mathbf{x}-\mathbf{x}_0\|_\infty \leq r$ (here $\|\ \|_\infty$ is the maximum norm), then $\|f(\mathbf{x}) - f(\mathbf{x}_0)\|_\infty \leq \varepsilon$, therefore $f(\mathbf{x}) \in N_\varepsilon(F_i)$.

Let $D_{\mathbf{x}_0, r} := \{\mathbf{x} \in X \mid \|\mathbf{x}-\mathbf{x}_0\|_\infty \leq r\}$, for $\mathbf{x} = (x^1, x^2, \ldots x^n) \in X$, we have

$$P\{\mathbf{x}+\mathbf{Z} \in D_{\mathbf{x}_0, r}\} = \prod_{k=1}^{n} \int_{x_0^k - x^k - r}^{x_0^k - x^k + r} \frac{1}{\sqrt{2\pi}\sigma} e^{-\frac{u^2}{2\sigma^2}} du.$$

Let $P_1(\mathbf{x}, \mathbf{x}_0) = P\{\mathbf{x}+\mathbf{Z} \in D_{\mathbf{x}_0, r}\}$, then $0 < P_1(\mathbf{x}, \mathbf{x}_0) < 1$.

Because $P_1(\mathbf{x}, \mathbf{x}_0)$ is continuous on compact set X, there exists $\mathbf{x}_1', \mathbf{x}_0' \in X$, such that

$$P_1(\mathbf{x}, \mathbf{x}_0) \geq P_1(\mathbf{x}_1', \mathbf{x}_0') = \min_{\mathbf{x}, \mathbf{x}_0 \in X} P_1(\mathbf{x}, \mathbf{x}_0), \text{ and } 0 < P_1(\mathbf{x}_1', \mathbf{x}_0') < 1.$$

Therefore

$$P\{A^{(n+1)} \cap N_\varepsilon(F_i) \neq \emptyset \mid A^{(n)} \cap N_\varepsilon(F_i) = \emptyset\} \geq P_1(\mathbf{x}_1', \mathbf{x}_0')$$

$$\beta_n^i = P\{A^{(n+1)} \cap N_\varepsilon(F_i) = \emptyset \mid A^{(n)} \cap N_\varepsilon(F_i) = \emptyset\}$$

$$\leq 1 - P_1(\mathbf{x}_1', \mathbf{x}_0') = c, c \in (0,1). \qquad \square$$

From the proof of Theorem 2, we know that if the Gaussian variation is replaced by Cauchy variation [20], Theorem 2 is still valid.

Furthermore, we have the following more general convergence theorem for the (μ+1)-MOEAs:

Theorem 3: Except for the variation, let all other assumptions remain the same as Theorem 2. Let the random variation vector be $\mathbf{Z} = (z_1, z_2, \ldots, z_n)$, where z_i ($i = 1, 2, \ldots n$) are the independently identically distributed random variables whose density function is $\varphi(x)$. If $\varphi(x)$ satisfies:

(1) $\varphi(x)$ is continuous on R;

(2) $\forall a, b \in R$, $a < b$, $\int_a^b \varphi(x) dx > 0$.

Then the (μ+1)-MOEA converges almost surely to Pareto-optimal front.

Proof: Similar to that of Theorem 2.

4 Conclusions and Future Work

Compared with single-objective evolutionary algorithms, the design and analysis of MOEAs are much more complicated. This paper has investigated the convergence properties of a simple pragmatic (μ +1)-MOEA based on grids [6,15]. We have established the conditions that guarantee the convergence of the algorithm, and proved that the (μ +1)-MOEA using either Gaussian variation or Cauchy variation is convergent. In more general, the proposed MOEA is proved to be convergent under the assumption that the variation parameter in the algorithm remains constant.

However, the convergent conditions presented in the paper do not hold for the algorithms with self-adaptation variation, which are widely applied in evolution strategy to improve convergence speed. This is one of our future works. Like the analysis in single-objective evolutionary algorithms [21,22], the limit behavior, time complexity, and dynamical behavior of MOEAs are also important topics in our future research.

References

1. C. A. C Coello, D. A. Van Veldhuizen, and G. B. Lamont: Evolutionary algorithms for solving multi-objctive problems. Norwell, MA: Kluwer (2002)
2. K. Deb: Multi-Objective Optimization Using Evolutionary Algorithms. Chichester, U.K.: Wiley (2001)
3. J. D. Schaffer: Multiple objective optimization with vector evaluated genetic algorithms. In: Grefenstte J J (ed.): Proceeding of an international conference on genetic algorithms and their applications. Pittsburgh PA: Morgan Kaufmann Publishers(1985)93-100
4. N. Srinivas, K. Deb: Multi-objective function optimization use non-dominated genetic algorithms. Evolutionary Computation, Vol.2(3): (1994)221-248
5. E. Zitzler, L. Thiele: Multiobjective evolutionary algorithms: a comparative case study and the strength Pareto approach. IEEE Transaction on Evolutionary Computation, Vol.3(4): (1999)257-271
6. J. D. Knowles, D. W. Corne: Approximating the nondominated front using the Pareto archived evolution strategy. Evolutionary Computation. Vol.8(2), (2000)149-172
7. K. Deb, S. Agrawal, A. Pratap, T. Meyarivan: A fast and elitist multi-objective genetic algorithms: NSGA- II . IEEE Transaction on Evolutionary Computation. Vol.6(2), (2002)182-197
8. H.-G.Beyer, H.-P.Schwefel, and I. Wegener: How to analysis evolutionary algorithms. Theoretical Computation Science, Vol.287, (2002)101-130
9. G.Rudolph: Convergence Properties of evolutionary algorithms. Kovac, Hamburg(1997)
10. A. Bienvetle, O. Francois: Global convergence for evolution strategies in spherical problems: some simple proofs and difficulties. Theoretical Computer Science, Vol.306 (2003)269-289
11. C. H. Guo, H. W. Tang: Global convergence properties of evolution strategies. Mathematica Numerica Sinica. Vol.23(1): (2001)106-110
12. G. Rudolph: On a multi-objective evolutionary algorithm and its convergence to the Pareto set. In: Proc. Fifth IEEE Conf. Evolutionary Computation, Anchorage AK (1998)511-516

13. G. Rudolph, A. Agapie: Convergence properties of some multi-objective evolutionary algorithms. In: Proceedings of the 2000 Congress on Evolutionary Computation (CEC2000), Piscataway NJ (2000)1010-1016
14. T. Hanne: On the convergence of multiobjective evolutionary algorithms. European Journal of Operational Research, Vol.117(3): (1999)553-564
15. M. Laumanns, L. Thiele, K. Deb, E. Zitzler: Combining Convergence and diversity in evolutionary multi-objective optimization. Evolutionary Computation. Vol.10(3): (2002)263-282
16. M. Laumanns, L. Thiele, and E. Zitzler: Running time analysis of multiobjcetive evolutionary algorithms on pseudo-boolean functions. IEEE Transaction on Evolutionary Computation, Vol.8, No.2, (2004)170-182
17. Deb K, Mohan M, Mishra S: A fast multi-objective evolutionary algorithm for finding well-spread Pareto-optimal solutions. Indian Institute of Technology Kanpur, KanGal Report: Number 2003002(2003)
18. H. P. Schwefel: Evolution and optimum seeking. John Wiley & Sons, New York(1995)
19. K. L. Chung: A course in probability. Academic Press, New York (1974)
20. X. Yao, Y. Liu, G. Lin: Evolutionary programming made faster. IEEE Transaction on Evolutionary Computation. Vol.3(2): (1999)82-102
21. J. He and X. Yao: From an individual to a population: An analysis of the first hitting time of population-based evolutionary algorithms. IEEE Transactions on Evolutionary Computation, Vol.6(5): (2002)495-511
22. J. He and X. Yao: Towards an analytic framework for analysing the computation time of evolutionary algorithms. Artificial Intelligence, Vol.145(1-2): (2003)59-97

Influence of Finite Population Size
–Extinction of Favorable Schemata–

Hiroshi Furutani, Makoto Sakamoto, and Susumu Katayama

Faculty of Engineering, University of Miyazaki,
Kibanadai, Miyazaki City, 889-2192 Japan

Abstract. Since genetic algorithms (GAs) treat a population of finite size, it is necessary to study stochastic fluctuations in evolution processes. In this study, we investigated the influence of genetic drift due to finite population size on the performance of a GA on the multiplicative landscape. There was large difference between numerical experiments with small population size and the prediction of deterministic model. It was observed in some experiments that favorable first order schemata were lost from the population. It was also noted that the population can be assumed to be in linkage equilibrium in the GA including crossover. Then we performed the theoretical investigation of frequencies of the first order schemata, and calculated their changes in time by using the Wright-Fisher model and diffusion equations. We showed that these mathematical theories reasonably predict various quantities including the ultimate extinction probability. We found that the extinction of favorable schemata is the most undesirable effect of genetic drift.

1 Introduction

In this paper, we study the influence of finite population size on the performance of genetic algorithms (GAs). We focus on the effect of genetic drift by the random sampling in the selection process. When we apply a GA to a given problem, we choose the population size N intuitively. We do not have any applicable theory to guide the choice of N. If we choose a small N to reduce the cost of calculations, there appears the problem of genetic drift. The main part of the effect of genetic drift may disappear by averaging repeated trials. However there are several cases in which its effect remains finite even after averaging. An example of such cases is a GA on the multiplicative landscape. If one uses a small N, the risk of poor performance becomes high by the undesirable effect of genetic drift.

The theoretical analysis of GAs with finite N is far more complicated than the deterministic approach assuming infinitely many N. The most representative approach is Markov chain analysis of Nix and Vose [1]. The Nix and Vose Markov model includes selection, mutation and crossover and can calculate the exact transition matrix. However, it is in general difficult to obtain an analytical expression of Markov process in closed form. Furthermore the dimension of the transition matrix increases exponentially with string length ℓ and population size N. This makes numerical simulations almost impossible for realistic values of ℓ and N. De Jong, Spears and Gordon investigated the transient behavior of GA by using the Nix and Vose model with small numbers of ℓ and N [2].

In population genetics, researchers also encountered this type of difficulties in treating the evolution of a finite population by Markov chain model [3]. They found another approach to get out of it, the diffusion model [4]. Fisher treated the simple case of no selection by the heat diffusion equation, in which he introduced the method of partial differential equations for the study of gene frequency distributions [5]. Wright also made a great contribution to this area. He introduced a general form of the heat diffusion equation, the Kolmogorov forward equation [6].

We apply their stochastic approaches to the present problem, and consider the evolution of first order schemata in the GA on the multiplicative landscape with the finite population size.

2 Mathematical Model

This study takes into account the processes of selection and crossover in GAs, and investigates the influence of finite population size. Though mutation is a very important operator for this kind of analysis, we neglect it to make this analysis simple. We use the fitness proportionate selection and uniform crossover. A population is assumed to evolve in discrete and non-overlapping generations.

An individual is represented by a binary string of fixed length ℓ, and there are $n = 2^\ell$ possible genotypes. The representation of an integer i is

$$i = <i(\ell), \cdots, i(1)> \quad (0 \leq i \leq n-1),$$

where $i(k) \in \{0, 1\}$. The ith genotype is identified with the integer i.

We use the frequency $N_i(t)$ and relative frequency $x_i(t)$ of the ith genotype at generation t. The population size N is assumed to be time-independent, and

$$N = \sum_{i=0}^{n-1} N_i(t).$$

The relative frequency $x_i(t)$ is given as a fraction of the ith genotype in a population

$$x_i(t) = N_i(t)/N.$$

2.1 Deterministic Evolution Equations

We derive here the deterministic evolution equations for selection and crossover. In proportionate selection, $x_i(t+1)$ is given in terms of $x_j(t)$

$$x_i(t+1) = \frac{f_i}{\bar{f}(t)} x_i(t) \quad (i = 0, \ldots, n-1), \tag{1}$$

where f_i is a fitness of the ith genotype, and $\bar{f}(t)$ the average fitness of the population

$$\bar{f}(t) \equiv \sum_{j=0}^{n-1} f_j\, x_j(t). \qquad (2)$$

To show equation (1) is under the action of selection, we use the notation

$$\widehat{S}x_i(t) = \frac{f_i}{\bar{f}(t)} x_i(t),$$

where $\widehat{S}x_i$ means the frequency x_i after selection.

2.2 Schema Theorem

A schema $\mathcal{H}$ is the set of all strings with certain defining values at fixed positions. We use the notation showing explicitly the order of schema k, the positions of defining bits, and their binary values,

$$\mathcal{H} = \mathcal{H}^{(k)}[i(b_1), i(b_2), \ldots, i(b_k)],$$

Here, $1 \leq b_1 < b_2 < \ldots < b_k \leq \ell$ are positions of defining bits. In the similar manner, the relative frequency $h(\mathcal{H})$ is given by

$$h(\mathcal{H}) = h^{(k)}[i(b_1), i(b_2), \ldots, i(b_k)].$$

We also use shorthand notations

$$h[1_k] = h^{(1)}[i(k) = 1], \quad h[0_k] = h^{(1)}[i(k) = 0].$$

In this analysis, the notion of linkage [15] is very important, and the second order linkage disequilibrium coefficient D is defined as

$$D[k, m] = h^{(2)}[i(k) = 1, i(m) = 1] - h[1_k]h[1_m]. \qquad (3)$$

When each gene evolves independently, a population is in linkage equilibrium, while if there are any correlations among genes at different loci, it is in linkage disequilibrium. When the population is in linkage equilibrium, all D coefficients are zero, $D[k, m] = 0$. In this state, the frequency of genotypes i is given in terms of the first order schema frequencies

$$x_i = \prod_{k=1}^{\ell} h[i(k)]. \qquad (4)$$

3 Deterministic Model

We consider the evolution of the GA on the multiplicative landscape in the deterministic model. We define the fitness function of multiplicative form as

$$f_i = \prod_{k=1}^{\ell} (1 + i(k)\, s). \quad (s \geq 0), \qquad (5)$$

where s is a parameter of the selection strength.

It is natural to assume that the population is in linkage equilibrium at $t = 0$, and the deterministic theory predicts that the population is in linkage equilibrium at all generations under the action of selection and crossover. Using equation (4), we have the average fitness in the product form

$$\bar{f}(t) = \prod_{k=1}^{\ell} \{h[0_k] + (1+s)h[1_k]\} = \prod_{k=1}^{\ell}(1 + s\,h[1_k]). \tag{6}$$

Then we may define the fitness function of the first order schemata

$$g_k = 1 + s\,h[1_k]. \tag{7}$$

To show the assumption of linkage equilibrium explicitly, we give

$$\bar{f}^{(\mathrm{eq})} = \prod_{k=1}^{\ell} g_k.$$

Under the assumption of linkage equilibrium, we can obtain the schema equation of the first order schemata for selection. The evolution equation of the first order schema $h[i(k)]$ is

$$\widehat{S}\,h[0_k](t) = \frac{h[0_k](t)}{h[0_k](t) + (1-s)h[1_k](t)}, \tag{8}$$

and

$$\widehat{S}\,h[1_k](t) = \frac{(1-s)\,h[1_k](t)}{h[0_k](t) + (1-s)h[1_k](t)}. \tag{9}$$

In the deterministic model, if a population is in linkage equilibrium, schemata after selection also satisfy the condition of linkage equilibrium, and the schemata after crossover are also in equilibrium. Thus, if the population is in linkage equilibrium at $t = 0$, then it is in equilibrium at all t.

4 Stochastic Model

4.1 Wright-Fisher Model

We review here the Wright-Fisher model for the evolution of a haploid population whose size remains constant at N. This model deals with the chromosome of one-locus two-allele type, or $\ell = 1$ with genotypes $i \in \{0, 1\}$. The number of the first genotype N_0 takes the values of $\{0, 1, \ldots, N\}$, and that of the second genotype is given by $N_1 = N - N_0$.

We consider the selection process of random sampling. Let us assume there are $N_1(t) = i$ copies of the first genotype at the current generation. If we randomly choose the offspring from the population, the probability $P(j|i)$ of

$N_1(t+1)$ taking the value of j from the possible values of $\{0,\ldots,N\}$ is given by the binomial distribution,

$$P(j|i) = \binom{N}{j}\left(\frac{i}{N}\right)^j\left(1-\frac{i}{N}\right)^{N-j}. \tag{10}$$

The probability $P(j|i)$ specifies the process of random sampling, and the future behavior of the process only depends on its current frequencies. Thus this process is a Markov chain. The states $i=0$ and $i=N$ are absorbing states, and other states are transient states. If the process enters either of the absorbing states, it will stay there forever. The state $i=N$ means the allele 1 is fixed while the allele 0 is lost in the population.

Let $q_i(t)$ be the probability that the population is in $N_1 = i$ at generation t. Then

$$\sum_{i=0}^{N} q_i(t) = 1,$$

and the process is described by

$$q_j(t+1) = \sum_{i=0}^{N} P(j|i)\, q_i(t). \tag{11}$$

The generalization of the Wright-Fisher model to a GA of $\ell = 1$ with different fitness values is straightforward. We define the fitness values as

$$f_i = \begin{cases} 1 & (i=0) \\ 1+s & (i=1). \end{cases}$$

We assume $s \geq 0$ and consider the maximization of the fitness, thus $i = 1$ is the favorable allele. The transition probability is given by

$$P(j|i) = \binom{N}{j} b^j (1-b)^{N-j}, \tag{12}$$

$$b = \frac{(1+s)i}{(1+s)i + N - i}.$$

The evolution of the system is given by equation (11). It is to be noted that both $N_1 = 0$ and $N_1 = N$ are also absorbing states, and there is a finite risk of the loss of favorable allele 1.

4.2 Diffusion Model

It is in general very difficult to solve evolution equation (11) even for the simple case of equation (10). In the field of theoretical population genetics, this serious problem is solved by the use of the diffusion model, where the Kolmogorov forward equation plays a fundamental role. The counterpart of the discrete evolution equation (11) with different fitness values (12) is

$$\frac{\partial \phi(y,t)}{\partial t} = \frac{1}{2}\frac{\partial^2}{\partial y^2}\{V(y)\phi(y,t)\} - \frac{\partial}{\partial y}\{M(y)\phi(y,t)\}, \tag{13}$$

where
$$V(y) = \frac{y(1-y)}{N}, \quad M(y) = sy(1-y).$$

Here we assume that the parameter s is small compared with 1, $s \ll 1$. The function $\phi(y,t)$ is a probability density that the relative frequency of the allele 1 becomes y at time t, corresponding to $q_i(t)$ in the Wright-Fisher model, and y is a continuous analogue of i/N. The generation t is also considered as a continuous variable.

We can derive an important property of the Kolmogorov forward equation (13). By replacing the time variable t by $\tau = t/N$, we have

$$\frac{\partial \phi(y,\tau)}{\partial \tau} = \frac{1}{2}\frac{\partial^2}{\partial y^2}\{y(1-y)\phi(y,\tau)\} - \frac{\partial}{\partial y}\{sNy(1-y)\phi(y,\tau)\}. \qquad (14)$$

This means the behavior of the solution $\phi(y,\tau)$ depends only on one parameter $S = sN$. Figure 1 demonstrates this fact by comparing probabilities of schema fixation and extinction given by Wright-Fisher model. Solutions for two sets of parameters ($N = 20, s = 0.05$) and ($N = 200, s = 0.005$), which have the same $S = sN$, show almost identical results of the probabilities.

There is another type of diffusion equation in stochastic theory. It describes the stochastic process retrospectively, and is called the backward Kolmogorov equation. It is used to derive the probabilities of fixation and extinction of alleles in population genetics,

$$\frac{\partial \psi(p,t)}{\partial t} = \frac{V(p)}{2}\frac{\partial^2 \psi(p,t)}{\partial p^2} + M(p)\frac{\partial \psi(p,t)}{\partial p}, \qquad (15)$$

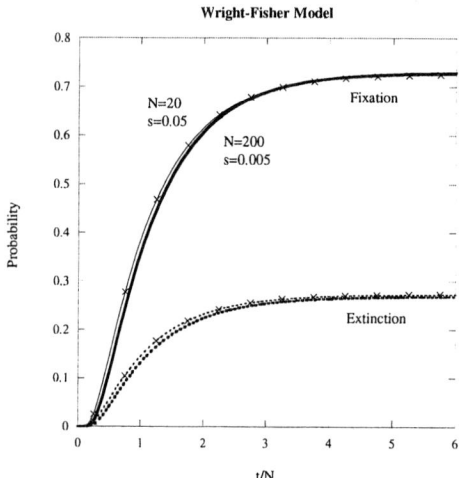

Fig. 1. Two solutions of Wright-Fisher model Fixation and extinction probabilities are shown for ($N = 20, s = 0.05$) and ($N = 200, s = 0.005$). Time scale is in $\tau = t/N$.

where p is the initial value of the relative frequency y at time $t = 0$. Solving equation(15) with the boundary conditions

$$\psi(0,t) = 0, \quad \psi(1,t) = 1,$$

we may obtain the probability that the allele 1 is fixed at time t. If we use another boundary conditions

$$\psi(0,t) = 1, \quad \psi(1,t) = 0,$$

$\psi(p,t)$ can be interpreted as the probability density of extinction.

In this study, we are interested in the probability of ultimate fixation denoted by

$$u(p) = \lim_{t \to \infty} \psi(p,t).$$

Since $\partial \psi(p,t)/\partial t = 0$ as $t \to \infty$ and using equation (15), we have

$$\frac{d^2 u(p)}{dp^2} + \frac{2M(p)}{V(p)} \frac{du(p)}{dp} = 0, \tag{16}$$

with the boundary conditions

$$u(0) = 0, \quad u(1) = 1.$$

Using $2M/V = 2Ns$, we obtain the solution

$$u(p) = \frac{1 - \exp(-2Nsp)}{1 - \exp(-2Ns)}. \tag{17}$$

The ultimate extinction probability $w(p)$ is given by

$$w(p) = 1 - u(p).$$

5 Numerical Results

We carried out GA calculations on the multiplicative landscape with the fitness proportionate selection. The results of numerical experiments were compared with the deterministic and stochastic models in the previous sections. The effect of crossover was given by uniform crossover with the crossover rates $\chi = 1$, and mutation was neglected. The string length was $\ell = 8$. The initial value of the first order schema was $h[1_k] = 1/2$. The calculations were performed repeatedly, and results were averaged over 1000 runs.

Figure 2 demonstrates the average fitness $\bar{f}(t)$ with three cases of N. We can observe strong N dependence of $\bar{f}(t)$. The worst case is $N = 20$, and the best one is $N = 200$. Since small N means the existence of large genetic drift, this result suggests the undesirable effect of genetic drift.

Figure 3 shows the frequencies of the first order schemata $h[1_k]$ with deterministic and stochastic predictions. We note that when N increases the result approaches to the deterministic model, which corresponds the case of $N = \infty$. If the population size is small, $N = 20$, $h[1_k]$ is only 0.6 even at large t. We also note that the predictions by Wright-Fisher model well reproduce the results of numerical experiments.

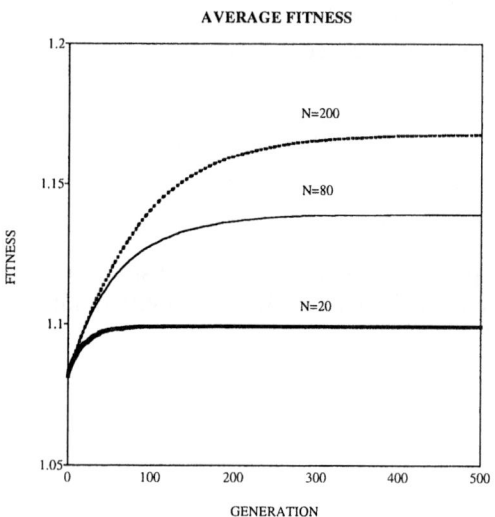

Fig. 2. Evolution of the average fitness $\bar{f}(t)$. $\ell = 8$, $s = 0.02$.

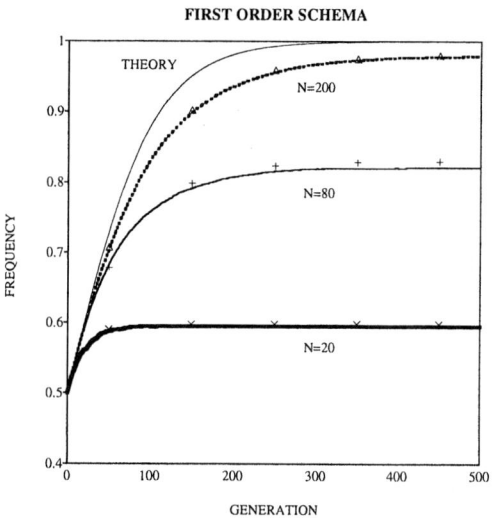

Fig. 3. Frequency of the first order schema. Symbols ×, + and △ are predictions of Wright-Fisher model with corresponding N. The solid line with THEORY represents the result of the deterministic model.

Figure 4 shows the extinction probabilities of the first order schema $h[1_k]$. This figure tells in the result of $N = 20$ that about 40% of the favorable schema is lost from the population by the genetic drift. On the other hand, with the large population size of $N = 200$, the extinction probability is very small, meaning the effect of genetic drift is very small. At $t = 500$, the extinction probabilities are 0.405, 0.179 and 0.020 for $N = 20$, 80 and 200, respectively. These results

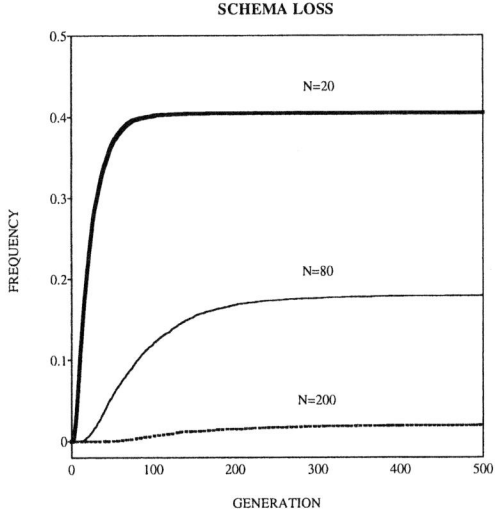

Fig. 4. Extinction Probability of the favorable schema

are consistent with the ultimate extinction probability $w(p) = 1 - u(p)$ given by equation (17) in the diffusion model. Theoretical values are $w(0.5) = 0.401$, 0.168 and 0.018 for $N = 20$, 80, and 200, respectively.

6 Summary

We studied the evolution of the GA on the multiplicative landscape by investigating the influence of genetic drift. Within the framework of the infinite population model, the assumption of linkage equilibrium holds at all generations if the initial state is at linkage equilibrium. Therefore, the system is completely determined by the first order schema frequencies $h[1_k]$.

In the GA calculation with crossover, the evolution of the first order schema $h[1_k]$ is well reproduced by the stochastic models; Wright-Fisher model and diffusion model. The average fitness $\bar{f}(t)$ has strong N-dependence, and genetic drift causes undesirable effect on it when N is small. The analysis of the first order schema shows that this problem is caused by the extinction of the favorable schema.

References

1. Nix, A. E., Vose, M. D.: Modelling Genetic Algorithm with Markov Chains. Annals of Mathematical and Artificial Intelligence. **5** (1992) 79–88
2. De Jong, K. A., Spears, W. M., Gordon, D. F.: Using Markov Chains to Analyze GAFOs. Foundations of Genetic Algorithms 3, (1995) 115–157
3. Ewens, J.W. J.: Mathematical Population Genetics. I. Theoretical Introduction, Second Edition. Springer-Verlag, New York (2004)

4. Crow, J. F., Kimura M.: An Introduction to Population Genetics Theory. Harper and Row, New York (1970)
5. Fisher, R. A.: On the Dominance Ratio. Proceedings of the Royal Society of Edinburgh. **42** (1922) 321–341
6. Wright, S.: Evolution in Menderian Populations. Genetics. **16** (1931) 97–159
7. Asoh, H., Mühlenbein, H.: On the Mean Convergence Time of Evolutionary Algorithms without Selection and Mutation. Parallel Problem Solving from Nature, Lecture Notes in Computer Science, **866**, Springer-Verlag, New York, (1994) 88-97
8. C. R. Stephens and H. Waelbroeck, *Evolutionary Computation*, **7**, 109 (1999).
9. M.D. Vose, *The Simple Genetic Algorithms*, (MIT Press, Cambridge, 1999).
10. H. Furutani, in *Foundations of Genetic Algorithms* 7, (Morgan Kaufmann, San Francisco, 2003), p.9.
11. H. Furutani, *Proceedings of the Simulated Evolution and Learning Conference, SEAL'00*, 2696 (2000) .
12. H. Furutani, *Proceedings of the Simulated Evolution and Learning Conference, SEAL'02*, 230 (2002).
13. H. Furutani, *Proceedings of the Genetic and Evolutionary Computation Conference, GECCO-2003*, Lecture Notes in Computer Science, **2723**, 934 (Springer-Verlag, New York, 2003).
14. R.A. Fisher, *The Genetical Theory of Natural Selection*, 2nd edition, (Dover, New York, 1958).
15. J. Maynard Smith, *Evolutionary Genetics*, 2nd edition, (Oxford University Press, Oxford, 1998).
16. H. Furutani, *Proceedings of the Genetic and Evolutionary Computation Conference, GECCO-2001*, 320 (Morgan Kaufmann, San Francisco, 2001).

A Theoretical Model and Convergence Analysis of Memetic Evolutionary Algorithms[*]

Xin Xu[1,2] and Han-gen He[1]

[1] Institute of Automation, National University of Defense Technology,
410073 Changsha, P.R. China
xuxin_mail@263.net
[2] School of Computer, National University of Defense Technology,
410073 Changsha, P.R. China

Abstract. Memetic evolutionary algorithms (MEAs) combine the global search of evolutionary learning methods and the fine-tune ability of local search methods so that they are orders of magnitude more accurate than traditional evolutionary algorithms in many problem domains. However, little work has been done on the mathematical model and convergence analysis of MEAs. In this paper, a theoretical model as well as the convergence analysis of a class of gradient-based MEAs is presented. The results of this paper are extensions of the research work on the abstract model and convergence analysis of general evolutionary algorithms. By modeling the local search of gradient methods as an abstract strong evolution operator, the theoretical framework for abstract memetic evolutionary algorithms is derived. Moreover, the global convergence theorems and the convergence rate estimations of gradient-based MEAs are also established.

1 Introduction

Evolutionary algorithms (EAs) are global search techniques derived from Darwin's theory of evolution by natural selection. The best-known examples of such simulated evolutionary algorithms include genetic algorithms (GAs), evolutionary programming (EP), and evolution strategies (ESs) [1]. Although these algorithms have been widely applied in global optimization problems, it is now well known that it is hard for an EA to fine tune the search in complex spaces. The main reason is that EAs update a population of potential solutions (called individuals) in a global search style so that there is no local search or learning during the life span of an individual. To solve the above problem, there have been growing interests in memetic evolutionary algorithms (MEAs) [2][3] that combine the global search ability of EAs with some kind of heuristic local search methods. In MEAs, learning occurs both in an evolutionary time-scale and in an individual's life-span time-scale. By combining EAs with different kinds of local search methods, various MEAs have been proposed and applied successfully to different complex problems such as TSP (Traveling Salesman

---

[*] Supported by the National Natural Science Foundation of China Under Grant 60303012, 60234030, Chinese Post-Doctor Science Foundation under Grant 200403500202, and A Project Supported by Scientific Research Fund of Hunan Provincial Education Department.

Problem) [2], the Quadratic Assignment Problem [4] and the graph partitioning problem [5], etc. Although the local search methods employed in MEAs are usually specific for the problems to be solved, many of them belong to a class of gradient-based local search methods that perform gradient descent search for individuals in the EA population [12][13]. Gradient-based local search has advantages in its search speed but suffers the problem of local minima. On the contrary, EAs are efficient in performing global search but with unsatisfactory fine-tune ability. Thus, gradient-based MEAs are promising to achieve better performance than either pure EAs or gradient search methods.

In spite of many successful applications of MEAs, little work has been done on the theoretical analysis of MEAs. The most fundamental theoretical issue related to MEAs as well as EAs is their convergence property, i.e., under what condition an MEA or EA will converge, and how fast it converges. Until now, there has been some research work on the convergence theory of EAs, which can be mainly classified into three categories, i.e., the simulated annealing approach [6], the Vose-Liepins model [7], and the stochastic model approach [8]. Although the above approaches provide theoretical analysis for certain kind of EAs, it is difficult to extend them from EAs to MEAs. In [9] and [10], a special class of memetic evolutionary algorithms called EPSAs (evolutionary pattern search algorithms) is presented and a probabilistic weak stationary point convergence theory is established for EPSAs. However, EPSAs are more closely related to adaptive EAs, where some adaptive mechanisms are introduced to modify the mutation or selection operators in EAs. In this paper, we will focus on more general MEAs that include individual learning and explicit local search such as the algorithms studied in [12] and [13].

Recently, an abstract model called abstract evolutionary algorithm (AEA) was presented for EAs [11], where the evolution was described by two fundamental operators, i.e., the selection and the evolution operator. In [11], several general convergence theorems and convergence rate estimations for the AEAs were established. The abstract model and the corresponding convergence theory can be applied to general EAs. Thus it may also provide a basis for theoretical analysis of MEAs. In this paper, by modeling the gradient-based local search as an abstract strong evolution operator, an abstract model for gradient-based MEAs is presented. Furthermore, the convergence theorems in [11] are extended from EAs to MEAs, which provides a basic theoretical analysis for gradient-based MEAs.

This paper is organized as follows. In Section 2, a framework for general gradient-based MEAs is presented. In Section 3, based on the theoretical results of AEAs, an abstract model for gradient-based MEAs is established and the convergence theorems in [11] are extended from AEAs to MEAs. Some conclusions are given in Section 4.

2 Gradient-Based MEAs

MEAs are commonly known as hybrid genetic algorithms. By hybrid, people mean that a local search stage takes place at some point of the "standard" evolutionary cycle composed of crossover-mutation-selection. Since EAs are global search methods and may be inefficient in fine-tuning, the local search stage is not merely a complement to the standard evolution cycle but is essential to the success of MEAs.

Although MEAs for different applications usually employ different local search methods, gradient-based methods are the most popular ones. As an important optimization technique, gradient search is efficient in its fast local searching speed. By the combination of EAs and various gradient search methods, there has been much research work on gradient-based MEAs and their successful applications in function approximation, machine-learning problems, etc [12][13]. However, little work has been done on the theoretical analysis of gradient-based MEAs. In this section, an unified framework for general gradient-based MEAs will be discussed. First, a pseudo-code that described the main process of gradient-based MEAs is shown as follows.

Algorithm 1: *Gradient-based MEA*
Begin
Generation number $t=0$;
Initialize: Control parameters: Population size M, Crossover rate Pc, Mutation rate Pm, Termination criterion;
Randomly generate an initial population $P(t)$;
Repeat
Apply gradient-based local search in the neighborhood of each individual;
Replace population $P(t)$ by a population $M(t)$ composed of the local search results of each individual;
Compute the fitness of each individual in $M(t)$;
Apply selection operator to $M(t)$, generate population $P'(t)$;
For population $P'(t)$, apply crossover and mutation operators, produce the population $P(t+1)$ of next generation;
$t=t+1$;
Until (Termination criterion fulfilled)
Return the best individual found in the evolution process;
End

In the above MEA, there is a local gradient-based search or learning process for each individual and the local search process is embedded in the standard selection-crossover-mutation process. The local search is carried out by gradient descent learning in the neighborhood of each individual and the global search is performed by the evolution operators including selection, crossover and mutation. The local gradient learning of each individual and the evolution cycle of the population are interleaved. Thus the hybrid algorithm can employ the advantages of both methods effectively and there have been several successful applications of the above gradient-based MEAs. For example, in [12], G-Prop was proposed to solve supervised learning problems in function approximation. The G-Prop algorithm combines genetic algorithms with back-propagation (BP) algorithms for neural networks and it can obtain a much higher degree of accuracy and generalization than conventional BP algorithms.

Despite the successful applications of gradient-based MEAs, their general model and convergence theory need to be further studied. In the next sections, based on the previous work on EAs, an abstract model and corresponding convergence theory will be established for gradient-based MEAs.

3 Theoretical Analysis of Gradient-Based MEAs

In [11], an abstract evolutionary algorithm (AEA) was proposed to unify most of the currently known EAs and the evolution was described as an abstract stochastic process composed of two fundamental operators: selection and evolution operators. Several convergence theorems for the AEA were also established. In this section, we will generalize the above results from EAs to MEAs by modeling the gradient-based local search as an evolution operator. First, a brief introduction on the theory of AEA [11] is presented in the following.

3.1 The AEA Model

Consider the optimization problem

$$\max\{g(x); x \in \Omega\} \quad (1)$$

where $g : \Omega \to R$ is the fitness function, and Ω is the feasible region. Assume that $g(x) \geq 0$ for any $x \in \Omega$. Since it is difficult or impossible to find an exact optimal solution x^* for the above problem, a satisfactory solution will be found in practice. The following gives the definition of a satisfactory set B, which includes all the satisfactory solutions.

Definition 1 (Satisfactory Set): A nonempty subset $B \subset \Omega$ is called a satisfactory set of the problem (1) if $g(a) > g(b)$ for any $a \in B$ and $b \in \Omega \setminus B$. The collection of all satisfactory sets of (1) is denoted by T.

In AEA, an individual is represented by an element of Ω. Ω^N is the population space, where N is the population size. The AEA model in [11] is a stochastic process composed of two independent stochastic operators: the abstract selection operators and the evolution operators, which are defined as follows.

Definition 2 (Selection Operator): Let M and X_M denote the optimal solution values and the optimal solution set in a population $X \in \Omega^N$, respectively, i.e., $M=\max\{g(x); x \in X\}$, $X_M=\{x \in X; g(x)=M\}$ for each $X \in \Omega^N$. $|Y|$ denotes the cardinality of a set Y, and $P[x]$ is the probability of a random variable x. A stochastic function $S : \Omega^N \to \Omega^N$ is an abstract selection operator if

1) $S(X) \subset X$ for any $X \in \Omega^N$

2) there is a positive constant p such that for each $X \in \Omega^N$ with $|X_M| < N$

$$P_S(X; |S(X)_M| > p + |X_M|) \neq 0 \quad (2)$$

3) for any fixed $p > 0$

$$P_S(X; |S(X)_M| > p)$$
$$\geq \inf\{P_S(X : |S(X)_M| > p); |X_M| = 1\} \quad (3)$$

Definition 3 (Evolution Operator): A stochastic function $E: \Omega^N \to \Omega^N$ is an abstract evolution operator if, for each $X \in \Omega^N$ and $B \subset T$

1) $P_E(X: E(X) \cap B \neq \phi) \neq 0$, whenever $X \cap B = \phi$ \hfill (4)

2) $P_E(X: E(X) \cap B = \phi) \neq 1$, whenever $X \cap B \neq \phi$ \hfill (5)

E is an abstract strong evolution operator if E additionally satisfies

3) $P_E(X: |E(X) \cap B| \geq |X \cap B|) \neq 0$ \hfill (6)

Based on the above three definitions, an abstract model AEA was proposed for general EAs in [11], which can be described as follows:

Definition 4 (AEA) [11]: An AEA is a stochastic process, deduced from a sequence of abstract selection operators $\{S(t): t \geq 1\}$ and evolution operators $\{E(t): t \geq 1\}$, where the population at time t is defined by

$$X^{(t)} = E(t) \circ S(t)(X^{(t-1)}) \quad (7)$$

By introducing the related characteristic parameters of the selection and evolution operators, i.e., the selection pressure Ps, the selection intensity Is, the aggregating rate A_E and the scattering rate S_E, several convergence theorems for AEA have been established. In the next section, we will extend the theoretical results from AEA to general gradient-based MEAs. For a detailed discussion on the theory of AEA, please refer to [11].

3.2 An Abstract Model for Gradient-Based MEAs

In gradient-based MEAs, a gradient learning process is embedded into the evolution process and a new evolutionary cycle, which combines gradient search with the standard selection-crossover-mutation global search, is constructed. Since the AEA model and its corresponding theory is applicable to general EAs, it deserves to be studied whether the AEA model can also be extended to the case of gradient-based MEAs. In the following discussion, we will present an abstract model for MEAs based on the AEA model. First, two formal definitions of the gradient-based local search operator are given as follows.

Definition 5 (Gradient-based Local Search Operator—Deterministic Case): A deterministic gradient-based local search operator is a mapping $G: \Omega^N \to \Omega^N$ such that

$$\forall x \in X, \quad g(G_x(X)) \geq g(x) \quad (8)$$

where $G_x(X)$ denotes the element in $G(X)$ that is mapped from x, i.e., $G_x(X)$ is the current best solutions found by gradient search in the neighborhood of x.

The above *Definition 5* only applies to gradient descent learning in deterministic case. However, in many cases, stochastic gradient descent search is usually employed.

Definition 6 (Gradient-based Local Search Operator—Stochastic Case): A stochastic gradient-based local search operator is a mapping $G: \Omega^N \to \Omega^N$ such that

$$\forall x \in X, \quad P_G[g(G_x(X)) \leq g(x)] \leq \varepsilon \tag{9}$$

where $\varepsilon > 0$ is a sufficient small number close to 0.

Since in practice, stochastic gradient search is usually used, we will focus our discussion on the stochastic case of gradient-based local search operator. Based on the definitions of stochastic gradient-based local search operator and the evolution operator, the following Lemma 1 holds.

Lemma 1: Suppose the satisfactory set B is composed of some solutions among the best of all local minima. Then the stochastic gradient-based local search operator G is an abstract strong evolution operator.

Proof: When $X \cap B = \phi$, since $G(X)$ is generated by stochastic gradient descent search, it is possible to find a element of the satisfactory set B in $G(X)$, i.e.,

$$P_G(X : G(X) \cap B \neq \phi) \neq 0 \tag{10}$$

When there is an element of B in X, based on the definition of G, the probability of removing it from X by G will be less than 1. Thus, the following holds.

$$P_G(X : G(X) \cap B = \phi) \neq 1 \tag{11}$$

Furthermore, it is possible to find more elements of B by stochastic gradient search G, i.e.,

$$P_E(X : |G(X) \cap B| \geq |X \cap B|) \neq 0 \tag{12}$$

Thus, from *Definition 4*, the stochastic gradient-based local search is an abstract strong evolution operator. □

From *Lemma 1* and the above definitions, an abstract model of gradient-based MEAs is presented as follows.

Definition 7 (Abstract model for gradient-based MEAs): A gradient-based MEA is a stochastic process, deduced by a sequence of abstract selection operators $\{S(t): t \geq 1\}$, stochastic gradient-based local search operators $\{G(t): t \geq 1\}$ and evolution operators $\{E(t): t \geq 1\}$, whose population at time t is defined by

$$X^{(t)} = E(t) \circ S(t) \circ G(t)(X^{(t-1)}) \tag{13}$$

where $X^{(0)}$ is the initial population randomly chosen from Ω^N.

3.3 Convergence Theorem for Gradient-Based MEAs

Now we have proposed an abstract model for gradient-based MEAs, which is derived by the AEA model for general EAs. We will show later that the convergence theorems of AEA can also be extended from EAs to MEAs based on gradient local search. First, the definition of convergence is introduced, which is also extended from AEA to MEAs.

Definition 8: An AEA or MEA is said to be quasi-convergent if

$$\lim_{t \to \infty} P[X^{(t)} \cap B \neq \phi] = 1 \qquad (14)$$

for each satisfactory set $B \in T$. The AEA or MEA is said to be convergent if

$$\lim_{t \to \infty} P[X^{(t)} \subset B] = 1 \qquad (15)$$

for each satisfactory set $B \in T$.

To establish the convergence theory of MEAs, we also need to define some characteristic parameters for the gradient local search operators as well as the evolution operators. The definitions of selection pressure P_{st} and selection intensity I_t in [11] can remain unchanged. However, we need several new definitions of aggregating rate, scattering rate and stability rate for evolution operators since they are combined with gradient-based local search operators. To simplify analysis, we will show the gradient-based local search operators can be unified with other standard evolution operators so that a generalized evolution operator using gradient local search is introduced. The following *Lemma 2* describes the results.

Lemma 2 (Unified Evolution Operators): The abstract model for gradient-based MEAs can be transformed to an equivalent AEA with the following unified evolution operator

$$E_U(t) = G(t+1) \circ E(t) \qquad (16)$$

Proof: As in Definition 7, at time t, the abstract model for gradient-based MEAs has a population with the following form

$$X^{(t)} = E(t) \circ S(t) \circ G(t)(X^{(t-1)}) \qquad (17)$$

Let $Y^0 = G(1)X^{(0)}$, $Y(t) = G(t+1)(X(t)), t > 0$, then

$$\begin{aligned} Y^{(t)} &= G(t+1) \circ E(t) \circ S(t)(Y^{(t-1)}) \\ &= E_U(t) \circ S(t)(Y^{(t-1)}) \end{aligned} \qquad (18)$$

Thus, the MEA with population $X(t)$ can be transformed to an equivalent AEA with population $Y(t)$. □

From *Lemma 1*, we know that the gradient-based local search operator $G(t)$ is an abstract evolution operator, thus the unified operator $E_U(t)$ is also an evolution operator defined by *Definition 3*. Then, based on *Lemma 2*, the characteristic parameters for evolution operators can be extended to the unified evolution operator $E_U(t)$. The following *Definition 9* describes the corresponding parameters of $E_U(t)$.

Definition 9: Let $E_U(t)$ be an unified abstract evolution operator, the aggregating rate A and the scattering rate S of $E_U(t)$ are positive real numbers such that

$$\begin{aligned} A &= \inf\{P(X : E(X) \cap B \neq \phi); X \cap B = \phi, B \in T\} \\ S &= \sup\{P(X : E(X) \cap B = \phi); |X \cap B| \geq r, B \in T\} \end{aligned} \qquad (19)$$

Let $X^{(t)}$, A_t, P_t, I_t and S_t denote the population, the aggregating rate, the selection pressure, the selection intensity and the scattering rate at time t. For detailed discussion on the selection pressure P_t and the selection intensity I_t, please refer to [11]. From the above analysis and definitions, the gradient-based MEA described by Definition 7 has the following convergence theorem.

Theorem 1 (Quasi-convergence): A gradient-based MEA is quasi-convergent if it satisfies the following conditions: there is an $m>0$ such that the selection pressure $P_t \geq m$ for each $t>0$

$$\lim_{t\to\infty}(1-I_t(1-S_t^{(m+1)}))/A_t = 0 \qquad (20)$$

$$\sum_{t=1}^{\infty} A_t = \infty \qquad (21)$$

The convergence speed estimation can be given by

$$P[X^{(t)} \cap B \neq \phi] > 1-\varepsilon \qquad (21)$$

for any $\varepsilon > 0$ and $t>R+T$, where R, T are integers such that $\prod_{t=R}^{R+T} A_t < \varepsilon/2$ and $(1-I_t(1-S_t^{(m+1)}))/A_t < \varepsilon/2$ whenever $t \geq R$.

The above theorem for the quasi-convergence of gradient-based MEA is different from that of general EAs in that the scattering rate and aggregating rate are defined for a unified evolution operator which combines the gradient-based local search operator and the conventional crossover and mutation operators. However, the proof in [11] can be directly applied here since the characteristic parameters of the unified evolution operator have the same expression as AEAs. Furthermore, the convergence theorem for strong evolution operator can also be established similarly.

4 Conclusion and Future Work

Gradient-based MEAs are hybrid algorithms that combine the local gradient learning with the global search of evolutionary methods. Compared to gradient learning methods, these hybrid algorithms have advantages in global convergence. On the other hand, they have better fine-tune ability than conventional EAs. In this paper, we studied the abstract model and convergence theory of gradient-based MEAs. The main contribution of this paper is that an abstract model and the corresponding convergence theorems for gradient-based MEAs are established by modeling the gradient local search as a strong evolution operator. The theoretical results in this paper are generalizations of the research work on EAs in [11]. Although the analysis is restricted to gradient-based MEAs, more theoretical work may be done for MEAs with other local search methods. Further work needs to be done to study the convergence rate of specific gradient-based MEAs both theoretically and empirically.

References

1. Bäck T.: Evolutionary Algorithms in Theory and Practice:Evolution Strategies, Evolutionary Programming, Genetic Algorithms. Oxford University Press, (1996)
2. Moscato, P. and Norman, M. G.:A Memetic Approach for the Traveling Salesman Problem: Implementation of a Computational Ecology for Combinatorial Optimization on Message-Passing Systems. In Valero, M., Onate, E., Jane, M., Larriba, J. L. and Suarez, B., editors, Parallel Computing and Transputer Applications, IOS Press, Amsterdam, The Netherlands, (1992) 177--186
3. Steenbeek, A. G., Marchiori, E. and Eiben, A. E.: Finding Balanced Graph Bi-partitions Using a Hybrid Genetic Algorithm. In Proceedings of the IEEE International Conference on Evolutionary Computation ICEC'98, IEEE Press, Piscataway, New Jersey, (1998) 90--95
4. Merz P. and Freisleben B.: Fitness Landscape Analysis and Memetic Algorithms for the Quadratic Assignment Problem. IEEE Transactions on Evolutionary Computation, 4(4), (2000) 337-352
5. Merz P. and Freisleben B.: Fitness Landscapes, Memetic Algorithms, and Greedy Operators for Graph Bipartitioning. Evolutionary Computation, 8(1), (2000) 61-91
6. Francois O.: Convergence in Simulated Evolution Algorithms. Complex Systems, Vol.10, (1996) 311-319
7. Koehler G.J.: A Proof of the Vose-Liepins Conjecture. Annals of Mathematics and Artificial Intelligence, Vol. 10, (1994) 409-422
8. Dawid H.: A Markov Chain Analysis of Genetic Algorithms with a State Dependent Fitness Function. Complex Systems, Vol. 8, (1994) 407-417
9. Hart, W.E.: A Convergence Analysis of Unconstrained and Bound Constrained Evolutionary Pattern Search. Evolutionary Computation, 9(1), (2001) 1-23
10. Hart, W.E.: Evolutionary Pattern Search Algorithms for Unconstrained and Linearly Constrained Optimization. IEEE Trans. Evolutionary Computation, 5(4), (2001) 388-397
11. Leung K.W., Duan Q.H., Xu Z.B., and Wong C.K.: A New Model of Simulated Evolutionary Computation—Convergence Analysis and Specifications. IEEE Trans. On Evolutionary Computation, Vol.5, No.1, (2001) 3-16
12. Castillo P.A., Merelo J.J., Rivas V., Romero G., Prieto A.: G-Prop: Global Optimization of Multilayer Perceptrons using GAs. Neurocomputing, Vol.35/1-4, (2000) 149-163
13. Xu X., H.G. He, and D.W. Hu. Evolutionary Adaptive-Critic Methods for Reinforcement Learning. In: Proc. of the IEEE Congress on Evolutionary Computation, IEEE Press, (2002) 1320--1325

New Quality Measures for Multiobjective Programming

Hong-yun Meng[1], Xiao-hua Zhang[2], and San-yang Liu[1]

[1] Dept.of Applied Math. Xidian University, China
mhyxdmath@hotmail.com
[2] Institute of Intelligent Information Processing, Xidian University, China
mzhangh@hotmail.com

Abstract. In the case of multiobjective evolutionary algorithm, the outcome is usually an approximation of the true Pareto Optimal set and how to evaluate the quality of the approximation of the Pareto-optimal set is very important. In this paper, improved measures are carried out to the approximation, uniformity and well extended for the approximation of the Pareto optimal set with the advantage of easy to operate. Finally, we apply our measures to the four multiobjective evolutionary algorithms that are representative of the state-of-the-art on the standard functions. Results indicate that the measures are highly competitive and can be conducted to the comparisons of the approximation set.

1 Introduction

We consider the following multiobjective programming problem:
$$\text{(MOP)} \quad \min_{x \in X} F(x) = (f_1(x), f_2(x), \cdots, f_l(x))$$
where $f_1(x), f_2(x), \cdots, f_l(x)$ are l objective functions, x is a variable vector in n dimensional space, and X is the feasible solution space.

Definition 1. (Pareto Dominance): A decision vector $x^1 \in X$ is said to dominate $x^2 \in X$ (denoted as $x^1 \preceq x^2$)iff $\forall i \in \{1, \cdots, l\}$, $f_i(x^1) \le f_i(x^2) \wedge \exists i \in \{1, \cdots, l\}$, $f_i(x^1) < f_i(x^2)$. If no other solution is strictly better than x^1, then x^1 is called a non-dominated solution(or Pareto-optimal solution). A MOP may have multiple non-dominated solutions, and the set of these solutions is called Pareto-optimal set. In the objective space, they constitute a Pareto frontier.

Definition 2. (Pareto filter): For set $I \subset X$, the Pareto filter of set I is defined as $Pareto(I) := \{x \mid x \in I, \not\exists y \in I, F(y) \preceq F(x)\}$.

Different algorithms may give different approximation sets of non-dominated solutions to the same multiobjective programming problem. To evaluate the quality of these algorithms, several quality measures have been used or proposed in the literatures [1-4], etc. However, almost all measures are compatible, but not complete [5]. In addition, most of them evaluate the approximation of a given algorithm by the minimum distance (or mean of minimum distance) with the real Pareto optimal set as a reference, but the real one is usually unknown. To this end, improved quality measures are proposed in the next section for MOP.

2 New Quality Measures for Multiobjective Programming

2.1 Quality Measure for the Approximation of the Pareto Optimal Set

Assume $P_1, P_2, \cdots, P_N$ are N approximation sets of the Pareto optimal set for N different algorithms to the same problem. Since the real Pareto optimal set is unknown, we let $U = P_1 \cup P_2 \cdots \cup P_N$ and take the $Pareto(U)$ as the real Pareto optimal set in this paper. The generational distance of set P_i is defined as $GD_i = \sqrt{\sum_{q \in P_i}(d_q^{P_i})^2} / |P_i|$, where the distance between any two solutions in the objective space to be $d_q^{P_i} = \min_{h \in Pareto(U)} d(q,h)$, and $|P_i|$ is the cardinality of P_i ($i = 1, \cdots, N$). If $GD_i < GD_j$ ($i, j = 1, \cdots, N$), then P_i is superior to P_j in approximation.

2.2 Quality Measure for the Uniformity of the Pareto Optimal Set

Different objective functions may have different orders of magnitude. To overcome this problem, we normalize each objective function $f_i(x)$ with U_i and L_i, where $U_i = \max_{x \in Pareto(U)} f_i(x)$, $L_i = \min_{x \in Pareto(U)} f_i(x)$ ($i = 1, \cdots, l$). For convenience, functions normalized are still denoted as $f_i(x)(i = 1, \cdots, l)$. To measure uniformity of a given nondominated solution set, Schott [6] used Spacing (SP) to measure the spread of approximation vectors throughout the nondominated vectors found so far. In this metric, a value of zero indicates all members of the Pareto front currently available are equidistantly spaced. However, it is not the usual case, such as Figure 1.

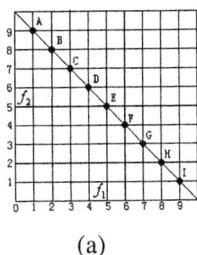
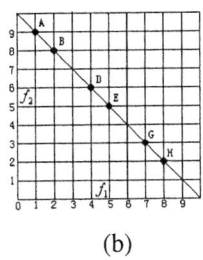

(a)   (b)

Fig. 1. Example with two given solution sets. (a) Solution set of P_1. The solutions in P_1 are uniformly scattered over the given portion of Pareto frontier. (b) Solution set of P_2. The solutions in P_2 are not uniformly scattered over the given portion of Pareto frontier.

We specify the Fig.1 in the following. Assume P_1={A,B,C,D,E,F,G,H,I} and P_2={A,B,D,E,G,H} are two approximation sets of the Pareto optimal set. From Fig.1, it is easy to see that set P_1 is uniform or equidistantly spaced, while P_2 is not. However, the Spacing metric for them is equal, i.e., $SP_1 = SP_2 = 0$. Hence, we think when the Spacing metrics of two solution sets are equal, but it can not indicate that the distributions of them are complete same. Furthermore, the Spacing metric of a given solution set is equal to zero is also not able to show the uniformity of approximation set. At the same time, if the uniformity of P_1 is superior to that of P_2, it can not assure $SP_1 < SP_2$, either. In the view of Zitzler [5], this measure is compatible, but not complete. What cause this is that the only nearest solution is concerned and other solutions in its neighborhood are neglected.

Let $P_1 = \{p_1^1, p_2^1, \cdots, p_N^1\}$, $P_2 = \{p_1^2, p_2^2, \cdots, p_M^2\}$ be two approximation sets of the Pareto optimal set by two different evolutionary algorithms, respectively. The main steps of our new measure for uniformity are the following.

Step 1. $k = 1$, $P_{New}^1 = \{P_1^1 = \{p_1^1\}, \ldots, P_N^1 = \{p_N^1\}\}$, $P_{New}^2 = \{P_1^2 = \{p_1^2\}, \ldots, P_N^2 = \{p_N^2\}\}$.

Step 2. Compute

$$d_i^1 = \min_{\substack{j=1,\cdots,i-1 \\ i+1,\cdots,N}} D(P_i^1, P_j^1), \quad \overline{d}_k^1 = \sum_{i=1}^N d_i^1 / N, \quad SP_k^1 = (\sum_{i=1}^N (1 - F(d_i^1, \overline{d}_k^1))^2 /(N-1))^{0.5},$$

$$d_i^2 = \min_{\substack{j=1,\cdots,i-1 \\ i+1,\cdots,M}} D(P_i^2, P_j^2), \quad \overline{d}_k^2 = \sum_{i=1}^M d_i^2 / M, \quad SP_k^2 = (\sum_{i=1}^M (1 - F(d_i^2, \overline{d}_k^2))^2 /(M-1))^{0.5}$$

where $F(x, y) = \begin{cases} x/y, & \text{if } x > y \\ y/x, & \text{esle} \end{cases}$, and $D(P, Q)$ is the distance in the objective space between any two solutions in set P and Q, respectively.

Step 3. If $SP_k^1 > SP_k^2$, then the uniformity of P_2 is superior to that of P_1. If $SP_k^1 < SP_k^2$, then the uniformity of P_1 is superior to that of P_2. else $SP_k^1 = SP_k^2$, let $D(P_l^1, P_m^1) = \min\{d_1^1, \cdots, d_N^1\}$ and take the union of P_l^1 and P_m^1, the outcome is $P_{New}^1 = \{P_1^1, P_2^1, \ldots, P_{N-1}^1\}$, the same to P_{New}^2. Let $k = k+1$, $N = N-1$, $M = M-1$. And if $k < \min(N-1, M-1)$, then go to Step2.

Step 4. If $SP_k^1 > SP_k^2$, then the uniformity of P_2 is superior to that of P_1; if $SP_k^1 < SP_k^2$, then P_1 is superior to that of P_2; else, let $SP_k^1 = SP_k^2$, then P_1 is as the same as P_2.

By the new measure, we compute the uniformity of two given sets P_1 in Fig.1 (a) and P_2 in Fig.1 (b). $SP_1^1 = SP_1^2 = 0$, while $SP_2^1 = 0, SP_2^2 = 0.3837 > 0$. Thus, P_1 outperforms P_2 in uniformity, which is fit with the fact in Fig.1. And it is easy to see that the new measure is in essence the concept of multi-scale from wavelet analysis.

2.3 Quality Measure for Well-Extended of the Pareto Optimal Set

To measure well-extended of the Pareto optimal set, we do it in the following.

(1) Construct reference solution set $P_r = \{F_1^1, \cdots, F_l^1\}$, in which each one is called reference solution and $F_i^1 = (L_1, \cdots, L_{i-1}, U_i, L_{i+1}, \cdots, L_l)$ ($i = 1, \cdots, l$). We wish the approximation set distribute uniformly between reference solutions.

(2) Define the distance in the objective space between a reference solution $p_r \in P_r$ to set P as $d_r^P = \min\{d(p_r, p) \mid p \in P\}$. A smaller d_r^P means P have a better well extended Pareto frontier. Hence, the extension of P is defined to be $EX = \sqrt{\sum (d_r^P)^2} / l$.

The results for the extension of sets P_1 and P_2 in Fig.1 by our measure are $EX_{P_1} = 0.0$, $EX_{P_2} = 0.7071$, which show the extension of P_1 is better than that of P_2.

3 Experiments and Discussion

To validate the feasibility and efficiency of the proposed measures, we conduct them on the four multiobjective evolutionary algorithms–SPEA,NSGA,NPGA and VEGA– with 30 independent runs for each of six standard functions ZDT1--ZDT6 from[2], in which the outcomes are all from http://www.tik.ee.ethz.ch/ ~zitzler/testdata.html/.

The simulation results in Table1 indicate that the approximation of the Pareto optimal set for SPEA is the best, and then is NSGA, VEGA and NPGA, which agrees with the fact and other measures for approximation. At the same time, the extension in descending order: SPEA, NSGA, NPGA, and VEGA. But in uniformity aspect, the SPEA is not the best, which results from the reason that in approximation set, there exist many vectors which are superposed together or very close to other vectors. Although the approximation of SPEA is better than that of NSGA, while solutions found by SPEA are very close. However, in uniformity aspect, NSGA is better than SPEA, and SPEA is the only algorithm that found a widely distributed Pareto frontier which makes explicit use of the concept of elitism. Furthermore, it is remarkable that VEGA outperforms NPGA mainly because of fewer solutions found by the former.

Table 1. Performance comparisons for the different algorithms

(a) Quality metrics of SPEA

QM	ZDT1	ZDT2	ZDT3	ZDT4	ZDT5	ZDT6
GD	0.000	0.000	0.000	0.000	0.000	0.000
EX	0.000	0.000	0.000	0.000	0.000	0.000
SP	5.858	4.495	15.18	26.45	1.014	1.874

(b) Quality metrics of NSGA

QM	ZDT1	ZDT2	ZDT3	ZDT4	ZDT5	ZDT6
GD	0.039	0.052	0.026	0.763	0.031	0.381
EX	0.109	0.258	0.139	1.270	6.447	0.739
SP	4.539	12.98	1.384	13.78	0.104	1.291

(c) Quality metrics of NPGA

QM	ZDT1	ZDT2	ZDT3	ZDT4	ZDT5	ZDT6
GD	0.216	0.298	0.198	3.413	0.209	0.980
EX	0.505	0.827	0.613	1.879	1.875	1.858
SP	4.034	3.823	6.923	0.269	0.786	1.503

(d) Quality metrics of VEGA

QM	ZDT1	ZDT2	ZDT3	ZDT4	ZDT5	ZDT6
GD	0.184	0.422	0.204	2.936	0.151	1.598
EX	0.529	0.756	0.639	3.298	7.065	1.654
SP	1.796	0.000	4.420	0.000	0.311	2.231

4 Conclusion and Future Work

In this paper, new quality measures are proposed with the advantage of easy to operate for the approximation, uniformity and well extended of an approximation set. However, how to construct compatible and complete measure also should be investigated. In addition, constrained and multiple(more than two) objective optimization problems are still deserved to consider.

References

1. Zitzler E. Evolutionary Algorithms for Multiobjective Optimization: Methods and Applications. Ph.D. Thesis, Swiss Federal Institute of Technology (ETH), Zurich, Switzerland, November, 1999.
2. Leung Y. W., Wang Y. P. U-Measure: a Quality Measure for Multiobjective Programming. IEEE Trans. Sys. Man Cybern. A, 33(3): 337-343, 2003.
3. Ishibuchi H. and Murata T, A Multiobjective Genetic Local Search Algorithm and its Application to Flowshop Scheduling. IEEE Trans. Sys. Man Cybern, C, 28, 392-403, 1998.
4. D.A.Van Veldhuizen and G.B. lamont. Multiobjective Evolutionary Algorithm Research: A history and analysis. Dept. Elec.Comput.Eng.,Graduate School of Eng., Air Force Inst.Technol.,Wright-Patterson AFB, OH.Tech.Rep.TR-98-03,1998.
5. Zitzler and Thiele. Performance Assessment of Multiobjective Optimizers: An Analysis and Review. IEEE Trans. On Evolutionary Computation,7(2), 117-132, 2003.
6. J.R. Schott. Fault tolerant design using single and multicriteria genetic algorithm optimization. M.S. thesis, Dept. Aeronautics and Astronautics, Massachusetts Inst. Technol., Cambridge, MA, May 1995.

An Orthogonal Dynamic Evolutionary Algorithm with Niches

Sanyou Zeng[1,2], Deyou Tang[1], Lishan Kang[3], Shuzhen Yao[2], and Lixin Ding[3]

[1] Dept. of Computer Science, Zhuzhou Institute of Technology,
412008 Zhuzhou, Hunan, P.R. China
sanyou-zeng@263.net
[2] Dept. of Computer Science, China University of GeoSciences,
430074 Wuhan, Hubei, P.R. China
[3] State Key Laboratory of Software Engineering, Wuhan University,
430072 Wuhan, Hubei, P.R. China

Abstract. A new dynamic evolutionary algorithm based on orthogonal design (denoted by **ODEA**) is proposed in present paper. Its population does not consist of individuals (solution vectors), but of niches, a properly small hyper-rectangle where orthogonal design method likely work well. Each niche selects the best solution found so far as its representative. And orthogonal design method is employed to find potentially good solution which is probably the representative in the niche. The niche mutation, the only genetic operator in this evolutionary algorithm, is guided by the representative of the niche, therefore, the fitness of the offspring is likely better than that of its father, furthermore, **ODEA** evolves fast. We employ a complex benchmark (moving peaks functions) testing the new approach and the numerical experiments show that **ODEA** performs much better than **SOS** [1].

1 Introduction

Most research in evolutionary computation focuses on optimization of static, non-changing problems. Many real world optimization problems however are actually dynamic, and optimization methods capable of continuously adapting solution to a changing environment are needed. And over the past years, a number of authors have addressed this problem in many different ways, as Branke surveyed in [2], [3], most of those could be grouped into the following categories:

1. The EA runs in standard fashion, but as soon as a change in the environment has detected, explicit actions are taken to facilitate the shift to the new optimum. Typical representatives of this approach are Hypermutation [4] or Variable Local Search [5].
2. Conergence is avoided all the time and it is hoped that a spread-out population can adapt to changes more easily. The random immigrants approach [6] or EAs using sharing or crowding mechanisms [7] belong into this group.
3. The EA is supplied with memory to be able to recall useful information from the past generations, which seems especially useful when the optimum

repeatedly returns to previous location. Memory based approaches can be divided into explicit memory with specific strategies for storing and retrieving information (see e.g. [8], [9], [10]) or implicit memory, where the EA is simply using a redundant representation (e.g. [11], [12], [13], [14], [15]).
4. Multiple subpopulations are used, some to track known local optima, some to search for new optima. The different subpopulations can maintain information about several promising regions of the search space, act as a kind of diverse, self-adaptation memory. Examples are [1], [16], [17], [18].

We restrict our attention in present paper to problems where fitness values on a small region and fitness landscapes before and after a change display some exploitable similarities. The mentioned approaches all tried to use landscape similarities before and after a change, but not fully employ those similarities in a small region. Orthogonal design [19] seems to have potentiality to make use of the similarities. Zeng, Kang and Ding [20] designed an orthogonal multi-objective evolutionary algorithm (OMOEA) for multi-objective optimization problems, OMOEA employed orthogonal design not only to search space evenly but also to find Pareto-optima statistically where fitness values on a small region were used.

In present paper, the proposed algorithm (denoted by **ODEA**) is a new dynamic evolutionary algorithm based on orthogonal design. Its population consists of niches, a properly small hyper-rectangle where orthogonal design method can work well. Each niche selects the best solution found so far as its representative, and orthogonal design method is employed to find potentially good solution which is probably the representative in the niche. The representative fitness is regarded as the fitness of the niche. The niche mutation operator is guided by its representative. Therefore, the fitness of the offspring is likely better than that of its father, and hence **ODEA** evolves fast. **ODEA** borrows some ideas from **SOS**. Some niches called watching niches watch over known peaks, and others called exploring niches find new peaks. The watching niches fully use the fitness similarities of the landscapes before and after a change, the exploring niches ensure global search, orthogonal design method makes good use of the fitness similarities over small region.

In the remainder of the paper, we briefly mention orthogonal design method and concept of niche in Section 2. Then, **ODEA** is suggested in Section 3. The next section presents numerical experiments. Finally, we outline the conclusions of present paper.

2 Preliminary

2.1 Orthogonal Design Method

We use an example to introduce the basic concept of experimental design methods. For more details, see [19]. The yield of a vegetable depends on: 1) the temperature, 2) the amount of fertilizer, and 3) the pH value of the soil. These three quantities are called the factors of the experiment. Each factor has three possible values shown in Table 1, and we say that each factor has three levels. To find the best combination of levels for a maximum yield, we can do one

Table 1. Experimental design problem with three factors and three levels per factor

	Factors		
Levels	Temperature	Amount of fertilizers	pH value
Level 1	$20°C$	$100g/m^2$	6
Level 2	$25°C$	$150g/m^2$	7
Level 3	$30°C$	$200g/m^2$	8

experiment for each combination, and then select the best one. In the above example, there are $3 \times 3 \times 3 = 27$ combinations. And hence there are 27 experiments. In general, when there are N factors and Q levels, there are Q^N combinations. When N and Q are large, it may not be possible to do all Q^N experiments. Therefore, it is desirable to sample a small, but representative set of combinations for experimentation. The orthogonal design was developed for the purpose [19]. Let $L_M(Q^N)$ be an orthogonal array for N factors and Q levels, where "L" denotes a Latin square and M the number of combination of levels. It has M rows, where every row represent a combination of levels. Applying orthogonal array $L_M(Q^N)$, we only select M combinations to be tested, where M may be much smaller than Q^N, For convenience, we denote $L_M(Q^N) = [a_{i,j}]_{M \times N}$ where the jth factor in the ith combination has level $a_{i,j}$ and $a_{i,j} \in \{1, 2, ..., Q\}$, and the corresponding yields of the M combinations by $[y_i]_{M \times 1}$, where the ith combination (experiment) has yield y_i. The following is an orthogonal array:

$$L_9(3^3) = \begin{bmatrix} 1 & 1 & 1 \\ 1 & 2 & 2 \\ 1 & 3 & 3 \\ 2 & 1 & 2 \\ 2 & 2 & 3 \\ 2 & 3 & 1 \\ 3 & 1 & 3 \\ 3 & 2 & 1 \\ 3 & 3 & 2 \end{bmatrix} \qquad (1)$$

In $L_9(3^3)$, there are three factors, three levels per factor, and nine combination of levels. The three factors have respective levels $1, 1, 1$ in the first combination, $1, 2, 2$ in the second combination, etc. We apply orthogonal array $L_9(3^3)$ to select nine combinations to be tested, and the nine combination and their yields are shown in Table 2. From the yields of the selected combinations, a promising solution can be obtained by statistical methods: calculate the mean value of the yield for each factor at each level, where each factor has a level with best mean value, choose the combination of the best levels as promising solution. For example, the mean yields for temperature at levels 1, 2 and 3 can be calculated by averaging yields for the experiments $1-2-3$, $4-5-6$ and $7-8-9$, respectively. The mean yields at different levels for other factors can be computed in a similar manner. The mean yields are shown in Table 3.

Table 2. Based on the orthogonal array $L_9(3^3)$, nine representative combinations for experimentation and their yields, where T denote temperature and F denotes amount of fertilizers

combination	Factors			yield
	$T(°C)$	$F(g/m^2)$	pH value	
1	1(20)	1(100)	1(6)	2.75
2	1(20)	2(150)	2(7)	4.52
3	1(20)	3(200)	3(8)	4.65
4	2(25)	1(100)	2(7)	4.60
5	2(25)	2(150)	3(8)	5.58
6	2(25)	3(200)	1(6)	4.10
7	3(30)	1(100)	3(8)	5.32
8	3(30)	2(150)	1(6)	4.10
9	3(30)	3(200)	2(7)	4.37

Table 3. The mean yields for each factor at different levels

Level	Mean yield		
	Temperature	Amount of fertilizers	pH value
Level1	3.97	4.22	3.65
Level2	4.76	4.73	4.50
Level3	4.60	4.37	5.18

From Table 3, we can see the best levels of temperature, amount of fertilizers and pH values are 25, 150 and 8 respectively, and therefore, we regard ($25°C$, $150g/m^2, 8$) as promising. Such solution may not really be optimal, for additive and quadratic models, however, orthogonal design has been proven optimal.

As we will explain, the proposed technique may require different orthogonal arrays for different optimization problems. Although many orthogonal arrays have been tabulated in the literature, it is impossible to store all of them for the proposed algorithm. We introduce an existed simple permutation method to construct a class of orthogonal arrays $L_M(Q^P)$ where Q is prime and $M = Q^J$, where J is a positive integer fulfilling

$$P = \frac{Q^J - 1}{Q - 1} \qquad (2)$$

Denote the jth column of the orthogonal array $[a_{i,j}]_{M \times P}$ by $\mathbf{a}_j$. Column $\mathbf{a}_j$ for $j = 1, 2, (Q^2-1)/(Q-1)+1, (Q^3-1)/(Q-1)+1, ..., (Q^{J-1}-1)/(Q-1)+1$ are called *basic columns*. And the others are called *nonbasic columns*. The algorithm first constructs the basic columns, and then constructs the nonbasic columns. The details are as follows.

Algorithm 1. *Construction of orthogonal array* $L_M(Q^P)$
//Construct the the basic columns as follows:
FOR $k = 1$ TO J
  $j = \frac{Q^{k-1}-1}{Q-1} + 1;$
  FOR $i = 1$ TO Q^J
    $a_{i,j} = \lfloor \frac{i-1}{Q^{J-k}} \rfloor \bmod Q;$
  ENDFOR
ENDFOR
//Construct the the nonbasic columns as follows:
FOR $k = 2$ TO J
  $j = \frac{Q^{k-1}-1}{Q-1} + 1;$
  FOR $s = 1$ TO $j-1$, $t = 1$ TO $Q-1$
    $\mathbf{a}_{j+(s-1)(Q-1)+t} = (\mathbf{a}_s \times t + \mathbf{a}_j) \bmod Q;$
  ENDFOR
ENDFOR
Increment $a_{i,j}$ by one for $-1 \leq i \leq M$ and $1 \leq j \leq P$; ♯

$L_M(Q^P)$ is the full size of the orthogonal array, which has P columns. For a problem with N decision variables, we discard the last $P - N$ columns of $L_M(Q^P)$ and get an orthogonal array $L_M(Q^N)$.

The proposed algorithm will require the mean value of the objective at each level of each factor. We denote the objective values of the orthogonal experiments by $[y_i]_{M \times 1}$ where the objective has the value y_i at the ith combination; the mean values by $[\Delta_{k,j}]_{Q \times N}$ where the objective has the mean value $\Delta_{k,j}$ at the kth level of the jth factor; and

$$\Delta_{k,j} = \frac{Q}{M} \sum_{a_{i,j}=k} y_i \qquad (3)$$

where the orthogonal array $L_M(Q^N)$ has the value $a_{i,j}$ at ith row and jth column. That is, the jth factor has level $a_{i,j}$ in the ith combination(experiment). The objective has value y_i at the ith combination, and $\sum_{a_{i,j}=k} y_i$ implies the sum of y_i where $\forall i$ satisfy $a_{i,j} = k$. The details of the algorithm are as follows

Algorithm 2. *Calculation of mean value* $[\Delta_{k,j}]_{Q \times N}$
$[\Delta_{k,j}]_{Q \times N} = [0]_{Q \times N};$
//Add up objective result for each factor at each level
  FOR $i = 1$ TO M, $j = 1$ TO N
    $q = a_{i,j}; \Delta_{q,j} = \Delta_{q,j} + y_i;$
  ENDFOR
//Average results for each factor at each level
  $[\Delta_{k,j}]_{Q \times N} = [\Delta_{k,j}]_{Q \times N} \times Q/M$ ♯

Each factor has its best level by the mean value matrix $[\Delta_{k,j}]_{Q \times N}$. Usually, the combination of the best levels is a good solution, for additive or quadratic model, it is optimal. The details of calculating the combination of the best levels are as follows.

Algorithm 3. *Calculation of potentially good combination* $[b_j]_{1 \times N}$
$\quad FOR\ j = 1\ TO\ N$
$\quad\quad b_j = arg \max_{i \in \{1,2,...,Q\}} \Delta_{i,j}$
$\quad ENDFOR$
$\quad Return\ \mathbf{b} = (b_1, b_2, ..., b_N);$ ♯

2.2 Niche

Suppose objective function is additive or quadratic on hyper-rectangle $\mathcal{W}$

$$\begin{array}{l} \mathcal{W} = \{\mathbf{x} = (x_1, x_2, ..., x_N) \mid l_j \le x_j \le u_j \} \\ j = 1, 2, ..., N \end{array} \quad (4)$$

then, orthogonal design method is optimal. We employ orthogonal design method to find the optimal solution on $\mathcal{W}$ as follows.

Quantize the range of component x_j in $\mathbf{x} = (x_1, x_2, ..., x_N)$ into Q levels: $x_{1,j}, x_{2,j}, ..., x_{Q,j}$, where x_j is called the jth factor. $x_{q,j}$ is given by

$$x_{q,j} = \begin{cases} l_j^{(n)} & q = 1 \\ l_j^{(n)} + (q-1)\delta_j & 2 \le q \le Q-1 \\ u_j^{(n)} & q = Q \end{cases} \quad (5)$$

$$where\ \delta_j = \frac{u_j^{(n)} - l_j^{(n)}}{Q-1}$$

In other words, the difference between two successive levels is the same. For convenience, denote $x_j = \{x_{1,j}, x_{2,j}, ..., x_{Q,j}\}$, and call $x_{q,j}$ the qth level of the jth factor. After quantization, x_j has Q possible values $x_{1,j}, x_{2,j}, ..., x_{Q,j}$. Suppose $[b_j]_{1 \times N}$ is yielded by Algorithm 3 where orthogonal design method is used, then the optimal solution stays in the neighbor of $[b_j]_{1 \times N}$

$$\begin{array}{l} \mathcal{W}' = \{\mathbf{x} = (x_1, x_2, ..., x_N) \mid b_j - \frac{\delta_j}{2} \le x_j \le b_j + \frac{\delta_j}{2} \} \\ j = 1, 2, ..., N \end{array} \quad (6)$$

that is, $[b_j]_{1 \times N}$ is close-to-optimal with error of b_j less than $\frac{\delta_j}{2}$. For yielding solution with higher precision, we need only to repeat above process on $\mathcal{W}'$ as on $\mathcal{W}$.

In general, objective function is not additive or quadratic on the search space $\mathcal{X}$

$$\begin{array}{l} \mathcal{X} = \{\mathbf{x} = (x_1, x_2, ..., x_N) \mid L_j \le x_j \le U_j \} \\ j = 1, 2, ..., N \end{array} \quad (7)$$

and the orthogonal design method does not work well on the whole search space. However, on a properly small hyper-rectangle $\mathcal{W}$ (cf. Equation 4), there may be no more than one peak of the search space $\mathcal{X}$ covered by $\mathcal{W}$ (that is, $\mathcal{W}$ coves no peak or only one peak), and the objective function may approximate additive or quadratic on $\mathcal{W}$. Therefore, the orthogonal design method may work well. Such hyper-rectangle $\mathcal{W}$, which covers no more than one peak of the search space $\mathcal{X}$, is called a **niche**, and orthogonal design method can be employed to find promising solution in niche $\mathcal{W}$.

3 New Algorithm

SOS [1] makes good use of landscape similarities before and after a change, but, it does not fully use the fitness similarities on a small region. **ODEA** borrows some ideas from **SOS** to make use of landscape similarities before and after a change ,and by orthogonal design method, it takes advantage of fitness similarities on a small region. **ODEA** uses niches, instead of multi-populations, so as to employ orthogonal design method. The population of this new algorithm does not consist of solution vectors (individual), but of niches. For evaluating fitness of a niche, each niche selects its best solution found so far as its **representative**, and the fitness value of the representative is regarded as that of the niche. Since orthogonal design method works well in niche, it is used to find a potentially good solution which is likely near the optimal solution in the niche. And the potentially good solution is probably the representative of the niche. Since the representative is likely to be close to optimal in its niche, we determine whether or not the niche covers a peak on the search space according to the position of the representative. If the representative stays inside the niche then we say the niche covers a peak, and if it stays at the boundary of the niche then we say the niche does not cover a peak yet.

Like **SOS**,**ODEA** divides its population into two groups, one group of niches is to watch over the known peaks, called **watching niches**, the other group is to explore new peaks, called **exploring niches**. Watching niches will fully use the landscape similarities before and after a change, while exploring niches benefit global search.

Mutation operator is the only genetic operator. The mutation of a watching niche is as follows: If the watching niche does not cover any peak, then it moves to its nearest peaks; if the niche covers a peak, then it shrinks to obtain a close-to-peak with higher precision. The mutation of an exploring niche is as follows: If the exploring niche does not cover any peak, then it moves to its nearest peaks; if the niche covers a peak, then it is inserted into watching group where a worse watching niche has to be deleted with consideration of diversity, and a new exploring niche has to be created. We will implement **ODEA** in the following.

Suppose there are K watching niches, denoted by $\mathcal{W}_1, \mathcal{W}_2, ..., \mathcal{W}_K$, L exploring niches, denoted by $\mathcal{E}_1, \mathcal{E}_2, ..., \mathcal{E}_L$; if not confused, the representative of each niche is denotes by s; we have a flag to sign whether or not a niche covers a peak, and denote the flag by identifier $PeakIsInside$ for each niche, without confused, the initial value $PeakIsInside = false$; the initial side length of niches is denoted by $d_1, d_2, ..., d_N$; the counter of generation is denoted t. The framework of **ODEA** is as follows.

Algorithm 4. *The framework of* **ODEA**
   //*Initiate.*
   FOR $i = 1$ TO K
      Randomly create initial watching niche $\mathcal{W}_i$;
      (cf. Algorithm 10);
      Calculate representative s for $\mathcal{W}_i$ *(cf. Algorithm 7);*
   ENDFOR
   FOR $i = 1$ TO L
      Randomly create initial exploring niche $\mathcal{E}_i$
      (cf. Algorithm 10);
      Calculate representative s for $\mathcal{E}_i$ *(cf. Algorithm 7);*
   ENDFOR
   $t = 0$;
   //*Begin evolving.*
   REPEAT
      FOR $i = 1$ TO K
         Mutate watching niche $\mathcal{W}_i$ *(cf. Algorithm 5);*
         IF(*having detected an environmental change*)
            Adjust all watching niches (cf. Algorithm 11);
         ENDIF
      ENDFOR
      FOR $i = 1$ TO L
         Mutate exploring niche $\mathcal{E}_i$ *(cf. Algorithm 6);*
         IF(*having detected an environmental change*)
            Adjust all watching niches (cf. Algorithm 11);
      END OF FOR
      $t = t + 1$;
   UNTIL *termination criterion*   ♮

Algorithm 5. *Mutate watching niche* $\mathcal{W}$.
   IF(*PeakIsInside* == *false*)//$\mathcal{W}$ *covers no peak.*
      Move $\mathcal{W}$; *(cf. Algorithm 8);*
      Calculate representative s for $\mathcal{W}$ *(cf. Algorithm 7);*
      IF(*s stays inside* $\mathcal{W}$) *PeakIsInside* = *true*;
   ELSE//$\mathcal{W}$ *covers a peak.*
      IF(*solution precision inferior to demand*)
         Shrink $\mathcal{W}$ *(cf. Algorithm 9);*
         Calculate representative s for $\mathcal{W}$ *(cf. Algorithm 7);*
      ENDIF
   ENDIF   ♮

Algorithm 6. *Mutate exploring niche* $\mathcal{E}$.
   IF(*PeakIsInside* == *false*)//$\mathcal{E}$ *covers no peak.*
      Move $\mathcal{E}$ *(cf. Algorithm 8);*
      Calculate representative s for $\mathcal{E}$ *(cf. Algorithm 7);*
   ELSE//$\mathcal{E}$ *covers a peak.*
      Insert $\mathcal{E}$ *into the group of watching niches;*

*Delete a worst watching niche
with consideration of diversity;
Randomly create a new searching niche $\mathcal{E}$
(cf. Algorithm 10);
Calculate representative s for $\mathcal{E}$ (cf. Algorithm 7);*
*ENDIF
IF(s stays inside $\mathcal{E}$) PeakIsInside = true;* ♯

Note: Deleting a worst niche with consideration of diversity means that if there exist two niches too close to each other in the watching group then delete one of them, else delete the worst niche.

The algorithm of calculating representative employs orthogonal design method. Suppose the dynamic function has N factors, and the range of each factor is quantized into Q levels. Executing Algorithm 1, we will get orthogonal array $L_M(Q^P)$. We require $P \geq N$ here. The details of calculating representative are as follows.

Algorithm 7. *Calculate representative for niche.*

1. *Execute Algorithm 1 to construct orthogonal array $L_M(Q^P)$;*
2. *Delete the last $P - N$ columns of $L_M(Q^P)$ to get $L_M(Q^N)$;*
3. *Using $L_M(Q^N)$, execute Algorithm 2 to construct array $[\Delta_{q,j}]_{Q \times N}$;*
4. *Execute Algorithm 3 to get a promising solution $\mathbf{b}$;*
5. *$s \leftarrow$ Best $\{\mathbf{b},$ the M combinations corresponding to $L_M(Q^N)\}$;* ♯

Note: In the case that orthogonal method fails, the step 5 in Algorithm 7 ensures that the representative is the best solution found so far in the niche.

Suppose niche $\mathcal{W}$ is as Equation 4, and niche $\mathcal{W}'$ is as follow.

$$\mathcal{W}' = \{\mathbf{x} = (x_1, x_2, ..., x_N) \mid l'_j \leq x_j \leq u'_j \ j = 1, 2, ..., N\}, \qquad (8)$$

The details of moving niche $\mathcal{W}$ to $\mathcal{W}'$ are as follows.

Algorithm 8. *Move niche $\mathcal{W}$ to $\mathcal{W}'$.*
*FOR $j = 1$ TO N
  IF($l_j \leq s_j \leq u_j$)
    $l'_j = s_j - \frac{u_j - l_j}{2}, u'_j = s_j + \frac{u_j - l_j}{2}$;
  IF($l_j = s_j$)
    $l'_j = s_j - \frac{(Q-2)*(u_j - l_j)}{Q-1}; u'_j = s_j + \frac{u_j - l_j}{Q-1}$,;
  IF($u_j = s_j$)
    $l'_j = s_j - \frac{u_j - l_j}{Q-1}; u'_j = s_j + \frac{(Q-2)*(u_j - l_j)}{Q-1}$;
END OF FOR
IF($\mathcal{W}'$ out of the problem search space)
  move it rightly into the problem search space;* ♯

Figure 1 depicts a move of niche.
The details of shrinking operator are as follows.

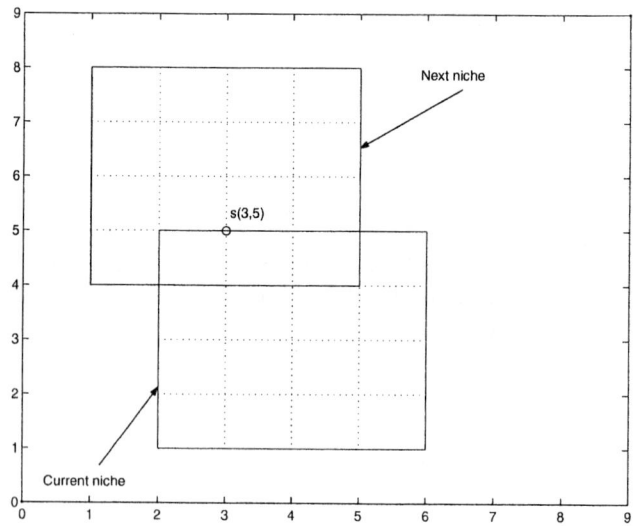

Fig. 1. An illustration of moving niche where $N = 2$ and $Q = 5$

Algorithm 9. *Shrink niche $\mathcal{W}$ to $\mathcal{W}'$*
FOR $j = 1$ TO N
$l'_j = s_j - \frac{u_j - l_j}{Q-1}, u'_j = s_j + \frac{u_j - l_j}{Q-1}$;
END OF FOR ♯

For creating initial niche, each side of the search space is parted into several equal portions, therefore, the search space is equally parted into units. Let the size of the unit be the size of the initial niche. Suppose the side length of the search space are $D_1, D_2, ..., D_N$ and they are parted into $Q_1, Q_2, ..., Q_N$ equal portions respectively, then the side length of the initial niche are $d_1 = \frac{D_1}{Q_1}, d_2 = \frac{D_2}{Q_2}, ..., d_N = \frac{D_N}{Q_N}$. Note that we hope initial niche coves no more peak for orthogonal design working well on the niche. The details of creating initial niche are as follows.

Algorithm 10. *Randomly create a niche*
Randomly pick a unit from the search space as an initial niche;
$PeakIsInside = false$; ♯

Once an environmental change takes place, all watching niches have to be adjusted while exploring niche need not to be adjusted. Thus adjusting operator executes just after a change and the detail is as follows.

Algorithm 11. *Adjusting watching niche $\mathcal{W}$*
FOR $j = 1$ TO N
$l_j = s_j - \frac{d_j}{2}, u_j = s_j + \frac{d_j}{2}$;
END OF FOR
IF($\mathcal{W}$ being out of original search space)
  Move $\mathcal{W}$ rightly into the search space; ♯

4 Experiments and Comparisons

4.1 Parameter Settings for ODEA

Four parameters need to be set in **ODEA**. The initial size of niche: $d_1, d_2, ..., d_N$, where $d_1 = \frac{D_1}{Q_1}, d_2 = \frac{D_2}{Q_2}, ..., d_N = \frac{D_N}{Q_N} d_1, d_2, ..., d_N$; the prime number of quantized levels: Q; parameter in orthogonal array (cf. Equation 2): J; the number of watching niches and exploring niches: K, L, therefore, the size of population is $K+L$. A niche should satisfy that it covers no more than one peak to ensure that **ODEA** works well. If the niche size is too big, then it might cover more than one peaks, therefore the representative calculated by Algorithm 7 would be poor and **ODEA** would fail to track the moving best. And if the niche size is too small, then exploring peak would be time-consuming because moving niche would be very slow. For determining $Q_1, Q_2, ..., Q_N$, the moving peaks function problem (cf. website: "http:// www.aifb.uni-karlsruhe.de/ jbr/ MovPeaks") is used to test **ODEA** and let $Q_1 = Q_2 = ... = Q_N = 11, 29, 53, 71, 97$ respectively. The results show that **ODEA** relatively works well when $Q_1 = Q_2 = ... = Q_N = 29$. For the level Q, we choose a small prime, because a big Q will increase the number of experiments $M = Q^J$, therefore the computations would increase, the default value $Q = 5$. We let parameter J be determined by both Q and number of dimension N. The used orthogonal array $L_M(Q^N)$ consists of the former N columns of the orthogonal array $L_M(Q^P)$ constructed by Algorithm 1, therefore it must be satisfied that $P \geq N$, i.e.

$$P = \frac{Q^J - 1}{Q - 1} \geq N. \qquad (9)$$

As J increases, the number of combinations Q^J increases exponentially, therefore we choose a smallest integer J which satisfies Equation (9). Thus J is a parameter determined internally, and need not be set outside **ODEA**. The default setting for $L = 1, K = 10$ (**SOS** has $L = 1$ and $K = 10$).

4.2 Test Function and Parameter Settings

Branke [8] suggested a problem called moving peaks function with a multidimensional landscape consisting of several peaks ,where the height, the width and the position of each peak are altered a little every time a change in environment occurs, and independently, Morrison and DeJong [22] has suggested a similar benchmark. For the details of the function, please visit website: "http:// www.aifb.uni-karlsruhe.de/ jbr/ MovPeaks". We choose moving peaks function as test problems. and unless stated otherwise, the default settings defining the benchmark are employed in the experiments and can be found in Table 4. An evaluation means that an individual is created and evaluated its fitness. Shift length s means that a peak **p** will move within its neighbor with radius s after next environment changes.

Table 4. Default settings for the moving peaks benchmark used in this paper, where f denotes change frequency, A denotes minimum and maximum allele value, H denotes minimum and maximum height of peaks, W denotes minimum and maximum peak width parameter, I denotes initial peak height for all peaks

Parameter	Value
Number of peaks p	10
f	every 5000 evaluations
height-severity	7.0
width-severity	1.0
peak shape	cone
basic function	no
shift length s	1.0
number of dimension	5
A	[0,100]
H	[30.0,70.0]
W	[1,12]
I	50.0

4.3 Comparison of ODEA with SOS

Let e_t be the difference between the optimum value and the value of the best individual in the population just before the tth environment change and let T be the number of environment changes, the off-line error is the average of all differences over the environment changes, i.e. $e = \frac{1}{T}\sum_{t=1}^{T} e_t$. For the results reported, we use an average over 50 runs of **ODEA**, each runs with a specific random seed and a specific instance of the problem. The offline errors after 500,000 evaluations in **ODEA** are compared with that in **SOS**. Table 5, 6, 7, 8 show the effects of peak movements, change frequency, changing the number of peaks and higher dimensionality on both **ODEA** and **SOS** respectively. All above results show that **ODEA** can track the moving best solution much better than **SOS**, therefore **ODEA** is an efficient approach.

Table 5. The offline error of both **ODEA** and **SOS** for different shift length

shift length	SOS	ODEA
1.0	4.01	1.95
2.0	5.12	2.23
3.0	6.54	2.38

4.4 Limitation of ODEA

That a niche covers no more than one peak ensures that **ODEA** can work well. However, if two peaks is too close, then the representative might be poor and

Table 6. The offline error of both **ODEA** and **SOS** for different number of individual evaluations between changes

evaluations between changes	SOS	ODEA
10000	3.62	1.81
5000	4.01	1.95
2500	4.93	2.19
1000	6.51	2.43
500	8.59	4.70

Table 7. The offline error of both **ODEA** and **SOS** for different number of peaks

number of peaks	SOS	ODEA
1	2.06	0.68
10	4.01	1.95
20	4.43	1.93
30	4.20	1.91
40	4.06	1.82
50	4.12	1.70
100	3.75	1.31
200	3.62	1.14

Table 8. The offline error of both **ODEA** and **SOS** on a Moving Peaks problem with 200 peaks and 20 dimensions

SOS	ODEA
12.67	4.09

ODEA would not track the moving best solution well; and if fitness values on small region and fitness landscapes before and after a change do not display any exploitable similarity in the problem, **ODEA** might works poorly.

5 Conclusion

ODEA is different from others. Its population does not consist of individuals, but of niches. Each niche selects the best solution found so far as its representative. And orthogonal design method is employed to find potentially good solution which is probably the representative in the niche. The niche mutation operator is conducted by its representative, therefore, **ODEA** evolves fast. **ODEA** borrows some ideas from **SOS**. Watching niches watch over known peaks, and exploring niches find new peaks. The watching niches fully use the fitness similarities of the landscapes before and after a change, and the exploring niches ensure global search. The numerical experiments show that **ODEA** performs much better than **SOS**.

Acknowledgment. This work is supported by The National Natural Science Foundation of China (No.s: 60473037, 60483081, 40275034, 60204001, 60133010) and by China Postdoctoral Science Foundation (No. 2003034505). And the author thanks Juergen Branke, Institute for Applied Computer Science and Formal Descriptiom Methods, University of Karlsruhe (TH), Karlsruhe, Germany, for his helpful suggestion on expressing the paper and choosing parameters for the algorithm.

References

1. J. Branke, T. Kaufler, C. Schmidt, and H. Schmeck. A multipopulation approach to dynamic optimization problems. Adaptive Computing in Design and Manufacturing. Springer, 2000.
2. J. Branke. Evolutionary approaches to dynamic optimization problems -Instruction and recent trends-. In J. Branke, editor, Proceedings of the Workshop on Evolutionary Algorithms for Dynamic Optimization Problems, pages 1-3. Chicago, USA, 2003.
3. J. Branke. Evolutionary Optimization in dynamic Environments. Kluwer Academic Publishers, 2002.
4. H. G. Cobb. An investigation into the use of hypermutation as adaptive operator in genetic algorithms having continuous, time-dependent nonstationary environments. Technical Report AIC-90-001, Naval Research Laboratory, Washington, USA, 1990.
5. F. Vavak, K. Jukes, and T. C. Fogarty. Adaptive combustion balancing in multiple burner boiler using a genetic algorithm with variable range of local search. In T. Bäck, editor. Seventh International Conference on Genetic Algorithms, pages 719-726. Morgan Kaufmann, 1997.
6. J. J. Grefenstette. Genetic algorithms for changing environments. In R. Maenner and B. Manderick, editors, Parallel Problem Solving from Nature 2, pages 137-144. North-Holland, 1992.
7. W. Cedeno and V. R. Vemuri. On the use niching for dynamic landscapes. In International Conference on Evolutionary Computation, pages 361-366. IEEE, 1997.
8. J. Branke. Memory enchanced evolutionary algorithms for changing optimization problems. In congress on Evolutionary Computation. CEC99, volume 3, pages 1875-1882. IEEE, 1999.
9. N. Mori, S. Imanishi, H. Kita, and Y. Nishikawa. Adaptation to changing environments by means of the memory based thermodynamical genetic algorithm. In T. Bäck, editor. Seventh International Conference on Genetic Algorithms, pages 299-306. Morgan Kaufmann, 1997.
10. C. L. Ramsey and J. J. Grefenstette. Case-based initialization of genetic algorithms. In S. Forrest, editor, Fifth International Conference on Genetic Algorithms, pages 84-91. Morgan Kaufmann, 1993.
11. D. Dasgupta and D. R. Mcgregor. Nonstationary function optimization using the structured genetic algorithm. In R. Männer and B. Manderick, editors, Parallel Problem Solving from Nature, pages 145-154. Elsevier Science Publisher, 1992.
12. D. E. Goldberg and R. E. Smith. Nonstationary function optimization using genetic algorithms with dominance and diploidy. In J. J. Grefenstette, editor, Second International Conference on Genetic Algorithms, pages 59-68. Lawrence Erlbaum Associates, 1987.

13. B. S. Hadad and C. F. Eick. Supporting polyploidy in genetic algorithms using dominace vector. In P. J. A. et al., editors, 6th International Conference on Evolutionary Programming, volume 1213 of LNCS, pages 223-234. Springer, 1997.
14. J. Lewis, E. Hart, and G. Ritchie. A comparison of dominance mechanisms and simple mutation on non-stationary problems. In A. E. Eiben, T. Bäck, M. Schoenauer, and H. P. Schwefel, editors, Parallel Problem Solving from Nature, volume 1498 of LNCS, pages 139-148. Springer, 1998.
15. C. Ryan. Diploidy without dominance. In J. T. Alander, editor, Third Nordic Workshop on Genetic Algorithms, pages 63-70, 1997.
16. J. Branke and H. Schmeck. Designing evolutionary algorithms for dynamic optimization problems. In S. Tsutsui and A. Ghosh, editors, Theory and application of Evolutionary Computation: Recent Trends, pages 239-262. Springer, 2002.
17. R. K. Ursem. Mutinational GAsptimization techniques in dynamic environments. In D. Whitley, D. Goldberg, E. Cantu-Paz, L. Spector, I. Parmee, and H. G. Beyer, editors, Genetic and Evolutionary Computation Conference, pages 19-26. Morgan Kaufmann, 2000.
18. M. Wineberg and F. Oppacher. Enchancing th GA's ability to cope with dynamic environments. In W. et al., editor, Genetic and Evolutionary Computation Conference, pages 3-10. Morgan Kaufmann, 2000.
19. Montgomery, D. C.. Design and Analysis of Experiments. 3rd ed. New York: Wiley, 1991.
20. Sanyou Y.Zeng, Lishan S.Kang, Lixing X.Ding. An Orthogonal Multi-objective Evolutionary Algorithm for Multi-objective Optimization Problems with Constraints. Evolutionary Computation. Vol.12No.1, pp77-98M, IT Press, 2004,.
21. J. Branke. Evolutionary algorithms for dynamic optimization problems - a survey. Technical Report 387, Institute AIFB University of Karlsruhe, February 1999.
22. R. W. Morrison and K. A. DeJong. A tes problem generator for nonstationary environments. In Congress on Evolutionary Computation, volume 3, pages 2047-2053.IEEE, 1999.

Fitness Sharing Genetic Algorithm with Self-adaptive Annealing Peaks Radii Control Method

Xinjie Yu

State Key Lab of Power Systems, Dept. of Electrical Engineering,
Tsinghua University, Beijing 100084, China
yuxj@tsinghua.edu.cn

Abstract. Fitness sharing genetic algorithm is one of the most common used methods to deal with multimodal optimization problems. The algorithm requires peaks radii as the predefined parameter. It is very difficult to guess peaks radii for designers and decision makers in the real world applications. A novel self-adaptive annealing peaks radii control method has been suggested in this paper to deal with the problem. Peaks radii are coded into chromosomes and evolved while fitness sharing genetic algorithm optimizes the problem. The empirical results tested on the benchmark problems show that fitness sharing genetic algorithm with self-adaptive annealing peaks radii control method can find and maintain nearly all peaks steadily. This method is especially suitable for the problems whose peaks radii are difficult to estimate beforehand.

1 Introduction

It is well known that design and decision making problems can all be considered as optimization problems. There are so many instances in engineering design that multiple optimal designs exist in solution space. Common optimization algorithms can at best find one optimal design. If designers and decision makers can make choices from multiple optimal designs and decisions, there will be remarkable enhancements in the efficiency and quality of designs and decisions.

As the representative of modern optimization algorithms, genetic algorithms have achieved successes in function optimization, knowledge acquisition, and system simulation [4]. The genetic operation is carried out with a group of individuals, so it is possible for genetic algorithms to maintain all peaks in multimodal optimization problems. However under the circumstance of finite population size and improper selective pressure, genetic algorithms can only converge to one solution [8].

Fitness sharing is an effective method which can maintain the population diversity of genetic algorithms to find multiple peaks in the solution space [2, 5]. In multimodal optimizing genetic algorithms, the sub-space around a peak in the solution space is usually named as a niche. Individuals around a peak constitute a species. Fitness sharing is to decrease the fitness of individuals in a species according to the scope of the niche. If there are too many individuals in a niche, their fitness will decrease dramatically, which can encourage the species with fewer individuals to survive. Standard fitness sharing genetic algorithm adopts fitness sharing method before the selection stage of genetic algorithms.

There are two difficulties in applying standard fitness sharing genetic algorithm in real world applications. One is that fitness sharing method needs peaks radii beforehand. In real world applications, it is very hard to estimate peaks radii of the multimodal optimization problems. The other is that every peak is supposed to have the same radius in fitness sharing method, which is not the true condition for real world applications.

Many improvements have been suggested to enhance the search ability and overcome the shortcomings of standard fitness sharing genetic algorithm. The representatives include clearing algorithm suggested by Petrowski [11], adaptive KMEAN cluster with fitness sharing algorithm suggested by Yin and Germay [13], dynamic niche sharing algorithm suggested by Miller and Shaw [10], adaptive niching algorithm suggested by Goldberg and Wang [6]. These algorithms either need minimal peak radius or the peak number in the solution space. They improve the performance of the standard fitness sharing genetic algorithms in different ways. Sareni and Krahenbuhl suggest that adaptive peaks radii control is a good method for fitness sharing algorithms, but there is no trail of optimization instances which have ever been reported [12].

Parameter control is very important in genetic algorithms research. Parameter control methods include optimal parameter tuning, deterministic parameter control, adaptive parameter control, and self-adaptive parameter control [3]. Among them, self-adaptive parameter control method, which utilizes GAs to tune the parameter in the optimization procedure, is the most flexible way of parameter control. Peaks radii are the key parameters in fitness sharing genetic algorithms. In this paper, we adopt the idea from simulated annealing algorithm and combine it with self-adaptive parameter control. Every individual has its own peak radius, which is coded into its chromosome as genes. The peaks radii are evolved in the problem optimization process. The procedure of the problem optimization is the procedure of peaks radii annealing. In this way, peaks radii are no longer the predetermined parameters of fitness sharing algorithms. They might be different in the population, which expands the applicable range of the algorithm.

In the next section, fitness sharing genetic algorithm with self-adaptive annealing peaks radii control method is described in detail. Section 3 investigates the suggested algorithm on several benchmark multimodal problems. Conclusions and discussions are given in section 4.

2 Self-adaptive Annealing Peaks Radii Control Method

In binary simple genetic algorithm, each decimal variable needs to be transferred to binary variables and combined with each other to form a chromosome. In the proposed algorithm, the peak radius of each individual is viewed as a variable, and needs to be coded and combined with other variables. The code length of the peak radius is *lsigma*.

The initialization of individuals is the same as the standard fitness sharing genetic algorithms. The peaks radii genes are put in the last part of the chromosome. If *lsigma* genes of the peak radius are all zero after initialization, special treatment is needed to ensure fitness sharing procedure can perform. In this case, we pick a peak radius gene randomly and set the value of the gene as 1, which ensures that the radius of peak will not be zero. Other steps of the algorithm can be expressed as follows.

Step one. Calculate the shared fitness of every individual. Suppose d_{ij} is the distance between individual i and individual j, then the sharing function $sh(d_{ij})$ can be calculated by using equation 1.

$$sh(d_{ij}) = \begin{cases} 1 - \left(d_{ij}/\sigma_i\right)^\alpha & d_{ij} < \sigma_i \\ 0 & \text{Otherwise} \end{cases} \quad (1)$$

where σ is the peak radius of the individual i, α is the parameter which controls the form of the sharing function, commonly equals to 1. After the sharing function value of each individual is calculated, niche count m of every individual can be calculated by using equation 2.

$$m_i = \sum_{j=1}^{N} sh(d_{ij}) \quad i = 1, 2, \cdots, N \quad (2)$$

where N is population size. It is obvious that if an individual has larger niche count, there are more individuals around it. The shared fitness of every individual can be calculated by using equation 3.

$$f'_i = f_i / m_i \quad i = 1, 2, \cdots, N \quad (3)$$

where f'_i is the shared fitness of the individual i and f_i is its raw fitness. The following selection stage uses the shared fitness.

Step two. Use the proper selection method to select N individuals from current population.

Step three. Perform crossover and mutation to generate new individuals until the new population size reaches N. The mating restriction strategy is adopted [2]. If an individual's peak radius changes to 0 after crossover and mutation, a random gene of the peak radius is selected and the value of that gene changes to 1.

Step four. Decide whether to stop the algorithm or not. If stop criteria are not fulfilled, go back to step one; otherwise, select the group with maximum fitness to be the peak sets, or use cluster analysis method to search niche centers from current population to find the peak sets.

There is no predefined parameter, such peaks radii or peak number, in the above method. The peak radius of each individual may evolve during the procedure of optimization. At the early stage of the algorithm, all kind of peaks radii may exist. Because peaks radii can affect the shared fitness of the individual and then affect the selective probability of the individual, those individuals whose fitness is relatively large and peak radius is relatively small have selection superiorities. The initialization of peaks radii is in a random way, so most of the individuals are with intermediate peaks radii in the beginning. The algorithm is quite similar to standard fitness sharing genetic algorithm. The difference is that the peak radius is a global parameter in standard fitness sharing genetic algorithm, which is predefined by the user. The algorithm can fully explore solution space and find the convergent area of peaks during this period. With the evolution goes on, better individuals will be found by GAs and peaks radii will undergo a simulated-annealing-like procedure. Peaks radii will decrease self-adaptively. At the late stage of the algorithm, with the effect of selective pressure and genetic operator, individuals with large fitness value and small peaks radii get flourishing. The algorithm is quite similar to crowding genetic algorithm [7]. The difference between them is that the offspring replace the parents according to the distance and the fitness in crowding genetic algorithm but the replacement takes place directly in the suggested algorithm. The algorithm can maintain population diversity and exploit the convergent area of peaks to locate them in this period.

3 Tests on the Novel Algorithm

In order to test the searching ability of fitness sharing genetic algorithm with self-adaptive annealing peaks radii control method, 6 benchmark multimodal problems are optimized [9].

3.1 The Description of the Benchmark Problems

Problem I can be expressed as follows:

$$F1(x) = \sin^6(5\pi x) \tag{4}$$

The domain of the problem is [0, 1]. There are 5 evenly distributed peaks. The peaks are at 0.100, 0.300, 0.500, 0.700, and 0.900 respectively. The heights of the peaks are all 1.0.

Problem II can be expressed as follows:

$$F2(x) = e^{-2(\ln 2)\left(\frac{x-0.1}{0.8}\right)^2} \sin^6(5\pi x) \tag{5}$$

The domain of the problem is [0, 1]. There are 5 evenly distributed peaks. The peaks are at 0.100, 0.300, 0.500, 0.700, and 0.900 respectively. The heights of the peaks are 1.000, 0.917, 0.707, 0.459, and 0.250 respectively. The ratio of the lowest peak height to the highest peak height is 0.25.

Problem III can be expressed as follows:

$$F3(x) = \sin^6\left[5\pi\left(x^{0.75} - 0.05\right)\right] \tag{6}$$

The domain of the problem is [0, 1]. There are 5 unevenly distributed peaks. The peaks are at 0.080, 0.247, 0.451, 0.681 and 0.934 respectively. The heights of the peaks are all 1.0.

Problem IV can be expressed as follows:

$$F4(x) = e^{-2(\ln 2)\left(\frac{x-0.08}{0.854}\right)^2} \sin^6\left[5\pi(x^{0.75} - 0.05)\right] \quad (7)$$

The domain of the problem is [0, 1]. There are 5 unevenly distributed peaks. The peaks are at 0.080, 0.247, 0.451, 0.681 and 0.934 respectively. The heights of the peaks are 1.000, 0.917, 0.707, 0.459, and 0.250 respectively. The ratio of the lowest peak height to the highest peak height is 0.25.

Problem V can be expressed as follows:

$$F5(x, y) = 2500 - (x^2 + y - 11)^2 - (x + y^2 - 7)^2 \quad (8)$$

The domain of the problem is [-6,6]*[-6,6]. There are 4 unevenly distributed peaks. The peaks are at (3.000, 2.000), (3.584, -1.848), (-3.779, -3.283), and (-2.805, 3.131). The heights of the peaks are all 2500.0.

Problem VI can be expressed as follows:

$$f(x_0, \cdots, x_{29}) = \sum_{i=0}^{4} u\left(\sum_{j=0}^{5} x_{6i+j}\right) \quad (9)$$

where $\forall x_k \in \{0,1\}, k = 0, \cdots, 29$, and the definition of $u(s)$ is:

$$u(s) = \begin{cases} 1 & s \in \{0,6\} \\ 0 & s \in \{1,5\} \\ 0.360384 & s \in \{2,4\} \\ 0.640576 & s = 3 \end{cases} \quad (10)$$

The problem is called the massively deceptive problem. It contains 10^6 peaks with only 32 global peaks. The reason of its massive deception is that (1) it has huge number of peaks and (2) global peaks are surrounded by local peaks. This benchmark problem is often used to test the performance of multimodal genetic algorithms. The global peaks are at (000000, 000000, 000000, 000000, 000000), (000000, 000000, 000000, 000000, 111111), ..., (111111, 111111, 111111, 111111, 111111). The heights of the global peaks are all 5.0.

3.2 The Parameters of the Algorithms

Table 1 lists the parameters for fitness sharing genetic algorithm with self-adaptive annealing peaks radii control method in the test problems.

Table 1. The parameters of the algorithm in test problems

Problem	I	II	III	IV	V	VI
Scale Type	No	No	No	No	Power Law	Power Law
Distance Metric	Euclidian	Euclidian	Euclidian	Euclidian	Euclidian	Hamming
Population Size	60	60	60	60	100	800
Maximum Generation	50	50	50	50	50	120
Chromosome Length	30+4	30+4	30+4	30+4	15+4	30+4
Convergence Criterion	$h<0.02$	$h<0.02$	$h<0.02$	$h<0.02$	$h<0.832$	At Peaks

where h is the distance between the individual and the real nearest peak. SUS selection [1] and single point crossover are adopted. The crossover probability is 0.9, and mutation probability is 0.05. *lsigma* is 4 in this paper, which is proved to be adequate for most problems. The mating restriction method is employed. The algorithms are implemented in MATLAB environment. The problems are optimized on an IBM compatible PC with Intel Pentium 4 2.4G CPU and 512M memories. The performance criterion for problem I, III, V, and VI is the number of global peaks maintained by the algorithm at the end of the optimization, for problem II and IV is the number of peaks maintained by the algorithm at the end of the optimization. The algorithm optimizes every problem 20 times. Then calculate the average of the performance.

3.3 The Results

The optimization results of fitness sharing genetic algorithm with self-adaptive annealing peaks radii control method are listed in Table 2.

Table 2. The optimization results of the algorithm

Problem	I	II	III	IV	V	VI
peaks found	4.86	4.88	4.78	4.80	4.00	32.00

Figure 1 shows the number of global peaks found by the suggested algorithm during the optimization procedure on the massively deceptive problem.

Problem I to IV represent the problems with or without uniformly distributed peaks. The peaks may be of the same height or not. Fitness sharing genetic algorithm with self-adaptive annealing peaks radii control method can change the peaks radii dynamically, thus find almost all peaks.

Problem V represents the problem with flat peaks, which needs power law scaling method to adjust shared fitness [14]. The algorithm suggested in this paper can find and maintain all peaks steadily.

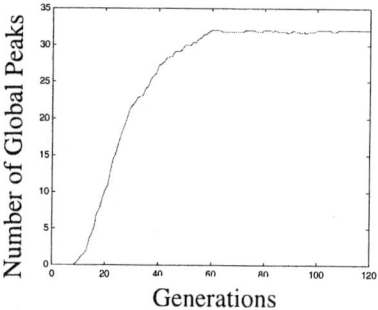

Fig. 1. Optimization result of problem VI

Problem VI is the massively deceptive problem. Simple genetic algorithm can either find local peaks only or converge to one global peak. Fitness sharing genetic algorithm with self-adaptive annealing peaks radii control method can find and maintain all the global peaks steadily with the help of power law scaling.

4 Conclusions and Discussions

A new self-adaptive annealing peaks radii control method is suggested in this paper. Combined with standard fitness sharing genetic algorithm, the method can find and maintain all peaks in the search space without the information of peaks radii or the number of peaks. Peaks radii are coded into chromosomes of the individuals, and undergo a simulated-annealing-like procedure during optimization procedure. The early stage of the algorithm is similar to standard fitness sharing genetic algorithm, and the late stage of the algorithm is similar to crowding genetic algorithm.

The optimization results of several benchmark multimodal problem show that fitness sharing genetic algorithm with self-adaptive annealing peaks radii control method is suitable for a wide range of multimodal problems. The suggested algorithm can be used to search for both all peaks and all global peaks. If all global peaks are needed, additional scaling method might be adopted to eliminate the local peaks.

The proposed algorithm is similar to crowding algorithm in late stage. So the population diversity can be preserved, but the convergence of all individuals to peaks cannot be pledged. If the distribution of individuals according to the peaks height is required, other local search or cluster analysis methods may be adopted to prompt convergence.

Further research may be carried out in the aspects of the relationship between population size, coding length of peaks radii and the optimization results of the algorithm; more extensive tests on the algorithm; and applications of the algorithm in real world problems.

References

1. Baker, J. E.: Reducing Bias and Inefficiency in the Selection Algorithm. In: Grefenstette, J.J. (eds.): Proceedings Of the Second International Conference on Genetic Algorithms and Their Applications. Hillsdale, NJ: Lawrence Erlbaum (1987) 14–21
2. Deb, K. and Goldberg, D.E.: An Investigation of Niche and Species Formation in Genetic Function Optimization. In: Schaffer, J.D. (eds.): Proceedings of the Third International Conference on Genetic Algorithms and their Applications. San Mateo, CA: Morgan Kaufmann (1989) 42–50
3. Eiben, E., Hiterding, R. and Michalewicz, Z.: Parameter Control in Evolutionary Algorithms. IEEE Transactions on Evolutionary Computation. Vol. 3, no.2, (1999) 124–141
4. Goldberg, D.E.: Genetic Algorithms in Search, Optimization, and Machine Learning. New York: Addison-Wesley (1989)
5. Goldberg, D.E. and Richardson J.: Genetic Algorithms with Sharing for Multimodal Function Optimization. In: Grefenstette, J.J. (eds.): Proceedings Of the Second International Conference on Genetic Algorithms and Their Applications. Hillsdale, NJ: Lawrence Erlbaum (1987) 41–49
6. Goldberg, D.E. and Wang, L.: Adaptive Niching via Coevolutionary Sharing. IlliGAL Report No. 97007. (1997)
7. Mahfoud, S.W.: Crossover Interactions among Niches. In: Proceedings of the first IEEE Conference on Evolutionary Computation. Piscataway, NJ: IEEE Press (1994) 188–193
8. Mahfoud, S.W.: Genetic Drift in Sharing Methods," In: Proceedings of the First IEEE Conference on Evolutionary Computation. Piscataway, NJ: IEEE Press (1994) 67–72
9. Mahfoud, S. W.: Niching Methods for Genetic Algorithms. Ph.D. Dissertation, University of Illinois, Urbana-Champaign (1995)
10. Miller, B.L. and Shaw, M. J.: Genetic Algorithms with Dynamic Niche Sharing for Multimodal Function Optimization. In: Proceedings of the third IEEE Conference on Evolutionary Computation. Piscataway, NJ: IEEE Press (1996) 786–791
11. Petrowski, A.: A Clearing Procedure as a Niching Method for Genetic Algorithms. In: Proceedings of the third IEEE Conference on Evolutionary Computation. Piscataway, NJ: IEEE Press (1996) 798–803
12. Sareni, B. and Krahenbuhl, L.: Fitness Sharing and Niching Methods Revisited. IEEE Transactions on Evolutionary Computation. Vol. 2, no. 3, (1998) 97–106
13. Yin, X. and Germay, N.: A Fast Genetic Algorithm with Sharing Scheme Using Cluster Analysis Methods in Multimodal Function Optimization. In: Albrecht, R.F. (eds.): Proceedings of International Conference on Artificial Neural Nets and Genetic Algorithms. New York, Springer-Verlag (1993) 450–457
14. Yu, X. and Wang, Z.: The Fitness Sharing Genetic Algorithms with Adaptive Power Law Scaling. System Engineering Theory and Practice. Vol. 22, no. 2, (2002) 42–28

A Novel Clustering Fitness Sharing Genetic Algorithm

Xinjie Yu

State Key Lab of Power Systems, Dept. of Electrical Engineering,
Tsinghua University, Beijing 100084, China
yuxj@tsinghua.edu.cn

Abstract. The hybrid multimodal optimization algorithm that combines a novel clustering method and fitness sharing method is presented in this paper. The only parameter required by the novel clustering method is the peak number. The clustering criteria include minimizing the square sum of the inner-group distance, maximizing the square sum of the inter-group distance, and the fitness value of the individuals. After each individual has been classified to the certain cluster, fitness sharing genetic algorithm is used to find multiple peaks simultaneously. The empirical study of the benchmark problems shows that the proposed method has satisfactory performance.

1 Introduction

Many real world optimization problems are multimodal in essence. Thus it is very convenient for product designers and decision makers to select one solution from several candidates. Though Simple Genetic Algorithm (SGA) has been proved very useful in optimization, machine learning and many other industrial application areas, it can only converge to a single peak in the search space [1, 2]. Theoretical analyses and numerical experiments show that with finite population size and weak selective pressure, the single convergence, named as genetic drift, may occur [3].

Fitness sharing genetic algorithm is one of the most useful methods for multimodal optimization problems, which reduces the individual's fitness value according to the distance between individuals [4]. Improvements on standard fitness sharing genetic algorithm include clearing procedure suggested by Petrowski [5], dynamic niche sharing suggested by Miller and Shaw [6], and adaptive niching via coevolutionary sharing suggested by Goldberg and Wang [7]. These algorithms need the peaks radii before performing fitness sharing method, which is hard to estimate for some problems.

The organization of this paper goes as follows. Section 2 surveys the clustering methods combined with fitness sharing genetic algorithms and presents the new clustering method. Section 3 studies the suggested approach by optimizing the benchmark multimodal problems. Conclusions appear in the last section.

2 The Novel Clustering Fitness Sharing Genetic Algorithm

2.1 Surveys on Clustering Methods for Fitness Sharing Genetic Algorithm

Both standard fitness sharing genetic algorithm and its improvements need to identify the centers and the peaks radii. Clustering methods have been used to grouping the data for a long time. Combining clustering methods with fitness sharing genetic algorithm may improve the adaptability and the speed of the algorithm.

Yin and Germay presented a fast genetic algorithm with sharing scheme using adaptive MacQueen's KMEAN clustering algorithm [8]. The adaptive KMEAN starts generating k initial centers of the cluster according to the fitness value of the individuals. Then the centers merge and receive new individuals using d_{min} and d_{max}.

In Lin, Liu and Yang's paper, a new cluster technique is proposed for automatic and adaptive identification of the locations and the sizes of the clusters in genetic algorithms with fitness sharing [9]. Although no cluster number and cluster radii are required, the algorithm needs several predefined parameters.

Torn's clustering method has been used by many researchers [10]. The method takes the best individual as the first cluster center. Hanagandi and Nikolaou use Torn's clustering method to do global optimization [11]. After several generations of GAs, Torn's clustering method is carried out and cluster centers are found.

2.2 The New Clustering Method

Every clustering method has its own cluster criteria. The cluster criteria adopted by the new clustering method contain the square sum of the inner-group distance and square sum of the inter-group distance [12].

Given N individuals and k clusters, the square sum of inner-group distance can be defined as follows:

$$J_1 = \sum_{j=1}^{k} \sum_{i=1}^{n_j} \left\| x_i - m_j \right\|^2 \tag{1}$$

where n_j is the number of individuals of the cluster j, x_i is the i'th individual in the cluster j, and m_j is the center of the cluster j. The smaller the inner-group distance criterion is, the better the clustering result is.

The square sum of the inter-group distance criterion can be defined as follows:

$$J_2 = \sum_{j=1}^{k} \left\| m_j - m \right\|^2 \tag{2}$$

where m is the center of the total individuals. The larger the inter-group distance criterion is, the better the clustering result is.

In this paper, only the multimodal optimization problems with equal fitness values of the peaks are concerned. The suggested clustering method combines minimizing the square sum of the inner-group distance, maximizing the square sum of the inter-group distance, and the fitness value information of individuals in an easy heuristic way. The novel clustering method need the number of peaks k beforehand and can be illustrated in Fig. 1.

The first part considers the fitness value information of individuals. The better the individual is, the earlier it will be treated. The second part tries to maximize the square sum of the inter-group distance and the third part tries to minimize the square sum of the inner-group distance. The last part combines the novel clustering method with the fitness sharing method.

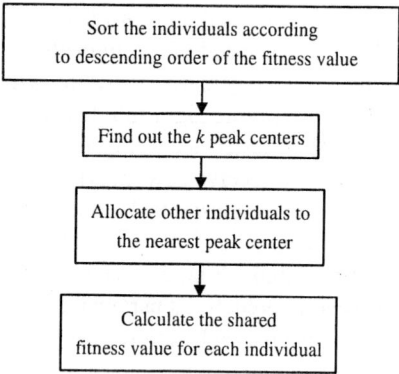

Fig. 1. The novel clustering method

The specific algorithm for finding the k peak centers can be expressed as follows:

1. The first individual is the first *confirmed* peak center, and mark it as *selected*.
2. Select k individuals which are not marked as selected orderly from the population.
3. Calculate the distances from the k individuals to the confirmed peak centers.
4. For each selected individual, appoint its *representative distance* as its nearest distance to the confirmed peak centers.
5. Select the largest representative distance from the k representative distances and point the corresponding individual as the next confirmed peak center, and mark it as selected
6. If the number of the confirmed peak centers is less than k, go to step 2.

The specific algorithm for allocating other individuals can be expressed as follows:

1. For each individual, which is not marked as selected, calculate its distances to the k confirmed peak centers.
2. Select the shortest distance and allocate the individual to the corresponding confirmed peak center, market the individual as *allocated*, and record which confirmed peak center it belongs to.
3. Go to step 1 until all the individuals are allocated.

In the novel clustering method, a niche is a peak. The specific algorithm for calculating the shared fitness value for each individual can be expressed as follows

1. For each niche, find out the number of individuals (m_i) in it. (Note that every individual can only be allocated to one niche.)
2. For each individual in that niche, its niche count is m_i, and its shared fitness value is f / m_i (f is its raw fitness value)
3. Go to step 1 until every individual gets its shared fitness value.

The time complexity of distance calculation of this method can be considered as follows. The number of distance calculation in finding the peak centers is $k+2k+\ldots+(k-1)k$.

The number of distance calculation in allocating individuals is $(N-1)k$. Generally speaking, $N>>k$, so the total time complexity of distance calculation is $O(Nk)$, which is the same as that of the adaptive KMEAN clustering method[8] and much less than $O(N^2)$ of the standard fitness sharing method [13]. Additional analyses show that the suggested method does not need steps to merge clusters and identify the cluster centers, so the total calculation time of the new method may be smaller than that of the adaptive KMEAN clustering method.

The predetermined parameter k is easy to obtain in some circumstance, especially when the problem is to calculate the root of algebraic equation. If there is not any clue about k, users can increase k continuously.

2.3 The Novel Clustering Fitness Sharing Genetic Algorithm

The novel clustering fitness sharing genetic algorithm can be illustrated in Fig. 2.

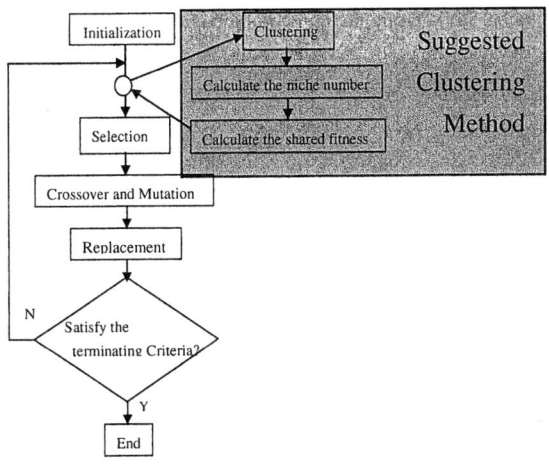

Fig. 2. The novel clustering fitness sharing genetic algorithm

3 Empirical Studies on the Suggested Algorithm

The algorithm is compared with other multimodal genetic algorithms using 3 benchmark problems. The algorithms include the standard fitness sharing (SH), the fitness sharing with adaptive KMEAN clustering method (KMEAN), the new clustering fitness sharing method (NEW).

3.1 Benchmark Problem Specification

Only maximization problems with same peak height are considered as the test problems. The sequence of problem represents the increase of multimodality.

Problem I can be expressed as follows [14]:

$$F1(x) = \sin^6\left[5\pi\left(x^{0.75} - 0.05\right)\right] \quad (3)$$

The domain of the problem is [0,1]. There are 5 unequally spaced peaks with same height. The maxima are located at x values of 0.080, 0.247, 0.451, 0.681, and 0.934. All peaks are of height 1.0.

Problem II can be expressed as follows [15]:

$$F2(x) = 2500 - \left(x(1)^2 + x(2) - 11\right)^2 - \left(x(1) + x(2)^2 - 7\right)^2 \quad (4)$$

The domain of the problem is [-6,6]*[-6,6]. There are 4 unequally spaced peaks with same height. The maxima are located at x values of (3.5844, -1.8481), (3,2), (-2.8051, 3.1313), and (-3.7793, -3.2832). All peaks are of height 2500.0.

Problem III is the massive deceptive problem and can be expressed as follows [16]:

$$f(x_0, \cdots, x_{29}) = \sum_{i=0}^{4} u\left(\sum_{j=0}^{5} x_{6i+j}\right) \quad (5)$$

where $\forall\, x_k \in \{0,1\}, k = 0, \cdots, 29$. $u(s)$ is defined as follows:

$$u(s) = \begin{cases} 1 & s \in \{0,6\} \\ 0 & s \in \{1,5\} \\ 0.360384 & s \in \{2,4\} \\ 0.640576 & s = 3 \end{cases} \quad (6)$$

The search space of the problem is of size 10^9, the number of peaks is of size 10^6, but the number of global peaks is only 32. Operations like crossover and mutation are likely to generate local peaks. The maxima of problem III are located at x values of (000000, 000000, 000000, 000000, 000000), ...,(111111, 111111, 111111, 111111, 111111). All peaks are of height 5.

These benchmark problems are the most common ones while testing the multimodal genetic algorithms. As can be seen from Section 2, the proposed clustering based fitness sharing genetic algorithm has no difficulty while scaling with increasing dimensions.

3.2 Parameters and Performance Criteria

To compare the three algorithms fairly, the parameters of each algorithm are set to be equal, as shown in Table 1. Mating restriction strategy is adopted in SH [13]. Twenty runs are carried out with different initial population generated at random and the average of these runs is taken for comparison.

Table 1. The parameters for the algorithms to solve 3 benchmark problems

Problem	I	II	III
Selection Type	SUS [17]	SUS [17]	SUS [17]
Crossover Type	Single Point	Single Point	Single Point
Crossover Probability	0.9	0.9	0.9
Mutation Probability	0.05	0.05	0.05
Scaling Type	No	Power Law Scaling[18]	Power Law Scaling[18]
Distance Type	Euclidean Distance	Euclidean Distance	Hamming Distance
Population Size	60	100	400
Maximum Generation	50	50	100
Chromosome Length	30	15	30
Sigma (SH)	0.1 [13]	4.2426 [13]	6 [16]
d_{min}, d_{max} (KMEAN)	0.05, 0.1 [8]	1.5, 3	2, 6
Initial Cluster Number (KMEAN)	5	4	32
Peak Number (NEW)	5	4	32
Run Time	20	20	20
Convergence Criterion	$h<0.02$	$h<0.832$	At Peaks

where h is the distance between the individual and the peak nearest to it.

Four performance criteria are used to evaluate the algorithms. The number of global peaks maintained by algorithms is criterion I. It is very clear that the larger the criterion I is, the better the algorithm is. The chi-square-like number is the criterion II [13]. Smaller chi-square-like number means more uniform distribution of the population. The number of individuals resided in the global peaks is the criterion III. The large number of criterion I and the large number of criterion III represent good solution. But the large number of the criterion III and the small number of criterion I represent premature convergence. The run time is the criterion IV, measured by second. The calculation is carried out with MATLAB on the computer with 466MHz Celeron CPU and 128MB memories. The less the run time is, the better the algorithm is.

3.3 Results

Table 2 lists the average results of 20 runs using 3 algorithms on 3 benchmark problems respectively.

Problem I represents the multimodal problem with different peaks radii, and it is quite easy to solve. So all three algorithms' results are nearly the same except the run time. SH's run time is almost two times of that of NEW, and KMEAN's run time is in intermediate level.

Problem II represents the multimodal problem with flat fitness landscape. KMEAN seems to be inconvenient for this kind of problem, and NEW is efficient and excellent. Although SH can find all the peaks, its run time is three times of that of NEW.

Table 2. The computation result of the algorithms

	Problem I			Problem II			Problem III		
Criteria	SH	KMEAN	NEW	SH	KMEAN	NEW	SH	KMEAN	NEW
I	4.8	4.6	4.8	4.0	3.6	3.9	31.9	2.0	30.9
II	3.7	3.9	3.0	5.8	8.3	3.0	12.1	79	7.0
III	45	44	52	53	33	82	260	400	345
IV	71.1	55.5	37.5	188.3	115.8	61.2	6046.2	3597.0	3941.7

Problem III represents the multimodal problem with massive deception, and is very hard to solve. SH achieves the best solution result but the run time cost is rather expensive. KMEAN can only find two global peaks because its search ability is weaker than the other two. NEW can maintain 30.9 global peaks with lower chi-squire-like criterion and less run time.

It is very clear that the overall champion is NEW. SH is good for its solution quality, but suffers from long run time. KMEAN is quicker than SH, but its search ability is weak.

4 Conclusions

In this paper, a novel clustering method based on the criteria of minimizing the inner-group distance and maximizing the inter-group distance has been presented. The clustering method also considers the fitness information of individuals and is very easy to combine with the standard fitness sharing genetic algorithm. Properties of the suggested clustering method are discussed as follows:

- The time complexity of distance calculation of the new clustering method is $O(Nk)$, which is the same as that of the adaptive KMEAN clustering method and much less than $O(N^2)$ of the standard fitness sharing method. The total calculation time of the new method is smaller than that of the adaptive KMEAN clustering method because it does not need to identify the cluster center and merge the clusters.
- The predetermined parameter of the new clustering method is the number of peaks, which is very convenient in some circumstances, especially in finding roots of algebraic equation.
- The solution quality of the novel clustering fitness sharing genetic algorithm is satisfactory for various kinds of multimodal benchmark problems.

References

1. Holland J.H.: Adaptation in Natural and Artificial Systems. Ann Arbor, MI: University of Michigan Press (1975)
2. Goldberg, D.E.: Genetic Algorithms in Search, Optimization, and Machine Learning. New York: Addison-Wesley (1989)
3. Mahfoud, S.W.: Genetic Drift in Sharing Methods," In: Proceedings of the First IEEE Conference on Evolutionary Computation. Piscataway, NJ: IEEE Press (1994) 67–72
4. Goldberg, D.E. and Richardson J.: Genetic Algorithms with Sharing for Multimodal Function Optimization. In: Grefenstette, J.J. (eds.): Proceedings Of the Second International Conference on Genetic Algorithms and Their Applications. Hillsdale, NJ: Lawrence Erlbaum (1987) 41–49
5. Petrowski, A.: A Clearing Procedure as a Niching Method for Genetic Algorithms. In: Proceedings of the third IEEE Conference on Evolutionary Computation. Piscataway, NJ: IEEE Press (1996) 798–803
6. Miller, B.L. and Shaw, M. J.: Genetic Algorithms with Dynamic Niche Sharing for Multimodal Function Optimization. In: Proceedings of the third IEEE Conference on Evolutionary Computation. Piscataway, NJ: IEEE Press (1996) 786–791
7. Goldberg, D.E. and Wang, L.: Adaptive Niching via Coevolutionary Sharing. IlliGAL Report No. 97007. (1997)
8. Yin, X. and Germay, N.: A Fast Genetic Algorithm with Sharing Scheme Using Cluster Analysis Methods in Multimodal Function Optimization. In: Albrecht, R.F. (eds.): Proceedings of International Conference on Artificial Neural Nets and Genetic Algorithms. New York, Springer-Verlag (1993) 450–457
9. Lin C.Y, Liu J.Y, and Yang Y.J.: Hybrid Multimodal Optimization with Clustering Genetic Strategies. Engineering Optimization (1998) 30: 263–280
10. Torn A.: A Search-clustering Approach to Global Optimization. In: Dixon, S. (eds.): Towards Global Optimization, Vol. 2. North-Holland (1978) 49–70
11. Hanagandi V. and Nikolaou M.: A Hybrid Approach to Global Optimization Using A Clustering Algorithm in A Genetic Search Framework. Computers Chem. Engng. (1998) 22(12): 1913–1925
12. Everitt B.S. Cluster Analysis. 3rd ed. New York. John Wiley & Sons (1993)
13. Deb, K. and Goldberg, D.E.: An Investigation of Niche and Species Formation in Genetic Function Optimization. In: Schaffer, J.D. (eds.): Proceedings of the Third International Conference on Genetic Algorithms and their Applications. San Mateo, CA: Morgan Kaufmann (1989) 42–50
14. Sareni, B. and Krahenbuhl, L.: Fitness Sharing and Niching Methods Revisited. IEEE Transactions on Evolutionary Computation. Vol. 2, no. 3, (1998) 97–106
15. Harik G.: Finding multimodal solutions using restricted tournament selection. In: Eshelman, L. (eds.): Proceedings of the 6th. International Conference on Genetic Algorithms. San Mateo, CA: Morgan Kaufmann (1995) 24–31
16. Goldberg D.E., Deb K., and Horn J.: Massive Multimodality, Deception, and Genetic Algorithms. In: Manner R. and Manderick B. (eds.): Proceedings of the Second Conference on Parallel Problem Solving from Nature. Amsterdam: North-Holland (1992) 15–25
17. Baker, J. E.: Reducing Bias and Inefficiency in the Selection Algorithm. In: Grefenstette, J.J. (eds.): Proceedings Of the Second International Conference on Genetic Algorithms and Their Applications. Hillsdale, NJ: Lawrence Erlbaum (1987) 14–21
18. Yu, X. and Wang, Z.: The Fitness Sharing Genetic Algorithms with Adaptive Power Law Scaling. System Engineering Theory and Practice. 2002. Vol. 22, no. 2, 42–28

Cooperative Co-evolutionary Differential Evolution for Function Optimization

Yan-jun Shi[1,3], Hong-fei Teng[2], and Zi-qiang Li[1,4]

[1] Department of Computer Science and Engineering, Dalian University of Technology
Dalian, P.R. China 116024
vsyj@yahoo.com
[2] School of Mechanical Engineering, Dalian University of Technology,
Dalian, P.R. China 116024
tenghf@dlut.edu.cn
[3] Key Laboratory for Precision and Non-traditional Machining Technology
of Ministry of Education, Dalian University of Technology,
Dalian, P.R. China 116024
vsyj@yahoo.com
[4] School of Information and Engineering, Xiangtan University
Xiangtan, P.R. China 411105
xtulzq@hotmail.com

Abstract. The differential evolution (DE) is a stochastic, population-based, and relatively unknown evolutionary algorithm for global optimization that has recently been successfully applied to many optimization problems. This paper presents a new variation on the DE algorithm, called the cooperative co-evolutionary differential evolution (CCDE). CCDE adopts the cooperative co-evolutionary architecture, which was proposed by Potter and had been successfully applied to genetic algorithm, to improve significantly the performance of the DE. Such improvement is achieved by partitioning a high-dimensional search space by splitting the solution vectors of DE into smaller vectors, then using multiple cooperating subpopulations (or smaller vectors) to co-evolve subcomponents of a solution. Applying the new DE algorithm to on 11 benchmark functions, we show that CCDE has a marked improvement in performance over the traditional DE and cooperative co-evolutionary genetic algorithm (CCGA).

1 Introduction

Evolutionary algorithms (EAs) are a class of nonlinear stochastic optimization approaches based on natural selection and Darwin's main principle: the fittest individuals reproduce and survive. EAs have many particular advantages over the traditional optimizer, e.g., global optimization, parallelism, robustness, and etc., which make EAs successfully applied in many difficult engineering problems. As a relatively new evolutionary algorithm, the differential evolution (DE), firstly proposed by Storn and Price [1], has shown great promise in many numerical real-world applications [2], [4]. Therefore, DE is one of the most attractive evolutionary optimizers for practical engineering problems. However, for problems with high-dimensional search space, like other EAs, DE also suffers from the "curse of dimensionality" [3], which implies that the complexity of problem-solving grows exponentially with the dimension of problem.

To solve such problems, in genetic algorithm (GA) community, Potter [7] proposed a cooperative co-evolutionary genetic algorithm (CCGA), which partitioned the search space by splitting the solution vectors into smaller vectors. Potter found that CCGA has a significant improvement in performance over the traditional GA when optimizing functions with 30 variables. For the problem decomposition, Potter took each function variable as a subcomponent, and did not investigate the other problem-decomposition methods. Subsequently, Sofge [8] extend Potter's models to evolution strategy (ES), called CCES, using a blended population. His work showed that CCES also offer advantages over the traditional ES on several functions with 2-dimensionality. Recently, Bergh [9] applied Potter's models to the PSO, called CPSO, and also reported a marked improvement in performance over the traditional PSO on 4 functions with 30 variables. Therefore, as a general cooperative co-evolutionary framework, Potter's models have been successfully applied to solve complex problems in different algorithms, e.g., GA, ES, and PSO. And casting the cooperative co-evolutionary architecture of Potter into DE may provide a more competitive solution. Besides, little work on DE using cooperative co-evolutionary architecture was reported until now.

Attempting to offer better performance in optimizing high-dimensional problems, this paper applies Potter's models to the DE algorithms, resulting in a new cooperative DE computational model, i.e., CCDE. CCDE also investigates the different decomposition methods of problems, which were not studied in Potter's work [7]. And the performance of the proposed CCDE is compared with that of the traditional DE and that of cooperative co-evolutionary genetic algorithm (CCGA). All algorithms were benchmarked on 11 commonly used optimization problems.

2 A Brief Overview of DE

The DE algorithm was introduced by Storn and Price in 1995 [1]. Since then, several schemes of the DE were proposed [4]. The particular version used in this paper is the *DE/rand/1/exp* version, which appears to be the most frequently used scheme [1], and is considered to be the basic version of DE. Therefore, the traditional DE mentioned in this paper would be considered as *DE/rand/1/exp*, which is briefly described as follows. For minimization problems, i.e., $\min f(\vec{x})$, DE starts to work with a population of N candidate solutions, i.e., $\vec{x}_{i,G}, i = 1, 2, ..., N$, where i indexes the population and G is the current generation. Like genetic algorithms, DE also has the mutation, crossover and selection operations.

For the mutation operation, a perturbed vector $\vec{v}_{i,G}$ is generated according to

$$\vec{v}_{i,G} = \vec{x}_{r1,G} + F(\vec{x}_{r2,G} - \vec{x}_{r3,G}) \tag{1}$$

with random indexes $r1, r2, r3 \in \{1, 2, ..., N\}$ and a scaling factor $F \in [0, 2]$.

For the crossover operation, the perturbed vector $\vec{v}_{i,G} = [v_{1i}, v_{2i}, ..., v_{Di}]$ and the target vector $\vec{x}_{i,G} = [x_{1i}, x_{2i}, ..., x_{Di}]$ both are used to generate a trial vector $\vec{x}'_{i,G} = [x'_{1i}, x'_{2i}, ..., x'_{Di}]$:

$$x'_{ji} = \begin{cases} v_{ji}, & \text{if } randb(j) \leq CR \text{ or } j = randr(i) \\ x_{ji}, & \text{if } randb(j) > CR \text{ and } j \neq randr(i) \end{cases}, \quad (2)$$

where $j \in [1, D]$, $randb(j) \in [0,1]$ is the jth evaluation of a uniform random number generator. $CR \in [0,1]$ is the crossover constant. $randr(i) \in \{1, 2, ...D\}$ is a randomly chosen index which ensures that $\vec{x}'_{i,G}$ gets at least one parameter from $\vec{v}_{i,G}$.

For selection operation, a greedy scheme is performed:

$$\vec{x}_{i,G+1} = \begin{cases} \vec{x}'_{i,G}, & \text{if } \Phi(\vec{x}'_{i,G}) < \Phi(\vec{x}_{i,G}) \\ \vec{x}_{i,G}, & \text{otherwise} \end{cases}, \quad (3)$$

where $\Phi(\vec{x})$ represents a fitness function.

Compared to other EAs, e.g., GA, ES, EP (evolutionary programming) [5], the DE needs less parameters, which only include N, F, and CR. Moreover, the main idea of DE is to create new offspring solutions from a weighed difference of parent solutions, and use a greedy selection scheme where the offspring only replaces the parent if it has a better fitness score.

3 Cooperative Co-evolutionary DE

As Potter's suggested [7], when applying cooperative co-evolutionary framework to solve a particular problem, a standard approach is to decompose the problem into subcomponents and assign each subcomponent to a subpopulation. These subpopulations are evolved by a particular EA and co-evolved simultaneously. To follow these suggestions, we propose the cooperative differential evolution, i.e., CCDE, which is described below in Fig. 1.

gen =0
for each subcomponent *S* **do**
   Population$_S$(gen) = randomly initialized population
   evaluation fitness of each individual in *Population$_S$(gen)*
endfor
while not terminated **do**
   gen = gen + 1
   for each subcomponent *S* **do**
     select *Representative$_S$(gen)* from *Population$_S$(gen-1)* based on fitness
   endfor
   for each subcomponent *S* **do**
     apply the mutation, crossover and selection operation of DE to *Population$_S$(gen)*
     evaluate fitness of individual in *Population$_S$(gen)* using *Representative$_S$(gen)*
   endfor
endwhile

Fig. 1. The cooperative evolutionary DE

As shown in Fig. 1, three key questions should be addressed to use CCDE successfully: (1) how to find a suitable problem-decomposition, (2) how to form a complete solution by assembling subcomponents evolved by subpopulations, and (3) how to evaluate fitness of the individuals who participate in the solution.

For the problem-decomposition, Potter used a static problem decomposition, which took each function variable as a separate subpopulation of individuals. This method of problem-decomposition is also applied in DE, called CCDE-O. Moreover, we present a new method of static decomposition to DE, called CCDE-H, which takes half of all the function variables as a subcomponent. For collaboration methods and fitness assignment in CCDE, early work [7] in the CCGA suggested two methods for selecting collaborators to evaluate fitness of individuals: (1) Select the best individuals from alternative subpopulations, as defined by fitness obtained from last evaluation, and (2) Select two individual (the best and a random one) and then evaluate both with the current individual and use the higher fitness value for the fitness score of current individual. For the functions with strongly interacting variables, the method (1) is not an accurate fitness assignment. Rather, the method (1) can simplify the computational environment and make us focus on the other aspects of cooperative co-evolution. Therefore, the method (1) is used in this paper. However, the method (2) will be addressed in later work for its importance to optimize functions with interaction between variables.

In conclusion, for a D-dimensional problem, CCDE decomposes the search space into two subpopulations (CCDE-H), or D subpopulations (CCDE-O), and then uses the best individuals from each subpopulation collaborating together for fitness evaluation. For each subpopulation being evolved, all the other subpopulation holds fixed. Subsequently, the subpopulations are each evolved in a round-robin fashion and perform mutation, crossover and selection operation of DE (see equation (1, 2, 3)) to obtain a final solution.

4 Experiments Studies

4.1 Numerical Benchmark Problems

To evaluate the proposed algorithms, we used a test suit of benchmark functions previously introduced by Yao [5], which are largely based on their popularity in the evolutionary computation (EC) community and provided for easier comparison. The dimensionality of problems originally varied from 2 to 30, we extended some functions with 100-dimensional variables to allow for comparison on more difficult problems. These functions and their parameters are listed in Table 1. Note that the functions with strongly interacting variables such as Rosenbrock function [5] were not listed here, and will be addressed on later work using different methods.

4.2 Experimental Setup

To compare the different optimizers, a fair time measure must be used. CCDE has lower overheads because it uses smaller vector. Hence, using cost time as a measure would be unfair to original DE. If the number of generations is used as a measure, it is

Table 1. The benchmark functions and their parameters used in our experimental studies, where n is the dimension of the function, , and f_{min} is the minimum value of the function

Benchmark functions	n	S	f_{min}
$f_1(\vec{x}) = \sum_{i=1}^{n} i^2 x_i^2$	30/100	$[-100,100]^n$	0
$f_2(\vec{x}) = \sum_{i=1}^{n} -x_i \sin(\sqrt{|x_i|})$	30/100	$[-500,500]^n$	-12569.5 / -41898.3
$f_3(\vec{x}) = \sum_{i=1}^{n} (x_i^2 - 10\cos(2\pi x_i) + 10)$	30/100	$[-5.12, 5.12]^n$	0
$f_4(\vec{x}) = 1 + \sum_{i=1}^{n} \frac{x_i^2}{4000} - \prod_{i=1}^{n} \cos(\frac{x_i}{\sqrt{i}})$	30/100	$[-100,100]^n$	0
$f_5(\vec{x}) = 20 - 20e^{-0.2\sqrt{\frac{1}{n}\sum_{i=1}^{n} x_i^2}} + e - e^{\frac{1}{n}\sum_{i=1}^{n} \cos(2\pi x_i)}$	30/100	$[-32,32]^n$	0
$f_6(\vec{x}) = -\sin(2x_0 - 0.5\pi) - 3\cos(x_1) - 0.5x_0$	2	$[-3.0, 3.0]^n$	-4.81681
$f_7(\vec{x}) = -\sin(x_0)\sin^{20}(\frac{x_0^2}{\pi}) - \cos(x_1)\cos^{20}(\frac{2x_1^2}{\pi})$	2	$[0, \pi]^n$	-1.8013
$f_8(\vec{x}) = x_0^2 - 0.3\cos(3\pi x_0) + 2x_1^2 - 0.4\cos(4\pi x_1) + 0.7$	2	$[-50,50]^n$	0
$f_9(\vec{x}) = \sum_{i=1}^{5} i\cos((i+1)x_0 + i) \sum_{i=1}^{5} i\cos((i+1)x_1 + i)$	2	$[-10,10]^n$	-186.731
$f_{10}(\vec{x}) = e^{\|-2\ln(2)(\frac{x_0-0.1}{0.8})^2\|} \|\sin(5\pi x_0)^6\| + 0.1\cos(500\pi x_0)^2 + e^{\|-2\ln(2)(\frac{x_1-0.1}{0.8})^2\|} \|\sin(5\pi x_1)^6\| + 0.1\cos(500\pi x_1)^2$	2	$[0,1]^n$	-2.2
$f_{11}(\vec{x}) = -\dfrac{1}{\frac{1}{500} + \sum_{i=1}^{25} \dfrac{1}{i + \sum_{i=1}^{n}(x_i - a_{ij})^6}} + 500$	2	$[-65.6, 65.6]^n$	-499.002

still unfair because DE and CCDE do the different amounts of work when optimizing the same problems. Considering that the number of function evaluations has a strong relationship with cost time and a weak relationship with overheads of optimizers itself, we used the number of function evaluations as a fair time measure in this paper.

All experiments were run for 10^6 function evaluations, or until the function value met a stopping threshold (see Table 1). Here, all results below 10^{-12} were reported as '0'. Moreover, each of experiments was run 50 times with different random seeds; the results reported are the averages calculated from all 50 runs.

As mentioned above, the DE has three parameters: (1) the size of the population (N), (2) the crossover constant (CR), and (3) the scaling factor (F). According to Ref. [1] the size of the population increases as the dimension of function increases. Hence, CCDE uses smaller N than that of the DE because of its smaller vector, and the same setting in the other parameters. As a result, in our experiments they were set to the following values: $N = 100$ (DE), $N = 50$ (CCDE), $CR = 0.8$, $F = 0.5$. These parameters follow the suggestion in other literature where they have been found empirically to provide good performance [1], [4].

The CCGA here used the same problem-decomposition as Potter [7]. That is, CCGA took each variable as a subpopulation. Each GA used real-coded representation, tournament selection, arithmetic crossover and Gaussian mutation [6]. Besides, the population N, crossover probability Pc and mutation probability Pm of CCGA was respectively set to 50, 0.9 and 0.03.

4.3 Results

The experiments were aimed to compare the convergence speed of DE, CCDE and CCGA. For simplification, CCGA was only tested on 100-dimensional functions. The term "convergence speed" is used here to mean that the optimizers succeeded in meeting a specified threshold using fewer than maximum assigned number of function evaluations (i.e., 10^6). Table 2 provides the following information: The "SR%" column lists the success rate, where success means that a run meets the threshold in less than 10^6 function evaluations. And the "Mean" column presents the averaged function evaluations, which were only calculated for the success run. When no success run is performed, "N/A" (not available) is used in "Mean" and "SD" (standard deviation) columns.

4.3.1 Functions of Dimensionality 30 or Less

Table 2 shows the results for the benchmark problems f_1-f_{11} with dimensionality 30 or less. For all the functions, the success rate ("SR%") of DE and CCDE-H was 100% in all the 50 runs. But the success rate of CCDE-O was 100% only on f_6-f_{11}. Note that the dimensionality of f_6-f_{11} is 2. For this case, CCDE-H and CCDE-O had the same calculated results because they use the same algorithms.

On functions f_1-f_5 with 30-dimensional variables, in successful runs, the split DE (CCDE-H and CCDE-O) significantly outperformed the traditional DE both in the averaged number of function evaluations need to meet the threshold and in the standard deviations. And these function evaluations used in both split DE was about 50% of the traditional DE. Although CCDE-H used more functions evaluations than that of

Table 2. Comparison between DE and CCDE on benchmark functions of dimensionality 30 or less, where "No." lists the benchmark functions used, "SR%" indicates the success rate found in all 50 runs, "Mean" is the averaged number of function evaluations needed to meet the threshold, and "SD" stands for the stardard deviation.

No.	SR%	DE Mean	SD	SR%	CCDE-H Mean	SD	SR%	CCDE-O Mean	SD
f_1	100	142425	1294	100	76656	722	88	66834	1015
f_2	100	226401	33551	100	91976	11789	18	79026	2596
f_3	100	221756	2838	100	117473	1796	12	82014	779
f_4	100	137277	3965	100	79325	6587	6	76637	3934
f_5	100	234675	1205	100	125666	1032	74	115193	1164
f_6	100	2246	243	100	979	146	100	979	146
f_7	100	2665	355	100	1193	216	100	1193	216
f_8	100	7373	290	100	3557	233	100	3557	233
f_9	100	23008	2954	100	3685	475	100	3685	475
f_{10}	100	6726	942	100	2056	327	100	2056	327
f_{11}	100	3352	1211	100	787	298	100	787	298

CCDE-O, CCDE-H was much better than CCDE-O in "SR%". Especially on f_4 that has a product term leading to interdependency between the variables, CCDE-O that each variable took one subpopulation only ran 6 times successfully in 50 runs.

For functions f_6-f_{11} with low dimensionality 2, each of runs was successful. In "Mean" and "SD" columns, CCDE and DE had the similar results to f_1-f_5. The largest improvement in performance occurred with f_9, which is composed of the two independent production terms. The split CCDE only took 3685 functions evaluations (16% of the traditional DE) to meet the threshold.

To draw a conclusion according to Table 2, CCDE has a marked improvement in performance over the traditional DE. Moreover, CCDE-H performed better than CCDE-O because of its much higher success rate.

4.3.2 Functions of Dimensionality 100

Table 3 shows the results for the benchmark problems f_1-f_5 with dimensionality 100. And Table 4 shows the corresponding success rate ("SR%") of above results. DE and CCDE-H was also 100% in all the 50 runs. But the success rate of CCDE-O in Table 3 was worse than that in Table 2. For f_2 and f_3 with 100 dimensional variables, no one successful run was done for CCDE-O. Besides, the success rate of CCGA was 100% on $f1$ and $f4$, but less than 50% on $f2$ and $f5$.

For the 100-dimensionality version of f_1-f_5, in successful runs, the CCDE-H also performed much better than the DE in Table 3. Interestingly, CCDE-H took much more functions evaluations than CCDE-O in Table 2. But in Table 3, the needed functions evaluations of CCDE-H is less than or equal to that of CCDE-O. Besides, CCDE-H outperformed CCGA except for $f4$, where CCDE-H and CCGA took almost the same function evaluations (2.5e^5).

Therefore, the CCDE-H still performed better than the DE and CCGA on 100-dimensional functions.

Table 3. Comparison between DE, CCDE and CCGA on benchmark functions of dimensionality 100, where "No." lists the benchmark functions used, "Mean" is the averaged number of function evaluations needed to meet the threshold, and "SD" stands for the standard deviation.

No.	DE Mean	DE SD	CCDE-H Mean	CCDE-H SD	CCDE-O Mean	CCDE-O SD	CCGA Mean	CCGA SD
f_1	512170	2363	290889	1775	273265	3181	480707	2699
f_2	1093720	330442	681837	357578	N/A	N/A	N/A	N/A
f_3	761475	4968	421945	3739	N/A	N/A	332038	127002
f_4	445859	2597	254769	4682	277611	7245	252889	981
f_5	792265	2544	447517	2147	448041	3769	718747	116114

Table 4. The corresponding success rate ("SR%") of the results in Table 3

No.	DE	CCDE-H	CCDE-O	CCGA
f_1	100	100	84	100
f_2	100	100	0	0
f_3	100	100	0	80
f_4	100	100	36	100
f_5	100	100	86	40

4.4 Discussion of Results

It is very clear from Table 2, Table 3 and Table 4 that the CCDE had improved the performance significantly of the DE for all the test functions with various dimensionalities. Moreover, for two variations of CCDE and CCGA, CCDE-H performed better than CCDE-O and CCGA.

Keep in mind that CCDE evolves each subpopulation (half of all function variables in CCDE-H, or each function variable in CCDE-O) in a round-robin fashion using the current best values from the other subpopulations. It is rather reasonable to hypothesize that CCDE-O would perform better than CCDE-H for its much more amount of subcomponents. Note that in Potter's experimental studies [7] this issue was not addressed. However, in our experimental studies the contrary results to the hypothesis were shown. For example, on f_3, each function variable as a subcomponent only achieved 12% successful runs, and with its dimensionality increase by 100 it even did not achieve one successful run.

Therefore, the proper decomposition of problems should be addressed. Too much subcomponent should not be used even if the dimensionality of problems is high. We believe that too much subcomponent needed lots of cooperation among these subcomponents so that performance of algorithm decreased. Furthermore, we can not hypothesize that a half of all the variables (CCDE-H) for a problem as a subcomponent is a best choice for decomposition of problem. Much work should been done for this issues on future research.

Besides, as computational basis of cooperative co-evolutionary algorithm, DE was reported to generally outperform the real-valued GA on many widely used benchmark problems in Ref. [1]. We believe that this report can give a clue why CCDE-H outperformed CCGA on 5 functions with 100-dimensionality.

Overall, the cooperative DE algorithms offer improved performance over the traditional DE and CCGA in our experiments, especially in terms of convergence speed.

5 Conclusion

This paper presented a method of casting differential evolution into a cooperative framework. This led up to a significant improvement in performance. On cooperative co-evolutionary framework originally proposed by Potter [7], we also extend his experiments using different decomposition methods of problems, i.e., CCDE-H. Our experimental studies demonstrated that the proposed problems decomposition adopted in CCDE-H has a better performance than that of CCDE-O and that of CCGA.

Several important properties of the split DE technique still remain to be investigated. It is not yet clear that our decomposition of problems is optimal for the split DE. Although the cooperative differential evolution outperformed the traditional DE on the 11 functions used in this paper, we can not declare that these new approaches to DE would be better for all the other problems, especially for those functions with many interacting variables. Furthermore, the theoretical analysis of CCDE will be provided in the next work to make cooperative co-evolutionary algorithms offer better performance.

Acknowledgements

This work is supported by the National Natural Science Foundation of P. R. China (Grant Nos. 60073036, 50275019 and 50335040) and Doctoral Specialty Foundation of Ministry of Education, P. R. China (Grant No. 20010141005).

References

1. Storn, R. and K. Price: DE - A simple and efficient heuristic for global optimization over continuous space. Journal of Global Optimization **4** (1997) 341-359.
2. Cruz, I.L.L., L.G.V. Willigenburg, and G.V. Straten: Efficient Differential Evolution algorithms for multimodal optimal control problems. Applied Soft Computing **3** (2003) 97-122.
3. Bellman R E. Adaptive Control Processes: A Guided Tour. Princeton University Press, Princeton, NJ (1961).
4. Storn, R.: System Design by Constraint Adaptation and Differential Evolution. IEEE Transactions On Evolutionary Computation **1** (1999) 22-34.
5. Yao, X. and Y. Liu: Evolutionary programming made faster. IEEE Transactions On Evolutionary Computation **2** (1999) 82-102.
6. Kenneth De Jong, Lawrence Fogel, Hans-Paul Schwefel: Handbook of Evolutionary Computation, vol., ed.: Oxford University Press (1997).
7. Potter, M.A. and K.A.D. Jong: A cooperative coevolutionary approach to function optimization. In: The Third Parallel Problem Solving From Nature (1994), 249-257.
8. Sofge, D., K.D. Jong, and A. Schultz: A blended population approach to cooperative coevoultion for decomposition of complex problems. In: Congress on Evolutionary Computation 2002 (CEC2002). IEEE Service Center (2002) 413-418.
9. Bergh, F.v.d. and A.P. Engelbrecht: A Cooperative Approach to Particle Swarm Optimization. IEEE Transactions On Evolutionary Computation **3** (2004) 225-239.

Optimal Design for Urban Mass Transit Network Based on Evolutionary Algorithms

Jianming Hu[1,2], Xi Shi[2], Jingyan Song[1,2], and Yangsheng Xu[2]

[1] Department of Automation, Tsinghua University,
Beijing 100084, China
{hujm, jysong}@mail.tsinghua.edu.cn
[2] Department of Automation and Computer-aided Engineering,
The Chinese University of Hong Kong, Shatin, Hong Kong
{xshi, ysxu}@acae.cuhk.edu.hk

Abstract. Optimal design for urban mass transit network is the precondition and basis to establish an effective public transportation system. Transit network optimization and headway optimization are two of the most important issues to be dealt with. In this paper, a transit network optimization model is firstly proposed to maximize the nonstop passenger flow. Moreover, this paper puts forwards the optimization model of headways for all the transit routes in the optimized network. Since all the two models can be boiled down to the NP-hard problem, two kinds of evolutionary algorithms, i.e., ant colony algorithm and improved genetic algorithm are introduced to solve the problems respectively. Finally, a case study in a typical city is introduced to explain the validity of the proposed methods.

1 Introduction

As we know, mass transit system plays a vital role in satisfying the trip demand of urban residents. In China mainland, advanced public transportation systems (APTS) have been implementing in many metropolitan cities.

In order to bring into play the advantages of APTS adequately, an effective and rational mass transit network must be planned in advance. Mass transit network planning is composed of four aspects, i.e., transit network design, working out timetable, determining the headway of each route and dispatching driver and steward. The mass transit network design is the basis and precondition because not only the designed transit network will determine the headway and the configuration of driver and steward, but also it should not be changed frequently once it is designed. Especially, if APTS is not implemented on a well-designed transit network, it will not perform well. Besides, headway optimization is another important work to do because headway is one of the most important parameters in the urban transit operation. Not only the public transportation company but also the passengers can benefit from the reasonable headways.

The review of the literature reveals that many researchers are always concerned about the studies on the optimization method. For the public transit network optimization problem, the conventional mathematical programming was proposed to solve the transit network optimization model by Steenbrink in 1974. Kochur and Hendrickson proposed that the analytic models can be used to simplify the transit network to deduce the optimal relationship among the parameters of transit system. The three stages method is introduced by Ceder and Wilson to design the transit network. Dubois et al. introduced the heuristic search method to built up the transit network generation model. Prof. Wang et al presented three transit network planning methods in their monograph. Prof. Gao et al proposed the a bi-level programming model for continuous equilibrium network design. Lin Boliang et al set up the non-linear 0-1 planning model for design the transit network. Han Yin presented PSO algorithm to adjust and optimize the transit network in 1999. Furth and Wilson established the model for assigning the frequencies in the given set of transit lines by optimizing the sum of the waiting time and travel time. Much more research fruits were achieved in the research field of headway optimization. The evolutionary algorithms such as neural network and genetic algorithm were used to solving the optimization problem. The genetic algorithm was applied to solve the scheduling problems by Chakroborty et al. Partha Chkroborty formulated the scheduling as an optimization problem of minimizing the overall transfer time and initial waiting time. Xu Jun Eberlein formulated the deadheading problem in transit operations control. Avishai Ceder addressed the problem of how to allocate vehicles efficiently for carrying out all of the trips in a given transit timetable. Stelios G. Efstathiadis introduced the SUPERBUS system which consisted of various modules for scheduling the public transport operations.

To sum up, there are two main ideas to study the optimal design of urban transit network. One is that the transit routes and their headways are determined simultaneously, the other is that transit network is firstly optimized, and then the headways of the transit routes are determined in another model. The author of this paper tends to the latter idea. The remainder of this paper is organized as follows. A transit network model is formulated firstly and an improved ant colony algorithm is introduced to solve the problem in Section II. Moreover, in Section III, a model is established to optimize the headways for the optimized transit network. An improved genetic algorithm is proposed to tackle with this NP-hard problem. A case study in Changchun is introduced to demonstrate the validity of the proposed models and algorithms in Section VI. A conclusion is drawn in the final section.

2 Modeling and Solving of Mass Transit Network Optimization

2.1 Transit Network Optimization Model

Urban mass transit network optimization model is built up according to the method named "lay out the routes in turn and build up the network via optimization" proposed by WANG, etc. The model is based on the following two assumptions:

(1) Don't add new terminals to the current transit network any more;
(2) Don't add new roads to the current transit network any more.

The two assumptions make sure that the optimized transit network is based on the current network status and the structure of the network is stationary. The transit network optimization model is presented as Equation (1).

$$\max \ f(x_{ij}) = \sum_{j=1}^{n}\sum_{i=1}^{n} SP_{ij} \cdot x_{ij}$$

$$s.t. \begin{cases} 5km \leq \sum_{j=1}^{n}\sum_{i=1}^{n} l_{ij} x_{ij} \leq 15km \\ q_x \leq 1.50 \\ Q_k < Q_k^{\max} \\ b_n \leq 1.5 \\ ATT < 3 \\ x_{ij} \in (0, 1) \end{cases} \quad (1)$$

The objective function $f(x_{ij})$ of this model is to maximize the nonstop passenger flow. In other words, the optimized transit network can make sure that most of the passengers will reach their destinations without transfer. x_{ij} is a Boolean decision-making variable, the value of "1" represents that the bus stop node (v_i, v_j) belongs to a certain transit route, while the value of "0" denotes (v_i, v_j) does NOT belong to a certain transit route. SP_{ij} denotes the passenger flow without transfer from bus stop node v_i to v_j in the network. l_{ij} means the length between two adjacent bus stop node v_i and v_j in the transit network. Accordingly, $L = \sum_{j=1}^{n}\sum_{i=1}^{n} l_{ij} x_{ij}$ calculates the length of a certain route. Since the model is proposed for the mass transit network optimization of a medium-sized or large-scale city, the length of a route is set to be 5 to 15 kilometers. q_x is defined as a nonlinear coefficient. It can be calculated with D_{od}/L, herein, D_{od} denotes the distance between the two terminus of the given route. Q_{sk} and $Q_k^{\max}$ represent the sth designed transverse passenger flow and the maximum transverse passenger flow for the kth route respectively. The computational method of $Q_k^{\max}$ is as Equation (2).

$$Q_k^{\max} = 60 C_x l_k X_{cr} / h_k \quad (2)$$

where, C_x is the capacity of a transit vehicle. In China, the values of C_x are stipulated as 72, 129, 120, 29 for a single bus, an articulated bus, a double-deck bus and an intermediate-size bus respectively. l_k is the load factor of route No. k, setting to be "0.85" and "0.6" in rush hour and ordinary time period respectively. X_{cr} is denoted as the reduplicated routes impact coefficient.

b_k means the asymmetric coefficient of transverse passenger flow of route No. k. ATT means the average times of transfer, which can be calculated with Equation (3).

$$ATT = \frac{\sum_{r=1}^{4}\sum_{j=1}^{N_s}\sum_{i=1}^{N_s} SP_{ij} \cdot T_{ij}^{(r-1)} \cdot r}{\sum_{j=1}^{N_s}\sum_{i=1}^{N_s} SP_{ij}} \quad (3)$$

where, T is a transfer matrix, r is the times of transfer. Generally speaking, if ATT is larger than 3, then the planning of the transit network is unreasonable.

Besides the constraints mentioned above, any planned transit route candidate should satisfy the following requirement as well. That is, both of the two terminals for any transit route should NOT be identical except for a circle route and any intermediate nodes should NOT be passed through twice in order to avoid forming sub-circles.

2.2 Optimization Method Based on Ant Colony Algorithm

As for the optimization method, this paper proposes a novel research thought. Instead of starting from the determined O-D pairs, this paper treats the start-point and the end-point as the same, then builds up the set of terminals with all the start-points and end-points. Starting from all the terminals, the optimal transit lines will be found out in turn via maximizing the non-stop passenger flow.

The mass transit network optimization problem has been proved as a *NP*-hard problem. Some traditional optimization methods are not suitable for dealing with it. In this paper, ant colony algorithm is firstly introduced to solve the transit network optimization problem.

In this paper, the process of searching food source from the nest is corresponding to the process of finding an optimal transit route from a certain terminal. The ants' nest is corresponding to the transit line terminal. One forthcoming step of an ant corresponds to the passenger's traveling from a bus stop node to the next one in the transit network. The pheromone that the ant leaves on the route is corresponding to the link weight changing from one status to the other in the transit network. Accordingly, the ant colony algorithm is applicable to optimize the urban mass transit network.

An artificial ant will be placed at each terminal node. The artificial ants are used to construct transit routes by choosing nodes (bus stops) successfully until each bus stop has been visited once. When a city is to be selected, two parameters, i.e., visibility and pheromone intensity denoted as η_{ij} and τ_{ij} respectively should be taken into consideration. The visibility means how promising a bus stop will be visited, while pheromone intensity is the intensity of arc (v_i, v_j), i.e., the nonstop passenger flow of a certain transit route. $\Delta\tau_{ij}$ is the quantity of pheromone left by the kth ant on arc (i, j). If arc (i, j) is on the optimal route, then $\Delta\tau_{ij}$ is equal to (Q/f_k), where, Q is a constant which can reflect the quantity of pheromone, and f_k is the objective function value, i.e., nonstop passenger flow. The pheromone intensity is updated according to Equation (4).

$$\tau_{ij}^{new} = \rho \cdot \tau_{ij}^{old} + \sum_k \Delta\tau_{ij}^k \tag{4}$$

where, ρ ($0 \le \rho \le 1$) is the persistence coefficient.

The probability p_0 is a predetermined parameter of the algorithm. With probability $(1-p_0)$ and the set of unvisited bus stops, denoted as Ω, a tour is successfully built by choosing the next customer v_j immediately after v_i according to a probability distribution determined as Equation (5).

$$p_{ij}^k = \begin{cases} \dfrac{[\tau_{ij}]^\alpha [\eta_{ij}]^\beta}{\sum_{h \in \Omega}[\tau_{ih}]^\alpha [\eta_{ih}]^\beta} & if \quad v_j \in \Omega \\ 0 & otherwise \end{cases} \quad (5)$$

where, α and β are two constants to be demarcated, which determine the relative importance degree of visibility and pheromone intensity.

The flow chart of headway optimization method based on improved genetic algorithm is shown in Figure 1.

3 Modeling and Solving of Headways

3.1 Transit Vehicle Headway Optimization Model

The mass transit vehicle headway optimization model is based on the following assumptions:

(1) The passengers arrive at the station at a constant rate r_k randomly.

(2) All the passengers waiting at the station get on the earliest transit vehicle, i.e., the vehicle size is enough.

(3) The transit vehicle can't wait for the passengers at the bus stations, i.e., the vehicle must go at once boarding or alighting.

(4) The transit vehicle must stop at all the stations even though there is no passenger boarding or alighting.

(5) The headway of a certain line is fixed for a certain period;

(6) The link travel time is only relative to the link length.

As we know, the transit operators want to put larger headway to reduce operation cost, while the passengers prefer smaller headway in order to reduce their waiting and transfer cost. Consequently, reducing the operators cost means increasing the passengers cost and vice versa. Minimizing the sum of the operators and passengers cost can achieve the maximum social benefit. The problem of headway optimization is formulated as a mathematical program.

The term a_{im}^k and d_{jm}^k represent the arrival time and the departure time of the mth vehicle at the kth station of the ith route respectively. L_{im}^k is the number of on-board passengers, and $L_{im}^k = L_{im}^{k-1}(1-q_k) + r_k(a_{im}^k - a_{i,m-1}^k)$, where, q_k is the alighting proportion at station k, r_k is the randomly arrival rate at the kth station. The term $\delta_{i,j}^{k,l}$ is a Boolean variable. The value of "0" means that the transfer between those two stations is not optimal or infeasible. $\omega_{i,j}^k$ is the transfer proportion from the ith route to the jth route at station k, and $0 < \omega_{i,j}^k < q_k < 1$, $v_w, v_o, v_t, O_i, \bar{a}, \bar{b}$ are parameters to be demarcated, stand for the user waiting cost, user on-board cost, user transfer cost, the variable operation cost, average alighting time per passenger and average boarding time

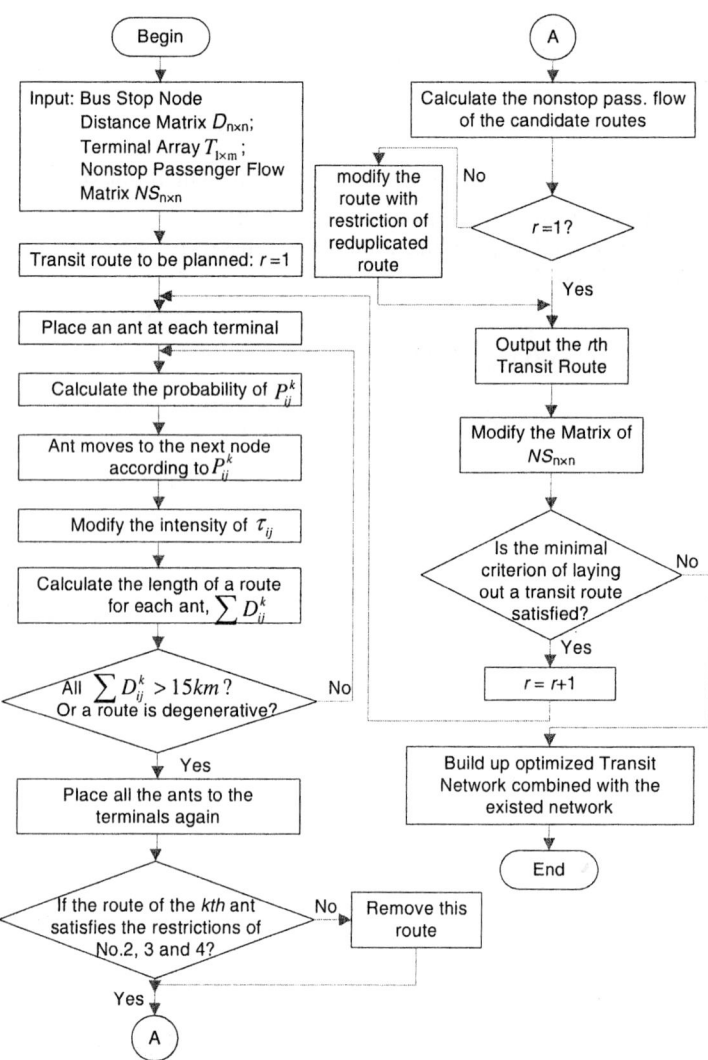

Fig. 1. Flow chart of transit network optimal design based on ant algorithm

per passenger respectively. T represents the maximum value of the departure time from the lth station of the jth transferred route minus the arrival time at the kth station of the ith route. M is an arbitrary large number. h_i and h_j denote the headways of the ith route and the jth route respectively. $D_{k-1,k}$ is the distance from station $(k-1)$ to station k. v_i and v_j are the speeds of the ith route and the jth route respectively, H is the time interval to be studied. Then, the number of dispatched vehicle is $60 \cdot H / h_i$. Then, the transit operation model is as follows:

$$\text{Min} \left\{ \frac{v_w}{2} \sum_{i,k} r_k h_i^2 + v_o \sum_{i,k,m} [D_{k-1,k} L_{i,m}^{k-1}/V_i + \right.$$
$$\left. (\overline{a} L_{i,m}^{k-1} q_k + \overline{b} r_k h_k L_{i,m}^{k-1}(1-q_k)] + v_t \sum_{i,j,k,l,m,n} \delta_{i,j}^{k,l}(d_{j,n}^l - a_{i,m}^k) L_{i,m}^{k-1} \omega_{i,j}^k + 60 \cdot H \sum_i \sum_k O_i D_{k-1,k}/h_i \right\} \quad (6)$$

$$s.t. \begin{cases} g_1 : d_{i,m}^k - a_{i,m}^k \le s_i^{\max}; & \forall i,k \\ g_2 : d_{i,m}^k - a_{i,m}^k \ge s_i^{\min}; & \forall i,k \\ g_3 : d_{j,n}^l - a_{i,m}^k + M(1-\delta_{i,j}^{k,l}) \ge 0; & \forall i,j,k,l,m,n, j \ne i \\ g_4 : \sum_l \delta_{i,j}^{k,l} = 1; & \forall i,j,k,l, j \ne i \\ g_5 : (d_{j,n}^l - a_{i,m}^k)\delta_{i,j}^{k,l} \le T; & \forall i,j,k,l,m,n, j \ne i \\ g_6 : a_{i,m}^k - a_{i,m-1}^k \le h_i; & \forall i,k,m \end{cases} \quad (7)$$

The objective function is to minimize the sum of the passengers and operators cost with four terms. The first term represents the total waiting cost for all the waiting passengers. The second one denotes the total on-board cost for all the in-vehicle passengers. The third term represents the total transfer cost for all the transfer passengers. The three cost components constitute the passenger total cost. And the fourth term represents the total variable operating cost for all the transit companies. The fixed cost is not added to the objective function because it is not subject to the travel time.

Constraint g_1 and g_2 state that the stopping time $d_{im}^k - a_{im}^k$ of the mth vehicle at station k of route i should be less than or equal to the maximum stopping time $s_i^{\max}$, greater than or equal to the minimum stopping time $s_i^{\min}$. Constraint g_3 and g_4 assure that only one transfer station is feasible from a special station of route i to another route j. Constraint g_5 specifies that the transfer time for all passengers is less than or equal to a maximum value of T. Constraint g_6 makes sure that the headway $(a_{i,m}^k - a_{i,m-1}^k)$ is less than or equal to the maximum bound h_i on difference in arrival time of two successive vehicles.

From the model we know that the objective function is dependent on the headways of all the transit lines and 0-1 variable $\delta_{i,j}^{k,l}$ in the transfer stops. The optimization model is a nonlinear program problem. Even though a few routes and vehicles are discussed, there are still a large number of variables and constraints. It is obviously infeasible to minimize the objective function by setting its partial derivatives with respect to the decision variables to "0". Improved genetic algorithms (IGA) are proposed to deal with the optimization problem.

3.2 Optimization Method Based on Improved Genetic Algorithm

Genetic algorithm is an efficient optimal solution searching algorithm based on the mechanics of natural selection and natural genetics. The global solutions can be found for both linear and nonlinear formulations. The optimal solution searching process is independent of the form of the objective function. It combined survival of the fittest

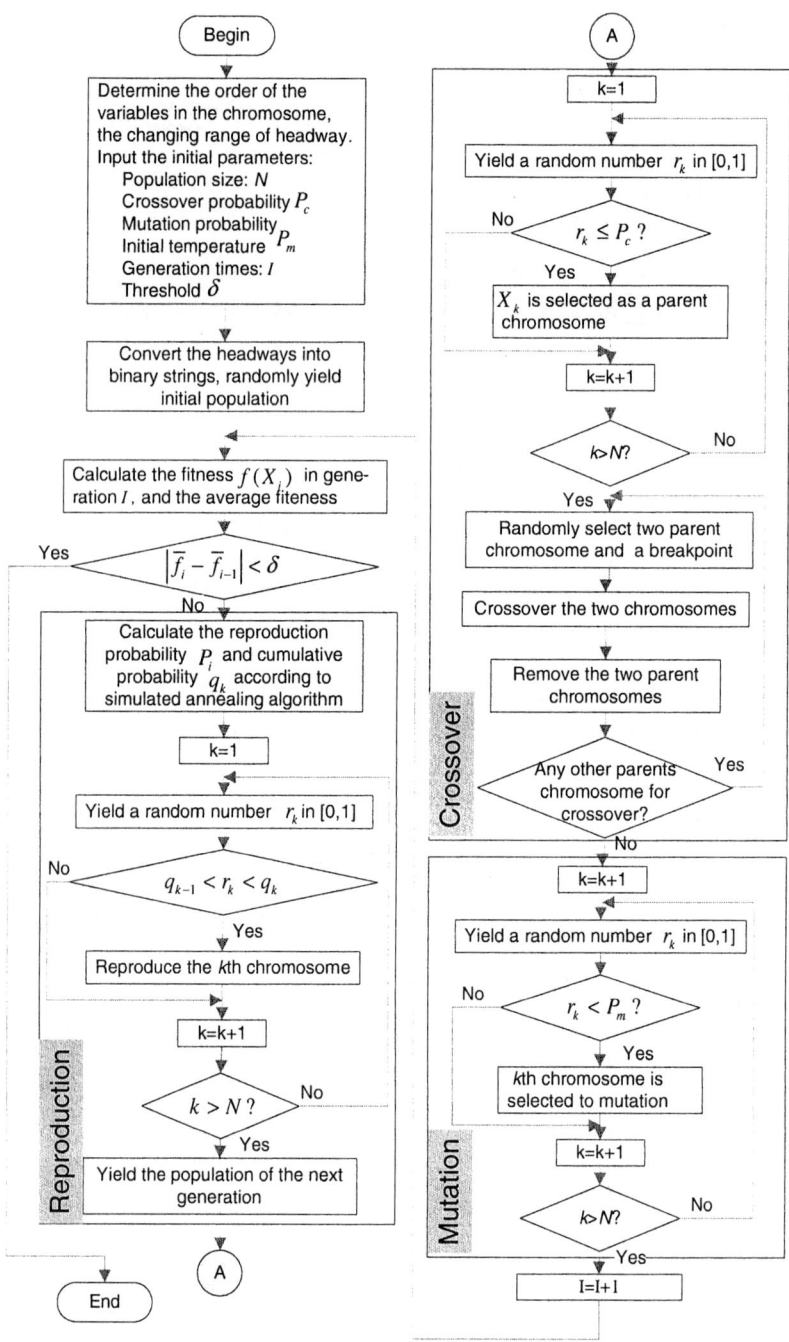

Fig. 2. Flow chart of headway optimization based on improved genetic algorithm

among string structures with a structured, yet randomized, information exchange to form a search algorithm. In each generation, a new set of artificial creatures (strings) is created using bits and pieces of the fittest of the old. Three commonly used operations are employed: reproduction, crossover, and mutation. These three operators are applied in turn to the solutions in the current generation during the search process.

However, the standard GA (SGA) has some defects such as premature convergence and low efficiency. An improved genetic algorithm is introduced to solve the problems, which embodies two aspects, i.e., reproduction operation and the judgment of break condition.

Simulated Annealing, another heuristic search algorithm is introduced to solve the premature problem in reproduction. Firstly, we compute the reproduction probability P_i of a certain chromosome in a certain population with $P_i = e^{f_i/T} / \sum_{i=1}^{N} e^{f_i/T}$, where, $T = T_0(0.99^{g-1})$, f_i is the fitness of ith chromosome, N is the population size, T_0 is the initial temperature, T is the temperature and g is the serial number of generation. Secondly, we calculate the cumulative q_k of each chromosome according to $q_k = \sum_{i=1}^{k} p_i (i=1,2,...,N)$. Finally, a random number r in interval [0,1] according to uniform distribution. If $r \leq q_1$ then select the first chromosome to reproduce, else if $q_{k-1} \leq r \leq q_k$, then select the rth chromosome to reproduce. A new generation comes into being by repeating N times. According to this method of reproduction, when the temperature is high, the reproduction probability with close fitness will be close. With the decreasing of the temperature, the difference of the reproduction probability will be enlarged. Thereby, the prevalence of the excellent individual will be more obvious. Thus, the method can solve not only the premature problem but also the problem of low evolution speed in the later period.

The classic method to judge the break condition is to determine a fixed generation in advance. This paper proposes to judge if the population has been mature and has no longer the evolution tendency. The algorithm will be stopped when the average individual fitness of the successive several generations is constant or less than an arbitrary small number.

The flow chart of headway optimization method based on improved genetic algorithm is shown in Figure 2.

4 Case Study

4.1 Optimal Design of Transit Network

Changchun is the capital city of Jilin Province, China. There were 115 transit routes, 904 buses, 1180 mini-buses in this city (2000). According to the survey on trip mode, 23.3 percent of inhabitants traveled by means of mass transit. Nevertheless, the profit of public transit company decreased year-by-year despite of the increasing subsidy from the government. Unreasonable transit network may be one of the most important reasons resulting in this phenomenon. The transit network optimization model and the solution method were successfully applied in Changchun city. The parameters used in the model and ant algorithm are demarcated as follows. $m = 49$, $Q=10000$, $\rho = 1$, $\alpha = 0.5$ and $\beta = -0.5$. The previous twenty transit routes planned are listed in Table 1. The percentage of nonstop passenger flow is approximate 40%.

Table 1. Previous Planned Twenty Transit Routes

Line NO.	Number of Stops	Length (Km)	Nonstop Passenger Flow	Line NO.	Number of Stops	Length (Km)	Nonstop Passenger Flow
1	16	14.84	26983	11	11	15.20	14016
2	14	14.36	23214	12	12	12.00	13326
3	14	11.20	22945	13	12	11.20	12429
4	15	14.16	19116	14	11	10.78	12401
5	11	10.56	18150	15	14	10.56	11882
6	16	10.40	18050	16	12	11.52	10130
7	15	10.88	15971	17	8	10.08	9812
8	11	10.56	15410	18	12	12.04	9265
9	11	10.24	15281	19	12	11.06	9104
10	11	10.20	14276	20	11	10.16	7964

4.2 Optimal Design of Headway

In this paper, MTR system of Hong Kong, as an example, are talked about to testify the effectiveness and validity of the proposed headway optimization method. The MTR system map is shown in Figure 3. The numbers beside the stations denote the real time numbers of passengers in waiting metros. The six lines are Island Line, Kwun Tong Line, Tsuen Wan Line, Tseung Kwan O Line, Tung Chung Line, Airport Express Line. There are 14 transfer stations, i.e., Hong Kong, Centrol, Admiralty, North Point, Quarry Bay, Yau Tong, Tiu Keng Leng, Yau Ma Tei, Monkok, Prince Edward, Kai King, Tsim Sha Tsui, Kowloon and Tsing Yi.

The average waiting, on-board and transfer time value is about 0.4 HKD/min (According to the statistics, GDP per capita in Hong Kong is 25,400USD in 2004). Variable operation cost is set to be 120HKD/min. The average boarding or alighting time is 0.2 second per passenger. The investigated time period is from 8.20 a.m. to 9:00 a.m. The running speed is 60km/hr. The maximal transfer time is 10min. The headways vary from 1min to 17min, and can be divided exactly by 0.5. Population size is 20, crossover probability is 0.95 and mutation probability is 0.005, δ is equal to 1. The arrival rates are not listed because of the restriction of paper length.

The simulation process lasts 40mins. The following are the optimization results using IGA. The optimal headways of the twelve lines (No.1 Island Line, No.3 Kwun Tong Line, No.5 Tsuen Wan Line, No.7 Tseung Kwan O Line, No.9 Tung Chung Line, No.11 Airport Express Line, No. 2, …No, 12 are the back lines) are 3min, 3min, 6min, 4min, 4min, 4min, 4min, 8min, 5min, 4min, 7min and 7min respectively,

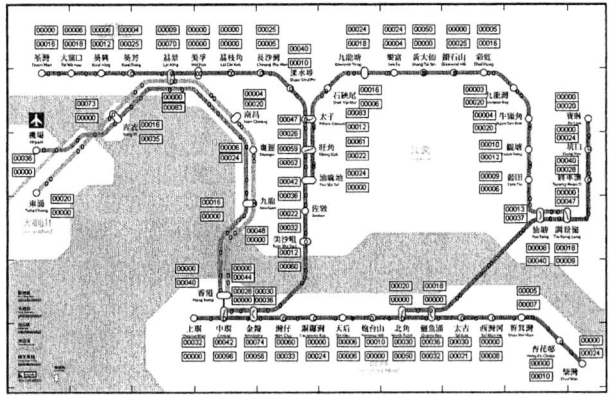

Fig. 3. Hong Kong MTR system map

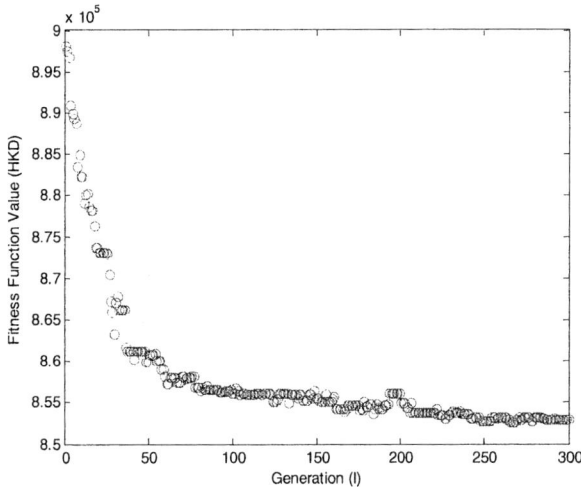

Fig. 4. The changing process of fitness function using improved genetic algorithm

minimum fitness is 854,302HKD. The total waiting, on-board, transfer, operator variable costs are 103,750, 653,750, 22,930, and 73,872 HKD respectively. The changing process of fitness function using IGA is illustrated in Figure 4.

5 Conclusion

Transit network optimization and headway optimization are two of the most important issues in urban public transport system operation and management. Many scholars all over the world attached importance to study them using many methods. Two optimization models are proposed at first. Based on the analysis, both the two problems can be boiled down to NP-hard problems. Two evolutionary algorithms, ant colony algorithm and genetic algorithm have been introduced to solve them. Flow charts of the two algorithms are presented as well. Finally, a case study testified the applicability and validity of the proposed methods.

Acknowledgement

This work is supported by NSFC under the grant 60374059.

References

1. Avishal Ceder : Transit Vehicle-Type Scheduling Problem, TRR 1503(1995)
2. Chakroborty, P., Deb, K., and Subrahmanyam, P.S. : Optimal Scheduling of Urban Transit Systems Using Genetic Algorithms, Journal of Transportation Engineering, Vol.121(6) (1995) 544-553
3. Jianming HU : Research on Critical Theories and Implementation Technologies of Advanced Public Transportation System, Ph.D. dissertation, Jilin University (2001)
4. Keiichi Uchimura, Hiro Takahashi, and Takashi Saitoh : Advanced public transit system routing and scheduling, IFAC Transportation Systems, Chania, Greece (1997) 753-758
5. Kurt Ker-Tshung Lee, Sharon H. F. Kuo, and Paul M. Schonfeld : Optimal mixed bus fleet for urban operations, TRR 1503 (1995)
6. Marco Dorigo, Gianni Di Caro and Luca M. Gambardella : Ant Algorithms for Discrete Optimization Art. Life. Vol.5, No.3 (1999) 137-172
7. Moazzem Hossain and Mir Zahid Hasan : Simulation of Bus Operation under Mixed Traffic Conditions, Proceedings of ICTTS'2000, Beijing (2000) 441-453
8. Omar Mekkaoui, Andre de Plama and robin Lindsey : Optimal Bus Timetables and Trip Timing Preferences, Proceedings of ICTTS'2000, Beijing (2000) 355-363
9. Richard J. Balling□JohnT.Tuber□Michael R.Brown and Kirsten Day : Multiobjective Urban Planning Using Genetic Algorithm, Journal of Urban Planning and Development, Vol.125(2) (1999) 82-99
10. S. B. Pattaik, S. Mohan, and V. M. Tom : Urban Bus Transit Route Network Design Using Genetic Algorithm, Journal of Transportation Engineering, Vol.124(4)(1998) 368-375
11. Stelios G. Efstathiadis, Dr.Nick Theophilopoulos : Flexible Dynamic scheduling for public transport, IFAC Transportation Systems, Chania, Greece(1997) 1207-1211
12. Wei WANG, Jiqian XU, Tao YANG and Xuhong LI et al : Urban Transportation Planning Theories and Applications, Publishing House of Southeast University, Nanjing (1998)

A Method for Solving Nonlinear Programming Models with All Fuzzy Coefficients Based on Genetic Algorithm[*]

Yexin Song[1], Yingchun Chen[2], and Xiaoping Wu[3]

[1] College of Sciences, Naval University of Engineering, Wuhan 430033, China
yxsong@21cn.com
[2] Huazhong University of Science and Technology, Wuhan 430074, China
chyc@21cn.com
[3] College of Electronic Engineering, Naval University of Engineering,
Wuhan 430033, China
wxp8@sohu.com

Abstract. This paper develops a novel method for solving a type of nonlinear programming model with all fuzzy coefficients (AFCNP). For a decision maker specified credibility level, by presenting the equivalent deterministic forms of fuzzy inequality constraints and fuzzy objective, the fuzzy model is converted into a crisp constrained nonlinear programming model with parameter (CPNP). An improved genetic algorithm is presented to solve the CPNP and obtain the crisp optimal solution of AFCNP for specified credibility level.

1 Introduction

Research on modeling and optimization methods for fuzzy nonlinear programming is very important in fuzzy optimization theory. Trappey et al. [1], Ali [2], Tang and Wang [3,4] have proposed and studied some types of fuzzy nonlinear programming problems. In this paper, we consider a type of nonlinear programming models with all fuzzy coefficients (AFCNP) as follows.

$$Max \ \tilde{f}(x) = \tilde{c}_1 y_1(x) \oplus \tilde{c}_2 y_2(x) \oplus \cdots \oplus \tilde{c}_n y_n(x) \quad (1)$$

$$s.t. \ \begin{cases} \tilde{a}_{i1} y_{i1}(x) \oplus \tilde{a}_{i2} y_{i2}(x) \oplus \cdots \oplus \tilde{a}_{in} y_{in}(x) \leq \tilde{b}_i, & i=1,2,\cdots,m, \quad (2)\\ x \geq 0. \quad (3) \end{cases}$$

where x is an n-dimensional vector of decision variables, $y_k(x), \forall k$, are real-valued nonlinear functions. For the sake of notational convenience, denote $y_k(x) = y_k$. Symbol $\oplus$ is the fuzzy addition operation (In case no misunderstanding occurs, instead of $\oplus$ symbol + may be used). $\tilde{c}_j, \tilde{a}_{ij}, i=1,2,\cdots,m, j=1,2,\cdots,n$, are modeled as trapezoidal fuzzy numbers, denote $\tilde{c}_j = (c_j^L, c_j^R, \underline{c}_j, \overline{c}_j)$, $\tilde{a}_{ij} = (a_{ij}^L, a_{ij}^R, \underline{a}_{ij}, \overline{a}_{ij})$, and $\tilde{b}_i, i=1,2,\cdots,m$, is modeled as a triangular fuzzy number, denote $\tilde{b}_i = (b_i, \underline{b}_i, \overline{b}_i)$.

In the following sections, for a DM specified credibility level, we first present an approach to transform the AFCNP into an equivalent deterministic form. Then, an improved genetic algorithm is presented to solve the crisp optimal solution of AFCNP.

---

[*] This work is supported by National Natural Science Foundation of China Grant #70471031.

2 Deterministic Transformation of AFCNP

For the sake of convenience in discussion, we first assume $y_k \geq 0$ for $\forall k$.

Suppose ε is the credibility level specified by the DM, for $\varepsilon \in [0,1]$, treating fuzzy inequality constraints (2) as fuzzy goals in exactly the same way as done in [5], these can be converted into equivalent deterministic forms as

$$\sum_{j=1}^{n}(a_{ij}^{R}+\overline{a}_{ij}(1-\varepsilon))y_{ij} \leq b_i + \overline{b}_i(1-\varepsilon), \quad \mu_i(\sum_{j=1}^{n} a_{ij}^{R} y_{ij}) \rightarrow Max, \quad i=1,2,\cdots,m. \quad (4)$$

The membership function $\mu_i(x)$ may be interpreted as the subjective evaluation of $\sum_{j=1}^{n} a_{ij}^{R} y_{ij}$ with regard to $\tilde{b}_i$. It can be appropriately represented by a linear function as

$$\mu_i(x) = \begin{cases} 1, & \sum_{j=1}^{n} a_{ij}^{R} y_{ij} \leq b_i, \\ 1-(\sum_{j=1}^{n} a_{ij}^{R} y_{ij} - b_i)/(\overline{b}_i(1-\varepsilon)), & b_i < \sum_{j=1}^{n} a_{ij}^{R} y_{ij} \leq b_i + \overline{b}_i(1-\varepsilon), \\ 0, & \sum_{j=1}^{n} a_{ij}^{R} y_{ij} > b_i + \overline{b}_i(1-\varepsilon). \end{cases} \quad (5)$$

Fuzzy objective (1) may be interpreted as in [5] as fuzzy goals. Let $\tilde{d} = (d, \underline{d}, \overline{d})$ be the fuzzy aspiration level specified by the DM for the fuzzy objective. Then we have

$$\tilde{f}(x) = \tilde{c}_1 y_1 \oplus \tilde{c}_2 y_2 \oplus \cdots \oplus \tilde{c}_n y_n \geq \tilde{d}. \quad (6)$$

This fuzzy inequality relation can be converted into an equivalent deterministic form as

$$\sum_{j=1}^{n}(c_j^{L}-\underline{c}_j(1-\varepsilon))y_j \geq d - \underline{d}(1-\varepsilon), \quad \mu_0(\sum_{j=1}^{n} c_j^{L} y_j) \rightarrow Max \quad (7)$$

The membership function $\mu_0(x)$ may be interpreted as the subjective evaluation of $\sum_{j=1}^{n} c_j^{L} y_j$ with regard to $\tilde{d}$. It can be defined by the following linear function

$$\mu_0(x) = \begin{cases} 1, & \sum_{j=1}^{n} c_j^{L} y_j \geq d, \\ 1-(d-\sum_{j=1}^{n} c_j^{L} y_j)/(\underline{d}(1-\varepsilon)), & d-\underline{d}(1-\varepsilon) \leq \sum_{j=1}^{n} c_j^{L} y_j < d, \\ 0, & \sum_{j=1}^{n} c_j^{L} y_j < d - \underline{d}(1-\varepsilon) \end{cases} \quad (8)$$

With the above treatment of the constraints and objective, AFCNP (1-3) can be rewritten as the following constrained nonlinear programming with parameter (CPNP).

$$\max \quad \alpha = \min\{\mu_0(x), \mu_i(x), i=1,2,\cdots,m.\}$$

$$\text{s.t.} \begin{cases} \sum_{j=1}^{n}(a_{ij}^{R}+\overline{a}_{ij}(1-\varepsilon))y_{ij} \leq b_{i}+\overline{b}_{i}(1-\varepsilon), & i=1,2,\cdots,m, \\ \sum_{j=1}^{n}(c_{j}^{L}-\underline{c}_{j}(1-\varepsilon))y_{j} \geq d-\underline{d}(1-\varepsilon), & x \geq 0. \end{cases} \quad (9)$$

Note: In this section, we first assume $y_k \geq 0$ for $\forall k$. But in many situations it does not hold, therefore we must consider more general assumptions. Based on the rule of real multiplication operation of trapezoidal fuzzy numbers, in situations in which y_k can be positive or negative, in place of $a_{ij}^{R}, \overline{a}_{ij}, c_{j}^{L}, \underline{c}_{j}$, we have

$$a_{ij}^{R} = \begin{cases} a_{ij}^{L} & y_k < 0, \\ a_{ij}^{R} & y_k \geq 0 \end{cases}, \quad \overline{a}_{ij} = \begin{cases} -\underline{a}_{ij} & y_k < 0, \\ \overline{a}_{ij} & y_k \geq 0 \end{cases}, \quad c_{j}^{L} = \begin{cases} c_{j}^{R} & y_k < 0, \\ c_{j}^{L} & y_k \geq 0 \end{cases}, \quad \underline{c}_{j} = \begin{cases} -\overline{c}_{j} & y_k < 0, \\ \underline{c}_{j} & y_k \geq 0. \end{cases}$$

3 Solving the Crisp Optimal Solution of AFCNP Based on GA

Let $(R^{p}(\varepsilon))^{+}$ be the feasible domain of model (9), denote

$$\widetilde{S} = \{(x, \mu_{\widetilde{S}}(x)) \mid x \in (R^{p}(\varepsilon))^{+}, \mu_{\widetilde{S}}(x) = \min\{\mu_{0}(x), \mu_{i}(x), i=1,2,\cdots,m\}\} \quad (10)$$

Definition 1. The fuzzy set $\widetilde{S}$ is the fuzzy optimal solution of AFCNP for specified credibility level ε.

Definition 2. Let $\alpha^{*} = \max\{\mu_{\widetilde{S}}(x) \mid x \in (R^{p}(\varepsilon))^{+}\}$, α^{*} is the best balance degree between the constraints and objective for the credibility level ε.

Definition 3. The maximizing decision $x^{*} = \{x \mid \mu_{\widetilde{S}}(x) = \alpha^{*}, x \in (R^{p}(\varepsilon))^{+}\}$ is the crisp optimal solution of AFCNP for specified credibility level ε.

According to above definitions, the crisp optimal solution of AFCNP for specified ε can be obtained by solving model (9).

In this section we use an improved GA to solve model (9). The basic idea is described as follows. First, select any small degree α_{0} (generally, $\alpha_{0}=0.05$ or 0.1), randomly produce an initial population with the size of N individuals, each individual is selected to reproduce children along the increment direction of $\mu_{0}(x)$ and $\mu_{i}(x), i=1,2,\cdots,m$, according to selection probability, depending on its fitness function value. For an individual with fitness function value less than α_{k-1} (the smallest fitness function value of the individual in (k-1)th generation), give it a less fitness function value by means of penalty so that it may have a smaller chance than others of being selected as a parent to reproduce children in the later generation. As the generation increases, the individual with less fitness function value gradually die out. After a number of generations, the individual's fitness function value reaches the optimum or near optimum.

Since there exist constrained conditions in model (9), we must consider whether the individual satisfies these constrains. For the individual which does not satisfy the constrains, give a penalty to its fitness function value so that it may have a smaller chance of being selected as a parent to reproduce children in the later generation.

Based on the above idea, for individual x, let

$$\mu_i'(x) = \max\{\mu_i(x) - \rho_i \max\{g_i(x),0\},0\}, \quad i = 0,1,2,\cdots,m. \tag{11}$$

where ρ_i is a penalty coefficient, and

$$g_0(x) = [d - \underline{d}(1-\varepsilon)] - \sum_{j=1}^{n}(c_j^L - \underline{c}_j(1-\varepsilon))y_j,$$

$$g_i(x) = \sum_{j=1}^{n}(a_{ij}^R + \overline{a}_{ij}(1-\varepsilon))y_{ij} - [b_i + \overline{b}_i(1-\varepsilon)], \quad i = 1,2,\cdots,m.$$

Denote $\mu_{\min}(x) = \min\{\mu_0'(x),\mu_1'(x),\cdots,\mu_m'(x)\}$. The fitness function of individual x^k in kth generation is defined as follows.

$$f(x^k) = \begin{cases} \mu_{\min}(x^k), & \text{if } \mu_{\min}(x^k) \geq \alpha_{k-1}, \\ \lambda\mu_{\min}(x^k), & \text{if } \mu_{\min}(x^k) < \alpha_{k-1}. \end{cases} \tag{12}$$

where $\lambda \in (0,1)$. From (11) and (12), it can be seen that for an individual which does not satisfy the constrains or whose membership degree is less than α_{k-1}, by giving it a smaller fitness function value, it will have little chance of being selected as a parent to reproduce children in the later generation.

4 Conclusion

In this paper a solving method is proposed for the AFCNP. By presenting the equivalent deterministic forms of fuzzy inequality constraints and objective, the fuzzy model is transformed into a CPNP model. The crisp optimal solution of AFCNP for specified credibility level is obtained by solving the CPNP using an improved genetic algorithm.

References

1. Trappey, J.F.C.: Fuzzy non-linear programming: theory and application in manufacturing. Int. J. of Production Research. 26 (1988) 957-985
2. Ali, F.M.: A differential equation approach to fuzzy non-linear programming problems. Fuzzy Sets and Systems. 93 (1998) 57-61
3. Tang, J., Wang, D., Fung, R.Y.K.: Model and method based on GA for non-linear programming problems with fuzzy objective and resources. Int. J. of System Science. 29 (1998) 907-913
4. Tang, J., Wang, D.: A non-symmetric model for fuzzy nonlinear programming problems with penalty coefficients. Computers and Operations Research. 24 (1997) 717-725
5. Mohan, C., Nguyen, H.T.: An interactive satisficing method for solving multiobjective mixed fuzzy-stochastic programming problems. Fuzzy Sets and Systems. 117 (2001) 61-79

An Evolutionary Algorithm Based on Stochastic Weighted Learning for Constrained Optimization

Jun Ye[1], Xiande Liu[1], and Lu Han[2]

[1] Optics Engineering Dept.,
Huazhong Univ. of Science & Tech.,
430074 Hubei, P.R. China
yejun_clinux@hotmail.com
[2] Electronics & Info. Engineering Dept.,
Huazhong Univ. of Science & Tech.,
430074 Hubei, P.R. China

Abstract. In this paper, we propose an evolutionary algorithm based on a single operator called stochastic weighted learning, i.e., each individual will learn from other individuals specified with stochastic weight coefficients in each generation, for constrained optimization. For handling equality and inequality constraints, the proposed algorithm introduces a learning rate adapting technique combined with a fitness comparison schema. Experiment results on a set of benchmark problems show the efficiency of the algorithm.

1 Introduction

Most engineering optimization problems include equality and/or inequality constraints, and recent years, evolutionary algorithms have received a lot of attention regarding their potential for solving effectively such constrained optimization problems (see [1], [2], [3] for a comprehensive survey).

In a previous work [4], we have introduced a new evolutionary algorithm based on a single operator called stochastic weighted learning for unconstrained optimization problems. The idea of the algorithm is very simple, i.e., in each generation each individual will learn from other individuals in the population specified with stochastic weight coefficients that represent the learning strength related to them. The similar strategy learning process can be commonly observed in the behavior of rational agents within economic environment, and the operator tries to mimic such process.

In this paper, we attempt to extend our algorithm to solve constrained optimization problems. Section 2 presents the basic structure of the proposed algorithm. Section 3 introduces a learning rate adapting technique combined with a fitness comparison schema for handling equality and inequality constraints. Section 4 presents the experimental results on a set of benchmark problems. Comparisons with other evolutionary algorithms are also included in this section. Finally, Section 5 concludes with a brief summary of the paper.

2 New Evolutionary Algorithm Based on Stochastic Weighted Learning

The general nonlinear programming problem can be formulated as follows:

$$\max f(x)$$
$$s.t. \begin{cases} g_j(x) \leq 0 & j=1,\ldots,p \\ h_j(x) = 0 & j=p+1,\ldots,q \end{cases} \quad (1)$$

where $x = (x_1, x_2, \ldots, x_n) \in R^n$, $x_i \in [x_i^l, x_i^u]$, $i = 1, 2, \ldots, n$, is n-dimensional real vector, $f(x)$ is the objective function, $g_j(x)$ is the jth inequality constraint, $h_j(x)$ is the jth equality constraint, and $D = \prod [x_i^l, x_i^u] \subseteq R^n$ defines the search space.

Unlike most EAs that have different selection strategies, mutation rules and crossover operators, the proposed algorithm uses only one operator that mimics the strategy learning process of rational agents to achieve the objective of optimization, therefore it is fairly simple and can be easily realized.

2.1 Individual Representation

Individual representation in the proposed algorithm is straightforward. Each individual in the population is represented only by its solution variables. We denote the ith individual in the tth generation by $x(t)_i$, where $i = 1, 2, \ldots, M$, M is the population size.

2.2 Stochastic Weighted Learning

In each generation, each individual will learn new strategy profile from other m individuals for next generation. In these m individuals, $(m - 1)$ individuals are randomly selected from the whole population and one is the best-fit individual in this generation. Each one of these m individuals is specified with a weight coefficient that represents the positive or negative learning strength related to that individual. We denote these weight coefficients by w_k, where $k = 1, 2, \ldots, m$, and they are satisfied the relation below:

$$\sum_{k=1}^{m} w_k = 1 \quad (2)$$

where $w_k \sim U(-1, 1)$. The strategy profile learned from these m individuals is then defined as follows:

$$x_i' = \sum_{k=1}^{m} w_k x(t)_k \quad (3)$$

where $i = 1, 2, \ldots, M$.

If a certain component of the strategy profile learned, say x'_{ij} (the jth component of x'_i), is outside the parametric bounds defined by the problem, the algorithm will use the arithmetical average of the corresponding components of these m individuals instead.

Each individual in the population will adopt the new strategy profile in next generation if the fitness of the new strategy profile is greater than its current one. Otherwise, it will hold the current strategy profile without any change.

2.3 Algorithm

We have already explained each element in our algorithm. The pseudocode of the proposed algorithm can be summarized as follows.

```
Procedure SWL
   t = 0;
   initialize x(0);
   while t < T do
      find the best-fit individual;
      for i = 1, 2, ..., M do
         randomly select (m-1) individuals and generate w_k;
         x•_i = sum[w_k x(t+1)_k], k = 1, 2, ..., m;
      end
      for i = 1, 2, ..., M do
         if fitness[x•_i] > fitness[x(t)_i] then
            x(t+1)_i = x•_i;
         else
            x(t+1)_i = x(t)_i;
         end
      end
      t = t + 1;
   end
end
```

3 Constraint Handling

Here we introduce a learning rate adapting technique combined with a fitness comparison schema for handling equality and inequality constraints.

3.1 Fitness Comparison

All equality constraints are converted into inequality constraints, $|h(x)| - \varepsilon \le 0$, where ε is the degree of tolerated violation. We define $v(x) = \max(v_1(x), \ldots, v_q(x))$, where $v_j(x)$ is:

$$v_j(x) = \begin{cases} \max(g_j(x), 0) & j = 1, \ldots, p \\ \max(|h_j(x)| - \varepsilon, 0) & j = p+1, \ldots, q \end{cases} \quad (4)$$

In the algorithm, the fitness of x_1 is greater than the fitness of x_2 if one of the conditions (a) $v(x_1) = 0$ and $v(x_2) = 0$ and $f(x_1) > f(x_2)$; or (b) $v(x_1) = 0$ and $v(x_2) > 0$; or (c) $v(x_1) > 0$ and $v(x_1) < v(x_2)$ is fulfilled. That is, if the both individuals are feasible, then the one with greater $f(x)$ is better; feasible individual is better than infeasible one; and if the both individuals are infeasible, then the one with less $v(x)$ is better.

3.2 Learning Rate Adapting

In every Δt generations, there are $\Delta t \times M$ times of tries for learning a better strategy profile. We denote the times of made-learning (the strategy profile learned is better than the current one) in these tries by s. The learning rate r is defined as:

$$r = s / (\Delta t \times M) \tag{5}$$

In the algorithm, the number of individuals that each individual will learn from, m will be adjusted adaptively within a predefined range $[m_1, m_2]$ along the evolution according to r, i.e., if $r < r_1$ and $m > m_1$, then $m = m - 1$; else if $r > r_2$ and $m < m_2$, then $m = m + 1$. (r_1 and r_2 are two predefined threshold values, $0 < r_1 < r_2 < 1$)

For the problems that have equality constraints, the degree of tolerated violation ε will be adjusted adaptively along the evolution according to r as well, i.e., if $r < r_1$, then $\varepsilon = \varepsilon / \alpha$; else if $r > r_2$, then $\varepsilon = \varepsilon \times \alpha$. ($\alpha$ is a predefined scaling factor, $0 < \alpha < 1$)

The idea is, start with an initial value $m^{(0)}$ (and $\varepsilon^{(0)}$ if have equality constraints), for every Δt generations, if the learning rate is lower than a certain level, then decrease m to speed up the learning process (and increase ε to enlarge the feasible domain); or if the learning rate is higher than a certain level, then increase m to slow down the learning process (and decrease ε to reduce the feasible domain).

4 Experimental Results

We use a set of benchmark problems G01 to G13 for testing the performance of the proposed algorithm. These problems are proposed in [1] and [5]. And for all test problems, the parameters are fixed to $M = 70$, $T = 5000$, $\Delta t = 10$, $r_1 = 0.01$, $r_2 = 0.03$, $m^{(0)} = 10$, $m_1 = 9$, $m_2 = 11$, $\varepsilon^{(0)} = 10$, $\alpha = 0.85$. These parameters were selected based on the experimental experience. A total number of 35 independent runs are executed for each problem, and each run involves 350000 function evaluations. Results are shown in Table 1.

The column indicated by "optimal" in Table 1 shows the known "optimal" solution for each problem. The three columns under caption "Fitness" give the best, mean, and worst objective value found, and the three columns under caption "Violation" give the minimal, mean, and maximal solution violations.

From the table, one may find that the algorithm has consistently found the "optimal" solutions for all problems in 35 runs except G02. And for problems G03, G05, G11 and G13 that have equality constraints, the solution violations are very low, compared with 1e-3 and 1e-4, the values of tolerated violation degree usually used by other evolutionary algorithms.

Table 2 shows the result of another experiment on problem G02 with the parameter settings of $M = 200$, $T = 12000$, $m^{(0)} = m_1 = m_2 = 11$. A total number of 35 independent runs are executed, and each run involves 2400000 function evaluations. As expected, with large population and suitable value m, the proposed algorithm can consistently found the optimal solutions for G02 in all runs.

Table 3 summarizes the comparison between our results and Runarsson and Xin Yao's results [6]. The results of [6] shown in Table 3 is the statistics of 30 independent

Table 1. Experimental Results on Benchmark Problems

	optimal	Fitness			Violation		
		Best	Mean	Worst	Best	Mean	Worst
G01	-15.000	-15.000	-15.000	-15.000	0	0	0
G02	-0.803619	-0.803619	-0.792695	-0.756970	0	0	0
G03	-1.000	-1.000	-1.000	-1.000	0	1.33e-17	2.22e-16
G04	-30665.539	-30665.539	-30665.539	-30665.539	0	0	0
G05	5126.498	5126.498	5126.498	5126.498	0	2.73e-13	4.55e-13
G06	-6961.814	-6961.814	-6961.814	-6961.814	0	0	0
G07	24.306	24.306	24.306	24.306	0	0	0
G08	-0.095825	-0.095825	-0.095825	-0.095825	0	0	0
G09	680.630	680.630	680.630	680.630	0	0	0
G10	7049.248	7049.248	7049.248	7049.248	0	0	0
G11	0.750	0.750	0.750	0.750	0	7.22e-17	1.11e-16
G12	-1.000000	-1.000000	-1.000000	-1.000000	0	0	0
G13	0.053950	0.053950	0.053950	0.053950	0	1.53e-15	4.88e-15

Table 2. Experimental Result on G02 with $M = 200$, $T = 12000$, $m^{(0)} = m_1 = m_2 = 11$

	optimal	Fitness			Violation		
		Best	Mean	Worst	Best	Mean	Worst
G02	-0.803619	-0.803619	-0.803619	-0.803619	0	0	0

Table 3. Comparison Between Our (Indicated by SWL) and Runarsson and Xin Yao's (Indicated by SR [6]) Algorithms

	optimal	Best		Mean		Worst	
		SWL	SR	SWL	SR	SWL	SR
G01	-15.000	-15.000	-15.000	-15.000	-15.000	-15.000	-15.000
G02	-0.803619	-0.803619	-0.803515	-0.792695	-0.781975	-0.756970	-0.726288
G03	-1.000	-1.000	-1.000	-1.000	-1.000	-1.000	-1.000
G04	-30665.539	-30665.539	-30665.539	-30665.539	-30665.539	-30665.539	-30665.539
G05	5126.498	5126.498	5126.497	5126.498	5128.881	5126.498	5142.472
G06	-6961.814	-6961.814	-6961.814	-6961.814	-6875.940	-6961.814	-6350.262
G07	24.306	24.306	24.307	24.306	24.374	24.306	24.642
G08	-0.095825	-0.095825	-0.095825	-0.095825	-0.095825	-0.095825	-0.095825
G09	680.630	680.630	680.630	680.630	680.656	680.630	680.763
G10	7049.248	7049.248	7049.316	7049.248	7559.192	7049.248	8835.655
G11	0.750	0.750	0.750	0.750	0.750	0.750	0.750
G12	-1.000000	-1.000000	-1.000000	-1.000000	-1.000000	-1.000000	-1.000000
G13	0.053950	0.053950	0.053957	0.053950	0.067543	0.053950	0.216915

runs and each run involves 350000 function evaluations. And for problems G03, G05, G11 and G13, the tolerated violation degree for equality constraints is fixed to 10^{-4}. From the table, one may find that the algorithm proposed in this paper outperforms that in [6] for all cases (the best solution found by [6] for G05 which is better than the "optimal" solution is a result of loose tolerated violation degree).

Table 4 and 5 summarizes the comparisons between our results and the more recent work [7]. The results of [7] shown in Table 4 and 5 is the statistics of 31 independent runs and each run involves 1500000 function evaluations. From the tables, one may find that the results of our algorithm are better not only in term of objective value but also in term of solution violations.

Table 4. Comparison Between Our (Indicated by SWL) and Hamida and Schoenauer's (Indicated by ASCHEA [7]) Algorithms

	optimal	Best		Median		Mean	
		SWL	ASCHEA	SWL	ASCHEA	SWL	ASCHEA
G01	-15.000	-15.000	-15	-15.000	-15	-15.000	-14.84
G02	-0.803619	-0.803619	-0.803614	-0.794885	-0.794568	-0.792695	-0.788950
G03	-1.000	-1.000	-1.000	-1.000	-0.999995	-1.000	-0.99997
G04	-30665.539	-30665.539	-30665.5	-30665.539	-30665.5	-30665.539	-30665.5
G05	5126.498	5126.498	5126.5	5126.498	5126.5	5126.498	5126.53
G06	-6961.814	-6961.814	-6961.81	-6961.814	-6961.81	-6961.814	-6961.81
G07	24.306	24.306	24.3323	24.306	24.6162	24.306	24.6636
G08	-0.095825	-0.095825	-0.095825	-0.095825	-0.095825	-0.095825	-0.095825
G09	680.630	680.630	680.630	680.630	680.635	680.630	680.641
G10	7049.248	7049.248	7049.42	7049.248	7272.19	7049.248	7615.2
G11	0.750	0.750	0.75	0.750	0.75	0.750	0.75
G12	-1.000000	-1.000000	-	-1.000000	-	-1.000000	-
G13	0.053950	0.053950	-	0.053950	-	0.053950	-

Table 5. Violation Comparison Between Our (Indicated by SWL) and Hamida and Schoenauer's (Indicated by ASCHEA [7]) Algorithms for G03, G05, G11 and G13

	Violation					
	Best		Mean		Worst	
	SWL	ASCHEA	SWL	ASCHEA	SWL	ASCHEA
G03	0	0	1.33e-17	1.8e-16	2.22e-16	2.22e-16
G05	0	1.6e-9	2.73e-13	2.61e-4	4.55e-13	0.008
G11	0	0	7.22e-17	1.87e-11	1.11e-16	4.46e-11
G13	0	-	1.53e-15	-	4.88e-15	-

5 Conclusion

This paper is a continuation of the study devoted to stochastic weighted learning, a new operator for EAs introduced in earlier work. By extending with a learning rate adapting technique and a fitness comparison schema, the evolutionary algorithm based on stochastic weighted learning can solve constrained optimization problems efficiently. The validity of the proposed algorithm was tested on a set of benchmark problems and the experimental results are very promising. From these results, we may conclude that the proposed algorithm seems to be a useful candidate for EAs.

References

1. Michalewicz, Z., Schoenauer, M.: Evolutionary Algorithm for Constrained Parameter Optimization Problems. Evolutionary Computation, 4(1) (1996) 1-32
2. Yao, X.: Evolutionary Computation: Theory and Applications. World Scientific, Singapore (1999)
3. Tan, K.C., Lim, M.H., Yao, X., Wang L.P. (eds.): Recent Advances in Simulated Evolution And Learning. World Scientific, Singapore (2004)
4. Jun, Y., Xiande, L., Lu, H.: An evolutionary algorithm based on stochastic weighted learning for continuous optimization. Proc. of 2003 IEEE International Conference on Neural Networks & Signal Processing, Nanjing, China (2003)
5. Koziel, S., Michalewicz, Z.: Evolutionary algorithms, homomorphous mapping and constrained parameter optimization. Evolutionary Computation, 7(1) (1999) 19-44
6. Runarsson, T.P., Yao, X.: Stochastic Ranking for Constrained Evolutionary Optimization, IEEE Trans. on Evolutionary Computation, Vol.4, No.3 (2000)
7. Hamida, S.B., Schoenauer, M.: ASCHEA: New results using adaptive segregational constraint handling. Proc. of the 2002 Congress on Evolutionary Computation (2002)

A Multi-cluster Grid Enabled Evolution Framework for Aerodynamic Airfoil Design Optimization

Hee-Khiang Ng[1], Dudy Lim[1], Yew-Soon Ong[1], Bu-Sung Lee[1],
Lars Freund[2], Shuja Parvez[2], and Bernhard Sendhoff[2]

[1] School of Computer Engineering
Nanyang Technological University, Nanyang Avenue, Singapore 639798
{mhkng, dlim, asysong, ebslee}@ntu.edu.sg
[2] Honda Research Institute Europe Gmbh
Carl-Legien-Strasse 30, 63073 Offenbach
shshgs01@fht-esslingen.de,
{lars.freund , bernhard.sendhoff]}@honda-ri.de

Abstract. Advances in grid computing have recently sparkled the research and development of Grid problem solving environments for complex design. Parallelism in the form of distributed computing is a growing trend, particularly so in the optimization of high-fidelity computationally expensive design problems in science and engineering. In this paper, we present a powerful and inexpensive grid enabled evolution framework for facilitating parallelism in hierarchical parallel evolutionary algorithms. By exploiting the grid evolution framework and a multi-level parallelization strategy of hierarchical parallel GAs, we present the evolutionary optimization of a realistic 2D aerodynamic airfoil structure. Further, we study the utility of hierarchical parallel GAs on two potential grid enabled evolution frameworks and analysis how it fares on a grid environment with multiple heterogeneous clusters, *i.e.*, clusters with differing specifications and processing nodes. From the results, it is possible to conclude that a grid enabled hierarchical parallel evolutionary algorithm is not mere hype but offers a credible alternative, providing significant speed-up to complex engineering design optimization.

1 Introduction

Genetic Algorithms (GA) represents one of the well-known modern stochastic search techniques inspired by the Neo-Darwinian theory of natural selection and evolution [1] and have been employed with great success for solving many complex engineering design problems [2-6]. The popularity of GAs lies in the ease of implementation and the ability to arrive close to the global optimum design. Another well-known strength of GAs is that sub-linear improvements in the search efficiency may be easily achieved by incorporating parallelism. Many studies on the parallelism of GAs have been made over the last decade [7-10], with many strategies introduced to date.

Recently, there has been a new paradigm shift in science and engineering towards the utilization of increasingly high-fidelity and accurate analysis codes in the design analysis and optimization processes which could take up many minutes to hours or even days of supercomputing time [11-13]. The high computational costs associated with the use of high-fidelity simulation models thus poses a serious impediment to the successful application of evolutionary algorithms (EAs) to engineering design optimization since EAs typically require many thousands of function evaluations to locate a near optimal solution.

Recent technologies in Grid computing [14-16] have therefore offered a fresh solution to this problem by enabling collaborative computing on an unprecedented scale via leveraging from geographically distributed computing resources. Here, we harness the idea of employing heterogeneous computing resources distributed in different design teams as a powerful technology to facilitate parallelism in evolutionary optimization. The use of Grid technologies in optimization can be found in [17-19].

In this paper, we present a scalable parallel evolutionary optimization framework for engineering design problems in a Grid infrastructure which we refer to as Grid Enabled Evolution (GEE). In particular, we consider the parallel evolutionary design optimization of 2D aerodynamic airfoil using the proposed GEE, where an optimal solution is sought for a particular configuration of flight speed given by the Mach number M_∞, and the angle of attack (AOA). The 2D aerodynamic airfoil design problem represents one of the most frequently tackled computationally expensive design problems in aeronautics. One major feature of GEE is the ability to harness computing clusters that spans across international boundaries, *i.e.*, computing clusters in Asia and Europe may be used simultaneously in the GEE. This is achieved by using standard Globus [20] and NetSolve [21] toolkits. In the GEE, the parallel evolution of multiple subpopulations are conducted across all computing clusters available on the Grid.

The rest of this paper is organized as follows. Section 2 describes the GEE framework while section 3 provides a brief description of the aerodynamic airfoil design problem we consider in this work. The empirical study is presented in section 4. Analysis of the multi-cluster GEE for hierarchical parallel evolutionary design optimization based on the result obtained from the experiments is also presented in the section. Finally section 5 concludes this paper.

2 Grid Enabled Evolutionary Framework

In this section, we present the architecture of the proposed GEE for complex engineering design optimization. Like any Grid computing setups, it would be necessary to first enable the software components as grid services so that they may be accessed within the Grid environment. Here, two grid services are created using our extended GridRPC technologies proposed in [22] for 'gridifying' existing applications. The first 'subpopulation-evolution' service is a composition of the standard GA evolutionary operators for evolving a GA subpopulation. On the other hand, the other 'airfoil-analysis' grid service is the gridified aerodynamic airfoil analysis code or the objective function of the GA for evaluating the subpopulation of chromosomes. Further for security reasons, we restrict the 'subpopulation evolution' service to be executed only on the master node of each cluster. This implies that the 'subpopulation-evolution' is developed as a Globus grid services capable of remote execution across unlimited computing clusters. In contrast, we consider the 'airfoil-analysis' as a NetSolve services that resides on all processing nodes of the clusters.

A PHGA algorithm using the GEE framework is outlined in Figure 1. Before the search starts, the services are deployed onto the clusters on the grid and registered with the resource agent. This enables the latter to search for the available computing resources and 'airfoil-analysis' service. The workflow of the Grid enabled evolutionary optimization framework is also depicted in Figure 2. The detail workflow of the GEE can be outlined as nine crucial stages and is depicted in Figure 3. The nine stages are described as follows:

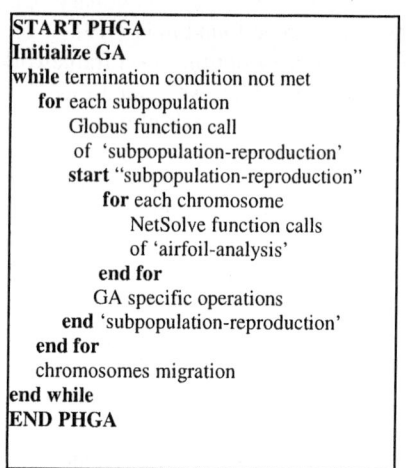

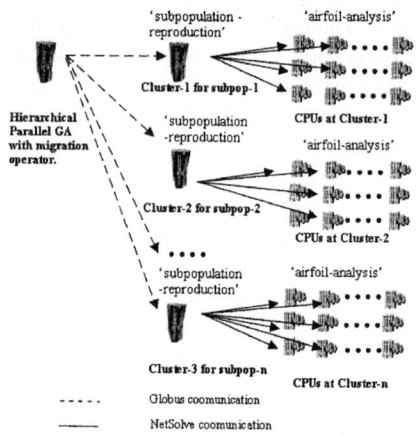

Fig. 1. PHGA algorithm using GEE framework

Fig. 2. Workflow of the Grid enabled evolutionary optimization framework

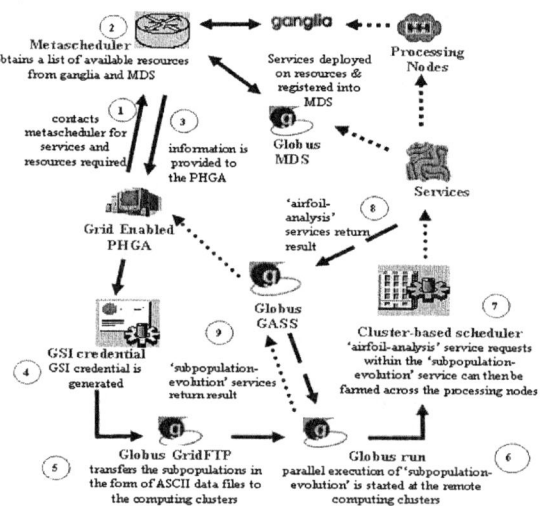

Fig. 3. GEE Workflow

1) Prior to the start of the evolutionary search, the grid enabled PHGA contacts the meta-scheduler, requesting for services and resources necessary required for conducting the evolution of the GA subpopulations.
2) The metascheduler [22] then obtains a list of the available resources together with their status of availability. Such status information is acquired from services provided by the Globus Monitoring and Discovery Service (MDS) and Ganglia monitoring toolkit [22-24].
3) These resources information and services are then provided to allow the PHGA to proceed with the parallel evolutionary search.
4) Upon obtaining the information in relation to the resources and services, the Grid Security Infrastructure (GSI) [25] credentials are subsequently generated. This forms the authentication or authority to use the computing resources available in the system.
5) The GridFTP [26] mechanism provided in the GEE then transfers the subpopulations in the form of ASCII data files to the computing clusters that has the correct services to perform genetic evolution and fitness evaluation.
6) Parallel evolution of the multiple subpopulations is then started at the remote computing clusters using the Globus job submission protocol.
7) Whenever the Globus Resource Allocation Manager (GRAM) [27] gatekeeper of a cluster receives a request to start the 'subpopulation-evolution' service, an instance of this service get instantiated on the master node of the cluster. Subsequently, the nested set of 'airfoil-analysis' service requests within the 'subpopulation-evolution' service can then be farmed across the processing nodes within the cluster using any cluster level local scheduler, for example, NetSolve, Sun Grid Engine [28], Condor [29] or others.
8) When the 'airfoil-analysis' services completed execution, the fitness values of the chromosomes are conveyed back to the 'subpopulation-evolution' service so that standard GA operations such as mutation, crossover and selection can take place.
9) Similarly when the 'subpopulation-evolution' services deployed across the remote clusters completes, the resultant evolved subpopulations are then marshaled back to the main PHGA program using the Global Access to Secondary Storage (GASS). The migration operation of the PHGA then proceeds. The process repeats until the termination condition is met.

3 Aerodynamic Airfoil Design Problem

In this section, we present a 2D aerodynamic airfoil design problem, particularly, the subsonic inverse pressure design problem used in our present study. The target pressure profile is generated from the NACA 0012 airfoil, which itself is the baseline shape. The airfoil geometry is characterized using 24 design variables as depicted in Figure 4. Hence, there exists for this problem a global solution corresponding to $z_1 = \ldots = z_{24} = 0$. The free-stream conditions in this problem are subsonic speed of Mach 0.5, and zero angle of attack (AOA), corresponding to symmetric pressure profiles on the upper and lower walls.

It is worth noting that the inverse problem constitutes a good test problem for validating the convergence property of GEE, since the optimal design is known in advance. At the same time, it facilitates our study on complex engineering design optimization problems of variable-fidelity. Secondly, the inverse design problem also has a practical purpose, as the designer generally has an idea of the desired pressure profile that yields good aerodynamic performance. For example, in transonic design, a shock front on the upper surface generally leads to undesirably high pressure drag that degrades the efficiency of the airfoil. A typical approach to inverse pressure design is to 'smoothen' the pressure distribution on the upper-surface in a way that maintains the area under the curve, so as to maintain the lift force generated by the airfoil. Thus, the inverse pressure design problem can be formulated as a minimization problem of the form:

$$I(w, S) = \frac{1}{2} \int_{wall} (p - p_d)^2 d\sigma \qquad (1)$$

subject to constraints.

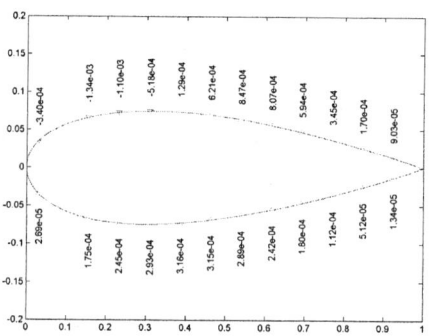

Fig. 4. A 2D airfoil geometry characterized using 24 design variables with the NACA 0012 as baseline

4 Empirical Study

In this section we present an empirical study of the PHGA using the GEE framework for complex engineering design, particularly, aerodynamic airfoil design optimization.

4.1 Experimental Setup

The control parameter of the PHGA are configured as follows: population size for every subpopulation is 80, crossover probability of 0.9, mutation probability of 0.1, migration period of 10 generations with 1 chromosome per migration phase, linear fitness scaling, elitism, and termination upon maximum number of generation 100. Further, three computing clusters used in our study and are listed in Table 1.

Table 1. Specifications of the clusters used

Cluster Name	No. of CPUs	CPU Clock	Memory	MFLOPS (average)
pdcc	28	PIV Xeon 3.6GHz	10G	920
pdpm	20	PIV Xeon 2.6GHz	10G	800
surya	21	PIII 450MHz PIII 550MHz PIII 733MHz	6G	150

The respective Million Floating Point Operations (MFLOPS) of the computing clusters are also tabulated in Table 1. The *pdcc* cluster has a significantly higher MFLOPS than the *surya* cluster. Clearly they are heterogeneous clusters and *pdcc* and *pdpm* are much more powerful clusters than *surya*.

4.2 Experimental Results and Analysis

Using 24 design variables and the cost function in equation 1, the PHGA with the GEE framework is applied for the optimization of the subsonic inverse pressure design problem described in section 4. Further we consider two separate analysis codes or variable-fidelity in our study. The low-fidelity and moderate-fidelity analysis codes considered here represent realistic computationally inexpensive and expensive design problems, respectively. The exact wall clock time for a single airfoil analysis on the three heterogeneous is summarized in Table 2. A single moderate-fidelity analysis of the airfoil geometry using an Euler CFD solver takes around 110 seconds on a Pentium III processor, while a low-fidelity takes around 10 seconds. From Table 2, it may also be observed that the time taken for each clusters to complete an analysis is clearly significantly different on the moderate-fidelity analysis code.

Table 2. Wall clock time to conduct a single of the variable-fidelity airfoil code on clusters on the clusters

Variable Fidelity	Low-fidelity Analysis code			Moderate-fidelity Analysis code		
Cluster	*surya*	*pdpm*	*pdcc*	*surya*	*pdpm*	*pdcc*
Wall Clock Time	10 s	9 s	8 s	110 s	54 s	37 s

For each set of experimental study, 10 PHGA runs using the GEE framework were conducted and the average of the runs are reported. The average wall clock time taken by the PHGA to complete a maximum of 100 generations on a GEE with single cluster or multiple clusters for 2 subpopulations is depicted in Figure 5. From these

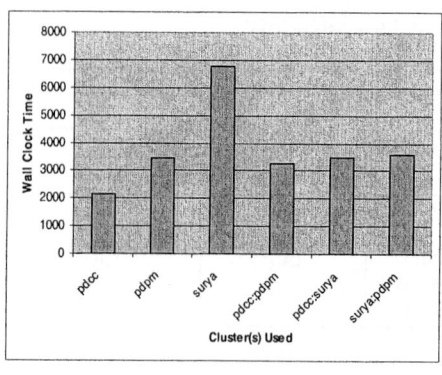 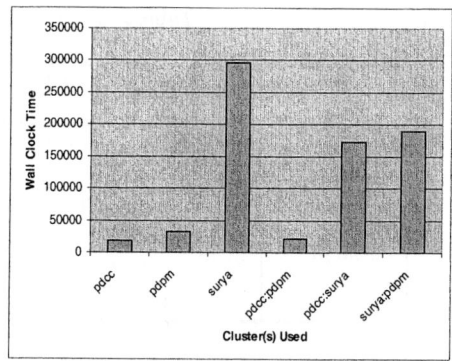

(a) Low-fidelity analysis code   (b) Moderate-fidelity analysis code

Fig. 5. Average wall clock time for PHGA-2 subpopulations using the GEE framework for variable-fidelity analysis code

results, the PHGA with 2 subpopulations and a GEE a single *pdcc* cluster appears to complete the maximum of 100 generations much earlier than all other single cluster or two-clusters combinations. This is because of our present restriction on the GEE which enforces a one-to-one mapping between subpopulations and computing clusters regardless of their specifications, *i.e.*, CPU clock, number of processing nodes, memory, MFLOP and etc. The effect is more evident on the Figure 5(b) than (a), due to the larger differences on the execution time to perform a single analysis of the moderate-fidelity analysis code on the three clusters.

Besides, due to the large differences in completion time by the clusters to complete the evolution of a subpopulation, all subpopulations have to wait for the slowest cluster to complete evaluations of all chromosomes and evolution before any migration operation may take place and proceed with the next generation. Hence, it appears proper parallelism and division of the subpopulations and chromosomes evaluations is crucial to the performance of the PHGA and GEE when operating on a heterogeneous computing cluster environment such as the grid. Here, to fully utilize the grid computing cluster resources for complex engineering design of computationally expensive optimization problems, dynamic bundling of chromosomes is proposed. Here we pool all chromosomes in the subpopulations together and submit chromosomes to clusters according to their specifications, for instance based on their MFLOPS and CPU numbers. In this way, more chromosomes are sent to the high-end clusters than to its lower-end counterparts. In our case, as the number of CPUs are all almost the same, i.e. varying from 20-28 CPUs for the three clusters (see Table 1), we consider only MFLOPS as the criterion for dynamic bundling. For instance, using the MFLOPS of the three heterogeneous clusters defined in Table 1, dynamic bundling is carried out as follows:

$$R_i = \frac{C_i}{\sum_{i=1}^{n} C_i} \times Pop \qquad (2)$$

where R_i = Ratio of chromosomes sent to cluster i.
  C_i = MFLOPS of cluster i.
  n = Total number of clusters to be used.

Using the GEE with dynamic bundling, the PHGA with 2 subpopulations is once again used for optimizing the airfoil design problem. Note that all other parameters are kept the same as previous experiments. Using two-clusters, *pdcc:surya* and *pdcc:pdpm*, the chromosomes are bundled as tabulated in Table 3 using equation (2).

Table 3. Chromosomes distribution ratio based on the MFLOPS of the clusters for 2 subpopulations (a total of 160 chromosomes)

Cluster Name	MFLOPS Ratio	Chromosomes Distribution Ratio
pdcc : *surya*	920:150	138:22
pdcc : *pdpm*	920:800	86:74

The average wall clock time of the experiments are depicted in Figure 6 and 7. It can be observed that with the use of the dynamic bundling GEE for PHGA optimization, the wall clock time is significantly improved on all the two-cluster combinations. This is because chromosomes are now sent to more powerful clusters for evaluations than their less powerful counterparts on the grid. In effect, it is possible to conclude that the use of the Grid and hence the proposed GEE for facilitating parallelism in PHGA can provide significant speed-up on the optimization search.

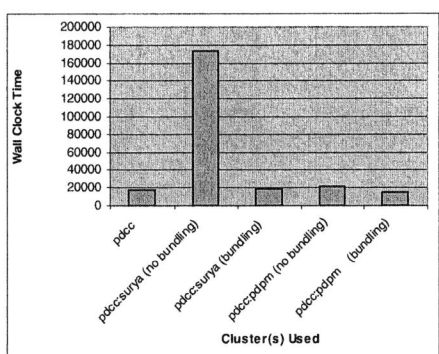

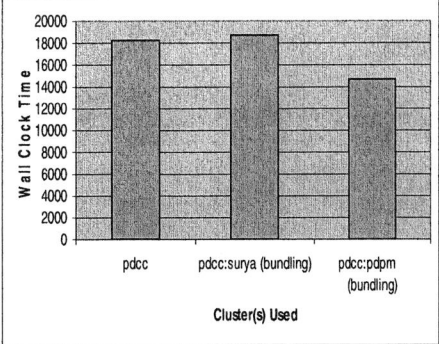

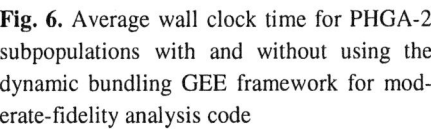

Fig. 6. Average wall clock time for PHGA-2 subpopulations with and without using the dynamic bundling GEE framework for moderate-fidelity analysis code

Fig. 7. Average wall clock time for PHGA-2 subpopulations using the dynamic bundling compared to without using dynamic bundling in a single fast cluster (*pdcc*)

5 Conclusions

In this paper, we have presented the Grid Enabled Evolution framework, which employs Grid computing technologies for facilitating parallelism in multi-population parallel GA optimization. Based on the experimental results obtained, an assessment and analysis of the GEE is performed. The negative consequences using of heterogeneous clusters in a realistic Grid environment based on a GEE with one-to-one mapping between subpopulations and computing clusters is discussed. Further, dynamic bundling based on the MFLOPS metric of the clusters is also proposed and demonstrated to provide significant speed-up in the PHGA optimization search. From our analysis, it is possible to conclude that a grid enabled hierarchical parallel evolutionary algorithm is not mere hype but does offers as a credible alternative for providing significant speed-up to complex engineering design optimization.

References

1. Goldberg D.E., "Genetic Algorithms in Search, Optimization and Machine Learning", 1989.
2. M. Olhofer, T. Arima, T. Sonoda and B. Sendhoff, "Optimization of a stator blade used in a transonic compressor cascade with evolution strategies", *Adaptive Computing in Design and Manufacture (ACDM)*, Springer Verlag, pp. 45-54, 2000.
3. P. Hajela, J. Lee., "Genetic algorithms in multidisciplinary rotor blade design", *Proceedings of 36th AIAA/ASME/ASCE/AHS/ASC Structures, Structural Dynamics and Material Conference*, New Orleans, pp. 2187-2197, 1995.
4. Y. S. Ong and A.J. Keane, "Meta-Lamarckian in Memetic Algorithm", *IEEE Trans. Evolutionary Computation*, Vol. 8, No. 2, pp. 99-110, April 2004.
5. I. C. Parmee., D. Cvetkovi., A. H. Watson, C. R. Bonham, "Multi objective satisfaction within an interactive evolutionary design environment", *Evolutionary Computation*, 2000.
6. P. B. Nair and A. J. Keane, "Passive Vibration Suppression of Flexible Space Structures via Optimal Geometric Redesign", *AIAA Journal* 39(7), pp. 1338-1346, 2001.
7. Baluja S., "The Evolution of Genetic Algorithms: Towards Massive Parallelism", *Machine Learning: Proceedings of the Tenth International Conference*, 1993.
8. Mariusz Nowostawski, Riccardo Poli, "Parallel Genetic Algorithm Taxonomy", *Proceedings of the Third International conference on knowledge-based intelligent information engineering systems (KES'99)*, pages 88-92, Adelaide, August 1999. IEEE.
9. Cantu-Paz E., "A Survey of Parallel Genetic Algorithms", *Calculateurs Paralleles, Reseaux et Systems Repartis* vol. 10 No. 2 pp. 141-171, 1998.
10. Baluja S., "The Evolution of Genetic Algorithms: Towards Massive Parallelism", *Machine Learning: Proceedings of the Tenth International Conference*, 1993.
11. Huyse L. et. al., "Aerodynamic Shape Optimization of Two-dimensional Airfoils Under Uncertain Operating Conditions", ICASE NASA Langley Research Centre, 2001.
12. Padula S.L. and Li W., "Robust Airfoil Optimization in High Resolution Design Space", ICASE NASA Langley Research Centre, 2002.
13. Ong Y.S., Lum K.Y., Nair P.B., Shi D.M. and Zhang Z.K., "Global Convergence of Unconstrained and Bound Constrained Surrogate-Assisted Evolutionary Search in Aerodynamic Shape Design Solvers", *IEEE Congress on Evolutionary Computation*, Special Session on Design Optimization with Evolutionary Computation", 2003.

14. Foster I. and Kesselman C., editors, "The Grid: Blueprint for a New Computing Infrastructure," Morgan Kaufman Publishers,1999.
15. Foster I., Kesselman C., and Tuecke S., "The Anatomy of the Grid: Enabling Scalable Virtual Organizations" , *International J. Supercomputer Applications*, vol. 15, no. 3, 2001.
16. Baker M., Buyya R., Laforenza D., "The Grid : International Efforts in Global Computing", *International Conference on Advances in Infrastructures for Electronic Business, Science, and Education on the Internet*, 2000.
17. Cox J., "Grid enabled optimisation and design search for engineering (Geodise)", in: NeSC Workshop on Applications and Testbeds on the Grid, 2002.
18. Parashar M. et. al., "Application of Grid-enabled Technologies for Solving Optimization Problems in Data-Driven Reservoir Studies", submitted to Elsevier Science, 2004.
19. Price A.R. et. al., "Tuning GENIE Earth System Model Components using a Grid Enabled Data Management System", School of Engineering Sciences, University of Soton, UK.
20. Foster I., "The Globus Toolkit for Grid Computing", *Proceedings of the 1st International Symposium on Cluster Computing and the Grid*, 2001.
21. Agrawal S., Dongarra J., Seymour K., Vadhiyar S., "NetSolve: past, present, and future; a look at a grid enabled server", 2002.
22. Ho Q.T., Cai W.T., and Ong Y.S., "Design and Implementation of An Efficient Multi-cluster GridRPC System", Cluster and Computing Grid, 2005.
23. Globus: Information Services/MDS, http://www-unix.globus.org/toolkit/mds.
24. Massie M., Chun B., and Culler D., "The Ganglia Distributed Monitoring System: Design, Implementation, and Experience", Technical report, University of California, Berkeley, 2003.
25. Tuecke S., "Grid Security Infrastructure (GSI) Roadmap", Internet Draft Document: draft-gridforum-gsi-roadmap-02.txt, 2001.
26. The Globus Project, "GridFTP Universal Data Transfer for the Grid", The Globus Project White Paper, 2000.
27. The Globus Resource Allocation Manager (GRAM) http://www-unix.globus.org/developer/resource-management.html.
28. Geer D., "Grid Computing Using the Sun Grid Engine", Technical Enterprises, Inc., 2003.
29. Frey J., Tannenbaum T., Livny M., Foster I., Tuecke S., "Condor-G: A Computation Management Agent for Multi-Institutional Grids", *Proceedings of the Tenth IEEE Symposium on High Performance Distributed Computing (HPDC10)*, 2001.

A Search Algorithm for Global Optimisation

S. Chen[1], X.X. Wang[2], and C.J. Harris[1]

[1] School of Electronics and Computer Science,
University of Southampton, Southampton SO17 1BJ, U.K
[2] Neural Computing Research Group, Aston University,
Birmingham B4 7ET, U.K

Abstract. This paper investigates a global search optimisation technique, referred to as the repeated weighted boosting search. The proposed optimisation algorithm is extremely simple and easy to implement. Heuristic explanation is given for the global search capability of this technique. Comparison is made with the two better known and widely used global search techniques, known as the genetic algorithm and adaptive simulated annealing. The effectiveness of the proposed algorithm as a global optimiser is investigated through several examples.

1 Introduction

Evolutionary and natural computation has always provided inspirations for global search optimisation techniques. Indeed, two of the best-known global optimisation algorithms are the genetic algorithm (GA) [1]-[3] and adaptive simulated annealing (ASA) [4]-[6]. The GA and ASA belong to a class of guided random search methods. The underlying mechanisms for guiding optimisation search process are, however, very different for the two methods. The GA is population based, and evolves a solution population according to the principles of the evolution of species in nature. The ASA by contrast evolves a single solution in the parameter space with certain guiding principles that imitate the random behaviour of molecules during the annealing process. It adopts a re-annealing scheme to speed up the search process and to make the optimisation process robust.

We experiment with a guided random search algorithm, which we refer to as the repeated weighted boosting search (RWBS). This algorithm is remarkably simple, requiring a minimum software programming effort and algorithmic tuning, in comparison with the GA or ASA. The basic process evolves a population of initially randomly chosen solutions by performing a convex combination of the potential solutions and replacing the worst member of the population with it until the process converges. The weightings used in the convex combination are adapted to reflect the "goodness" of corresponding potential solutions using the idea from boosting [7]-[9]. The process is repeated a number of "generations" to improve the probability of finding a global optimal solution. An elitist strategy is adopted by retaining the best solution found in the current generation in the initial population of the next generation. Several examples are included to demonstrate the effectiveness of this RWBS algorithm as a global optimisation tool and to compare it with the GA and ASA in terms of convergence speed.

The generic optimisation problem considered is defined by

$$\min_{\mathbf{u} \in \mathcal{U}} J(\mathbf{u}) \qquad (1)$$

where $\mathbf{u} = [u_1 \cdots u_n]^T$ is the n-dimensional parameter vector to be optimised, and $\mathcal{U}$ defines the feasible set. The cost function $J(\mathbf{u})$ can be multimodal and nonsmooth.

2 The Proposed Guided Random Search Method

A simple and effective strategy for forming a global optimiser is called the multistart [10]. A local optimiser is first defined. By repeating the local optimiser multiple times with some random sampling initialisation, a global search algorithm is formed. We adopt this strategy in deriving the RWBS algorithm.

2.1 Weighted Boosting Search as a Local Optimiser

Consider a population of P_S points, $\mathbf{u}_i \in \mathcal{U}$ for $1 \leq i \leq P_S$. Let $\mathbf{u}_{\text{best}} = \arg \min J(\mathbf{u})$ and $\mathbf{u}_{\text{worst}} = \arg \max J(\mathbf{u})$, where $\mathbf{u} \in \{\mathbf{u}_i, 1 \leq i \leq P_S\}$. Now a $(P_S + 1)$th point is generated by performing a convex combination of $\mathbf{u}_i$, $1 \leq i \leq P_S$, as

$$\mathbf{u}_{P_S+1} = \sum_{i=1}^{P_S} \delta_i \mathbf{u}_i \qquad (2)$$

where the weightings satisfy $\delta_i \geq 0$ and $\sum_{i=1}^{P_S} \delta_i = 1$. The point $\mathbf{u}_{P_S+1}$ is always within the convex hull defined by $\mathbf{u}_i$, $1 \leq i \leq P_S$. A mirror image of $\mathbf{u}_{P_S+1}$ is then generated with respect to $\mathbf{u}_{\text{best}}$ and along the direction defined by $\mathbf{u}_{\text{best}} - \mathbf{u}_{P_S+1}$ as

$$\mathbf{u}_{P_S+2} = \mathbf{u}_{\text{best}} + (\mathbf{u}_{\text{best}} - \mathbf{u}_{P_S+1}) \qquad (3)$$

According to their cost function values, the best of $\mathbf{u}_{P_S+1}$ and $\mathbf{u}_{P_S+2}$ then replaces $\mathbf{u}_{\text{worst}}$. The process is iterated until the population converges. The convergence is assumed if $\|\mathbf{u}_{P_S+1} - \mathbf{u}_{P_S+2}\| < \xi_B$, where the small $\xi_B > 0$ defines search accuracy.

The weightings δ_i, $1 \leq i \leq P_S$, should reflect the "goodness" of $\mathbf{u}_i$, and the process should be capable of self-learning these weightings. We modify the AdaBoost algorithm [8] to adapt the weightings δ_i, $1 \leq i \leq P_S$. Let t denote the iteration index, and give the initial weightings $\delta_i(0) = \frac{1}{P_S}$, $1 \leq i \leq P_S$. Further denote $J_i = J(\mathbf{u}_i)$ and $\bar{J}_i = J_i / \sum_{j=1}^{P_S} J_j$, $1 \leq i \leq P_S$. Then the weightings are updated according to

$$\tilde{\delta}_i(t) = \begin{cases} \delta_i(t-1)\beta_t^{\bar{J}_i}, & \text{for } \beta_t \leq 1 \\ \delta_i(t-1)\beta_t^{1-\bar{J}_i}, & \text{for } \beta_t > 1 \end{cases} \qquad (4)$$

$$\delta_i(t) = \frac{\tilde{\delta}_i(t)}{\sum_{j=1}^{P_S} \tilde{\delta}_j(t)}, \quad 1 \leq i \leq P_S \qquad (5)$$

where

$$\beta_t = \frac{\eta_t}{1-\eta_t}, \quad \eta_t = \sum_{i=1}^{P_S} \delta_i(t-1)\bar{J}_i \qquad (6)$$

The weighted boosting search (WBS) is a local optimiser that finds an optimal solution within the convex region defined by the initial population. This capability can be explained heuristically using the theory of weak learnability [7],[8]. The members of the population $\mathbf{u}_i$, $1 \leq i \leq P_S$, can be seen to be produced by a "weak learner", as they are generated "cheaply" and do not guarantee certain optimal property. Schapire [7] showed that any weak learning procedure can be efficiently transformed (boosted) into a strong learning procedure with certain optimal property. In our case, this optimal property is the ability of finding an optimal point within the defined search region.

2.2 Repeated Weighted Boosting Search as a Global Optimiser

The WBS is a local optimiser, as the solution obtained depends on the initial choice of population. We "convert" it to a global search algorithm by repeating it N_G times or "generations" with a random sampling initialization equipping with an elitist mechanism. The resulting global optimiser, the RWBS algorithm, is summarised as follows.

- **Loop: generations** For $g = 1 : N_G$
  - Initialise the population by setting $\mathbf{u}_1^{(g)} = \mathbf{u}_{\text{best}}^{(g-1)}$ and randomly generating rest of the population members $\mathbf{u}_i^{(g)}$, $2 \leq i \leq P_S$, where $\mathbf{u}_{\text{best}}^{(g-1)}$ denotes the solution found in the previous generation. If $g = 1$, $\mathbf{u}_1^{(g)}$ is also randomly chosen
  - Call the WBS to find a solution $\mathbf{u}_{\text{best}}^{(g)}$
- **End of generation loop**

The appropriate values for P_S, N_G and ξ_B depends on the dimension of $\mathbf{u}$ and how hard the objective function to be optimised. Generally, these algorithmic parameters have to be found empirically, just as in any other global search algorithm. The elitist initialisation is useful, as it keeps the information obtained by the previous search generation, which otherwise would be lost due to the randomly sampling initialisation. Note that for the iterative procedure of the WBS, there is no need for every members of the population to converge to a (local) minimum, and it is sufficient to locate where the minimum lies. Thus, ξ_B can be set to a relatively large value. This makes the search efficient, achieving convergence with a small number of the cost function evaluations. It should be obvious, although the formal proof is still required, that with sufficient number of generations, the algorithm will guarantee to find a global optimal solution, since the parameter space will be searched sufficiently. In a variety of optimisation applications, we have found that the RWBS is efficient in finding global optimal solutions and achieve a similar convergence speed as the GA and ASA, in terms of the required total number of the cost function evaluations. The RWBS algorithm has additional advantage of being very simple, needing a minimum programming effort and having few algorithmic parameters that require tuning, in comparison with the GA and ASA.

3 Optimisation Applications

Example 1. The cost function to be optimised is depicted in Fig. 1 (a). Uniformly random sampling in $[-8, 8]$ was adopted for population initialisation. With $P_S = 4$,

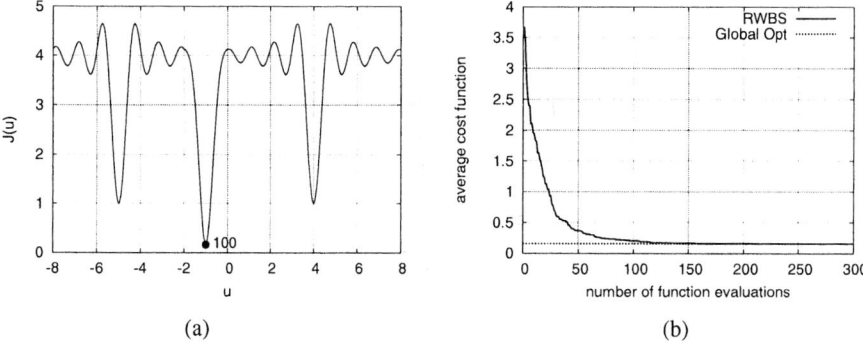

Fig. 1. One-dimensional multimodal function minimisation using the RWBS: (a) cost function, where number 100 beside the point in the graph indicates convergence to the global minimum in all the 100 experiments, and (b) convergence performance averaged over 100 experiments.

$\xi_B = 0.02$ as well as $N_G > 6$, the RWBS algorithm consistently converged to the global minimum point at $u = -1$ in all the 100 experiments conducted, as can be seen from the convergence performance shown in Fig. 1 (b). The averaged number of cost function evaluations required for the algorithm to converge to the global optimal solution is around 100, which is consistent with what can be achieved using GA and ASA for this type of one-dimensional optimisation.

Example 2. The IIR filter with transfer function $H_M(z)$ was used to identify the system with transfer function $H_S(z)$ by minimising the mean square error (MSE) $J(\mathbf{u})$, where

$$H_S(z) = \frac{0.05 - 0.4z^{-1}}{1 - 1.1314z^{-1} + 0.25z^{-2}}, \; H_M(z) = \frac{a_0}{1 + b_1 z^{-1}} \tag{7}$$

and $\mathbf{u} = [a_0 \; b_1]^T$. When the system input is white and the noise is absent, the MSE cost function has a global minimum at $\mathbf{u}_{\text{global}} = [-0.311 \; -0.906]^T$ with the value of the normalised MSE 0.2772 and a local minimum at $\mathbf{u}_{\text{local}} = [0.114 \; 0.519]^T$ with the normalised MSE value 0.9762 [11]. In the population initialisation, the parameters were uniformly randomly chosen as $(a_0, b_1) \in (-1.0, 1.0) \times (-0.999, 0.999)$. It was found empirically that $P_S = 4$, $\xi_B = 0.05$ $N_G > 15$ were appropriate, and Fig. 2 (a) depicts convergence performance of the RWBS algorithm averaged over 100 experiments. The previous study [6] applied the ASA to this example. The result of using the ASA is reproduced in Fig. 2 (b) for comparison. The distribution of the solutions obtained in 100 experiments by the RWBS algorithm is shown in Fig. 3.

Example 3. For this 2nd-order IIR filter design, the system and filter transfer functions are given by

$$H_S(z) = \frac{-0.3 + 0.4z^{-1} - 0.5z^{-2}}{1 - 1.2z^{-1} + 0.5z^{-2} - 0.1z^{-3}}, \; H_M(z) = \frac{a_0 + a_1 z^{-1}}{1 + b_1 z^{-1} + b_2 z^{-2}} \tag{8}$$

respectively. In the simulation, the system input was a uniformly distributed white sequence, taking values from $(-1, 1)$, and the signal to noise ratio was SNR=30 dB.

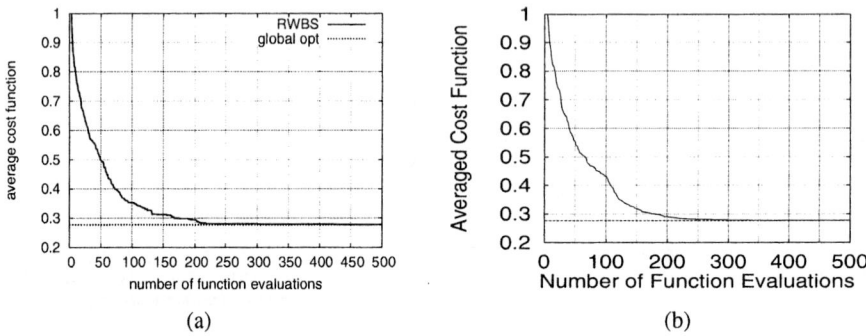

Fig. 2. Convergence performance averaged over 100 experiments for the 1st-order IIR filter design: (a) using the RWBS, and (b) using the ASA.

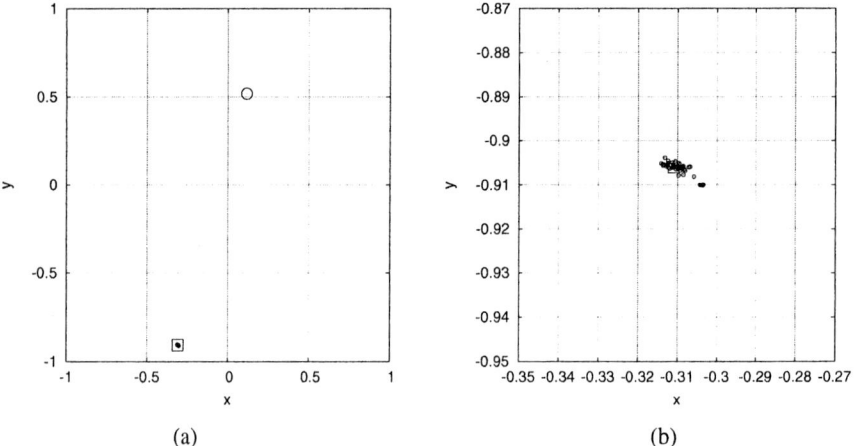

Fig. 3. Distribution of solutions (a_0, b_1) (small circles) obtained in 100 experiments for the 1st-order IIR filter design by the RWBS: (a) showing the entire search space, and (b) zooming in the global minimum, where large square indicate the global minimum and large circle the local minimum.

The data length used in calculating the MSE cost function was 2000. The MSE for this example was multi-modal and the gradient-based algorithm performed poorly as was demonstrated clearly in [6]. In the actual optimisation, the lattice form of the IIR filter was used, and the filter coefficient vector used in optimisation was $\mathbf{u} = [a_0\ a_1\ \kappa_0\ \kappa_1]^T$, where κ_0 and κ_1 are the lattice-form reflection coefficients. In the population initialisation, the parameters were uniformly randomly chosen as $a_i \in (-1.0, 1.0)$ and $\kappa_i \in (-0.999, 0.999)$ for $i = 0, 1$. It was found out that $N_B = 10$, $\xi_B = 0.05$ and $N_G > 20$ were appropriate for the RWBS algorithm, and Fig. 4 (a) depicts convergence performance of the RWBS algorithm averaged over 500 experiments. In [6], convergence performance using the ASA was obtained by averaging over 100 experiments, and this result is also re-plotted in Fig. 4 (b) as a comparison. The distribution

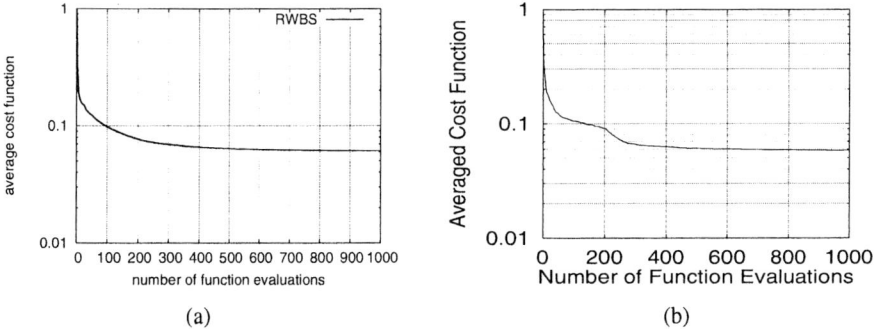

Fig. 4. Convergence performance for the 2nd-order IIR filter design: (a) using the RWBS averaged over 500 experiments, and (b) using the ASA averaged over 100 experiments.

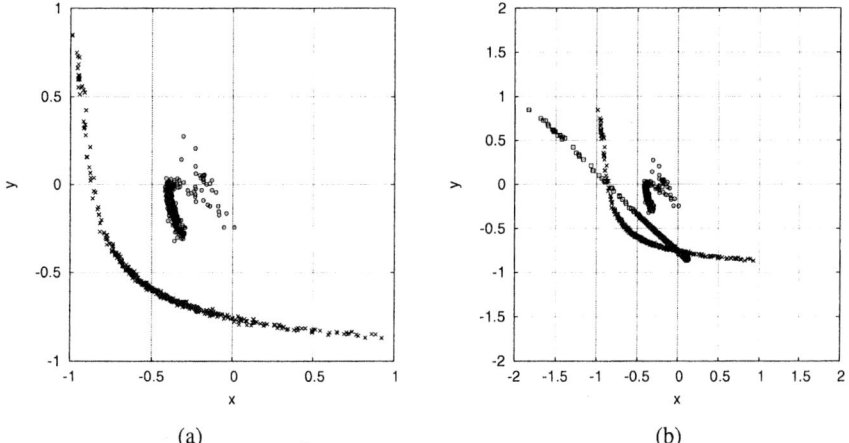

Fig. 5. Distribution of the solutions obtained in 500 experiments for the 2nd-order IIR filter design by the RWBS: (a) showing (a_0, a_1) as circles and (κ_0, κ_1) as crosses, and (b) showing (a_0, a_1) as circles, (b_1, b_2) as squares, and (κ_0, κ_1) as crosses.

of the solutions obtained in 500 experiments by the RWBS is illustrated in Fig. 5. It is clear that for this example there are infinitely many global minima, and the global minimum solutions for (b_1, b_2) form a one-dimensional space.

Example 4. Consider a blind joint maximum likelihood (ML) channel estimation and data detection for the single-input multiple-output (SIMO) system that employs a single transmitter antenna and $L \ (> 1)$ receiver antennas. In a SIMO system, the symbol-rate sampled antennas' outputs $x_l(k)$, $1 \leq l \leq L$, are given by

$$x_l(k) = \sum_{i=0}^{n_c-1} c_{i,l} s(k-i) + n_l(k) \tag{9}$$

where $n_l(k)$ is the complex-valued Gaussian white noise associated with the lth channel and $E[|n_l(k)|^2] = 2\sigma_n^2$, $\{s(k)\}$ is the transmitted symbol sequence taking values from the quadrature phase shift keying (QPSK) symbol set $\{\pm 1 \pm j\}$, and $c_{i,l}$ are the channel impulse response (CIR) taps associated with the lth receive antenna. Let

$$\begin{aligned} \mathbf{x} &= [x_1(1)\, x_1(2) \cdots x_1(N)\, x_2(1) \cdots x_L(1)\, x_L(2) \cdots x_L(N)]^T \\ \mathbf{s} &= [s(-n_c+2) \cdots s(0)\, s(1) \cdots s(N)]^T \\ \mathbf{c} &= [c_{0,1}\, c_{1,1} \cdots c_{n_c-1,1}\, c_{0,2} \cdots c_{0,L}\, c_{1,L} \cdots c_{n_c-1,L}]^T \end{aligned} \qquad (10)$$

be the vector of $N \times L$ received signal samples, the corresponding transmitted data sequence and the vector of the SIMO CIRs, respectively. The probability density function of the received data vector $\mathbf{x}$ conditioned on $\mathbf{c}$ and $\mathbf{s}$ is

$$p(\mathbf{x}|\mathbf{c},\mathbf{s}) = \frac{1}{(2\pi\sigma_n^2)^{NL}} e^{-\frac{1}{2\sigma_n^2}\sum_{k=1}^{N}\sum_{l=1}^{L}\left|x_l(k) - \sum_{i=0}^{n_c-1} c_{i,l} s(k-i)\right|^2} \qquad (11)$$

The joint ML estimate of $\mathbf{c}$ and $\mathbf{s}$ is obtained by maximising $p(\mathbf{x}|\mathbf{c},\mathbf{s})$ over $\mathbf{c}$ and $\mathbf{s}$ jointly. Equivalently, the joint ML estimate is the minimum of the cost function

$$J_{\mathrm{ML}}(\hat{\mathbf{c}},\hat{\mathbf{s}}) = \frac{1}{N}\sum_{k=1}^{N}\sum_{l=1}^{L}\left|x_l(k) - \sum_{i=0}^{n_c-1}\hat{c}_{i,l}\hat{s}(k-i)\right|^2 \qquad (12)$$

The joint minimisation process $(\hat{\mathbf{c}}^*, \hat{\mathbf{s}}^*) = \arg\left[\min_{\hat{\mathbf{c}},\hat{\mathbf{s}}} J_{\mathrm{ML}}(\hat{\mathbf{c}},\hat{\mathbf{s}})\right]$ can be solved iteratively first over the data sequences $\hat{\mathbf{s}}$ and then over all the possible channels $\hat{\mathbf{c}}$:

$$(\hat{\mathbf{c}}^*, \hat{\mathbf{s}}^*) = \arg\left[\min_{\hat{\mathbf{c}}} \left(\min_{\hat{\mathbf{s}}} J_{\mathrm{ML}}(\hat{\mathbf{c}},\hat{\mathbf{s}})\right)\right] \qquad (13)$$

The inner optimisation can readily be carried out using the Viterbi algorithm (VA). We employ the RWBS algorithm to perform the outer optimisation task, and the proposed blind joint ML optimisation scheme can be summarised as follows.

Outer level Optimisation. The RWBS searches the SIMO channel parameter space to find a global optimal estimate $\hat{\mathbf{c}}^*$ by minimising the MSE $J_{\mathrm{MSE}}(\hat{\mathbf{c}}) = J_{\mathrm{ML}}(\hat{\mathbf{c}}, \tilde{\mathbf{s}}^*)$.
Inner level optimisation. Given the channel estimate $\hat{\mathbf{c}}$, the VA provides the ML decoded data sequence $\tilde{\mathbf{s}}^*$, and feeds back the corresponding value of the likelihood metric $J_{\mathrm{ML}}(\hat{\mathbf{c}}, \tilde{\mathbf{s}}^*)$ to the upper level.

The SIMO CIRs, listed in Table 1, were simulated with the data length $N = 50$. In practice, the value of $J_{\mathrm{MSE}}(\hat{\mathbf{c}})$ is all that the upper level optimiser can see, and the convergence of the algorithm can only be observed through this MSE. In simulation, the performance of the algorithm can also be assessed by the mean tap error defined as

$$\mathrm{MTE} = \|\mathbf{c} - a \cdot \hat{\mathbf{c}}\|^2 \qquad (14)$$

where

$$a = \begin{cases} \pm 1, & \text{if } \hat{\mathbf{c}} \to \pm \mathbf{c} \\ \mp j, & \text{if } \hat{\mathbf{c}} \to \pm j\mathbf{c} \end{cases} \qquad (15)$$

Table 1. The simulated SIMO system

l	Channel impulse response		
1	0.365-0.274j	0.730+0.183j	-0.440+0.176j
2	0.278+0.238j	-0.636+0.104j	0.667-0.074j
3	-0.639+0.249j	-0.517-0.308j	0.365+0.183j
4	-0.154+0.693j	-0.539-0.077j	0.268-0.358j

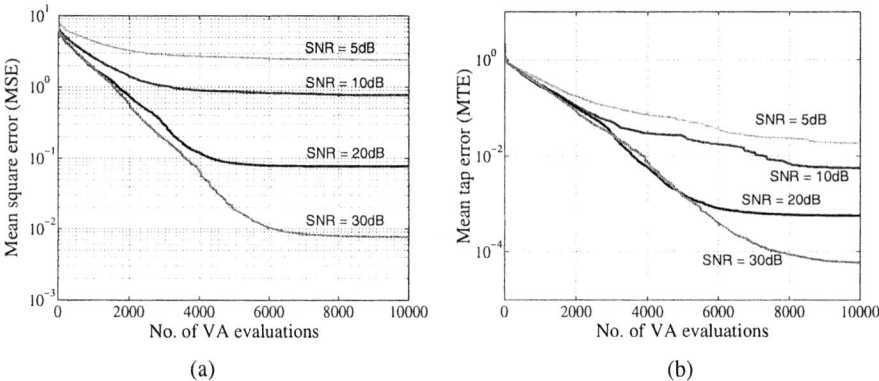

Fig. 6. Convergence performance of blind joint ML estimation using the RWBS averaged over 50 runs: (a) MSE and (b) MTE against number of VA evaluations.

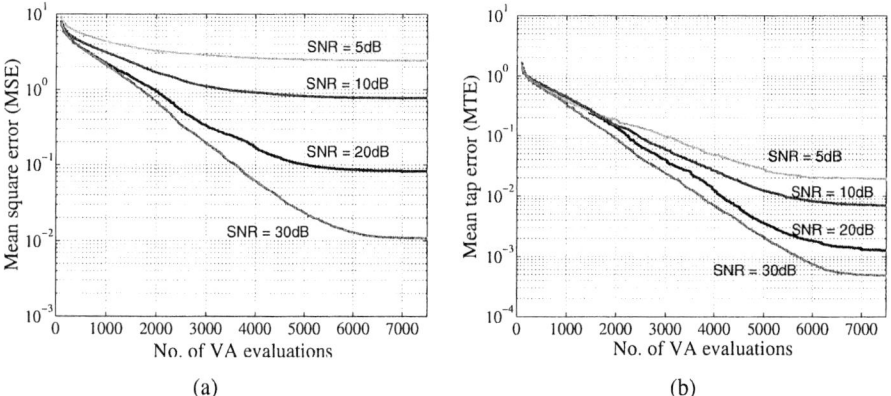

Fig. 7. Convergence performance of blind joint ML estimation using the GA averaged over 50 runs: (a) MSE and (b) MTE against number of VA evaluations.

Note that since $(\hat{\mathbf{c}}^*, \hat{\mathbf{s}}^*)$, $(-\hat{\mathbf{c}}^*, -\hat{\mathbf{s}}^*)$, $(-j\hat{\mathbf{c}}^*, +j\hat{\mathbf{s}}^*)$ and $(+j\hat{\mathbf{c}}^*, -j\hat{\mathbf{s}}^*)$ are all the solutions of the joint ML estimation problem, the channel estimate $\hat{\mathbf{c}}$ can converges to $\mathbf{c}$, $-\mathbf{c}$, $j\mathbf{c}$ or $-j\mathbf{c}$. Fig. 6 shows the evolutions of the MSE and MTE averaged over 50 runs and for different values of signal to noise ratio (SNR), obtained by the blind joint ML optimisation scheme using the RWBS. From Fig. 6, it can be seen that the MSE converged to the noise floor. We also investigated using the GA to perform the upper-level optimisation, and the results obtained by this GA-based blind joint ML estimation scheme are presented in Fig. 7. It is worth pointing out that the dimension of the search space was $n = 24$ for this example.

4 Conclusions

A guided random search optimisation algorithm has been proposed. The local optimiser in this global search method evolves a population of the potential solutions by forming a convex combination of the solution population with boosting adaptation. A repeating loop involving a combined elitist and random sampling initialisation strategy is adopted to guarantee a fast global convergence. The proposed guided random search method, referred to as the RWBS, is remarkably simple, involving minimum software programming effort and having very few algorithmic parameters that require tuning. The versatility of the proposed method has been demonstrated using several examples, and the results obtained show that the proposed global search algorithm is as efficient as the GA and ASA in terms of global convergence speed, characterised by the total number of cost function evaluations required to attend a global optimal solution.

Acknowledgement

S. Chen wish to thank the support of the United Kingdom Royal Academy of Engineering.

References

1. J.H. Holland, *Adaptation in Natural and Artificial Systems*. University of Michigan Press: Ann Arbor, MI, 1975.
2. D.E. Goldberg, *Genetic Algorithms in Search, Optimization and Machine Learning*. Addison Wesley: Reading, MA, 1989.
3. L. Davis, Ed., *Handbook of Genetic Algorithms*. Van Nostrand Reinhold: New York, 1991.
4. A. Corana, M. Marchesi, C. Martini and S. Ridella, "Minimizing multimodal functions of continuous variables with the simulated annealing algorithm," *ACM Trans. Mathematical Software*, Vol.13, No.3, pp.262–280, 1987.
5. L. Ingber and B. Rosen, "Genetic algorithms and very fast simulated reannealing: a comparison," *Mathematical and Computer Modelling*, Vol.16, No.11, pp.87–100, 1992.
6. S. Chen and B.L. Luk, "Adaptive simulated annealing for optimization in signal processing applications," *Signal Processing*, Vol.79, No.1, pp.117–128, 1999.
7. R.E. Schapire, "The strength of weak learnability," *Machine Learning*, Vol.5, No.2, pp.197–227, 1990.
8. Y. Freund and R.E. Schapire, "A decision-theoretic generalization of on-line learning and an application to boosting," *J. Computer and System Sciences*, Vol.55, No.1, pp.119–139, 1997.
9. R. Meir and G. Rätsch, "An introduction to boosting and leveraging," in: S. Mendelson and A. Smola, eds., *Advanced Lectures in Machine Learning*. Springer Verlag, 2003, pp.119–184.
10. F. Schoen, "Stochastic techniques for global optimization: a survey of recent advances," *J. Global Optimization*, Vol.1, pp.207–228, 1991.
11. J.J. Shynk, "Adaptive IIR filtering," *IEEE ASSP Magazine*, pp.4–21, April 1989.

Selection, Space and Diversity: What Can Biological Speciation Tell Us About the Evolution of Modularity?

Suzanne Sadedin

School of Computer Science and Software Engineering, Monash University,
Vic. 3800, Australia
suzanne.sadedin@gmail.com

Abstract. Modularity is a widespread form of organization in complex systems, but its origins are poorly understood. Here, I discuss the causes and consequences of modularity in evolutionary systems. Almost all living organisms engage in sexual exchange of genes, and those that do so are organized into discrete modules we call species. Gene exchange occurs within, but not between, species. This genetic segregation allows organisms to adapt to different niches and environments, and thereby evolve complex and long-lasting ecosystems. The process that generates such modularity, speciation, is therefore the key to understanding the diversity of life. Speciation theory is a highly developed topic within population genetics and evolutionary theory. I discuss some lessons from recent progress in speciation theory for our understanding of diversification and modularity in complex systems more generally, including possible applications in genetic algorithms, artificial life and social engineering.

1 Introduction

Many systems exhibit modular structure. By this I mean that their underlying units interact within discrete subsystems, rather than with the system as a whole (a number of other definitions are possible, mostly related to engineering and therefore less relevant to understanding natural systems [1-4]). Such modular structures appear to be a very general consequence of adaptive evolution at a wide range of scales[1,5-7]. By allowing differentiation of components within complex systems, modular structure is a key factor in the behavior of complex systems[1-4]. However, the principles governing the origins of modular structure in complex systems remain poorly understood [3,4]. Here, I discuss the evolutionary origins of one of the best-studied forms of modularity in nature, the biological species, and its implications for our understanding of ecological and evolutionary systems. It is shown that the evolution of genetic modularity has some important lessons for our understanding of modularity and diversification in complex systems in general.

1.1 What Is Modularity?

A system can be described as modular when its components form hierarchically organized, interacting subsystems[1-4]. For example, a road traffic system can be decomposed into interacting vehicles in a spatial environment, and each vehicle can then be decomposed into wheels, engines, brakes, each of which can itself be broken down into lower-level components, ultimately to the level of subatomic particles. Thus, modules are units within a system that are themselves composed of lower level units. Secondly, these lower level units interact primarily within their own module, and their sole significant effect with regard to understanding the system is to induce a state change of that module[2,3]. The module as a whole interacts with other modules, depending on its state. In this sense, each module can be considered as a "black box" for the purpose of understanding the functioning of the system at a higher level. We need know nothing about interactions at the subatomic, atomic or molecular levels, or even the behavior of the braking and acceleration systems, in order to understand traffic dynamics. We can collapse all of these subsystems into an attribute of each car – its speed – without losing any generality in our understanding of traffic dynamics.

It should be noted that modularity is relative to the system we are interested in. Cars are modular relative to traffic dynamics. They are not necessarily modular relative to air flow, magnetism, pollution, or many other features.

1.2 Complex Systems, Network Theory, Emergence and Modularity

The terms complexity and emergence should be mentioned because they are commonly used to describe systems that exhibit modularity [3-6, 8]. Systems that are composed of a large number of interacting units are often called "complex systems", especially when the behavior of the units is not always uniform and leads to different or surprising outcomes at larger scales [3-6, 8]. The latter phenomenon is sometimes termed emergence [8-9]. In practice these definitions are subjective. They describe our perception of system behavior, rather than an objective attribute of the system.

For example, a table is not usually considered a complex system, but it is composed of many units (atoms), the behavior of these atoms is not always uniform (they are usually, but not always, maintained in a stable configuration), and they have a collective outcome which might sometimes surprise us (the table mostly holds things up, but sometimes breaks or falls over).

Defining complex systems in terms of modularity does not resolve the definition problem: many systems that are not widely considered complex are modular with regard to some function. A table can be decomposed into modules (legs, nails and surface), each of which can be decomposed further, but whose underlying structure is generally irrelevant to understanding the system of table behaviour. As long as we understand that the table legs support (or fail to support) the table surface, we do not need to understand whether they are made of steel or wood. Thus, modularity is not a measure of complexity, although it is a common feature of systems usually described as complex.

It is often useful to view systems as networks of interacting elements [10-11]. From this perspective, modules are highly connected subsystems that share few connections with other such subsystems [11]. In network theory highly connected subsystems are termed clusters, and clustering can be measured as a continuous parameter [10-11]. In modular systems, connections within modules are qualitatively different from connections between modules [10]. This is not necessarily the case in clustering systems. Thus, modules are clusters, but not all clusters are modules. Clustering behaviour can be generated quite easily in networks, especially through scale-free growth patterns [10-11]. However, known growth patterns do not generate the functional differentiation that is observed in modular systems [11].

2 Species as Modules

The definition suggested above implies that modules are not objective phenomena, but exist only in relation to a system. Therefore, in deciding whether species are modules, we must first specify the system within which they might form modules. I will discuss two possible systems, ecology and evolution, and the commonalities between them.

2.1 Species as Ecological Modules

Species are not clearly modular in an ecological sense. Animals and plants interact with their environment as separate individuals, not as an aggregate of their species. Although the outcomes of these individual interactions may be viewed from an aggregate perspective, the aggregate view may be a human construction rather than a natural feature of the system.

We can draw a food web that describes which species eats which within a certain ecosystem, for example, foxes eat rabbits. Such a drawing is a usable hierarchical abstraction of the relationships between different organisms. However, it may be a mistake to assume that such an abstraction actually reflects an underlying modular structure. The fox species as a whole does not eat the rabbit species as a whole: rather, individual fox units eat individual rabbit units. Thus the interaction between rabbits and foxes is an interaction between many distinct units of two basic types, rather than an interaction between modules. The principle that units within a module interact primarily with one another, rather than with units belonging to other modules, appears to be violated.

Although rabbits and foxes are not modular in this sense, there may nonetheless be a system of interactions between the rabbit and fox species which can be understood from a modular perspective. It may not matter that individual foxes eat individual rabbits if there is an efficient way to summaries the interactions between all rabbits and all foxes with respect to the system in which we are interested. The assumption that ecological interactions can be summarized in this way is necessary for notions such as ecosystems and food webs to have any validity beyond mere description.

2.2 Consequences of Species Modularity in Ecology

There is a tension in ecological literature between these two viewpoints. The ecosystem view sees species as modules existing in tightly coupled interactions with other species [12-19]. In contrast, neutral theory sees species as aggregates of individuals, all separately interacting [20-21]. In the neutral view, food webs are descriptions of how interactions generally happen to occur, but they do not describe a system that can be analyzed in any meaningful way, because the interactions between individuals overwhelm interactions happening at the species level. In the ecosystem view, interactions can be meaningfully analyzed at the species level. The ecosystem view tends to assume that species interactions attain some form of dynamic equilibrium, in which each species plays a consistent role, while neutral theory focuses on non-equilibrium dynamics [22-23]. In their most extreme form, ecosystem models take the form of the

Gaia hypothesis, which proposes that ecosystems form self-sustaining complex adaptive systems [24-26].

The debate about whether species form ecological modules is far from resolved: current empirical evidence suggests that both neutral and ecosystem dynamics are important [27]. The ecological literature contains good examples of both highly specialized ecological feedback loops, and non-equilibrium neutral ecological dynamics, and few large-scale data sets are capable of distinguishing between the two models. Perhaps we need a theory that can unify these perspectives, allowing species to have varying degrees of modularity.

2.3 Species as Evolutionary Modules

At the evolutionary level, the view of species as modules is less dubious. Evolutionary systems are constituted by the interactions that determine the movement of genes within populations. Sexual reproduction implies that genes do not remain in fixed relationships with one another: instead, genes move into a new genetic environment every time sexual reproduction occurs. We term the net movement of genes within natural populations gene flow [28].

Gene flow occurs within, but not between, species. In 1942, Ernst Mayr proposed his biological species concept, which states, in its short form:

"Species are groups of actually or potentially interbreeding natural populations, which are reproductively isolated from other such groups." [28]

Much subsequent debate has centered on what exactly reproductive isolation might entail [29-30]. However, Mayr's essential concept that species are units defined by the limits of gene flow is widely accepted and often regarded as one of the major advances of evolutionary theory during the 20th century.

Gene flow occurs slowly, over generations. Day to day interactions between individuals are therefore not as important to gene flow as they are to ecology. What is important for gene flow is the average outcome from those interactions. For example, to understand cheetah population dynamics, we need to understand not only that cheetahs eat gazelles, but that competition from lions and hyenas limits the spatial range cheetahs can occupy; that gazelles rely on pasture, which is also spatially and seasonally limited, and numerous other interactions. However, to understand the evolutionary impact of cheetahs on gazelles, we need to know only the average impact of the cheetah gene pool on the gazelle gene pool: cheetahs generate a net selection pressure on gazelles, and vice versa. In this sense, treating species as modules from an evolutionary perspective is much more clearly justifiable than treating species as modules from an ecological perspective.

2.4 Punctuated Equilibrium and Species Modularity

The view that species function as evolutionary modules potentially has some major consequences for our understanding of evolution. This is reflected in the great debate between neo-Darwinian and punctuated equilibrium theorists. Species modularity opens the door for the controversial process of selection at multiple scales, a necessary component of punctuated equilibrium as championed by Gould [31].

The view that selection can operate at the level of species as well as individuals is often regarded as nonsensical in neo-Darwinian theory for the following reason [32]. Selection at the species level occurs on a vastly slower timescale than selection at the individual level. It is, therefore, comparatively very weak. Moreover, most genes that are advantageous at the species level are also advantageous for the individual. Therefore, any consequences of species selection are likely to be trivial, and overwhelmed by selection at the level of the individual. This makes species-level selection in general untestable and therefore unscientific [32].

Gould, on the other hand, argued that after some form of perturbation, species rapidly evolve to an equilibrium state in nature [31]. Evolution to equilibrium is governed by natural selection at the individual level, as argued by the neo-Darwinian theorists. However, adaptive variations should percolate through a population quite rapidly even with weak selection, and mutations are rare. Therefore, most of the time, there will be no significant variation in adaptive traits, and therefore no natural selection. Species will remain in an equilibrium evolutionary state, unable to evolve new adaptations because the necessary variation is absent. However, they will compete with other species for space and resources, and species with superior design features will ultimately drive less efficiently adapted ones to extinction. Thus in Gould's model, selection occurs primarily at the species level.

Part of the confusion between these two viewpoints results from a conflation of scales [33]. Neo-Darwinians are interested in relating quantifiable population genetic processes to observable current evolutionary processes. Therefore, they tend to regard macroscopic evolution as something that cannot be studied in anything more than a historical sense. Paleontologists, on the other hand, are interested in the processes that generate the fossil record. The fossil record reflects only a tiny proportion of species, and only limited aspects of those species. This limitation means that paleontologists are intensely interested in the processes that generate macroscopic structures in evolution – about which neo-Darwinian theory has very little to say.

We can caricature this debate, with even-handed unfairness to both sides, as follows. Suppose a tree-dwelling mammal species has split into two forms. One of these forms has skin-flaps that are useful for aerodynamic control during leaps between trees. The other has bristles that perform the same function. Neo-Darwinians are interested in the gene-level selection process that leads to bristle and skin flap production, and the process of diversification that means bristly animals lack skin-flaps, and vice versa. Paleontologists are interested in the processes that determine whether, in the long term, animals with skin-flaps become abundant and diverse, and ultimately produce new adaptations, while animals with bristles disappear. From the paleontological perspective, it therefore makes sense to think about whether skin flaps are selected over bristles, that is, whether skin flaps are ultimately a better or worse path to aerodynamic control. This is species-level selection because there is no gene-level competition between skin-flaps and bristles: they occur in separate evolutionary lineages. From the neo-Darwinian perspective, such analysis appears excessively speculative: species with skin flaps may have succeeded while species with bristles went extinct for any number of reasons, which may or may not have anything to do with skin flaps.

However, this difference of scale also leads to a philosophical divergence that permeates the interaction between evolutionary biology and other disciplines. If species are discrete, relatively stable units, occasionally passing through brief but dramatic periods of diversification and adaptation, then the ecosystem view becomes highly plausible. If, on the other hand, species are loose, fluctuating aggregations of genes, maintained by competing feedback processes but in a state of permanent disequilibrium, then ecosystems make far less sense. The more modular our perception of species, the more we move towards the punctuated equilibrium side of the debate; the less modular, the more we are inclined to the neo-Darwinian view. Table 1 summarizes this dispute.

Table 1. Consequences of modular and non-modular views of species

Aspect	Modular view	Non-modular view
Species interactions	Tightly coupled, no significant variation within species (specialists)	Loose and interchangeable (generalists)
Ecological dynamics	Equilibrium, self-maintaining, generally stable	Non-equilibrium, illusion of stability caused by limited human perspective
Food webs	Accurate representations of system dynamics that can be analyzed in their own right	Descriptive snapshots of what is happening at a certain time and place
Environment	Stable/predictable (except at boundaries)	Unstable/unpredictable
Evolution	Punctuated equilibrium	Gradualist

3 How Do Species Form?

Understanding speciation is one of the major theoretical challenges of evolutionary biology [28]. Among sexually reproducing organisms, genetic recombination continually breaks down associations between genes, so that genes that are mutually incompatible, even if harmless in themselves, are unlikely to persist within a sexual population. Consequently, through recombination, a high degree of self-compatibility is thought to be maintained within sexual populations. Speciation requires that this homogenizing force of gene flow be overcome. Gene flow can be restricted either by the spatial environment or by genetic changes; genetic changes are almost always required at some point (except possibly in the case of *Wolbachia* bacterial infection [34]). However, the importance of spatial isolation has been disputed throughout the history of speciation theory.

3.1 Isolation in Space

Geographic isolation (allopatry) can cause genetic divergence, because genes that could become incompatible together can evolve freely in separated populations [28]. Provided spatial separation continues for a sufficient number of generations, genetic drift and possibly founder effects and natural selection acting on the separated populations inevitably lead to the evolution of such incompatibilities between the two populations [35-36]. The evolution of co-adapted gene complexes through natural selection occurs separately within each population. Mate choice systems may also diverge when populations are spatially separated, such that hybridization does not occur when contact between populations is resumed. Eventually, the populations reach a point where successful interbreeding no longer occurs when they are once again in contact; mating between members of different populations may not occur, or hybrids may be ecologically or behaviorally impaired, inviable, or sterile. This process is referred to as allopatric speciation [28].

The converse possibility is sympatric speciation, in which reproductive isolation evolves within populations sharing a single habitat area [28]. Speciation without spatial separation remains controversial because no single, widespread mechanism opposes the homogenizing force of genetic recombination. However, recent theoretical work, as well as evidence from a variety of natural populations, shows that speciation without spatial isolation can and almost certainly does occur, albeit under relatively restrictive conditions [37].

In most cases that have been studied, it appears that spatial isolation is neither absolute nor insignificant [38-39]. Rather, genetic discontinuities occur within continuous populations where gene flow is restricted. In general, it is unclear whether hybridizing populations were previously completely geographically isolated, but have resumed contact before the evolution of complete reproductive isolation, or have always been in limited contact, as the geographic patterns produced by the two histories are usually indistinguishable [38]. Gene flow can be restricted geographically by a partial barrier, such as a mountain range that crosses a large proportion of the species range, a channel between a continent and an island, an area of sub-optimal habitat, or an ecotone with a strong selection gradient.

3.2 Isolation Without Space

There are, in addition to geographic barriers, potential barriers to gene flow that do not require any population-level geographic separation. These factors increase the probability of a member of a particular population mating with a member of its own population rather than another population. Positive assortative mating, the tendency for like to mate with like, is commonly observed and can be caused by a variety of factors such as:

- sexual competition: for example among calanoid copepods larger males are more successful in competing for access to preferred larger females;
- temporal differentiation, such as differentiation of flowering times in plants [40], or daily cycles of pheromone release in aphids [41];
- microhabitat differentiation, for example in pea aphids that prefer different feeding substrates, and tend to mate where they feed [42];
- learned social preferences. Zebrafish prefer shoaling partners whose pigmentation matches that of their early experience and tend to mate with their shoaling partners [43]. Similarly vocalizations used by both male and female crows are thought to contribute to assortative mating through homotypic flocking [44];
- sexual imprinting, where offspring learn mating preferences and displays from their parents [45].

Such limitations on gene flow are likely to occur in a wide range of populations. However, they seem, in themselves, unlikely to be sufficient to lead to speciation by drift alone. There are theoretical arguments [46] that gene flow must be extremely low in order for incipient species to persist. Two selective mechanisms can lead to strong genetic divergence in populations with little or no spatial isolation. These are disruptive ecological selection and sexual selection.

3.3 Ecological Speciation

Ecological speciation, which proposes that speciation results from disruptive natural selection, is generally accepted despite a lack of strong empirical data distinguishing between ecological and non-selection-based mechanisms of speciation [37, 47]. The reason for this acceptance is that models suggest that ecological speciation is highly likely and will occur very rapidly under very general conditions even in sympatry [39,48-50], provided it is combined with sexual selection (see below). In contrast, speciation by drift is expected to be slow even in optimum conditions and likely to be prevented altogether in spatially connected populations because it requires that two incompatible alleles be simultaneously present, but not ubiquitous in populations [39,51]. Because the average time between the origin and extinction or fixation of neutral incompatibility-causing alleles is likely to be orders of magnitude smaller than the mutation rate, simultaneous coexistence of such alleles is thought to be relatively unlikely [39]. However, inclusion of a spatial dimension in modeling may considerably modify this prediction because it can result in the indefinite persistence of neutral genetic variation.

3.4 Isolation by Sexual Selection

The possibility of speciation by sexual selection was first considered by Fisher in 1930 [52]. Sexual selection was first proposed by Darwin in 1871 as an explanation for conspicuous sexual advertisements by male animals, such as peacock tails [53]. If, by chance, a proportion of a population happens to prefer a certain arbitrary trait for mating, then individuals possessing that trait will be chosen as mates more often, and consequently produce more offspring, than individuals who lack the trait. Moreover, these offspring will have a high probability of inheriting not only the trait, but the preference as well. Thus both the preference and the trait automatically become adaptive and associated with one another. In this way an initially arbitrary mating preference can generate rapid positive feedback between selection on traits and selection on mating preferences. This positive feedback process is potentially a cause of rapid and powerful evolutionary change (termed "runaway sexual selection") [52]. From a complex systems perspective, sexual selection is self-organizing within a population through the non-linearity of the selective process.

If sexual selection can lead to mating preferences and traits diverging between populations, then speciation might be self-organizing. This is an idea many researchers find appealing. In addition to sexual selection speciation models that assume populations have limited spatial interactions [54-55], several recent models have developed the concept of speciation by sexual selection without spatial isolation. However, there are strong constraints on the generality of this idea [56-58] and field evidence is ambiguous [59]. The view that runaway sexual selection contributes to speciation events that also involve other forms of genetic divergence is less controversial [60]. In this model, speciation is initiated by ecological divergence or drift in geographic isolation, but selection against hybridization initiates runaway sexual selection for divergent mate choice systems when the populations are in contact.

A much-debated question, whose resolution is required as part of a general theory of speciation involving sexual selection, is how preferences can be maintained in the face of realistic costs to mate choice, a problem termed the "paradox of the lek". As sexual selection proceeds, variation in display traits disappears, and positive selection for preferences consequently ceases. One model shows that costly preferences can be maintained when display traits are costly also and dependent on many loci [62]. In addition, it has been found that costly mating preferences and varying displays and preferences were usually maintained in a spatially explicit model provided the optimum male phenotype varied between localities [63].

Despite this theoretical problem, the evidence that sexual selection contributes greatly to speciation is unambiguous. In areas where populations hybridize, the parental populations retain a separate genetic identity only when different mate choice systems have evolved [64]. Species that share the same environment tend to discriminate more strongly against potential mates belonging to the other species than do species that live in different environments [65]. Indeed, some reviewers argue that divergence of mate choice systems is virtually essential for speciation [66].

3.5 Summary of Speciation Theory

Modes of speciation can be broadly classified in two ways.

1. By the spatial arrangement and consequent level of interaction of speciating populations. This includes:
   - Allopatric (no interaction);
   - Parapatric (interaction across a linear interface);
   - Sympatric (populations interact without geographic restriction).
2. By the mechanism driving speciation. Mechanisms include
   - Genetic drift (includes founder and chromosomal speciation, and speciation by chance accumulation of genetic incompatibilities);
   - Sexual selection (termed reinforcement when combined with another mechanism);
   - Disruptive natural selection on ecological traits (with or without a spatially varying component);
   - Disruptive natural selection acting on mate choice system traits. This scenario can simplify the evolution of prezygotic isolation.

Any of the above mechanisms can in principle be combined with any spatial arrangement. More than one mechanism may operate in the same speciation event, and spatial arrangements may change over time [38]. This makes empirical testing of models difficult. Most models agree that speciation should be most likely in populations with greater spatial separation (but see [56, 67]), and where there is natural and/or sexual selection rather than drift alone. In addition, empirical evidence strongly suggests that sexual selection is usually important, if not essential, for speciation [64-66].

4 What Can Speciation Teach Us About Module Formation?

Several of the findings discussed above have more general implications for the study of modularity in natural and artificial systems.

- Modularity has important consequences. I have tried to show how the question of whether species are modules, and of what systems, is central to a major dichotomy in current evolutionary and ecological thinking.
- Modules arise in genetic systems mainly through selection pressure, not through passive drift. This selection can be generated either internally (through sexual selection) or externally (through disruptive selection in the environment).
- Sexual selection is more powerful than natural selection in inducing modularity.
- Inclusion of spatial dimensions greatly facilitates evolution of modularity. Under most conditions, populations that are not distributed in some form of spatial environment will not form discrete modules.
- The absence of ecological competition is not always a good thing for module formation. In fact, if diverging populations are not permitted to evolve separate mate choice, ecological competition between them enhances their persistence by preventing spatial coexistence (Sadedin, in prep.).

4.1 Applications

A much-studied problem in the use of evolutionary algorithms is how to maintain variation in evolving solution populations to widely explore solution space and avoid convergence on local optima, while also allowing rapid adaptation [68-69]. Incorporating sexual selection and spatial dimensions in evolutionary algorithms may help in balancing these needs, permitting different solutions to take different evolutionary paths in problem-solving within the same domain.

Researchers in artificial life have sought to evolve ecologies that share the diversity of coexisting genetic modules seen in real biological systems. A common mistake in artificial life has been to assume that coexistence of different genetic modules will occur if separate ecological niches are created, that is, niche differentiation is a sufficient condition for speciation [70-72]. In fact, genetic recombination will tend to eliminate one evolving module unless spatial geometry and/or sexual selection are incorporated [54-58].

Conversely, it has often been assumed that separate niches, or separate adaptive peaks, are necessary for the evolution of differentiated modules [73-75]. This is not so. Diversification is entirely possible in connected spatial environments without separate ecological niches; indeed, separate niches may inhibit evolutionary diversification unless sexual selection is included [76-78].

In this paper I have considered the origin of modularity in biological genetic systems. It is possible, however, that other modular evolving systems have similar dynamics. One application may be in the self-segregation of human cultural groups.

Within cultural groups, ideas, attitudes and beliefs are exchanged and evolve over time. Incompatible views are often eliminated due to cognitive dissonance. Exchange of views between cultural groups is relatively restricted. Thus in an extreme form, cultures may form social modules. The exchange of ideas within, but not between, cultural groups may be analogous to the exchange of genes within, but not between, species [32]. If so, then speciation research may help us to understand the dynamics of social conflict and cultural diversity.

Very high social connectivity (i.e., high levels of communication) might prevent the evolution of co-adapted sets of ideas forming discrete social modules. This could reduce the global exploration of parameter space by human thought, thereby hindering human creativity. On the other hand, a lack of connectivity may lead to incompatibilities which manifest themselves as hostilities. The effects of this idea for technological innovation have been explored by [4].

Spatial isolation is clearly a factor in cultural diversification and module formation. Human social networks often display small-world dynamics, meaning that the connection distance between individuals is much smaller than geometric measures would suggest [79]. Although small-world dynamics often facilitate clustering, they also enhance information transmission [12-13, 80-81]. Small-world dynamics may therefore mitigate against formation of social modules, especially in modern societies with electronic communication.

A form of sexual selection may also operate within cultural modules, and enhance their isolation. This could occur through the promotion of signals of cultural allegiance. For example, a symbol of religious adherence is likely to be associated with a preferential receptivity to ideas originating in the same religious group. This could lead to the evolution of isolated subcultures even within highly socially connected environments. Manipulation of the evolution of such allegiance signals, and of dimensions of spatial isolation, may be an effective way to regulate cultural modularity.

References

1. Simon, H.: The Sciences of the Artificial. MIT Press, Cambridge (1996)
2. Baldwin, C., Clark, K.: Design Rules: The Power of Modularity. MIT Press, Cambridge (1999)
3. Fleming, L., Sorenson, O.: Technology as a complex adaptive system: evidence from patent data. Research Policy, 30 (2001) 1019-1039
4. Ethiraj, S.K., Levinthal, D.A.: Modularity and Innovation in Complex Systems. http://ssrn.com/abstract=459920
5. Wagner, G.P.: Adaptation and the modular design of organisms. In: Advances in Artificial Life. Springer-Verlag, New York (1995) 317–328
6. Wagner, G., Altenberg, L.: Perspective: Complex adaptations and the evolution of evolvability. Evolution **50** (1996) 967–976
7. Sperber, D.: In defense of massive modularity. In: Dupoux, E. Language, Brain and Cognitive Development: Essays in Honor of Jacques Mehler. MIT Press, Cambridge (2002) 47-57
8. Green, D.G., Sadedin, S.: Interactions matter—complexity in landscapes and ecosystems. Ecological Complexity (2005) in press
9. Green, D.G.: Emergent behaviour in biological systems. In: Green, D.G., Bossomaier, T. (eds.): Complex Systems: from Biology to Computation. IOS Press, Amsterdam (1993) 24-35

10. Ravasz, E., Somera, A.L., Mongru, D.A. Oltvai, Z.N.,, Barabási, A.L.: Hierarchical Organization of Modularity in Metabolic Networks. Science **297** (2002) 1551-1555
11. Radicchi, F., Castellano, C., Cecconi, F., Loreto, V., Parisi, D.: Defining and identifying communities in networks. Proc. Natl. Acad. Sci. USA **101** (2004) 2658–2663
12. Montoya, J.M., Solé, R.V.: Small world patterns in food webs. J. Theor. Biol. **214** (2002) 405–412
13. Watts, D.J., Strogatz, S.H.: Collective dynamics of 'small-world' networks. Nature **393** (1998) 440–442
14. Krause, A.E., Frank, K.A., Mason, D.M., Ulanowicz, R.E., Taylor, W.W.: Compartments revealed in food-web structure. Nature **426** (2003) 282–285
15. Newth, D., Lawrence, J., Green, D.G.: Emergent organization in dynamic networks. In: Namatame, A., Green, D., Aruka, Y., Sato, H. (eds.): Complex Systems 2002. Chuo University, Tokyo (2002) 229–237
16. Solé, R.V., Levin, S.: Preface. Philos. Trans. R. Soc. Lond. B **357** (2002) 617–618
17. Solé, R.V., Alonso, D., McKane, A.: Self-organized instability in complex ecosystems. Philos. Trans. R. Soc. Lond. B **357** (2002) 667–681
18. Levin, S.: Ecosystems and the biosphere as complex adaptive systems. Ecosystems **1** (1998) 431–436
19. McGill, B.J.: A test of the unified neutral theory of biodiversity. Nature **422** (2003) 881–885
20. Hubbell, S.: The Unified Neutral Theory of Biodiversity and Biogeography. Princeton University Press, Princeton (2001)
21. Volkov, I., Banavar, J.R., Hubbell, S.P., Maritan, A.: Neutral theory and relative species abundance in ecology. Nature **424** (2003) 1035–1037
22. Naeem, S.: The world according to niche. Trends Ecol. Evol. **18** (2003) 323–324
23. Nee, S., Stone, G.: The end of the beginning for neutral theory. Trends Ecol. Evol. **18** (2003) 433–434
24. Lovelock, J.E.: The Ages of Gaia. W.W. Norton and Company, New York (1998)
25. Kleidon, A.: Testing the effect of life on earth's functioning: how Gaian is Earth? Climatic Change **52** (2002) 383–389
26. Lenton, T.M., van Oijen, M.: Gaia as a complex adaptive system. Philos. Trans. R. Soc. Lond. B **357** (2002) 683–695
27. Poulin, R., Guegan, J.-F.: Nestedness, anti-nestedness, and the relationship between prevalence and intensity in ectoparasite assemblages of marine fish: a spatial model of species coexistence. Int. J. Parasitol. **30** (2000) 1147–1152
28. Mayr, E.: Systematics and the origin of species. Columbia University Press, N.Y. (1942)
29. Avise, J.C., Walker, D.: Abandon all species concepts? A response. Conservation Genetics **1** (2000) 77-80
30. Hendry, A.P., Wenburg, J.K., Bentzen, P., Volk, E.C., Quinn, T.P.: Rapid evolution of reproductive isolation in the wild: evidence from introduced salmon. Science **290** (2000) 516-518
31. Gould, S.J.: The Structure of Evolutionary Theory. Bellknap Press, Cambridge (2002)
32. Dawkins, R.: The Selfish Gene. Oxford University Press, New York (1976)
33. Gould, S.J., Eldredge, N.: Punctuated equilibrium comes of age. Nature **366** (1993) 223
34. Bordenstein, S.R., O'Hara, F.P., Werren, J.H.: Wolbachia-induced incompatibility precedes other hybrid incompatibilities in Nasonia. Nature **409** (2001) 707 – 710
35. Orr, H.A.: The population genetics of speciation: the evolution of hybrid incompatibilities. Genetics **139** (1995) 1805-1813

36. Turelli, M., Barton, N.H., Coyne, J.A.: Theory and speciation. Trends Ecol. Evol. **16** (2001) 330-342
37. Via, S.: Sympatric speciation in animals: the ugly duckling grows up. Trends Ecol. Evol. **16** (2001) 318-390
38. Endler, J.A.: Geographic Variation, Speciation and Clines. Princeton University Press, Princeton (1977)
39. Gavrilets, S.: Models of speciation: what have we learned in 40 years? Evolution **57** (2003) 2197-2215
40. Crosby, J.L.: The evolution of genetic discontinuity: computer models of the selection of barriers to interbreeding between subspecies. Heredity **25** (1970) 253-297
41. Guldemond, J.A., Dixon, A.F.G.: Specificity and daily cycle of release of sex pheromones inaphids: A case of reinforcement? Biol. J. Linn. Soc. **52** (1994) 287-303
42. Via, S., Hawthorne, D.J.: The genetic architecture of ecological specialization: correlated gene effects on host use and habitat choice in pea aphids. Am. Nat. **159** (2002) S76-S88
43. Engeszer, R.E., Ryan, M.J., Parichy, D.M.: Learned social preference in zebrafish. Current Biology **14** (2004) 881-884
44. Palestrini, C., Rolando, A.: Differential calls by carrion and hooded crows (Corvus corone corone and C. c. cornix) in the Alpine hybrid zone. Bird Study **43** (1996) 364–370
45. Irwin, D.E., Price, T.: Sexual imprinting, learning and speciation. Heredity **82** (1999) 247-354
46. Spencer, H.G., McArdle, B.H., Lambert, D.M.: A theoretical investigation of speciation by reinforcement. Am. Nat. **128** (1986) 241-262
47. Schluter, D. Trends Ecol. Evol. **16** (2001) 372-380
48. Dieckmann, U., Doebeli, M.: On the origin of species by sympatric speciation. Nature **400** (1999) 354-357
49. Doebeli, M., Dieckmann, U.: Evolutionary branching and sympatric speciation caused by different types of ecological interactions. Am. Nat. **156** (2000) S77-S101
50. Kondrashov, A.S., Kondrashov, F.A.: Interactions among quantitative traits in the course of sympatric speciation. Nature **400** (1999) 351-354
51. Gavrilets, S.: Waiting time to parapatric speciation. Proc. Royal Soc. Lond. B **256** (2000) 2483-2492
52. Fisher, R.A.: The Genetical Theory of Natural Selection. Clarendon Press, Oxford (1930)
53. Darwin, C.: The Descent of Man, and Selection in Relation to Sex. Murray, London. (1871)
54. Lande, R.: Models of speciation by sexual selection on polygenic traits. Proc. Natl. Acad. Sci. U. S. A. **78** (1981) 3721-3725
55. Lande, R.: Rapid origin of sexual isolation and character divergence in a cline. Evolution **36** (1982) 213-223
56. Higashi, M. Takimoto, G., Yamamura, N.: Sympatric speciation by sexual selection. Nature **402** (1999) 523-526
57. Takimoto, G., Higashi, M., Yamamura, N.: A deterministic genetic model for sympatric speciation by sexual selection. Evolution **54** (2000) 1870–1881
58. Kawata, M., Yoshimura, J.: Speciation by sexual selection in hybridizing populations without viability selection. Evol. Ecol. Res. **2** (2000) 897-909
59. Panhuis, T.M., Butlin, R. Zuk, M., Tregenza, T.: Sexual selection and speciation. Trends Ecol. Evol. **16** (2001) 364-371
60. Dobzhansky, T.: Genetics and the Origin of Species. Columbia University Press, New York (1937)

61. Lerena, P.: Sexual preferences: dimension and complexity. Proceedings of the Sixth International Conference of the Society for Adaptive Behavior. From Animals to Animats 6, MIT Press, Paris (2000)
62. Tomkins, J.L., Radwan, J., Kotiaho, J.S., Tregenza, T.: Genic capture and resolving the lek paradox. Trends Ecol. Evol. **19** (2004) 323-328
63. Day, T.: Sexual selection and the evolution of costly female preferences: spatial effects. Evolution **54** (2000) 715-730
64. Jiggins, C.D., Mallet, J.: Bimodal hybrid zones and speciation. Trends Ecol. Evol. **15** (2000) 250-255
65. Howard, D.J.: Reinforcement: origin, dynamics and fate of an evolutionary hypothesis. In: Harrison, R.G. (ed.): Hybrid Zones and the Evolutionary Process. Oxford University Press, New York (1993) 46-69
66. Kirkpatrick, M., Ravigné, V.: Speciation by natural and sexual selection: models and experiments. Am. Nat. **159** (2002) S22–S35
67. Kirkpatrick, M.: Reinforcement and divergence under assortative mating. Proc. R. Soc. Lond. B **267** (2000) 1649-1655
68. Fontana, W., Schnabl, W., Schuster, P.: Physical aspects of evolutionary optimization and adaptation. Phys. Rev. A **40** (1989) 3301–3321
69. Cantú-Paz, E., Kamath, C.: On the use of evolutionary algorithms in data mining. In: Abbass, H.A., Sarker, R.A., Newton, C.S. (eds.): Data Mining: A Heuristic Approach. Idea Group Publishing (2001)
70. Ray, T.S.: An approach to the synthesis of life. In: Langton, C., Taylor, C., Farmer, J.D., Rasmussen, S. (eds.): Artificial Life II. Santa Fe Institute Studies in the Sciences of Complexity, vol. X. Addison-Wesley, Redwood City CA (1991) 371–408
71. Adami, C.: 1994. On modeling life. Artificial Life I (1994) 429–438
72. Adami, C., Yirdaw, R., Seki, R.: Critical exponent of species-size distribution in evolution. In: Adami, C., Belew, R., Kitano, H. Taylor, C. (eds.): Artificial Life VI (1998) 221–227
73. Wilke, C.O., Adami, C.: Interaction between directional epistasis and average mutational effects. Proc. R. Soc. Lond. B **268** (2001) 1469–1474
74. Wilke, C.O., Wang, J.L., Ofria, C., Lenski, R.E., Adami, C.: Evolution of digital organisms at high mutation rate leads to survival of the flattest. Nature **412** (2001) 331–333
75. Ofria, C., Wilke, C.O.: Avida: a software platform for research in computational evolutionary biology. Artificial Life **10** (2004) 191–229
76. Barton, N.H.: The dynamics of hybrid zones. Heredity **43** (1979) 341-359
77. Barton, N.H., Hewitt, G.M.: Analysis of hybrid zones. Ann. Rev. Ecol. Syst. **16** (1985) 113-48
78. Sadedin, S. in prep. Niche differentiation destabilises tension zones.
79. Barabasi, A.-L., Albert, R., Jeong, H.: Scale-free characteristics of random networks: the topology of the world-wide web. Physica A **281** (2000) 69–77
80. Marchiori, M., Latora, V.: Harmony in the small world. Physica A **285** (2000) 539–546
81. Farkas, I., Derenyi, I., Jeong, H., Neda, Z., Oltvai, Z.N., Ravasz, E., Schubert, A., Barabasi, A.-L., Vicsek, T.: Networks in life: scaling properties and eigenvalue spectra. Physica A **314** (2002) 25–34

On Evolutionary Optimization of Large Problems Using Small Populations

Yaochu Jin, Markus Olhofer, and Bernhard Sendhoff

Honda Research Institute Europe, Carl-Legien-Str. 30,
63073 Offenbach/Main, Germany
yaochu.jin@honda-ri.de

Abstract. Small populations are very desirable for reducing the required computational resources in evolutionary optimization of complex real-world problems. Unfortunately, the search performance of small populations often reduces dramatically in a large search space. To addresses this problem, a method to find an optimal search dimension for small populations is suggested in this paper. The basic idea is that the evolutionary algorithm starts with a small search dimension and then the search dimension is increased during the optimization. The search dimension will continue to increase if an increase in the search dimension improves the search performance. Otherwise, the search dimension will be decreased and then kept constant. Through empirical studies on a test problem with an infinite search dimension, we show that the proposed algorithm is able to find the search dimension that is the most efficient for the given population size.

1 Introduction

To reduce the computational time in solving expensive optimization problems using evolutionary algorithms, a commonly adopted approach is to parallelize the fitness evaluation process so that each individual is evaluated on a separate machine. In this case, use of a relatively small population size will be very helpful in reducing the computational cost for the evolutionary optimization.

Unfortunately, we are left in a dilemma when we use small populations for solving complex real-world problems. On the one hand, many real-world optimization problems, e.g., design optimization where splines are used to describe the geometry of a structure [1], have a very large number of design parameters. On the other hand, the search efficiency decreases seriously when small populations are used to optimize problems with a high search dimension.

Two approaches could be employed to alleviate, if not solve, the difficulty mentioned above. One method is to develop an efficient evolutionary algorithm with a small population size whose performance is less sensitive to the search dimension. One good example is the derandomized evolution strategy with covariance matrix adaptation (CMA-ES) [2], which has shown to be robust on various unimodal test functions. Nevertheless, the search efficiency of the CMA-ES still greatly depends on the population size. A conclusion from empirical studies is that the population size should be scaled between linear and cubic with the problem dimension to locate the global optimum [3].

Another method is to adapt the search dimension to the population size in use. To this end, an adaptive coding scheme has been suggested where the CMA-ES is employed in aerodynamic shape optimization [4]. The basic idea is to encode the number of parameters to be optimized (the search dimension) in the chromosome and to mutate during the optimization. One issue that arises in the adaptive coding scheme is that the self-adaptation of the evolution strategy can be disturbed due to the mutation in the search dimension, which is harmful to the search performance. One measure to address this problem is to ensure that the mutations are neutral, i.e., the shape of the geometry will be kept the same before and after a new point is inserted in the spline representation.

In this paper, we will explicitly monitor the performance change after the search dimension is increased. If the increase in the search dimension is beneficial, the search dimension will be further increased. Otherwise, the search dimension will be decreased and then will be kept constant until the end of the optimization. To minimize the disturbance on the self-adaptation mechanism, the dimension is increased only by 1 in each change in dimension. Through simulations on various population sizes, it is shown that our method is able to find an optimal or nearly optimal search dimension for the given population size on a test problem with an infinite search dimension.

The test problem used in this study will be briefly described in Section 2. The search capacity of the CMA-ES with regard to the population size on the test problem are investigated empirically in Section 3. The algorithm to find the optimal search dimension is given in Section 4 and a number of simulations are conducted in Section 5, where we show that the algorithm is able to find the optimal or sub-optimal search dimension for different population sizes. Conclusion and further research topics are discussed in Section 6.

2 Test Problem

The test problem used in this study is very simple. However, it serves our purpose well where an infinitely large search dimension is needed theoretically. We consider the approximation of a one-dimensional function using a Taylor series. If a function $f(x)$ has continuous derivatives, then this function can be expanded as follows:

$$f(x) = f(a) + f'(a)(x-a) + \frac{f''(a)(x-a)^2}{2!} + \cdots + \frac{f^{(n)}(a)(x-a)^n}{n!} + R_n, \quad (1)$$

where R_n is the remainder after $n+1$ terms defined by:

$$R_n = \int_a^x f^{(n+1)}(u) \frac{(x-u)^n}{n!} du$$
$$= \frac{f^{(n+1)}(\xi)(x-a)^{n+1}}{(n+1)!}, \quad (2)$$

where $a < \xi < x$. When this expansion converges over a certain range of x, i.e., $\lim_{n \to} R_n = 0$, then the expansion is known as em Taylor Series of function $f(x)$ about a. For example, the Taylor expansion of sine function is as follows:

$$\sin(x) = x - \frac{x^3}{3!} + \frac{x^5}{5!} - \frac{x^7}{7!} + \cdots, -\infty < x < \infty. \quad (3)$$

The optimization problem is to find the coefficients of the Taylor series by minimizing the squared approximation error:

$$E(x) = (\sum_{i=0}^{n} a_i x^i - \sin(x))^2, \quad (4)$$

where x is the point about which the Taylor series is expanded, $a_i, i = 0, 1, 2, \cdots, n$ is the number of terms of the Taylor series. Theoretically, an infinite search dimension is needed to realize a perfect approximation of a sinusoidal function using Taylor series. To estimate the approximation error reliably, we sample 100 points uniformly within the range of $0 \le x \le 1$:

$$E = \sum_{j=1}^{100} E(x_j). \quad (5)$$

An interesting fact in the above test function is that the influence of each term on the function value decreases as the order increases. Thus, terms in the Taylor expansion are added in the search algorithm from lower orders to higher ones. This is reasonable because in optimization of real-world problems, we try to account for at first the most important factors and then try to include those with minor influence.

3 Search Efficiency of Small EAs

As we mentioned in the Introduction, the derandomized evolution strategy with covariance matrix adaptation (CMA-ES) proposed in [5] was designed for small populations. It has shown to be efficient on a large number of unimodal optimization problems, particularly on ill-conditioned and non-separable problems [2]. In the (μ, λ)-CMA-ES without recombination, the λ offspring of generation $g + 1$ is generated as follows:

$$\mathbf{x}_k^{(g+1)} = \mathbf{x}_j^{(g)} + \sigma^{(g)} \mathbf{B}^{(g)} \mathbf{D}^g \mathbf{z}_k^{(g+1)}, \; j = 1, \cdots, \mu; \; k = 1, \cdots, \lambda, \quad (6)$$

where k is randomly chosen from the μ selected parents, $\mathbf{z}$ is an n-dimensional (n is the search dimension) vector of normally distributed random numbers with expectation zero and identity covariance matrix, $\mathbf{BD}\,(\mathbf{BD})^T = \mathbf{C}$ is the covariance matrix. During the evolution, the covariance matrix is updated as follows:

$$\mathbf{C}^{(g+1)} = (1 - c_{\text{cov}})\mathbf{C}^{(g)} + c_{\text{cov}} \mathbf{p}_\mathbf{C}^{(g+1)} \left(\mathbf{p}_\mathbf{C}^{(g+1)}\right)^T, \quad (7)$$

where $\mathbf{p}_C^{(g+1)}$ is known as the evolution path calculated by:

$$\mathbf{p}_C^{(g+1)} = (1 - c_C)\mathbf{p}_C^{(g)} + \sqrt{c_C \cdot (2 - c_C)}\mathbf{B}^{(g)}\mathbf{D}^{(g)}\mathbf{z}_k^{(g)}. \tag{8}$$

The adaptation of the global step-size $\sigma^{(g+1)}$ is calculated by:

$$\sigma^{(g+1)} = \sigma^{(g)} \exp\left(\frac{1}{d_\sigma} \frac{\|\mathbf{p}_\sigma^{(g)}\| - \hat{chi}_n}{\hat{\chi}_n}\right), \tag{9}$$

where $\hat{\chi}_n$ is the expected length of a $(\mathbf{0}, \mathbf{I})$-normally distributed random vector and can be approximated by $\sqrt{n}(1 - \frac{1}{4n} - \frac{1}{21n^2})$, d_σ is a damping coefficient, and $\mathbf{p}_\sigma^{(g+1)}$ is a "conjugate" evolution path:

$$\mathbf{p}_\sigma^{(g+1)} = (1 - c_\sigma)\mathbf{p}_\sigma^{(g)} + \sqrt{c_\sigma \cdot (2 - c_\sigma)}\mathbf{B}^{(g)}\mathbf{z}_k^{(g)}. \tag{10}$$

The default parameter setting suggested in [2] is as follows:

$$c_C = \frac{4}{n+4}, \ c_{cov} = \frac{2}{(n+\sqrt{2})^2}, \ c_\sigma = \frac{4}{n+4}, d_\sigma = c_\sigma^{-1} + 1. \tag{11}$$

In this study, a slightly modified variant of the algorithm presented in [5] has been adopted, where a separate covariance matrix is maintained for each parent individual. Though the CMA-ES is designed for small populations, recent studies have found that CMA-ESs with a large population can improve the search performance significantly [3,6].

However, little work has been reported on what is the optimal search dimension for a CMA-ES with a small population size when the theoretic search dimension is very large or even infinite. In the following, we investigate the search performance of CMA-ES with small populations on the test problem described in Section 2. In our simulations, the CMA-ES without recombination has been adopted and a maximum of 2000 generations are run for search dimensions 5, 7, $\cdots$, 47, 49. For each search dimension, the results are averaged over 50 independent runs. The results from a (1, 4)-CMA-ES and a (2, 10)-CMA-ES are presented in Figures 1 and 2, respectively.

From Fig. 1, we can see that the search performance of the (1, 4)-CMA-ES heavily depends on the search dimension. For a search dimension smaller than 7, the approximation error is quite large due to the limited number of free parameters. The minimal approximation error (0.002936) is achieved when the search dimension is 11, where the approximation error is mostly smaller than 0.01. When the search dimension further increases, the search performance degrades seriously due to the limited search capacity of the (1,4)-CMA-ES.

Similar simulations are carried out for the (2, 10)-CMA-ES. The minimal approximation error (0.000003) is achieved when the search dimension is 11. This implies that the (1, 4)-CMA-ES failed to locate the global optimum for an eleven-dimensional optimization problem in 50 runs. Even the (2, 10)-CMA-ES is able to locate the best found solution only once in the 50 runs. These results indicate that the search efficiency of CMA-ES with small populations is

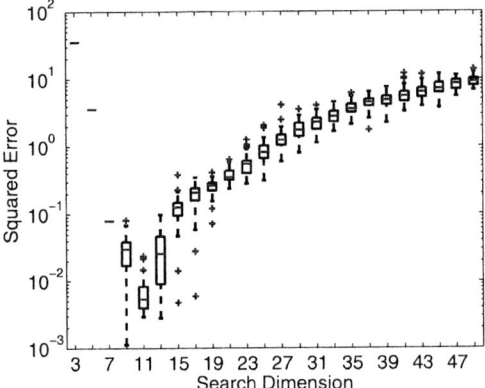

Fig. 1. Search performance of the (1,4)-CMA-ES for search dimensions ranging from 3 to 49. Results averaged over 50 runs.

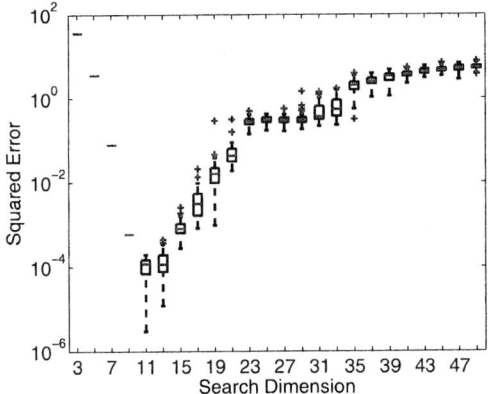

Fig. 2. Search performance of the (2, 10)-CMA-ES for search dimensions ranging from 3 to 49. Results averaged over 50 runs.

limited even for a relatively low dimensional problem. Meanwhile, as in the (1, 4)-CMA-ES case, the search performance becomes worse when the search dimension increases, though not as serious as the (1, 4)-CMA-ES. Again, there is an optimal search dimension where the (2, 10)-CMA-ES achieves the best performance and the search performance is acceptable when the search dimension is from 9 up to 17 (approximation error smaller than 0.01).

4 Adaptation of Search Dimension

It can be seen from the results in the previous section that there is an optimal search dimension for a given population size that is able to achieve the minimal

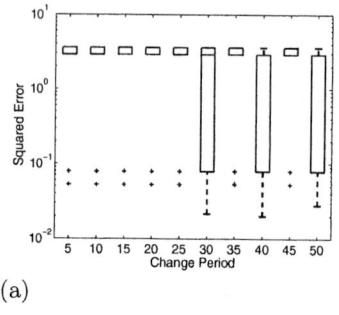
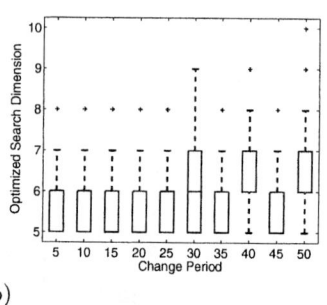

Fig. 3. Adaptation of search dimension for (1, 4)-CMA-ES with various change periods. The design parameters are randomly re-initialized during dimension changes. (a) The best fitness value, and (b) the optimized search dimension. Results averaged over 50 runs.

approximation error. The optimal search dimension is unknown beforehand and is presumably dependent on the population size and the problem at hand.

In this section, we suggest a simple approach to address this problem by adapting the search dimension during the optimization to find an approximately optimal search dimension for a given population size. The basic idea is to start the optimization from a relatively low search dimension and let the search dimension increase in every k generations during the optimization. k is called *change period*. To determine whether an increase in search dimension is beneficial, we compare the best fitness values before and after dimension increase. Assume the best (minimal in this work) fitness values before and after an increase in search dimension are $PBest$ and $CBest$, respectively. Note that $CBest$ is the best fitness value after k generations with an increased search dimension. The increase in search dimension is considered to be beneficial if $CBest$ is smaller than $Pbest$ for minimization problems. If an increase in dimension is regarded as beneficial, then the search dimension will be further increased by one. Otherwise, the search dimension will be decreased by one and fixed until the end of the optimization.

To implement the above idea, the change period k needs to be determined. We conduct simulations to investigate the influence of this parameter on the adaptation performance. Another parameter to be determined is the initial search dimension. This parameter should depend on the problem at hand. In our simulations, the initial dimension is set to 5.

When the search dimension is increased, we have the following three alternatives:

- Re-initialize all design parameters randomly;
- Inherit the value for existing design parameters and initialize new design parameter randomly;
- Inherit the value for existing design parameters and set the new parameter to zero, so that the fitness function does not change after the inclusion of the new dimension.

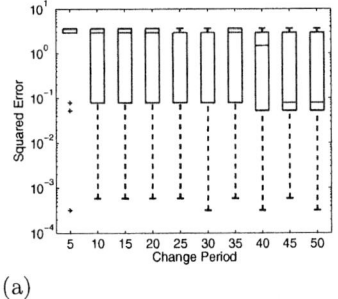
(a)
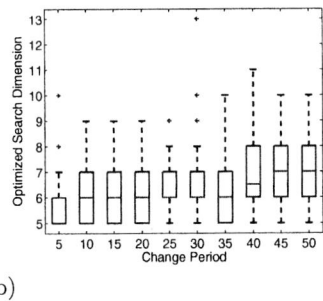
(b)

Fig. 4. Adaptation of search dimension for (2, 10)-CMA-ES with various change periods. The design parameters are randomly re-initialized during dimension changes. (a) The best fitness value, and (b) the optimized search dimension. Results averaged over 50 runs.

We test the performance of the suggested algorithm for 10 change periods, i.e., $k = 5, 10, 15, 20, 25, 30, 35, 40, 45, 50$. The results where all design parameters are randomly initialized are presented in Figures 7 and 8, respectively. Again, 50 runs are conducted for each k.

From Fig. 3 and Fig. 4, we see that neither the (1, 4)-CMA-ES nor the (2, 10)-CMA-ES shows acceptable performance. The search dimension is largely underestimated for all tested change periods. A much larger change period is not practical, since an overly large period will unfavorably increase the needed computational time. Thus, we conclude that randomly re-initialize the design parameters is undesirable in adopting an adaptive search dimension.

The next idea to try out is to inherit the value for each existing design parameter and then initialize the newly added design variable randomly. The simulation results are shown in Figures 5 and 6, respectively. We notice that the performance has been improved significantly. For the (1, 4)-CMA-ES, the per-

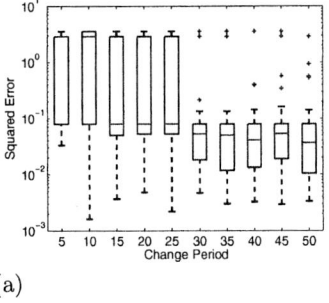
(a)
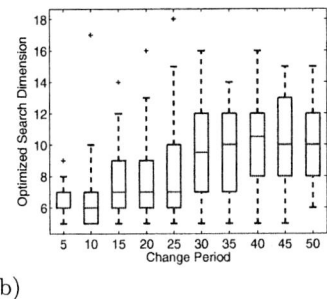
(b)

Fig. 5. Adaptation of search dimension for (1, 4)-CMA-ES with various change periods. The value of the existing design parameters are inherited and the new one is randomly initialized during dimension change. (a) The best fitness value, and (b) the optimized search dimension. Results averaged over 50 runs.

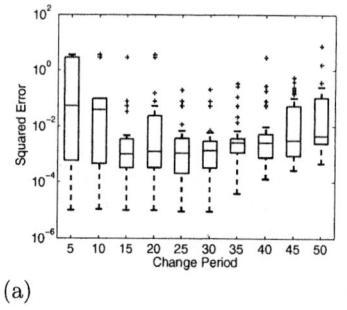
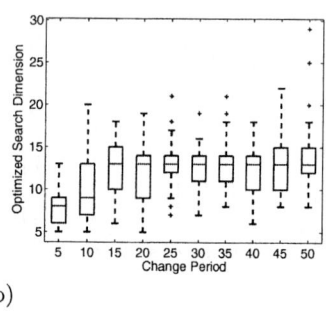

Fig. 6. Adaptation of search dimension for (2, 10)-CMA-ES with various change periods. The value of the existing design parameters are inherited and the new one is randomly initialized during dimension changes. (a) The best fitness value, and (b) the optimized search dimension. Results averaged over 50 runs.

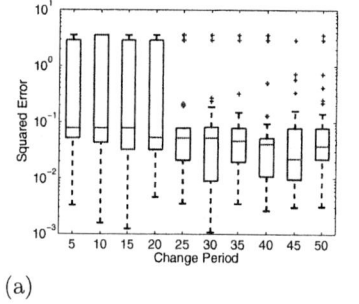
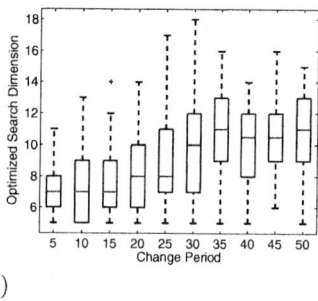

Fig. 7. Adaptation of search dimension for (1, 4)-CMA-ES with various change periods. The value of the existing design parameters are inherited and the new one is set to zero during dimension changes. (a) The best fitness value, and (b) the optimized search dimension. Results averaged over 50 runs.

formance is quite good when the change period is between 30 and 50, where the optimized search dimension is between 9 and 11 on average, which are optimal or sub-optimal if we refer to the empirical results shown in Fig. 1. Similar conclusion can be made to the results obtained for the (2, 10)-CMA-ES. However, the performance of the algorithm seems more robust against the change period in that satisfying performance has been achieved when the change period varies from 15 to 50, where the estimated optimal search dimension is 13 on average, which is one of the optimal search dimension as shown in Fig. 2.

Finally, we investigate the performance of the algorithm when we initialize the newly added design parameter to 0, which in this example makes the inclusion of the new search dimension neutral to the fitness value. Such neutral mutations have shown to be essential to the success of adaptive coding when splines are used for geometry description in design optimization [4]. Comparing

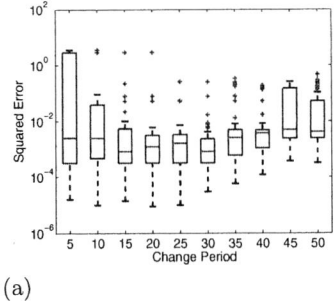 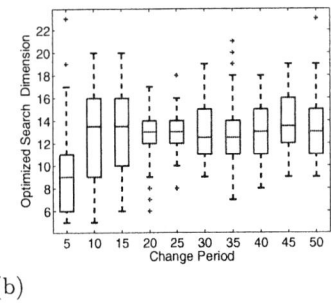

Fig. 8. Adaptation of search dimension for (2, 10)-CMA-ES with various change periods. The value of the existing design parameters are inherited and the new one is set to zero during dimension changes. (a) The best fitness value, and (b) the optimized search dimension. Results averaged over 50 runs.

the results in Fig. 5 and those in Fig. 7 regarding the (1, 4)-CMA-ES, we see that minor improvements have been achieved, particularly when the change period is small.

5 Conclusions

Evolutionary optimization of large problems with evolutionary algorithms with a small population is a challenging topic. To efficiently optimize possibly infinite large problems using small populations, a method to adapt the search dimension has been suggested in this paper. The basic idea is that for small populations, we should start from a relatively low search dimension and then increase it gradually during the optimization. The increase in search dimension should continue until performance improvement cannot be achieved in a number of generations after the dimension increase. In this case, the search dimension is decreased by one and and kept constant till the end of the optimization. From our empirical studies, the change period should be between 20 to 50 generations. A too small change period is not desirable because the algorithm needs some time to find the potential improvement after an increase in dimension. Neither is a large change period preferred because a larger change period tends to increase the computational time rapidly.

It is found essential for the success of our algorithm that the value of the existing design parameters should be inherited after an increase in search dimension. This result is consistent with the findings reported in the literature that *a priori* knowledge is beneficial in enhancing the performance of evolutionary algorithms [7].

The strategy parameters are randomly re-initialized during dimension changes in this work, which may not be optimal for evolution strategies. It will be one of our future work to investigate the influence of re-initialization of strategy parameters on the performance of our algorithm using a dynamic search dimension.

References

1. Jin, Y., Olhofer, M., Sendhoff, B.: A framework for evolutionary optimization with approximate fitness functions. IEEE Transactions on Evolutionary Computation. **6** (2002) 481–494
2. Hansen N., Ostermeier A.: Completely derandomized self-adaptation in evolution strategies. Evolutionary Computation **9** (2001) 159–195
3. Hansen, N., Kern S.: Evaluating the CMA evolution strategy on multimodal test functions. Parallel Problem Solving from Nature, Vol. 3242. Springer (2004) 282–291
4. Olhofer, M., Jin, Y., Sendhoff, B.: Adaptive encoding for aerodynamic shape optimization using evolution strategies. Congress on Evolutionary Computation (2001) 576–583
5. Hansen, N., Ostermeier, A.: Adapting arbitrary normal mutation distributions in evolution strategies: The covariance Matrix Adaptation. IEEE Conf. on Evolutionary Computation (1996) 312–317
6. Hansen, N., Müller, S., Koumoutsakos, P.: Reducing the time complexity of the derandomized evolution startegy with covariance matrix adaptation (CMA-ES). Evolutionary Computation. **11** (2003) 1–18
7. Jin, Y. (ed.): Knowledge Incorporation in Evolutionary Computation. Springer, Berlin Heidelberg (2005)

Reaction-Driven Membrane Systems

Luca Bianco, Federico Fontana, and Vincenzo Manca

University of Verona, Department of Computer Science,
15 strada Le Grazie - 37134 Verona, Italy
{bianco, fontana}@sci.univr.it
vincenzo.manca@univr.it

Abstract. Membrane systems are gaining a prominent role in the modeling of biochemical processes and cellular dynamics. We associate specific reactivity values to the production rules in a way to be able to tune their rewriting activity, according to the kinetic and state-dependent parameters of the physical system. We come up with an algorithm that exhibits a good degree of versatility, meanwhile it gives an answer to the problem of representing oscillatory biological and biochemical phenomena, so far mostly treated with differential mathematical tools, by means of symbolic rewriting. Results from simulations of the Lotka-Volterra's predator-prey population dynamics envision application of this algorithm in biochemical dynamics of interest.

1 Introduction

Besides their connections with formal language theory, membrane systems often use to be applied to the analysis of biological processes [1,2,3,4]. In particular, *P systems* have come useful provided their capability to represent several structural aspects of the cell along with many intra- and extra-cellular communication mechanisms: dynamic rewriting by means of P systems has already led to alternative representations of different biological phenomena and to new models of important pathological processes [3,4].

By our side we have developed a P system-based algorithm in which rules are specified along with *reactivities*, respectively denoting the "power" of a production rule to process elements such as chemical reactants, bio-molecules and so on [5]. The performances shown in the simulation of the Lotka-Volterra population dynamics foster potential practical application of this algorithm in critical open problems dealt with by computational systems biology.

2 The Algorithm

For the sake of brevity, in this paper the algorithm is formalized for the case of just one membrane [2]. So, let us consider a P system Π working on the alphabet $\mathcal{A} = \{X, Y, \ldots, Z\}$, provided with rules $r, s, \ldots, w \in R$.

The algorithm requires, firstly, to recognize the *state* of the system. This state, along with constant factors (depending, for instance, on chemical kinetic parameters), is used to compute specific functions called *reaction maps*. Once we have the values assumed by such maps at hand we normalize them consistently with the available resources (i.e., *objects* in the P system), meanwhile *limiting* these values to avoid to over-consume objects. Finally, a simple stochastic method is employed to decide how to treat individual objects in the system, for which the procedure so far described cannot take a definite decision. This situation occurs when reaction maps ask for partitioning one or more objects into fractional parts of them.

About the definition of state, we postulate that at every discrete time t we can read the type and number of objects within the membrane system. More formally the state at time t is identified by a function $q_t : \mathcal{A} \longrightarrow \mathbb{N}$: for instance, $q_t(X)$ gives the amount of objects X available in the system at time t. The set of all states assumed along time by the system is given by $Q = \{q_t \mid t \in \mathbb{N}\}$: this set contains the complete information on the system evolution.

About the definition of reaction maps (one for each rule), let a reaction map give the reactivity that the corresponding rule has when the system is in a given state. In formal terms, for each rule r we define a reaction map $F_r : Q \longrightarrow \mathbb{R}$ that maps states into non-negative real numbers. Since the state is defined at any temporal step, the application of a reaction map F_r ultimately results in a non-negative real number that we will take as the *reactivity of r in q_t*.

Such maps allow for a wide choice of possible definitions depending on the biological phenomenon under analysis. As an example, consider a membrane system having an alphabet made of five symbols, $\mathcal{A} = \{A, B, C, D, E\}$, and two rules: $r : ABB \rightarrow AC$, and $s : AE \rightarrow BD$.

Possible structures of the reaction maps might be, for instance, reactivities driven by the *law of mass action* tuned by constant kinetic parameters, k_r and k_s, as well as reactivities depending on an external promoter, like an enzyme capable of activating the reaction. The two possibilities are shown in (1), respectively in the left and right column:

$$
\begin{array}{ll}
F_r = k_r\, q_t(A) q_t(B) & F_r = q_t(D) \\
F_s = k_s\, q_t(A) q_t(E) & F_s = \{q_t(D)\}^2
\end{array}
\quad (1)
$$

2.1 Reaction Weights, Limitation and Rounding, and State Transition

Reaction maps are proportionally weighted among rules by means of *reaction weights*. Every reaction weight gives, for each symbol, a population a rule applies to in order to proportionally consume the corresponding objects. By denoting with $\alpha(i)$ the ith symbol in a string α, with $|\alpha|$ the length of the same string, and with $|\alpha|_X$ the number of occurrences of X in α, then we define the reaction weight $W_r(\alpha_r(i))$ for $r : \alpha_r \rightarrow \beta_r$ with respect to the symbol $\alpha_r(i)$.

Normalization can be expressed in quantitative terms if we think that all rules co-operate, each one with its own reactivity, to consume all available objects. Thus, it must be:

$$\sum_{\rho \in R \mid X \in \alpha_\rho} W_\rho(X) = 1 \quad \forall X \in \mathcal{A} \qquad (2)$$

that is, for each symbol the sum of the reaction weights made over the rules containing that symbol in their left part equals unity.

Holding this constraint, we can define the reaction weights for each $r \in R$ as

$$W_r(\alpha_r(i)) = \frac{F_r}{\sum_{\rho \in R \mid \alpha_r(i) \in \alpha_\rho} F_\rho} \quad , \quad i = 1, \ldots, |\alpha_r| \tag{3}$$

Similarly to what happens in (2), here we sum at the denominator over the rules containing the symbol $\alpha_r(i)$ in their left part.

Every rule cannot consume more than the amount of the (reactant) object, *taken with its own multiplicity in the reaction*, whose availability in the system is lowest. Thus, we have to limit the application of every rule by minimizing among all reactant symbols participating to it:

$$\Lambda_r = \min_{i=1,\ldots,|\alpha_r|} \left\{ W_r(\alpha_r(i)) \frac{q_t(\alpha_r(i))}{|\alpha_r|_{\alpha_r(i)}} \right\}. \tag{4}$$

Still, Λ_r is a real number. As opposite to this, a genuine object-based rewriting system must restrict the rule application domain to integer values. We choose the following policy: for every rule, compute $\overline{\Lambda}_r$ by comparing the fractional part of Λ_r to a random variable v_r defined between 0 and 1; choose the floor of Λ_r if this fraction is smaller, the ceiling otherwise. In the simulation of the Lotka-Volterra dynamics v_r can be chosen to have a uniform distribution.

The proposed rounding policy does not prevent from potentially exceeding the available resources in the system. To avoid this we check that $\sum_{r \in R} \overline{\Lambda}_r |\alpha_r|_X \leq q_t(X) \forall X \in \mathcal{A}$, otherwise the set of minima must be computed again.

In conclusion, for every symbol $X \in \mathcal{A}$ the change $\Delta_r(X)$ in the number of objects due to r is equal to the *stoichiometric factor* of r, equal to $|\beta_r|_X - |\alpha_r|_X$, times the value $\overline{\Lambda}_r$: $\Delta_r(X) = \overline{\Lambda}_r (|\beta_r|_X - |\alpha_r|_X)$. It descends that for every symbol $X \in \mathcal{A}$ the state evolves according to the following formula:

$$q_{t+1}(X) = q_t(X) + \sum_{r \in R} \Delta_r(X). \tag{5}$$

3 Simulation: Lotka-Volterra Dynamics

The classic Lotka-Volterra population dynamics [5] can be described by a simple set of rewriting rules in which X are preys and Y predators: $r : X \to XX$ accounts for prey reproduction, $s : XY \to YY$ for predator reproduction, and finally $t : Y \to \lambda$ accounts for predator death.

We tune the activity of every rule by selecting proper reactivity kinetic constants k_r, k_s, and k_t, proportional to the rate of reproduction and death of both predators and preys. Moreover we postulate F_s to be proportional to the maximum number between preys and predators: $F_r = k_r$, $F_s = k_s \max\{q_t(X), q_t(Y)\}$, $F_t = k_t$. Finally we add *transparent rules* [5] accounting for preys that are not

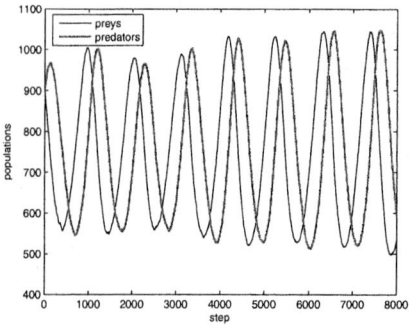 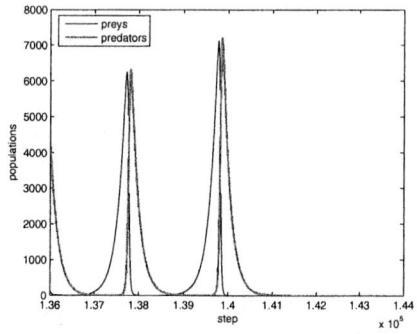

Fig. 1. Predator-prey initial dynamics (left) and after 136000 observation slots (right)

reproducing or being consumed and for predators that are not eating or dieing, respectively: $u : X \to X$ and $v : Y \to Y$, with $F_u = k_u$ and $F_v = k_v$.

Plots of the dynamic behavior of the predator-prey model are depicted in Figure 1. These plots come out when we set $k_r = k_t = 3 \cdot 10^{-2}$, $k_s = 4 \cdot 10^{-5}$, and $k_u = k_v = 5$ along with initial conditions $q_t(X) = q_t(Y) = 900$.

The oscillation can evolve to the death of both species, as in this case, or to the death of the predators solely. The long-term evolution in fact depends on single events taking place when few individuals, either preys or predators, are present in the system. Such a long-term behavior emphasizes the importance of a careful description of not only the reactivities, but also the relationships existing between individuals: the nature of these relationships can completely change the overall system evolution.

References

1. Rozenberg, G., Salomaa, A., eds.: Handbook of Formal Languages. Springer-Verlag, Berlin, Germany (1997)
2. Păun, G.: Membrane Computing. An Introduction. Springer, Berlin, Germany (2002)
3. Bianco, L., Fontana, F., Franco, G., Manca, V.: P systems for biological dynamics. In Ciobanu, G., Păun, G., Pérez-Jiménez, M.J., eds.: Applications of Membrane Computing. Springer, Berlin, Germany (2005) To appear.
4. Mauri, G., Păun, G., Pérez-Jiménez, M.J., Rozenberg, G., Salomaa, A., eds.: Membrane Computing, 5th International Workshop, WMC 2004, Milan, Italy, June 14-16, 2004, Revised Selected and Invited Papers. In Mauri, G., Păun, G., Pérez-Jiménez, M.J., Rozenberg, G., Salomaa, A., eds.: Workshop on Membrane Computing. Volume 3365 of Lecture Notes in Computer Science., Springer (2005)
5. Bianco, L., Fontana, F., Manca, V.: Metabolic algorithm with time-varying reaction maps. In: Proc. of the Third Brainstorming Week on Membrane Computing (BWMC 2005), Sevilla, Spain (2005) 43–62

A Genetic Algorithm Based Method for Molecular Docking

Chun-lian Li[1], Yu Sun[2], Dong-yun Long[1], and Xi-cheng Wang[3]

[1] School of Computer Science and Technology,
Changchun University,
Changchun 130022, China
[2] Institute of Special Education,
Changchun University, Changchun 130022, China
[3] State Key Laboratory of Analysis for Industrial Equipment,
Dalian University of Technology,
Dalian 116023, China
chdlichl@sina.com

Abstract. The essential of Molecular docking problem is to find the optimum conformation of ligand bound with the receptor at its active site. Most cases the optimum conformation has the lowest interaction energy. So the molecular docking problem can be treated as a minimization problem. An entropy-based evolution model for molecular docking is proposed in this paper. The model of molecular docking is based on a multi-population genetic algorithm. Two molecular docking processes are investigated to demonstrate the efficiency of the proposed model.

1 Introduction

The molecular docking problem is generally cast as a problem of finding the low-energy binding modes of a small molecule or ligand based on the "lock and key mechanism", within the active site of a macromolecule, or receptor, whose structure is known. It plays an important role in drug design, which is demonstrated by the vast amount of literature devoted to the optimization methods for molecular docking design since the pioneering work of Kuntz et al. [1]. Protein-ligand docking for drug molecular design is an ideal approach to virtual screening, i.e., to search large sets of compounds for putative new lead structure. A fundamental problem with molecular docking is that orientation space is very large and grows combinatorial with the number of degrees of freedom of the interacting molecules. Therefore, simpler and efficient methods are continuously being studied into. An entropy-based model of molecular docking is here presented, and a multi-population genetic algorithm is used to solve optimization problem of molecular conformation for protein-ligand docking.

2 Entropy-Based Genetic Model of Molecular Docking

Molecular docking is actually a problem of finding the conformation of ligand with the lowest interaction energy. An entropy-based evolutionary model for molecular docking is constructed as follows

$$\begin{cases} \min \ -\sum_{j=1}^{m} p_j F(\mathbf{x}) \\ \min \ H = -\sum_{j=1}^{m} p_j \ln(p_j) \\ s.t. \ \sum_{j=1}^{m} p_j = 1, \ p_j \in [0,1] \end{cases} \quad (1)$$

where H is the information entropy, p_j is here defined as a probability that the optimal solution occurs in the population j. $F(\mathbf{x})$ is intermolecular interaction energy

$$F(\mathbf{x}) = \sum_{i=1}^{lig} \sum_{j=1}^{rec} \left(\frac{A_{ij}}{r_{ij}^a} - \frac{B_{ij}}{r_{ij}^b} + 332.0 \frac{q_i q_j}{Dr_{ij}} \right) \quad (2)$$

where each term is a double sum over ligand atoms i and receptor atoms j, r_{ij} is distance between atom i in ligand and atom j in receptor, A_{ij}, B_{ij} are Van der waals repulsion and attraction parameters, a, b are Van der waals repulsion and attraction exponents, q_i, q_j are point charges on atoms i and j, D is dielectric function, and 332.0 is factor that converts the electrostatic energy into kilocalories per mole. In the protein-ligand docking process, the binding free energy (2) should be transferred to related to the ligand atoms' Cartesian coordinates only to reduce the computing complexity. This method is based on the pre-calculated energy grid [2]. So as a matter of fact, the equation used in the real optimization can be expressed as follows [3,4]

$$\begin{aligned} \text{Min} \quad & F(\mathbf{x}) = f(T_x, T_y, T_z, R_x, R_y, R_z, T_{b1}, \cdots, T_{bn}) \\ s.t. \quad & \underline{X} \leq T_x \leq \overline{X} \\ & \underline{Y} \leq T_y \leq \overline{Y} \\ & \underline{Z} \leq T_z \leq \overline{Z} \\ & -\pi \leq angle \leq \pi, \\ & angle = R_x, R_y, R_z, T_{b1}, \cdots, T_{bn} \end{aligned} \quad (3)$$

where design variables $T_{b1}, \cdots, T_{bn}$ are the torsion angles of the rotatable bonds for flexible ligand docking, $T_x, T_y, T_z, R_x, R_y, R_z$, are the position coordinates and rotational angles of the anchor for the matching-based orientation search, and objective function E is intermolecular interaction energy.

It means that the optimal conformation of flexible ligand is formed by the translation (T_x, T_y, T_z), rotation (R_x, R_y, R_z) and the torsion motions (T_{bi}, i=1,2, ···, n, n is the number of torsion bonds). The former six variables are the six degrees of freedom for rigid body, it can also be seemed as the orientation of the ligand. T_{bi} is the angle of the ith flexible bond. For GA, each chromosome consists of the above three design variables that represent a ligand in a particular conformation and orientation. The design space of (T_x, T_y, T_z) must be limited in the spheres space of the receptor. A Circum-cuboid of the sphere space is here used to confine the rigid body's coordinates, which can greatly avoid the computational complexity of resolving the actual boundary. The rest variables are allowed to vary between $-\pi$ and π rad.

3 The Genetic Approach

In this paper, an information entropy-based searching technique developed in prior work [5] is used to perform optimization. Design space is defined as initial searching space. M populations with N members are generated in the given space. After two generations are independently evolved in each population, searching space of each population except for the worst one is narrowed according to a coefficient calculated through the application of information entropy (See [5] for detail).

This GA is in binary coded and in each generation, there are three main genetic operators: selection, crossover and mutation. Selection is performed by an integer-decimal method. Crossover is executed by two-point rule, which firstly selecting two individuals as the parents from the current population, then selected randomly two cutting sites, swap 0s and 1s of the strings between the cutting sites of the mating pairs. As to another operator, a uniform mutation is employed to protect against the loss of some useful genetic information, and may help design to get out of local optimization solution. The process of mutation is to select simply a few strings from the population according to probability P_m and change the value of 0s or 1s on each chosen string in terms of some rule.

When taking the elitist maintaining, simple GA can convergent to its optimal solution at probability 1. So, an elitist maintaining mechanism is designed in the proposed GA. It is common for GA to involve a few decades and even more than several hundreds generations before finding the global solution. So a lot of historic information will be generated during the evolutionary process. Among them, we considered most is the elitist of all the populations in each generation. In this paper, the information of the best individual is recorded first in the former generation, then compare with the best one of current generation, and the absolute excellent individual up to now is stored in the contemporary as the elitist. Iterate this process in every generation till the convergence is reached. The final elitist is the solution to the optimization problem.

4 Application

To test the efficiency of the molecular docking, two docking examples are investigated. The first is, the protein-ligand docking process between sc-558 and its

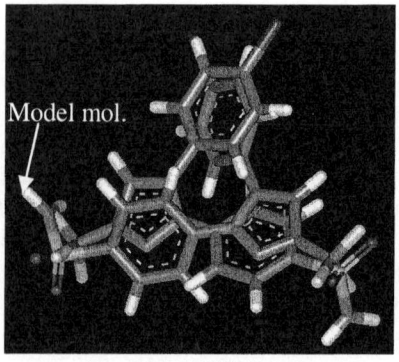
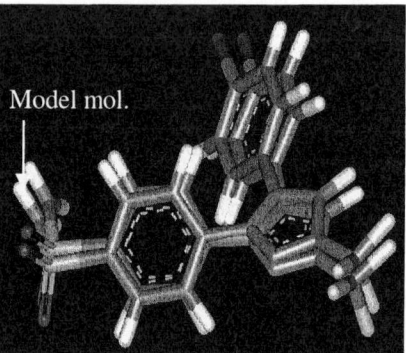

(a) Get by DOCK5 program (b) Get by the proposed method

Fig. 1. Cox-2 result conformations against the model molecule

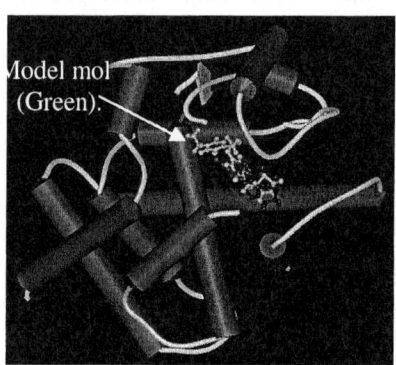
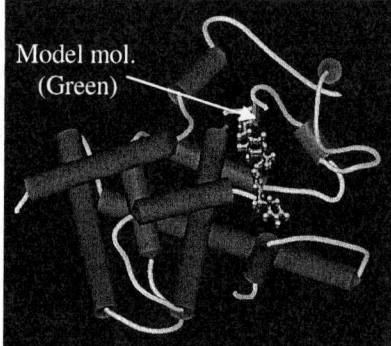

(a) Get by DOCK5 program (b) Get by the proposed method

Fig. 2. PPARλ result conformations against the model molecule and its receptor

receptor in known cyclooxygenase-2 (COX-2) inhibitors, and the second is one of the peroxisome proliferator-activated receptors (PPARs) –PPARλ and small molecule: pioglitazone. In both cases, docking program runs at the same environment (Pentium® 4 CPU 2.4GHz, 256 MB ram, Red hat linux 7.1). In the first example, the docking results are: energy score of the best conformation obtained by the proposed method is –2.0 kcal/mol with 2.91 seconds against the result of 187.7 kcal/mol with 68 seconds got by DOCK5.0.0 program [6]. In the second example, the docking results are: energy score of the best conformation obtained by the proposed method is -32.5 kcal/mol with 2.56s seconds against the result of –17 kcal/mol with 172.2 seconds got by DOCK5.0.0 program. Fig.1 and Fig.2 show the result conformations against the model molecule.

5 Conclusions

The use of docking as a virtual screening tool is more challenging than using it as a ligand design tool. It has to be developed so that docking algorithms can find the correct binding mode of a compound by effectively sampling its available conformational and orientational space in the binding pocket within 10 seconds of central processing unit (CPU) time. To date, the best performing docking algorithms take about 1-3 min of CPU time for a ligand-protein docking experiment [7]. An evolutionary design model of molecular conformation for PLD is presented in this paper. The application examples show that the proposed design model and method are suitable for drug molecular design, and can get good accuracy and efficiency.

Acknowledgements

The authors gratefully acknowledge financial support for this work from the National Natural Science Foundation (10272030) and the Subsidized by the Special Funds for Major State Basic Research Project (G1999032805) of China. Additionally, appreciate the Kuntz group (UCSF) for supplying DOCK program.

References

1. I. D. Kuntz, J. M. Blaney, S. J. Oatley, and R. L. Langridge, A Geometric Approach to Macromolecule-Ligand Interactions. J. Mol. Biol., 161:269-288,1982.
2. E. C. Meng, B. K. Shoichet, I. D. Kuntz. Automated Docking with Grid-Based Energy Evaluation. J. Comput. Chem. **13(4)**:505-524,1992.
3. Li chun-lian, Wang Xi-cheng, Zhao Jin-cheng, Li Wen, Yu En-sheng, A Parallel Computing of Drug Molecular Docking Design, International Conference on Parallel Algorithms and Computing Environments (ICPACE)□2003:229-231
4. Li chunlian, Wang xicheng, Zhao jincheng, Drug molecular docking design based on optimal conformation search, Computers and Applied Chemistry, vol.21 (2), 2004
5. Li chun-lian, Wang Xi-cheng, Zhao Jin-cheng, et al. An Information Entropy-based Multi-population Genetic Algorithm. Journal of Dalian University of Technology, vol.44(4):589-593, 2004(in Chinese)
6. DOCK5.0.0. Demetri Moustakas. Kuntz Laboratory, UCSF, 4,15,2002.
7. I. Muegge, M. Rarey. Small molecular docking and scoring. In Reviews in computational chemistry, K. B. Lipkowitz and D. B. Boyd, Eds., VCH Publishers, New York, 2001, Vol.17:1-60

A New Encoding Scheme to Improve the Performance of Protein Structural Class Prediction

Zhen-Hui Zhang[1], Zheng-Hua Wang[2], and Yong-Xian Wang[2]

[1] Institute of Science, National University of Defense Technology,
410073 Changsha, China
zhangzhenhui2000@163.com
[2] Institute of Computer, National University of Defense Technology,
410073 Changsha, China
yongxian_wang@yahoo.com

Abstract. Based on the concept of coarse-grained description, a new encoding scheme with grouped weight for protein sequence is presented in this paper. By integrating the new scheme with the component-coupled algorithm, the overall prediction accuracy of protein structural class is significantly improved. For the same training dataset consisting of 359 proteins, the overall prediction accuracy achieved by the new method is 7% higher than that based solely on the amino-acid composition for the jackknife test. Especially for $\alpha+\beta$ the increase of prediction accuracy can achieve 15%. For the jackknife test, the overall prediction accuracy by the proposed scheme can reach 91.09%, which implies that a significant improvement has been achieved by making full use of the information contained in the protein sequence. Furthermore, the experimental analysis shows that the improvement depends on the size of the training dataset and the number of groups.

1 Introduction

It is generally accepted that protein structure is determined by its amino acid sequence [1] and that the knowledge of protein structures plays an important role in understanding their functions. Understanding the relation between amino acid sequence and three-dimensional protein structure is one of the major goals of contemporary molecular biology. A priori knowledge of protein structural classes has become quite useful from both an experimental and theoretical point of view. The concept of protein structural classes was proposed by Levitt and Chothia more than 20 years ago [2]. According to this concept, a protein is usually classified into one of the following structural classes: all-α, all-β, α/β and $\alpha + \beta$. The structural class of a protein presents an intuitive description of its overall folding and the restrictions of the structural class have a high impact on its secondary and tertiary structure prediction [3]. Some researchers have claimed that the knowledge of structural classes might be used to decrease the complexity of searching conformational space during energy optimization, and provide useful information for a heuristic approach to find the tertiary structure of a protein. Owing to the importance and the relative simplicity of structural class prediction, considerable attention has been focused on this problem during the past years [3-11].

Historically, Nishikawa's found [4] that structural classes of proteins correlate strongly with amino acid composition. It marked the onset of algorithm developments aimed at predicting the structural class of a protein from its amino acid composition solely. There have been a number of algorithms about this topic, such as the least Hamming distance, the least Euclidian distance, the discriminate analysis, the vector decomposition, the component-coupled algorithm, and fuzzy structural vectors. Although the amino-acid composition is very convenient to calculate, the full information contained in the protein sequence is reduced considerably. The prediction accuracy is limited by the amino-acid composition-based approach. It is the aim of this study to overcome this drawback.

Based on the concept of coarse-grained description, a protein sequence was reduced to a few of binary sequences, which we named characteristic sequences. For each characteristic sequence, a canonical weight function was introduced to realize the grouped weight encoding of protein sequence. We name this new encoding approach of protein sequence as EBGW (Encoding Based on Grouped Weight) approach. Integrating the new scheme (EBGW) with the component-coupled algorithm, it shows that the overall prediction accuracy of protein structural class is significantly improved. Furthermore, the methodology presented here might be useful for other studies of protein structure.

2 Methods

For many quite different things, we can treat them as one if they have some same characters. This is the main idea of coarse-grained and was applied to DNA sequence analysis in [12]. It is well known that the three-dimensional structure of protein is more conservative than its protein sequence. In the process of folding, the insertion, deletion or permutation of single amino acid residue may not destroy the three-dimensional structure. The most important influencing factor of protein folding is the unique character of amino acid residue. Thus ,in the following, we present a new encdoing scheme (named EBGW) of amino acid sequence based on the different character of amino acid residue and coarse-grained idea.

2.1 EBGW of Protein Sequence

Considering the hydrophobicity and charged character, we can divide the 20 amino acid residues into four different classes as follows [13]:

neuter and non-polarity residue	C1={G,A,V,L,I,M,P,F,W}
neuter and polarity residue	C2={Q,N,S,T,Y,C}
acidic residue	C3={D,E}
alkalescence residue	C4={H,K,R}

Thus, we can get three combinations, each of which can partition the 20 amino acid residues into two disjoint group: C1+C2 vs C3+C4, or C1+C3 vs C2+C4, and C1+C4 vs C2+C3.

Definition 1. *(Characteristic Sequence) Let $A(n) = a_1 a_2 \cdots a_n$ be a protein sequence, we can transform it into three binary sequences by three homomorphic maps $\Phi_i(A(n)) = \Phi_i(a_1)\Phi_i(a_2)\cdots\Phi_i(a_n)$ $(i = 1, 2, 3)$ which are defined as follows:*

$$\Phi_1(a_j) = \begin{cases} 1 & if\ a_j \in C1 \cup C2 \\ 0 & if\ a_j \in C3 \cup C4 \end{cases} \quad (j = 1, 2, \cdots, n) \tag{1}$$

$$\Phi_2(a_j) = \begin{cases} 1 & if\ a_j \in C1 \cup C3 \\ 0 & if\ a_j \in C2 \cup C4 \end{cases} \quad (j = 1, 2, \cdots, n) \tag{2}$$

$$\Phi_3(a_j) = \begin{cases} 1 & if\ a_j \in C1 \cup C4 \\ 0 & if\ a_j \in C2 \cup C3 \end{cases} \quad (j = 1, 2, \cdots, n) \tag{3}$$

Denote $H(n)^i = \Phi_i(A(n)) = h_1^i h_2^i \cdots h_n^i$ $(i = 1, 2, 3)$, we call $H(n)^1, H(n)^2, H(n)^3$ as 1-, 2- and 3-characteristic sequences of the protein sequence, respectively.

For simplicity, in the following text we denote $H(n) = h_1 h_2 \cdots h_n$ as any characteristic sequence of three defined above.

Definition 2. *(Weight) Let $H(n) = h_1 h_2 \cdots h_n$ be a characteristic sequence, the weight of $H(n)$ is defined as the enumeration of digit 1 in $H(n)$.*

We can see that the weight of characteristic sequence is dependent on the sequence length. So it could not be applied to the comparison or analysis of sequences with different lengths.

Definition 3. *(Canonical Weight) Let $H(n) = h_1 h_2 \cdots h_n$ be a characteristic sequence, the canonical weight $w(n)$ is defined as the frequency of digit 1 occurs in $H(n)$, that is $w(n) = p/n$, where p is the weight of $H(n)$.*

Definition 4. *(Encoding Based on Grouped Weight) Let $H(n) = h_1 h_2 \cdots h_n$ be a characteristic sequence, assume L be a positive integer, we can partition $H(n)$ into L pieces of subsequence. The process of subsequence partitioning can refer to Figure 1. From Figure 1 we know that the length of each subsequence is progressive increase. Let $H(\lfloor kn/L \rfloor)$ $(k = 1, 2, \cdots, L)$ be subsequences of $H(n)$ whose length are $\lfloor kn/L \rfloor$ $(k = 1, 2, \cdots, L)$, where $\lfloor \bullet \rfloor$ is the operation returning a number down to the nearest integer, and $w(\lfloor kn/L \rfloor)$ $(k = 1, 2, \cdots, L)$ be the canonical weight of $H(\lfloor kn/L \rfloor)$ $(k = 1, 2, \cdots, L)$, we can get $W = [w(\lfloor n/L \rfloor), w(\lfloor 2n/L \rfloor), \cdots w(\lfloor Ln/L \rfloor)]$ which we call as the EBGW string of characteristic sequence $H(n)$.*

Thus, given a protein sequence $A(n) = a_1 a_2 \cdots a_n$, we can transform it into three characteristic sequences $H(n)^1, H(n)^2, H(n)^3$ by using definition 1.

$H(n)$ 1010110010111100110100100001000101001101101011100001010101111011111
$H(10)$ 1010110010
$H(21)$ 101011001011110011010
$H(32)$ 10101100101111001101001000010001
$H(43)$ 1010110010111100110100100001000101001101101
$H(54)$ 101011001011110011010010000100010100110110101110000101
$H(65)$ 1010110010111100110100100001000101001101101011100001010101111011111

n=65 L=6 length of subsequence is 10,21,32,43,54,65 respectively

Fig. 1. Partitioning subsequence of characteristic sequence

For each characteristic sequence $H(n)^i (i = 1, 2, 3)$, it can be encoded into a L-dimension vector $W^i (i = 1, 2, 3)$ with definition 4. That is, we can transform a protein sequence into a 3L-dimension vector $X = [W^1, W^2, W^3] = [x_1, x_2, \cdots x_{3L}]$, we call x as the EBGW string of protein sequence A.

In EBGW approach, characteristic sequence is introduced based on the concept of coarse-grained. It reflects the distribution of residues with the same unique characteristic and portrays the essence of protein sequence. Although the amino-acid composition is very convenient to calculate, the information contained in the protein sequence is reduced considerably. In EBGW approach, grouping presented can contain more information in the protein sequence. If grouping based on the amino acid composition, a protein sequence can be transformed into a 20L-dimension vector, where L is the number of groups. However, grouping based on characteristic sequence, a protein sequence can be transformed into a 3L-dimension vector. The computational complexity is largely decreased. From definition 4, we know that the larger the value of L used, the more information of EBGW approach contained, and the higher accuracy of test reached. On the other hand, information may be less when L equals the length of protein sequence. So the optimal value of L should be carefully chosen for different dataset.

2.2 Component-Coupled Algorithm

Suppose there are N proteins forming a set S, i.e.

$$S = S^\alpha \cup S^\beta \cup S^{\alpha+\beta} \cup S^{\alpha/\beta} \quad (4)$$

where the subset S^α consists of only all-α proteins, the subset S^β consists of only all-β proteins, and so forth. According to the EBGW approach, any protein in the set S corresponds to a vector (or a point) in the 3L-dimension space, i.e.

$$X_k^\xi = [x_{k,1}^\xi, x_{k,2}^\xi, \cdots, x_{k,3L}^\xi] \quad (k = 1, 2, \cdots, N_\xi) \quad (5)$$

where $\xi = \alpha, \beta, \alpha + \beta, \alpha/\beta$ denotes one of the four different structural classes and N_ξ is the number of proteins in the subset ξ.

The standard vector for the subset S^ξ is defined by

$$X^\xi = [x_1^\xi, x_2^\xi, \cdots, x_{3L}^\xi] \tag{6}$$

where

$$x_i^\xi = \frac{1}{N_\xi} \sum_{k=1}^{N_\xi} x_{k,i}^\xi \quad i = 1, 2, \cdots 3L \tag{7}$$

Suppose X is a protein whose structural class is to be predicted. It can be either one of the N proteins in the set S or a protein outside it. It also corresponds to a point $[x_1, x_2, \cdots x_{3L}]$ in the 3L-dimension space with EBGW approach.

The component-coupled algorithm is based on the squared Mahalanobis distance, defined by

$$F_M^2(X, X^\xi) = (X - X^\xi)C_\xi^{-1}(X - X^\xi)^T + \ln K_\xi \tag{8}$$

where $C_\xi = (c_{i,j}^\xi)_{3L \times 3L}$ is a covariance matrix given by

$$C_\xi = \begin{bmatrix} c_{1,1}^\xi & c_{1,2}^\xi & \cdots & c_{1,3L}^\xi \\ c_{2,1}^\xi & c_{2,2}^\xi & \cdots & c_{2,3L}^\xi \\ \vdots & \vdots & \ddots & \vdots \\ c_{3L,1}^\xi & c_{3L,2}^\xi & \cdots & c_{3L,3L}^\xi \end{bmatrix}$$

and the superscript T is the transposition operator; C_ξ^{-1} is the inverse matrix of C_ξ. The matrix elements $C_{i,j}^\xi$ are given by

$$c_{i,j}^\xi = \frac{1}{N_\xi - 1} \sum_{k=1}^{N_\xi} [x_{k,i}^\xi - x_i^\xi][x_{k,j}^\xi - x_j^\xi] \quad (i, j = 1, 2, \cdots 3L) \tag{9}$$

K_ξ is the product of all positive eigenvalues of C_ξ. The target protein X is predicted to be the structural class for which the corresponding Mahalanobis distance has the least value, as can be formulated as follow

$$F_M^2(X, X^\lambda) = \min \left\{ F_M^2(X, X^\alpha), F_M^2(X, X^\beta), F_M^2(X, X^{\alpha+\beta}), F_M^2(X, X^{\alpha/\beta}) \right\} \tag{10}$$

where λ can be $\alpha, \beta, \alpha/\beta$ or $\alpha+\beta$ and the superscript λ in Equation (10) will give the subset (or structural class) to which the predicted protein X should belong.

2.3 Evaluation of the Prediction Results

In order to assess the accuracy of a prediction algorithm, the sensitivity for each type is calculated according to Baldi et al [14]. Evaluating a given prediction method is a common but quite subtle problem. Usually, a prediction method is evaluated by the prediction results for a training data set and testing data set, respectively. According to the statistical terminology, the former is called a test of resubstitution reflecting the self-consistency, and the latter is a test of cross-validation reflecting the extrapolating effectiveness of the algorithm studied. As is well known, the single-test-set analysis, sub-sampling and jackknife analysis are the three methods often used for cross-validation examination[5]. In the single-test-set examination, the selection of a testing dataset is arbitrary, and the accuracy thus obtained lacks an objective criterion unless the training database is an ideal one and the testing dataset is sufficiently large. Another approach for cross-validation is sub-sampling analysis, according to which a given dataset is divided into a training set and a testing set. However, how to divide the whole dataset into a training set and a testing set is a serious problem. The number of possible divisions might be extremely large. In comparison with the single-set-test examination and the sub-sampling analysis, the jackknife test, also called the leave-one-out test seems to be most effective. In the jackknife test, each domain in the dataset is singled out in turn as a test domain and all the rule-parameters are determined from the remaining domains. Hence the memorization effects that are included in the resubstitution tests can be completely removed. During the process of jackknife analysis, both the training and testing datasets are actually open, and a domain will in turn move from each to the other. Both tests of resubstitution and jackknife are used to evaluate the new prediction method proposed here.

3 Results and Discussion

3.1 Dataset

To facilitate the comparison between our approach and the amino-acid composition- based approach, the same datasets and algorithm used by Chou and Maggiora [5] are used here. In their work several datasets were selected from structural classification of proteins (SCOP) [15] for the study of a four-class prediction. These datasets consist of 253, 359, 225 and 510 proteins respectively. The datasets T359 and T253 are mainly used here for comparison. Furthermore, the datasets T225 and T510 are also used as a practical application. The Protein DataBank codes of these proteins are referred to [5], and the constructions of all the datasets are listed in Table 1.

Table 1. Datasets used in this paper

Dataset	The number of sequences in different classes				Total
	$all - \alpha$	$all - \beta$	α/β	$\alpha + \beta$	
T253	63	58	61	71	253
T225	61	45	56	63	225
T359	82	85	99	93	359
T510	109	130	135	136	510

3.2 Prediction Results

The prediction results for dataset T359 are listed in Table 2. For convenience, we abbreviate the two approaches as follows: AAC, the amino acid composition-based approach; EBGW, encode based on grouped weight approach. In the following tables, we also abbreviate Resb and Jack as the Resubstitution test and the jackknife test respectively. As seen from Table 2, the overall prediction accuracy achieved by EBGW is 5% higher than AAC for the Resubstitution test. Meanwhile, the overall prediction accuracy achieved by EBGW is about 7% higher than AAC for the jackknife test. As the jackknife test is thought of a rigorous cross-validation, the improvement of the overall prediction accuracy for the jackknife test is considered remarkable. Carefully analysis the data in Table 2, we find that the prediction accuracy for each class is improved. Especially for the protein structure class of $\alpha + \beta$ the increase of prediction accuracy can achieve about 15%. Note that the above results for EBGW approach is dependent on the datasets and the number of groups L adopted (L=13 here). We will discuss this point as well as several other points below.

Table 2. Prediction results for dataset T359 using EBGW (L=13)

Method/test	Prediction accuracy for each class				Overall accuracy
	$all - \alpha$	$all - \beta$	α/β	$\alpha + \beta$	
EBGW/Resb	100%	100%	100%	98.92%	**99.72%**
AAC[5]/Resb	93.90%	94.12%	95.96%	93.55%	94.43%
EBGW/Jack	95.12%	85.88%	89.90%	93.55%	**91.09%**
AAC[5]/Jack	89.02%	83.53%	85.86%	78.49%	84.12%

3.3 The Optimal Choice of the Number of Groups

The number of groups is denoted as L in definition 4. Usually, the larger the value of L is used, the higher the accuracy of the resubstitution test can get. However, our study shows that a great number of groups do not always lead to a better prediction result for the jackknife test. For the dataset T359 we find that L=13 leads to the highest prediction accuracy of jackknife test, i.e. 327/359=91.09%, while for the dataset T510 we find that L= 14 is the best choice. We should point out that the optimal L value is dependent on the dataset. For the different datasets discuss here, the optimal L value are found to vary from 7 to 14 (see Table 2-6).

3.4 The Impact of the Size of Dataset to the Prediction Accuracy

We also try to discover how the size of dataset can affect the prediction accuracy. A smaller dataset consisting of 253 proteins was used early in Chou et al [5], which has less overlap with those of dataset T359. The same prediction was performed for dataset T253, the results are shown in Table 4(L=8). The overall prediction accuracy of the resubstitution test for EBGW is about 0.79% higher

Table 3. Optimal choice of the number of groups for dataset T359

L	Prediction accuracy for each class in jackknife test				Overall accuracy
	$all - \alpha$	$all - \beta$	α/β	$\alpha + \beta$	
10	87.80%	82.35%	86.87%	89.25%	86.63%
11	91.46%	85.88%	80.81%	92.47%	87.47%
12	90.24%	83.53%	88.89%	91.40%	88.58%
13	95.12%	85.88%	89.90%	93.55%	**91.09%**
14	98.78%	83.53%	87.88%	88.17%	89.42%
15	98.78%	72.94%	87.88%	88.17%	86.91%

than that for AAC, whereas the overall prediction accuracy of the jackknife test for EBGW is about 2.77% higher than that for AAC. Because the component-coupled algorithm needs more training data to make its prediction mechanism work properly, the decrease in the improvement (from 7% to about 3%) may be caused by the smaller size of the dataset T253. We should point out that in the case of the smaller dataset T253, the optimal number of groups used is changed, here we find that L=8 leads to the highest overall prediction accuracy.

Table 4. Prediction results for dataset T253 using EBGW (L=8)

Method/test	Prediction accuracy for each class				Overall accuracy
	$all - \alpha$	$all - \beta$	α/β	$\alpha + \beta$	
EBGW/Resb	90.48%	98.28%	96.72%	98.59%	**96.05%**
AAC[5]/Resb	95.24%	93.10%	98.36%	94.37%	95.26%
EBGW/Jack	82.54%	75.86%	75.41%	91.55%	**81.82%**
AAC[5]/Jack	84.13%	79.31%	70.49%	81.69%	79.05%

To test the new approach for a larger dataset, another dataset, which was used in Chou [5], consisting of 510 proteins extracted from SCOP is used here. Performing exactly the same prediction as for the dataset T359, the detailed prediction results are shown in Table 5 (L=14). The overall prediction accuracy of the jackknife test for EBGW is 91.96%, indicating that a higher overall prediction accuracy is achieved with EBGW approach. This prediction confirms again the point of view that in order to work properly, the new method needs a much larger training dataset.

Table 5. Prediction results for dataset T510 using EBGW (L=14)

Method/test	Prediction accuracy for each class				Overall accuracy
	$all - \alpha$	$all - \beta$	α/β	$\alpha + \beta$	
EBGW/Resb	100%	100%	99.26%	100%	**99.80%**
EBGW/Jack	91.74%	88.46%	91.11%	96.32%	**91.96%**

3.5 Application

The prediction quality of EBGW approach can be improved has been demonstrated above through both resubstitution and jackknife tests. Here, a practical application is presented to indicate the consistency of this kind of improvement.

The procedure consists of the following two steps: (1) constructing a training dataset from which the prediction-rule-parameters are derived; (2) constructing an independent testing dataset for which the prediction is performed using the parameters derived from the training dataset. Another two datasets, which used in Chou [5], consisting of 225 and 510 proteins extracted from SCOP are used here as training dataset and testing dataset respectively. By following the same prediction procedure, the structural classes of the 510 proteins in the testing dataset can be predicted based on the parameters derived from the 225 proteins in the training dataset. The prediction results are summarized in Table 6, from which it can be seen that the overall prediction rate of correct prediction for the independent testing dataset by EBGW approach is about 3% higher than those by AAC approach. This is consistent with the jackknife test results demonstrated in the previous section.

Table 6. Prediction results for dataset T510 as testing dataset using EBGW (L=11)

Method	Prediction accuracy for each class				Overall accuracy
	$all - \alpha$	$all - \beta$	α/β	$\alpha + \beta$	
EBGW	82.57%	93.08%	85.93%	94.85%	89.41%
AAC[5]	74.31%	90.00%	91.85%	87.50%	86.47%

4 Conclusions

Instead of the approach based on amino acid composition solely, a new encoding scheme named EBGW is presented in this paper. Applying EBGW approach to some non-redundant datasets with component-coupled algorithm, considerable improvements in the overall prediction accuracy are achieved compared with the AAC approach. The experiment results show that EBGW approach is convenient to calculate and provides an effective tool to extract valuable information from protein sequences, which may be a useful tool in other assignment problems in proteomics and genome research.

References

1. Anfinsen C.B: Principles that govern the folding of protein chains. Science. **181** (1973) 223-230
2. Levitt M, Chothia C: Structure patterns in globular proteins. Nature. **262** (1976) 552-557
3. Chou K.C, Zhang C.T: Prediction of protein structural classes. Crit.Rev.Biochem.Mol.Biol. **30** (1995) 275-349

4. Nakashima H, Nishikawa K, Ooi T: The folding type of a protein is relevant to the amino acid composition. J.Biochem. **99** (1986) 152-162
5. Chou K.C, Maggiora G.M: Domain structural class prediction. Protein Engineering.**11**(1998) 523-538
6. Bu W.S, Feng Z.P, Zhang Z.D, Zhang C.T: Prediction of protein (domain) structural classes based on amino-acid index. Eur. J. Biochem.**266** (1999) 1043-1049
7. Li X.Q, Luo L.F: The definition and recognition of protein structural class. Progress in Biochemistry and Biophysics. **29**(2002) 124-127
8. Li X.Q, Luo L.F: The recognition of protein structural class. Progress in Biochemistry and Biophysics.**29** (2002) 938-941
9. Wang Z.X, Yuan Z: How good is prediction of protein structural class by the component-coupled method?. Proteins.**38** (2000) 165-175
10. Cai Y.D, Liu X.J, Xu X.B, Zhou G.P: Support Vector Machines for predicting protein structural class. BMC Bioinformatics. **2**(2001) 3
11. Luo R.Y, Feng Z.P, Liu J.K: Prediction of protein structural class by amino acid and ploypeptide composition. Eur.J.Biochem. **269**(2002) 4219-4225
12. He P.A, Wang J: Numerical characterization of DNA primary sequence. Internet Electronic Journal of Molecular Design. **1** (2002) 668-674
13. Lin J.C, Yang K.C: Biochemistry. Shenyang: liaoning science and technology press. (1996) 6-7
14. Baldi P, Brunak S, Chauvin Y, Andersen C.A, Nielsen H: Assessing the accuracy of prediction algorithms for classification: an overview. Bioinformatics.**16** (2000) 412-424
15. Loredana L.C, Steven E.B, Tim J.P.H, Cyrus C, Alexey G.M: SCOP dataset in 2002: refinements accommodate structural genomics. Nucleic Acids Research. **30**(2002) 264-267

DNA Computing Approach to Construction of Semantic Model

Yusei Tsuboi, Zuwairie Ibrahim, Nobuyuki Kasai, and Osamu Ono

Institute of Applied DNA Computing
Graduate School of Science & Technology, Meiji University
1-1-1 Higashimita, Tama-ku, Kawasaki-shi
Kanagawa 214-8571, Japan
Phone: +81-44-934-7289, Fax: +81-44-934-7909
{tsuboi, zuwairie, ce55024, ono}@isc.meiji.ac.jp

Abstract. In this paper, after a new DNA-based semantic model is theoretically proposed, the preliminary experiment on construction of the small test model is successfully done. This model, referred to as *'semantic model based on molecular computing'* (SMC) has the structure of a graph formed by the set of all (attribute, attribute values) pairs contained in the set of represented objects, plus a tag node for each object. Each path in the network, from an initial object-representing tag node to a terminal node represents the object named on the tag. Input of a set of input strands will result in the formation of object-representing dsDNAs via parallel self-assembly, from encoded ssDNAs representing both attributes and attribute values (nodes), as directed by ssDNA splinting strands representing relations (edges) in the network. The proposed model is rather suitable for knowledge representation in order to store vast amount of information with high density. The proposed model will appears as an interaction between AI and biomolecular computing research fields, and will be further extended for several AI applications

1 Introduction

Baum [1] first proposed an idea of constructing DNA-based memory. Some related experimental work has been reported. In their reports, instead of encoding data into {0, 1} bit in case of conventional memory, the data is encoded as {A, T, C, G} base sequences then it is stored in DNA strands, but they never sufficiently compensate for the way to arrange knowledge information for representing an object in DNA strands, which makes it difficult for human to understand any information instinctively.

Semantic networks or nets are graphic notations for representing knowledge in patterns of interconnected nodes and edges. Computer implementations of semantic networks were first developed for artificial intelligence (AI) and machine translation, but earlier versions have long been used in philosophy, psychology, and linguistics. Brain information processing often involves comparing concepts. There are various ways of assessing concept similarity, which vary depending on adopted models of knowledge representation. In featural representations, concepts are represented by sets of features. In Quillian's model of semantic memory [8], concepts are represented by the relationship name via links. Links are labeled by the name of the relationship and are assigned criteriality tags that attest to the importance of link. In artificial computer implementations, criteriality tags are numerical values the represent the degree of association between concept pairs (i.e., how often the link is traversed), and the nature of the association. There are many variations of semantic networks, but all can be categorize into either one of the six categories: definitional, assertional, implicational, executable, learning, and hybrid [3]. The detail of such categories is not covered in this paper. The point of our study is in the structure of semantic networks.

In semantic networks, a basic structure of relations between two objects is described with nodes, directed edges and labels as shown in Figure 1. The nodes denote "object" and the directed edge denotes the relations. Semantic network is a set of objects described by such structures. The nodes and edges are changeable under the situations of various representations. It is easy for man to intuitively understand meanings of the object with network structures. The graph of the semantic network potentially realizes reasonable knowledge representation.

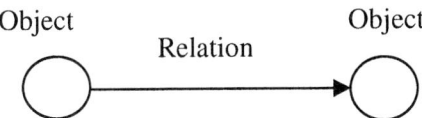

Fig. 1. A standard structure of a semantic network: the nodes denote objects and the directed edge denotes relation between the two objects.

It is considered that one method of approaching a memory with power near to that of human is to construct a semantic network model based on molecular computing. However it is difficult to apply existing semantic networks because duplex DNA structures forced them to limit capacity of knowledge representation. It seems a new semantic model like a network will be required for DNA computing approach.

In this paper, we design a semantic model derived from semantic networks for implementation with DNA. A set of semantic information is stored in single-stranded (ss) or double-stranded (ds) DNAs. These strands will form linear dsDNA by using DNA computing techniques.

2 Semantic Model Based on Molecular Computing

In this section, from theoretical points of view, we propose a DNA-based semantic model that is graphically described in the straightforward manner. Then, the model is represented by DNA sequences for an experimental approach.

2.1 Model

Some researches have been trying to solve simple problems on semantic networks using AI technique. Therefore it was conceivable that early semantic network was done using papers and pencils. When researchers realize the need to represent bigger problem domain, computers software were designed to overcome the limitation inherent in the conventional methods. These graphical notions were ultimately transferred on to computers using software specific data structures to represent nodes and edges. We produce another way by using DNA-based computers to implement such semantic networks.

In our consideration, however, it is almost impossible to implement existing semantic networks by using DNA computing techniques, because DNA's duplex structure limits representations of them heavily. Thus, instead of using the standard existing semantic network described in the section 1, we create a new semantic model such a network in order to enable to use the DNA computing techniques. Such a model has to be created to maintain the concept of an existing semantic network as much as possible. The way to make the semantic model is described as follows.

First, a tag as a name of an object is set to an initial node in the graph. After we determine the number and the kinds of the attribute of the object, both the attribute and attribute value are sequentially set to another node following by the tag node. Second, a directed edge is connected between (attribute, attribute value) pair nodes. Figure 2 shows a basic structure of this. It is imperative to transform complicated graphs into simpler ones. An AND/OR graph enables the reduction of graph size, and facilitates easy understanding. The relation between the nodes and edges is represented using a new defined AND/OR graph. A directed edge in the terminal direction is sequentially connected between the nodes except for the following case (AND). If there are two nodes which have same attributes but different attribute values, each of directive edges is connected in parallel (OR). Each edge denotes only connection between the nodes in the directed graph. Finally, labels are attached to the nodes, such as '(Tag: O)' and '(Attribute: A, Attribute Value: V)'.

The nodes denote either a name of the object or both the attribute and the attribute values. In short, one path from an initial node to a terminal node means one object named on the tag. We define this graph as a knowledge representation model. The model represents an object, as reasoned out by the combinations between the nodes connected by the edges. For example, Figure 3 illustrates this object representation in the context of object X (named via the tag). An overall graph is then formed by the union of a set of such basic objects, each of which is described in similar, simple fashion. Figure 4 shows an example of such a network. We name such a graph a *semantic model based on molecular computing* (SMC). An SMC contains all attributes common to every object as well as each attribute value. Attribute layers consist of attribute values, lined up. If an object has no value of a certain attribute, the attribute value is assigned '*no value*', such a question of 'What is water's shape?' An object is expressed by the list representation style as follows,

$$\{<O, A_i, V_{ji}> | i=1, 2,\ldots, m; j=1,2,\ldots, n\}$$

Although an attribute generally corresponds to an attribute value with one to one, in the SMC the attribute is allowed to have one or more attribute values.

For example, object X such as Figure 3 is,

$$<\text{Object } X, A_1, V_{11}>$$

$$<\text{Object } X, A_2, V_{12}>$$

$< \text{Object X}, A_2, V_{22}>$

$< \text{Object X}, A_3, V_{13}>$

$<\text{Object X}, A_3, V_{23}>$

A_2 has two attribute values, V_{12} and V_{22}. And also, A_3 has two attribute values, V_{13} and V_{23}.

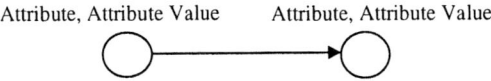

Fig. 2. A basic structure of the semantic model proposed: the nodes except for the tag node denote both attributes and attribute values. The directed edge merely is connected between the two nodes.

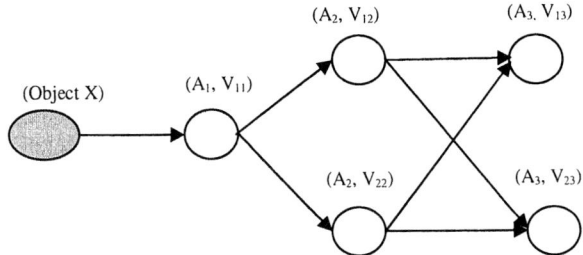

Fig. 3. A simple object model of X; the three determined attributes are A_1, A_2, and A_3

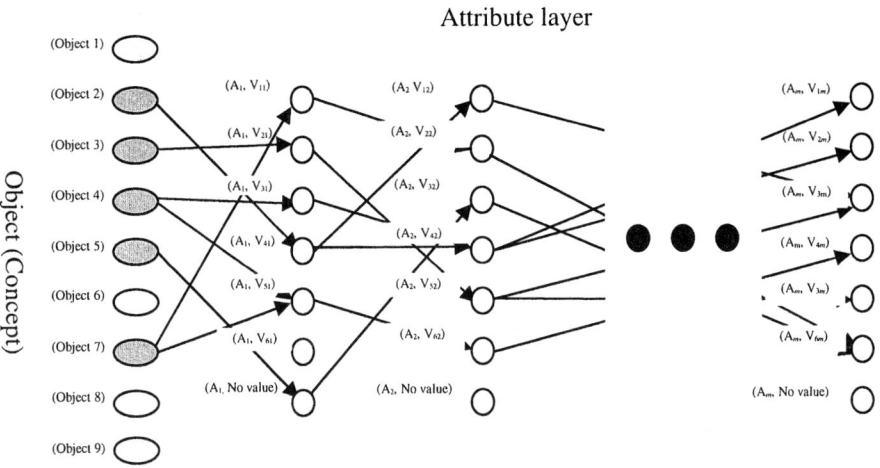

Fig. 4. A semantic model based on molecular computing (SMC), which collectively models a set of objects, given a total number of attribute layers, m.

2.2 DNA Representation

Each of the nodes and edges within an SMC may be represented by a DNA strand, as follows. First, each node is mapped onto a unique, ssDNA oligonucleotide, in a DNA library of strands. In the DNA library, a row shows attributes, a column shows attribute values and each DNA sequence is designed. The DNA sequences are assigned by 20 oligonucleotides. Here, an important thing is that every sequence is designed according to these relations to prevent mishybiridization via other unmatching sequences. The sequences used are designed by DNA Sequence Generator [2] that is a program for the design of DNA sequences useful for DNA computing, nanotechnology and the design of DNA Arrays. Second, each edge is mapped by following the Adleman [6] scheme. Finally, the overall strands are respectively represented by the size which suits the end of the DNA pieces of the initial or the terminal exactly. In this way, the semantic model of each object is represented by DNA strands. Figure 5 shows one of paths shown for object X model in Figure 3, as represented by a set of ssDNA ((Object X)→(A_1, V_{11})→(A_2, V_{12})→(A_3, V_{13})).

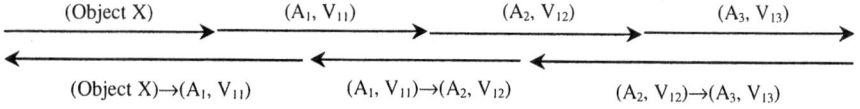

Fig. 5. One of the DNA paths of the graph (Object X) in Figure 3. The arrowhead indicates the 3' hydroxyl end.

3 Experimental Construction of DNA-Based Semantic Model

The SMC is theoretically described in the section 2. It is essential to implement SMC to verify our theory. The target model is Figure 3, a small SMC graph. Every path from the initial node to the terminal node in this model is represented by a set of ssDNA. The ssDNAs of tag node and the edges within the set are synthesized as *knowledge based molecules*. The sequences substantially used are shown in Table 1. The ssDNAs representing label (A_1, V_{11}), (A_2, V_{12}), and (A_3, V_{13}) is synthesized as an *input molecule* to be combined with the DNA library. The sequences are shown in Table 2.

Knowledge based molecules are first inserted into a test tube, followed by addition of the input molecules, in addition to appropriate volume of distilled water, were mixed. The mixture was heated to 94 ℃ and then hybridized by slowly cooled to 16 ℃ at 1 ℃ per minutes. The reaction mixture was then subjected to a ligation. For a ligation, 50μl of the reaction mixtures, T4 DNA ligase (4unlts/μl, TOYOBO, Japan), ligation buffer (10×reaction buffer for LGA, TOYOBO, Japan), and ATP (100mM, TOYOBO, Japan). The total reaction volume was 56μl. The reaction mixture was incubated at 16 ℃ for 16 hours. The schematic diagram of this process is shown in Figure 6.

The only DNAs representing the test model are efficiently amplified with PCR to surely obtain correct dsDNA length for a next operation, gel electrophoresis. Although the PCR needs two primers of sequences properly designed for the template DNAs, it is

Table 1. The sequences synthesized for knowledge based molecules

Label	Sequence (5'→ 3')
(Object X)	AAAGCTCGTCGTTTAAGGAA
(Object X) → (A_1, V_{11})	AGTAGGCTTCTTCCTTAAACGACGAGCTTT
(A_1, V_{11}) → (A_2, V_{12})	AATCACGATACGCAGAGTAC
(A_1, V_{11}) → (A_2, V_{22})	TACGTGGCTGCGCAGAGTAC
(A_2, V_{12}) → (A_3, V_{13})	CTTATCAGTTCGATTGGGTATCCACCTCCA
(A_2, V_{12}) → (A_3, V_{23})	GAGCCCCCTCCGTTGACCGATCCACCTCCA
(A_2, V_{22}) → (A_3, V_{13})	CTTATCAGTTCGATTGGGTACTAGCTCTAC
(A_2, V_{22}) → (A_3, V_{23})	GAGCCCCCTCCGTTGACCGACTAGCTCTAC

Table 2. The sequences synthesized for input molecules

Label	Sequence (5' → 3')
(A_1, V_{11})	GAAGCCTACTGTACTCTGCG
(A_2, V_{12})	TATCGTGATTTGGAGGTGGA
(A_3, V_{13})	TACCCAATCGAACTGATAAG

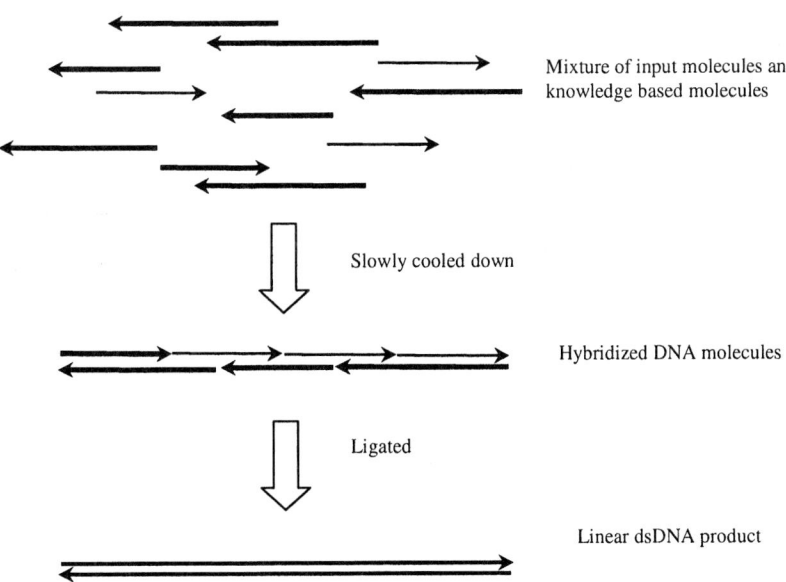

Fig. 6. Schematic diagram of hybridization & ligation process. The thick arrows denote the knowledge based molecules. The thin arrows denote the input molecules.

possible to design them by the sequences assigned by the initial node and the terminal node. As for this experiment, the sequences used as primers are 5'TTCCTTAAA CGACGAGCTTT3' and 5'CTTATCAGTTCGATTGGGTA3'. The PCR is performed in a 25μl solution including 13.875μl distilled water, 2.5μl for each primers, 1μl template, 2.5μl 10×KOD dash buffer (TOYOBO, Japan), 0.125μl KOD dash (TOYOBO, Japan), and 2.5μl dNTP (TOYOBO, Japan) for 25 cycle at 94 for 30 seconds, at 55 for 30 seconds, and at 74 seconds for 10 seconds.

4 Result and Discussion

The PCR products are subjected to gel electrophoresis to determine the presence of the correct dsDNAs, which then appear as discrete bands on the gel. The correct dsDNA length, denoted as L_S, is given by the simple relation:

$$L\_S = L\_D\,(m+1),$$

where L_D is the length of each synthesized DNA fragment. Now L_D is length of 20-mer assignedd by the DNA library, and $m = 3$, then L_D is 80 bp (base pair). The gel is stained by SYBR GOLD (Molecular probes). After gel electrophoresis was executed for 35 minutes, the gel image was captured as shown in Figure 7. In the lane 1 the dsDNAs of 80 bp clearly appeared on the gel. The result explains that the small test model is successfully constructed with DNA molecules.

In AI research fields, some work has been focusing on how to arrange and store a set of knowledge in memories. By semantic models composed of nodes and edges, not logical rules, a certain object is administered by a tag node linking (attribute, attribute value) pair nodes. It might have difficulties treating complicated representation only by (attribute, attribute value) pairs. However, the proposed model has much advantage over the logical rule approaches. By picking the nodes up, it is possible to reach for the object at a stretch. Human can understand and recognize the context of the object smoothly compared with other models [1][4][5][7] when he sees the model. If individual objects have common (attribute, attribute value) pair nodes, they can share them, which enable to reduce the vain synthesis of such overlap sequences. Moreover, knowledge representation capacity of this model is very higher, because the SMC is represented by both attributes and attribute values with a concept of AND/OR graph.

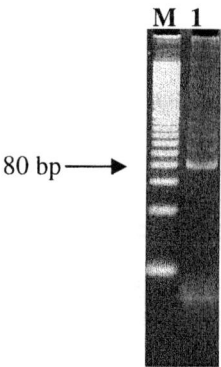

Fig. 7. The result of the gel electrophoresis on 10% polyacrylamide gel. The product amplified by PCR is in lane 1. Lane M denotes 20 bp ladder.

Therefore, we believe that the proposed one is very suitable for semantic memories with DNA molecules. In the future work, to achieve reliable performance, the optimization of some parameters, such as reaction-temperature, oligonucleotide concentrations, reaction time, etc. will be experimentally tested when a larger complex model is implemented. The proposed model will appears as an interaction between AI and biomolecular computing research fields, and will be further extended for several AI applications.

Acknowledgements

The research was financially supported by the Sasakawa Scientific Research Grant from The Japan Science Society. The second author would like to thank Universiti Teknologi Malaysia for a study leave.

References

1. E. B. Baum: How to Build an Associative Memory Vastly Larger than the Brain, Science 268 (1995), pp.583-585.
2. F. Udo, S. Sam, B. Wolfgang, and R. Hilmar, DNA sequence generator: A Program for the Construction of DNA Sequences, Proc. of the Seventh International Workshop on DNA Based Computers (2001), pp.21-32.
3. J. F. Sowa: Sematic Networks, http://www.jfsowa.com/pubs/semnet.htm. (2005).
4. J. H. Rief: Parallel Molecular Computation, Models and Simulations, Proc. of the 7th Annual Symaposium on Parallel Algorithms and Architectures (1995), pp.213-223.
5. J. H. Reif, H. T. LaBean, M. Pirrung, V. S. Rana,, B. Guo, C. Kingsford, G. S. Wickham: Experimental Construction of Very Large Scale DNA Databases with Associative Search Capability, The 10th International Workshop on DNA Based Computers, Revised Papers, Lecture Notes in Computer Science 2943 (2002), pp. 231-247.
6. L. M. Adleman: Molecular Computation of Solutions to Combinatorial Problems, Science 266 (1994), pp.583-585.
7. M. Arita, M Hagiya, and A. Suyama: Joining and Rotating Data with Molecules, Proc. of IEEE International Conference on Evolutionary Computation (1997), pp.243-248.
8. M. R. Quillian, and M. Minsky: Semantic Memory, Semantic Information Processing, MIT Press, Cambridge, MA. (1968), pp.216-270.

DNA Computing for Complex Scheduling Problem

Mohd Saufee Muhammad, Zuwairie Ibrahim, Satomi Ueda,
Osamu Ono, and Marzuki Khalid

Institute of Applied DNA Computing, Meiji University,
1-1-1 Higashi-Mita, Tama-Ku, Kawasaki-Shi, Kanagawa-Ken 214-8571, Japan
{msaufee, zuwairie, satomixx, ono}@isc.meiji.ac.jp,
marzuki@utmkl.utm.my
http://www.isc.meiji.ac.jp/~i3erabc/IADC.html

Abstract. Interest in DNA computing has increased overwhelmly since Adleman successfully demonstrated its capability to solve Hamiltonian Path Problem (HPP). Many research results of similar combinatorial problems which are mainly in the realm of computer science and mathematics have been presented. In this paper, implementation ideas and methods to solve an engineering related combinatorial problem using this DNA computing approach is presented. The objective is to find an optimal path for a complex elevator scheduling problem of an 8-storey building with 3 elevators. Each of the elevator traveled path is represented by DNA sequence of specific length that represent elevator's traveling time in a proportional way based on certain initial conditions such as present and destination floors, and hall calls for an elevator from a floor. The proposed ideas and methods show promising results that DNA computing approach can be well-suited for solving such real-world application in the near future.

1 Introduction

In 1994, Adleman [1] demonstrated the practical possibility of using molecules of Deoxyribonucleic Acid or DNA as a medium for computation. In his experiment, Adleman successfully solved a directed Hamiltonian Path Problem (HPP) using the tools of biomolecular engineering. Adleman [2] created DNA strands to represent an airplane flight from each of the seven cities, and then combined them to produce every possible route. Given its vast parallelism, the DNA strands yielded 10^9 answers in less than one second.

DNA computation relies on devising algorithms that solve problems using the encoded information in the sequence of oligonucleotides that make up DNA's double helix – the bases Adenine, Guanine, Thymine, and Cytosine (A, G, T, and C, respectively) and then breaking and making new bonds between them to reach the answer.

Research on DNA application to solve engineering problem however has not been very well establish. In this paper DNA computing technique to solve such problem is proposed. Since DNA computing is very suitable to solve combinatorial problems, an elevator scheduling problem is chosen to be solved using this computing technique. The elevator scheduling problem involves finding an optimal path, or in other word, finding the shortest path for the travel path of the elevators for a building with certain number of elevators and floors. However, this problem is a complex combinatorial problem since certain criteria need to be fulfilled for the problem solution such as initial elevator position, its destinations and hall calls made for an elevator.

As mentioned, the elevator scheduling problem involves finding the elevator shortest travel path. Hence, current research works on DNA computing techniques for solving shortest path is being reviewed. Among others, Nayaranan and Zorbalas [3] proposed a constant proportional length-based DNA computing technique for solving Traveling Salesman Problem (TSP) or shortest path HPP. Yamamoto *et al.* [4] proposed a concentration-controlled DNA computing to accomplish local search for the shortest path problem. Lee *et al.* [5] proposed a DNA computing technique based on temperature gradient to solve the TSP problem. Ibrahim *et al.* [6] on the other hand proposed a direct-proportional length-based DNA computing for shortest path problem. The proposed method for the finding the optimal path of the elevator scheduling problem based on one of the shortest path method is presented in detail in this paper.

2 Biomolecular Operations of DNA

DNA computing involves biomolecular operations to manipulate the DNA strands by DNA synthesis, polymerase chain reaction (PCR), ligation, parallel overlap assembly (POA) and gel electrophoresis operations that are described as follows.

DNA Synthesis. DNA synthesis or replication is the process of copying a double-stranded DNA strand. Presently, a test tube containing approximately 10^{18} DNA molecules are available from commercial DNA synthesis companies at a reasonable price.

Polymerase Chain Reaction (PCR). PCR is an incredibly sensitive copying machine for DNA. DNA strands can be copied exponentially using PCR. PCR proceeds in cycles of 3 steps at different temperatures as illustrated in Fig. 1 [7]. These steps are denaturation (95°C), involves separation of the double strand template, annealing (55°C) where primers are 'annealed' to both the single strands ends and extension (75°C) process where polymerase enzymes are used to extend the primers into replicas of the template. This sequence is repeated causing an exponential growth in the number of templates.

Ligation. Ligation is often invoked after an annealing operation to concatenate strands of DNA. Although it is possible to use some ligase enzymes to concatenate free-floating double-stranded DNA, it is more efficient to allow single strands to anneal together, connecting up series of single-strand fragments, and then use a ligase to seal the covalent bonds between adjacent fragments, as shown in Fig. 2 [8].

Parallel Overlapping Assembly (POA). POA is a method for initial pool generation to solve weighted graph problems. This method is introduced by Stemmer [9] to facilitate *in vitro* mutagenesis. Kaplan *et al.* [10] successfully applied this method to

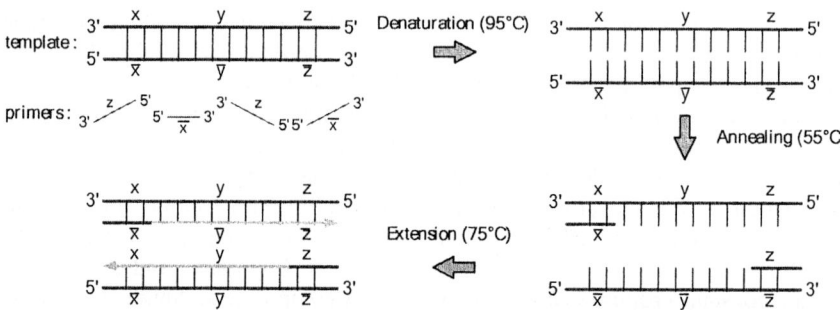

Fig. 1. One cycle of PCR

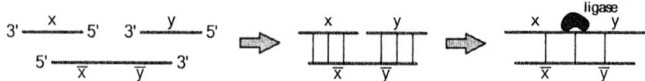

Fig. 2. Ligation process

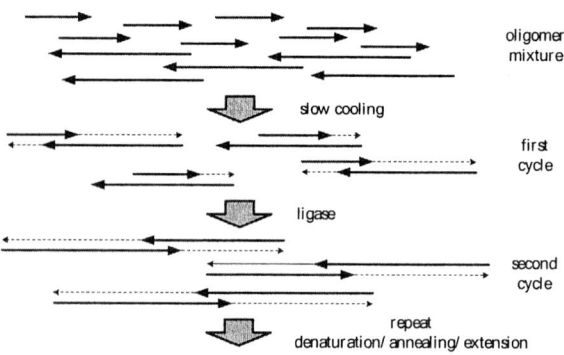

Fig. 3. Parallel overlapping assembly (POA) for initial pool generation. The continuous arrows represent the synthesized oligos which are the input to the computation. The dotted arrows represent the elongated part during polymerization. The arrowhead indicates the 3' end.

generate initial pool consisting of binary numbers to solve maximal clique problem. POA involves thermal cycle where during the thermal cycle, the position strings in one of the oligo is annealed to the complementary strings of the next oligo. In the presence of polymerase enzyme, the oligo 3' end side is extended to form a longer double stranded DNA as depicted in Fig. 3 [11]. A data pool consisting of all possible combinations are thus produced after a number of thermal cycles.

Gel Electrophoresis. Gel electrophoresis is a technique for separating DNA strands according to its length through a gel in an electrical field based on the fact that DNA is negatively charged [12]. As the separation process continues the separation between the larger and smaller fragments increases as depicted in Fig. 4 [13, 14].

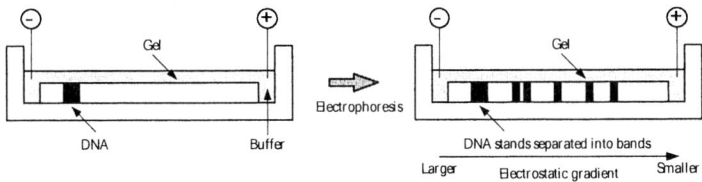

Fig. 4. Gel electrophoresis process

3 Elevator Scheduling Problem

Typically, a building consists of N floors with a total of M elevators. An example of elevator situation at an instance of a time can be illustrated as in Table 1.

The elevator travel path can be represented as a weighted graph problem. This is done by representing the elevator position at floor 1, 2, 3, ... , $N-2$, $N-1$, N with nodes V_1, V_2, V_3, ... , V_{N-2}, V_{N-1}, V_N respectively. The graph of all possible travel paths of one of the elevator is constructed as shown in Fig. 5.

Table 1. Elevator situation at an instance of time

Floor No	Elevator 1	Elevator 2	...	Elevator $M-1$	Elevator M	Hall Call
N			...	$(N-3, 7, 3)$		
$N-1$	$(N-2, 4, 1)$		...			↑
$N-2$			...			↓
:	:	:	:	:	:	:
3		$(4, 6, N-2)$	...			↑
2			...		$(5, 8, N-1)$	↓
1			...			

The weight between nodes can be represented as

$$\omega_{|j-i|} = (|j-i|)T_T + T_S \qquad (1)$$

where

$\qquad i$ — elevator present floor position
$\qquad j$ — elevator destination floor position
$\qquad |j-i|$ — total number of floors of elevator movement
$\qquad T_T$ — elevator traveling time between two consecutive floors
$\qquad T_S$ — elevator stopping time at a floor

The output of the graph, given by sum of the graph weights thus represents the total traveling time of the elevator, i.e.

$$G(E) = \sum_{|j-i|=1}^{N-1} \omega_{|j-i|} \qquad (2)$$

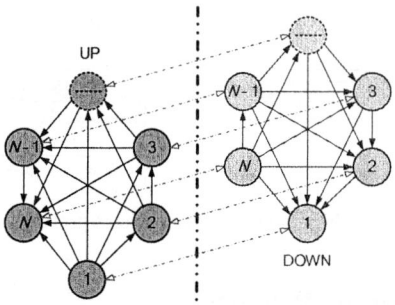

Fig. 5. Graph of all possible travel paths of an elevator

For a building with M elevators, M similar graphs as shown in Fig. 5 can be duplicated representing all M elevators travel paths. The total traveling time of all the elevators can thus be calculated by summing up each of the elevators traveling time as

$$G(E_1, E_2, \cdots, E_{M-1}, E_M) = G(E_1) + G(E_2) + \cdots + G(E_{M-1}) + G(E_M) \tag{3}$$

The optimal travel path is thus given by the minimum total traveling time of all the elevators with all initial conditions and requirements satisfied, i.e.

$$\text{Optimal Travel Path} = G(E_1, E_2, \ldots, E_{M-1}, E_M)_{min} \tag{4}$$

Let us consider a building with 3 elevators and 8 floors. Elevator A is presently at 1st floor and its destination is 4th and 5th floor, elevator B is presently at 6th floor and its destination is 3rd and 2nd floor, and elevator C is presently at 3rd floor and its destination is 6th and 8th floor. There are hall calls at 4th floor going up, and hall calls at 5th floor going down, as illustrated in Table 2.

Table 2. Elevator position for elevator scheduling problem example

Floor No	Elevator A	Elevator B	Elevator C	Hall Call
8				
7				
6		(3, 2)		
5				↓
4				↑
3			(6, 8)	
2				
1	(4, 5)			

The solution to this elevator scheduling problem is to find the optimal travel path for all the elevators that fulfill all initial conditions and requirements defined. Therefore, it is necessary to calculate the total output of the graphs $G(A, B, C)$. The optimal travel path will thus be given by the minimum graph output among all the graph output for all possible travel paths of elevator A, B and C.

4 DNA Computing to Solve Elevator Scheduling Problem

A method proposed by [6] to solve the shortest path problem is being applied to solve the elevator scheduling problem. Using this method, the weights between every node are encoded by oligonucleotide length in a proportional way to represent the elevator's traveling time between floors. A number of steps are performed for the computation process that is discussed below.

Step 1. The elevator position are represented as nodes V_1, V_2, V_3, V_4, V_5, V_6, V_7, V_8 and V_1', V_2', V_3', V_4', V_5', V_6', V_7', V_8' for upward and downward movements respectively representing all the 8 floor positions in the building.

Step 2. The weights between nodes are assigned in such a way that it will directly represent the elevator's traveling time between the floors. Since the building consists of 8 floors, the maximum number of floors that the elevator can travel is $(8-1) = 7$ floors. Now, assuming that $T_T = 5$ sec, $T_S = 15$ sec, and representing every 5 sec with 10 units, we have form (1)

$$\omega_0 = 0(5) + 15 = 15 \text{ sec} = 30 \quad , \quad \omega_1 = 1(5) + 15 = 20 \text{ sec} = 40$$
$$\omega_2 = 2(5) + 15 = 25 \text{ sec} = 50 \quad , \quad \omega_3 = 3(5) + 15 = 30 \text{ sec} = 60$$
$$\omega_4 = 4(5) + 15 = 35 \text{ sec} = 70 \quad , \quad \omega_5 = 5(5) + 15 = 40 \text{ sec} = 80$$
$$\omega_6 = 6(5) + 15 = 45 \text{ sec} = 90 \quad , \quad \omega_7 = 7(5) + 15 = 50 \text{ sec} = 100$$

Step 3. Construct a graph with its corresponding weight representing all possible travel path combinations of each elevator that fulfill all the required initial conditions and requirements as shown in Fig. 6. Note that all possible end paths of elevator A are joined with the start path of elevator B. Similarly, all possible end paths of elevator B are joined with the start path of elevator C. This is done in order that the total output of the graph $G(A, B, C)$ representing the travel path of all the elevators can be calculated.

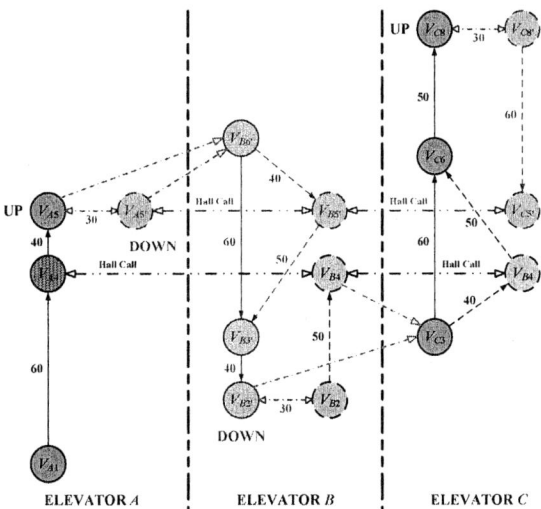

Fig. 6. Graph of all possible travel path combinations of elevators A, B and C

Table 3. DNA sequence for nodes (elevator floor position)

Upward Movement	20-mer Sequence (5'–3') V_{ia}	V_{ib}	GC%	T_m (°C)
V_1	TCATCCTCCC	GTCATTAACT	0.45	59.35
V_2	TTGGCTAAGG	AAGTCGGTAG	0.50	59.32
V_3	GCTCTAAGCT	AGTATCGCGG	0.55	59.24
V_4	CAATACTGCG	CGAATGTTAC	0.45	59.20
V_5	AAATACCAAA	AACATGCCGT	0.35	59.19
V_6	ATAGGGGGGA	CATATCCAAT	0.45	59.19
V_7	CTAATTCTGC	AAACCACACG	0.45	59.18
V_8	AATTTGGGTG	GACCGTAGTA	0.45	59.16
Downward Movement	20-mer Sequence (5'–3') V_{ia}	V_{ib}	GC%	T_m (°C)
$V_{8'}$	ACGGAGTCAA	GTGAATAGCC	0.50	59.15
$V_{7'}$	GGGCTTGATT	GTTCTGAGTT	0.45	59.13
$V_{6'}$	CACATAGACT	GGGGGTTACC	0.55	59.12
$V_{5'}$	GAAGGGGCTC	AAAGTCATAA	0.45	59.11
$V_{4'}$	AACTCGCCTA	GAACTGCCTA	0.50	59.09
$V_{3'}$	CAATATGCTT	TCCGGCTTAT	0.40	59.05
$V_{2'}$	ATCCCAATTA	TGGGTCTCAA	0.40	59.04
$V_{1'}$	CTACTCCCCA	CTCCACAGTT	0.55	59.01

Step 4. Assign a unique DNA sequence for each of the node (elevator floor position) and its direction. Using available software for DNA sequence design named DNASequenceGenerator [15], the sequence is generated as shown in Table 3. The GC contents (GC%) and melting temperature (T_m) of each sequence is also shown in the table. Note that V_i is separated into half-5 end V_{ia} and half-3 end V_{ib}.

Step 5. Synthesize the oligos for every path in the graph according to the following rules [6] so that the oligos length will directly represent the weight between the nodes

(i) If i is a start node and j is an intermediate node, synthesize the oligo as
$V_{iab}(20) + W_{ij}(\omega_{ij} - 30) + V_{ja}(20)$
(ii) If i is an intermediate node and j is an end node, synthesize the oligo as
$V_{ib}(20) + W_{ij}(\omega_{ij} - 30) + V_{jab}(20)$
(iii) If i and j are both intermediate nodes, synthesize the oligo as
$V_{ib}(20) + W_{ij}(\omega_{ij} - 20) + V_{ja}(20)$

where V denotes the DNA sequence for node, W denotes the DNA sequence for weight, ω denotes the weight value, and '+' denotes a 'join' between the DNA sequence. All the synthesized oligos based on the stated rules are shown in Table 4.

Table 4. DNA sequence for path between nodes

Node Path	DNA Sequence (5' – 3')		
	V_i	W_{ij}	V_j
$V_1 \to V_4$	TCATCCTCCC GTCATTAACT	30	CAATACTGCG
$V_2 \to V_4$	AAGTCGGTAG	20	CAATACTGCG CGAATGTTAC
$V_3 \to V_4$	GCTCTAAGCT AGTATCGCGG	10	CAATACTGCG
$V_3 \to V_6$	GCTCTAAGCT AGTATCGCGG	30	ATAGGGGGGA
$V_4 \to V_5$	CGAATGTTAC	10	AAATACCAAA AACATGCCGT
$V_4 \to V_5$	CGAATGTTAC	20	AAATACCAAA
$V_5 \to V_{5'}$	AACATGCCGT	0	GAAGGGGCTC AAAGTCATAA
$V_6 \to V_8$	CATATCCAAT	20	AATTTGGGTG GACCGTAGTA
$V_6 \to V_8$	CATATCCAAT	30	AATTTGGGTG
$V_8 \to V_{8'}$	GACCGTAGTA	10	ACGGAGTCAA
$V_8 \to V_{5'}$	GTGAATAGCC	30	GAAGGGGCTC AAAGTCATAA
$V_6 \to V_{5'}$	CACATAGACT GGGGGTTACC	10	GAAGGGGCTC
$V_6 \to V_{3'}$	CACATAGACT GGGGGTTACC	30	CAATATGCTT
$V_5 \to V_{3'}$	AAAGTCATAA	30	CAATATGCTT
$V_3 \to V_{2'}$	TCCGGCTTAT	10	ATCCCAATTA TGGGTCTCAA
$V_3 \to V_{2'}$	TCCGGCTTAT	20	ATCCCAATTA
$V_2 \to V_2$	TGGGTCTCAA	10	TTGGCTAAGG

Step 6. All the synthesized oligos are then poured into a test tube for initial pool generation. POA is used to for the initial pool generation as suggested by Lee et al. [11] who demonstrated that POA is a more efficient and economical initial pool generation method for weighted graph problems. POA operation is similar to PCR; the only difference is that POA operates without the use of primers. As PCR, one cycle consists of three steps: hybridization, extension, and denaturation. During the annealing step, the temperature is decreased slowly so that partial hybridization is allowed to occur at respective locations. The extension on the other hand is applied with the presence of polymerase enzyme and the polymerization can be done from 5' to 3' direction. The generated double stranded DNA molecules are then separated by denaturation step. This can be done by increasing the temperature until the double stranded DNA molecules are separated to become single stranded DNA molecules.

From the graph of Fig. 6, the total output of the graph representing the travel path of each elevator A, B and C with either elevator A, B and C answering the hall calls can be calculated. The calculations performed verifies that the optimal path is $V_{A1} \to V_{A4} \to V_{A5} \to V_{A5'}$ for elevator A, $V_{B6'} \to V_{B3'} \to V_{B2'}$ for elevator B and $V_{C3} \to V_{C6} \to V_{C8}$ for elevator C with a total output $G(A, B, C) = 340$.

Fig. 7 illustrates the oligos involved in the generation of this optimal path. Note that at the same time, all other combinations of travel paths are also generated in the same manner.

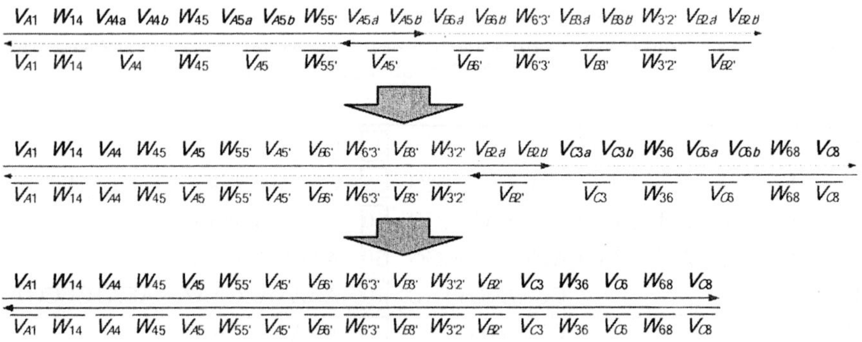

V_{A1} W_{14} V_{A4a} V_{A4b} W_{45} V_{A5a} V_{A5b} $W_{55'}$ $V_{A5'a}$ $V_{A5'b}$ $V_{B6'a}$ $V_{B6'b}$ $W_{63'}$ $V_{B3'a}$ $V_{B3'b}$ $W_{32'}$ $V_{B2'a}$ $V_{B2'b}$

V_{A1} W_{14} V_{A4} W_{45} V_{A5} $W_{55'}$ $V_{A5'}$ $V_{B6'}$ $W_{63'}$ $V_{B3'}$ $W_{32'}$ $V_{B2'}$

⬇

V_{A1} W_{14} V_{A4} W_{45} V_{A5} $W_{55'}$ $V_{A5'}$ $V_{B6'}$ $W_{63'}$ $V_{B3'}$ $W_{32'}$ $V_{B2'a}$ $V_{B2'b}$ V_{C3a} V_{C3b} W_{36} V_{C6a} V_{C6b} W_{68} V_{C8}

V_{A1} W_{14} V_{A4} W_{45} V_{A5} $W_{55'}$ $V_{A5'}$ $V_{B6'}$ $W_{63'}$ $V_{B3'}$ $W_{32'}$ $V_{B2'}$ V_{C3} W_{36} V_{C6} W_{68} V_{C8}

⬇

V_{A1} W_{14} V_{A4} W_{45} V_{A5} $W_{55'}$ $V_{A5'}$ $V_{B6'}$ $W_{63'}$ $V_{B3'}$ $W_{32'}$ $V_{B2'}$ V_{C3} W_{36} V_{C6} W_{68} V_{C8}

V_{A1} W_{14} V_{A4} W_{45} V_{A5} $W_{55'}$ $V_{A5'}$ $V_{B6'}$ $W_{63'}$ $V_{B3'}$ $W_{32'}$ $V_{B2'}$ V_{C3} W_{36} V_{C6} W_{68} V_{C8}

Fig. 7. DNA duplex based on POA method representing elevator's optimal path $V_{A1} \to V_{A4} \to V_{A5} \to V_{A5'} \to V_{B6'} \to V_{B3'} \to V_{B2'} \to V_{C3} \to V_{C6} \to V_{C8}$. The 3' end is indicated by the arrowhead.

Step 7. At this stage, an initial pool of solution is produced. The optimal path combinations among many other alternative path combinations of the problem have to be filtered. This filtering process copies the target DNA duplex exponentially using the PCR process by amplifying all the DNA molecules containing start node V_{A1} and end node V_{C8}. Numerous amount of DNA strands representing the start node V_{A1} and end node V_{C8} passing through all possible travel path combinations will be presented once the PCR operation is accomplished. Finally, gel electrophoresis is then performed onto the output solution of the PCR. The DNA molecules will be separated according to its length during this operation. The bands of gel electrophoresis are then analyzed, and the DNA duplex representing the shortest path starting from V_{A1} and end node V_{C8} will be extracted to represent the required solution of the problem.

5 Conclusions

In this paper, ideas and implementation methods to solve an elevator scheduling problem using DNA computing has been presented and discussed in details. DNA computing application towards solving this type of engineering problem has been shown to be achievable and applicable. It is expected from experimental results that the shortest DNA sequence length will represent the required optimal path for the elevator scheduling problem. With the successful confirmation of the expected result, the applicability of DNA computing could be extended into many more complex problems of this type of nature. Hence, the applicability of DNA computing could be extended into greater fields of other engineering related problems.

References

1. Adleman, L.M.: Molecular Computation of Solutions to Combinatorial Problems. Science, Vol. 266 (1994) 1021-1024
2. Adleman, L.M.: Computing with DNA. Scientific American (1998) 34-41
3. Narayanan, A., Zorbalas, S.: DNA Algorithms for Computing Shortest Paths. Proceedings of Genetic Programming, (1998) 718-723

4. Yamamoto, Y., Kameda, A., Matsuura, N., Shiba, T., Kawazoe, Y., Ahochi, A.: Local Search by Concentration-Controlled DNA Computing. International Journal of Computational Intelligence and Applications, Vol. 2 (2002) 447-455
5. Lee, J.Y., Shin, S.Y., Augh, S.J., Park, T.H., Zhang, B.T.: Temperature Gradient-Based DNA Computing for Graph Problems with Weighted Edges. Lecture Notes in Computer Science, Springer-Verlag, Vol. 2568 (2003) 73-84
6. Ibrahim, Z., Tsuboi, Y., Ono, O., Khalid, M.: Direct-Proportional Length-Based DNA Computing for Shortest Path Problem. International Journal of Computer Science and Applications, Vol. 1, Issue 1 (2004) 46-60
7. Fitch, J. P.: Engineering Introduction to Biotechnology. SPIE Press (2001)
8. Zucca, M.: DNA Based Computational Models. PhD Thesis, Politecnico Di Torino, Italy (2000)
9. Stemmer, W.P.: DNA Shuffling by Random Fragmentation and Reassembly: In Vitro Recombination for Molecular Evolution. Proc. Natl. Acad. Sci. U.S.A., Vol. 91 (1994) 10747-10751
10. Kaplan, P.D., Ouyang, Q., Thaler, D.S., Libchaber, A.: Parallel Overlap Assembly for the Construction of Computational DNA Libraries. Journal of Theoretical Biology, Vol. 188, Issue 3 (1997) 333-341
11. Lee, J.Y., Lim, H.W., Yoo, S.I., Zhang, B.T., Park, T.H.: Efficient Initial Pool Generation for Weighted Graph Problems Using Parallel Overlap Assembly. Preliminary Proceeding of the 10th International Meeting on DNA Computing (2004) 357-364
12. Paun, G., Rozenberg, G., Salomaa, A.,: DNA Computing: New Computing Paradigms. Lecture Notes in Computer Science, Springer-Verlag, Vol. 1644 (1998) 106-118
13. Amos, M.: DNA Computation. PhD Thesis, The University of Warwick, UK (1997)
14. Yamamoto, Y., Kameda, A., Matsuura, N., Shiba, T., Kawazoe, Y., Ahochi, A.: A Separation Method for DNA Computing Based on Concentration Control. New Generation Computing, Vol. 20, No. 3 (2002) 251-262
15. Udo, F., Sam, S., Wolfgang, B., Hilmar, R.: DNASequenceGenerator: A Program for the Construction of DNA Sequences. Proceedings of the Seventh International Workshop on DNA Based Computers (2001) 23-32

On Designing DNA Databases for the Storage and Retrieval of Digital Signals

Sotirios A. Tsaftaris and Aggelos K. Katsaggelos

Department of Electrical and Computer Engineering,
Northwestern University, 2145 Sheridan Rd., Evanston, IL 60208, USA
{stsaft, aggk}@ece.northwestern.edu

Abstract. In this paper we propose a procedure for the storage and retrieval of digital signals utilizing DNA. Digital signals are encoded in DNA sequences that satisfy among other constraints the Noise Tolerance Constraint (NTC) that we have previously introduced. NTC takes into account the presence of noise in digital signals by exploiting the annealing between non-perfect complementary sequences. We discuss various issues arising from the development of DNA-based database solutions (i) *in vitro* (in test tubes, or other materials) for short-term storage and (ii) *in vivo* (inside organisms) for long-term storage. We discuss the benefits and drawbacks of each scheme and its effects on the codeword design problem and performance. We also propose a new way of constructing the database elements such that a short-term database can be converted into a long term one and vice versa without the need for a re-synthesis. The latter improves efficiency and reduces the cost of a long-term database.

1 Introduction

The history of DNA as an information storage and processing medium begins with Adleman's work on DNA-based solutions of the Hamiltonian path problem [1]. Subsequently, Baum proposed building a DNA database capable of storing and retrieving digital information [2].

Using DNA to solve a computationally hard digital signal processing problem was presented in [9, 11], where a DNA based solution to the disparity estimation problem was given.

DNA offers significant advantages when compared to other media for storing digital signals or data, in general. The DNA molecule, especially in its double stranded form, is very stable, compact, and inexpensive. Polymerase Chain Reaction (PCR) is an economical and efficient way to replicate databases. Querying the database can be implemented with a plethora of techniques. In digital databases the query time increases proportionally to the size of the database. However, in DNA databases when annealing is used as a search mechanism, the querying time is independent of the database size when the target molecules have equal concentrations.

As with any DNA computing application, the first step is to find reliable mechanisms for encoding digital signals into DNA sequences, also known as the codeword design problem. In our problem, the encoding has to be such that it enables content-based searches and at the same time limits the possibility of errors during retrieval. Furthermore, in the case of digital signals where perfect matches are almost impossible due to noise or the nature of the signals, the encoding scheme needs to allow for and account for imperfect matches. To accomplish this we introduced a new constraint, the Noise Tolerance Constraint (NTC) [9, 11].

The second step is to decide on the structure of the storage elements each of which has unique properties and characteristics. DNA databases consist of a collection of elements. Usually each element has a unique address (or index) block, which uniquely identifies (and therefore enables the retrieval of) a usually larger information-carrying block (data block).

The third step is to decide on the host environment of the database. It can be a test tube, a polymer, or even a living organism. Each host offers unique capabilities but at the same time imposes constraints on the information capacity, database longevity, and ease of use. Finally, input and output methods need to be chosen. Some input (information storage) and output (information retrieval) methods are faster than others.

The steps mentioned above are not independent. For example, the choice of host and database element has a large impact on the codeword design problem and the capabilities of the database.

In this paper we briefly describe the codeword design problem (section 2) and propose and analyze possible schemes for database construction, storage, and retrieval. In section 3 we present the state of the art in database element design and suggest a modification that can relax the constraints on codeword design. In section 4 we discuss short-term databases and their performance and present an input/output protocol. In section 5 we repeat the task for a long-term database but also emphasize the construction of a long-term database from a short-term version. Finally, in section 6 we conclude this paper.

2 The Codeword Design Problem

In most DNA computing applications only perfect hybridizations are acceptable. In our case, we want to design the DNA codewords such that the melting temperature between DNA words is *inversely proportional to the absolute difference* between the encoded signal values. To accomplish this, we have introduced a new constraint, the *Noise (or inexact match) Tolerance Constraint (NTC)* [9, 10, 11]. According to the NTC, duplexes formed by codewords assigned to neighboring signal values must

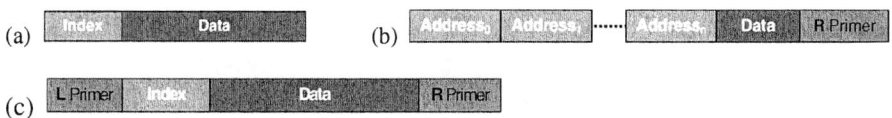

Fig. 1. Commonly used database elements (DE): (a) An index-data DE; (b) An address based DNA DE approach; (c) A DNA DE with left and right primers added for easy replication. All single border rectangles represent single stranded sequences.

have high (similar) melting temperatures, while duplexes outside this neighborhood must have melting temperatures lower than a predefined temperature threshold. In our case, we combine the NTC with other commonly used constraints, such as the self-complementarity, consecutive bases, GC content, frame-shift, and the reverse complement constraints. Another useful constraint is the illegal code constraint, that is, all codewords must not contain any word belonging to a set of illegal codes. In many cases recognition sites of enzymes are such codes. To solve this constrained optimization problem we have developed a random generate and test algorithm [10] and an iterative algorithm with stochastic non-improving steps [12].

3 Database Elements

3.1 State of the Art

The capabilities of a DNA database are highly dependent on the selection of the DNA database elements (DE). The sequences are created in such a way that it is clear which part is the entry identifier and which is the data. Database elements are then synthesized and mixed together to form the database.

Various designs of database element have been proposed in the literature. In Fig. 1 we illustrate some of the most commonly used ones. Baum [2] was the first to suggest the index-data approach (Fig. 1(a)) in building DNA memories. The left part is the index that identifies the data, which appear on the right. The index part of different DEs should be very dissimilar. Using even this simple DE with the appropriate encoding of information and annealing, database searches are possible.

As suggested in the introduction, using DNA to store information and annealing to perform the search is highly beneficial. A search of a database with a given query will return all the DEs that contain the query information. Although such feasibility is available with today's computers, the search time in a computer database is dependent on the size of the database (number of DEs). In a DNA database, the search time is not dependent on the number of the DEs but on the concentration of the DEs instead. Furthermore, a query search not only will return the DEs that match the query, but will provide information on the number of matching instances and their quality (strength), a feature very useful for signal processing applications [11].

Another possible DE structure is the address-data one shown in Fig. 1(b). This design was used in [6] for the implementation of a hierarchical DNA memory based on nested PCR, termed Nested Primer Molecular Memory (NPMM). The advantages of this approach are the theoretically unlimited scalability and capacity of the DNA database. An obvious disadvantage is that the lengths of DEs may differ, thus complicating the extraction of information.

Fig. 2. A DNA database element with a separation element (SEP) between the index and data parts. Double border rectangles represent double stranded sequences.

Ordinary DEs can be retrofitted (before synthesis) with unique left and right primers at each end shown in Fig. 1(c). A PCR procedure applied to the database with primers, defined as the complements of the L and R primer sites, can easily replicate the whole database, thus reducing replication and distribution costs.

3.2 Proposed Design

When single stranded DNA DEs are used, the index and data have to be designed in such a way that an index query will not hybridize within the data part and vice versa. Such specificity falls in the category of the illegal code constraint, but unfortunately has its limitations (section 2).

Let us assume K different DEs are needed to carry digital signals (N integer values). In this case we have to (i) define the primers L and R, (ii) find K unique and highly dissimilar indices, and (iii) find a mapping between digital values and DNA sequences (N different sequences). A reasonable path for designing the system will be to first decide on the primers and then find the K unique indices using a codeword design algorithm with high Hamming distance as one of the constraints. Consecutively, data codewords will be designed to satisfy the illegal code constraint with illegal codes the K indices and the primers.

For large databases, such a procedure can be rather daunting. In Fig. 2 a different approach on DE design is shown, where the DEs are double stranded sequences with a separator sequence in the middle (labeled in the figure as SEP). With this approach, the design of the indices and the mapping can be separated and index sequences can actually be similar to data codewords. The idea is that the part needed for a search is exposed (single stranded, correct direction) upon request. For example, for a search in the data part, only that part is exposed. Furthermore, the parts can be exposed with different DNA direction. For example, the index part can be exposed in the 3' to 5' direction, thus requiring a query in the 5' to 3' direction, while the data part can be exposed in the 5' to 3' direction requiring a query in the 3' to 5' direction.

A similar idea was presented in [5] using hairpin formations of DNA as a conformational addressing mechanism. In this case, data access could be given after the addressing was complete, which is not exactly sought after in our research.

Our current design suggests the recognition site of a nicking enzyme as a separator sequence. Nicking enzymes are restriction enzymes that introduce an incision in one of the single strands instead of cutting the double stranded sequence in two parts. Our scope is to use a combination of nicking enzymes and two types of exonucleases. An appropriate exonuclease can be applied to expose the sequence in the desired direction for processing.

In this case the constraints for the codeword design problem are augmented with the addition of the recognition site as another illegal code.

4 Short Term Storage

We have previously discussed various DEs and their properties. Here we propose a possible platform for short-term storage and retrieval of digital signals. DNA sequences can be either kept in liquid form placed in test tubes, freeze-dried to save volume, or even placed within an exotic substance.

We have focused our attention on DEs of the form shown in Fig. 1(c) and Fig. 2. For added security, the database can be mixed with random genetic material as in [3]. To guarantee correct separation and amplification of the database, the primers need to be highly dissimilar compared to the genetic material.

4.1 Input-Output

There are many ways to implement a query search. Overall it requires the synthesis of the *query strand*, introduction of the query in the database solution and detection of the hybridization event using one of several spectroscopic techniques, i.e., fluorescent labels attached to the query strand.

In the case where a simple yes or no answer (whether the query can be found in the database or not) is needed, a change in the fluorescent response will indicate success.

If, in addition, we want to know the elements in which a match was found, affinity purification or Fluorescence Activated Cell Sorting (FACS, a technique that allows the separation of fluorescence activated molecules) can separate the strands that had a match. For affinity purification, query strands should be attached to beads. For FACS, query strands should be fluorescently labeled. Assuming the existence of a DNA chip (microarray) with all the indices immobilized in spots, placing a sample of the washed solution onto the chip will return the index. If the position of a match is sough after, a laboratory procedure would include a PCR step using as primer the query strand followed by a gel electrophoresis and a DNA sequencing step.

4.2 Performance

To evaluate the performance of a DNA database, three factors have to be evaluated: (a) speed, (b) information capacity and scalability of the database, and (c) accuracy.

Speed

The biggest advantage of a DNA approach is that search speed is constant for any database size and that multiple searches can take place in parallel. Speed is estimated by the amount of time a query strand needs to react such that a high detectable concentration of outcomes can be guaranteed. The time spent for extracting the outcomes is not accounted for. In order for the constant speed assumption to hold, DEs must have equal concentrations and the query strands must be in excess.

The key to constant speed is that a query search using DNA annealing is, in fact, a competitive hybridization. This means that for a given high concentration of DEs, the best match will find the query in a given amount of time. Following the proposed DE design, this is relatively easy since only a PCR amplification step is needed. It is clear that there is a trade-off between speed and molar concentrations. If speed is a concern and a constant search time is sought after, an increase in the database concentration is needed. On the other hand, if volume is a concern then a higher reaction time is needed resulting in a reduction in speed.

Capacity and Scalability

Information capacity is a critical component of a database, although in many cases, capacity is a function of speed and accuracy. The study of information capacity in

DNA databases has to be coupled with the accuracy of the database. The scalability of the database depends on the available indices.

Accuracy
Although the scope of the codeword and index design algorithms is to find sequences that will not cause hybridization errors, the models used to simulate hybridization procedures have inherent statistical errors. It is therefore expected that outcomes of *in vitro* database searches will have some errors. The most important sources of errors are: hybridization errors, polymerase errors, enzymatic errors, extraction errors, and human errors.

5 Long Term Storage

For long-term storage, we propose the insertion of the database in living organisms following the insertion technique used in [13]. The choice of the hosting organism depends on various parameters, such as mutation rate, capacity, maintenance cost, and others.

5.1 Proposed Database Element Construction

To embed a sequence in the genome of an organism the message sequence (in our case the database) is encapsulated between two extraction primers, the L and R keys. The primers are used to extract the database from the organism's genome using a PCR procedure. The L and R keys need to be (i) highly dissimilar compared to the genome of the organism for extraction and (ii) include multiple repetitions of STOP codons to protect the organism [7].

In [13] the message was pre-synthesized and was part of the overall embedding sequence. In our case, the message is either the whole or a part of the database consisting of concatenations of DEs shown in the previous section. Following the same approach, the construction of a long-term version of our database would require the re-synthesis of the whole database as a big linear molecule, which is rather inefficient and uneconomical.

Here we propose a slight modification of the DEs used for short-term storage to accommodate further long-term storage applications with minimal laboratory work. Furthermore, using only two laboratory operations, the database extracted from an organism is converted to the short-term equivalent and the same information retrieval procedures can be applied.

The proposed modification affects only the design of the L and R primers used to encapsulate the DEs. The primers are designed such that when two DEs are concatenated, they create the recognition site, RS, of a restriction enzyme as shown in Fig. 3.

As shown in Fig. 3, with the addition of the restriction enzyme, the concatenated database constructed from DEs is transformed into individual DEs with sticky ends. To transform the DEs into their original single stranded form, only the addition of a 3'→5' exonuclease is needed.

(a)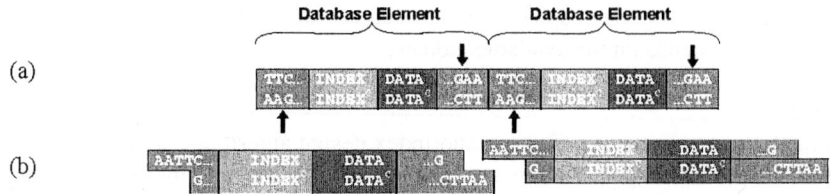

(b)

Fig. 3. Transformation from a long database strand (a) to individual database elements with sticky ends by adding a restriction enzyme (b).

(a)
(b)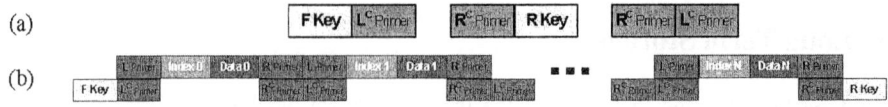

Fig. 4. (a) The "helper strands." (b) Molecular self-assembly of database elements for long term storage with the addition of complementary helper strands.

If the DEs have a separator sequence in the middle, the double stranded form is adequate. Consequently, only an exonuclease that digests single stranded parts is needed to eliminate the sticky ends.

To construct a long concatenation of DEs from a given short-term database, "helper strands" are employed. The "helper strands" are illustrated in Fig. 4(a), where the F and R keys are the extraction primers, and R^C and L^C are the complements of the L and R primers.

When the "helper strands" are added to a solution containing DEs in the form of Fig. 1(c), molecular self-assembly will follow, which will create formations similar to the one illustrated in Fig. 4(b). With the addition of ligase, each formation will be joined at the hybridized parts, and long, partially single stranded molecules composed of DEs are obtained.

Clearly, the self-assembly will happen at random, and it is not guaranteed that each formation will contain at least one copy of each DE in the database. With gel electrophoresis, the molecules can be sorted according to length, and a subset D of those with the longer length can be finally selected, with the expectation that in D, at least one copy of each DE is present. In the performance section, we will further discuss this issue.

Overall the problem of codeword design does not change significantly. In this case the only difference is the design of the L and R keys and the L and R primers and the addition of the restriction site RS, the keys and the primers as illegal codes in the design problem.

5.2 Input Output

Here we assume that a short-term storage solution is already available and the DEs conform to the constraints listed in the previous paragraph. This conformation assumes prior knowledge of the hosting organism. The procedure for acquiring a long-term storage from a short-term storage solution that follows the appropriate DE structure involves: mixing the helper strands with a sample of the solution, extracting the self-assembled strands, converting them into cloning vectors, and inserting them in the organism.

To extract information from the organism, the procedure requires extracting the genetic material, amplifying the database using PCR and the L/R keys, and cutting the long strands into DEs with the restriction enzyme.

5.3 Performance

Since most of the discussion of section 4.2 is applicable here, we will only mention some further considerations.

Speed
Transformation between short-term and long-term is a tedious one-time event; hence, it is not considered as overhead. Search performance will be the same as in the short-term case.

Capacity
The capacity in this case is also affected by the design of the database due to the self-assembly process, and the organism itself. The construction of the database is based on stochastic molecular self-assembly. To increase the probability of inclusion of at least one DE in the cloning vector, high redundancy is needed. Multiple vectors of high dissimilarity need to be formed and inserted into different populations of organisms. With high probability, this mixture of organisms will contain all DEs. A second issue is the capacity of the organism itself. Certain limits and workarounds exist and are available throughout the literature of recombinant libraries [8].

Accuracy
The long-term storage is comprised of the following major components: (1) database creation (DEs to self-assembled strands), (2) database insertion (cloning vectors), (3) database maintenance (maintaining the organism), (4) database extraction, and (5) information retrieval. Each component introduces possible errors.

In (1) the errors are introduced from the random creation of the self-assembled strands, which leads to ambiguity in the final molar concentration of the DEs in (4).

In (2) the error arises from the event of unsuccessful insertion. To minimize its probability, multiple clones are inserted into multiple copies of the organism.

Component (3) introduces a very important source of errors, namely mutations. Organisms, especially bacteria, evolve very fast. To minimize the probability of such an error, an organism with low mutation rates should be chosen and redundancy should be exploited by inserting the same information into multiple bacteria.

In (4) enzymatic reactions are used that have certain success rates.

Finally in (5) the same sources of errors as in the short-term case apply. They are amplified by the fact that molar concentrations are random variables.

6 Concluding Remarks

In this paper we proposed various approaches towards the DNA-based storage and retrieval of digital signals. We considered two different approaches: one for short-term storage and one for long-term storage. For short-term storage, the database is kept in test tubes or other materials, whereas for long-term storage, the database is inserted inside an organism.

As a search mechanism we use the annealing property of DNA. To perform searches based on signal similarity, we stressed the importance of the Noise Tolerance Constraint, which was previously established.

We argued that a DNA based approach offers significant advantages when compared to traditional computer based techniques.

For database construction, we analyzed and compared various forms of its elements and identified the necessary changes in the codeword design problem. For each form, we provided an analysis of materials and equipment needed and also laid out procedures for database creation, replication, maintenance, and information extraction. We also proposed a procedure that can be used to transform one database form to another, thus avoiding re-synthesis costs. Finally, for each storage solution, we discussed performance issues, identified problems, and proposed a framework for simulation.

Although our goal is to offer a demonstrational small scale *in vitro* DNA database, in order to reduce laboratory costs we are in the process of implementing an *in silico* DNA database equivalent. This equivalent simulates various procedures, such as target-to-primer hybridization (already implemented in [9]), PCR, and bead based searches, and will be used to measure and improve the performance of the database. Laboratory experiments are planned to commence after the completion of the simulations.

Acknowledgements

The authors would like to thank Prof. Osamu Ono and Zuwairie Ibrahim for their invitation to participate in this session. We are also grateful to Prof. Papoutsakis and Dr. Paredes for their help with our laboratory work. Finally Mr. Tsaftaris would like to thank the *Alexander S. Onassis* public benefit foundation for their financial support.

References

1. L. Adleman, Molecular computation of solutions to combinatorial problems, Science, vol. 266, no. 5187, pp.1021–1024, 1994.
2. E.B. Baum, Building an associative memory vastly larger than the brain, Science, vol. 268, no. 5210, pp.583-585, 1995.
3. C.T. Clelland, V. Risca, and C. Bancroft, Hiding messages in DNA microdots, Nature, vol. 399, no. 6736, pp. 533–534, 1999.
4. H. Kakavand, D. O'Brien, A. Hassibi, and T.H. Lee, Maximum a Posteriori (MAP) Estimator for Polymerase Chain Reaction (PCR) Processes, In Proc. of 26th Int. Conf. of IEEE Engineering in Medicine and Biology, 2004.

5. Kameda, M. Yamamoto, H. Uejima, M. Hagiya, K. Sakamoto, and A. Ohuchi, Conformational addressing using the hairpin structure of single-strand DNA, In Revised Papers from DNA Computing, 9th International Workshop on DNA-Based Computers, Lecture Notes in Computer Science, Springer-Verlag, vol. 2943, pp. 219–224, 2004.
6. S. Kashiwamura, M. Yamamoto, A. Kameda, T. Shiba, and A. Ohuchi, Hierarchical DNA Memory Based on Nested PCR, In Revised papers from DNA Computing: Eighth Int'l Meeting on DNA Based Computers, Lecture Notes in Computer Science, vol. 2568, pp. 112–123, Springer-Verlag, 2003
7. Y. Ozawa, S. Hanaoka, R. Saito, and M. Tomita, Differences of Translation Termination Sites Among the Three Stop Codons, in Asai, K. and Miyano, S. and Takagi, T. (eds.), Genome Informatics 1999, vol. 10, pp. 328-329, Universal Academy Press, Tokyo, 1999.
8. K. She, So you want to Work with Giants: The BAC Vector, BioTeach Journal, vol. 1, Fall 2003, available online at http://www.bioteach.ubc.ca.
9. S.A. Tsaftaris, DNA-based Digital Signal Processing, M.S. Thesis, Northwestern University, Dept. of Electrical and Computer Engineering, June 2003.
10. S.A. Tsaftaris, A.K. Katsaggelos, T.N. Pappas and E.T. Papoutsakis, DNA based matching of digital signals, in Proc. IEEE Int. Conf. on Acoustics, Speech, and Signal Processing, vol. 5, Montreal, Quebec, Canada, pp. 581-584, 2004.
11. S.A. Tsaftaris, A.K. Katsaggelos, T.N. Pappas and E.T. Papoutsakis, How can DNA-computing be applied in digital signal processing?, IEEE Signal Processing Mag., vol. 21, no. 6, pp. 57-61, 2004.
12. S.A. Tsaftaris and A.K. Katsaggelos, A New Codeword Design Algorithm for DNA-Based Storage and Retrieval of Digital Signals, Pre-Proceedings of the 11th International Meeting on DNA Computing, June 6-9, London, Canada, 2005.
13. P.C. Wong, K. Wong, and H. Foote, Organic Data Memory Using the DNA Approach, Communications of the ACM, vol. 46, no. 1, 2003.

Composite Module Analyst: Tool for Prediction of DNA Transcription Regulation. Testing on Simulated Data

Tatiana Konovalova[1], Tagir Valeev[2], Evgeny Cheremushkin[2], and Alexander Kel[3],

[1] Institue of Citology and Genetics, 10, Lavrentev ave,
630090 Novosibirsk, Russia
tanya@biorainbow.com
[2] A.P. Ershov's Institute of Informatics Systems, 6, Lavrentiev ave,
630090 Novosibirsk, Russia
[3] BIOBASE GmbH, Halchtersche Str. 33, D-38304 Wolfenbüttel, Germany

Abstract. Functionally related genes involved in the same molecular-genetic, biochemical, or physiological process are often regulated coordinately Such regulation is provided by precisely organized binding of a multiplicity of spe cial proteins- transcription factors to their target sites (cis-elements) in regulatory regions of genes. Cis-element combinations provide a structural basis for the generation of unique patterns of gene expression. Here we present new method based on genetic algorithm for prediction of class-specific composite modules in promoters of functionally related or coexpressed genes and it's testing on simulated data.

1 Introduction

Massive application of microarray measurements of gene expression is a common route in the current studies of disease mechanisms. Hundred of genes are revealed whose change of expression is associated with the disease. But changed expression of these genes often represents just an "echo" of real molecular processes in the cells. Still, the available means of analysis and interpretation of these mechanisms are very limited.

Regulation of gene expression is accomplished through binding of transcription factors (TFs) to distinct regions of DNA. It is clear by now that combinations of transcription factors rather than single transcription factors drive gene transcription and define its specificity. At the level of DNA, the blueprints for assembling of such variable TF complexes on promoter regions may be seen as specific combinations of TF binding sites located in close proximity to each other. We call such structures "composite regulatory modules".

For revealing class-specific composite modules in promoters of functionally related or coexpressed genes we developed Composite Module Analyst - an integrated computational method for causal interpretation of gene expression data. It analysis microarray data and proposes complexes of transcription factors.

2 Data and Method

In this study we used library of about 500 positional weight matrices (PWMs) from TRANSFAC®, that is a database on gene regulation [1].

We define a composite module (CM) as a set of individual PWMs and pairs of PWMs that are characteristic for co-regulated promoters. CMs are characterized by the following parameters: K, the number of individual PWMs in the module, R, the number of pairs of PWMs, cut-off value $q_{cut-off}^{(k)}$, relative impact values $\phi^{(k)}$ maximal number of best matches $\kappa^{(k)}$ that were assigned to every weight matrix k (k=1,K), as well as cut-off value $q_{cut-off}^{(r)}$, relative impact values $\phi^{(r)}$ and maximal $d_{max}^{(r)}$ and minimal $d_{min}^{(r)}$ distances that were assigned to every matrix pair r (r=1,R) in the CM. Matrices are selected to be included into the CM by the program from a profile, containing all or some part of TRANSFAC PWMs. A composite module score (CM score) is calculated for all sequences X according to the following equation:

$$F_{CM}(x) = \sum_{k=1,K} \phi^{(k)} \times \sum_{i=1}^{\kappa^{(k)}} q_i^{(k)}(x) + \sum_{r=1,R} \phi^{(r)} \times (q_1^{(r)}(x) + q_2^{(r)}(x)), \quad (1)$$

where $q_i^{(k)}(X) < q_{cut-off}^{(k)}$ and $q_{1,2}^{(r)}(X) < q_{cut-off}^{(r)}$; and distance between matches of two matrices of a pair (r) : $d_{min}^{(r)} < d^{(r)} < d_{max}^{(r)}$.

We define Score of CM as weighted sum of several components: correlation between F distribution and the expression profile, statistical significance (t-test), false positive and false negative errors, correlation between distribution of the F function over the set of sequences and the normal distribution, penalty on the number of parameters.

Search for the CM with the optimum score is made with the help of genetic algorithm. It takes as an input two sets of promoters (the set of promoters of differentially expressed genes – changed; and a set of promoters of genes whose expression does not differ significantly between experiment and control - unchanged) or set of promoters and relative expressions and a set of PWMs for transcription factors.

First program generates the set of random CM according for defined parameters. They are considered as "organisms" subjected to mutations, recombination, selection, and multiplication. During the number of iterations program optimizes set of matrices selected, their cut-offs, the relative impact, maximum number of best matches and some optional parameters such as site orientation and distance range in pairs. The output of the program is the best discriminative CM with the optimized parameters.

3 CMA Testing on the Simulated Data

First we did initial testing of the ability of the program to reveal *combinations of single matrices* with the goal to restrict space of genetic algorithm parameters. We saw that with increase of matrixes library size quality falls linearly, but increasing number of iterations it is possible to achieve 100 % of recognition quality; Population size to number of iterations ratio should be between 0.01 and 1, optimal selection and mutation levels are 40 % and 0.5, respectively.

Taking in account these results we performed further testing.

Table 1. Testing of ability of CMA program to reveal an implanted combination of 3 sites in the window of 200bp. Sites were implanted into sets of 300 sequences of the length 1000bp and were compared with the random sets of 700 sequences. Scores of the implanted sites are high (optimum to reduce false positive) or low (optimum to reduce false negative). Part of the set with the implanted sites (P) varies from 30% till 90%. +++ indicates that all implanted matrices were revealed, ++– that only 2 were found.

Site scores	Probability of site insertion		
	0.9	0.6	0.3
High	+++	+++	+++
Low	+++	++–	++–

The result of this simulation shows that the CMA program was able to determine implanted matrices correctly in most cases.

Microarray data usually contains much noise and has no clear differentiation between changed and unchanged genes, expression values vary a lot. In order to test the ability of our method to deal with various *patterns of expression* we generated test data with different values of expression increase and dispersion. The result of this simulation (see Table 2) shows that the CMA was able to reveal correct complex in cases where $\Delta e < e$ or $\Delta e \sim e$, though score of the complex is decreasing. In case when $\Delta e > e$ only 2 implanted matrices were present in the best CM. Correct CM also was present in the population, but its score was slight lower.

Table 2. Testing of ability of CMA program to reveal an implanted CM with different expression parameters. CM that consisted of 3 matrices where implanted in to the set of 1000 random sequences where 1/3 were considered as «changed genes». Three tests with different ratio of expression increase (e) on changed genes to the dispersion (Δe) of expression are considered. +++ indicates that all implanted matrices were revealed, ++– that only 2 were found.

Expresion parameters	CM Score	CM
$\Delta e < e$	0,6	+++
$\Delta e \sim e$	0,4	+++
$\Delta e > e$	0,3	++–

Next we test the functionality of the program on revealing *pairs* of matrices that reflect composite elements composed of two closely situated sites. After one pair was implanted in to the set of random sequences, we searched for different types of complexes (see Table 3). When preset module contains one or several pairs, method was able to correctly detect the implanted CM structure – it founds one and only one pair as the best complex. In case we search for either one pair or 2 matrices, implanted matrices were revealed not as pair but as single matrices. It should be noted that in case when insertion probability of sites is low – correct module structure appears.

Table 3. Testing of ability of CMA program to reveal an implanted pair of matrices. Sites were implanted into sets of 300 sequences of the length 1000bp and were compared with the random sets of 700 sequences. (++) indicates that pair was found, ++ that single matrices were revealed.

Searched CM Structure	Probability of site insertion		
	0,9	0,6	0,3
1 pair	(++)	(++)	(++)
1-3 pair	(++)	(++)	(++)
0-1 pair, 0-2 single matrices	+ +	++	(++)

4 Discussion

In this paper we describe a method for analysis and interpretation of gene expression data.

Recently, a number of approaches identifying composite motifs that help to discover new regulatory sites for yet unknown transcription factors, were described. But an "*ab initio*" motif finding method is limited by the length of sequences and may not be suitable for the analysis of long regulatory regions of higher eukaryotic organisms. A valuable source to identify transcription factor binding sites is the TRANSFAC® database[1]. Novel methods have been developed that utilizes this information [2],[3]. In comparison with them our method has several advantages, such as ability to work with microarray experiments; optimisation of not only matrix sets, but also cutoff values for each matrix; search for pairs of matrices, selecting best distance and orientation.

Testing on simulated data shows that our method is able to correctly reveal CM that is overrepresented in the set of sequences and can be used to analyze data and propose factors are playing key role in transcriptional regulation in the given experiment.

References

1. Matys V, Fricke E, Geffers R et al.: TRANSFAC: transcriptional regulation, from patterns to profiles. Nucleic Acids Res. Vol. 31(2003) 3576-3579.
2. Kel-Margoulis, O.V., Ivanova, T.G., Wingender, E., Kel, A.E.: Automatic annotation of genomic regulatory sequences by searching for composite clusters. Pac Symp Biocomput. (2002) 187-198.
3. Aerts, S., Thijs, G., Coessens B., Staes, M., Moreau, Y., De Moor, B., :TOUCAN : Deciphering the Cis-Regulatory Logic of Coregulated Genes. Nucl Acids Res, Vol. 31 (2003) 1753-1764.

Simulation and Visualization for DNA Computing in Microreactors

Danny van Noort[1], Yuan Hong[2],
Joseph Ibershoff[2], and Jerzy W. Jaromczyk[2]

[1] Biointelligence Lab., School of Computer Science and Engineering,
Seoul National University, San 56-1, Sinlim-dong, Gwanak-gu,
Seoul 151-742, Korea
danny@bi.snu.ac.kr
[2] Department of Computer Science, University of Kentucky,
Lexington, KY 40506, USA
jurek@cs.uky.edu

Abstract. A simulation program is a useful tool to predict the hybridization error propagated through a microfluidic system. This paper shows the hybridization event between solution strands and capture probes. The program provides a Graphical User Interface that allows the user to insert parameters as well as to observe results showing critical values and additional visualization of the simulation process. The program and its interface have been developed in Java, making it platform independent and web-based.

1 Introduction

DNA computering is very promising because it is closely connected to the biological world and can therefore have applications in biotechnology, such as medical diagnostics and drug lead-compound optimization. Research on operations with biomolecules can give a better insight into biological systems, while information processing and construction at molecular level can give rise to new computing paradigms and insights into nanobiotechnology.

Microfluidic networks can be incorporated as an information carrier in a DNA computing scheme. The advantages of microfluidics are the small volumes (in the pico-liter range) of DNA solution needed and the speed of reactions. When using fluidic valves and micro pumps, the flow can be (re-)directed [1]. The channels are like the wires in an electronic circuit, transporting the information from one operator to another, to fluidic flip-flops, i.e. logical operators.

The objective of this ongoing research is to develop a simulation environment to perform DNA-computing in a network of microreactors and to measure the effects of propagating errors. In this paper we will show the results of negative selection in one selection module, or microreactor. The objective of the simulation is to determine the parameters for optimal uptake of ssDNA from the solution and minimize the propagation of an erroneous strand. The simulator will be modular, so that objects and parameters of the process can be easily updated or changed. Furthermore, it is developed in Java to make it platform independent and web-based. Beyond its primary role to predict the hybridization error thus enhancing the laboratory infrastructure, the program can serve as a teaching aid and learning guide for DNA.

In this work the flows are considered laminar, i.e. there is no mixing of flows.

2 Selection Procedure

The basic operation is the selection from a sequence space $\{S_i\}$ of a single stranded DNA (ssDNA), i.e. a word, consisting of 15 nt (nucleotide) sections representing bits, as defined in computer science (Fig. 1). A 15 nt complementary capture probe (CP; complementary bit) is immobilized to the surface of beads (with a diameter in the range of 5-10 μm). Hybridization between these two is a selection, a YES or NO, i.e. a logic operation.

It is clear from the above that logic operators can be defined with these selection procedures. A NOT operation corresponds to a negative selection which discards S_k from the sequence space $\{S_i\}$ [2], while the retention of a certain member S_k corresponds to a positive selection [3]. Two selectors in sequence will

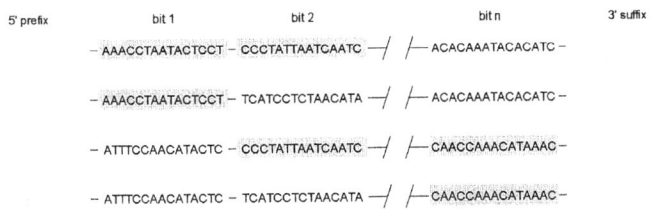

Fig. 1. Examples of possible words of n-bits. Each bit can consist of 15 nucleotides. Furthermore, each bit is unique and should not hybridize to other bits nor to itself.

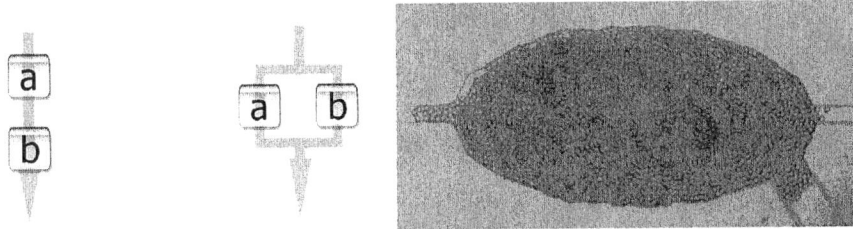

Fig. 2. An AND operation can be made by having two selectors in sequence (*left*), while an OR operation is made by two selectors in parallel. (*right*)

Fig. 3. A microreactor filled with beads. The reactor and the diagonal bead delivery channel has a depth of 15 μm, while the horizontal flow channel has a depth of 5 μm and effectively functions as a bead barrier.

perform an AND operation, while two selectors in parallel will perform an OR operation (Figure 2).

The advantage of positive selection is that there is a minimal amount of unwanted DNA, while the advantage of negative selection is the simplicity of operation and control, however with higher error rate. In the latter case it is possible to re-run the solution over the (regenerated) CP's as to optimize the purity of the DNA template solution. However, in this simulation we want to minimize this error.

The microreactor is completely packed with these beads and the solution with ssDNA words flows in between the beads (Figure 3).

3 Factors Deciding the Rate of Hybridization

Hybridization depends on the following factors:

1. *The size of the reactor.* The larger the reactor the more beads can be held. This means more CP and a larger uptake. However, the larger the reactor the longer the diffusion time and thus the reaction time.
2. *The size of the beads.* The larger the beads the more CP's there are per bead. However, the packing of beads is an issue as well. This determines the amount of beads that can be held in the reactor. Smaller beads have a higher packing density. This factor determines the uptake of ssDNA. Here, we presume that the packing is not ideal, i.e. close packing, but rather stacked with the dimension of their enveloping cube.
3. *The concentration and volume of ssDNA.* The higher the concentration of ssDNA the faster and higher the uptake. The laws of chemical reactions dictate this. However, there is a problem connected to this. A certain volume is injected in the channels. Over time there is a diffusion taking place at the interface between the ssDNA and the carrier buffer. In this case timing is important. But with a suitable carrier buffer (e.g. Fluorinert, Hampton Research, USA) this problem can be eliminated, since there will be no diffusion. In this case just the volume is important. A larger volume of ssDNA takes more time to flow through a reactor, while it will saturate the CP's faster when at the same concentration. The best results will be gained by a small volume and high concentration of ssDNA.
4. *The concentration of CP.* The concentration of the CP's depends on the immobilization capacity of the bead. Each size or sort bead has a different capacity of binding, specified by the manufacturer. Typically the CP's have a biotin end that binds irreversibly to the streptavidin functionalized beads.
5. *Flow velocity.* The speed that the ssDNA passes the beads dictates the time the ssDNA remains in the reactor. The reaction between the CP and ssDNA occurs in a certain time. The faster the velocity, the faster the DNA computer but the shorter the interaction time between the CP and ssDNA.
6. *Environmental conditions (pH, salt concentration, temperature).* Besides the sequence of the DNA, environmental conditions determine the hybridization rate. The pH, salt concentration and temperature determine the melting

temperature. The melting temperature (T_m) is that T where half of the concentration of double stranded DNA is dissociated. The environmental conditions are important as they control the reaction rate as well.

However, in the here presented program we will only consider the reactor size, flow volume and velocity, and the concentration of the DNA strands as input parameters. To include the environmental conditions requires a more complex model, which will not be considered here. This will presented elsewhere.

4 Method

The simulation of a single selection module (i.e. microreactor) is based on compartmentalization. The module is divided in compartments of volume V. The smaller the compartments, the closer the model will be to a continuous model. The DNA solution is presumed to flow in a plug, so no diffusion is assumed. The plug is then divided in compartments with the same volume V as in the modules (Figure 4). Time and total volume decide the accuracy of the selection. The uptake of the ssDNA is calculated in a static fashion, which in principle means that the flow is stopped and started with time intervals depending on the flow velocity and the size of the compartment.

The objective of negative selection is to uptake all the ssDNA not wanted. In every compartment the uptake of ssDNA was calculated and that information was passed on to the next, in the direction of the flow. Furthermore, the error rate was calculated in case of negative selection.

One should be aware that if the binding capacity of the beads in a microreactor is insufficient to remove the vast majority of incorrect candidates, then they will flow through to the next selection module, contributing to the overall error rate.

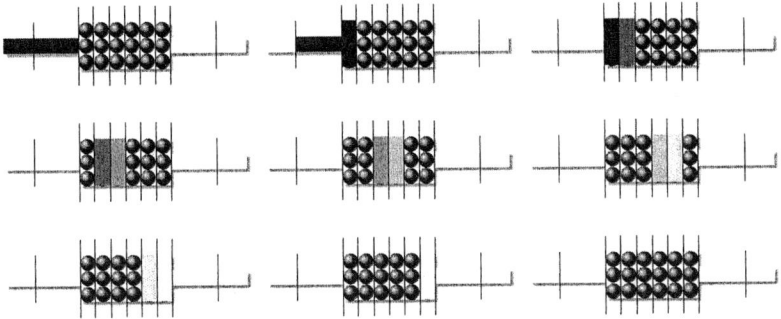

Fig. 4. A schematic of the flow of a plug with ssDNA though a compartmentalized microreactor filled with beads. The sequence of the figures is from left to right and top to bottom. In this example the volume of the plug corresponds to two compartments.

To find appropriate DNA concentrations and flow rates for the solution containing the bit library, the adsorption rate of the ssDNA molecule to beads with the CP's was calculated. Since the number of molecules involved is sufficiently large ($\sim 10^{10}$), it is possible to use deterministic and continuous, rather than stochastic, equations. It is assumed that annealing of two ssDNA molecules follows second-order reaction kinetics:

$$[W] + [C] \xrightarrow{k} [WC] \tag{1}$$

where $[W]$ is the concentration of the ssDNA in solution $\{S_i\}$ and $[C]$ is the concentration of the CP. From eq.1 we can derive the following about the decrease of the concentration of $\{S_i\}$ and concentration of the CP, i.e. the binding capacity.

$$W_{i+1} = \frac{\varepsilon W_i (W_i - C_i)}{\varepsilon W_i - C_i} \tag{2}$$

$$C_{i+1} = \frac{C_i (W_i - C_i)}{\varepsilon W_i - C_i} \tag{3}$$

$$\varepsilon = e^{kt(W_i - C_i)} \tag{4}$$

where i is the compartment, k is the second-order rate constant and t is the duration of the incubation.

5 The Program

The program that carries the simulation has a typical structure of the Model-View-Controller design pattern [5]. The screenshot of the interface of the simulation program is shown in Figure 5 and it illustrates that the window is divided into three major components. The first part is responsible for controls and input parameters. The middle area displays the schematic animation of the flow through the microreactor. The third part contains text and graphs of the simulation results.

The program has a total of eight input parameters that can be set:

1. *Reactor volume.* This is the total free space available for flow of ssDNA solution (i.e. it does not include the volume consumed by beads). This corresponds to the "the size of the reactor" (item (1) in the "factors deciding the rate of hybridization" section of this paper).
2. *ssDNA volume.* This is the volume of ssDNA solution that will flow through the reactor. Note that in this model the ratio of these two volumes is all that is important, not the values themselves. This corresponds to the volume factor described in "the concentration and volume of ssDNA" (item (3) in the "factors deciding the rate of hybridization" section of this paper).
3. *Reactor flow time.* This is the total time it will take solution to flow to the end of the reactor after it enters the front of the reactor; in other words, this is the flow time for n compartments of solution, not for the entire plug. This corresponds to "flow velocity" (item (5) in the "factors deciding the rate of hybridization" section of this paper).

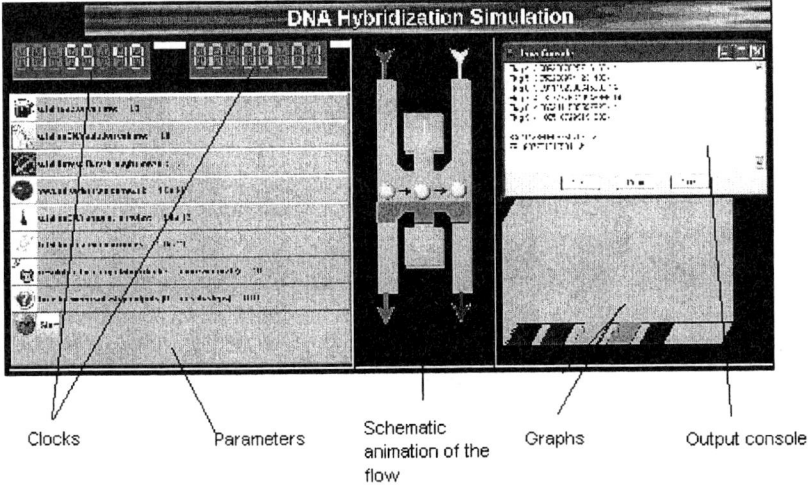

Fig. 5. A screenshot of the GUI with input and output components

4. *Rate constant.* This is the second-order rate constant k described in the above equations; this value specifies how quickly hybridization occurs when ssDNA is in the presence of CP in the microreactor. However, since this value may be different for different microreactors, it is necessary to allow the user to specify this.
5. *ssDNA amount.* This specifies the total amount of ssDNA present in the solution, in moles. This is used with ssDNA volume to calculate the concentration factor described in "the concentration and volume of ssDNA" (item (3) in the "factors deciding the rate of hybridization" section of this paper).
6. *Bind capacity.* This specifies the total amount of ssDNA that can theoretically be bound within the microreactor. If this value is less than the ssDNA amount, then error (ssDNA left behind) will be at least (ssDNA amount − bind capacity), which is the minimum possible error. Reactor volume and bind capacity are used together to calculate "the concentration of CP" (item (4) in the "factors deciding the rate of hybridization" section of this paper). This parameter depends on the binding capacity as specified by the manufacturer of the beads, as well as the number of beads.
7. *Resolution.* This specifies the granularity of calculation for the simulation; higher values will require more computation time, but will yield more accurate results. The smaller of reactor volume or ssDNA volume will be represented by resolution compartments; the larger will be represented by however many compartments necessary to yield the appropriate relative volume. Unless many significant figures are necessary in the result, a value of about 10 is appropriate.
8. *Sub-steps.* Each compartment of the plug remains in each compartment of the reactor for a certain amount of time; sub-steps is a the number of times output data should be produced during each static step. So, if each plug

compartment remains stationary for 0.1 seconds, and sub-steps is 10 seconds, then sub-step values will be generated every 0.01 seconds during each stationary step. A sub-step value of 0 will cause no sub-step values to be produced, resulting in 1 set of output values each time the plug moves forward one compartment in the reactor.

The output consists of ssDNA values for each plug compartment and CP values for each compartment organized in four ways:

1. The concentration of ssDNA present in a particular plug compartment over time, for each plug compartment.
2. The concentration of CP present in a particular reactor compartment over time, for each reactor compartment.
3. The concentration of CP "observed" by a particular plug compartment over time, for each plug compartment. This data has discontinuities resulting from movement of the plug compartment into a new reactor compartment.
4. The concentration of ssDNA present in a particular reactor compartment over time, for each reactor compartment. This data has discontinuities similar to those of (3), resulting from movement of a new plug compartment into the reactor compartment.

Two of these four are illustrated in Figures 6 and 7.

The behavior of the data in the two charts above is as expected; both show sections that resemble e^{-x} exponential decay. However, additional useful information can be obtained from viewing them in series rather than in parallel, as in the charts below. The first illustrates that although the points of compartment movement are noticeable, the function as a whole very closely resembles the expected exponential decay; this implies that large compartment resolution is not necessary to achieve accurate results. The second illustrates the behavior of the final CP value of a reactor compartment just before the first plug compartment leaves it; this line very closely resembles a $n - e^{-x}$ exponentially decaying increase.

6 Simulation Results

Using this simulator makes it possible to determine an appropriate amount of ssDNA and an appropriate flow rate to give a desired error rate for negative selection in a given microreactor. Error for negative selection is the total amount of ssDNA that did not bind in the microreactor - in other words, the total ssDNA left at the end of the simulation. Achieving low error requires a balance of flow rate and the amount of ssDNA used. Letting the ssDNA move more slowly through the microreactor decreases the error, but requires more time for a computation; reducing the amount of ssDNA used also decreases the error, but restricts computation by allowing only smaller libraries of solutions.

Let us assume the target error rate is 10% or less (smaller may be desired for a system involving several microreactors). To examine the effect of each

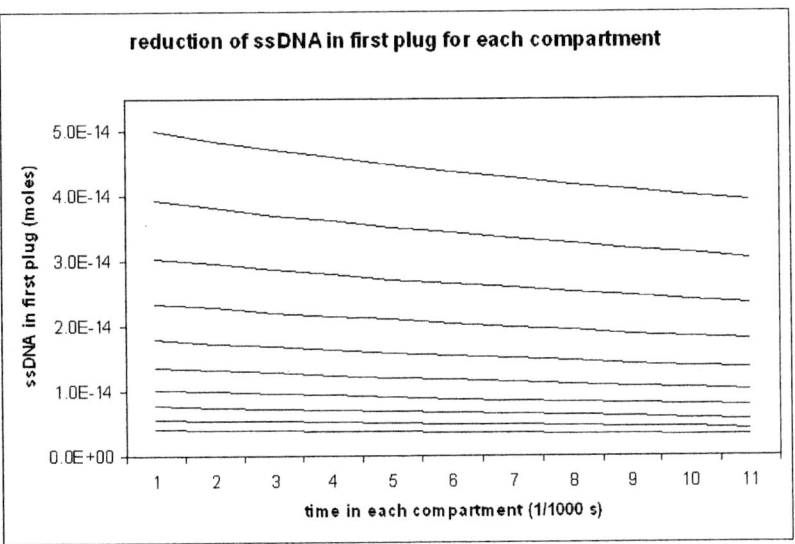

Fig. 6. Reduction of ssDNA in the first plug for each compartment. This corresponds to output (1) described above for the leading plug compartment, with 10 reactor compartments and 10 sub-steps (point 11 of a line matches point 1 of the next line). Each point is one sub-step; each line is a different reactor compartment.

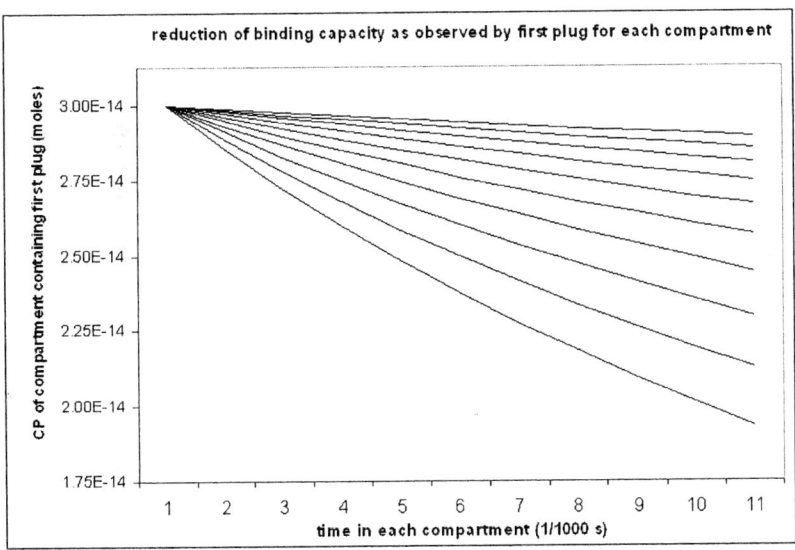

Fig. 7. Reduction of the binding capacity as observed by the first plug for each compartment. This corresponds to output (3) above for the leading plug compartment, with 10 reactor compartments and 10 sub-steps. Each point is one sub-step; each line is a different reactor compartment.

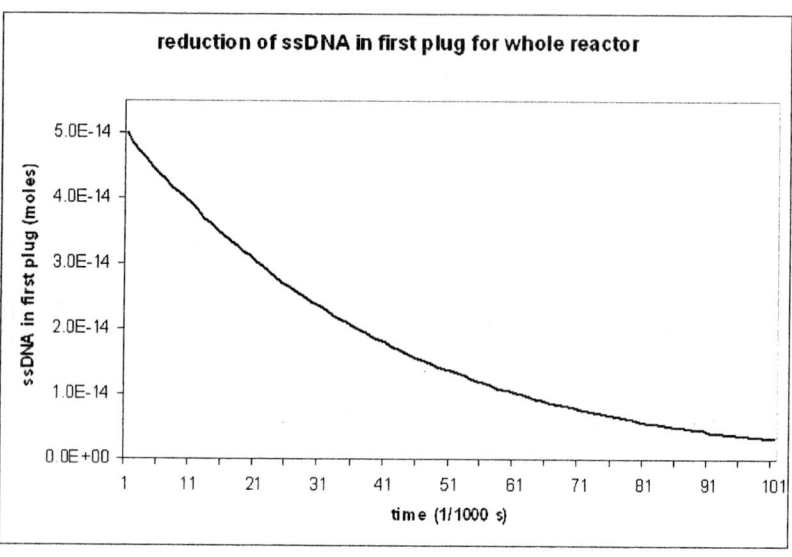

Fig. 8. Reduction of ssDNA in the first plug for the whole reactor. Concatenation of the 10 lines shown in Figure 6, to show the desired approximate smoothness of the overall curve; although the curve appears smooth, it is piecewise. The connections are at 11, 21, 31, etc. and correspond to times when the plug compartment moves from one reactor compartment to the next.

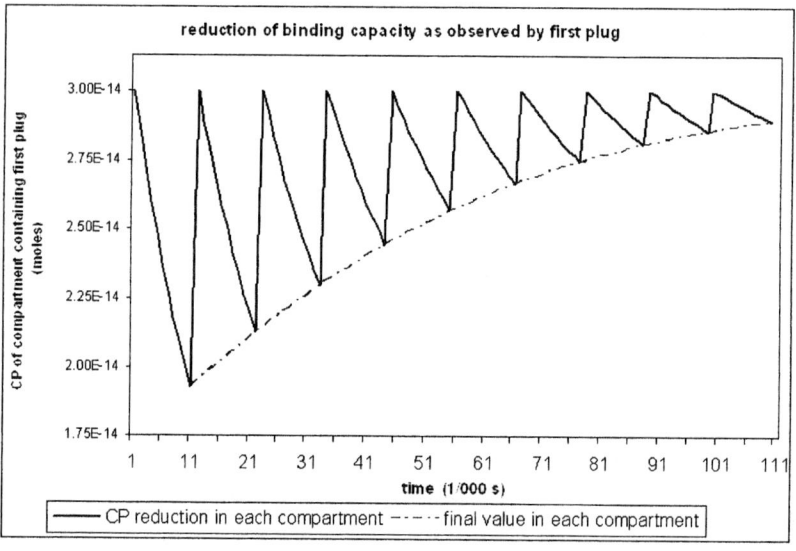

Fig. 9. Reduction of the binding capacity as observed by the first plug. Concatenation of the 10 lines shown in Figure 7, to show the curve presented by the final values from each reactor compartment (connected linearly with the dotted line).

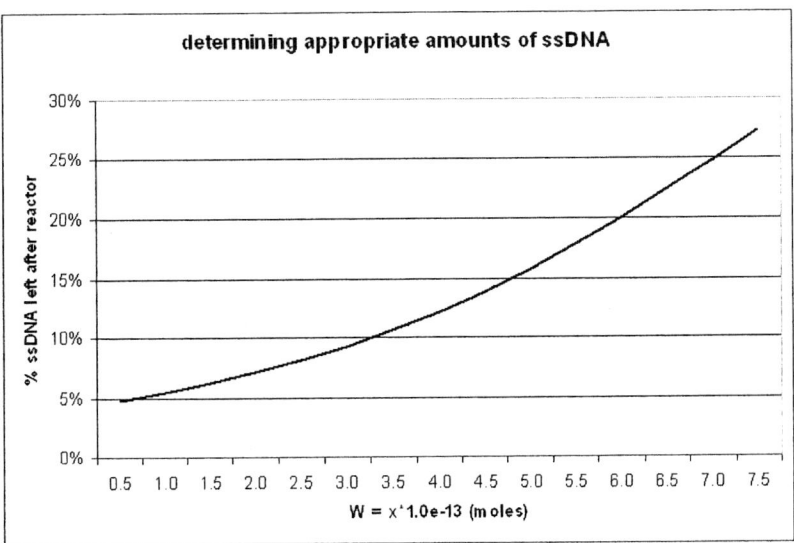

Fig. 10. This curve shows how changes to the initial amount of ssDNA (ssDNA concentration) affect the percent error rate for negative selection (i.e. the percent of ssDNA which is left in solution after passing through the reactor). Similar charts can be used to choose values of ssDNA concentration that will yield a desired acceptable error rate.

parameter, two sets of simulations were performed, each varying one parameter and holding all others constant. The result of each set is shown in a chart below.

For the simulations varying amount of ssDNA, the following parameters were held constant: the reactor volume and ssDNA volume were set to 10; time in reactor was 0.5 seconds; rate constant was 1.0e14; binding capacity was 6.3e-13; computation resolution was 10.

The result shows that, under these conditions, ssDNA concentration must be less than ~3.25e-13 (just over half the binding capacity) to achieve an error rate under 10%. It also shows that to achieve further decreases in error rate, significant (undesirable) reductions in ssDNA are required.

For the simulations varying time in reactor, the following parameters were held constant: the reactor volume and ssDNA volume were set to 10; rate constant was 1.0e14; amount of ssDNA was 6.0e-13; binding capacity was 6.3e-13; computation resolution was 10.

The result shows that, under these conditions, time in reactor must be greater than ~1 second to achieve an error rate under 10%. It also shows that further decreases in error rate are easily achievable through further increase in time, even though the ssDNA amount and bind capacity are very close.

One additional use of simulation is to help determine microreactor intrinsics. For instance, assume that the second-order rate constant (k in the equations introduced earlier) for a particular microreactor and environmental conditions is not known. By running a microreactor flow, measuring the resulting ssDNA, and then comparing to simulation, approximate values for this constant can be

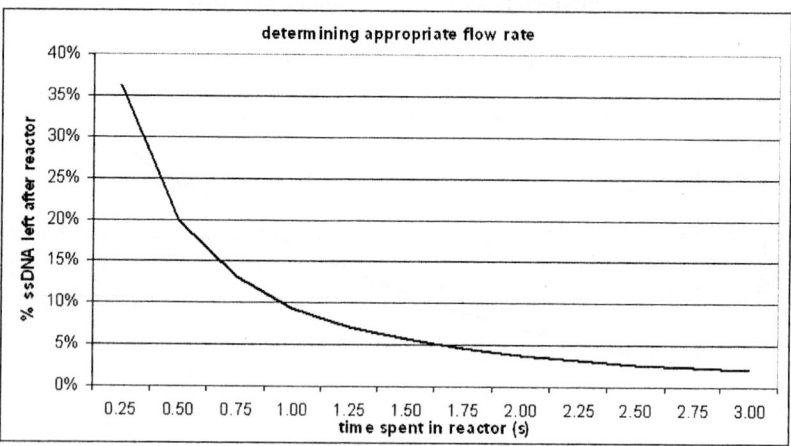

Fig. 11. This curve shows how changes to the time spent in the reactor (reactor flow time) affect the percent error rate for negative selection (i.e. the percent of ssDNA which is left in solution after passing through the reactor). Similar charts can be used to choose values of reactor flow time that will yield a desired acceptable error rate.

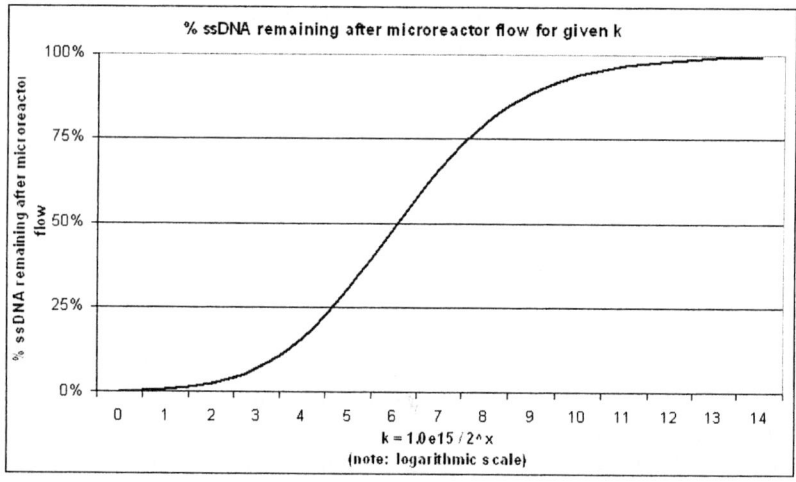

Fig. 12. This chart shows how the second-order rate constant (k) influences binding of ssDNA in the reactor. (Note that the x-axis is logarithmic.) Similar charts can be used to experimentally determine and/or verify the value of k for a given microreactor combined with specific environmental conditions; this would be done by matching observed results with a point on the curve, to yield an estimate k.

determined. An example set of simulations varying the rate constant is shown in the chart below; using this chart to work backwards and determine an approximate value for the rate constant would be a simple task. Multiple experiment/simulation pairs would help improve accuracy of the resulting estimate.

7 Conclusions

Simulation of binding activities in microreactors proves to be a useful tool, not only in DNA computing, but also in any other application utilizing microfluidic systems. Additionally to predicting the hybridization error propagated through a microfluidic system, the model can be extended to compute the fraction of strands that actually hybridizes. This, in turn, may help to relax the simplifying assumptions used in the analysis of microreactor-based computations. This will require provisions for operations such as a flushing, in order to accommodate simulations for multiple plugs. Beyond its primary role to predict the hybridization error the program can serve as a teaching aid and learning guide for DNA computing thanks to its GUI and visualization features.

Further development the simulation will comprise of a cascading network of microreactors, while it will also parse a Boolean expression in a minimal number of selection modules and OR functions. It is known that OR functions give rise to errors [4].

Acknowledgements

D. van Noort would like to acknowledge the support from the Molecular Evolutionary Computing (MEC) project of the Korean Ministry of Commerce, Industry and Energy, and the National Research Laboratory (NRL) Program from the Korean Ministry of Science and Technology. J. W. Jaromczyk acknowledges the support by the Kentucky Biomedical Research Infrastructure Network, funded by grant 2P20RR016481-04 from the National Center for Research Resources (subcontract to a grant awarded to N. Cooper from the University of Louisville).

References

1. van Noort, D., Tang Z.-L. and Landweber, L. F.: Fully controllable microfluidics for molecular computers. JALA 9, (2004)
2. van Noort, D., Wagler, P. and McCaskill, J. S.: The role of microreactors in molecular computing. Smart Mater. Struct. 11, (2002) 756–760
3. McCaskill, J. S.: Optically programming DNA computing in microflow reactors. BioSystems 59, (2001) 125–138.
4. Livestone, M. S. and Landweber L. F.: Mathematical considerations in the design of microreactor-based DNA computers. LNCS 2943, (2004) 180–189.
5. E. Gamma, R. Helm, R. Johnson, J. Vlissides.: Design Patterns: Elements of Reusable Object-Oriented Software. Addison-Wesley, (1995).

A Novel Ant Clustering Algorithm with Digraph[*]

Ling Chen[1,2], Li Tu[1], and Hongjian Chen[1]

[1] Department of Computer Science, Yangzhou University,
Yangzhou 225009, China
[2] National Key Lab of Novel Software Tech, Nanjing University,
Nanjing 210093, China
lchen@yzcn.net

Abstract. A novel adaptive ant colony clustering algorithm based on digraph (A^3CD) is presented. Inspired by the swarm intelligence shown through the social insects' self-organizing behavior, in A^3CD we assign acceptance weights on the directed edges of a pheromone digraph. The weights of the digraph is adaptively updated by the pheromone left by ants in the seeking process. Finally, strong connected components are extracted as clusters under a certain threshold. A^3CD has been implemented and tested on several clustering benchmarks and real datasets to compare the performance with the classical K-means clustering algorithm and LF algorithm which is also based on ACO. Experimental results show that our algorithm is easier to implement, more efficient and performs faster and has better clustering quality than other methods.

1 Introduction

Clustering is a very important problem in data mining. Cluster analysis has found many extensive applications including classification of coals[1], toxicity testing[2], discovering of clusters in DNA dinucleotides[3], etc.

Social insects(e.g. birds, bee, fish, ants etc.) have high swarm intelligence[4-5]. Among the social insects' many behaviors, the most widely recognized is the ants' ability to work as a group in order to finish a task that cannot be finished by a single ant. By simulating ant's swarm intelligence, M.Dorigo et al. first advanced the ant colony optimization algorithm(ACO)[6-8] to solve several discrete optimization problems. In ACO, artificial ants are created to emulate the real ants in the process of seeking food and information exchanging. The successful simulation has been applied to TSP problem[9], system fault detecting [10], sequential ordering[11], job-shop scheduling [12,13], quadratic assignment problem[14], frequency assignment problem [15] network routing[16], network load balancing [17], graph color[18], robotics [19] and other combinational optimization problems [20-21].

Based on the behavior of ants' piling corpses, researchers have applied artificial ant colony to data clustering which is an important task in data mining. Deneubourg et al

---

[*] Supported in part by the National Natural Science Foundation under grant No. 60473012, Science Foundation of Educational Commission Jiangsu Province.

first proposed a basic model (BM)[22] to explain the ants' corpses piling phenomenon and presented an clustering algorithm based on this model. LF algorithm, which is presented by and named after Lumer and Faieta [23], is an other ant colony clustering algorithm which is based on BM algorithm. In LF algorithm, a formula to measure the similarity between two data objects is defined. BM and LF have become well-known models that have been extensively used in different applications [24-27]. Kuntz et al [24-26] successfully applied and improved the LF algorithm for graph partitioning and other related problems. Ramos et al[27] and Handl et al[27] recently applied the LF algorithm to text clustering and reported promising results. Holland et al[19] applied the LF algorithm to robotics.

Since artificial ants in BM and LF perform large amount of random idle moves before they pick up or drop a datum, large amount of repetition occurs during the random idle move, which increases the computational time cost greatly. We notice that ants will also volatilize a kind of chemical odor called pheromone when they encounter each other or in the process of seeking their fellows. Based on this kind of odor ant i may exclude or attract ant j, however, on the opposite way, ant j is possible to attract or expel ant i. Enlightened by this fact, we propose a novel adaptive ant colony clustering algorithm based on digraph(A^3CD). In A^3CD, we first apply weights of rejection and acceptance between the data to form a completed digraph in which the vertexes represent the data and the initial weight of each edge between vertexes is the weights of acceptance between the data. Artificial ants travel on the graph and deposits pheromone on the edges they passed. In each step, the artificial ant selects the next vertex according to the acceptance weight in digraph and some heuristic information. The pheromone on each edge of the digraph will be updated with the artificial ants' adaptive movements. Some adaptive strategies are also presented to speed up the clustering greatly. The more similar data objects are, the higher the quantity of pheromone may be deposited on the edge between their vertexes. Finally, making full use of the quantity of pheromone on each edge, we omit some connections whose pheromone value is less than a certain threshold to get a new digraph. Then, the strong connected components of the new digraph forms the finial data clusters. A^3CD has been implemented and tested on several clustering benchmarks and real datasets to compare the performance with the classical K-means clustering algorithm and LF algorithm which is also based on ACO. Experimental results show that our algorithm is easier to implement, more efficient, faster and has better clustering quality than other methods.

2 Ant Clustering Algorithm with Digraph

2.1 The Framework of the Algorithm of A^3CD

Including three stages, the framework of the proposed algorithm A^3CD is as follows.

Algorithm: Adaptive Ant Clustering Algorithm With Digraph (A^3CD)
```
Begin
  Stage1:
    Initialize parameters: minC ,m, ε, γ, α,β ;
    Initialize the pheromone digraph;
```

```
      For each ant do
         Chooses an initial data item to visit randomly;
      End for
   Stage2:
      While (not termination) do      /*500 interations*/
         For each ant k do
            While (allowed_k not empty) do
               Compute p function;
               Select the next data item to visit;
               Update allowed_k;
            End do
            Reset allowed_k;
         End for
         Update the pheromone on each edge in the digraph;
         Adaptively update the value of α,β ;
      End do
   Stage3:
      Transfer the pheromone digraph to another digraph by
         omitting the edges whose pheromone value is less
         than ε ;
      Find out the strong connected components of the up-
         dated digraph as clusters;
      Join the small cluster whose data number is less than
         minC with the nearest cluster;
End
```

2.2 The Initialization of Pheromone Digraph

The first stage of the algorithm constructs the weighted digraph. The acceptance weight assigned on the edges of the digraph can be computed from the attribute distance between the data items.

Definition 1. The Set of Data Items

A set of n data items is defined as $S = (O, A)$ where,

$O = \{object_1, object_2, ...object_n\}$ represents the set data objects,

$A = \{A_1, A_2, ... A_r\}$ represents the attributes of data objects, where

$\forall i, i \in (1,2,...n)$, $\exists a_{ik}, k \in (1,2,...r)$ denotes the attribute A_k of $object_i$.

Although the values of different attributes possibly are not with the same data type, it is possible to quantify them into a standard metric. Therefore, each data item $object_i$ could be denoted as a r-dimension vector $(a_{i1}, a_{i2}, ...a_{ir})$, $i \in \{1,2,...n\}$.

Definition 2. The Attribute Distance Between Data Items

For two data items $object_i$ and $object_j$, $d(object_i, object_j)$ is defined as their attribute distance, i.e. the dissimilarity between $object_i$ and $object_j$:

$$d(object_i, object_j) = \sqrt{\sum_{k=1}^{r}(p_k a_{ik} - p_k a_{jk})^2}, i, j = 1,2,...n \ . \quad (2.1)$$

Definition 3. The Mean Distance and the Shortest Distance

We use $d_{mean}(object_i)$ to denote the mean distance from $object_i$ to all the other data items, namely

$$d_{mean}(object_i) = \frac{1}{n-1}\sum_{j=1}^{n} d(object_i, object_j) \ . \tag{2.2}$$

We also denote the shortest distance from $object_i$ to all the other data items as $d_{min}(object_i)$

$$d_{min}(object_i) = \min_{1 \leq j \leq n, j \neq i} d(object_i, object_j) \ . \tag{2.3}$$

Definition 4. The Acceptance Weights

For two data items $object_i$ and $object_j$, the acceptance weights for $object_i$ to $object_j$ is defined as Equation 2.4.

$$accept_i(object_j) = \frac{d_{min}(object_i) + d_{mean}(object_i)}{d(object_i, object_j)}, (i, j = 1,2...n) \ . \tag{2.4}$$

From the definition we can see that the more similar two data objects are, the greater acceptance weight to each other will be. We also can see that acceptance weight between two data objects is not symmetric, namely, normally $accept_j(object_i)$ is also not equal to $accept_i(object_j)$.

According to the definitions above, we could form a weighed digraph where each vertex represents a data object. Denote the weight of the directed edge from the vertexes representing data objects $object_i$ to $object_j$ as $\tau_{ij}(0)$. This value will be updated in every step of the clustering by the pheromone deposited by the ants passing it. Its initial value $\tau_{ij}(0)$ is set as the acceptance weight:

$$\tau_{ij}(0) = accept_i(object_j) \ ;$$

In traditional ant colony algorithm, pheromone at all edges are usually initialized as zero. This is not helpful for ants to choose path at the early stages. However, in A^3CD the proposed initial pheromone value set on the digraph is much important for ants' latter movements and the efficiency of algorithm's execution. Based on this initial value, in the latter stages the ants will update this pheromone digraph for the final clustering. Our experiment results show that this will not cause any sensitivity in the procedure of optimization.

2.3 The Probability Function

In stage 2 of the algorithm A^3CD, a certain probability function is computed for the ant_k to select the next vertex. When an ant on data item i select the next one as its destination, the most similar data item should have the largest probability to be chosen. Therefore, we measure the similarity between data objects by pheromone between them. The next data item j to be visited by ant k is determined as follows:

$$j = \begin{cases} \arg\max_{u=allowed_k(t)}[\tau_{iu}^{\alpha}(t)\eta_{iu}^{\beta}] & \text{when } q \leq q_0 \\ \text{selected by probability } p_{ij}^k(t), & \text{otherwise} \end{cases} \quad (2.5)$$

Here q_0 is a constant. In each step a random number $q \in [0,1]$ is generated. If $q \leq q_0$, the ant selects the vertex connected by the edge with the largest amount of pheromone. Otherwise, data item j is chosen by the probability defined as follows.

$$p_{ij}^k(t) = \begin{cases} \dfrac{\tau_{ij}^{\alpha}(t)\eta_{ij}^{\beta}(t)}{\sum_{r \in allowed_k} \tau_{ir}^{\alpha}(t)\eta_{ir}^{\beta}(t)} & j \in allowed_k \\ 0 & \text{otherwise} \end{cases} \quad (2.6)$$

2.4 Heuristic Function

The heuristic function η_{ij} in (2.6) is a problem dependent function that measures the "quality" of the edge (i,j) which connects the vertexes i and j representing the two data objects. It is given by the following formula.

$$\eta_{ij} = 1/d(object_i, object_j) . \quad (2.7)$$

2.5 Pheromone Updating

In stage 2 of the algorithm, based on the following formula, pheromone on edge (i,j) is updated on the paths the ants just passed after each iteration.

$$\tau_{ij}(t+1) = (1-\rho) \cdot \tau_{ij}(t) + \sum_{k=1}^{m} \Delta \tau_{ij}^k . \quad (2.8)$$

Here constant $\rho \in (0.1)$ is the coefficient of evaporation. $\Delta \tau_{ij}^k$ is the increment of τ_{ij} by ant k, which is defined as:

$$\Delta \tau_{ij}^k = \begin{cases} Q/d(object_i, object_j), & \text{if ant k passes the path i - j} \\ 0, & \text{otherwise} \end{cases} \quad (2.9)$$

Here Q is a constant. From the formulas above, it is easy to see that the more ants pass through an edge, the more pheromone deposited on it, and the two vertexes connected by the edge will have more probability to be included in the same strong connected component of the weighted digraph constructed in the third stage of the algorithm.

2.6 Adaptive Update of the Parameters: α, β

The second stage of the algorithm consists the step of updating the value of parameters α, β which determine the relative influence of the trail strength τ_{ij} and the heuristic information η_{ij}. At the initial stage of the algorithm, the pheromone value on each edge is relatively small. To speedup the convergence, the value of α should be relatively large. After some iterations, the pheromone values on the edges are increased, the value of β should be relatively large. Therefore, the algorithm updates the value of α, β as follows:

$$\alpha = \log^{1+\delta}, \quad \beta = \frac{1}{\alpha}. \tag{2.10}$$

Here, $\delta = \dfrac{\sum_{i=1}^{n}\sum_{j=1,j\neq i}^{n}|\tau_{ave} - \tau_{ij}|}{n(n-1)}$ and $\tau_{ave} = \dfrac{\sum_{i=1}^{n}\sum_{j=1,j\neq i}^{n}\tau_{ij}}{n(n-1)}$. δ is the pheromone distributing weight to measure the distribution of pheromone on the digraph and τ_{ave} is defined as the average amount of pheromone on the pheromone digraph.

By adjusting the value of α, β adaptively, the algorithm can accelerate the convergence and also can avoid local convergence and precocity.

3 Computational Results and Discussion

In this section, we show the test results on the ant-based clustering data benchmark and several real data sets to compare our method with that of K-means and LF algorithm. The algorithms are tested on Pentium 1.7G. The basic parameters are set as $m=n/2$, $\rho=0.05$, $q_0=0.95$.

3.1 Test on Randomly Generated Data Sets

We test randomly generated data sets with 40, 300 and 600 data items respectively.

First we test a data set with four data types each of which consists of 10 two-dimensional data (x,y) which belong to four classes as shown in Fig. 1, Here x and y obey normal distribution $N(u,\sigma^2)$. The normal distributions of the four types of data (x,y) are [N(0.2,0.12), N(0.2,0.12)], [N(0.6,0.12), N(0.2,0.12)], [N(0.2,0.12), N(0.6,0.12)], [N(0.6,0.12), N(0.6,0.12)], respectively.

Fig. 2 shows the initial pheromone digraph of this data set of 40 data items. The pheromone digraph obtained after 50 iterations of A^3CD is then modified by omitting the edges whose pheromone value is less than $\varepsilon = 1.95$. The modified digraph is shown in Fig. 3

As shown in Fig. 4, four strong connected components of the modified digraph are computed which form the finial clusters.

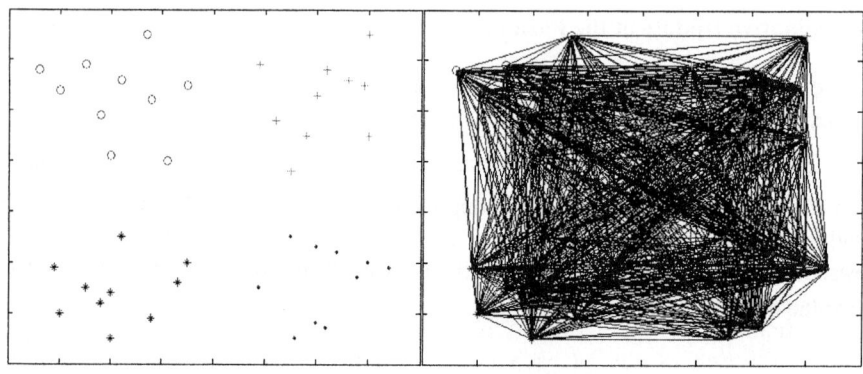

Fig. 1. The initial data sets   **Fig. 2.** The initial pheromone digraph

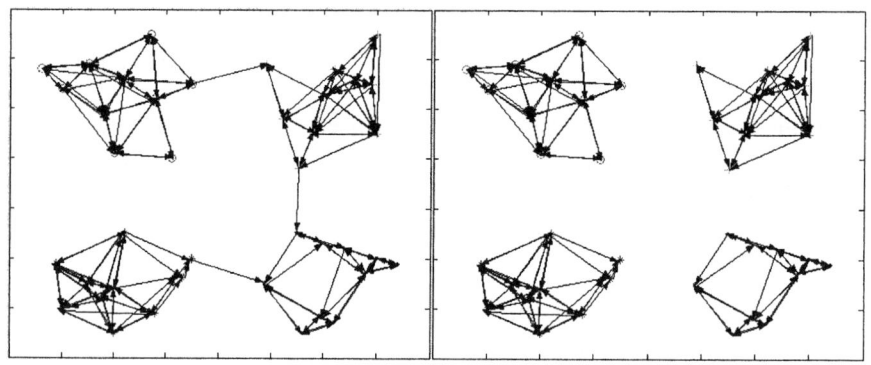

Fig. 3. The modified pheromone digraph (after 50 iterations)   **Fig. 4.** The finial strong connected components

In addition, we also test on data sets with 300 and 600 data items. Each data set has two attributes and three classes. In each class, data items are generated at random in distributions of [N(0.2,0.12), N(0.2,0.12)], [N(0.9,0.12), N(0.2,0.12)], [N(0.5,0.12), N(0.9,0.12)] respectively. The average results of 100 trails on these two types of data sets are as shown in Table 1.

Table 1. The results of three algorithms on artificial studies

Clustering Algorithms	300 data items		600 data items	
	Error rate	Time cost(s)	Error rate	Time cost(s)
K-Means	0	120.30	2.67%	250.32
LF	0	145.08	1.95%	352.55
A^3CD	0	60.21	0.37%	121.83

From Table 1, we can see that A³CD costs much less computational time than K-means and LF algorithm in terms of error rate and time cost.

3.2 Experiments on Real Data Bases Benchmarks

We test K-means, LF and A³CD using the real data set benchmarks of Iris, Wine and Glass. In the most trials, LF possibly finds correct clusters only after 15000 iterations, and K-means still shows an unsatisfied average error rate. However, A³CD could successfully form clustering after 500 iterations. Therefore, we set the parameter t_{max} the maximum iterations of LF algorithm as 15000, and those for A³CD as 500. Results of 100 trials of each algorithm on the three data sets are shown in Table 2 to Table 4.

Table 2. The comparison of three algorithms on Iris data sets

Parameters	Algorithms		
	K-Means (k=3)	LF (15000iterations)	A³CD (500iterations)
Number of clusters	3	3	3
Max error numbers	15	13	9
Min error numbers	5	4	4
Average number of errors	7.35	6.65	4.48
Average error rate	4.90%	4.43%	2.98%
Time cost (s)	45.57	64.15	23.30

Table 3. The comparison of three algorithms on Wine data sets

Parameters	Algorithms		
	K-Means (k=3)	LF (15000iterations)	A³CD (500iterations)
Number of clusters	3	3	3
Max error numbers	18	16	10
Min error numbers	4	3	2
Average number of errors	6.12	6.95	3.45
Average error rate	3.43%	3.90%	1.93%
Time cost (s)	104.10	99.51	36.13

Table 4. The comparison of three algorithms on Glass data sets

Parameters	Algorithms		
	K-Means (k=3)	LF (15000iterations)	A^3CD (500iterations)
Number of clusters	6	6	6
Max error numbers	17	14	11
Min error numbers	9	7	6
Average number of errors	12.15	10.31	7.82
Average error rate	5.67%	4.68%	3.65%
Time cost (s)	100.22	119.54	45.24

It can easily be seen from Table 2 that A^3CD require less iterations and hence less computation time than K-means and LF. The table also show the error rates of A^3CD is much lower, which means the clustering quality of A^3CD is much better than the other two algorithms.

From the test results above, it is obvious that the time cost of LF is quite large, mainly because ants spend large amount of time in searching for data and have difficulty to drop its data in data-rich environment. The parameters in LF algorithm, especially the parameter α, are difficult to set and can affect the quality of clustering results. A^3CD not only has advantages of simple, directness, dynamic, visible, but also offers self-adaptive adjustment to important parameters and process isolated data directly and effectively. Compared to LF algorithm, A^3CD algorithm is more effective and requires much less computation time.

4 Conclusion

A novel adaptive ant clustering algorithm A^3CD which is based on digraph is presented in this paper. In A^3CD, each data is represented by a vertex in the digraph. In the process of clustering, the edges connecting vertexes with more similarity have more probability to be selected by the ants and will has more pheromone to be deposited on. When the pheromone are increased and updated, the clusters could be obtained by finding the strong connection components on the pheromone digraph. By analyzing the effect of each parameter, we proposed effective strategies for the ants selecting the edge, updating the pheromone, and adjusting the parameters adaptively to speed up the clustering procedure and to improve the clustering quality in A^3CD. Experimental results on standard clustering benchmarks demonstrate significant improvement in both computation time and clustering quality over K-means and LF algorithm.

References

1. Kaufman, L., Pierreux,A., Rousseuw, P., Derde, M.P., Detaecernier, M.R., Massart, D.L., Platbrood, G.: Clustering on a Microcomputer with an Application to the Classification of Coals, Analytica Chimica Acta, 153 (1983) 257–260.

2. Lawson, R.G., Jurs, P.C.: Cluster Analysis of Acrylates to Guide Sampling for Toxicity Testing. Journal of Chemical Information and Computer Science, 30 (1) (1990)137–144.
3. Beckers, M.L.M., Melssen, W.J., Buydens, L.M.C.: A self-organizing feature map for clustering nucleic acids. Application to a data matrix containing A-DNA and B-DNA dinucleotides. Comput. Chem., 21 (1997)377–390.
4. Kennedy, J., Eberhart, R.C.: Swarm Intelligence. Morgan Kaufmann Publishers, San Francisco CA (2001).
5. Bonabeau, E., Dorigo, M., Théraulaz, G.: Swarm Intelligence: From Natural to Artificial Systems. Santa Fe Institute in the Sciences of the Complexity. Oxford University Press, Oxford New York (1999).
6. Dorigo, M., Maniezzo, V., Colomi, A.: Ant system :Optimization by a colony of cooperating agents. IEEE Transactions on Systems, Man and Cybernetics-Part B, 26(1) (1996) 29–41.
7. Dorigo, M., Gambardella, L.M.: Ant colony system: a cooperative learning approach to the traveling salesman problem. IEEE Trans. On Evolutionary Computation, 1(1) (1997) 53–66.
8. Stutzle, T., Hoos, H.: MAX-MIN Ant systems. Future Generation Computer Sytems, 16(2000) 889–914.
9. Dorigo, M., Gambardella, L.M.: Ant colonies for the traveling salesman problem. BioSystems, 43(2) (1997) 73–81.
10. Chang, C.S., Tian, L., Wen, F.S.: A new approach to fault section in power systems using Ant System. Electric Power Systems Research, 49(1) (1999) 63–70.
11. Gambardella, L.M., Dorigo, M.: HAS-SOP: An Hybrid Ant System for the Sequential Ordering Problem. Tech. Rep. No. IDSIA 97-11, IDSIA, Lugano Switzerland (1997).
12. Colorni, A., Dorigo, M., Maniezzo, V.: Ant colony system for job-shop scheduling. Belgian J. of Operations Research Statistics and Computer Science, 34(1) (1994) 39–53.
13. Bonabeau, E., Sobkowski, A., Théraulaz, G., Denebourg, J.L.: Adaptive Task Allocation Inspired by a Model of Division of Labor in Social Insects. In: Lundh, D. et al. (eds.): Biocomputing and Emergent Computation: Proceedings of BCEC'97 (1997) 36–45.
14. Maniezzo, V.: Exact and approximate nondiministic tree search procedures for the quaratic assignment problem. INFORMS J. Comput, 11 (1999) 358–369.
15. Maniezzo, V., Carbonaro, A.: An ANTS heuristic for the frequency assignment problem. Future Generation Computer Systems, 16 (2000) 927–935.
16. Di Caro, G., Dorigo, M.: Distributed Reinforcement Agents for Adaptive Routing in Communication Networks. Third European Workshop on Reinforcement Learning, Rennes (F), October 13–14 (1997).
17. Schoonderwoerd, R., Holland, O., Bruten, J.: Ant-like agents for load balancing in telecommunications networks. Proc.of Agents'97. Marina del Rey,CA: ACM Press, (1997) 209–216.
18. Costa, D., Hertz, A.: Ants can colour graphs. J. of the Opnl.Res.Soc.48(3) (1997) 295–305.
19. Holland, O.E., Melhuish, C.: Stigmergy, self-organization, and sorting in collective robotics. Artificial Life, 5 (1999) 173–202.
20. Kuntz, P., Layzell, P., Snyder, D.: A colony of ant-like agents for partitioning in VLSI technology. In: Husbands, P., Harvey, I.(eds.): Proceedings of the Fourth European Conference on Artificial Life, MIT Press, Cambridge MA (1997) 412–424.
21. Kuntz, P., Snyder, D.: New results on ant-based heuristic for highlighting the organization of large graphs. In: Proceedings of the 1999 Congress or Evolutionary Computation, IEEE Press, Piscataway NJ (1999) 1451–1458.

22. Deneubourg, J.L., Goss, S., Franks, N., Sendova-Franks, A., Detrain, C., Chretien, L.: The Dynamic of Collective Sorting Robot-like Ants and Ant-like Robots. In: Meyer, J.A., Wilson, S.W. (eds.): SAB'90-1st Conf. On Simulation of Adaptive Behavior: From Animals to Animats, Mit press, (1991) 356–365.
23. Lumer, E., Faieta, B.: Diversity and adaptation in populations of clustering ants. In: Meyer, J.A., Wilson, S.W. (eds.): Proceedings of the Third International Conference on Simulation of Adaptive Behavior: From Animates, Vol.3. MIT Press/ Bradford Books, Cambridge MA (1994) 501–508.
24. Kuntz, P., Snyers, D., Layzell, P.: A stochastic heuristic for visualizing graph clusters in a bi-dimensional space prior to partitioning. Journal of Heuristics, 5 (1999) 327–351.
25. Kuntz, P., Layzell, P., Snyder, D.: A colony of ant-like agents for partitioning in VLSI technology. In: Husbands, P., Harvey, I. (eds.): Proceedings of the Fourth European Conference on Artificial Life, MIT Press, Cambridge MA (1997) 412–424.
26. Kuntz, P., Snyder, D.: New results on ant-based heuristic for highlighting the organization of large graphs. In: Proceedings of the 1999 Congress or Evolutionary Computation, IEEE Press, Piscataway. NJ (1999) 1451–1458.
27. Handl, J., Meyer, B.: Improved ant-based clustering and sorting in a document retrievalinterface. PPSN.VII, LNCS. 2439 (2002).

Ant Colony Search Algorithms for Optimal Packing Problem

Wen Peng, Ruofeng Tong, Min Tang, and Jinxiang Dong

State Key Laboratory of CAD & CG, Zhejiang University,
Hangzhou 310027
{pengwen, trf, tang_m, djx}@zju.edu.cn

Abstract. Ant Colony optimization takes inspiration from the behavior of real ant colony to solve optimization problems. This paper presents a parallel model for ant colony to solve the optimal packing problem. The problem is represented by a directed graph so that the objective of the original problem becomes to find the shortest closed circuit on the graph under the problem-specific constraints. A number of artificial ants are distributed on the graph and communicate with one another through the pheromone trails which are a form of the long-term memory guiding the future exploration of the graph. The algorithm supports the parallel computation and facilitates quick convergence to the optimal solution. The performance of the proposed method as compared to those of the genetic-based approaches is very promising.

1 Introduction

Many heuristic methods currently used in combinatorial optimization are inspired by adaptive natural behaviors or natural systems, such as genetic algorithms, simulated annealing, neural networks, etc. Ant colony algorithms belong to this class of biologically inspired heuristic. The basic idea is to imitate the cooperative behavior of ant colonies, which can be used to solve several discrete combinatorial optimization problems within a reasonable amount of time. Ant Colony (AC), a novel population-based approach, was proposed by Dorigo [1]. AC has achieved widespread success in solving different optimization problems (the vehicle routing problem [2], the machine tool tardiness problem [3] and the multiple objective JIT sequencing problem [4]).

The packing problems, aiming at improving the utilization and reducing the cost, arise frequently in many manufacture such as garment cutting [5] and facility layout design [6]. However, an exhaustive search for the packing from the given set of data will result in an exponential complexity. Fortunately, there exist some global search heuristic algorithms which can educe solutions very close to the global optimal one in a relative short time. Jakobs' 1996 implementation of genetic algorithm is used as a basic heuristic method in order to solve the packing problem [7]. Chen provides a new way to represent the sheet and part geometry, in which the irregularity of shape does not affect the computation complexity [8]. In addition, some improved genetic algorithm [9,10] and Han's neural network [11] both show the superiority of the technique.

Our aim is to develop a parallel model for AC to solve the optimal packing problem. AC can make algorithm amenable to parallel implementations, compared with other approaches, for its distinct feature -- distributed computation. The proposed parallel algorithm can obtain the optimal solution in a reasonably shorter period of time.

2 Ant Colony for Combinatorial Optimization

The ant colony algorithms have been introduced with Dorigo's Ph.D. They are based on the principle that by using very simple communication mechanisms, an ant group is able to find the shortest path between any two points. During their trips a chemical trail (pheromone) is left on the ground. The role of this trail is to guide the other ants towards the target point. For one ant, the path is chosen according to the quantity of pheromone. Furthermore, this chemical substance has a decreasing action over time, and the quantity left by one ant depends on the amount of food found and the number of ants using this trail. As illustrated in Fig. 1, when facing an obstacle, there is an equal probability for every ant to choose the left or right path. As the left trail is shorter than the right one and so requires less travel time, it will end up with higher level of pheromone. More ants take the left path, higher pheromone trail is.

The general principles for the AC simulation of real ant behavior are as follows.

(1) *Initialization*. The initialization of the AC includes two parts: the problem graph representation and the initial ant distribution. *First*, the underlying problem should be represented in terms of a graph, G = <N,E>, where N denotes the set of nodes, and E the set of edges. The graph is connected, but not necessarily complete, such that the feasible solutions to the original problem correspond to paths on the graph which satisfy problem-domain constraints. *Second*, a number of ants are arbitrarily placed on the nodes chosen randomly. Then each of the distributed ants will perform a tour on the graph by constructing a path according to the node transition rule described next.

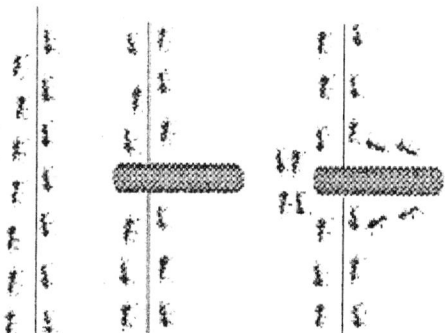

Fig. 1. Ants face an obstacle. When facing an obstacle, there is an equal probability for every ant to choose the left or right path. As the left trail is shorter than the right one and so requires less travel time, it will end up with higher level of pheromone. More ants take the left path, higher pheromone trail is.

(2) *Node transition rule.* The ants move from node to node based on a node transition rule. According to the problem-domain constraints, some nodes could be marked as inaccessible for a walking ant. The node transition rule is probabilistic. For the kth ant on node i, the selection of the next node j to follow is according to the node transition probability:

$$p_{ij}^k = \begin{cases} \dfrac{(\tau_{ij})^\alpha (\eta_{ij})^\beta}{\sum_{h \notin tabu_k} (\tau_{ih})^\alpha (\eta_{ih})^\beta} & \text{if } j \notin tabu_k \\ 0 & otherwise \end{cases} \quad (1)$$

where τ_{ij} is the intensity of pheromone laid on edge (i,j), η_{ij} is the value of visibility of edge (i,j), α and β are control parameters, and $tabu_k$ means the set of currently inaccessible nodes for the kth ant according to the problem-domain constraints. The intensity of pheromone laid on edge (i,j) reflecting the previous experience of the ants about this edge is shared memory which provides indirect communication between the ants. Pheromone information provides a global view about the selection of the edge based on a quality measure of the solution constructed afterward. On the other hand, the value of visibility is determined by a greedy heuristic method for the original problem which considers only the local information on edge (i,j) such as the length of it. Parameters α and β control the relative contribution between the two types of measures mentioned above. Therefore, the node transition rule given by Eq. (1) is trade-off between the search of intensification and diversification.

(3) *Pheromone updating rule.* The ant keeps walking through edges to different nodes by iteratively applying the node transition rule until a solution to the original problem is constructed. We define that a cycle of the AC algorithm is completed when every ant has constructed a solution. At the end of each cycle, the intensity of pheromone trails on each edge is updated by the pheromone updating rule:

$$\tau_{ij} \leftarrow \rho \tau_{ij} + \sum_{k=1}^{m} \Delta \tau_{ij}^k \quad (2)$$

where $\rho \in (0,1)$ is the persistence rate of previous trails, $\Delta \tau_{ij}^k$ is the amount of pheromone laid edge (i,j) by the kth ant at the current cycle, and m is the number of distributed ants. In a real ant system, shorter paths will retain more quantities of pheromone; analogously, in the AC, the paths corresponding to fitter solutions should receive more pheromone quantities and become more attractive in the next cycle. Hence, if we define L_k, the total length of the kth ant in a cycle, as the fitness value of the solution, then $\Delta \tau_{ij}^k$ can be given by

$$\Delta \tau_{ij}^k = \begin{cases} \dfrac{Q}{L_k} & \text{if edge } (i,j) \text{ is traversed by} \\ & \text{the } k\text{th ant at this cycle} \\ 0 & otherwise \end{cases} \quad (3)$$

where Q is a constant.

(4) *Stopping criterion.* The stopping criterion of the AC algorithm could be the maximal number of running cycles or the CPU time limit.

3 Ant Colony for the Optimal Packing Problem

In this section, we first give the problem definition of the optimal packing, and then describe how we modify the AC algorithm and apply it to the problem.

3.1 Problem Definition

The packing problem, which is generally described as an optimization problem, aims at finding the optimal layout that satisfies certain given constraints. Given a finite set of polygons $P=\{p_1,p_2,\ldots,p_n\}$, and a two dimensional strip S with width Ws and infinite height, it is to place all the elements in P on S and make a layout with the constraints about the overlap (p_i and p_j ($i \neq j$)don't overlap) and overhang (p_i(i=1,2,...,n) is located within the S) such that the used height of S is minimized.

In this paper, the sequence Seq of the polygons and each polygon's rotation θ are essential parameters to determine a layout, so the packing problems can be divided into two parts: finding the packing parameters values and transforming them into a layout. AC as a combinatorial optimization method is used to search the optimal packing parameters values, then the heuristic approach BLF (bottom-left-fill) is used for determining the exact layout under the fixed packing parameters value and computing the height of strip. Therefore, the packing problem is defined as:

$$\min\{H \mid H = BLF(Seq, \theta)\} \qquad (4)$$

(Seq, θ) result from AC

3.2 Graph Representation

To apply the AC, the underlying problem should be represented in terms of a directed graph, G=<N,E>, which can avoid the ants walking backward. Apparently, for optimal packing problem, each polygon p_i should be represented as a node of the graph, N=P. We represent the edge E as $\overrightarrow{(p_i, p_j, \theta_k, M_l)}$, where θ is the basic rotation of the polygon p_j, and M is one of eight mirror images of the polygon [10], as shown in Fig.2. $\overrightarrow{h(p_i, p_j, \theta_k, M_l)}$ is defined the height of the edge $\overrightarrow{(p_i, p_j, \theta_k, M_l)}$, in Fig.3.

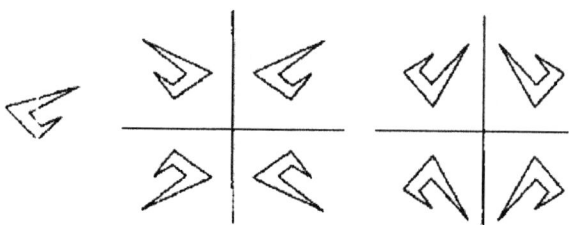

Fig. 2. The original polygon and its mirror images

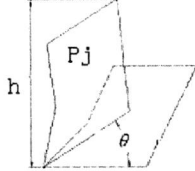

Fig. 3. The height (h) of the edge $\overrightarrow{(p_i, p_j, \theta_k, M_l)}$ is the vertical dimension of the polygon P_j

There are many edges between two nodes in our graph, which differs from AC. Now, the problem of optimal packing is equivalent to finding a closed circuit, which satisfies the lowest height by BLF, on the directed graph.

3.3 Node Transition Rule

The node transition rule is a probabilistic one determined by the pheromone intensity τ_{ijkl} and the visibility value η_{ijkl} of the corresponding edge. In the proposed method, τ_{ijkl} is equally initialized to any small constant positive value, and is gradually updated at the end of each cycle according to the average quality of the solution that involve this edge. On the other hand, the value of η_{ijkl} is determined by a greedy heuristic method, which encourages the ants to walk to the lowest height edge in order to construct the lowest height layout. This can be accomplished by setting $\eta_{ijkl} = 1/h(p_i, p_j, \theta_k, M_l)$.

We now define the transition probability from node i to node j through directed edge $\overrightarrow{(p_i, p_j, \theta_k, M_l)}$ as

$$p_{ijkl}(t) = \begin{cases} \dfrac{[\tau_{ijkl}(t)]^\alpha [\eta_{ijkl}]^\beta}{\sum\limits_{allowed\_list} [\tau_{ijkl}(t)]^\alpha [\eta_{ijkl}]^\beta} & \text{if } j \in allowed\_list \\ 0 & \text{otherwise} \end{cases} \quad (5)$$

where *allowed_list* are the accessible nodes by walking ants, and the means of other symbols are same to the Eq. (1).

3.4 Pheromone Updating Rule

The intensity of pheromone trails of an edge is updated at the end of each cycle by the average quality of the solutions that traverse along this edge. We simply apply and modify Eqs. (2) and (3) to update pheromone intensity.

$$\tau_{ijkl} \leftarrow \rho.\tau_{ijkl} + \sum_{s=1}^{m} \Delta\tau_{ijkl}^s \quad (6)$$

$$\Delta \tau_{ijkl}^s = \begin{cases} \dfrac{Q}{H_s} & \text{if the sth ant walk } \overrightarrow{(p_i, p_j, \theta_k, M_l)} \\ 0 & \text{otherwise} \end{cases} \quad (7)$$

where H_s is the height of the layout by sth ant at current cycle.

3.5 Ant Colony for the Optimal Packing

According to the given definitions as above, the packing algorithm based on ant colony is described as following.

Input:
m: the number of ants.
MAX_CYCLE: the maximal number of running cycles.
1: Construct the directed graph G=<N,E> as described in Subsection 3.2 Set NC=1 (NC is the cycles counter), $\tau_{ijkl}(t) = c$ (c is constant), $H_{global\_best} = \infty$ (H_{global_best} saves the lowest height of the strip). Compute η_{ijkl} on every edge $\overrightarrow{(p_i, p_j, \theta_k, M_l)}$.
2: For every ant do
    Select a starting node.
    Repeat
        Move to next node according to the node transition rule using Eq. (5).
    until a closed tour is completed.
    //a closed tours is completed when the ant arrives at the starting node again.
3: According to BLF, find out the best optimal layout among the m tours obtained at step2, say Hcurrent_best.
4: If Hcurrent_best < Hglobal_best, then Hglobal_best = Hcurrent_best.
5: For every directed edge $\overrightarrow{(p_i, p_j, \theta_k, M_l)}$ do
    Update the pheromone intensity using Eqs. (6) and (7).
6: If (NC = MAX_CYCLE), then output Hglobal_best and strop; otherwise, NC = NC + 1 and goto step2.

4 Parallel Ant Colony

To solve efficiently large optimization problems, a parallel model of ant colony has been developed. The programming style used is a synchronous master/workers paradigm. The master initializes all kinds of data as stated in section 3.5 step1, and then sends the graph information including the trail density τ_{ijkl} and the visibility η_{ijkl} to workers. With the graph information, the worker takes charge of searching for a tour composed of the edge and computing the height of the strip using BLF. The parallel algorithm works as follows Fig. 4. Each worker returns the height of the strip and the tour visited to the master, which later updates the intensity of trail on the edge and controls the flow of the algorithm. By this way all the workers can implement parallel packing by sharing the information from the master.

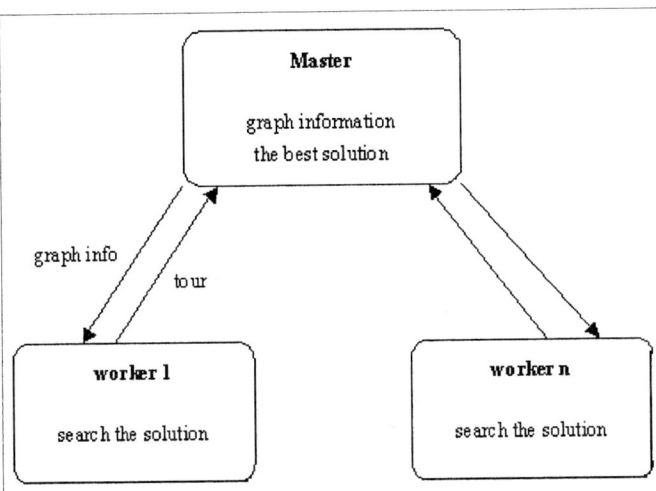

Fig. 4. Synchronous master/workers model for parallel ant colony. The master initializes all kinds of data and the worker takes charge of searching for a tour composed of the edge and computing the height of the strip using BLF.

5 Experimental Results

The proposed algorithm has been programmed in VC++ language, and run in Windows 2000 Professional. In all solutions, we set the width of the strip 600mm, $\alpha = 1.0$, $\beta = 2.0$ and $\rho = 0.9$.

5.1 The Visibility η

As mentioned in Eq.(5), the probability of choosing edge is a trade-off between visibility and trail intensity. Since the intensity of trail, changing continually, is uncontrollable, the visibility should be attached much importance. The visibility η is set $1/d$ in AC, where d is the length of the path. So we set $\eta_{ijkl} = 1/h(p_i, p_j, \theta_k, M_l)$ by analogy, which indicates that the edge with lower height, that is to say, the lower polygons should be chosen with high probability.

However, it may be not a good choice because all the lower (generally smaller) polygons have been packed and there are no smaller polygons to fill the gaps formed by the bigger ones, which leads to a high and loose layout for the gaps are left unused and dead. In view of this case, the area of the polygons is taken into consideration, $\eta_{ijkl} = Sp_j / h(p_i, p_j, \theta_k, M_l)$ (Sp_j is the area of the polygon Pj), so that the bigger polygons take priority of the smaller ones in packing and the latter can squash into the gaps.

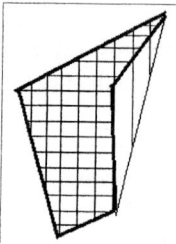

Fig. 5. The bold lines represent the polygon. The Horizontal lines represent its area and the vertical lines represent its concave area.

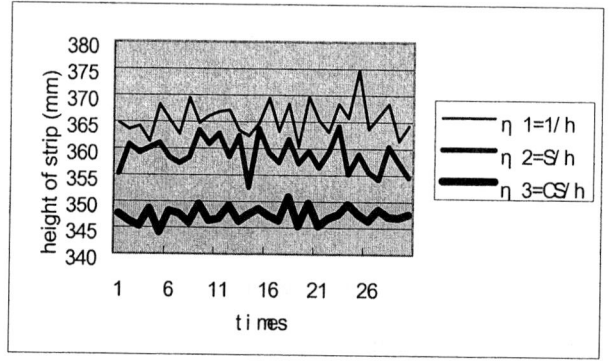

Fig. 6. Height obtained with different visibility η

Nevertheless it is still incapable of packing those extremely concave polygons with big size but small area as shown in Fig. 5. So we choose the convex area as a measurement to judge the size of the polygons and set $\eta_{ijkl} = CSp_j / \overrightarrow{h(p_i, p_j, \theta_k, M_l)}$ (CSp_j is the convex area of the polygon Pj), under which those polygons bigger in size and lower in height are packed prior to others so that smaller ones can fill the gaps.

We conduct the experiments with three different visibilities, as above-mentioned, thirty times separately. The results, as shown in Fig.6, prove our analysis so we put the η 3 into practice in the following experiments.

5.2 Comparison with Other Algorithms

In this section we compare the efficiency of our algorithm to those of the other two algorithms, both genetic algorithm [7] and genetic simulated annealing [8]. With variable number of the blocks, we complete four examples whose results are listed in Table 1 and the patterns from example 3 are shown in Fig 7. In our algorithm, 10 workers are used to search the solutions. It is indicated from the results that our algorithm can converge more quickly to the better solutions because of the parallel implementation.

Table 1. Results from the different algorithms

Examples		Genetic algorithm	Genetic simulated annealing	Our algorithm
Example 1: 15 blocks	Time (hour)	9.5	10.1	2.4
	Height of strip(mm)	287.45	284.67	280.21
Example 2: 20 blocks	Time (hour)	11.6	12.5	3.2
	Height of strip(mm)	326.70	320.02	309.46
Example 3: 25 blocks	Time (hour)	14.0	14.8	4.1
	Height of strip(mm)	349.57	347.26	340.67
Example 4: 30 blocks	Time (hour)	16.8	17.3	5.2
	Height of strip(mm)	395.43	389.33	378.62

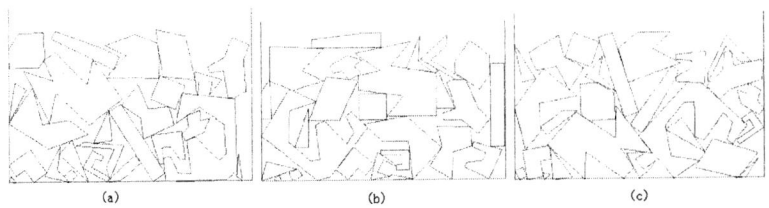

Fig. 7. The results. (a) result from genetic algorithm, (b) result from genetic simulated annealing, (c) result from our algorithm.

6 Summary

In this paper we have developed a powerful and robust algorithm for the packing problem, which combines the AC with the heuristic approach BLF. The proposed algorithm supports parallel computation and facilitates quick convergence to the optimal solution. The experimental result demonstrates that our algorithm can search the solution space more effectively and obtain the optimal solution in a reasonably shorter period of time.

Acknowledgements

The project is supported by the Natural Science Foundation (No.M603129) of Zhejiang Province, China and the Education Bureau (No.20030267) of Zhejiang Province, China.

References

1. Dorigo, M.: Optimization, learning and natural algorithms. Ph.D. Thesis, Italy (1992).
2. Bullnheimer, B. Hartl, R. F., Strauss, C.: Applying the ant system to the vehicle routing problem. In the Second Metaheuristics International Conference, France (1997).

3. Bauer, A., Bullnheimer, B. Hartl, RF: An ant colony optimization approach for the single machine tool tardiness problem. Proceeding of the Congress on Evolutionary Computation (1999) 1445-1450
4. McMullen, PR.: An ant colony optimization approach to addressing a JIT sequencing problem with multiple objectives. Artificial Intelligence (2001) 309-317
5. Leo Ho Wai Yeung, Wallace, K. S. Tang.: A Hybrid Genetic Approach for Garment Cutting in the Clothing Industry. IEEE Transaction on Industrial Electronics (2003), vol. 50.
6. Kado, K., Ross, P. Come, D.: A study of genetic algorithm hybrids for facility layout problem. Proceeding of the 6th International Conference Genetic Algorithm (1995) 498-505.
7. Jakobs, S.: On genetic algorithms for the packing problems. European Journal of Operational Research (1996) 165-188.
8. Chen Yong, Tang Min, Tong Ruofeng, Dong Jinxiang.: Packing of Polygons Using Genetic Simulated Annealing Algorithm. Journal of CAD & CG (2003), Vol, 15 598-603, 609.
9. Ramesh, Babu, A, Ramesh Babu N.: Effective nesting of rectangular parts in multiple rectangular sheets using genetic and heuristic algorithms. International Journal of Production Research (1999) 1925-1643.
10. Martens, J.: Two genetic algorithms to solve a layout problem in the fashion industry. European Journal of Operational Research (2004) 304-322.
11. Han, G.: Two-stage approach for nesting in two-dimensional cutting problems using neural network and simulated annealing. Journal of Engineering Manufacture (1996) 509-519.

Adaptive Parallel Ant Colony Algorithm

Ling Chen[1,2] and Chunfang Zhang[1]

[1] Department of Computer Science, Yangzhou University,
225009 Yangzhou, China
[2] National Key Lab of Novel Software Tech, Nanjing University,
210093 Nanjing, China
lchen@yzcn.net

Abstract. An adaptive parallel ant colony optimization is presented by improving the critical factor influencing the performance of the parallel algorithm. We propose two different strategies for information exchange between processors: selection based on sorting and on difference, which make each processor choose another processor to communicate and update the pheromone adaptively. In order to increase the ability of search and avoid early convergence, we also propose a method of adjusting the time interval of information exchange adaptively according to the diversity of the solutions. These techniques are applied to the traveling salesman problem on the massive parallel processors (MPP) Dawn 2000. Experimental results show that our algorithm has high convergence speed, high speedup and efficiency.

1 Introduction

Among the social insects' many behaviors, the most widely recognized is the ants' ability to work as a group in order to finish a task that cannot be finished by a single ant. Inspired by this effect of ant colony, M.Dorigo et al. first advanced an ant colony system and the ant colony optimization algorithm (ACO)[1-3] to solve several discrete optimization problems. ACO has also been applied to TSP problem[4], system fault detecting[5], sequential ordering[6], job-shop scheduling[7,8], quadratic assignment problem[9], frequency assignment problem[10] and other combinational optimization problems[11-16].

Though ACO usually can find a satisfactory result of the problem within a certain period of time, it becomes more difficult to speedup the algorithm when the complexity of the problem increases. Ant colony algorithm has its natural parallelism which is very suitable for implementing on the large-scale parallel computer. Some results on parallel ant colony algorithms have been reported recently. B.Buklnheimer[17] proposed two parallelization strategies of synchronous and asynchronous. Talbi[18] presented a synchronous fine grained parallel ant colony algorithm in master/servant fashion combined with local tabu search, and applied this algorithm to solve quadratic assignment problem (QAP). D.A.L.Piriyakumar[19] introduced an asynchronous parallel Max-Min ant colony algorithm associated with the local search strategy. M.Randall[20] introduced a synchronous parallel strategy which assigns only one ant on each processor. By modifying the classical ACO, D. Merkle[21] first proposed a parallel ant colony algorithm on reconfigurable processor arrays. M.Dorigo[22] advanced a parallel ant colony algorithm on the hyper-cube architecture by modifying the rule of updating the pheromone so as to limit the pheromone values within the range of [0,1].

In this paper, we present an efficient adaptive parallel ant colony algorithm (APACA). We also propose two different strategies for information exchange between processors: selection based on sorting and on difference, which made each processor choose another processor to communicate and update the pheromone adaptively. In order to increase the ability of search and avoid early convergence, we also propose a method of adjusting the time interval adaptively according to the diversity of the solutions. These techniques are applied to the traveling salesman problem on the massive parallel processors (MPP) Dawn 2000. Experimental results show that our algorithm has high convergence speed, high speedup and efficiency.

2 The Adaptive Parallel Ant Colony Algorithm

In our adaptive parallel ant colony algorithm (APACA), M ants are divided equally into P groups which are allocated into P processors. The ants in each group search for the best solution in its own processor independently. To prevent the sub colony in a single processor from converging into the local optimal solution, information of the groups, i.e. processors, should be exchanged when a certain condition is satisfied. We present two adaptive strategies of information exchange and one method for setting the time interval.

2.1 Adaptive Strategies of Information Exchange Between Processors

By information exchange, each processor makes full use of the information come from other processors to update pheromone matrix and continues to search for the best solution. Such information exchange plays an important role in APACA, it may enhance the probability of getting the optimum solution. We propose two strategies for information exchange which enable each processor to choose a processor to exchange information adaptively according to its fitness. These two strategies offer a direction for each processor in further searching towards the optimal solution.

(1) The Strategy of Information Exchange Based on Fitness Sorting

We denote the average and maximum fitness of solutions on processor i on current iteration as $f_{ave}(i)$ and $f_{max}(i)$ respectively, i.e. $f_{ave}(i) = \dfrac{1}{N_i} \sum_{k=1}^{N_i} f(i,k)$, $f_{max}(i) = \max\limits_{1 \le k \le N_i} \{f(i,k)\}$, here N_i is the number of ants on processor i, $f(i,k)$ is the fitness of ant k. In every information exchange step, the average fitness $f_{ave}(i)$ of every processor is sorted in descent order. Suppose the indices of the processors after such sorting are $rank_1, rank_2, \ldots, rank_P$ The processor of number $rank_i$ ($i \in [1, 2 \ldots P]$) chooses the processor of number $rank_{P+1-i}$ to exchange information as shown in Fig.1.

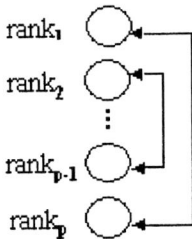

Fig. 1. The strategy for information exchange based on sorting

After the processor of number $rank_i$ ($i \in [1, 2 \ldots P]$) receives the best solution from processor of number $rank_{P+1-i}$, the elements $\tau(j,k)$ of its pheromone matrix is updated by equations (1)、(2)、(3):

$$\tau(j,k) = (1-\xi) \cdot \tau(j,k) + \xi \cdot \left[(1-\frac{rank_i}{P}) \cdot \Delta\tau(j,k) + \frac{rank_i}{P} \Delta\tau^*(j,k) \right]. \quad (1)$$

where

$$\Delta\tau(j,k) = \begin{cases} Q_1 / L(rank_i) & \text{the trail } (j,k) \text{ consists of the best tour of ant which gets the solution } f_{\max}(rank_i) \text{ on processor } rank_i \\ 0 & \text{otherwise} \end{cases} \quad (2)$$

$$\Delta\tau^*(j,k) = \begin{cases} \dfrac{Q_1}{L(rank_{P+1-i})} & \text{the trail } (j,k) \text{ consists of the best tour of ant which gets the solution } f_{\max}(rank_{P+1-i}) \text{ on processor } rank_{P+1-i} \\ 0 & \text{otherwise} \end{cases} \quad (3)$$

In (1), $\xi \in (0, 1)$ is the evaporation coefficient. $L(rank_i)$ and $L(rank_{P+1-i})$ are the lengths of the best tours on processor $rank_i$ and $rank_{P+1-i}$ in current iteration.

It can easily be seen from (1) that the solutions of processor $rank_i$ and $rank_{P+1-i}$ have the different influence on the pheromone updating for the best tour. If average fitness of processor $rank_i$ is relatively low, then $\dfrac{rank_i}{P}$ will be high. This will enable processor $rank_i$ to make full use of the information from the processor $rank_{P+1-i}$ with high average fitness so as to increase the pheromone on the best trail which is helpful to accelerate the speed of optimization in processor $rank_i$. On the other hand, by getting information from other processors, the processor with higher average fitness can extend the searching space and increase the diversity of the solutions.

(2) The Strategy of Information Exchange Based on Difference
In this strategy, each processor chooses the processor with the most different best solution. We use $diff(i, j)$ to denote the difference between the best solutions of processor i and processor j. Let $best(i)$ be the best solution of processor i and a_{ik} be the kth city of $best(i)$. Then $diff(i, j)$ is defined as:

$$diff(i,j) = \sum_{k=1}^{n} x(i,j,k), \quad where: x(i,j,k) = \begin{cases} 0 & if\ a_{ik} = a_{jk} \\ 1 & otherwise \end{cases} \quad (4)$$

Processor i should choose processor j according to (5).

$$j = \arg\max_{\substack{1 \leq k \leq P \\ k \notin tabu}} \left\{ \frac{diff(i,k)}{L(k)} \right\}. \quad (5)$$

where $tabu$ is the set of processors that have not been chosen, $L(k)$ is the length of the best tour that processor k gets. Then processor i update the pheromone matrix with the information from processor j:

$$\tau(u,v) = (1-\lambda) \cdot \tau(u,v) + \lambda \cdot [\Delta\tau(u,v) + \Delta\tau'(u,v)]. \quad (6)$$

where

$$\Delta\tau(u,v) = \begin{cases} \dfrac{Q_2 \cdot \sum_{k=1}^{P} diff(i,k)}{L(i)} & \begin{array}{l} if\ the\ ant\ that\ gets\ the\ solution\ best(i) \\ on\ processor\ i\ travels\ on\ edge\ (u,v) \end{array} \\ 0 & otherwise \end{cases} \quad (7)$$

$$\Delta\tau'(u,v) = \begin{cases} \dfrac{Q_2 \cdot \sum_{k=1}^{P} diff(j,k)}{L(j)} & \begin{array}{l} if\ the\ ant\ that\ gets\ the\ solution\ best(j) \\ on\ processor\ j\ travels\ on\ edge\ (u,v) \end{array} \\ 0 & otherwise \end{cases} \quad (8)$$

Here $\lambda \in (0,1)$ is the pheromone evaporation efficient of processor i, and Q_2 is a positive constant. $L(i)$ and $L(j)$ are the lengths of the best tours processor i and j have respectively since the start of algorithm.

Since the strategy of information exchange based on difference enables each processor chooses its partner by their fitness and difference, each processor will exchange information with the processor which has the most dissimilarity and high fitness. This enables both of the processors update its pheromone referencing the information of the best trail of its partner and evolve towards the optimum solution while keeping the diversity of the solutions to avoid premature.

2.2 Adjust the Time Interval of Information Exchange Adaptively

The time interval of the adjacent information exchanges could affect the performance of the parallel ant algorithm greatly. To adjust the time interval of information exchange adaptively according to the diversity of solutions, a criterion to measure the diversity of the solutions should be defined. Let N_i be the number of ants on processor i and the fitness of its N_i solutions be $f(i,1), f(i,2), \ldots f(i,N_i)$. $f_{ave}(i)$. We denote the average and maximum fitness of these solutions as $f_{ave}(i)$ and $f_{max}(i)$ respectively, i.e. $f_{ave}(i) = \frac{1}{N_i}\sum_{k=1}^{N_i} f(i,k)$, $f_{max}(i) = \max_{1 \le k \le N_i}\{f(i,k)\}$. The gap between $f_{ave}(i)$ and $f_{max}(i)$ reflects the distributing of solutions. The less the gap between average and maximum fitness is, the more concentrated the solutions are. Using $\triangle_i$ to denote the degree of diversity of solutions on processor i, and *Diver* to denote the degree of diversity of solutions of all processors, they are defined as (10). Here P is the number of processor.

$$\triangle_i = f_{ave}(i) / f_{max}(i) , \qquad Diver = \frac{1}{P} \cdot \sum_{i=1}^{P} \triangle_i . \qquad (9)$$

Here P is the number of processor. Since $\triangle_i$ and *Diver* reflects the local and global diversities respectively, smaller $\triangle_i$ indicates poor diversity of solutions on processor i while smaller *Diver* indicates poor diversity of solutions of the processors in the whole system. The time interval of information exchange is determined as follows:

$$interval = 5 - [\frac{1}{1+\exp(-k_1 \cdot Diver)} - 0.85] \cdot k \cdot \qquad (10)$$

where k and k_1 are positive constants. When *Diver* becomes smaller, solutions of the processors in the whole system lack of diversity, so the time interval of information exchange should be reduced in order to frequently interchange the best solutions within the processors to prevent local convergence. On the other hand, when *Diver* value increases, solutions of the processors become well diversified, are we so the interval can be increased appropriately in order to reduce the overhead of communication.

3 The Outline of APACA

We describe the framework of our adaptive parallel ant colony optimization using MPI subroutines. In the description, we let N be the number of cities, m be the number of ants on each processor, *NCMAX* be the number of total iteration, *optimum* be the best solution of problem.

Algorithm1: Adaptive Parallel Ant Colony Algorithm.

```
{/*each processor gets its rank and the total number of
   processors*/
    MPI_Comm_rank(MPI_COMM_WORLD,&mid);
    MPI_Comm_size(MPI_COMM_WORLD,&size);
    m=N/size;
 /*root processor computes distance matrix and broadcasts
   the result to other processor*/
    if (mid= =0)
       { read the coordinate of every city from the file;
         compute the distance between the cities;
       }
    MPI_Bcast(distance,N*N,MPI_DOUBLE,0,MPI_COMM_WORLD);
 /*each processor initialize the pheromone matrix */
    initialize the pheromone matrix;
    initialize the value of interval;
    i=0;
    while (i<NCMAX)
    {  i=i+interval;
    /*each processor runs the ACO independently*/
       for(j=0;j<interval;j++)
       { for (each ant)
           for (each city)
              { find the next city;
                update the pheromone matrix locally;
              }
         iteration_best=the best solution of the m ants;
         compare  the   iteration_best_cost   with   the
         best_cost, determine the best solution;
         update the pheromone matrix globally;
       }
    /*when satisfy the condition, information exchange is
      taken between the processors, every processor com-
      putes local diversity, sends the best solution and
      local diversity to root processor*/
       calculate the local_diver;
       MPI_Gather(&best_cost,1,MPI_DOUBLE,buffer1,1,MPI_
       DOUBLE,0,MPI_COMM_WORLD);
       MPI_Gather(&local_diver,1,MPI_DOUBLE,buffer2,1,
       MPI_DOUBLE,0,MPI_COMM_WORLD);
    /*exchange information and update the pheromone ma-
      trix*/
       if (mid= =0)
            determine the communication_object for each
            processor according to section 4.1,store the
            communication_object in buffer3;
       MPI_Scatter(buffer3,1,MPI_DOUBLE,&communication_
       object,1,MPI_DOUBLE,0,MPI_COMM_WORLD);
       update the pheromone matrix from the communica-
       tion_object;
    /*compute the new interval of information exchange*/
       if (mid= =0)
            interval=calculate the new interval according
            to section 4.2;
       MPI_Bcast(&interval,1,MPI_DOUBLE,0,MPI_COMM_WORLD);
    }
```

```
/*get the best solution of all processor: optimum*/
  MPI_Allreduce(&best_cost,&optimum,1,MPI_DOUBLE,MPI_MIN,
  MPI_COMM_WORLD);
}
```

4 Experimental Results and Analysis

In this section, we show the test results of our parallel ant algorithm on the TSP benchmarks from the library TSPLIB[23] on the massive parallel processors Dawn 2000 using MPI (C bounding). The parameters in the test are set as follows: $\rho = \gamma = \xi = \lambda = 0.1$, $\alpha = 1$, $\beta = 2$, $k=16$, $k_1=0.5$, the number of ants is equal to the number of cities, the number of processors is 6. Our experiment performs 50 trials on each problem and 2000 iterations on each trial. The experimental results are shown in Table 1 where five TSP problems are tested and the results are compared with that of classical ACO algorithm and Circular-PACA(the strategy for information exchange is "Circular exchange of locally best solutions"[24]). In table 1, Sort-APACA stands for APACA which determine the time interval of information exchange based on fitness sorting, while Diff-APACA based on difference.

Table 1. The comparison result of ACO, Circular-PACA, Sort-APACA and Diff-APACA

Problem	Algorithm	Best value	Average value	The number of trials reaching the best solution	Time (s)
eil51	ACO	434.18	438.34	42	49.58
	Circular-PACA	426.21	432.49	48	12.64
	Sort-APACA	426.21	426.21	50	9.14
	Diff-APACA	426.21	426.21	50	9.36
eil76	ACO	559.70	563.82	43	82.67
	Circular-PACA	538.37	550.16	46	21.42
	Sort-APACA	538.37	539.98	49	14.79
	Diff-APACA	538.37	538.37	50	15.01
kroA100	ACO	21684.64	21786.29	36	90.88
	Circular-PACA	21282.44	21375.13	41	23.17
	Sort-APACA	21282.44	21288.52	46	15.45
	Diff-APACA	21282.44	21285.16	48	15.76
d198	ACO	16826.60	16915.53	40	118.42
	Circular-PACA	15794.72	15936.57	43	29.48.
	Sort-APACA	15780.03	15784.61	46	19.96
	Diff-APACA	15780.03	15782.97	48	20.14
Lin318	ACO	43003.69	43127.47	37	200.63
	Circular-PACA	42037.68	42517.06	42	43.87
	Sort-APACA	42029.14	42033.95	47	33.74
	Diff-APACA	42029.14	42032.52	47	34.21

It can easily be seen from Table 1 that Sort-APACA and Diff-APACA have more chance to reach the theoretical optimums and their average value (the length of the shortest path) of the best solutions are much smaller than that of classical ACO and Circular-PACA. This means our parallel algorithms has higher optimization ability while their computation time are reduced due to the parallel computation. Compared to Circular-PACA, two strategies for information exchange we present enhance the probability of getting the optimum solution as the result of choosing the exchange object adaptively. The reason for APACA's high optimization ability is that it can accelerate the convergence by dividing the ants into smaller groups allocated in the processors and can avoid premature and adaptively adjust the diversity of solutions by information exchange.

Fig.2 shows the speedup of various TSP benchmark problems using Diff-APACA. From Fig.2 we can see that the speedup of our algorithm can not increase linearly with the increasing of processor exactly, due to the overhead of communication which increases the total time of algorithm. This is in conformity with the Amdahl's Law. The results show that problems with small size can not get high speedup since the communication overhead is relatively larger than the computations. However, the speedup is increased in the large size problems. For instance, the speedup of problem lin318 is much greater than that of problem eil51.

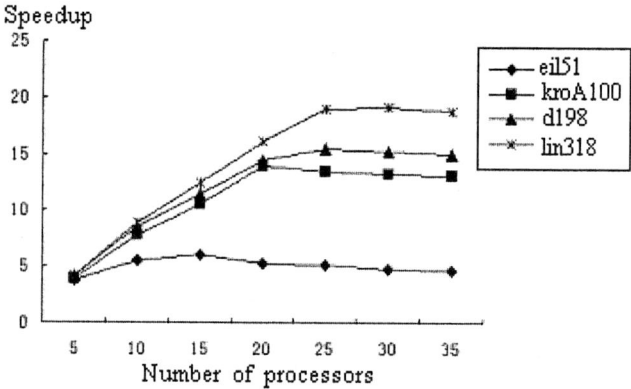

Fig. 2. Speedup on different problem

Table 2. The comparison result of different interval of information exchange

Problem Interval	eil76		kroA100		d198	
	Best value	Time(s)	Best value	Time(s)	Best value	Time(s)
3	545.41	14.03	21285.44	15.43	15783.73	19.85
5	546.97	14.00	21290.65	15.36	15788.67	19.15
7	550.83	13.97	21299.59	15.18	15799.41	19.07
9	554.71.	13.85	21302.19	14.96	15801.89	18.94
Diff-APACA	544.37	14.79	21282.44	15.45	15780.03	19.96

We also test the problems using the different time interval of information exchange and the results is shown in Table 2. It can be seen in Table 2 that if fixed time interval is adopted, longer time interval requires less communication overhead and hence the time cost can be reduced. On the other hand, since the best solutions cannot be exchanged frequently, this could affect the search ability of the algorithm.

Compared with other parallel algorithms with fixed time interval of information exchange, our adaptive parallel ant algorithm with variable time interval has higher optimization ability. It can keep balance between the diversity of solutions and the convergence of algorithm. Figure.3 shows the result of our test on the problem kroA100 to compare the performance of our Diff-APACA with the fixed time interval algorithm. From Figure.3 we can see that the evolutionary process of our algorithm converges after only 1000 iterations. After reaching the best solution, the curve is flat and constrained within a narrow scope around the best solution. But the curve of the algorithm with fixed time interval fluctuates even after 2000 iterations. This shows our algorithm is more stable and effective than other parallel ant algorithms.

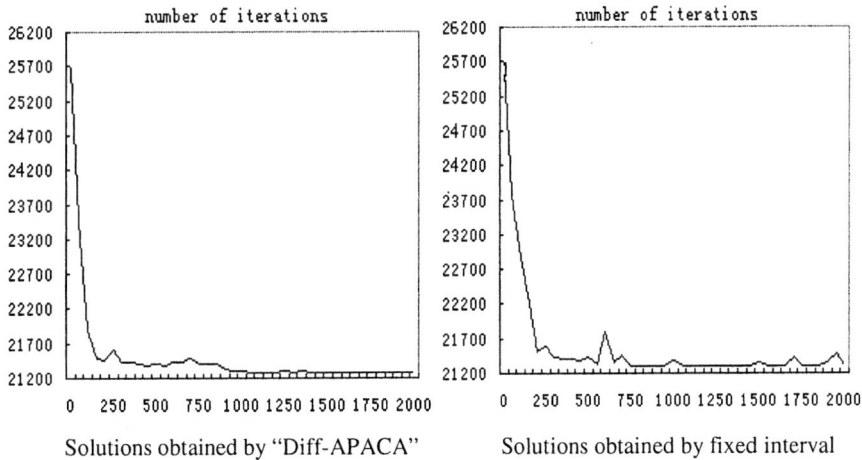

Fig. 3. The evolutionary process of the best solution for kroA100 problem

5 Conclusion

The performance of parallel ant colony algorithm can be affected by the strategy of method and the time interval of information exchange. An adaptive parallel ant colony optimization is presented by improving these two critical factors to improve the performance of the algorithm. We propose two different strategies for information exchange between processors: selection based on sorting and on difference. These two strategies make each processor choose another processor to communicate and update the pheromone adaptively, and offer a direction for each processor in further searching towards the optimal solution. We also propose a method of adjusting the time interval adaptively according to the diversity of the solutions in order to increase the ability of search and avoid early convergence. Experimental results show that our algorithm has high convergence speed, high speedup, stability and efficiency than other parallel ant algorithms.

References

1. Dorigo, M., Maniezzo, V., Colomi, A.: Ant system: Optimization by a colony of cooperating agents. IEEE Transactions on Systems, Man and Cybernetics-Part B, Vol. 26(1), (1996) 29-41
2. Dorigo, M., Gambardella, L.M.: Ant colony system: a cooperative learning approach to the traveling salesman problem. IEEE Transaction. On Evolutionary Computation, Vol. 1(1), (1997) 53-66
3. Stutzle, T., Hoos, H.: MAX-MIN Ant systems. Future Generation Computer Systems, Vol. 16, (2000) 889-914
4. Dorigo, M., Gambardella, L.M.: Ant colonies for the traveling salesman problem. BioSystems , Vol. 43(2), (1997) 73-81
5. Chang, C.S., Tian, L., Wen, F.S.: A new approach to fault section in power systems using Ant System. Electric Power Systems Research , Vol. 49(1), (1999) 63-70
6. Gambardella, L.M., Dorigo, M.: HAS-SOP: An Hybrid Ant System for the Sequential Ordering Problem. Tech. Rep. No. IDSIA 97-11, IDSIA, Lugano, Switzerland (1997)
7. Colorni, A. Dorigo, M, Maniezzo, V.: Ant colony system for job-shop scheduling. Belgian J. of Operations Research Statistics and Computer Science, Vol. 34(1), (1994) 39-53
8. Bonabeau, E., Sobkowski, A., Théraulaz, G., Denebourg, J..L.: Adaptive Task Allocation Inspired by a Model of Division of Labor in Social Insects. in Lundh, D. et al. (Eds.):Biocomputing and Emergent Computation: Proceedings of BCEC'97 (1997) 36-45
9. Maniezzo, V.: Exact and approximate nonditerministic tree search procedures for the quadratic assignment problem. Informs Journal of Computer, Vol. 11(4), (1999) 358-369
10. Maniezzo,V., Carbonaro, A.: An ANTS heuristic for the frequency assignment problem. Future Generation Computer Systems, Vol. 16. (2000) 927-935
11. Di Caro, G., Dorigo, M.: AntNet: A mobile agents approach to adaptive routing. Technical Report, IRIDIA/97-12, IRIDIA, Universite Libre de Bruxelles, Belgium (1997)
12. Schoonderwoerd, R., Holland, O., ruten, J.: Ant-like agents for load balancing in telecommunications networks. Proc.of Agents'97, Marina del Rey,CA:ACM Press (1997) 209-216.
13. Costa, D., Hertz , A.: Ants can colour graphs. Journal of the Operational.Research Society, Vol. 48(3), (1997) 295-305
14. Holland, O.E., Melhuish, C.: Stigmergy, self-organization, and sorting in collective robotics. Artificial Life, Vol. 5, (1999) 173-202
15. Kuntz, P., Layzell, P., Snyder, D.: A colony of ant-like agents for partitioning in VLSI technology. in: P. Husbands, I. Harvey(Eds.), Proceedings of the Fourth European Conference on Artificial Life, MIT Press, Cambridge, MA (1997) 417-424
16. Kuntz, P., Snyder, D.: New results on ant-based heuristic for highlighting the organization of large graphs. in: Proceedings of the 1999 Congress or Evolutionary Computation, IEEE Press, Piscataway, NJ (1999) 1451-1458
17. Bullnheimer, B., Kotsis, G., Steauss, C.: Parallelization strategies for the ant system. High Performance and Algorithms and Software in Nonlinear Optimization, Applied Optimization , Vol. 24, (1998) 87-100

18. Talbi, E-G., Roux, O., Fonlupt, C., Robilard, D.: Parallel ant colonies for the quadratic assignment problem. Future Generation Computer Systems, Vol. 17, (2001) 441-449
19. Piriyakumar, D.A.L., Levi, P.: A new approach to exploiting parallelism in ant colony optimization. Proceedings of 2002 International Symposium on Micromechatronics and Human Science, (2002) 237-243
20. Randall, M., Lewis, A.: A parallel implementation of ant colony optimization. Parallel and Distributed Computing, Vol. 62, (2002) 1421-1432
21. Merkle, D., Middendorf, M.: Fast ant colony optimization on runtime reconfigurable processor arrays. Genetic Programming and Evolvable Machine, Vol. 3, (2002) 345-361
22. Blum, C., Dorigo, M.: The Hyper - Cube framework for ant colony optimization. IEEE Transactions on SMC, Vol. 34(2), (2004) 1161-1172
23. TSPLIB WebPage, http://www.iwr.uni-heidelberg.de/groups/comopt/software/TSPLIB95/tsp/
24. Middendorf, M., Reischle, F., Schmeck, H.: Multi colony ant algorithms. Heuristics, Vol. 8, (2002) 305-320

Hierarchical Image Segmentation Using Ant Colony and Chemical Computing Approach

Pooyan Khajehpour, Caro Lucas, and Babak N. Araabi

Control and Intelligent Processing Center of Excellence,
Department of Electrical and Computer Engineering,
University of Tehran, Tehran, Iran
School of Cognitive Science,
Institute for Studies in Theoretical Physics and Mathematics, Tehran, Iran
p.khajehpour@ece.ut.ac.ir, lucas@ipm.ir, araabi@ut.ac.ir

Abstract. This paper presents a new method for hierarchical image segmentation. The hierarchical structure is represented by a binary tree with the main image as its root. At the lower levels, each node stands as one image segment, which is described by a weighted graph and may be divided into two new segments at the next level through a specific cut. Graph bi-sectioning is done by the self organizing property of ant systems. Ants are free to wander over one image segment graph to find the best cut on it. When an ant finds a suitable cut, it returns to its colony and leaves a proper value of pheromone over its trail to attract other ants to that cut. By using the Chemical Computing approach in this paper, it is assumed the mobile hormones (pheromone) are secreted which can diffuse around initial positions and attract more ants to the found cut. The advantages of this assumption are reducing the noise effects and improving the convergence speed of ants to find a new selected image segment, which can be seen in the practical results.

1 Introduction

Image processing algorithms play a key role in many applications in Robotics and Automation. One of the most applicable algorithms in this field is image segmentation which is usually used to detect objects of an image. Segmentation subdivides an image into its constituent regions or objects. Many image processing approaches can be found in literature and Image Processing text books like: edge linking and boundary detection, thresholding, region based methods and morphological watersheds [16].

Segmentation of nontrivial images is one of the most difficult tasks in Image Processing. Although this process is very common in applications, single general algorithm that would work well for all of them does not exist. Thus finding a general method for Image Segmentation seems very crucial.

For this purpose, in this paper a general graph theoretical representation of the problem is introduced initially. There are some previous works in literature use the graph theoretical approach for solving Segmentation problem [4], [5], [16].

In the next section finding of minimum mean cut problem will be discussed as the main graph theoretical problem. This problem is very complicated and like many other graph problems requires a long processing time. To resolve this problem a natural computation approach is used.

The self organizing property of artificial ants is used to deal with the common combinatorial graph problems. In this case ants are employed to solve the famous graph partitioning problem. Ant colony systems are described in Section 3. There are some similar approaches which utilize ant colony optimization to solve graph theoretical problems in the literature [1].

A new approach to graph bi-sectioning problem is developed by the concept of artificial ant colony described in Section 4 and the related algorithm is discussed next.

Hormone based behavior for ant colonies is presented in Section 5, results a novel advancement in ants' performance to solve the problem. Finally the simulation results are shown in Section 6.

2 Graph Theoretical Representation

Many graph theoretical approaches proposed for data clustering can be used in image segmentation algorithms. Commonly known techniques include single-link and complete-link hierarchical algorithms discussed in [2].

This paper presents a hierarchical tree for image representation and an image segmentation algorithm that constructs this tree. The root node of the representation is the full image, and the leaf nodes are the smallest possible segments of the main image. Though there are some approaches which construct this tree in bottom-up direction [3], in this paper the top-down approach is chosen.

Each node of the tree is one big segment of the main image. The goal is to find the best cut on the equivalent graph of each segment and possibly divide it into two smaller segments.

2.1 Equivalent Graph

Suppose a graph G(V,E) with one vertex over each pixel. Each vertex is connected to its four closest neighbors by a simple undirected edge. The weight of the edge which connects u and v is the amount of similarity value between them which is a Gaussian function [4] and calculated by (1):

$$w(u,v) = e^{-\frac{\left(D_{u,v}^R\right)^2 + \left(D_{u,v}^G\right)^2 + \left(D_{u,v}^B\right)^2}{\sigma^2}} \quad (1)$$

Where $D_{u,v}$ is the edge strength computed separately for R, G and B of an RGB color image. The value of $D_{u,v}$ is the differences between the pixel pair, and between the pixel pair in their vicinity by applying the masks shown in Fig.1. This method is described in [5] in more detail. By using these masks the resulted $D_{u,v}$ values will be smoother.

A 2-way cut of G partitions its vertices (V) into two subsets A and B such that (2) is satisfied.

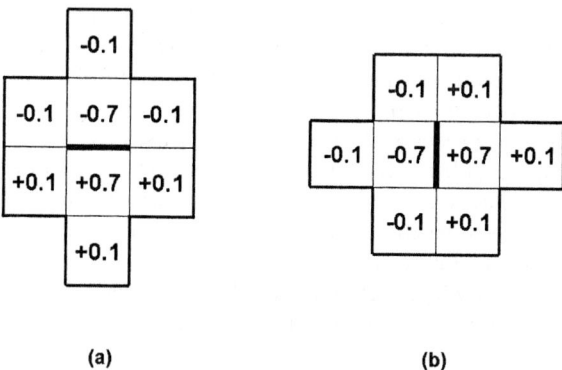

Fig. 1. Masks for computing edge strength: (a) for horizontal edges; (b) for vertical edges

$$A \cup B = V$$
$$A \cap B = \emptyset \tag{2}$$

Then the cut edges are defined as the set of edges that cross from A to B. Similarly the cut cost function is defined by (3):

$$c(a,b \mid f) = \sum_{u \in A, v \in B, (u,v) \in E} f \tag{3}$$

If G' is the dual graph of the planer graph G, it can be shown [4] that a 2-way cut set in G is equal to a simple circle in G'.

2.2 Suitable Cut

Finding a suitable cut in a graph is the key to the proper be-sectioning of one segment into two. There are some definitions which describe the suitable cut in the literature, for example minimum cut [5] and minimum normalized cut [6]. The minimum mean cut is chosen for this paper to describe the suitable cut. The mean-cut cost function is defined by (4):

$$\overline{c}(A, B) = \frac{c(A, B \mid w(u,v))}{c(A, B \mid 1)} \tag{4}$$

In other words, by referring to the described duality property, it can be said that finding a simple circle in dual graph with the minimum average weight on its edges, would be the main goal of graph bi-sectioning.

3 Ant Colony System

Real ants can find the shortest path to food by leaving a pheromone (chemical) trail as they walk. Other ants follow the pheromone trail to food. Ants that happen to pick the shorter path will create a stronger trail of pheromone than the ones choosing a longer path. Since stronger pheromone attracts ants better, more and more ants choose the shorter path, until finally all ants have found the shortest path. This is the main idea of artificial ant colony [14].

Artificial ants behave very similar to the real ants; they select the next vertex by a weighted probability that is a function of the strength of the pheromone laid on the path and the distance of that vertex. The probability that one ant will travel from vertex u to vertex v is given by (5):

$$p_u(v) = \frac{t(u,v)/w(u,v)}{\sum_{(u,q) \in E} t(u,q)/w(u,q)} \quad (5)$$

To force an artificial ant to move more deterministically, a constant probability P is supposed. With the probability of P, ant will take the heuristic selection by (6):

$$v = Arg \left[\max_{(u,q) \in E} \{t(u,q)/w(u,q)\} \right] \quad (6)$$

A problem that may happen at this stage is the premature convergence of ants towards a local optimal solution because of the high amount of left virtual pheromone on the field. To avoid this case, pheromone evaporation is implemented which means pheromone disappears after a period of time by a constant rate.

4 Proposed Ant Colony System for Image Segmentation

Ant colonies have in recent years been widely used as prototypes of multi-agent systems with stigmergic communication, where the building up of positive or negative emotions are modeled via chemicals deposited by individual agents based on perceived outcomes of their past actions. The activities of a colony are very complicated and different from the behavior of its individual ants. A colony's cooperative behavior exceeds the sum of its individual member's actions. This phenomenon is called emergence.

On the other hand, the intelligence of a neural network appears from the cooperative behavior of neurons. Each individual neuron is able to do only very limited operations but it can be seen than though each individual neuron works slowly, the brain can process quickly and finds a solution by cooperation of its neurons in parallel.

Observations show that the self-organization of neurons in the brain and ants in a swarm is very similar [10]. Employing the features of such systems can lead to an important development in image processing systems e.g. [11], where perceptive capabilities can emerge and advance from the interaction of many simple local actions.

4.1 Artificial Ant's Behavior

To use artificial ants in image segmentation some natural habits and definitions in ant's real life should be modeled and defined initially:

1. The aim is defined by finding the image segments instead of food source. Image segment is a proper cut in the image or equivalent circle in its dual graph; thus, the aim is changed to find the proper circle in the dual graph which can be modeled by searching for boundary of one piece of food and circle around it.
2. Each ant has a memory that contains its traveled path on the graph. In this way an ant can recognize the circles in its path.
3. The amount of pheromone an ant leaves over the edges is proportional to the mean-cut cost of the segment the ant has found. This proposition leads the ants to find the minimum mean cut finally.
4. To find the smoother boundaries, the forward move is more probable compared to turning right or left. Backward move is not allowed.
5. To avoid finding small segments, minimum circle length is constrained and circles with shorter lengths are removed from ant's memory. This length is the function of the segment's hierarchical level and area.

In this manner the ant's general behavior will change. It can find the shortest path to more food by leaving a pheromone on its path, and therefore attract other ants to the same path. As more amount of food in a shorter distance is reached a stronger pheromone trail is left behind. Because of stronger pheromone, more ants choose this path until finally all ants find the shortest path to the most food.

4.2 Algorithm

For each level of hierarchy, all segments with an area greater than the minimum required area are checked by the ant colony segmentation algorithm.

```
Hierarchical_Segmentation (Graph)

  For Level = 0 to Max_Level
    For Segment = 1 to 2Level-1
      If Area(Segment) > Min_Area
        Ant_Colony_Segmentation(Segment, Level);
      End If
    End
  End

End.
```

Because the requirements will change by the level of hierarchy, a particular segment independently may or may not be divided at each separate level of hierarchy.

In the ant colony segmentation algorithm, for each segment the border nodes are specified and the ant colony is put out of the border line. Then ants enter the segment from any random border node.

Each ant has a specified duration of life. If it finds any suitable circle in a segment with the mentioned rules, it returns to the colony and leaves an amount of pheromone over the edges in proportion to the food, otherwise it will die.

During an iteration, all ants would return to the colony or die. Then the best circle will be kept and the pheromone over the entire graph evaporates [15]. The pseudo code of this algorithm is presented below:

```
Ant_Colony_segmentation(Segment, Level)
  Put the ants randomly over the border line;
  For Iteration = 1 to Max_Iteration
    For time = 1 to Ant_Life
      For Ant = 1 to Number_of_Ants
        If not Reached(Ant)
          Move(Ant);
        If Reached(Ant)
          Return to colony and leave pheromone;
          Compare found circle with the Best_Answer
          and take the better one;
        End If
      End If
    End
  End

  Evaporate(Pheromone);
  HighLight(Best_Answer);
End

If Best_Answer satisfies the condition(Level)
  Divide(Segment);
End If

End.
```

With respect to the described rules, function Move(Ant) forces the ant to move to the next node of the graph and updates its memory. Finding a non-valid circle, it removes the circle from ant's memory, otherwise the Reach function returns true.

After each iteration, the pheromone will evaporate, and the Best_Answer will be reinforced to attract more ants. After a couple of iterations the solution should converge and the best circle with the minimum mean-cut cost will be found. If the circle is a valid cut, the segment will be divided into two segments. The Divide function will divide the segment with Segment label into two other segments with the labels of 2*Segment and 2*Segment+1.

5 Chemical Computing and Hormones

Each individual ant has a simple behavior in a way that it only finds simple paths on its own and can not solve complex problems. Better paths are found as the emergent result of the global cooperation among ants in the colony.

In populations of cells or insects, every individual may release chemical hormones. [12]. The cooperation is obtained through this unstable chemical hormone, called pheromone. The hormone system is equivalent to an artificial chemistry without any reactions, so that hormones just carry information and do not process it [13]. These hormones diffuse and have the Stigmergic effect on the medium. The chemical composition of the hormones represents an activity pattern of population which can be considered as public emotion or distributed knowledge in the system.

Real ants can smell the pheromone from a particular distance. But all generic ant colony algorithms are implemented in a way that ants must be on the pheromone to sense it. The novel idea here is to consider pheromone as a moving hormone in the graph. In other words, the graph is a medium for pheromone and the pheromone will be diffused.

Suppose a graph, whose edge can be simulated by a vein and whose pheromone is a hormone carried by blood to other parts. This movement can be simulated as a simple diffusion; therefore, the algorithm must be changed in this way:

```
Ant_Colony_segmentation(Segment, Level)
    ...
    For Iteration = 1 to Max_Iteration
        ...
        ...
        Evaporate(Pheromone);
        HighLight(Best_Answer);
        Diffusion(Pheromone);
    End

    If Best_Answer satisfies the condition(Level)
        Divide(Segment);
    End If
End.
```

Using this change, after each iteration, the pheromone of each edge diffuses to its neighbor edges, which will enable the ants to smell a weaker amount of pheromone from further distances in the next iterations and stimulates them to follow the smell. In this way the algorithm would converge sooner.

6 Simulation Results

To observe the results of this method, a Matlab program is written. Simulation is started using 10 ants and 30 iterations, depicted in Fig. 2 (a) as the main image; the weighted graph is shown in Fig. 2 (b). The final results are shown in Fig. 5.

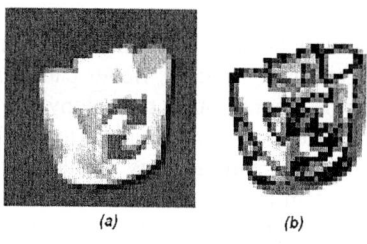

Fig. 2. Main image (a) and weights (b)

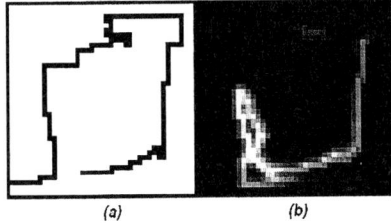

Fig. 3. Sample ant's path (a) pheromoneafter 10 iteration (b)

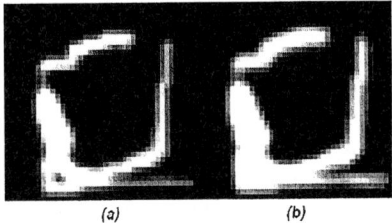

Fig. 4. Pheromone after 20 iteration (a) pheromoneafter 30 iteration (b)

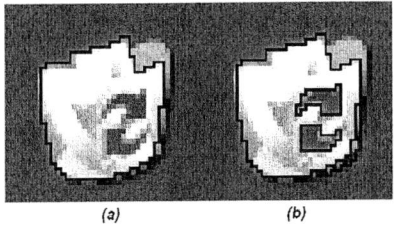

Fig. 5. Segmentation at level = 0 (a) segmentation at level = 2 (b)

The pheromone field is shown in Fig. 3 and Fig. 4. The effect of diffusion can be observed clearly. After 30 iterations the pheromone almost fills the entire segment's border neighborhood.

7 Summary and Conclusion

In this paper hierarchical clustering method is used as the main algorithm for image segmentation. Then the problem is fully described from the graph theoretical point of view and some solving methods are referred for this purpose. The general solution for these kinds of graph theoretical problems is too complex that Artificial Intelligence methods are used instead.

For this reason, a new approach to ant colony systems is developed to solve the problem. The differences between this method and the previous methods in ACO are also described. The main difference is about pheromone concept; in this approach the hormone concept is applied instead of the usual pheromone notion in the ant colony system to obtain a better performance of ants' behavior.

This method is inspired from and works very similar to the cooperation of individuals (e.g. ants, neurons etc.) in nature, where coordination is achieved without excessive planning and full rationality. This method of achieving intelligence is thus at the borderline between behavioral and cognitive approaches, and can be used for other pattern recognition and image processing applications.

Acknowledgements

The first author (Pooyan Khajehpour) wishes to express his gratitude to Pantea Alirezazadeh for her time and assistance on writing of this paper. The author would also like to thank Saied Haidarian for his critical review of this paper.

References

1. Langham, A.E., Grant, P.W.: Using Competing Ant Colonies to Solve k–way Partitioning Problems with Foraging and Raiding Strategies. Proceedings of the 5th European Conference on Advances in Artificial Life (1999) 621-625
2. Hubert, L.J.: Some Application of Graph Theory to Clustering. PSYCHOMETRIKA, Vol. 39, No. 3 (1974)
3. Yu, W., Fritts, J., Sun, F.: A Hierarchical Image Segmentation Algorithm. In Proc. ICME'02 (2002) 221–224
4. Wang, S., Siskind, J.M.: Image Segmentation with the Minimum Mean Cut. ICME'02 (2002) 221-224
5. Wu, Z., Leahy, R.: An Optimal Graph Theoretic Approach to Data Clustering: Theory and Its Application to Image Segmentation. IEEE Trans. On Pattern Analysis and Machine Intelligence, vol. 15, N 11 (1993) 1101–1113
6. Duarte, A., Sánchez1, Á., Fernández, F., Montemayor, A.S., Pantrigo, J.J.: Top-Down Evolutionary Image Segmentation using a Hierarchical Social Metaheuristic. EvoWorkshops 2004, Applications of Evolutionary Computing (EVOIASP 2004)
7. Dorigo, M., Gambardella, L.M.: Ant colonies for the traveling salesman problem. BioSytems (1997)
8. Bell, J.E., McMullen, P.R.: Ant colony optimization techniques for the vehicle routing problem. ELSEVIER (2004)
9. Sim, K.M., Sun, W.H.: Ant Colony Optimization for Routing and Load-Balancing: Survey and New Directions. IEEE Transactions on Systems, Man, and Cybernetics—Part A: Systems and Humans, Vol. 33, No. 5 (2003)
10. Ramos, V., Almeida, F.: Artificial Ant Colonies in Digital Image Habitats – A Mass Behavior Effect Study on Pattern Recognition. Proceeding of ANTS'2000, 2nd International Workshop on Ant Algorithms: From Ant Colonies to Artificial Ants (2000)
11. Isaacs, J., Watkins, R., Petrone, J., Foo, S.: Ant Colony Systems Toolbox. Military and Aerospace Programmable Logic Device International Conference (2003)
12. Adamatzky, A.: Computing in Nonlinear Media and Automata Collectives. Intelligent Autonomous System Laboratory, University of the West of England, Bristol, UK (2001)
13. Dittrich, P., Ziegler, J., Banzhaf, W.: Artificial Chemistries – A Review. Artificial Life, Vol. 7 (2001) 225-275
14. Dorigo, M., Stutzle, T.: Ant Colony Optimization. MIT Press (2004)
15. Jones, M.T.: Artificial Intelligence Application Programming. Charles River Media (2003)
16. Gonzalez, R.C., Woods, R.E.: Digital Image Processing. 2nd edn. Prentice Hall (2002)

Optimization of Container Load Sequencing by a Hybrid of Ant Colony Optimization and Tabu Search*

Yong Hwan Lee[1], Jaeho Kang[2], Kwang Ryel Ryu[2], and Kap Hwan Kim[3]

[1] SK Teletech, Twenty-first FL. Star Tower 737 Yeoksam-dong,
Kangnam-gu, Seoul, Korea
yhlee1@skteletech.com
[2] Department of Computer Engineering, Pusan National University,
San 30, Jangjeon-dong, Kumjeong-gu, Busan, Korea
{jhkang, krryu}@pusan.ac.kr
[3] Department of Industrial Engineering, Pusan National University,
San 30, Jangjeon-dong, Kumjeong-gu, Busan, Korea
kapkim@pusan.ac.kr

Abstract. Many algorithms that solve optimization problems are being developed and used. However, large and complex optimization problems still exist, and it is often difficult to obtain the desired results with one of these algorithms alone. This paper applies tabu search and ant colony optimization method to the container load sequencing problem. We also propose a hybrid algorithm, which can combine the merits of these two algorithms by running them alternately. Experiments have shown that the proposed hybrid algorithm is superior to both tabu search and ant colony optimization individually.

1 Introduction

Since most of the real world optimization problems have a very large search space, it is impossible to explore the entire search space comprehensively. Therefore, many researchers have tried to find acceptable solutions by seeing only part of the search space and they have developed various algorithms. Existing optimization algorithms could be divided into point-to-point search methods and population-based search methods. Point-to-point local search algorithms, such as hill-climbing search, simulated annealing, and tabu search, can find a solution quickly but they tend to become trapped in local optima. In contrast, population-based search algorithms, such as the genetic algorithm and ant colony optimization, have excellent global searching ability but they take a long time to find the final solution. In general, the difficulty of a given optimization problem is determined by its solution landscape. Many optimization problems have a complex

---

* This work was supported by "Research Center for Logistics Information Technology (LIT)" hosted by Korean Ministry of Education & Human Resources Development.

and irregular solution landscape imposed by accompanying constraints. Therefore, it is difficult for local search algorithms to find a good solution especially when the quality of a solution varies abruptly with little change of the solution. Conversely, global search algorithms are good at finding the plausible areas for the optimal solution but are slow in converging to the optimal solution because of its lack of useful local information. Optimization problems are gradually becoming larger and more complex, and it is difficult to obtain the desired results in a limited time using only one of the available search algorithms. To overcome such problems, many researchers are trying to produce better results by combining search algorithms. In this paper, we describe the application of tabu search and ant colony optimization to the container load sequencing problem and propose a hybrid algorithm combining the merits of both algorithms. Experiments have shown that our hybrid algorithm is superior to both tabu search and ant colony optimization individually.

The next section describes the problem of container load sequencing. Section 3 presents the implementation details of ant colony optimization, tabu search, and the hybrid scheme. Section 4 compares test results of the three algorithms, and finally Section 5 gives some conclusions.

2 Container Load Sequencing Problem

2.1 Container Loading in a Terminal

In a container terminal, the efficiency of container loading operation is highly dependent on the sequence of export containers that a quay crane (QC) loads onto a ship. The order of containers should be in such a way that the target slots in the ship are filled in a consecutive manner whenever possible so that we can minimize back and forth movements of the QC. Also, since the export containers are usually stacked in many different parts of the container yard, a good load sequence can help minimizing the travel distance of the transfer cranes (TC) which operate in the yard to retrieve the stacked containers. Moreover, when multiple QCs are operating for a ship, there can arise interferences between the TCs each of which is assigned to work for a QC. The efficiency goes down when interference occurs because one of the TCs must stop its operation.

Figure 1 shows a part of a container terminal in which two QCs are assigned to a ship for loading. The yard storage space is divided into multiple blocks. A block consists of many yard-bays each of which typically has four tiers and six rows of individual containers. Each QC is assigned a TC to retrieve the containers to be loaded. For a QC to load a container onto a ship, the TC assigned to the QC moves to the target yard-bay, picks up the selected container, and loads it onto a waiting yard tractor (YT). Then, the YT transports the container to the QC. Since there are two QCs working simultaneously in this illustration, two separate load sequences must be determined.

The load planning at a terminal begins by receiving from a shipping company a work instruction, otherwise called a load profile, for each ship. As illustrated in Fig. 1, a load profile shows cross-sectional views of the ship-bays with several

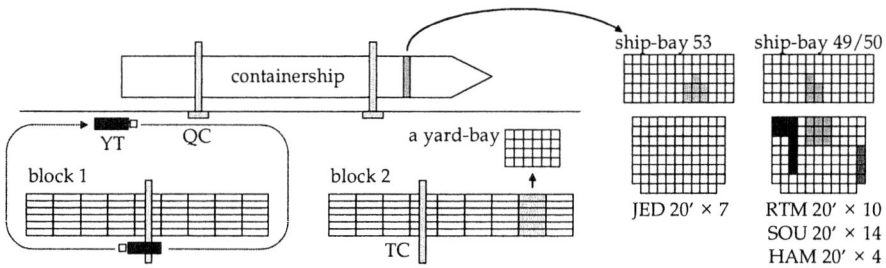

Fig. 1. An illustration of container handling in a yard with a load profile (cross-sectional views) of a container ship

clusters of cells color-coded (actually shaded at different gray levels in this figure). Each cell in the figure represents a slot where a container can be placed. A color-coded cluster represents a group of container slots of the same type, i.e., of the same length with the same destination port. Under each cross-sectional view are written each cluster's destination code, the length, and the number of containers in it. Based on this load profile and the availability of QCs, the load sequence at the ship-bay level called a QC work schedule is determined. In typical QC work schedules, the QCs usually work on ship-bays in a consecutive order. A major consideration here is given to the prevention of interference between the adjacent QCs.

2.2 Construction of Clusters and Cluster-Level Load Sequencing

Once QC work schedules are completed, the load sequence of containers for each ship-bay must be determined. We take a hierarchical approach to its solution to cope with the complexity of the problem. The containers are grouped into clusters, which are sets of containers of the same type (size and destination), and then the sequencing is performed in two separate stages. In the first stage, the overall sequence of the clusters is determined. In the second stage, the order of the individual containers within each cluster is determined. The ordering problem of individual containers in the second stage is simple, as the number of containers in a single cluster is relatively small. We used a beam search algorithm to solve this problem [1]. This paper examines the method of solving the cluster-level sequencing for the first stage.

An obvious ordering constraint in a ship-bay is that the containers should be loaded to the slots from the bottom to the top. Therefore, in our algorithm, each color-coded cluster is further divided into smaller groups for the flexibility of the load operation under this ordering constraint. Figure 2 shows an example of our cluster subdivision. We start with the four different clusters as shown in Fig. 2 (a). Note that clusters A and C are considered different even though their slots are for the same type of containers. Cluster A in Fig. 2 (a) is subdivided into two smaller clusters 1 and 2 in Fig. 2 (c) because cluster 2 is constrained to be loaded after cluster 6 while cluster 1 can be loaded at any time. If cluster

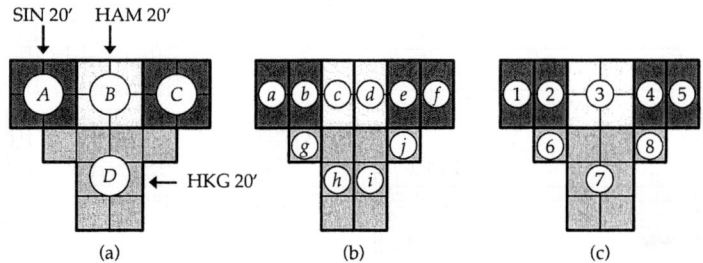

Fig. 2. An example of ship-cluster subdivision

A were not divided, all the container slots in cluster A should be constrained to be loaded after cluster 6.

The cluster subdivision in our algorithm begins by first dividing all the clusters into independent columns as shown in Fig. 2 (b). Then the adjacent columns of the same type are merged together if they are under the same ordering constraint with other columns below and above to restrict the number of possible solutions. Note that there exist partial ordering constraints among different clusters in a ship-bay, and there can be many possible linear orderings of these clusters under the ordering constraints.

The containers to be loaded are stacked in many different parts of the yard, again in clusters of the same type. Figure 3 illustrates a small part of a yard map showing the locations of some yard-bays storing the clusters to be loaded. Since the TC does not need to make any travel to retrieve containers in the same yard-bay, containers of the same type in one yard-bay are treated as one cluster even when they are stacked in separate groups. The clusters in the yard must be associated with the clusters of the same type in the ship before they can actually be loaded. This association is not necessarily one-to-one because the associated clusters may have different number of containers. For the ship clusters in the example of Fig. 2 (c), 6, 7, 8, 1, 2, 3, 4, 5 could be one good load sequence which does not violate the ordering constraint. If we associate the yard clusters with these ship clusters, the sequence can be represented as (Y3, 6), (Y3, 7), (Y3, 8), (Y1, 1), (Y1, 2), (Y2, 3), (Y1, 4), (Y1, 5). In this case the TC travels from yard-bay 10 to 3 and then back to 8. If we had a different sequence (Y3, 6), (Y3, 7), (Y3, 8), (Y2, 3), (Y1, 1), (Y1, 2), (Y1, 4), (Y1, 5) instead, the travel distance of the TC could have been shorter because the TC visits the yard-bays in consecutive order. Unlike in this example, multiple yard clusters could also be associated with a single ship cluster. In general, the association is $N : M$. The remaining containers of the yard clusters will be loaded later when the QC works for other ship-bays.

In our load sequencing algorithm, we search for a good sequence of yard clusters while associating them with the ship clusters without violating the ordering constraints of each ship-bay. When there are multiple QCs operating for a ship and thus multiple TCs one for each QC, we find a sequence for each QC (or equivalently for each TC). In doing so, we not only try to minimize the overall

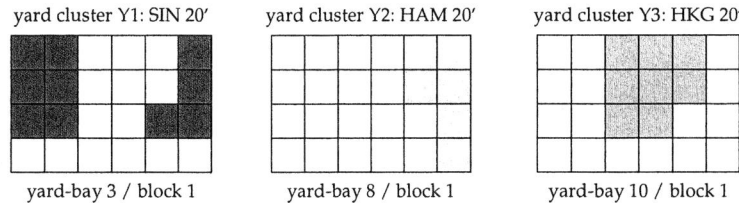

Fig. 3. A yard map showing yard-bays with different clusters of containers

travel distance of the TCs but also minimize interferences among different TCs. Interference of TCs is detected when any two TCs approach to each other within a predetermined distance.

For a more detailed introduction to load planning and crane work scheduling, refer to [2,3] and [4,5], respectively. There were some previous works for solving the load sequencing problem [6,7]. They attempted to minimize the travel cost of TCs or straddle carriers assuming that the cluster-level loading sequence is given.

3 Implementation Details

3.1 Ant Colony Optimization

The task of load sequencing can be viewed as finding an appropriate order of yard clusters that should be visited by the TC assigned to each QC. The order of yard clusters is constrained by the ordering constraints of the associated ship clusters in a ship-bay. Suppose, for example, we want to determine the order of yard clusters of Fig. 3 when the associated ship clusters are those shown in the ship-bay of Fig. 2 (c). Since any one of the ship clusters 1, 5, 6, 7, and 8 can be the first to be loaded, the first yard cluster to be loaded would be either Y1 or Y3. One possible load sequence starting from Y1 could be (Y1, 1), (Y3, 6), (Y3, 7), (Y3, 8), (Y1, 2), (Y2, 3), (Y1, 4), (Y1, 5), which is obviously not a good one because the TC must travel back and forth repeatedly. In general, there are multiple yard clusters from which the TC can start the loading operation. For any of these starting yard clusters, there are again multiple choices of yard clusters to visit next, and so on.

Figure 4 shows our ant algorithm implemented for load sequencing. When there are q QCs operating for a ship, q different load sequences must be determined, one for each QC. To find a load sequence for a QC, a population of m ants is randomly distributed to those yard clusters that are eligible for being the first in the load sequence to be found. Then, each ant independently moves on to the next cluster and then to the next and so on, until it completes the tour corresponding to a load sequence. How an ant chooses the next cluster to visit is governed by a probabilistic rule depending on the amount of pheromone laid and the visibility. The visibility in our implementation is inversely proportional to the distance to the next candidate cluster to visit. Once all the ants complete the tour with each ant having the path of its tour recorded in its memory, they

```
for t = 1 to n  { n: the number of epochs }
  for j = 1 to q  { q: the number of QCs }
    Randomly distribute m ants to the yard clusters
      that can become the first in the sequence for the jth QC;
    for k = 1 to m
      repeat until ant k completes the tour
        Probabilistically select the next yard cluster to visit;
      Record the complete tour in the memory of ant k;
    for k = 1 to m
      Evaluate the tour record generated by ant k;
    Select the best σ ants;
    for k = 1 to σ
      Update the pheromone quantity on the path of ant k;
```

Fig. 4. The ant algorithm for load sequencing

are again randomly distributed to the possible starting yard clusters in the load sequence for the next QC. While a tour is being pursued, the ant cannot visit the yard clusters that were already visited by itself in the current tour or in any previous tours unless those clusters still have remaining containers to be loaded. When the first embedded **for** loop of our algorithm is completed, each ant will have a record of tours for all the QCs. This means that we are given m different candidate solutions for our load sequencing problem.

The next step is to evaluate the cost of each of these candidate solutions. Each candidate solution consists of q tours. Although, in our algorithm, each ant finds a series of q tours in sequence, these q tours are typically executed in parallel by the TCs in the yard. Therefore, the cost of a candidate solution is the lowest when the total travel distance of all the q TCs is the shortest and if there occurs minimal number of interferences between TCs. Based on the evaluation result of all the candidate solutions, the amount of pheromone is determined and laid on some of the promising paths. After the evaluation and pheromone laying is done, the whole process repeats all over again continuing on to the next epochs. The movement of ants in each epoch is influenced by the pheromone trail laid on various paths in the previous epochs. We applied the elitist strategy to encourage the ants to be attracted more to the paths of the best-so-far solution, thus allowing more intensive search of the area that appears to be promising [8,9]. We also used the ranking scheme to prevent the search from becoming directionless in later stages [8]. General descriptions on ant colony optimization can be found in [10,11].

3.2 Tabu Search

Tabu search is another meta-heuristic algorithm popularly used to solve optimization problems [12,13,14]. To apply tabu search to the load sequencing

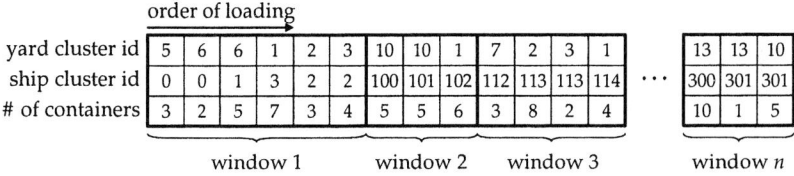

Fig. 5. Representation of a candidate solution

problem, we represent a candidate solution in the form of a list of columns as in Fig. 5. Each column is an ordered triple (yard cluster id, ship cluster id, number of containers) which represents a yard cluster and its associated ship cluster with the number of containers assigned to this association. The order of the columns corresponds to the order of loading. In this example, three containers of yard cluster 5 are first loaded to ship cluster 0, and then two containers of yard cluster 6 are loaded to ship cluster 0, and so on. A set of consecutive columns constitutes a window and the consecutive windows constitute the whole list. Each window corresponds to a ship-bay.

An initial solution for the search to start with is generated by a separate greedy search. The neighbors are generated by swapping the yard and ship cluster associations and/or by swapping the order of ship clusters. Too many neighbors are generated if all possible swappings are applied in all possible ways to a current solution. Therefore, our algorithm proceeds in two alternating phases: the intra-window phase and the inter-window phase. In the intra-window phase, each window is processed one by one starting from the first window. In each window, all possible yard cluster swapping and column swapping (and also column swapping followed by yard cluster swapping) are tried to generate neighbors. The best of these neighbors is chosen to become the next current solution and the same process iterates until no improvement is observed for a certain number of iterations. Then, the search moves to the next window and so on until all the windows are processed. Then, our tabu search switches to the inter-window phase. Here again, all possible inter-window swapping of yard clusters are examined to generate neighbors and the search iterates until no improvement is observed for a certain number of iterations. Since each of these phases provides a context for further improvement to be made in the subsequent phase, the search continues by alternately switching to these two phases. The search terminates if no improvement can be made in two consecutive phases.

3.3 Hybrid Scheme

Our hybrid search method starts with ant colony optimization, which runs for only a given number of epochs. The best solution found by ant colony optimization is used as the initial solution for the subsequent tabu search. If the tabu search becomes stuck at a local optimum, it is transformed to an elitist ant for a new round of ant colony optimization, and so on. We found this type of hybrid search efficiently mix the strengths of ant colony optimization and tabu search. Figure 6 illustrates the execution flow of the proposed hybrid search algorithm.

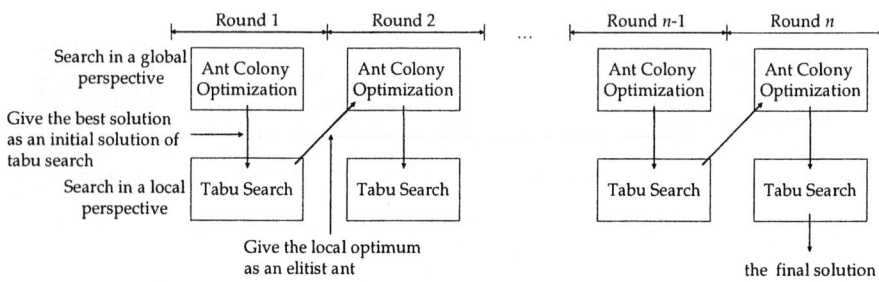

Fig. 6. The execution flow of the proposed hybrid search algorithm

4 Experimental Results

The dataset used for the experiments consists of six different loading scenarios of various scale as shown in Table 1. The cost of a load sequence found is evaluated by taking into account the travel distances of all the working TCs, the setup cost of each TC after every movement, and the cost of interference between the TCs. Table 2 compares the performance of ant colony optimization, tabu search and hybrid search on various sized problems. Since the ant colony optimization and hybrid search are non-deterministic, they were run five times on each problem and the results were averaged. Hybrid-1 is an implementation of hybrid search that only runs one round, and Hybrid-10 is another implementation of hybrid search that runs up to 10 rounds. However, ant colony optimizations of the two hybrid implementations ran for the same number of epochs for fair comparison. This means that if ant colony optimization of Hybrid-1 ran for 100 epochs then that of Hybrid-10 ran for 10 epochs in each round.

First, we compare the performance of tabu search and ant colony optimization. It can be seen that ant colony optimization gives lower cost solutions than tabu search when the problem size is large, while demanding much more CPU time than tabu search. Tabu search, although very fast, becomes stuck at a local optimum solution when the problem is large. One possible reason for these phenomena may be the limitation of the neighbor generation mechanism. Although swapping multiple clusters simultaneously is often the only means of removing some of the TC interferences in a given situation, it is prohibited in our implementation because it leads to a combinatorial explosion of the number of neighbors generated.

Table 1. Data set used for the experiments

Data set	1	2	3	4	5	6
# of containers	313	618	653	1012	1304	1334
# of QCs	2	3	3	4	3	4
# of ship clusters	39	171	257	300	549	514
# of yard clusters	36	116	116	223	219	350

Table 2. Comparison of solution qualities of ant colony optimization, tabu search, and hybrid search. Numbers in parentheses are elapsed CPU times in seconds.

Data set	1	2	3	4	5	6
TS	744 (3)	8666 (10)	5716 (15)	15377 (23)	21090 (43)	27478 (53)
ACO	744 (23)	7381 (349)	5001 (617)	12114 (1579)	15308 (3909)	24696 (3299)
Hybrid-1	744 (14)	7318 (179)	4755 (316)	11718 (801)	14311 (1976)	22668 (1676)
Hybrid-10	743 (14)	7211 (223)	4692 (392)	11280 (1020)	14004 (2276)	22452 (2389)

Next, we compare the performance of ant colony optimization and hybrid searches. Two versions of hybrid search found better solutions than ant colony optimization in less CPU time on all datasets except dataset 1 on which they found the same quality solutions. As the problem becomes larger, the performance gap between hybrid and non-hybrid searches becomes larger. We also note that Hybrid-10 has generally superior performance to Hybrid-1. These experimental results show that a hybrid search properly combined can have both the global search ability of ant colony optimization and the rapid local convergence of tabu search.

5 Conclusions

This paper describes meta-heuristic approaches for solving the load sequence problem of export containers at a container terminal. The load sequencing algorithms have been implemented by using ant colony optimization and tabu search. The experimental results show that it is difficult to obtain satisfactory results in both solution quality and search time when only a single search algorithm is used, whether it is a local search method or a global search method. To overcome this limitation, we propose a hybrid search combining the strengths of both algorithms. As a result, we obtained better solutions than either algorithm in a comparatively short time.

References

1. Kim, K. H., Kang, J. S., Ryu, K. R.: A Beam Search Algorithm for the Load Sequencing of Outbound Containers in Port Container Terminals. OR Spectrum (**26**) (2004) 93–116
2. Beliech, D. E.: A proposed method for efficient pre-load planning for containerized cargo ships. Master's Thesis, Naval Postgraduate School, Monterey, California (1974)
3. Cho, D. W.: Development of a Methodology for Containership Load Planning. Ph.D. Dissertation, Oregon State University (1982)
4. Daganzo, C. F.: The Crane Scheduling Problem, Transp. Res. B. **23B(3)** (1989) 159–175
5. Peterkofsky, R. I., Daganzo, C. F.: A Branch and Bound Solution Method for the Crane Scheduling Problem. Transp. Res. B. **24B(3)** (1990) 159–172

6. Kim, K. H., Kim, K. Y.: Routing straddle carriers for the loading operation of containers using a beam search algorithm. Computers and Industrial Engineering **36(1)** (1999) 109–136
7. Kim, K. H., Kim, K. Y.: An optimal routing algorithm for a transfer crane in port con-tainer terminals. Transportation Science **33(1)** (1999) 17–33
8. Bullnheimer, B., Hartl, R. F., Strauss, C.: A New Rank Based Version of the Ant System: A Computational Study. Central European Journal for Operational Research and Economics **7(1)** (1999) 25–38, 1999.
9. Dorigo, M., Maniezzo V., Colorni, A.: The Ant System: Optimization by a colony of cooperation agents. IEEE Transaction on System, Man, and Cybernetics-Part B **26(1)** (1996) 1–13
10. Colorni, A., Dorigo, M., Malffioli, F., Maniezzo, V., Righini, G., Trubian, M.: Heuristics from Nature for Hard Combinatorial Problems. International Transactions in Operational Research **3(1)** (1996) 1–21
11. Colorni, A., Dorigo, M., Maniezzo, V.: Distributed Optimization by Ant Colonies. Proceeding of European Conference on Artificial Life, Paris, France (1991) 134–142
12. Glover, F., Laguna, M.: Tabu search. Kluwer Academic Publishers (1997)
13. Glover, F.: Tabu Search Part I. ORSA Journal of Computing **1** (1989) 190–206
14. Glover, F.: Tabu Search Part II. ORSA Journal of Computing **2** (1989) 4–32

A Novel Ant Colony System Based on Minimum 1-Tree and Hybrid Mutation for TSP

Chao-Xue Wang, Du-Wu Cui, Zhu-Rong Wang, and Duo Chen

School of Computer Science and Engineering,
Xi'an University of Technology, Xi'an 710048, China
Wbllw@126.com, cuidw@xaut.edu.cn

Abstract. By applying a candidate set strategy based on minimum 1-tree and a self-adaptive hybrid mutation operator to the ant colony system, a novel ant colony system for TSP (MMACS) is proposed. Under the condition that all the edges in the global optimal tour are nearly all contained in the candidate sets, the candidate set strategy based on minimum 1-tree can limit the selection scope of ants at each step to six cities and thus substantially reduce the size of search space. Meanwhile, the self-adaptive hybrid mutation operator that consists of inversion mutation, insertion mutation and swap mutation can effectively prevent MMACS from being trapped in local optimal areas. The simulation of TSP shows that MMACS can avoid the premature convergence phenomenon effectively while greatly increasing the convergence speed. Although MMACS takes TSP as an example for explaining its mechanism, its ideas can be used for other related algorithms.

1 Introduction

The traveling salesman problem (TSP) is a well-known NP-hard problem. Not only is it broadly applicable to a variety of routing and scheduling problem, but it is also usually considered as a standard test-bed for novel algorithmic ideas such as simulated annealing (SA) [1], tabu search (TS) [2,3], evolutionary algorithms (EC) including genetic algorithms (GA) [4,5], ant colony optimization (ACO) [6,7,8] and so on. Owing to the approximation of TSP, ACO has become one of the most efficient algorithms for TSP [7, 9].

Since ACO is a constructive meta-heuristic, where a solution is probabilistically built by iteratively adding solution elements to partial solutions and at each step ants consider the entire set of possible elements before choosing just one, the vast majority of an ant algorithm's runtime is devoted to evaluating the utility of reachable elements. Hence, in order to reduce the runtimes and improve algorithm's convergence speed efficiently, the candidate set strategy that ants select from the narrowed set first and only if there are no feasible candidates are the remaining cities considered becomes an important strategy in ACO [10]. The most commonly used candidate set strategy for TSP in ACO is the candidate set strategy based on the nearest neighbor (CSNN), in which a set of the S nearest cities is maintained for each city, for example, the algorithms in Ref. [7, 9] use CSNN ($S=15$ or 20), the algorithm in Ref. [11] uses CSNN ($S=n/w$, n is the total number of cities for TSP, w is a variable parameter varying with n). When candidate set strategy is adopted in ACO, the total number of global optimal solution's edges contained in candidate sets and the limiting extent of candidate sets to the selection scope of ants, which vary with the difference of the candidate set strategy, will greatly influence the performance of ACO.

Estimating the lower bound for TSP by minimum 1-tree was introduced in Ref. [12], and the error between this lower bound and the length of global optimal tour doesn't exceed 10%. A *a-nearness* was used for a measure reflecting the chance of a given edge being a member of minimum 1-tree in Ref. [13]. On the basis of further investigation into minimum 1-tree and the *a-nearness*, a candidate set strategy based on minimum 1-tree (CSMT) is built in this paper. The theoretical analysis and test results of TSP demonstrate the edges in global optimal tour are nearly all contained in candidate sets ($S=6$, S is the cardinal number of candidate set) when CSMT is adopted, and CSMT ($S=6$) is superior to CSNN ($S=20$). To the shortage of search being possibly trapped in the local optimal area as the locality of CSMT, a self-adaptive hybrid mutation operator (SHMO) that consists of inversion mutation, inserting mutation and swap mutation is designed. By applying CSMT and SHMO to ant colony system (ACS) [7], a novel ant colony system for TSP (MMACS) is proposed. The main ideas underlying this algorithm are to give full play to the role of guidance function of domain knowledge, hybridization of ACS and GA, and integration of various operators. The simulation tests of TSP show that MMACS can not only greatly increase convergence speed but also improve the quality of solution.

The rest of this paper are organized as follows. Section 2 describes ACS. Section 3 presents our proposed MMACS, which focuses on CSMT and SHMO. Section 4 illustrates and analyses the simulation of TSP for comparisons of MMACS with the algorithms in Ref. [7, 11]. Section 5 makes a conclusion for this paper.

2 The Ant Colony System

The ACO algorithm has been inspired by the collective behavior of real ant colonies, in particular, by their foraging behavior. The main idea of this algorithm is the indirect communication of ants based on pheromone trails, which are one kind of distributed numeric information that is modified by the ants to reflect their experience while solving a particular problem. The first ACO algorithm proposed is ant system (AS) [6], and since then Dorigo and other researchers have introduced many improved ACO algorithm based on AS, among which ACS has better performance and is a representative of ACO algorithms. In the following, we take TSP as an example to explain this algorithm.

Informally, ACS works as follows: m ants are initially positioned on n cities chosen randomly. Each ant builds a tour by repeatedly applying a state transition rule. While constructing its tour, an ant also modifies the amount of pheromone on the visited edges by applying a local updating rule. Once all ants have terminated their tour, the amount of pheromone on edges is modified again by applying a global updating rule. The pseudo-code for this algorithm is shown in Fig.1. In the following we discuss the state transition rule, the local updating rule, and the global updating rule [7].

```
Initialize the pheromone on all edges
Set parameters
Loop /* at this level each loop is called an iteration */
    Each ant is positioned on a starting node
    Loop /* at this level each loop is called a step */
        Each ant applies a state transition rule to incrementally build a solution
        and a local updating rule
    Until all ants have built a complete solution
    A global updating rule is applied
Until End_condition
```

Fig. 1. The pseudo-code of ACS

2.1 The ACS State Transition Rule

When building a tour in ACS, an ant k at the current position of city i chooses the next city j to move to by applying the state transition rule of Eq. (1).

$$j = \begin{cases} \arg\max_{u \in J_k(t)} \{\tau_{iu}(t)[\eta_{iu}]^\beta\}, & \text{if } q \leq q_0 \text{ (exploitation)} \\ J, & \text{otherwise (biased exploration)} \end{cases} \quad (1)$$

where $\tau_{iu}(t)$ is the pheromone level on edge (i, u) at the t-th step, $\eta_{iu} = 1/d_{iu}$ is the inverse of the distance d_{iu} from city i to city u, $J_k(t)$ is the set of cities that remain to be visited by ant k at the t-th step. Also, β is a parameter that determines the relative importance of pheromone versus distance ($\beta > 0$), q is a random number uniformly distributed in $[0...1]$, and q_0 is a parameter ($0 \leq q_0 \leq 1$) that determines the relative importance of exploitation versus exploration. In addition, J is a random variable selected according to the probability distribution, called a random-proportional rule [6], given in Eq. (2).

$$p_{ij}^k(t) = \begin{cases} \dfrac{\tau_{ij}(t) \cdot [\eta_{ij}]^\beta}{\sum_{u \in J_k(t)} \tau_{iu}(t) \cdot [\eta_{iu}]^\beta}, & \text{if } j \in J_k(t) \\ 0, & \text{otherwise} \end{cases} \quad (2)$$

where $p_{ij}^k(t)$ is the probability with which ant k in city i chooses to move to the city j at the t-th step.

The state transition rule resulting from Eqs. (1) and (2) is called pseudo-random-proportional rule, which favors transitions toward cities connected by short edges and with a large amount of pheromone. Every time an ant in city i has to choose a city j to move to, it samples a random number q. If $q \leq q_0$ then the best edge, according to Eq. (1), is chosen (exploitation), otherwise an edge is chosen according to Eq. (2) (biased exploration).

2.2 The ACS Local Updating Rule

While building a tour of TSP, ants visit edges and change their pheromone level by applying the local updating rule of Eq.(3)

$$\tau_{ij}(t+1) \leftarrow \tau_{ij}(t)(1-\rho) + \rho\tau_o \tag{3}$$

where ρ denotes the local pheromone decay parameter ($0 < \rho < 1$), τ_0 denotes the initial pheromone level on each edge.

The effect of local updating rule is to make the desirability of edges change dynamically in order to shuffle the tour. If ants explore different paths, then there is a higher probability that one of them will find an improving solution than they all search in a narrow neighborhood of the previous best tour. Every time an ant constructs a path, the local updating rule will make its visit edges' pheromone diminish and become less attractive. Hence, the cities in one ant's tour will be chosen with a lower probability in building other ants' tours. As a result, ants will favor the exploration of edges not yet visited and prevent converging to a common path.

2.3 The ACS Global Updating Rule

Once all ants have completed their tours, the pheromone level is updated by applying the global updating rule of Eq. (4)

$$\tau_{ij}(t+1) \leftarrow (1-\alpha)\tau_{ij}(t) + \alpha \nabla \tau_{ij} \tag{4}$$

where $\nabla \tau_{ij} = \begin{cases} (L_{gb})^{-1}, & \text{if edge}(i,j) \in \text{the best-tour} \\ 0, & \text{otherwise} \end{cases}$, α is global pheromone decay parameter($0 < \alpha < 1$), and L_{ab} is the length of best tour from the beginning of the trial.

The global updating is intended to provide a greater amount of pheromone to shorter tours so as to make the search more directed. Eq. (4) dictates that only those edges belonging to the best tour will receive reinforcement.

3 A Novel Ant Colony Algorithm Based on Minimum 1-Tree and Hybrid Mutation for TSP

The pseudo-code of MMACS is shown in Fig.2, where Con_Max denotes the iterations when SHMO can be applied. In the following, CSMT and SHMO will be described in detail.

```
Initialize the pheromone on all edges
Set parameters
Constructing CSMT (k=6)
Loop /* at this level each loop is called an iteration */
    Each ant is positioned on a starting node
    Loop /* at this level each loop is called a step */
        Each ant applies a state transition rule with CSMT (k=6) to incrementally
        build a solution and a local updating rule
    Until all ants have built a complete solution
    A global updating rule is applied
    SHMO is applied to the current best solution when iterations >=Con_Max
Until End_condition
```

Fig. 2. The pseudo-code of MMACS

3.1 The Candidate Set Strategy Based on Minimum 1-Tree

Estimating the lower bound for TSP by minimum 1-tree was introduced in Ref. [12], and the error between this lower bound and the length of global optimal tour doesn't exceed 10%. Therefore, minimum 1-tree seems to be well suited as a basis of measuring the probability of an edge belonging to a global optimal tour: edges that belong, or 'nearly belong', to a minimum 1-tree, stand a good chance of also belonging to a global optimal tour. Conversely, edges that are 'far from' belonging to a minimum 1-tree have a low probability of also belonging to a global optimal tour. A $\alpha-nearness$ was used for a measure reflecting the chances of a given edge being a member of Minimum 1-tree in Ref. [13]. On the basis of further investigation into minimum 1-tree and the $\alpha-nearness$, CSMT (S=6) is applied to ACS. The method of constructing CSMT can be described briefly in the following:

Step 1: For each city of TSP, calculate the $\alpha-nearness$ of the n-1 edges incident to this city (n is the total number of cities).

Step 2: Let $\alpha(i, j)$ denote the $\alpha-nearness$ of edge $(i, j)(i=1,...,n, j \neq i, j=1,...,n)$. For each city of TSP, arrange the n-1 edges incident to this city according to their $\alpha-nearness$ in descending order. Then, the S cities that are another end node of the S top edges make up of candidate set of this city ($S=1,..., n-1$).

On the basis of investigating the impact of various S value to the quality of CSMT, $S=6$ is found out an appropriate value. A comparison of the percentage of their edges shared with the global optimal tour for 23 instances of TSP from TSPLIB between CSNN ($S=20$) and CSMT ($S=6$) is shown in Fig.3, where the average percentage of the former is 99.38% while the later is 99.91%. Of course, constructing CSMT creates an overhead, but this overhead can be accepted since its time complexity and space complexity can be limited to $O(n^2)$ and $O(n)$ respectively. Generally speaking, CSMT ($S=6$) is superior to CSNN ($S=20$).

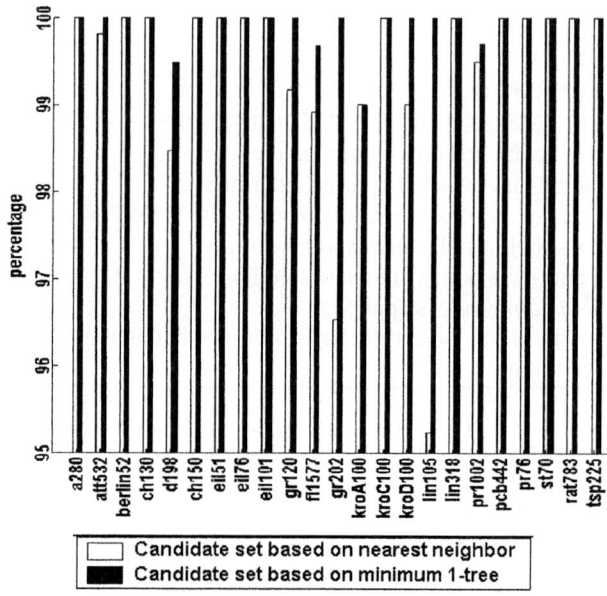

Fig. 3. A comparison of the quality of two kinds of candidate set

3.2 The Self-adaptive Hybrid Mutation Operator

If CSMT (S =6) is adopted in ACS, this algorithm will quickly find out local optimal solutions. However, it is likely to take enough long time to find out the global optimal solution, and sometimes this algorithm can only converge to a local optimal solution.

As we all know, mutation operator can keep the diversity of population and prevent search from being trapped in the local optimal area in genetic algorithm (GA). The commonly used mutation operators for TSP have inversion, insertion, and swap, whose neighborhood search scopes are two edges, tree edges and four edges respectively. A measure of search difficulty, fitness distance correlation (FDC) was introduced in Ref. [14], and there exists a high and positive FDC for TSP, which indicates that the smaller the solution cost is, the closer are the solutions – on average – to a global optimal solution [15]. Hereby there is often a small quantity of different edges between a local optimal solution and the global optimal solution or a better local optimal solution, namely we possibly find out a better local optimal solution or the global optimum so long as a small quantity of edges are changed. On the other hand, a local optimal solution with respect to one mutation operator is not necessary for another, but the global optimal solution with respect to all mutation operators is the same one.

Based on the consideration above, a self-adaptive hybrid mutation operator (SHMO), which is self-adaptively assembled with the inversion operator, inserting operator and swap operator, is designed in this paper. This operator can self-adaptively adjust the size of neighborhood search scope, keep the diversity of solutions and improve the global search ability of ACS efficiently. In MMACS, when the algorithm population has evolved for many iterations and the search will possibly be in stagnation, this operator is applied to the current best solution. Suppose the algorithm has evolved for Con_Max iterations and the search will possibly be in stagnation and the current best tour is $(b_1b_2...b_i...b_j...b_n)$, and then the pseudo-code of SHMO can be given in Fig.4.

```
Begin
   for(i=1;i<n-1;i++)
   {
      for(j=i+2;j<n+1;j++)
      {
        if (j-i=n-1)break;
        if (after the path between b_i and b_j is reversed,
            tour's length is reduced)
        {
         reverse the path between b_{i+1} and b_j;
         continue;
        }
        else if (after city b_j is inserted behind city b_i,
                tour's length is reduced)
        {
         insert city b_j behind city b_i;
         continue;
        }
        else if (after city b_i and b_j is swapped,
                tour's length is reduced)
        {
         swap city b_i and b_j;
        }
      }
   }
End
```

Fig. 4. The pseudo-code of SHMO

4 Simulations and Analysis

MMACS is realized in VC6.0 and run on a PC (CPU Pentium4 2.4GHz, 256 MB memory) with Windows 2000 Operating System. Many instances of TSP from TSPLIB are used in simulation, and perfect results are achieved. In all experiments the numeric parameters, except when indicated differently, are set to the following values: $m=2\sim10$, $Con\_Max=3\sim15$, $\beta=2, q=0.7\sim0.9, a=0.1\sim0.2, r=0.1\sim0.2, \tau_0 = (nL_{nn})^{-1}$. ($L_{nn}$ is the tour length produced by the nearest neighbor heuristic [16]).

4.1 The Comparisons Between MMACS and the Algorithm in the Later Reference

An ant colony optimization algorithm based on mutation and dynamic pheromone updating (NDMACO), which adopted CSNN ($S = n/w$, n is the total number of cities for TSP, w is a variable parameter varying with n) and a unique mutation scheme, was introduced in Ref. [11]. In order to compare MMACS with NDMACO, some instances of TSP that are the same as ones used in NDMACO are chosen in simulation. Comparisons of the final solution and convergence number and convergence time between MMACS and NDMACO are shown in Table.1 (test results of NDMACO are directly taken from Ref. [11]) and Table.2 respectively. It can be seen that MMACS not only finds out the global optimal solutions for the four instances of TSP but also has very quick convergence speed while NDMACO only finds out the local optimal solutions for Pr107.tsp and D198.tsp.

Table 1. A comparison of the final solution and convergence number between MMACS and NDMACO

Name	Optimum	Best length of MMACS	Best length of NDMACO	Convergence number of MMACS	Convergence number of NDMACO
Eil51	426	426	426	5	7
Berlin52	7542	7542	7542	4	11
Pr107	44303	44303	44383	8	330
D198	15780	15780	15796	71	800

Table 2. A comparison of convergence time between MMACS and NDMACO

Name	Convergence time of MMACS(s)	Convergence time of NDMACO(s)
Eil51	0.001	0.02
Berlin52	0.001	0.02
Pr107	0.02	0.6

4.2 The Comparison Between MMACS and ACS

MMACS and ACS are tested on five hard and large-scaled TSP respectively, and the experimental results are shown in Table.3, where each experiment consists of at least 20 trials; and the experimental results of ACS are directly taken from Ref. [7]. It can be seen from Table.3 that MMACS makes not only the quality of solutions better than ACS but also the speed of convergence hundreds of times faster than ACS.

Table 3. A comparison between MMACS and ACS

Name	Optimum (1)	MMACS best integer length (2)	MMACS number of tours generated to best	MMACS average integer length	Relative error (2)−(1) (1)	ACS best integer length (3)	ACS number of tours generated to best	ACS average integer length	Relative error (3)−(1) (1)
D198	15780	15780	213	15785	0%	15888	585000	16054	0.68%
Pcb442	50779	50779	3100	50912	0%	51268	595000	51690	0.96%
Att532	27686	27705	16520	27729	0.07%	28174	830658	28523	1.67%
Rat783	8806	8830	17310	8851	0.27%	9015	991276	9066	2.37%
Fl1577	22249	22323	10900	22375	0.34%	22977	942000	23163	3.48%

4.3 The Analysis of Diversity

MMACS about the variation of tour length with iteration is shown in Fig.5. It can be seen that the best solution has verged on a local optimal solution after having evolved for 18 iterations, and then the global optimal solution is obtained after having evolved for about 50 iterations. In the meantime, the average tour length has been in shaking at random all the time, and it has been able to keep a certain distance with the best tour length. Therefore, MMACS can greatly reduce the size of search space and improve the convergence speed after CSMT is adopted; meanwhile SHMO commendably maintains the diversity of solutions. This is one of the reasons why MMACS has the good ability of global optimization while the convergence speed has been improved greatly.

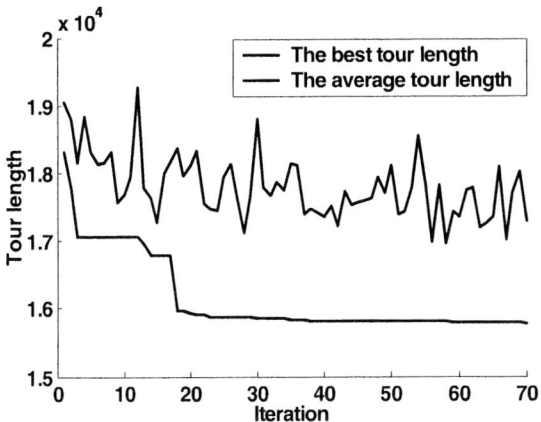

Fig. 5. The variation of best tour length and average tour length with iteration for d198.tsp

5 Conclusions

Although the global optimal solution is not a subset of CSMT ($S=6$), CSMT ($S=6$) contains the edges of the global optimal solution at high probability. MMACS adopts CSMT ($S=6$) to make the search scope reduced from $n(n-1)/2$ to $6n$, thus the search time of this algorithm is reduced greatly. To the shortage that this algorithm is possibly trapped in local optimal solution caused by the locality of CSMT ($S=6$), the algorithm designs SHMO by combining the inversion operator, inserting operator and swap operator, and thus introduces the mechanism of diversity and improves the global search ability of the algorithm. The results of simulation show that MMACS is efficient.

One of the main ideas underlying this algorithm is to give full play to the role of guidance of domain knowledge [17], by which an efficient CSMT is obtained. Another idea is hybridization of meta-heuristics and integration of various operators, namely, mixing and hybridizing is often better than purity [18], by which a self-adaptive search hybrid mutation operator from genetic algorithm is designed and then applied to ACS. Although MMACS takes TSP as an example for explaining its mechanism, its ideas can be used for other related algorithms.

References

1. Lo, C.C., Hus, C.C.: Annealing Framework with Learning Memory. IEEE Transactions on System, Man, Cybernetics, Part A (1998) 28(5) 1-13
2. Glover, F.: Tabu Search-Part I. ORSA Journal on Computing (1998) 1(3)190-206
3. Glover, F.: Tabu Search-Part II. ORSA Journal on Computing (1990) 2(1) 4-32
4. Jog, P., Suh, J. Y., Gucht, D. V.: The Effects of Population Size, Heuristic Crossover and Local Improvement on a Genetic Algorithm for the Traveling Salesman Problem. In Proc of the 3rd Int Conf on Genetic Algorithms (1989) 110–115
5. Jiao, L.C., Wang, L.: A Novel Genetic Algorithm Based on Immunity. IEEE Transactions on Systems, Man, and Cybernetics, Part A: Systems and Humans (2000) 30(5)552–561
6. Colormi, A., Dorigo, M., Manieaao, V.: Distributed Optimization by Ant Colonies. In Varela, F. and Bourgine, P. (eds.): Proc of the First European Conf On Artificial Life. Paris, France, Elsevier Publishing (1991) 134–142
7. Dorigo, M., Gambardella, L. M.: Ant Colony System: A Cooperative Learning Approach to the Traveling Salesman Problem. IEEE Trans on Evolutionary Computation (1997) 1(1) 53–66
8. Dorigo, M. and Di Caro, G.: The Ant Colony Optimization Meta-heuristic. In Corne, D., Dorigo, M., Glover, F. (eds.): New Ideas in Optimization. McGraw-Hill, London, UK (1999) 11–32
9. Stützle, T., Hoos, H.: MAX-MIN Ant System and Local Search for the Traveling Salesman Problem. In: IEEE Int'l Conf. on Evolutionary Computation. Indianapolis: IEEE Press (1997) 309–314
10. Randall, M. and Montgomery, J.: Candidate Set Strategies for Ant Colony Optimization. School of Information Technology, Bond University, Australia, Technical Report TR02-04 (2002)
11. Zhu, Q. B., Yang, Z. J.: An Ant Colony Optimization Algorithm Based on Mutation and Dynamic Pheromone Updating. Journal of Software (2004) 15(2) 185–192 (In Chinese).
12. Volgenant, T., Jonker, R.: The Symmetric Traveling Salesman Problem and Edge Exchanges i Minima l-Trees. European Journal of Operational Research 12 (1983) 394–403
13. Yang, H., Kang, L.S. and Chen, Y.P.: A Gene-Based Genetic Algorithm for TSP. Chinese Journal of Computers (2003) 26(12)1753–1758(in Chinese)
14. Jones, T. and Forrest, S.: Fitness Distance Correlation as a Measure of Problem Difficulty for Genetic Algorithms. In Eshelman, L.J. (eds.): Proceedings of the 6th International Conference on Genetic Algorithms. Morgan Kaufman, San Francisco, CA, USA (1995) 184–192
15. Merz, P. and Freisleben, B.: Fitness Landscapes and Memetic Algorithm Design. In Corne, D., Dorigo, M., Glover, F. (eds.): New Ideas in Optimization. McGraw-Hill, London, UK (1999) 245-260
16. Rosenkrantz, D. J., Stearns, R. E. and Lewis, P. M.: An Analysis of Several Heuristics for the Traveling Salesman Problem. SIAM Journal on Computing (1977) 6(3) 563–581
17. Wolpert, D. H., Macready, W. G.: No Free Lunch Theorems for Optimization. IEEE Trans on Evolutionary Computation (1997) 1 (1) 67– 82
18. Blum, C. and Roli, A.: Metaheuristics in Combinatorial Optimization: Overview and Conceptual Comparison. ACM Computing Surveys (2003) 35(3) 268–308

Author Index

Ahmad, Muhammad Bilal II-43
Akin, Erhan III-787
Alatas, Bilal III-787
Almeida, Gustavo Maia de III-313
Amin, Hesham H. I-456
An, Wensen I-546
Anh, Vo III-337
Aoki, Terumasa II-622
Araabi, Babak N. II-1250
Arita, Jun II-165
Asiedu, Baffour Kojo III-903
Asiimwe, Alex Jessey III-968
Aydin, Serkan III-703

Baba, Sapiyan I-893
Bae, Hyeon I-1160, II-564
Bae, SungMin II-530
Bai, JianCong III-74
Bai, Lin II-780
Baicher, Gurvinder S. III-877
Balescu, Catalin III-1300
Bao, Leilei III-988
Bao, Zhejing I-688
Barbosa, Helio J.C. II-941
Bea, Hae-Ryong III-1182
Belatreche, A. I-420
Bertoni, Alberto III-235
Bi, D. II-266, II-592
Bianco, Luca II-1155
Bin, Guang-yu I-1031, III-646
Bingul, Zafer III-1304
Bolat, Bülent I-110
Bonfim, Danilo Mattos I-1275
Borne, Pierre III-259
Bu, Nan II-165
Butun, Erhan II-204
Byun, Kwang-Sub II-85

Čada, Josef I-1234
Cai, Guangchao III-915
Cai, Jiamei I-1117
Cai, Yici III-181
Cai, Yunze I-51, I-528, I-582, II-175
Cai, Zhiping II-913

Cai, Zixing III-1308
Campadelli, Paola III-235
Cao, Chunhong I-783, II-139
Cao, Qixin III-535, III-723
Cao, Xianqing III-1162
Cao, Yijia II-895
Cao, Zuoliang III-984
Carvalho, Andre C.P.L.F. I-1189
Chai, Tianyou II-214
Chambers, J.A. I-199
Chang, Chia-Lan II-735
Chang, Chuan-Wei II-296
Chang, Hui-Chen III-1172
Chang, HuiYou III-74
Chang, Min Hyuk II-43
Chang, Pei-Chann I-364, II-983, III-205
Chang, Ping-Teng I-619
Chang, Ray-I I-1224
Chang, Yongmin I-850
Chau, Kwokwing III-1152
Chen, Chen-Tung I-619
Chen, Chih-Ming III-1186
Chen, Chongcheng III-1051
Chen, Chunlin II-686
Chen, Duo II-1269
Chen, G.L III-1060
Chen, Gang II-37, II-270
Chen, Guangzhu III-444
Chen, Guochu II-610, III-515
Chen, Haixu III-938
Chen, Hongjian II-1218
Chen, Huanwen III-384
Chen, Jiah-Shing II-735, III-798
Chen, Jin-Long III-1186
Chen, Jing II-539
Chen, Ke II-656
Chen, Liangzhou I-679
Chen, Ling II-1218, II-1239
Chen, Qian III-490
Chen, Qingzhan III-782
Chen, S. II-1122
Chen, Shengda III-1235
Chen, Shengyong I-332
Chen, Shi-Fu III-855

Chen, Shiming II-913
Chen, Shu-Heng III-612
Chen, Shuang I-101
Chen, Tianping I-245
Chen, Tieming I-1117
Chen, Xin III-628
Chen, Xinghuan III-57
Chen, Xuefeng II-324
Chen, Yan Qiu II-705, III-822, III-845
Chen, Yanmin I-947
Chen, Ying-Chun III-482
Chen, Yingchun II-1101
Chen, Yong II-890
Chen, Yun Wen II-705
Chen, Zehua II-945
Chen, Zhao-Qian II-55
Chen, Zhong II-1
Chen, Zong-Ming II-425
Chen, Zonghai II-686
Cheng, Chun-Tian III-453, III-1152
Cheng, Kuo-Hsiang III-1186
Cheng, Lixin I-470
Cheng, Yinglei III-215
Cheng, Zhihong III-444
Cheremushkin, Evgeny II-1202
Chi, Huisheng I-167
Chien, Shu-Yen II-296
Chiu, David II-306
Cho, Daehyeon I-536
Cho, Eun-kyung III-1069
Cho, Yeon-Jin I-1009
Cho, Yeun-Jin I-1002
Choi, Dong-Seong I-797
Choi, Jinsung II-552
Choi, Jonghwa I-1185, II-552
Choi, Wonil I-850
Chu, Ming-Hui II-296
Chu, Tianguang I-769
Chua, Ming-Hui II-296
Chun, Jong Hoon II-43
Chunjie, Yang I-696
Cong, Shuang I-773
Cooper, Leon N. I-71, I-554, I-877
Copper, J. I-1039
Corchado, Emilio I-778
Cui, Baotong I-1
Cui, Du-Wu II-1269, III-86
Cui, Zhihua III-255, III-467
Cukic, Bojan I-750

Dai, Hongwei III-332
Dai, Yuewei III-976
Damiance, Antonio P.G., Jr. I-1189
Dang, Chuangyin III-392
Dang, Yan I-956
Daoying, Pi I-696
de Carvalho, Luis A.V. II-941
de Castro, Leandro Nunes I-1275, I-1279
Demir, Ibrahim II-648
Deng, Fei-Qi I-1150
Deng, Weihong I-915
Ding, Hongkai I-119
Ding, Juling II-804
Ding, Lixin II-1049
Ding, Zhan I-835
Dixit, Vikas III-1242
Do, Tien Dung II-849
Dong, Chaojun I-340
Dong, Daoyi II-686
Dong, Jin-xiang III-48
Dong, Jingxin II-105
Dong, Jinxiang II-1229
Dong, Min I-397
Dong, Qiming II-185
Dong, Xiuming III-374
Du, Haifeng II-826, II-876, II-931, III-399
Du, Shihong III-1261, III-1274
Du, Wenli II-631
Du, Ying I-480
Du, Yuping III-592
Duan, Ganglong I-640

Ebecken, Nelson F.F. III-245
Egan, G.F. I-1057
Elena, José Manuel II-147
Engin, Seref N. II-648
Eom, Il Kyu II-400
Erfidan, Tarık II-204
Estevam, R. Hruschka Jr. III-245
Eto, Tsuyoshi I-439
Everly, R.D. I-1039

Fan, FuHua II-493
Fan, Hong I-476
Fan, Muhui II-592
Fan, Zhi-Gang II-396
Fang, Bin III-663
Fang, Yi II-135
Farkaš, Igor II-676

Feng, Chen I-793, I-1256
Feng, Chunbo III-698
Feng, Ding I-25
Feng, Du I-679
Feng, Guangzeng III-457
Feng, Guiyu I-209, I-675
Feng, Guorui I-720
Feng, Jiuchao II-332
Feng, Li III-374
Feng, Naiqin III-562
Feng, Xiao-Yue II-698
Figueredo, Grazziela P. II-941
Fong, Alvis C.M. II-849
Fontana, Federico II-1155
Freeman, Walter J. I-378
Freund, Lars II-1112
Fu, Chaojin I-664
Fu, Duan III-1128
Fu, Xiao II-627
Fu, Y.X. III-668
Fu, Zetian II-352
Fujii, Robert H. I-456
Fukumura, Naohiro I-313
Furutani, Hiroshi II-1025

Gao, Hai-Hua I-565, II-21, II-89
Gao, Pingan III-1308
Gao, Xieping I-358, I-783, II-139
Gao, Ying II-386
Ge, Weimin III-984
Ge, Yang III-553
Geem, Zong Woo III-741, III-751
Germen, Emin I-353
Glackin, B. I-420
Goebels, Andreas II-744
Goëffon, Adrien III-678
Göksu, Hüseyin II-618, III-1242
Gong, Dengcai II-602
Gong, Ling I-925
Gong, Maoguo I-449, II-826, III-399, III-768
Gong, Zhiwei III-1251
Górriz, J.M. III-863
Gou, Jin III-490
Gowri, S. III-361
Gu, Faji I-1052
Gu, Xingsheng II-880
Guan, Qiu I-332, II-795
Guan, Xinping II-75
Guan, Yi I-947

Guang, Cheng II-338
Guangli, Liu I-650
Günes, Salih II-830
Guo, Hongbo II-957
Guo, Huawei I-679
Guo, Jun I-915
Guo, Lei III-698
Guo, Ya-Jun III-28
Guo, Zhenhe II-867

Hakl, František I-1234
Ham, Fredric M. I-1100
Han, Cheon-woo I-797
Han, Dongil II-328
Han, Jianghong III-782
Han, Jong-Hye I-850
Han, Lansheng III-903
Han, Lu II-1105
Han, Ray P.S. III-269
Han, Soowhan I-1100
Hang, D. I-1057
Hao, Fei I-769
Hao, Jin-Kao III-678
Hao, Zhifeng III-137, III-1257
Harris, C.J. II-1122
Hayward, Serge I-1214
He, Han-gen II-1035
He, Jun II-1015, III-279, III-323
He, Lianlian III-636, III-668
He, Mi I-508
He, Pilian I-692
He, Shengjun III-915
He, Wenxiu III-782
He, Wuhong II-931
He, Xiaoguang I-187
He, Yinghao II-12
He, Yuguo III-434
He, Yunhui II-71
He, Yuyao I-273
He, Zhengjia II-324
He, Zhenya I-683
Heckman, C. I-1039
Herbert, Joseph I-129
Herrero, Álvaro I-778
Hlaváček, Marek I-1234
Ho, Daniel W.C. I-730
Hong, Chao-Fu III-11
Hong, Gye Hang II-710
Hong, Keongho I-789
Hong, Kwang-Seok I-1179

Hong, Qin I-264
Hong, Sang Jeen I-1113
Hong, Wei-Chiang I-619, I-668
Hong, Xianlong III-181
Hong, Yuan II-1206
Hong, Zhang I-499
Hooke, J. I-1039
Hosoi, Satoshi II-438
Hou, Chong II-876
Hou, Cuiqin III-768
Hou, Kunpeng II-483
Hou, Yanfeng III-1216
Hou, Yimin III-873
Hou, Yunxian II-352
Hou, Zeng-Guang III-622
Hruschka, Eduardo R. III-245
Hsu, Chi-I III-812
Hsu, Hao-Hsuan II-859
Hsu, Pei Lun III-812
Hsu, Yuan Lin III-812
Hu, Chunfeng II-65
Hu, Chunhua II-234
Hu, Dewen I-101, I-209, I-675, I-700, III-1128
Hu, Guangshu III-654
Hu, Hong I-91, I-1039
Hu, Huaqiang I-835
Hu, Jiani I-915
Hu, Jianming II-1089
Hu, Qiao II-324
Hu, Qinghua III-1190
Hu, Shigeng I-740
Hu, Tao II-352
Hu, Tingliang II-234
Hu, Weisheng III-102
Hu, Xiaomin II-592
Hu, Zhi-kun III-477
Hu, Zhonghui I-528, II-175
Hua, Yong II-12
Huang, Gaoming I-683
Huang, Hai III-772, III-1142
Huang, Han III-137
Huang, Houkuan III-323
Huang, Min I-1
Huang, Wanping III-289
Huang, Wentao I-449, II-826
Huang, Xiyue II-890
Huang, Xuemei II-800
Huang, Xueyuan II-913
Huang, Ya-Chi III-612

Huang, Yan-Xin II-698
Huang, Yu-Ying I-668
Huh, Sung-Hoe III-1099
Hui, Siu Cheung II-849
Hui-zhong, Yang I-25
Hwang, Changha I-512, I-521, I-536, II-306
Hwang, Su-Young I-797

Ibershoff, Joseph II-1206
Ibrahim, Zuwairie II-1174, II-1182
Ichikawa, Michinori I-293
Im, Kwang Hyuk II-530
Iwata, Atsushi III-1006

Jaromczyk, Jerzy W. II-1206
Jeon, In Ja II-764, III-356
Jeon, Jun-Cheol III-348
Jeong, Eunhwa I-789
Jeong, EunSung II-764
Jeong, Kee S. I-818
Jeong, Ok-Ran I-850
Ji, Guangrong I-793, I-1256
Jia, Sen II-391
Jian, Gong II-338
Jiang, Chunhong I-985
Jiang, Michael I-750
Jiang, Minghu I-1140
Jiang, Minghui I-740
Jiang, Weijin I-139, I-345
Jiang, Xiaoyue III-215
Jiang, Yaping II-800
Jiang, Zefei I-608
Jianmin, Han I-336
Jianying, Xie I-44
Jiao, Licheng I-449, II-780, II-826, II-839, II-876, II-905, II-931, III-366, III-399, III-768, III-925
Jie, Liu I-254
Jin, Dongming III-1022
Jin, Qiao III-1089
Jin, Wuyin I-390
Jin, Xiaogang I-1209
Jin, Xiaoguang II-584
Jin, Yaochu II-1145
Jin, Yaohui III-102
Jing, Guixia II-376
Jing, Ling I-217
Jiskra, Jan III-841
Jiuzhen, Liang I-336

Jordan, R.   I-1039
Juang, Yau-Tarng   III-1172
Jun, Feng   I-33
Jun, Liu   I-44
Jun-an, Lu   I-254
Jung, In-Sung   I-888
Jung, Jo Nam   II-109
Jwo, Dah-Jing   II-425

Kala, Keerthi Laal   III-1015
Kang, Hyun-Ho   III-962
Kang, Jaeho   II-1259
Kang, Kyung-Woo   II-543
Kang, Lishan   II-1049
Kang, Yuan   II-296
Karwowski, Waldemar   III-1216
Kasai, Nobuyuki   II-1174
Katayama, Susumu   II-1025
Kato, Tsuyoshi   II-963
Katsaggelos, Aggelos K.   II-1192
Kaya, Mehmet Ali   II-618
Ke, Hengyu   II-210
Kel, Alexander   II-1202
Khajehpour, Pooyan   II-1250
Khalid, Marzuki   II-1182
Kikuchi, H.   III-684
Kim, Chang-Suk   III-1182
Kim, Dong-Hyun   III-1044
Kim, Dongwon   III-1099
Kim, DuckSool   II-714
Kim, Eun Ju   II-155
Kim, Hang-Joon   II-543
Kim, Ho-Joon   III-1178
Kim, Hyeoncheol   I-1002, I-1009
Kim, Hyun-jung   I-1247
Kim, Hyung-Bum   I-1027
Kim, Jinsu   III-1044
Kim, Jong-Bin   III-1032
Kim, Jong-Min   II-224
Kim, Ju Han   I-965
Kim, Kap Hwan   II-1259
Kim, Kee-Won   III-348
Kim, Kwang-Baek   I-237, III-1182
Kim, Myung Won   II-155
Kim, Nam H.   I-818
Kim, Pan-Koo   I-1027
Kim, Seong-Whan   II-451
Kim, Sun   II-636
Kim, Sung-il   I-797
Kim, Sungshin   I-1160, II-564

Kim, Tae Hyun   II-530
Kim, Tae Hyung   II-400
Kim, Won-sik   I-797
Kim, Woong Myung   I-760
Kim, Yong-Kab   III-1044
Kim, Yoo Shin   II-400
Kim, Young-Joong   III-1079
Knidel, Helder   I-1279
Kobayashi, Kunikazu   I-439
Kodaz, Halife   II-830
Kökçe, Ali   II-618
Kong, Min   I-15
Konovalova, Tatiana   II-1202
Kou, Jisong   III-37, III-943
Kouh, Jen-Shaing   I-1224
Kramer, Oliver   II-744
Krishnamurthy, E.V.   II-784
Ku, Dae-Sung   III-1032
Kuremoto, Takashi   I-439
Kwon, Ki-Ryong   III-962
Kwon, Young-hee   III-1069

Lai, Chien-Yuan   III-205
Lai, Kin Keung   I-382
Lai, Liang-Bin   I-1224
Lai, Yungang   III-782
Lam, Kin-man   II-7
Lan, Shu   I-33
Lee, Bu-Sung   II-1112
Lee, Byung C.   I-818
Lee, Chung K.   I-818
Lee, Dong-Un   I-237
Lee, Hak-Sung   II-328
Lee, Hsuan-Shih   III-1290
Lee, Hyon Soo   I-760
Lee, Jang Hee   II-710
Lee, Jay   III-535
Lee, Jongkeuk   I-1100
Lee, KangWoo   I-855
Lee, Kwangeui   I-1100
Lee, Myung-jin   I-797
Lee, Sang-Ho   I-965
Lee, Sun-young   I-797
Lee, Sungyoung   II-101
Lee, Woo-Gul   I-797
Lee, Yong Hwan   II-1259
Lee, Yunsik   I-1113
León, Carlos   II-147
Li, BiCheng   II-37
Li, Bin   III-1261

Li, Chun-lian   II-1159, III-93
Li, Chunshien   III-1186
Li, Fu-ming   II-992
Li, G.Q.   III-668
Li, Guang   I-378, I-411, I-1052
Li, Guodong   I-773
Li, Guoyou   I-397
Li, Haifeng   III-972
Li, Hejun   II-185
Li, Hong   I-952
Li, Hong-Nan   III-1089
Li, Hua   II-483
Li, Huiguang   I-397
Li, Hui-Xian   III-453
Li, Jianyu   I-867
Li, Jing   I-293, II-931
Li, Meiyi   III-1308
Li, Ming   I-209, I-675
Li, Minqiang   III-37, III-171, III-185, III-808, III-943
Li, Na-na   I-1047
Li, Qingyong   I-903, III-496
Li, Ruonan   III-654
Li, Shanbin   II-242
Li, Shaoqian   II-316
Li, Tao   II-800, II-804
Li, Tianpeng   III-948
Li, Wei   I-995
Li, Wenhui   III-938
Li, Wu-Jun   II-55
Li, Xiao feng   III-505
Li, Xiaobin   II-922
Li, Xiaohong   II-584
Li, Xiaoming   III-808
Li, Xiu   II-574
Li, Xu   I-378, I-1121
Li, Xu-yong   III-68
Li, Xue-yan   I-1047
Li, Xuewei   III-309
Li, Xuming   II-468
Li, Xunming   II-602
Li, Yangmin   III-628, III-1109
Li, Ye   II-175
Li, Yijun   II-123
Li, Ying   III-215
Li, Yinglu   II-627
Li, Yongming   III-1132
Li, Yuan   I-1132
Li, Yuangui   I-528, II-175
Li, Yuanyuan   II-774

Li, Yunfeng   II-119
Li, Zeng-Zhi   III-602, III-883
Li, Zhanhuai   III-1001
Li, Zhengxue   I-720
Li, Zhishu   III-444
Li, Zhong-Wei   I-1132
Li, Zi-qiang   II-1080
Li, Zongmin   II-483
Lian, Hui-Cheng   II-438
Liang, Min   II-316
Liang, Yan-Chun   II-698
Liang, Yanchun   III-137, III-1226, III-1257
Liao, Benjamin Penyang   III-798
Liao, Guisheng   III-1, III-893
Liao, Shasha   I-1140
Liao, Zaiyi   III-1205
Liebman, M.N.   I-1039
Lim, Dudy   II-1112
Lim, Heuseok   I-844
Lim, Karam   I-797
Lim, Myo-Taeg   III-1079
Lim, Sehun   I-1270
Lim, Soonja   III-1044
Lin, Chun-Cheng   II-859
Lin, Dacheng   I-903
Lin, Dan   III-171, III-185, III-808, III-943
Lin, Jian-Yi   III-1152
Lin, Jianning   III-225
Lin, Mu-Hua   III-11
Lin, Pan   III-873
Lin, Qian   I-390
Lin, Zuoquan   I-825
Liu, AnFei   II-37
Liu, Benyong   I-660
Liu, Bin   III-181
Liu, Chen-Hao   I-364, II-983, III-205
Liu, Chongyang   III-1
Liu, Dang-hui   II-7
Liu, Ding   II-922
Liu, Dong   II-75
Liu, Fang   II-780
Liu, Feng   II-316
Liu, Feng-yu   III-1280
Liu, Guangjie   III-976
Liu, Guangyuan   III-1231
Liu, Hongbing   I-592
Liu, Hua-Yong   III-28
Liu, Hui   III-903

Liu, Ji II-863
Liu, Jing III-366, III-543, III-925
Liu, Juan III-636
Liu, Jun I-411
Liu, Li II-135
Liu, Lianggui III-457
Liu, Lin III-980
Liu, Ping II-185
Liu, Renren III-1251
Liu, San-yang II-1044
Liu, Shumei III-566
Liu, Wanquan I-1057, III-1198
Liu, Wenhuang II-574
Liu, Xiande II-1105
Liu, Xianghui II-913
Liu, Xiaodong III-1198
Liu, Xiaojie II-804
Liu, Xueliang II-376
Liu, Yan I-750
Liu, Yanjuan III-1235
Liu, Ye III-761
Liu, Yilin II-690
Liu, Yong I-149
Liu, Yongpan III-219
Liu, Yuan-Liang II-296
Liu, Yugang III-1109
Liu, Yuling III-958
Liu, Yutian III-449
Liu, Zhiyong I-340
Liu, Zhongshu III-772
Long, Dong-yun II-1159
Lou, Zhengguo I-411
Lou, Zhenguo I-378
Lu, Bao-Liang I-293, I-303, II-396, II-438
Lu, Bin II-826, III-399, III-768
Lu, Guihua III-129
Lu, Hongtao II-28
Lu, Huifang I-720
Lu, Jiang III-592
Lu, Jiwen I-640
Lu, Qi-Shao I-480, I-1199
Lu, Wenkai II-410
Lu, Yiyu II-584
Lucas, Caro II-1250
Luo, Bin II-55
Luo, H. III-684
Luo, Rong III-219
Luo, Siwei I-322, I-710, I-867
Luo, Yanbin III-1132

Lu-ping, Fang I-499
Lv, Qiang I-81

Ma, Longhua III-289
Ma, Xiaojiang II-81
Maeda, Michiharu I-283, II-361, II-415
Maguire, L.P I-420
Manca, Vincenzo II-1155
Mao, Keji III-782
Mao, Zong-yuan I-601
Marras, William S. III-1216
Matsugu, Masakazu III-1006
Matsuka, Toshihiko I-933
Matsuoka, Kiyotoshi II-274
Maul, Tomás I-893
Mayumi, Oyama-Higa I-811
McGinnity, T.M. I-420
Meng, Fan II-371
Meng, Hong-yun II-1044
Meng, Qingchun II-1005
Meng, Yu III-938
Miao, Gang II-81
Miao, Shouhong III-723
Miao, Tiejun I-811
Mills, Ashley II-666
Min, Zhao I-374
Miyajima, Hiromi I-283, II-361, II-415
Mohanasundaram, K.M. III-572
Monedero, Iñigo II-147
Montaño, Juan C. II-147
Morie, Takashi III-1006
Mozhiwen I-33
Mu, Weisong II-352
Muhammad, Mohd Saufee II-1182
Murthy, V.K. II-784

Nagao, Tomoharu III-566
Nakayama, Hirotaka III-409
Nam, Kichun I-844, I-850
Nam, Mi Young II-109
Nan, Guofang III-943
Narayanan, M. Rajaram III-361
Neagu, Daniel III-1300
Nepomuceno, Erivelton Geraldo III-313
Neskovic, Predrag I-71, I-554, I-877
Ng, Hee-Khiang II-1112
Nguyen, Duc-Hoai I-1113
Nguyen, Ha-Nam I-1017
Nhat, Vo Dinh Minh II-101
Nian, Rui I-793, I-1256

Nie, Weike II-839
Nie, Yinling II-839
Niu, Xiao-hui I-1047
Niu, Xiaoxiao I-592
Nomura, Osamu III-1006
Nowinski, Wieslaw L. I-1065

Obayashi, Masanao I-439
Oh, Heung-Bum I-1009
Ohn, Syng-Yup I-1017
Ohyama, Norifumi II-274
Ok, Sooyol II-714
Olhofer, Markus II-1145
Ong, Yew-Soon II-1112
Önkal-Engin, Güleda II-648
Ono, Osamu II-1174, II-1182
Ooshima, Masataka II-274
Ou, Ling II-814
Ou, Zongying II-119, III-688

Pai, Ping-Feng I-619, I-668
Palaniappan, K. III-1132
Palmes, Paulito P. III-1119
Pan, Chen II-135
Pan, Li III-934
Pan, Zhigeng III-1051
Pappalardo, Francesco III-161
Park, Chang-Hyun II-85
Park, Chun-Ja III-1069
Park, Dong-Chul I-1113, I-1266
Park, Gwi-Tae III-1099
Park, Hyun Jin II-451
Park, Hyun-Soo II-543
Park, Jaehyun I-1017
Park, Jong-An I-1027, II-43
Park, Jong-won III-1069
Park, Kinam I-844
Park, Kyu-Sik I-1017
Park, Kyungdo I-1247, II-636
Park, Moon-sung III-1069
Park, Sang Chan II-530
Park, Seoung-Kyu II-224
Park, Taesu I-1027
Park, Yongjin III-741
Park, Youn J. I-818
Park, Young-Ran III-962
Parsopoulos, K.E. III-582
Parvez, Shuja II-1112
Pei, Xiao-mei I-1031, III-646
Pei, Xiaomei II-376

Peng, Jing III-194
Peng, Tao II-690
Peng, Wei I-835
Peng, Wen II-1229
Peng, Xiao-qi III-477
Pi, Daoying I-688, I-706, I-716
Pi, Xiongjun I-1035, I-1043
Pigg, Paul III-1242
Polat, Kemal II-830
Posenato, Roberto III-235
Priesterjahn, Steffen II-744
Puntonet, C.G. III-863
Pyun, Jae Young II-43

Qi, Huan III-482
Qi, Ming II-51
Qian, Feng II-631
Qian, Jixin III-289, III-948
Qian, Yuntao II-391
Qin, Guoqiang III-592
Qin, Qiming III-1261, III-1274
Qin, Zheng II-756, III-592
Qin-ye, Tong I-499
Qiu, Jiang I-952
Qiu, Yuhui III-562
Qiu, Zulian I-340

Rameshkumar, K. III-572
Ravi, S. III-361
Ren, Quanmin II-81
Ren, Xinhua II-774
Rhee, Phill Kyu II-109, II-764, III-356
Richer, Jean-Michel III-678
Ríos, Sebastián A. II-622
Rocha e Silva, Valceres Vieira III-313
Rojas, F. III-863
Rong, Lili III-151
Ropero, Jorge II-147
Rowlands, Hefin III-877
Rubo, Zhang III-553
Ruizhi, Sun I-650
Ryu, Joung Woo II-155
Ryu, Kwang Ryel II-1259

Sadedin, Suzanne II-1131
Sahan, Seral II-830
Sáiz, José Manuel I-778
Sakamoto, Makoto II-1025
Sang, Enfang I-199
Sasaki, S. III-684

Sendhoff, Bernhard II-1112, II-1145
Sengupta, Biswa I-429
Seo, Kyung-Sik I-1027
Seo, Sam-Jun III-1099
Seok, Kyung Ha I-536
Shang, Fu hua III-505
Shang, Jincheng III-374
Shang, Lin III-855
Shen, Hong-yuan III-477
Shen, Lan-sun I-975, II-7
Shen, Xisheng I-470
Shen, Xueqin I-692
Shen, Yi I-740
Shen, Zhenyao III-129
Shi, Feng I-1047, III-636
Shi, Haixiang I-1080
Shi, Jun III-496
Shi, Lukui I-692
Shi, Min I-229
Shi, Wenkang I-679
Shi, Xi II-1089
Shi, Xiangquan II-508
Shi, Yan-jun II-1080
Shi, Yuexiang III-1308
Shi, Zhiping III-496
Shi, Zhongzhi I-903, III-496
Shigei, Noritaka II-361, II-415
Shi-hua, Luo I-374
Shim, JeongYon I-1170
Shim, Jooyong I-512, I-521
Shin, Dongil I-1185, II-552
Shin, Dongkyoo I-1185, II-552
Shin, Jeong-Hoon I-1179
Shin, Kyung-shik I-1247, II-636
Shin, Sang-Uk III-962
Shou-jue, Wang I-264
Shriver, C.D. I-1039
Sim, Kwee-Bo I-237, II-85, III-713
Smutek, Daniel III-841
So, Yeon-hee I-797
Soh, W-S. I-1057
Sohn, Insuk II-306
Soke, Alev III-1304
Somiari, R. I-1039
Somiari, S.B. I-1039
Song III-1089
Song, Chonghui II-214
Song, Gangbing III-1089
Song, Hong II-863, III-602
Song, Jingyan II-1089

Song, Shiji I-470
Song, Weiwei III-972
Song, Xiao-yu II-992
Song, Yexin II-1101
Srinivas, M.B. III-1015
Su, Guangda I-985
Su, Juanhua II-185
Su, Tao III-893
Su, Tieming III-688
Su, Xiao-hong I-213
Suenaga, Masaya I-283
Sun, Changping I-397
Sun, Changyin II-602
Sun, Jiancheng I-573
Sun, Jigui III-434
Sun, Jun III-543
Sun, Lin-yan III-911
Sun, Shiliang II-652
Sun, Wei II-190
Sun, Xin-yu III-911
Sun, Xingming III-958, III-968
Sun, Yanguang I-546
Sun, Yi II-12
Sun, Ying-Guang III-1152
Sun, Youxian I-688, I-706, I-716, II-242, II-292
Sun, Yu II-1159, III-93
Sun, Zengqi II-234, II-252, II-262, III-141
Sun, Zhengxing I-655
Sun, Zonghai II-292
Sung, HyunSeong II-451
Sureerattanan, Nidapan I-157
Sureerattanan, Songyot I-157
Suresh, R.K. III-572
Szeto, Kwok Yip III-112

Takikawa, Erina II-438
Tan, E.C. I-975
Tan, Guanzheng III-915
Tan, Min III-622
Tan, Ying II-476, II-493, II-501, II-867
Tang, Chang-jie III-194
Tang, Deyou II-1049
Tang, Enyi I-655
Tang, Min II-1229, III-48
Tang, Renyuan III-1162
Tang, Xiaojun I-806
Tang, Xiaowei I-1052
Tang, Xusheng III-688

Tang, Yinggan II-75
Tang, Yiyuan I-1052
Tang, Yuan Yan III-663
Tang, Zhe II-252
Tao, Hai-hong III-893
Tao, Jun III-761
Taylor, Meinwen III-877
Temeltas, Hakan III-703
Teng, Hong-fei II-1080
Tesař, Ludvík III-841
Thapa, Devinder I-888
Tiňo, Peter II-666, II-676
Tian, Jie I-187
Tian, Lian-fang I-601
Tian, Shengfeng III-323
Tian, Zheng II-371
Ting, Ching-Jung III-205
Toh, C.K. III-525
Tong, Ruofeng II-1229
Tong, Weimin II-123
Tsaftaris, Sotirios A. II-1192
Tseng, Chung-Li III-741
Tsuboi, Yusei II-1174
Tsuji, Toshio II-165
Tu, Li II-1218

Ueda, Satomi II-1182
Uno, Yoji I-313
Usui, Shiro I-1074, III-1119

Valeev, Tagir II-1202
Valenzuela, O. III-863
van Noort, Danny II-1206
Velásquez, Juan D. II-622
Vera, Eduardo S. II-622
Von Zuben, Fernando J. I-1279
Vrahatis, M.N. III-582

Wakaki, Keitaro I-313
Wan, Jinming III-332
Wan, Qiong III-855
Wang, Ai-guo III-93
Wang, Bin II-410, III-822
Wang, Chao-Xue II-1269, III-86
Wang, Chaoyong III-1226
Wang, Chen III-845
Wang, Chong-Jun II-55
Wang, Dingsheng Luo Xinhao I-167
Wang, Fang III-562, III-622
Wang, G.L. II-266

Wang, Gang I-700
Wang, Gi-Nam I-888
Wang, Guizeng II-95
Wang, Guo-Xin III-1089
Wang, Guoqiang II-119
Wang, Hai III-883
Wang, Hai-Xia I-1199
Wang, Haijun I-405
Wang, He-Jun I-1150
Wang, Hong III-171, III-185
Wang, Honggang III-22
Wang, Hongguang III-727
Wang, Hui I-716, III-219
Wang, Jigang I-71, I-554
Wang, Jinwei III-976
Wang, Jun-nian III-477
Wang, Le I-378
Wang, Lei II-839, III-86
Wang, Lifang III-467
Wang, Ling III-417, III-832
Wang, Lipo I-1080
Wang, Long I-769, III-424
Wang, Longhui III-636
Wang, Lunwen II-501
Wang, Nong I-217
Wang, Qiao III-1261, III-1274
Wang, Qing-Yun I-1199
Wang, Qingquan III-151
Wang, Rubin I-490
Wang, Shan-Shan III-482
Wang, Shi-min I-480
Wang, Shitong III-1128
Wang, Shouyang I-382
Wang, Shuqing II-270
Wang, Shuxun III-972
Wang, Song II-574
Wang, Tong III-938
Wang, W. I-199
Wang, Wanliang I-332, II-795
Wang, Weihong I-1209
Wang, Weizhi III-1022
Wang, X.X. II-1122
Wang, Xi-cheng II-1159, III-93
Wang, Xiaodong I-221
Wang, Xiaofan II-283
Wang, Xiaolong I-947
Wang, Xihuai II-196
Wang, Xin III-525
Wang, Xinfei II-584
Wang, Xing-Yu I-565, II-21, II-89

Wang, Xiufeng II-978
Wang, Ya-dong I-213
Wang, Yan II-12, II-698
Wang, Yaonan II-190
Wang, Yen-Nien II-859
Wang, Yen-Wen I-364, II-983, III-205
Wang, Yong I-565
Wang, Yong-Xian II-1164
Wang, Yongcheng I-925
Wang, Yongqiang II-292
Wang, Yuping III-392
Wang, Zhanshan I-61
Wang, Zheng-Hua II-1164
Wang, Zhijie I-476
Wang, Zhiquan III-976
Wang, Zhizhong III-1142
Wang, Zhu-Rong II-1269, III-86
Wang, Zilei I-1090
Wang, Ziqiang II-727, II-822
Wanlin, Gao I-650
Watanabe, Atsushi II-274
Wei, Ding II-338
Wei, Li I-601
Wei, Xiaopeng I-405
Wei, Yaobing I-390
Wei, Yunbing I-332
Wei, Zhi II-592
Wei, Zhiqiang II-1005
Weijun, Li I-264
Weimer, Alexander II-744
Weizhong, Guo I-44
Wen, Quan III-972
Wen, Wanhui III-1231
Wen, Xiangjun I-51, I-582
Woo, Kwang Bang I-1160, II-564
Wu, Chunguo III-137, III-1226, III-1257
Wu, Fangfang I-608
Wu, Hao III-417
Wu, Huizhong III-225
Wu, Jianping II-105
Wu, Kai-Gui II-814
Wu, Lenan II-468
Wu, Qing I-692
Wu, Qingliang III-761
Wu, QingXiang I-420
Wu, Qiongshui II-210
Wu, Tihua I-397
Wu, Wei I-720, III-772
Wu, Xiaoping II-1101
Wu, Xihong I-167

Wu, Yadong III-332
Wu, Yan III-1
Wu, Ying I-390, I-508
Wu, Yiqiang I-8
Wu, Yong III-958
Wu, Yun III-120
Wu, Zhong-Fu II-814

Xi, Hongsheng I-1090
Xia, Feng II-242
Xiang, Zheng I-573
Xiang-guan, Liu I-374
Xiao, Fen I-783, II-139
Xiao, Jian I-101
Xiao, Jianmei II-196
Xiao, Yunshi I-119
Xiaolong, Deng I-44
Xie, Gang II-945
Xie, Guangming III-424
Xie, Hongbo III-1142
Xie, Jun II-951
Xie, Keming II-945, II-951, II-957
Xie, Li I-386
Xie, Lijuan III-384
Xie, Qihong III-57
Xie, Sheng-Li I-839
Xie, Shengli I-229, II-386, II-442
Xie, Xiaogang III-1235
Xie, Zongxia III-1190
Xin-guang, Shao I-25
Xiong, Shengwu I-592
Xiong, Zhangliang II-508
Xu, Bin II-520
Xu, Chen I-264
Xu, Chunlin II-800
Xu, De III-622
Xu, Fen III-1251
Xu, Haixia II-371
Xu, Jian III-505, III-1280
Xu, Jianxue I-508
Xu, Jin I-1031, II-376, III-646
Xu, Jinhua I-730
Xu, Junqin III-299
Xu, Min III-1128
Xu, Wenbo III-543
Xu, Xiaoming I-51, I-582, II-175
Xu, Xin I-700, II-1035
Xu, Xinli II-795
Xu, Xinying II-945
Xu, Xiuling I-221

Xu, Yangsheng II-1089
Xu, Yubin III-22
Xu, Yuelei I-449
Xu, Yuhui I-139, I-345
Xu, Yusheng I-139, I-345
Xu, Zhenhao II-880
Xu, Zhiwei I-750
Xue, Juan III-68
Xue, Q. II-266
Xue, Xiangyang III-525
Xue, Xiaoping I-466

Yan, Gaowei II-951
Yan, Haifeng III-444
Yan, Shaoze III-632
Yan, Weidong III-980
Yan, Xiao-Ke I-1150
Yan, Xin III-980
Yan, Xiong III-181
Yang, Bo I-213
Yang, C.F. II-557
Yang, Chunyan II-214
Yang, Hai-Dong I-1150
Yang, Hsiao-Fang III-11
Yang, Huazhong III-219
Yang, Hui II-214
Yang, Hui-Hua I-565, II-21, II-89
Yang, Hwan-Seok II-224
Yang, Hyun-Seung III-1178
Yang, Jian I-322
Yang, Jiangang III-490
Yang, Jie II-95
Yang, Jing I-1132
Yang, Jun III-120
Yang, Jun-an II-461
Yang, Kongyu II-978
Yang, Li-ying II-756
Yang, Luxi I-683
Yang, Pin II-804
Yang, Qing II-442
Yang, Shun-Lin I-668
Yang, Shuzhong I-710
Yang, Wenlu I-1043
Yang, Xiaohua III-129
Yang, Xiaowei III-137, III-1257
Yang, Xin I-187
Yang, Xiyang I-225
Yang, Xuhua I-332
Yang, Yipeng III-1274
Yang, Yong III-873

Yang, YonQing I-15
Yang, Zheng Rong I-179
Yang, Zhifeng III-129
Yang, Zhixia I-217
Yang, Zhuo I-806
Yao, JingTao I-129
Yao, Shuzhen II-1049
Yao, Xin III-279
Yasuda, Hiroshi II-622
Yazhu, Qiu I-33
Ye, Bin II-895
Ye, Hao II-95
Ye, Jun II-1105
Ye, Mao II-557
Ye, Xiuzi I-835
Ye, Zhongfu II-461
Yi, Bian I-264
Yi, Yang III-74
Yibo, Zhang I-696
Yim, Hyungwook I-844
Yin, Bo II-1005
Yin, Changming III-384
Yin, Chao-wan II-992
Yin, Chuanhuan III-323
Yin, Jianping II-65, II-913
Yin, Junsong I-101
Yin, Ling I-1052
Yin, Xiao-chuan II-539
Yokoyama, Ryuichi III-313
Yoo, Kee-Young II-512, III-348
Yoo, Sun K. I-818
Yoon, Eun-Jun II-512
Yoon, Han-Ul III-713
Yoon, Hye-Sung I-965
Yoon, Mi-sun I-797
Yoon, Min III-409
You, Jing III-1280
You, Xinge III-663
Young, Natasha I-179
Youxian, Sun I-696
Yu, Changjie II-262
Yu, Daren III-1190
Yu, Fusheng I-225
Yu, Jin-shou I-81
Yu, Jinshou I-630, II-610, III-515, III-832
Yu, Lean I-382
Yu, Qizhi III-1051
Yu, Wei I-490
Yu, Xinjie II-1064, II-1072

Author Index

Yu, Zhenhua II-627
Yu, Zu-Guo III-337
Yuan, Chang-an III-194
Yuan, Hong I-952
Yuan, Lin I-199, III-1001
Yue, Jiguang I-119
Yun, Jung-Hyun III-1032
Yun, Sung-Hyun I-797
Yun, Yeboon III-409
Yusof, Azwina I-893
Yıldırım, Tülay I-110

Zeng, Jianchao III-22, III-255, III-467
Zeng, Libo II-210
Zeng, Qingdong III-915
Zeng, Sanyou II-1049
Zeng, Zhigang I-664
Zhan, Tao III-602, III-883
Zhang, Changjiang I-221
Zhang, Changshui II-652
Zhang, Chunfang II-1239
Zhang, Chunkai I-91
Zhang, Dan II-863, III-602, III-883
Zhang, Defu III-1235
Zhang, Dexian II-727, II-822
Zhang, Dongmo I-956
Zhang, Erhu I-640
Zhang, Feng III-873
Zhang, Gang II-957
Zhang, Guomin II-65
Zhang, Haoran I-221
Zhang, Hongbo II-210
Zhang, Huaguang I-61
Zhang, Huidang I-273
Zhang, Jian II-266, III-112
Zhang, Jiang III-309
Zhang, Jianming II-270
Zhang, Jian-Pei I-1132
Zhang, Jihui III-299
Zhang, Jing I-660, I-1052, III-194
Zhang, Jingjing III-102
Zhang, Jun I-358, I-783, II-139, II-592
Zhang, Lei III-535
Zhang, Ling II-501
Zhang, Liqing I-1043
Zhang, Lisha I-655
Zhang, Min II-476, III-668
Zhang, Qiang I-405
Zhang, Qing-Guo III-28
Zhang, Sanyuan I-835
Zhang, Shuai III-1300
Zhang, Shui-ping II-539
Zhang, Taiyi I-573
Zhang, Tao I-806
Zhang, Wei III-28
Zhang, Weidong I-528
Zhang, Wen III-449
Zhang, Wenquan I-8
Zhang, Xianfei II-37
Zhang, Xiangrong II-905
Zhang, XianMing II-1
Zhang, Xiao-hua II-1044
Zhang, Xiaoshuan II-352
Zhang, Xiufeng II-774
Zhang, Xuanping III-592
Zhang, Xudong III-654
Zhang, Y.S. III-1060
Zhang, Yan III-938
Zhang, Yanning III-215
Zhang, Yanxin II-283
Zhang, Ye I-8
Zhang, Yuanzhen II-483
Zhang, Yulei I-956
Zhang, Yuming III-723
Zhang, Yuntao I-925
Zhang, Z.Z. III-668
Zhang, Zhen-Hui II-1164
Zhang, Zhengwei II-95
Zhang, Zhijie I-952
Zhang, Zhousuo II-324
Zhao, Bin II-461
Zhao, Bo II-895
Zhao, Guoying I-740
Zhao, Hai I-303
Zhao, Hengping I-630
Zhao, Jian II-346
Zhao, Jieyu II-432
Zhao, Jin-cheng II-1159
Zhao, Jing II-557
Zhao, Jun III-948
Zhao, Keyou III-698
Zhao, Li II-71
Zhao, Liang I-1189
Zhao, Liping I-956
Zhao, Mingyang III-727
Zhao, Pengfei III-688
Zhao, Qiang III-632
Zhao, Qijun II-28
Zhao, Qin II-346
Zhao, Rongchun III-215

Zhao, Wencang   I-793, I-1256
Zhao, Xi   III-137
Zhao, Xinyu   I-825
Zhao, Xue-long   III-1280
Zhao, Yinliang   I-608
Zhao, Yu   I-1090, II-584
Zhao, Zhefeng   II-957
Zhao, Zhi-Hong   III-855
Zhao, Zhilong   III-980
Zhao, Zijiang   III-444
Zheng, ChongXun   I-1031, II-376, III-646, III-873
Zheng, Da-zhong   III-417
Zheng, Hong   II-210, III-934
Zheng, Ji   III-525
Zheng, Jin-hua   III-68
Zheng, Shiqin   II-978
Zheng, Yi   I-8
Zheng, Yisong   I-773
Zhexin, Cao   II-316
Zhi, Qiang   II-316
Zhong, Jiang   II-814
Zhong, Weicai   III-366, III-925
Zhong, Weimin   I-706
Zhong, Xiang-Ping   II-55
Zhou, Changjiu   II-252
Zhou, Chun-Guang   II-698
Zhou, Dongsheng   I-405
Zhou, Jian   III-120, III-684
Zhou, Jiping   III-727
Zhou, Li-Quan   III-337
Zhou, Lifang   III-289
Zhou, Ming-quan   II-346

Zhou, Qiang   III-181
Zhou, Shude   III-141
Zhou, Wen-Gang   II-698
Zhou, Xiaoyang   III-374
Zhou, Ying   II-814
Zhou, Yuanfeng   II-105
Zhou, Yuanpai   III-269
Zhou, Yuren   II-1015
Zhou, Zhi-Heng   I-839
Zhou, Zhong   III-772
Zhou, Zongtan   I-101, I-209, I-675
Zhu, Chengzhi   II-895
Zhu, Daqi   I-15
Zhu, En   II-65
Zhu, Jia   III-93
Zhu, Jianguang   III-1162
Zhu, Jihong   II-234, II-262
Zhu, Qingsheng   III-57
Zhu, Xinglong   III-727
Zhu, Xue-feng   I-995
Zhu, Yan-fei   I-601
Zhu, Yun-long   II-992
Zhu, Zheng-Zhou   II-814
Zhu, Zhengyu   III-57
Zi, Yanyang   II-324
Zou, Cairong   II-71
Zou, Henghui   III-996
Zou, Hengming   III-988, III-996, III-1001
Zou, Qi   I-867
Zribi, Nozha   III-259
Zuo, Wanli   II-690
Zuo, Wen-ming   II-51
Zurada, Jacek M.   III-1216

Lecture Notes in Computer Science

For information about Vols. 1–3537

please contact your bookseller or Springer

Vol. 3659: J.R. Rao, B. Sunar (Eds.), Cryptographic Hardware and Embedded Systems – CHES 2005. XIV, 458 pages. 2005.

Vol. 3654: S. Jajodia, D. Wijesekera (Eds.), Data and Applications Security XIX. X, 353 pages. 2005.

Vol. 3653: M. Abadi, L.d. Alfaro (Eds.), CONCUR 2005 – Concurrency Theory. XIV, 578 pages. 2005.

Vol. 3649: W.M.P. van der Aalst, B. Benatallah, F. Casati, F. Curbera (Eds.), Business Process Management. XII, 472 pages. 2005.

Vol. 3639: P. Godefroid (Ed.), Model Checking Software. XI, 289 pages. 2005.

Vol. 3638: A. Butz, B. Fisher, A. Krüger, P. Olivier (Eds.), Smart Graphics. XI, 269 pages. 2005.

Vol. 3636: M.J. Blesa, C. Blum, A. Roli, M. Sampels (Eds.), Hybrid Metaheuristics. XII, 155 pages. 2005.

Vol. 3634: L. Ong (Ed.), Computer Science Logic. XI, 567 pages. 2005.

Vol. 3633: C. Bauzer Medeiros, M. Egenhofer, E. Bertino (Eds.), Advances in Spatial and Temporal Databases. XIII, 433 pages. 2005.

Vol. 3632: R. Nieuwenhuis (Ed.), Automated Deduction – CADE-20. XIII, 459 pages. 2005. (Subseries LNAI).

Vol. 3627: C. Jacob, M.L. Pilat, P.J. Bentley, J. Timmis (Eds.), Artificial Immune Systems. XII, 500 pages. 2005.

Vol. 3626: B. Ganter, G. Stumme, R. Wille (Eds.), Formal Concept Analysis. X, 349 pages. 2005. (Subseries LNAI).

Vol. 3625: S. Kramer, B. Pfahringer (Eds.), Inductive Logic Programming. XIII, 427 pages. 2005. (Subseries LNAI).

Vol. 3624: C. Chekuri, K. Jansen, J.D.P. Rolim, L. Trevisan (Eds.), Approximation, Randomization and Combinatorial Optimization. XI, 495 pages. 2005.

Vol. 3623: M. Liśkiewicz, R. Reischuk (Eds.), Fundamentals of Computation Theory. XV, 576 pages. 2005.

Vol. 3621: V. Shoup (Ed.), Advances in Cryptology – CRYPTO 2005. XI, 568 pages. 2005.

Vol. 3620: H. Muñoz-Avila, F. Ricci (Eds.), Case-Based Reasoning Research and Development. XV, 654 pages. 2005. (Subseries LNAI).

Vol. 3619: X. Lu, W. Zhao (Eds.), Networking and Mobile Computing. XXIV, 1299 pages. 2005.

Vol. 3615: B. Ludäscher, L. Raschid (Eds.), Data Integration in the Life Sciences. XII, 344 pages. 2005. (Subseries LNBI).

Vol. 3614: L. Wang, Y. Jin (Eds.), Fuzzy Systems and Knowledge Discovery, Part II. XLI, 1314 pages. 2005. (Subseries LNAI).

Vol. 3613: L. Wang, Y. Jin (Eds.), Fuzzy Systems and Knowledge Discovery, Part I. XLI, 1334 pages. 2005. (Subseries LNAI).

Vol. 3612: L. Wang, K. Chen, Y. S. Ong (Eds.), Advances in Natural Computation, Part III. LXI, 1326 pages. 2005.

Vol. 3611: L. Wang, K. Chen, Y. S. Ong (Eds.), Advances in Natural Computation, Part II. LXI, 1292 pages. 2005.

Vol. 3610: L. Wang, K. Chen, Y. S. Ong (Eds.), Advances in Natural Computation, Part I. LXI, 1302 pages. 2005.

Vol. 3608: F. Dehne, A. López-Ortiz, J.-R. Sack (Eds.), Algorithms and Data Structures. XIV, 446 pages. 2005.

Vol. 3607: J.-D. Zucker, L. Saitta (Eds.), Abstraction, Reformulation and Approximation. XII, 376 pages. 2005. (Subseries LNAI).

Vol. 3606: V. Malyshkin (Ed.), Parallel Computing Technologies. XII, 470 pages. 2005.

Vol. 3603: J. Hurd, T. Melham (Eds.), Theorem Proving in Higher Order Logics. IX, 409 pages. 2005.

Vol. 3602: R. Eigenmann, Z. Li, S.P. Midkiff (Eds.), Languages and Compilers for High Performance Computing. IX, 486 pages. 2005.

Vol. 3599: U. Aßmann, M. Aksit, A. Rensink (Eds.), Model Driven Architecture. X, 235 pages. 2005.

Vol. 3598: H. Murakami, H. Nakashima, H. Tokuda, M. Yasumura, Ubiquitous Computing Systems. XIII, 275 pages. 2005.

Vol. 3597: S. Shimojo, S. Ichii, T.W. Ling, K.-H. Song (Eds.), Web and Communication Technologies and Internet-Related Social Issues - HSI 2005. XIX, 368 pages. 2005.

Vol. 3596: F. Dau, M.-L. Mugnier, G. Stumme (Eds.), Conceptual Structures: Common Semantics for Sharing Knowledge. XI, 467 pages. 2005. (Subseries LNAI).

Vol. 3595: L. Wang (Ed.), Computing and Combinatorics. XVI, 995 pages. 2005.

Vol. 3594: J.C. Setubal, S. Verjovski-Almeida (Eds.), Advances in Bioinformatics and Computational Biology. XIV, 258 pages. 2005. (Subseries LNBI).

Vol. 3593: V. Mařík, R. W. Brennan, M. Pěchouček (Eds.), Holonic and Multi-Agent Systems for Manufacturing. XI, 269 pages. 2005. (Subseries LNAI).

Vol. 3592: S. Katsikas, J. Lopez, G. Pernul (Eds.), Trust, Privacy and Security in Digital Business. XII, 332 pages. 2005.

Vol. 3591: M.A. Wimmer, R. Traunmüller, Å. Grönlund, K.V. Andersen (Eds.), Electronic Government. XIII, 317 pages. 2005.

Vol. 3587: P. Perner, A. Imiya (Eds.), Machine Learning and Data Mining in Pattern Recognition. XVII, 695 pages. 2005. (Subseries LNAI).

Vol. 3586: A.P. Black (Ed.), ECOOP 2005 - Object-Oriented Programming. XVII, 631 pages. 2005.

Vol. 3584: X. Li, S. Wang, Z.Y. Dong (Eds.), Advanced Data Mining and Applications. XIX, 835 pages. 2005. (Subseries LNAI).

Vol. 3583: R.W. H. Lau, Q. Li, R. Cheung, W. Liu (Eds.), Advances in Web-Based Learning – ICWL 2005. XIV, 420 pages. 2005.

Vol. 3582: J. Fitzgerald, I.J. Hayes, A. Tarlecki (Eds.), FM 2005: Formal Methods. XIV, 558 pages. 2005.

Vol. 3581: S. Miksch, J. Hunter, E. Keravnou (Eds.), Artificial Intelligence in Medicine. XVII, 547 pages. 2005. (Subseries LNAI).

Vol. 3580: L. Caires, G.F. Italiano, L. Monteiro, C. Palamidessi, M. Yung (Eds.), Automata, Languages and Programming. XXV, 1477 pages. 2005.

Vol. 3579: D. Lowe, M. Gaedke (Eds.), Web Engineering. XXII, 633 pages. 2005.

Vol. 3578: M. Gallagher, J. Hogan, F. Maire (Eds.), Intelligent Data Engineering and Automated Learning - IDEAL 2005. XVI, 599 pages. 2005.

Vol. 3577: R. Falcone, S. Barber, J. Sabater-Mir, M.P. Singh (Eds.), Trusting Agents for Trusting Electronic Societies. VIII, 235 pages. 2005. (Subseries LNAI).

Vol. 3576: K. Etessami, S.K. Rajamani (Eds.), Computer Aided Verification. XV, 564 pages. 2005.

Vol. 3575: S. Wermter, G. Palm, M. Elshaw (Eds.), Biomimetic Neural Learning for Intelligent Robots. IX, 383 pages. 2005. (Subseries LNAI).

Vol. 3574: C. Boyd, J.M. González Nieto (Eds.), Information Security and Privacy. XIII, 586 pages. 2005.

Vol. 3573: S. Etalle (Ed.), Logic Based Program Synthesis and Transformation. VIII, 279 pages. 2005.

Vol. 3572: C. De Felice, A. Restivo (Eds.), Developments in Language Theory. XI, 409 pages. 2005.

Vol. 3571: L. Godo (Ed.), Symbolic and Quantitative Approaches to Reasoning with Uncertainty. XVI, 1028 pages. 2005. (Subseries LNAI).

Vol. 3570: A. S. Patrick, M. Yung (Eds.), Financial Cryptography and Data Security. XII, 376 pages. 2005.

Vol. 3569: F. Bacchus, T. Walsh (Eds.), Theory and Applications of Satisfiability Testing. XII, 492 pages. 2005.

Vol. 3568: W.-K. Leow, M.S. Lew, T.-S. Chua, W.-Y. Ma, L. Chaisorn, E.M. Bakker (Eds.), Image and Video Retrieval. XVII, 672 pages. 2005.

Vol. 3567: M. Jackson, D. Nelson, S. Stirk (Eds.), Database: Enterprise, Skills and Innovation. XII, 185 pages. 2005.

Vol. 3566: J.-P. Banâtre, P. Fradet, J.-L. Giavitto, O. Michel (Eds.), Unconventional Programming Paradigms. XI, 367 pages. 2005.

Vol. 3565: G.E. Christensen, M. Sonka (Eds.), Information Processing in Medical Imaging. XXI, 777 pages. 2005.

Vol. 3564: N. Eisinger, J. Małuszyński (Eds.), Reasoning Web. IX, 319 pages. 2005.

Vol. 3562: J. Mira, J.R. Álvarez (Eds.), Artificial Intelligence and Knowledge Engineering Applications: A Bioinspired Approach, Part II. XXIV, 636 pages. 2005.

Vol. 3561: J. Mira, J.R. Álvarez (Eds.), Mechanisms, Symbols, and Models Underlying Cognition, Part I. XXIV, 532 pages. 2005.

Vol. 3560: V.K. Prasanna, S. Iyengar, P.G. Spirakis, M. Welsh (Eds.), Distributed Computing in Sensor Systems. XV, 423 pages. 2005.

Vol. 3559: P. Auer, R. Meir (Eds.), Learning Theory. XI, 692 pages. 2005. (Subseries LNAI).

Vol. 3558: V. Torra, Y. Narukawa, S. Miyamoto (Eds.), Modeling Decisions for Artificial Intelligence. XII, 470 pages. 2005. (Subseries LNAI).

Vol. 3557: H. Gilbert, H. Handschuh (Eds.), Fast Software Encryption. XI, 443 pages. 2005.

Vol. 3556: H. Baumeister, M. Marchesi, M. Holcombe (Eds.), Extreme Programming and Agile Processes in Software Engineering. XIV, 332 pages. 2005.

Vol. 3555: T. Vardanega, A.J. Wellings (Eds.), Reliable Software Technology – Ada-Europe 2005. XV, 273 pages. 2005.

Vol. 3554: A. Dey, B. Kokinov, D. Leake, R. Turner (Eds.), Modeling and Using Context. XIV, 572 pages. 2005. (Subseries LNAI).

Vol. 3553: T.D. Hämäläinen, A.D. Pimentel, J. Takala, S. Vassiliadis (Eds.), Embedded Computer Systems: Architectures, Modeling, and Simulation. XV, 476 pages. 2005.

Vol. 3552: H. de Meer, N. Bhatti (Eds.), Quality of Service – IWQoS 2005. XVIII, 400 pages. 2005.

Vol. 3551: T. Härder, W. Lehner (Eds.), Data Management in a Connected World. XIX, 371 pages. 2005.

Vol. 3548: K. Julisch, C. Kruegel (Eds.), Intrusion and Malware Detection and Vulnerability Assessment. X, 241 pages. 2005.

Vol. 3547: F. Bomarius, S. Komi-Sirviö (Eds.), Product Focused Software Process Improvement. XIII, 588 pages. 2005.

Vol. 3546: T. Kanade, A. Jain, N.K. Ratha (Eds.), Audio- and Video-Based Biometric Person Authentication. XX, 1134 pages. 2005.

Vol. 3544: T. Higashino (Ed.), Principles of Distributed Systems. XII, 460 pages. 2005.

Vol. 3543: L. Kutvonen, N. Alonistioti (Eds.), Distributed Applications and Interoperable Systems. XI, 235 pages. 2005.

Vol. 3542: H.H. Hoos, D.G. Mitchell (Eds.), Theory and Applications of Satisfiability Testing. XIII, 393 pages. 2005.

Vol. 3541: N.C. Oza, R. Polikar, J. Kittler, F. Roli (Eds.), Multiple Classifier Systems. XII, 430 pages. 2005.

Vol. 3540: H. Kalviainen, J. Parkkinen, A. Kaarna (Eds.), Image Analysis. XXII, 1270 pages. 2005.

Vol. 3539: K. Morik, J.-F. Boulicaut, A. Siebes (Eds.), Local Pattern Detection. XI, 233 pages. 2005. (Subseries LNAI).

Vol. 3538: L. Ardissono, P. Brna, A. Mitrovic (Eds.), User Modeling 2005. XVI, 533 pages. 2005. (Subseries LNAI).

Lecture Notes in Computer Science 3611

Commenced Publication in 1973
Founding and Former Series Editors:
Gerhard Goos, Juris Hartmanis, and Jan van Leeuwen

Editorial Board

David Hutchison
  Lancaster University, UK
Takeo Kanade
  Carnegie Mellon University, Pittsburgh, PA, USA
Josef Kittler
  University of Surrey, Guildford, UK
Jon M. Kleinberg
  Cornell University, Ithaca, NY, USA
Friedemann Mattern
  ETH Zurich, Switzerland
John C. Mitchell
  Stanford University, CA, USA
Moni Naor
  Weizmann Institute of Science, Rehovot, Israel
Oscar Nierstrasz
  University of Bern, Switzerland
C. Pandu Rangan
  Indian Institute of Technology, Madras, India
Bernhard Steffen
  University of Dortmund, Germany
Madhu Sudan
  Massachusetts Institute of Technology, MA, USA
Demetri Terzopoulos
  New York University, NY, USA
Doug Tygar
  University of California, Berkeley, CA, USA
Moshe Y. Vardi
  Rice University, Houston, TX, USA
Gerhard Weikum
  Max-Planck Institute of Computer Science, Saarbruecken, Germany